Not For Tourists Guide™ to **NEW YORK CITY**

Not For Tourists, Inc

2009

published and designed by:
Not For Tourists, Inc
NFT_{TM}—Not For Tourists_{TM} Guide to New York City 2009
www.notfortourists.com

Publisher
Jane Pirone

Information Design
Jane Pirone
Rob Tallia
Ben Bray
Scot Covey

Managing Editor
Craig Nelson

Database Manager
Ben Bray

City Editors
Krikor Daglian
Soraya Victory

Writing and Editing
Deena Campbell
Krikor Daglian
Michael Dale
Jessica Feder-Birnbaum
Rebecca Katherine Hirsch
Craig Nelson
Jennifer Keeney Sendrow

Alex Sinclair
Rob Tallia
Soraya Victory

Contributors
Yuki Endo
Judith-Noëlle Lamb
Patricia Glowinski
Brett Pacheco
KC Sharp

Research
Melissa Burgos
Ben Bray
Bethany Covey
Michael Dale
Lea Garrett

Graphic Design/ Production
Scot Covey
Bethany Covey
Yumi Endo
Aaron Schielke
Carolyn Thomas

Editorial Interns
Rebecca Katherine Hirsch
Allison Dedianko

Proofing
Sho Spaeth

Sales & Marketing
Sarah Hocevar
Erin Hodson
Annie Holt
Sho Spaeth
Jennifer Wong

Official NFT Mascots
Lulu & Beni

Ex-Elevator Man
Mr. Lee

Web Guru
Juan Molinari

Printed in China
ISBN#978-0-9814887-0-7 $16.95
Copyright © 2008 by Not For Tourists, Inc.

Every effort has been made to ensure that the information in this book is as up-to-date as possible at press time. However, many details are liable to change—as we have learned. The publishers cannot accept responsibility for any consequences arising from the use of this book.

Not For Tourists does not solicit individuals, organizations, or businesses for listings inclusion in our guides, nor do we accept payment for inclusion into the editorial portion of our book; the advertising sections, however, are exempt from this policy. We always welcome communications from anyone regarding ANYTHING having to do with our books; please visit us on our website at www.notfortourists.com for appropriate contact information.

Dear NFT User,

You know you're a real New Yorker when…you know that an empty subway car on an otherwise packed train is to be avoided, and you know why; a tourist stops you to ask for directions and you know where he's going before he even opens his mouth; you think 300 square feet constitutes an apartment fit to live in—with another person; you know you live in the greatest city in existence, and just can't stop reminding the rest of the world.

Whether you're a native New Yorker, a fresh-faced transplant, or a day-tripper who simply wants to experience the non-touristy side of NYC, you need a guidebook. And not the big clunky kind with a glossy photo cover that screams, "I'm a tourist, take advantage of me!" You need a sleek, elegant one fit for a local—which means black. And it has to come from people who know the streets of this city better than anyone because they eat, drink, shop, walk, bike, drive, and live in every one of its neighborhoods. Whether you're an NFT veteran or virgin, you just won't be able to put down the 2009 edition, fortified with 30 more pages of priceless content. Sink your teeth into thousands of updated listings and info you otherwise don't even realize you need until it's too late, like closing times for restaurant kitchens. And now we've got four maps for every single neighborhood (Essentials, Sundries, Entertainment, and Transportation), and larger type throughout. You'll never miss a detail, whether you're hunting for the best beers on the Upper West Side, or just trying to get home from Battery Park City.

As you savor each and every fabulous page of this nifty black book, know that this urban Bible results from the collaboration of many talented souls. The contributors and the mighty NFT staff continue to draw on the expertise and energy of these folks to create the ultimate guide to life in NYC. Without them and their passion, we'd just be a bunch of headless chickens running around trying to make sense of this town. Our sincere appreciation goes out to them.

Be sure to check out our fabulous website, www.notfortourists.com, where you can sign up for our weekly newsletters and shop 'til you drop. You can also read "On Our Radar" articles about livin' it up in New York and cruise through our online database with over 60,000 listings. And to all of you New Yorkers out there who want to let us know that we neglected to mention a killer bar, left out the best Cubano sandwich around, or missed a stellar indie boutique, visit the site and drop us a line.

Here's to knowing this city inside and out,

Jane, Rob, Craig, Krikor, and Soraya

The Bronx

Central Park

Hudson River

East River

Upper
New York
Bay

Table of Contents

Subway Map/Bus Map
foldout, last page

Map 1 • **Financial District**

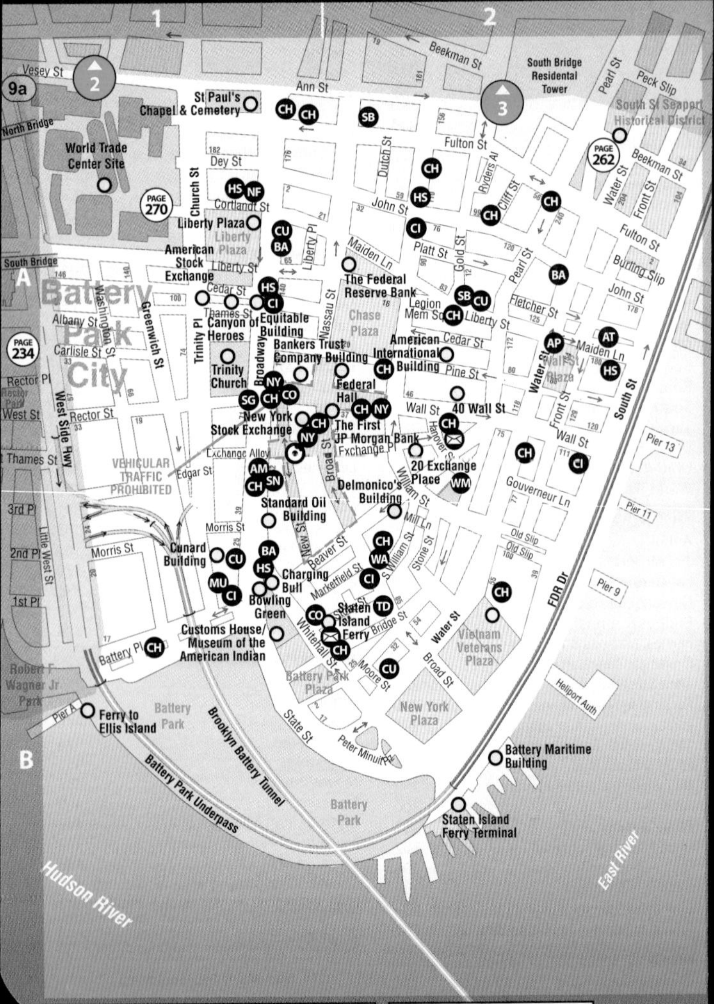

1

2

Vesey St

9a

North Bridge

Beekman St

South Bridge
Residential
Tower

Peck Slip

Pearl St

South St Seaport
Historical District

Ann St

Dey St

CH CH

St Paul's
Chapel & Cemetery

SB

Fulton St

PAGE
262

Beekman St

Water St

Front St

World Trade
Center Site

PAGE
270

Church St

Dutch St

Ryders Al

CH

John St

HS

Fulton St

HS NF

Cortlandt St

Liberty Plaza

CU

American
Stock
Exchange

BA

Liberty Pl

Liberty
Plaza

Maiden Ln

CI

Platt St

CH

Gold St

CH

CI

Pearl St

Building Slip

John St

BA

Battery
Park
City

Albany St

Washington St

Greenwich St

Cedar St

HS

Trinity Pl

Broadway

Thames St

Canyon
of Heroes

Equitable
Building

Nassau St

Chase
Plaza

The Federal
Reserve Bank

Legion
Mem Sq

SB CU

CH Liberty St

Cedar St

AP

HS

AT

Maiden Ln

Fletcher St

Carlisle St

PAGE
234

Rector Pl

Trinity Church

Bankers Trust
Company Building

American
International
Building

Pine St

Water St

Front St

Rector St

West St

SG

NY
CO

Federal
Hall

CH

CH NY

Wall St

40 Wall St

CH

West Side Hwy

3rd Pl

2nd Pl

1st Pl

West St

New York
Stock Exchange

The First
JP Morgan Bank
Exchange Pl

NY
CO

NY

Pier 13

Thames St

VEHICULAR
TRAFFIC
PROHIBITED

Edgar St

Exchange Alley

AM
SN

Standard Oil
Building

20 Exchange
Place

Hanover Sq

South St

CH

Wall St

CI

Gouverneur Ln

WM

Pier 11

Morris St

Cunard
Building

Morris St

BA

Delmonico's
Building

William St

Mill Ln

Old Slip

Old Slip

FDR Dr

Pier 9

CU

HS

Charging
Bull

Beaver St

S William St

Stone St

MU

CI

Bowling
Green

Marketfield St

WA

CH

Whitehall St

Customs House/
Museum of the
American Indian

CO

Staten
Island
Ferry

TD

Water St

Broad St

CU

Battery Park
Underpass

CH

CH

Bridge St

Battery Park
Plaza

Pearl St

Vietnam
Veterans
Plaza

Heliport Auth

CH

New York
Plaza

Robert F
Wagner Jr
Park

Battery Pl

Pier A

Ferry to
Ellis Island

Battery
Park

Brooklyn Battery Tunnel

State St

Peter Minuit Pl

Battery Maritime
Building

Battery
Park

Staten Island
Ferry Terminal

East River

Hudson River

N

B

A

| 1/4 mile | .25 km |

Here's where Gotham City got its name. From the seaport to Battery Park, from the looming skyscrapers to the eerie sense of quiet cash, downtown is alive with history, tradition, and young, hungry VIPs. One-up 'em, Clark Kent—you know where the true ROIs are hidden down here.

Bagels

• **Champs** • 70 Exchange Pl [New]

$ Banks

AM • Amalgamated • 52 Broadway [Exchange Pl]
AP • Apple • Wall St Plz [Maiden Ln]
AT • Atlantic • 15 Maiden Ln [Liberty Pl]
BA • Bank of America • 150 Broadway [Liberty]
BA • Bank of America • 29 Broadway [Morris St]
BA • Bank of America (ATM) • 175 Water St [John St]
NY • Bank of New York • 20 Broad St [Exchange]
NY • Bank of New York • 1 Wall St [Broadway]
CH • Chase • 1 Chase Plz [Pine St]
CH • Chase • 20 Broad St [Nassau St]
CH • Chase • 214 Broadway [Fulton St]
CH • Chase • 42 Broadway [Morris St]
CH • Chase • 45 Wall St [Broadway]
CH • Chase • 55 Water St [Hanover Sq]
CH • Chase (ATM) • 1 Wall St [Broadway]
CH • Chase (ATM) • 1 Whitehall St [Stone St]
CH • Chase (ATM) • 130 William St [Fulton St]
CH • Chase (ATM) • 147 Fulton St [Broadway]
CH • Chase (ATM) • 17 Battery Pl [Washington]
CH • Chase (ATM) • 40 Fulton St [Pearl St]
CH • Chase (ATM) • 45 Pine St [William St]
CH • Chase (ATM) • 60 Wall St [Hanover St]
CH • Chase (ATM) • 67 Broad St [Marketfield St]
CH • Chase (ATM) • 80 Maiden Ln [Gold St]
CH • Chase (ATM) • 95 Wall St [Water St]
CH • Chase (ATM) • 99 John St [Cliff St]
CI • Citibank • 1 Broadway [Battery Pl]
CI • Citibank • 111 Wall St [Front St]
CI • Citibank • 120 Broadway [Cedar St]
CI • Citibank (ATM) • 100 William St [Platt St]
CI • Citibank (ATM) • 80 Broad St [S William St]
CO • Commerce • 2 Wall St [Broadway]
CO • Commerce (ATM) • Staten Island Ferry • 1 Whitehall St [Stone St]
HS • HSBC • 100 Maiden Ln [Pearl St]
HS • HSBC • 110 William St [John St]
HS • HSBC • 120 Broadway [Cedar St]
HS • HSBC • 26 Broadway [Morris St]
HS • HSBC (ATM) • 22 Cortlandt St [Cortlandt]
CU • Lower East Side People's Federal Credit Union (ATM) • 160 Broadway [Maiden Ln]
CU • Lower East Side People's Federal Credit Union (ATM) • McDonald's •6 Water St [Moore]
CU • Lower East Side People's Federal Credit Union (ATM) • McDonald's • 90 Maiden Ln [Pearl St]
CU • Municipal Credit Union (ATM) • 2 Broadway [Stone St]

NF • North Fork • 176 Broadway [Cortlandt St]
SG • Signature • 71 Broadway [Rector St]
SB • Sovereign • 2 Gold St [Liberty St]
SB • Sovereign (ATM) • CVS • 129 Fulton St [Nassau St]
SN • Sterling National • 42 Broadway [Morris]
TD • TD Banknorth • 90 Broad St [Stone St]
WA • Wachovia (ATM) • 75 Broad St [S William]
WM • Washington Mutual • 10 Hanover Sq [Pearl St]

O Landmarks

• **20 Exchange Place** • 20 Exchange Pl [William]
• **40 Wall St** • 40 Wall St [William]
• **American International Building** • 70 Pine St [Pearl]
• **American Stock Exchange** • 86 Trinity Pl [Thames]
• **Bankers Trust Company Building** • 16 Wall St [Nassau]
• **Battery Maritime Building** • 10 South St [Broad]
• **Bowling Green** • Broadway & State St
• **Canyon of Heroes** • Broadway b/w Bowling Green & City Hall Park
• **Charging Bull** • Bowling Green Park
• **Cunard Building** • 25 Broadway [Morris]
• **Customs House/Museum of the American Indian** • 1 Bowling Green [State]
• **Delmonico's Building** • 56 Beaver St [S William]
• **Ferry to Ellis Island** • Battery Park
• **Equitable Building** • 120 Broadway [Cedar]
• **Federal Hall** • 26 Wall St [Broad]
• **The Federal Reserve Bank** • 33 Liberty St [William]
• **The First JP Morgan Bank** • 23 Wall St [Broad]
• **Liberty Plaza** • Trinity Pl & Cedar St
• **New York Stock Exchange** • 20 Broad St [Exchange Pl]
• **South Street Seaport** • South St [Fulton]
• **St Paul's Chapel & Cemetery** • Broadway & Fulton St
• **Standard Oil Building** • 26 Broadway [Morris]
• **Staten Island Ferry** • 1 Whitehall St [Stone]
• **Trinity Church** • Broadway & Wall St
• **Vietnam Veterans Plaza** • Coenties Slip & Water St
• **World Trade Center Site** • Church St & Vesey St

 Post Offices

• **Wall Street Retail** • 1 Hanover St [Wall St]
• **Whitehall Retail** • 1 Whitehall St [Stone St]

Map 1 · **Financial District**

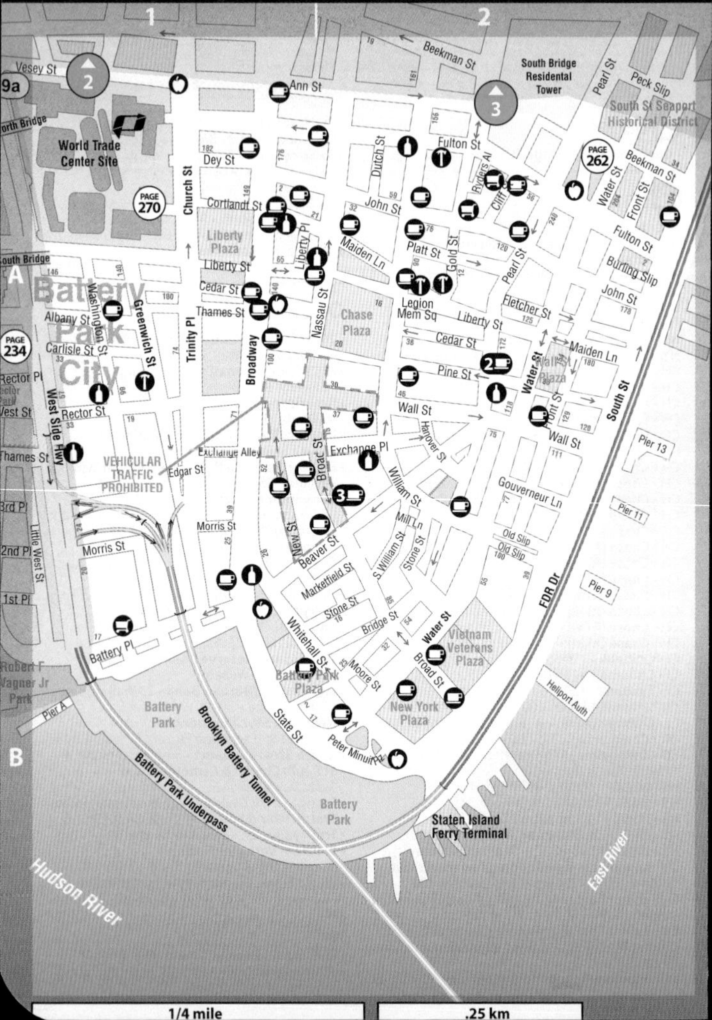

Hudson River

East River

World Trade Center Site

PAGE 270

South Bridge Residental Tower

South St Seaport Historical District

PAGE 262

Battery Park City

PAGE 234

Chase Plaza

Legion Mem Sq

VEHICULAR TRAFFIC PROHIBITED

Battery Park

Brooklyn Battery Tunnel

Battery Park Underpass

Staten Island Ferry Terminal

Vietnam Veterans Plaza

New York Plaza

Bowling Green Plaza

Heliport Auth

Pier 13

Pier 11

Pier 9

FDR Dr

Streets: Vesey St, North Bridge, South Bridge, Ann St, Beekman St, Peck Slip, Pearl St, Dey St, Church St, Cortlandt St, Fulton St, Dutch St, John St, Water St, Front St, Liberty St, Platt St, Gold St, Cliff St, Burling Slip, Maiden Ln, Nassau St, Cedar St, Pine St, William St, Wall St, Exchange Pl, Broadway, Beaver St, Morris St, Stone St, Bridge St, Whitehall St, State St, Battery Pl, Peter Minuit Pl, Old Slip, Gouverneur Ln, South St, Trinity Pl, Greenwich St, West Side Hwy, Rector St, Carlisle St, Albany St, Thames St, Marketfield St, Broad St

1/4 mile   .25 km

Down here, businesses are more apt to be open during the week. Also, not really the place to go for unusual, non-chain stores, with the exception of some fine wine and hardware purveyors (note: please don't drink and drill).

☕ Coffee

- **Andrew's Coffee Shop** • 116 John St [Pearl]
- **Ashby's** • 120 Broadway [Cedar]
- **Au Bon Pain** • 1 State St Plz [Whitehall]
- **Au Bon Pain** • 222 Broadway [Ann]
- **Au Bon Pain** • 60 Broad St [Beaver]
- **Au Bon Pain** • 80 Pine St [Pearl]
- **Café Toda** • 180 Broadway [Cortlandt St]
- **Cosi** • 54 Pine St [William]
- **Cosi** • 55 Broad St [Beaver]
- **Dean & DeLuca Café** • 100 Broadway [Pine]
- **Dunkin' Donuts** • 1 New York Plz
- **Dunkin' Donuts** • 139 Fulton St [Nassau]
- **Dunkin' Donuts** • New York Stock Exchange Cafeteria • 20 Broad St [Exchange Pl]
- **Dunkin' Donuts** • 40 Broad St [Exchange Pl]
- **Dunkin' Donuts** • 48 New St [Exchange Pl]
- **Dunkin' Donuts** • 50 Fulton St [Cliff]
- **Dunkin' Donuts** • 89 South St [Beekman]
- **Klatch** • 9 Maiden Ln [B'way]
- **Lane Café** • 75 Maiden Ln [William]
- **Roxy Coffee Shop** • 20 John St [Nassau]
- **Seaport Café** • 89 South St [Beekman]
- **Seattle Coffee Roasters** • 110 William St [John]
- **Starbucks** • 1 Battery Park Plz [B'way]
- **Starbucks** • 100 Wall St [Water]
- **Starbucks** • 100 William St [Platt]
- **Starbucks** • 110 Pearl St [William]
- **Starbucks** • 115 Broadway [Thames]
- **Starbucks** • 165 Broadway [Cortlandt]
- **Starbucks** • 195 Broadway [Dey]
- **Starbucks** • 2 Broadway [Beaver]
- **Starbucks** • 3 New York Plz [Broad]
- **Starbucks** • 45 Wall St [William]
- **Starbucks** • 55 Broad St [Beaver]
- **Starbucks** • 55 Liberty St [Nassau]
- **Starbucks** • 80 Pine St [Pearl]
- **Starbucks** • 85 West St [Vesey]

🌀 Farmers Markets

- **Bowling Green Greenmarket (Tues & Thurs 8 am–5 pm, Year Round)** • Battery Park Pl & Broadway
- **Cedar Street Greenmarket (Tues & Thurs 8 am–6 pm, Aug–Dec)** • Broadway & Cedar St
- **Downtown PATH (Tues & Thurs 8 am–6 pm Apr–Dec)** • Vesey St & Church St
- **South Street Seaport (Tues 8 am–5 pm May–Nov)** • Fulton b/w Water & Pearl Sts
- **Staten Island Ferry Whitehall Terminal (Tues 8 am–7 pm, Year Round)** • South St & Whitehall St

🔧 Hardware Stores

- **Dick's Hardware** • 9 Gold St [Maiden Ln]
- **Fulton Supply & Hardware** • 74 Fulton St [Edens Aly]
- **Whitehall Hardware** • 102 Greenwich St [Rector]
- **Wolff Hardware** • 75 Maiden Ln [William]

🍾 Liquor Stores

- **Famous Wines & Spirits** • 40 Exchange Pl [William]
- **Fulton Wines & Spirits** • 110 Fulton St [Dutch]
- **The Greene Grape Downtown** • 55 Liberty St [Nassau]
- **Maiden Lane Wines & Liquors** • 6 Maiden Ln [B'way]
- **New York Wine Exchange** • 9 Broadway [Morris]
- **Water Street Wine & Spirit** • 79 Pine St [Pearl]
- **West Street Wine & Spirits** • 56 West St [Rector]
- **West Street Wine & Spirits Outlet Inc** • 33 Rector St [Wash]

🛒 Supermarkets

- **Amish Market** • 17 Battery Pl [West St]
- **Associated** • 77 Fulton St [Front]
- **Jubilee Marketplace** • 99 John St [Cliff] ⊘

Map 1 · **Financial District**

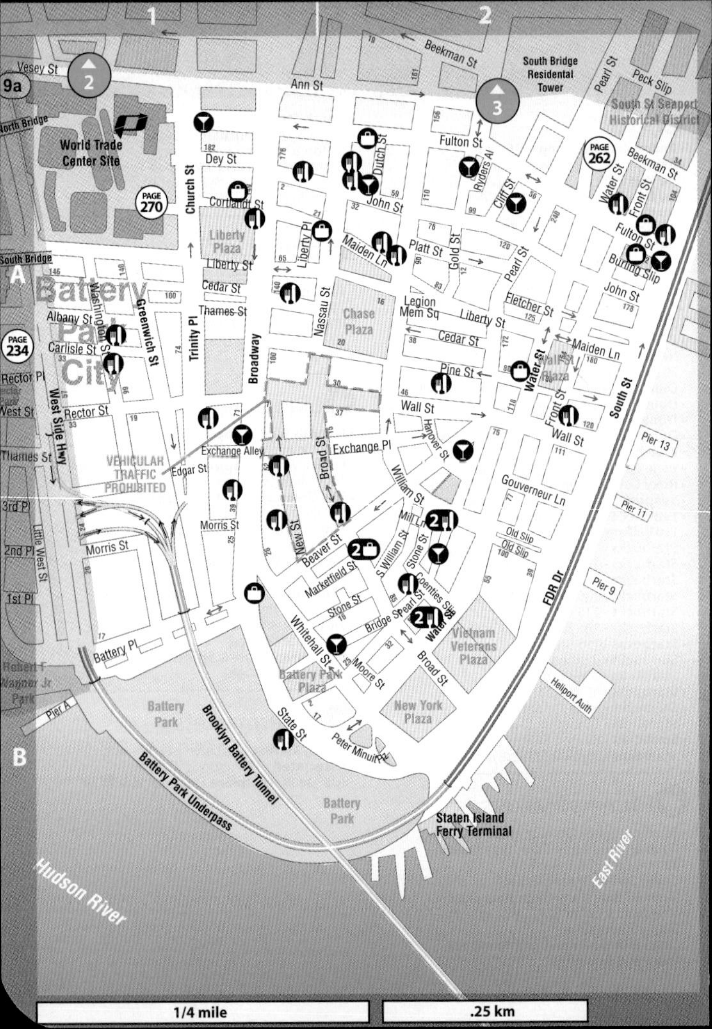

N

9a
PAGE 270
PAGE 234
PAGE 262

1

2

2

3

Vesey St
North Bridge
Ann St
Beekman St
South Bridge Residential Tower
Pearl St
Peck Slip
South St Seaport Historical District
Fulton St
Dey St
World Trade Center Site
Church St
Cortlandt St
Dutch St
John St
Ryders Al
Cliff St
Water St
Front St
Fulton St
Beekman St
Liberty Plaza
Liberty Pl
Maiden Ln
Platt St
Gold St
Pearl St
Burling Slip
Liberty St
Cedar St
Nassau St
Chase Plaza
John St
Thames St
Fletcher St
Maiden Ln
South St
Battery Park City
Albany St
Trinity Pl
Broadway
Legion Mem Sq
Liberty St
Water St
Carlisle St
Cedar St
Pine St
Rector Pl
West St
Rector St
Wall St
Front St
Wall St
Pier 13
Thames St
West Side Hwy
Exchange Alley
Exchange Pl
Hanover St
Pier 11
3rd Pl
Edgar St
Broad St
William St
Gouverneur Ln
FDR Dr
2nd Pl
Morris St
New St
Mill Ln
Old Slip
Pier 9
1st Pl
Morris St
Beaver St
S William St
Stone St
Old Slip
VEHICULAH TRAFFIC PROHIBITED
Marketfield St
Bridge St
Pearl St
Stone St
Whitehall St
S William St
Beaver St
Wall St
Battery Pl
Battery Park Plaza
Moore St
Broad St
Vietnam Veterans Plaza
Robert F Wagner Jr Park
Bridge St
Pier A
State St
New York Plaza
Heliport Auth
Peter Minuit Pl
Heliport Auth
Brooklyn Battery Tunnel
Battery Park
Battery Park Underpass
Battery Park
Staten Island Ferry Terminal
East River

Hudson River

East River

Not much of a destination for nightlife, but some life can be found around Stone Street, with Wall Street champs favoring Ulysses for after-work fun, and the Battery Gardens for upscale power lunching. Adrienne's raises the bar for pizza in the nabe, though the Grotto still satisfies for a quick slice.

🕶 Nightlife

- **Heartland Brewery** • 93 South St [Fulton]
- **John Street Bar & Grill** •
  17 John St [Nassau]
- **Killarney Rose** • 80 Beaver St [Pearl]
- **Liquid Assets** • Millennium Hilton Hotel • 55 Church St [Fulton]
- **Papoo's** • 55 Broadway [Exchange Aly]
- **Ryan Maguire's Ale House** •
  28 Cliff St [Fulton]
- **Ryan's Sports Bar & Restaurant** •
  46 Gold St [Fulton]
- **Ulysses** • 95 Pearl St [Hanover Sq]
- **Whitehorse Tavern** • 25 Bridge St [Whitehall]

🛍 Shopping

- **Barclay Rex** • 75 Broad St [S William]
- **Century 21** • 22 Cortlandt St [B'way]
- **Christopher Norman Chocolates** •
  60 New St [Exchange Pl]
- **Flowers of the World** • 80 Pine St [Pearl]
- **Godiva Chocolatier** • 33 Maiden Ln [Nassau]
- **Radio Shack** • 114 Fulton St [Dutch]
- **Radio Shack** • 9 Broadway [Morris]
- **South Street Seaport** • 19 Fulton St [South]
- **The World of Golf** • 74 Broad St [Marketfield]
- **Yankees Clubhouse Shop** • 8 Fulton St [South]

🍴 Restaurants

- **Adrienne's** • 54 Stone St [S William]
- **Battery Gardens** • Battery Park,
  across from 17 State St [Pearl]
- **Bayard's** • 1 Hanover Sq [Pearl]
- **Burritoville** • 36 Water St [Coenties Aly]
- **Cosi Sandwich Bar** • 54 Pine St [William]
- **Cosi Sandwich Bar** • 55 Broad St [Beaver]
- **Daily Soup** • 41 John St [Nassau]
- **Financier Patisserie** • 62 Stone St [Mill Ln]
- **Giovanni's Atrium** •
  100 Washington St [Rector]
- **Grotto Pizzeria** • 69 New St [Beaver]
- **Heartland Brewery** • 93 South St [Fulton]
- **Lemongrass Grill** • 84 William St [Maiden Ln]
- **Les Halles** • 15 John St [B'way]
- **Papoo's** • 55 Broadway [Exchange Aly]
- **Red** • 19 Fulton St [South]
- **Rosario's** • 38 Pearl St [Moore]
- **Roy's New York** • Marriott Financial Ctr • 130 Washington St [Albany]
- **Sophie's** • 73 New St [Beaver]
- **St Maggie's Café** • 120 Wall St [Front]
- **Zaitzeff** • 72 Nassau St [John]
- **Zeytuna** • 59 Maiden Ln [William]

Map 1 · **Financial District**

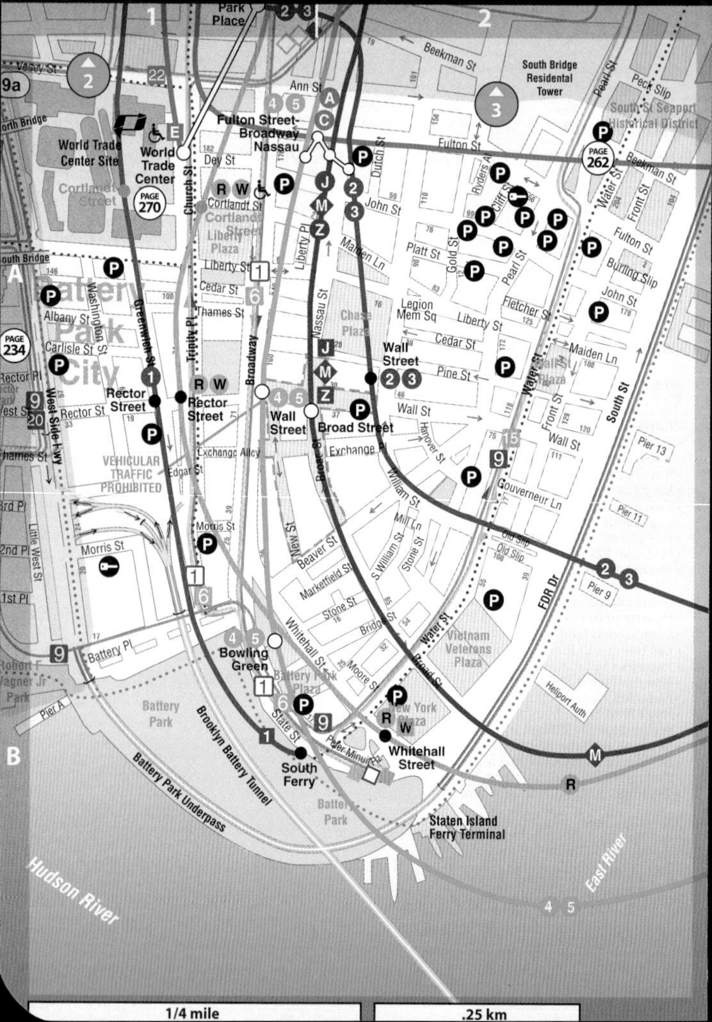

N

Park Place

Beekman St

South Bridge Residential Tower

South St Seaport Historical District

9a

2

Vesey St

22

North Bridge

Ann St

Fulton Street-Broadway Nassau

Dey St

World Trade Center Site

E

World Trade Center
PAGE 270

R W

Cortlandt St

Cortlandt Library Plaza

Liberty St

Cedar St

Thames St

Fulton St

PAGE 262

Water St

Front St

Beekman St

Peck Slip

Pearl St

Dutch St

John St

Ryders Alley

Cliff St

Gold St

Platt St

Fulton St

Burling Slip

Fletcher St

John St

Maiden Ln

Legion Mem Sq

Liberty St

Cedar St

Pine St

Pearl St

Chase Plaza

Maiden Ln

PAGE 234

Battery Park City

Albany St

Carlisle St

Rector St

Rector Place

R W

Rector Street

West St

Rector St

West St

Greenwich St

Trinity Pl

Thames St

3rd Pl

VEHICULAR TRAFFIC PROHIBITED

Edgar St

Exchange Alley

Broadway

Nassau St

Wall Street

Broad Street

J M Z

Wall Street

2 3

Pine St

Wall St

William St

Front St

South St

Pier 13

Maiden Ln

Water St

Gouverneur Ln

Pier 11

2 3

Pier 9

FDR Dr

2nd Pl

1st Pl

Morris St

Morris St

Beaver St

Marketfield St

Stone St

S William St

Mill Ln

Stone St

Bridge St

Whitehall St

Water St

Old Slip

Vietnam Veterans Plaza

Helipad

Heliport Auth

9

Battery Pl

Robert F Wagner Jr

Pier A

Bowling Green

4 5

Battery Park Plaza

State St

1

New York Plaza

R W

Whitehall Street

Battery Park Underpass

Brooklyn Battery Tunnel

Pier Minuets

9

South Ferry

1

Battery Park

Staten Island Ferry Terminal

M

R

4 5

Hudson River

East River

| 1/4 mile | .25 km |

Transportation

Attempting to drive—or park—during the day can be maddening, but you can check out the lots underneath the FDR if you really must. Subways are, as usual, your best bet. The plans for the new transit hub on Fulton Street become less grand with every hour.

Subways

1 .... Rector St
1 .... South Ferry
2 **3** .... Wall St
4 **5** .... Bowling Green
4 **5** .... Wall St
2 **3** **4** **5** **A** **C** **J** **M** **Z** .... Fulton St-Broadway-Nassau St
E .... World Trade Center
J **M** **Z** .... Broad St
R **W** .... Rector St
R **W** .... Whitehall St-South Ferry

 PATH

• World Trade Center Site

Bus Lines

1 .... Fifth/Madison Aves
15 .... First/Second Aves
20 .. Riverdale/246th St via Henry Hudson Pky
22 .... Madison/Chambers St
6 .... Seventh Ave/Broadway/Sixth Ave
9 .... Ave B/East Broadway

Bike Lanes

• • • • Recommended Route

• • • • Greenway

 Car Rental

• **Enterprise** • 56 Fulton St [Cliff]
• **Hertz** • 20 Morris St [Wash]

Parking

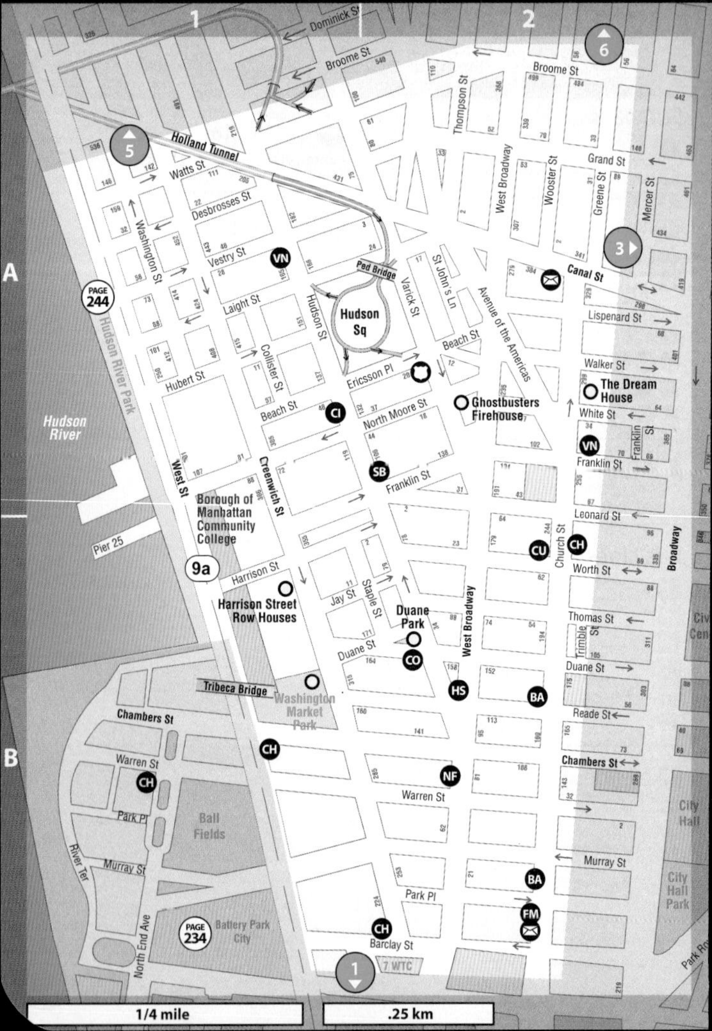

Map 2 · **TriBeCa**

Dominick St

Broome St

Holland Tunnel

Watts St

Desbrosses St

Vestry St

Laight St

Hudson Sq

Collister St

Hubert St

Beach St

Greenwich St

Borough of Manhattan Community College

Harrison St

Harrison Street Row Houses

Duane Park

Tribeca Bridge

Washington Market Park

Chambers St

Warren St

Park Pl

Murray St

Ball Fields

Battery Park City

North End Ave

River Ter

Broome St

Thompson St

West Broadway

Wooster St

Greene St

Mercer St

Grand St

Canal St

Lispenard St

Walker St

The Dream House

White St

Franklin St

Franklin St

Leonard St

Church St

Broadway

Worth St

Thomas St

Trimble

Duane St

Reade St

Chambers St

Warren St

Murray St

Park Pl

Barclay St

7 WTC

Civic Cen

City Hall

City Hall Park

St John's Ln

Varick St

Beach St

Avenue of the Americas

Ericsson Pl

North Moore St

Ghostbusters Firehouse

Franklin St

West Broadway

Jay St

Staple St

Duane St

Hudson St

1/4 mile   .25 km

Two luxuries most New Yorkers lack make the Triangle-Below-Canal sing: lofts and families. While you're waiting for your record to go platinum and The Right Person to divvy out a series of lifetime one-liners, roll by, stay, and gawk. You'll find your own luxurious tune someday, rockstar.

Banks

BA • Bank of America • 100 Church St [Park Pl]
BA • Bank of America (ATM) •
168 Church St [Reade St]
CH • Chase • 101 Barclay St [Greenwich St]
CH • Chase • 65 Worth St [Church St]
CH • Chase (ATM) • 199 Chambers St [West St]
CH • Chase (ATM) • Duane Reade •
325 N End Ave [Warren St]
CI • Citibank • 127 Hudson St [Beach St]
CO • Commerce • 25 Hudson St [Duane St]
EM • Emigrant • 110 Church St [Park Pl]
HS • HSBC • 110 West Broadway [Reade St]
CU • Municipal Credit Union (ATM) •
40 Worth St [Church St]
NF • North Fork •
90 West Broadway [Chambers St]
SB • Sovereign • 108 Hudson St [Franklin St]
VN • Valley National • 170 Hudson St [Vestry St]
VN • Valley National • 90 Franklin St [Church St]

Landmarks

• **The Dream House** • 275 Church St [White]
• **Duane Park** • Duane St & Hudson St
• **Ghostbusters Firehouse** •
14 N Moore St [Varick]
• **Harrison Street Row Houses** •
Harrison St & Greenwich St
• **Washington Market Park** •
Greenwich St [Chambers]

 Police

• **1st Precinct** • 16 Ericsson Pl [Varick]

Post Offices

• **Canal Street** • 350 Canal St [Church]
• **Church Street** • 90 Church St [Barclay]

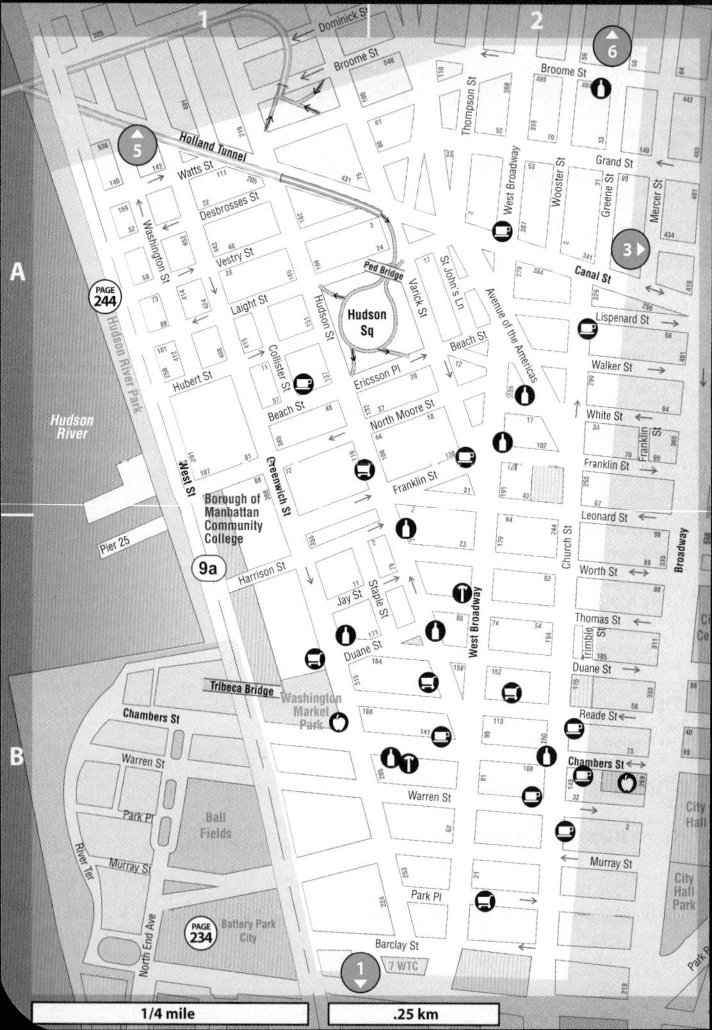

Map 2 · TriBeCa

1

2

6

5

Dominick St

Broome St

Holland Tunnel

Broome St

Watts St

Grand St

Thompson St

West Broadway

Wooster St

Greene St

Mercer St

Desbrosses St

Vestry St

Canal St

3

Ped Bridge

Varick St

St John's Ln

Avenue of the Americas

Lispenard St

Laight St

Hudson Sq

Walker St

Hudson St

Beach St

White St

Collister St

Ericsson Pl

Franklin St

Beach St

North Moore St

Franklin St

Leonard St

Greenwich St

Borough of Manhattan Community College

Harrison St

Worth St

Church St

Broadway

Pier 25

Hudson River

Hudson River Park

N St

9a

Jay St

Staple St

Duane St

Thomas St

Trimble Pl

Duane St

West Broadway

Tribeca Bridge

Washington Market Park

Reade St

Chambers St

Chambers St

Warren St

Warren St

Murray St

Park Pl

Ball Fields

River Ter

Park Pl

Murray St

City Hall

City Hall Park

North End Ave

Battery Park City

Barclay St

7 WTC

1

PAGE 244

PAGE 234

1/4 mile

.25 km

A

B

A well served area, though stores are scarce as you get closer to the Holland Tunnel. Fresh produce is no problem for much of the year, with farmers markets on Wednesdays and Saturdays in Washington Market Park, along with a Friday one in City Hall Park.

Coffee

- **Dunkin' Donuts** • 100 Chambers St [Church]
- **Dunkin' Donuts** • 130 Church St [Murray]
- **Dunkin' Donuts** • 381 Canal St [W B'way]
- **Pecan** • 130 Franklin St [W B'way]
- **Starbucks** • 125 Chambers St [W B'way]
- **Westside Coffee Shop II** •
  323 Church St [Lispenard]
- **Zoie's Coffee Shop** • 49 Beach St [Collister]

Farmers Markets

- **City Hall Park (Fri 8am–5pm, Jun–Nov)** •
  Broadway b/w Chambers St & Warren St
- **Tribeca (Wed 8 am–3 pm, Apr–Dec;
  Sat 8 am–3 pm, Year Round)** •
  Greenwich St b/w Chambers & Duane

Hardware Stores

- **Ace Hardware** •
  160 West Broadway [Worth]
- **Tribeca Hardware True Value** •
  154 Chambers St [W B'way]

Liquor Stores

- **Brite Buy Wines & Spirits** •
  11 Sixth Ave [White]
- **Chambers Street Wines** •
  160 Chambers St [Greenwich St]
- **City Hall Wines & Spirits** •
  108 Chambers St [Church]
- **Downtown Liquor Store** •
  90 Hudson St [Leonard]
- **Hudson Wine & Spirits** •
  165 Hudson St [Laight]
- **Tribeca Wine Merchants (Wine only)** •
  40 Hudson St [Duane]
- **Tribeca Wines** • 327 Greenwich St [Duane]
- **Vinovino** • 211 West Broadway [Franklin]
- **Vintage New York (Wine only)** •
  482 Broome St [Wooster]

Supermarkets

- **Amish Market** • 53 Park Pl [W B'way]
- **Bell Bates Natural Foods** •
  97 Reade St [Church]
- **Food Emporium** • 316 Greenwich St [Duane]
- **Jin Market** • 111 Hudson St [N Moore] ⊘
- **Morgan's Market** • 13 Hudson St [Reade]

Map 2 · **TriBeCa**

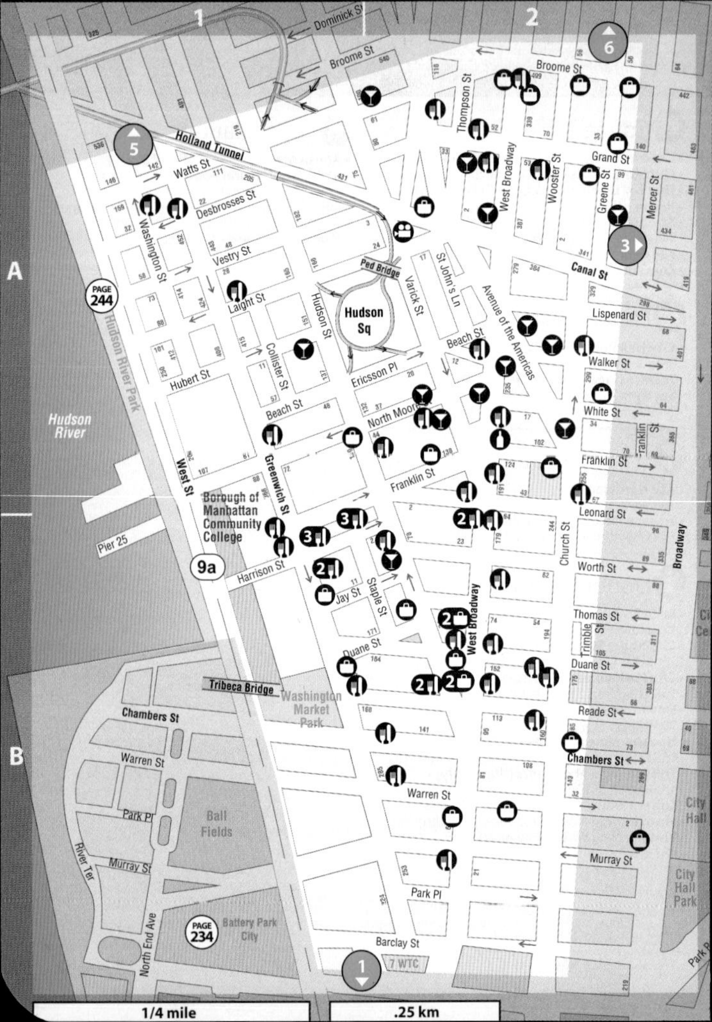

1

2

6

5 Holland Tunnel

Dominick St

Broome St

Broome St

Grand St

Thompson St

West Broadway

Wooster St

Greene St

Mercer St

Watts St

Desbrosses St

Vestry St

Canal St

3

Laight St

Hudson St

Collister St

Hubert St

Beach St

Greenwich St

Ericsson Pl

North Moore St

Franklin St

West St

Washington St

Varick St

St John's Ln

Beach St

Avenue of the Americas

Lispenard St

Walker St

White St

Franklin St

Leonard St

Worth St

Franklin St

Broadway

Hudson Sq

Ped Bridge

PAGE 244

Hudson River

Hudson River Park

Pier 25

9a

Borough of Manhattan Community College

Harrison St

3

3

2

2

2

Staple St

Jay St

Duane St

West Broadway

2

2

2

Church St

Thomas St

Trimble Pl

Duane St

Reade St

Chambers St

Tribeca Bridge

Washington Market Park

Chambers St

Warren St

Park Pl

Ball Fields

Murray St

River Ter

Warren St

Murray St

City Hall

City Hall Park

2

Park Pl

Barclay St

PAGE 234

Battery Park City

North End Ave

1

7 WTC

1/4 mile

.25 km

A

B

For arts, TriBeCa rocks—the film festival every year, the MELA Foundation's "Dream House," several galleries, and experimental music at Roulette. Stalwart bars such as Puffy's and Walker's can effectively wet your whistle while you're waiting to win the lotto so you can eat at Nobu.

 Movie Theaters

- **Tribeca Cinemas** • 54 Varick St [Laight]
- **Makor** • 200 Hudson St [Vestry]

Nightlife

- **Brandy Library** • 25 N Moore St [W B'way]
- **Bubble Lounge** • 228 West Broadway [White]
- **Church Lounge** • Tribeca Grand Hotel • 25 Walker St [Church]
- **Circa Tabac** • 32 Watts St [Sullivan]
- **Lucky Strike** • 59 Grand St [W B'way]
- **Naked Lunch** • 17 Thompson St [Grand]
- **Nancy Whisky Pub** • 1 Lispenard St [W B'way]
- **Puffy's Tavern** • 81 Hudson St [Harrison]
- **Roulette** • 20 Greene St [Canal]
- **Soho Grand Hotel** • 310 West Broadway [Canal]
- **The Tank** • 279 Church St [White St]
- **Tribeca Tavern & Café** • 247 West Broadway [Beach]
- **Walker's** • 16 N Moore St [W B'way]

Restaurants

- **Acapella** • 1 Hudson St [Chambers St]
- **Azafran** • 77 Warren St [W B'way]
- **Bouley** • 120 West Broadway [Duane]
- **Bread Tribeca** • 301 Church St [Walker]
- **Bubby's** • 120 Hudson St [N Moore]
- **Café Noir** • 32 Grand St [Thompson]
- **Capsouto Freres** • 451 Washington St [Watts]
- **Centrico** • 211 West Broadway [Franklin]
- **Chanterelle** • 2 Harrison St [Hudson]
- **City Hall** • 131 Duane St [Church]
- **Cupping Room Café** • 359 West Broadway [Broome]
- **Danube** • 30 Hudson St [Duane]
- **Duane Park Café** • 157 Duane St [Hudson]
- **Dylan Prime** • 62 Laight St [Greenwich St]
- **Edward's** • 136 West Broadway [Duane]
- **Estancia 460** • 460 Greenwich St [Watts]
- **Flor de Sol** • 361 Greenwich St [Harrison]
- **fresh** • 105 Reade St [W B'way]
- **The Harrison** • 355 Greenwich St [Harrison]
- **Il Giglio** • 81 Warren St [Greenwich St]
- **Ivy's Bistro** • 385 Greenwich St [N Moore]
- **Kitchenette** • 156 Chambers St [Centre]
- **Kori** • 253 Church St [Leonard]
- **Landmarc** • 179 West Broadway [Leonard]
- **Lupe's East LA Kitchen** •

110 Sixth Ave [Sullivan]

- **Montrachet** • 239 West Broadway [White]
- **Nobu** • 105 Hudson St [Franklin]
- **Nobu, Next Door** • 105 Hudson St [Franklin]
- **Odeon** • 145 West Broadway [Thomas]
- **Pakistan Tea House** • 176 Church St [Reade]
- **Palacinka** • 28 Grand St [Thompson]
- **Square Diner** • 33 Leonard St [W B'way]
- **Thalassa** • 179 Franklin St [Hudson]
- **Tribeca Grill** • 375 Greenwich St [Franklin]
- **Viet Café** • 345 Greenwich St [Jay]
- **Walker's** • 16 N Moore St [W B'way]
- **Yaffa's** • 353 Greenwich St [Harrison]
- **Zutto** • 77 Hudson St [Harrison]

Shopping

- **Babylicious** • 51 Hudson St [Thomas]
- **Balloon Saloon** • 133 West Broadway [Duane]
- **Bazzini** • 339 Greenwich St [Jay]
- **Boffi SoHo** • 31 1/2 Greene St [Grand]
- **Canal Street Bicycles** • 417 Canal St [6th Av]
- **Duane Park Patisserie** • 179 Duane St [Staple]
- **Gotham Bikes** • 112 West Broadway [Duane]
- **Issey Miyake** • 119 Hudson St [N Moore]
- **Jack Spade** • 56 Greene St [Broome]
- **Janovic** • 136 Church St [Warren]
- **Kings Pharmacy** • 5 Hudson St [Chambers]
- **Korin Japanese Trading** • 57 Warren St [W B'way]
- **Let There Be Neon** • 38 White St [Church]
- **Lucky Brand Dungarees** • 38 Greene St [Grand]
- **MarieBelle's Fine Treats & Chocolates** • 484 Broome St [Wooster]
- **New York Nautical** • 158 Duane St [Thomas]
- **Oliver Peoples** • 366 West Broadway [Watts]
- **Shoofly** • 42 Hudson St [Thomas]
- **Steven Alan** • 103 Franklin St [Church]
- **Urban Archaeology** • 143 Franklin St [W B'way]
- **We Are Nuts About Nuts** • 165 Church St [Chambers]
- **What Comes Around Goes Around** • 351 West Broadway [Broome]
- **Willner Chemists** • 253 Broadway [Murray]

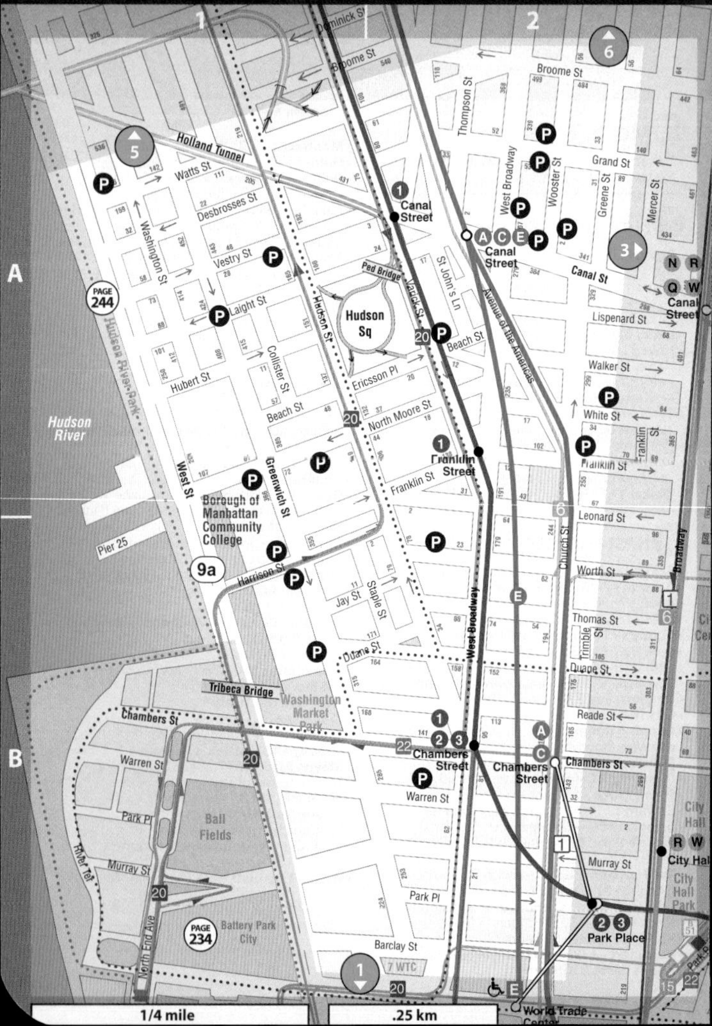

Map 2 · **TriBeCa**

N

2

6

Minnick St

Broome St

Holland Tunnel

5

Watts St

P

Thompson St

Broome St

West Broadway

Wooster St

Grand St

P

P

Greene St

Mercer St

Desbrosses St

Washington St

Vestry St

Canal
Street

P

St John's Ln

A C E
Canal
Street

P

P

P

3

N R
Q W
Canal
Street

Laight St

P

Hudson
Sq

Ped Bridge

Avenue of the Americas

Lispenard St

Walker St

White St

P

Collister St

Hubert St

Beach St

Ericsson Pl

North Moore St

20

Beach St

20

Franklin St

Franklin St

Franklin
Street

Leonard St

Church St

P

Greenwich St

P

West St

Borough of
Manhattan
Community
College

P

Harrison St

P

Jay St

Staple St

P

Worth St

E

Thomas St

Trimble Pl

9a

Pier 25

Hudson River Park

Hudson River

PAGE
244

Duane St

P

Tribeca Bridge

Chambers St

Washington
Market
Park

Chambers
Street

22

1

2 3

A
C
Chambers
Street

Chambers St

Warren St

Warren St

P

Reade St

Ball
Fields

20

Park Pl

Murray St

Murray St

1

R W
City Hall

City
Hall

City
Hall
Park

20

PAGE
234

Park Pl

Battery Park
City

Barclay St

1

20

7 WTC

2 3
Park Place

E

World Trade

Ce

1/4 mile   .25 km

Transportation

Moving around and parking in TriBeCa, especially in its northwest corner, isn't too bad. But the closer you get to City Hall and the WTC site the more of a pain it is to find anything, especially during the week. Still, it's a lot better than many other NYC neighborhoods.

Subways

2 3 .... Park Pl
1 2 3 .... Chambers St
1 ....Canal St
1 .... Franklin St
A C .... Chambers St
A C E .... Canal St
R W .... City Hall

Bus Lines

1 .... Broadway
20 .... Abingdon Sq
22 .... Seventh Ave/Sixth Ave/Broadway
6 .... Seventh Ave/Broadway/Sixth Ave

Bike Lanes

- • • • Recommended Route
- • • • Greenway

 Parking

21

Map 3 • **City Hall / Chinatown**

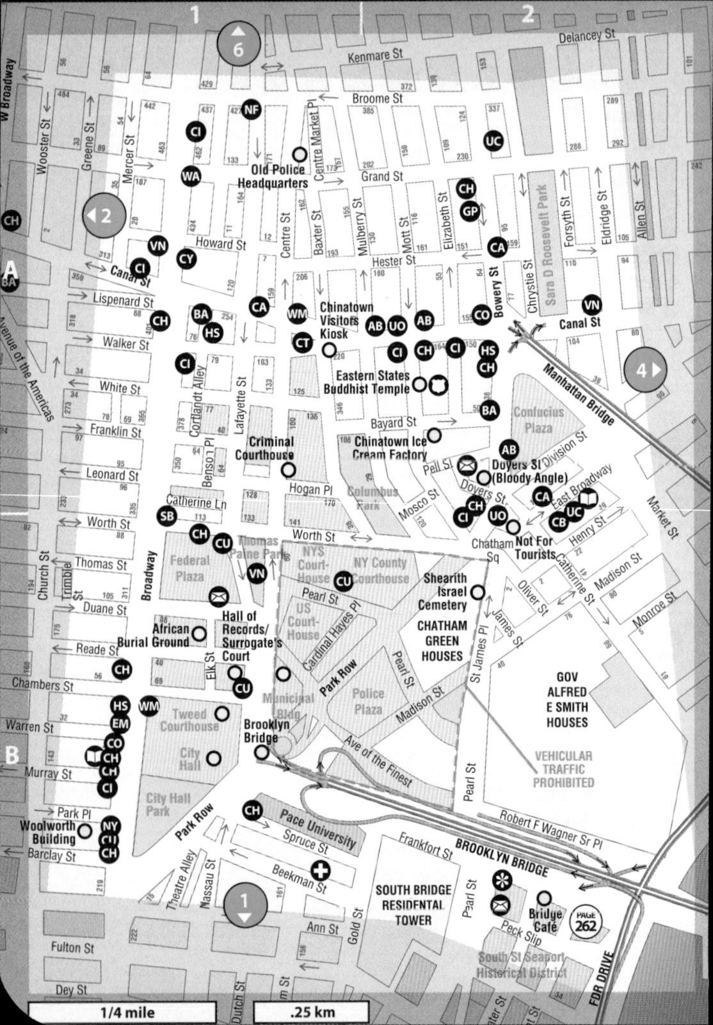

6

Delancey St

Kenmare St

Broome St

Central Market Pl

NF

CI

WA

Old Police
Headquarters

Grand St

UC

2

W Broadway

Wooster St

Greene St

Mercer St

429

484

442

437

463

462

187

133

372

385

202

230

337

289

292

CH

GP

Howard St

VN

CI

CY

12

Centre St

Baxter St

Mulberry St

Mott St

Elizabeth St

Hester St

165

151

CA

Bowery St

Chrystie St

Forsyth St

Eldridge St

Allen St

Sara D Roosevelt Park

A

CH

BA

Canal St

Lispenard St

BA

HS

CA

Chinatown
Visitors
Kiosk

WM

CT

AB

UO

AB

CI

CH

HS

CH

VN

Canal St

Walker St

CH

CI

White St

Cortlandt Alley

Benson Pl

193

125

136

266

Eastern States
Buddhist Temple

Manhattan Bridge

Franklin St

Lafayette St

Leonard St

Worth St

Bayard St

Chinatown Ice
Cream Factory

Pell St

BA

Confucius
Plaza

Division St

Criminal
Courthouse

Columbus
Park

Mosco St

Hogan Pl

AB

Doyers St
(Bloody Angle)

East Broadway

Market St

SB

Catherine Ln

113

128

141

Worth St

Chatham
Sq

CI

CH

UO

CI

CB

UC

Not For
Tourists

Henry St

CU

Thomas
Paine Park

NYS
Court-
House

VN

NY County
Courthouse

CU

Shearith
Israel
Cemetery

Pearl St

Catherine St

Madison St

Monroe St

African
Burial Ground

Hall of
Records/
Surrogate's
Court

US
Court-House

Cardinal Hayes Pl

Park Row

CHATHAM
GREEN
HOUSES

James St

St James Pl

Broadway

Elk St

Pearl St

Police
Plaza

Madison St

GOV
ALFRED
E SMITH
HOUSES

Oliver St

CH

Chambers St

HS

EM

CO

CH

CH

CI

WM

Tweed
Courthouse

CU

Municipal
Bldg

Brooklyn
Bridge

Ave of the Finest

Robert F Wagner Sr Pl

VEHICULAR
TRAFFIC
PROHIBITED

B

Warren St

Murray St

Park Pl

Woolworth
Building

NY
CI
CI

City Hall

City Hall
Park

Park Row

CH

Pace University

Spruce St

BROOKLYN BRIDGE

Pearl St

Theatre Alley

Nassau St

Beekman St

Frankfort St

SOUTH BRIDGE
RESIDENTAL
TOWER

Peck Slip

Bridge
Café

PAGE
262

1

Fulton St

Ann St

Gold St

William St

South St Seaport
Historical District

FDR DRIVE

Dey St

Dutch St

| 1/4 mile | | .25 km | |

The post office on Doyers Street always has a hellish line—it's worth going somewhere else. Canal Street is the major tourist site, but it's where we buy our $10 knock-offs. Columbus Park recently received a nice makeover and remains New York's Chinese Chess "hotspot." Head to East Broadway under the Manhattan Bridge to see the real Chinatown.

$ Banks

AB • Abacus • 181 Canal St [Mott St]
AB • Abacus • 6 Bowery [Doyers St]
BA • Bank of America • 260 Canal St [Lafayette]
BA • Bank of America • 261 Broadway [Warren]
BA • Bank of America • 50 Bayard St [Elizabeth]
NY • Bank of New York • 233 Broadway [Park]
CY • Cathay • 129 Lafayette St [Howard St]
CY • Cathay • 16 East Broadway [Catherine St]
CY • Cathay • 45 East Broadway [Market St]
CH • Chase • 180 Canal St [Mott St]
CH • Chase • 2 Bowery [Doyers St]
CH • Chase • 231 Grand St [Bowery]
CH • Chase • 253 Broadway [Murray St]
CH • Chase • 280 Broadway [Reade St]
CH • Chase • 407 Broadway [Lispenard St]
CH • Chase (ATM) • 1 Pace Plz [Spruce St]
CH • Chase (ATM) • 111 Worth St [Lafayette St]
CH • Chase (ATM) • 250 Broadway [Murray St]
CH • Chase (ATM) • 280 Broadway [Reade St]
CH • Chase (ATM) • 305 Broadway [Duane St]
CH • Chase (ATM) • 50 Bowery [Canal St]
CH • Chase (ATM) • 233 Broadway [Park Pl]
CT • Chinatrust • 208 Canal St [Mulberry St]
CI • Citibank • 164 Canal St [Elizabeth St]
CI • Citibank • 184 Canal St [Mott St]
CI • Citibank • 2 Mott St [Chatham Sq]
CI • Citibank • 250 Broadway [Murray St]
CI • Citibank • 309 Canal St [Mercer St]
CI • Citibank • 476 Broadway [Broome St]
CI • Citibank (ATM) • 396 Broadway [Walker St]
CO • Commerce • 155 Canal St [Bowery]
CO • Commerce • 258 Broadway [Warren St]
EM • Emigrant • 261 Broadway [Chambers St]
HS • HSBC • 11 East Broadway [Catherine St]
HS • HSBC • 254 Canal St [Lafayette St]
HS • HSBC • 265 Broadway [Lispenard St]
HS • HSBC • 58 Bowery [Canal St]
CU • Lower East Side People's Federal Credit Union (ATM) • 26 Federal Plz [Worth St]
CU • Municipal Credit Union • 2 Lafayette St [Reade St]
NF • North Fork • 116 Bowery [Grand St]
NF • North Fork • 200 Lafayette St [Broome St]
SB • Sovereign • 336 Broadway [Worth St]
UC • United Commercial • 131 Bowery [Grand]
UC • United Commercial • 245 Canal St [Lafayette St]
UC • United Commercial • 27 East Broadway [Catherine St]
UC • United Commercial • 77 Bowery [Canal St]
UO • United Orient • 10 Chatham Sq [Catherine St]
UO • United Orient • 185 Canal St [Mott St]
CU • US Courthouse Federal Credit Union • 233 Broadway [Barclay St]
CU • US Courthouse Federal Credit Union (ATM) • 500 Pearl St [Centre St]
VN • Valley National • 434 Broadway [Howard]
VN • Valley National • 93 Canal St [Eldridge St]
WA • Wachovia • 463 Broadway [Grand St]
WM • WaMu • 221 Canal St [Baxter St]
WM • WaMu • 270 Broadway [Chambers St]

✿ Community Gardens

➕ Emergency Rooms

• **NYU Downtown** • 170 William St [Ann]

○ Landmarks

• **African Burial Ground** • Duane St & Broadway
• **Bridge Café** • 279 Water St [Dover]
• **Brooklyn Bridge** • Chambers St & Centre St
• **Chinatown Ice Cream Factory** • 65 Bayard St
• **Chinatown Visitors Kiosk** • Canal & Baxter
• **City Hall** • Park Row & Broadway
• **Criminal Courthouse** • 100 Centre St
• **Doyers Street (Bloody Angle)** • Doyers St
• **Eastern States Buddhist Temple** • 64 Mott St
• **Hall of Records/Surrogate's Court** • Chambers St & Park Row
• **Municipal Building** • Chambers St & Park Row
• **Not For Tourists** • 2 East Broadway
• **Old Police Headquarters** • 240 Centre St
• **Shearith Israel Cemetery** • 55 St James Pl
• **Tweed Courthouse** • Chambers St & Broadway
• **Woolworth Building** • 233 Broadway [Park Pl]

📖 Libraries

• **Chatham Square** • 33 E Broadway [Catherine]
• **New Amsterdam** • 9 Murray St [Broadway]

👮 Police

• **5th Precinct** • 19 Elizabeth St [Canal]

✉ Post Offices

• **Chinatown** • 6 Doyers St [Bowery]
• **Peck Slip** • 1 Peck Slip [Pearl]
• **Federal Plaza** • 26 Federal Plz [Worth St]

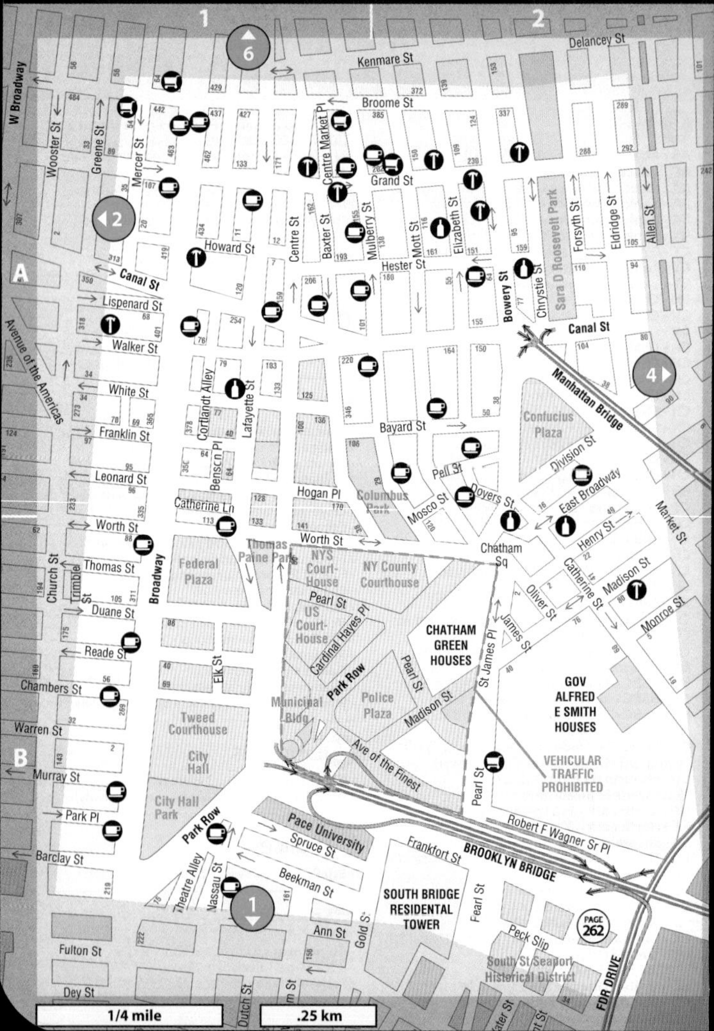

Map 3 · **City Hall / Chinatown**

N

1   2

6

Kenmare St

Delancey St

W Broadway

Wooster St

Greene St

Mercer St

Broome St

Centre Market Pl

Grand St

Centre St

Baxter St

Mulberry St

Mott St

Elizabeth St

Bowery St

Chrystie St

Forsyth St

Eldridge St

Allen St

Sara D Roosevelt Park

2

Howard St

A

Canal St

Lispenard St

Walker St

White St

Franklin St

Leonard St

Worth St

Cortlandt Alley

Benson Pl

Lafayette St

Hester St

Bayard St

Pell St

Mosco St

Doyers St

Hogan Pl

Columbus

Canal St

Manhattan Bridge

4

Confucius Plaza

Division St

East Broadway

Henry St

Market St

Avenue of the Americas

Church St

Trimble Pl

Broadway

Thomas St

Duane St

Reade St

Chambers St

Warren St

Catherine Ln

Federal Plaza

Thomas Paine Park

NYS Court-House

NY County Courthouse

Pearl St

US Court-House

Cardinal Hayes Pl

Park Row

Elk St

Worth St

Chatham Sq

Catherine St

Madison St

Monroe St

Oliver St

James St

St James Pl

CHATHAM GREEN HOUSES

Police Plaza

Madison St

GOV ALFRED E SMITH HOUSES

B

Murray St

Park Pl

Barclay St

Tweed Courthouse

City Hall

City Hall Park

Municipal Bldg

Pearl St

Ave of the Finest

VEHICULAR TRAFFIC PROHIBITED

Park Row

Theatre Alley

Nassau St

Pace University

Spruce St

Beekman St

Ann St

Gold St

Fulton St

Dutch St

Dey St

1

SOUTH BRIDGE RESIDENTIAL TOWER

Frankfort St

BROOKLYN BRIDGE

Robert F Wagner Sr Pl

Pearl St

Peck Slip

Fearl St

South St Seaport Historical District

FDR DRIVE

PAGE 262

1/4 mile   .25 km

Sundries

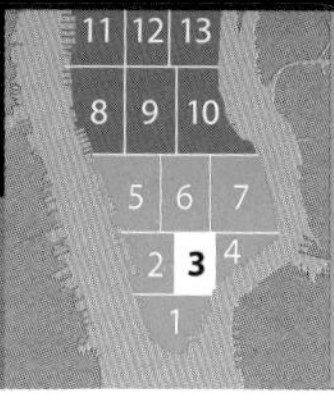

11 12 13
8 9 10
5 6 7
2 **3** 4
1

Map 3

The Bowery is still the epicenter of discount kitchen supplies and lighting fixtures and you'll find some good hardware stores here. Café life is quite alive here, with your choice of Little Italy, "NoLita," and Chinatown versions.

Coffee

- **Blue Spoon Coffee** • 76 Chambers St [B'way]
- **Café Palermo** • 148 Mulberry St [Grand]
- **Caffe Del Arte** • 143 Mulberry St [Grand]
- **Dunkin' Donuts** • 132 Nassau St [Beekman]
- **Dunkin' Donuts** • 250 Broadway [Murray]
- **Dunkin' Donuts** • 321 Broadway [Thomas]
- **Dunkin' Donuts** • 42 Mulberry St [Mosco]
- **Ferrara Café** • 195 Grand St [Mulberry]
- **Green Tea Café** • 45 Mott St [Bayard]
- **Ho Wong Coffee House** • 146 Hester St [Elizabeth]
- **Kam Hing Coffee Shop** • 119 Baxter St [Hester]
- **Los Punito Café** • 117 Mulberry St [Hester]
- **Mee Sum Coffee Shop** • 26 Pell St [Doyers]
- **Mei Lai Wah Coffee House** • 64 Bayard St [Mott]
- **Miro Café** • 474 Broadway [Grand]
- **Nom Wah Tea Parlor** • 13 Doyers St [Chatham Sq]
- **Qq Café** • 50 East Broadway [Market]
- **Sambuca's Café & Desserts** • 105 Mulberry St [Canal]
- **Starbucks** • 111 Worth St [Lafayette]
- **Starbucks** • 233 Broadway [Park Pl]
- **Starbucks** • 241 Canal St [Centre]
- **Starbucks** • 291 Broadway [Reade]
- **Starbucks** • 38 Park Row [Beekman]
- **Starbucks** • 405 Broadway [Walker]
- **Starbucks** • 471 Broadway [Grand]
- **Ten Ren Tea Time** • 79 Mott St [Canal]

Liquor Stores

- **Chez Choi Liquor & Wine** • 49 Chrystie St [Hester]
- **Elizabeth Street Wine & Liquor** • 86 Elizabeth St [Hester]
- **Sun Wai Liquor Store** • 17 East Broadway [Catherine St]
- **Walker Liquors** • 101 Lafayette St [Walker]
- **Wine Wo Liquor Discount** • 12 Chatham Sq [E B'way]

Supermarkets

- **C-Town** • 5 St James Pl [Pearl]
- **Gourmet Garage** • 453 Broome St [Mercer]
- **Italian Food Center** • 186 Grand St [Mulberry]

Hardware Stores

- **Centre Plumbing & Hardware Supply** • 233 Centre St [Grand]
- **Design Source** • 115 Bowery [Grand]
- **Eastern Tool & Supply** • 428 Broadway [Howard]
- **Karlee Hardware** • 98 Madison St [Catherine St]
- **Kessler Hardware & MFG** • 229 Grand St [Bowery]
- **Lendy Hardware** • 176 Grand St [Baxter]
- **OK Hardware** • 438 Broome St [B'way]
- **T&Y Hardware** • 101 Chrystie St [Grand]
- **Walker Supply** • 61 Walker St [B'way]

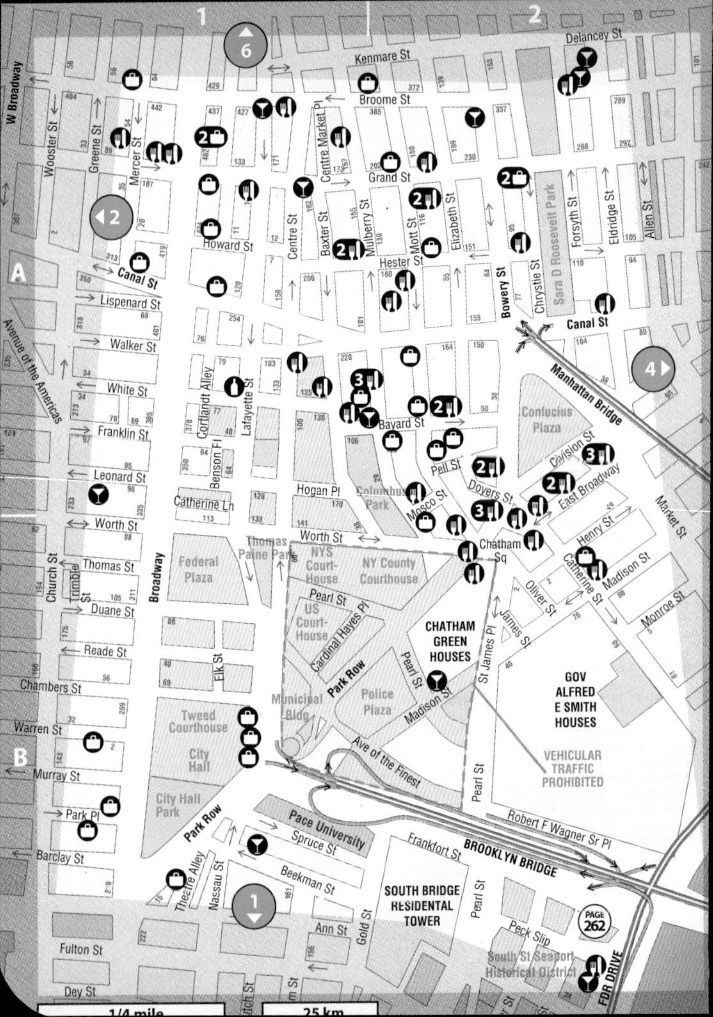

Map 3 · **City Hall / Chinatown**

The crab soup dumplings at Joe's Shanghai are essential Chinatown eats. For Vietnamese, Pho Viet Huong; Thai, Pongsri; Chinese, New Green Bo; Seafood, Fuleen; Banh Mi, Saigon (in the back of a jewelry store of course). If you're not in the mood for Asian, try the greasy grub at Cup & Saucer. Four words for dessert: Chinatown Ice Cream Factory.

Nightlife

- **The Beekman Pub** • 15 Beekman St [Nassau]
- **Capitale** • 130 Bowery [Grand]
- **Experimental Intermedia** • 224 Centre St [Grand]
- **Happy Ending** • 302 Broome St [Forsyth]
- **Knitting Factory** • 74 Leonard St [Church]
- **Martignetti Downstairs (Belgrade)** • 1 Cleveland Pl [Broome]
- **Metropolitan Improvement Company** • 3 Madison St [Ave of the Finest]
- **Milk & Honey** • 134 Eldridge St [Broome]
- **The Paris Café** • 119 South St [Peck Slip]
- **Winnie's** • 104 Bayard St [Mulberry]

Restaurants

- **Baby O Pizza** • 225 Park Row [Pearl St]
- **Big Wong King** • 67 Mott St [Bayard]
- **Bridge Café** • 279 Water St [Dover]
- **Buddha Boddhai** • 5 Mott St [Worth]
- **Cendrillon** • 45 Mercer St [Grand]
- **Cong Ly** • 124 Hester St [Chrystie]
- **Cup & Saucer** • 89 Canal St [Eldridge]
- **Despana** • 408 Broome St [Centre]
- **Dim Sum Go Go** • 5 East Broadway [Catherine St]
- **Drew's Place** • 100 Forsyth St [Broome]
- **East Corner Wonton** • 70 East Broadway [Market St]
- **Everest Pancake and Coffee House** • 22 Chatham Sq [E B'way]
- **Excellent Dumpling House** • 111 Lafayette St [Canal]
- **Food Shing** • 2 East Broadway [Chatham Sq]
- **Fried Dumpling** • 106 Mosco St [Mulberry]
- **Fuleen Seafood** • 11 Division St [Catherine St]
- **Il Palazzo** • 151 Mulberry St [Grand]
- **Joe's Shanghai** • 9 Pell St [Bowery]
- **L'Ecole** • 462 Broadway [Grand]
- **Le Pain Quotidien** • 100 Grand St [Mercer]
- **Mandarin Court** • 61 Mott St [Bayard]
- **Mark Joseph Steakhouse** • 261 Water St [Peck Slip]
- **May Wah Fast Food** • 190 Hester St [Baxter]
- **Mei Lai Wah Coffee House** • 64 Bayard St [Mott St]
- **New Green Bo Restaurant** • 66 Bayard St [Mott]
- **New York Noodle Town** • 28 Bowery [Bayard]
- **Nha Trang** • 87 Baxter St [White]
- **Parigot** • 155 Grand St [Lafayette]
- **The Paris Café** • 119 South St [Peck Slip]
- **Pho Viet Huong** • 73 Mulberry St [Bayard]
- **Ping's** • 22 Mott St [Mosco]
- **Pongsri Thai** • 106 Bayard St [Mulberry]
- **Positano** • 122 Mulberry St [Hester]
- **Saigon Banh Mi** • 138 Mott St [Grand]
- **Sanur Restaurant** • 18 Doyers St [Bowery]
- **Shing's Food Shop** • Catherine St b/w Madison St & Henry St
- **Triple Eight Palace** • 88 East Broadway [Forsyth]
- **Wo Hop** • 17 Mott St [Mosco]
- **Xin Jiang Kebab Cart** • Market St b/w Division St & East Broadway

Shopping

- **Aji Ichiban** • 167 Hester St [Mott]
- **Bangkok Center Grocery** • 104 Mosco St [Mulberry]
- **Catherine Street Meat Market** • 21 Catherine St [Henry]
- **The Changing Room** • 3 Centre St [Chambers]
- **Chinatown Ice Cream Factory** • 65 Bayard St [Mott]
- **Fay Da Bakery** • 83 Mott St [Canal]
- **Fountain Pen Hospital** • 10 Warren St [B'way]
- **GS Food Market** • 250 Grand St [Chrystie]
- **Hong Keung Seafood & Meat Market** • 75 Mulberry St [Bayard]
- **J&R Music & Computer World** • 33 Park Row [Beekman]
- **Kate Spade** • 454 Broome St [Mercer]
- **Lung Moon Bakery** • 83 Mulberry St [Canal]
- **Mitchell's Place** • 15 Park Pl [B'way]
- **New Age Designer** • 38 Mott St [Pell]
- **New Beef King** • 89 Bayard St [Mulberry]
- **The New York City Store** • 1 Centre St [Chambers]
- **No 6** • 6 Centre St [Chambers]
- **Opening Ceremony** • 35 Howard St [Crosby]
- **Papabubble** • 380 Broome St [Mulberry St]
- **Pearl Paint** • 308 Canal St [Mercer]
- **Pearl River Mart** • 477 Broadway [Broome]
- **SoHo Art Materials** • 127 Grand St [Crosby]
- **Tan My My Market** • 249 Grand St [Chrystie]
- **Tent & Trails** • 21 Park Pl [Church]
- **Unimax** • 269 Canal St [Cortlandt Aly]
- **Yellow Rat Bastard** • 478 Broadway [Broome]

Map 3 • City Hall / Chinatown

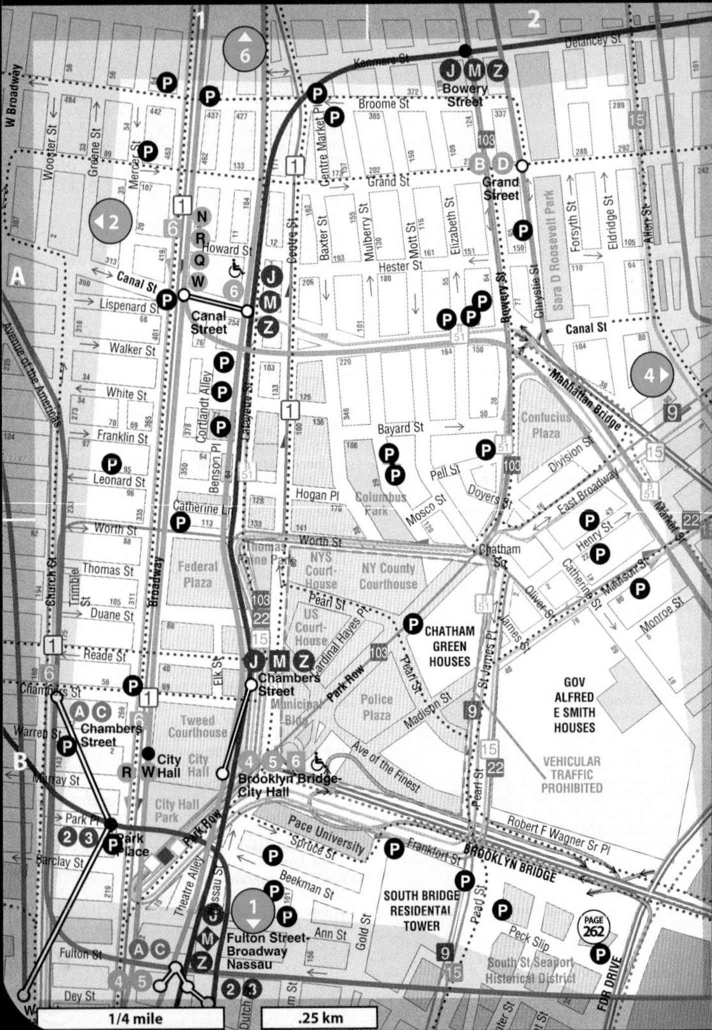

W Broadway
Wooster St
Greene St
Mercer St
Broadway
Lafayette St
Centre St
Centre Market Pl
Baxter St
Mulberry St
Mott St
Elizabeth St
Bowery St
Chrystie St
Forsyth St
Eldridge St
Allen St
Sara D Roosevelt Park
Kenmare St
Delancey St
Broome St
Grand St
Howard St
Hester St
Canal St
Lispenard St
Walker St
White St
Franklin St
Leonard St
Catherine Ln
Worth St
Thomas St
Duane St
Reade St
Chambers St
Warren St
Murray St
Park Pl
Barclay St
Fulton St
Dey St
Avenue of the Americas
Church St
Trimble Pl
Cortlandt Alley
Benson Pl
Elk St
Hogan Pl
Bayard St
Pell St
Doyers St
Mosco St
Columbus Park
Thomas Paine Park
Federal Plaza
NYS Court-House
NY County Courthouse
US Court-House
Cardinal Hayes Pl
Pearl St
Park Row
Municipal Bldg
Police Plaza
Madison St
Ave of the Finest
Chatham Sq
Confucius Plaza
Manhattan Bridge
Division St
East Broadway
Henry St
Market St
Oliver St
Catherine St
Madison St
Monroe St
James St
St James Pl
CHATHAM GREEN HOUSES
GOV ALFRED E SMITH HOUSES
VEHICULAR TRAFFIC PROHIBITED
Tweed Courthouse
City Hall
City Hall Park
Pace University
Spruce St
Frankfort St
Robert F Wagner Sr Pl
BROOKLYN BRIDGE
Theatre Alley
Nassau St
Beekman St
Ann St
Gold St
SOUTH BRIDGE RESIDENTAI TOWER
Peck Slip
South St Seaport Historical District
FDR DRIVE
Dutch St
Bowery Street
Grand Street
Canal Street
Chambers Street
City Hall
Park Place
Brooklyn Bridge-City Hall
Fulton Street-Broadway Nassau
PAGE 262
1/4 mile
.25 km

Transportation

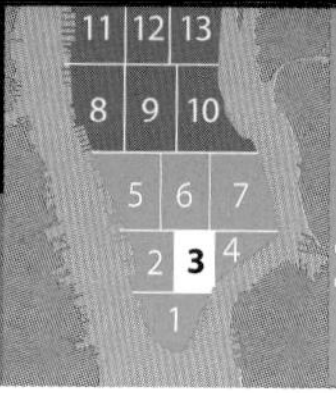

11	12	13
8	9	10
5	6	7
2	**3**	4
	1	

Map 3

The Brooklyn Bridge is best approached from Pearl Street. Be careful about driving east on Canal Street—you have to make a right on Bowery or else you'll drive over the Manhattan Bridge. (Canal Street is one-way going west between Bowery and Chrystie.) Forget about street parking during the day.

Subways

2 3 .... Park Pl

4 5 6 J M Z

.....Brooklyn Bridge-City Hall-Chambers St

B D .... Grand St

6 J M Z N Q R W ...... Canal St

R W .... City Hall

J M Z .... Bowery St

A C .... Chambers St

2 3 4 5 A C J M Z

.... Fulton St/Broadway

Bus Lines

1 .... Broadway/Centre St

103 .... Bowery/Park Row

15 .... East Broadway/Park Row

22 .... Chambers/Madison St

6 .... Church St/Broadway

9 .... Park Row

6 51 .... Lafayette/Canal Sts

Bike Lanes

- • • • Marked Bike Lane
- • • • Recommended Route
- • • • Greenway

P Parking

Map 4 · **Lower East Side**

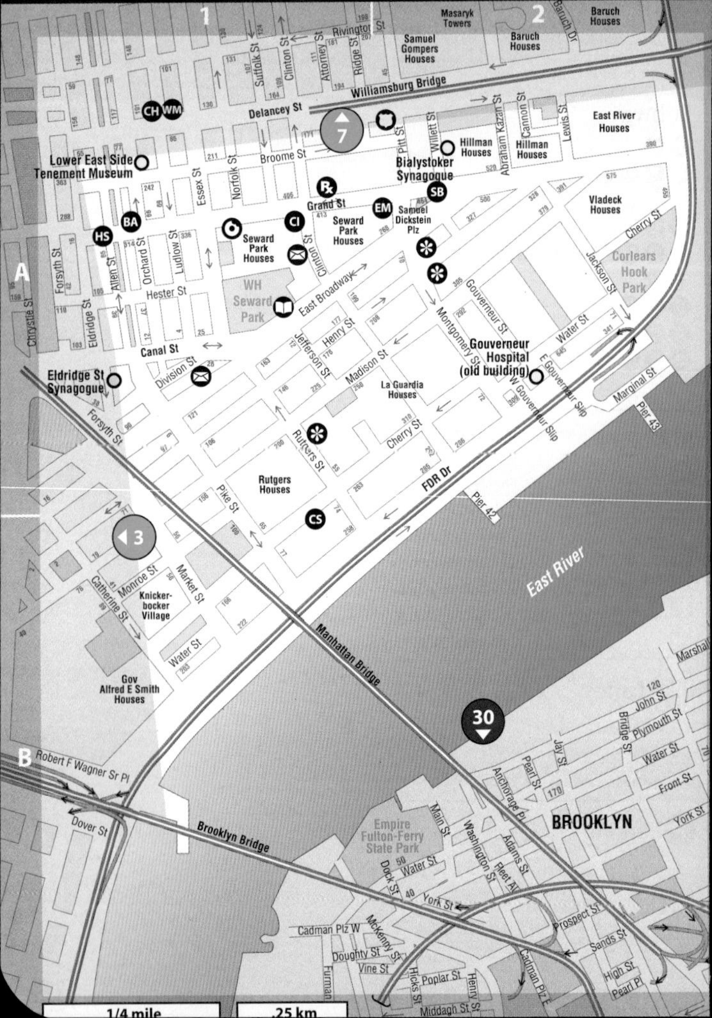

⊗ N

1

2

Masaryk Towers

Baruch Houses

Baruch Dr

Samuel Gompers Houses

Rivington St

Williamsburg Bridge

Delancey St

7

Broome St

Hillman Houses

Hillman Houses

East River Houses

CH WM

Lower East Side Tenement Museum

℞

Grand St

Bialystoker Synagogue

Essex St

Norfolk St

Suffolk St

Clinton St

Attorney St

Ridge St

Pitt St

Willett St

Sheriff St

Columbia St

Abraham Kazan St

HS

BA

CI

Seward Park Houses

EM

Samuel Dickstein Plz

SB

Vladeck Houses

Cherry St

Seward Park Houses

✳

Orchard St

Ludlow St

Hester St

WH Seward Park

East Broadway

✳

Gouverneur St

Montgomery St

Jackson St

Corlears Hook Park

A

Eldridge St

Allen St

Canal St

Division St

✉

Jefferson St

Clinton St

Henry St

Madison St

La Guardia Houses

Cherry St

Gouverneur Hospital (old building)

Water St

Gouverneur Slip

Marginal St

Eldridge St Synagogue

Forsyth St

✳

Rutgers St

FDR Dr

Pier 36

3

Market St

Pike St

Rutgers Houses

CS

Manhattan Bridge

East River

Monroe St

Catherine St

Knickerbocker Village

Water St

30

Gov Alfred E Smith Houses

Jay St

Plymouth St

Water St

120

John St

Marshall

Bridge St

B

Robert F Wagner Sr Pl

Pearl St

Anchorage Pl

Adams St

Washington St

Front St

BROOKLYN

Dover St

Brooklyn Bridge

Empire Fulton-Ferry State Park

Dock St

Water St

York St

Main St

Prospect St

Sands St

High St

Cadman Plz W

McKenney St

York St

48

Doughty St

Vine St

Cadman Plz

Henry St

Hicks St

Poplar St

Middagh St

Furman St

Cranberry St

Pearl Pl

1/4 mile

.25 km

Essentials

Encroached upon by Chinatown from the south and the hip, new Lower East Side from the north, this area holds onto its heritage with a few remaining synagogues and old school food vendors. A logical next area for gentrification (if the abundance of public housing doesn't deter the money), for now it's a nice mash-up.

 24-Hour Pharmacies
• **Rite Aid** • 408 Grand St [Clinton] ♿

 Bagels
• **Kossar's Bagels and Bialys** •
367 Grand St [Essex]

$ Banks
BA • Bank of America •
318 Grand St [Orchard St]
CS • CFS Bank • 227 Cherry St [Rutgers Slip]
CH • Chase (ATM) • Duane Reade •
98 Delancey St [Ludlow St]
CI • Citibank • 411 Grand St [Clinton St]
EM • Emigrant •
465 Grand St [Samuel Dickstein Plz]
HS • HSBC • 307 Grand St [Allen St]
SB • Sovereign (ATM) • 500 Grand St [Willett St]
WM • Washington Mutual •
104 Delancey St [Ludlow St]

✹ Community Gardens

O Landmarks
• **Bialystoker Synagogue** •
7 Bialystoker Pl [Grand]
• **Eldridge Street Synagogue** •
12 Eldridge St [Division]
• **Gouverneur Hospital** •
Gouverneur Slip & Water St
• **Lower East Side Tenement Museum** •
90 Orchard St [Broome]

Libraries
• **Seward Park** • 192 East Broadway [Jefferson]

O Police
• **7th Precinct** • 19 1/2 Pitt St [Broome]

 Post Offices
• **Knickerbocker** • 128 East Broadway [Pike]
• **Pitt Station** • 185 Clinton St [Grand]

Map 4 • **Lower East Side**

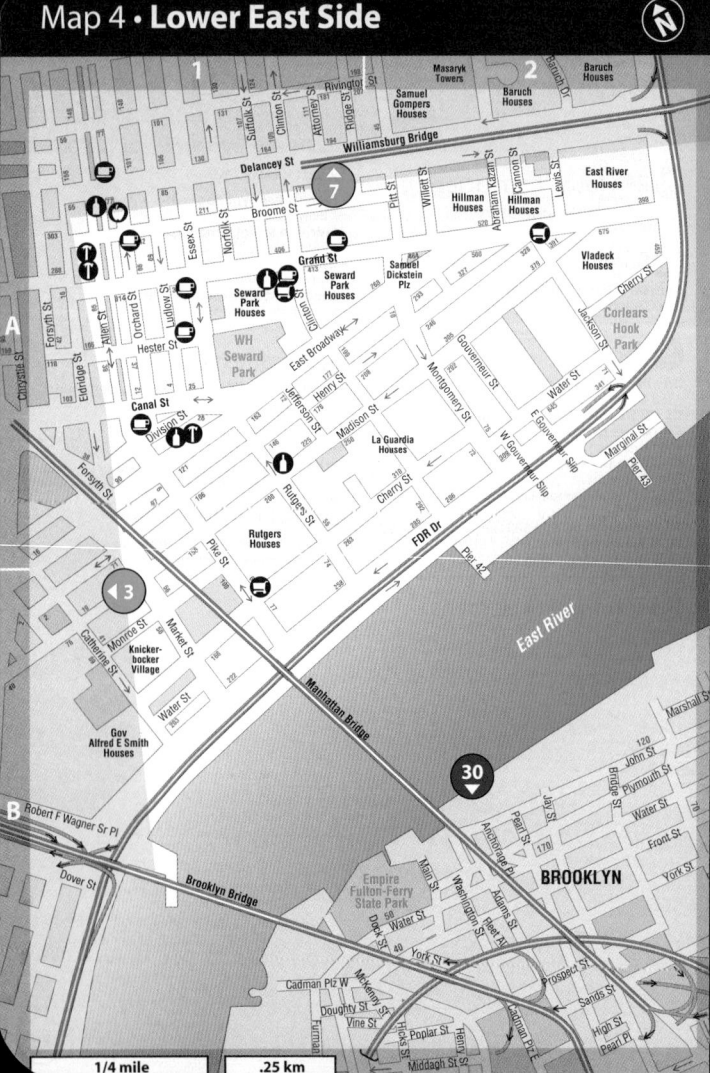

Sundries

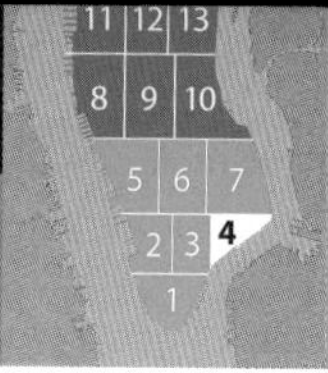

11 | 12 | 13
8 | 9 | 10
5 | 6 | 7
2 | 3 | **4**
1

Map 4

Hit Brown Café, 88 Orchard or Flowers Café for coffee and bites to eat. The supermarkets here tend to be more basic than in other neighborhoods, but there is a greenmarket on Orchard Street on Sundays.

Coffee

• **88 Orchard** • 88 Orchard St [Broome]
• **Brown Café** • 61 Hester St [Ludlow St]
• **Flowers Café** • 355 Grand St [Essex]
• **Full City Coffee** • 409 Grand St [Clinton]
• **Happy Café** • 8 Allen St [Canal]
• **Roots & Vine** • 409 Grand St [Attorney]
• **Starbucks** • 80 Delancey St [Allen]

Farmers Markets

• **Orchard Street (Sun 9 am–5pm July 9–Nov)**
  • Orchard St b/w Broome & Delancey Sts

Hardware Stores

• **International Electrical** • 77 Allen St [Grand]
• **New York Home Center True Value** •
  71 Allen St [Grand]
• **Tom's Hardware** •
  154 East Broadway [Rutgers]

Liquor Stores

• **Madison Liquor** • 195 Madison St [Rutgers]
• **Seward Park Liquors** • 393 Grand St [Suffolk]
• **Wedding Banquet Liquor** •
  135 Division St [Canal]
• **Wing Tak Liquor** • 101 Allen St [Delancey]

Supermarkets

• **Fine Fare** • 175 Clinton St [Grand]
• **Fine Fare** • 545 Grand St [Jackson]
• **Pathmark** • 227 Cherry St [Rutgers Slip] ⊗

Map 4 · **Lower East Side**

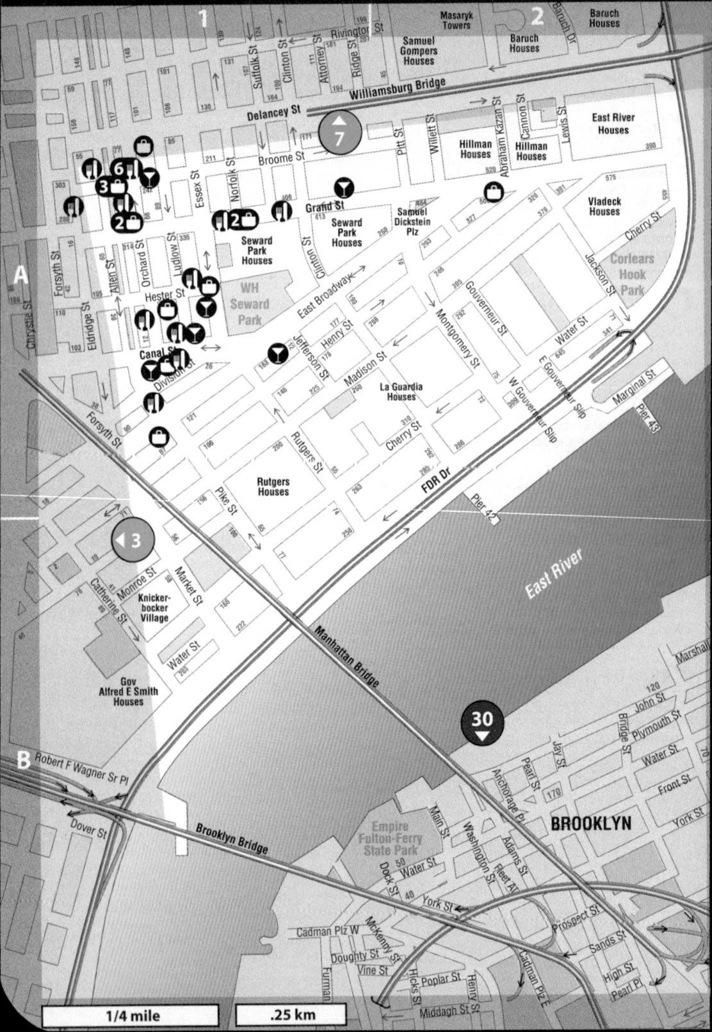

1

2

Masaryk Towers

Baruch Houses

Baruch Dr

Samuel Gompers Houses

Williamsburg Bridge

Delancey St

7

East River Houses

Broome St

Hillman Houses

Hillman Houses

Vladeck Houses

Grand St

Seward Park Houses

Samuel Dickstein Plz

Cherry St

Corlears Hook Park

A

Seward Park Houses

WH Seward Park

East Broadway

Jackson St

Hester St

Henry St

Madison St

Montgomery St

Water St

Marginal St

Canal St

Jefferson St

La Guardia Houses

Division St

Rutgers St

Cherry St

FDR Dr

Pier 42

Pike St

Rutgers Houses

Manhattan Bridge

East River

3

Monroe St

Market St

Knicker-bocker Village

Water St

Gov Alfred E Smith Houses

30

B

Robert F Wagner Sr Pl

BROOKLYN

Brooklyn Bridge

Dover St

Empire Fulton-Ferry State Park

Cadman Plz W

York St

Prospect St

Front St

York St

Doughty St

Vine St

Poplar St

Henry St

Middagh St

| 1/4 mile | .25 km |

The tide of hipness is sweeping down Allen, Orchard, and Ludlow Streets, but some old timers remain. For amazing bagels and bialys, head straight to Kossar's. Something sweeter awaits you at the Doughnut Plant. If you like your cuisine a little more Euro-hip, try Les Enfants Terribles or Bacaro.

Nightlife

- **Bacaro** • 136 Division St [Ludlow St]
- **Bar 169** • 169 East Broadway [Rutgers]
- **Clandestino** • 35 Canal St [Ludlow]
- **Good World** • 3 Orchard St [Canal]
- **King Size** • 21 Essex St [Canal]
- **Lolita** • 266 Broome St [Allen]
- **Roots & Vine** • 409 Grand St [Attorney]

Restaurants

- **88 Orchard** • 88 Orchard St [Broome]
- **Bacaro** • 136 Division St [Ludlow St]
- **Barrio Chino** • 253 Broome St [Orchard]
- **Brown Café** • 61 Hester St [Ludlow St]
- **Congee Village** • 100 Allen St [Delancey]
- **Dumpling House** • 118 Eldridge St [Broome]
- **Good World** • 3 Orchard St [Canal]
- **Il Laboratorio del Gelato** • 95 Orchard St [Broome]
- **Kossar's Bagels and Bialys** • 367 Grand St [Essex]
- **Les Enfants Terribles** • 37 Canal St [Ludlow]
- **Little Giant** • 85 Orchard St [Broome]
- **Noah's Arc** • 399 Grand St [Suffolk]
- **Pho Bang** • 3 Pike St [Division]
- **Sticky Rice** • 85 Orchard St [Broome]

Shopping

- **Babycakes** • 248 Broome St [Ludlow]
- **Doughnut Plant** • 379 Grand St [Norfolk]
- **Hong Kong Supermarket** • 109 East Broadway [Pike]
- **Il Laboratorio del Gelato** • 95 Orchard St [Broome]
- **Joe's Fabric Warehouse** • 102 Orchard St [Delancey]
- **Kossar's Bagels and Bialys** • 367 Grand St [Essex]
- **Mendel Goldberg Fabrics** • 72 Hester St [Orchard]
- **Moishe's Kosher Bake Shop** • 504 Grand St [E B'way]
- **Pippin** • 72 Orchard St [Grand]
- **Project 8** • 138 Division St [Ludlow St]
- **Sweet Life** • 63 Hester St [Ludlow]
- **Tahir** • 75 Orchard St [Grand]
- **Zarin Fabrics** • 314 Grand St [Allen]

Map 4 • Lower East Side

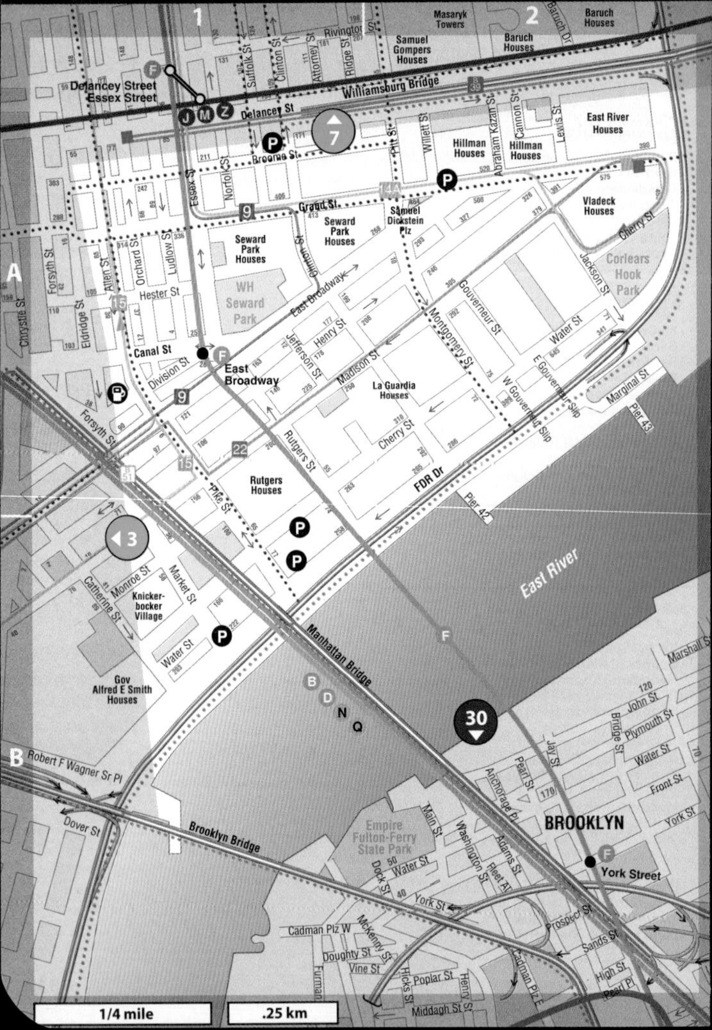

N

1

2

Masaryk Towers

Baruch Houses

Samuel Gompers Houses

Baruch Dr

Rivington St

Stanton St

Suffolk St

Clinton St

Attorney St

Ridge St

Pitt St

Willett St

Abraham Kazan St

Cannon St

Lewis St

Delancey Street
Essex Street

J M Z

Williamsburg Bridge

Delancey St

East River Houses

7

P

Broome St

Norfolk St

Hillman Houses

Hillman Houses

9

Grand St

Seward Park Houses

Samuel Dickstein Plz

P

4A

Cherry St

Vladeck Houses

Essex St

Ludlow St

Orchard St

Allen St

A

15

Hester St

Seward Park Houses

East Broadway

Columbia St

Gouverneur St

Montgomery St

Jackson St

Corlears Hook Park

Forsyth St

Eldridge St

Canal St

WH Seward Park

Division St

F

East Broadway

Henry St

Jefferson St

Madison St

La Guardia Houses

Water St

Marginal St

Pier 42

P

9

East River

Rutgers St

Cherry St

W Gouverneur Slip

E Gouverneur Slip

15

22

Rutgers Houses

FDR Dr

3

Monroe St

Market St

Pike St

Madison St

Knicker-bocker Village

P

P

Manhattan Bridge

F

P

Water St

Gov Alfred E Smith Houses

B

D

N

Q

30

Robert F Wagner Sr Pl

Dover St

Brooklyn Bridge

Empire Fulton Ferry State Park

Main St

Plymouth St

Water St

Front St

BROOKLYN

John St

Marshall St

Jay St

Bridge St

Pearl St

York St

Washington St

Adams St

Dock St

Water St

Front St

York St

F

York Street

Cadman Plz W

McKenney St

Doughty St

Vine St

Poplar St

Hicks St

Prospect St

Sands St

High St

Pearl St

Furman St

Middagh St

1/4 mile

.25 km

Transportation

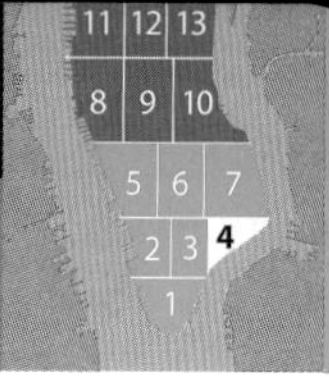

11 12 13
8 9 10
5 6 7
2 3 4
1

Not exactly a transit hub, though the F train has the benefit of hitting the West Side, Midtown, and the Upper East Side, as well as Queens (as long as you've got some time). Abundant opportunities exist for walking, biking, and blading. The Williamsburg and Manhattan bridges are open to pedestrian traffic and boast great views.

Subways

F .... East Broadway

F .... York St

F J M Z .... Delancey St-Essex St

Bus Lines

14 .... Grand St

15 .... Allen St

22 .... Madison St

9 .... East Broadway/Essex St

B51 .... Forsyth St

Bike Lanes

• • • • Recommended Route

• • • • Greenway

Gas Stations

• **Mobil** • 2 Pike St [Division] 24

Parking

Map 5 · **West Village**

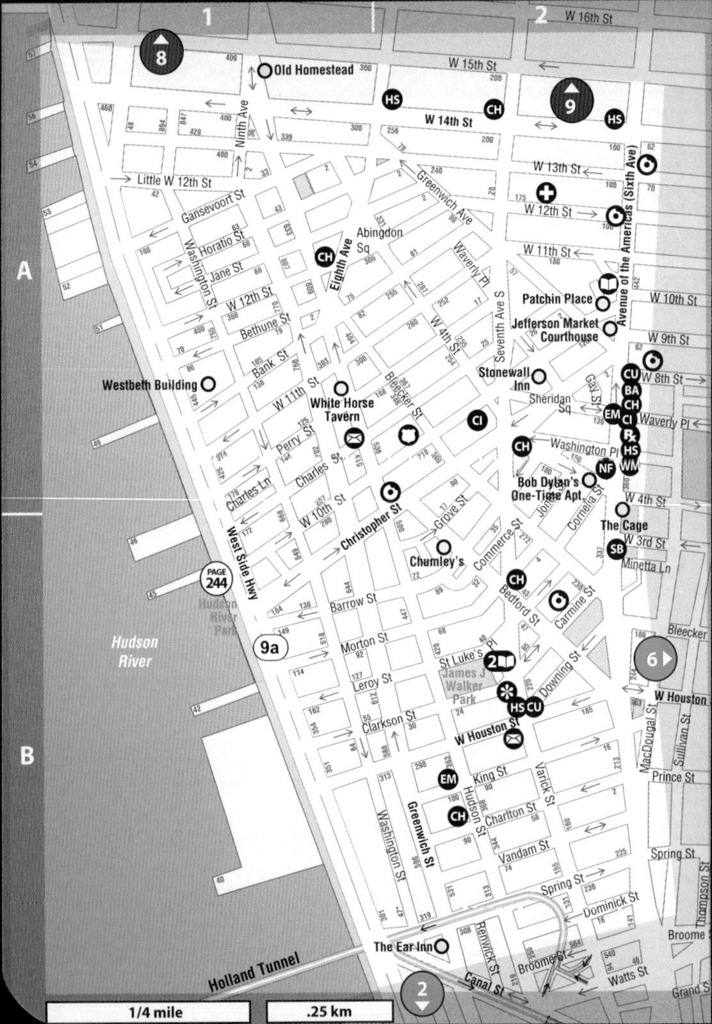

N

1

2

W 16th St

8

W 15th St

Old Homestead

Ninth Ave

406

300

200

HS

W 14th St

CH

9

HS

W 13th St

Avenue of the Americas (Sixth Ave)

100

62

78

Little W 12th St

W 12th St

175

100

Greenwich Ave

Gansevoort St

W 11th St

Horatio St

Abingdon Sq

Jane St

Eighth Ave

CH

W 10th St

A

Washington St

Waverly Pl

Patchin Place

W 12th St

Jefferson Market Courthouse

W 9th St

Bethune St

Seventh Ave S

W 4th St

Bank St

W 11th St

Westbeth Building

Stonewall Inn

CU
BA
CH
EM
CI
Rx
HS
WM

Perry St

White Horse Tavern

Bleecker St

Sheridan Sq

Waverly Pl

W 8th St

CH

CI

Washington Pl

Charles Ln

Charles St

CH

NF

Bob Dylan's One-Time Apt.

W 4th St

Jones St

Christopher St

W 10th St

Cornelia St

The Cage

SB

W 3rd St

Grove St

Minetta Ln

Commerce St

Chumley's

Bedford St

CH

Barrow St

Carmine St

Bleecker

6

PAGE 244

Hudson River Park

9a

Morton St

St Luke's Pl

2

St Christopher St

James J Walker Park

Leroy St

Downing St

MacDougal St

Sullivan St

Hudson River

Clarkson St

HS CU

W Houston St

W Houston St

Prince St

B

EM

King St

Varick St

Charlton St

Hudson St

CH

Spring St

Vandam St

Greenwich St

Washington St

Spring St

Dominick St

Broome

Renwick St

The Ear Inn

Thompson St

Watts St

Holland Tunnel

2

Canal St

Broome St

Essentials

11 12 13
8 9 10
5 6 7
2 3 4
1

Map 5

Let's all collectively thank our local deities for Jane Jacobs. If you don't know who she is, we can't help you---but you can hopefully ask at Chumley's, if it ever opens again. To the north, the fashion-raw meat dichotomy continues, though $800 shoes seem to be winning.

 24-Hour Pharmacies

• **Duane Reade** • 378 Sixth Ave [Waverly] ☼

Bagels

• **Bagel Buffet** • 406 Sixth Ave [8th]
• **Bagels on the Square** • 7 Carmine St [6th Av]
• **Famous Bagels Buffet** •
  510 Ave of the Americas [13th]
• **Hudson Bagels** • 502 Hudson St [Christopher]
• **Murray's Bagels** • 500 Sixth Ave [13th]

Banks

BA • Bank of America (ATM) •
  390 Sixth Ave [W 8th St]
CH • Chase • 158 W 14th St [Seventh Ave]
CH • Chase • 204 W 4th St [Barrow St]
CH • Chase • 302 W 12th St [Eighth Ave]
CH • Chase • 345 Hudson St [Charlton St]
CH • Chase (ATM) • Duane Reade •
  29 Seventh Ave [Bedford St]
CH • Chase (ATM) • Duane Reade •
  378 Sixth Ave [Waverly Pl]
CI • Citibank (ATM) • 364 Sixth Ave [Waverly Pl]
CI • Citibank (ATM) •
  75 Christopher St [W 4th St]
EM • Emigrant • 375 Hudson St [W Houston St]
EM • Emigrant • 395 Sixth Ave [W 8th St]
HS • HSBC • 101 W 14th St [Sixth Ave]
HS • HSBC • 207 Varick St [Downing St]
HS • HSBC • 354 Sixth Ave [Washington Pl]
HS • HSBC • 80 Eighth Ave [W 14th St]
**CU • Lower East Side People's Federal Credit
  Union (ATM)** • McDonald's •
  208 Varick St [W Houston St]
**CU • Lower East Side People's Federal Credit
  Union (ATM)** • McDonald's •
  405 Sixth Ave [W 8th St]
NF • North Fork • 347 Sixth Ave [W 4th St]
SB • Sovereign (ATM) • CVS •
  307 Sixth Ave [Minetta Ln]
WM • Washington Mutual •
  340 Sixth Ave [W 4th St]

Community Gardens

Emergency Rooms

• **St Vincent's** • 170 W 12th St [7th Av]

Landmarks

• **Bob Dylan's One-Time Apartment** •
  161 W 4th St [Cornelia]
• **The Cage (basketball court)** •
  320 Sixth Ave at W 4th St
• **Chumley's** • 86 Bedford St [Barrow]
• **The Ear Inn** • 326 Spring St [Greenwich St]
• **Jefferson Market Courthouse** •
  425 Sixth Ave [10th]
• **Old Homestead** • 56 Ninth Ave [14th]
• **Patchin Place** •
  W 10th St b/w Sixth Ave & Greenwich Ave
• **Stonewall Inn** • 53 Christopher St [7th Av]
• **Westbeth Building** •
  Washington St & Bethune St
• **White Horse Tavern** • 567 Hudson St [11th]

 Libraries

• **Early Childhood Resource & Information
  Center** • 66 Leroy St [7th Ave S]
• **Hudson Park** • 66 Leroy St [Hudson]
• **Jefferson Market Courthouse** •
  425 Sixth Ave [10th]

 Police

• **6th Precinct** • 233 W 10th St [Bleecker]

Post Offices

• **Village** • 201 Varick St [Houston]
• **West Village** • 527 Hudson St [Charles]

Map 5 • **West Village**

N

1

2

W 16th St

8

W 15th St

W 14th St

9

Ninth Ave

Little W 12th St

Greenwich Ave

W 13th St

Gansevoort St

W 12th St

Horatio St

Abingdon Sq

W 11th St

Jane St

Eighth Ave

Waverly Pl

Avenue of the Americas (Sixth Ave)

W 10th St

Washington St

A

W 12th St

Bethune St

W 4th St

W 9th St

Bank St

Seventh Ave S

W 8th St

W 11th St

Sheridan Sq

Waverly Pl

Perry St

Washington Pl

Bleecker St

Charles Ln

Charles St

Grove St

W 4th St

Jones St

Cornelia St

W 10th St

Christopher St

Commerce St

W 3rd St

Minetta Ln

PAGE 244

Barrow St

Bedford St

Hudson River Park

West Side Hwy

Morton St

Carmine St

Bleecker St

6

9a

Leroy St

St Luke's Pl

Downing St

W Houston St

Hudson River

Clarkson St

James J Walker Park

W Houston St

Greenwich St

King St

Charlton St

Vandam St

MacDougal St

Sullivan St

Prince St

B

Hudson St

Varick St

Spring St

Washington St

Vandam St

Spring St

Thompson St

Dominick St

Broome St

Watts St

Renwick St

Canal St

Grand St

Holland Tunnel

2

1/4 mile   .25 km

Sundries

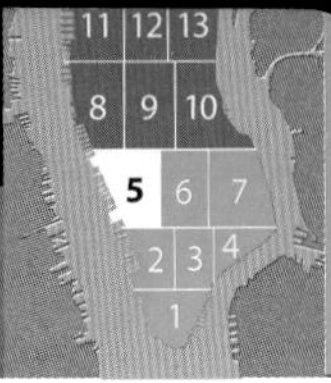

It may be difficult to navigate, but the West Village, with its beautiful brownstones on tree-lined streets, is full of hidden gems. Stop by Joe or Doma for some coffee then stroll along Hudson River Park and take in the posh, new architecture mixed with the brick structures from a bygone era. Lovely.

☕ Coffee

- **Café 201** • 201 Varick St [Houston]
- **CC's Café** • 496 Hudson St [Christopher]
- **Chocolate Bar** • 48 Eighth Ave [4th]
- **Coffee Sweet Heart** • 69 Eighth Ave [13th]
- **Cosi** • 504 Sixth Ave [13th]
- **Doma** • 17 Perry St [Waverly]
- **Dub Café** • 348 W 14th St [Hudson St]
- **Dunkin' Donuts** • 395 Hudson St [Clarkson]
- **Dunkin' Donuts** • 536 Sixth Ave [14th]
- **Dunkin' Donuts** • 75 Christopher St [4th]
- **Dunkin' Donuts** • 175 Varick St [Charlton St]
- **Dunkin' Donuts** • 215 W 14th St [7th Ave]
- **The Grey Dog's Coffee** •
  33 Carmine St [Bedford]
- **Grounded** • 28 Jane St [4th]
- **Hudson Coffee Bar** • 350 Hudson St [Charlton]
- **Joe: The Art of Coffee** • 141 Waverly Pl [Gay]
- **Le Gamin Café** • 522 Hudson St [10th]
- **Millers Tea Room** •
  113 Christopher St [Bedford]
- **Porto Rico Importing** •
  201 Bleecker St [MacDougal]
- **Rocco's** • 243 Bleecker St [Leroy]
- **Sant Ambroeus** • 259 W 4th St [Perry]
- **sNice** • 45 Eighth Ave [4th]
- **Starbucks** • 150 Varick St [Vandam]
- **Starbucks** • 345 Hudson St [Charlton]
- **Starbucks** • 378 Sixth Ave [Waverly]
- **Starbucks** • 510 Sixth Ave [13th]
- **Starbucks** • 518 Hudson St [10th]
- **Starbucks** • 72 Grove St [4th]
- **Starbucks** • 93 Greenwich Ave [Bank]
- **Sucelt Coffee Shop** • 200 W 14th St [7th Ave]
- **Sweet Life Café** •
  147 Christopher St [Greenwich St]

🌱 Farmers Markets

- **Abingdon Square (Sat 8 am–2 pm, year round)** • W 12th St & Hudson St
- **South Village Greenmarket (Sun 8 am–4 pm, July–Nov)** •
  6th Ave & Downing St

🔧 Hardware Stores

- **Barney's Hardware** • 467 Sixth Ave [11th]
- **Blaustein Paint & Hardware** •
  304 Bleecker St [Barrow]
- **Garber Hardware** • 710 Greenwich St [Charles]
- **Greenwich Locksmiths** •
  56 Seventh Ave S [Commerce]
- **Hardware Mart True Value** •
  140 W 14th St [6th Av]
- **Janovic** • 161 Sixth Ave [Spring St]
- **Lock-It Hardware** • 59 Carmine St [Bedford]

🍾 Liquor Stores

- **Casa Oliveira Wines & Liquors** •
  98 Seventh Ave S [Grove St]
- **Christopher Street Liquor Shoppe** •
  45 Christopher St [Grove St]
- **Golden Rule Wine & Liquor** •
  457 Hudson St [Barrow]
- **Imperial Liquors** • 579 Hudson St [Bank]
- **Manley's Liquor Store** • 35 Eighth Ave [4th]
- **North Village Liquors** • 254 W 14th St [7th Av]
- **Pop the Cork Wine Merchant** •
  168 Seventh Ave S [Waverly]
- **Sea Grape Wine & Spirits** •
  512 Hudson St [10th]
- **Spirits of Carmine** • 52 Carmine St [Bedford]
- **Village Vintner** • 448 Sixth Ave [10th]
- **Village Wine & Spirits** • 486 Sixth Ave [12th]
- **Vinvino Wine** • 56 King St [Varick]
- **Waverly Wine & Liquor** •
  135 Waverly Pl [6th Av]
- **Wines by Com (Wine only)** • 23 Jones St [4th]

🛒 Supermarkets

- **Associated** • 255 W 14th St [8th Av]
- **Balducci's** • 81 Eighth Ave [14th]
- **Citarella** • 424 Sixth Ave [9th]
- **D'Agostino** • 666 Greenwich St [Christopher]
- **D'Agostino** • 790 Greenwich St [Bethune]
- **Food Emporium** • 475 Sixth Ave [12th]
- **Gourmet Garage** •
  117 Seventh Ave S [Christopher]
- **Gristedes** • 3 Sheridan Sq [Barrow]
- **Gristedes** • 585 Hudson St [Bank]
- **Western Beef** • 403 W 14th St [9th Av]

Map 5

Map 5 • **West Village**

N

1

2 W 16th St

W 15th St

8

3

400

300

W 14th St

9

Ninth Ave

429

Little W 12th St

42

W 13th St

100

Gansevoort St

Abingdon
Sq

Greenwich Ave

W 12th St

200

Horatio St

Waverly Pl

W 11th St

2

Avenue of the Americas (Sixth Ave)

A

Jane St

Eighth Ave

W 12th St

W 10th St

W 9th St

Bethune St

4th St

Seventh Ave S

2

Bank St

Bleecker St

3

Sheridan
Sq

W 8th St

W 11th St

Waverly Pl

Perry St

Washington Pl

Charles St

Charles Ln

2

2

Jones St

W 4th St

W 10th St

2

Grove St

2

W 3rd St

Christopher St

Commerce St

Cornelia St

Minetta Ln

3

Barrow St

Bedford St

Carmine St

Bleecker St

PAGE
244

Hudson
River
Park

Morton St

Carmine St

5

6

9a

Leroy St

St. Luke's
Pl

James J
Walker
Park

Downing St

WEST SIDE HWY

Clarkson St

Hudson
River

W Houston St

W Houston St

King St

Vandam St

MacDougal St

Sullivan St

B

Greenwich St

Washington St

Charlton St

Hudson St

Prince St

Spring St

Vandam St

Spring St

Dominick St

Broome St

Holland Tunnel

Canal St

2

Watts St

Grand St

Thompson St

1/4 mile   .25 km

Map 5

Entertainment

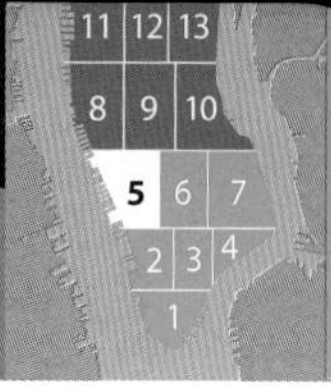

What can we say? Movies = Film Forum, IFC; Trendy = Spotted Pig; Burgers = Corner Bistro; Pizza = Joe's, John's; Cheese = Murray's; Jazz = Village Vanguard; Classic Bar = The Ear Inn. We mourn the passing of the warm, homey, and brilliant Florent. Rest in Peace.

Movie Theaters

- **Film Forum** • 209 W Houston St [Varick]
- **IFC Center** • 323 Sixth Ave [3rd]

Nightlife

- **Ara** • 24 Ninth Ave [W 13th St]
- **Art Bar** • 52 Eighth Ave [4th]
- **Arthur's Tavern** • 57 Grove St [Bleecker]
- **Automatic Slims** • 733 Washington St [Bank]
- **Duplex** • 61 Christopher St [7th Av]
- **The Ear Inn** • 326 Spring St [Greenwich St]
- **Employees Only** • 510 Hudson St [10th]
- **The Four-Faced Liar** • 165 W 4th St [Cornelia]
- **Gaslight Lounge** • 400 W 14th St [9th Av]
- **Henrietta Hudson** • 438 Hudson St [Morton]
- **Hudson Bar and Books** • 636 Hudson St [Horatio]
- **Johnny's Bar** • 90 Greenwich Ave [12th]
- **Kettle of Fish** • 59 Christopher St [7th Av]
- **Lotus** • 409 W 14th St [9th Av]
- **The Otherroom** • 143 Perry St [Wash]
- **SOB's** • 204 Varick St [Houston]
- **Stonewall Inn** • 53 Christopher St [7th Av]
- **Turks and Frogs** • 323 W 11th St [Greenwich St]
- **Village Vanguard** • 178 Seventh Ave S [Perry]
- **Vol de Nuit** • 148 W 4th St [6th Av]
- **White Horse Tavern** • 567 Hudson St [11th]

Restaurants

- **AOC** • 314 Bleecker St [Grove St]
- **Aquagrill** • 210 Spring St [Sullivan]
- **August** • 359 Bleecker St [Charles]
- **Blue Ribbon Bakery** • 33 Downing St [Bedford]
- **Café Asean** • 117 W 10th St [Patchin Pl]
- **Corner Bistro** • 331 W 4th St [Horatio]
- **Da Andrea** • 557 Hudson St [Perry]
- **Diablo Royale** • 189 W 10th St [4th]
- **Ditch Plains** • 29 Bedford St [Downing]
- **Do Hwa** • 55 Carmine St [Bedford]
- **Employees Only** • 510 Hudson St [10th]
- **Fatty Crab** • 643 Hudson St [Gansevoort]
- **French Roast** • 78 W 11th St [6th Av] ☺
- **GoBo** • 401 Ave of the Americas [8th]
- **Home** • 20 Cornelia St [4th]
- **Ivo & Lulu** • 558 Broome St [Varick]
- **Joe's Pizza** • 7 Carmine St [Bleecker]
- **John's Pizzeria** • 278 Bleecker St [Jones]
- **Karahi** • 118 Christopher St [Bleecker]

- **Little Havana** • 30 Cornelia St [6th Av]
- **Mary's Fish Camp** • 64 Charles St [4th]
- **Mercadito** • 100 Seventh Ave S [Grove St]
- **One If By Land, TIBS** • 17 Barrow St [Bleecker]
- **Paris Commune** • 99 Bank St [Greenwich St]
- **Pastis** • 9 Ninth Ave [Little W 12th]
- **Pearl Oyster Bar** • 18 Cornelia St [4th]
- **Po** • 31 Cornelia St [4th]
- **Provence** • 38 MacDougal St [King St]
- **Souen** • 210 Sixth Ave [Prince]
- **Spotted Pig** • 314 W 11th St [Greenwich St]
- **Taïm** • 222 Waverly Pl [Perry St]
- **Tea & Sympathy** • 108 Greenwich Ave [13th]
- **Wallse** • 344 W 11th St [Washington St]
- **The Waverly Inn** • 16 Bank St [Waverly]
- **Yama** • 38 Carmine St [Bedford]

Shopping

- **Alexander McQueen** • 417 W 14th St [9th Av]
- **Alphabets** • 47 Greenwich Ave [Charles]
- **Bleecker Street Records** • 239 Bleecker St [Leroy]
- **CO Bigelow Chemists** • 414 Sixth Ave [9th]
- **Diane von Furstenberg** • 874 Washington St [W 14th St]
- **Faicco's Pork Store** • 260 Bleecker St [Cornelia]
- **Flight 001** • 96 Greenwich Ave [Jane]
- **Geppetto's Toy Box** • 10 Christopher St [Gay]
- **Health & Harmony** • 470 Hudson St [Barrow]
- **Jacques Torres Chocolate Haven** • 350 Hudson St [Charlton]
- **Jeffrey** • 449 W 14th St [Wash]
- **The Leather Man** • 111 Christopher St [Bedford]
- **Little Pie Company** • 407 W 14th St [9th Av]
- **Murray's Cheese Shop** • 254 Bleecker St [Leroy]
- **Mxyplyzyk** • 125 Greenwich Ave [13th]
- **Myers of Keswick** • 634 Hudson St [Horatio]
- **O Ottomanelli's & Sons** • 285 Bleecker St [Jones]
- **Porto Rico Importing Company** • 201 Bleecker St [MacDougal]
- **Rebel Rebel Records** • 319 Bleecker St [Christopher]
- **Scott Jordan Furniture** • 137 Varick St [Spring]
- **Stella McCartney** • 429 W 14th St [Greene]
- **Vitra** • 29 Ninth Ave [13th]

Map 5 • West Village

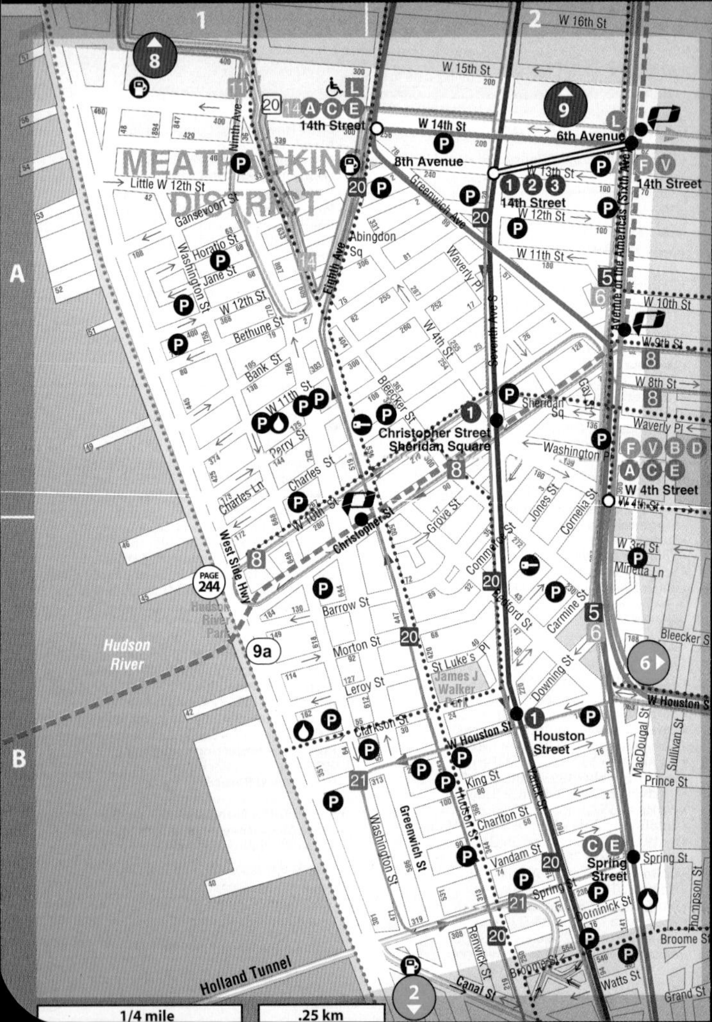

MEATPACKING DISTRICT
W 16th St
W 15th St
W 14th St
14th Street
8th Avenue
6th Avenue
14th Street
W 13th St
14th Street
W 12th St
W 11th St
W 10th St
W 9th St
W 8th St
Waverly Pl
Washington Pl
W 4th Street
W 4th St
W 3rd St
Minetta Ln
Bleecker St
W Houston St
Little W 12th St
Gansevoort St
Horatio St
Jane St
W 12th St
Bethune St
Bank St
W 11th St
Perry St
Charles St
Charles Ln
W 10th St
Christopher St
Christopher Street Sheridan Square
Sheridan Sq
Gay St
Jones St
Cornelia St
Grove St
Commerce St
Bedford St
Carmine St
Barrow St
Morton St
Leroy St
St Luke's Pl
James J Walker Park
Downing St
Clarkson St
W Houston St
Houston Street
King St
Charlton St
Vandam St
Spring St
Spring Street
Dominick St
Broome St
Watts St
Grand St
Canal St
Holland Tunnel
Prince St
MacDougal St
Sullivan St
Thompson St
Ninth Ave
Eighth Ave
Abingdon Sq
Greenwich Ave
Waverly Pl
W 4th St
Bleecker St
Seventh Ave S
Avenue of the Americas (Sixth Ave)
Washington St
West Side Hwy
Hudson St
Greenwich St
Washington St
Renwick St
Varick St
Hudson River
Hudson River Park
PAGE 244
9a
A
B
1
2
8
9
6
1/4 mile
.25 km

The one way streets even get the locals turned around. Parking is notoriously difficult except for on Thompson, Sullivan, and West 3rd during weekday evenings. Biking is a pleasant alternative. Use the West 4th Street subway rather than Christopher Street just to have an excuse to watch basketball at the Cage.

Subways

① ② ③ Ⓕ Ⓥ Ⓛ ...... 14th St-Sixth Ave
① .... Christopher St-Sheridan Sq
① .... Houston St
Ⓐ Ⓒ Ⓔ Ⓕ Ⓥ Ⓑ Ⓓ .... W 4th St
Ⓐ Ⓒ Ⓔ Ⓛ .... 14th St-Eighth Ave
Ⓖ Ⓔ .... Spring St

Bus Lines

11 .... Ninth Ave/Tenth Ave
14 .... 14th St Crosstown
20 .... Abingdon Sq
20 .. Seventh Ave/Eighth Ave/Central Park West
21 .... Houston St Crosstown
5 .... Fifth Ave/Sixth Ave/Riverside Dr
6 .... Seventh Ave/Sixth Ave/Broadway
8 .... 8th St/9th St Crosstown

Bike Lanes

• • • Marked Bike Lane

• • • Recommended Route

• • • Greenway

PATH

• **14 St** • 14th St & Sixth Ave
• **9th St** • 9th St & Sixth Ave
• **Christopher St** • Christopher St & Hudson St

Car Rental

• **Big Apple Rent-A-Car** •
575 Washington St [W Houston]
• **Dollar** • 99 Charles St [Bleecker]
• **Hertz** • 18 Morton St [7th Av]

Car Washes

• **Apple Management** • 332 W 11th St [Wash]
• **Lage Car Wash** • 124 Sixth Ave [Sullivan]
• **Village Car Wash & Lube** •
160 Leroy St [Wash]

Gas Stations

• **Lukoil** • 63 Eighth Ave [13th] ☯
• **Mobil** • 290 West St [Canal]

Parking

Map 6 • **Washington Sq / NYU / NoHo / SoHo**

W 16th St
E 16th St
W 15th St
E 15th St
Union Square
9
W 14th St
E 14th St
CH CO
CU CO
10
New School
PAGE 250
AM
Rx
W 13th St
E 13th St
Con Edison Building
AP
Rx
CH
AP
WM
The Strand Bookstore
W 12th St
E 12th St
Salmagundi Club
W 11th St
Grace Church
BA
Site of Weathermen Explosion
11th Pl
St Mark's-in-the-Bowery Church
W 10th St
E 10th St
CH
CO
Mark Twain House
W 9th St
CU
Rx
BA
CH
Stuyvesant St
NF
CH
CU
HS
W 8th St
SB
Wanamaker's
Washington Mews
The Alamo (The Cube)
Gem Spa
WM
St Marks Pl
Washington Sq N
Waverly Pl
Asch Building
Washington Pl
CH
BA
The Public Theater
Cooper Union
E 7th St
EM
Cooper Square
E 6th St
Washington Square
PAGE 252
Colonnade Row
Old Merchant's House
E 5th St
BA
7
W 4th St
CH
E 4th St
Great Jones Fire House
NYU
W 3rd St
CO
Great Jones St
New York Marble Cemetery
CI
Washington Square Village
James Aly
Joey Ramone Place
Bond St
E 2nd St
SB
Bleecker St
Silver Towers
CH
Bayard-Condict Building
CBGB & OMFUG
E 1st St
CH
W Houston St
E Houston St
E Houston St
HS NF
BA Rx
Milano's
SOHO
Jersey St
Singer Building
Prince St
Spring St
CH
3
Broome St

1/4 mile   .25 km

Essentials

11	12	13
8	9	10
5	**6**	7
	2	3	4
		1	

Map 6

Hipsters and NYU students may reign near Astor Place, but this downtown kingdom is suited for all styles. Lofts soar and narrow cobblestone side streets give way to taxis speeding down The Bowery. A cool indifference permeates the air while the epic line at Trader Joe's keeps growing.

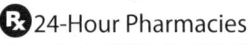 24-Hour Pharmacies

• **Duane Reade** • 123 Third Ave [14th] ♿
• **Duane Reade** • 24 E 14th St [University] ♿
• **Duane Reade** • 598 Broadway [Houston] ♿
• **Duane Reade** • 769 Broadway [9th] ♿
• **Walgreen's** • 145 Fourth Ave [13th] ♿

Bagels

• **Bagel Bob's** • 51 University Pl [10th]
• **The Bagel Café** • 2 St Marks Pl [3rd Av]
• **Giant Bagel Shop** • 120 University Pl [13th]

$ Banks

AM • **Amalgamated** • 10 E 14th St [5th Av]
AP • **Apple** • 4 Irving Pl [E 14th St]
AP • **Apple (ATM)** • 145 Fourth Ave [E 13th St]
BA • **Bank of America** • 589 Broadway
BA • **Bank of America** • 72 Second Ave
BA • **Bank of America** • 770 Broadway
BA • **Bank of America (ATM)** • 66 Third Ave
BA • **Bank of America (ATM)** • 742 Broadway
CH • **Chase** • 156 Second Ave [E 10th St]
CH • **Chase** • 26 Astor Pl [Lafayette St]
CH • **Chase** • 32 University Pl [E 9th St]
CH • **Chase** • 525 Broadway [Spring St]
CH • **Chase** • 623 Broadway [W Houston St]
CH • **Chase** • 785 Broadway [E 10th St]
CH • **Chase** • 90 Fifth Ave [W 15th St]
CH • **Chase (ATM)** • 46 Third Ave [E 10th St]
CH • **Chase (ATM)** • 125 Third Ave [E 14th St]
CH • **Chase (ATM)** • 144 Bleecker St [LaGuardia]
CH • **Chase (ATM)** • 24 E 14th St [University Pl]
CH • **Chase (ATM)** • 4 W 4th St [Broadway]
CH • **Chase (ATM)** • 598 Broadway [E Houston St]
CH • **Chase (ATM)** • 636 Broadway [Bleecker St]
CH • **Chase (ATM)** • 761 Broadway [E 8th St]
CI • **Citibank** • 555 LaGuardia Pl [W 3rd St]
CO • **Commerce** • 47 Third Ave [E 10th St]
CO • **Commerce** • 666 Broadway [Bond St]
CO • **Commerce** • 90 Fifth Ave [W 15th St]
EM • **Emigrant** • 105 Second Ave [E 6th St]
HS • **HSBC** • 599 Broadway [W Houston St]
HS • **HSBC** • 769 Broadway [E 9th St]
CU • **Lower East Side People's Federal Credit Union (ATM)** • 13 E 8th St [Fifth Ave]
CU • **Lower East Side People's Federal Credit Union (ATM)** • 7 W 14th St [Fifth Ave]
NF • **North Fork** • 159 Second Ave [E 10th St]
NF • **North Fork** • 594 Broadway [E Houston St]
SB • **Sovereign** • 43 E 8th St [Greene St]
SB • **Sovereign (ATM)** • CVS • 158 Bleecker St [Thompson St]

WM • **WaMu** • 130 Second Ave [St Marks Pl]
WM • **WaMu** • 57 Bond St [Bowery]
WM • **WaMu** • 835 Broadway [E 13th St]

 Community Gardens

Emergency Rooms

• **New York Eye & Ear Infirmary** • 310 E 14th St [2nd Av]

Landmarks

• **The Alamo (The Cube)** • Astor Pl & Fourth Ave
• **Asch Building** • 23-29 Washington Pl [Greene]
• **Bayard-Condict Building** • 65 Bleecker St
• **Colonnade Row** • 428 Lafayette St [Astor Pl]
• **Con Edison Building** • 145 E 14th St [Irving]
• **Cooper Union** • 30 Cooper Sq [Bowery]
• **Former location of CBGB** • 315 Bowery
• **Gem Spa** • 131 Second Ave [St Marks]
• **Grace Church** • 802 Broadway [11th]
• **Great Jones Fire House** • Great Jones St
• **Joey Ramone Place** • Bowery & E 2nd St
• **Mark Twain House** • 14 W 10th St [5th Av]
• **Milano's** • 51 E 14th St [Mott]
• **New York Marble Cemetery** • 41 Second Ave
• **Old Merchant's House** • 29 E 4th St [Lafayette]
• **The Public Theater** • 425 Lafayette St [Astor Pl]
• **Salmagundi Club** • 47 Fifth Ave [12th]
• **Singer Building** • 561 Broadway [Prince]
• **Site of the Weathermen Explosion** • 18 W 11th St [5th Av]
• **St Mark's-in-the-Bowery Church** • 131 E 10th St [3rd Av]
• **The Strand Bookstore** • 828 Broadway [12th]
• **Wanamaker's** • Broadway & E 8th St
• **Washington Mews** • University Pl (entrance)
• **Washington Square Park** • Washington Sq

Libraries

• **Mulberry** • 10 Jersey St [Mulberry St]
• **Ottendorfer** • 135 Second Ave [9th]

Post Offices

• **Cooper** • 93 Fourth Ave [11th]
• **Patchin** • 70 W 10th St [6th Av]
• **Prince** • 124 Greene St [Prince]

Map 6 • **Washington Sq / NYU / NoHo / SoHo**

1
2

Union Sq W
Union Sq E

PAGE 266

Union Square

Rutherford Pl
Stuyvesant Square
N D Pertman Pl

W 16th St
E 16th St

W 15th St
E 15th St

9

W 14th St
E 14th St

10

New School
PAGE 250

W 13th St
E 13th St

W 12th St
E 12th St

A

W 11th St
E 11th St

Fifth Ave
University Pl

W 10th St
E 10th St

W 9th St
E 9th St

Fourth Ave
Third Ave
Stuyvesant St
Second Ave
First Ave

St Marks Pl

W 8th St
E 8th St

MacDougal Aly
Washington Aly

Waverly Pl
Astor Pl

E 7th St

Cooper Square
E 6th St

Washington Square N
Washington Pl

Schevchenko Pl
E 5th St

PAGE 252
Washington Square

Washington Sq S
W 4th St

Broadway
E 4th St

Lafayette St
E 4th St

7

NYU
W 3rd St

Shinbone Aly
Great Jones St
E 3rd St

Washington Square Village

James Aly
Bond St
NoHo
E 2nd St

Bleecker St
Bowery
E 1st St

Silver Towers
Mercer St

W Houston St
E Houston St
E Houston St

MacDougal St
Sullivan St
Thompson St
LaGuardia Pl

5
B

Jersey St
Mott St
Stanton St

Charlton St
Prince St
Sara D Roosevelt Park
Chrystie St
Forsyth St
Eldridge St
Allen St
Rivington St

SOHO

Vandam St
West Broadway
Wooster St
Greene St
Mercer St
Crosby St
Cleveland Pl
Mulberry St
Elizabeth St

Spring St
Spring St

Minetta St
MacDougal St

Dominick St
Kenmare St
Delancey St

Broome St
Broome St
Centre St

3

1/4 mile
.25 km

Game for a jolt? Forgo the chain coffee shops and dive instead into the pool of unique java offerings such as Mudspot, Joe, Caffe Reggio, Think, Gimme Coffee, or Housing Works. For a different kind of buzz, try Astor Wines or Warehouse Wines.

☕ Coffee

- **Anyway Café** • 34 E 2nd St [2nd Av]
- **Aroma** • 160 Wooster St [W Houston]
- **Atlas Café** • 73 Second Ave [4th]
- **Au Bon Pain** • 58 E 8th St [Mercer]
- **Au Bon Pain** • 684 Broadway [3rd]
- **Bite** • 335 Lafayette St [Bleecker St]
- **Café Angelique** • 68 Bleecker St [Crosby]
- **Café Gitane** • 242 Mott St [Prince]
- **Caffe Dante** • 79 MacDougal St [Bleecker]
- **Caffe Pane e Cioccolato** • 10 Waverly Pl [Mercer]
- **Caffe Reggio** • 119 MacDougal St [3rd]
- **Coffee Master** • 13 E 4th St [Lafayette]
- **Cosi** • 841 Broadway [13th]
- **Cremcaffe** • 65 Second Ave [4th]
- **Cuppa Cuppa** • 75 E 4th St [2nd Av]
- **Dean & Deluca** • 560 Broadway [Prince]
- **Dean & DeLuca Café** • 75 University Pl [11th]
- **Dunkin' Donuts** • 110 E 14th St [Irving]
- **Dunkin' Donuts** • 166 Second Ave [11th]
- **Dunkin' Donuts** • 218 E 14th St [3rd Av]
- **Gimme Coffee** • 228 Mott St [Prince]
- **Hiroko's** • 75 Thompson St [Spring]
- **Housing Works Used Book Café** • 126 Crosby St [Jersey]
- **J&B Express** • 123 W 3rd St [MacDougal]
- **Joe: The Art of Coffee** • 9 E 13th St [5th Av]
- **L'Angolo Café** • 108 W Houston St [Thompson]
- **La Lanterna di Vittorio** • 129 MacDougal St [3rd]
- **Le Petite Café** • 156 Spring St [W B'way]
- **Mission Café** • 82 Second Ave [5th]
- **Moxa** • 552 LaGuardia St [3rd]
- **Mudspot** • 307 E 9th St [2nd Av]
- **News Bar** • 107 University Pl [E 13th]
- **Once Upon A Tart** • 135 Sullivan St [Prince]
- **Open Pantry** • 184 Second Ave [12th]
- **Oren's Daily Roast** • 31 Waverly Pl [Greene]
- **Podunk** • 231 E 5th St [3rd Av]
- **Porto Rico Importing** • 107 Thompson St [Prince]
- **Porto Rico Importing** • 40 St Marks Pl [2nd Av]
- **Saint's Alp Tea House** • 39 Third Ave [9th]
- **Starbucks** • 13 Astor Pl [B'way]
- **Starbucks** • 145 Second Ave [9th]
- **Starbucks** • 21 E 8th St [University]
- **Starbucks** • 45 W 4th St [Wash Sq E]
- **Starbucks** • 51 Astor Pl [4th Av]
- **Starbucks** • 665 Broadway [Bond]
- **Starbucks** • 72 Spring St [Lafayette]
- **Tea Spot** • 127 MacDougal St [3rd]
- **Think** • 1 Bleecker St [Bowery]
- **Think** • 248 Mercer St [3rd]
- **Thompson Café** • 68 Thompson St [Broome]

🌿 Farmers Markets

- **St Mark's Church** (Tues 8 am–7pm, Jun–Dec) • E 10th St & Second Ave

🔧 Hardware Stores

- **Ace Hardware** • 130 Fourth Ave [13th]
- **Allied Hardware** • 59 Second Ave [3rd]
- **Bowery Homes Supplies** 55 Bond St [Bowery]
- **Brickman Outlets** • 125 W 3rd St [MacDougal]
- **East Hardware** • 79 Third Ave [12th]
- **Home Locksmith** • 229 E 14th St [3rd Av]
- **Mott Hardware** • 186 Mott St [Kenmare]
- **Shapiro Hardware** • 63 Bleecker St [Lafayette]
- **TS Hardware** • 52 E 8th St [Mercer]

🍾 Liquor Stores

- **Anthony Liquors** • 52 Spring St [Mulberry]
- **Astor Wines & Spirits** • 399 Lafayette St [4th]
- **B&S Zeeman** • 47 University Pl [9th]
- **Crossroads Wine** • 55 W 14th St [5th Av]
- **Elizabeth & Vine** • 253 Elizabeth St [Houston]
- **Miat Liquor Store** • 166 Second Ave [11th]
- **New Beers Distributors** • 167 Chrystie St [Rivington]
- **Soho Wine** • 461 West Broadway [Houston]
- **Spring Street Wine Shop** • 187 Spring St [Thompson]
- **Thompson Wine** • 222 Thompson St [3rd]
- **Trader Joe's** • 138 E 14th St [Irving]
- **Union Square Wine** • 140 Fourth Ave [13th]
- **Warehouse Wines** • 735 Broadway [Astor Pl]
- **Washington Square Wines** • 545 LaGuardia St [3rd]
- **Wine Therapy** • 171 Elizabeth St [Spring]

🛒 Supermarkets

- **Associated** • 130 Bleecker St [LaGuardia]
- **D'Agostino** • 64 University Pl [11th]
- **Dean & DeLuca** • 560 Broadway [Prince]
- **Garden of Eden** • 7 E 14th St [5th Av]
- **Gristedes** • 246 Mercer St [3rd]
- **Gristedes** • 25 University Pl [8th]
- **Gristedes** • 333 E 14th St [2nd Av]
- **Gristedes** • 5 W 14th St [5th Av]
- **Met Food** • 107 Second Ave [6th]
- **Met Food** • 251 Mulberry St [Prince]
- **Trader Joe's** • 142 E 14th St [Irving]
- **Whole Foods** • 4 Union Sq S [University]

49

Map 6 • **Washington Sq / NYU / NoHo / SoHo**

Union Sq W

E 16th St

W 16th St

PAGE 266

Rutherford Pl

Stuyvesant Square

N D Perlman Pl

Union Sq E

W 15th St

E 15th St

W 14th St

9

E 14th St

10

New School

PAGE 250

W 13th St

E 13th St

W 12th St

E 12th St

Stuyvesant St

W 11th St

E 11th St

First Ave

W 10th St

E 10th St

Second Ave

A

W 9th St

E 9th St

Fifth Ave

University Pl

W 8th St

E 8th St

Third Ave

MacDougal Aly

Washington Aly

Fourth Ave

Astor Pl

St Marks Pl

T Shevchenko Pl

E 7th St

Waverly Pl

Washington Sq N

Washington Pl

E 6th St

Washington Square

PAGE 252

Washington Sq E

Broadway

Cooper Square

E 5th St

Washington Sq S

W 4th St

E 4th St

7

Ave of the Americas

NYU

W 3rd St

NOHO

E 3rd St

Shinbone Aly

Lafayette St

Great Jones St

Washington Square Village

James Aly

Bond St

E 2nd St

Minetta Ln

Bowery

Bleecker St

4

Mercer St

E 1st St

Silver Towers

LaGuardia Pl

Thompson St

Sullivan St

MacDougal St

W Houston St

E Houston St

E Houston St

5

SOHO

Stanton St

Jersey St

Prince St

Sara D Roosevelt Park

Forsyth St

Eldridge St

Allen St

West Broadway

Wooster St

Greene St

Mercer St

Crosby St

Mulberry St

Mott St

Elizabeth St

Chrystie St

Rivington St

Charlton St

Vandam St

Spring St

Cleveland Pl

Delancey St

Spring St

Dominick St

3

Kenmare St

Broome St

3

Broome St

Centre St

Map 6

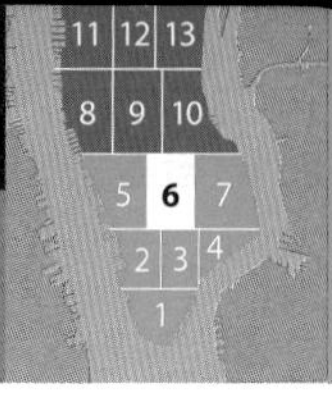

The streets boast eats, drinks, and boutiques galore. Post-grads get flirty at Sweet and Vicious, the literary set holes up in the KGB, and everyone else piles in at Milano's. Like to see and be seen? Do brunch at Balthazar wearing some outrageously kicks from Prada.

Movie Theaters

- **AMC Loews Village VII** • 66 Third Ave [11th]
- **Angelika** • 18 W Houston St [Mercer]
- **Anthology Film Archives** • 32 Second Ave [2nd]
- **Cinema Village** • 22 E 12th St [University]
- **City Cinemas: Village East** • 181 2nd Ave [12th]
- **Landmark Sunshine Cinema** •
  141 E Houston St [Eldridge]
- **NYU Cantor Film Center** • 36 E 8th St [Greene]
- **Quad Cinema** • 34 W 13th St [5th Av]
- **Regal Union Square 14** • 850 Broadway [14th]

Nightlife

- **Beauty Bar** • 231 E 14th St [3rd Av]
- **Blue & Gold** • 79 E 7th St [1st Av]
- **Bowery Ballroom** • 6 Delancey St [Bowery]
- **Bowery Poetry Club** • 308 Bowery [1st]
- **Decibel** • 240 E 9th St [2nd Av]
- **Fanelli's** • 94 Prince St [Mercer]
- **Grassroots Tavern** • 20 St Marks Pl [2nd Av]
- **Holiday Lounge** • 75 St Marks Pl [1st Av]
- **Joe's Pub** • 425 Lafayette St [Astor Pl]
- **KGB** • 85 E 4th St [2nd Av]
- **Marion's Continental** • 354 Bowery [Great Jones]
- **Mars Bar** • 25 E 1st St [2nd Av]
- **Milady's** • 160 Prince St [Thompson]
- **Milano's** • 51 E Houston [Mott]
- **Nevada Smith's** • 74 Third Ave [11th]
- **Pravda** • 281 Lafayette St [Prince]
- **Red Bench** • 107 Sullivan St [Spring]
- **Rififi** • 332 E 11th St [2nd Av]
- **Sweet & Vicious** • 5 Spring St [Bowery]
- **Webster Hall** • 125 E 11th St [4th Av]

Restaurants

- **12 Chairs** • 56 MacDougal St [King]
- **9th St Market** • 337 E 9th St [2nd Av]
- **Arturo's** • 106 W Houston St [Thompson]
- **Babbo** • 110 Waverly Pl [MacDougal]
- **Balthazar** • 80 Spring St [Crosby]
- **Blue Hill** • 75 Washington Pl [MacDougal]
- **Blue Ribbon** • 97 Sullivan St [Spring]
- **Café Colonial** • 276 Elizabeth St [Houston]
- **Café Habana** • 17 Prince St [Elizabeth]
- **Eight Mile Creek** • 240 Mulberry St [Prince]
- **Five Points** • 31 Great Jones St [Lafayette]
- **Frank** • 88 Second Ave [5th]
- **Freemans** • End of Freeman Aly [Rivington]
- **Ghenet** • 284 Mulberry St [Houston]
- **Hampton Chutney** • 68 Prince St [Crosby]
- **Hummus Place** • 99 MacDougal St [Bleecker]
- **Il Mulino** • 86 W 3rd St [Thompson]

- **Jeollado** • 116 E 4th St [1st Av]
- **John's of 12th Street** • 302 E 12th St [2nd Av]
- **Jules** • 65 St Marks Pl [1st Av]
- **La Esquina** • 106 Kenmare St [Cleveland]
- **Lahore** • 132 Crosby St [Houston] ◌
- **Mara's Homemade** • 342 E 6th St [2nd Av]
- **Olive's** • 120 Prince St [Wooster]
- **Paul's Palace** • 131 Second Ave [St Marks]
- **Pepe Rosso** • 149 Sullivan St [Houston]
- **Prune** • 54 E 1st St [1st Av]
- **Sammy's Roumanian** •
  157 Chrystie St [Delancey]
- **Strip House** • 13 E 12th St [5th Av]
- **Temple** • 81 St Marks Pl [1st Av]
- **Ukranian East Village Restaurant** •
  140 Second Av [E 9th St]
- **Una Pizzeria Napoletana** • 349 E 12th St [1st]
- **Veselka** • 144 Second Ave [9th] ◌

Shopping

- **Apple Store SoHo** • 103 Prince St [Greene]
- **Black Hound New York** • 170 Second Ave [11th]
- **Cinema Nolita** • 202 Elizabeth St [Prince St]
- **Daily 235** • 235 Elizabeth St [Prince]
- **East Village Cheese** • 40 Third Ave [10th]
- **East Village Music** • 85 E 4th St [2nd Av]
- **EMS** • 591 Broadway [Houston]
- **Global Table** • 107 Sullivan St [Spring]
- **Grand Daisy Bakery** • 73 Sullivan St [Spring]
- **Jam Paper & Envelope** • 135 Third Ave [15th]
- **Joe's Dairy** • 156 Sullivan St [Houston]
- **Kar'ikter** • 19 Prince St [Elizabeth]
- **Kee's Chocolates** • 80 Thompson St [Spring St]
- **Kiehl's** • 109 Third Ave [13th]
- **Kim's Video** • 6 St Marks Pl [3rd Av]
- **Lighting by Gregory** • 158 Bowery [Delancey]
- **Lord Willy's** • 223 Mott St [Prince]
- **The Market NYC** • 268 Mulberry St [Prince]
- **MOMA Design Store** • 81 Spring St [Crosby]
- **Moishe's Bake Shop** • 115 Second Ave [E 7th St]
- **Moss** • 150 Greene St [Prince]
- **Nancy Koltes** • 31 Spring St [Mott]
- **National Wholesale Liquidators** •
  632 Broadway [Bleecker]
- **New York Central Art Supply** • 62 3rd Ave [11th]
- **Other Music** • 15 E 4th St [Lafayette]
- **Otto Tootsi Plohound** • 273 Lafayette St [Prince]
- **Pino's Prime Meats** • 149 Sullivan St [Prince St]
- **Prada** • 575 Broadway [Prince]
- **Pylones** • 69 Spring St [Lafayette]
- **Saint Mark's Comics** • 11 St Marks Pl [3rd Av]
- **Stereo Exchange** • 627 Broadway [Bleecker]
- **Taschen** • 107 Greene St [Prince]
- **Uniqlo** • 546 Broadway [Spring]

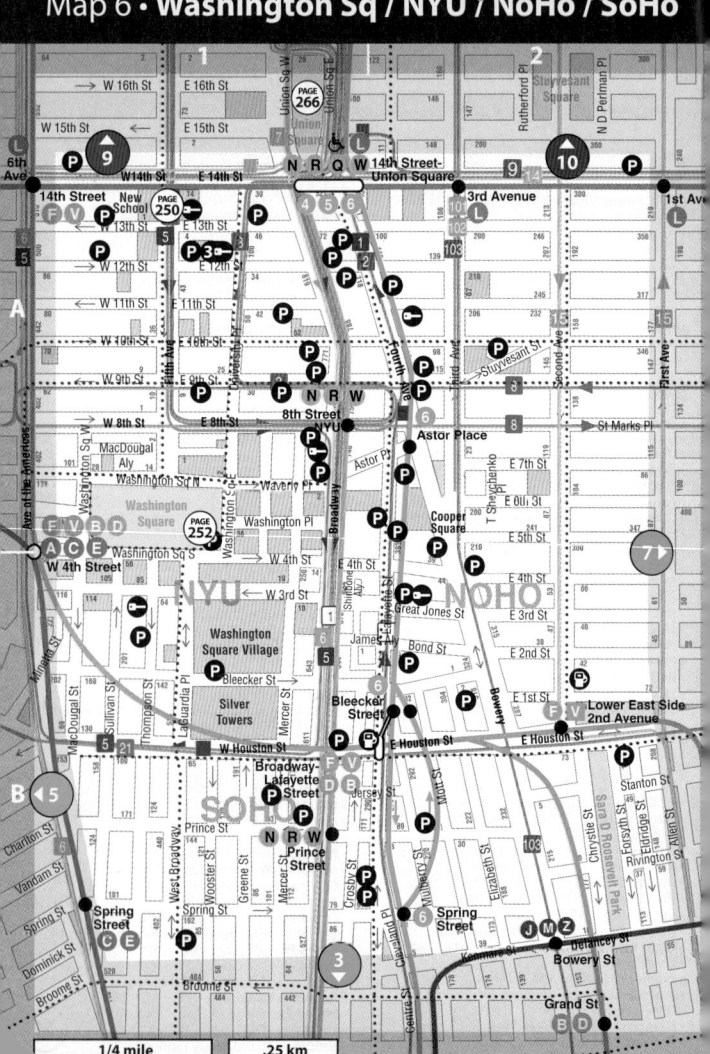

Map 6 · **Washington Sq / NYU / NoHo / SoHo**

Transportation

Considering how exciting and vibrant this section of the city is, parking should be way worse than it is. For biking, use Lafayette Street to go north and either Fifth Avenue or Second Avenue to go south. You can transfer to the BDFV subway from the 6 only going downtown—weird.

Subways

6 .... Astor Pl
6 .... Bleecker St
6 .... Spring St
F V .... Second Ave
B D F V .... Broadway-Lafayette St
J M Z .... Bowery
L .... Third Ave
4 5 6 L N Q R W
.... 14th St-Union Sq
N R W .... 8th St-NYU
N R W .... Prince St
C E .... Spring St

Bus Lines

1 .... Fifth/Madison Aves
101 . Third Ave/Lexington Ave/Amsterdam Ave
102 .. Third Ave/Lexington Ave/Malcolm X Blvd
103 .... Third Ave/Lexington Ave
14 .... 14th St Crosstown
15 .... First/Second Aves
2 .... Fifth/Madison Aves/Powell Blvd
21 .... Houston St/Avenue C
3 ...... Fifth/Madison Aves/St Nicholas Ave
5 .... Fifth Ave/Sixth Ave/Riverside Dr
6 .... Seventh Ave/Sixth Ave/Broadway
7 .... Columbus Ave/Amsterdam Ave
Lenox Ave/Sixth/Seventh Aves/Broadway
8 .... 8th/9th Sts Crosstown
9 .... Ave B/East Broadway

Bike Lanes

- • • • Marked Bike Lane
- • • • Recommended Route

Car Rental

- **Action Car Rental** • 741 Broadway [Astor Pl]
- **Alamo** • 19 E 12th St [University]
- **American Rent-A-Car** •
  33 Great Jones St [Lafayette]
- **Avis** • 68 E 11th St [B'way]
- **Enterprise** • 221 Thompson St [Bleecker]
- **Hertz** • 12 E 13th St [5th Av]
- **National/Alamo** • 21 E 12th St [University]

Gas Stations

- **BP Amoco** • 21 E Houston St [Crosby]
- **Exxon** • 24 Second Ave [1st] ⊗

Parking

Map 7 • East Village / Lower East Side

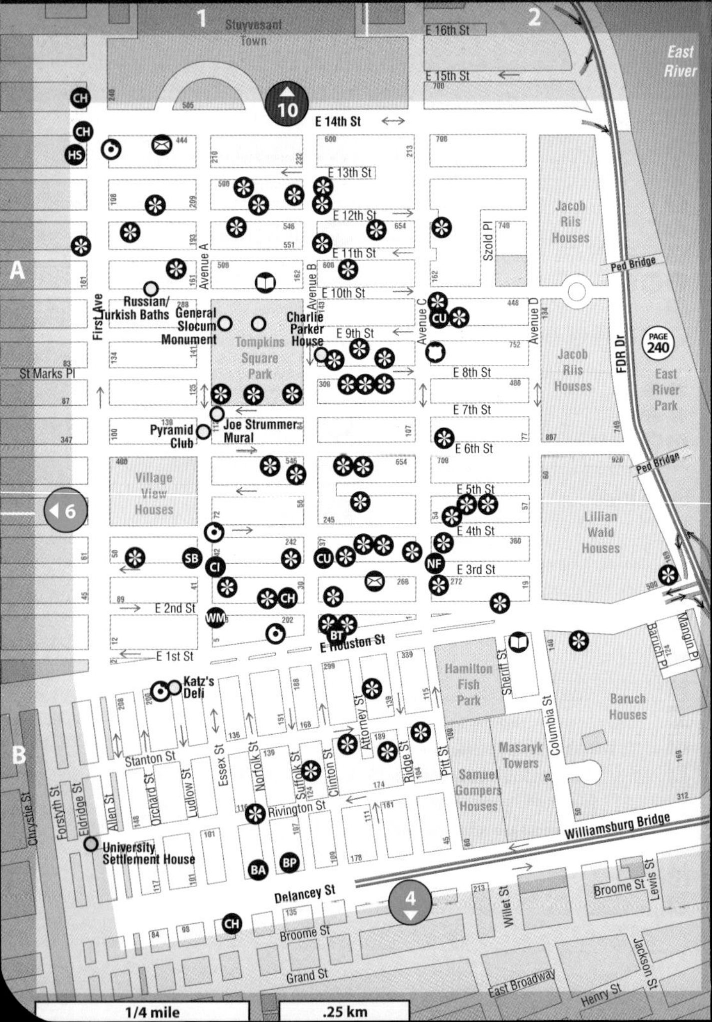

Stuyvesant Town

East River

E 16th St

E 15th St

E 14th St

E 13th St

E 12th St

E 11th St

E 10th St

E 9th St

E 8th St

E 7th St

E 6th St

E 5th St

E 4th St

E 3rd St

E 2nd St

E 1st St

E Houston St

First Ave

Avenue A

Avenue B

Avenue C

Avenue D

Szold Pl

FDR Dr

Jacob Riis Houses

Jacob Riis Houses

East River Park

Lillian Wald Houses

Ped Bridge

Ped Bridge

PAGE 240

St Marks Pl

Russian/Turkish Baths

General Slocum Monument

Charlie Parker House

Tompkins Square Park

Pyramid Club

Joe Strummer Mural

Village View Houses

Katz's Deli

University Settlement House

Stanton St

Rivington St

Delancey St

Broome St

Grand St

East Broadway

Henry St

Chrystie St

Forsyth St

Eldridge St

Allen St

Orchard St

Ludlow St

Essex St

Norfolk St

Suffolk St

Clinton St

Attorney St

Ridge St

Pitt St

Sheriff St

Columbia St

Willet St

Baruch Pl

Mangin St

Lewis St

Hamilton Fish Park

Baruch Houses

Masaryk Towers

Samuel Gompers Houses

Williamsburg Bridge

1/4 mile

.25 km

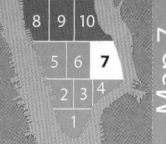

Essentials

Map 7

Though old-timers say this area is irrevocably wrecked, we're still partial to the LES and, especially, the East Village. The small-scale feel, excellent food and drink, and never-ending reserve of small, cool shops make things pretty sweet in Map 7. We still don't understand why it's so much dirtier than the West Village though.

⊙ Bagels

- **535 Self** • 203 E Houston St [Ludlow]
- **Bagel Zone** • 50 Ave A [4th]
- **David's Bagels** • 228 First Ave [14th]
- **Houston's Bagel & Grill** •
283 E Houston St [Clinton]

$ Banks

BP • **Banco Popular** •
134 Delancey St [Norfolk St]
BP • **Banco Popular** • 310 E Houston St [Ave B]
BA • **Bank of America** •
126 Delancey St [Norfolk St]
CH • **Chase** • 109 Delancey St [Essex St]
CH • **Chase** • 255 First Ave [E 15th St]
CH • **Chase (ATM)** • Duane Reade •
194 E 2nd St [Ave B]
CH • **Chase (ATM)** • Duane Reade •
237 First Ave [E 14th St]
CI • **Citibank** • 50 Ave A [E 4th St]
HS • **HSBC** • 245 First Ave [E 15th St]
CU • **Lower East Side People's Federal
Credit Union** • 134 Ave C [E 9th St]
CU • **Lower East Side People's Federal
Credit Union** • 37 Ave B [E 3rd St]
NF • **North Fork** • 273 E 3rd St [Ave C]
SB • **Sovereign** • 57 Ave A [E 4th St]
WM • **Washington Mutual** • 20 Ave A [E 2nd St]

❋ Community Gardens

○ Landmarks

- **Charlie Parker House** •
151 Ave B & 10th St
- **General Slocum Monument** •
Tompkins Sq Park [Av A]
- **Joe Strummer Memorial** •
112 Ave A [E 7th St]
- **Katz's Deli** • 205 E Houston St [Ludlow]
- **Pyramid Club** • 101 Ave A [7th]
- **Russian and Turkish Baths** •
268 E 10th St [1st Av]
- **Tompkins Square Park** • Ave A & E 9th St
- **University Settlement House** •
184 Eldridge St [Rivington]

🏛 Libraries

- **Hamilton Fish Park** •
415 E Houston St [Columbia]
- **Tompkins Square** • 331 E 10th St [Av B]

👮 Police

- **9th Precinct** • 130 Avenue C [8th]

✉ Post Offices

- **Peter Stuyvesant** • 432 E 14th St [1st Av]
- **Tompkins Square** • 244 E 3rd St [Av C]

55

Map 7 · **East Village / Lower East Side**

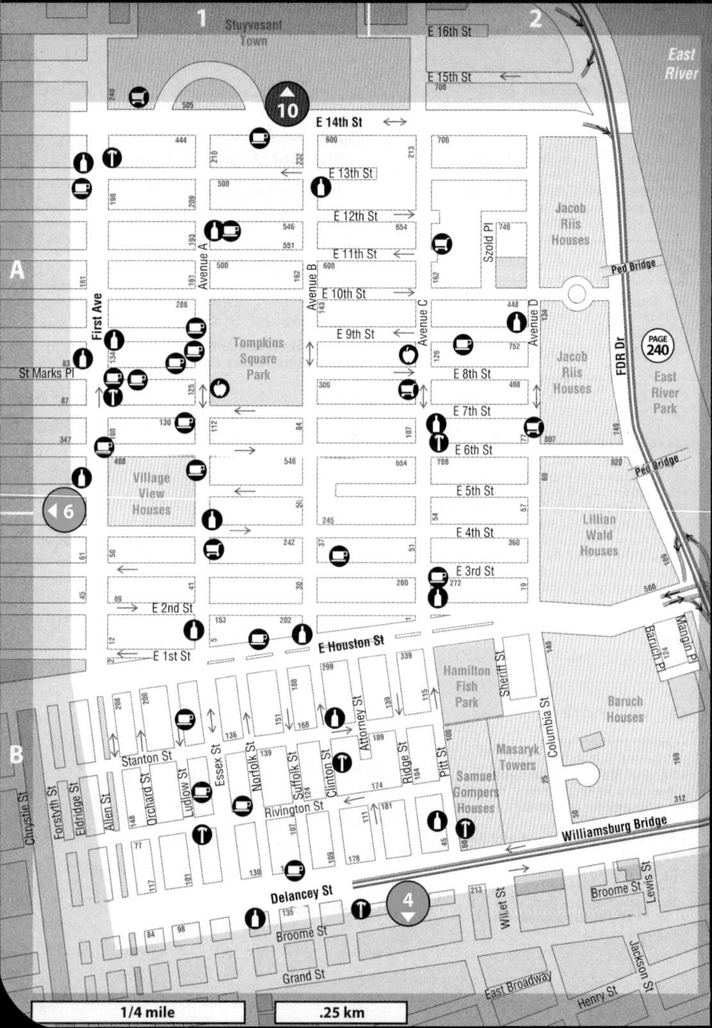

1

Stuyvesant
Town

E 16th St

2

East
River

E 15th St

740

509

10

E 14th St

444

210

222

600

E 13th St

713

706

706

198

299

500

E 12th St

654

746

Jacob Riis
Houses

593

546

551

E 11th St

Szold Pl

Ped Bridge

A

181

Avenue A

500

162

E 10th St

600

Avenue B

448

288

E 9th St

Avenue C

126

752

Avenue D

134

St Marks Pl

E 8th St

468

East
River
Park

93

125

300

187

807

87

136

112

84

E 7th St

920

347

460

546

E 6th St

708

Jacob Riis
Houses

FDR Dr

148

Village
View
Houses

561

E 5th St

54

57

Lillian
Wald
Houses

6

61

50

242

37

51

360

E 4th St

Ped Bridge

681

45

89

41

30

268

19

E 3rd St

272

508

E 2nd St

5

153

202

654

E 1st St

E Houston St

299

339

Hamilton
Fish
Park

148

Baruch
Houses

Mangin Pl

Baruch Pl

B

268

260

136

198

151

168

115

Sheriff St

Columbia St

Masaryk
Towers

312

Stanton St

148

Essex St

Norfolk St

Suffolk St

Clinton St

Ridge St

Pitt St

Samuel
Gompers
Houses

Allen St

Orchard St

Ludlow St

Rivington St

174

181

77

169

146

Williamsburg Bridge

Chrystie St

Forsyth St

Eldridge St

117

178

Willet St

Delancey St

4

64

98

135

213

Broome St

Broome St

Lewis St

Jackson St

Grand St

East Broadway

Henry St

| 1/4 mile | .25 km |

Want to know what kind of people live in this area? Check out the number of coffee shops, pet stores, and liquor shops. Some sundry recommendations: Saifee for hardware, Café Pick Me Up for coffee, Sympathy for the Kettle for tea, and Alphabet City Wine Co. for wine.

Coffee

- **9th Street Espresso** • 700 E 9th St [Av C]
- **Abraço** • 86 E 7th St [1st Av]
- **The Bean** • 49 1/2 First Ave [3rd]
- **Café Pick Me Up** • 145 Ave A [9th]
- **Ciao for Now** • 504 E 12th St [Av A]
- **Flea Market Café** • 131 Ave A [St Marks]
- **Dunkin' Donuts** • 100 First Ave [6th]
- **Dunkin' Donuts** • 140 Delancey St [Suffolk]
- **Dunkin' Donuts** • 215 First Ave [13th]
- **Dunkin' Donuts** • 250 E Houston St [Norfolk]
- **Dynasty Restaurant & Coffee Shop** • 600 E 14th St [Av B]
- **Hopscotch Café** • 139 Ave A [9th]
- **Lalita Java Limited** • 210 E 3rd St [Av B]
- **Le Gamin Café** • 536 E 5th St [Av A]
- **Live Juice** • 85 Ave A [6th]
- **Maria's Café** • 32 Ave C [3rd]
- **Pink Pony Café** • 176 Ludlow St [E Houston]
- **Rush Hour** • 134 Ludlow St [Rivington]
- **Simone Espresso & Wine Bar** • 134 First Ave [St Marks]
- **Sugar Sweet Sunshine Bakery** • 126 Rivington St [Norfolk St]
- **Sympathy for the Kettle** • 109 St Marks Pl [1st Av]

Farmers Markets

- **Lower East Side Girls Club Farmers Market (Wed 11 am–7 pm, Jul 1–Oct 31)** • Ave C b/w 8th St & 9th St
- **Tompkins Square Park (Sun 8 am–6 pm, year round)** • E 7th St & Ave A

Hardware Stores

- **Ace Hardware** • 55 First Ave [3rd]
- **CHP Hardware** • 96 Ave C [6th]
- **H&W Hardware** • 220 First Ave [13th]
- **HH Hardware** • 111 Rivington St [Essex]
- **Rosa Hardware** • 85 Pitt St [Rivington]
- **Rothstein Hardware** • 56 Clinton St [Rivington]
- **Saifee Hardware** • 114 First Ave [7th]

Liquor Stores

- **6 Avenue B Liquors** • 6 Ave B [2nd]
- **Alphabet City Wine Company** • 100 Ave C [E 7th St]
- **Avenue A Wine & Liquor** • 196 Ave A [12th]
- **Bee Liquors** • 225 Ave B [13th]
- **De Vino** • 30 Clinton St [Stanton]
- **Discovery Wines** • 10 Ave A [Houston]
- **East Village Wines** • 138 First Ave [St Marks]
- **Gary's Liquor** • 141 Essex St [Rivington]
- **Jade Fountain Liquor** • 123 Delancey St [Norfolk]
- **Loon Chun Liquor** • 47 Pitt St [Delancey]
- **Marty's Liquors** • 133 Ave D [9th]
- **Nizga Liquors** • 58 Ave A [4th]
- **Sale Price Liquor** • 24 Ave C [3rd]
- **Tinto Fino** • 85 First Ave [5th]
- **Wines on 1st** • 224 First Ave [13th]

Supermarkets

- **Associated** • 123 Ave C [8th]
- **Associated** • 409 E 14th St [1st Av]
- **C-Town** • 188 Ave C [12th]
- **Compare** • 71 Ave D [6th]
- **Key Food** • 43 Columbia St [Delancey]
- **Key Food** • 52 Ave A [4th] ♿

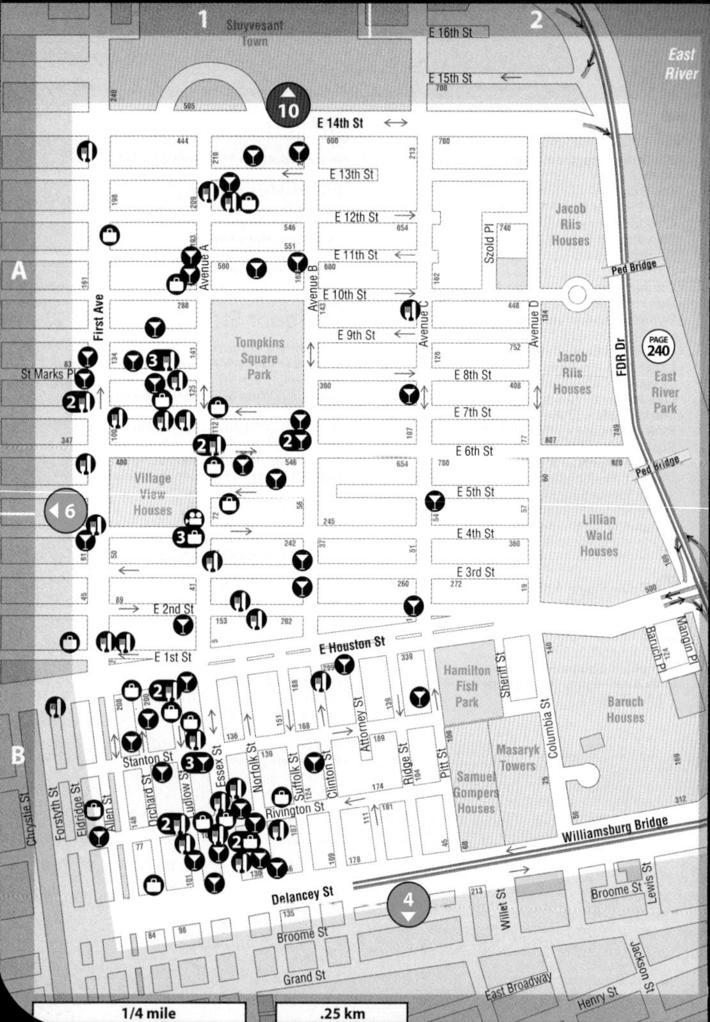

Map 7 • East Village / Lower East Side

1 Stuyvesant Town

2

East River

E 16th St

E 15th St

10 E 14th St

E 13th St

E 12th St

Jacob Riis Houses

E 11th St

Szold Pl

E 10th St

Ped Bridge

A E 9th St

First Ave

Avenue A

Avenue B

Avenue C

Avenue D

St Marks Pl

E 8th St

Jacob Riis Houses

FDR Dr

PAGE 240

East River Park

Tompkins Square Park

E 7th St

E 6th St

Ped Bridge

Village View Houses

E 5th St

Lillian Wald Houses

6

E 4th St

E 3rd St

E 2nd St

E 1st St

E Houston St

Hamilton Fish Park

Baruch Houses

Mangin Pl

Baruch Pl

Stanton St

Essex St

Attorney St

Ridge St

Pitt St

Sheriff St

Columbia St

Masaryk Towers

Chrystie St

Forsyth St

Eldridge St

Allen St

Orchard St

Ludlow St

Norfolk St

Suffolk St

Clinton St

Samuel Gompers Houses

Williamsburg Bridge

Rivington St

Delancey St

4

Willet St

Broome St

Lewis St

Jackson St

Broome St

Grand St

East Broadway

Henry St

1/4 mile   .25 km

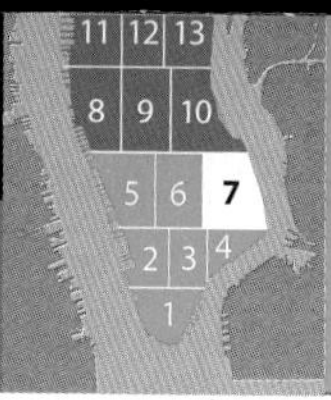

Entertainment

11 | 12 | 13
8 | 9 | 10
5 | 6 | **7**
2 | 3 | 4
1

Map 7

A million great restaurants. All the bars below are great (unless we say it ain't), but you'll usually find us at Joe's, 2A, Bua, 7B, or Heathers. Also, a great area for gifts—between Alphabets, Exit 9, Lancelotti, and Economy Candy, you're bound to find that perfect something. If not, try Babeland.

🎭 Movie Theaters

• **Two Boots Pioneer Theater** • 155 E 3rd St [Av A]

🎯 Nightlife

• **2A** • 25 Ave A [2nd]
• **7B (Horseshoe Bar)** • 108 Ave B [7th]
• **Ace Bar** • 531 E 5th St [Av A]
• **Arlene's Grocery** • 95 Stanton St [Ludlow]
• **Back Room** • 102 Norfolk St [Delancey]
• **Barramundi** • 67 Clinton St [Rivington]
• **Bua** • 122 St Marks Pl [1st Av]
• **Cake Shop** • 152 Ludlow St [Stanton]
• **Dark Room** • 165 Ludlow St [Stanton]
• **Heathers** • 506 E 13th St [Av A]
• **Hi-Fi** • 169 Ave A [11th]
• **I Coppi** • 432 E 9th St [1st Av]
• **Joe's Bar** • 520 E 6th St [Av A]
• **Lakeside Lounge** • 162 Ave B [10th]
• **The Magician** • 118 Rivington St [Essex]
• **Mama's Bar** • 34 Ave B [E 3rd St]
• **Manitoba's** • 99 Ave B [6th]
• **Marshall Stack** • 66 Rivington St [Allen St]
• **Max Fish** • 178 Ludlow St [Stanton]
• **Mercury Lounge** • 217 E Houston St [Essex]
• **Mona's** • 224 Ave B [13th]
• **Motor City** • 127 Ludlow St [Rivington]
• **NuBlu** • 62 Ave C [5th]
• **Nuyorican Poet's Café** • 236 E 3rd St [Av C]
• **Parkside Lounge** • 317 E Houston St [Attorney]
• **The Stone** • Ave C & E 2nd St [2nd]
• **Ten Degrees** • 121 St Marks Pl [1st Av]
• **Verlaine** • 110 Rivington St [Essex]
• **Welcome to the Johnsons** •
123 Rivington St [Essex]
• **Zum Schneider** • 107 Ave C [7th]

🍴 Restaurants

• **7A** • 109 Ave A [7th] ⊘
• **Banjara** • 97 First Ave [6th]
• **Bereket Turkish Kebab House** •
187 E Houston St [Orchard]
• **Big Arc Chicken** • 233 First Ave [E 14th St] ⊘
• **Boca Chica** • 13 First Ave [1st]
• **Caracas Arepa Bar** • 91 E 7th St [1st Av]
• **Clinton St Baking Company** •
4 Clinton St [Houston]
• **Dok Suni's** • 119 First Ave [7th]
• **El Castillo de Jaqua** • 113 Rivington St [Essex]
• **El Sombrero** • 108 Stanton St [Ludlow]
• **Esashi** • 32 Ave A [3rd]

• **Il Posto Accanto** • 190 E 2nd St [Av B]
• **inoteca** • 98 Rivington St [Ludlow]
• **Katz's Deli** • 205 E Houston St [Ludlow]
• **Kuma Inn** • 113 Ludlow St [Delancey]
• **Kura Sushi** • 67 First Ave [4th]
• **Le Pere Pinard** • 175 Ludlow St [Stanton]
• **Luzzo's** • 211 First Ave [13th]
• **Mama's Food Shop** • 200 E 3rd St [Av B]
• **Momofuku Noodle Bar** • 163 First Ave [10th]
• **Nicky's Vietnamese Sandwiches** •
150 E 2nd St [Av A]
• **Odessa** • 119 Ave A [St Marks] ⊘
• **Old Devil Moon** • 511 E 12th St [Av A]
• **Pylos** • 128 E 7th St [Av A]
• **Royale** • 157 Ave C [10th]
• **Schiller's Liquor Bar** • 131 Rivington St [Norfolk]
• **Shopsin's** • 120 Essex St [Rivington]
• **Sidewalk** • 94 Ave A [6th]
• **Sigiri** • 91 First Ave [6th]
• **St Dymphna's** • 118 St Marks Pl [1st Av]
• **Takahachi** • 85 Ave A [6th]
• **Tasting Room** • 72 E 1st St [1st Av]
• **Teany** • 90 Rivington St [Orchard]

🛍 Shopping

• **Alphabets** • 115 Ave A [7th]
• **Babeland** • 94 Rivington St [Ludlow]
• **Dowel Quality Products** • 91 First Ave [6th]
• **Earthmatters** • 177 Ludlow St [Stanton]
• **Economy Candy** • 108 Rivington St [Essex]
• **Essex Street Market** • 120 Essex St [Rivington]
• **Etherea** • 66 Ave A [5th]
• **Exit 9** • 64 Ave A [5th]
• **First Flight Music** • 174 First Ave [11th]
• **Lancelotti** • 66 Ave A [5th]
• **Ludlow Guitars** • 164 Ludlow St [Stanton]
• **Masturbakers** • 511 E 12th St [Av A]
• **The Paris Apartment** • 70 E 1st St [1st Av]
• **Russ & Daughters** • 179 E Houston St [Orchard]
• **Saxelby Cheesemongers** •
120 Essex St [Rivington]
• **Tiny Living** • 125 E 7th St [Av A]
• **Yonah Schimmel's Knishery** •
137 E Houston St [Forsyth]

Map 7 · **East Village / Lower East Side**

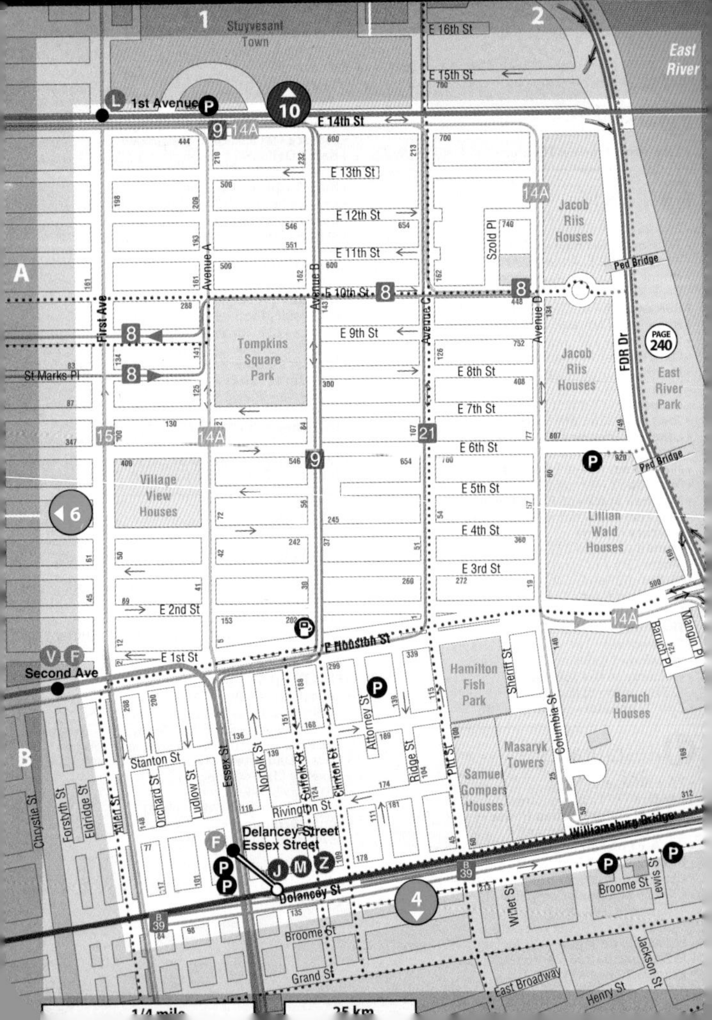

Stuyvesant
Town

East
River

E 16th St

E 15th St
760

1st Avenue

10

E 14th St

9 14A

444

210

292

E 13th St

660

213

700

198

200

500

E 12th St

654

14A

Jacob
Riis
Houses

Szold Pl

746

Ped Bridge

546

551

A

Avenue A

500

E 11th St

162

First Ave

288

E 10th St

8

8

448

FDR Dr

PAGE
240

Tompkins
Square
Park

E 9th St

Avenue B

752

8

Jacob
Riis
Houses

East
River
Park

St Marks Pl

134

8

E 8th St

126

408

77

87

E 7th St

107

15

100

347

130

14A

546

654

21

E 6th St

760

920

P

9

E 5th St

Village
View
Houses

72

55

245

54

360

51

Lillian
Wald
Houses

50

242

27

E 4th St

272

41

E 3rd St

19

500

14A

153

E 2nd St

266

V F

Second Ave

266

E 1st St

E Houston St

339

Hamilton
Fish
Park

Sheriff St

Baruch
Houses

Mangin St

200

290

P

299

188

Attorney St

140

Columbia St

318

136

160

Stanton St

189

Pitt St

194

Masaryk
Towers

Williamsburg Bridge

Christie St

Forsyth St

Eldridge St

Allen St

Orchard St

Ludlow St

Essex St

Norfolk St

Suffolk St

Clinton St

174

Ridge St

184

181

Samuel
Gompers
Houses

Rivington St

111

26

B

F

Delancey Street
Essex Street

178

P
P
P

J M Z

Delancey St

4

P
P

Broome St

Lewis St

Jackson St

Broome St

64

96

Willet St

B
39

Grand St

East Broadway

Henry St

6

1/4 mile

.25 km

Transportation

Map 7

11	12	13
8	9	10
5	6	**7**
2	3	4
	1	

Subway lines frame this area, but most residents only use them for getting to work. The streets are more "griddy" here, so driving is less confusing than to the west, but there's always plenty of traffic, especially on weekends when Avenue A becomes a parking lot.

Subways

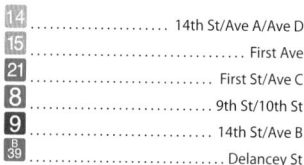

F J M Z	Delancey St-Essex St
L	First Ave
F V	Second Ave

Bus Lines

14	14th St/Ave A/Ave D
15	First Ave
21	First St/Ave C
8	9th St/10th St
9	14th St/Ave B
8 39	Delancey St

Bike Lanes

- • • • Marked Bike Lane
- • • • Recommended Route
- • • • Greenway

 Gas Stations

• **Mobil** • 253 E 2nd St [Av C] ⌚

Ⓟ Parking

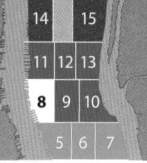
It's not just for artists with money and wealthy gay boys. We know two lesbians here as well. Then toss in the Javits Center, Chelsea Market, Chelsea Piers, and the art galleries. Throw in a diversified nightlife scene and some surprisingly serene streets lined with trees and brownstones, and you've got yourself a neighborhood.

℞ 24-Hour Pharmacies

• **Duane Reade** • 460 Eighth Ave [33rd] ⏱

◉ Bagels

• **Murray's Bagels** • 242 Eighth Ave [22nd]
• **Ruthy's** • Chelsea Market • 75 Ninth Ave [16th]

$ Banks

BA • Bank of America (ATM) •
244 Eighth Ave [W 22nd St]
BA • Bank of America (ATM) •
312 W 34th St [Eighth Ave]
BA • Bank of America (ATM) • Loews •
320 W 34th St [Eighth Ave]
CH • Chase • 475 W 23rd St [Tenth Ave]
CH • Chase (ATM) • Duane Reade •
1 Penn Plz [W 31st St]
CH • Chase (ATM) • 238 Eighth Ave [W 22nd St]
CH • Chase (ATM) • Duane Reade •
315 W 23rd St [Eighth Ave]
CH • Chase (ATM) • Duane Reade •
322 Eighth Ave [W 26th St]
CH • Chase (ATM) • 460 Eighth Ave [W 33rd St]
CI • Citibank • 322 W 23rd St [Eighth Ave]
CI • Citibank (ATM) •
111 Eighth Ave [W 16th St]
CI • Citibank (ATM) • Chelsea Market •
322 W 23rd St [Eighth Ave]
CI • Citibank (ATM) • 88 Tenth Ave [W 16th St]
**CU • Lower East Side People's Federal Credit
Union (ATM)** • McDonald's •
335 Eighth Ave [W 27th St]
MA • Marathon • 250 Ninth Ave [W 25th St]
NF • North Fork • 520 Eighth Ave [W 36th St]
PN • PNC (ATM) • Tommy Hilfiger, 6th Flr •
601 W 26th St [Eleventh Ave]
CU • Skyline Federal Credit Union •
350 W 31st St [Ninth Ave]
SB • Sovereign (ATM) • CVS •
272 Eighth Ave [W 24th St]
WA • Wachovia • 66 Ninth Ave [W 15th St]
WM • Washington Mutual •
111 Eighth Ave [W 16th St]
WM • Washington Mutual •
601 Eighth Ave [W 39th St]

◎ Landmarks

• **Chelsea Market** • 75 Ninth Ave [16th]
• **The Frying Pan** • Pier 63 [23rd]
• **General Theological Seminary •**
175 Ninth Ave [20th]
• **High Line Elevated Railroad •**
Gansevoort to 34th St, west of Tenth Ave
• **JA Farley Post Office** • 441 Eighth Ave [31st]
• **Jacob K Javits Convention Center •**
36th St & Eleventh Ave
• **Starrett-Lehigh Building •**
27th St & Eleventh Ave

🔵 Police

• **Mid-Town South** • 357 W 35th St [9th Av]

✉ Post Offices

• **James A Farley** • 421 Eighth Ave [31st] ⏱
• **London Terrace** • 234 Tenth Ave [24th]
• **Port Authority** • 309 W 15th St [9th Av]

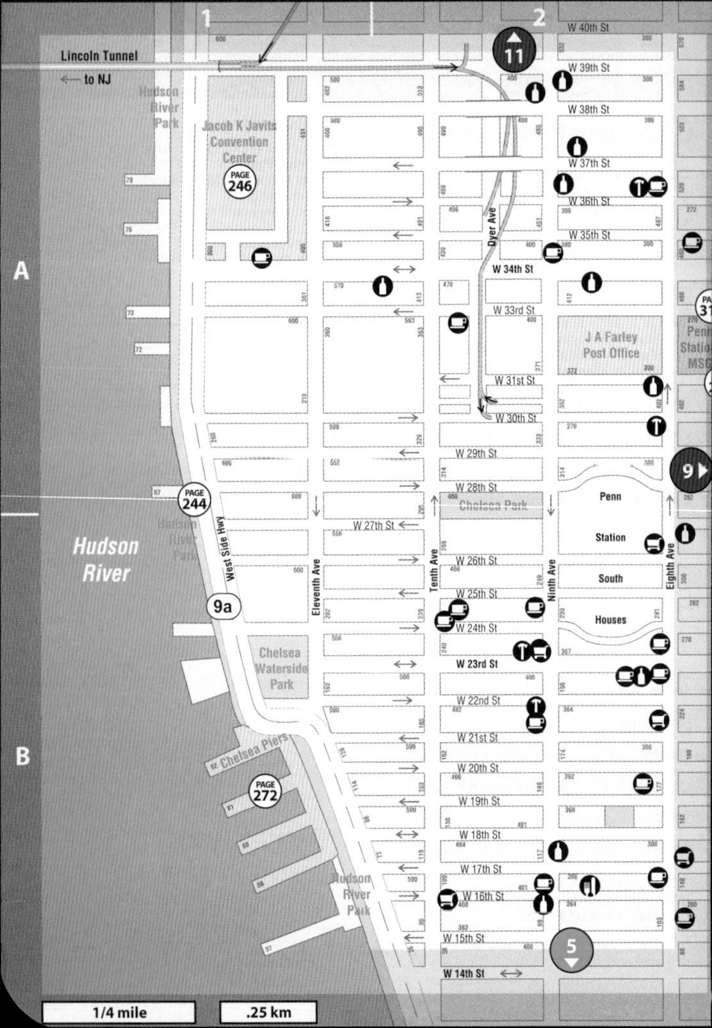

Map 8 · Chelsea

N

W 40th St

Lincoln Tunnel
← to NJ

Hudson River Park

Jacob K Javits Convention Center

PAGE 246

W 39th St

W 38th St

W 37th St

W 36th St

W 35th St

W 34th St

W 33rd St

W 31st St

W 30th St

W 29th St

W 28th St

W 27th St

W 26th St

W 25th St

W 24th St

W 23rd St

W 22nd St

W 21st St

W 20th St

W 19th St

W 18th St

W 17th St

W 16th St

W 15th St

W 14th St

Dyer Ave

J A Farley Post Office

Penn Station MSG

Penn Station

South Houses

Hudson River

West Side Hwy

Hudson River Park

PAGE 244

9a

Chelsea Waterside Park

Chelsea Piers

PAGE 272

Hudson River Park

Eleventh Ave

Tenth Ave

Ninth Ave

Eighth Ave

Chelsea Park

A

B

PAGE 31

9

5

11

1/4 mile   .25 km

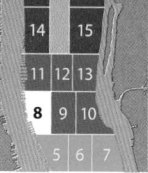
Even if you planned to just pick up a couple basic items, the aforementioned Chelsea Market will suck you in for hours. Diners like Empire or Tick Tock (see Entertainment) will comfort you at any hour, and your sweet tooth will find no shortage of homes in the area, starting with Choux Factory and Billy's Bakery.

Coffee

- **254 Snack Shop Corp** •
  254 Tenth Ave [25th]
- **Billy's Bakery** • 184 Ninth Ave [21st]
- **Choux Factory** • 316 W 23rd St [8th Av]
- **Dunkin' Donuts** •
  269 Eighth Ave [24th]
- **Dunkin' Donuts** •
  525 Eighth Ave [36th]
- **Dunkin' Donuts** •
  243 Ninth Ave [25th]
- **From Earth To You Gourmet Café** •
  252 Tenth Ave [25th]
- **Paradise Café & Muffins** •
  139 Eighth Ave [17th]
- **Starbucks** • 124 Eighth Ave [16th]
- **Starbucks** • 177 Eighth Ave [19th]
- **Starbucks** • 255 Eighth Ave [23rd]
- **Starbucks** • 300 W 23rd St [8th Av]
- **Starbucks** • 450 W 33rd St [10th Av]
- **Starbucks** • 494 Eighth Ave [35th]
- **Starbucks** • 655 W 34th St [11th Av]
- **Starbucks** • 76 Ninth Ave [16th]
- **The Sun Gourmet Deli** •
  440 Ninth Ave [34th]

Hardware Stores

- **Hardware Depot** •
  399 Eighth Ave [30th]
- **MJ Hardware & Electric** •
  315 W 36th St [8th Av]
- **NF Hardware** • 219 Ninth Ave [24th]
- **Scheman & Grant** •
  545 Eighth Ave [37th]
- **True Value Hardware** •
  191 Ninth Ave [22nd]

Liquor Stores

- **34th Street Winery** •
  460 W 34th St [10th Av]
- **Banville & Jones Wine Merchants (Wine Only)** • 545 W 34th St [10th Av]
- **Cambridge Wine & Liquor** •
  594 Eighth Ave [39th]
- **Chelsea Liquor** • 114 Ninth Ave [17th]
- **Chelsea Wine Vault** • Chelsea Market •
  75 Ninth Ave [16th]
- **DeLauren Wines & Liquors** •
  332 Eighth Ave [26th]
- **London Terrace Liquor** •
  221 Ninth Ave [24th]
- **Nrs Wine & Liquor** •
  414 Eighth Ave [31st]
- **Philippe Wine & Liquor** •
  312 W 23rd St [8th Av]
- **US Wine & Liquor** • 486 Ninth Ave [37th]

Supermarkets

- **D'Agostino** • 257 W 17th St [8th Av]
- **Gristedes** • 221 Eighth Ave [21st]
- **Gristedes** • 225 Ninth Ave [24th]
- **Gristedes** • 307 W 26th St [8th Av]
- **Western Beef** • 431 W 16th St [10th Av]

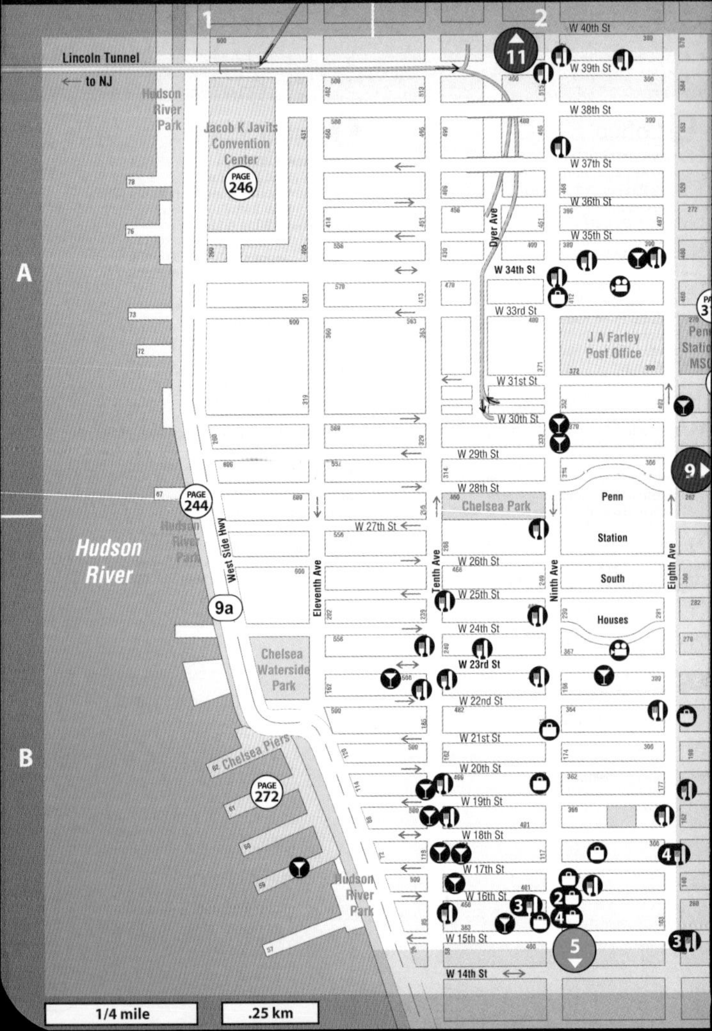

Map 8 · Chelsea

W 40th St

Lincoln Tunnel
← to NJ

W 39th St

W 38th St

Hudson
River
Park

Jacob K Javits
Convention
Center

**PAGE
246**

W 37th St

W 36th St

W 35th St

Dyer Ave

W 34th St

A

W 33rd St

J A Farley
Post Office

W 31st St

W 30th St

W 29th St

**PAGE
244**

W 28th St

Chelsea Park

Penn

Hudson
River
Park

Hudson
River

West Side Hwy

W 27th St

Station

South

9a

W 26th St

Tenth Ave

Ninth Ave

Eighth Ave

W 25th St

Houses

W 24th St

9

Chelsea
Waterside
Park

W 23rd St

Eleventh Ave

W 22nd St

B

W 21st St

Chelsea Piers

W 20th St

**PAGE
272**

W 19th St

W 18th St

W 17th St

Hudson
River
Park

W 16th St

3

2

W 15th St

3

5

W 14th St

1/4 mile   .25 km

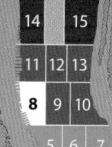

14 15
11 12 13
8 9 10
5 6 7

If the gay paradise along Eighth in southern Chelsea isn't for you, no matter. You can gallery hop in the 20s b/w Tenth and Eleventh, and dine at the delicious Cookshop. Too mellow? Go pubbing at Half King (note the cool apartment/studio space above) or clubbing wherever you spy velvet ropes.

Movie Theaters

- **AMC 34th Street 14** •
  312 W 34th St [8th Av]
- **Clearview's Chelsea West** •
  333 W 23rd St [8th Av]

Nightlife

- **Billymark's West** • 332 Ninth Ave [29th]
- **Chelsea Brewing Company** •
  Pier 59 [17th]
- **Gym Sports Bar** • 167 Eighth Ave [19th]
- **Half King** • 505 W 23rd St [10th Av]
- **Hammerstein Ballroom** •
  311 W 34th St [8th Av]
- **Highline Ballroom** • 431 W 16th St [10th Av]
- **The Kitchen** • 512 W 19th St [10th Av]
- **Molly Wee Pub** • 402 Eighth Ave [30th]
- **The Park** • 118 Tenth Ave [17th]
- **Passerby** • 436 W 15th St [9th Av]
- **Red Rock West** • 457 W 17th St [10th Av]
- **West Side Tavern** • 360 W 23rd St [9th Av]

Restaurants

- **202 Café** • Chelsea Market •
  75 Ninth Ave [16th]
- **Better Burger Chelsea** •
  178 Eighth Ave [19th]
- **Blue Moon Mexican Café** •
  150 Eighth Ave [17th]
- **Buddakan** • Chelsea Market •
  75 Ninth Ave [16th]
- **Burritoville** • 352 W 39th St [9th Av]
- **Cola's Italian** • 148 Eighth Ave [17th]
- **Cookshop** • 156 Tenth Ave [20th]
- **Casa Cupcake** • 545 Ninth Ave [39th]
- **El Quinto Pino** • 401 W 24th St [9th Av]
- **Empire Diner** • 210 Tenth Ave [22nd] ⌂
- **Frank's Restaurant** •
  410 W 16th St [9th Av]
- **Grand Sichuan Int'l** •
  229 Ninth Ave [24th]
- **Havana Chelsea** • 190 Eighth Ave [20th]
- **La Luncheonette–Jean Francois** •
  130 Tenth Ave [18th]
- **La Taza de Oro** • 96 Eighth Ave [15th]
- **Manganaro Foods** • 488 Ninth Ave [37th]
- **Matsuri** • Maritime Hotel •
  369 W 16th St [9th Av]
- **Moonstruck Diner** • 400 W 23rd St [9th Av]

- **Morimoto** • 88 Tenth Ave [16th]
- **Pepe Giallo** • 253 Tenth Ave [25th]
- **Pomodoro** • 518 Ninth Ave [39th]
- **The Red Cat** • 227 Tenth Ave [23rd]
- **Sandwich Planet** • 534 Ninth Ave [40th]
- **Skylight Diner** • 402 W 34th St [9th Av] ⌂
- **Soul Fixin's** • 371 W 34th St [9th Av]
- **Swich** • 104 Eighth Ave [15th]
- **Tia Pol** • 205 Tenth Ave [22nd]
- **Tick Tock Diner** • 481 Eighth Ave [34th] ⌂
- **Tour** • 102 Eighth Ave [15th]
- **Viceroy** • 160 Eighth Ave [18th]

Shopping

- **B&H Photo** • 420 Ninth Ave [33rd]
- **Billy's Bakery** • 184 Ninth Ave [21st]
- **Brooklyn Industries** • 161 Ninth Ave [19th]
- **Buon Italia** • Chelsea Market •
  75 Ninth Ave [16th]
- **Chelsea Garden Center** •
  499 Tenth Ave [38th]
- **Chelsea Market Baskets** •
  75 Ninth Ave [16th]
- **Chelsea Wholesale Flower Market** • Chelsea
  Market • 75 Ninth Ave [16th]
- **Eleni's** • Chelsea Market •
  75 Ninth Ave [16th]
- **Fat Witch Bakery** • Chelsea Market •
  75 Ninth Ave [16th]
- **Find Outlet** • 361 W 17th St [9th Av]
- **Gerry's** • 110 Ninth Ave [17th]
- **Kitchen Market** • 218 Eighth Ave [21st]
- **Ronnybrook Milk Bar** • 75 Ninth Ave [15th]

Map 8 · **Chelsea**

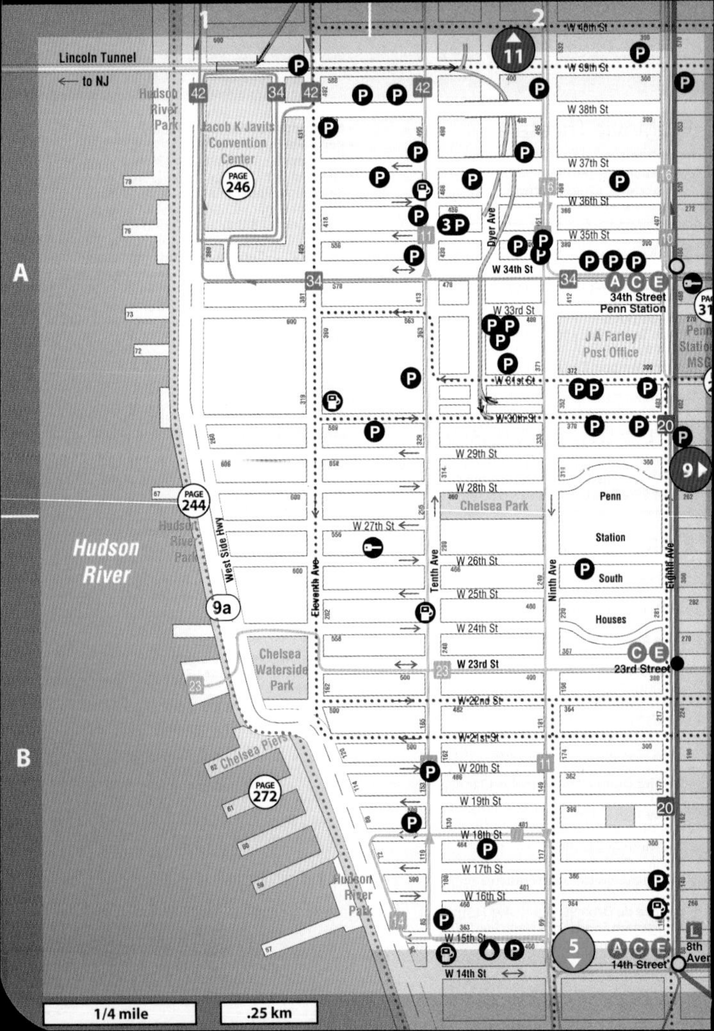

Lincoln Tunnel
← to NJ

W 40th St
W 39th St
W 38th St
W 37th St
W 36th St
W 35th St
W 34th St
W 33rd St
W 31st St
W 30th St
W 29th St
W 28th St
W 27th St
W 26th St
W 25th St
W 24th St
W 23rd St
W 22nd St
W 21st St
W 20th St
W 19th St
W 18th St
W 17th St
W 16th St
W 15th St
W 14th St

Jacob K Javits
Convention Center
PAGE 246

Hudson River Park

Hudson River

West Side Hwy

Eleventh Ave

Tenth Ave

Ninth Ave

Eighth Ave

Dyer Ave

J A Farley Post Office

Chelsea Park

Penn Station

South Houses

Chelsea Waterside Park

Chelsea Pier

PAGE 244

PAGE 272

Hudson River Park

34th Street Penn Station
A C E

23rd Street
C E

14th Street
A C E
8th Ave

1/4 mile   .25 km

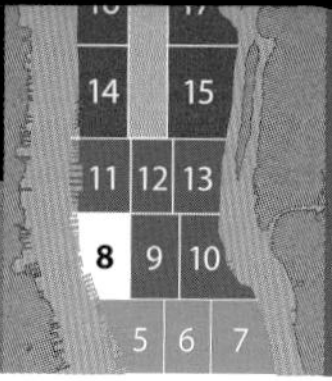

Map 8

Transportation

No subway west of Eighth Avenue. Maybe someday. Take cross-town buses at 14th, 23rd, and 34th Streets if you're too cheap for a cab. Or just walk---it's usually faster anyway. You've got Penn Station and PATH trains if you really must leave the island. Cyclists and bladers have easy access from the path along the river.

Subways

A C E .... 34th St-Penn Station
A C E L .... 14th St/Eighth Ave
C E .... 23rd St

Bus Lines

10 20 Seventh Ave/Eighth Ave/Central Park W
11 .... Ninth Ave/Tenth Ave
14 .... 14th St Crosstown
16 ....34th St Crosstown
23 ....23rd St Crosstown
34 ....34th St Crosstown
42 .... 42nd St Crosstown

Bike Lanes

- • • • Marked Bike Lanes
- • • • Recommended Route
- • • • Greenway

Car Rental

- **Chelsea Rental** • 549 W 26th St [10th Av]
- **Hertz** • 1 Penn Plz [31st]

Car Washes

- **10th Ave Car Wash** • 70 Tenth Ave [15th]

Gas Stations

- **BP Amoco** • 466 Tenth Ave [36th]
- **Exxon** • 110 Eighth Ave [15th] ☼
- **Getty / Lukoil** • 239 Tenth Ave [24th] ☼
- **Mobil** • 309 Eleventh Ave [30th] ☼
- **Mobil** • 70 Tenth Ave [15th] ☼

Parking

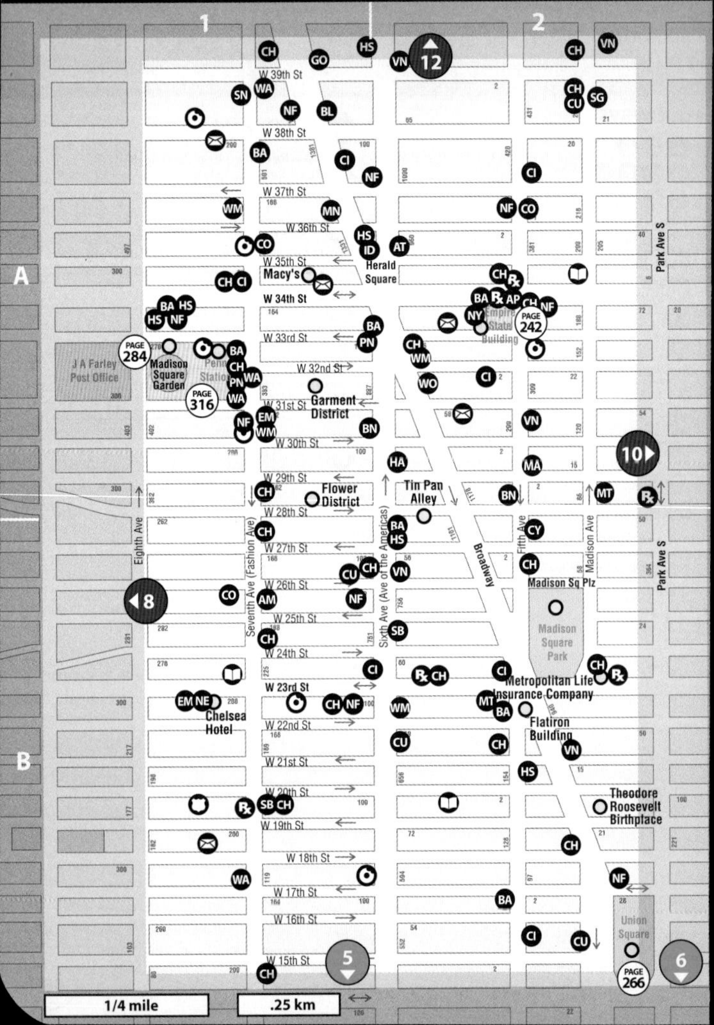

Map 9 · Flatiron / Lower Midtown

1

2

W 39th St
CH
GO
HS
VN
12
CH
VN

W 38th St
SN
WA
NF
BL
CH
CU
SG

BA
CI
NF
CI

W 37th St
WM
MN
NF
CO

W 36th St
CO
HS
ID
AT
CH Rx
BA Rx AP
CH NF
NY
AP

A

Macy's
Herald Square
CH CI
Empire State Building
PAGE 242

W 34th St
BA HS
HS NF
BA
PN
CH
WM
WO
CI
MA

W 33rd St
PAGE 284
Madison Square Garden
PAGE 316
Penn Station
BA
PN
WA
VN

Garment District
NF
EM
WM
BN

HA
10

W 29th St
CH
Flower District
Tin Pan Alley
BN
MT
Rx

W 28th St
CH
CY

W 27th St
CH
BA
HS
VN
CH
Madison Sq Plz

8

W 26th St
CU
CO
AM
NF
SB
Madison Square Park
CH Rx

W 24th St
Rx CH
CI
Metropolitan Life Insurance Company
CH Rx

W 23rd St
EM NE
CH NF
WM
M1
BA
Flatiron Building
VN

Chelsea Hotel
W 22nd St
CU
CH

B

W 21st St
HS

W 20th St
Theodore Roosevelt Birthplace

Rx
SB CH

W 19th St

W 18th St
WA
BA
NF

W 17th St

W 16th St
CI
CU

W 15th St
CH
5
Union Square
PAGE 266
6

1/4 mile   .25 km

Eighth Ave
Seventh Ave (Fashion Ave)
Sixth Ave (Ave of the Americas)
Broadway
Fifth Ave
Madison Ave
Park Ave S

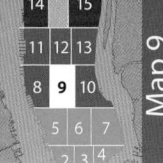

We guarantee you'll visit this area when your cousins from Iowa visit. Top-notch restaurants, the Empire State Building, and curiosities like the Chelsea Hotel make it irresistible to tourists. The neighborhood also constitutes an appropriate cross-section of the city, from pretty (Madison Square Park) to gritty (anywhere near Penn Station).

Rx 24-Hour Pharmacies
• **Duane Reade** • 153 Seventh Ave [19th] ♿
• **Duane Reade** • 358 Fifth Ave [34th] ♿
• **Duane Reade** • 401 Park Ave S [28th] ♿
• **Duane Reade** • 71 W 23rd St [6th Av] ♿
• **Walgreen's** • 33 E 23rd St [Madison] ♿
• **Walgreen's** • 350 Fifth Ave [34th] ♿

Bagels
• **23rd Street Bagel** • 170 W 23rd St [7th Av]
• **Bagel Maven** • 362 Seventh Ave [30th]
• **Bagels & Co** • 243 W 38th St [7th Av]
• **Bread Factory Café** • 470 Seventh Ave [35th]
• **Brooklyn Bagel** • 319 Fifth Ave [32nd]
• **Hot & Crusty** • 10B Penn Station (lower level)
• **New York City Bagel** • 601 Sixth Ave [17th]

$ Banks
AM • Amalgamated
AP • Apple
AT • Atlantic
BL • Bank Leumi
BA • Bank of America
NY • Bank of New York
BN • Broadway National
CY • Cathay
CH • Chase
CI • Citibank
CO • Commerce
EM • Emigrant
GO • Gotham Bank of New York
HA • Habib American
HS • HSBC
ID • IDB
CU • Lower East Side People's Federal Credit
    Union (ATM)
MA • Marathon
MT • M&T
MN • Metropolitan National
CU • Montauk Credit Union
NE • NorthEast Community Bank
NF • North Fork
PN • PNC
SG • Signature
SB • Sovereign
SN • Sterling National
VN • Valley National
WA • Wachovia
WM • Washington Mutual
WO • Woori America

Landmarks
• **Chelsea Hotel** • 222 West 23rd St [7th Av]
• **Empire State Building** • 34th St & Fifth Ave
• **Flatiron Building** • 175 Fifth Ave [22nd]
• **Flower District** •
  28th St b/w Sixth & Seventh Aves
• **Garment District** •
  West 30s south of Herald Square
• **Macy's** • 151 W 34th St [7th Av]
• **Madison Square Garden** • 4 Penn Plz [31st]
• **Madison Square Park** • 23rd St & Broadway
• **Metropolitan Life Insurance Co** •
  1 Madison Ave [23rd]
• **Penn Station** • 31st St & Eighth Ave
• **Theodore Roosevelt Birthplace** •
  28 E 20th St [B'way]
• **Tin Pan Alley** •
  W 28th St b/w Sixth Ave & Broadway
• **Union Square** • 14th St–Union Sq

Libraries
• **Andrew Heiskell Braille & Talking Book
  Library** • 40 W 20th St [5th Av]
• **Muhlenberg** • 209 W 23rd St [7th Av]
• **Science, Industry, and Business Library** •
  188 Madison Ave [34th]

Police
• **10th Precinct** • 230 W 20th St [7th Av]

Post Offices
• **Empire State** • 19 W 33rd St [5th Av]
• **Greeley Square** • 39 W 31st St [B'way]
• **Midtown** • 223 W 38th St [7th Av]
• **Old Chelsea** • 217 W 18th St [7th Av]
• **Station 138 (Macy's)** • 151 W 34th St [7th Av]

Map 9 • Flatiron / Lower Midtown

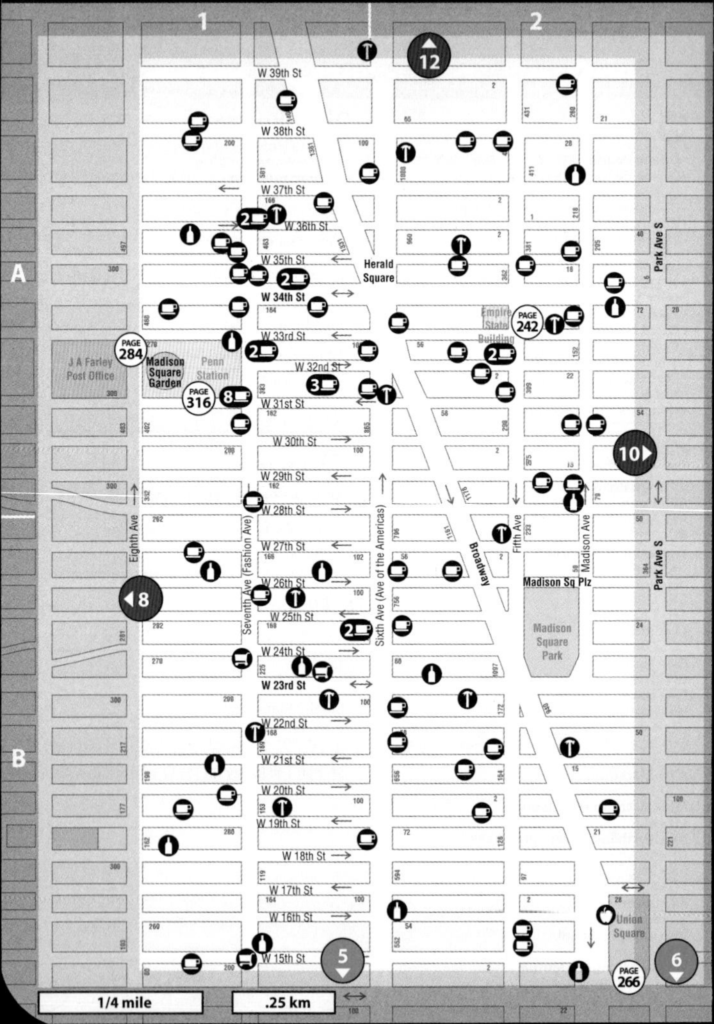

1

2

W 39th St

W 38th St

W 37th St

W 36th St

W 35th St

W 34th St

Herald
Square

W 33rd St

W 32nd St

W 31st St

W 30th St

W 29th St

W 28th St

W 27th St

W 26th St

W 25th St

W 24th St

W 23rd St

W 22nd St

W 21st St

W 20th St

W 19th St

W 18th St

W 17th St

W 16th St

W 15th St

A

B

J A Farley
Post Office

Madison
Square
Garden

Penn
Station

PAGE
284

PAGE
316

Empire
State
Building

PAGE
242

Eighth Ave

Seventh Ave (Fashion Ave)

Sixth Ave (Ave of the Americas)

Broadway

Fifth Ave

Madison Ave

Park Ave S

Park Ave S

Madison Sq Plz

Madison
Square
Park

Union
Square

PAGE
266

12

10

8

5

6

1/4 mile

.25 km

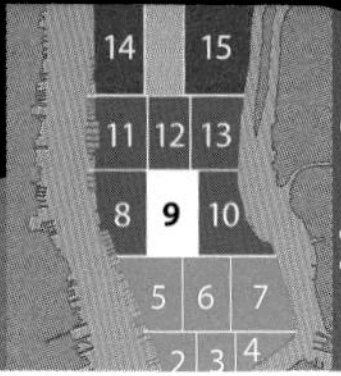

Sundries

Map 9

The Flower District ain't what it used to be, but the Garment District still has its charms (and chaos). Sixth Avenue resembles a strip mall, but small art and photo shops along the side streets take the sting out of running errands. Pop into Café Grumpy for a jolt.

Coffee

- **Andrew's Coffee** • 246 W 38th St [7th Av]
- **Andrew's Coffee** • 463 Seventh Ave [35th]
- **Anesis Café** • 42 W 35th St [5th Av]
- **Antique Café** • 234 W 27th St [7th Av]
- **Antique Café** • 55 W 26th St [6th Av]
- **Au Bon Pain** • 151 W 34th St [7th Av]
- **Au Bon Pain** • 420 Fifth Ave [38th]
- **Au Bon Pain** • 73 Fifth Ave [15th]
- **The Bread Factory Café** • 470 7th Ave [35th]
- **Café 34** • 250 W 34th St [7th Av]
- **Café Express** • 138 W 32nd St [6th Av]
- **Café Beyond** • 620 Sixth Ave [18th]
- **Café Bonjour** • 20 E 39th St [Madison]
- **Café Grumpy** • 224 W 20th St [7th Av]
- **Café Muse** • 43 W 32nd St [B'way]
- **Café Pom Pom** • 169 W 32nd St [7th Av]
- **Coco Moka Café** • 2 Penn Plz [31st]
- **Cosi** • 498 Seventh Ave [37th]
- **Cosi** • 700 Sixth Ave [22nd]
- **Dunkin' Donuts** • 1 Penn Plz [34th]
- **Dunkin' Donuts** • 1286 Broadway [33rd]
- **Dunkin' Donuts** • 152 W 31st St [6th Av]
- **Dunkin' Donuts** • 2 Penn Plz [31st]
- **Dunkin' Donuts** • 289 Seventh Ave [26th]
- **Dunkin' Donuts** • 302 Fifth Ave [31st]
- **Dunkin' Donuts** • 401 Seventh Ave [32nd]
- **Dunkin' Donuts** • 51 E 34th St [Madison]
- **Dunkin' Donuts** • 80 Madison Ave [28th]
- **Elemental Foods** • 259 W 19th St [8th Av]
- **Europa Café** • 11 Penn Plz [31st]
- **Guy & Gallard** • 1001 Sixth Ave [37th]
- **Guy & Gallard** • 180 Madison Ave [34th]
- **Guy & Gallard** • 245 W 38th St [7th Av]
- **Guy & Gallard** • 469 Seventh Ave [35th]
- **Guy & Gallard** • 475 Park Ave S [31st]
- **Guy & Gallard** • 339 Seventh Ave [29th]
- **Harrie's Coffee Shop** • 1407 Broadway [38th]
- **Jamie's** • 164 Madison Ave [33rd]
- **Keko Café** • 121 Madison Ave [30th]
- **Le Café Catering Deli** • 1 Penn Plz [34th] ⊕
- **Le Gamin Café** • 258 W 15th St [8th Av]
- **News Bar** • 2 W 19th St [5th Av]
- **Primo Cappachino** • Penn Station LIRR
- **Seattle Coffee Roasters** • 202 W 34th St [7th]
- **Starbucks** • 1372 Broadway [37th]
- **Starbucks** • 261 Fifth Ave [29th]
- **Starbucks** • 330 Fifth Ave [33rd]
- **Starbucks** • 334 Fifth Ave [33rd]
- **Starbucks** • 373 Fifth Ave [35th]
- **Starbucks** • 200 Madison Ave [35th]
- **Starbucks** • 1 Penn Plz [34th St]
- **Starbucks** • 1 Penn Plz (Concourse) [34th]
- **Starbucks** • 370 Seventh Ave [30th]
- **Starbucks** • 450 Seventh Ave [35th]
- **Starbucks** • 462 Seventh Ave [35th]
- **Starbucks** • 525 Seventh Ave [38th]
- **Starbucks** • 684 Sixth Ave [21st]
- **Starbucks** • 750 Sixth Ave [25th]
- **Starbucks** • 776 Sixth Ave [26th]
- **Starbucks** • 875 Sixth Ave [31st]
- **Starbucks** • 906 Sixth Ave [32nd]
- **Starbucks** • 41 Union Sq W [16th]
- **Starbucks** • 4 W 21st St [5th Av]
- **Starbucks** • 151 W 34th St [7th Av]
- **Subtle Tea** • 121 Madison Ave [30th]
- **Takken America** • 38 W 38th St [5th Av]
- **West Front Store** • 28 W 32nd St [5th Av]

Farmers Market

- **Union Square Greenmarket**
  (Mon, Wed, Fri & Sat 8am–6pm, year round)
  • E 17th St & B'way

Hardware Stores

- **727 Hardware** • 727 Sixth Ave [24th]
- **Adco Hardware** • 23 W 35th St [5th Av]
- **Admore Hardware** • 11 E 33rd St [5th Av]
- **B&N Hardware** • 12 W 19th St [5th Av]
- **Central Hardware** • 1055 Sixth Ave [40th]
- **Elm Hardware** • 884 Sixth Ave [32nd]
- **Home Depot** • 40 W 23rd St [5th Av]
- **J&M Hardware** • 19 E 21st St [B'way]
- **KDM Hardware** • 147 W 26th St [6th Av]
- **Kove Brothers Hardware** • 189 7th Ave [21st]
- **Whitey's Hardware** • 244 Fifth Ave [28th]

Liquor Stores

- **A&J Kessler Liquors** • 23 E 28th St [Madison]
- **Baron Francois** • 236 W 26th St [7th Av]
- **Burgundy Wine Co** • 143 W 26th St [6th Av]
- **Chelsea Wine Cellar** • 200 W 21st St [7th Av]
- **Harry's Liquors** • 270 W 36th St [8th Av]
- **House of Cheers** • 261 W 18th St [8th Av]
- **Landmark Wine & Spirit** • 167 W 23rd St [7th]
- **Lewis-Kaye Wines** • 60 E 34th St [Madison]
- **Madison Ave Liquors** • 244 Madison [38th]
- **Manor House Liquor** • 61 W 23rd St [6th Av]
- **Old Chelsea Wine** • 86 Seventh Ave [15th]
- **Penn Wine & Spirits** • Penn Station LIRR Level
- **Wine Gallery** • 576 Sixth Ave [16th]

Supermarkets

- **Garden of Eden** • 162 W 23rd St [7th Av]
- **Westside Market** • 77 Seventh Ave [15th]
- **Whole Foods** • 250 Seventh Ave [24th]

Map 9 • **Flatiron / Lower Midtown**

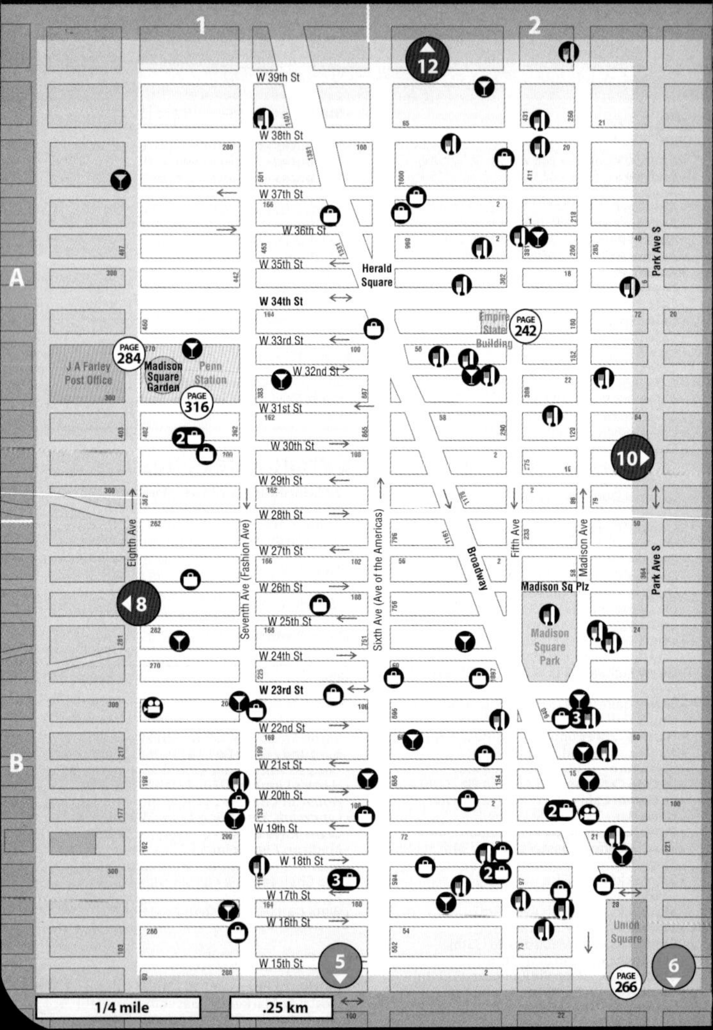

1

2

12

W 39th St

W 38th St

W 37th St

W 36th St

W 35th St

A

Herald
Square

W 34th St

W 33rd St

PAGE
242

Empire
State
Building

W 32nd St

PAGE
284

J A Farley
Post Office

Madison
Square
Garden

Penn
Station

W 31st St

PAGE
316

W 30th St

2

W 29th St

W 28th St

10

W 27th St

Eighth Ave

Seventh Ave (Fashion Ave)

Sixth Ave (Ave of the Americas)

Broadway

Fifth Ave

Madison Ave

Park Ave S

W 26th St

8

W 25th St

W 24th St

Madison Sq Plz

W 23rd St

Madison
Square
Park

W 22nd St

3

B

W 21st St

W 20th St

W 19th St

2

W 18th St

3

2

W 17th St

W 16th St

Union
Square

W 15th St

PAGE
266

5

6

1/4 mile

.25 km

Entertainment

Map 9

Yes, you can try the acclaimed Gramercy Tavern, but you must eat in Koreatown (32nd Street b/w Broadway & Fifth Ave). Definitely check for special events at Madison Square Park (like the popular jumbotron telecasts of the U.S. Open), then pick up a BLT from Eisenberg's, or brave the Shake Shack line. Or both.

Movie Theaters

- **AMC 19th Street** • 890 Broadway [19th]
- **Clearview's Chelsea** • 260 W 23rd St [8th Av]

Nightlife

- **Avalon** • 660 Sixth Ave [20th]
- **Club Shelter** • 20 W 39th St [5th Av]
- **Cutting Room** • 19 W 24th St [B'way]
- **Live Bait** • 14 E 23rd St [Madison]
- **Merchants** • 112 Seventh Ave [17th]
- **Metropolitan Room** • 34 W 22nd St [6th Av]
- **Old Town Bar & Restaurant** •
  45 E 18th St [B'way]
- **Peter McManus** • 152 Seventh Ave [19th]
- **Rebel** • 251 W 30th St [B'way]
- **Silver Swan** • 41 E 20th St [B'way]
- **Sky Bar at La Quinta** • 17 W 32nd St [B'way]
- **Splash Bar** • 50 W 17th St [6th Av]
- **Under The Volcano** • 12 E 36th St [Madison]
- **Wakamba Cocktail Lounge** •
  543 Eighth Ave [37th]

Restaurants

- **Ben's NY Kosher** • 209 W 38th St [7th Av]
- **BLT Fish** • 21 W 17th St [5th Av]
- **Borough Food and Drink** •
  12 E 22nd St [Broadway]
- **Butterfield 8** • 5 E 38th St [5th Av]
- **Chat 'n Chew** • 10 E 16th St [5th Av]
- **City Bakery** • 3 W 18th St [8th Av]
- **Coffee Shop** • 29 Union Sq W [16th]
- **Craft** • 43 E 19th St [B'way]
- **Eisenberg's Sandwich Shop** •
  174 Fifth Ave [22nd]
- **Eleven Madison Park** • 11 Madison Ave [24th]
- **Evergreen Shanghai Restaurant** •
  10 E 38th St [5th Av]
- **Gramercy Tavern** • 42 E 20th St [B'way]
- **Hangawi** • 12 E 32nd St [5th Av]
- **Kang Suh** • 1250 Broadway [32nd] ⊕
- **Koryodang** • 31 W 32nd St [6th Av]
- **Kunjip** • 9 W 32nd St [B'way] ⊕
- **Le Zie 2000** • 172 Seventh Ave [20th]
- **Mendy's Kosher Deli** • 61 E 34th St [Madison]
- **Olympic Pita** • 58 W 38th St [6th Av]
- **Republic** • 37 Union Sq W [16th]
- **RUB BBQ** • 208 W 23rd St [7th Av]
- **Salute!** • 270 Madison Ave [40th]
- **Seoul Garden** • 34 W 32nd St [Madison]

- **Shake Shack** • Madison Sq Park
- **Tabla** • 11 Madison Ave [24th]
- **Tamarind** • 41 E 22nd St [B'way]
- **Tocqueville** • 1 E 15th St [5th Av]
- **Toledo** • 6 E 36th St [5th Av]
- **Union Square Café** • 21 E 16th St [5th Av]
- **Woo Chon** • 8 W 36th St [5th Av] ⊕

Shopping

- **17 at 17 Thrift Shop** •
  17 W 17th St [5th Av]
- **30th Street Guitars** •
  236 W 30th St [7th Av]
- **ABC Carpet & Home** • 888 Broadway [19th]
- **Abracadabra** • 19 W 21st St [5th Av]
- **Academy Records** • 12 W 18th St [5th Av]
- **Adorama Camera** • 42 W 18th St [5th Av]
- **Al Friedman** • 44 W 18th St [5th Av]
- **Angel Street Thrift Shop** •
  118 W 17th St [6th Av]
- **Ariston** • 110 W 17th St [6th Av]
- **Capitol Fishing Tackle** • 132 W 36th St [B'way]
- **Chelsea Flea Market** • 112 W 25th St [6th Av]
- **The City Quilter** • 133 W 25th St [6th]
- **Cupcake Café** • 18 W 18th St [5th Av]
- **The Family Jewels** • 130 W 23rd St [6th Av]
- **Fisch For The Hip** • 153 W 18th St [7th Av]
- **Fish's Eddy** • 889 Broadway [19th]
- **Housing Works Thrift Shop** •
  143 W 17th St [6th Av]
- **Janovic** • 215 Seventh Ave [22nd]
- **Jazz Record Center** • 236 W 26th St [7th Av]
- **Loehmann's** • 101 Seventh Ave [16th]
- **Lord & Taylor** • 424 Fifth Ave [38th]
- **Lush Cosmetics** • 1293 Broadway [33rd]
- **M&J Trimmings** • 1008 Sixth Ave [38th]
- **Macy's** • 151 W 34th St [7th Av]
- **Mandler's, The Original Sausage Co** •
  26 E 17th St [B'way]
- **Otto Tootsi Plohound** • 137 Fifth Ave [20th]
- **Paragon Sporting Goods** •
  867 Broadway [18th]
- **Pleasure Chest** • 156 Seventh Ave [19th]
- **Rogue Music** • 251 W 30th St [7th Av]
- **Sam Flax** • 12 W 20th St [5th Av]
- **Space Kiddets** • 26 E 22nd St [B'way]
- **Tekserve** • 119 W 23rd St [6th Av]
- **Toho Shoji** • 990 Sixth Ave [37th]

Map 9 · Flatiron / Lower Midtown

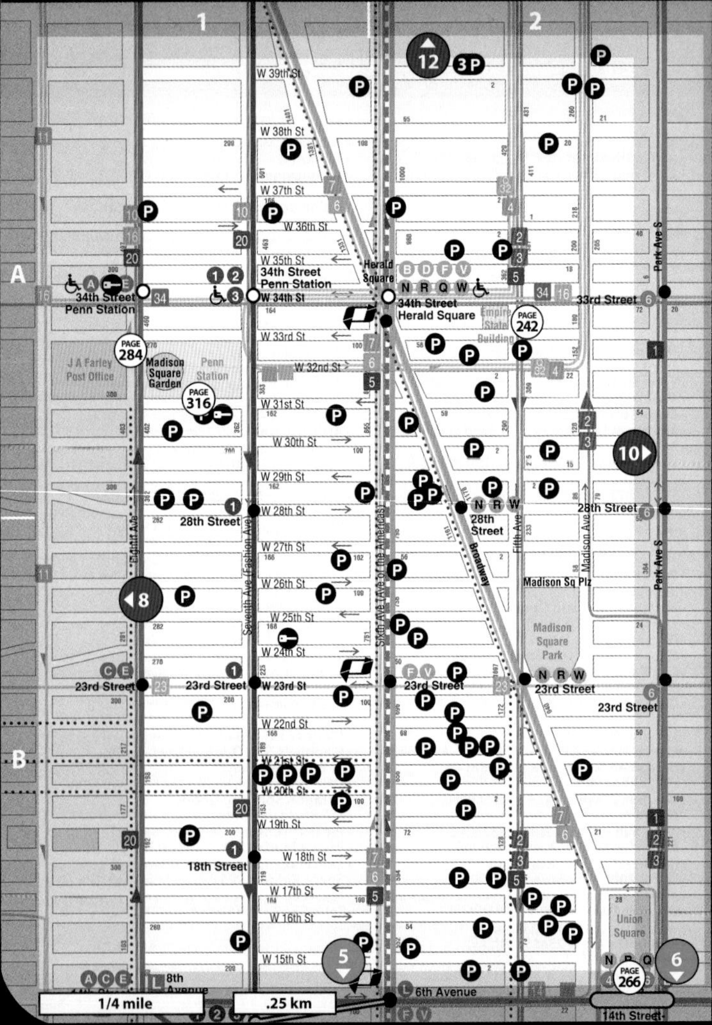

1   2

W 39th St

12   3P

W 38th St

W 37th St

W 36th St

W 35th St

34th Street Penn Station

Herald Square

34th Street Herald Square

W 34th St

B D F V

Herald Square

Empire State Building

PAGE 242

A

34th Street Penn Station

34

33rd Street

J A Farley Post Office

PAGE 284

Madison Square Garden

Penn Station

PAGE 316

W 33rd St

W 32nd St

W 31st St

W 30th St

W 29th St

W 28th St

28th Street

28th Street

N R W

28th Street

28th Street

10

W 27th St

W 26th St

W 25th St

W 24th St

Madison Sq Plz

Madison Square Park

8

C E

23rd Street

23rd Street

W 23rd St

23rd Street

F V

23rd Street

N R W

23rd Street

23rd Street

B

W 22nd St

W 21st St

W 20th St

W 19th St

18th Street

W 18th St

W 17th St

W 16th St

W 15th St

Union Square

PAGE 266

N R Q

6

5

6th Avenue

8th Avenue

A C E

1/4 mile   .25 km

14th Street

Seventh Ave (Fashion Ave)

Sixth Ave (Avenue of the Americas)

Broadway

Fifth Ave

Madison Ave

Park Ave S

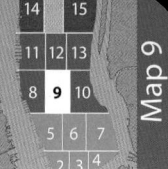

Parking during the day and on weekends is extremely difficult, and the trickle-down effect of Lincoln Tunnel traffic makes driving a nightmare anyway. But few areas boast better subway access. If you're headed downtown or to Brooklyn from Herald Square, we think Q stands for "quickest train ever."

Subways

1 2 3 .... 34th St-Penn Station
1 .... 18th St
1 .... 23rd St
1 .... 28th St
A C E .... 14th St
A C E .... 34th St-Penn Station
C E .... 23rd St
B D F V N Q R W
.... 34th St-Herald Sq
F V .... 23rd St
R W .... 23rd St
R W .... 28th St

Bus Lines

10 20 .... Seventh Ave/Eighth Ave
(Central Park West)/Frederick Douglass Blvd
16 .... 34th St Crosstown
1 2 3 .... Fifth Ave/Madison Ave
23 .... 23rd St Crosstown
4 .... Fifth Ave/Madison Ave/Broadway
5 .... Fifth Ave/Sixth Ave/Riverdale Dr
6 .... Seventh Ave/Broadway/Sixth Ave
7 .... Columbus Ave/Amsterdam Ave/
Lenox Ave/Sixth Ave/Seventh Ave/Broadway
11 .... Ninth Ave/Tenth Ave
32 ....Penn Station/Jackson Heights, Queens

Bike Lanes

• • • Marked Bike Lanes

• • • Recommended Route

PATH

• **23 St** • 23rd St & Sixth Ave
• **33 St** • 33rd St & Sixth Ave

Car Rental

• **Avis** • 220 W 31st St [7th Av]
• **Enterprise** • 106 W 24th St [6th Av]
• **Hertz** • 323 W 34th St [8th Av]

Parking

Map 10 · **Murray Hill / Gramercy**

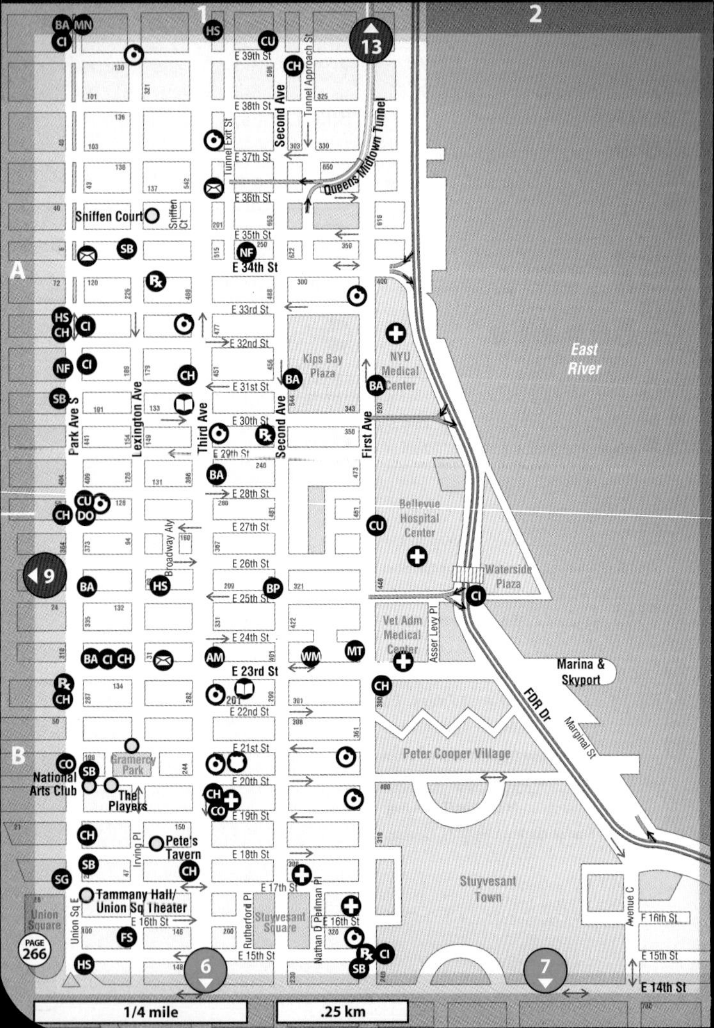

1

2

13

E 39th St

E 38th St

E 37th St

E 36th St

E 35th St

E 34th St

E 33rd St

E 32nd St

E 31st St

E 30th St

E 29th St

E 28th St

E 27th St

E 26th St

E 25th St

E 24th St

E 23rd St

E 22nd St

E 21st St

E 20th St

E 19th St

E 18th St

E 17th St

E 16th St

E 15th St

E 14th St

Second Ave

First Ave

Third Ave

Lexington Ave

Park Ave S

Tunnel Exit St

Tunnel Approach St

Queens Midtown Tunnel

Broadway Alley

Irving Pl

Union Sq

Rutherford Pl

Nathan D Perlman Pl

Asser Levy Pl

Marginal St

FDR Dr

Avenue C

E 16th St

E 15th St

E 14th St

Shiffen Court

Shiffen Ct

Kips Bay Plaza

NYU Medical Center

East River

Bellevue Hospital Center

Waterside Plaza

Vet Adm Medical Center

Marina & Skyport

Peter Cooper Village

Stuyvesant Town

National Arts Club

Gramercy Park

The Players

Pete's Tavern

Tammany Hall/ Union Sq theater

Stuyvesant Square

9

6

7

1/4 mile   .25 km

Friendly residents of drab condo developments mix with quirky SVA students and businessmen. Gramercy Park is pastoral and beautiful if you're lucky enough to get the key. Keep an eye out for interesting architecture like The Players. Six major hospitals in case of an accident. You'll get used to the sirens.

℞ 24-Hour Pharmacies

- **CVS Pharmacy** • 253 First Ave [15th] ♿
- **Duane Reade** • 155 E 34th St [Lex] ♿
- **Duane Reade** • 300 Park Ave S [23rd] ♿
- **Rite Aid** • 542 Second Ave [30th] ♿

⊙ Bagels

- **A&K Bagels** • 246 Third Ave [20th]
- **Bagel du Jour** • 478 Third Ave [33rd]
- **Bagel & Schmear** • 116 E 28th St [Lex]
- **Bagelry** • 429 Third Ave [30th]
- **Bagels & More** • 331 Lexington Ave [39th]
- **Daniel's Bagels** • 569 Third Ave [38th]
- **David's Bagels** • 331 First Ave [19th]
- **Ess-A-Bagel** • 359 First Ave [21st]
- **La Bagel** • 263 First Ave [15th]
- **New York Bagel** • 587 First Ave [34th]
- **Pick-a-Bagel** • 297 Third Ave [22nd]

$ Banks

AM • Amalgamated
BP • Banco Popular
BA • Bank of America
CH • Chase
CI • Citibank
CO • Commerce
DO • Doral
FS • Flushing Savings
HS • HSBC
CU • Lower East Side People's Federal Credit Union
MT • M&T
MA • Marathon
MN • Metropolitan National
CU • Municipal Credit Union
NF • North Fork
SG • Signature
SB • Sovereign
WM • Washington Mutual

➕ Emergency Rooms

- **Bellevue Hospital Center** • 462 First Ave [27th]
- **Beth Israel Medical Center** • 281 First Ave [16th]
- **Cabrini Medical Center** • 227 E 19th St [3rd Av]
- **Hospital for Joint Diseases** • 301 E 17th St [2nd Av]
- **NYU Medical Center: Tisch** • 560 First Ave [33rd]
- **VA Hospital** • 423 E 23rd St [1st Av]

○ Landmarks

- **Gramercy Park** • Irving Pl & 20th St
- **National Arts Club** • 15 Gramercy Park S [20th]
- **Pete's Tavern** • 129 E 18th St [Irving]
- **The Players** • 16 Gramercy Park S [20th]
- **Sniffen Court** • 36th St & Third Ave
- **Tammany Hall/Union Sq Theater** • 100 E 17th St [Park]

 Libraries

- **Epiphany** • 228 E 23rd St [3rd Av]
- **Kips Bay** • 446 Third Ave [31st]

○ Police

- **13th Precinct** • 230 E 21st St [3rd Av]

 Post Offices

- **Madison Square** • 149 E 23rd St [Lex]
- **Murray Hill** • 205 E 36th St [3rd Av]
- **Murray Hill Finance** • 115 E 34th St [Park]

Map 10 · **Murray Hill / Gramercy**

1

2

13

E 39th St

Tunnel Approach St

Second Ave

Tunnel Exit St

E 38th St

E 37th St

Queens Midtown Tunnel

E 36th St

Shriffen Ct

E 35th St

E 34th St

A

E 33rd St

E 32nd St

Kips Bay Plaza

NYU Medical Center

East River

E 31st St

Lexington Ave

Park Ave S

Third Ave

E 30th St

Second Ave

First Ave

E 29th St

E 28th St

Bellevue Hospital Center

E 27th St

9

Broadway

E 26th St

E 25th St

Waterside Plaza

E 24th St

Vet Adm Medical Center

Asser Levy Pl

E 23rd St

Marina & Skyport

E 22nd St

FDR Dr

Marginal St

B

E 21st St

Peter Cooper Village

Gramercy Park

E 20th St

Irving Pl

E 19th St

E 18th St

E 17th St

Stuyvesant Town

Union Sq E

Rutherford Pl

E 16th St

Nathan D Perlman Pl

Stuyvesant Square

16th St

Avenue C

E 16th St

PAGE 266

E 16th St

E 15th St

E 15th St

6

7

E 14th St

1/4 mile

.25 km

Sundries

14	15
11	12	13
8	9	**10**
5	6	7

Map 10

71 Irving is a welcome reprieve from the Starbucks saturation. Saturday's farmers market on 33rd beats its more crowded Union Square counterpart. Sweat it out at one of the ubiquitous New York Sports Clubs before cruising the meat market bars on First Avenue. Finish off with Dunkin' Donuts.

 Coffee

- **71 Irving** • 71 Irving Pl [19th]
- **Au Bon Pain** • 6 Union Sq E [14th]
- **Au Bon Pain** • 600 Third Ave [39th]
- **Brasil Coffee House** • 161 Lexington Ave [30th]
- **Cosi** • 257 Park Ave S [20th]
- **Cosi** • 461 Park Ave S [31st]
- **Dean & Deluca Café** • 576 Second Ave [32nd]
- **Delectica** • 564 Third Ave [37th]
- **Dip Café** • 416 Third Ave [29th]
- **Dunkin' Donuts** • 127 E 23rd St [Lex]
- **Dunkin' Donuts** • 152 W 34th St [7th Av]
- **Dunkin' Donuts** • 266 First Ave [15th]
- **Dunkin' Donuts** • 243 Third Ave [20th]
- **Dunkin' Donuts** • 355 Third Ave [26th]
- **Dunkin' Donuts** • 361 First Ave [21st]
- **Dunkin' Donuts** • 412 Third Ave [29th]
- **Dunkin' Donuts** • 455 Park Ave S [31st]
- **Dunkin' Donuts** • 476 Second Ave [27th]
- **Dunkin' Donuts** • 567 Third Ave [38th]
- **Dunkin' Donuts** • 601 Second Ave [33rd]
- **Franchia Teahouse** • 12 Park Ave [35th]
- **Gregorys Coffee** • 327 Park Ave S [24th]
- **Guy & Gallard** • 120 E 34th St [Lex]
- **Lady Mendl's Tea Salon** • 56 Irving Pl [17th]
- **Oren's Daily Roast** • 434 Third Ave [30th]
- **Plaza de Café** • 61 Lexington Ave [25th]
- **Push Café** • 294 Third Ave [22nd]
- **Starbucks** • 10 Union Sq E [15th]
- **Starbucks** • 145 Third Ave [15th]
- **Starbucks** • 286 First Ave [17th]
- **Starbucks** • 296 Third Ave [22nd]
- **Starbucks** • 3 Park Ave [33rd]
- **Starbucks** • 304 Park Ave S [23rd]
- **Starbucks** • 395 Third Ave [28th]
- **Starbucks** • 424 Park Ave S [29th]
- **Starbucks** • 585 Second Ave [32nd]
- **Starbucks** • 90 Park Ave [40th]
- **Sunburst** • 206 Third Ave [18th]
- **Trevi Coffee Shop** • 48 Union Sq E [16th]

Farmers Markets

- **26th St/Phipps Houses (Tues, 8am–5pm, July 11–Nov)** • E 26th St b/w Second Ave & Mt Carmel Pl
- **Murray Hill (Sat 8am–5pm, Jun–Dec)** • Second Ave & E 33rd St

Hardware Stores

- **Gurell Hardware** • 132 E 28th St [Lex]
- **HomeFront** • 202 E 29th St [3rd Av]
- **Lumber Boys** • 698 Second Ave [38th]
- **Lumberland Hardware** • 368 Third Ave [27th]
- **Render Hardware True Value** • 485 Third Ave [33rd]
- **Simon's Hardware & Bath** • 421 Third Ave [29th]
- **Town & Village Hardware** • 337 First Ave [20th]
- **Vercesi Hardware** • 152 E 23rd St [Lex]
- **Warshaw Hardware** • 248 Third Ave [20th]
- **Z Locksmith & Hardware** • 347 Third Ave [25th]

Liquor Stores

- **111 Lex Liquors** • 111 Lexington Ave [28th]
- **America's Wine Shop** • 398 Third Ave [28th]
- **First Avenue Wine** • 383 First Ave [23rd]
- **Flynn Winfield Liquor** • 558 Third Ave [37th]
- **Frank's Liquor Shop** • 46 Union Sq E [16th]
- **Gramercy Park Wines** • 104 E 23rd St [Park]
- **House of Wine** • 250 E 34th St [2nd Av]
- **HS Wine & Liquor** • 161 Third Ave [16th]
- **Italian Wine Merchants** • 108 E 16th St [Union Sq E]
- **Murray Hill Wine** • 516 Third Ave [35th]
- **New Gramercy Liquors** • 279 Third Ave [21st]
- **Quality House** • 2 Park Ave [33rd]
- **Royal Wine Merchants** • 25 Waterside Plz [26th]
- **Stuyvesant Square Liquors** • 333 Second Ave [19th]
- **Vino** • 121 E 27th St [Lex]
- **Welcome Wine** • 424 Second Ave [24th]
- **Windsor Wine Shop** • 474 Third Ave [32nd]
- **Wine Shop** • 345 Lexington Ave [40th]
- **World Wine** • 705 Second Ave [38th]
- **Zeichner Wine & Liquor** • 279 First Ave [16th]

Supermarkets

- **Associated** • 278 Park Ave S [22nd]
- **Associated** • 311 E 23rd St [2nd Av]
- **D'Agostino** • 341 Third Ave [25th]
- **D'Agostino** • 528 Third Ave [35th]
- **D'Agostino** • 578 Third Ave [38th]
- **Food Emporium** • 10 Union Sq E [15th]
- **Food Emporium** • 200 E 32nd St [3rd Av]
- **Gristedes** • 25 Waterside Plz [26th]
- **Gristedes** • 355 First Ave [21st]
- **Gristedes** • 512 Second Ave [29th]
- **Gristedes** • 549 Third Ave [36th]
- **Met Food** • 180 Third Ave [17th]

Map 10 · **Murray Hill / Gramercy**

2

1

13

E 39th St

E 38th St

E 37th St

Second Ave

Tunnel Approach St

Tunnel Exit St

E 36th St

Queens Midtown Tunnel

E 35th St

3

E 34th St

A

E 33rd St

E 32nd St

Kips Bay Plaza

NYU Medical Center

East River

Sniffen Ct

E 31st St

E 30th St

Lexington Ave

Third Ave

Second Ave

First Ave

2

E 29th St

2

Park Ave S

E 28th St

4

2

3

E 27th St

2

Broadway Ave

2

E 26th St

Bellevue Hospital Center

E 25th St

Waterside Plaza

◄ 9

E 24th St

Vet Adm Medical Center

Asser Levy Pl

E 23rd St

Marina & Skyport

E 22nd St

Gramercy Park

E 21st St

FDR Dr

Marginal St

B

E 20th St

Peter Cooper Village

E 19th St

Irving Pl

E 18th St

E 17th St

Rutherford Pl

Stuyvesant Square

Nathan D Perlman Pl

E 16th St

Stuyvesant Town

Union Sq E

E 16th St

Avenue C

E 16th St

PAGE 266

E 15th St

E 15th St

6

7

E 14th St

1/4 mile

.25 km

Entertainment

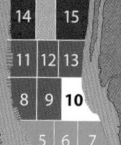

Map 10

It ain't called Curry Hill for nothing. Sample Indian food at Chennai Garden or Tiffin Wallah. Blue Smoke is an amazing jazz and BBQ joint. Molly's is Irish heaven for beer lovers. Head to Pete's Tavern for whiskey and history. Hooray for the return of the Second Avenue Deli. On 33rd Street, of course.

🎬 Movie Theaters
- **Loews Kips Bay** • 570 Second Ave [31st]
- **The Scandinavia House** • 58 Park Ave [38th]

🍸 Nightlife
- **Falite Irish Whiskey Bar** •
  531 Second Ave [29th]
- **The Filmore New York at Irving Plaza** •
  17 Irving Pl [15th]
- **The Jazz Standard** • 116 E 27th St [Lex]
- **McSwiggan's** • 393 Second Ave [23rd]
- **Molly's** • 287 Third Ave [22nd]
- **Paddy Reilly's Music Bar** •
  519 Second Ave [29th]
- **Pete's Tavern** • 129 E 18th St [Irving]
- **Revival** • 129 E 15th St [Irving]
- **Pug Uglies** • 257 Third Ave [20th]
- **Rocky Sullivan's** • 129 Lexington Ave [29th]
- **Rodeo** • 375 Third Ave [27th]
- **Rolf's** • 281 Third Ave [22nd]
- **Waterfront Ale House** •
  540 Second Ave [30th]
- **Whiskey River** • 575 Second Ave [32nd]

🍴 Restaurants
- **Angelo & Maxie's** • 233 Park Ave S [19th]
- **Artisanal** • 2 Park Ave [32nd]
- **Bar Jamon** • 52 Irving Pl [17th]
- **BLT Prime** • 111 E 22nd St [Park]
- **Blue Smoke** • 116 E 27th St [Park]
- **Burger Joint** • 241 Third Ave [20th]
- **Butai** • 115 E 18th St [Irving]
- **Carl's Steaks** • 507 Third Ave [34th]
- **Chennai Garden** • 129 E 27th St [Lex]
- **Chinese Mirch** • 120 Lexington Ave [28th]
- **Curry Leaf** • 99 Lexington Ave [27th]
- **El Parador Café** • 325 E 34th St [2nd Av]
- **Friend of a Farmer** • 77 Irving Pl [19th]
- **Gemini Diner** • 641 Second Ave [35th] ♿
- **Gramercy Restaurant** • 184 Third Ave [17th] ♿
- **Haandi** • 113 Lexington Ave [28th]
- **I Trulli** • 122 E 27th St [Lex]
- **Jess Bakery** • 221 E 23rd St [3rd Av]
- **L'aanam** • 393 Third Ave [28th]
- **L'Express** • 249 Park Ave S [20th] ♿
- **La Posada** • 364 Third Ave [26th]
- **Latin Corner** • 507 Third Ave [34th]
- **Les Halles** • 411 Park Ave S [29th]
- **Mark Café** • 125 E 23rd St [2nd Av]
- **Mee's Noodle Shop & Grill** •
  547 Second Ave [30th St]
- **Mexico Lindo** • 459 Second Ave [26th]
- **Novità** • 102 E 22nd St [Park Av S]
- **Paquitos** • 160 E 28th St [Lex]
- **Penelope** • 159 Lexington Ave [30th]
- **Pongal** • 110 Lexington Ave [28th]
- **Pongsri Thai** • 311 Second Ave [18th]
- **Posto** • 310 Second Ave [18th]
- **Rare Bar & Grill** •
  Shelbourne Murray Hill Hotel •
  303 Lexington Ave [37th]
- **Resto** • 111 E 29th St [Park Av S]
- **Rice** • 115 Lexington Ave [28th]
- **Sarge's Deli** • 548 Third Ave [37th] ♿
- **Second Avenue Deli** •
  162 E 33rd St [Lexington Av]
- **Tiffin Wallah** • 127 E 28th St [Lexington Av]
- **Totonno's Pizzeria Napolitano** •
  462 Second Ave [26th]
- **Turkish Kitchen** • 386 Third Ave [28th]
- **Water Club** • East River at 30th St
- **Zen Palate** • 34 Union Sq E [16th]

🛍 Shopping
- **City Opera Thrift Shop** •
  222 E 23rd St [3rd Av]
- **Foods of India** • 121 Lexington Ave [28th]
- **Homefront Kids/Kids Cuts** •
  202 E 29th St [3rd Av]
- **Housing Works Thrift Shop** •
  157 E 23rd St [Lex]
- **Kalustyan's** • 123 Lexington Ave [28th]
- **La Mazou Cheese** • 370 Third Ave [27th]
- **Ligne Roset** • 250 Park Ave S [20th]
- **Max Nass Inc.** • 118 E 28th St [Lexington Av]
- **NKNY Neera Sari Palace** •
  131 Lexington Ave [29th]
- **Nemo Tile Company** • 48 E 21st St [B'way]
- **Om Sari Palace** • 134 E 27th St [Lexington Av]
- **Pookie & Sebastian** • 541 Third Ave [36th]
- **Quark Spy** • 240 E 29th St [3rd Av]
- **Shambhala** • 655 Second Ave [36th]
- **Todaro Bros.** • 555 Third Ave [31st]
- **Urban Angler** • 206 Fifth Ave [25th]

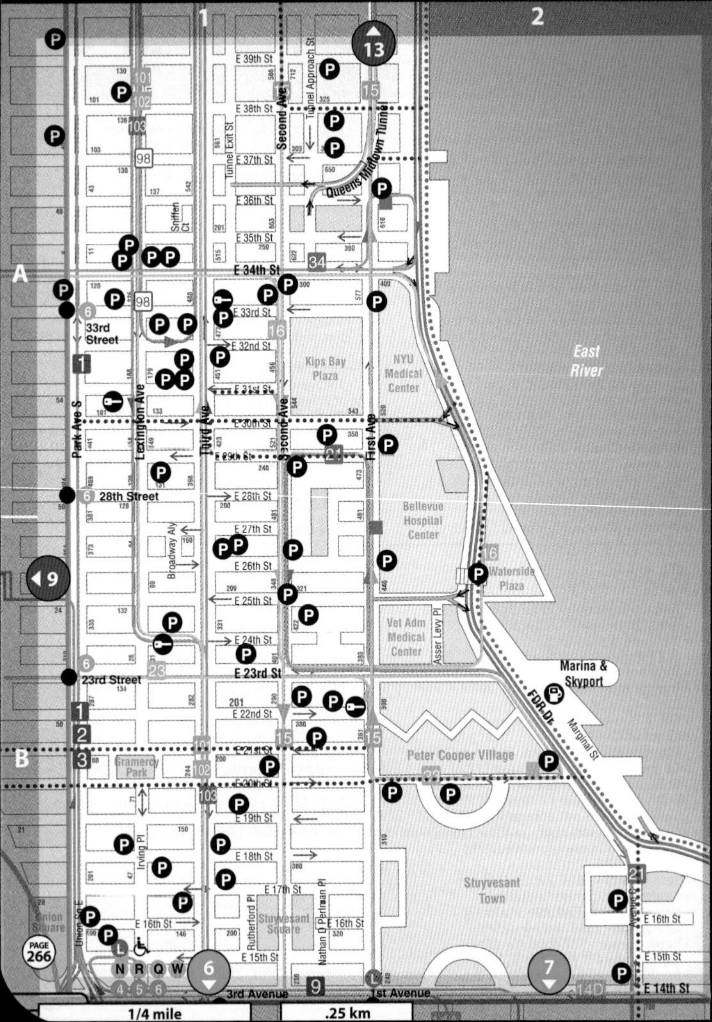

Map 10 · **Murray Hill / Gramercy**

1

2

13

15

E 39th St

E 38th St

Tunnel Approach St

Second Ave

Tunnel Exit St

E 37th St

Queens Midtown Tunnel

E 35th St

E 34th St

34

A

120

33rd
Street

98

Lexington Ave

Third Ave

E 33rd St

16

E 32nd St

Kips Bay
Plaza

NYU
Medical
Center

East
River

Park Ave S

E 30th St

Second Ave

27

First Ave

E 28th St

28th Street

9

Broadway Alley

E 27th St

E 26th St

Bellevue
Hospital
Center

E 25th St

E 24th St

16

Waterside
Plaza

Asser Levy Pl

Vet Adm
Medical
Center

23rd Street

23

E 23rd St

E 22nd St

Marina &
Skyport

15

15

Peter Cooper Village

FDR Dr

Magnat St

Gramercy
Park

102

109

E 20th St

E 19th St

E 18th St

Irving Pl

E 17th St

Rutherford Pl

Nathan D Perlman Pl

Stuyvesant
Square

16th St

Stuyvesant
Town

21

E 16th St

E 16th St

E 15th St

Union
Square

PAGE
266

N R Q W

4 5 6

6

3rd Avenue

9

1st Avenue

7

14 D

E 14th St

1/4 mile

.25 km

Transportation

Map 10

14	15	
11	12	13
8	9	**10**
5	6	7

We're still skeptical about the Second Avenue subway line, especially after the transit strike. Too many broken promises. Walk if the weather's nice. Otherwise, take uptown buses on First & Third or downtown buses on Second & Lexington. Or just cab it. And bring an umbrella.

Subways

6	....	23rd St
6	....	28th St
6	....	33rd St
4 5 6 L N Q R W	......	14th St
L	....	First Ave
L	....	Third Ave

Bus Lines

1 2 3	....	Fifth Ave/Madison Ave
101	....	Third Ave/Lexington Ave
102	....	Third Ave/Lexington Ave
103	....	Third Ave/Lexington Ave
9	....	Avenue B/East Broadway
14	....	14th St Crosstown
34	....	34th St Crosstown
15	....	First Ave/Second Ave
16	....	34th St Crosstown
21	....	Houston St Crosstown
23	....	23rd St Crosstown
98	....	Third Ave/Lexington Ave

Bike Lanes

- • • • Marked Bike Lanes
- • • • Recommended Route
- • • • Greenway

Car Rental

- **Action Car Rental** • 200 E 33rd St [3rd Av]
- **Dollar** • 329 E 22nd St [2nd Av]
- **Hertz** • 150 E 24th St [Lexington Av]
- **National/Alamo** • 142 E 31st St [Lex]

Gas Stations

- **Gulf** • E 23rd St & E River Dr

Parking

Map 11 · **Hell's Kitchen**

N

1   2

W 60th St

W 59th St

PAGE 248
Time Warner Center

Columbus Circle

CH

W 58th St

Rx

14

HS

W 57th St

CH

W 56th St

A

W 55th St

CH

W 54th St

12

W 53rd St

Dewitt Clinton Park

W 52nd St

Hudson River

W 51st St

PAGE 244

CH

W 50th St

CH

W 49th St

W 48th St

West Side Hwy

Hudson River Park

Eleventh Ave

Tenth Ave

W 47th St

Ninth Ave

Eighth Ave

W 46th St

Restaurant Row

W 45th St

W 44th St

B

W 43rd St

W 42nd St

SB CH
Theatre Row

CI

HS

CO

CI

W 41st St

Dyer Ave

PAGE 319
Port Authority Bus Terminal

8

The Annex/
Hell's Kitchen Flea Market

W 39th St

Lincoln Tunnel

W 40th St

W 38th St

Jacob K Javits Convention Center

PAGE 246

W 37th St

| 1/4 mile | .25 km |

Essentials

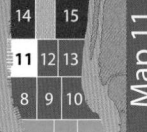

Though often underappreciated, this storied neighborhood enjoys proximity to some of Manhattan's featured destinations (Central Park, Lincoln Center, Columbus Circle, Carnegie Hall, Theatre Row, to name a few), and conveniences like bona fide grocery stores and great local eateries. Join us in refusing to call the area "Clinton," as real estate brokers and taxi maps do.

24-Hour Pharmacies
• **CVS Pharmacy** • 400 W 58th St [9th Av] ⏰

Bagels
• **Bread Factory Café** • 600 Ninth Ave [43rd]
• **H&H Bagels** • 639 W 46th St [11th Av] ⏰

Banks
CH • **Chase** • 471 W 42nd St [Tenth Ave]
CH • **Chase** • 839 Ninth Ave [W 55th St]
CH • **Chase (ATM)** • Duane Reade • 4 Amsterdam Ave [W 59th St]
CH • **Chase (ATM)** • 603 W 50th St [11th Av]
CH • **Chase (ATM)** • Duane Reade • 721 Ninth Ave [W 49th St]
CH • **Chase (ATM)** • Duane Reade • 524 W 57th St [11th Av]
CI • **Citibank** • 401 W 42nd St [Ninth Ave]
CI • **Citibank (ATM)** • 7-Eleven • 345 W 42nd St [Eighth Ave]
CO • **Commerce** • 582 Ninth Ave [W 42nd St]
HS • **HSBC** • 330 W 42nd St [Eighth Ave]
HS • **HSBC** • 601 W 57th St [Eleventh Ave]
SB • **Sovereign (ATM)** • CVS • 500 W 42nd St [Tenth Ave]

Community Gardens

Emergency Rooms
• **St Luke's Roosevelt Hospital Center** • 1000 Tenth Ave [59th]
• **St Vincent's Midtown** • 415 W 51st St [9th Av]

Landmarks
• **The Annex/Hell's Kitchen Flea Market** • W 39th St b/w Ninth Ave & Tenth Ave
• **Restaurant Row** • 46th St b/w Eighth & Ninth Aves
• **Theatre Row** • 42nd St b/w Ninth & Tenth Aves

Libraries
• **Columbus** • 742 Tenth Ave [51st]

Police
• **Mid-Town North** • 306 W 54th St [8th Av]

Post Offices
• **Radio City** • 322 W 52nd St [8th Av]
• **Times Square** • 340 W 42nd St [8th Av]

Map 11 · **Hell's Kitchen**

Columbus Circle

Time Warner Center

PAGE 248

HENRY HUDSON PKWY

W 60th St
W 59th St
W 58th St
W 57th St
W 56th St
W 55th St
W 54th St
W 53rd St
W 52nd St
W 51st St
W 50th St
W 49th St
W 48th St
W 47th St
W 46th St
W 45th St
W 44th St
W 42nd St
W 41st St
W 40th St
W 39th St
W 38th St
W 37th ST

W 43rd St

14

12

8

Dewitt Clinton Park

Hudson River

West Side Hwy

Hudson River Park

Eleventh Ave

Tenth Ave

Ninth Ave

Eighth Ave

Dyer Ave

Lincoln Tunnel

Jacob K Javits Convention Center

Port Authority Bus Terminal

PAGE 244

PAGE 246

PAGE 319

A

B

1

2

1/4 mile   .25 km

Sundries

Map 11

Flesh, flesh and more human flesh. Just kidding. It's not 1845. Try The Bread Factory with its bountiful loaves. Hudson River Park was made for jogging. And no trip to the bastion of hell would be complete without a stop at the Amish Market. Fresh Amish made daily.

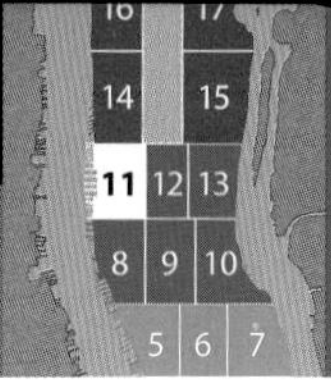

Coffee

- **The Bread Factory Café** •
  600 Ninth Ave [43rd]
- **Café Ole** • 453 W 54th St [10th Av]
- **The Coffee Pot** • 350 W 49th St [9th Av]
- **Dunkin' Donuts** • 580 Ninth Ave [42nd]
- **Dunkin' Donuts** • 815 Tenth Ave [54th]
- **Empire Coffee & Tea** • 568 Ninth Ave [41st]
- **Felix Coffee Shop** • 630 Tenth Ave [45th]
- **Flame Coffee House** •
  893 Ninth Ave [58th]
- **Starbucks** • 322 W 57th St [8th Av]
- **Starbucks** • 325 W 49th St [8th Av]
- **Starbucks** • 555 W 42nd St [11th Av]
- **Starbucks** • 593 Ninth Ave [43rd]
- **Starbucks** • 682 Ninth Ave [47th]

Farmers Markets

- **43rd St/Hell's Kitchen**
  (Sat 8am–5pm, Jul–Nov) •
  W 43rd St b/w Ninth Ave & Tenth Ave
- **57th Street (Wed 8 am–6 pm Apr–Dec; Sat 8**
  am–6 pm, Year Round) •
  W 57th St & Ninth Ave

Hardware Stores

- **Columbus Hardware** • 852 Ninth Ave [56th]
- **Garden Hardware & Supply** •
  701 Tenth Ave [48th]
- **HT Sales** • 718 Tenth Ave [49th]
- **Metropolitan Lumber & Hardware** •
  617 Eleventh Ave [46th]
- **Straight Hardware & Supply** •
  590 Ninth Ave [43rd]

Liquor Stores

- **54 Wine & Spirits** • 408 W 55th St [9th Av]
- **860 Ninth Liquors** • 860 Ninth Ave [56th]
- **B&G Wine & Liquor Store** •
  507 W 42nd St [10th Av]
- **Manhattan Plaza Winery** •
  589 Ninth Ave [42nd]
- **Ninth Avenue Vintner** • 669 Ninth Ave [46th]
- **Ninth Avenue Wine & Liquor** •
  474 Ninth Ave [37th]
- **Ray & Frank Liquor Store** •
  706 Ninth Ave [48th]
- **West 57th Street Wine & Spirit** •
  344 W 57th St [8th Av]

Supermarkets

- **Amish Market** • 731 Ninth Ave [50th]
- **Associated** • 917 Ninth Ave [58th]
- **D'Agostino** • 353 W 57th St [9th Av]
- **D'Agostino** • 815 Tenth Ave [54th]
- **Food Emporium** • 452 W 43rd St [10th Av]

Map 11 · Hell's Kitchen

N

W 60th St

W 59th St

W 58th St

W 57th St

W 56th St

W 55th St

W 54th St

W 53rd St

W 52nd St

W 51st St

W 50th Ct

W 49th St

W 48th St

W 47th St

W 46th St

W 45th St

W 44th St

W 43rd St

W 42nd St

W 41st St

W 40th St

W 39th St

W 38th St

W 37th ST

Columbus Circle

PAGE 248

Time Warner Center

Dewitt Clinton Park

Hudson River

PAGE 244

West Side Hwy

Hudson River Park

Eleventh Ave

Tenth Ave

Ninth Ave

Eighth Ave

Dyer Ave

Port Authority Bus Terminal

PAGE 319

Lincoln Tunnel

Jacob K Javits Convention Center

PAGE 246

14

12

8

1/4 mile

.25 km

Looking for a scene? The Hudson Hotel Library should do the trick. Otherwise, focus on casual and delicious eats, like Gazala Place and Nizza. Keep an eye out for the much anticipated reopening of the Museum of Arts and Design, in its new home in the redesigned 2 Columbus Circle.

Nightlife

- **Birdland** • 315 W 44th St [8th Av]
- **Don't Tell Mama** • 343 W 46th St [8th Av]
- **House of Brews** • 363 W 46th St [9th Av]
- **Hudson Hotel Library** • 356 W 58th St [9th Av]
- **Rudy's Bar & Grill** • 627 Ninth Ave [44th]
- **Vintage** • 753 Ninth Ave [51st]
- **Xth** • 642 Tenth Ave [45th]

Restaurants

- **99 Cent Pizza** • 569 Ninth Ave [41st]
- **Afghan Kebab House** • 764 Ninth Ave [51st]
- **Arriba Arriba Mexican Restaurant** • 762 Ninth Ave [51st]
- **Breeze** • 661 Ninth Ave [46th]
- **Burrito Box** • 885 Ninth Ave [57th]
- **Casellula** • 401 W 52nd St [9th Av]
- **Chili Thai** • 712 Ninth Ave [49th]
- **Churruscaria Plataforma** • 316 W 49th St [8th Av]
- **Daisy May's BBQ USA** • 623 Eleventh Ave [46th]
- **Don Giovanni** • 358 W 44th St [9th Av]
- **Eatery** • 798 Ninth Ave [53rd]
- **Empanada Mama** • 763 Ninth Ave [51st]
- **etcetera etcetera** • 352 W 44th St [9th Av]
- **Gazala Place** • 709 Ninth Ave [48th]
- **Grand Sichuan Int'l** • 745 Ninth Ave [50th]
- **Hallo Berlin** • 626 Tenth Ave [45th]
- **Hell's Kitchen** • 679 Ninth Ave [47th]
- **Hudson Cafeteria** • Hudson Hotel • 356 W 58th St [9th Av]
- **Island Burgers 'N Shakes** • 766 Ninth Ave [51st]
- **Joe Allen** • 326 W 46th St [8th Av]
- **Little Pie Company** • 424 W 43rd St [9th Av]
- **Marseille** • 630 Ninth Ave [44th]
- **Meskerem** • 468 W 47th St [10th Av]
- **Morningstar** • 401 W 57th St [9th Av] ⊗
- **Nizza** • 630 Ninth Ave [45th]
- **The Nook** • 746 Ninth Ave [50th]
- **Old San Juan** • 765 Ninth Ave [51st]
- **Piece of Chicken** • 630 Ninth Ave [44th]
- **Puttanesca** • 859 Ninth Ave [56th]
- **Ralph's** • 862 Ninth Ave [56th]
- **Say Cheese** • 649 Ninth Ave [51st]
- **Shorty's** • 576 Ninth Ave [42nd]
- **Taboon** • 773 Tenth Ave [52nd]
- **Tony Luke's** • 576 Ninth Ave [42nd]
- **Tout Va Bien** • 311 W 51st St [8th Av]
- **Turkish Cuisine** • 631 Ninth Ave [44th]
- **Vice Versa** • 325 W 51st St [8th Av]
- **Zen Palate** • 663 Ninth Ave [46th]

Shopping

- **Amy's Bread** • 672 Ninth Ave [47th]
- **Annex/Hell's Kitchen Flea Market** • W 39th St b/w Ninth Ave & Tenth Ave
- **Chelsea Garden Center** • 580 11th Ave [38th]
- **Coup de Coeur** • 609 Ninth Ave [43rd]
- **Delphinium** • 358 W 47th St [9th Av]
- **Delphinium Home** • 653 Ninth Ave [46th]
- **Janovic** • 771 Ninth Ave [52nd]
- **Little Pie Company** • 424 W 43rd St [9th Av]
- **Lyd** • 405 W 44th St [9th Av]
- **Metro Bicycles** • 360 W 47th St [9th Av]
- **Ninth Avenue International** • 543 Ninth Ave [40th]
- **Pan Aqua Diving** • 460 W 43rd St [10th Av]
- **Poseidon Bakery** • 629 Ninth Ave [44th]
- **Radio Shack** • 333 W 57th St [8th Av]
- **Sea Breeze** • 541 Ninth Ave [40th]

Map 11 · Hell's Kitchen

W 60th St

W 59th St

Time Warner Center

W 58th St

Columbus Circle

W 57th St

W 56th St

W 55th St

W 54th St

W 53rd St

Dewitt Clinton Park

W 52nd St

Hudson River

W 51st St

West Side Hwy

W 50th St

50th Street

W 49th St

Hudson River Park

Eleventh Ave

Tenth Ave

Ninth Ave

W 48th St

W 47th St

W 46th St

W 45th St

W 44th St

W 43rd St

W 42nd St

42nd Street Port Authority Bus Terminal

Port Authority Bus Terminal

W 41st St

Dyer Ave

W 40th St

Lincoln Tunnel

W 39th St

Jacob K Javits Convention Center

W 38th St

1/4 mile   .25 km

W 37th St

PAGE 248

PAGE 244

PAGE 319

PAGE 246

Transportation

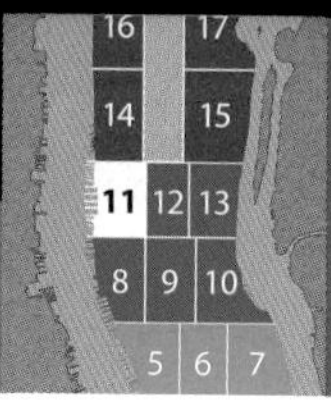

Map 11

There is no escaping Lincoln Tunnel traffic, and if you have to enter it, expect diabolical signage and obstructions. Walking beats the buses, weather permitting. Avoid the West Side Highway at rush hour. Take advantage of multiple subway lines (A-C-E and the 1), including a few that make the rare, underground cross-town voyage (N-R-W).

Subways

Ⓒ Ⓔ ....50th St

Ⓐ Ⓒ Ⓔ 42nd St/Port Authority Bus Terminal

Ⓐ Ⓒ Ⓑ Ⓓ ❶ ......59th St/Columbus Cir

Bus Lines

11	.... Ninth Ave/Tenth Ave
16	.... 34th St Crosstown
27	.... 49th St/50th St Crosstown
31	.... 57th St Crosstown
42	.... 42nd St Crosstown
50	.... 49th St/50th St Crosstown
57	.... 57th St Crosstown
104	..........................Broadway/42nd St

Bike Lanes

- • • • Marked Bike Lanes
- • • • Recommended Route
- • • • Greenway

Car Rental

- **All-State Auto Rental** •
  540 W 44th St [10th Av]
- **Autorent Car Rental** • 415 W 45th St [9th Av]
- **Avis** • 515 W 43rd St [10th Av]
- **Courier Car Rental** • 537 Tenth Ave [40th]
- **Enterprise** • 667 Eleventh Ave [48th]

Car Washes

- **New York Car Wash** • 625 Eleventh Ave [46th]
- **Westside Highway Car Wash** •
  638 W 47th St [11th Av]

Gas Stations

- **Hess** • 502 W 45th St [10th Av] ⊗
- **Mobil** • 718 Eleventh Ave [51st] ⊗

Parking

Map 12 · Midtown

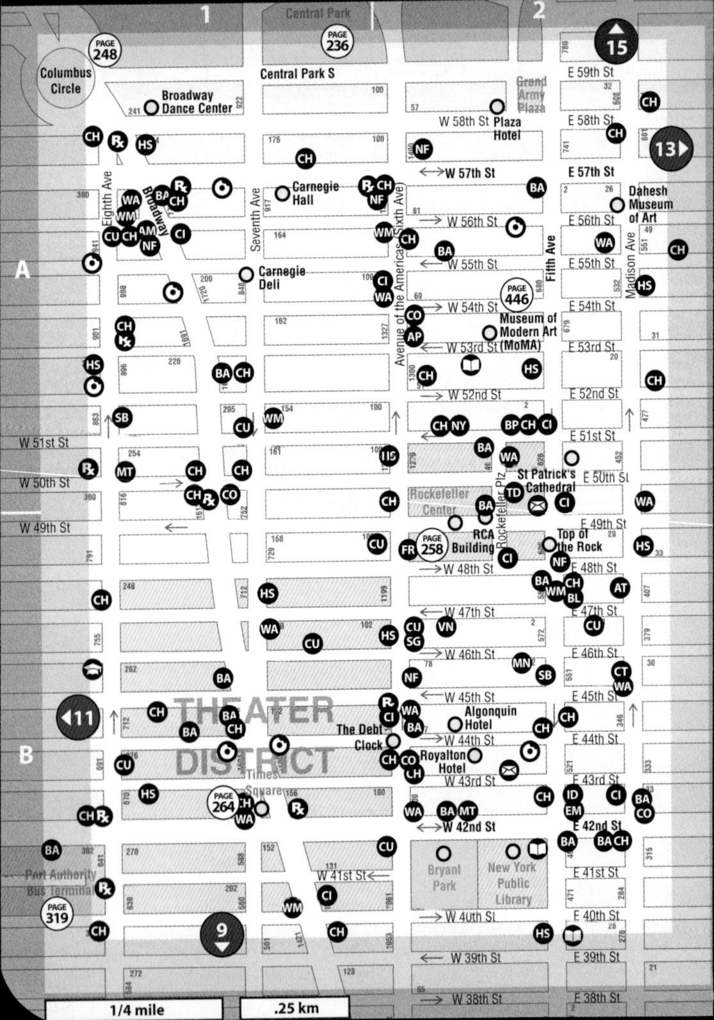

Central Park

1   2

PAGE 248

PAGE 236

Columbus Circle

Central Park S

Broadway Dance Center

E 59th St

15

E 58th St

Grand Army Plaza

Plaza Hotel

W 58th St

13

W 57th St

E 57th St

Dahesh Museum of Art

Carnegie Hall

W 56th St

E 56th St

Madison Ave

Fifth Ave

W 55th St

E 55th St

Carnegie Deli

W 54th St

PAGE 446

E 54th St

Museum of Modern Art (MoMA)

W 53rd St

E 53rd St

Avenue of the Americas (Sixth Ave)

Seventh Ave

Eighth Ave

Broadway

W 52nd St

E 52nd St

W 51st St

W 51st St

E 51st St

St Patrick's Cathedral

W 50th St

E 50th St

W 49th St

Rockefeller Center

W 48th St

RCA Building

PAGE 258

Top of the Rock

E 49th St

E 48th St

Rockefeller Plz

W 47th St

E 47th St

W 46th St

E 46th St

W 45th St

E 45th St

THEATER DISTRICT

The Debt Clock

Algonquin Hotel

W 44th St

E 44th St

Royalton Hotel

W 43rd St

E 43rd St

Times Square

PAGE 264

11

W 42nd St

E 42nd St

W 41st St

Bryant Park

New York Public Library

E 41st St

Port Authority Bus Terminal

PAGE 319

W 4uth St

E 40th St

9

W 39th St

E 39th St

W 38th St

E 38th St

1/4 mile   .25 km

Welcome to the heart of the city. It's got some of the finest art (MoMA), the biggest businesses (bank headquarters abound), the brightest lights (Times Square), a world-famous hotel (the Plaza) and cathedral (St. Patrick's), and a pair of the most iconic animal statues ever (the lions guarding the Public Library). Hello, New York.

24-Hour Pharmacies

- **Duane Reade** • 100 W 57th St [6th Av] ⊛
- **Duane Reade** • 1150 Sixth Ave [45th] ⊛
- **Duane Reade** • 1627 Broadway [50th]
- **Duane Reade** • 224 W 57th St [B'way] ⊛
- **Duane Reade** • 250 W 57th St [8th Av] ⊛
- **Duane Reade** • 4 Times Sq [43rd] ⊛
- **Duane Reade** • 625 Eighth Ave [40th] ⊛
- **Duane Reade** • 661 Eighth Ave [42nd] ⊛
- **Duane Reade** • 900 Eighth Ave [54th] ⊛
- **Rite Aid** • 301 W 50th St [8th Av] ⊛

Bagels

- **44th Street Bagel** • 22 W 44th St [5th Av]
- **Bagel Stix** • 891 Eighth Ave [53rd]
- **Bagel-N-Bean** • 1710 Broadway [54th]
- **Bread Factory Café** • 935 Eighth Ave [55th]
- **Pick-a-Bagel** • 200 W 57th St [7th Av]
- **Times Square Bagels** • 200 W 44th St [7th]
- **Torino Deli** • 22 W 56th St [5th Av]

Banks

AM • **Amalgamated**
AP • **Apple**
AT • **Atlantic**
BP • **Banco Popular**
BL • **Bank Leumi**
BA • **Bank of America**
NY • **Bank of New York**
CH • **Chase**
CL • **Chiba**
CT • **Chinatrust**
CI • **Citibank**
CO • **Commerce**
EM • **Emigrant**
FR • **First Republic**
HS • **HSBC**
ID • **IDB**
CU • **Lower East Side People's Federal Credit Union**
MT • **M&T**
MN • **Metropolitan National**
NF • **North Fork**
SG • **Signature**
SB • **Sovereign**
TD • **TD Banknorth**
VN • **Valley National**
WA • **Wachovia**
WM • **Washington Mutual**

Landmarks

- **Algonquin Hotel** • 59 W 44th St [6th Av]
- **Broadway Dance Center** • 221 W 57th St, 5th Fl [B'way]
- **Bryant Park** • 42nd St & Sixth Ave
- **Carnegie Deli** • 854 Seventh Ave [55th]
- **Carnegie Hall** • 154 W 57th St [7th Av]
- **Dahesh Museum of Art** • 580 Madison Ave [57th]
- **The Debt Clock** • Sixth Ave & 44th St
- **Museum of Modern Art (MoMA)** • 11 W 53rd St [5th Av]
- **New York Public Library** • Fifth Ave & 42nd St
- **Plaza Hotel** • 768 Fifth Ave [58th]
- **RCA Building** • 30 Rockefeller Plz [49th]
- **Rockefeller Center** • 600 Fifth Ave [48th]
- **Royalton Hotel** • 44th St b/w Fifth Ave & Sixth Ave
- **St Patrick's Cathedral** • Fifth Ave & 50th St
- **Times Square** • 42nd St-Times Sq [7th Av]
- **Top of the Rock** • 600 Fifth Ave [48th]

Libraries

- **Donnell Library Center** • 20 W 53rd St [5th]
- **Humanities & Social Sciences Library** • 42nd St & Fifth Ave
- **Mid-Manhattan Library** • 455 Fifth Ave [40th]

Post Offices

- **Bryant** • 23 W 43rd St [5th Av]
- **Rockefeller Center** • 610 Fifth Ave [49th St]

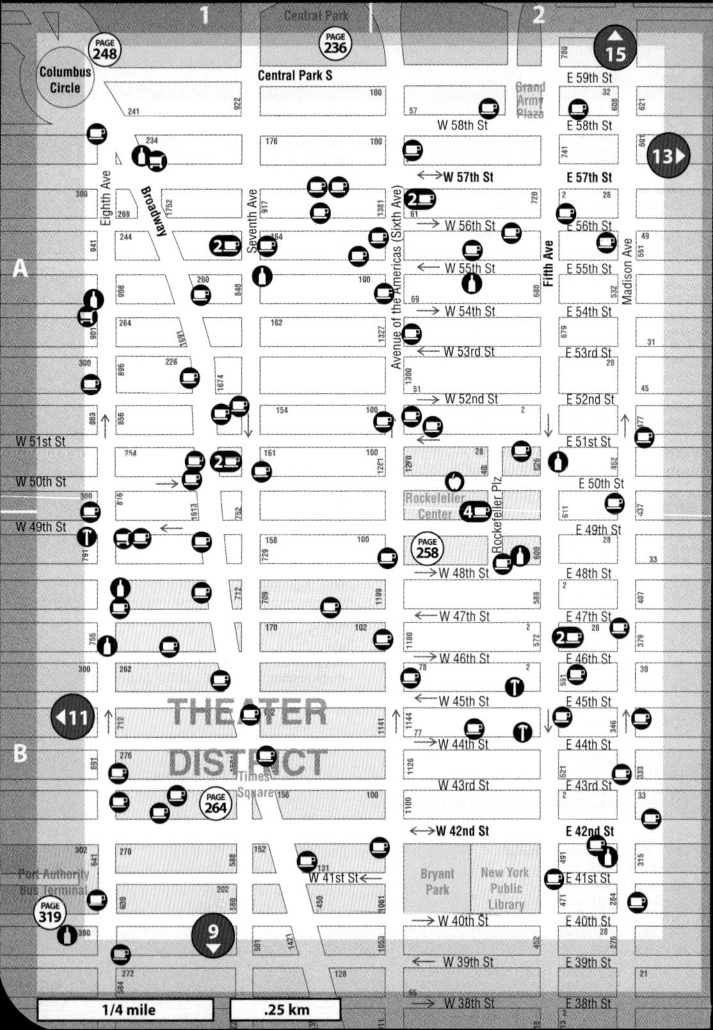

Map 12 • Midtown

PAGE 248
PAGE 236
PAGE 258
PAGE 264
PAGE 319

Columbus Circle

Central Park

Central Park S

Grand Army Plaza

E 59th St
E 58th St
W 58th St
E 57th St
W 57th St
E 56th St
W 56th St
E 55th St
W 55th St
E 54th St
W 54th St
E 53rd St
W 53rd St
E 52nd St
W 52nd St
E 51st St
W 51st St
E 50th St
W 50th St
E 49th St
W 49th St
E 48th St
W 48th St
E 47th St
W 47th St
E 46th St
W 46th St
E 45th St
W 45th St
E 44th St
W 44th St
E 43rd St
W 43rd St
E 42nd St
W 42nd St
E 41st St
W 41st St
E 40th St
W 40th St
E 39th St
W 39th St
E 38th St
W 38th St

Eighth Ave
Broadway
Seventh Ave
Avenue of the Americas (Sixth Ave)
Fifth Ave
Madison Ave

Rockefeller Plz

Rockefeller Center

THEATER DISTRICT

Times Square

Bryant Park

New York Public Library

Port Authority Bus Terminal

15
13
11
9

1/4 mile
.25 km

People actually live here (not just the ones who never leave the office), so you can easily find the basics. For a cut above, enjoy a true Italian espresso at Zibetto or a taste of Sweden at Fika. Summertime brings the Greenmarket to Rockefeller Center too.

Coffee

- **Au Bon Pain** • 1211 Sixth Ave [48th]
- **Au Bon Pain** • 125 W 55th St [6th Av]
- **Au Bon Pain** • 1251 Sixth Ave [50th]
- **Au Bon Pain** • 16 E 44th St [Madison]
- **Au Bon Pain** • 444 Madison Ave [50th]
- **Au Bon Pain** • 625 Eighth Ave [41st]
- **Bistro New York International** •
  1285 Ave of the Americas [51st]
- **Café Metro** • 625 Eighth Ave [40th]
- **City Chow** • 1633 Broadway [50th]
- **Cosi** • 11 W 42nd St [5th Av]
- **Cosi** • 1633 Broadway [50th]
- **Cosi** • 61 W 48th St [6th Av]
- **Crestanello Gran Café Italiano** •
  475 Fifth Ave [41st]
- **Cyber Café** • 250 W 49th St [B'way]
- **Dean & DeLuca Café** • 235 W 46th St [B'way]
- **Dean & DeLuca Café** • 9 Rockefeller Plz [48th]
- **Dunkin' Donuts** • 30 Rockefeller Plz [49th]
- **Dunkin' Donuts** • 55 W 55th St [6th Av]
- **Dunkin' Donuts** • 6 E 46th St [5th Av]
- **Dunkin' Donuts** • 761 Seventh Ave [50th]
- **Europan** • 672 Eighth Ave [43rd]
- **Evergreen Coffee Shop Restaurant** •
  145 W 47th St [6th Av]
- **Fika** • 41 W 58th St [5th Av]
- **Fluffy's Café & Bakery** • 855 Seventh Ave [55th]
- **La Parisiene Coffee** • 910 Seventh Ave [58th]
- **Lucky Star Café** • 250 W 43rd St [7th Av]
- **Oren's Daily Roast** • 33 E 58th St [Madison]
- **Philips Coffee** • 155 W 56th St [7th Av]
- **Red Flame Coffee Shop** • 67 W 44th St [6th Av]
- **Roy Bean** • 38 W 56th St [5th Av]
- **Seattle Coffee** • 1634 Broadway [50th]
- **Sixth Avenue Café** • 1414 Sixth Ave[58th]
- **Starbucks** • 1100 Sixth Ave [42nd]
- **Starbucks** • 1166 Sixth Ave [45th]
- **Starbucks** • 1185 Sixth Ave [46th]
- **Starbucks** • 120 W 56th St [6th Av]
- **Starbucks** • 1290 Sixth Ave [52nd]
- **Starbucks** • 1320 Sixth Ave [53rd]
- **Starbucks** • 1345 Sixth Ave [54th]
- **Starbucks** • 1380 Sixth Ave [56th]
- **Starbucks** • 142 W 57th St [6th Av]
- **Starbucks** • 1460 Broadway [42nd]
- **Starbucks** • 1500 Broadway [43rd]
- **Starbucks** • 1530 Broadway [45th]
- **Starbucks** • Marriott - 1535 Broadway [45th]
- **Starbucks** • 156 W 52nd St [7th Av]
- **Starbucks** • 1585 Broadway [48th]
- **Starbucks** • 1602 Broadway [49th]
- **Starbucks** • 1656 Broadway [51st]
- **Starbucks** • 1675 Broadway [52nd]
- **Starbucks** • 1710 Broadway [54th]
- **Starbucks** • 251 W 42nd St [8th Av]
- **Starbucks** • 295 Madison Ave [41st]
- **Starbucks** • 30 Rockefeller Plz [49th]
- **Starbucks** • 330 Madison Ave [43rd]
- **Starbucks** • 335 Madison Ave [43rd]
- **Starbucks** • 4 Columbus Cir [8th Av]
- **Starbucks** • 400 Madison Ave [48th]
- **Starbucks** • 45 E 51st St [Madison]
- **Starbucks** • 545 Fifth Ave [45th]
- **Starbucks** • 550 Madison Ave [55th]
- **Starbucks** • 565 Fifth Ave [46th]
- **Starbucks** • 575 Fifth Ave [47th]
- **Starbucks** • 600 Sixth Ave [39th]
- **Starbucks** • 684 Eighth Ave [43rd]
- **Starbucks** • 725 Fifth Ave [56th]
- **Starbucks** • 750 Seventh Ave [50th]
- **Starbucks** • 770 Eighth Ave [47th]
- **Starbucks** • 825 Fifth Ave [50th]
- **Starbucks** • 870 Seventh Ave [56th]
- **Starbucks** • 871 Eighth Ave [52nd]
- **Teresa's Gourmet Coffee Bar** •
  51 W 51st St [Rockefeller Plz]
- **Zibetto** • 1385 Sixth Ave [56th]

Farmers Markets

- **Rockefeller Center (Thur, Fri & Sat, 8 am–6 am, Jul–Aug)** • Rockefeller Plz & 50th St

Hardware Stores

- **New Hippodrome Hardware** •
  23 W 45th St [5th Av]
- **New Hippodrome True Value Hardware** •
  10 E 44th St [5th Av]

Liquor Stores

- **Athens Wine** • 302 W 40th St [8th Av]
- **Carnegie Spirits & Wine** • 849 7th Ave [54th]
- **Columbus Circle Wine** • 1780 B'way [57th]
- **Fifty Fifth Street** • 40 W 55th St [5th Av]
- **Morrell & Co Wine** • 1 Rockefeller Plz [48th]
- **Park Avenue Liquor** • 292 Madison Ave [41st]
- **Reidy Wine & Liquor** • 762 Eighth Ave [47th]
- **Shon 45 Liquors Inc** • 840 Eighth Ave [51st]
- **Westerly Liquors** • 921 Eighth Ave [55th]

Supermarkets

- **Associated** • 225 W 57th St [B'way]
- **Food Emporium** • 810 Eighth Ave [49th]
- **Gristedes** • 907 Eighth Ave [54th] ⊕

Map 12 • **Midtown**

Entertainment

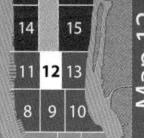

Map 12

Short on bargains, long on options. Shopping at Bergdorf epitomizes stylish New York, and even the English approve of their high tea. If you can afford them, Aquavit, The Modern, and Per Se make for some fine dining. If not, join the regulars at Jimmy's Corner for a shot and a beer.

Movie Theaters
• **AMC Empire 25** • 234 W 42nd St [7th Av]
• **Bryant Park Summer Film Festival (outdoors)** • Bryant Park, b/w 40th & 42nd Sts
• **Clearview's Ziegfeld** • 141 W 54th St [6th Av]
• **MOMA** • 11 W 53rd St [5th Av]
• **Paley Center for Media** • 25 W 52nd St [5th Av]
• **Paris Theatre** • 4 W 58th St [5th Av]
• **Regal 42nd Street E Walk** • 247 W 42nd St [7th Av]

Nightlife
• **Blue Bar** • 59 W 44th St [6th Av]
• **China Club** • 268 W 47th St [8th Av]
• **Flute** • 205 W 54th St [7th Av]
• **Iridium** • 1650 Broadway [51st]
• **Jimmy's Corner** • 140 W 44th St [B'way]
• **Oak Room** • 59 W 44th St [6th Av]
• **Paramount Bar** • 235 W 46th St [B'way]
• **Roseland** • 239 W 52nd St [B'way]
• **The Royalton** • 44 W 44th St [5th Av]
• **Russian Vodka Room** • 265 W 52nd St [8th Av]
• **St Andrews** • 120 W 44th St [6th Av]
• **Town Hall** • 123 W 43rd St [6th Av]

Restaurants
• **21 Club** • 21 W 52nd St [5th Av]
• **Aquavit** • 13 W 54th St [5th Av]
• **BG** • 754 Fifth Ave [57th]
• **Brasserie 8 1/2** • 9 W 57th St [5th Av]
• **Burger Joint** • Parker Meridien • 119 W 56th St [6th Av]
• **Carnegie Deli** • 854 Seventh Ave [55th]
• **Gallagher's Steak House** • 228 W 52nd St [B'way]
• **Haru** • 205 W 43rd St [7th Av]
• **Joe's Shanghai** • 24 W 56th St [5th Av]
• **La Bonne Soupe** • 48 W 55th St [5th Av]
• **Le Bernardin** • 155 W 51st St [7th Av]
• **Metro Marche** • 625 Eighth Ave [40th]
• **The Modern** • 9 W 53rd St [5th Av]
• **Molyvos** • 871 Seventh Ave [56th]
• **Mont Blanc** • 315 W 48th St [8th Av]
• **Nation Restaurant & Bar** • 12 W 45th St [5th Av]
• **Per Se** • Time Warner Center • 10 Columbus Cir [58th]
• **Shelly's New York** • 41 W 57th St [5th Av]
• **Spanky's BBQ** • 127 W 43rd St [6th Av]
• **Virgil's Real BBQ** • 152 W 44th St [6th Av]
• **wichcraft** • Bryant Park, Sixth Ave b/w 40th St & 42nd St

Shopping
• **Apple Store** • 767 Fifth Ave [59th]
• **Baccarat** • 625 Madison Ave [59th]
• **Bergdorf Goodman** • 754 Fifth Ave [57th]
• **Burberry** • 9 E 57th St [5th Av]
• **Chanel** • 15 E 57th St [5th Av]
• **Colony Music** • 1619 Broadway [49th]
• **Drummer's World** • 151 W 46th St [6th Av]
• **Ermenegildo Zegna** • 543 Madison Ave [52nd]
• **FAO Schwarz** • 767 Fifth Ave [59th]
• **Felissimo** • 10 W 56th St [5th Av]
• **Henri Bendel** • 712 Fifth Ave [56th]
• **Joseph Patelson Music House** • 160 W 56th St [7th Av]
• **Kate's Paperie** • 140 W 57th St [6th Av]
• **Klavierhaus** • 211 W 58th St [7th Av]
• **Manny's Music** • 156 W 48th St [7th Av]
• **Mets Clubhouse Shop** • 11 W 42nd St [5th Av]
• **Mikimoto** • 730 Fifth Ave [57th]
• **MoMA Design Store** • 44 W 53rd St [5th Av]
• **Museum of Arts and Design Shop** • 40 W 53rd St [5th Av]
• **Paul Stuart** • Madison Ave & 45th St
• **Petrossian Boutique** • 911 Seventh Ave [58th]
• **Roberto's Woodwind Repair Shop** • 146 W 46th St [6th Av]
• **Saks Fifth Avenue** • 611 Fifth Ave [49th]
• **Sam Ash** • 160 W 48th St [7th Av]
• **Smythson of Bond Street** • 4 W 57th St [5th Av]
• **Steinway and Sons** • 109 W 57th St [6th Av]
• **Takashimaya** • 693 Fifth Ave [54th]
• **Tiffany & Co** • 727 Fifth Ave [56th]

Map 12 · Midtown

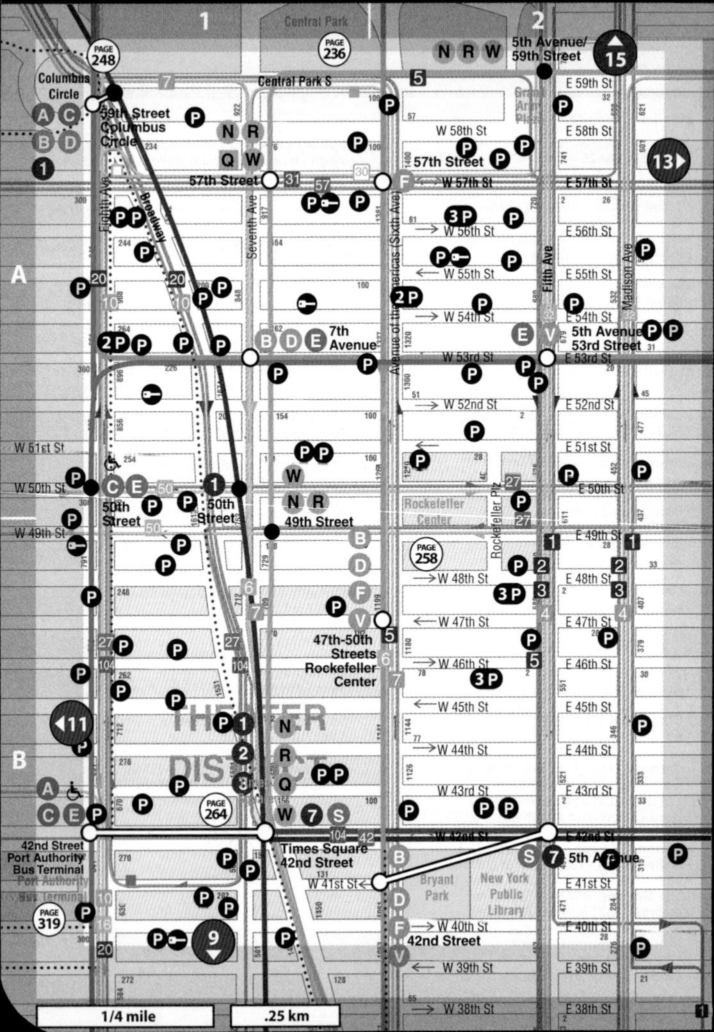

You can't NOT get to Midtown. Almost every subway line stops here. There are plenty of parking lots, but between their fees and the traffic, it's never worth it. Your feet and a Metro Card will suffice, we promise.

Subways

1 ....50th St
1 **A** **C** **B** **D** ......59th St-Columbus Cir
A **C** **E** .... 42nd St/Port Authority
B **D** **E** ....Seventh Ave
B **D** **F** **V** 47th St-50th St/Rockefeller Ctr
7 **B** **D** **F** **V** **S** ..... 42th St/Fifth Ave
C **E** .... 50th St
E **V** ....Fifth Ave/53rd St
F .... 57th St
1 **2** **3** **7** **N** **Q** **R** **W** **S**
.............................Times Sq/42th St
N **R** **Q** **W** .... 57th St
N **R** **W** .... 49th St
N **R** **W** .... Fifth Ave/59th St

Bike Lanes

- • • • Marked Bike Lanes
- • • • Recommended Route

Car Rental

- **Avis** • 153 W 54th St [6th Av]
- **Budget** • 304 W 49th St [8th Av]
- **Dollar** • 263 W 52nd St [B'way]
- **Hertz** • 126 W 55th St [6th Av]
- **Hertz** • 152 W 57th St [7th Av]
- **National/Alamo** • 252 W 40th St [7th Av]

Parking

Bus Lines

1 **2** **3** **4** .... Fifth Ave/Madison Ave
10 **20** .... Seventh Ave/Eighth Ave
(Central Park West)/Frederick Douglass Blvd
104 .... Broadway/42nd St
16 .... 34th St Crosstown
27 .... 49th St/50th St Crosstown
30 .... 57th St /72nd St Crosstown
31 .... York Ave/57th St
42 .... 42nd St Crosstown
5 .... Fifth Ave/Sixth Ave/Riverside Dr
50 .... 49th St/50th St Crosstown
57 .... 57th St Crosstown
6 .... Seventh Ave/Broadway/Sixth Ave
7 .... Columbus Ave/Amsterdam Ave/
Lenox Ave/Sixth Ave/Seventh Ave/Broadway
Q32 ... Penn Station/Jackson Heights, Queens

Map 13 • **East Midtown**

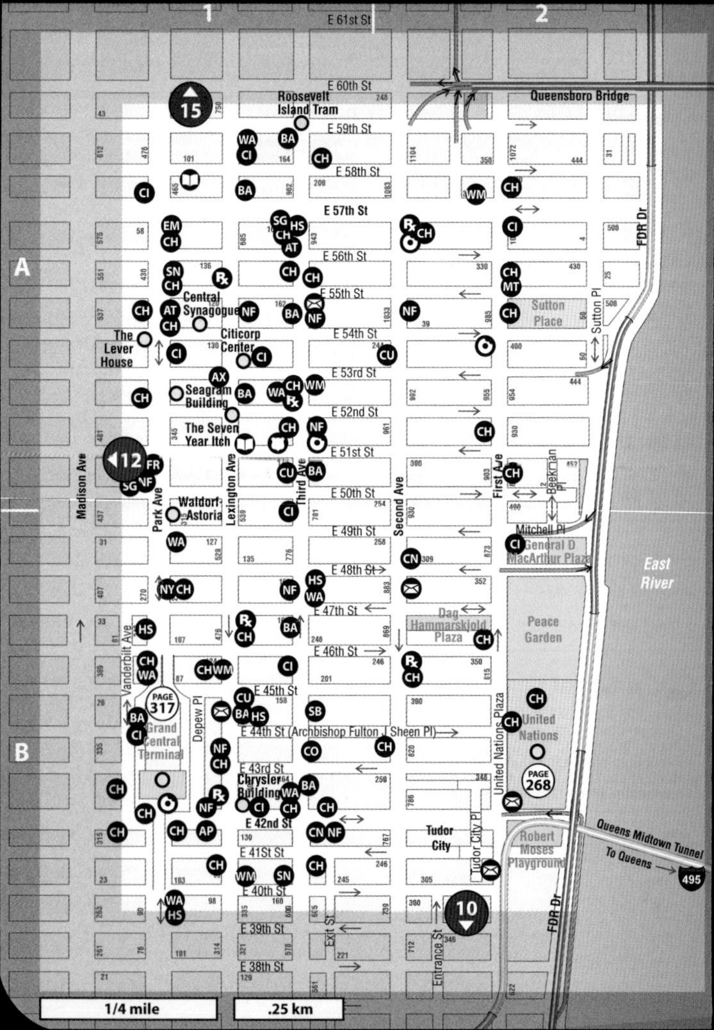

E 61st St

1

2

Queensboro Bridge

E 60th St

Roosevelt
Island Tram

15

E 59th St

E 58th St

E 57th St

E 56th St

Central
Synagogue

E 55th St

E 54th St

Citicorp
Center

The
Lever
House

Seagram
Building

E 53rd St

E 52nd St

The Seven
Year Itch

E 51st St

112

Waldorf-
Astoria

E 50th St

E 49th St

E 48th St

E 47th St

E 46th St

Dag
Hammarskjold
Plaza

PAGE
317

Grand
Central
Terminal

E 45th St

E 44th St (Archbishop Fulton J Sheen Pl)

E 43rd St

Chrysler
Building

E 42nd St

E 41st St

E 40th St

E 39th St

E 38th St

Sutton
Place

FDR Dr

General D
MacArthur Plaza

Mitchell Pl

Beekman Pl

East
River

Peace
Garden

United
Nations

PAGE
268

Tudor City

Robert
Moses
Playground

Queens Midtown Tunnel

To Queens

495

10

Madison Ave

Park Ave

Lexington Ave

Third Ave

Second Ave

First Ave

Vanderbilt Ave

Depew Pl

Tudor City Pl

United Nations Plaza

Exit St

Entrance St

FDR Dr

1/4 mile

.25 km

N

East Midtown has multiple personality disorder—in a good way. It's got the tranquility of elegant Sutton Place, the rowdy nightlife along Second Avenue, the commuter bustle of Grand Central Terminal, and the international crowd around the U.N. Not to mention the legendary architecture (the Chrysler and Seagram buildings, to name a few.)

24-Hour Pharmacies

- **CVS Pharmacy** • 630 Lexington Ave [54th] ☺
- **Duane Reade** • 1076 Second Ave [57th] ☺
- **Duane Reade** • 405 Lexington Ave [42nd] ☺
- **Duane Reade** • 485 Lexington Ave [46th] ☺
- **Duane Reade** • 852 Second Ave [45th] ☺
- **Duane Reade** • 866 Third Ave [53rd] ☺

Bagels

- **Ess-A-Bagel** • 831 Third Ave [51st]
- **Hot & Crusty** • 84 E 42nd St [Park]
- **Jumbo Bagels & Bialys** •
  1070 Second Ave [56th]
- **Tal Bagels** • 977 First Ave [54th]

Banks

AX • **AmEx Travel Related Services**
AP • **Apple**
AT • **Atlantic**
BA • **Bank of America**
NY • **Bank of New York**
CH • **Chase Ave**
CI • **Citibank**
CO • **Commerce**
CN • **Country Bank]**
EM • **Emigrant**
FR • **First Republic**
HS • **HSBC**
CU • **Lower East Side People's Federal Credit
      Union**
MT • **M&T**
NF • **North Fork**
SG • **Signature**
SB • **Sovereign**
SN • **Sterling National**
WA • **Wachovia**
WM • **Washington Mutual**

Landmarks

- **Central Synagogue** • 123 E 55th St [Lex]
- **Chrysler Building** • 405 Lexington Ave [42nd]
- **Citicorp Center** • 153 E 53rd St [Lex]
- **Grand Central Terminal** • 42nd St
- **The Lever House** • 390 Park Ave [54th]
- **Roosevelt Island Tram** •
  E 59th St & Second Ave
- **Seagram Building** • 375 Park Ave [53rd]
- **The Seven Year Itch** •
  E 52nd St & Lexington Ave
- **United Nations** •
  First Ave b/w 42nd & 48th Sts
- **Waldorf-Astoria** • 301 Park Ave [49th]

Libraries

- **58th St** • 127 E 58th St [Lex]
- **Terence Cardinal Cooke-Cathedral** •
  560 Lexington Ave [50th]

Police

- **17th Precinct** • 167 E 51st St [3rd Av]

Post Offices

- **Dag Hammarskjold** • 884 Second Ave [47th]
- **Franklin D Roosevelt** • 909 Third Ave [55th]
- **Grand Central Station** •
  450 Lexington Ave [45th]
- **United Nations** • 405 E 42nd St [1st Ave]

Map 13 · **East Midtown**

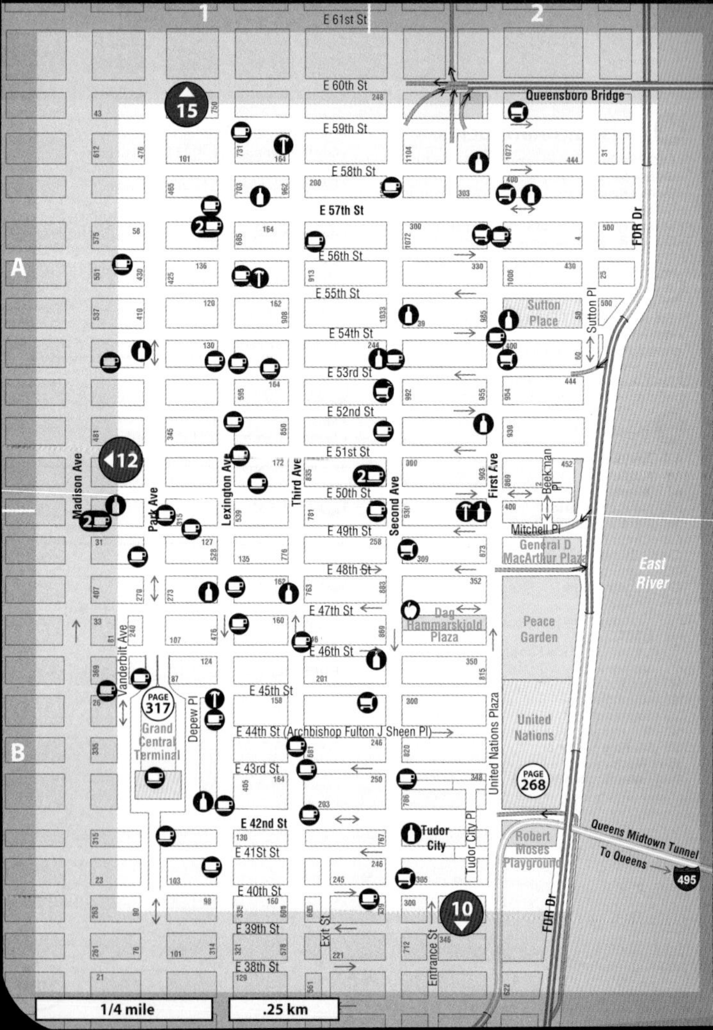

1 **2**

E 61st St

E 60th St

Queensboro Bridge

E 59th St

E 58th St

E 57th St

E 56th St

E 55th St

A

E 54th St

Sutton Place

E 53rd St

E 52nd St

E 51st St

E 50th St

E 49th St

First Ave

Mitchell Pl

General D
MacArthur Plaza

East
River

E 48th St

E 47th St

Dag
Hammarskjold
Plaza

Peace
Garden

E 46th St

E 45th St

PAGE
317

Grand
Central
Terminal

E 44th St (Archbishop Fulton J Sheen Pl)

United Nations Plaza

United
Nations

B

E 43rd St

PAGE
268

E 42nd St

Tudor City

Robert
Moses
Playground

Queens Midtown Tunnel
To Queens

495

E 41st St

E 40th St

10

E 39th St

E 38th St

Madison Ave

Park Ave

Lexington Ave

Third Ave

Second Ave

Vanderbilt Ave

Depew Pl

Tudor City Pl

Exit St

Entrance St

FDR Dr

Sutton Pl

Beekman Pl

15

12

1/4 mile

.25 km

N

More than the sum of its infinite ethnically dissimilar UN delegates, East Midtown is brimming with chain donuts (Dunkin'), coffee (Starbucks) and the ghosts of long-gone East River slaughterhouses. Ogle the riches in Tudor City. Meet a friend at Dag Hammarskjold Plaza. Something about all that emptiness really frees a man to say what's on his mind.

 Coffee

- **Au Bon Pain** • 600 Lexington Ave [52nd]
- **Bistro 300** • 49 E 49th St [Madison]
- **Buttercup Bake Shop** • 973 Second Ave [52nd]
- **Cosi** • 38 E 45th St [Madison]
- **Cosi** • 60 E 56th St [Madison]
- **Cosi** • 685 Third Ave [43rd]
- **Dunkin' Donuts** • 1024 First Ave [56th]
- **Dunkin' Donuts** • 1093 Second Ave [58th]
- **Dunkin' Donuts** • 153 E 53rd St [Lex]
- **Dunkin' Donuts** • 250 E 40th St [Tunnel Exit]
- **Dunkin' Donuts** • 47 E 42nd St [Madison]
- **Dunkin' Donuts** • 800 Second Ave [43rd]
- **Ing Direct** • 45 E 49th St [Madison]
- **Mambi Lounge** • 933 Second Ave [50th]
- **Manhattan Espresso HD** • 146 E 49th St [Lex]
- **Morningstar Café** • 949 Second Ave [50th]
- **NY Luncheonette** • 135 E 50th St [Lex]
- **Oren's Daily Roast** • Grand Central Market • 105 E 42nd St [Park]
- **Palace Restaurant Coffee House** • 122 E 57th St [Lex]
- **Starbucks** • Grand Central • 107 E 43rd St [Lex]
- **Starbucks** • 116 E 57th St [Park]
- **Starbucks** • 125 Park Ave [41st]
- **Starbucks** • 135 E 57th St [Lex]
- **Starbucks** • 150 E 42nd St [Lex]
- **Starbucks** • 230 Park Ave [46th]
- **Starbucks** • 280 Park Ave [48th]
- **Starbucks** • Waldorf Astoria • 301 Park Ave [49th]
- **Starbucks** • 360 Lexington Ave [40th]
- **Starbucks** • 400 E 54th St [1st Av]
- **Starbucks** • 450 Lexington Ave [45th]
- **Starbucks** • 511 Lexington Ave [48th]
- **Starbucks** • 55 E 53rd St [Madison]
- **Starbucks** • 560 Lexington Ave [50th]
- **Starbucks** • 599 Lexington Ave [52nd]
- **Starbucks** • 630 Lexington Ave [54th]
- **Starbucks** • 639 Third Ave [41st]
- **Starbucks** • 655 Lexington Ave [55th]
- **Starbucks** • 685 Third Ave [43rd]
- **Starbucks** • 731 Lexington Ave [59th]
- **Starbucks** • 757 Third Ave [47th]
- **Starbucks** • 943 Second Ave [50th]
- **Starbucks** • Grand Central Station, Track 35

Farmers Markets

- **Dag Hammarskjold Plaza (Wed 8 am–6 pm, Year Round)** • E 47th St & Second Ave

Hardware Stores

- **55th Street Hardware** • 155 E 55th St [Lex]
- **Home Depot** • 980 Third Ave [59th]
- **Midtown Hardware** • 155 E 45th St [Lex]
- **Walbaum** • 881 First Ave [50th]

Liquor Stores

- **Ambassador Wines & Spirits** • 1020 Second Ave [54th]
- **American First Liquors** • 1059 First Ave [58th]
- **Beekman Liquors** • 500 Lexington Ave [47th]
- **Crush Wine & Spirits** • 153 E 57th St [Lex]
- **Diplomat Wine & Spirits** • 939 Second Ave [50th]
- **First Avenue Vintner** • 984 First Ave [54th]
- **Grande Harvest Wines** • 107 E 42nd St [Park]
- **Jeffrey Wine & Liquors** • 939 First Ave [52nd]
- **Midtown Wine & Liquor Shop** • 44 E 50th St [Madison]
- **Schumer's Wine & Liquors** • 59 E 54th St [Madison]
- **Sussex Wine & Spirits** • 300 E 42nd St [2nd Av]
- **Sutton Wine Shop** • 403 E 57th St [1st Av]
- **Turtle Bay Liquors** • 855 Second Ave [46th]
- **UN Liquor** • 885 First Ave [50th]
- **Viski Wines & Liquor** • 764 Third Ave [47th]

Supermarkets

- **Amish Market** • 240 E 45th St [3rd Av]
- **Associated** • 908 Second Ave [48th]
- **D'Agostino** • 1031 First Ave [57th]
- **D'Agostino** • 966 First Ave [53rd]
- **Food Emporium** • 405 E 59th St [1st Av]
- **Food Emporium** • 969 Second Ave [51st]
- **Gristedes** • 1052 First Ave [57th]
- **Gristedes** • 748 Second Ave [40th]

Map 13 · East Midtown

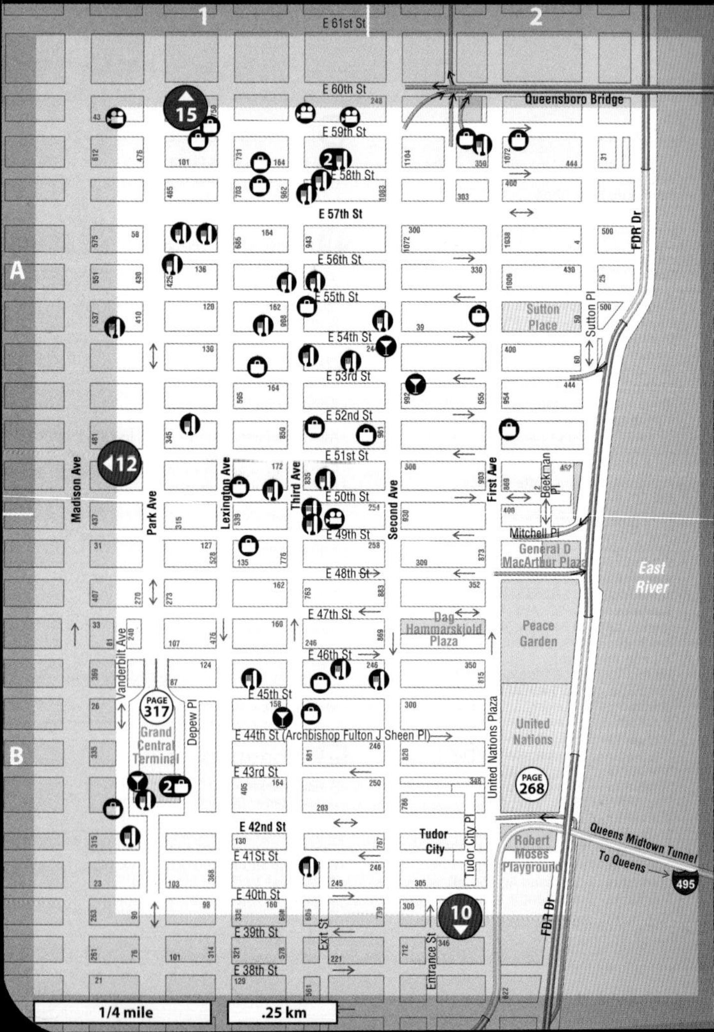

E 61st St

E 60th St

E 59th St

E 58th St

E 57th St

E 56th St

E 55th St

E 54th St

E 53rd St

E 52nd St

E 51st St

E 50th St

E 49th St

E 48th St

E 47th St

E 46th St

E 45th St

E 44th St (Archbishop Fulton J Sheen Pl)

E 43rd St

E 42nd St

E 41st St

E 40th St

E 39th St

E 38th St

Madison Ave

Park Ave

Vanderbilt Ave

Lexington Ave

Depew Pl

Third Ave

Exit St

Second Ave

First Ave

Sutton Pl

Beekman Pl

Mitchell Pl

United Nations Plaza

Tudor City Pl

Entrance St

FDR Dr

Queensboro Bridge

Sutton Place

General D MacArthur Plaza

Dag Hammarskjold Plaza

Peace Garden

United Nations

East River

Grand Central Terminal

PAGE 317

PAGE 268

Tudor City

Robert Moses Playground

Queens Midtown Tunnel

To Queens

495

15

12

10

1/4 mile

.25 km

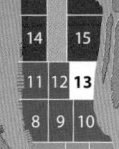

For a great night out without the downtown throngs, indulge in dinner at Vong or Rosa Mexicano (don't be fooled by their color, the special pomegranate margaritas pack a punch). And don't miss the burger at P.J. Clarke's, a New York institution. RIP to local fav Fubar, destroyed in the horrible crane accident.

Movie Theaters

- **City Cinemas 1, 2, 3** • 1001 Third Ave [60th]
- **French Institute** • 55 E 59th St [Madison]
- **The ImaginAsian** • 239 E 59th St [3rd Av]
- **Instituto Cervantes** • 211 E 49th St [3rd Av]

Nightlife

- **Blarney Stone** • 710 Third Ave [45th]
- **The Campbell Apartment** • Grand Central Terminal
- **Metro 53** • 307 E 53rd St [2nd Av]
- **Sutton Place** • 1015 Second Ave [54th]

Restaurants

- **BLT Steak** • 106 E 57th St [Park]
- **Caffé Buon Gusto** • 1009 Second Ave [53rd]
- **Chola** • 232 E 58th St [3rd Av]
- **Cosi Sandwich Bar** • 60 E 56th St [Madison]
- **Dawat** • 210 E 58th St [3rd Av]
- **Docks Oyster Bar** • 633 Third Ave [41st]
- **F&B** • 150 E 52nd St [Lex]
- **Felidia** • 243 E 58th St [3rd Av]
- **Four Seasons** • 99 E 52nd St [Park]
- **March** • 405 E 58th St [1st Av]
- **Menchanko-tei** • 131 E 45th St [Lex]
- **Nikki** • 151 E 50th St [Lex]
- **Oceana** • 55 E 54th St [Madison]
- **Opia** • 130 E 57th St [Lexington Av]
- **Organic Harvest Café** • 235 E 53rd St [3rd Av]
- **Oyster Bar** • Grand Central, Lower Level
- **Palm** • 837 Second Ave [45th]
- **Pershing Square** • 90 E 42nd St [Vanderbilt]
- **PJ Clarke's** • 915 Third Ave [55th]
- **Rosa Mexicano** • 1063 First Ave [58th]
- **Sidecar** • 205 E 55th St [3rd Av]
- **Shun Lee Palace** • 155 E 55th St [Lex]
- **Smith & Wollensky** • 797 Third Ave [49th]
- **Sparks Steak House** • 210 E 46th St [3rd Av]
- **Taksim** • 100 Second Ave [54th]
- **Vong** • 200 E 54th St [3rd Av]
- **Wollensky's Grill** • 205 E 49th St [3rd Av]
- **Yuva** • 230 E 58th St [3rd Av]

Shopping

- **A&D Building** • 150 E 58th St [Lex]
- **Alkit Pro Camera** • 227 E 45th St [3rd Av]
- **Bridge Kitchenware** • 711 Third Ave [45th]
- **Buttercup Bake Shop** • 973 Second Ave [52nd]
- **Godiva Chocolatier** • 560 Lexington Ave [50th]
- **Ideal Cheese** • 942 First Ave [52nd]
- **Innovative Audio** • 150 E 58th St [Lex]
- **New York Transit Museum** • Grand Central, Main Concourse
- **New York Vintage Club** • 346 E 59th St [1st Av]
- **Nicola's Specialty Emporium** • 997 First Ave [55th]
- **Pottery Barn** • 127 E 59th St [Lex]
- **Radio Shack** • 940 Third Ave [57th]
- **Sam Flax** • 900 Third Ave [55th]
- **Sports Authority** • 845 Third Ave [51st]
- **Terence Conran Shop** • 407 E 59th St [1st Av]
- **The World of Golf** • 147 E 47th St [Lex]
- **Yankee Clubhouse Shop** • 110 E 59th St [Park]
- **Zaro's Bread Basket** • 89 E 42nd St [Vanderbilt]

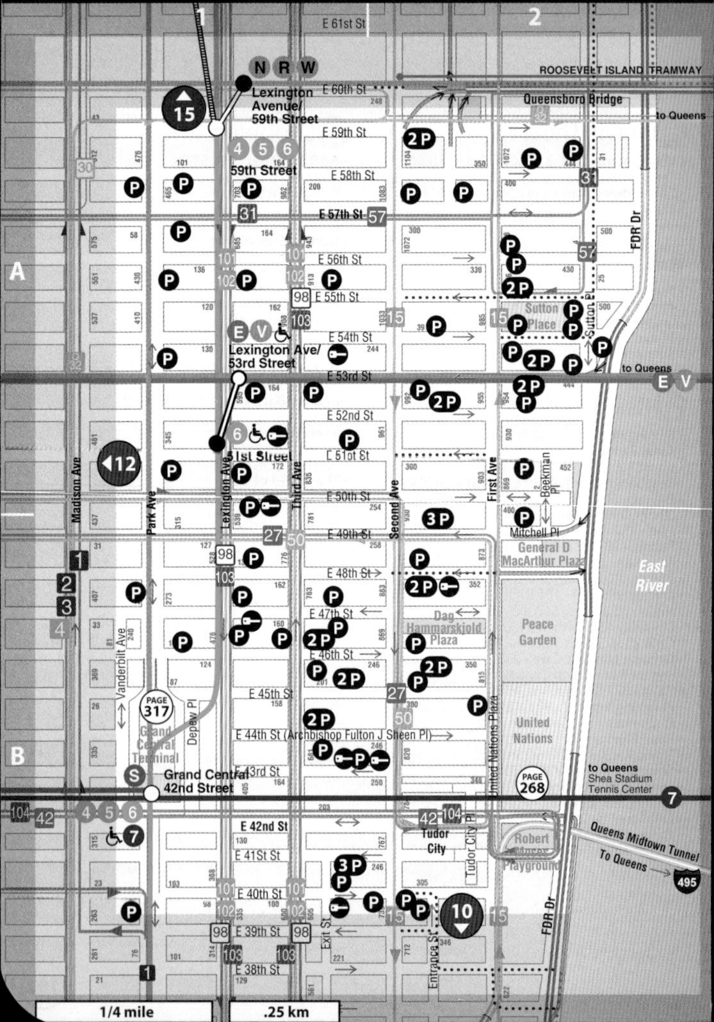

Map 13 · East Midtown

E 61st St

N R W

Lexington Avenue/59th Street

Roosevelt Island Tramway

Queensboro Bridge

to Queens

E 60th St

4 5 6

59th Street

E 59th St

E 58th St

E 57th St

FDR Dr

E 56th St

E V

Lexington Ave/53rd Street

E 55th St

E 54th St

Sutton Place

E 53rd St

to Queens

E V

E 52nd St

6

51st Street

E 51st St

Beekman Pl

12

Madison Ave

Park Ave

Lexington Ave

Third Ave

Second Ave

First Ave

E 50th St

Mitchell Pl

E 49th St

General D MacArthur Plaza

East River

E 48th St

E 47th St

Dag Hammarskjold Plaza

Peace Garden

E 46th St

E 45th St

27

50

United Nations

E 44th St (Archbishop Fulton J Sheen Pl)

PAGE 317

Grand Central Terminal

Vanderbilt Ave

Depew Pl

to Queens
Shea Stadium
Tennis Center

PAGE 268

S

Grand Central
42nd Street

3rd St

E 42nd St

7

Tudor City

Robert Moses Playground

Queens Midtown Tunnel

To Queens

495

E 41st St

E 40th St

Tudor City Pl

E 39th St

Exit St

Entrance St

FDR Dr

E 38th St

10

1/4 mile

.25 km

Access to multiple subway lines, the FDR and the Queensboro Bridge are pluses for getting in and out of the area. But you'll have to get used to the obstacles around the bridge (for pedestrians and vehicles), and the frequent motorcades of visiting dignitaries. Don't forget to wave.

Subways

4 5 6 N R W Lexington Ave-59th St
6 E V . . . . . 51st St-Lexington Ave-53rd St
4 5 6 7 S . . . . Grand Central-42nd St

Bus Lines

1 2 3 4 . . . . Fifth Ave/Madison Ave
104 . . . . Broadway
15 . . . . First Ave/Second Ave
27 50 . . . . 49th St/50th St Crosstown
30 . . . . 72nd St/57th St Crosstown
31 . . . . York Ave/57th St
42 . . . . 42nd St Crosstown
57 . . . . 57th St Crosstown
57 . . . Washington Heights/Midtown Limited
98 101 102 103 . . . . . . Third Ave/Lexington Ave
📍 . . . . Queens-to-Midtown

Bike Lanes

- • • • Marked Bike Lanes
- • • • Recommended Route
- • • • Greenway

🚗 Car Rental

- **Avis** • 217 E 43rd St [3rd Av]
- **Avis** • 240 E 54th St [3rd Av]
- **Budget** • 225 E 43rd St [3rd Av]
- **Enterprise** • 135 E 47th St [Lex]
- **Hertz** • 222 E 40th St [Tunnel Exit]
- **Hertz** • 310 E 48th St [2nd Av]
- **National/Alamo** • 138 E 50th St [Lex]
- **Prestige Car Rental** • 151 E 51st St [Lex]

🅿 Parking

Map 14 • **Upper West Side (Lower)**

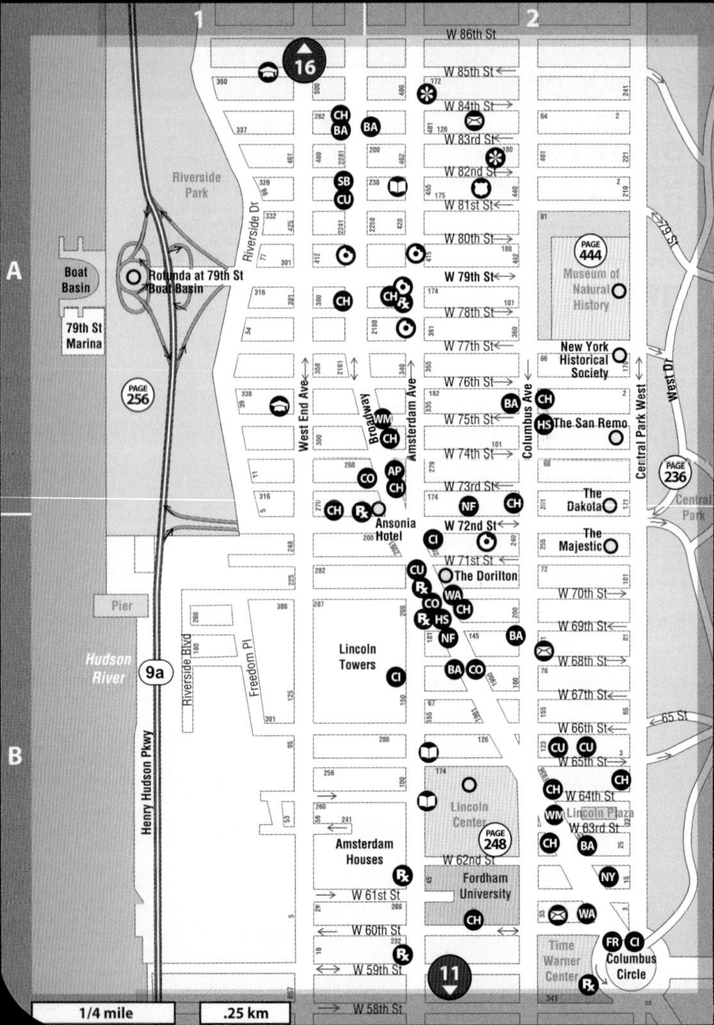

N

W 86th St

1

2

350

16

W 85th St

172

337

282 CH
BA

BA

480 485

W 84th St

200

402

W 83rd St

461 481 480

SB
CU

230

432 440

420

W 82nd St

W 81st St

Riverside Park

Riverside Dr

320

301

425 430

412

W 80th St

100

316

301

304

CH

CH
Rx

174

W 79th St

PAGE
444

Museum of
Natural
History

A

Boat
Basin

Rounda at 79th St
Boat Basin

79th St
Marina

2100

301

W 78th St

101

W 77th St

66

New York
Historical
Society

PAGE
256

358 362

2181

CH

338

300

WM

Broadway

Amsterdam Ave

West End Ave

348

335

162

BA

CH

CH
HS

The San Remo

Columbus Ave

W 76th St

W 75th St

W 74th St

290

CO

AP
CH

278

174

101

NF

CH

The Dakota

Central Park West

West Dr

PAGE
236

Central
Park

270

CH
Rx

Ansonia
Hotel

200

CI

240

W 73rd St

W 72nd St

The
Majestic

282

CU
Rx
CO
Rx

The Dorilton

WA
HS

72

W 71st St

W 70th St

101

Hudson
River

9a

Riverside Blvd

Freedom Pl

287

200

NF

BA

145

W 69th St

78

W 68th St

Pier

Lincoln
Towers

CI

BA
CO

W 67th St

W 66th St

65 St

B

200

126

CU
CU

256

174

CH

CH

Lincoln
Center

PAGE
248

W 64th St

WM Lincoln Plaza
W 63rd St

CH

BA

Amsterdam
Houses

Rx

280

241

Fordham
University

W 62nd St

NY

W 61st St

280

CH

WA

W 60th St

232

W 59th St

FR
CI

Columbus
Circle

Time
Warner
Center

Rx

11

W 58th St

1/4 mile   .25 km

Essentials

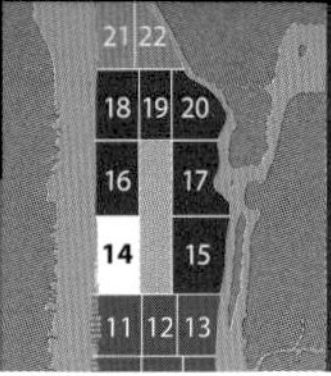

Map 14

21 22
18 19 20
16 17
14 15
11 12 13

Wynton Marsalis's Jazz at Lincoln Center and The American Museum of Natural History are the draw within this gentrified strip of chain boutiques, but the gorgeous tree-and brownstone-lined residential streets that lead you to Central Park (east) or Riverside Drive (west) offer a perennial New York vibe.

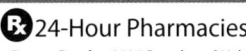

24-Hour Pharmacies

- **Duane Reade** • 2025 Broadway [69th] ⊕
- **Duane Reade** • 253 W 72nd St [West End] ⊕
- **Duane Reade** • 380 Amsterdam Ave [78th] ⊕
- **Duane Reade** • 4 Amsterdam Ave [59th] ⊕
- **Duane Reade** • 4 Columbus Cir [8th Av] ⊕
- **Rite Aid** • 210 Amsterdam Ave [70th] ⊕

Bagels

- **Bagel Talk** • 368 Amsterdam Ave [78th]
- **Bagels & Co** • 396 Amsterdam Ave [79th]
- **H&H Bagels** • 2239 Broadway [80th] ⊕
- **Pick-A-Bagel** • 130 W 72nd St [Columbus]

Banks

AP • Apple • 2100 Broadway [73rd St]
BA • Bank of America •
1886 Broadway [62nd St]
BA • Bank of America (ATM) •
192 Columbus Ave [69th St]
BA • Bank of America (ATM) •
1998 Broadway [68th St]
BA • Bank of America (ATM) •
2301 Broadway [83rd St]
BA • Bank of America (ATM) •
2310 Broadway [84th St]
BA • Bank of America (ATM) •
334 Columbus Ave [76th St]
NY • Bank of New York •
47 W 62nd St [B'way]
CH • Chase • 1 Lincoln Plz [63rd St]
CH • Chase • 2030 Broadway [70th St]
CH • Chase • 2099 Broadway [73rd St]
CH • Chase • 2219 Broadway [79th St]
CH • Chase • 260 Columbus Ave [72nd St]
CH • Chase • 335 Columbus Ave [76th St]
CH • Chase (ATM) • 1889 Broadway [62nd St]
CH • Chase (ATM) • 263 W 72nd St [West End Av]
CH • Chase (ATM) • 2025 Broadway [70th St]
CH • Chase (ATM) • 2150 Broadway [76th St]
CH • Chase (ATM) • 2307 Broadway [83rd St]
CH • Chase (ATM) • 380 Amsterdam Ave [78th]
CH • Chase (ATM) • 47 W 62nd St [Broadway]
CH • Chase (ATM) • 124 W 60th St [Columbus Av]
CI • Citibank • 162 Amsterdam Ave [67th St]
CI • Citibank • 170 W 72nd St [Amsterdam Av]
CI • Citibank • 4 Columbus Cir [8th Av]
CO • Commerce • 1995 Broadway [68th St]
CO • Commerce • 2109 Broadway [73rd St]
FR • First Republic • 10 Columbus Cir [B'way]
HS • HSBC • 2025 Broadway [W 69th St]
HS • HSBC • 301 Columbus Ave [W 74th St]
CU • Lower East Side People's Federal Credit Union (ATM) • 2049 Broadway [W 71st St]
CU • Lower East Side People's Federal Credit Union (ATM) • 2259 Broadway [W 81st St]
NF • North Fork • 175 W 72nd St [Amsterdam]
NF • North Fork • 2025 Broadway [69th St]
SB • Sovereign • 2275 Broadway [82nd St]
WA • Wachovia • 2040 Broadway [70th St]
WA • Wachovia (ATM) •
1841 Broadway [60th St]
WM • Washington Mutual •
1900 Broadway [63rd St]
WM • Washington Mutual •
2139 Broadway [75th St]

Community Gardens

Landmarks

- **Ansonia Hotel** • 2109 Broadway [73rd]
- **The Dakota** • Central Park W & W 72nd St
- **The Dorilton** • Broadway & 71st St
- **Lincoln Center** • Broadway & 64th St
- **The Majestic** • 115 Central Park W [71st]
- **American Museum of Natural History** • Central Park W & 79th St
- **New York Historical Society** • 2 W 77th St [CPW]
- **Rotunda at 79th St Boat Basin** • W 79th St [Riverside Dr]
- **The San Remo** • Central Park W & 74th St

Libraries

- **New York Public Library for the Performing Arts** • 40 Lincoln Center Plz [65th]
- **Riverside** • 127 Amsterdam Ave [65th]
- **St Agnes** • 444 Amsterdam Ave [81st]

Police

- **20th Precinct** • 120 W 82nd St [Columbus]

Post Offices

- **Ansonia** • 178 Columbus Ave [68th]
- **Columbus Circle** • 27 W 60th St [B'way]
- **Planetarium** • 127 W 83rd St [Columbus]

(111)

Map 14 • **Upper West Side (Lower)**

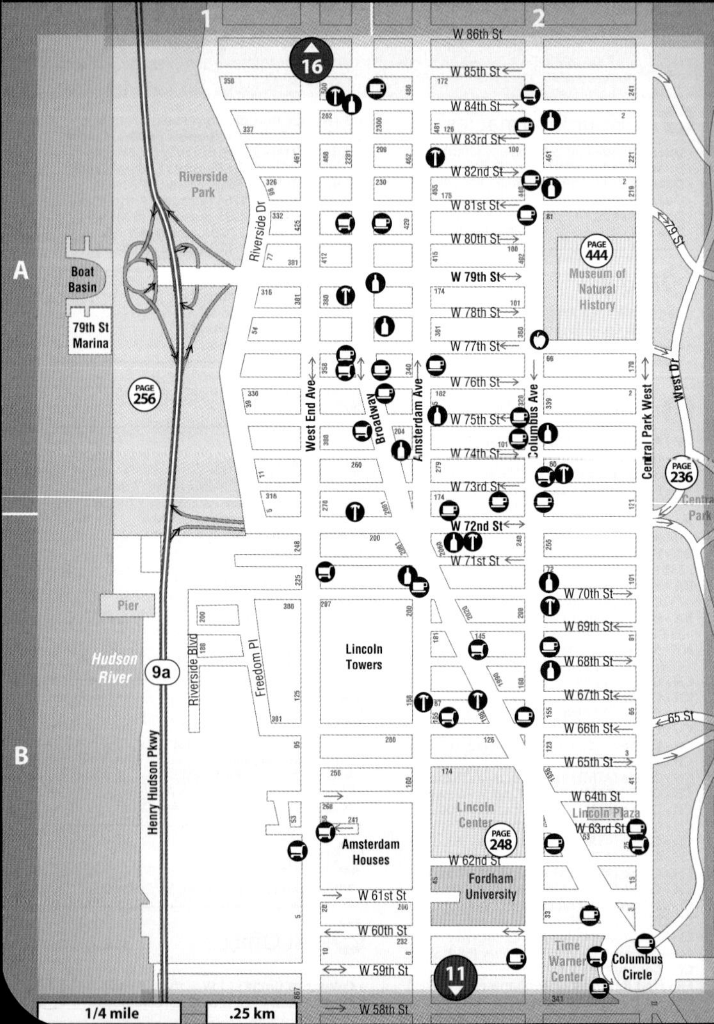

1
2

W 86th St

16

W 85th St

W 84th St

W 83rd St

W 82nd St

W 81st St

W 80th St

Riverside Park

W 79th St

A

Boat
Basin

79th St
Marina

W 78th St

W 77th St

**PAGE
256**

West End Ave

Broadway

Amsterdam Ave

W 76th St

W 75th St

W 74th St

W 73rd St

W 72nd St

W 71st St

**PAGE
444**
Museum of
Natural
History

Columbus Ave

Central Park West

West Dr

**PAGE
236**

Central
Park

W 70th St

W 69th St

Pier

Hudson
River

9a

Riverside Blvd

Freedom Pl

Lincoln
Towers

W 68th St

W 67th St

W 66th St

W 65th St

B

W 64th St

Lincoln
Center

**PAGE
248**

W 63rd St

W 62nd St

Lincoln Plaza

Amsterdam
Houses

Fordham
University

W 61st St

W 60th St

W 59th St

Time
Warner
Center

Columbus
Circle

11

W 58th St

1/4 mile   .25 km

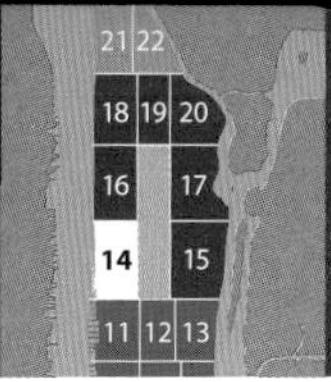

Sundries

Map 14

21 22
18 19 20
16   17
14   15
11 12 13

It's all about the chow. Head to Fairway, Citarella, and Zabar's and shop 'til you drop like a real Manhattanite, but steer clear of their carts at rush hour! 67 Wine & Spirits will dazzle you with choice and the chocolate cupcake at Buttercup Bake Shop is divine.

Coffee

- **Alice's Tea Cup** • 102 W 73rd St [Columbus]
- **Beard Papa** • 2167 Broadway [76th]
- **Buttercup Bake Shop** •
  141 W 72nd St [Columbus]
- **Columbus Bakery** • 474 Columbus Ave [83rd]
- **Columbus Café** • 87 Columbus Ave [63rd]
- **Cosi** • 2160 Broadway [76th]
- **Dean & DeLuca** • 10 Columbus Cir [B'way]
- **Edgar's Café** • 255 W 84th St [B'way]
- **Elixir Juice Bar** • 10 Columbus Cir [B'way]
- **International Café** • 5 W 63rd St [CPW]
- **Lenny's Café** • 302 Columbus Ave [74th]
- **New World Coffee** • 416 Columbus Ave [80th]
- **Starbucks** • 152 Columbus Ave [67th]
- **Starbucks** • 1841 Broadway [60th]
- **Starbucks** • 1889 Broadway [63rd]
- **Starbucks** • 2 Columbus Ave [59th]
- **Starbucks** • 2045 Broadway [70th]
- **Starbucks** • 2140 Broadway [75th]
- **Starbucks** • 2252 Broadway [81st]
- **Starbucks** • 267 Columbus Ave [72nd]
- **Starbucks** • 338 Columbus Ave [76th]
- **Starbucks** • 444 Columbus Ave [81st]

Farmers Markets

- **77th Street (Sun 10 am–5 pm, Year Round)** •
  W 77th St & Columbus Ave
- **Tucker Square (Thurs & Sat 8 am–5 pm, Year Round)** • W 66th St & Columbus Ave

Hardware Stores

- **A&I Hardware** • 207 Columbus Ave [69th]
- **Amsterdam Hardware** •
  147 Amsterdam Ave [66th]
- **Beacon Paint & Wallpaper** •
  371 Amsterdam Ave [78th]
- **Ben Franklin True Value Hardware** •
  2193 Broadway [78th]
- **Berg Hardware & Houseware** •
  239 W 72nd St [B'way]
- **Gartner's Hardware** •
  134 W 72nd St [Columbus]
- **Gracious Home** • 1992 Broadway [68th]
- **Klosty Hardware** • 471 Amsterdam Ave [83rd]
- **Supreme Hardware & Supply** •
  65 W 73rd St [Columbus]

Liquor Stores

- **67 Wine & Spirits** • 179 Columbus Ave [68th]
- **79th Street Wine & Spirits** •
  230 W 79th St [B'way]
- **Acker Merrall** • 160 W 72nd St [Amsterdam]
- **Bacchus Wine Made Simple (Wine only)** •
  2056 Broadway [71st]
- **Beacon Wines & Spirits** •
  2120 Broadway [74th]
- **Candlelight Wine** • 2315 Broadway [84th]
- **Central Wine & Liquor Store** •
  227 Columbus Ave [70th]
- **Ehrlich Liquor Store** •
  222 Amsterdam Ave [70th]
- **Nancy's Wines** • 313 Columbus Ave [75th]
- **Pour** • 321 Amsterdam Ave [75th]
- **Rose Wine & Liquor** • 449 Columbus Ave [81st]
- **West Side Wine & Spirits Shop** •
  481 Columbus Ave [83rd]

Supermarkets

- **Balducci's** • 155 W 66th St [B'way]
- **Citarella** • 2135 Broadway [75th]
- **Fairway** • 2127 Broadway [74th]
- **Food Emporium** • 2008 Broadway [69th]
- **Gristedes** • 25 Central Park W [63rd]
- **Gristedes** • 504 Columbus Ave [84th]
- **Gristedes** • 80 West End Ave [63rd]
- **Pioneer** • 289 Columbus Ave [73rd]
- **Western Beef** • 75 West End Ave [63rd]
- **Westside Market** • 2171 Broadway [77th]
- **Whole Foods** • 10 Columbus Cir [8th Av]
- **Zabar's** • 2245 Broadway [80th]

Map 14 · **Upper West Side (Lower)**

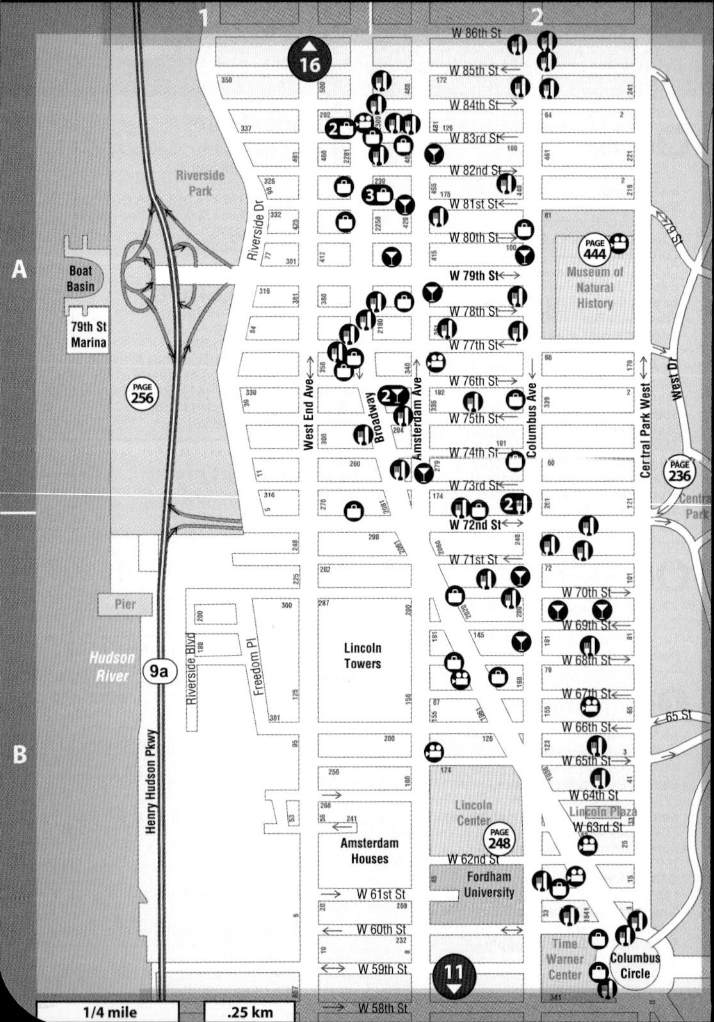

1

2

N

W 86th St←

W 85th St←

350

172

W 84th St←

337

126

W 83rd St←

2

Riverside Park

106

226

W 82nd St←

230

175

W 81st St←

3

322

W 80th St←

100

PAGE
444

323

W 79th St←

Museum of
Natural
History

A

Boat
Basin

319

W 78th St←

79th St
Marina

280

W 77th St←

66

361

W 76th St←

PAGE
256

330

W 75th St←

PAGE
236

101

W 74th St←

2

260

W 73rd St←

Central
Park

2

316

174

W 72nd St←

270

208

Pier

282

W 71st St←

72

300

287

W 70th St←

Hudson
River

9a

Lincoln
Towers

208

191

W 69th St←

145

W 68th St←

87

126

W 67th St←

155

W 66th St←

250

123

65 St

B

200

W 65th St←

266

174

W 64th St←

Lincoln
Plaza

241

Lincoln
Center

PAGE
248

W 63rd St

25

Amsterdam
Houses

Fordham
University

W 62nd St

15

W 61st St

208

W 60th St

237

Time
Warner
Center

Columbus
Circle

W 59th St

11

341

W 58th St

1/4 mile

.25 km

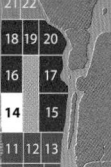

Treat yourself to an authentic gelato at Grom. Bars abound but pick wisely. P&G and Dublin House are dives from the past; spot real celebs at Café Luxembourg's bar. See the Allman Brothers at the Beacon for a New York spring ritual. Chow down on a good burger at Big Nick's.

🎬 Movie Theaters

- **AMC 84th St 6** • 2310 Broadway [84th]
- **AMC Lincoln Square 13** • 1998 Broadway [68th]
- **American Museum of Natural History IMAX** • Central Park W & 79th St
- **Clearview's 62nd & Broadway** • 1871 Broadway [61st]
- **Jewish Community Center in Manhattan** • 334 Amsterdam Ave [77th]
- **Lincoln Plaza Cinemas** • 1886 Broadway [63rd]
- **Walter Reade Theater** • 70 Lincoln Plz [65th]

🍸 Nightlife

- **Beacon Theater** • 2124 Broadway [74th]
- **Café Des Artistes** • 1 W 67th St [CPW]
- **Dead Poet** • 450 Amsterdam Ave [82nd]
- **Dublin House** • 225 W 79th St [B'way]
- **Emerald Inn** • 205 Columbus Ave [69th]
- **The Evelyn Lounge** • 380 Columbus Ave [78th]
- **Hi Life Bar & Grill** • 477 Amsterdam Ave [83rd]
- **Jake's Dilemma** • 430 Amsterdam Ave [81st]
- **P&G** • 279 Amsterdam Ave [73rd]
- **Yogi's** • 2156 Broadway [76th]

🍴 Restaurants

- **Artie's Deli** • 2290 Broadway [83rd]
- **Asiate** • 80 Columbus Cir, 35th fl [B'way]
- **Big Nick's** • 2175 Broadway [77th] ☺
- **Café Lalo** • 201 W 83rd St [Amsterdam]
- **Café Luxembourg** • 200 W 70th St [Columbus]
- **Café Rhonda** • 249 Columbus Ave [71st]
- **'cesca** • 164 W 75th St [Amsterdam]
- **Crumbs** • 321 Amsterdam Ave [75th]
- **Epices du Traiteur** • 103 W 70th St [Columbus]
- **Fairway Café** • 2127 Broadway [74th]
- **The Firehouse** • 522 Columbus Ave [85th]
- **French Roast** • 2340 Broadway [85th] ☺
- **Gabriel's** • 11 W 60th St [B'way]
- **Gari** • 370 Columbus Ave [78th]
- **Garlic Bob's** • 508 Columbus Ave [84th]
- **Good Enough to Eat** • 483 Amsterdam Ave [83rd]
- **Gray's Papaya** • 2090 Broadway [71st] ☺
- **Jacques-Imo's NYC** • 366 Columbus Ave [77th]
- **Jean-Luc** • 507 Columbus Ave [84th]
- **Josie's** • 300 Amsterdam Ave [74th]
- **Kefi** • 505 Columbus Ave [84th]
- **Kinoko** • 165 W 72nd St [Amsterdam]
- **La Caridad 78** • 2199 Broadway [78th]
- **Le Pain Quotidien** • 50 W 72nd St [CPW]
- **Manhattan Diner** • 2180 Broadway [77th] ☺
- **Ouest** • 2315 Broadway [84th]
- **Nougatine** • Trump International Hotel • 1 Central Park W [Columbus Cir]
- **Picholine** • 35 W 64th St [CPW]
- **Rain** • 100 W 82nd St [Columbus]
- **Rosa Mexicano** • 61 Columbus Ave [62nd]
- **Ruby Foo's Dim Sum & Sushi Palace** • 2182 Broadway [77th]
- **Santa Fe** • 73 W 71st St [Columbus]
- **Sarabeth's** • 423 Amsterdam Ave [80th]
- **Vince and Eddie's** • 70 W 68th St [Columbus]
- **Whole Foods Café** • Time Warner Center • 10 Columbus Cir, downstairs [B'way]

🛍 Shopping

- **Allan & Suzi** • 416 Amsterdam Ave [80th]
- **Alphabets** • 2284 Broadway [82nd]
- **Blades Board & Skate** • 156 W 72nd St [Columbus]
- **Bruce Frank** • 215 W 83rd St [Amsterdam]
- **Bruno the King of Ravioli** • 2204 Broadway [78th]
- **Claire's Accessories** • 2267 Broadway [81st]
- **Gracious Home** • 1992 Broadway [68th]
- **Grandaisy Bakery** • 176 W 72nd St [Amsterdam]
- **Grom** • 2165 Broadway [76th]
- **Harry's Shoes** • 2299 Broadway [83rd]
- **Housing Works Thrift Shop** • 306 Columbus Ave [74th]
- **Laytner's Linens** • 2270 Broadway [82nd]
- **Patagonia** • 426 Columbus Ave [81st]
- **Pookie & Sebastian** • 322 Columbus Ave [75th]
- **Townshop** • 2273 Broadway [82nd]
- **Tumi** • 10 Columbus Cir [B'way]
- **West Side Records** • 233 W 72nd St [B'way]
- **Yarn Co** • 2274 Broadway [82nd]
- **Zabar's** • 2245 Broadway [80th]

Map 14 · **Upper West Side (Lower)**

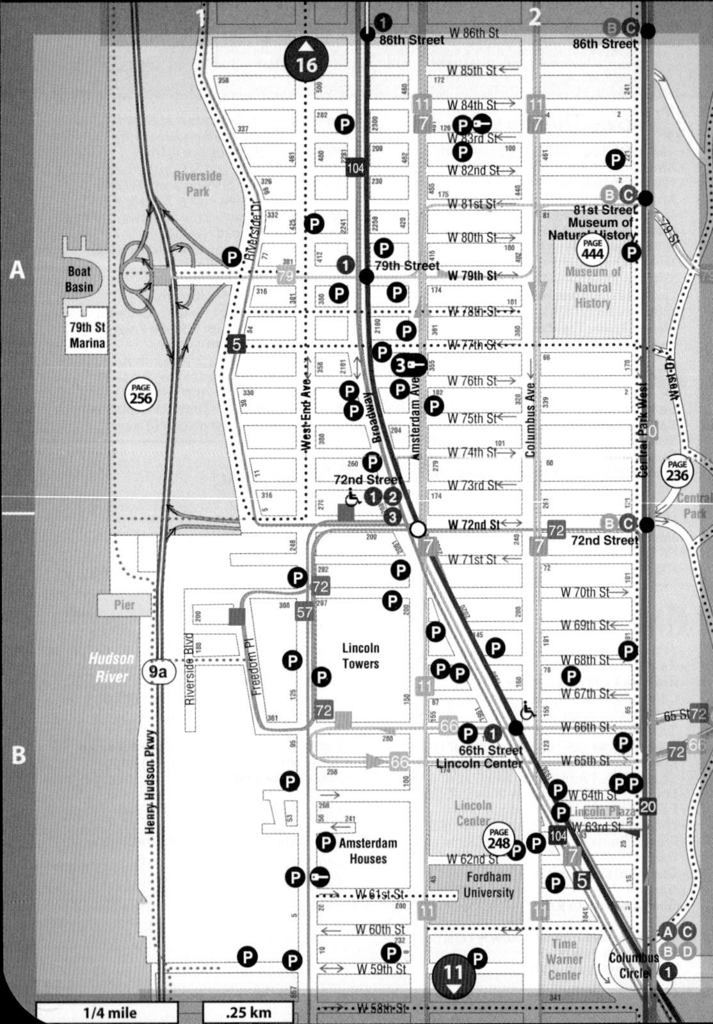

1

2

W 86th St
86th Street

86th Street

W 85th St

W 84th St

W 83rd St

W 82nd St

81st Street
Museum of
Natural
History
PAGE
444

Riverside Park

W 81st St

W 80th St

Museum of
Natural
History

W 79th St
79th Street

W 78th St

W 77th St

Boat
Basin

W 76th St

79th St
Marina

West End Ave

Broadway

Amsterdam Ave

Columbus Ave

W 75th St

W 74th St

W 73rd St

72nd Street

72nd Street

W 72nd St

W 71st St

Pier

W 70th St

Hudson
River

9a

Lincoln
Towers

W 69th St

W 68th St

Riverside Blvd

Freedom Pl

W 67th St

W 66th St
66th Street
Lincoln Center

Henry Hudson Pkwy

Lincoln
Center
PAGE
248

W 65th St

W 64th St
Lincoln Plaza

W 63rd St

Amsterdam Houses

Fordham University

W 62nd St

W 61st St

W 60th St

Time
Warner
Center

Columbus
Circle

W 59th St

W 58th St

1/4 mile   .25 km

Transportation

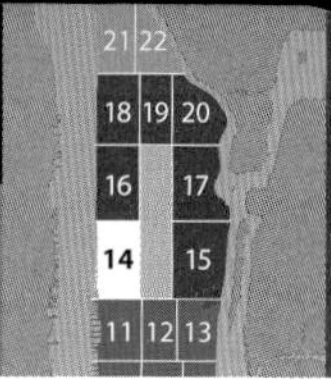

Map 14

21 22
18 19 20
16 17
14 15
11 12 13

Take the crosstown bus at 65th or 79th Streets, though your feet are faster. Broadway is the speedy route north while Columbus lights are synchronized south. Parking is scarce but eagle eyes will spot the 2-hour meters in the West 70s around Broadway, and on West 72nd.

Subways

1 2 3 .... 72nd St

1 .... 66th St-Lincoln Center

1 .... 79th St

1 A C B D .... Columbus Circle

B C .... 72nd St

B C .... 81st St-Museum of Natural History

Bus Lines

10 20 Seventh Ave/Eighth Ave/Douglass Blvd

104 .... Broadway/42nd St

11 .... Ninth Ave/Tenth Ave

5 .... Fifth Ave/Sixth Ave/Riverside Dr

57 .... 57th St Crosstown

66 .... 66th St/67th St Crosstown

7 .... Columbus Ave/Amsterdam Ave/
Lenox Ave/Sixth Ave/Broadway

72 .... 72nd St Crosstown

79 .... 79th St Crosstown

Bike Lanes

• • • Marked Bike Lanes

• • • Recommended Route

• • • Greenway

Car Rental

- **Avis** • 216 W 76th St [B'way]
- **Enterprise** • 147 W 83rd St [Columbus]
- **Hertz** • 210 W 77th St [Amsterdam]
- **National/Alamo** • 219 W 77th St [B'way]
- **Prestige Car Rental** • 55 West End Ave [62nd]

P Parking

Map 15 · **Upper East Side (Lower)**

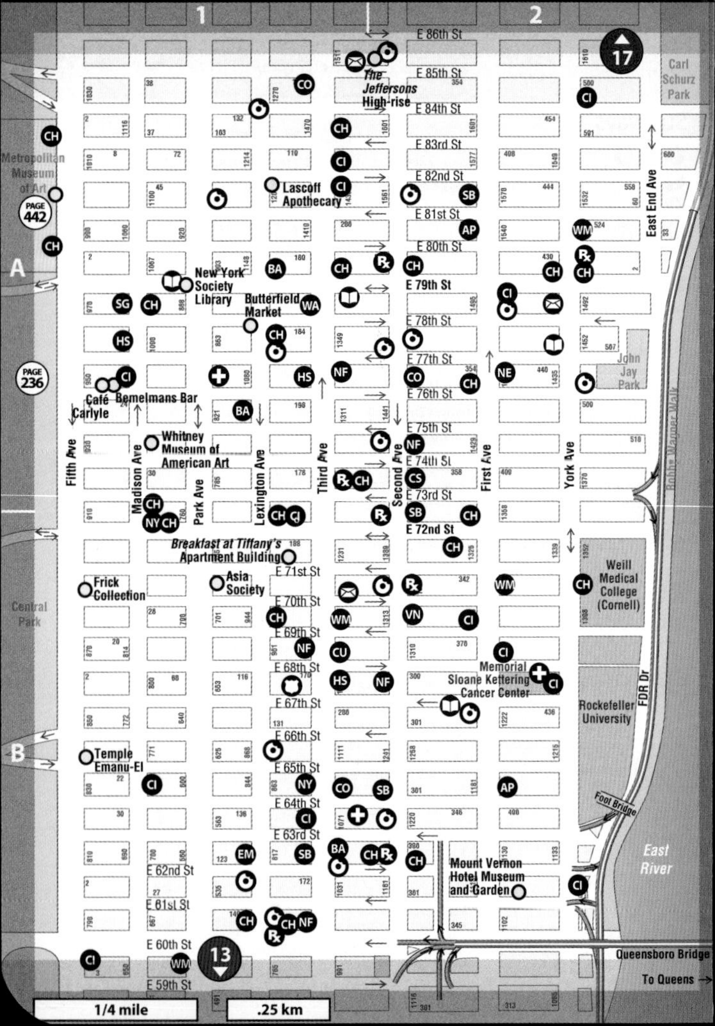

N

17

E 86th St

E 85th St

The Jeffersons High-rise

E 84th St

CO

E 83rd St

CH

E 82nd St

CI

SB

Lascoff Apothecary

CI

E 81st St

AP

WM

Metropolitan Museum of Art

PAGE 442

CH

E 80th St

CH

CH

RX

CH

E 79th St

SG CH

New York Society Library

BA

CI

Butterfield Market

WA

HS

E 78th St

CH

East End Ave

Carl Schurz Park

PAGE 236

HS

CI

Café Carlyle

Bemelmans Bar

CH

CO

NE

E 77th St

NF

CH

E 76th St

BA

Whitney Museum of American Art

NF

E 75th St

E 74th St

NF

RX CH

John Jay Park

Fifth Ave

Madison Ave

Park Ave

Lexington Ave

Third Ave

Second Ave

First Ave

York Ave

CH

NY CH

CH CI

E 73rd St

SB

RX

CH

E 72nd St

Breakfast at Tiffany's Apartment Building

Frick Collection

Asia Society

E 71st St

WM

RX

WM

Weill Medical College (Cornell)

E 70th St

NF

WM

VN

CI

E 69th St

CU

Rockefeller University

E 68th St

HS

NF

Memorial Sloane Kettering Cancer Center

E 67th St

E 66th St

Temple Emanu-El

CI

E 65th St

NY

CO

SB

AP

E 64th St

FOR Dr

Central Park

EM

SB

071

E 63rd St

BA RX

CH

E 62nd St

Foot Bridge

E 61st St

Mount Vernon Hotel Museum and Garden

CI

East River

CH

CH NF

RX

E 60th St

CI

WM

13

E 59th St

Queensboro Bridge

To Queens →

1/4 mile | .25 km

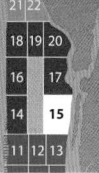
Culture, money, class, museums, and ladies who lunch make up the "silk stocking district." The Frick Collection is an insight into the homes that lined Fifth Avenue before the high rises took over. Don't miss the polar bear, penguins, or timeless Delacorte clock at the Central Park Zoo—an oasis in the middle of the urban zoo.

24-Hour Pharmacies

- **CVS Pharmacy** • 1396 Second Ave [72nd] ⚷
- **Duane Reade** • 1191 Second Ave [63rd] ⚷
- **Duane Reade** • 1279 Third Ave [73rd]
- **Duane Reade** • 1345 First Ave [72nd] ⚷
- **Duane Reade** • 1498 York Ave [79th] ⚷
- **Duane Reade** • 773 Lexington Ave [60th] ⚷
- **Rite Aid** • 1535 Second Ave [80th] ⚷
- **Walgreen's** • 1328 Second Ave [70th] ⚷

Bagels

- **Bagel Shoppe** • 1421 Second Ave [74th]
- **Bagels & Co** • 1428 York Ave [76th]
- **Bagelworks** • 1229 First Ave [67th]
- **Bread Factory Café** • 785 Lexington Ave [62nd]
- **Eastside Bagel** • 1496 First Ave [78th]
- **H&H** • 1551 Second Ave [81st]
- **Hot & Crusty** • 1201 Second Ave [63rd]
- **Hot & Tasty Bagels** • 1323 Second Ave [70th]
- **Monsieur Bagel** • 874 Lexington Ave [66th]
- **Pick A Bagel** • 1101 Lexington Ave [77th]
- **Pick A Bagel** • 1475 Second Ave [77th]
- **Tal Bagel** • 1228 Lexington Ave [83rd]

Banks

AP • **Apple**
BA • **Bank of America**
NY • **Bank of New York**
CH • **Chase**
CI • **Citibank**
CS • **City and Suburban FSB**
CO • **Commerce**
EM • **Emigrant**
HS • **HSBC**
CU • **Lower East Side People's Federal Credit Union**
NF • **North Fork**
NE • **NorthEast Community Bank**
SG • **Signature**
SB • **Sovereign**
VN • **Valley National**
WA • **Wachovia**
WM • **Washington Mutual**

Emergency Rooms

- **Lenox Hill** • 110 E 77th St [Park]
- **Manhattan Eye, Ear & Throat** • 210 E 64th St [3rd Av]
- **New York Presbyterian–Weill Cornell Medical Center** • 525 E 68th St [York Av]

Landmarks

- **Asia Society** • 725 Park Ave
- **Bemelmans Bar** • Carlyle Hotel • 35 E 76th St [Madison]
- *Breakfast at Tiffany's* **Apartment Building** • 1 69 E 71st St [Lexington]
- **Butterfield Market** • 1114 Lexington Ave [78th]
- **Café Carlyle** • Carlyle Hotel • 35 E 76th St [Madison]
- **Frick Collection** • 1 E 70th St [5th Av]
- *The Jeffersons* **High-rise** • 185 E 85th St [3rd Av]
- **Lascoff Apothecary** • 1209 Lexington Ave [82nd]
- **Metropolitan Museum of Art** • 1000 Fifth Ave [81st]
- **Mount Vernon Hotel Museum and Garden** • 421 E 61st St [1st Av]
- **New York Society Library** • 53 E 79th St [Madison]
- **Temple Emanu-El** • 1 E 65th St [5th Av]
- **Whitney Museum of American Art** • 945 Madison Ave [75th]

Libraries

- **67th St** • 328 E 67th St [2nd Av]
- **New York Society Library** • 53 E 79th St [Madison]
- **Webster** • 1465 York Ave [78th]
- **Yorkville** • 222 E 79th St [3rd Av]

Police

- **19th Precinct** • 153 E 67th St [Lexington Ave]

Post Offices

- **Cherokee** • 1483 York Ave [79th]
- **Gracie** • 229 E 85th St [3rd Av]
- **Lenox Hill** • 217 E 70th St [3rd Av]

Map 15 • Upper East Side (Lower)

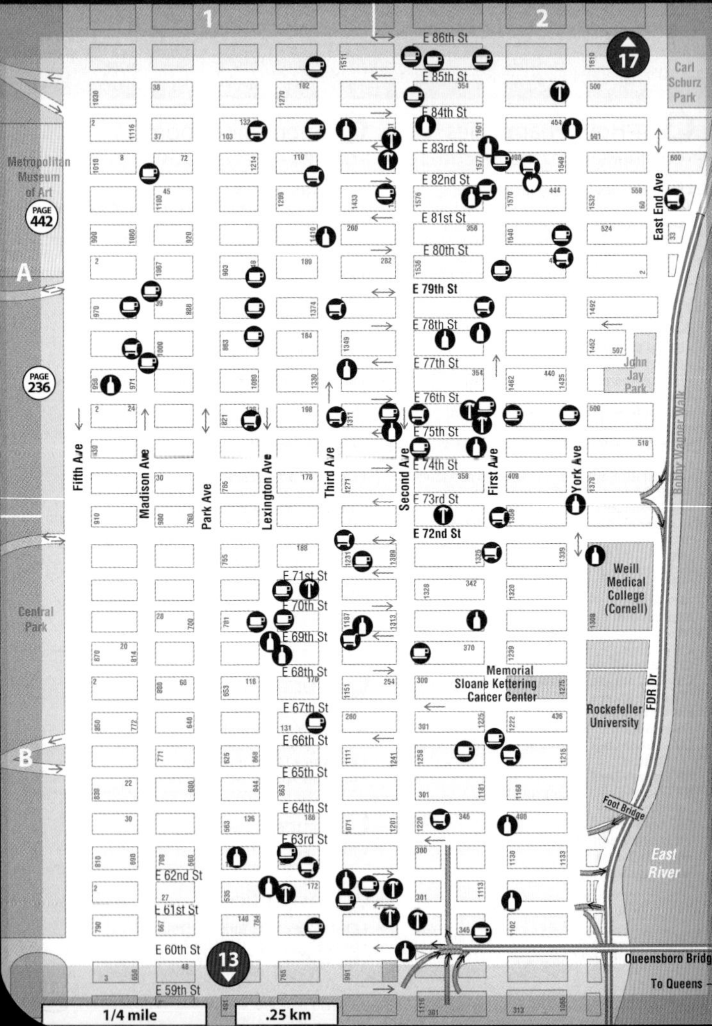
1
2
A
B
17
13
PAGE 442
PAGE 236
E 86th St
E 85th St
E 84th St
E 83rd St
E 82nd St
E 81st St
E 80th St
E 79th St
E 78th St
E 77th St
E 76th St
E 75th St
E 74th St
E 73rd St
E 72nd St
E 71st St
E 70th St
E 69th St
E 68th St
E 67th St
E 66th St
E 65th St
E 64th St
E 63rd St
E 62nd St
E 61st St
E 60th St
E 59th St
Fifth Ave
Madison Ave
Park Ave
Lexington Ave
Third Ave
Second Ave
First Ave
York Ave
East End Ave
FDR Dr
Bobby Wagner Walk
Metropolitan Museum of Art
Central Park
Carl Schurz Park
John Jay Park
Weill Medical College (Cornell)
Memorial Sloane Kettering Cancer Center
Rockefeller University
Foot Bridge
East River
Queensboro Bridg
To Queens
1/4 mile
.25 km

Sundries

Map 15

21 22
18 19 20
16 17
14 15
11 12 13

If you have the bucks, Agata & Valentina and Eli's are great places to shop for dinner. Indulge in a "Brooklyn Blackout" cake from Two Little Red Hens or stroke your laptop keys all day long at M Rohrs, a classic UES coffeehouse.

Coffee

- **Anneliese's Pastries** • 1516 First Ave [79th]
- **Beanocchio Café** • 1413 York Ave [75th]
- **The Bread Factory Café** • 785 Lexington [61st]
- **Cafe Bacio** • 1223 Third Ave [71st]
- **City Chow Café** • 140 E 63rd St [Lex]
- **DT UT** • 1626 Second Ave [84th]
- **Dunkin' Donuts** • 1225 First Ave [66th]
- **Dunkin' Donuts** • 1433 Second Ave [75th]
- **Dunkin' Donuts** • 1593 First Ave [83rd]
- **First Avenue Coffee Shop** • 1433 First Ave [75th]
- **Gotham Coffee House** • 1298 2nd Ave [68th]
- **Java Girl** • 348 E 66th St [2nd Av]
- **M Rohrs** • 310 E 86th St [2nd Av]
- **Nectar Coffee Shop** • 1022 Madison Ave [79th]
- **Nectar Coffee Shop** • 1090 Madison [82nd]
- **Neil's Coffee Shop** • 961 Lexington Ave [70th]
- **Oren's Daily Roast** • 1144 Lexington Ave [79th]
- **Oren's Daily Roast** • 1574 First Ave [82nd]
- **Oren's Daily Roast** • 985 Lexington Ave [71st]
- **Corrado Bread & Pastry** • 960 Lexington [70th]
- **Sicaffe** • 964 Lexington Ave [70th]
- **Starbucks** • 1021 Third Ave [61st]
- **Starbucks** • 1102 First Ave [60th]
- **Starbucks** • 1117 Lexington Ave [78th]
- **Starbucks** • 1128 Third Ave [66th]
- **Starbucks** • 1261 Lexington Ave [85th]
- **Starbucks** • 1445 First Ave [75th]
- **Starbucks** • 1449 Second Ave [75th]
- **Starbucks** • 1488 Third Ave [84th]
- **Starbucks** • 1515 York Ave [80th]
- **Starbucks** • 1559 Second Ave [81st]
- **Starbucks** • 1631 First Ave [85th]
- **Telegraphe Café** • 260 E 72nd St [2nd Av]
- **Tramway Coffee** • 1143 Second Ave [59th]
- **Two Little Red Hens** • 1652 Second Ave [86th]
- **Viand Coffee Shop** • 1011 Madison Ave [78th]

Farmers Markets

- **St Stephen's Greenmarket (Sat 9 am–3 pm, July–Nov)** • E 82nd St b/w First Ave & York Ave

Hardware Stores

- **ATB Locksmith & Hardware** • 1603 York Ave [85th]
- **Eastside Hardware** • 1175 Second Ave [62nd]
- **Gracious Home** • 1220 Third Ave [71st]
- **Home Plus** • 1400 Second Ave [73rd]
- **Kraft Hardware** • 315 E 62nd St [2nd Av]
- **Lexington Hardware** • 797 Lexington [62nd]
- **New York Paint** • 1593 Second Ave [83rd]
- **Queensboro Hardware** • 1157 2nd Ave [61st]
- **Rainbow Ace Hardware** • 1449 First Ave [75th]
- **S&V General Supply** • 1450 First Ave [75th]
- **Thalco Maintenance Supply** • 1462 Second Ave [76th]

Liquor Stores

- **76 Liquors** • 1473 First Ave [77th]
- **Aulden Cellars** • 1334 York Ave [71st]
- **Big Apple Wine** • 1408 Second Ave [73rd]
- **City Liquor** • 1145 Second Ave [60th]
- **Cork and Bottle** • 1158 First Ave [63rd]
- **Crown Wine** • z1587 Second Ave [82nd]
- **Drink** • 235 E 69th St [2nd Av]
- **East River Liquors** • 1364 York Ave [73rd]
- **Eli's** • 1415 Third Ave [80th]
- **Embassy Liquors** • 796 Lexington Ave [62nd]
- **Garnet Wines** • 929 Lexington Ave [69th]
- **Gracies Wine** • 1577 York Ave [84th]
- **In Vino Veritas** • 1375 First Ave [73rd]
- **Lumers Fine Wines** • 1479 Third Ave [83rd]
- **McCabe's Wines** • 1347 Third Ave [77th]
- **Morrell Wine Exchange** • 1035 3rd Ave [62nd]
- **Rosenthal Wine** • 318 E 84th St [2nd Av]
- **Vintage Grape** • 1479 Third Ave [84th]
- **Windsor Wine Shop** • 1103 First Ave [61st]
- **The Wine Shop** • 1585 First Ave [83rd]
- **Woody Liquor** • 1450 Second Ave [76th]
- **York Wines & Spirits** • 1291 First Ave [70th]

Supermarkets

- **Agata & Valentina** • 1505 First Ave [79th]
- **Associated** • 1565 First Ave [81st]
- **Citarella** • 1313 Third Ave [75th]
- **D'Agostino** • 1074 Lexington Ave [76th]
- **D'Agostino** • 1233 Lexington Ave [84th]
- **D'Agostino** • 1507 York Ave [80th]
- **Eli's Manhattan** • 1411 Third Ave [80th]
- **Food Emporium** • 1066 Third Ave [63rd]
- **Food Emporium** • 1175 Third Ave [68th]
- **Food Emporium** • 1331 First Ave [71st]
- **Food Emporium** • 1450 Third Ave [82nd]
- **Gourmet Garage East** • 301 E 64th St [2nd Av]
- **Grace's Marketplace** • 1237 Third Ave [71st]
- **Gristedes** • 1208 First Ave [65th]
- **Gristedes** • 1350 First Ave [72nd]
- **Gristedes** • 1365 Third Ave [78th]
- **Gristedes** • 1446 Second Ave [75th] ⊗
- **Gristedes** • 40 East End Ave [81st]
- **Health Nuts** • 1208 Second Ave [63rd]

Map 15 • **Upper East Side (Lower)**

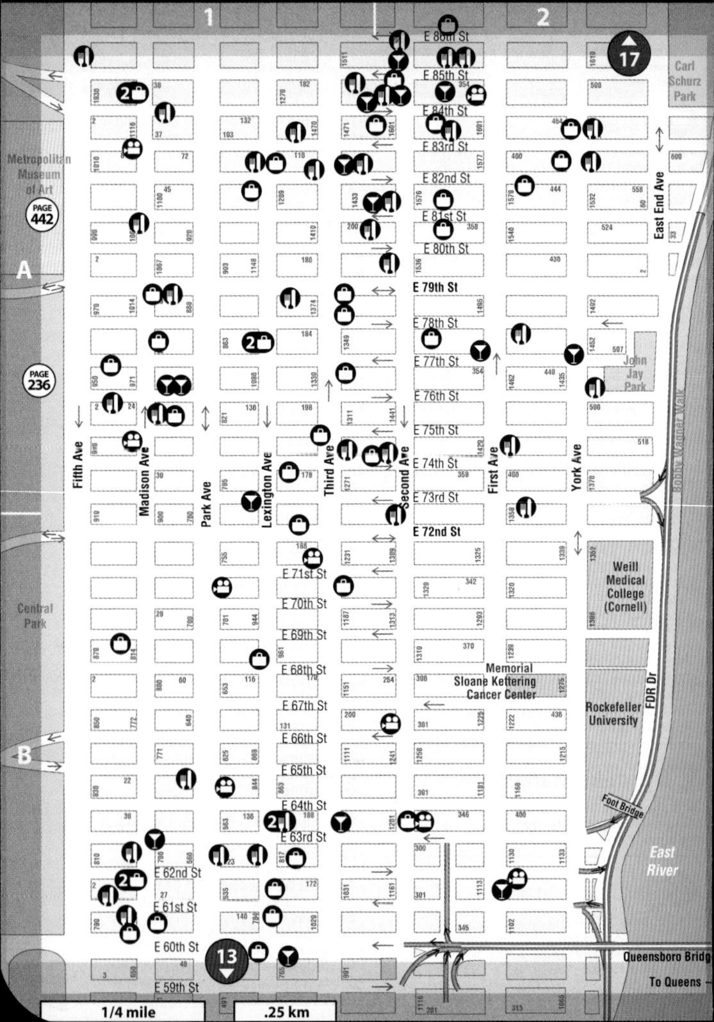

N

1

2

17

Carl
Schurz
Park

E 86th St

E 85th St

E 84th St

E 83rd St

E 82nd St

E 81st St

E 80th St

Metropolitan
Museum
of Art
PAGE
442

East End Ave

PAGE
236

E 79th St

E 78th St

E 77th St

E 76th St

E 75th St

E 74th St

E 73rd St

E 72nd St

John
Jay
Park

A

Fifth Ave

Madison Ave

Park Ave

Lexington Ave

Third Ave

Second Ave

First Ave

York Ave

E 71st St

E 70th St

E 69th St

E 68th St

E 67th St

E 66th St

E 65th St

E 64th St

E 63rd St

E 62nd St

E 61st St

E 60th St

Central
Park

Weill
Medical
College
(Cornell)

Memorial
Sloane Kettering
Cancer Center

Rockefeller
University

FDR Dr

B

Foot Bridge

East
River

13

Queensboro Bridg
To Queens

E 59th St

1/4 mile

.25 km

Skip the chains and buy your toothbrush at Lascoff Apothecary. Old-time New York is Bemelmans Bar at the legendary Café Carlyle. Burger nirvana can be reached at JG Melon. Free chips for the masses at Ryan's Daughter, and free grime for the regulars at the Subway Inn.

Movie Theaters

- **AMC 72nd Street East** • 1230 Third Ave [71st]
- **The Asia Society** • 725 Park Ave [70th]
- **Clearview's Beekman One & Two** • 1271 Second Ave [67th]
- **Clearview's First & 62nd Street** • 400 E 62nd St [1st Av]
- **Czech Center** • 1109 Madison Ave [83rd]
- **UA 64th and 2nd** • 1210 Second Ave [64th]
- **UA East 85th Street** • 1629 First Ave [85th]
- **Whitney Museum Theater** • 945 Madison Ave [75th]

Nightlife

- **Accademia di Vino** • 1081 Third Ave [63rd]
- **The Bar at Etats-Unis** • 247 E 81st St [3rd Av]
- **Bemelmans Bar** • 35 E 76th St [Madison]
- **Brandy's Piano Bar** • 235 E 84th St [3rd Av]
- **Café Carlyle** • 35 E 76th St [Madison]
- **Club Macanudo** • 26 E 63rd St [Madison]
- **Feinstein's at the Regency** • 540 Park Ave [61st]
- **Finnegan's Wake** • 1361 First Ave [73rd]
- **Lexington Bar & Books** • 1020 Lexington Ave [73rd]
- **Pudding Stone's Wine Bar** • 1457 Third Ave [82nd]
- **Ryan's Daughter** • 350 E 85th St [2nd Av]
- **Subway Inn** • 143 E 60th St [Lex]
- **Trinity Pub** • 299 E 84th St [2nd Av]
- **Vudu** • 1487 First Ave [78th]

Restaurants

- **Burger Heaven** • 804 Lexington Ave [62nd]
- **Burke Bar Café** • 150 E 59th St [Lex]
- **Burke in the Box at Bloomingdale's** • 150 E 59th St [Lex]
- **Café Boulud** • 20 E 76th St [Madison]
- **Café Mingala** • 1393 Second Ave [73rd]
- **Candle 79** • 154 E 79th St [Lex]
- **Candle Café** • 1307 Third Ave [75th]
- **Donguri** • 309 E 83rd St [2nd Av]
- **EAT** • 1064 Madison Ave [81st]
- **Elio's** • 1621 Second Ave [84th]
- **Etats-Unis** • 242 E 81st St [3rd Av]
- **Ethiopian Restaurant** • 1582 York Ave [83rd]
- **Heidelberg** • 1648 Second Ave [86th]
- **Indian Tandoor Oven Restaurant** • 175 E 83rd St [3rd Av]
- **Jacque's Brasserie** • 204 E 85th St [3rd Av]
- **JG Melon** • 1291 Third Ave [73rd]
- **JoJo** • 160 E 64th St [Lex]
- **Lexington Candy Shop/Luncheonette** • 1226 Lexington Ave [83rd]
- **Malaga** • 406 E 73rd St [1st Av]
- **Neue Galerie** • 1048 Fifth Ave [85th]
- **Park Avenue Café** • 100 E 63rd St [Park]
- **Payard Patisserie & Bistro** • 1032 Lexington Ave [74th]
- **Pintaile's Pizza** • 1577 York Ave [84th]
- **Poke** • 343 E 85th St [2nd Av]

Shopping

- **Arthritis Thrift Shop** • 1383 Third Ave [79th]
- **Barneys New York** • 660 Madison Ave [61st]
- **Beneath** • 265 E 78th St [2nd Av]
- **Bis Designer Resale** • 1134 Madison Ave, 2nd Fl [84th]
- **Black Orchid Bookshop** • 303 E 81st St [2nd Av]
- **Housing Works Thrift Shop** • 202 E 77th St [3rd Av]
- **J Leon Lascoff & Son Apothecaries** • 1209 Lexington Ave [82nd]
- **Just Bulbs** • 220 E 60th St [5th Av]
- **Kate's Paperie** • 1282 Third Ave [74th]
- **Lascoff Apothecary** • 1209 Lexington Ave [82nd]
- **Logos Bookstore** • 1575 York Ave [84th]
- **Lyric Hi-Fi** • 1221 Lexington Ave [83rd]
- **Martine's Chocolates too** • 400 E 82nd St [1st Av]
- **Myla** • 20 E 69th St [Madison]
- **Oldies, Goldies & Moldies** • 1609 Second Ave [84th]
- **Orwasher's** • 308 E 78th St [2nd Av]
- **Ottomanelli Brothers** • 1549 York Ave [82nd]
- **Pookie & Sebastian** • 1488 Second Ave [77th]
- **Pylones** • 842 Lexington Ave [64th]
- **Radio Shack** • 1477 Third Ave [83rd]
- **The Shoe Box** • 1349 Third Ave [77th]
- **Steuben** • 667 Madison Ave [61st]
- **Sylvia Pines Uniquities** • 1102 Lexington Ave [77th]
- **Tender Buttons** • 143 E 62nd St [Lex]
- **Two Little Red Hens** • 1652 Second Ave [86th]
- **Venture Stationers** • 1156 Madison Ave [85th]
- **Vintage Collections** • 147 E 72nd St, 2nd Fl [Lex]
- **William Poll** • 1051 Lexington Ave [75th]
- **The Woolgathering** • 318 E 84th St [2nd Av]
- **Yorkville Meat Emporium** • 1560 Second Ave [81st]
- **Zitomer** • 969 Madison Ave [76th]

Map 15 · **Upper East Side (Lower)**

Transportation

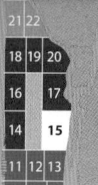

Map 15

Parking is extremely difficult during the day due to the number of schools in this area. It gets a bit better (but not much) at night, especially in the upper 70s and lower 80s near the FDR. Thankfully, buses on Fifth run almost by the minute and the Lexington Avenue line is showing renewed vigor.

Subways

6	68th St-Hunter College
6	77th St
4 5 6	86th St
F	Lexington Ave/63rd St
N R W	Fifth Ave/59th St
4 5 6 N R W	Lexington Ave/59th St

Bus Lines

1 2 3	Fifth Ave/Madison Ave
101 102 103	Third Ave/Lexington Ave
15	First Ave/Second Ave
30	72nd St/57th St Crosstown
31	York Ave/57th St Crosstown
4	Fifth Ave/Madison Ave/Broadway
66	67th St/68th St Crosstown
72	72nd St Crosstown
79	79th St Crosstown
98	Washington Heights/Midtown

Car Rental

- **Avis** • 310 E 64th St [2nd Av]
- **Enterprise** • 403 E 65th St [1st Av]
- **Hertz** • 327 E 64th St [2nd Av]
- **Hertz** • Carlyle Hotel • 355 E 76th St [1st Av]
- **National/Alamo** • 305 E 80th St [2nd Av]

Gas Stations

- **Mobil** • 1132 York Ave [61st] ⏱

Parking

Bike Lanes

- • • • Marked Bike Lanes
- • • • Recommended Route
- • • • Greenway

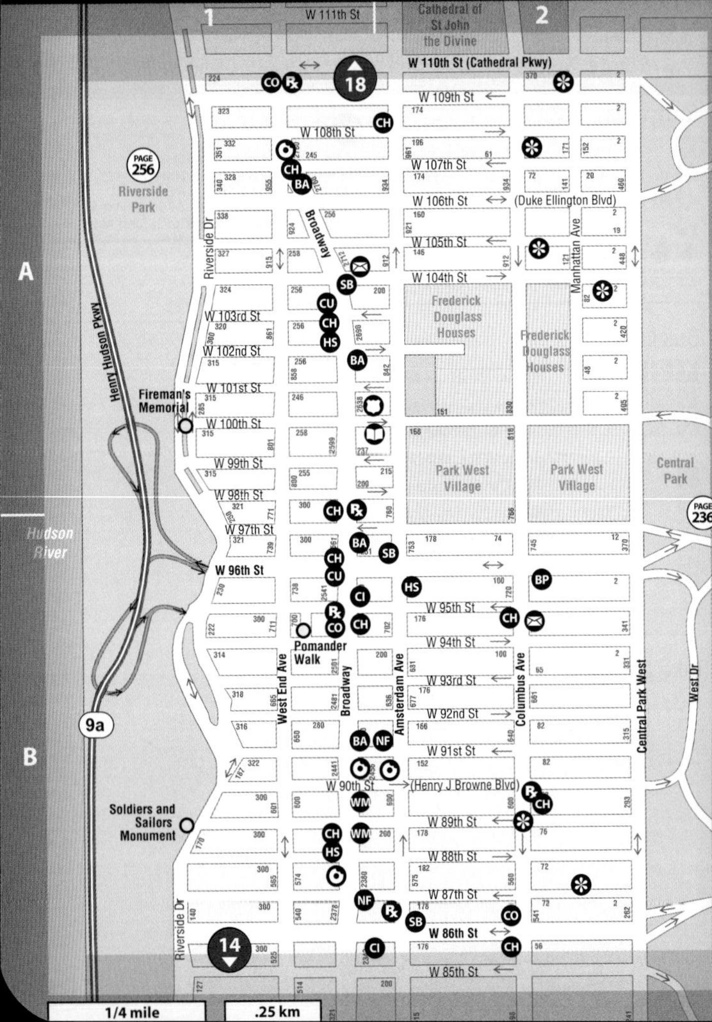

Map 16 · **Upper West Side (Upper)**

W 111th St

Cathedral of
St John
the Divine

1   2

W 110th St (Cathedral Pkwy)

224   CO   Rx   ▲ 18   378   ✳

W 109th St

323   174

W 108th St   196   ✳   171

361 332   245   W 107th St   61   171

340 328 555   W 106th St   141   20   466

338   256   (Duke Ellington Blvd)

PAGE
256

Riverside Park

327   258   934   W 105th St   148   ✳   448   19

324   256   256   200   W 104th St

CU   SB   ✳

W 103rd St   256   Frederick
320   256   CH   Douglass
315   HS   Houses

W 102nd St   256   Frederick
BA   Douglass
Houses

Fireman's
Memorial

246   151

315

W 101st St   315   258   2598

W 100th St   315   801   237

258   255   158   818

W 99th St   321   255   215   200

W 98th St   321   300   CH   Rx   Park West   Park West
Village   Village

W 97th St   321   738   300   BA   SB   178   74   745   12

W 96th St   739   738   CH   CU   100   100   BP

Pomander   CI   702   W 95th St   176   HS   770   341
Walk   Rx CO   760   CH

222   771   W 94th St   100   341

314   200   W 93rd St   681   55   651   82

318   655   2491   W 92nd St   176   640

W 91st St   166   82   315

BA   NF   152   82

W 90th St   (Henry J Browne Blvd)

WM   178   608   RX

CH   WM   W 89th St   ✳   76

HS   W 88th St   72

308   574   W 87th St   182   676   560   72   ✳

380   540   2376   Rx   W 86th St   176   SB   CO   56

▼ 14   308   CI   W 85th St   200   CH

9a

Hudson
River

Soldiers and
Sailors
Monument

Central
Park

PAGE
236

West Dr

Central Park West

Columbus Ave

Amsterdam Ave

Broadway

West End Ave

Riverside Dr

Manhattan Ave

Riverside Dr

Henry Hudson Pkwy

A

B

1/4 mile   .25 km

How do you get a quiet neighborhood in Manhattan? Put it between two major parks (Riverside and Central) far enough uptown. Some are rich and some are less rich up here, but all enjoy the slower pace of the beautiful streets and not-so-hidden gems like Pomander Walk.

24-Hour Pharmacies

- **CVS Pharmacy** • 540 Amsterdam Ave [86th] ☼
- **Duane Reade** • 2522 Broadway [94th] ☼
- **Duane Reade** • 2589 Broadway [98th] ☼
- **Duane Reade** • 609 Columbus Ave [89th] ☼
- **Rite Aid** • 2833 Broadway [110th] ☼

Bagels

- **Absolute Bagels** • 2788 Broadway [108th]
- **Bagel Basket** • 618 Amsterdam Ave [90th]
- **Hot & Crusty** • 2387 Broadway [88th]
- **Tal Bagels** • 2446 Broadway [90th]

$ Banks

BP • Banco Popular •
90 W 96th St [Columbus Ave]
BA • Bank of America •
2574 Broadway [W 97th St]
BA • Bank of America •
2770 Broadway [W 107th St]
BA • Bank of America (ATM) •
2461 Broadway [W 91st St]
BA • Bank of America (ATM) •
2680 Broadway [W 102nd St]
CH • Chase • 2551 Broadway [W 96th St]
CH • Chase • 59 W 86th St [Columbus Ave]
CH • Chase (ATM) • Duane Reade •
201 W 108th St [Amsterdam Ave]
CH • Chase (ATM) • Duane Reade •
2407 Broadway [W 88th St]
CH • Chase (ATM) • Duane Reade •
2522 Broadway [W 94th St]
CH • Chase (ATM) • Duane Reade •
2589 Broadway [W 97th St]
CH • Chase (ATM) • Duane Reade •
2683 Broadway [W 102nd St]
CH • Chase (ATM) • Duane Reade •
2760 Broadway [W 106th St]
CH • Chase (ATM) • Duane Reade •
609 Columbus Ave [W 90th St]
CH • Chase (ATM) • Duane Reade •
700 Columbus Ave [W 94th St]
CI • Citibank • 2350 Broadway [W 85th St]
CI • Citibank • 2560 Broadway [W 96th St]
CO • Commerce • 2521 Broadway [94th St]
CO • Commerce • 2831 Broadway [110th St]
CO • Commerce • 535 Columbus Ave [86th St]
HS • HSBC • 2411 Broadway [88th St]
HS • HSBC • 2681 Broadway [102nd St]

HS • HSBC • 739 Amsterdam Ave [96th St]
CU • Lower East Side People's Federal Credit Union (ATM) • McDonald's •
2549 Broadway [96th St]
CU • Lower East Side People's Federal Credit Union (ATM) •
W 103rd St & Broadway
NF • North Fork •
215 W 91st St [Amsterdam Av]
NF • North Fork •
2379 Broadway [87th St]
SB • Sovereign •
2700 Broadway [103rd St]
SB • Sovereign (ATM) • CVS •
540 Amsterdam Ave [W 86th St]
SB • Sovereign (ATM) • CVS •
743 Amsterdam Ave [W 96th St]
WM • Washington Mutual •
2438 Broadway [90th St]
WM • Washington Mutual •
2554 Broadway [W 96th St]

Community Gardens

Landmarks

- **Fireman's Memorial** •
W 100th St & Riverside Dr
- **Pomander Walk** •
261 W 94th St [B'way]
- **Soldiers and Sailors Monument** •
Riverside Dr & 89th St

Libraries

- **Bloomingdale** •
150 W 100th St [Columbus]

Police

- **24th Precinct** •
151 W 100th St [Amsterdam]

Post Offices

- **Cathedral** • 215 W 104th St [Amsterdam]
- **Park West** • 700 Columbus Ave [94th]

Map 16 · **Upper West Side (Upper)**

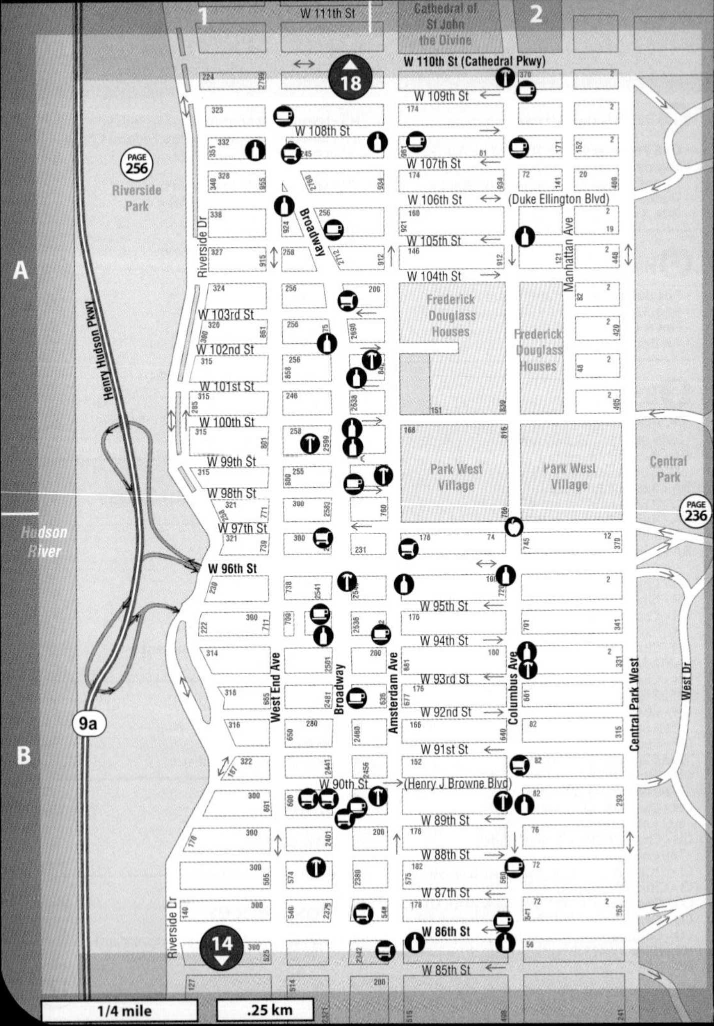

1　**2**

W 111th St

Cathedral of
St John
the Divine

PAGE
256

Riverside
Park

W 110th St (Cathedral Pkwy)

18

224

W 109th St

174

332

W 108th St

W 107th St

174

340　328

W 106th St (Duke Ellington Blvd)

336

W 105th St

146

W 104th St

324

Frederick
Douglass
Houses

Riverside Dr

Broadway

W 103rd St

328

W 102nd St

315

Frederick
Douglass
Houses

W 101st St

315

W 100th St

315

Manhattan Ave

W 99th St

315

W 98th St

321

Park West
Village

Park West
Village

Hudson
River

W 97th St

321

PAGE
236

W 96th St

259

W 95th St

176

Central
Park

227

314

W 94th St

W 93rd St

176

9a

318

W 92nd St

166

West End Ave

Broadway

Amsterdam Ave

Columbus Ave

Central Park West

West Dr

316

W 91st St

322

W 90th St (Henry J Browne Blvd)

300

W 89th St

360

W 88th St

308

W 87th St

300

Riverside Dr

W 86th St

14

W 85th St

| 1/4 mile | | .25 km |

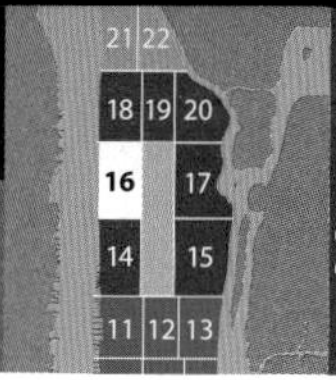

Sundries

Map 16

21 22
18 19 20
16 17
14 15
11 12 13

Shop the year-round 97th Street farmers market for fresh goods. Afterwards take a break at the classic Three Star Coffee Shop. Or do like the Parisian and peruse the goods at Silver Moon. For challah, smoked fish, or prepared meals, Kosher Marketplace is your connection (just not on the Sabbath).

 Coffee

- **108 Mini Café** • 196 W 108th St [Amsterdam]
- **Dunkin' Donuts** • 2424 Broadway [89th]
- **La Negrita** • 999 Columbus Ave [109th]
- **Silver Moon Bakery** •
  2740 Broadway [105th]
- **Sip** • 998 Amsterdam Ave [109th]
- **Starbucks** • 2498 Broadway [93rd]
- **Starbucks** • 2521 Broadway [94th]
- **Starbucks** • 2600 Broadway [98th]
- **Starbucks** • 540 Columbus Ave [86th]
- **Three Star Coffee Shop** •
  541 Columbus Ave [86th]
- **Westway Café** • 2800 Broadway [108th]
- **Zanny's Café** • 975 Columbus Ave [108th]

Farmers Markets

- **97th Street (Fri, 8 am–2 pm, Year Round)** •
  W 97th St & Columbus Ave
- **Stranger's Gate (Sat 8 am–3 pm, Jul–Nov)** •
  W 106th St & Central Park W

Hardware Stores

- **Ace Hardware** • 610 Columbus Ave [90th]
- **Aquarius Hardware & Houseware** •
  601 Amsterdam Ave [89th]
- **Broadway Home Center** •
  2672 Broadway [102nd]
- **C&S Hardware** • 788 Amsterdam Ave [98th]
- **Columbus Distributors** •
  687 Columbus Ave [93rd]
- **Garcia Hardware Store** •
  995 Columbus Ave [109th]
- **Grand Metro Home Centers** •
  2554 Broadway [96th]
- **Mike's Lumber Store** • 254 W 88th St [B'way]
- **World Houseware** • 2617 Broadway [99th]

Liquor Stores

- **86th Corner Wine & Liquor** •
  536 Columbus Ave [86th]
- **Adel Wine & Liquor** •
  925 Columbus Ave [105th]
- **Best Liquor & Wine** • 2648 Broadway [100th]
- **Columbus Avenue Wine & Spirits** •
  730 Columbus Ave [96th]
- **Gotham Wines And Liquors** •
  2517 Broadway [94th]
- **H&H Broadway Wine Center** •
  2669 Broadway [102nd]
- **Hong Liquor Store** • 2616 Broadway [99th]
- **Martin Brothers Liquor Store** •
  2781 Broadway [107th]
- **Mitchell's Wine & Liquor Store** •
  200 W 86th St [Amsterdam]
- **Polanco Liquor Store** •
  948 Amsterdam Ave [107th]
- **Riverside Liquor** • 2746 Broadway [106th]
- **Roma Discount Wine & Liquor** •
  737 Amsterdam Ave [96th]
- **Turin Wines & Liquors** •
  609 Columbus Ave [90th]
- **Vintage New York (Wine only)** •
  2492 Broadway [93rd]
- **Westlane Wines & Liquor** •
  689 Columbus Ave [93rd]
- **Wine Place** • 2406 Broadway [88th]

Supermarkets

- **Associated** • 755 Amsterdam Ave [97th]
- **D'Agostino** • 633 Columbus Ave [91st]
- **Food Emporium** • 2415 Broadway [89th]
- **Garden of Eden** • 2780 Broadway [107th]
- **Gourmet Garage West** • 2567 Broadway [96th]
- **Gristedes** • 251 W 86th St [B'way]
- **Gristedes** • 2704 Broadway [104th] ⊕
- **Gristedes Mega Store** •
  262 W 96th St [B'way] ⊕
- **Kosher Marketplace** • 2442 Broadway [90th]
- **Met Food** • 530 Amsterdam Ave [86th]

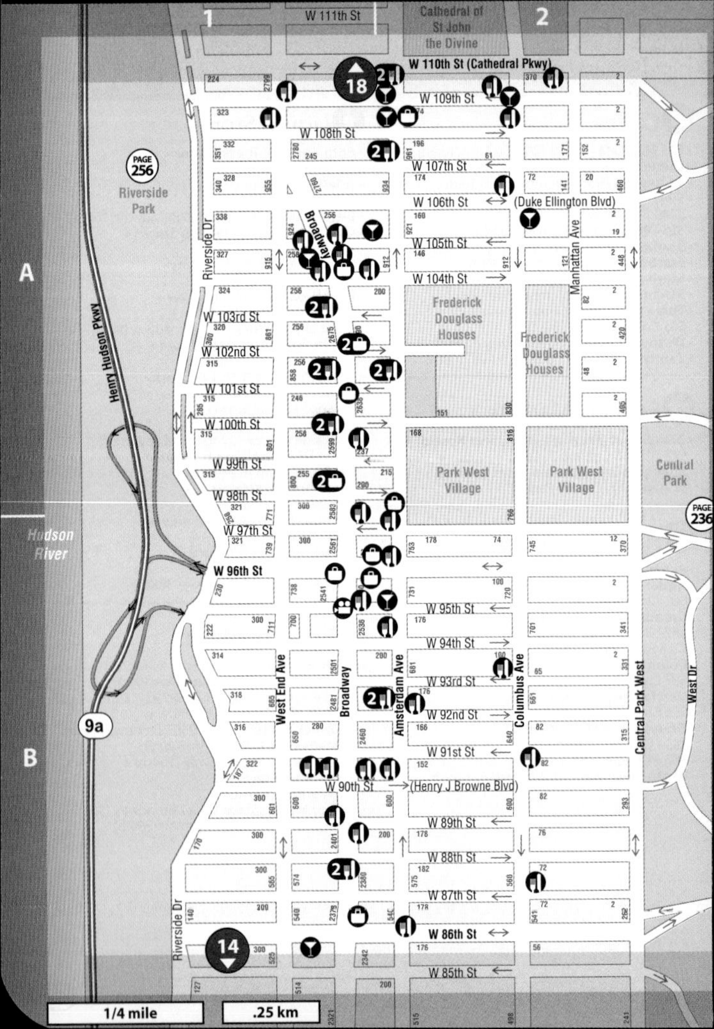

Map 16 • Upper West Side (Upper)

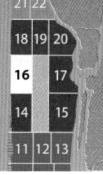
Get up early and chow on some sturgeon at Barney Greengrass for the ultimate NYC breakfast. Pretend you live Downtown and dine at A. When darkness falls head to Smoke for one of the city's most intimate jazz spots. Or meet your friends at La Negrita, a fantastic neighborhood bar.

Movie Theaters

• **Leonard Nimoy Thalia** •
2537 Broadway [95th]

Nightlife

• **Abbey Pub** • 237 W 105th St [B'way]
• **Broadway Dive** • 2662 Broadway [101st]
• **The Ding Dong Lounge** •
929 Columbus Ave [105th]
• **Dive Bar** • 732 Amsterdam Ave [96th]
• **La Negrita** • 999 Columbus Ave [109th]
• **The Parlour** • 250 W 86th St [B'way]
• **Sip** • 998 Amsterdam Ave [109th]
• **Smoke** • 2751 Broadway [106th]

Restaurants

• **A** • 947 Columbus Ave [106th]
• **AIX Brasserie** • 2398 Broadway [88th]
• **Alouette** • 2588 Broadway [98th]
• **Asiakan** • 710 Amsterdam Ave [94th]
• **Awash** • 947 Amsterdam Ave [106th]
• **Barney Greengrass** •
541 Amsterdam Ave [86th]
• **Bella Luna** • 584 Columbus Ave [86th]
• **Café Con Leche** •
726 Amsterdam Ave [96th]
• **Café du Soleil** • 2723 Broadway [104th]
• **Carmine's** • 2450 Broadway [91st]
• **City Diner** • 2441 Broadway [90th]
• **Crepes on Columbus** •
990 Columbus Ave [109th]
• **Docks Oyster Bar** • 2427 Broadway [90th]
• **El Malecon** •
764 Amsterdam Ave [97th]
• **Flor de Mayo** • 2651 Broadway [101st]
• **Gabriela's** • 688 Columbus Ave [94th]
• **Gennaro** • 665 Amsterdam Ave [92nd]
• **Georgia's Bake Shop** • 2418 Broadway [89th]
• **Giovanni's** • 1011 Columbus Ave [109th]
• **Henry's** • 2745 Broadway [105th]
• **Indus Valley** • 2636 Broadway [100th]
• **Jerusalem Restaurant** •
2715 Broadway [104th]
• **Krik Krak** • 844 Amsterdam Ave [101st]
• **Lemongrass Grill** • 2534 Broadway [95th]
• **Lime Leaf** • 2799 Broadway [108th]
• **Malasia Grill** • 224 W 104th St [Broadway]
• **Mary Ann's** • 2452 Broadway [91st]

• **Metisse** • 239 W 105th St [Broadway]
• **Metro Diner** • 2641 Broadway [100th]
• **Miss Mamie's Spoonbread Too** •
366 W 110th St [Manhattan]
• **Pizzabolla** • 654 Amsterdam Ave [105th]
• **Popover Café** • 551 Amsterdam Ave [87th]
• **Rack'n Soul** • 2818 Broadway [109th]
• **Restaurant Broadway** •
2664 Broadway [101st]
• **Roti Roll Bombay Frankie** •
994 Amsterdam Ave [109th]
• **Royal Kabob & Curry** •
2701 Broadway [103rd]
• **Saigon Grill** • 620 Amsterdam Ave [90th]
• **Sal & Carmine's Pizza** •
2671 Broadway [102nd]
• **Talia's Steakhouse** •
668 Amsterdam Ave [93rd]
• **Taqueria Y Fonda La Mexicana** •
968 Amsterdam Ave [108th]
• **Thai Market** • 960 Amsterdam Ave [107th]
• **Tokyo Pop** • 2728 Broadway [104th]
• **Trattoria Pesce & Pasta** •
625 Columbus Ave [91st]
• **Turkuaz** • 2637 Broadway [100th]

Shopping

• **Banana Republic** • 2360 Broadway [86th]
• **Ben & Jerry's** • 2722 Broadway [104th]
• **Gothic Cabinet Craft** •
2652 Broadway [101st]
• **Gourmet Garage** • 2567 Broadway [87th]
• **Health Nuts** • 2611 Broadway [99th]
• **Janovic** • 2680 Broadway [102nd]
• **Joon's Fine Seafood** •
774 Amsterdam Ave [98th]
• **Metro Bicycles** • 231 W 96th St [B'way]
• **Mugi Pottery** •
993 Amsterdam Ave [109th]
• **New York Flowers & Plant Shed** •
209 W 96th St [Amsterdam]
• **Planet Kids** • 2688 Broadway [103rd]
• **Regional** • 2607 Broadway [98th]

Map 16 · **Upper West Side (Upper)**

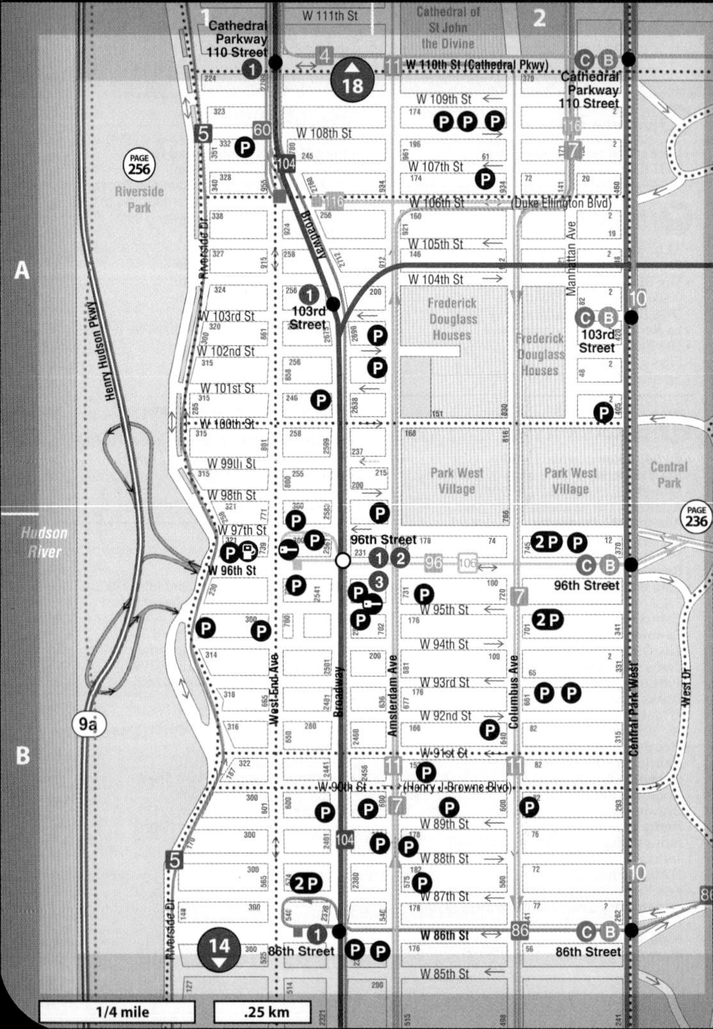

The 96th Street Transverse is by far the best way to cross Central Park. Of course, cutting through the park at this point allows you to enjoy the quiet rolling hills north of the Reservoir. And isn't it nice that the Upper West Side has two separate subway lines?

Subways

1 **2** **3**	96th St
1	103rd St
1	Cathedral Parkway-110th St
1	86th St
B **C**	103rd St
B **C**	Cathedral Parkway-110th St
B **C**	86th St
B **C**	96th St

Bus Lines

10	Seventh Ave/Central Park W
104	Broadway
106	106th St Crosstown
11	Columbus Ave/Amsterdam Ave
116	116th St Crosstown
5	Fifth Ave/Sixth Ave/Riverside Dr
60	LaGuardia Airport
7	Columbus Ave/Amsterdam Ave
86	86th St Crosstown
96	96th St Crosstown

Bike Lanes

- • • • Marked Bike Lanes
- • • • Recommended Route
- • • • Greenway

Car Rental

- **AAMCAR** • 315 W 96th St [West End]
- **Hertz** • 214 W 95th St [Amsterdam]

Gas Stations

- **Exxon** • 303 W 96th St [West End] Φ

Parking

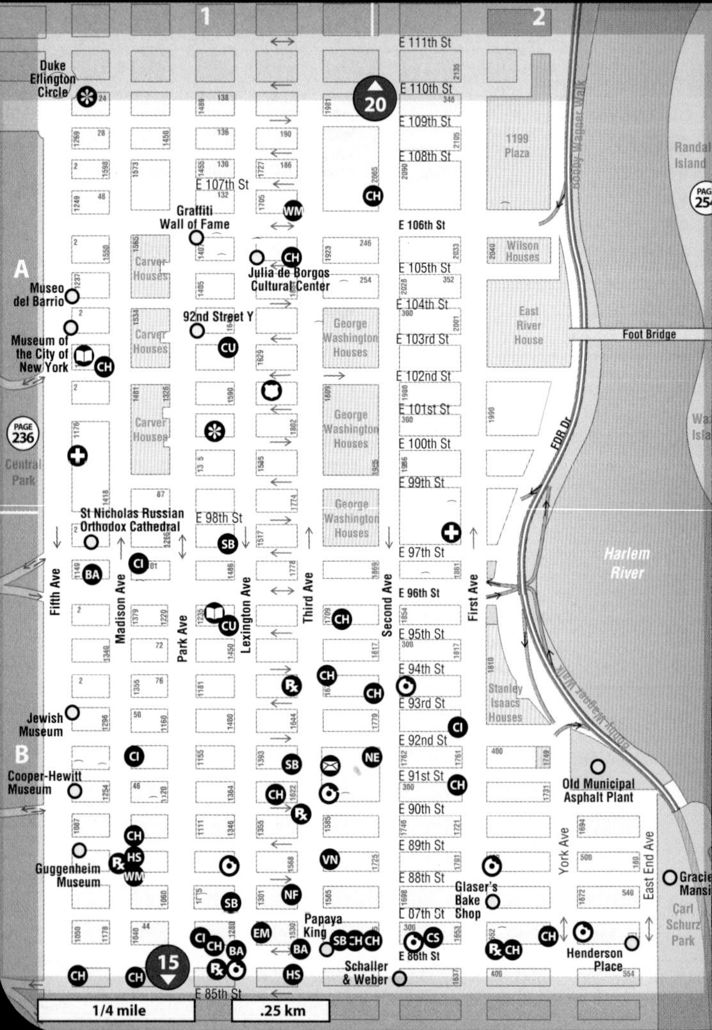

Map 17 · **Upper East Side / East Harlem**

E 111th St

E 110th St 20

E 109th St

1199 Plaza

E 108th St

CH

WM

Graffiti Wall of Fame

E 107th St

E 106th St

Wilson Houses

Duke Ellington Circle

Carver Houses

CH

Julia de Burgos Cultural Center

E 105th St

A

Museo del Barrio

92nd Street Y

CU

E 104th St

East River House

Foot Bridge

Museum of the City of New York

CH

George Washington Houses

E 103rd St

Carver Houses

E 102nd St

E 101st St

PAGE 236

George Washington Houses

E 100th St

Central Park

Carver Houses

E 99th St

George Washington Houses

Harlem River

St Nicholas Russian Orthodox Cathedral

E 98th St

SB

E 97th St

BA

CI

CU

E 96th St

Fifth Ave

Madison Ave

Park Ave

Lexington Ave

Third Ave

Second Ave

First Ave

E 95th St

E 94th St

Rx

E 93rd St

CH

CI

Jewish Museum

E 92nd St

Stanley Isaacs Houses

Old Municipal Asphalt Plant

CI

E 91st St

SB

NE

B

Cooper-Hewitt Museum

CH

Rx

E 90th St

E 89th St

York Ave

East End Ave

CH

HS

VN

Guggenheim Museum

Rx

WM

SB

NF

E 88th St

Glaser's Bake Shop

Gracie Mansion

Papaya King

E 87th St

CS

Rx

CH

CH

Carl Schurz Park

CI

CI

BA

EM

BA

SB

CH

CH

Henderson Place

CH

15

Rx

HS

Schaller & Weber

E 86th St

CH

CH

E 85th St

1/4 mile   .25 km

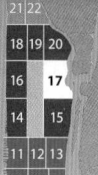
The 92nd Street Y is the place to catch some of the coolest lectures and readings in town. The nabe itself is home to a variety of folks, including recent college grads, seniors, young families, and Wall Streeters. Despite the continual sprout of residential high-rises, many relatively affordable walk-ups still exist.

℞ 24-Hour Pharmacies

- **CVS Pharmacy** • 1622 Third Ave [91st] ⊕
- **Duane Reade** • 1231 Madison Ave [88th] ⊕
- **Duane Reade** • 125 E 86th St [Park] ⊕
- **Duane Reade** • 1675 Third Ave [94th] ⊕
- **Duane Reade** • 401 E 86th St [1st Av] ⊕

Bagels

- **Bagel Bob's** • 1638 York Ave [86th]
- **Bagel Express** • 1804 Second Ave [93rd]
- **Bagel Mill** • 1700 First Ave [88th]
- **Corner Bagel Market** • 1324 Lexington [88th]
- **Hot & Crusty** • E 86th St & Lexington Ave
- **New York Hot Bagel** • 1585 Third Ave [89th]
- **Tal Bagels** • 333 E 86th St [2nd Av]

$ Banks

- BA • **Bank of America** • 1276 Lexington [86th]
- BA • **Bank of America** • 1538 Third Ave [86th St]
- BA • **Bank of America** • 21 E 96th St [5th Av]
- CH • **Chase** • 12 F 86th St [5th Av]
- CH • **Chase** • 126 E 86th St [Lexington Av]
- CH • **Chase** • 181 E 90th St [3rd Av]
- CH • **Chase** • 2065 Second Ave [106th St]
- CH • **Chase** • 255 E 86th St [2nd Av]
- CH • **Chase** • 453 E 86th St [York Av]
- CH • **Chase (ATM)** • 1231 Madison Ave [89th St]
- CH • **Chase (ATM)** • 125 E 86th St [Park Av]
- CH • **Chase (ATM)** • 1490 Madison Ave [102nd]
- CH • **Chase (ATM)** • 1637 York Ave [86th]
- CH • **Chase (ATM)** • 1675 Third Ave [94th St]
- CH • **Chase (ATM)** • 1749 First Ave [91st St]
- CH • **Chase (ATM)** • 1801 Second Ave [93rd]
- CH • **Chase (ATM)** • 1915 Third Ave [106th]
- CH • **Chase (ATM)** • 205 E 95th St [3rd Av]
- CH • **Chase (ATM)** • 251 E 86th St [3rd Av]
- CH • **Chase (ATM)** • 401 E 86th St [1st Av]
- CI • **Citibank** • 123 E 86th St [Lexington Ave]
- CI • **Citibank** • 1275 Madison Ave [91st St]
- CI • **Citibank** • 1391 Madison Ave [97th St]
- CI • **Citibank** • 1781 First Ave [91st St]
- EM • **Emigrant** • 1270 Lexington Ave [86th St]
- HS • **HSBC** • 186 E 86th St [3rd Av]
- HS • **HSBC** • 45 E 89th St [Madison Av]
- CU • **Lower East Side People's Federal Credit Union (ATM)** • 1476 Lexington Ave [95th St]
- CU • **Lower East Side People's Federal Credit Union (ATM)** • 1635 Lexington Ave [103rd St]
- NF • **North Fork** • 1536 Third Ave [86th St]
- NE • **NorthEast Bank** • 1751 Second Ave [91st St]
- RS • **Ridgewood Savings Bank** • 345 E 86th St [2nd Av]
- SB • **Sovereign** • 225 E 86th St [3rd Av]
- SB • **Sovereign (ATM)** • 1294 Lexington [87th]
- SB • **Sovereign (ATM)** • 1500 Lexington [97th]
- SB • **Sovereign (ATM)** • 1622 Third Ave [91st]
- VN • **Valley National** • 1569 Third Ave [88th]
- WM • **WaMu** • 1221 Madison Ave [88th St]
- WM • **WaMu** • 1924 Third Ave [106th St]

Community Gardens

- **103rd Street Garden** • 105 E 103rd St [Park Av]

Emergency Rooms

- **Metropolitan** • 1901 First Ave [97th]
- **Mt Sinai Medical Center** • 1190 5th Ave [101st]

Landmarks

- **92nd Street Y** • 1395 Lexington Ave [92nd]
- **Cooper-Hewitt National Design Museum** • 2 E 91st St [5th Av]
- **Glaser's Bake Shop** • 1670 First Ave [87th]
- **Gracie Mansion** • Carl Schulz Park & 88th St
- **Graffiti Wall of Fame** • E 106th St & Park Ave
- **Guggenheim Museum** • 1071 Fifth Ave [88th]
- **Henderson Place** • East End Ave & E 86th St
- **Jewish Museum** • 1109 Fifth Ave [92nd]
- **Julia de Borgos Cultural Center** • 1680 Lexington Ave [105th]
- **Museo del Barrio** • Fifth Ave & 104th St
- **Museum of the City of New York** • Fifth Ave & 103rd St
- **Old Municipal Asphalt Plant** • 90th St & FDR
- **Papaya King** • 179 E 86th St [3rd Av]
- **Schaller & Weber** • 1654 Second Ave [86th]
- **St Nicholas Russian Orthodox Cathedral** • 15 E 97th St [5th Av]

Libraries

- **96th Street** • 112 E 96th St [Park]
- **New York Academy of Medicine Library** • 1216 Fifth Ave [102nd]

Police

- **23rd Precinct** • 162 E 102nd St [3rd Av]

Post Offices

- **Yorkville** • 1617 Third Ave [91st]

135

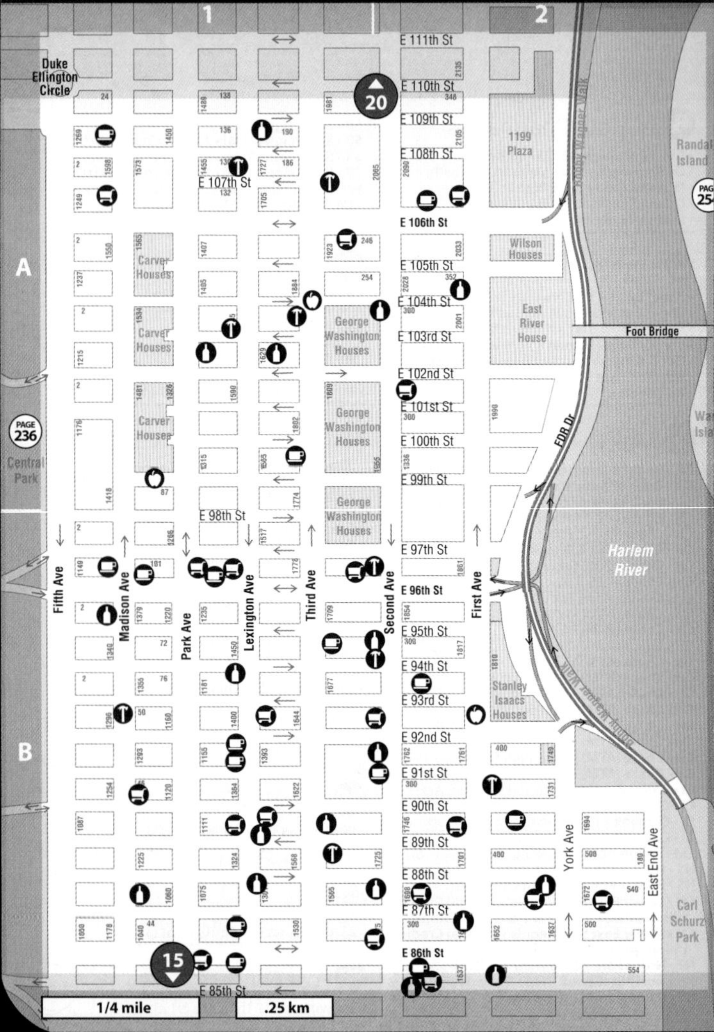

Map 17 · **Upper East Side / East Harlem**

N

1

2

E 111th St

Duke
Ellington
Circle

E 110th St

E 109th St

▲
20

E 108th St

1199
Plaza

Randal
Island

PAGE
25

E 107th St

E 106th St

E 105th St

Wilson
Houses

Carver
Houses

E 104th St

George
Washington
Houses

E 103rd St

East
River
House

Foot Bridge

A

Carver
Houses

E 102nd St

E 101st St

George
Washington
Houses

E 100th St

PAGE
236

Carver
Houses

E 99th St

George
Washington
Houses

Central
Park

E 98th St

E 97th St

Harlem
River

E 96th St

Fifth Ave

Madison Ave

E 95th St

Park Ave

Lexington Ave

Third Ave

E 94th St

Second Ave

First Ave

E 93rd St

Stanley
Isaacs
Houses

E 92nd St

B

E 91st St

E 90th St

E 89th St

York Ave

East End Ave

E 88th St

E 87th St

Carl
Schurz
Park

E 86th St

▼
15

E 85th St

1/4 mile

.25 km

Sundries

Map 17

21 22
18 19 20
16 **17**
14 15
11 12 13

For home improvement projects, Wankel's is your best bet. When cocktail party planning, Mister Wright will hook you up. Decent supermarkets are scarce above 96th, so stop by Gourmet Garage on your way home or take your chances at the local bodega.

Coffee

- **Dunkin' Donuts** • 1276 Lexington Ave [86th]
- **Dunkin' Donuts** • 1391 Madison Ave [97th]
- **Dunkin' Donuts** • 1392 Lexington Ave [92nd]
- **Dunkin' Donuts** • 1630 Madison Ave [109th]
- **Dunkin' Donuts** • 1760 Second Ave [92nd]
- **Dunkin' Donuts** • 345 E 93rd St [2nd Av]
- **El Castillo Coffee Shop** •
  344 E 106th St [2nd Av]
- **Juliano Gourmet Coffee** •
  1378 Lexington Ave [91st]
- **Just in Time Café** • 119 E 96th St [Park]
- **Starbucks** • 120 E 87th St [Park]
- **Starbucks** • 1378 Madison Ave [96th]
- **Starbucks** • 1642 Third Ave [92nd]
- **Starbucks** • 400 E 90th St [1st Av]
- **Viand Coffee Shop** • 300 E 86th St [2nd Av]

Farmers Markets

- **Mt Sinai Hospital (Fri 8 am–5 pm, July–Nov)** •
  E 99th St b/w Madison Av & Park Av
- **92nd St (Sun 9 am–5 pm, July–Nov)** •
  First Ave b/w 92nd St & 93rd St
- **East Harlem/Union Settlement Farmers Market (Thu 8 am–4 pm, Jul 6–Nov 16)** •
  E 104th St & Third Ave

Hardware Stores

- **Century Lumber** • 1875 Second Ave [96th]
- **El Barrio Hardware** • 1876 Third Ave [104th]
- **Feldman's Housewares** •
  1304 Madison Ave [92nd]
- **Johnny's Hardware** •
  1708 Lexington Ave [107th]
- **K&G Hardware & Supply** •
  401 E 90th St [1st Av]
- **Morales Brothers Hardware** •
  1959 Third Ave [108th]
- **Rainbow Ace Hardware** •
  1815 Second Ave [94th]
- **Wankel's Hardware & Paint** •
  1573 Third Ave [88th]

Liquor Stores

- **86th Street Wine & Liquor** •
  306 E 86th St [2nd Av]
- **Best Cellars (Wine only)** •
  1291 Lexington Ave [97th]

- **East 87th Street Wine Traders** •
  1693 Second Ave [88th]
- **Edwin's Wines & Liquors** •
  176 E 103rd St [3rd Av]
- **Explorers Wines & Liquors** •
  1755 Lexington Ave [107th]
- **House of J&H** • 2073 Second Ave [106th]
- **K&D Wines & Spirits** •
  1366 Madison Ave [96th]
- **Mercedes Liquor Store** • 102 E 103rd St [Park]
- **Mister Wright** • 1593 Third Ave [90th]
- **Normandie Wines (Wine only)** •
  1834 Second Ave [95th]
- **Park East Liquors** • 1657 York Ave [87th]
- **Rivera Liquor Store** • 2025 First Ave [105th]
- **Uptown Wine Shop (Wine only)** •
  1361 Lexington Ave [90th]
- **West Coast Wine & Liquor** •
  1440 Lexington Ave [94th]
- **Wine Lovers Wines & Spirits** •
  1752 Second Ave [91st]
- **Yorkshire Wines & Spirits** •
  1646 First Ave [86th]

Supermarkets

- **Associated** • 1486 Lexington Ave [96th]
- **Associated** • 1588 Madison Ave [107th]
- **Associated** • 1968 Second Ave [101st]
- **C-Town** • 1721 First Ave [89th]
- **Food Emporium** • 1211 Madison Ave [87th]
- **Food Emporium** • 1660 Second Ave [86th]
- **Gourmet Garage** • 1245 Park Ave [96th]
- **Gristedes** • 120 E 86th St [Park]
- **Gristedes** • 1343 Lexington Ave [89th]
- **Gristedes** • 1356 Lexington Ave [90th]
- **Gristedes** • 1637 York Ave [86th]
- **Gristedes** • 1644 York Ave [86th]
- **Gristedes** • 202 E 96th St [3rd Av]
- **Gristedes Mega Store** •
  350 E 86th St [2nd Av] ⊕
- **Key Food** • 1769 Second Ave [92nd]
- **Met Food** • 235 E 106th St [3rd Av]
- **Pioneer** • 1407 Lexington Ave [92nd]
- **Pioneer** • 2076 First Ave [106th]

Map 17 · **Upper East Side / East Harlem**

Duke
Ellington
Circle

E 111th St
E 110th St
E 109th St
E 108th St
E 107th St
E 106th St
E 105th St
E 104th St
E 103rd St
E 102nd St
E 101st St
E 100th St
E 99th St
E 98th St
E 97th St
E 96th St
E 95th St
E 94th St
E 93rd St
E 92nd St
E 91st St
E 90th St
E 89th St
E 88th St
E 87th St
E 86th St
E 85th St

1199 Plaza

Randalls
Island

PAGE 254

Wilson
Houses

East
River
House

Foot Bridge

Ward
Island

Harlem
River

Carver
Houses

George
Washington
Houses

Stanley
Isaacs
Houses

Carl
Schurz
Park

PAGE 236

Central
Park

Fifth Ave
Madison Ave
Park Ave
Lexington Ave
Third Ave
Second Ave
First Ave
York Ave
East End Ave

FDR Dr

20

15

1/4 mile
.25 km

Entertainment

Map 17

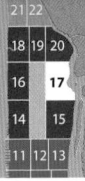

Elaine's—an old favorite—carries on as new superstars Peri Ela, Sfoglia and Café D'Alsace make their mark. For a taste of Spanish Harlem head north, to La Fonda Boricua or El Paso. And no weekend is complete without a visit to Glaser's Bake Shop—going strong for 106 years.

Movie Theaters

• **92nd Street Y** • 1395 Lexington Ave [92nd]
• **AMC Orpheum 7** • 1538 Third Ave [87th]
• **City Cinemas: East 86th Street** •
210 E 86th St [3rd Av]
• **Guggenheim Museum Movie Theater** •
1071 Fifth Ave [88th]

Nightlife

• **Auction House** • 300 E 89th St [2nd Av]
• **Caruto's** • 1701 Lexington Ave [106th]
• **Cavatappo Wine Bar** • 1728 Second Ave [90th]
• **FB Lounge** • 172 E 106th St [Lexington Av]
• **Kinsale Tavern** • 1672 Third Ave [94th]
• **Marty O'Brien's** • 1696 Second Ave [88th]
• **Phil Hughes** • 1682 First Ave [88th]
• **Rathbones Pub** • 1702 Second Ave [88th]
• **Reif's Tavern** • 302 E 92nd St [2nd Av]
• **Tool Box** • 1742 Second Ave [91st]

Restaurants

• **Bella Cucina** • 1293 Lexington Ave [87th]
• **Café D'Alsace** • 1695 Second Ave [88th]
• **Carino** • 1710 Second Ave [89th]
• **Chef Ho's Peking Duck Grill** •
1720 Second Ave [89th]
• **Choux Factory** • 1685 First Ave [87th]
• **Corner Bakery** • 1659 Third Ave [93rd]
• **El Paso Taqueria** • 1642 Lexington Ave [104th]
• **Elaine's** • 1703 Second Ave [88th]
• **GK Triple A Diner** • 2061 Third Ave [106th]
• **Ithaka** • 308 E 86th St [2nd Av]
• **Itzocan Bistro** • 1575 Lexington Ave [100th]
• **Jackson Hole** • 1270 Madison Ave [91st] ♿
• **Joy Burger Bar** • 1567 Lexington Ave [100th]
• **Kebap G** • 1830 Second Ave [94th]
• **La Fonda Boricua** • 169 E 106th St [Lex]
• **La Isla Restaurant** • 1883 Third Ave [103rd]
• **Luca Restaurant** • 1712 First Ave [89th]
• **Nick's Restaurant & Pizzeria** •
1814 Second Ave [94th]
• **Nina's Argentinean Pizzeria** •
1750 Second Ave [91st]
• **Papaya King** • 179 E 86th St [3rd Av]
• **Peri Ela** • 1361 Lexington Ave [90th]
• **Petak's** • 1246 Madison Ave [90th]
• **Piatto D'Oro I** • 349 E 109th St [2nd Av]
• **Pinocchio** • 1748 First Ave [91st]
• **Pintaile's Pizza** • 26 E 91st St [5th Av]
• **Pio Pio** • 1746 First Ave [91st]

• **Sabora Mexico** • 1744 First Ave [90th]
• **Sarabeth's** • 1295 Madison Ave [92nd]
• **Sfoglia** • 1402 Lexington Ave [92nd]
• **Viand** • 300 E 86th St [2nd Av] ♿
• **White Castle** • 351 E 103rd St [1st Av]
• **Zebu Grill** • 305 E 92nd St [2nd Av]

Shopping

• **Blacker & Kooby** • 1204 Madison Ave [88th]
• **Blades Board & Skate** •
156 W 72nd St [Columbus]
• **Blue Tree** • 1283 Madison Ave [91st]
• **Capezio** • 1651 Third Ave [92nd]
• **Caravan 91** • 128 E 91st St [Lex]
• **The Children's General Store** •
168 E 91st St [Lex]
• **Ciao Bella Gelato** • 27 E 92nd St [Madison]
• **Cooper-Hewitt National Design Museum
Shop** • 2 E 91st St [5th Av]
• **Coup de Coeur** • 1628 Third Ave [91st]
• **Doyle New York** • 175 E 87th St [3rd Av]
• **Eli's Vinegar Factory** • 431 E 91st St [1st Av]
• **Exotic Fragrances** • 1645 Lexington Ave [104]
• **Glaser's Bake Shop** • 1670 First Ave [87th]
• **Housing Works Thrift Shop** •
1730 Second Ave [90th]
• **Kessie & Co** • 163 E 87th St [Lex]
• **La Tropezienne** • 2131 First Ave [110th]
• **Laytner's Linens** • 237 E 86th St [3rd Av]
• **MAD Vintage Couture & Designer Resale** •
167 E 87th St [Lex]
• **Nellie M Boutique** •
1309 Lexington Ave [88th]
• **New York Replacement Parts** •
1456 Lexington Ave [94th]
• **Orva** • 155 E 86th St [Lex]
• **Pickles, Olives Etc** • 1647 First Ave [86th]
• **Rincon Musical** • 1936 Third Ave [107th]
• **Samba Bakery** • 165 E 106th St [Lex]
• **Schaller & Weber** • 1654 Second Ave [86th]
• **Schatzie's Prime Meats** •
1200 Madison Ave [87th]
• **Shatzi The Shop** • 243 E 86th St [3rd Av]
• **Soccer Sport Supply** • 1745 First Ave [90th]
• **Spence-Chapin Thrift Shop** •
1850 Second Ave [96th]
• **Super Runners Shop** •
1337 Lexington Ave [89th]
• **Tito's Plastic Covers** •
1642 Lexington Ave [104th]
• **Williams-Sonoma** • 1175 Madison Ave [86th]

Map 17 · Upper East Side / East Harlem

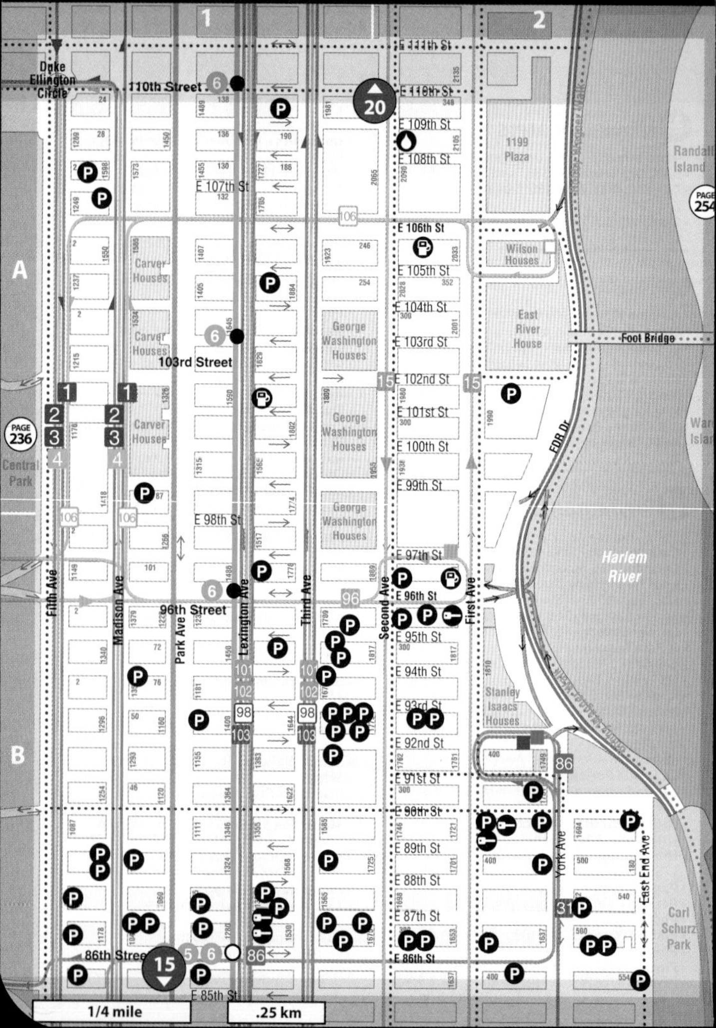

E 111th St

110th Street

6

20

E 110th St

E 109th St

E 108th St

1199 Plaza

Randall Island

PAGE 254

E 107th St

Carver Houses

E 106th St

E 105th St

Wilson Houses

Carver Houses

E 104th St

E 103rd St

East River House

6

103rd Street

George Washington Houses

E 102nd St

15

15

E 101st St

1

1

George Washington Houses

E 100th St

PAGE 236

2

2

3

3

E 99th St

4

4

George Washington Houses

E 98th St

Central Park

Harlem River

E 97th St

6

96th Street

96

E 96th St

Second Ave

First Ave

E 95th St

E 94th St

E 93rd St

98

98

Stanley Isaacs Houses

E 92nd St

E 91st St

86

E 90th St

E 89th St

York Ave

E 88th St

E 87th St

31

Carl Schurz Park

East End Ave

86th Street

15

86

E 86th St

E 85th St

Fifth Ave

Madison Ave

Park Ave

Lexington Ave

Third Ave

FDR Dr

Ward Island

Foot Bridge

Duke Ellington Circle

1/4 mile

.25 km

Transportation

Map 17

21	22	
18	19	20
16	**17**	
14		15
11	12	13

The construction is finally underway for the much-anticipated Second Avenue Subway—hope for a population that, for generations, has schlepped all the way to Lex just to sardine itself on the East Side's sole subway line. But don't hold your breath—the T-line won't be complete until at least 2013.

Subways

4 5 6	86th St
6	96th St
6	103rd St
6	110th St

Bus Lines

1 2 3	Fifth Ave/Madison Ave
101	Third Ave/Lexington Ave
102	Third Ave/Lexington Ave
103	Third Ave/Lexington Ave
106	96th St/106th St Crosstown
15	First Ave/Second Ave
31	York Ave/57th St
4	Fifth Ave/Madison Ave/Broadway
86	86th St Crosstown
96	96th St Crosstown
98	Washington Heights/Midtown

Bike Lanes

- • • • Marked Bike Lanes
- • • • Recommended Route
- • • • Greenway

Car Rental

- **Avis** • 420 E 90th St [1st Av]
- **Budget** • 152 E 87th St [Lex]
- **Dollar** • 160 E 87th St [Lex]
- **Enterprise** • 1833 First Ave [95th]
- **Hertz** • 412 E 90th St [1st Av]

Car Washes

- **LMC Car Wash** • 334 E 109th St [2nd Av]

Gas Stations

- **Getty** • 348 E 106th St [1st Av] ⊗
- **Shell** • 1599 Lexington Ave [101st] ⊗
- **Shell** • 1855 First Ave [96th] ⊗

Parking

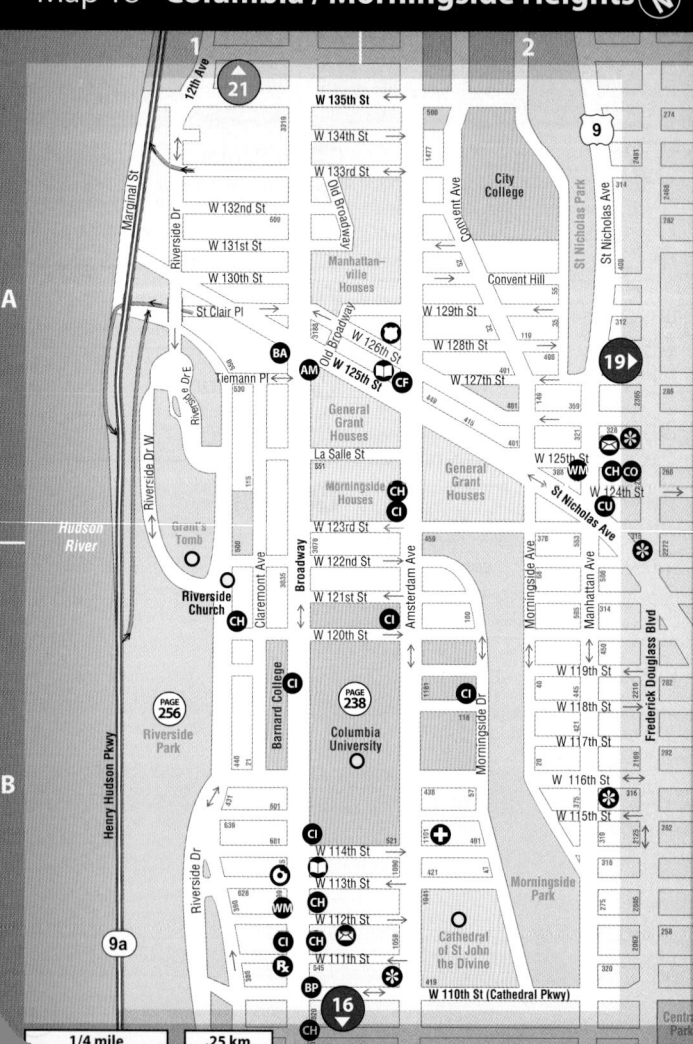

Map 18 • Columbia / Morningside Heights ⒩

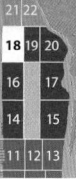
Quick—visit before Columbia fully takes over! There are still a few places that show the old (and gritty) neighborhood of the Gershwins and the Beats (before they were THE Beats). Have a picnic at Grant's Tomb before exploring the breathtaking Cathedral of St. John the Divine.

24-Hour Pharmacies
• **Duane Reade** • 2864 Broadway [111th] ☑

Bagels
• **Nussbaum & Wu** • 2897 Broadway [113th]

Banks
AM • Amalgamated •
564 W 125th St [Old Broadway]
BP • Banco Popular •
2852 Broadway [W 111th St]
BA • Bank of America (ATM) •
580 W 125th St [Broadway]
CF • Carver Federal Savings (ATM) •
503 W 125th St [Amsterdam Ave]
CH • Chase • 2824 Broadway [W 109th St]
CH • Chase (ATM) • Duane Reade •
2864 Broadway [W 111th St]
CH • Chase (ATM) •
2898 Broadway [W 113th St]
CH • Chase (ATM) •
475 Riverside Dr [W 120th St]
CI • Citibank •
1310 Amsterdam Ave [La Salle St]
CI • Citibank • 2861 Broadway [W 111th St]
CI • Citibank (ATM) •
Columbia Barnes & Noble •
2922 Broadway [W 114th St]
CI • Citibank (ATM) • Barnard College •
3009 Broadway [W 119th St]
CI • Citibank (ATM) •
School of International Affairs •
420 W 118th St [Morningside Dr]
CI • Citibank (ATM) •
525 W 120th St [Amsterdam Ave]
CO • Commerce •
300 W 125th St [Frederick Douglass Blvd]
CU • Municipal Credit Union (ATM) •
280 St Nicholas Ave [W 124th St]
WM • Washington Mutual •
2875 Broadway [W 112th St]
WM • Washington Mutual •
350 W 125th St [St. Nicholas Ave]

Community Gardens

Emergency Rooms
• **St Luke's** • 1111 Amsterdam Ave [115th]

Landmarks
• **Cathedral of St John the Divine** •
112th St & Amsterdam Ave
• **Columbia University** • 116th St & Broadway
• **Grant's Tomb** • 122nd St & Riverside Dr
• **Riverside Church** • 490 Riverside Dr [122nd]

Libraries
• **George Bruce** • 518 W 125th St [Amsterdam]
• **Morningside Heights Library** •
2900 Broadway [113th]

Police
• **26th Precinct** • 520 W 126th St [Amsterdam]

Post Offices
• **Columbia University** •
534 W 112th St [Amsterdam]
• **Manhattanville** • 365 W 125th St [Manhattan]

Map 18 · **Columbia / Morningside Heights**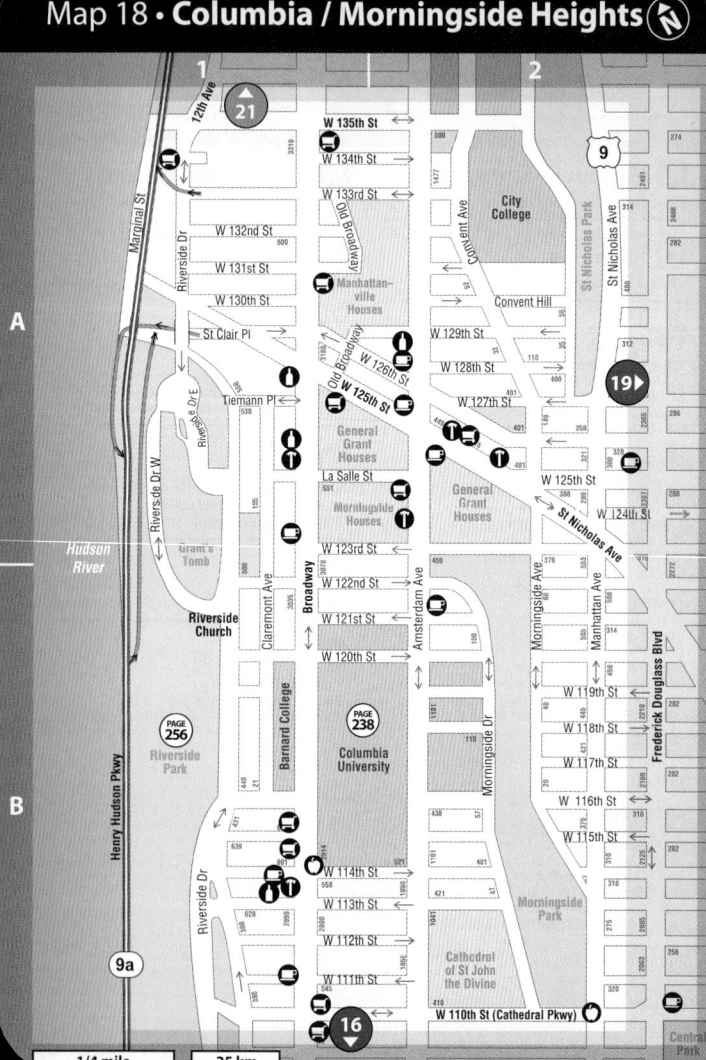

For coffee, toiletries, and such, it's quickest to shop Broadway south of 116th Street. Try Oren's for a good cuppa joe. Options thin out as you head north or east. The one exception is the magnificent, cold storage maze— a.k.a. Fairway.

Coffee

- **Café Fresh** • 1241 Amsterdam Ave [121st]
- **Chokolat Patisserie** • 3111 Broadway [123rd]
- **Dunkin' Donuts** •
  1342 Amsterdam Ave [125th]
- **Dunkin' Donuts** • 321 W 125th St [F Douglass]
- **Jimbo's Coffee Shop** •
  1345 Amsterdam Ave [125th]
- **Oren's Daily Roast** • 2882 Broadway [112th]
- **Pino's Café** • 501 W 125th St [Amsterdam]
- **Saurin Parke Café** • 301 W 110th St [CPW]
- **Starbucks** • 2853 Broadway [111th]
- **Starbucks** • 2929 Broadway [115th]

Farmers Markets

- **Columbia**
  (Thu & Sun 8 am–6 pm, Year Round) •
  Broadway b/w 114 & 115th Sts
- **Morningside Park Farmers Market**
  (Sat 9 am–5 pm, April 8–Dec 16) •
  W 110th St & Manhattan Ave

Hardware Stores

- **Clinton Supply** •
  1256 Amsterdam Ave [122nd]
- **Columbia Hardware** • 2905 Broadway [113th]
- **Philip Glick Supply** •
  421 W 125th St [F Douglass]
- **TriBoro Hardware** •
  433 W 125th St [Morningside Av]
- **University Houseware and Hardware** •
  2901 Broadway [113th]

Liquor Stores

- **Amsterdam Liquor Mart** •
  1356 Amsterdam Ave [126th]
- **Caro Wines & Liquor** •
  3139 Broadway [La Salle]
- **International Wines and Spirits** •
  2903 Broadway [113th]
- **Wine & Liquors Authority** •
  574 W 125th St [B'way]

Supermarkets

- **Associated** • 1440 Amsterdam Ave [131st]
- **Associated** • 2943 Broadway [115th]
- **C-Town** • 3320 Broadway [134th]
- **C-Town** • 560 W 125th St [Old B'way]
- **Citarella** • 461 W 125th St [Amsterdam]
- **D'Agostino** • 2828 Broadway [110th]
- **Fairway Market** • 2328 Twelfth Ave [133rd]
- **Met Food** • 1316 Amsterdam Ave [La Salle]
- **Morton Williams** • 2941 Broadway [115th]
- **Westside Market** • 2840 Broadway [110th]

Map 18 · Columbia / Morningside Heights

1   2

12th Ave

21

W 135th St

W 134th St

W 133rd St

Old Broadway

W 132nd St

Riverside Dr

W 131st St

W 130th St

St Clair Pl

Manhattan-
ville
Houses

City
College

Convent Ave

St Nicholas Park

9

Convent Hill

W 129th St

W 128th St

W 127th St

Tiemann Pl

Old Broadway

W 125th St

W 126th St

General
Grant
Houses

La Salle St

Morningside
Houses

General
Grant
Houses

19

St Nicholas Ave

W 125th St

W 124th St

Hudson
River

Grant's
Tomb

Riverside Dr W

W 123rd St

W 122nd St

3

Claremont Ave

Broadway

Amsterdam Ave

Morningside Ave

Manhattan Ave

Frederick Douglass Blvd

Riverside Church

W 121st St

W 120th St

W 119th St

W 118th St

W 117th St

PAGE
256

Riverside
Park

Barnard College

PAGE
238

Columbia
University

Morningside Dr

W 116th St

W 115th St

Henry Hudson Pkwy

2

Riverside Dr

2

3

2

W 114th St

W 113th St

W 112th St

W 111th St

Morningside
Park

Cathedral
of St John
the Divine

4

16

9a

W 110th St (Cathedral Pkwy)

Central
Park

1/4 mile   .25 km

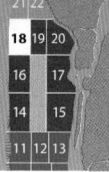

Meet your professor at Hungarian Pastry Shop (for sugared and caffeinated goods), bring your uncle to Dinosaur Bar-B-Que (they have real fire), and take your date to the Cotton Club (for jazz). Failed an exam? The cheap drinks at 1020 will cheer you up.

Movie Theaters

- **Italian Academy** •
1161 Amsterdam Ave [117th]

Nightlife

- **1020 Bar** • 1020 Amsterdam Ave [110th]
- **Cotton Club** • 656 W 125th St [St Clair Pl]
- **Heights Bar & Grill** • 2867 Broadway [112th]
- **Saurin Parke Café** • 301 W 110th St [CPW]
- **Soundz Lounge** •
3155 Broadway [Tiemann Pl]

Restaurants

- **Amir's Falafel** • 2911 Broadway [113th]
- **Bistro Ten 18** • 1018 Amsterdam Ave [110th]
- **Café Swish** • 2955 Broadway [115th]
- **Deluxe Diner** • 2896 Broadway [113th]
- **Dinosaur Bar-B-Que** • 646 W 131st St [B'way]
- **Havana Central** • 2911 Broadway [114th]
- **The Heights Bar & Grill** •
286? Broadway [111th]
- **Hungarian Pastry Shop** •
1030 Amsterdam Ave [111th]
- **Kitchenette** • 1272 Amsterdam Ave [123rd]
- **Koronet Pizza** • 2848 Broadway [111th]
- **Le Monde** • 2885 Broadway [112th]
- **M&G Soul Food Diner** •
383 W 125th St [Morningside Av]
- **Massawa** • 1239 Amsterdam Ave [121st]
- **Max SoHa** • 1274 Amsterdam Ave [123rd]
- **Mill Korean** • 2895 Broadway [113th]
- **Ollie's** • 2957 Broadway [116th]
- **P + W Sandwich Shop** •
1030 Amsterdam Ave [111th]
- **Pisticci** • 125 La Salle St [B'way]
- **Sezz Medi'** • 1260 Amsterdam Ave [122nd]
- **Symposium** • 544 W 113th St [Amsterdam]
- **Terrace in the Sky** •
400 W 119th St [Morningside Dr]
- **Toast** • 3157 Broadway [La Salle]
- **Tom's Restaurant** • 2880 Broadway [112th]
- **Tomo Sushi** • 2850 Broadway [111th]
- **V&T Pizzeria** • 1024 Amsterdam Ave [110th]

Shopping

- **Aunt Meriam's** •
435 W 125th St [Morningside Av]
- **El Mundo** • 3300 Broadway [133rd]
- **JAS Mart** • 2847 Broadway [111th]
- **Kim's Mediapolis** • 2906 Broadway [114th]
- **Book Culture** • 536 W 112th St [Amsterdam]
- **Mondel Chocolates** • 2913 Broadway [114th]
- **Pinkberry** • 2873 Broadway [112th]

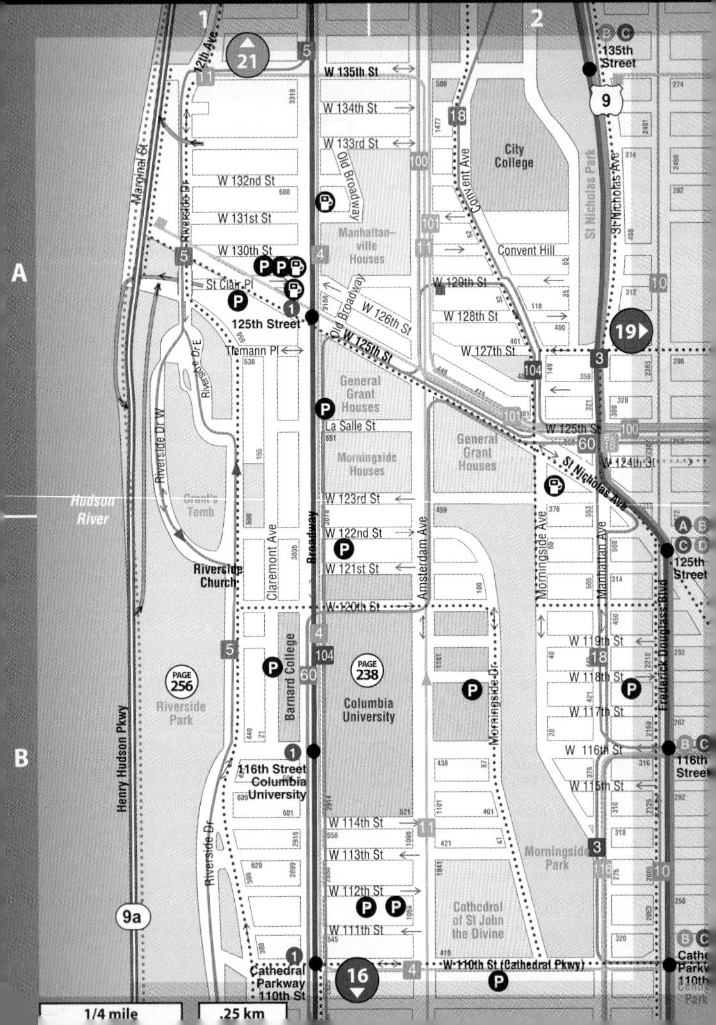

Map 18 · **Columbia / Morningside Heights** Ⓝ

1

12th Ave

Manhattan St

Riverside Dr

21

5

W 135th St

W 134th St

W 133rd St

Old Broadway

W 132nd St

W 131st St

W 130th St

Manhattan-
ville
Houses

A

St Clair Pl

P P P

5

4

125th Street

Tiemann Pl

Riverside Dr E

Riverside Dr W

Old Broadway

W 126th St

W 125th St

2

Convent Ave

City
College

13

Convent Hill

St Nicholas Park

St Nicholas Ave

9

135th
Street
B C

W 129th St

W 128th St

W 127th St

19

3

General
Grant
Houses

P

La Salle St

Morningside
Houses

General
Grant
Houses

W 125th St

104

103

St Nicholas Ave

60

100

W 124th St

**Hudson
River**

Grant's
Tomb

Riverside
Church

Claremont Ave

Broadway

W 123rd St

W 122nd St

P

W 121st St

W 120th St

Amsterdam Ave

P

Morningside Ave

Morningside Dr

Manhattan Ave

P

Frederick Douglass Blvd

125th
Street
A B
C D

B

Henry Hudson Pkwy

Riverside Park

PAGE
256

5

P

Barnard College

4

104

60

PAGE
238

Columbia
University

W 119th St

18

W 118th St

W 117th St

P

3

116th
Street
B C

W 116th St

W 115th St

1

116th Street
Columbia
University

Riverside Dr

W 114th St

W 113th St

11

Morningside
Park

10

W 112th St

P P

Cathedral
of St John
the Divine

9a

1

Cathedral
Parkway
110th St

16

4

W 110th St (Cathedral Pkwy)

P

Cathe
Parkw
110th
B C

1/4 mile

.25 km

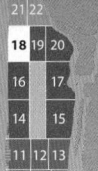
This may be the easiest neighborhood in Manhattan to park in, but take that with a grain of salt. Riverside Drive remains a smart (and beautiful) alternative to the congested West Side Highway. The local 1 subway never keeps you waiting long, but the B and C only offer limited service.

Subways

1 .... 116th St Columbia University
1 .... 125th St
1 .... Cathedral Pkwy (110th St)
A C B D .... 125th St
B C .... Cathedral Pkwy (110th St)
B C .... 116th St
B C .... 135th St

Bus Lines

100 .... 86th St Crosstown
101 .... 96th St Crosstown
104 .... 106th St Crosstown
11 .... Columbus Ave/Amsterdam Ave
18 .... Convent Ave
3 .... Fifth Ave/Madison Ave
4 .... Fifth Ave/Sixth Ave/Riverside Dr
5 .... Columbus Ave/Amsterdam Ave
Bx15 .... 116th St Crosstown

Bike Lanes

• • • Marked Bike Lanes
• • • Recommended Route
• • • Greenway

 Gas Stations

• **Independent** • 619 W 125th St [129th] ℗
• **Mobil** • 3260 Broadway [131st] ℗
• **Shell** • 117 Morningside Ave [124th]
• **Shell** • 3225 Broadway [129th]

Parking

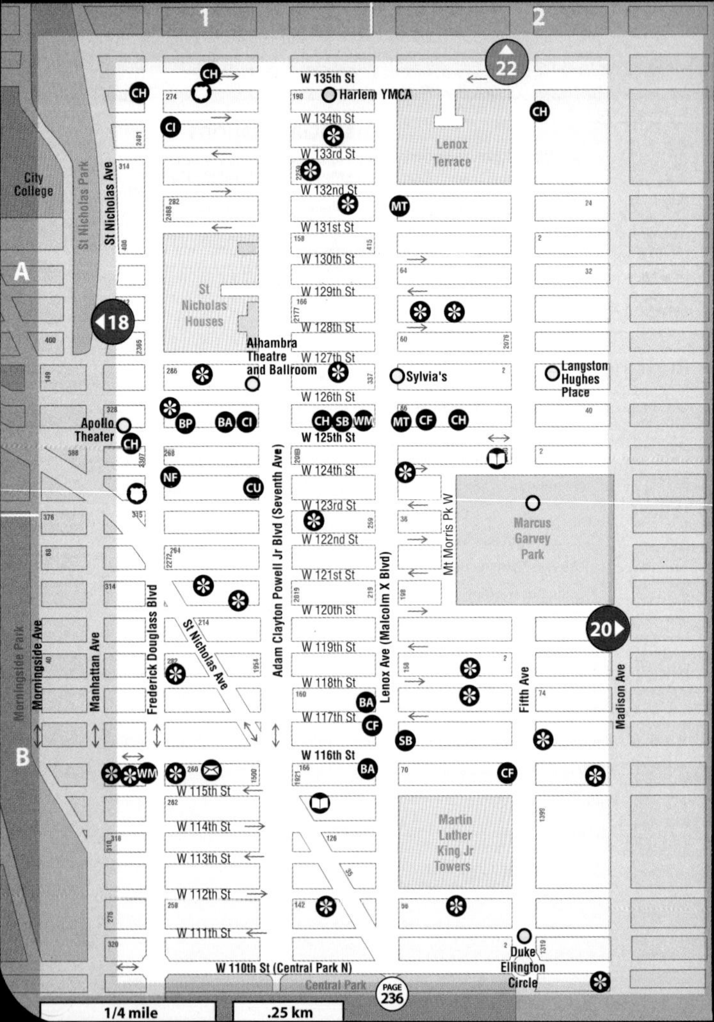

Map 19 · Harlem (Lower)

City College

St Nicholas Park

Morningside Park

Manhattan Ave

Frederick Douglass Blvd

St Nicholas Ave

Adam Clayton Powell Jr Blvd (Seventh Ave)

Lenox Ave (Malcolm X Blvd)

Mt Morris Pk W

Fifth Ave

Madison Ave

◀18

▲22

20▶

W 135th St
Harlem YMCA
W 134th St
W 133rd St
W 132nd St
W 131st St
W 130th St
W 129th St
W 128th St
W 127th St
Alhambra Theatre and Ballroom
W 126th St
Sylvia's
Langston Hughes Place
W 125th St
Apollo Theater
W 124th St
W 123rd St
W 122nd St
W 121st St
W 120th St
W 119th St
W 118th St
W 117th St
W 116th St
W 115th St
W 114th St
W 113th St
W 112th St
W 111th St
W 110th St (Central Park N)

Lenox Terrace

St Nicholas Houses

Marcus Garvey Park

Martin Luther King Jr Towers

Duke Ellington Circle

Central Park

PAGE 236

CH CI BP BA CI CH SB WM MT CF CH NF CU MT CF SB BA WM

1/4 mile   .25 km

Essentials

Map 19

The lifeline of this neighborhood is 125th Street, a thoroughfare known for the Apollo, a zillion stores, and players strutting their stuff. With some of the tastiest grub in town, bargains lining the streets, and locals who keep it real, Harlem is a nabe for New Yorkers who like a little gruff. But a recent rezoning may change it all. Stay tuned.

💲 Banks

BP • Banco Popular •
231 W 125th St [Seventh Ave]
BA • Bank of America •
106 W 117th St [Lenox Ave]
BA • Bank of America •
215 W 125th St [Seventh Ave]
BA • Bank of America (ATM) •
102 W 116th St [Lenox Ave]
CF • Carver Federal Savings •
142 Lenox Ave [W 117th St]
CF • Carver Federal Savings •
75 W 125th St [Lenox Ave]
CF • Carver Federal Savings (ATM) •
1400 Fifth Ave [W 115th St]
CH • Chase • 2218 Fifth Ave [W 135th St]
CH • Chase •
300 W 135th St [Frederick Douglass Blvd]
CH • Chase •
322 W 125th St [Frederick Douglass Blvd]
CH • Chase • 55 W 125th St [Lenox Ave]
CH • Chase (ATM) • Duane Reade •
135 E 125th St [Lexington Ave]
CH • Chase (ATM) •
251 W 135th St [Frederick Douglass Blvd]
CH • Chase (ATM) • Duane Reade •
322 W 125th St [St. Nicholas Ave]
CI • Citibank • 201 W 125th St [Seventh Ave]
CI • Citibank •
2518 Frederick Douglass Blvd [W 134th St]
CU • Lower East Side People's Federal Credit Union •
2052 Adam Clayton Powell Jr Blvd [W 123rd St]
MT • M&T • 310 Lenox Ave [W 131st St]
NF • North Fork •
2310 Frederick Douglass Blvd [W 124th St]
SB • Sovereign (ATM) •
CVS •115 W 125th St [Lenox Ave]
SB • Sovereign (ATM) •
CVS •130 Lenox Ave [W 116th St]
WM • Washington Mutual •
105 W 125th St [Lenox Ave]
WM • Washington Mutual •
2149 Frederick Douglass Blvd [W 116th St]

❊ Community Gardens

⭕ Landmarks

• **Alhambra Theatre and Ballroom •**
2116 Adam Clayton Powell Jr Blvd [121st]
• **Apollo Theater •** 253 W 125th St [F Douglass]
• **Duke Ellington Circle •** 110th St & Fifth Ave
• **Harlem YMCA •** 180 W 135th St [Lenox]
• **Langston Hughes Place •**
20 E 127th St [5th Av]
• **Marcus Garvey Park •**
E 120–124th Sts & Madison Ave
• **Sylvia's •** 328 Lenox Ave [126th]

📖 Libraries

• **115th Street •** 203 W 115th St [7th Av]
• **Harlem •** 9 W 124th St [5th Av]

🛡 Police

• **28th Precinct •**
2271 Frederick Douglass Blvd [122nd]
• **32nd Precinct •** 250 W 135th St [7th Av]

✉ Post Offices

• **Morningside •** 232 W 116th St [7th Av]

151

Map 19 · **Harlem (Lower)**

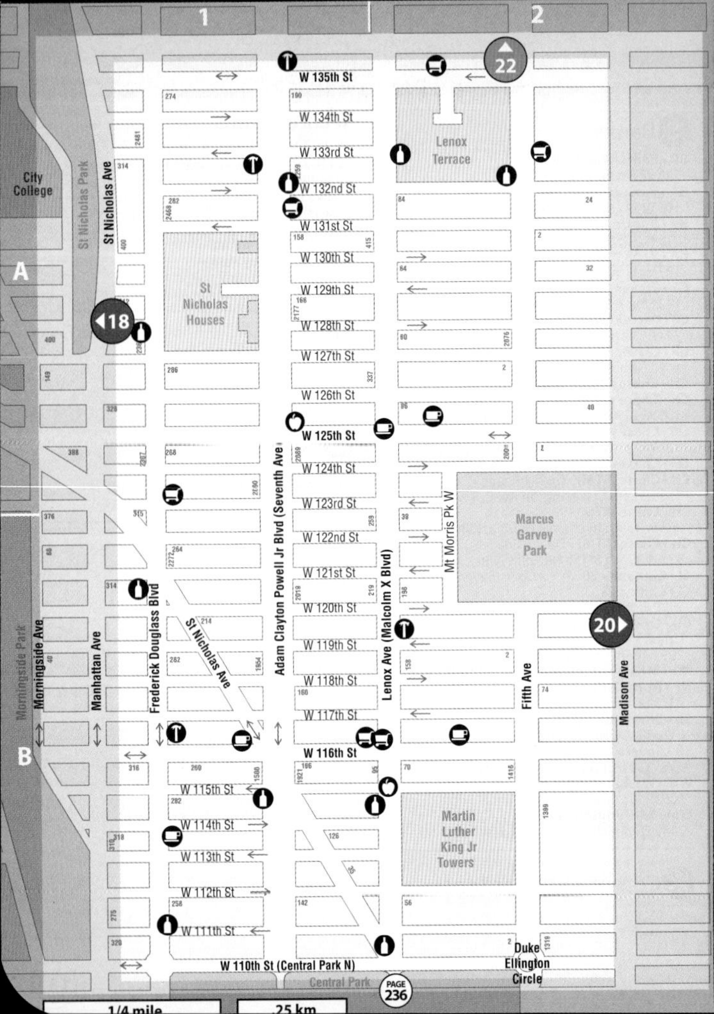

1
2

W 135th St
W 134th St
W 133rd St
W 132nd St
W 131st St
W 130th St
W 129th St
W 128th St
W 127th St
W 126th St
W 125th St
W 124th St
W 123rd St
W 122nd St
W 121st St
W 120th St
W 119th St
W 118th St
W 117th St
W 116th St
W 115th St
W 114th St
W 113th St
W 112th St
W 111th St
W 110th St (Central Park N)

Lenox Terrace

City College

St Nicholas Park

St Nicholas Houses

Marcus Garvey Park

Martin Luther King Jr Towers

Central Park

Duke Ellington Circle

Morningside Park

Morningside Ave
Manhattan Ave
Frederick Douglass Blvd
St Nicholas Ave
Adam Clayton Powell Jr Blvd (Seventh Ave)
Lenox Ave (Malcolm X Blvd)
Mt Morris Pk W
Fifth Ave
Madison Ave

A

B

22
118
20

PAGE 236

1/4 mile
.25 km

Yes, there is a Starbucks here, but for a bunch of your non-caffeinated needs just stroll up and down 125th. It's all here—from a farmers market to guys selling shea butter products and incense on the street.

Coffee

- **Dunkin' Donuts** • 105 W 125th St [Lenox]
- **Dunkin' Donuts** • 53 W 116th St [Lenox]
- **Farafena Coffee Shop** •
  219 W 116th St [St Nicholas]
- **Society Coffee & Juice** •
  2104 Frederick Douglass Blvd [114th]
- **Starbucks** • 77 W 125th St [Lenox]

Farmers Markets

- **Harlem Renaissance Lenox Ave Farmers Market**
  (Sat 8 am–4 pm Jul 8–Nov 18) •
  Lenox Ave b/w 114th & 115th St
- **Harlem Renaissance State Office Bldg Farmers Market (Tues 8 am–4 pm, Jul 11–Nov 21)** •
  W 125th St & Adam Clayton Powell Jr Blvd

Hardware Stores

- **Concordia Electrical & Plumbing** •
  2297 Adam Clayton Powell Jr Blvd [135th]
- **Garcia Brothers Hardware** •
  2258 Seventh Ave [133rd]
- **United Hardware** •
  2160 Frederick Douglass Blvd [117th]
- **Virgo Houseware & Hardware** •
  188 Lenox Ave [119th]

Liquor Stores

- **467 Lenox Liquors** • 467 Lenox Ave [133rd]
- **A&D Liquor** • 23 Lenox Ave [111th]
- **D&L Liquor** • 2178 Fifth Ave [132nd]
- **Fred's Wine & Liquors** • 77 Lenox Ave [114th]
- **Grand Liquors** •
  2049 Frederick Douglass Blvd [111th]
- **Harlem Retail Wine & Liquor** •
  1902 Adam Clayton Powell Jr Blvd [115th]
- **Harlem Vintage** •
  2235 Frederick Douglass Blvd [121st]
- **Olympic Wine and Liquor** •
  2391 Frederick Douglass Blvd [128th]
- **Palace Liquors** •
  2215 Adam Clayton Powell Jr Blvd [131st]

Supermarkets

- **Associated** •
  2296 Frederick Douglass Blvd [123rd]
- **Associated** • 448 Lenox Ave [132nd]
- **C-Town** •
  2217 Adam Clayton Powell Jr Blvd [131st]
- **C-Town** • 238 W 116th St [7th Av]
- **C-Town** • 24 W 135th St [Lenox]
- **Pioneer** • 136 Lenox Ave [117th]

Map 19 · **Harlem (Lower)**

N

1

2

22

W 135th St

274

W 134th St

2481

Lenox
Terrace

314

W 133rd St

W 132nd St

2358

3468

W 131st St

158

1415

W 130th St

84

24

480

2

A

W 129th St

166

W 128th St

2177

64

32

400

2385

286

W 127th St

2570

337

W 126th St

480

328

W 125th St

2

3

2

388

2089

2586

250

W 124th St

376

2000

W 123rd St

315

258

38

W 122nd St

Marcus
Garvey
Park

2272

264

314

W 121st St

2319

214

W 120th St

350

St Nicholas Houses
St
Nicholas
Houses

W 119th St

2

20

St Nicholas Ave

100

W 118th St

7

W 117th St

74

St Nicholas Ave

Frederick Douglass Blvd

Manhattan Ave

Adam Clayton Powell Jr Blvd (Seventh Ave)

Lenox Ave (Malcolm X Blvd)

Mt Morris Pkw

Fifth Ave

Madison Ave

Morningside Park

W 116th St

316

260

1600

1601

85

W 115th St

282

70

W 114th St

136

Martin
Luther
King Jr
Towers

1399

318

W 113th St

275

258

142

W 112th St

58

320

W 111th St

2319

W 110th St (Central Park N)

Duke
Ellington
Circle

City
College

18

St Nicholas Park

Central Park

1/4 mile

.25 km

For the best in down-home cooking, Amy Ruth's is the place to go. Try the pork chops and order them swimming. Zoma serves up good Ethiopian, Settepani bakes fresh pastries, and the Malcolm Shabazz Harlem Market offers an incredible selection of African products (music, clothing, and art).

Movie Theaters
• **AMC Magic Johnson Harlem 9** •
2309 Frederick Douglass Blvd [124th]

Nightlife
• **Apollo Theater** • 253 W 125th St [F Douglass]
• **The Den** • 2150 Fifth Ave [132nd]
• **Lenox Lounge** • 288 Lenox Ave [124th]
• **Moca Bar & Grill** •
2210 Frederick Douglass Blvd [119th]
• **Woodshed** •
2236 Adam Clayton Powell Jr Blvd [131st]

Restaurants
• **African Kine Restaurant** •
256 W 116th St [F Douglass]
• **Amy Ruth's** • 113 W 116th St [Lenox]
• **Ginger Restaurant** • 1400 Fifth Ave [115th]
• **IHOP** •
2294 Adam Clayton Powell Jr Blvd [135th]
• **Keur Sokhna** • 225 W 116th St [7th Av]
• **Le Baobab** • 120 W 116th St [Lenox]
• **Manna's Too** • 486 Lenox Ave [134th]
• **Native** • 161 Lenox Ave [18th]
• **Papaya King** • 121 W 125th St [Lenox]
• **Piatto D'Oro II** • 1 E 118th St [5th Av]
• **Slice of Harlem** • 308 Lenox Ave [125th]
• **Sylvia's** • 328 Lenox Ave [126th]
• **Yvonne Yvonne** • 301 W 135th St [F Douglass]
• **Zoma** • 2084 Frederick Douglass Blvd [113th]

Shopping
• **The Body Shop** • 1 E 125th St [5th Av]
• **Carol's Daughter** • 24 W 125th St [5th Av]
• **Champs** • 208 W 125th St [7th Av]
• **Dr Jay's Harlem NYC** •
256 W 125th St [F Douglass]
• **Grandma's Place** • 84 W 120th St [Lenox]
• **H&M** • 125 W 125th St [Lenox]
• **Harlem Underground Clothing** •
20 E 125th St [5th Av]
• **Harlemade** • 174 Lenox Ave [119th]
• **Hats by Bunn** • 2283 Seventh Ave [134th]
• **Hue-Man** •
2319 Frederick Douglass Blvd [125th]
• **Jimmy Jazz** • 132 W 125th St [Lenox]
• **MAC Cosmetics** • 202 W 125th St [7th Av]
• **Malcolm Shabazz Harlem Market** •
58 W 116th St [Lenox]
• **N Boutique** • 114 W 116th St [Lenox]
• **Nubian Heritage** • 2037 Fifth Ave [126th]
• **Settepani** • 196 Lenox Ave [120th]
• **Studio Museum of Harlem Gift Shop** •
144 W 125th St [Lenox]
• **Xukuma** • 11 E 125th St [5th Av]

Map 19 · Harlem (Lower)

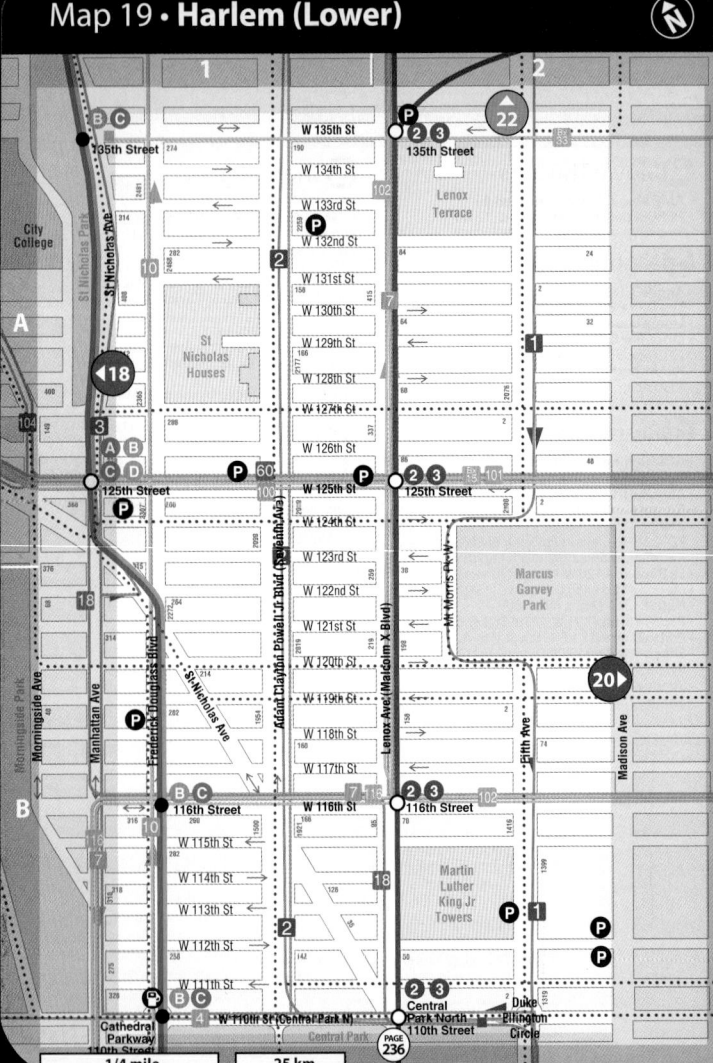

1/4 mile

.25 km

Transportation

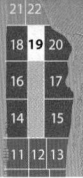

Do not use 125th unless you like to sit in your car a lot and look at people moving faster than you. Use 135th or 110th instead. And if you're heading west, 126th Street is a beautiful alternative, river to river. St. Nicholas Avenue has a nice bike path along its route.

Subways

🄶🄷 .... 116th St
🄶🄷 .... 125th St
🄶🄷 .... 135th St
🄶🄷 .... Central Park N (110th St)
🄱🄒 .... Cathedral Pkwy (110th St)
🄱🄒 .... 116th St
🄱🄒 .... 135th St
🄐🄒🄑🄓 ....125th St

Bus Lines

1 .... Fifth Ave/Madison Ave
10 .... Seventh Ave/Eighth Ave/
.... Frederick Douglass Blvd
100 ..... Amsterdam Ave/Broadway/125th St
101 . Third Ave/Lexington Ave/Amsterdam Ave
102 .. Third Ave/Lexington Ave/Malcolm X Blvd
116 .... 116th St Crosstown
2 .... Fifth Ave/Madison Ave/Powell Blvd
4 .... Fifth Ave/Madison Ave/Broadway
60 .... LaGuardia Airport via 125th St
7 .... Columbus Ave/Amsterdam Ave/
Lenox Ave/Sixth Ave/Seventh Ave/
Broadway
15 .... 125th St Crosstown
33 .... 135th St Crosstown

Bike Lanes

• • • Marked Bike Lanes
• • • Recommended Route

 Gas Stations

• **Exxon** • 2040 Frederick Douglass Blvd [111th] ⚙

🅿 Parking

Map 19

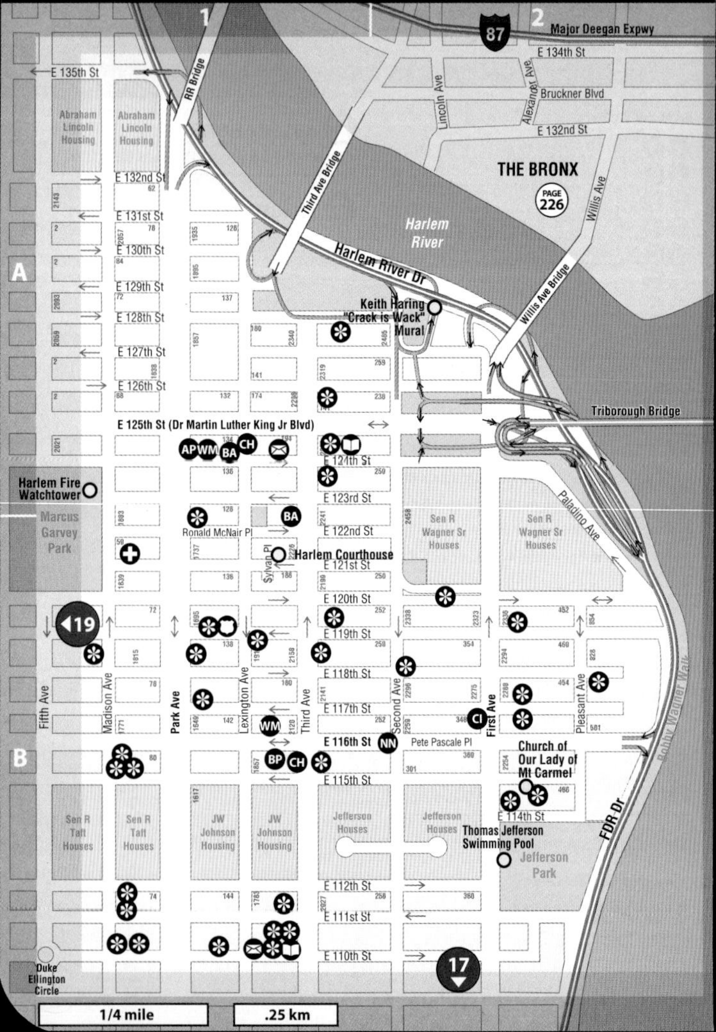

Map 20 · **El Barrio / East Harlem**

THE BRONX
PAGE 226

Harlem River

E 135th St

Abraham Lincoln Housing

Abraham Lincoln Housing

RR Bridge

E 134th St
Major Deegan Expwy

87

E 132nd St

Bruckner Blvd

Lincoln Ave

Alexander Ave

Willis Ave

E 132nd St
E 131st St
E 130th St
E 129th St
E 128th St
E 127th St
E 126th St

Third Ave Bridge

Harlem River Dr

Keith Haring "Crack is Wack" Mural

Willis Ave Bridge

Triborough Bridge

A

E 125th St (Dr Martin Luther King Jr Blvd)

AP WM BA CH

Harlem Fire Watchtower

Marcus Garvey Park

E 124th St
E 123rd St

BA

E 122nd St

Ronald McNair Pl

Harlem Courthouse

Sylvan Pl

E 121st St

Sen R Wagner Sr Houses

Sen R Wagner Sr Houses

Paladino Ave

◄19

E 120th St
E 119th St
E 118th St
E 117th St

Fifth Ave

Madison Ave

Park Ave

Lexington Ave

Third Ave

Second Ave

First Ave

Pleasant Ave

FDR Dr

CI

B

WM

E 116th St

NN

Pete Pascale Pl

BP CH

E 115th St

Church of Our Lady of Mt Carmel

Sen R Taft Houses

Sen R Taft Houses

JW Johnson Housing

JW Johnson Housing

Jefferson Houses

Jefferson Houses

Thomas Jefferson Swimming Pool

E 114th St

Jefferson Park

E 112th St
E 111th St
E 110th St

Duke Ellington Circle

17

1/4 mile   .25 km

1   2

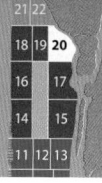

El Barrio is incredibly rich and vibrant in history and culture. Puerto Rican, African-American, Mexican, Dominican, Italian…it's all here. Abundant community gardens provide locals with the perfect summer chill out spots. Exploring this neighborhood is highly recommended.

$ Banks

AP • Apple • 124 E 125th St [Park Ave]
BP • Banco Popular •
164 E 116th St [Lexington Ave]
BA • Bank of America •
157 E 125th St [Lexington Ave]
BA • Bank of America (ATM) •
2250 Third Ave [E 122nd St]
CH • Chase • 160 E 125th St [Lexington Ave]
CH • Chase (ATM) • 2108 Third Ave [E 115th St]
CI • Citibank • 2261 First Ave [E 116th St]
NN • New York National •
2256 Second Ave [E 116th St]
WM • Washington Mutual •
103 E 125th St [Park Ave]
WM • Washington Mutual •
179 E 116th St [Third Ave]

✴ Community Gardens

✚ Emergency Rooms

• **North General •** 1879 Madison Ave [122nd]

○ Landmarks

• **Church of Our Lady of Mt Carmel •**
448 E 115th St [1st Av]
• **Harlem Courthouse •** 170 E 121st St [Lex]
• **Harlem Fire Watchtower •**
Marcus Garvey Park
• **Keith Haring "Crack is Wack" Mural •**
Second Ave & 127th St
• **Thomas Jefferson Swimming Pool •**
2180 First Ave [112th]

📖 Libraries

• **125th St •** 224 E 125th St [3rd Av]
• **Aguilar •** 174 E 110th St [Lex]

🚓 Police

• **25th Precinct •** 120 E 119th St [Park]

✉ Post Offices

• **Oscar Garcia Rivera •** 153 E 110th St [Lex]
• **Triborough •** 167 E 124th St [Lex]

Map 20 · **El Barrio / East Harlem**

N

1
2

87 Major Deegan Expwy

E 135th St
E 134th St

RR Bridge

Lincoln Ave

Alexander Ave

Bruckner Blvd

E 132nd St

Abraham
Lincoln
Housing

Abraham
Lincoln
Housing

THE BRONX

PAGE
226

Willis Ave

2745

E 132nd St
62

E 131st St
78

1995

126

*Harlem
River*

E 130th St
64

1885

Third Ave Bridge

A

2003

E 129th St
72

137

Harlem River Dr

2540

E 128th St
70

186

2319

259

2405

Willis Ave Bridge

2969

E 127th St

1657

1038

2206

132

2206

141

230

Triborough Bridge

2021

E 126th St

194

E 125th St (Dr Martin Luther King Jr Blvd)

134

250

Palladino Ave

5883

136

E 124th St

E 123rd St

2741

Ronald McNair Pl

Sen R
Wagner Sr
Houses

Sen R
Wagner Sr
Houses

**Marcus
Garvey
Park**

58

1839

136

E 122nd St

2480

Sylvan Pl

2218

E 121st St

2189

250

Fifth Ave

73

E 120th St

452

138

1915

2158

E 119th St

2523

250

354

460

864

119

1815

79

80

E 118th St

100

2294

829

Madison Ave

Park Ave

1606

E 117th St

2275

454

2398

Lexington Ave

1857

Third Ave

Second Ave

2298

First Ave

360

2254

Pleasant Ave

591

E 116th St

B

Pete Pascale Pl

E 115th St

466

Sen R
Taft
Houses

Sen R
Taft
Houses

JW
Johnson
Housing

JW
Johnson
Housing

Jefferson
Houses

Jefferson
Houses

E 114th St

FDR Dr

74

144

1788

E 112th St

250

2027

369

**Jefferson
Park**

E 111th St

Robert F Kennedy Bridge

Duke
Ellington
Circle

17

E 110th St

1/4 mile   .25 km

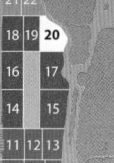
We're still hoping someone comes along to revive the historic public market La Marqueta. In the meantime, there are plenty of average supermarkets to fill your grocery needs. The Harlem Tea Room is the top destination for caffeine lovers.

Coffee

- **Central Minimarket** • 2165 First Ave [112th]
- **Dunkin' Donuts** • 159 E 116th St [Lex]
- **Dunkin' Donuts** • 2083 Lexington Ave [126th]
- **Dunkin' Donuts** • 2258 First Ave [116th]
- **Dunkin' Donuts** • 255 E 125th St [2nd Av]
- **The Harlem Tea Room** •
  1793 Madison Ave [117th]
- **Julia's Coffee Shop** • 242 E 116th St [3rd Av]
- **Kahlua's Café** • 2117 Third Ave [116th]
- **L&T Coffee Shop** • 2265 First Ave [116th]

Farmers Markets

- **La Marqueta (Sat 8 am–6 pm July–Oct)** •
  E 115th St & Park Ave

Hardware Stores

- **B&B Supply & Hardware** •
  2338 Second Ave [120th]
- **F&F Hardware** • 156 E 112th St [Madison]
- **N&J Locksmith & Hardware** •
  100 E 116th St [Park Av]
- **SM Hardware** • 2139 Third Ave [117th]

Liquor Stores

- **115 R & P Beer Distributors** •
  77 E 115th St [Park]
- **249 E 115th Liquor** • 249 E 115th St [2nd Av]
- **IC Liquors** • 2255 First Ave [116th]
- **Lexington Wine and Liquor** •
  2010 Lexington Ave [122nd]
- **Madison Avenue Wine** •
  1793 Madison Ave [117th]
- **Third Avenue Liquors** •
  2030 Third Ave [112th]
- **Uptown Wine Pantry** •
  63 E 125th St [Madison]

Supermarkets

- **Associated** • 125 E 116th St [Park]
- **Associated** • 160 E 110th St [Lex]
- **Associated** • 2212 Third Ave [121st]
- **Compare** • 309 E 115th St [2nd Av]
- **Pathmark** • 160 F 125th St [Lex]
- **Pioneer** • 1666 Madison Ave [111th]

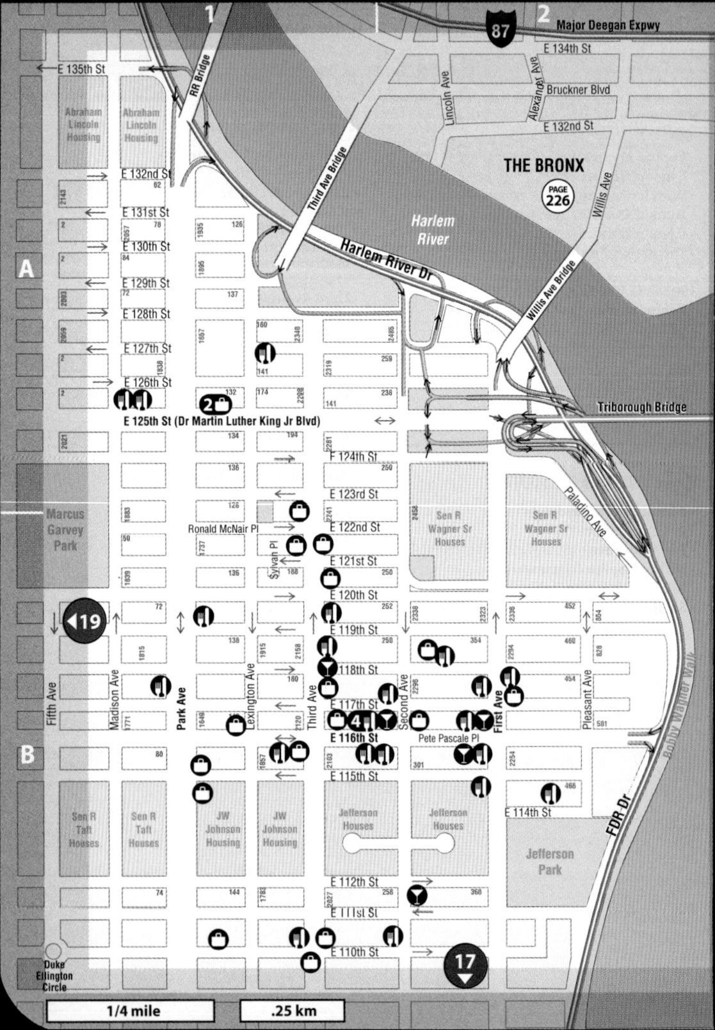

Map 20 · **El Barrio / East Harlem**

N

1   2 87 Major Deegan Expwy

E 135th St

RR Bridge

E 134th St

Abraham
Lincoln
Housing

Abraham
Lincoln
Housing

E 132nd St

E 132nd St

Lincoln Ave

Alexander Ave

Bruckner Blvd

E 131st St

E 130th St

Third Ave Bridge

THE BRONX

PAGE
226

Harlem
River

Willis Ave

E 129th St

Harlem River Dr

E 128th St

A

E 127th St

E 126th St

Willis Ave Bridge

E 125th St (Dr Martin Luther King Jr Blvd)

Triborough Bridge

E 124th St

E 123rd St

Marcus
Garvey
Park

Ronald McNair Pl

E 122nd St

Sen R
Wagner Sr
Houses

Sen R
Wagner Sr
Houses

Palladino Ave

Sylvan Pl

E 121st St

E 120th St

119

E 119th St

Madison Ave

Park Ave

Lexington Ave

E 118th St

E 117th St

Second Ave

First Ave

Pleasant Ave

4

E 116th St

Pete Pascale Pl

Third Ave

E 115th St

Fifth Ave

B

E 114th St

FDR Dr

Harlem River Dr

Sen R
Taft
Houses

Sen R
Taft
Houses

JW
Johnson
Housing

JW
Johnson
Housing

Jefferson
Houses

Jefferson
Houses

Jefferson
Park

E 112th St

E 111th St

E 110th St

Duke
Ellington
Circle

17

| 1/4 mile | .25 km |

Patsy's pizza really is the "original" New York thin-crust pizza, and Rao's is another New York restaurant you'll never get into. 116th Street is a budget culinary destination (try Taco Mix, Sandy, or El Nuevo Caridad). Nightlife picks: Camaradas, Dexy's, and Orbit East Harlem.

Nightlife

- **Café Creole** • 2167 Third Ave [118th]
- **Camaradas** • 2241 First Ave [115th]
- **Dexy's Lounge** • 2171 Second Ave [112th]
- **Mojitos** • 227 E 116th St [3rd Av]
- **Orbit East Harlem** • 2257 First Ave [116th]
- **Ragg's Pub** • 101 E 119th St [Park Ave]

Restaurants

- **A Taste of Seafood** • 59 E 125th St [Madison]
- **Café Creole** • 2167 Third Ave [118th]
- **Camaradas** • 2241 First Ave [115th]
- **Caminito** • 1664 Park Ave [117th]
- **Casa de los Tacos** • 2277 First Ave [116th]
- **Cuchifritos** • 168 E 116th St [Lex]
- **El Nuevo Caridad** • 2257 Second Ave [116th]
- **El Paso Taqueria** • 237 E 116th St [3rd Ave]
- **El Tapatio Mexican Restaurant** •
  209 E 116th St [3rd Av]
- **Golden Crust** • 2085 Lexington Ave [126th]
- **L&T Coffee Shop** • 2265 First Ave [116th]
- **La Hacienda** • 219 E 116th St [3rd Av]
- **Manna** • 51 E 125th St [Madison]
- **Mojitos** • 227 E 116th St [3rd Av]
- **Orbit East Harlem** • 2257 First Ave [116th]
- **Patsy's Pizzeria** • 2287 First Ave [118th]
- **Pee Dee Steakhouse** • 2006 Third Ave [110th]
- **Polash Indian Cuisine Restaurant** •
  2179 Third Ave [119th]
- **Rao's** • 455 E 114th St [1st Av]
- **Ricardo Steakhouse** •
  2145 Second Ave [110th]
- **Sandy Restaurant** • 2261 Second Ave [116th]
- **Taco Mix** • 236 E 116 St [3rd Av] ⊗
- **Treichville West African Cuisine** •
  339 E 118th St [2nd Av]

Shopping

- **American Outlet Superstore** •
  2226 Third Ave [121st]
- **Capri Bakery** • 186 E 116th St [3rd Av]
- **Casa Latina Music Store** • 151 E 116th St [Lex]
- **Casablanca Meat Market** •
  127 E 110th St [Park]
- **The Children's Place** • 163 E 125th St [Lex]
- **Don Paco Lopez Panaderia** •
  2129 Third Ave [116th]
- **Eagle Tile & Home Center** •
  2254 Second Ave [116th]
- **Everything Must Go** • 2281 First Ave [117th]
- **Gothic Cabinet Craft** • 2268 Third Ave [123rd]
- **La Marqueta** • 1607 Park Ave [112th]
- **Lore Upholstery Shop** •
  2201 Third Ave [120th]
- **Motherhood Maternity** • 163 E 125th St [Lex]
- **Payless Shoe Source** • 2143 Third Ave [117th]
- **R&S Strauss Auto** • 2005 Third Ave [110th]
- **VIM** • 2239 Third Ave [122nd]
- **Young's Fish Market** • 2004 Third Ave [110th]

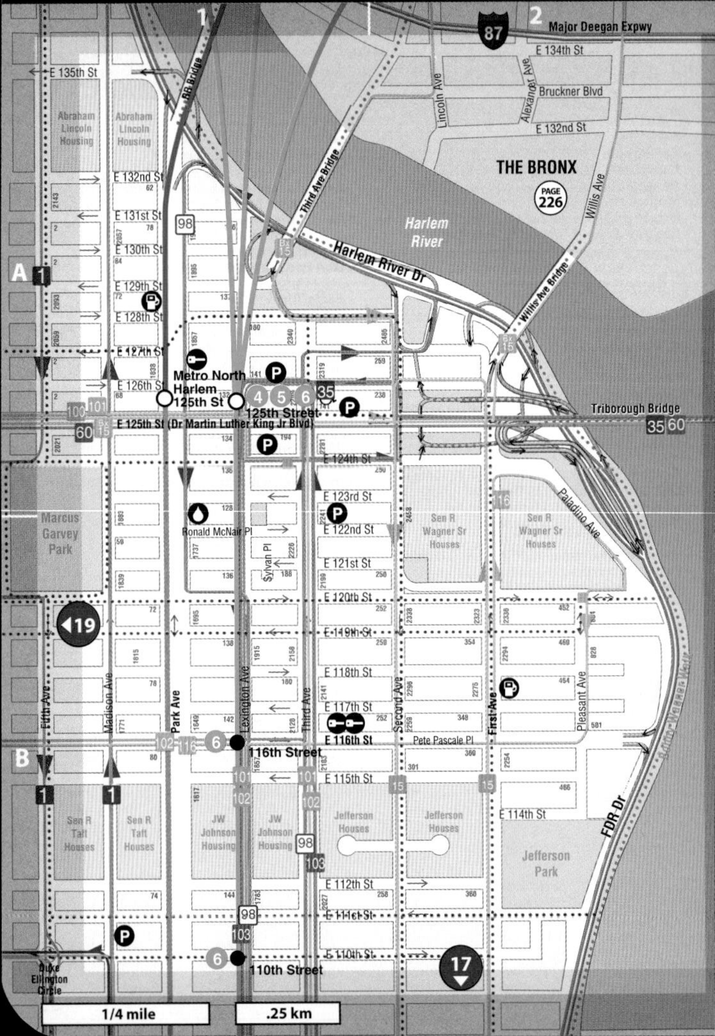

Map 20 · **El Barrio / East Harlem**

N

E 135th St

THE BRONX
PAGE
226

87 — 2 Major Deegan Expwy

E 134th St

Bruckner Blvd

E 132nd St

RR Ridge

Abraham
Lincoln
Housing

Abraham
Lincoln
Housing

E 132nd St

E 131st St

E 130th St

E 129th St

98

Third Ave Bridge

Lincoln Ave

Alexander Ave

Willis Ave

*Harlem
River*

Harlem River Dr

Willis Ave Bridge

A 1

E 128th St

P

E 127th St

E 126th St

Metro North
Harlem
125th St

E 125th St

109 101

60

125th Street

P

E 125th St (Dr Martin Luther King Jr Blvd)

4 4 5 6 35

238

Triborough Bridge

35 60

Palladino Ave

E 124th St

E 123rd St

P

E 122nd St

Sen R
Wagner Sr
Houses

Sen R
Wagner Sr
Houses

Marcus
Garvey
Park

Ronald McNair Pl

E 121st St

E 120th St

19

Fifth Ave

Madison Ave

Park Ave

Sylvan Pl

Lexington Ave

E 119th St

E 118th St

E 117th St

Third Ave

Second Ave

First Ave

Pleasant Ave

E 116th St

Pete Pascale Pl

B 1

102 116

6

116th Street

101

102

E 115th St

15

15

FDR Dr

Sen R Taft
Houses

Sen R Taft
Houses

JW
Johnson
Housing

JW
Johnson
Housing

98

Jefferson
Houses

Jefferson
Houses

E 114th St

Jefferson
Park

E 112th St

P

E 111th St

98

103

6

110th Street

Duke
Ellington
Circle

17

1/4 mile	.25 km

Transportation

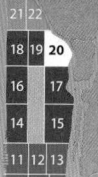

Map 20

The best route to the Triborough is to go up Third Avenue and make a right on 124th Street. Parking shouldn't be too much of a problem. Catch the M60 bus on 125th Street for La Guardia Airport. Tired of Grand Central? Try the Metro-North Station at 125th and Park.

Subways

6	................................110th St
6	................................116th St
4 5 6	.... 125th St

Bus Lines

1	.... Fifth/Madison Aves
101	. Third Ave/Lexington Ave/Amsterdam Ave
102	.. Third Ave/Lexington Ave/Malcolm X Blvd
103	.... Third/Lexington Aves
116	.... 116th St Crosstown
15	.... First Ave/Second Ave
35	.... Randall's Island/Ward Island
60	.... LaGuardia Airport
98	.... Washington Heights/Midtown
BX15	.... 125th St Crosstown

Bike Lanes

- • • • Marked Bike Lanes
- • • • Recommended Route
- • • • Greenway

Car Rental

- **A-Value Rent-A-Car** • 1851 Park Ave [126th]
- **Autorent Car Rental** • 220 E 117th St [3rd Av]
- **Enterprise** • 220 E 117th St [3rd Av]

Car Washes

- **NY Car Spa** • 1767 Park Ave [123rd]

Gas Stations

- **Gulf** • 1890 Park Ave [129th]
- **Shell** • 2276 First Ave [117th] ⌀

Parking

Map 21 · **Manhattanville / Hamilton Heights**

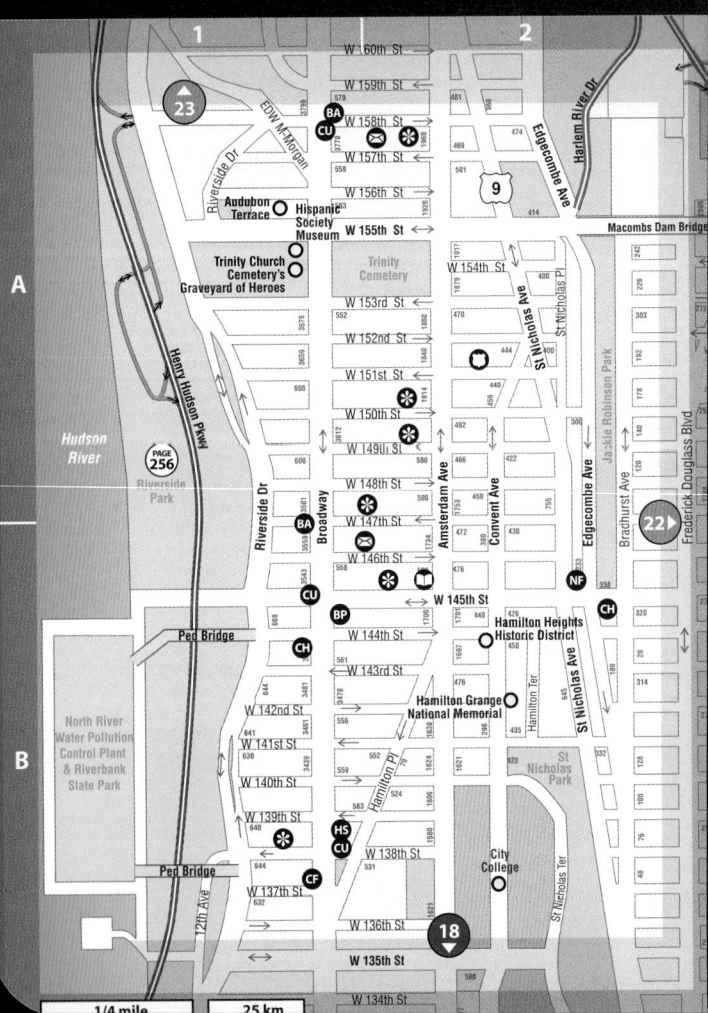

Essentials

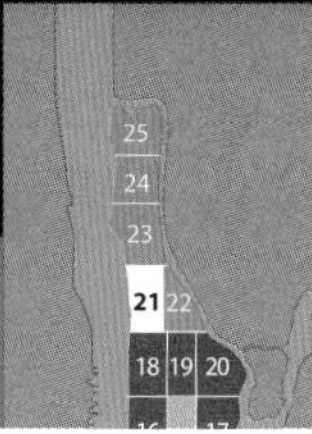

Map 21

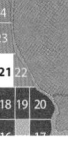

This closely knit community maintains its traditional essence with its neo-Gothic City College, gorgeous ethnic garb, memorial gardens, and, of course, breathtaking brownstones.

Banks

BP • Banco Popular •
3540 Broadway [W 145th St]
BA • Bank of America (ATM) •
3579B Broadway [147th St]
BA • Bank of America (ATM) •
3800 Broadway [158th St]
CF • Carver Federal Savings (ATM) •
3381 Broadway [137th St]
CH • Chase • 330 W 145th St [Edgecombe Ave]
CH • Chase • 3515 Broadway [144th St]
HS • HSBC • 3418 Broadway [139th St]
CU • Lower East Side People's Federal Credit Union (ATM) • McDonald's •
3410 Broadway [139th St]
CU • Lower East Side People's Federal Credit Union (ATM) • McDonald's •
3543 Broadway [145th St]
CU • Lower East Side People's Federal Credit Union (ATM) • McDonald's •
3794 Broadway [158th St]
NF • North Fork • 700 St Nicholas Ave [145th St]

Community Gardens

Landmarks

- **Audubon Terrace •** Broadway & W 155th St
- **City College •**
Convent Ave b/w W 130th St & W 141st St
- **Hamilton Grange National Memorial •**
287 Convent Ave [142nd]
- **Hamilton Heights Historic District •**
W 141st b/w W 145th St & Convent Ave
- **Hispanic Society Museum •**
613 W 155th St [B'way]
- **Trinity Church Cemetery's Graveyard of Heroes •** 3699 Broadway [153rd]

Libraries

- **Hamilton Grange •**
503 W 145th St [Amsterdam]

Police

- **30th Precinct •** 451 W 151st St [Convent]

Post Offices

- **Fort Washington •** 556 W 158th St [Broadway]
- **Hamilton Grange •**
521 W 146th St [Amsterdam]

Map 21 • **Manhattanville / Hamilton Heights**

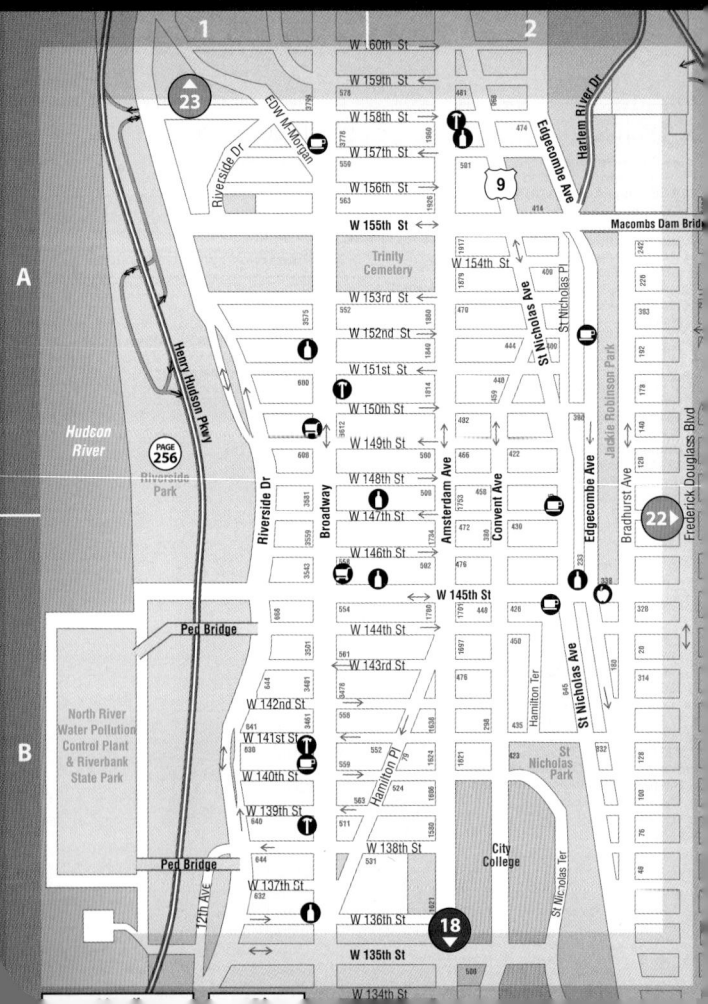

Sugar Hill is sweet, just like Café Bonjour's cakes and tasty treats. But nothing compares to Grass Roots Farmers Market delectable delights or the Coffee Shop in Hamilton Heights. Find everything you need in Manhattanville or visit St. Nicholas Park and just sit still.

Coffee

- **Astron Coffee Shop** • 3795 Broadway [158th]
- **Café Bonjour** • 741 St. Nicholas Ave [147th]
- **Coffee Shop** • 398 W 145th St [Convent]
- **Dunkin' Donuts** • 3455 Broadway [141st]
- **OC Bakery & Café** •
  375 Edgecombe Ave [152nd]

Farmers Markets

- **Grass Roots Farmers Market
  (Sat 9 am–4 pm Jul 1–Nov 25)** •
  W 145th St & Edgecombe Ave

Hardware Stores

- **Cohen & Cohen** •
  1982 Amsterdam Ave [158th]
- **Felix Supply** • 3650 Broadway [150th]
- **O&J Hardware** • 3405 Broadway [138th]
- **Westside Home Center** •
  3447 Broadway [141st]

Liquor Stores

- **2001 Liquor** • 3671 Broadway [152nd]
- **Brand's Liquor** • 550 W 145th St [Amsterdam]
- **JOCL Liquor Store** • 561 W 147th St [B'way]
- **Jumasol Liquors** •
  1963 Amsterdam Ave [157th]
- **Reliable Wine & Liquor Shop** •
  3375 Broadway [137th]
- **Unity Liquors** • 708 St Nicholas Ave [146th]

Supermarkets

- **C-Town** • 3550 Broadway [146th]
- **C-Town** • 3632 Broadway [149th]

169

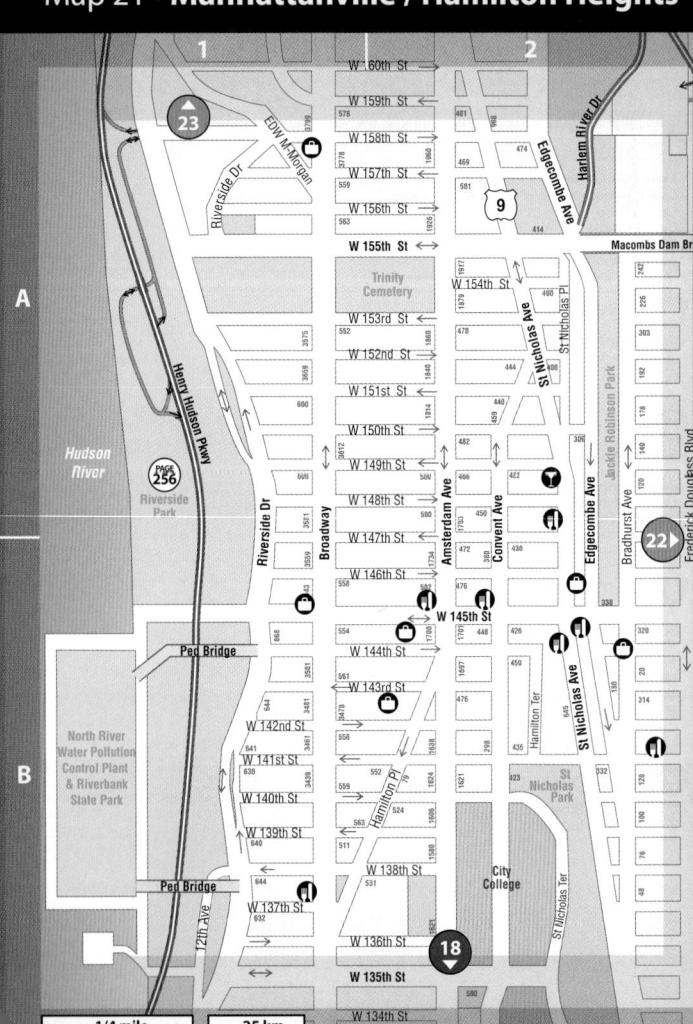

Map 21 • Manhattanville / Hamilton Heights

1

2

W 160th St

W 159th St

23

578

481

W 158th St

3578

1960

469

474

W 157th St

559

Edgecombe Ave

W 156th St

563

1928

581

9

EDW M Morgan

W 155th St

Riverside Dr

414

Hartem River Dr

Macombs Dam Bri

A

Trinity
Cemetery

W 154th St

1976

490

242

225

W 153rd St

552

678

303

W 152nd St

3658

1868
1848

444

408

192

Henry Hudson Pkwy

3600

W 151st St

1814

440

178

St Nicholas Ave

St Nicholas Pl

W 150th St

3612

600

482

306

140

W 149th St

500

466

422

120

Hudson
River

PAGE
256

Riverside
Park

9

Riverside Dr

3531

W 148th St

580

450

Convent Ave

Amsterdam Ave

Edgecombe Ave

Jackie Robinson Park

Bradhurst Ave

Frederick Douglass Blvd

22

W 147th St

3559

472

300

638

W 146th St

556

1734

Broadway

W 145th St

1700

476

1709

448

330

320

554

554

W 144th St

3581

561

W 143rd St

3478

426

450

20

314

Hamilton Ter

St Nicholas Ave

188

W 142nd St

644

3461

476

W 141st St

641
630

556

1628

298

435

128

332

Hamilton Pl

W 140th St

552
559

1624

1621

180

423

St
Nicholas
Park

W 139th St

563

524
1580

76

640

511

Ped Bridge

North River
Water Pollution
Control Plant
& Riverbank
State Park

12th Ave

W 138th St

644

531

1625

City
College

W 137th St

632

Ped Bridge

St Nicholas Ter

18

W 136th St

B

W 135th St

580

W 134th St

471

1/4 mile

.25 km

Map 21

Entertainment

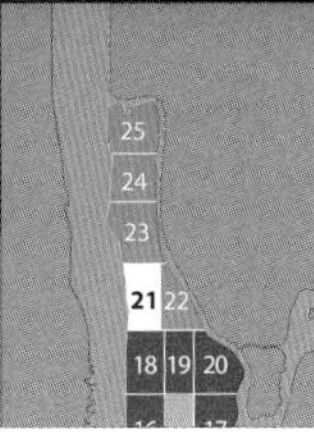

Find threads at SOH-Straight Out of Harlem Creative Outlet and then show off your goodies at Baton Rouge. Queen of Sheeba is perfect for Middle Eastern cravings, and smack your lips on New Caporal Fried Chicken. If you're ready for fine dining take a seat at Café Largo, but bring wine. And don't miss St. Nick's, one of the best jazz joints in the universe.

Nightlife

- **St Nick's Pub** • 773 St Nicholas Ave [149th]

Restaurants

- **Baton Rouge** • 458 W 145th St [Convent Av]
- **Café Largo** • 3387 Broadway [137th]
- **Devin's Fish & Chips** •
  747 St Nicholas Ave [147th]
- **Jesus Taco** • 501 W 145th St [Amsterdam]
- **New Caporal Fried Chicken** •
  3772 Broadway [157th] ⌀
- **Queen of Sheeba** •
  317 W 141st St [F Douglass]
- **Raw Soul** • 348 W 145th St [Edgecombe]
- **Sunshine Jamaican Restaurant** •
  695 St Nicholas Ave [145th]

Shopping

- **The Adventist Care Center** •
  528 W 145th St [Amsterdam]
- **B-Jays USA** • 540 W 143rd St [Hamilton Pl]
- **El Mundo** • 3791 Broadway [158th]
- **Foot Locker** • 3549 Broadway [146th]
- **SOH-Straight Out of Harlem Creative Outlet** • 704 St Nicholas Ave [145th]
- **VIM** • 508 W 145th St [Amsterdam]

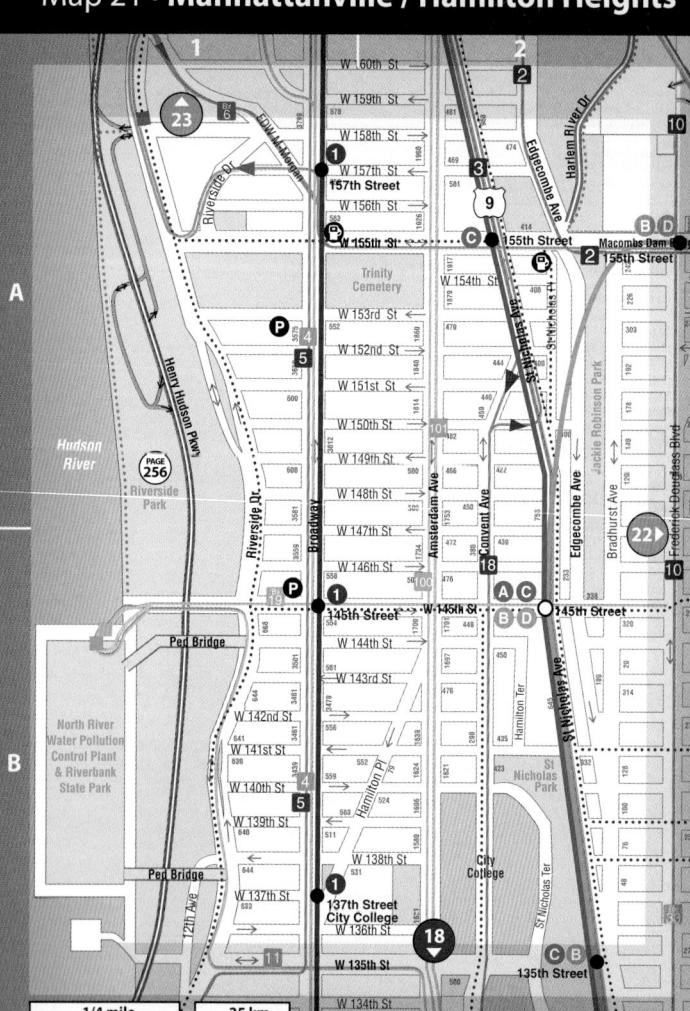

Map 21 • Manhattanville / Hamilton Heights

Transportation

Despite the fact that the signs outside the 135th and 155th Street stations list the A and C trains, the A train stops only during late nights, when it runs local. Drivers take note: Riverside Drive can be a viable alternative to the Henry Hudson during rush hour.

Subways

①	.... 137th St-City College
①	...................................145th St
①	...................................157th St
Ⓐ Ⓒ Ⓑ Ⓓ	.... 145th St
Ⓑ Ⓒ	.... 135th St
Ⓑ Ⓓ	.... 155th St
Ⓒ	...............................155th St

Bus Lines

100	.... Amsterdam Ave/Broadway/125th St
101	.................Third Ave/Lexington Ave/
	Broadway/125th St
11	....................Ninth (Columbus)/
	Tenth (Amsterdam Ave)/Convent Ave
18	.... Convent Ave
2	.... Fifth Ave/Madison Ave/Powell Blvd
3	... Fifth Ave/Madison Ave/St Nicholas Blvd
4	.... Fifth Ave/Madison Ave/Broadway
5	.... Fifth Ave/Sixth Ave/Riverside Dr
Bx 19	.... 145th St Crosstown

Bike Lanes

- • • • Marked Bike Lanes
- • • • Recommended Route
- • • • Greenway

ⓅGas Stations

- **Getty** • 155 St Nicholas Ave [118th] ⚙
- **Mobil** • 3740 Broadway [156th] ⚙

ⓅParking

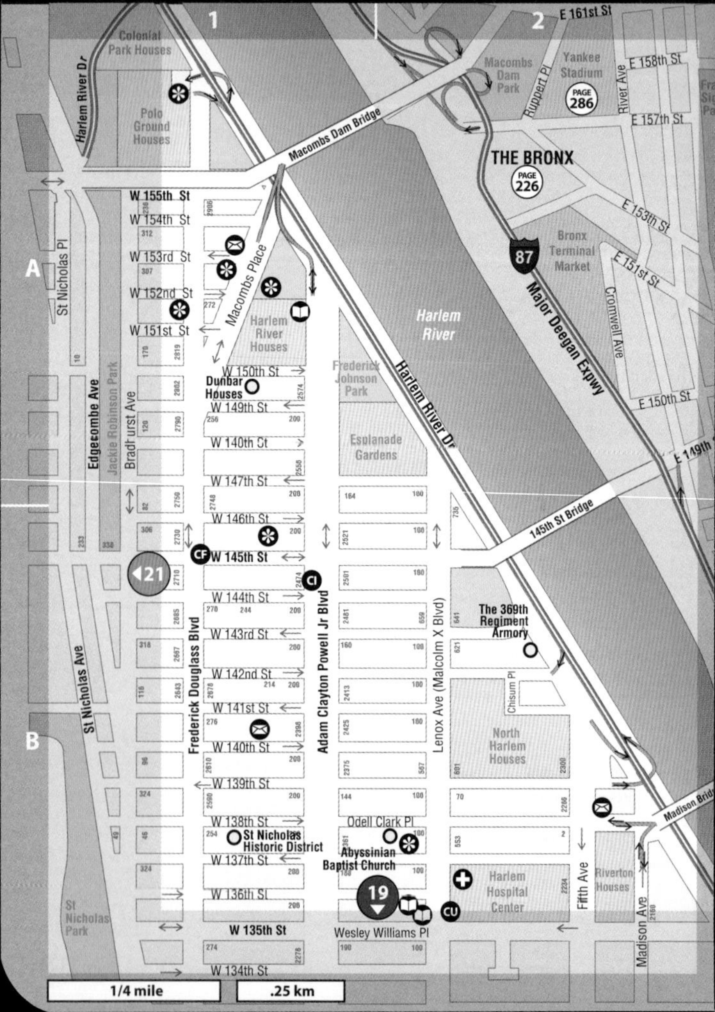

Map 22 · **Harlem (Upper)**

1

2

E 161st St

Harlem River Dr

Colonial
Park Houses

Macombs
Dam Park

Ruppert Pl

Yankee
Stadium

PAGE
286

River Ave

E 158th St

E 157th St

Fre
Sid
Ha

Polo
Ground
Houses

Macombs Dam Bridge

THE BRONX

PAGE
226

E 153rd St

87

Bronx
Terminal
Market

Cromwell Ave

Major Deegan Expwy

E 151st St

W 155th St

St Nicholas Pl

A

W 154th St

312

Macombs Place

W 153rd St

307

Edgecombe Ave

Jackie Robinson Park

Bradhurst Ave

W 152nd St

272

W 151st St

176

2919

Harlem
River
Houses

W 150th St

Frederick
Johnson
Park

Harlem
River

E 150th St

E 149th St

Dunbar
Houses

W 149th St

2574

256

W 148th St

2568

Esplanade
Gardens

2748

W 147th St

208

82

2768

W 146th St

306

200

164

100

100

2732

2021

2730

CF W 145th St

2724

145th St Bridge

735

St Nicholas Ave

21

2710

2685

278 244

2974

CI

W 144th St

2507

100

Adam Clayton Powell Jr Blvd

218

W 143rd St

260

2461

Lenox Ave (Malcolm X Blvd)

The 369th
Regiment
Armory

641

116

2978

W 142nd St

214

160

621

Chisum Pl

276

2966

W 141st St

2425

100

2930

W 140th St

2375

100

North
Harlem
Houses

2560

W 139th St

200

597

324

W 138th St

144

70

2096

Fifth Ave

Madison Bridge

48

254

St Nicholas
Historic District

Odell Clark Pl

2881

553

2

Madison Ave

324

W 137th St

Abyssinian
Baptist Church

Harlem
Hospital
Center

Riverton
Houses

2100

St
Nicholas
Park

274

W 136th St

208

19

2278

W 135th St

190

100

CU

Wesley Williams Pl

W 134th St

1/4 mile

.25 km

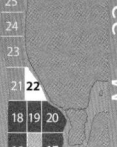
Upper Harlem is the center of black culture in New York. There are many historic buildings to visit, including New York's oldest black congregation, Abyssinian Baptist Church, and the Schomburg Center for Research in Black Culture which has resources documenting the history of African descent.

$ Banks

CF • Carver Federal Savings •
300 W 145th St [Frederick Douglass Blvd]
CI • Citibank •
2481 Adam Clayton Powell Jr Blvd [W 144th St]
CU • Municipal Credit Union (ATM) •
Harlem Hospital •506 Lenox Ave [W 135th St]

Community Gardens

Emergency Rooms

• **Harlem Hospital Center •**
506 Lenox Ave [135th]

O Landmarks

• **The 369th Regiment Armory •**
2366 Fifth Ave [142nd]
• **Abyssinian Baptist Church •**
132 Odell Clark Pl [Lenox]
• **The Dunbar Houses •**
Frederick Douglass Blvd & W 149th St
• **St Nicholas Historic District •**
202 W 138th St [7th Av]

Libraries

• **Countee Cullen •** 104 W 136th St [Lenox]
• **Macomb's Bridge •**
2650 Adam Clayton Powell Jr Blvd [152nd]
• **Schomburg Center for Research in Black Culture •** 515 Malcolm X Blvd [136th]

Post Offices

• **College Station •** 217 W 140th St [7th Av]
• **Colonial Park •** 99 Macombs Pl [154th]
• **Lincolnton •** 2265 Fifth Ave [138th]

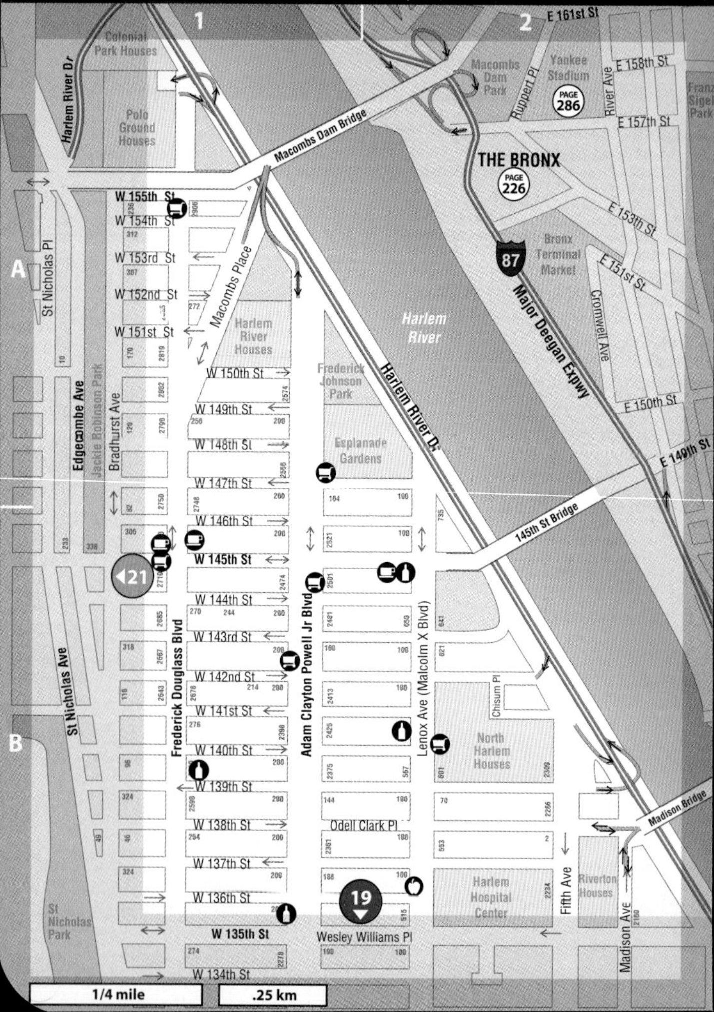

Map 22 · **Harlem (Upper)**

1

2 E 161st St

Colonial
Park Houses

E 158th St

Harlem River Dr.

Macombs
Dam Park

Ruppert Pl

Yankee
Stadium

River Ave

E 157th St

Franz
Sigel

Polo
Ground
Houses

PAGE
286

E 153rd St

Macombs Dam Bridge

THE BRONX

PAGE
226

St Nicholas Pl

W 155th St

W 154th St
312

87

Bronx
Terminal
Market

E 151st St

Cromwell Ave

A

W 153rd St
307

Macombs Place

W 152nd St

Harlem
River
Houses

Harlem
River

Major Deegan Expwy

E 150th St

W 151st St
170   2919

W 150th St   2574

18

Edgecombe Ave

W 149th St
258   200

Frederick
Johnson
Park

Harlem River Dr.

E 149th St

Bradhurst Ave

Jackie Robinson Park

2902

2796

W 148th St
200

Esplanade
Gardens

735

2748

W 147th St
164   100

2760

W 146th St
100

62

◀21

305
2718

W 145th St
2521

100

Frederick Douglass Blvd

2885

318

W 144th St
270   244   2474

Adam Clayton Powell Jr Blvd

2581

2567

2967

W 143rd St

W 142nd St
214   2481

Lenox Ave (Malcolm X Blvd)

2413

641

Chisum Pl

116   2643

276

W 141st St
2398   2425

2425

B

90

W 140th St
200   2375   567

North
Harlem
Houses

2006

324

2599

W 139th St
200

W 138th St
294   200

144   190

70

Fifth Ave

2006

Madison Bridge

63

324

W 137th St
200

Odell Clark Pl
2361   190   1553   2

Riverton
Houses

St
Nicholas
Park

W 136th St
180   186

**19
▼**

2034

Harlem
Hospital
Center

Madison Ave

274   2218

W 135th St
190   190

915

Wesley Williams Pl

W 134th St

1/4 mile	.25 km

Gentrification: the little word with the huge effects may have turned Harlem upside down, but with the Lenox Avenue and State Office Building Farmers Market on location, upper Harlem flips on the right side!

Coffee

• **Dunkin' Donuts** • 110 W 145th St [Lenox]
• **Dunkin' Donuts** •
  2730 Frederick Douglass Blvd [145th]
• **Starbucks** •
  301 W 145th St [Ferderick Douglass Blvd]

Farmers Markets

• **Harlem Hospital (Thu 8 am–5 pm Jul–Nov)** •
  Lenox Ave b/w 136th & 137th Sts

Liquor Stores

• **All-Rite Liquors** •
  2651 Frederick Douglass Blvd [142nd]
• **Friedland Wine & Liquor Store** •
  605 Lenox Ave [141st]
• **Harlem Discount Liquors** •
  2302 Adam Clayton Powell Jr Blvd [135th]
• **Luis Liquor** • 108 W 145th St [Lenox]

Supermarkets

• **Associated** • 2444 Seventh Ave [142nd]
• **Associated** •
  2927 Frederick Douglass Blvd [155th]
• **Met Food** •
  2541 Adam Clayton Powell Jr Blvd [147th]
• **Met Food** • 592 Lenox Ave [140th]
• **Pathmark** • 300 W 145th St [F Douglass] ♿
• **Pioneer** •
  2497 Adam Clayton Powell Jr Blvd [145th]

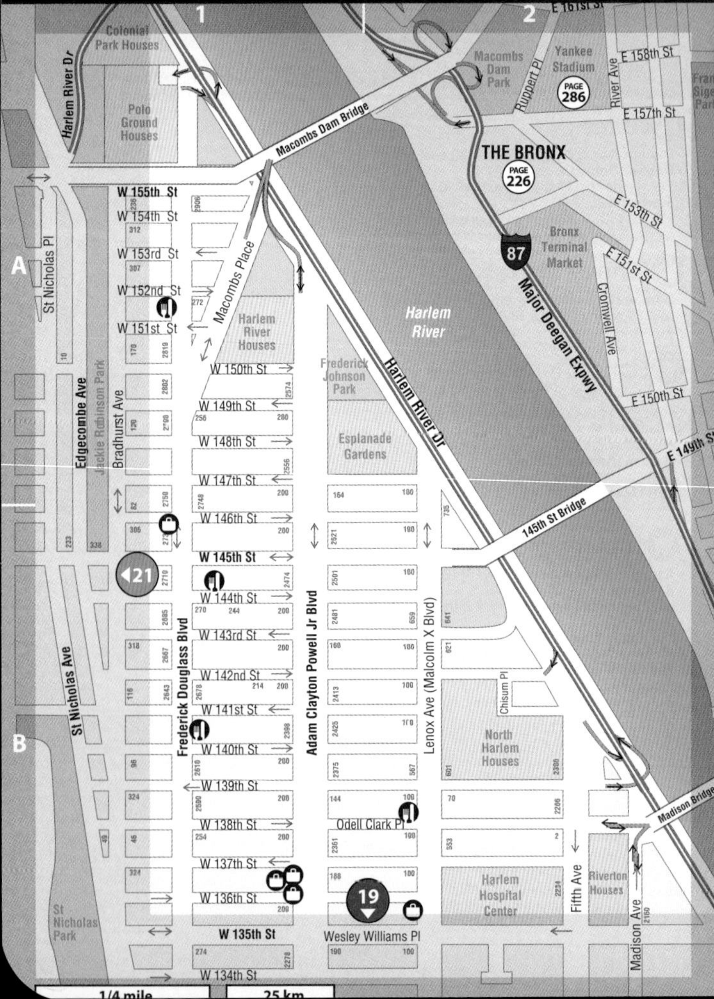

Map 22 · **Harlem (Upper)**

1

2

E 161st St

Colonial
Park Houses

Harlem River Dr

Polo
Ground
Houses

Macombs
Dam Park

Yankee
Stadium
PAGE
286

E 158th St

River Ave

E 157th St

Franz
Sigel
Park

Macombs Dam Bridge

THE BRONX
PAGE
226

E 153rd St

W 155th St

W 154th St

W 153rd St

W 152nd St

87

Bronx
Terminal
Market

Cromwell Ave

E 151st St

Macombs Place

St Nicholas Pl

A

W 151st St

Harlem
River
Houses

E 150th St

W 150th St

Frederick
Johnson
Park

Harlem River

Major Deegan Expwy

Harlem River Dr

E 149th St

Edgecombe Ave

Jackie Robinson Park

Bradhurst Ave

W 149th St

W 148th St

Esplanade
Gardens

W 147th St

W 146th St

W 145th St

145th St Bridge

‹21

W 144th St

W 143rd St

W 142nd St

Adam Clayton Powell Jr Blvd

Lenox Ave (Malcolm X Blvd)

W 141st St

Frederick Douglass Blvd

Chisum Pl

St Nicholas Ave

B

W 140th St

W 139th St

North
Harlem
Houses

Madison Bridge

W 138th St

Odell Clark Pl

Fifth Ave

Riverton
Houses

W 137th St

Harlem
Hospital
Center

Madison Ave

W 136th St

19 ▼

St
Nicholas
Park

W 135th St

Wesley Williams Pl

W 134th St

1/4 mile

25 km

145th and Adam Clayton Powell serve as the main arteries for this area, so be sure to check out Miss Maude's on Lenox for lunch or Charles' Southern-Style for classic fried chicken. Feel like shopping? Study denimology at the Denim Library and get fashionable at the B Oyama Homme.

 Restaurants

- **Charles' Southern-Style Kitchen •**
  2839 Frederick Douglass Blvd [151st]
- **Londel's Supper Club •**
  2620 Frederick Douglass Blvd [140th]
- **Margie's Red Rose •**
  275 W 144th St [F Douglass]
- **Miss Maude's •** 547 Lenox Ave [138th]

 Shopping

- **B Oyama Homme •** 2330 Seventh Ave [137th]
- **Baskin-Robbins •**
  2730 Frederick Douglass Blvd [145th]
- **Denim Library •** 2326 Seventh Ave [137th]
- **Montgomery's •** 2312 Seventh Ave [136th]
- **New York Public Library Shop •**
  Schomburg Ctr • 515 Lenox Ave [136th]

Map 22 · **Harlem (Upper)**

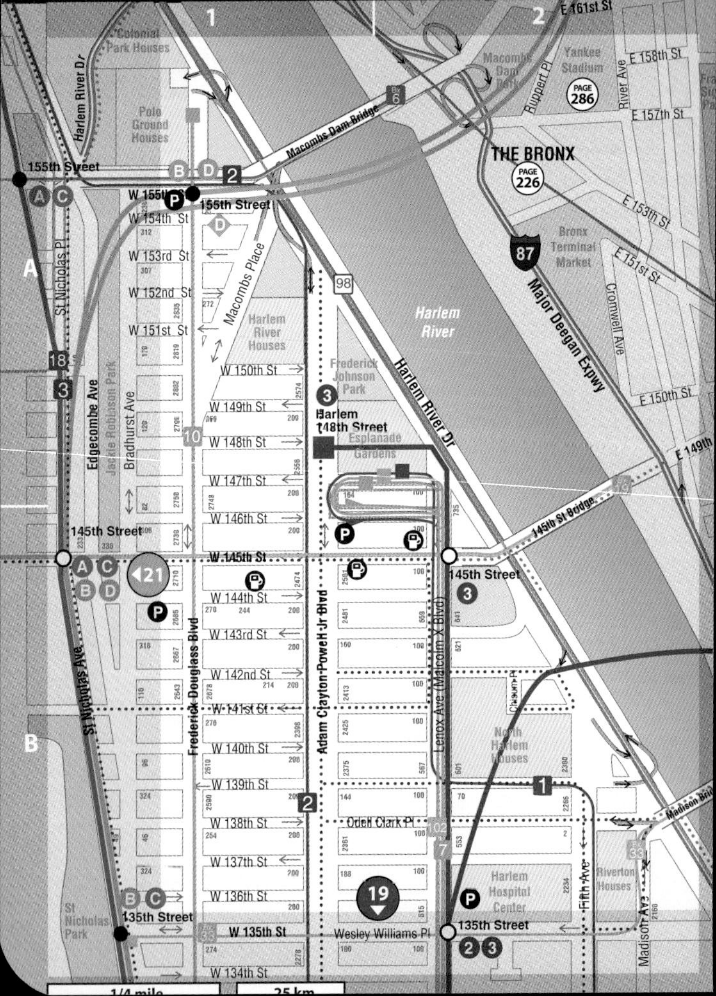

N

1

2

E 161st St

Colonial
Park Houses

Harlem River Dr

E 158th St

Macombs
Dam Park

Ruppert Pl

Yankee
Stadium

E 157th St

River Ave

PAGE
286

Polo
Ground
Houses

6

Macombs Dam Bridge

THE BRONX

PAGE
226

E 153rd St

Bronx
Terminal
Market

E 151st St

Cromwell Ave

155th Street

B D

2

A C

W 155th

155th Street

D

W 154th St

312

W 153rd St

357

Macombs Place

W 152nd St

272

W 151st St

178

Harlem
River
Houses

2910

87

98

Major Deegan Expwy

Harlem
River

E 150th St

St Nicholas Pl

Edgecombe Ave

Jackie Robinson Park

Bradhurst Ave

A

18

3

W 150th St

129

2574

Frederick
Johnson
Park

Harlem River Dr

E 149th St

170

W 149th St

200

2802

289

3

Harlem
148th Street

Esplanade
Gardens

145th St Bridge

2750

W 148th St

200

2308

10

W 147th St

164

100

735

62

2749

W 146th St

200

145th Street

A C

2738

506

538

W 145th St

2716

21

44

W 144th St

276

2474

2481

200

1609

641

P

145th Street

3

B D

P

St Nicholas Ave

Frederick Douglass Blvd

Adam Clayton Powell Jr Blvd

Lenox Ave (Malcolm X) Blvd

2605

276

W 143rd St

200

318

2567

W 142nd St

214

200

4413

567

601

156

2390

W 141st St

276

North
Harlem
Houses

2610

W 140th St

2375

3980

324

W 139th St

144

100

70

1

2266

254

W 138th St

200

2

324

W 137th St

200

Odell Clark Pl

102

7

553

Riverton
Houses

19

Harlem
Hospital
Center

Fifth Ave

B C

W 136th St

200

P

135th Street

St
Nicholas
Park

274

W 135th St

Wesley Williams Pl

2 3

Madison Ave

Madison Bridge

190

100

W 134th St

1/4 mile

.25 km

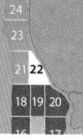
Driving is actually negotiable on all streets, and there's usually plenty of parking if you circle the block. With quick access to the FDR and the 145th Street Bridge, it's a good place to pull off and explore.

Subways

② ③	135th St
③	145th St
③	Harlem-148th St
Ⓐ Ⓒ Ⓑ Ⓓ	145th St
Ⓐ Ⓒ	155th St
Ⓑ Ⓒ	135th St
Ⓑ Ⓓ	155th St

Bus Lines

1	Fifth Ave/Madison Ave
10	Seventh Ave/Eighth Ave (Central Park West)/Frederick Douglass Blvd
102	Third Ave/Lexington Ave/Malcolm X Blvd
2	Fifth Ave/Madison Ave/Powell Blvd
7	Columbus Ave/Amsterdam Ave/ Sixth Ave/Seventh Ave/Broadway
98	Washington Heights/Midtown
M19	145th St Crosstown
M33	135th St Crosstown
Bx6	E 161st St/E 163rd St

Bike Lanes

- • • • Marked Bike Lanes
- • • • Recommended Route
- • • • Greenway

 Gas Stations

- **Hess** • 120 W 145th St [Lenox] ⌚
- **Mobil** • 150 W 145th St [Lenox] ⌚
- **Shell** • 232 W 145th St [7th Av] ⌚

Ⓟ Parking

Map 23 · **Washington Heights**

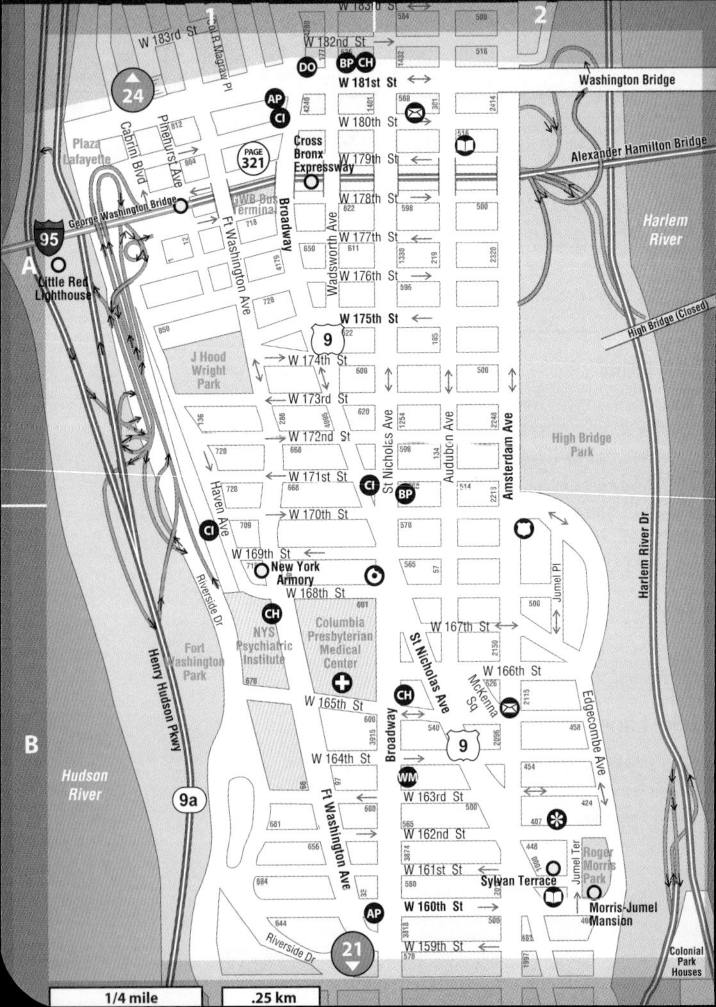

W 183rd St
W 182nd St
1
2

DO
BP CH
W 181st St
AP CI
W 180th St
Washington Bridge

Plaza Lafayette
24

Pinehurst Ave
Cabrini Blvd

Alexander Hamilton Bridge

PAGE 321

Cross Bronx Expressway
W 179th St
W 178th St

Harlem River

George Washington Bridge

FWB Bus Terminal
Broadway

Ft Washington Ave
Wadsworth Ave

W 177th St
W 176th St

95

A

Little Red Lighthouse

W 175th St
9

High Bridge (Closed)

W 174th St
W 173rd St

J Hood Wright Park

W 172nd St
W 171st St

High Bridge Park

St Nicholas Ave
Audubon Ave
Amsterdam Ave

Haven Ave

BP

C

W 170th St
W 169th St

New York Armory

W 168th St

Jumel Pl
Harlem River Dr

Columbia Presbyterian Medical Center

CH
NYS Psychiatric Institute

W 167th St
W 166th St

St Nicholas Ave
McKenna St
Edgecombe Ave

Riverside Dr

Fort Washington Park

+
W 165th St

CH
9
Broadway

W 164th St

B

Henry Hudson Pkwy

Hudson River

9a

WM
W 163rd St
W 162nd St

454
424

W 161st St

448

Jumel Ter

Roger Morris Park

Sylvan Terrace
Morris-Jumel Mansion

AP
W 160th St
W 159th St

Riverside Dr
21

Colonial Park Houses

1/4 mile
.25 km

Essentials

Map 23

They didn't name a musical after the 'Heights' for nothing. This northern tip of Manhattan is the Central America-cum-hardware capital of New York. Complete with bodegas and shops with building materials and home improvement tools, the Heights gets you high off fun and hard work.

Bagels
• **Mike's Bagels** • 4003 Broadway [168th]

Banks
AP • Apple • 3815 Broadway [W 159th St]
AP • Apple • 706 W 181st St [Broadway]
BP • Banco Popular •
1200 St Nicholas Ave [W 170th St]
BP • Banco Popular •
615 W 181st St [St Nicholas Ave]
CH • Chase • 1421 St Nicholas Ave [W 181st St]
CH • Chase •
180 Ft Washington Ave [W 168th St]
CH • Chase • 3940 Broadway [W 165th St]
CI • Citibank • 4249 Broadway [W 180th St]
CI • Citibank (ATM) •
4058 Broadway [W 171st St]
CI • Citibank (ATM) •
60 Haven Ave [W 170th St]
DO • Doral • 4246 Broadway [W 180th St]
WM • Washington Mutual •
3910 Broadway [W 164th St]

Community Gardens

Emergency Rooms
• **New York-Presbyterian Hospital/Columbia University Medical Center** •
622 W 168th St [B'way]

Landmarks
• **Cross Bronx Expressway** • n/a
• **George Washington Bridge** •
W 178th St [Henry Hudson]
• **Little Red Lighthouse** •
under the George Washington Bridge [178th]
• **Morris-Jumel Mansion** •
Edgecombe Ave & 161st St
• **New York Armory** •
216 Ft Washington Ave [169th]
• **Sylvan Terrace** •
b/w Jumel Ter & St Nicholas Ave

Libraries
• **Fort Washington** • 535 W 179th St [Audubon]
• **Washington Heights** •
1000 St Nicholas Ave [160th]

Police
• **33rd Precinct** • 2207 Amsterdam Ave [170th]

Post Offices
• **Audubon** • 511 W 165th St [Amsterdam]
• **Sergeant Riayan A Tejeda** •
555 W 180th St [Audubon]

Map 23 · **Washington Heights**

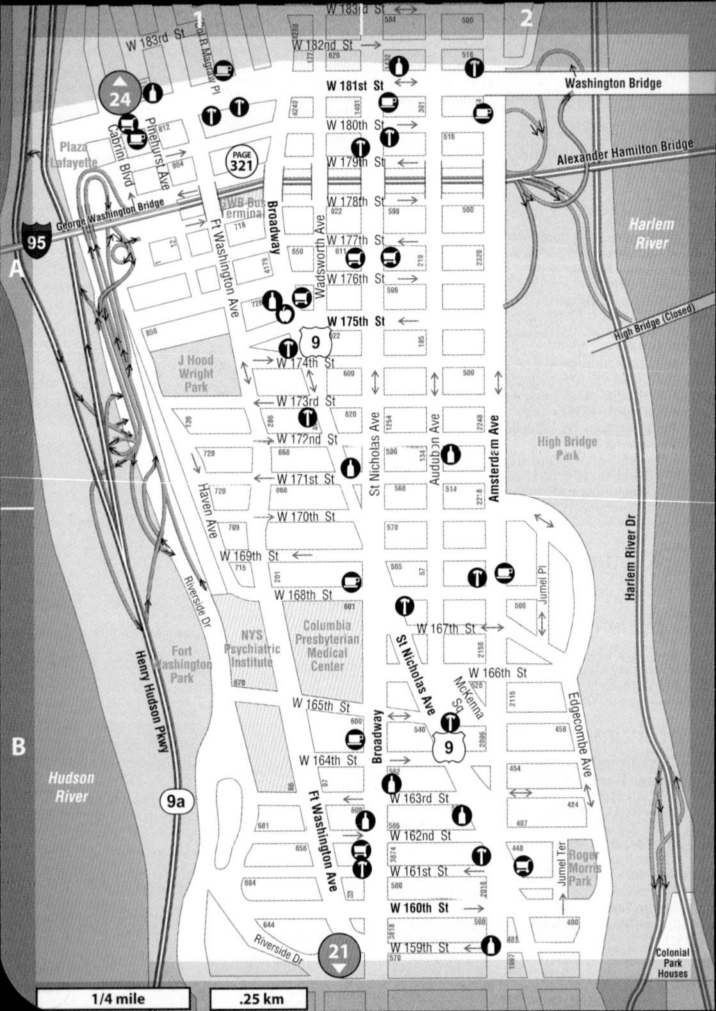

W 183rd St

W 183rd St

W 182nd St

24

W 181st St

Plaza
Lafayette

W 180th St

PAGE
321

W 179th St

Washington Bridge

GWB Bus
Terminal

Alexander Hamilton Bridge

Pinehurst Ave

Cabrini Blvd

Ft Washington Ave

Broadway

Wadsworth Ave

W 178th St

**Harlem
River**

George Washington Bridge

W 177th St

95

W 176th St

W 175th St

9

W 174th St

High Bridge (Closed)

J Hood
Wright
Park

W 173rd St

W 172nd St

St Nicholas Ave

Audubon Ave

Amsterdam Ave

**High Bridge
Park**

W 171st St

W 170th St

Haven Ave

W 169th St

W 168th St

Harlem River Dr

Riverside Dr

NYS
Psychiatric
Institute

W 167th St

Jumel Pl

Columbia
Presbyterian
Medical
Center

St Nicholas Ave

W 166th St

McKenna

Henry Hudson Pkwy

Fort
Washington
Park

W 165th St

B

Broadway

Edgecombe Ave

9

**Hudson
River**

W 164th St

9a

Ft Washington Ave

W 163rd St

W 162nd St

Jumel Ter

W 161st St

**Roger
Morris
Park**

W 160th St

W 159th St

Riverside Dr

21

**Colonial
Park
Houses**

1/4 mile

.25 km

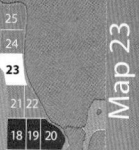

Map 23

The Heights is now facing a cultural and economic makeover. While there, experience your own renaissance by going green and organic at Karrot Cabrini and snagging all the wines you can for under $20 at Cabrini Wines & Liquors.

☕ Coffee

- **Chris Coffee Shop** •
  500 W 168th St [Amsterdam]
- **Dunkin' Donuts** •
  1206 St Nicholas Ave [170th]
- **Dunkin' Donuts** •
  1416 St Nicholas Ave [181st]
- **Dunkin' Donuts** •
  2420 Amsterdam Ave [181st]
- **Dunkin' Donuts** •
  728 W 181st St [Col R Magaw]
- **Jodie's Coffee Shop** • 3915 Broadway [164th]
- **Jou Jou** • 603 W 168th St [B'way]
- **Starbucks** • 803 W 181st St [Ft Wash]
- **X Caffe** • 3952 Broadway [165th]

🍎 Farmers Markets

- **175th Street**
  (Thurs, 8 am–6 pm, June–Nov) •
  W 175th St & Broadway

🔧 Hardware Stores

- **3841 Hardware** • 3841 Broadway [160th]
- **756 Hardware** • 756 W 181st St [Col R Magaw]
- **AHS Hardware** • 2416 Amsterdam Ave [180th]
- **AT Mini Hardware** •
  1388 St Nicholas Ave [180th]
- **Chavin Hardware** •
  1348 St Nicholas Ave [177th]
- **E&T Hardware** • 4087 Broadway [172nd]
- **Ernesto's Hardware Store** •
  2180 Amsterdam Ave [168th]
- **EZ Open Hardware** •
  2304 Amsterdam Ave [174th]
- **Ferreteria Hardware** •
  1087 St Nicholas Ave [164th]
- **Nunez Hardware** • 4147 Broadway [175th]
- **Taveras Hardware** •
  2029 Amsterdam Ave [161st]
- **Washington Heights Hardware** •
  736 W 181st St [Col R Magaw]

🍾 Liquor Stores

- **Cabrini Wines & Liquors** •
  831 W 181st St [Cabrini]
- **Galicia Liquors** • 3906 Broadway [158th]
- **Guadalupe Barbara** • 4084 Broadway [172nd]
- **Heights Liquor Supermarket** •
  547 W 181st St [Audubon]
- **In Good Spirits** • 3879 Broadway [162nd]
- **Mora Liquor** • 2001 Amsterdam Ave [159th]
- **O&J Liquors** • 1045 St Nicholas Ave [162nd]
- **Vargas Liquor Store** •
  114 Audubon Ave [171st]

🛒 Supermarkets

- **Associated** • 3871 Broadway [162nd]
- **Bravo Supermarket** •
  1331 St Nicholas Ave [177th]
- **C-Town** • 1016 St Nicholas Ave [161st]
- **C-Town** • 1314 St Nicholas Ave [176th]
- **Gristedes** • 4037 Broadway [170th]
- **Karrot Cabrini** • 854 W 181st St [Cabrini]

Map 23 · **Washington Heights**

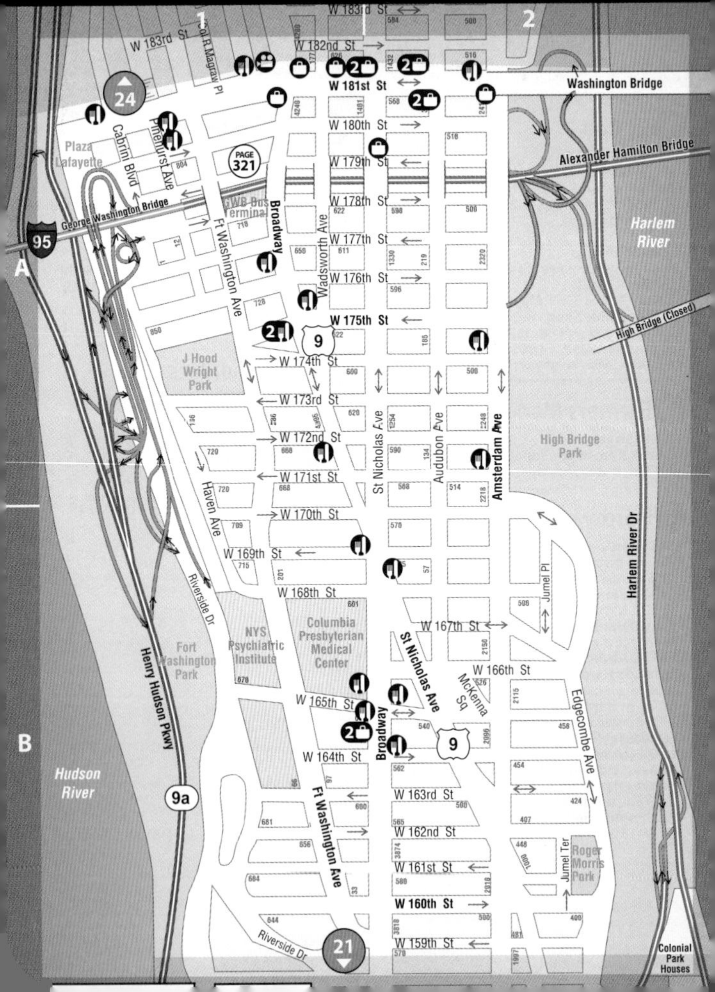

W 183rd St

W 182nd St

W 181st St

Washington Bridge

W 180th St

Alexander Hamilton Bridge

W 179th St

W 178th St

Harlem River

W 177th St

Plaza Lafayette

Cabrini Blvd

Pinehurst Ave

PAGE 321

GWB Bus Terminal

Broadway

Wadsworth Ave

W 176th St

W 175th St

9

W 174th St

J Hood Wright Park

High Bridge (Closed)

95

George Washington Bridge

Ft Washington Ave

W 173rd St

W 172nd St

St Nicholas Ave

Audubon Ave

Amsterdam Ave

High Bridge Park

Haven Ave

W 171st St

W 170th St

Harlem River Dr

W 169th St

Riverside Dr

W 168th St

Fort Washington Park

NYS Psychiatric Institute

Columbia Presbyterian Medical Center

W 167th St

Jumel Pl

W 166th St

McKenna Sq

Edgecombe Ave

9a

W 165th St

St Nicholas Ave

Hudson River

Broadway

9

W 164th St

W 163rd St

W 162nd St

Ft Washington Ave

Jumel Ter

Roger Morris Park

W 161st St

W 160th St

Henry Hudson Pkwy

21

Riverside Dr

W 159th St

Colonial Park Houses

24

Entertainment

Map 23

Take a stroll down 181st and get slayed by the lively sounds and chaos of the neighborhood. The restaurants are primarily Dominican, but you can get All-American at Dallas BBQ or enjoy Dominican and Chinese at Jimmy Oro Restaurant.

Movie Theaters
• **New Coliseum Theatre** •
701 W 181st St [B'way]

Restaurants
• **Aqua Marina** • 4060 Broadway [171st]
• **Carrot Top Pastries** • 3931 Broadway [165th]
• **Coogan's** • 4015 Broadway [169th]
• **Dallas BBQ** • 3956 Broadway [166th]
• **El Conde Steak House** •
4139 Broadway [175th]
• **El Malecon** • 4141 Broadway [175th] ⊕
• **El Ranchito** • 4129 Broadway [175th]
• **Genesis** • 511 W 181st St [Amsterdam Av]
• **Hispaniola** • 839 W 181st St [Cabrini]
• **Jesse's Place** • 812 W 181st St [Pinehurst]
• **Jimmy Oro Restaurant** •
711 W 181st St [B'way]
• **Parrilla** • 3920 Broadway [164th]
• **Reme Restaurant** • 4021 Broadway [169th]
• **Restaurant Tenares** •
2306 Amsterdam Ave [161st]
• **Taino Restaurant** •
2228 Amsterdam Ave [171st]
• **Tipico Dominicano** •
4177 Broadway [177th] ⊕

Shopping
• **Baskin-Robbins** •
728 W 181st St [Col R Magaw]
• **Carrot Top Pastries** • 3931 Broadway [165th]
• **The Children's Place** •
600 W 181st St [St Nicholas]
• **Chung Haeum** • 566 W 181st St [Audubon Av]
• **Fever** • 1387 St Nicholas Ave [180th]
• **Foot Locker** • 621 W 181st St [St Nicholas]
• **FootCo** • 1422 St Nicholas Ave [181st]
• **Goodwill Industries** •
512 W 181st St [Amsterdam]
• **Modell's** • 606 W 181st St [St Nicholas]
• **Payless Shoe Source** •
556 W 181st St [Audubon]
• **Planet Girls** • 3923 Broadway [164th]
• **Santana Banana** •
661 W 181st St [Wadsworth]
• **Tribeca** • 655 W 181st St [Wadsworth]
• **VIM** • 561 W 181st St [Audubon]

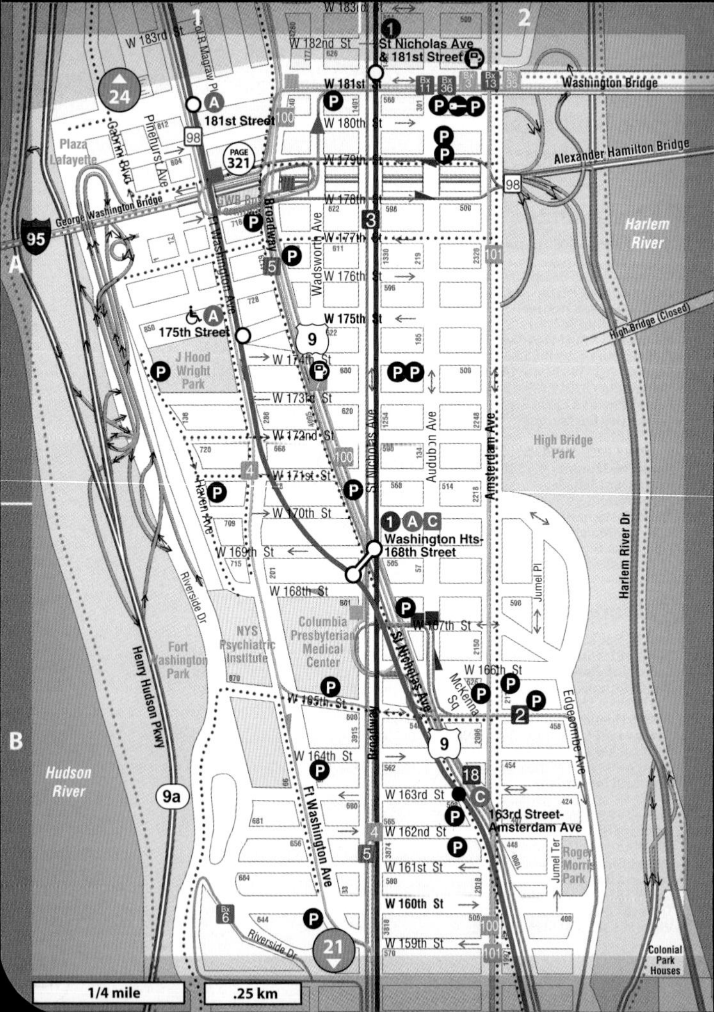

Map 23 · Washington Heights

W 183rd St

W 182nd St

St Nicholas Ave & 181st Street

W 181st St

Washington Bridge

A 181st Street

PAGE 321

W 180th St

W 179th St

Alexander Hamilton Bridge

George Washington Bridge

W 178th St

Harlem River

95

A

W 177th St

Wadsworth Ave

W 176th St

High Bridge (Closed)

W 175th St

A 175th Street

9

J Hood Wright Park

W 174th St

W 173rd St

W 172nd St

High Bridge Park

4 W 171st St

Audubon Ave

Amsterdam Ave

Harlem River Dr

W 170th St

W 169th St

1 A C Washington Hts-168th Street

W 168th St

NYS Psychiatric Institute

Fort Washington Park

Columbia Presbyterian Medical Center

Jumel Pl

W 167th St

W 166th St

Riverside Dr

McKellar Sq

W 165th St

9

2

Hudson River

W 164th St

Edgecombe Ave

B

9a

W 163rd St

18

C 163rd Street-Amsterdam Ave

W 162nd St

Fort Washington Ave

4

5

W 161st St

Jumel Ter

Roger Morris Park

W 160th St

W 159th St

Riverside Dr

6

21

Colonial Park Houses

1/4 mile   .25 km

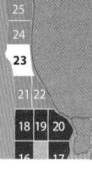

As you may note, this area acts as a hub for the GWB and the Cross Bronx Expressway. When on the main roads, just pay attention to where you're going. Use Amsterdam or St. Nick's for north-south travel. Once on the little streets, parking won't be too difficult.

Subways

① .... St Nicholas Ave &181st St
Ⓐ .... 175th St
Ⓐ .... 181st St
① **Ⓐ** **Ⓒ** .... 168th St-Washington Hts
Ⓒ .... 163rd St-Amsterdam Ave

Bus Lines

100 .... Amsterdam Ave/Broadway/125th St
101 . Third and Lexington Aves/Malcolm X Blvd
18 .... Convent Ave
2 .... Fifth and Madison Aves/
Adam Clayton Powell Jr Blvd
3 .. Fifth and Madison Aves/St Nicholas Ave
4 .... Fifth and Madison Aves/Broadway
5 .... Fifth Ave/Sixth Ave/Riverside Dr
98 .... Washington Heights/Midtown
Bx 11 .... to Southern Blvd via 170th St
Bx 13 .... to Yankee Stadium via Ogden Ave
Bx 3 .... to Riverdale, 238th St-Broadway
Bx 35 .... to West Farms Rd via 167th St
Bx 36 to Olmstead Ave/Randall Ave via 180th St
Bx 7 .... Riverdale Ave/Broadway

Bike Lanes

- • • • Marked Bike Lanes
- • • • Recommended Route
- • • • Greenway

 ## Car Rental

• **Uptown Car Rental** • 506 W 181st St [Amsterdam]

Gas Stations

• **Shell** • 2420 Amsterdam Ave [181st] ⌖
• **Shell** • 4116 Broadway [174th]

Parking

Map 24 · **Fort George / Fort Tryon**

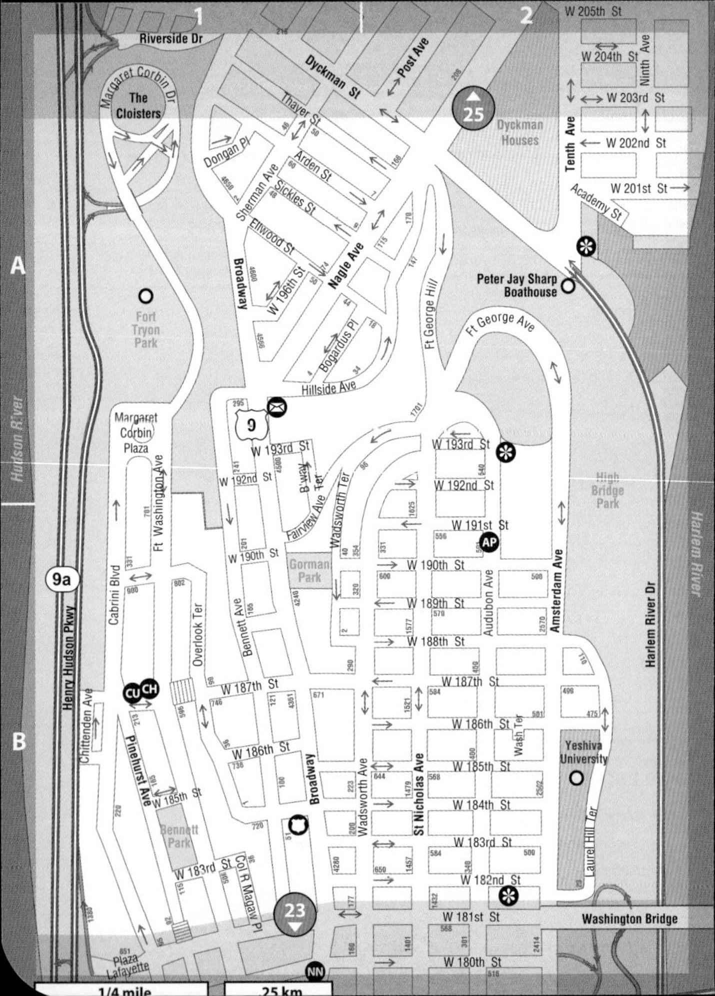

Riverside Dr

W 205th St
W 204th St
Ninth Ave
W 203rd St
Tenth Ave
W 202nd St
W 201st St
Academy St

Dyckman St
Post Ave

Thayer St

Dyckman Houses

25

Arden St
Dongan Pl
Sherman Ave
Sickles St

The Cloisters

Margaret Corbin Dr

Ellwood St

Broadway

W 196th St

Nagle Ave

Peter Jay Sharp Boathouse

Fort Tryon Park

Bogardus Pl

Ft George Hill

Ft George Ave

Hillside Ave

High Bridge Park

Hudson River

Harlem River

9

Margaret Corbin Plaza

W 193rd St
W 192nd St

W 193rd St
W 192nd St

Ft Washington Ave

B'way

Wadsworth Ter

Fairview Ave

W 191st St

W 190th St

AP

Cabrini Blvd

Gorman Park

W 190th St

Audubon Ave

Amsterdam Ave

9a

Bennett Ave

W 189th St
W 188th St

Overlook Ter

W 187th St

W 187th St

CU CH

W 186th St

Wadsworth Ave

St Nicholas Ave

Wadit Ter

Harlem River Dr

Chittenden Ave

Pinehurst Ave

Broadway

W 186th St
W 185th St
W 184th St
W 183rd St

Yeshiva University

Bennett Park

W 185th St

Laurel Hill Ter

Col R Magaw Pl

W 183rd St

W 182nd St

23

W 181st St

Washington Bridge

Plaza Lafayette

W 180th St

NN

1/4 mile
25 km

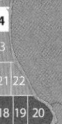
This quaint little town is great for epic walks, and one of the only places in Manhattan that's still got its lovely lady lumps. The curvy streets in the center are best—extremely steep as scarily winding. Fort Tryon Park is a must-see for soaking in greenery and awesome river views.

Banks

AP • Apple (ATM) • Isabella Geriatric Center •
515 Audubon Ave [W 191st St]
CH • Chase •
596 Ft Washington Ave [W 187th St]
**CU • Lower East Side People's Federal
Credit Union (ATM)** • Parikh News •
814 W 187th St [Pinehurst Ave]
NN • New York National •
4211 Broadway [W 179th St]

Community Gardens

O Landmarks

• **Fort Tryon Park** • Ft Washington Ave
• **Peter Jay Sharp Boathouse** •
Swindler Cove Park
• **Yeshiva University Main Building (Zysman
Hall)** • Amsterdam Ave & W 187th St

 Police

• **34th Precinct** • 4295 Broadway [184th]

Post Offices

• **Fort George** • 4558 Broadway [Hillside]

Map 24 • **Fort George / Fort Tryon**

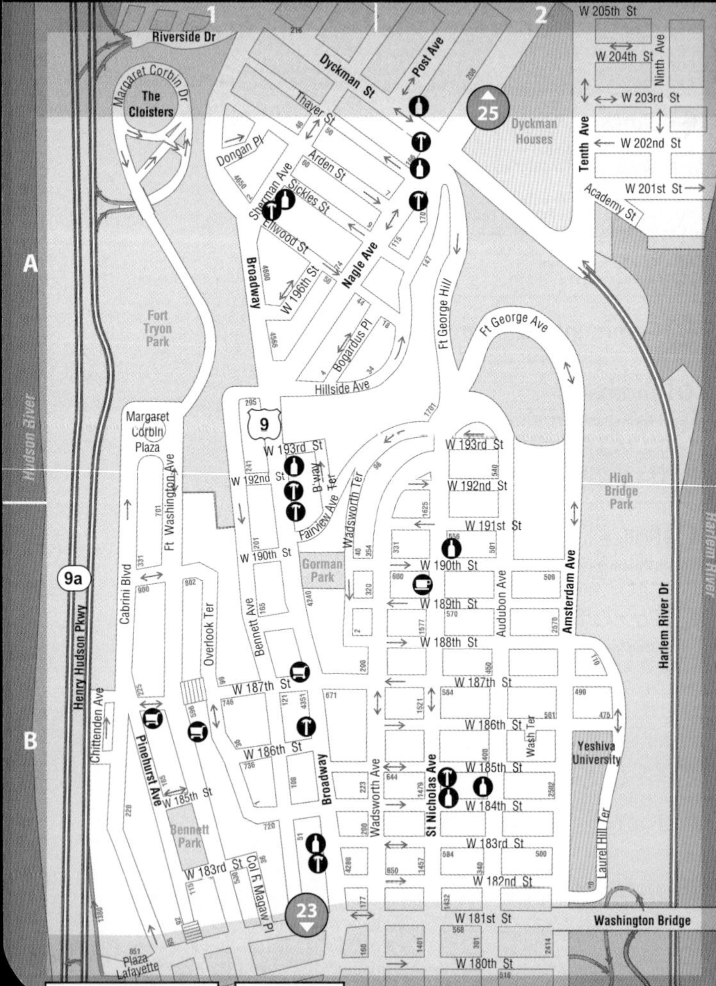

Riverside Dr

1

2

W 205th St

W 204th St

Ninth Ave

Dyckman St

Post Ave

W 203rd St

Tenth Ave

W 202nd St

Dyckman Houses

25

Academy St

W 201st St

Margaret Corbin Dr

The Cloisters

Thayer St

Dongan Pl

Arden St

Sherman Ave

Sickles St

Ellwood St

W 196th St

Naple Ave

Broadway

Fort Tryon Park

Bogardus Pl

Hillside Ave

Ft George Hill

Ft George Ave

Margaret Corbin Plaza

9

W 193rd St

B-way

W 192nd St

Fairview Ave Ter

Wadsworth Ter

W 193rd St

W 192nd St

High Bridge Park

W 191st St

Ft Washington Ave

W 190th St

W 190th St

Audubon Ave

Amsterdam Ave

9a

Cabrini Blvd

Overlook Ter

Bennett Ave

Gorman Park

W 189th St

W 188th St

W 187th St

W 187th St

Wash Ter

Henry Hudson Pkwy

Chittenden Ave

Pinehurst Ave

W 186th St

W 185th St

Wadsworth Ave

W 186th St

St Nicholas Ave

Yeshiva University

B

Bennett Park

W 183rd St

Broadway

W 185th St

W 184th St

W 183rd St

Laurel Hill Ter

Harlem River Dr

Plaza Lafayette

23

W 181st St

W 180th St

W 182nd St

Washington Bridge

Hudson River

Harlem River

A

1/4 mile

.25 km

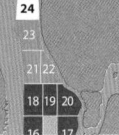
Fort George/Fort Tryon is the name given to the area south of Dyckman Street. Only a 25-minute subway ride from midtown, this area is filled with tree-lined streets and neighborhood shops and eateries.

Coffee

- **Angela's Coffee Shop** •
  805 W 187th St [Ft Wash]
- **Dunkin' Donuts** •
  1599 St Nicholas Ave [190th]

Hardware Stores

- **Apex Supply** • 4580 Broadway [196th]
- **Blue Bell Lumber** • 4309 Broadway [184th]
- **Century Hardware** • 4309 Broadway [184th]
- **Nagle Hardware Store** •
  145 Nagle Ave [Arden]
- **St Nicholas Hardware** •
  1488 St Nicholas Ave [185th]
- **Supreme Hardware** • 106 Dyckman St [Nagle]
- **Victor Hardware Store** •
  25 Sherman Ave [Sickles]
- **VNJ Hardware** • 4476 Broadway [192nd]

Liquor Stores

- **185th Street Liquor Store** •
  4329 Broadway [184th]
- **Alex's Liquor Store** •
  1598 St Nicholas Ave [190th]
- **Dyckman Liquors** • 121 Dyckman St [Post]
- **J&P Discount Liquors** •
  377 Audubon Ave [184th]
- **New York Liquors** • 154 Nagle Ave [Thayer]
- **Sanchez Liquors** •
  4500 Broadway Bsmt [192nd]
- **Sherman Liquor** • 25 Sherman Ave [Sickles]
- **Yuan & Yuan Wine & Liquors** •
  1492 St Nicholas Ave [185th]

Supermarkets

- **Associated** • 592 Ft Washington Ave [187th]
- **Frank's Meat Market** •
  807 W 187th St [Ft Wash]
- **Key Food** • 4365 Broadway [187th]

Restaurants

- **107 West** • 811 W 187th St [Ft Wash]
- **Bleu Evolution** • 808 W 187th St [Ft Wash]
- **Caridad Restaurant** • 4311 Broadway [184th]
- **New Leaf Café** •
  1 Margaret Corbin Dr [Henry Hudson]
- **Rancho Jubilee** • 1 Nagle Ave [Hillside]

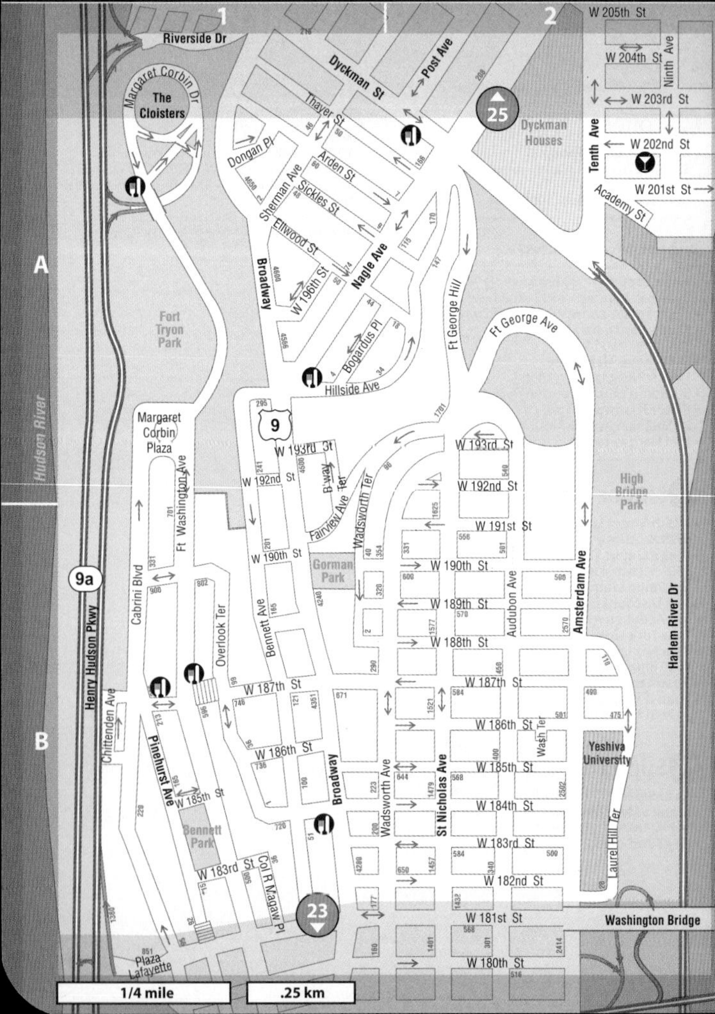

Map 24 · **Fort George / Fort Tryon**

N

W 205th St

Riverside Dr

Dyckman St

Post Ave

W 204th St

Ninth Ave

25

W 203rd St

Thayer St

Dyckman
Houses

Tenth Ave

W 202nd St

Arden St

Dongan Pl

W 201st St

The
Cloisters

Sherman Ave

Sickles St

Academy St

Margaret Corbin Dr

Elwood St

Nagle Ave

A

W 196th St

Ft George Hill

Broadway

Fort Tryon
Park

Ft George Ave

Bogardus Pl

Hillside Ave

9

W 193rd St

W 193rd St

High
Bridge
Park

B-way

Margaret
Corbin
Plaza

W 192nd St

Fairview Ave Ter

W 192nd St

Wadsworth Ave

Hudson River

W 191st St

Ft Washington Ave

W 190th St

W 190th St

9a

Cabrini Blvd

Bennett Ave

Audubon Ave

W 189th St

Amsterdam Ave

Gorman
Park

W 188th St

Overlook Ter

W 187th St

W 187th St

Henry Hudson Pkwy

Wash Ter

B

Chittenden Ave

W 186th St

W 186th Ter

Yeshiva
University

W 185th St

Pinehurst Ave

W 165th St

Wadsworth Ave

St Nicholas Ave

W 184th St

Broadway

Laurel Hill Ter

W 183rd St

Col R Magaw Pl

Harlem River Dr

Bennett
Park

W 183rd St

23

Washington Bridge

Plaza
Lafayette

W 181st St

W 180th St

1/4 mile   .25 km

This is a quiet residential neighborhood that welcomes families of all types, so expect kid-friendly restaurants and bars where everybody knows your name. Couples and crowds of singles agree on one thing: in season, the New Leaf Café is the best spot for drinks or dinner with a side of sunset.

Nightlife

• **Umbrella Bar & Lounge** •
  440 W 202nd St [9th Av]

Restaurants

• **107 West** • 811 W 187th St [Ft Wash]
• **809 Sangria Bar** • 112 Dyckman St [Nagle Av]
• **Bleu Evolution** • 808 W 187th St [Ft Wash]
• **Caridad Restaurant** • 4311 Broadway [184th]
• **New Leaf Café** •
  1 Margaret Corbin Dr [Henry Hudson]
• **Rancho Jubilee** • 1 Nagle Ave [Hillside]

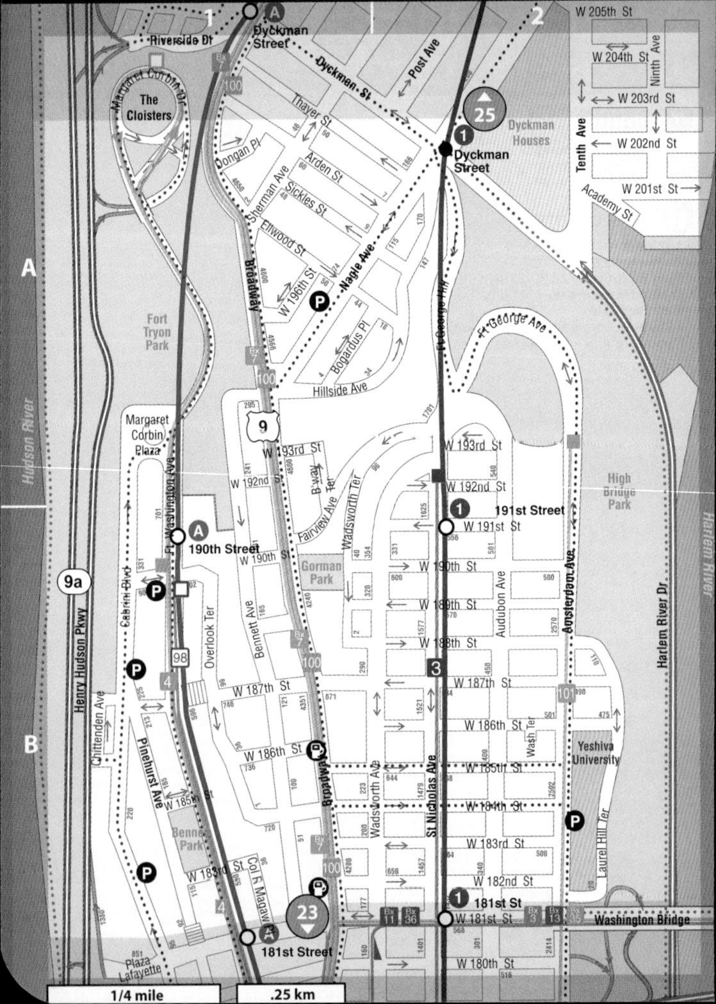

Map 24 · **Fort George / Fort Tryon**

N

1

2

Riverside Dr

Dyckman Street

Dyckman St

Post Ave

W 205th St

W 204th St

Ninth Ave

W 203rd St

Tenth Ave

W 202nd St

W 201st St

Academy St

Margaret Corbin Dr

The Cloisters

Thayer St

Arden St

Sickles St

Sherman Ave

Dongan Pl

100

Dyckman Houses

25

1 Dyckman Street

Elwood St

Nagle Ave

Broadway

W 196th St

P

Boradius Pl

Fort George Ave

Fort George Ave

Hillside Ave

Fort Tryon Park

Margaret Corbin Plaza

100

9

298

241

W 193rd St

W 192nd St

B-way

Fairview Ave

Wadsworth Ter

W 193rd St

W 192nd St

High Bridge Park

A 190th Street

Ft Washington Ave

701

W 190th Ter

Gorman Park

Overlook Ter

W 190th St

1 191st Street
W 191st St

Audubon Ave

Amsterdam Ave

Harlem River Dr

9a

Henry Hudson Pkwy

Cabrini Blvd

P

4

98

Bennett Ave

W 189th St

W 188th St

3

Wadsworth Ave

W 187th St

W 186th St

Wash Ter

101

Hudson River

Harlem River

Chittenden Ave

A

B

P

Pinehurst Ave

W 186th St

W 185th St

100

Broadway

P

Wadsworth Ave

St Nicholas Ave

W 185th St

W 184th St

W 183rd St

Yeshiva University

Laurel Hill Ter

P

Bennett Park

Col. Magaw Pl

W 182nd St

P

23

100

4

1 181st Street
W 181st St

Plaza Lafayette

A 181st Street

W 180th St

Washington Bridge

1/4 mile   .25 km

Transportation

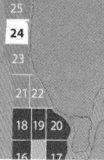

Map 24

Passing through via Broadway or St. Nick's is easy, but navigating the narrow streets can be rough. Parking is a notorious problem so get used to driving in circles. On a warm spring day, walking from the 190th A stop to the Cloisters is the best commute around.

Subways

1	181st St
1	191st St
1	Dyckman St
A	181st St
A	190th St
A	Dyckman St

Bus Lines

100	Broadway
100	Amsterdam Ave
3	St Nicholas Ave
4	Ft Washington Ave
98	Ft Washington Ave
7	Broadway

Bike Lanes

- • • • Marked Bike Lanes
- • • • Recommended Route
- • • • Greenway

 Gas Stations

- **BP** • 4353 Broadway [186th]
- **Rammco Service Station** •
  4275 Broadway [182nd]

Parking

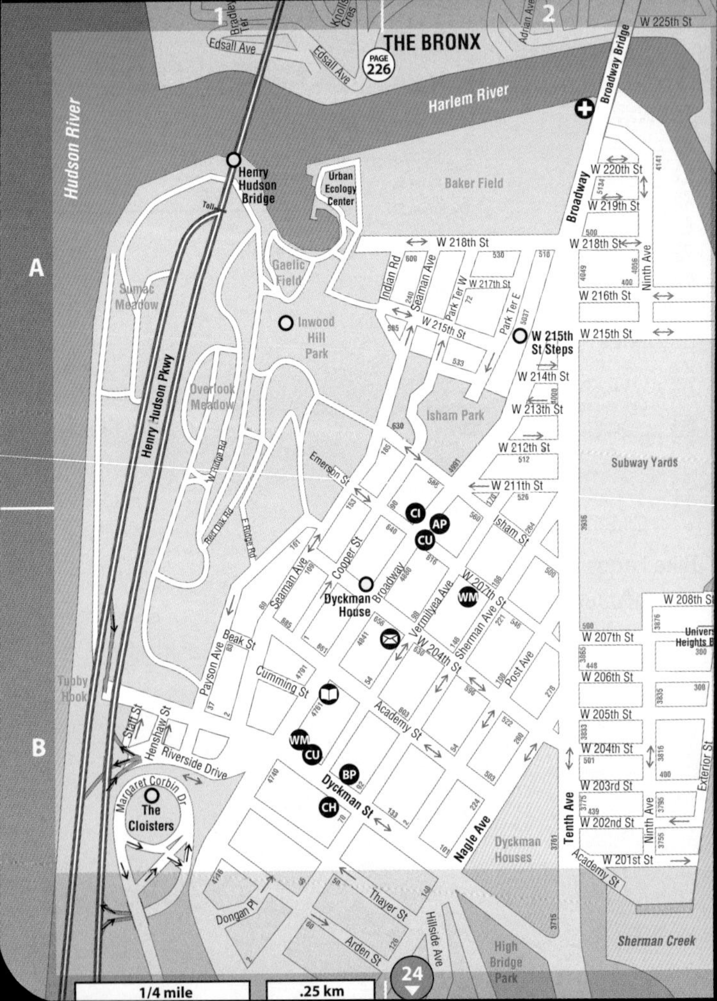

Map 25 • **Inwood**

THE BRONX

PAGE
226

Hudson River

Harlem River

Edsall Ave

Bradley
Edsall Ave

Adrian Ave

W 225th St

Broadway Bridge

W 220th St

Broadway

W 219th St

W 218th St

W 216th St

Ninth Ave

Henry Hudson
Bridge

Urban
Ecology
Center

Baker Field

Sumac
Meadow

Gaelic
Field

Indian Rd

Seaman Ave

W 218th St

W 217th St

Park Ter W

Park Ter E

W 215th St

W 217th St

W 215th St Steps

W 214th St

W 213th St

W 215th St

Inwood
Hill Park

Overlook
Meadow

Isham Park

W 212th St

Subway Yards

Emerson St

W 211th St

CI

AP

CU

Cooper St

Seaman Ave

Broadway

Dyckman
House

Vermilyea Ave

Isham St

WM

W 207th St

W 206th St

W 207th St

University
Heights B

Beak St

Payson Ave

Cumming St

W 204th St

Sherman Ave

Post Ave

Academy St

W 205th St

W 204th St

W 203rd St

WM

CU

BP

CH

Dyckman St

Nagle Ave

W 202nd St

W 201st St

Ninth Ave

Tenth Ave

Academy St

Exterior S

Margaret Corbin Dr

The
Cloisters

Riverside Drive

Dyckman
Houses

Tubby
Hook

Dongan Pl

Thayer St

Arden St

Hillside Ave

High
Bridge
Park

Sherman Creek

24

1/4 mile   .25 km

The end of Manhattan is filled with views for everyone---the iconic, breath-taking view from the Henry Hudson Bridge, and although dilapidated, catch a view of the last remaining Dutch farmhouse, Dyckman House. Also the Cloisters---home to an outdoor café with 15th-century carvings---hosts regular concerts of medieval music.

$ Banks

AP • Apple • 4950 Broadway [W 207th St]
BP • Banco Popular •
175 Dyckman St [Sherman Ave]
CH • Chase • 172 Dyckman St [Sherman Ave]
CI • Citibank • 4949 Broadway [W 207th St]
**CU • Lower East Side People's Federal
Credit Union (ATM)** • McDonald's •
208 Dyckman St [Vermilyea Ave]
**CU • Lower East Side People's Federal Credit
Union (ATM)** • McDonald's •
608 W 207th St [Broadway]
WM • Washington Mutual •
211 Dyckman St [Broadway]
WM • Washington Mutual •
570 W 207th St [Vermilyea Av]

➕ Emergency Rooms

• **New York-Presbyterian Hospital Allen
Pavilion** • 5141 Broadway [220th]

◯ Landmarks

• **The Cloisters** • Ft Tryon Park
• **Dyckman House** • 4881 Broadway [204th]
• **Henry Hudson Bridge** • n/a
• **Inwood Hill Park** • n/a
• **West 215th St Steps** • W 215th St [Park Ter E]

📖 Libraries

• **Inwood** • 4790 Broadway [Cumming]

✉ Post Offices

• **Inwood Post Office** • 90 Vermilyea Ave [204th]

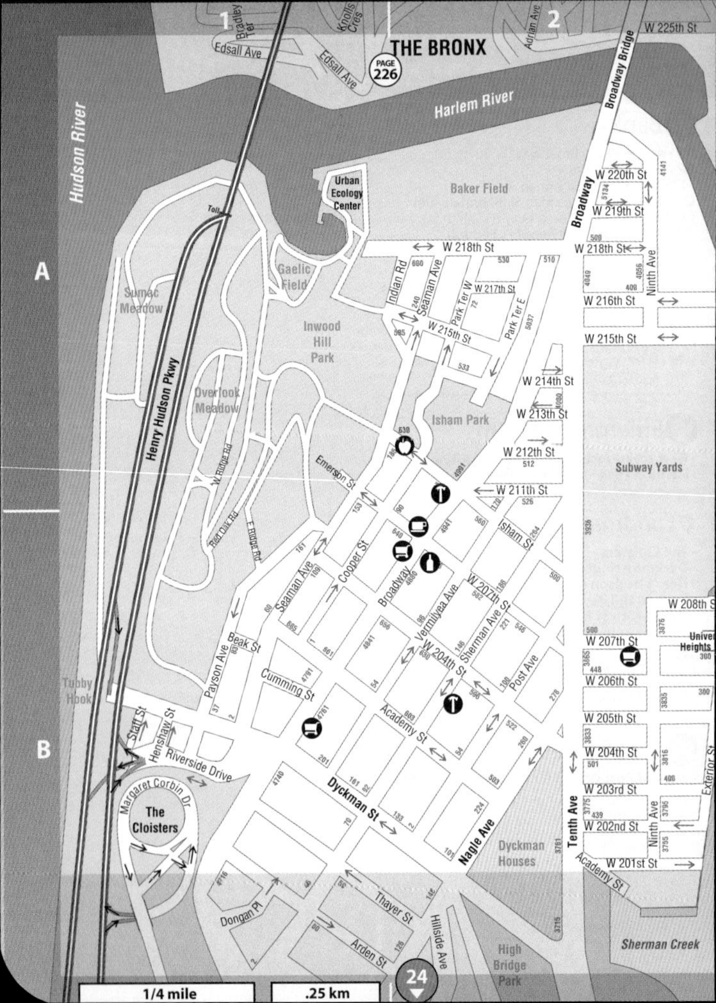

Map 25 · **Inwood**

THE BRONX

PAGE 226

W 225th St

Edsall Ave

Edsall Ave

Adrian Ave

Broadway Bridge

Harlem River

Hudson River

Henry Hudson Pkwy

Sumac Meadow

Overlook Meadow

W Ridge Rd

Tubby Hook

Toll

Urban Ecology Center

Baker Field

Gaelic Field

Inwood Hill Park

Indian Rd

Seaman Ave

Park Ter W

Park Ter E

W 218th St

W 217th St

W 216th St

W 215th St

Isham Park

W 214th St

W 213th St

Isham St

W 212th St

W 211th St

Emerson St

Cooper St

Broadway

Ninth Ave

W 220th St

W 219th St

Ninth Ave

Subway Yards

Seaman Ave

Payson Ave

Beak St

Cumming St

Vermilyea Ave

Sherman Ave

Post Ave

W 204th St

Academy St

W 208th St

W 207th St

W 206th St

W 205th St

W 204th St

W 203rd St

W 202nd St

W 201st St

Academy St

Tenth Ave

Ninth Ave

University Heights

Exterior St

Dyckman St

Riverside Drive

Staff St

Henshaw St

Margaret Corbin Dr

The Cloisters

Dongan Pl

Thayer St

Arden St

Hillside Ave

Maple Ave

Dyckman Houses

High Bridge Park

Sherman Creek

1/4 mile   .25 km

24

Because of the hilly geography and the interruption of the street grid, Inwood can be a bit disconnected from Manhattan. But fear not: common city must-haves are prevalent, like C-town, Pathmark, liquor shops, and hardware stores.

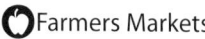 Farmers Markets

- **Inwood (Sat 8 am–3 pm, Year Round)** •
Isham St b/w Seaman Ave & Cooper St

Hardware Stores

- **Dick's Hardware** • 4947 Broadway [207th]
- **Inwood Paint & Hardware** •
165 Sherman Ave [204th]

Liquor Stores

- **PJ Liquor Warehouse** •
4898 Broadway [204th]

Supermarkets

- **C-Town** • 4918 Broadway [207th]
- **Fine Fare** • 4776 Broadway [Dyckman]
- **Pathmark** • 410 W 207th St [9th Av] ⓓ

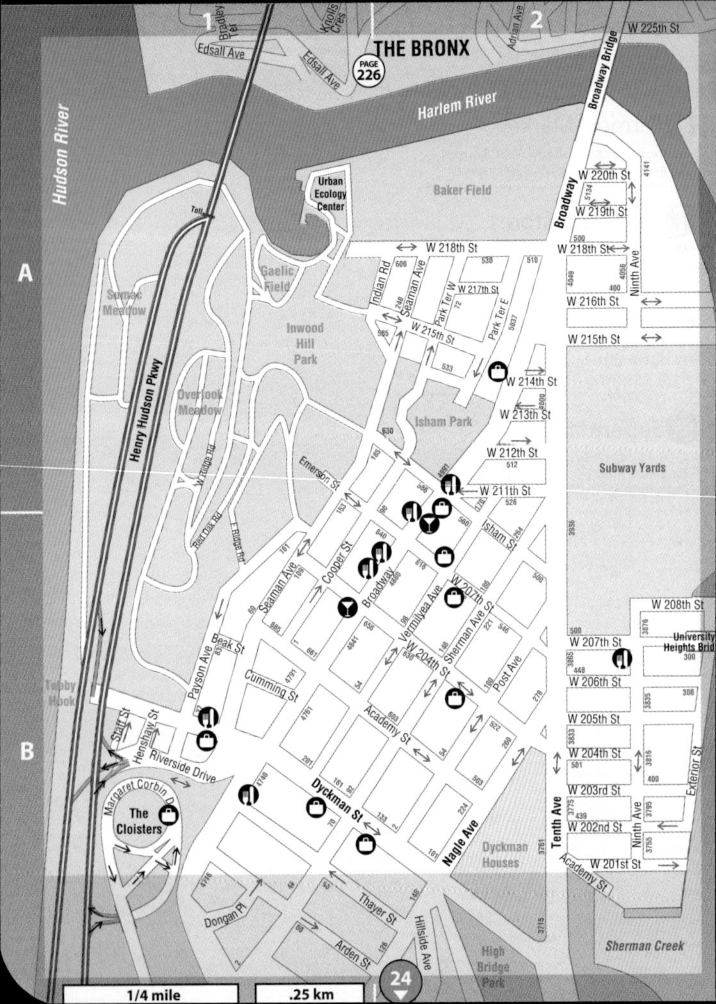

Map 25 • **Inwood**

THE BRONX
PAGE
226

Harlem River

Hudson River

Edsall Ave

W 225th St

Broadway Bridge

Broadway

W 220th St

W 219th St

W 218th St

Ninth Ave

Baker Field

Urban Ecology Center

Gaelic Field

Indian Rd

Seaman Ave

Park Terr W

Park Terr E

W 218th St

W 217th St

W 216th St

Inwood Hill Park

W 215th St

W 214th St

W 213th St

Overlook Meadow

Sunset Meadow

Isham Park

W 212th St

W 211th St

Subway Yards

Emerson St

Henry Hudson Pkwy

Spuyten Duyvil Pkwy

Cooper St

Seaman Ave

Broadway

Vermilyea Ave

Isham St

Sherman Ave

W 207th St

W 208th St

W 207th St

University Heights Bridge

Bleak St

Payson Ave

Cumming St

Academy St

Post Ave

Tenth Ave

Exterior St

W 206th St

W 205th St

W 204th St

W 203rd St

W 202nd St

W 201st St

Ninth Ave

Tubby Hook

Riverside Drive

Dyckman St

Nagle Ave

Staff St

Henshaw St

Margaret Corbin Dr

The Cloisters

Dongan Pl

Thayer St

Arden St

Hillside Ave

Dyckman Houses

High Bridge Park

Sherman Creek

1/4 mile

.25 km

24

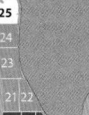
Ride your bike through Inwood Hill Park and after working up an appetite, grab a bite to eat at Grandpa's Brick Oven Pizza. And if you didn't grab a few flowers for your loved one at the park, be sure to do so at K&R Florist—they're the best in town!

Nightlife

- **Keenan's Bar** • 4878 Broadway [204th]
- **Piper's Kilt** • 4944 Broadway [207th]

Restaurants

- **Capitol Restaurant** • 4933 Broadway [207th]
- **Garden Café** • 4961 Broadway [Isham St]
- **Grandpa's Brick Oven Pizza** •
  4973 Broadway [Isham]
- **Mamajua Café** • 247 Dyckman St [Seaman Av]
- **Mr Seafood** • 3842 Ninth Ave [206th] ⊕
- **Park Terrace Bistro** •
  4959 Broadway [Isham St]
- **Tacos Puebla** • 5-22 W 207th St [Sherman]

Shopping

- **Carrot Top Pastries** • 5025 Broadway [214th]
- **The Cloisters Museum Store** • Ft Tryon Park
- **Foot Locker** • 146 Dyckman St [Sherman]
- **K&R Florist** • 4953 Broadway [207th]
- **Radio Shack** • 180 Dyckman St [Vermilyea]
- **Radio Shack** • 576 W 207th St [Vermilyea]
- **Tread Bike Shop** • 250 Dyckman St [B'way]
- **VIM** • 565 W 207th St [Vermilyea]

Map 25 · Inwood

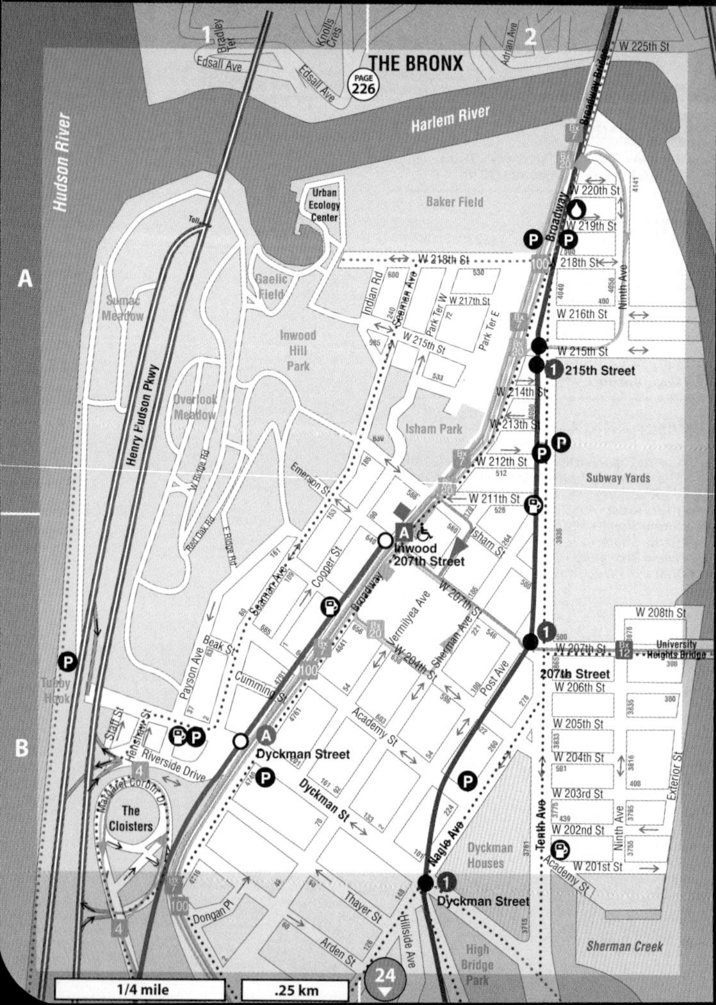

THE BRONX

PAGE 226

Hudson River

Harlem River

Knolls Cres

Bradley Ter
Edsall Ave
Indian Ave

W 225th St

Broadway

W 220th St
W 219th St
4141

218th St

Urban
Ecology
Center

Baker Field

W 218th St

Ninth Ave
W 217th St
W 216th St

Indian Rd

Park Ter W

Gaelic
Field

1 215th Street
W 215th St
W 214th St

W 213th St

Sumac
Meadow

Inwood
Hill
Park

Isham Park

W 212th St

Subway Yards

W 211th St

Henry Hudson Pkwy

Overlook
Meadow

Emerson St

Seaman Ave

Cooper St

Isham Street

W Eagle Ave

Payson Ave

Beak St

Cummin...

Broadway

Inwood
207th Street

Terminuel Ave

Sherman Ave

W 207th St
207th Street
W 206th St

1

University
Heights
Bridge

Post Ave

W 208th St

Exterior St

W 205th St

Academy St

W 204th St

Ninth Ave

W 203rd St

Tenth Ave

P Tubby
Hook

Seaman Ave

Beak St

Riverside Drive

A Dyckman Street

Dyckman St

Nagle Ave

W 202nd St
W 201st St

Academy St

Sherman Creek

The
Cloisters

Dongan Pl

Thayer St

Arden St

Dyckman
Houses

1 Dyckman Street

High
Bridge
Park

Hillside Ave

24

1/4 mile   .25 km

Transportation

Map 25

25
24
23
21 22
18 19 20

Inwood's main local thoroughfare is Broadway, but between the A and the 1, Inwood is very accessible via public transportation. When driving, it's a short hop off the Hudson pre-toll; take the Dyckman exit. Parking is generally available on the side streets, and the traffic condition is typical—i.e. crazed.

Subways

1	215th St
1	207th St
A	Dyckman St
A	Inwood-207th St

Bus Lines

100	Amsterdam Ave/Broadway/125th St
4	Fifth/Madison Aves/Broadway
Bx 12	Riverdale/263rd St via Riverdale Ave
Bx 20	Riverdale/246th St via Henry Hudson Pky
Bx 7	Riverdale Ave/Broadway

Bike Lanes

- • • • Marked Bike Lanes
- • • • Recommended Route
- • • • Greenway

Car Washes

- **Broadway Bridge Car Wash** •
  5134 Broadway [220th]

Gas Stations

- **BP** • 3936 Tenth Ave [Sherman] ⚙
- **Getty** • 4880 Broadway [204th] ⚙
- **Getty / Lukoil** • 242 Dyckman St [Seaman] ⚙
- **Shell** • 3761 Tenth Ave [201st] ⚙

Parking

Map 26 · Astoria

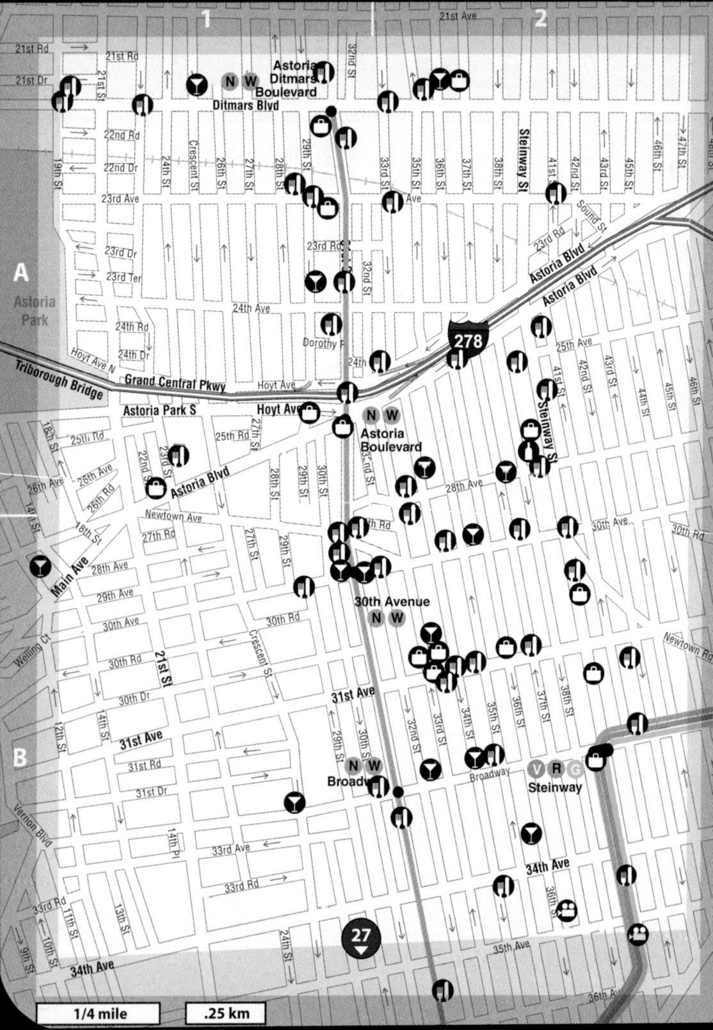

Map 26 · Astoria

21st Rd
21st Dr

21st Ave

21st Ave

21st Rd
21st Dr

22nd Rd
22nd Dr
22nd Ave

Astoria
Ditmars
Boulevard
Ditmars Blvd

23rd Dr
23rd Ter

Astoria
Park

24th Ave
24th Rd
24th Dr

Triborough Bridge

Grand Central Pkwy
Hoyt Ave
Astoria Park S   Hoyt Ave

Astoria Blvd
Astoria Blvd

278

Astoria
Boulevard

25th Rd
25th Ave
26th Ave
26th St

Main Ave N

Astoria Blvd

Newtown Ave
27th Ave
28th Ave
29th Ave
30th Ave
30th Rd
30th Dr

21st St

31st Ave
31st Rd
31st Dr

31st Ave

30th Avenue

Broadway

Broadway

Steinway

33rd Ave
33rd Rd

34th Ave

34th Ave

35th Ave

36th Ave

27

1/4 mile   .25 km

17
26
27

The Irish have their wonderful way at the Rover and Gilbey's, the cool kids congregate at The Sparrow and Crescent Lounge, but a summer night in the Beer Garden is an experience all its own. There's always something worth seeing at the Museum of the Moving Image.

Movie Theaters

- **Museum of the Moving Image** ·
  36-01 35th Ave
- **UA Kaufman Studios Cinema 14** ·
  35-30 38th St

Nightlife

- **Avenue Café** · 35-27 30th Ave
- **Bohemian Hall & Beer Garden** ·
  29-19 24th Ave
- **Brick Café** · 30-95 33rd Ave
- **Café Bar** · 32-90 36th St
- **Crescent Lounge** · 32-05 Crescent St
- **Cronin & Phelan** · 38-14 Broadway
- **Fatty's Café** · 25-01 Ditmars Blvd
- **Gibney's Tavern** · 32-01 Broadway
- **Hell Gate Social** · 12-21 Astoria Blvd
- **Irish Rover** · 37-18 28th Ave
- **Mary McGuire's** · 38-04 Broadway
- **McCaffrey & Burke** · 28-54 31st St
- **McCann's Pub & Grill** ·
  36-15 Ditmars Blvd
- **Rendezvous** · 34-13 Broadway
- **Rapture** · 34-27 28th Ave
- **The Sparrow** · 24-01 29th St

Restaurants

- **Agnanti** · 19-06 Ditmars Blvd
- **Aliada** · 29-19 Broadway
- **Athens Café** · 32-07 30th Ave
- **Bartolino's** · 34-15 Broadway
- **Chirping Chicken** · 30-91 21st St
- **Christos Steak House** · 41-08 23rd Ave
- **Churrascaria Girassol** · 33-18 28th Ave
- **Dhaka Café Jhill** · 35-55 31st St
- **Djardan** · 34-04 31st Ave
- **Elias Corner** · 24-02 31st St
- **Favela** · 33-18 28th Ave
- **Grand Café** · 37-01 30th Ave
- **Indigo** · 28-50 31st St
- **JJ's Restaurant** · 37-05 31st Ave
- **Jour et Nuit** · 28-04 Steinway St
- **Kabab Café** · 25-12 Steinway St
- **La Espiga II** · 32-44 31st St
- **Latin Cabana Restaurant** ·
  34-44 Steinway St ⊕
- **Lil Bistro 33** · 19-33 Ditmars Blvd
- **Mombar** · 25-22 Steinway St

- **Neptune Diner** · 31-05 Astoria Blvd ⊕
- **Original Mexican Food Deli** ·
  30-11 29th St
- **Ovelia** · 34-01 30th St
- **Papa's Empanadas** · 25-51 Steinway St
- **Philoxenia** · 32-07 Astoria Blvd N
- **Poodam Thai Cuisine** · 44-19 Broadway
- **Rizzo's Pizza** · 30-13 Steinway St
- **Sabry's** · 24-25 Steinway St
- **S'Agapo** · 34-21 34th St
- **Sabor Tropical** · 36-18 30th Ave
- **Sal, Chris, and Charlie Deli** ·
  33-12 23rd Ave
- **San Antonio II** · 36-20 Astoria Blvd S
- **Seven One Eight** · 35-01 Ditmars Blvd
- **Stamatis** · 29-12 23rd Ave
- **Telly's Taverna** · 28-13 23rd Ave
- **Tokyo Japanese Restaurant** ·
  31-05 24th Ave
- **Tony's Souvlaki Opa!** · 28-44 31st St
- **Trattoria L'Incontro** · 21-76 31st St
- **Uncle George's Greek Tavern** ·
  33-19 Broadway
- **Walima** · 31-06 42nd St
- **Watawa** · 33-10 Ditmars Blvd
- **Zenon** · 34-10 31st Ave
- **Zlata Praha** · 28-48 31st St

Shopping

- **Candy Plum** · 30-98 36th St
- **Easy Pickins** · 31-27 Steinway St
- **El Mundo Discount** · 32-40 Steinway St
- **The Furniture Market** ·
  22-08 Astoria Blvd
- **Jolson's Wines & Liquors** · 22-24 31st St
- **Laziza of New York Pastries** ·
  25-78 Steinway St
- **Loveday 31** · 33-06 31st Ave
- **Martha's Country Bakery** ·
  36-21 Ditmars Blvd
- **Mediterranean Foods** · 23-18 31st St
- **Rose & Joe's Italian Bakery** ·
  22-40 31st St
- **The Second Best** · 30-07 Astoria Blvd
- **Thessalikon Pastry Shop** ·
  33-21 31st Ave
- **Titan Foods** · 25-56 31st St
- **Venzini** · 30-64 Steinway St

Map 27 · **Long Island City**

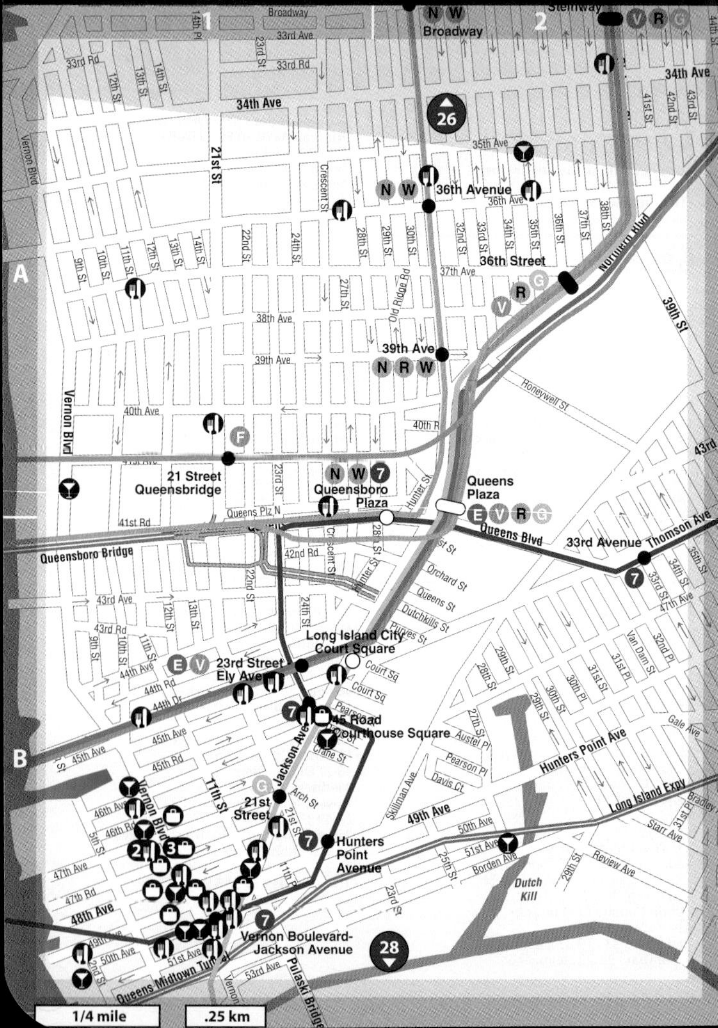

Broadway

Steinway

Broadway

34th Ave

34th Ave

26

35th Ave

36th Avenue

21st St

Crescent St

Hunters Pt

36th Ave

36th St

36th Street

Van Dam St

Bridge Rd

37th Ave

38th Ave

Honeywell St

39th Ave

39th St

21 Street Queensbridge

Vernon Blvd

40th Ave

40th Ave

Queens Plz N

41st Rd

Queensboro Plaza

Queens Plaza

Queens Blvd

33rd Avenue Thomson Ave

Queensboro Bridge

42nd Rd

Orchard St

Dutchkills St

43rd Ave

44th Ave

23rd Street Ely Ave

Long Island City Court Square

Court Sq

45th Ave

Page

Courthouse Square

Crane St

Austell Pl

Hunters Point Ave

45th Rd

46th Ave

Jackson Ave

Vernon Blvd

21st Street

Arch St

Pearson Pl

Davis Ct

Long Island Expy

Starr Ave

47th Ave

Skillman Ave

49th Ave

Hunters Point Avenue

Review Ave

48th Ave

Borden Ave

Dutch Kill

Vernon Boulevard-Jackson Avenue

Queens Midtown Tunnel

53rd Ave

Pulaski Bridge

28

1/4 mile   .25 km

Entertainment

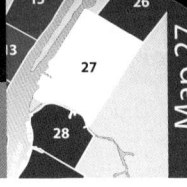

Map 27

Meet the neighbors at Dominie's, watch the game at P.J.'s, get cozy at LIC Bar, and, in summertime, relax on the sand at Water Taxi Beach. Art-o-Mat sells quirky local souvenirs. Devour Mario's Italian hero and McReilly's burgers. Tournesol, Manducatis, and Bella Via are classics, but wacky newcomer Lucky Mojo's is also worth a bite.

🌙 Nightlife

- **The Cave** · 10-93 Jackson Ave
- **Domaine Bar a Vins** · 50-04 Vernon Blvd
- **Dominie's Hoek** · 48-17 Vernon Blvd
- **LIC Bar** · 45-58 Vernon Blvd
- **Lounge 47** · 47-10 Vernon Blvd
- **McReilly's** · 46-42 Vernon Blvd
- **PJ Leahy's** · 50-02 Vernon Blvd
- **Shannon Pot** · 45-06 Davis St
- **Sunswick Limited** · 35-02 35th St
- **Water Taxi Beach Harry's** · 203 Borden Ave

🍴 Restaurants

- **43rd Avenue Diner / 5 Stars Punjabi** · 13-15 43rd Ave
- **Bella Via** · 47-46 Vernon Blvd
- **Blend** · 47-04 Vernon Blvd
- **Bricktown Bagel Café** · 51-06 Vernon Blvd
- **Brooks 1890 Restaurant** · 24-28 Jackson Ave ♿
- **Bulgara Restaurant** · 3710 11th St
- **Café Henri** · 10-10 50th Ave
- **Cassino** · 47-18 Vernon Blvd
- **Court Square Diner** · 45-30 23rd St ♿
- **Cup Diner** · 35-01 36th St
- **Dorian Café** · 10-01 50th Ave
- **El Sitio** · 35-55 31st St
- **Halal Meat Cart** · 34th Ave & Steinway St
- **Jackson Ave Steakhouse** · 12-23 Jackson Ave
- **Junior's Café** · 46-18 Vernon Blvd
- **Las Vegas Diner** · 44-62 21st St
- **Lucky Mojo's** · 516 51st Ave
- **Malagueta** · 25-35 36th Ave
- **Manducatis** · 13-27 Jackson Ave
- **Manetta's** · 10-76 Jackson Ave
- **Masso** · 47-25 Vernon Blvd
- **Pimenton** · 21-50 44th Dr
- **Queens Coffee Shop** · 25-15 Queens Plz N
- **Riverview Restaurant** · 201 50th Ave
- **Roti Boti Restaurant** · 27-09 21st St ♿
- **Tournesol** · 50-12 Vernon Blvd
- **Tuk Tuk** · 49-06 Vernon Blvd
- **Water's Edge** · 44th Dr & East River

🛍 Shopping

- **Art-o-Mat** · 46-46 Vernon Blvd
- **City Dog Lounge** · 49-02 Vernon Blvd
- **Greenmarket** · 48th Ave b/w 5th St & Vernon Blvd
- **Hunter's Point Wines & Spirits** · 47-07 Vernon Blvd
- **Mario's** · 47-23 Vernon Blvd
- **Network Video** · 22-42 Jackson Ave
- **Next Level Floral Design** · 47-30 Vernon Blvd
- **Purple Pumpkin** · 47-14 Vernon Blvd
- **Slovak-Czech Varieties** · 10-59 Jackson Ave
- **Spokesman Cycles** · 49-04 Vernon Blvd
- **Subdivision** · 48-18 Vernon Blvd
- **Vine Wine (Wine only)** · 12-09 Jackson Ave

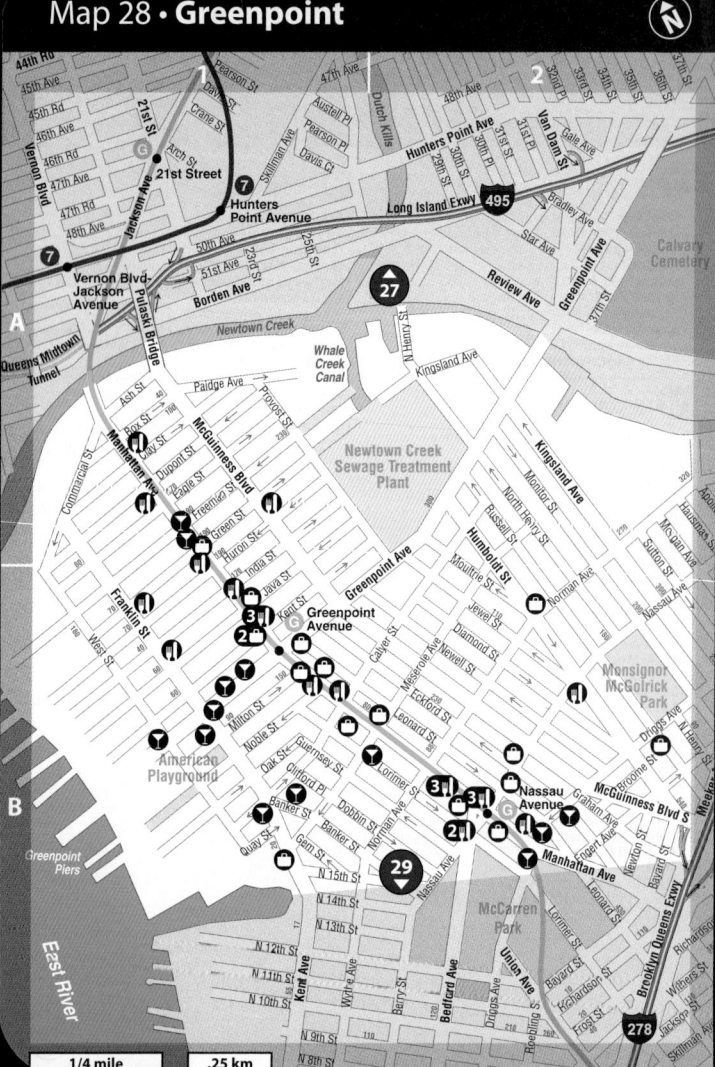

Map 28 · **Greenpoint**

1/4 mile .25 km

Entertainment

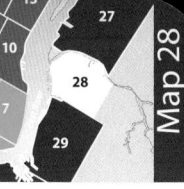

Map 28

The Pencil Factory remains the nightlife favorite of a certain demographic; Polish dance clubs cater to another. Where Wedel's churns out fancy Polish chocolates, legions of Manhattan Avenue meat markets slash out infinite slabs of bloody flesh. The Thing's got everything you never thought would merit a thrift store.

Nightlife

- **Black Rabbit** • 91 Greenpoint Ave [Franklin]
- **Coco 66** • 66 Greenpoint Ave [Franklin]
- **The Diamond** • 43 Franklin St [Calyer]
- **Enid's** • 560 Manhattan Ave [Driggs]
- **Europa** • 98 Meserole Ave [Manhattan]
- **Jack O'Neil's** • 130 Franklin St [Milton]
- **Lost and Found** • 113 Franklin St [Greenpoint]
- **The Mark Bar** • 1025 Manhattan Ave [Green]
- **Matchless** •557 Manhattan Ave [Driggs]
- **Pencil Factory** • 142 Franklin St [Greenpoint]
- **Red Star** • 37 Greenpoint Ave [West]
- **Studio B** • 259 Banker St [Meserole]
- **Tommy's Tavern** •
  1041 Manhattan Ave [Freeman]
- **Warsaw** • 261 Driggs Ave [Eckford]

Restaurants

- **Acapulco Deli & Restaurant** •
  1116 Manhattan Ave [Clay]
- **Amarin Café** • 617 Manhattan Ave [Nassau]
- **Baldo's Pizza** • 175 Nassau Ave [Diamond]
- **Brooklyn Label** • 180 Franklin St [Java]
- **Casanova** • 338 McGuinness Blvd [Green]
- **Christina's** • 853 Manhattan Ave [Noble]
- **Dami's** • 931 Manhattan Ave [Kent St]
- **Divine Follie Café** •
  929 Manhattan Ave [Kent St]
- **Enid's** • 560 Manhattan Ave [Driggs]
- **Erb** • 681 Manhattan Ave [Norman]
- **Fresca Tortilla** • 620 Manhattan Ave [Nassau]
- **God Bless Deli** • 818 Manhattan Ave [Calyer] ⊘
- **Johnny's Café** • 632 Manhattan Ave [Nassau]
- **Lamb & Jaffey** • 1073 Manhattan Ave [Eagle]
- **Lomzynianka** • 646 Manhattan Ave [Nassau]
- **Manhattan 3 Decker** •
  695 Manhattan Ave [Norman]
- **Monsignor's** • 905 Lorimer St [Nassau]
- **Old Poland Restaurant** •
  190 Nassau Ave [Humboldt]
- **OTT** • 970 Manhattan Ave [India]
- **Queen's Hideaway** • 222 Franklin St [Green]
- **Relax** • 68 Newell St [Nassau]
- **San Diego** • 999 Manhattan Ave [Huron]
- **Sapporo Haru** • 622 Manhattan Ave [Nassau]
- **Thai Café** • 925 Manhattan Ave [Kent St]
- **Valdiano** • 659 Manhattan Ave [Bedford]

Shopping

- **Alter** • 109 Franklin St [Greenpoint]
- **Brooklynski** • 145 Driggs Ave [Russell]
- **Chopin Chemists** •
  911 Manhattan Ave [Kent St]
- **Dee & Dee** • 777 Manhattan Ave [Meserole]
- **Film Noir** • 10 Bedford Ave [Manhattan]
- **The Garden** • 921 Manhattan Ave [Kent St]
- **Mini Me** • 123 Nassau Ave [Eckford]
- **Petland Discounts** •
  846 Manhattan Ave [Noble]
- **Photoplay** • 928 Manhattan Ave [Kent St]
- **Polam** • 952 Manhattan Ave [Java]
- **Pop's Popular Clothing** •
  7 Franklin St [Meserole]
- **Sikorski Meat** • 603 Manhattan Ave [Nassau]
- **Steve's Meat Market** •
  104 Nassau Ave [Leonard]
- **Syrena Bakery** • 207 Norman Ave [Humboldt]
- **The Thing** • 1001 Manhattan Ave [Huron]
- **Uncle Louie G's** •
  172 Greenpoint Ave [Leonard]
- **Wedel** • 772 Manhattan Ave [Meserole]
- **Wizard Electroland** •
  863 Manhattan Ave [Milton]

Map 29 · **Williamsburg**

McGuinness Blvd S.

Nassau Avenue

Manhattan Ave

McCarren Park

Graham Avenue

Bedford Avenue

Lorimer Street

Metropolitan Avenue

Metropolitan Ave

Grand Ave

Hewes Street

Marcy Avenue

Washington Plaza

Williamsburg Bridge

Broadway

East River

Bedford Ave

Kent Ave

Navy Yard

Walabout Channel

Flushing Ave

| 1/4 mile | .25 km |

Ententainment

Map 29

You want it, it's here. Carnivores flock to Luger and Fette Sau, beer-lovers throw 'em back at Spuyten Duyvil and Radegast, while Barcade gives joystick junkies their fix. Live music? Pete's Candy Store, Luna Lounge, or Music Hall should do it for ya. And Brooklyn's first new bowling alley in 50 years, The Gutter, was worth the wait.

Nightlife

• **The Abbey** • 536 Driggs Ave [N 8th]
• **Alligator Lounge** •
  600 Metropolitan Ave [Lorimer]
• **Barcade** • 388 Union Ave [Ainslie]
• **Bembe** • 81 S 6th St [Berry]
• **Black Betty** •
  366 Metropolitan Ave [Havemeyer]
• **Charleston** • 174 Bedford Ave [N 7th]
• **Clem's** • 264 Grand St [Roebling]
• **Daddy's** • 437 Graham Ave [Frost]
• **East River Bar** • 97 S 6th St [Berry]
• **Greenpoint Tavern** • 188 Bedford Ave [N 7th]
• **The Gutter** • 200 N 14th St [Wythe
• **Iona** • 180 Grand St [Bedford]
• **Larry Lawrence** • 295 Grand St [Havemeyer]
• **The Levee** • 212 Berry St [Metropolitan]
• **Luna Lounge** •
  361 Metropolitan Ave [Havemeyer]
• **Mugs Ale House** • 125 Bedford Ave [N 10th]
• **Music Hall of Williamsburg** •
  66 N 6th [Kent Ave]
• **Pete's Candy Store** •
  709 Lorimer St [Richardson]
• **Radegast Hall & Biergarten** •
  113 N 3rd St [Berry]
• **Royal Oak** • 594 Union Ave [Richardson]
• **Savalas** • 285 Bedford Ave [S 1st]
• **Spuyten Duyvil** •
  359 Metropolitan Ave [Havemeyer]
• **Trash** • 256 Grand St [Roebling]
• **Turkey's Nest** • 94 Bedford Ave [N 12th]
• **Union Pool** • 484 Union Ave [Rodney]
• **Zebulon** • 258 Wythe Ave [N 3rd]

Restaurants

• **Acqua Santa** • 556 Driggs Ave [N 7th]
• **Anna Maria Pizza** • 179 Bedford Ave [N 7th]
• **Bacci & Abbracci** • 204 Grand St [Driggs]
• **Blackbird Parlour** • 197 Bedford Ave [N 6th St]
• **Bonita** • 338 Bedford Ave [S 3rd]
• **Bozu** • 296 Grand St [Havemeyer]
• **Diner** • 85 Broadway [Berry]
• **Dokebi** • 199 Grand St [Driggs]
• **Dressler** • 149 Broadway [Bedford]
• **DuMont** • 432 Union Ave [Devoe]
• **DuMont Burger** • 314 Bedford Ave [S 1st]
• **Fada** • 530 Driggs Ave [N 8th]
• **Fette Sau** • 354 Metropolitan Ave [Roebling]
• **Juliette** • 135 N 5th St [Bedford]
• **Kate's Brooklyn Joint** • 295 Berry St [S 2nd]
• **Lola's** • 454 Graham Ave [Richardson]
• **Marlow & Sons** • 81 Broadway [Berry]

• **Moto** • 394 Broadway [Hopper]
• **Oasis** • 161 N 7th St [Bedford]
• **Peter Luger Steak House** •
  178 Broadway [Driggs]
• **Pies N Thighs** • 351 Kent Ave [S 5th]
• **PT** • 331 Bedford Ave [S 3rd]
• **Radegast Hall & Biergarten** •
  113 N 3rd St [Berry]
• **Raymund's Place** • 124 Bedford Ave [N 10th]
• **Relish** • 225 Wythe St [S 3rd]
• **Roebling Tea Room** •
  143 Roebling St [Metropolitan]
• **Sparky's/Egg** • 135A N 5th St [Bedford]
• **Taco Chulo** • 318 Grand St [Havemeyer]
• **Teddy's Bar and Grill** • 96 Berry St [N 8th]
• **Yola's Café** • 542 Metropolitan Ave [Union]

Shopping

• **Academy Records** • 96 N 6th St [Wythe]
• **Amarcord Vintage Fashion** •
  223 Bedford Ave [N 4th]
• **Artist & Craftsman** •
  761 Metropolitan Ave [Graham]
• **Beacon's Closet** • 88 N 11th St [Wythe]
• **Bedford Cheese Shop** •
  229 Bedford Ave [N 5th]
• **The Brooklyn Kitchen** •
  616 Lorimer St [Skillman]
• **Built By Wendy** • 46 N 6th St [Kent Ave]
• **Earwax Records** • 218 Bedford Ave [N 5th]
• **Emily's Pork Store** • 426 Graham Ave [Withers]
• **Future Perfect** • 115 N 6th St [Berry]
• **Houndstooth** • 485 Driggs Ave [N 10th]
• **KCDC Skateshop** • 90 N 11th St [Wythe]
• **The Mini-Market** • 218 Bedford Ave [N 5th]
• **Model T Meats** • 404 Graham Ave [Withers]
• **Moon River Chattel** • 62 Grand St [Wythe]
• **Otte** • 132 N 5th St [Bedford]
• **Passout Record Shop** • 131 Grand St [Berry]
• **Pegasus** • 355 Bedford Ave [S 4th]
• **Roulette** • 188 Havemeyer St [S 3rd]
• **Scandinavian Grace** • 197 N 9th St [Bedford]
• **Sodafine** • 119 Grand St [Myrtle]
• **Soundfix** • 110 Bedford Ave [N 11th]
• **Spoonbill & Sugartown** •
  218 Bedford Ave [N 5th]
• **Sprout** • 44 Grand St [Kent Ave]
• **Spuyten Devil Grocery** •
  132 N 5th St [Bedford]
• **Treehouse** • 430 Graham Ave [Frost]
• **Two Jakes** • 320 Wythe Ave [Grand]
• **Ugly Luggage** • 214 Bedford Ave [N 5th St]
• **Videology** • 308 Bedford Ave [S 1st St]
• **Yoko Devereaux** • 338 Broadway [Keap]

213

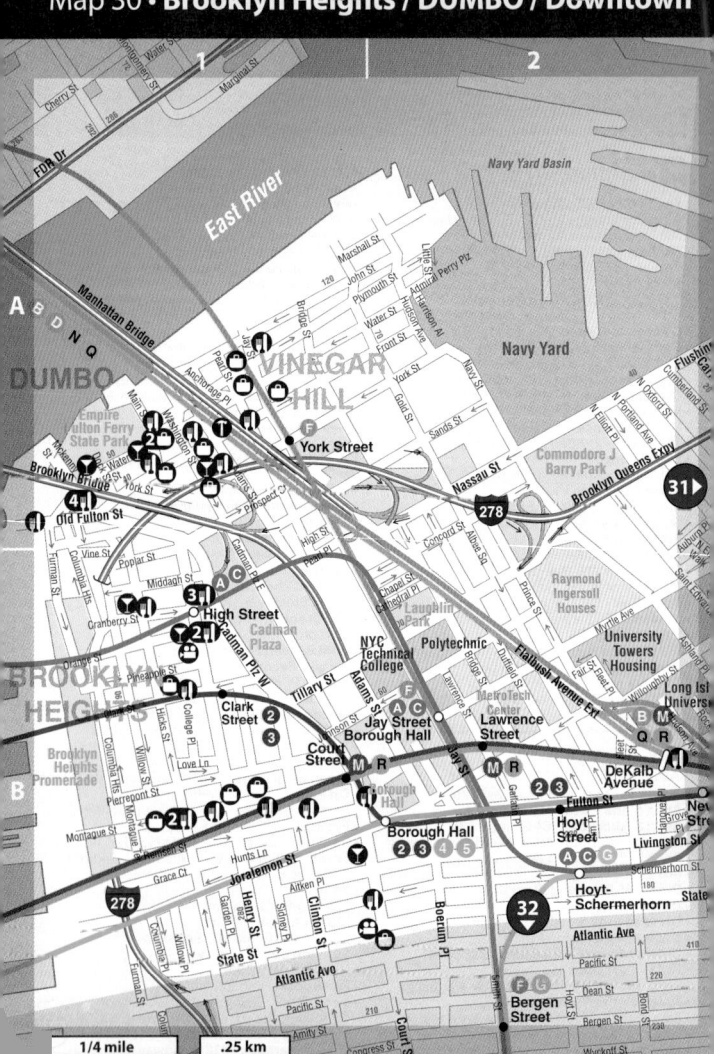

Map 30 • **Brooklyn Heights / DUMBO / Downtown**

Entertainment

Map 30

Old-world Henry's End is at the top of our list for food, but also check out ultrahip Superfine, friendly Noodle Pudding, and posh gastropub Jack the Horse. For culture, St. Ann's is the place. For chocolate, two words: Jacques Torres. When Tim and Jason move in together, they accessorize at West Elm.

🎬 Movie Theaters

• **Pavilion Brooklyn Heights** •
70 Henry St [Orange]
• **Regal/UA Court Street** •
108 Court St [State]

🍸 Nightlife

• **68 Jay Street Bar** • 68 Jay St [Front St]
• **Henry St Ale House** • 62 Henry St [Cranberry]
• **Jack the Horse Tavern** •
66 Hicks St [Cranberry]
• **Low Bar** • 81 Washington St [York]
• **Okeefe's** • 62 Court St [Livingston]
• **St Ann's Warehouse** •
38 Water St [Dock St]
• **Water Street Bar** • 66 Water St [Main]

🍴 Restaurants

• **Bubby's** • 1 Main St [Plymouth]
• **Curry Leaf** • 151 Remsen St [Clinton]
• **DUMBO General Store** • 111 Front St [Adams]
• **Fascati Pizzeria** • 80 Henry St [Orange]
• **Five Front** • 5 Front St [Old Fulton]
• **Five Guys** • 138 Montague St [Hicks]
• **Grimaldi's** • 19 Old Fulton St [Doughty]
• **Hale & Hearty Soup** • 32 Court St [Remsen]
• **Heights Café** • 84 Montague St [Hicks]
• **Henry's End** • 44 Henry St [Middagh]
• **Jack the Horse Tavern** •
66 Hicks St [Cranberry]
• **Junior's Restaurant** •
386 Flatbush Ave [St Johns]
• **Miso** • 40 Main St [Front St]
• **Noodle Pudding** • 38 Henry St [Middagh]
• **Pete's Downtown** • 2 Water St [Old Fulton]
• **The Plant** • 25 Jay St [Plymouth]
• **Queen Ristorante** •
84 Court St [Livingston]
• **Rice** • 81 Washington St [York]
• **River Café** • 1 Water St [Old Fulton]
• **Siggy's Good Food** •
76 Henry St [Orange]
• **Superfine** • 126 Front St [Pearl St]
• **Sushi California** • 71 Clark St [Henry]
• **Thai 101** • 101 Montague St [Hicks]
• **Theresa's** • 80 Montague St [Hicks]
• **Toro Restaurant** • 1 Front St [Old Fulton]

🛍 Shopping

• **Almondine Bakery** • 85 Water St [Main]
• **Design Within Reach** •
76 Montague St [Hicks]
• **Halcyon** • 57 Pearl St [Water]
• **Half Pint** • 55 Washington St [Front St]
• **Heights Prime Meats** • 59 Clark St [Henry]
• **Jacques Torres Chocolate** •
66 Water St [Main]
• **Lassen & Hennigs** • 114 Montague St [Henry]
• **Montague Street VIdeo** •
143 Montague St [Clinton St]
• **New Balance Store** • 125 Court St [State]
• **Pomme** • 81 Washington St [York]
• **Recycle-A-Bicycle** • 35 Pearl St [Plymouth St]
• **Stewart/Stand** • 165 Front St [Jay]
• **West Elm** • 75 Front St [Main]
• **Wonk** • 68 Jay St [Front St]

Map 31 • Fort Greene / Clinton Hill

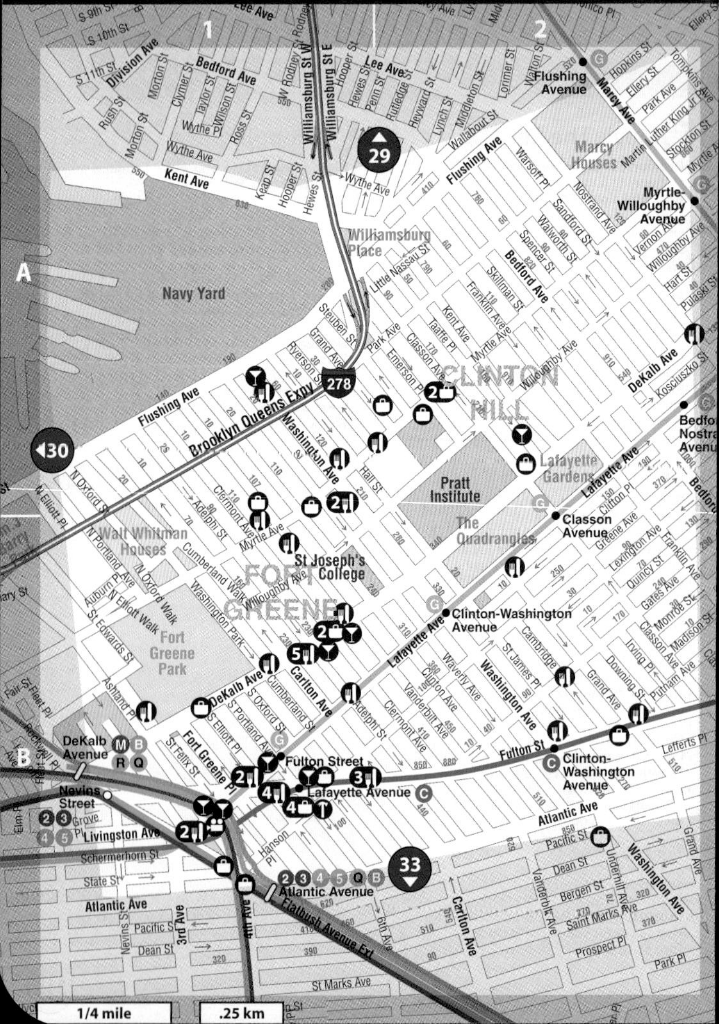

Entertainment

Map 31

Well, it's missing a cheese shop (supposedly coming soon) and a rock club, but that's about it—check out cool eats and Afro beats at Grand Dakar, friendly French at Chez Oskar, pre-BAM Austrian at Thomas Beisl, killer cheap Mexican at Castro's, posh Italian at Locanda, and short rib heaven at Smoke Joint.

🎬 Movie Theaters
- **BAM Rose Cinemas** • BAM • 30 Lafayette Ave [St Felix]

🍸 Nightlife
- **The Alibi** • 242 Dekalb Ave
- **BAMcafé** • 30 Lafayette Ave [Ashland]
- **Frank's Lounge** • 660 Fulton St [S Elliott Pl]
- **Grand Dakar** • 285 Grand Ave [Clifton]
- **Moe's** • 80 Lafayette Ave [S Portland]
- **Reign Bar & Lounge** • 46 Washington Ave [Flushing]
- **Sputnik** • 262 Taaffe Pl [DeKalb]
- **Stonehome Wine Bar** • 87 Lafayette Ave [S Portland]
- **Thomas Beisl** • 25 Lafayette Ave [Ashland]

🍴 Restaurants
- **1 Greene Sushi and Sashimi** • 1 Greene Ave [Fulton]
- **67 Burger** • 67 Lafayette Ave [S Elliott Pl]
- **BAMcafé** • 30 Lafayette Ave [Ashland]
- **Black Iris** • 228 DeKalb Ave [Clermont]
- **Café Lafayette** • 99 S Portland Ave [Fulton]
- **Castro's Restaurant** • 511 Myrtle Ave [Grand]
- **Chez Lola** • 387 Myrtle Ave [Clermont]
- **Chez Oskar** • 211 DeKalb Ave [Adelphi]
- **Choice Market** • 318 Lafayette Ave [Grand]
- **Grand Dakar** • 285 Grand Ave [Clifton]
- **Habana Outpost** • 757 Fulton St [S Portland]
- **Ici** • 246 DeKalb Ave [Vanderbilt]
- **Kush** • 17 Putnam Ave [Grand]
- **Locanda Vini & Olii** • 129 Gates Ave [Cambridge]
- **LouLou** • 222 DeKalb Ave [Clermont]
- **Luz** • 177 Vanderbilt Ave [Myrtle]
- **Madiba** • 195 DeKalb Ave [Carlton]
- **Maggie Brown** • 455 Myrtle Ave [Wash Ave]
- **Mojito Restaurant** • 82 Washington Ave [Park]
- **Night of the Cookers** • 767 Fulton St [S Oxford]
- **Olea** • 171 Lafayette Ave [Adelphi]
- **Pequena** • 86 S Portland Ave [Lafayette]
- **Red Bamboo** • 271 Adelphi St [Adelphi]
- **Rice** • 166 DeKalb Ave [Cumberland]
- **Ruthie's Restaurant** • 96 DeKalb Ave [Ashland]
- **Scopello** • 63 Lafayette Ave [S Elliott Pl]
- **The Smoke Joint** • 87 S Elliott Pl [Lafayette]
- **Soule** • 920 Fulton St [Wash Ave]
- **Thai 101** • 455 Myrtle Ave [Wash Ave]
- **Thomas Beisl** • 25 Lafayette Ave [Ashland]
- **Zaytoons** • 472 Myrtle Ave [Wash Ave]

🛍 Shopping
- **Atlantic Terminal Mall** • Atlantic Ave & Flatbush Ave
- **Bargains R Us** • 976 Fulton St [Grand]
- **Blue Bass Vintage** • 431 DeKalb Ave [Classon]
- **Cake Man Raven Confectionary** • 708 Fulton St [Hanson]
- **Carol's Daughter** • 1 S Elliot Pl [DeKalb]
- **Dope Jams** • 580 Myrtle Ave
- **Frosted Moon** • 154 Vanderbilt Ave [Myrtle]
- **The Greene Grape** • 765 Fulton St [S Oxford]
- **Gureje** • 886 Pacific St [Underhill]
- **Kiki's Pet Spa** • 239 DeKalb Ave [Vanderbilt]
- **Malchijah Hats** • 225 DeKalb Ave [Clermont]
- **The Midtown Greenhouse Garden Center** • 115 Flatbush Ave [Hanson]
- **My Little India** • 96 S Elliot Pl [Fulton]
- **Owa African Market** • 434 Myrtle Ave [Waverly]
- **Pratt Institute Bookstore** • 550 Myrtle Ave [Emerson Pl]
- **Target** • Atlantic Terminal • 139 Flatbush Ave [Atlantic]
- **White Elephant Gallery** • 572 Myrtle Ave [Classon]
- **Yu Interiors** • 15 Greene Ave [Cumberland]

Map 32 • BoCoCa / Red Hook

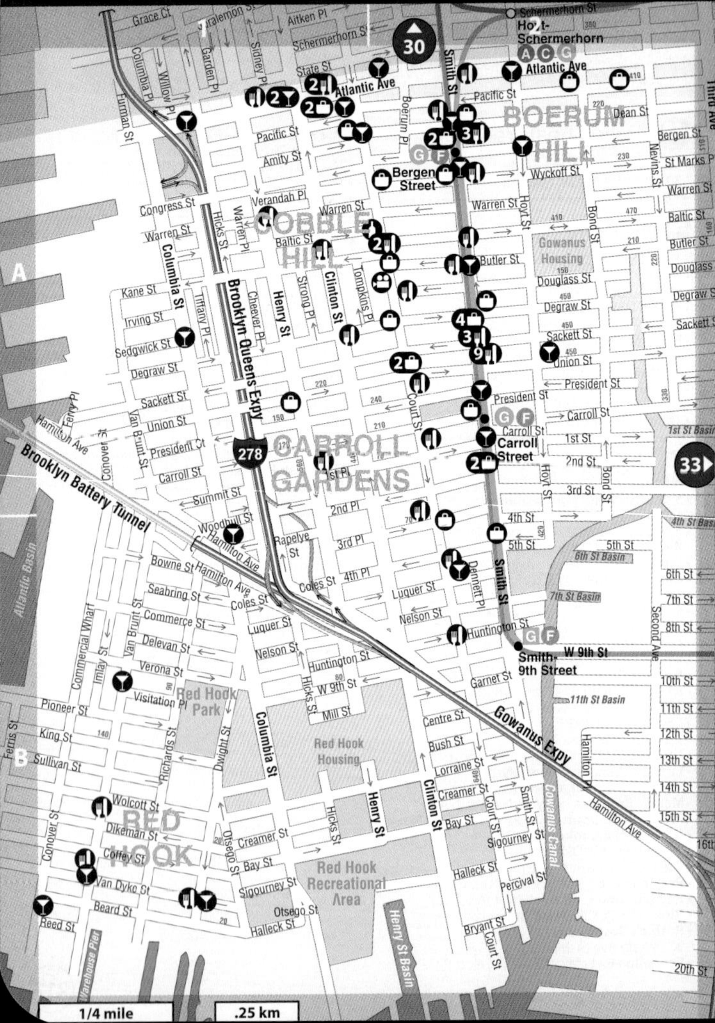

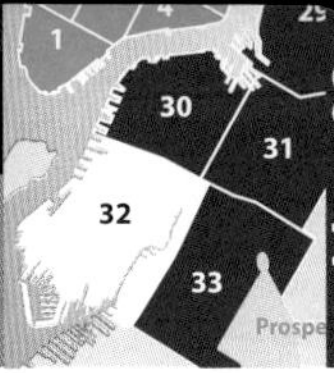

Entertainment

Map 32

The saturation of shops and restaurants on Court and Smith Streets is complete—seven Thai restaurants between the two, for instance. And CG West (Columbia Street) and Red Hook aren't too far behind, as standouts Alma, Good Fork, and Red Hook Bait & Tackle show. But don't forget Sunny's!

🎬 Movie Theaters

- **Cobble Hill Cinemas** • 265 Court St [Butler]

🍸 Nightlife

- **Abilene** • 442 Court St [3rd Pl]
- **Black Mountain Wine House** • 415 Union St [Hoyt]
- **Boat** • 175 Smith St [Wyckoff]
- **Brazen Head** • 228 Atlantic Ave [Court]
- **Brooklyn Inn** • 148 Hoyt St [Bergen]
- **Brooklyn Social** • 335 Smith St [Carroll]
- **Cody's Bar & Grill** • 154 Court St [Dean]
- **Downtown Bar & Grill** • 160 Court St [Amity]
- **Floyd** • 131 Atlantic Ave [Henry]
- **Gowanus Yacht Club** • 323 Smith [President]
- **Issue Project Room** • 232 3rd St [3rd Ave]
- **Kili** • 81 Hoyt St [State]
- **Last Exit** • 136 Atlantic Ave [Henry]
- **Montero Bar and Grill** • 73 Atlantic [Hicks]
- **Moonshine** • 317 Columbia St [Hicks]
- **PJ Hanley's** • 449 Court St [4th Pl]
- **Red Hook Bait & Tackle** • 320 Van Brunt St [Pioneer]
- **Rocky Sullivan's** • 34 Van Dyke St [Dwight]
- **Sugar Lounge** • 147A Columbia St [Kane]
- **Sunny's** • 253 Conover St [Reed]
- **Tini's Wine Bar & Cafe** • 414 Van Brunt St [Coffey]
- **Waterfront Ale House** • 155 Atlantic [Clinton]

🍴 Restaurants

- **Alma** • 187 Columbia St [Degraw]
- **Atlantic Chip Shop** • 129 Atlantic Ave [Henry]
- **Bar Tabac** • 128 Smith St [Dean]
- **Bocca Lupo** • 391 Henry St [Warren St]
- **Caserta Vecchia** • 155 Smith St [Bergen]
- **Chance** • 223 Smith St [Butler]
- **Chestnut** • 271 Smith St [DeGraw]
- **Chicory** • 243 DeGraw St [Clinton]
- **Cubana Café** • 272 Smith St [Degraw]
- **El Nuevo Portal** • 217 Smith St [Butler]
- **Ferdinando's Focacceria Restaurant** • 151 Union St [Hicks]
- **Fragole** • 394 Court St [Carroll]
- **Frankie's 457** • 457 Court St [Luquer]
- **The Good Fork** • 391 Van Brunt St [Coffey]

- **The Grocery** • 288 Smith St [Sackett]
- **Hadramout** • 172 Atlantic Ave [Clinton]
- **Hanco's** • 85 Bergen St [Smith]
- **Hope & Anchor** • 347 Van Brunt St [Wolcott]
- **Joya** • 215 Court St [Warren St]
- **Ki Sushi** • 122 Smith St [Dean]
- **Le Petite Café** • 502 Court St [Nelson]
- **Liberty Heights Tap Room** • 34 Van Dyke St [Dwight]
- **Lucali** • 575 Henry St [Carroll]
- **Panino'teca 275** • 275 Smith St [Sackett]
- **Patois** • 255 Smith St [Degraw]
- **Quercy** • 242 Court St [Baltic]
- **Sam's Restaurant** • 238 Court St [Baltic]
- **Saul** • 140 Smith St [Bergen]
- **Sherwood Café/Robin des Bois** • 195 Smith St [Warren]
- **Soul Spot** • 302 Atlantic Ave [Smith]
- **Yemen Café** • 176 Atlantic Ave [Clinton]
- **Zaytoons** • 283 Smith St [Sackett]

🛍 Shopping

- **A Cook's Companion** • 197 Atlantic Ave [Court]
- **Adam's Fresh Bakery by Design** • 144 Smith St [Bergen]
- **American Beer Distributors** • 256 Court St [Kane]
- **Blue Marble** • 420 Atlantic Ave [Bond]
- **Book Court** • 163 Court St [Dean]
- **Butter** • 389 Atlantic Ave [Bond]
- **Caputo's Fine Foods** • 460 Court St [3rd Pl]
- **D'Amico Foods** • 309 Court St [Degraw]
- **Environment337** • 337 Smith St [Carroll]
- **Exit 9** • 127 Smith St [Dean]
- **Fish Tales** • 296 Smith St [Union]
- **Flight 001** • 132 Smith St [Dean]
- **Marquet Patisserie** • 221 Court St [Warren]
- **Mazzola Bakery** • 192 Union St [Henry]
- **Refinery** • 254 Smith St [Douglass]
- **Rocketship** • 208 Smith St [Baltic]
- **Sahadi Importing Company** • 187 Atlantic Ave [Court]
- **Staubitz Meat Market** • 222 Court St [Baltic]
- **Stinky** • 261 Smith St [Degraw]
- **Swallow** • 361 Smith St [2nd]

Atlantic Ave
31

State St
Pacific St
Pacific Street
M N R D
Dean St
Bergen St
Bergen Street
2 3
St Mark's Pl
Prospect Pl
Warren St
Baltic St
Third Ave
Butler St
Douglass St
Degraw St
Sackett St
Union Street
M R
1st St Basin
32
4th St Basin
Whitwell Pl
Denton Pl
Fifth Avenue
Sixth Ave

Dean St
Bergen St
St Mark's Ave
7th Avenue
Park Pl

PROSPECT
HEIGHTS

Pacific St
Washington Ave
Grand Ave

Sterling Pl
St Johns Pl
Lincoln Pl

Plaza St E
Butler Pl
Lindenth Ave

Brooklyn
Botanic
Garden

Flatbush Ave

Prospect Pl
Sterling Pl
St Johns Pl
Lincoln Pl
Berkeley Pl
Union St
President St
Carroll St
Garfield Pl
1st St
2nd St
3rd St
4th St
5th St
6th St
7th St
8th St

Seventh Ave
Eighth Ave

Grand Army
Plaza
Grand Army Plz

Polhemus Pl
Fiske Pl
Montgomery Pl

PARK
SLOPE

West Dr
East Dr

Prospect
Park

4th Avenue-
9th Street
M F
R

9th St
7th Avenue
10th St
11th St
12th St
13th St
14th St
15th St
16th St

Fifth Avenue
Sixth Ave
Seventh Ave
Eighth Ave

Prospect Park W

F

15th Street-
Prospect Park
F

Prospect Park SW

W Lake Dr

WINDSOR
TERRACE

Tenth Ave
Sherman St
11th Ave

Prospect
Avenue
M R
278

Prospect Expy
17th St
18th St
27

Jackson Pl
Webster Pl
Calder Pl
Windsor Pl

Prospect Ave

Fuller Pl
17th St
Howard Pl
Prospect Park W

1/4 mile   .25 km

As if 7th and 5th Avenues didn't have enough already, now 4th (Sheep Station, Cherry Tree, etc.) gets into the act. Top food abounds—Applewood, Franny's, Blue Ribbon, Stone Park—as does great nabe hangouts Beast, The Gate, and Flatbush Farm. For live acts, head to Barbes, Southpaw, and Union Hall.

Movie Theaters

- **Pavilion Movie Theatres** •
188 Prospect Park W [Greenwood]

Nightlife

- **Bar Toto** • 411 11th St [6th Ave]
- **Barbes** • 376 9th St [6th Ave]
- **Buttermilk** • 577 Fifth Ave [16th]
- **Canal Bar** • 270 Third Ave [President St]
- **Cherry Tree** • 65 4th Ave [Bergen St]
- **Commonwealth** • 497 5th Ave [12th St]
- **Flatbush Farm** •
76 St Marks Ave [Flatbush Ave]
- **Freddy's Bar and Backroom** •
485 Dean St [6th Ave]
- **Fourth Avenue Pub** • 76 4th Ave [Bergen St]
- **The Gate** • 321 Fifth Ave [3rd St]
- **Ginger's** • 363 Fifth Ave [5th]
- **Great Lakes** • 284 Fifth Ave [1st St]
- **Good Coffeehouse Music Parlor** •
53 Prospect Park West [2nd St]
- **Hank's Saloon** • 46 Third Ave [Atlantic]
- **Lighthouse Tavern** • 243 Fifth Ave [Carroll]
- **Loki Lounge** • 304 Fifth Ave [2nd]
- **O'Connor's** • 39 Fifth Ave [Bergen]
- **Pacific Standard** • 82 Fourth Ave [St Marks Pl]
- **Park Slope Ale House** • 356 Sixth Ave [5th]
- **Patio Lounge** • 179 Fifth Ave [Berkeley]
- **Puppet's Jazz Bar** • 294 Fifth Ave [1st]
- **Soda** • 629 Vanderbilt Ave [Prospect Pl]
- **Southpaw** • 125 Fifth Ave [Sterling]
- **Timboo's** • 477 5th Ave [11th St]
- **Union Hall** • 202 Union St [5th Ave]

Restaurants

- **12th Street Bar and Grill** •
1123 Eighth Ave [11th]
- **2nd Street Café** • 189 Seventh Ave [2nd]
- **Al Di La Trattoria** • 248 Fifth Ave [Carroll]
- **Amorina** • 624 Vanderbilt Ave [Propect Pl]
- **Anthony's** • 426 Seventh Ave [14th]
- **Applewood** • 501 11th St [7th Ave]
- **Beast** • 638 Bergen St [Vanderbilt]
- **Belleville** • 332 Fifth Ave [3rd St]
- **Blue Ribbon Brooklyn** • 280 Fifth Ave [1st St]
- **Bogota Latin Bistro** • 141 Fifth Ave [St Johns]
- **Bonnie's Grill** • 278 Fifth Ave [1st St]
- **Brooklyn Fish Camp** •
162 Fifth Ave [Douglass]
- **ChipShop** • 383 Fifth Ave [6th]
- **Convivium Osteria** • 68 Fifth Ave [St Marks Pl]
- **Cousin John's Café and Bakery** •
70 Seventh Ave [Lincoln]
- **Dizzy's** • 511 Eighth Ave [5th St]
- **Elora's** • 272 Prospect Park W [17th]
- **Flatbush Farm** •
76 St Marks Ave [Flatbush Ave]
- **Franny's** • 295 Flatbush Ave [Prospect Pl]
- **Garden Café** •
620 Vanderbilt Ave [Prospect Pl]
- **Gen Restaurant** •
659 Washington Ave [St Marks Ave]
- **Jpan Sushi** • 287 5th Ave [1st St]
- **Kinara** • 473 Fifth Ave [11th]
- **La Taqueria** • 72 Seventh Ave [Berkeley]
- **The Minnow** • 442 9th St [7th Ave]
- **Mitchell's Soul Food** •
617 Vanderbilt Ave [St Marks Ave]
- **Moim** • 206 Garfield Pl [7th Ave]
- **Nana** • 155 Fifth Ave [Lincoln]
- **Noo Na** • 565 Vanderbilt Ave [Pacific St]
- **Olive Vine Café** • 54 Seventh Ave [St Johns]
- **Red Hot** • 349 Seventh Ave [10th]
- **Rose Water** • 787 Union St [6th Ave]
- **Sheep Station** • 149 4th Ave [Douglass]
- **Stone Park Café** • 324 Fifth Ave [3rd St]
- **Sushi Tatsu** • 347 Flatbush Ave [Sterling]
- **Tom's** • 782 Washington Ave [Sterling]
- **Watana** • 420 7th Ave [14th]

Shopping

- **3R Living** • 276 Fifth Ave [Garfield]
- **Artesana Home** • 170 Seventh Ave [1st St]
- **Beacon's Closet** • 220 Fifth Ave [President]
- **Bierkraft** • 191 5th Ave [Berkeley Pl]
- **Bird** • 430 Seventh Ave [14th]
- **Brooklyn Superhero Supply** •
372 Fifth Ave [6th Ave]
- **Buttercup's PAW-tisserie** • 63 5th Ave [10th]
- **Clay Pot** • 162 Seventh Ave [Garfield]
- **Fabrica** • 619 Vanderbilt Ave [Prospect Pl]
- **JackRabbit Sports** •
151 Seventh Ave [Garfield]
- **Leaf and Bean** • 83 Seventh Ave [Berkeley]
- **Loom** • 115 Seventh Ave [President]
- **Mostly Modern** • 383 Seventh Ave [12th]
- **Movable Feast** • 284 Prospect Park W [18th]
- **Nancy Nancy** • 244 Fifth Ave [Carroll]
- **Rare Device** • 453 Seventh Ave [16th]
- **Root Stock & Quade** •
297 Seventh Ave [7th St]
- **Somethin' Else** • 294 Fifth Ave [1st St]
- **Stitch Therapy** • 176 Lincoln Pl [7th Ave]
- **Trailer Park** • 77 Sterling Pl [6th Ave]
- **Uncle Louie G's** • 741 Union St [6th Ave]

Map 34 · Hoboken

N

13th St

14th St
Viaduct

13th St

12th St

Hoboken
Historical
Museum

Hoboken North
Ferries

to Pier 78
38th St

1400

1200

500   400   300

Monroe St
Madison St
Jefferson St
Adams St
Grand St
Clinton St
Willow Ave
Park Ave
Garden St
Bloomfield St
Washington St
Hudson St

11th St

1000

A

JFK
Stadium

Columbus
Park

10th St

Elysian
Park

HOBOKEN

9th St

200

100

8th St

Hudson
River

7th St

Stevens
Institute of
Technology

Castle Point Ter

Sinatra Dr

Willow
Terrace

6th St

600

Frank Sinatra's
Childhood House
Location

5th St

200   100

4

River St

Stevens
Park

4th St

Church
Square
Park

3

2

Court St

Hudson St

3rd St

Clinton St

2

Harrison St
Jackson St
Monroe St
Madison St
Jefferson St
Adams St
Grand St
Willow Ave
Park Ave
Garden St
Bloomfield St

2nd St

2

River St

Sinatra Dr

To Pier 78
38th St

B

1st St

3

Pier A
Park

Newark St

100   84

Hoboken
Terminal

PAGE
299

Hoboken
South
Ferries

2

Hudson Pl

Paterson St

Observer Hwy

Hoboken

PATH/NJ Transit/
Light Rail

To World
Financial
Center

Newark Ave

Manila Ave

Luis M Marin Blvd

565   563

PAGE
311

To Pier A
Wall St

To Pier 11
Wall St

35

PATH

1/4 mile   .25 km

It's only a short trip from the Village by PATH or ferry, but Hoboken feels more like an upscale college town. The salty longshoremen have moved on to that great pier in the sky, or at least to a members-only social club in town, leaving the waterfront to parkland, luxury condos, and many, many yuppies. Best bets for explorers are the raw clams at Biggies, beer and brats at Helmer's, and margaritas at East LA.

○ Landmarks

- **Elysian Park** • n/a
- **Frank Sinatra's Childhood House Location** • 415 Monroe St [4th St]
- **Hoboken Historical Museum** • 1301 Hudson St [13th St]
- **Hoboken Terminal** • 1 Hudson Pl [River St]
- **Willow Terrace** • 6th & 7th St b/w Willow Ave & Clinton St

 Nightlife

- **City Bistro** • 56 14th St [Washington St]
- **Leo's Grandezvous** • 200 Grand St [2nd St]
- **Maxwell's** • 1039 Washington St [10th St]
- **Oddfellows** • 80 River St [Newark St]

🍴 Restaurants

- **Amanda's** • 908 Washington St [9th St]
- **Arthur's Tavern** • 237 Washington St [2nd St]
- **Baja** • 104 14th St [Washington St]
- **Bangkok City** • 335 Washington St [3rd St]
- **Biggies Clam Bar** • 318 Madison St [3rd St]
- **Brass Rail** • 135 Washington St [1st St]
- **Cucharamama** • 233 Clinton St [2nd St]
- **Delfino's** • 500 Jefferson St [5th St]
- **East LA** • 508 Washington St [5th St]
- **Far Side Bar & Grill** • 531 Washington St [5th St]
- **Frankie & Johnnie's** • 163 14th St [Bloomfield St]
- **Gaslight** • 400 Adams St [4th St]
- **Helmer's** • 1036 Washington St [10th St]
- **Hoboken Gourmet Company** • 423 Washington St [4th St]
- **Karma Kafe** • 505 Washington St [5th St]
- **La Isla** • 104 Washington St [1st St]
- **Oddfellows Restaurant** • 80 River St [Warren St]
- **Robongi** • 520 Washington St [5th St]
- **Sushi Lounge** • 200 Hudson St [2nd St]
- **Trattoria Saporito** • 328 Washington St [3rd St]
- **Zafra** • 301 Willow Ave [3rd St]

🛍 Shopping

- **Big Fun Toys** • 602 Washington St [6th St]
- **City Paint & Hardware** • 130 Washington St [1st St]
- **Galatea** • 1224 Washington St [12th St]
- **Hoboken Farmboy** • 127 Washington St [1st St]
- **Kings Fresh Ideas** • 1212 Shipyard Ln [12th St]
- **Kings Fresh Ideas** • 333 River St [3rd St]
- **Lisa's Italian Deli** • 901 Park Ave [9th St]
- **Peper** • 1028 Washington St [10th St]
- **Sobsey's Produce** • 92 Bloomfield St [Newark St]
- **Sparrow Wine and Liquor** • 1224 Shipyard Ln [12th St]
- **Sparrow Wine and Liquor** • 126 Washington St [1st St]
- **Tunes New & Used CDs** • 225 Washington St [2nd St]
- **Yes I Do** • 312 Washington St [3rd St]

Map 35 • **Jersey City**

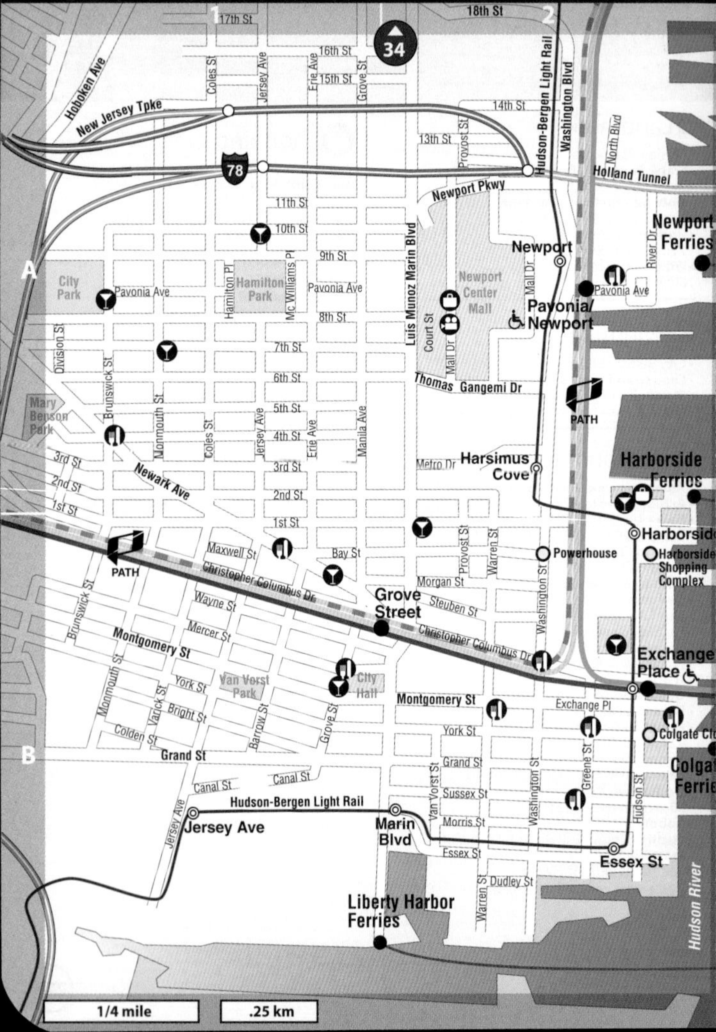

N

17th St
18th St
16th St
15th St
14th St
13th St
11th St
10th St
9th St
8th St
7th St
6th St
5th St
4th St
3rd St
2nd St
1st St

34
78

Hoboken Ave
New Jersey Tpke
Coles St
Jersey Ave
Erie St
Grove St
Provost St
Washington Blvd
North Blvd
Hudson-Bergen Light Rail
Holland Tunnel

Newport Pkwy

Newport
Newport Ferries
River Dr
Pavonia Ave
Mall Dr

Luis Munoz Marin Blvd
Court St
Mall Dr
Newport Center Mall

Pavonia/ Newport

City Park
Pavonia Ave
Hamilton Pl
McWilliams Pl
Pavonia Ave

Thomas Gangemi Dr

Division St
Brunswick St
Monmouth St
Coles St
Jersey Ave
Erie St
Manila Ave

Metro Dr
Harsimus Cove

PATH

Harborside Ferries
Harborside
Harborside Shopping Complex

Mary Benson Park
3rd St
2nd St
1st St
Newark Ave

Maxwell St
Bay St

Provost St
Warren St
Powerhouse
Washington St

PATH
Christopher Columbus Dr
Wayne St
Mercer St
Morgan St
Steuben St

Grove Street
Christopher Columbus Dr

Brunswick St
Montgomery St

Van Vorst Park
City Hall

Montgomery St
York St

Washington St
Exchange Place
Exchange Pl
Greene St

Colgate Clo
Colgate Ferrie

Monmouth St
Varick St
Bright St
Colden St
Grand St

Grove St
Barrow St

Grand St
Sussex St

Hudson St

Canal St
Canal St
Hudson-Bergen Light Rail

Jersey Ave
Jersey Ave

Marin Blvd
Morris St
Essex St

Essex St

Van Vorst St
Warren St
Dudley St

Liberty Harbor Ferries

Hudson River

1/4 mile   .25 km

Map 35

Jersey City has a siren song that lures dissatisfied New Yorkers to its mall-studded shores. First it came for the artists, then for our young families and yuppies. Next it came for our offices and suburbanites. Maybe you should start hanging out at Marco and Pepe's right now and be done with it. White Mana's is a bona fide landmark, after all, and we love Morgan's octopus platter, Ibby's falafel, Fatburger's L.A. grease...

○ Landmarks

- **Colgate Clock** • 30 Hudson St [Essex St]
- **Harborside Shopping Complex** • n/a
- **Powerhouse** • 344 Washington St [Bay St]
- **White Mana** • 470 Tonnele Ave [Bleecker St]

😀 Movie Theaters

- **AMC Newport Center 11** •
  30 Mall Dr W [Thomas Gangemi Dr]

🍸 Nightlife

- **Hamilton Park Ale House** •
  708 Jersey Ave [10th St]
- **Lamp Post Bar and Grille** •
  382 2nd St [Brunswick St]
- **LITM** • 140 Newark Ave [Grove St]
- **The Merchant** •
  279 Grove St [Montgomery St]
- **PJ Ryan's** • 172 1st St [Luiz Munoz Marin Blvd]
- **White Star** • 230 Brunswick St [Pavonia Ave]

🍴 Restaurants

- **Amelia's Bistro** • 187 Warren St [Essex St]
- **Beechwood Cafe** • 290 Grove St [Mercer St]
- **Fatburger** •
  286 Washington St [Christopher Columbus St]
- **Ibby's** • 303 Grove St [Wayne St]
- **Iron Monkey** • 97 Greene St [York St]
- **It's Greek to Me** •
  194 Newark Ave [Jersey Ave]
- **Kitchen Café** • 60 Sussex St [Greene St]
- **Komegashi** • 103 Montgomery St [Warren St]
- **Komegashi Too** • 99 Pavonia Ave [River Dr S]
- **Light Horse Tavern** •
  199 Washington St [Morris St]
- **Madame Claude** • 364 4th St [4th St]
- **Marco and Pepe** • 289 Grove St [Mercer St]
- **Morgan Seafood** •
  2801 John F Kennedy Blvd [Sip Ave]
- **Presto's Restaurant** •
  199 Warren St [Morris St]
- **Rosie Radigans** •
  10 Exchange Pl, Lobby [Hudson St]
- **Saigon Café** • 188 Newark Ave [Jersey Ave]
- **Sri Ganesh** • 809 Newark Ave [Liberty Ave]
- **White Mana** • 470 Tonnele Ave [Bleecker St]

🛍 Shopping

- **Harborside Shopping Complex** • n/a
- **Newport Center Mall** •
  30 Mall Dr W [Thomas Gangemi Dr]
- **Patel Snacks** • 785 Newark Ave [Herpert Pl]

Westchester

87

6

9

Woodlawn

Van Cortlandt
Golf Course

2

Baychester Ave

Wakefield
E 233rd St

Seton
Falls
Park

New England Pkwy

Pelham
Bay
Park

Shore Rd

11

Orchard
Beach

Hunters
Island

Ca
Islar

Eastchester

13

Co-Op
City

Rodman
Neck

Hutchinson River Pkwy

5

Wave Hill

Van Cortlandt
Park

Woodlawn
Cemetery

7

Jerome Ave

Williamsbridge

Gun Hill Rd

Haffen
Park

95

Baychester

Eastchester
Bay

Pelham
Bay
Park

Mosholu Pkwy

Norwood

Mosholu Pkwy

2

Bedford
Park

Boston Rd

BRONX

Bronx and Pelham Expwy

Williams Bridge Rd

Morris
Park

695

4

Riverdale

Marble
Hill

New York
Botanical

8

Pelham
Bay

Bruckner Expwy

Henry
Hudson
Bridge

18

Kings-
bridge
Heights

Webster Ave

Fordham
University

Bronx
Park

5

Williams Bridge Rd

E Tremont Ave

295

Thro
N

University
Heights
Bridge

University
Heights

Belmont

19

Bronx
Zoo

10

East
Tremont

Bronx River

Parkchester

Cross Bronx Expwy

St Raymond's
Cemetery

Ferry
Point
Park

678

Henry Hudson Pkwy

Morris
Heights

Tremont

E Tremont Ave

West
Farms

95

278

Castle
Hill

Washington
Bridge

2

Cross Bronx Expwy

Claremont

Crotona
Park

Sheridan Expwy

895

Bruckner Expwy

17

Castle
Hill

Locomotive Ave

Bronx
Whitestone
Bridge

Hamilton
Bridge

3

Grand Concourse

Third Ave

Claremont
Village

Morrisania

Boston Rd

Soundview

Clason
Point

Bronx
River

Sound View Park

Hudson
River

Harlem River

20

B
D

E 161 St

6

Hunts Point

**Flushing
Bay**

9A

Macombs
Dam Bridge

87

Yankee
Stadium

1

15

16

Longwood

St Mary's
Park

Bruckner Blvd

Bruckner Expwy

Riker's
Island

3

145 St
Bridge

E 149th St

14

Mott Haven

Madison Ave
Bridge

6

Port
Morris

3rd Ave
Bridge

Willis Ave
Bridge

Triborough
Bridge

Park Ave

A
C
B
D

1
2
3

4
5
6

MANHATTAN

QUEENS

278

Don't be afraid of the Boogie Down Bronx. Decades of entrenched poverty and poor urban planning once frayed many neighborhoods, but the borough today is no longer the burning wreck your parents warned you about years ago.

Communities

Belmont's Arthur Avenue **3** is still an authentic Little Italy even though many businesses now belong to Albanians. Woodlawn **9** is home to many Irish immigrants and it's got the pubs to prove it. With 15,372 units, towering Co-op City **13** is rightly called a city within the city; it even has its own mall! The Mott Haven **14** and Longwood **15** historic districts boast beautiful homes, but "The Hub" **16** features the grand architecture of the past conveniently filled with the discount shopping of today. For antiques, visit the cobblestone corridor of Bruckner Boulevard **17** at Alexander Avenue. Some of the city's grandest homes sit in the wooded environs of Riverdale **4**, while City Island **12** resembles nothing so much as a New England fishing village crossed with a New Jersey suburb.

Culture

The New York Botanical Garden **8** and the Bronx Zoo **10** are justly famous, well worth whatever effort it may take to get there. For a beautiful view of the Hudson and the Palisades beyond, choose the botanical garden and historic estate Wave Hill **5** or the quirky Hall of Fame for Great Americans **2** featuring 98 bronze busts of notable citizens in a grand outdoor colonnade. Explore your inner Goth at historic Woodlawn Cemetery **7** or Poe Cottage **18**, the American poet's final home. The recently expanded Bronx Museum of the Arts **20** is the best place to check out contemporary work from artists of African, Asian, and Latin American descent.

Sports

This year we'll cheer and jeer our way through the Yanks' first season in their new digs, creatively named "New Yankee Stadium" as of press time. They paved the House that Ruth built and put up a parking lot. You simply can't call yourself a New Yorker until you've taken in an afternoon game at Yankee Stadium **1**. Van Cortlandt Park **6** offers playgrounds, ball fields, tennis and basketball courts, hiking trails, stables for horseback riding, and one of golf's classic courses, "Vanny."

Nature

The restoration of the Bronx River **19** coincides with the improvement of green spaces throughout the borough. Pelham Bay Park **11** is the city's largest at 2,764 acres, offering many recreational opportunities in addition to the Thomas Pell Wildlife Sanctuary, two nature centers, and immensely popular Orchard Beach.

Food

Belmont:
- Dominick's, 2335 Arthur Ave, 718-733-2807 Famous, old-school Italian-American where there are no menus and no set prices.
- Full Moon, 602 East 187th St, 718-584-3451—Wonderful pizza and calzones.
- Roberto Restaurant, 603 Crescent Ave, 718-733-9503— Classic fare, rumored to be the best around.
- Arthur Avenue Retail Market, 2344 Arthur Ave—Get all the right ingredients for home-cooked Italian meals.

City Island:
- Johnny's Reef, 2 City Island Ave, 718-885-2090—Local favorite for fresh, inexpensive seafood.
- Le Refuge Inn, 620 City Island Ave, 718-885-2478— Excellent French prix fixe meals in a historic B&B.

Riverdale:
- Riverdale Garden, 4574 Manhattan College Pkwy, 718-884-5232—Upscale American and Continental food in a beautiful setting.
- An Beal Bocht, 445 West 238th St, 718-884-7127—Café/bar/coffee shop hangout for the hip, young, and Irish.
- S&S Cheesecake, 222 West 238th St, 718-549-3888— Forget Junior's, this is the city's best.

The Hub:
- In God We Trust, 441 E 153rd St, 718-401-3595—A café within a dry goods shop serving authentic Ghanaian food.

University Heights:
- African-American Restaurant, 1987 University Ave, 718-731-8595—24-hour diner serving soul food alongside traditional Ghanaian specialties.
- Ebe Ye Yie, 2364 Jerome Ave, 718-563-6064—Hearty Ghanaian meals.

Concourse Village:
- The Feeding Tree, 892 Gerard Ave, 718-293-5025— Delicious Jamaican food close to Yankee Stadium.

Kingsbridge:
- El Economico, 5589 Broadway, 718-796-4851—Home-style Puerto Rican meals.

Pelham Bay:
- Louie & Ernie's, 1300 Crosby Ave, 718-829-6230—Their thin-crust pizza is the best in the borough.

Bruckner Boulevard:
- Rinconcito Mexicano, 381 East 138th St, 718-401-8314— A great little place for tortas and tacos

Landmarks

1. Yankee Stadium
2. Hall of Fame for Great Americans
3. Arthur Avenue
4. Riverdale
5. Wave Hill
6. Van Cortlandt Park
7. Woodlawn Cemetery
8. New York Botanical Garden
9. Woodlawn
10. Bronx Zoo
11. Pelham Bay Park
12. City Island
13. Co-op City
14. Mott Haven
15. Longwood
16. The Hub
17. Bruckner Boulevard
18. Poe Cottage
19. Bronx River
20. Bronx Museum of the Arts

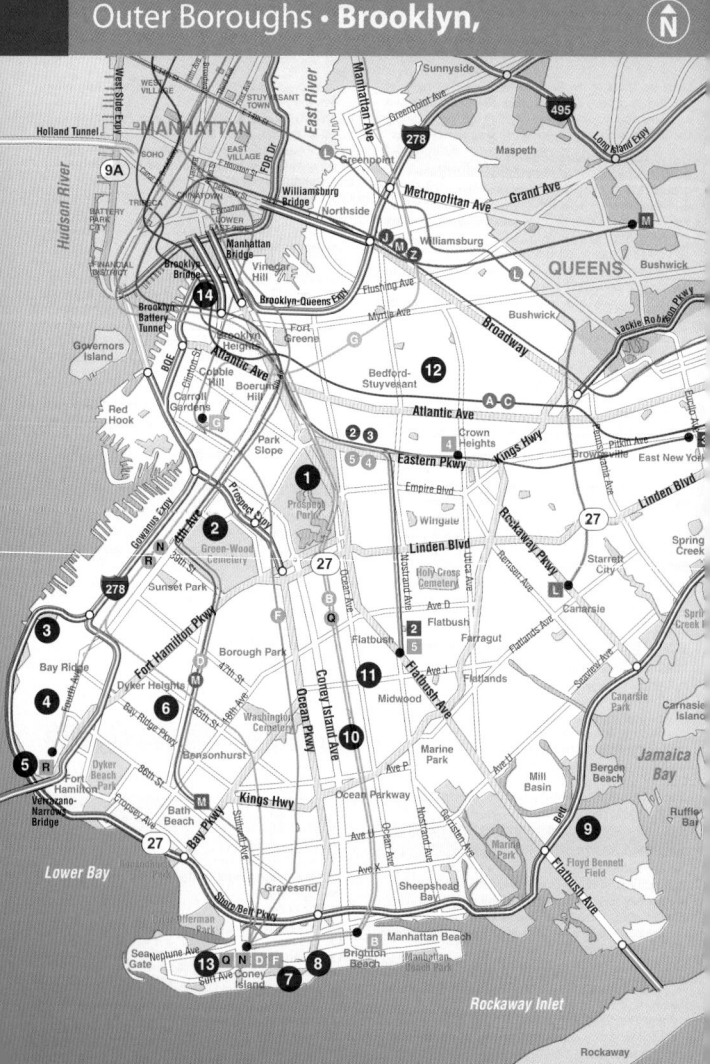

Until "The Great Mistake of 1898," Brooklyn was its own thriving city. Today, the Borough of Kings could still make a damn fine city all on its own. Although Manhattan will most likely overshadow Brooklyn for all of eternity, in recent years Brooklyn has begun to receive more than its fair share of attention. As Manhattan loses its neighborhood flavor while rents continue to soar, Brooklyn's popularity is at an all-time high. Scores of recent college grads, immigrants, ex-Manhattanites, and even celebrities are calling Brooklyn home. Along with the residential boom, Brooklyn has bloomed into a cultural and entertainment mecca, with top-notch restaurants, a thriving art and film scene, and plenty of unique shops. Throw in a bunch of cool bars, mind-blowing cultural diversity, and some of the city's best urban parks, and you get what may be the best place to live on the planet.

Communities

As the largest borough by population (over 2.5 million!), Brooklyn holds a special place as one of the nation's most important urban areas. As many as one in four people can trace their roots here! In Brooklyn, you can find pretty much any type of community—for better or for worse. As gentrification marches deeper into Brooklyn, the borough is changing fast. Neighborhoods most likely to see their first baby boutiques open soon include Red Hook, East Williamsburg, Prospect-Lefferts Gardens, and Crown Heights.

The first thing you notice when looking at Brooklyn on a map is the sheer size of it. Yet much of Brooklyn is largely unknown to most New Yorkers. Yes, Brooklyn Heights, Williamsburg, and Park Slope are nice communities that are fun to explore. However, if you've never ventured further out into Brooklyn than the obligatory trip to Coney Island, you're missing some fantastic neighborhoods. For instance, Bay Ridge **4** has beautiful single-family homes with its western edge, a killer view of the Verrazano Bridge, and a host of excellent shops and restaurants. Dyker Heights **6** is composed of almost all single-family homes, many of which go all-out with Christmas light displays during the holiday season. Brighton Beach **8** continues to be a haven for many Russian expatriates. The quiet, tree-lined streets of both Ocean Parkway **10** and Midwood **11** can make one forget all about the hustle and bustle of downtown Brooklyn, or downtown anywhere else for that matter. Finally, Bedford-Stuyvesant **12** has a host of cool public buildings, fun eateries, and beautiful brownstones.

Sports

No, the Dodgers are never coming back. This is still hard for many older Brooklynites to accept and accounts for much of the nostalgia that is still associated with the borough. If you can get beyond the fact that Ebbets Field is now a giant concrete housing complex, then you will enjoy spending a fine summer evening watching the Cyclones at Coney Island. Kensington Stables in Prospect Park provides lessons for wannabe equestrians. If you can never let go, then join the Brooklyn Kickball League to relive the happier moments of your childhood.

Attractions

There are plenty of reasons to dislike Coney Island **7**, imminent redevelopment notwithstanding, but they're simply not good enough when you stack them up against the Cyclone, the Wonder Wheel, Nathan's, Totonno's, the beach, the freaks, and *The Warriors*. Close by is the Aquarium **13**. Nature trails, parked blimps, views of the water, and scenic marinas all make historical Floyd Bennett Field **9** a worthwhile trip. For more beautiful views, you can check out Owl's Point Park **3** in Bay Ridge, or the parking lot underneath the Verrazano-Narrows Bridge **5** (located right off the Shore Parkway). The Verrazano might not be New York's most beautiful bridge, but it's hands-down the most awe-inspiring. Both Green-Wood Cemetery **2** and Prospect Park **1** provide enough greenery to keep you happy until you get to Yosemite. Finally, Brooklyn Heights **14** is the most beautiful residential neighborhood in all of New York. Don't believe us? Go stand on the corner of Willow and Orange Streets.

Food

Here are some restaurants in some of the outlying areas of Brooklyn: See pages 210 to 221 for other Brooklyn eateries.
Bay Ridge: Tuscany Grill, 8620 Third Ave, 718-921-5633—The gorgonzola steak is a must.
Coney Island: Totonno Pizzeria Napolitano, 1524 Neptune Ave, 718-372-8606—Paper-thin pizza. Bizarre hours.
Midwood: DiFara's Pizzeria, E 15th St & Ave J, 718-258-1367—Dirty, cheap, disgusting…awesome!
Sunset Park: Nyonya, 5223 Eighth Ave, 718-633-0808—Good quality Malaysian.
Sheepshead Bay: Randazzo's Clam Bar, 2017 Emmons Avenue, 718-615-0010—Essential summer dining.

Landmarks

1 Prospect Park	6 Dyker Heights	11 Midwood
2 Green-Wood Cemetery	7 Coney Island	12 Bedford-Stuyvesant
3 Owl's Point Park	8 Brighton Beach	13 New York Aquarium
4 Bay Ridge	9 Floyd Bennett Field	14 Brooklyn Heights
5 Verrazano-Narrows Bridge	10 Ocean Parkway	

N
MANHATTAN
Flushing Bay
Whitestone Bridge
Throgs Neck Bridge
Triborough Bridge
College Point
Whitestone
Cross Island Pkwy
LaGuardia Airport
Steinway
East Elmhurst
Flushing
Bayside
Douglaston
Queensboro Bridge
Astoria
Astoria Blvd
Grand Central Pkwy
Whitestone Expy
Northern Blvd
Utopia Pkwy
Francis Lewis Blvd
Clearview Expy
Long Island City
Jackson Heights
Flushing Meadows
Auburndale
Long Island Expy
Woodside
Kissena Park
Queens Blvd
Corona
Fresh Meadows
Floral Park
Sunnyside
Queens Expy
Elmhurst
Van Wyck Expy
Main St
Brooklyn
Queens Village
Grand Ave
Maspeth
Forest Hills
Hillside Ave
Hollis
Metropolitan Ave
Jamaica
Kew Gardens
Jamaica Ave
Bushwick
Forest Park
QUEENS
Cambria Heights
Broadway
Richmond Hill
South Jamaica
Woodhaven
St Albans
Atlantic Ave
Merrick Blvd
Springfield Blvd
Jackie
Ozone Park
Laurelton Pkwy
Rockaway Blvd
Conduit Ave
Springfield Gardens
Laurelton
Belt Pkwy
BROOKLYN
Kings Hwy
Linden Blvd
Bel
Cross Bay Blvd
Howard Beach
Rosedale
John F Kennedy International Airport
Airtrain
Rockaway Pkwy
Gateway National Recreation Area
Broad Channel
Far Rockaway
Somerville
Beach Channel Dr
Cross Bay Veterans Memorial Bridge
Jamaica Bay
Marine Parkway Bridge
Rockaway Beach
Atlantic Ocean
Lower New York Bay
Roxbury
Belle Harbor
Breezy Point
Rockaway Point

Outer Boroughs · **Queens**

Local publications declared Queens the next big thing years ago. We'll go on record: Queens will never be cool. But it will have affordable rents, easy subway access, cheap bars, and fantastic restaurants by the bushel. If that's not enough for you, have fun living in Jersey City, suckers!

Communities

From the stately Tudor homes of Forest Hills **28** gardens to the hip-hop beat of Jamaica Avenue **11**, Queens has it all. Eastern Queens tends towards suburbia, while the communities along the borough's southern border often include active industrial districts. All things Asian can be found in Flushing **20**, the city's largest Chinatown. Sunnyside **21** and Woodside **22** are home to Irish and Mexican immigrants alike, making it easy to find a proper pint and a fabulous taco on the same block. Jackson Heights' **6** 74th Street is Little India, while 82nd Street holds South and Central American businesses. Corona **23** blends old-school Italian-American delis with Latino dance clubs. Elmhurst **24** has attracted Asian, Southeast Asian, and South American immigrants to set up shop on its crowded streets. Island Broad Channel **12** feels like a sleepy village, while the Rockaways **13** offer the only surfing beaches in the city.

Culture

Fans of contemporary art have long known P.S.1 **4** is the place to be, especially during its summer weekend WarmUp parties. The Noguchi Museum **3**, dedicated to the work of the Japanese-American sculptor, and neighboring Socrates Sculpture Park **2**, a waterfront space with changing exhibitions, are less known. The Fischer Landau Center **25** is almost entirely unknown despite its world-class collection of modern art. Movie buffs should look for repertory screenings at the American Museum of the Moving Image **5**. The delightfully kitschy Louis Armstrong House **26** is a must-stop for jazz lovers. In Flushing Meadows-Corona Park, the New York Hall of Science **8** beckons the geeky kid in all of us with its hands-on exhibits while the Queens Museum of Art's **9** scale model of the entire city will wow even the most jaded New Yorkers.

Sports

In 2009, the Mets inaugurate a brand new place to make memories of exquisite disappointment, Jackie Robinson...err, sorry, kids... Citi Field. Enjoy the ersatz Ebbets Field façade. Feel free to root for the visiting team if you like—Mets supporters are far more subdued than their Yankee rivals. The U.S. Open takes place right across the street at the National Tennis Center. **7** See girls gone wild when our local ladies, The Queens of Pain, compete in the Gotham Girls Roller Derby league. Get out of that cruddy OTB and see the ponies live at the Aqueduct Racetrack **14**. Hitch a ride to Rockaway Beach **13** for swimming and surfing or paddle out in a kayak on loan from the Long Island City Community Boathouse **27**. Astoria Pool **1** is the city's largest with room for 3,000 swimmers. For bowling, all-night Whitestone Lanes **18** is the place to be.

Nature

Gantry State Park's **29** spacious piers attract strollers and urban fishermen alike with panoramic views of the Manhattan skyline, and a major park expansion is currently underway. The Jamaica Bay Wildlife Refuge **15** in Gateway National Recreation Area is internationally known for bird-watching. The Queens Zoo **19** is small but interesting, housing only animals native to North America. Flushing Meadows-Corona Park **30** is designed for active recreation, but Alley Pond Park **16** and Forest Park **17** have wooded trails perfect for wandering.

Food

Entire books have been written on where to eat in Queens (none as good as NFT, natch!), so these are just a handful of suggestions:
Corona: Leo's Latticini (a.k.a. Mama's), 46-02 104th St, 718-898-6639—Insanely good Italian sandwiches that pair well with dessert from the Lemon Ice King, 52-02 108th Street, 718-699-5133, just a few blocks away.
Forest Hills: Salut, 63-42 108th St, 718-275-6860—Order lots of lamb at this Kosher Uzbek gem.
Sunnyside: De Mole, 45-02 48th Ave, 718-392-2161—BYOB with fresh, simply prepared Mexican food.
Bayside: Uncle Jack's, 39-40 Bell Blvd, 718-229-1100—Mayor Bloomberg's favorite steakhouse serves up fine flesh.
Flushing: Spicy and Tasty, 39-07 Prince Street, 718-359-1601—The name of this Sichuan place is entirely accurate.
Woodside:
• Spicy Mina, 64-23 Broadway, 718-205-2340—Authentic Bangladeshi/Indian food superior to the blander fare of 74th Street.
• Sripaphai, 64-13 39th Ave, 718-899-9599—Easily the best Thai food in the city.
• La Flor, 53-02 Roosevelt Ave, 718-426-8023—Fantastic neighborhood café with Mexican-inflected dishes.
Elmhurst: Minangasli, 86-10 Whitney Ave, 718-429-8207—Delicious, inexpensive Indonesian fare.

Landmarks

1 Astoria Pool
2 Socrates Sculpture Park
3 Noguchi Museum
4 P.S.1 Art Museum
5 American Museum of the Moving Image
6 Jackson Heights
7 US Open/National Tennis Center
8 Hall of Science
9 Queens Museum of Art
10 Shea Stadium
11 Jamaica
12 Broad Channel
13 The Rockaways
14 Aqueduct Racetrack
15 Jamaica Bay Wildlife Refuge
16 Alley Pond Park
17 Forest Park
18 Whitestone Lanes
19 Queens Zoo
20 Flushing
21 Sunnyside
22 Woodside
23 Corona
24 Elmhurst
25 Fischer Landau Center
26 Louis Armstrong House
27 Long Island City Community Boathouse
28 Forest Hills
29 Gantry State Park
30 Flushing Meadows-Corona Park

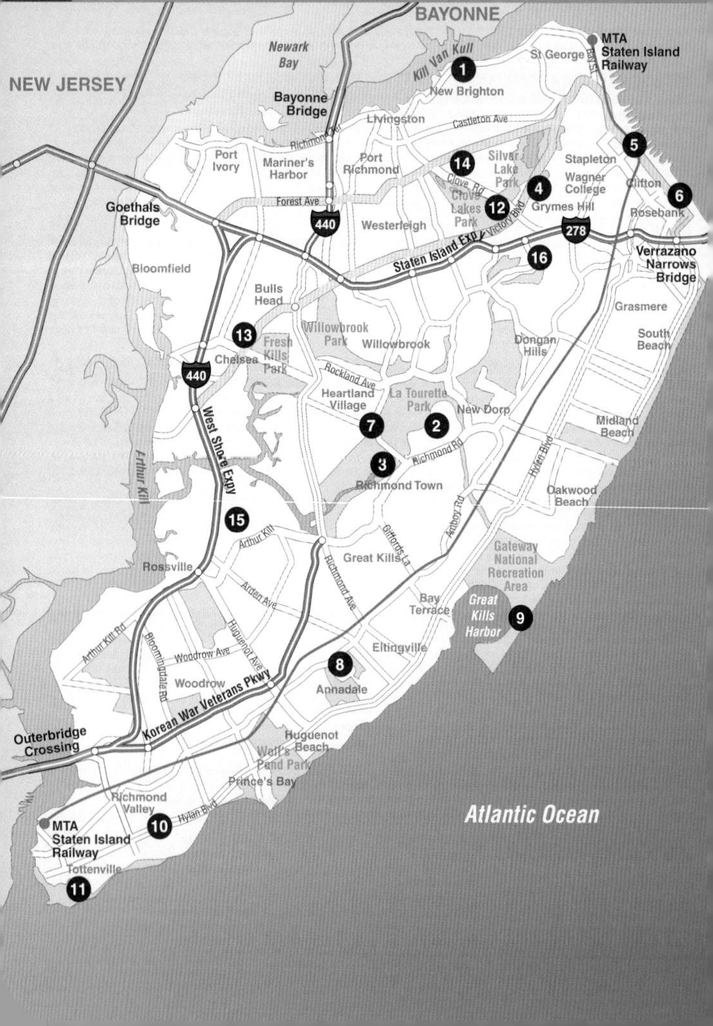

BAYONNE

Newark Bay

NEW JERSEY

Kill Van Kull

St George

MTA
Staten Island
Railway

1

New Brighton

Bayonne Bridge

Livingston

Castleton Ave

Port Ivory

Mariner's Harbor

Port Richmond

Silver Lake Park

14

Clove Rd

Stapleton

5

Clove Lakes Park

12

4

Wagner College

Clifton

6

Grymes Hill

Rosebank

Goethals Bridge

Forest Ave

Westerleigh

Staten Island Exp

Victory Blvd

16

278

Verrazano Narrows Bridge

Bloomfield

Grasmere

Bulls Head

Willowbrook Park

Willowbrook

Dongan Hills

South Beach

13

Chelsea

Fresh Kills Park

440

Rockland Ave

Heartland Village

La Tourette Park

7

2

New Dorp

Midland Beach

3

Richmond Rd

Richmond Town

Arthur Kill

Oakwood Beach

West Shore Expy

15

Arthur Kill

Great Kills

Richmond Ave

Bay Terrace

Gateway National Recreation Area

9

Great Kills Harbor

Arden Ave

Eltingville

Woodrow Ave

Hylan Blvd

Amboy Rd

Woodrow

8

Annadale

Korean War Veterans Pkwy

Bloomingdale Rd

Huguenot

Wolf's Beach Pond Park

Prince's Bay

Atlantic Ocean

Outerbridge Crossing

Arthur Kill Rd

Richmond Valley

Hylan Blvd

10

MTA
Staten Island
Railway

11

Tottenville

Staten Island, of thee we sing! Don't let the sight of yabbos with fake tans and gelled hair hold you back from exploring, lest you miss out on heaps of excellent pizza, the wildflower meadows at Mount Loretto, the windows on the past at Historic Richmond Town, the small-town charm of minor league baseball at St. George, and the striking design of the Chinese Scholars' Garden at Snug Harbor. It's high time you pulled your head out of your borough and hitched a ride on the ferry.

Culture

1 **Snug Harbor Cultural Center**, 1000 Richmond Ter, 718-448-2500. A former sailors' home transformed to a waterfront arts complex, Snug Harbor's 83 acres include classrooms, studio spaces, performance venues, galleries, three museums, and a truly noteworthy botanical garden. Call to learn about cultural events and exhibits on site.

2 **Jacques Marchais Museum of Tibetan Art**, 338 Lighthouse Ave, 718-987-3500. A world-class collection of Tibetan art, courtesy of former New York art collector Edna Coblentz, who had the surprising French pseudonym Jacques Marchais.

3 **Historic Richmondtown**, 441 Clark Ave, 718-351-1611. Get back to old-timey times visiting restored homes from the 17th to the 19th centuries, most populated by costumed guides. Great for kids and adults who want to learn how to churn butter/forge metal.

4 **Wagner College**, 1 Campus Rd, 718-390-3100. Wagner's tranquil hilltop location rewards visitors with beautiful views of the serene surroundings, but its best feature is the planetarium.

5 **Staten Island Village Hall**, 111 Canal St. Last remaining village hall building in Staten Island, a reminder of the borough's rural past.

6 **Alice Austen House**, 2 Hylan Blvd, 718-816-4506. Alice Austen was an early twentieth-century amateur photographer, and now she's got a museum and a ferry boat named after her. Go figure. Some of her 8,000 images are on view at her house, which has a great view of lower New York Harbor.

Nature

7 **The Staten Island Greenbelt**, 200 Nevada Ave, 718-667-2165. This 2,500-acre swath of land (comprising several different parks) in the center of the island contains a golf course, a hospital, a scout camp, several graveyards, and plenty of wooded areas that remain relatively undeveloped and can be accessed only by walking trails. A good starting point is High Rock Park. Panoramic views abound.

8 **Blue Heron Park**, 222 Poillon Ave, 718-967-3542. This quiet, 147-acre park has a fantastic Nature Center and plenty of ponds, wetlands, and streams to explore. Noted for bird-watching, hence the name.

9 **Great Kills Park**, 718-987-6790. Part of the Gateway National Recreation Area, Great Kills boasts clean beaches, a marina, and a nature preserve.

10 **Mount Loretto Unique Area**, 6450 Hylan Blvd, 718-482-7287. Flourishing wetlands, grasslands, and beaches all rolled into one serenely beautiful waterfront park. Mysterious sculptures dot the beach.

11 **Conference House Park**, 7455 Hylan Blvd, 718-984-0415. The historic house is worth a look, but watching the sunset from the restored waterfront pavilion is a must. You'll also find NYC's very own "South Pole" on the beach here.

12 **Clove Lakes Park**, Clove Rd and Victory Blvd, 311. Who needs Central Park? Check out these romantic rowboats on the lake in summer.

13 **Fresh Kills Park**, off Route 440. Former landfill, now a park. Sorta. They're working on it. Free tours by appointment.

Other

14 **110/120 Longfellow Road**. Celebrate one of the greatest American films without having to schlep to Sicily. This address is where the Corleone family held court in *The Godfather*.

15 **Ship Graveyard**, at Arthur Kill Rd and Rossville Ave. These ships of the damned make a perfect backdrop for Goth photo shoots.

16 **Staten Island Zoo**, 614 Broadway, 718-442-3100. Kids will go wild here, near the stunning Clove Lakes Park. Be sure to bring them to the vampire bat feedings.

Food

Snug Harbor:
RH Tugs, 1115 Richmond Ter, 718-447-6369. Standard bar food, but views of Kill Van Kull mean lots of hot tug and tanker action.

Tompkinsville:
New Asha, 322 Victory Blvd Ave, 718-420-0649. Great Sri Lankan food on the cheap. Spicy!

Port Richmond:
Denino's, 524 Port Richmond Ave, 718-442-9401. Some of the best pizza in town. Afterward, cross the street to Ralph's Famous for Italian ices.

Dongan Hills:
Lee's Tavern, 60 Hancock St, 718-667-9749. Great bar with great pizza—get the fresh mozzarella.

Grant City:
Nunzio's, 2155 Hylan Blvd, 718-667-964?. More great pizza. Notice a theme here?

Tottenville:
Gentile's, 5266 Arthur Kill Rd, 718-966-9005. Classic red sauce Italian-American dishes big enough for three.
Egger's Ice Cream Parlor, 7437 Amboy Rd, 718-605-9335. Old time ice cream and sweets. Kids love it.

Driving In / Through Staten Island

To visit Staten Island, one must either drive/take a bus/take a cab over the Verrazano Bridge ($9 toll) from Bay Ridge, Brooklyn, or catch the ferry from Lower Manhattan. If you elect to do the latter, you'll find myriad buses departing from the St. George side of the ferry as well as the terminal of the Staten Island Railway, ready to whisk you all the way down to Tottenville and back with one swipe of the Metrocard (literally—it's free to get on and off anyplace other than St. George). To reach New Jersey via Staten Island, take the Verrazano to the Staten Island Expressway (Route 278) to Route 440 to the Outerbridge Crossing, and you're almost halfway to Princeton or the Jersey shore. However…the Staten Island Expressway often gets jammed. Two scenic, though not really quicker, alternatives: one, take Hylan Boulevard all the way south to almost the southwest tip of Staten Island, and then cut up to the Outerbridge Crossing; two, take Richmond Terrace around the north shore and cross to New Jersey at the Goethals Bridge. Remember, neither is really faster, but at least you'll be moving.

General Information

Battery Park Parks Conservancy:
212-267-9700
Websites:
www.lowermanhattan.info
www.bpcparks.org
www.bpcdogs.org

Overview

The closest thing to suburbia around here. Welcome to Battery Park City—a master-planned community reminiscent of *Pleasantville*. Originally the brainchild of Nelson Rockefeller, this urban experiment transformed a WTC construction landfill into a 92-acre planned enclave on the southwestern tip of Manhattan. As space in Manhattan continues to disappear into the stratosphere (literally, the only way to build is up), the idea of BPC requires a doubletake. It's about making public spaces (about 30% of those 92 acres) work within private entities. Imagine taking Central Park, cutting it up, and saying, "Here, your neighborhood can have a chunk of it, and that street down there, and that street over there, too." Admit it: walking among private, commercial spaces day in and day out is enough to make anyone claustrophobic (thank you, Financial District). In BPC you walk through spacious parks with weird statues and brick pavers all on your way to work, the grocery store, the gym, or the movie theater. BPC will have you asking: "What's outside Battery Park City?"

Those looking for all-night eateries and party spots should pass it up, but if you've got kids this is the place for you. Many NY families—roughly 25,000 people—occupy the 40% of BPC that's dedicated residential space, including a future-forward "green" building, the Solaire. Robert F. Wagner Jr. and Rector are good choices for a picnic; The Esplanade or South Cove to walk along the Hudson; Nelson A. Rockefeller to play frisbee; North Cove to park your yacht; Teardrop Park for the kids.

Seeing: Amazing sculptures by Bourgeois, Otterness, Puryear, Dine, and Cragg. Inspired architecture: Stuyvesant High School, Siah Armajani's Tribeca Bridge, Kevin Roche's Museum of Jewish Heritage, Caesar Pelli's Winter Garden, and the World Financial Center. If you like things nice, neat, and compartmentalized, this 'hood is for you.

Bagels

• Pick A Bagel • Embassy Suites • 102 North End Ave [Vesey]

Banks

BA • Bank of America (ATM) •
3 World Financial Center [Vesey St]
BA • Bank of America (ATM) • 4 World Financial Ctr [Vesey St]
CH • Chase • 331 South End Ave [Albany St]
HS • HSBC (ATM) • NY Mercantile Exchange •
1 N End Ave [Vesey St]

Car Rental

• Avis • 345 South End Ave [Albany]

Coffee

• Au Bon Pain • WFC • 200 Liberty St [West St]
• Cosi • 200 Vesey St [West St]
• Financier Patisserie • 220 Vesey St [W Side Hwy]
• Starbucks • 3 World Financial Ctr • 250 Vesey St [W Side Hwy]

Community Gardens

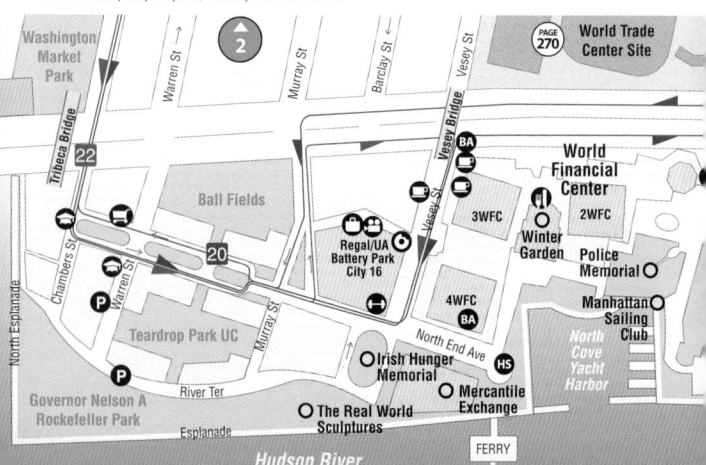

Parks & Places · **Battery Park City**

Gyms

- **Battery Park Swim & Fitness Center** ·
  375 South End Ave [Liberty]
- **Liberty Club MCB** · 200 Rector Pl [South End]
- **NYSC** · 102 North End Ave [Vesey]

Landmarks

- **The Irish Hunger Memorial** · Vesey St & North End Ave
- **Manhattan Sailing Club** · North Cove
  (Liberty St & North End Ave)
- **Mercantile Exchange** · 1 North End Ave [Vesey]
- **Museum of Jewish Heritage** · 36 Battery Pl [Little West]
- **Police Memorial** · Liberty St & South End Ave
- **The Real World Sculptures** · n/a
- **Skyscraper Museum** · 39 Battery Pl [Little West]
- **Winter Garden** · 37 Vesey St [Church]

Liquor Stores

- **Bulls & Bears Winery** · 309 South End Ave [Albany]

Movie Theaters

- **Regal Battery Park City 16** · Embassy Suites ·
  102 North End Ave [Vesey]

Nightlife

- **Rise Bar** · Ritz Carlton · 2 West St [Little West]

Parking

Pet Shops

- **Le Pet Spa** · 300 Rector Pl [South End]

Restaurants

- **Gigino at Wagner Park** · 20 Battery Pl [Wash]
- **Grill Room** · WFC · 225 Liberty St [W Side Hwy]
- **Picasso Pizza** · 303 South End Ave [Albany]
- **PJ Clarke's** · 4 World Financial Ctr [Vesey]
- **Samantha's Fine Foods** · 235 South End Ave [Rector Pl]
- **Steamer's Landing** · 375 South End Ave [Liberty]
- **Zen** · 311 South End Ave [Albany]

Schools

- **PS 89** · 201 Warren St [Clinton]
- **Stuyvesant High** · 345 Chambers St [North End]

Shopping

- **DSW Shoe Warehouse** · 102 North End Ave [Vesey]

Supermarkets

- **Gourmet Heaven** · 450 North End Ave [Chambers]
- **Gristedes** · 315 South End Ave [Albany]
- **Gristedes** · 71 South End Ave [W Thames]

Video Rental

- **Video Room** · 300 Rector Pl [South End]

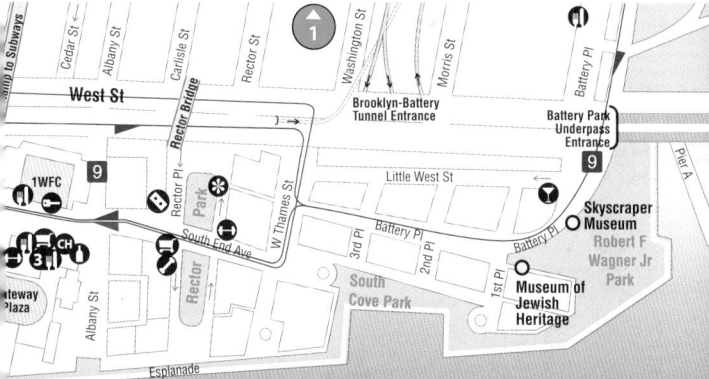

General Information

Website: www.centralparknyc.org
Central Park Conservancy: 212-310-6600
Shakespeare in the Park: 212-539-8750

Overview

For continued mental health that doesn't require a therapist, look no further than a mind-clearing walk through New York's blessed Central Park. Leave stressful car noise and concrete behind to find relative quiet and soft ground. Wandering aimlessly through the 843 acres (worth more than an estimated $528 billion), you'll discover many isolated corners and hiding places, despite the fact that 25 million people visit every year. On any given day, you'll see people disco roller-skating, playing jazz, juggling, walking their dogs, running, making out, meditating, playing softball, whining through soccer practice, getting married, picnicking, and playing chess.

Designed by Frederick Law Olmsted and Calvert Vaux in the 1850s, Central Park has a diverse mix of attractions. Walking tours are offered by the Central Park Conservancy (www.centralparknyc.org), and you can always hail a horse-drawn carriage or bike taxi for a ride through the park if you want to look like a true tourist.

Practicalities

Central Park is easily accessible by subway, since the Ⓐ Ⓒ Ⓑ Ⓓ Ⓝ Ⓡ Ⓠ Ⓦ ❶ ❷ ❸ trains all circle the park. Parking along CPW is harder, so try side streets. Unless you're heading to the park for a big concert, a softball game, or Shakespeare in the Park, walking or

hanging out (especially alone!) in the park at night is not recommended.

Nature

If you think people-watching in Times Square is good, wait until you check out the avian eye candy around here. More than 275 species of birds have been spotted in Central Park. The Ramble **27** is a good place to see them. There are an amazing number of both plant and animal species that inhabit the park, including the creatures housed in its two zoos **4** & **8**. In 2006, a wily coyote captivated New Yorkers with a guest appearance in the park until its successful capture. A good source of information on all of the park's flora and fauna is schoolteacher Leslie Day's website, www.nysite.com/nature/index.htm.

Architecture & Sculpture

Central Park was designed to thrill visitors at every turn. The Bethesda Fountain **11**, designed by Emma Stebbins, is one of the main attractions of the park. Don't miss the view of Turtle Pond from Belvedere Castle **16** (home of the Central Park Learning Center). The Arsenal **5** is a wonderful ivy-clad building that houses the Parks Department headquarters. Two of the most notable sculptures in the park are Alice in Wonderland **15** and the Obelisk **19**. Oh, and one other tiny point of interest…the Metropolitan Museum of Art **24** also happens to be in the park.

Open Spaces

New Yorkers covet space. Since they rarely get it in their apartments, they rely on large open areas such

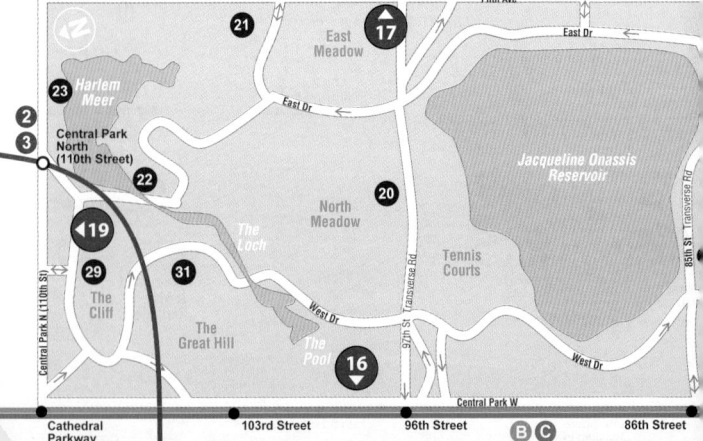

as Strawberry Fields **10**, the Great Lawn **26**, and Sheep Meadow **28**. The Ramble **27** and the Cliff **29** are still heavily forested and are good for hiking around, but don't go near them after dark. When it snows, you can find great sledding on Cedar Hill **30**, which is otherwise perfect for picnicking and sunbathing.

Performance

In warmer weather, Central Park is a microcosm of the great cultural attractions New York has to offer. The Delacorte Theater **18** is the home of Shakespeare in the Park, a New York tradition begun by famous director Joseph Papp. SummerStage **9** is now an extremely popular concert venue for all types of music, including the occasional killer rock concert. Opera companies and classical philharmonics also show up in the park frequently, as does the odd mega-star (Beastie Boys, Diana Ross, etc.). If you crave something truly outlandish, try the loinclothed Thoth, a self-proclaimed emotional hermaphrodite who plays the violin and sings in his own language, under the Angel Tunnel by the Bethesda Fountain **11**.

Sports

Rollerblading and roller skating are very popular (not just at the Roller Skating Rink **7**—see www.centralparkskate. com, www.cpdsa.org, www.skatecity.com), as is jogging, especially around the reservoir (1.57 mi). The Great Lawn **26** boasts beautiful softball fields. Central Park has 30 tennis courts (if you make a reservation, you can walk right on to the clay court with tennis shoes only—212-280-0205), fishing at Harlem Meer, gondola rides and boat rentals at the Loeb Boathouse **13**, model boat rentals at the Chess & Checkers House **25**, two ice-skating rinks **1** & **22**, croquet and lawn bowling just north of Sheep Meadow **28**, and rock-climbing lessons at the North Meadow Rec Center **20**. You will also see volleyball, basketball, skateboarding, bicycling, and many pick-up soccer, frisbee, football, and kill-the-carrier games to join. During heavy snows, bust out your snowboard, cross-country skis, or homemade sled. Finally, Central Park is where the NYC Marathon ends each year.

Landmarks

1 Wollman Rink
2 Carousel
3 The Dairy
4 Central Park Zoo
5 The Arsenal
6 Tavern on the Green
7 Roller Skating Rink
8 Children's Zoo
9 SummerStage
10 Strawberry Fields
11 Bethesda Fountain
12 Bow Bridge
13 Loeb Boathouse
14 Model Boat Racing
15 Alice in Wonderland
16 Belvedere Castle
17 Shakespeare Gardens
18 Delacorte Theater
19 The Obelisk
20 North Meadow Recreation Center
21 Conservatory Garden
22 Lasker Rink
23 Dana Discovery Center
24 Metropolitan Museum of Art
25 Chess & Checkers House
26 The Great Lawn
27 The Ramble
28 Sheep Meadow
29 The Cliff
30 Cedar Hill
31 The Great Hill

Police Precinct 86th St & Transverse Rd

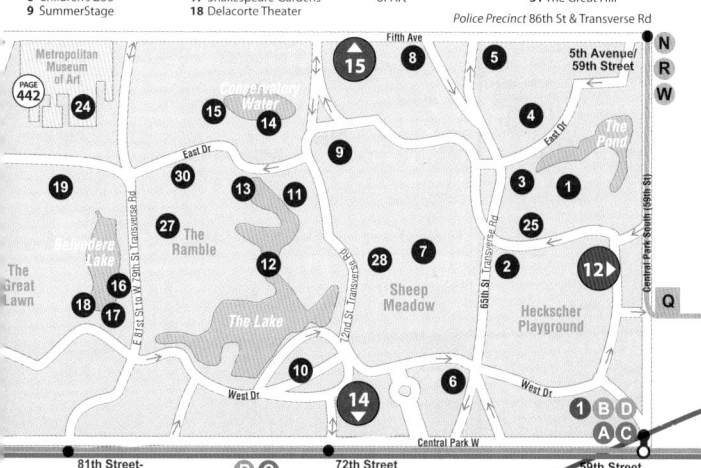

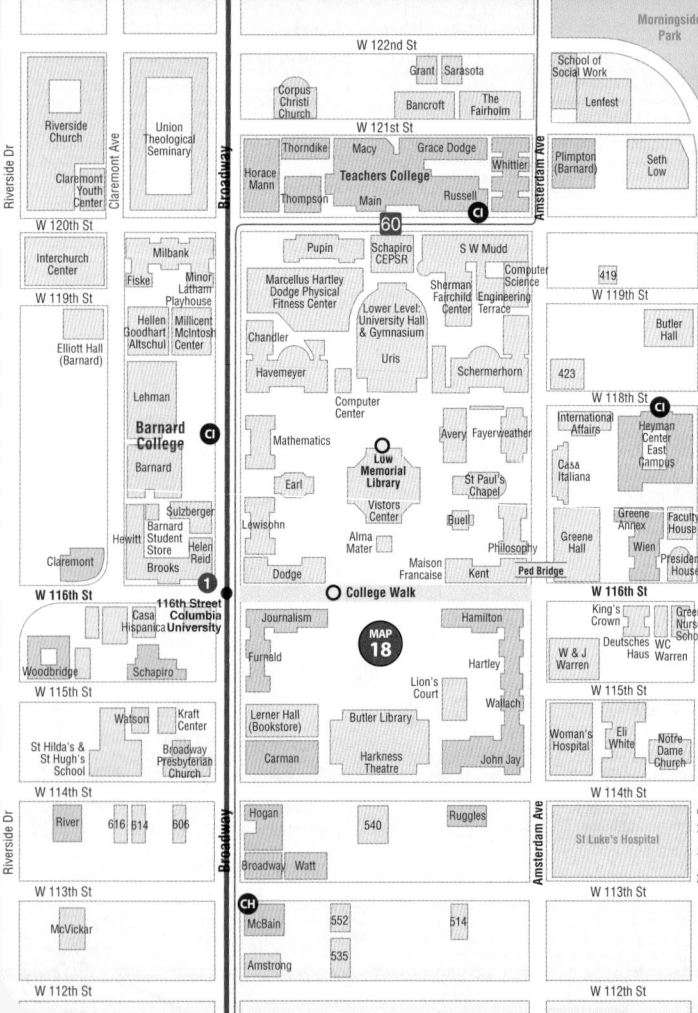

General Information

NFT Map:	18
Morningside Heights:	2960 Broadway & 116th St
Medical Center:	601 W 168th St
Phone:	212-854-1754
Website:	www.columbia.edu
Students Enrolled:	23,813
Endowment:	Market value as of June 30, 2005 $5.191 billion

Overview

Yearning for those carefree days spent debating nihilism in the quad and wearing pajamas in public? Look no further than a quick trip to the New York City Ivy League haven of Columbia University. Unlike the other collegiate institutions that pepper Manhattan's real estate, Columbia's campus has a real pastoral feel. The main campus, located in Morningside Heights, spans six blocks between Broadway and Amsterdam avenues. Most of the undergraduate classes are held here, along with several of the graduate schools. Other graduate schools, including the Law School and School of International and Public Affairs, are close by on Amsterdam Avenue. The main libraries, Miller Theater, and St. Paul's Chapel are also located on the Morningside Heights campus. You can even get your intramural fix on a few fields for frisbee-throwing and pick-up soccer games.

Founded in 1754 as King's College, Columbia University is one of the country's most prestigious academic institutions. The university is well known for its core curriculum, a program of requirements that gives students an introduction to the most influential works in literature, philosophy, science, and other disciplines. It also prepares them for the rigors of those pesky dinner parties.

After residing in two different downtown locations, Columbia moved to its present campus (designed by McKim, Mead, and White) in 1897. Low Library remains the focal point of the campus as does the Alma Mater statue in front—a landmark that continues to inspire student superstitions (find the hidden owl and you might be the next valedictorian) thanks to a thwarted plot to blow it up by the radical Weather Underground in the '60s. Students line the stairs in front of the library on sunny days, eating lunch and chatting with classmates. Columbia even has its own spooky network of underground tunnels (third largest in the world) that date back to the old Morningside mental asylum and were utilized by students and police during the 1968 strike.

Town/gown relations in Morningside Heights are complicated, and getting more so by the day. While Columbia students consistently show local businesses the money, it's not enough to keep community members from freaking every time the university discusses new construction projects. The most famous of these struggles came in response to Columbia's plans to build a gymnasium in Morningside Park. New and contentious proposals, recently approved, to expand the university into Manhattanville (the area north of 125th Street), are still causing tension and fear of evictions, and the debate between the university and old-time residents continues.

Columbia's medical school was the first in the nation. The school is affiliated with the Columbia-Presbyterian Medical Center in Washington Heights and encompasses the graduate schools of medicine, dentistry, nursing, and public health. Columbia is the only Ivy League university with a journalism school, which was founded at the bequest of Joseph Pulitzer in 1912. (The prize is still administered there.) The school is also affiliated with Barnard College, Jewish Theological Seminary, Teachers College, and Union Theological Seminary.

Numerous movies have been filmed on or around the campus including *Ghostbusters*, *Hannah and Her Sisters*, and *Spiderman I* and *II*. Most recently, Scarlett Johansson was spotted while shooting *The Nanny Diaries*.

Notable alums and faculty include artists James Cagney, Art Garfunkel, Georgia O'Keeffe, Rodgers and Hammerstein, Paul Robeson, and Twyla Tharp; critic Lionel Trilling; baseball player Lou Gehrig; and writers Isaac Asimov, Joseph Heller, Carson McCullers, Eudora Welty, Zora Neale Hurston, and Herman Wouk. Business alumni include Warren Buffet, Alfred Knopf, Joseph Pulitzer, and Milton Friedman, while politicians Madeline Albright, Dwight Eisenhower, Alexander Hamilton, Robert Moses, Franklin Delano Roosevelt, and Teddy Roosevelt all graced the university's classrooms. In the field of law, Benjamin Cardozo, Ruth Bader Ginsburg, Charles Evans Hughes, and John Jay called Columbia home, and Stephen Jay Gould, Margaret Mead, and Benjamin Spock make the list of notable science alumni.

Tuition

Columbia undergraduate tuition for 2007-08 was $35,516. Graduate school fees vary by college. We certainly hope a loaded family member or friend is picking up the tab.

Sports

The Columbia Marching Band plays "Roar, Lion, Roar" after every touchdown, but their instruments remain tragically roarless most of the time. The Lions almost set the record for straight losses by a major college football team when they dropped 44 consecutive games between 1983 and 1988. Not much has changed—their 1-9 record in 2007 was par for the course. The Lions play their mostly Ivy League opponents at Lawrence A. Wein Stadium (Baker Field), located way up at the top of Manhattan.

Columbia excels in other sports including crew, fencing, golf, tennis, and sailing (silver spoon not included). The university is represented by 29 men's and women's teams in the NCAA Division I. It also has the oldest wrestling team in the country.

Culture on Campus

The ire evoked by its controversial anti-immigration speech, when students stormed the stage, pales when compared to Columbia's invitation last year to Iranian president Mahmoud Ahmadinejad to participate in a debate. Good or bad, it created much hype and put the campus in the spotlight for a day or two. Columbia does, however, feature plenty of other less volatile dance, film, music, theater, lectures, readings, and talks. Venues include: the Macy Gallery at the Teacher's College, which exhibits works by a variety of artists, including faculty and children's artwork; the fabulous Miller Theatre at 2960 Broadway, which primarily features musical performances and lectures; the computer-run Postcrypt Art Gallery in the basement of St. Paul's Chapel; the Theatre of the Riverside Church for theatrical performances from their top-rated graduate program; and the Wallach Art Gallery on the 8th floor of Schermerhorn Hall, featuring art and architecture exhibits. Check the website for a calendar of events. And bring your rubber bullets, just in case.

Phone Numbers

Morningside Campus	212-854-1754
Medical Center	212-305-2500
Visitors Center	212-854-4900
Public Affairs	212-854-2037
University Development and Alumni Relations	877-854-ALUM(2586)
Library Information	212-854-3533
Graduate School of Architecture, Planning, and Preservation	212-854-3414
School of the Arts	212-854-2875
Graduate School of Arts and Sciences	212-854-4737
School of Dental and Oral Surgery	212-305-6726
School of Engineering	212-854-2993
School of General Studies	212-854-2772
School of International and Public Affairs	212-854-5406
Graduate School of Journalism	212-854-8608
School of Law	212-854-2640
School of Nursing	212-305-5756
School of Public Health	212-305-4797
School of Social Work	212-851-2300

Overview

East River Park is a long, thin slice of land, sandwiched between the FDR Drive and the East River, and running from Montgomery Street up to 12th Street. Built in the late 1930s as part of the FDR Drive, the park's recent refurbishments have made its sporting facilities some of the best Manhattan has to offer. The East River Esplanade, a walkway encircling many parts of the East Side, is a constant work-in-progress. The overall plan is to someday create one continuous green stretch from Maine to Florida, part of the highly ambitious East Coast Greenway project (www.greenway.org). But first we'll see if we can get East River Park to stretch as far as the UN. (Initial city plans are aiming to grow the park from Battery Park to Harlem.)

Attractions

No one would ever mistake East River Park for Battery Park, but to its credit, the city has made great improvements, cleaning and buffing it 'til it almost shines. The park comes alive in the summer and on weekends, when hundreds of families barbeque in the areas between the athletic fields, blaring music and eating to their hearts' content. Others take leisurely strolls or jogs along the East River Esplanade, which offers dramatic views of the river and Brooklyn. Many have turned the park's unused areas into unofficial dog runs, places for pick-up games of ultimate frisbee or soccer, and sunbathing areas. And aside from bathing beauties, you'll even find fishermen waiting patiently for striped bass (not that we have to tell you, but nothing caught in the East River should be eaten—while the water quality has improved dramatically, it's still full of pollutants).

Sports

The sports facilities at East River Park have undergone heavy reconstruction. The park now includes facilities for football, softball, basketball, soccer, tennis, and even cricket. Thankfully, many of the fields have been resurfaced with a resilient synthetic turf—a smart move given the amount of use the park gets by all the different sports leagues.

Facilities

There are three bathroom facilities located in the park—one at the tennis courts, one at the soccer/track field, and one up in the northern part of the park by the playground. The reconstruction has provided East River Park with new benches, game tables, a harbor seals spray sprinkler with animal art,

and new water fountains. Aside from the occasional guy with a cart full of cold drinks, there are no food or drink options close by. Your best bet is to arrive at the park with any supplies you might need—if that's too difficult, try a bodega on Avenue D.

Safety

East River Park is relatively safe, especially during the daytime, but we would not recommend hanging out there—or in any other city park, for that matter—after dark, even if you're just passing through.

Esoterica

Built in 1941, the Corlears Hook Pavilion was the original home of Joseph Papp's Shakespeare in the Park. However, it closed in 1973, and has never quite returned to its glory days. Plans for the fancy $3.5 million amphitheater/restaurant that was to replace the sad-looking, abandoned, graffiti-covered Corlears Hook Pavilion band shell have been canned. A less ambitious reconstruction took place in 2001, however, and with new seating, a renovated band shell, and a good scrubbing, the facility is currently open for use.

How to Get There

Two FDR Drive exits will get you very close to East River Park—the Houston Street exit and the Grand Street exit. Technically, cars are not allowed in the park. There is some parking available at the extreme south end of the park by Jackson Street off the access road, but it's hard to get to and poorly marked. Plan to find street parking just west of the FDR and cross over on a footbridge.

If you are taking the subway, you'd better have your hiking boots on—the fact that the closest subways (the J M Z F at Delancey/Essex St and the L at First Ave) are so far away (at least four avenue blocks) is one of the reasons East River Park has stayed mainly a neighborhood park. Fortunately, if you're into buses, the 21, 14, and 8 get you pretty close. Regardless of the bus or subway lines, you will have to cross one of the five pedestrian bridges that traverse the FDR Drive, unless you approach via the East River Esplanade.

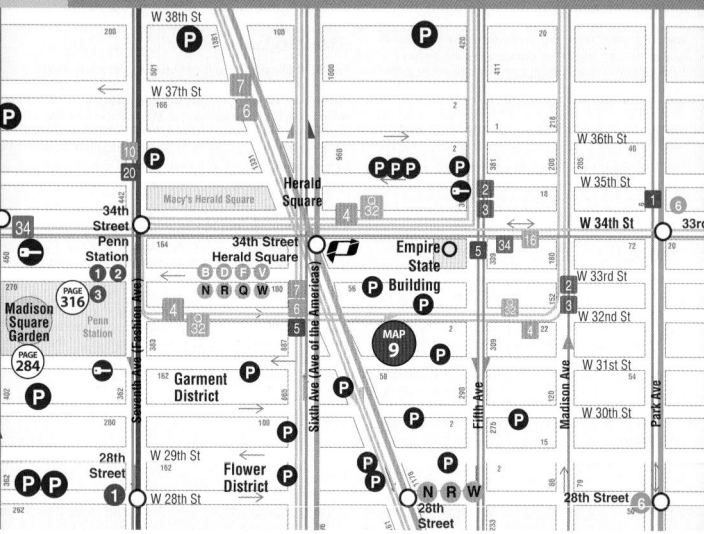

General Information

NFT Map:	9
Address:	350 Fifth Ave (& 34th St)
Phone:	212-736-3100
Website:	www.esbnyc.com
Observatory Hours:	Open daily 365 days a year 8 am–2 am. Last elevators go up at 1:15 am
Observatory Admission:	$19 for adults, $16 for children aged 12–17, seniors, military with ID, and $13 children aged 6–11. Toddlers (under 5) and military personnel in uniform get in free.

Overview

There may not be a gorilla climbing it, but if you don't already know the Empire State Building, the jig is up, Mac. Put down the NFT and back away slooowly. You're not a true Manhattanite. So, folks, how did the giant end up perching on our block? In 1930, at the hands of raw men compounding raw material day after day, four-and-a-half stories were erected per week. Those ravaged from the Depression and eager to put their minds to work built the 1,500-foot structure in just 14 months, way ahead of schedule.

A year later, it served as an ambassador to visiting dignitaries like Queen Elizabeth and, years later, your Aunt Elizabeth. These days it is one of New York City's (and the world's) most famous landmarks. Movies have been shot there. Big shots work there. And you can take plenty of snapshots from the reason-you-go-there-observation-deck on the 86th floor. No trick questions asked. Some New Yorkers think it's hip to have never been to the Empire State Building. These people are idiots. Whether you choose to go during the day or at night, it's a totally different but amazing experience either way.

The Lights

As far away as downtown and all the way uptown, the lights of the Empire State Building soar above the clouds, signifying an international holiday and/or an interminable disease. On the 86th floor, a man with binoculars and a direct line to the lighting engineers waits. His raison d'être? Close-flying flocks of birds. One phone call, and the lights go out, lest the poor suckers smash their beaks and plunge to their death from the mesmerizing lights. True story.

Lighting Schedule (for updates/changes, check www.esbnyc.com)

- January · Martin Luther King, Jr. Day
- January · March of Dimes
- January–February · Lunar New Year
- February 14 · Valentine's Day
- February · President's Day
- February · Westminster Kennel Club
- February · Swisspeaks Festival for Switzerland
- February · World Cup Archery Championship
- March 17 · St. Patrick's Day
- March · Greek Independence Day
- March · Equal Parents Day/ Children's Rights
- March · Wales/St. David's Day
- March · Oscar Week in NYC
- March · Colon Cancer Awareness
- March · Red Cross Month
- March–April · Spring/Easter Week
- April · Earth Day
- April · Child Abuse Prevention
- April · National Osteoporosis Society
- April · Rain Forest Day
- April · Israel Independence Day
- April · Dutch Queen's Day
- April · Tartan Day
- May · Muscular Dystrophy
- May · Armed Forces Day
- May · Memorial Day
- May · Police Memorial Day
- May · Fire Department Memorial Day
- May · Haitian Culture Awareness
- June 14 · Flag Day
- June · Portugal Day
- June · NYC Triathlon
- June · Stonewall Anniversary/ Gay Pride
- July 4 · Independence Day
- July · Bahamas Independence Day
- July · Bastille Day
- July · Peru Independence
- July · Columbia Heritage & Independence
- August · US Open

- August · Jamaica Independence Day
- August · India Independence Day
- August · Pakistan Independence Day
- September · Mexico Independence Day
- September · Labor Day
- September · Brazil Independence Day
- September · Pulaski Day
- September · Race for the Cure
- September · Switzerland admitted to the UN
- September · Qatar Independence
- September · Fleet Week/Support our Servicemen and Servicewomen/ Memorial for 9/11
- September · Feast of San Gennaro
- October · Breast Cancer Awareness
- October · German Reunification Day
- October · Columbus Day
- October 24 · United Nations Day
- October · Big Apple Circus
- October · Pennant/World Series win for the Yankees
- October · Pennant/World Series win for the Mets [Ha!]
- October · NY Knicks Opening Day
- October–November · Autumn
- October · Walk to End Domestic Violence
- November · NYC Marathon
- November · Veterans' Day
- November · Alzheimer's Awareness
- December · First night of Hanukkah
- December · "Day Without Art/Night Without Lights"/AIDS Awareness
- December–January 7 (with interruptions) · Holiday Season

Parks & Places · **Hudson River Park**

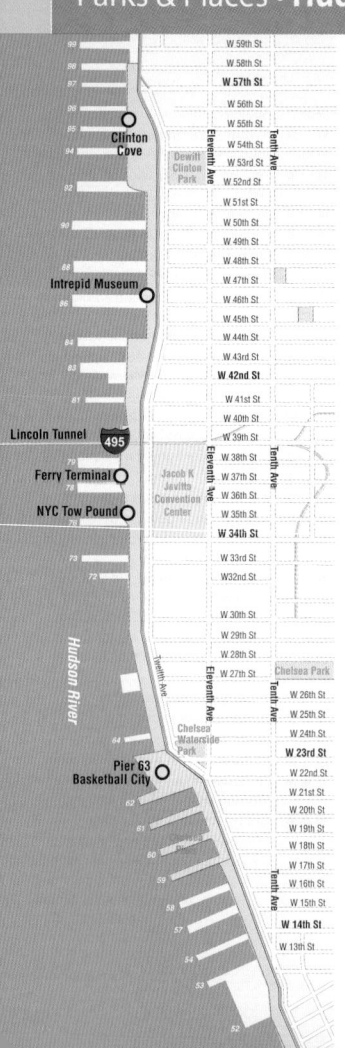

General Information

Hudson River
Park Trust: 212-627-2020
Websites: www.hudsonriverpark.org
                             www.friendsofhudsonriverpark.org

Overview

West Side Highway trapeze artists? Hudson River Park may not ring a bell, but those high-flyers just may. They're part of the 550-acre, up-and-coming $330-million park development along the south and southwest coastline of Manhattan, from Battery Place to West 59th. Rivaling the 800 acres of public lawn in Midtown, Hudson River Park is quickly becoming downtown's Central Park. Just think length, not width. And think trapezes and half pipes, not zoos.

Born of the Hudson River Park Act in 1998, the Hudson River Park Trust focuses on preserving the natural, historical, and ecological environment, while alleviating dire sanitary conditions, expanding public access to the river, and promoting water-based recreation. Translated check-off list: save the whales, er...um, American eel; remember the sailors; clean the water; dredge the plastic baggies and random boots; build pretty lookout areas; give the people something more to do than look at water.

As part of the New York State Significant Coastal Fish and Wildlife Habitat, 400 acres of the total 550 thrive as estuarine sanctuary. This means the seventy fish species (there are fish in the Hudson?) and thirty bird species on the waterfront won't go belly up or beak down with all the marine preservation. Thanks to this effort, you'll be able to enjoy the winter flounder, white perch, owls, hawks, and songbirds for generations to come. (That's fantastic! Bob, tell them what else they've won...) What downtown, nature-loving, organic-eating savers of the planet have won is in what they've lost. As a mandate, office buildings, hotels, casino gambling boats, and manufacturing plants are prohibited from the HRP, as are residences (sorry, no water-front property next to your yacht) and jet skis (better to leave them in the Caymans).

Art

From exhibition to permanent collection, HRP takes its culture cue from the surrounding downtown art scene of TriBeCa, SoHo, and Chelsea. You were probably one of the thousands waiting in line to see *Ashes and Snow*, Gregory Colbert's rendition of the interactions between animals and humans took form in the temporary Nomadic Museum on Pier 54. Or maybe you checked out Malcolm Cochran's *Private Passage* on Clinton Cove (55th–57th St). Similar to your late-night antics, you peered into a gigantic wine bottle. There, from portholes carved on the sides, you could see the interior of the stateroom of the Queen Mary. Or, hearkening back to an early time, the *Shadow of the Lusitania*. Justen Ladda recreated the shadow of the famous ship on the south side of Pier 54 (also home to reconstructed historic ships, not just their shadows), its original docking place, with glass and planters. A more permanent piece in HRP: *Salinity Gradient* in TriBeCa. Paver stones spanning 2000 feet take the shape of Hudson marine creatures. Striped bass included. Not impressed? HRP Trust hired different designers for each segment of the five-mile park, with only the esplanade and waterfront railing as universal pieces. Check out the landscape design of each segment. The *Intrepid* at the Sea-Air-Space Museum (vintage airplanes and sleek, modern jets) at Pier 86 (middle 40s) is temporarily on leave, but is anticipated to return in 2008.

Attractions

Season-specific events are held year-round at HRP. During the summer, experience fight-night basics on Pier 54 for Rumble on the River with live blood splattering with each KO. Sundays in the summer host Moon Dances on Pier 25 with free dance lessons before live New York bands play. Wednesday and Fridays in the summer boast River Flicks on Pier 54 and Pier 25 with throwback films like *The Goonies*. Pier of Fear is mainly a Halloween party for the kiddies, but if you're still down with dressing up as the *Scream* guy, hey, no one will stop you. Nature centers are next on the list of HRP's formidable repertoire of attractions.

Sports

Think of sports in terms of piers. You already know about ritzy Chelsea Piers, but soon enough "Pier 40" or "Pier 63" will also become vernacular to sports freaks. And there are far less expensive piers beyond CP. Most crucial to athletic-minded souls, a five-mile running/biking/blading path that threads through the piers. It's a miniature divided highway—smooth, simple, and super crowded during peak times (early evening and weekends). You'll find sunbathing lawns throughout (the most sport some will ever do). Pier 40: three and a half ball fields. Area south of Houston: three tennis courts. Mini-golf. Batting cages. Skateboard park. Beach volleyball. Trapeze lessons. Pier 40, CP, Pier 63, Pier 96: free kayaking. Those are the highlights; for more that's up your particular sports alley, check out the website.

How to Get There

Hmmm. How to most efficiently make your way through all the concrete to the shoreline? The ❶ and Ⓐ Ⓒ Ⓔ between Chambers and 59th Streets will get you the closest. Go west 'til you hit water. You're there.

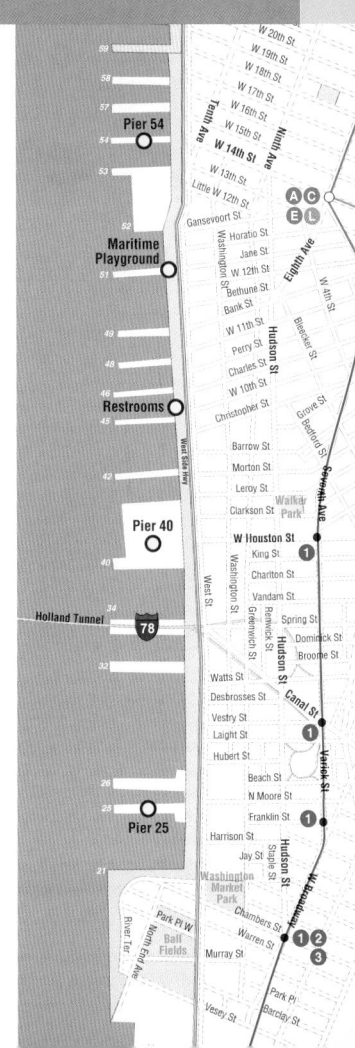

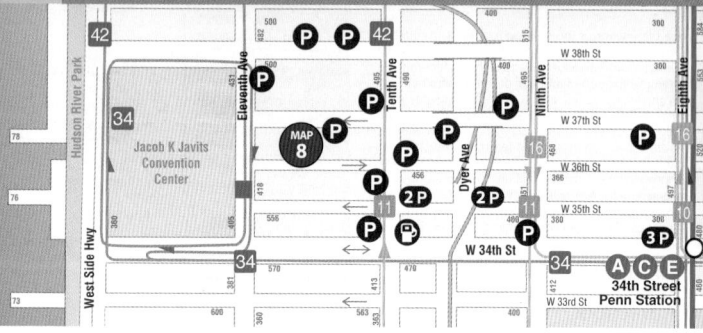

LEVEL ONE

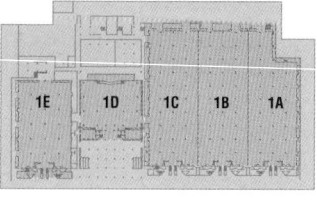

1E 1D 1C 1B 1A

LEVEL TWO

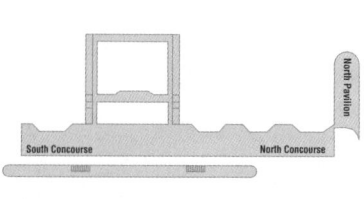

South Concourse North Concourse North Pavilion

LEVEL THREE

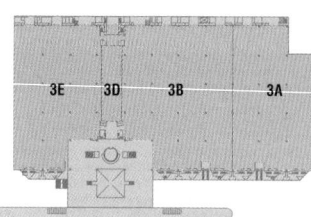

3E 3D 3B 3A

LEVEL FOUR

River Pavilion Galleria 4E Terrace Lounge

General Information

NFT Map: 8
Address: 655 W 34th St
Website: www.javitscenter.com
Phone Number: 212-216-2000
Fax Number: 212-216-2588

Overview

The Jacob K. Javits Center, designed by James Ingo Freed and completed in 1986, is a massive glass-and-steel behemoth of a convention hall next to the Hudson River between 34th and 38th Streets. It was built with the purpose of providing a place for big trade shows, conventions, and expositions, but its true purpose is clearly to annoy anyone who has to go there, since it's in the middle of nowhere with no subway link. Dissatisfaction with the convention center has brewed for a number of years, with complaints ranging from the aesthetic (big ugly box) to the practical (lack of space). Various plans have been proposed over the years to expand the center up or over the adjoining west side rail yards, and overhaul the building's facade. The Javits even got dragged into the Jets stadium fiasco, but seems to have emerged with some concrete progress towards a revamping: in late-2006, ground was broken on an expansion that would more than double the size of the Center. Shockingly, the election of a new governor (Spitzer), and resignation of a governor due to prostitution allegations (Spitzer again) has resulted in a re-evaluation of the plans. When discovered that most of the $1.6 billion budget would go towards fixing—not expanding—the project was essentially nixed.

ATMs

CH · Chase · Level One
CH · Chase · Level Three

Services

Coat/Luggage Check
Concierge Services
FedEx Kinko's Office and Print Center
First Aid
Hudson News
Information
Lost and Found
Mailboxes Etc
Shoeshine
Wi-Fi (hourly, daily, and show plans available)

Food

The food at the Javits Center is, of course, rapaciously expensive, and, if you're exhibiting, usually sold out by 2:30 in the afternoon. Our suggestion is to look for people handing out Chinese food menus and have them deliver to your booth. (And yes, they take credit cards. And yes, it's bad Chinese food.)

Level 1
Boar's Head Deli
Caliente Cab Company
Carvel Ice Cream Bakery
Feast of the Dragon
Gourmet Coffee Bar
Market Fair/Korean Deli Buffet
Nathan's
Villa Cucina Italiana
Villa Pizza

Level 3
The Bakery
Boar's Head Deli
Carvels
Caliente Cab Company
Dai Kichi Sushi
The Dining Car
Feast of the Dragon
Go Gourmet
The Grille
Villa Pizza

North Concourse
New York Pretzel
Panini

How to Get There— Mass Transit

Until they extend that 7 train, there's no direct subway access to the center. The closest subway stop is at 34th Street/Penn Station, but even that's a good 4- to 5-block hike away. You can also take the buses from the 42nd Street 42 and 34th Street 34 subway stops, which will both drop you off right outside the center.

There are also numerous shuttle buses that run to various participating hotels and other locales free of charge for convention goers. Schedules and routes vary for each convention, so ask at the information desk on the first floor.

From New Jersey, the NY Waterway operates ferries from Weehawken, Hoboken, and Jersey City that ship you across the Hudson River to 39th Street and Twelfth Avenue in 15 minutes or less, dropping you just one block from the Javits Center. The ferries leave every 15–30 minutes during peak hours. Call 1-800-53-FERRY or go to www.nywaterway.com for a schedule and more information.

Lincoln Center / Columbus Circle

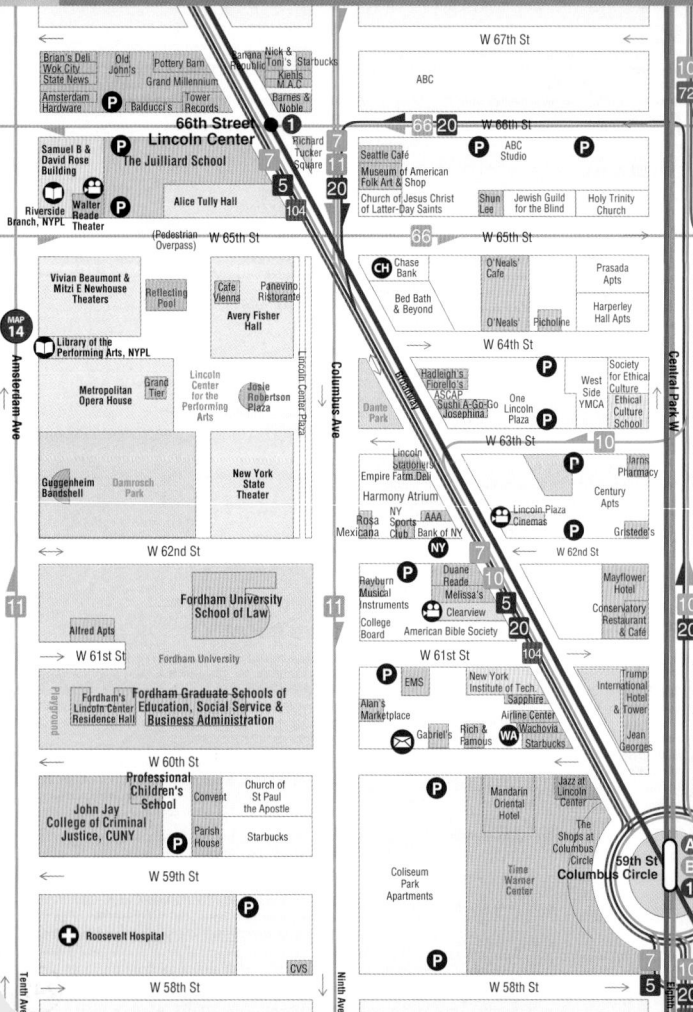

General Information

Website:	www.lincolncenter.org
General Information:	212-546-2656 (212-LINCOLN)
Customer Service:	212-875-5456
Alice Tully Hall:	212-875-5050
Avery Fisher Hall:	212-875-5030
The Chamber Music Society:	212-875-5775
Film Society of Lincoln Center:	212-875-5610
Guided Tours:	212-875-5350
Jazz at Lincoln Center:	212-258-9800
The Julliard School:	212-799-5000
Lincoln Center Theater:	212-362-7600
The Metropolitan Opera House:	212-362-6000
New York City Ballet:	212-870-5500
New York City Opera:	212-870-5630

New York Philharmonic:	212-875-5656
New York State Theater:	212-870-5570
Parking Garage:	212-874-9021
Walter Reade Theater:	212-875-5600
Ticket Purchase Phone Numbers	
Alice Tully Hall:	212-721-5050
Avery Fisher Hall:	212-721-5030
CenterCharge:	212-721-6500
Film Society of Lincoln Center:	212-496-3809
MovieFone, Walter Reade Theater:	212-777-FILM
TeleCharge, Lincoln Center Theater:	212-239-6200
Ticketmaster, New York State Theater:	212-307-4100
Ticketmaster, Met & Ballet:	212-362-6000

Overview

Sometimes, the typical dinner-and-drinks can color only so many nights before you crave a more…let's say, cultured experience. Cue Lincoln Center. As one of Manhattan's most romantic spots, its stages have felt soft pirouettes of ballet slippers from the NYC Ballet, vibrations from sopranos in the Metropolitan Opera, and tap-tap-tap from the soles of trumpet-players. Culture, indeed. This four-square-block area borders on cultural obscenity. Better leave dinner-and-drinks to the pre-show. However, visual aesthetic doesn't start and stop onstage. Lincoln Center also showcases some of the city's signature art and architectural gems: Henry Moore's *Reclining Figure* is the centerpiece of the reflecting pool, and Marc Chagall's murals grace the foyer of the Metropolitan Opera House. Philip Johnson's Plaza Fountain anchors the entire center, creating an intimate space where New Yorkers can go to forget about their appallingly high rents and pretend they're in the scene from *Moonstruck* where Cher and Nicholas Cage meet to see *La Bohème*.

Who Lives Where

A mecca of tulle, tin, and strings, Lincoln Center houses companies upon troupes upon societies. Matching the performing group to the building means you won't end up watching *Swan Lake* when you should be listening to Mozart. The most confusing part about Lincoln Center is that "Lincoln Center Theater" is two theaters—the Vivian Beaumont and the Mitzi E. Newhouse theaters. Jazz at Lincoln Center moved into the Frederick P. Rose Hall in the AOL/Time Warner Center.

American Ballet Theater — Metropolitan Opera House
Chamber Music Society — Alice Tully Hall
(which will be closed for renovations during the 2007–08 season. The Society's home that season will be The Concert Hall at the New York Society for Ethical Culture)
Film Society of Lincoln Center — Walter Reade Theater
Jazz at Lincoln Center — Frederick P. Rose Hall
Julliard Orchestra & Symphony — Alice Tully Hall
Metropolitan Opera Company — Metropolitan Opera House

Lincoln Center Theater — Vivian Beaumont Theater and Mitzi E. Newhouse Theater
Mostly Mozart Festival — Avery Fisher Hall
New York City Ballet — New York State Theater
New York City Opera — New York State Theater
New York Philharmonic — Avery Fisher Hall
School of American Ballet — Samuel B. and David Rose Building

Columbus Circle

Okay, okay, the real reason you head to Columbus Circle is for Whole Foods. This mothership, inside one of the closest things to a shopping mall in NYC, anchors the Time Warner Center and the Mandarin Oriental Hotel, which, by the way, has pillows on which your out-of-town guests will not sleep, unless they own a small kingdom. Ditto for eating at Per Se ($250 per person, plus drinks). Other highlights for us common folk include Thomas Keller's Bouchon Bakery, a Borders bookstore, and the Samsung UnStore, where you can check your email for free. The Trump International Hotel and Tower soars nearby. Nougatine, of Jean-Georges fame, features as its premier lunch spot…ahh…the other reason you go to Columbus Circle.

How to Get There

Lincoln Center is right off Broadway and only a few blocks north of Columbus Circle, which makes getting there easy. The closest subway is the 66th Street ❶ stop, which has an exit right on the edge of the center. It's also an easy walk from the trains that roll into Columbus Circle. If you prefer above-ground transportation, the ❺ ❼ ❿ ⓫ ⓴ Ⓜ bus lines all stop within one block of Lincoln Center. There is also a parking lot underneath the complex for those bent on driving.

W 16th St

E 16th St

1

Union Sq W

Union Sq E

W 15th St

E 15th St

2

Union Square

N R Q W
4 5 6 L

F V L

L

14th Street **W14th St**

Union Sq. E 14th St

3rd Ave

5
6
7

4 3

W 13th St

E 13th St

8

9 10
11
12

W 12th St

E 12th St

13

14
15

W 11th St

E 11th St

Broadway

Fourth Ave

16

W 10th St

E 10th St

Ave of the Americas

Fifth Ave

University Pl

W 9th St

E 9th St

Third Ave

17

W 8th St

E 8th St

N R W

8th Street

6

Astor Place

Astor Place

MacDougal Aly

Washington Mews

F V B D
A C E

Washington Sq N

Waverly Pl

Washington Square

Washington Sq E

Washington Pl

Washington Sq W

W. 4th St.

Washington Sq S

W 4th St

W 3rd St

Bleecker St

Bowery

Minetta St

MacDougal St

Sullivan St

Thompson St

LaGuardia Pl

Mercer St

St

1. 31 Union Sq. W.
   Residence Hall
2. 8 E. 16th St./ 79 Fifth Ave.
3. 25 E. 13th St.
4. Albert List Academic Center
   65 Fifth Ave.
5. 80 Fifth Ave.
6. 72 Fifth Ave.
7. Arnold Hall
   55 W. 13th St.
8. 118 W. 13th St.
   Residence Hall
9. 2 W. 13th St.
10. 70 Fifth Ave.
11. 68 Fifth Ave.
12. 66 Fifth Ave.
13. Loeb Hall
    135 E. 12th St.
14. Alvin Johnson/
    J.M. Kaplan Building
    66 W. 12th St.
15. Eugene Lang College
    65 W. 11th St.
16. 64 W. 11th St.
17. 5 W. 8th St.
    Marlton House

F V B D

W Houston St

E Houston St

Parks & Places • **The New School**

General Information

NFT Map: 5 & 6
Phone: 212-229-5600
Website: www.newschool.edu
Enrollment: 9,300

Overview

The graffiti logoed New School University, formerly The New School for Social Research, is a legendary progressive university located around Greenwich Village, housing eight major divisions, a world-renowned think tank and the backdrop for Project Runway. Founded in 1919 as a refuge for intellectual nonconformists (including historian Charles Beard, philosopher John Dewey, and several former Columbia professors), the New School credits its philosophy the fusing of American intellectual rigor and European critical thought.

The university annually enrolls 9,300 students within eight undergraduate and graduate divisions, including Parsons The New School for Design, Milano The New School for Management and Urban Policy, Eugene Lang College The New School for Liberal Arts, Mannes College The New School for Music, The New School for Drama, The New School for General Studies, The New School for Social Research, and The New School for Jazz and Contemporary Music.

Recent contentions include the 2006 graduation ceremony involvement of John McCain who "does not reflect the values upon which the university was founded," the switching of the longtime six-sided shield logo to the current capital-lettered orange graffiti one, and the end of the university's involvement with Bravo program Inside the Actor's Studio. Alright, maybe there weren't any contentions involved in the illustrious/ridiculed James Lipton vehicle transferring o'er to Pace University, but it was a move that we feel deserved mention.

On a final note, the current New School for Social Research, formerly the Graduate Faculty of Political and Social Science, formerly the University in Exile was a division founded as haven for dismissed teachers from totalitarian regimes in Europe. Original members included psychologist Erich Fromm and political philosopher Leo Strauss. Quite a lineage with most more recent graduates as Sufjan Stevens and Marc Jacobs have to contend.

Tuition

Varies on the program. See website for details.
http://www.newschool.edu/tuition/06/parsons.html

Culture on Campus

Parsons is always showcasing something or other, from student shows to MoMa-presented conferences to fine arts lectures. The John L. Tischman Auditorium is the egg-shaped art deco venue for the masses. The quad courtyard, between buildings on 12th and 13th Streets, is the closest thing to a college campus. Otherwise, there's the city.

Transportation

All the subways that Union Square has to offer! N, Q, R, W, 4, 5, 6 and the L.

General Phone Numbers

Student Financial Services (Mannes) 212-580-0210
Career Development 212-229-1324
Counseling Services. 212-229-1671
Financial Aid 212-229-8930
Food Services. 212-229-5161
Health Education 212-229-5687
Health Services 212-598-4796
HEOP 212-229-8996
Student Housing. 212-229-5459
Intercultural Support. 212-229-8996
International Student Services. 212-229-5592
International Student Services (Mannes) . . . 212-580-0210
Student Ombuds. 212-229-8996
Registrar. 212-229-5620
Registration (Mannes) 212-580-0210
Student Development 212-229-5687
Student Financial Services. 212-229-8930
Student Rights & Responsibilites. 212-229-5349
Fogelman Library 212-229-5307
Gimbel Library 212-229-8914
Scherman Library 212-580-0210

Residence Hall Phone Numbers

Loeb Hall 212-229-1167
Marlton House 212-473-7014
Union Square 212-229-5343
William Street. 646-414-0216
13th Street. 646-414-2671
Security (24 Hours) 212-229-7001

Academic Phone Numbers

The New School for General Studies 212-998-8040
Milano The New School for
Management and Urban Policy. 212-998-3011
Parsons The New School for Design. 212-998-6060
Eugene Lang College The New School
for Liberal Arts 212-263-7300
The New School for Social Research 212-998-7200
Mannes College The New School
for Music 212-998-7200
The New School for Drama 212-998-0100
The New School for Jazz and
Contemporary Music. 212-998-1800

Parks & Places · **New York University**

1. Carlyle Court
2. Coral Towers
3. Thirteenth St Residence Hall
4. 145 Fourth Avenue
5. University Hall
6. Palladium Hall
7. 113 University Place
8. 838 Broadway
9. 7 E 12th Street
10. Casa Italiana Zerilli-Marimò
11. Third Avenue North Residence Hall
12. Rubin Residence Hall
13. Brontman Center
14. Brittany Residence Hall
15. Lillian Vernon Center for International Affairs

16. Alumni Hall
17. Barney Building
18. 19 University Place
19. Cantor Film Center
20. 10 Astor Place
21. Deutches Haus
22. Glucksman Ireland House
23. Institute of French Studies/ La Maison Française
24. Weinstein Center for Student Living
25. Undergraduate Admissions
26. One-Half Fifth Avenue
27. 1-6 Washington Square North
    - School of Social Work
    - Graduate School of Arts and Science
28. Rufus D Smith Hall
29. Seventh Street Residence
30. 111, 113A Second Avenue

31. Silver Center Block
    - Silver Center for Arts and Science
    - Waverly Building
    - Brown Building
32. Kimball Block
    - Kimball Hall
    - Torch Club
    - Reprographic Services
    - 285 Mercer Street

33. Broadway Block
    - 715 Broadway
    - 719 Broadway
    - 721 Broadway
    - 1 Washington Place
    - 3 Washington Place
    - 5 Washington Place
34. NYU Health Center
35. 411 Lafayette Street

36. 48 Cooper Square
37. Hayden Residence Hall
38. Education Block
    - Pless Hall
    - Pless Annex
    - NYU Bookstore
    - East Building
    - Faye's @ the Square
    - Goddard Hall
39. Student Services Block
    - 25 West Fourth Street
    - Moses Center for Students with Disabilities
    - 242 Greene Street
    - 14, 14A Washington Place
    - Carter Hall
    - 8 Washington Place
    - 269 Mercer Street
40. Meyer Block
    - Meyer Hall
    - Psychology Block
41. Provincetown Playhouse
    - Layering Program
42. Vanderbilt Hall
43. Judson Block
    - Kevorkian Center
    - Skirball Department
    - King Juan Carlos I Center

44. Catholic Center at NYU
45. Kimmel Center for University Life
    - Skirball Center for the Performing Arts
46. Bobst Library
47. Schwartz Plaza
48. Shimkin Hall
    - Gould Welcome Center
49. Kaufman Management Center
50. Tisch Hall
51. Courant Institute
52. D'Agostino Hall
53. 561 La Guardia Place
54. Mercer Street Residence
55.

58. 530 La Guardia Place
59. Off-Campus Housing
60. Second Street Residence
61. University Plaza
62. Silver Towers
63. Coles Sports and Recreation Center
64. 194 Mercer Street
65. Puck Building
    - Wagner Graduate School of Public Service

General Information

NFT Map: 6
Phone: 212-998-1212
Website: www.nyu.edu
Enrollment: 50,917

Overview

Founded in 1831, the nation's largest private university sprawls throughout Manhattan, though its most recognizable buildings border Washington Square. Total enrollment is just over 50,000, about 20,000 of whom are undergraduates, and all of whom are more culturally savvy than any 10 other generic college students.

The expansion of NYU during recent years has not been welcomed by local residents. Some Village folks blame NYU's sprawl for higher rents and diminished quirkiness. On the other hand, the students are a financial boom for businesses in the area, and many historical buildings (such as the row houses on Washington Square) are owned and kept in good condition by the university.

NYU comprises fourteen colleges, schools, and faculties, including the well-regarded Stern School of Business, the School of Law, and the Tisch School of Arts. It also has a school of Continuing and Professional Studies, with offerings in publishing, real estate, and just about every other city-centric industry you could imagine. 34,944 people applied to NYU for undergraduate school last year; just over 28% were accepted. And listen up, boys, 61% of those enrolled last year were female.

Unfortunately, the Chick-fil-A within the Weinstein Hall dining facility closed a few years ago. We're still in mourning.

Tuition

Tuition costs roughly $33,740 for undergrads, while graduate schools generally charge by points taken (except for Stern, which costs nearly $20,000 per semester). Check the NYU website for specific tuition information.

Sports

NYU isn't big on athletics. They don't have a football team. (Where would they play anyway?) It does have a number of other sports teams, though. The school competes in Division III and its mascot is the Bobcat, although all of their teams are nicknamed the Violets. Go figure.

Culture on Campus

The Grey Art Gallery usually has something cool (www.nyu.edu/greyart), and the new Skirball Center for the Performing Arts hosts live performances (www.skirballcenter.nyu.edu). NYU doesn't host nearly as many events as decent liberal arts schools in the middle of nowhere. Why bother? It's in Greenwich Village, surrounded by some of the world's best rock and jazz clubs, and on the same island as 700+ art galleries, thousands of restaurants, and tons of revival and new cinema. This is both the blessing and the curse of NYU—no true "campus," but situated in the middle of the greatest cultural square mileage in the world.

Transportation

NYU runs its own campus transportation service for students, faculty, staff, and alumni with school ID cards. They run 7 am to 2 am weekdays and 10 am to 2 am weekends.

Route A: 200 Water St (South Street Seaport) to 715 Broadway (near 4th St), stopping at the Lafayette and Broome Street dorms on the way.
Route B: Woolworth Building to 715 Broadway, passing through the same areas as Route A.
Route C: 715 Broadway loop, passing through SoHo, NoHo, and the East Village.
Route D: 715 Broadway loop through the West Village.
Route E: Midtown Center (SCPS near 42nd St and Fifth Ave) to 715 Broadway, stopping at the NYU Medical Center on the east side and passing through the Gramercy Park area.

General Phone Numbers

Gould Welcome Center: 212-998-INFO (4636)
NYU Protection and
 Transportation Services 212-998-2222
Undergraduate Admissions: 212-998-4500
Financial Aid: 212-998-4444
University Registrar: 212-998-4800
University Employment Office: 212-998-1250
Student Health Services: 212-443-1000
Kimmel Center for University Life: 212-998-4900
Bobst Library: 212-998-2500
Coles Sports Center: 212-998-2020
NYU Card: 212-443-CARD (2273)

Academic Phone Numbers

All undergraduate programs: 212-998-4500
Summer Session: 212-998-2292
Dental School : 212-998-9800
Steinhardt School of Education: 212-998-5000
Ehrenkranz School of Social Work: 212-998-5910
Gallatin School of Individualized Study: 212-998-7370
Graduate School of Arts & Science: 212-998-8040
Graduate Computer Science: 212-998-3011
Law School: 212-998-6060
School of Medicine: 212-263-7300
School of Continuing and Professional
 Studies Degree Program: 212-998-7200
School of Continuing and Professional
 Studies Real Estate Institute: 212-998-7200
School of Continuing and Professional
 Studies Non-Credit Program: 212-998-7171
Stern School of Business: 212-998-0100
Tisch School of the Arts: 212-998-1800
Wagner School of Public Service: 212-998-7414

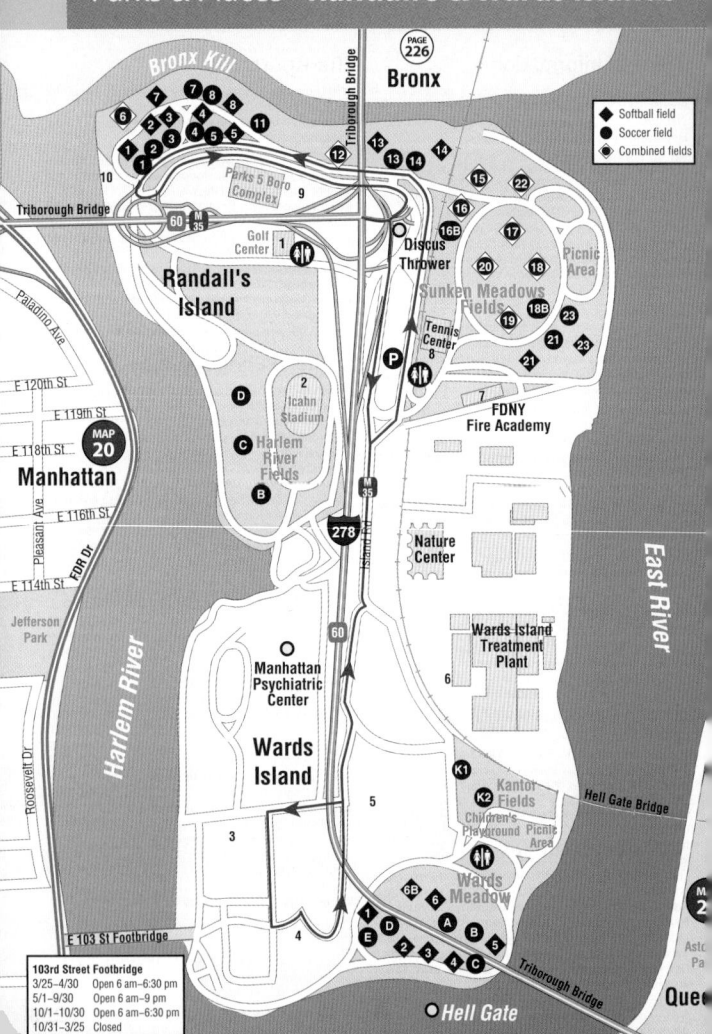

Bronx Kill

PAGE
226

Bronx

◆ Softball field
● Soccer field
◉ Combined fields

Triborough Bridge

Parks 5 Boro Complex

Golf Center

Randall's Island

Triborough Bridge

Discus Thrower

Sunken Meadows Fields

Picnic Area

Tennis Center

FDNY Fire Academy

Paladino Ave

E 120th St

E 119th St

E 118th St

MAP
20

Manhattan

Pleasant Ave

E 116th St

Jefferson Park

Roosevelt Dr

Harlem River

FDR Dr

E 114th St

D

C

B

Icahn Stadium

Harlem River Fields

Nature Center

Manhattan Psychiatric Center

Wards Island

Wards Island Treatment Plant

East River

Hell Gate Bridge

K1

K2

Kantor Fields

Children's Playground Picnic Area

Wards Meadow

6B 6

1 D A

E 2 B 5

4 C

E 103 St Footbridge

Triborough Bridge

Queens

Astoria Park

○ Hell Gate

103rd Street Footbridge
3/25–4/30   Open 6 am–6:30 pm
5/1–9/30   Open 6 am–9 pm
10/1–10/30 Open 6 am–6:30 pm
10/31–3/25 Closed

General Information

Randall's Island Sports Foundation: 212-830-7722; www.risf.org

Overview

Most New Yorkers associate Randall's Island solely with the Triborough Bridge, not realizing the island has 440 acres of parkland for public use. In fact, Randall's and Wards Islands, connected by landfill, contain some of Manhattan's best athletic fields and parks. Originally conceived of and built by the infamous Robert Moses, Randall's and Wards Island Park is now administered by the Randall's Island Sports Foundation. Their mission is to continue to improve and upgrade the park for the residents of New York City.

Phase I of their very big plan included replacing Downing Stadium with the state-of-the-art Icahn Track & Field Stadium and the adjacent amphitheater for concerts. The Foundation is also improving all bike and pedestrian trails. Future phases include adding a cricket field and ferry service, and there are even plans for a fancy water park opening sometime in the near future. Recently, controversial plans for a water park and the private use of athletic fields fell apart under community pressure. Hopefully part of any future plans will include some food facilities. As it is, the only food available is the snack bar in the golf center and the lunch trucks scattered around Icahn Stadium and the Fire Training Center. In the meantime, do what the locals do—pack a picnic and head to the island for a mellow weekend outing.

Just south of Wards Island lies Hell Gate, a treacherous body of water where the Harlem and East Rivers meet. Many commercial and private vessels have come to grief in this stretch of water.

How to Get There

By Car: Take the Triborough Bridge, exit left to Randall's Island. There's a $4.50 toll to get on the island with your car. It's free to leave!

By Subway/Bus: From Manhattan: take the **4 5 6** train to 125th Street, then transfer on the corner of 125th Street and Lexington Avenue for the **35** bus to Randall's Island. There's a bus about every 40 minutes during the day. From Queens: take the **Q** from 61st Street-Woodside.

By Foot: A pedestrian footbridge at 103rd Street was built by Robert Moses in the '50s to provide Harlem residents access to the recreational facilities of the parks after then-City Council President Newbold Morris criticized the lack of facilities in Harlem. Today, the bridge is open only during summer daylight hours. See timetable on map.

1 **Randall's Island Golf Center** • 212-427-5689 • The golf center on Randall's Island has a driving range open year-round with 80 heated stalls, along with two 18-hole mini-golf courses, nine batting cages, and a snack bar. A weekend shuttle service is available every hour on the hour, 10 am–5 pm from Manhattan (86th Street and Third Avenue) costs $10 round-trip. Summer hours are 6 am–11 pm Tuesday–Sunday and 11 am–11 pm on Mondays, with off-season hours from 8 am–8 pm Tuesday–Sunday and 1 pm–8 pm on Mondays.

2 **Icahn Track & Field Stadium** • 212- 860-1899 x101• Named for financier Carl Icahn, the 10,000-seat stadium is the only state-of-the-art outdoor track and field venue in New York City with a 400-meter running track and a regulation-size soccer field.

3 **Supportive Employment Center** • 212-534-3866

4 **Charles H. Gay Shelter Care Center for Men** • Volunteers of America - Greater New York • 212-369-8900 • www.voa-gny.org

5 **Odyssey House Drug Rehab Center** • Mabon Building • 212-426-6677

6 **DEP Water Pollution Control Plant** • 718-595-6600 • www.ci.nyc.ny.us/html/dep/html/drainage.html

7 **Fire Department Training Center** •
The NYC Fire Academy is located on 27 acres of landfill on the east side of Randall's Island. In an effort to keep the city's "bravest" in shape, the academy utilizes the easily accessible 68 acres of parkland for physical fitness programs. The ultra-cool training facility includes 11 Universal Studios–like buildings for simulations training, a 200,000 gallon water supply tank, gasoline and diesel fuel pumps, and a 300-car parking lot. In addition, the New York Transit Authority installed tracks and subway cars for learning and developing techniques to battle subway fires and other emergencies. It's really too bad they don't sell tickets and offer tours!

8 **Tennis Center** • 212- 427-6150 • 11 outdoor courts. Indoor courts heated for winter use.

9 **Robert Moses Building** • We're sure many an urban planning student has made a pilgrimage here.

10 **NYPD** • They launch cool-looking police boats from here.

General Information

Website:
   www.nycparks.org or www.riversideparkfund.org
Riverside Park Administrator
   (212) 408-0264
79th Street Boat Basin - Public Marina
   (212) 496-2105

Overview

If Sally Struthers taught you anything about saving the world and you still can't get to that darned developing country, your ticket to heaven awaits at Riverside Park. Pick a program and you're saved: Sponsor a Bench or Sponsor a Tree. Yes, apparently crabapple (or "crab apple" otherwise risking the tongue twister, "crap-abble") and London plane trees need your desperate help. For years, they've been subject to the cruelty of noxious gases from passing cars and dogs' territorial marks, but you, even you, cannot justify lovesick children carving hearts and initials in their bark. You may even remember those poor, diseased-looking trees, like cobras shedding their skins, bark peeling to reveal a lighter inner bark. Light bulb on yet? Those are London plane trees (no diseases involved). And don't forget those benches suffering the wrath of a million deadweights, as they stop to rest their walking feet. Surely, even Sally herself doesn't discriminate against the most deserving.

After you've sponsored your new friend, revel in the four miles of pure, parkalicious plain. Spanning from 72nd to 158th Street, Riverside Park was designed in 1875 by Frederick Law Olmsted. It was expanded and adapted for active recreational use during the early 20th Century without losing too much of its charm. In 1980, the New York City Landmarks Preservation Commission crowned Riverside Park between 72nd and 125th a "scenic landmark."

Things to do along 300 acres of green goodness: Walk. Run. Cycle. Skate. Kayak. Play ball, any ball. Throw in a couple of dog walkers, and sure as sugar, you've got yourself a bona fide park (see Hudson River Park, Battery Park City, Central Park for reference).

Parks & Places • Riverside Park

Sights & Sounds

North waterfront between 147th and 152nd streets: It's a looker. To excite the secret Oscar slave in you, head to the Crabapple Grove at 91st for a self-guided tour of *You've Got Mail*, where Tom Hanks finally met Meg Ryan (as if they didn't know each other the whole time). While you're there, check out the Garden for All Seasons. You can take a guess at what kind of garden that is. Whistle wet not? Take a gander at the American elms that surreptitiously line Riverside Drive. Remember what it's like to have trees—real trees—where you live. Or, if you're so over the tree thing, the Soldiers' and Sailors' Monument at 89th gives homage to Civil War heroes from New York and gives you +1 in preparing for that all-important tavern trivia game. Same goes for Grant's Tomb at 122nd, an intriguing monument, especially with Jazz Mobile (an offshoot of T-Mobile and Jazz at Lincoln Center…) strumming serious beats on a lazy summer day. Who knew the key to heaven's gates was in your backyard?

Swing a Ring

Located at Riverside Park's Hudson Beach (W 105th St), Swing a Ring is a unique fitness apparatus that exists only in New York City (lucky us) and Santa Monica. There's a set for adults and a set for ankle-biters. It's free, permanent, open year-round, and virtually indestructible (read: won't be destroyed by wayward youth with too much spare time on their hands). Each May there's a "Swing a Ring Day" celebration featuring expert instruction for adults and youngsters. For more information about the rings and special events, visit www.swingaring.com. Once you try it, you'll never stop swinging! (Well, not until the big guy with the lycra bicycle shorts wants a turn.) For those whose swinging only extends to an ice cold Corona with a passable burger to wash it down, the tables at the Hudson Beach Café, overlooking the swing set, offer a scenic (and more sedentary) view of the action.

Practicalities

Take the ❶ ❷ ❸ train to any stop between 72nd and 157th and it's just a short walk west to Riverside Park. Or just drive along Riverside Drive and park (no pun intended). And hey, be safe. Don't hang out there alone after dark.

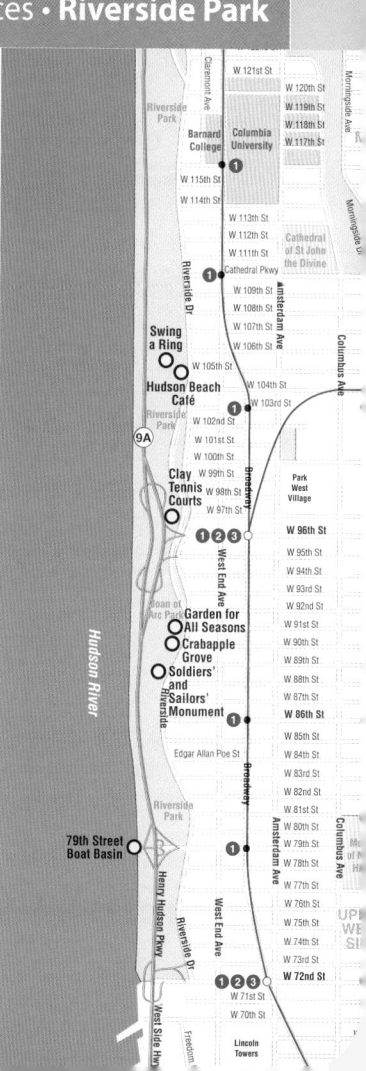

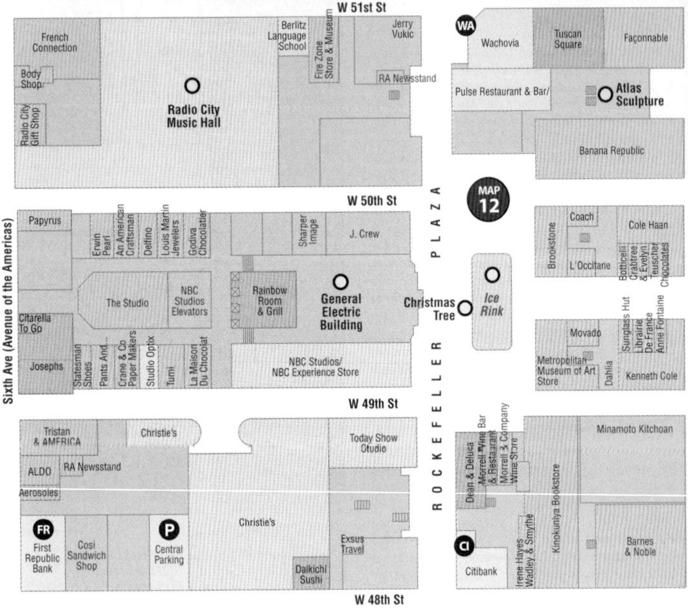

W 51st St

French Connection

Body Shop

Radio City Gift Shop

Berlitz Language School

Fire Zone Store & Museum

Jerry Vukic

RA Newsstand

Radio City Music Hall

WA — Wachovia

Tuscan Square

Façonnable

Pulse Restaurant & Bar/

Atlas Sculpture

Banana Republic

W 50th St

MAP 12

Papyrus

Erwin Pearl

An American Craftsman

Delfino

Louis Martin Jewelers

Godiva Chocolatier

Sharper Image

J. Crew

Citarella (To Go)

The Studio

Josephs

Statesman Stationers

Pants And...

Crane & Co Paper Makers

Studio Optix

Tumi

La Maison Du Chocolat

NBC Studios Elevators

Rainbow Room & Grill

General Electric Building

Christmas Tree

Ice Rink

Brookstone

Coach

Cole Haan

L'Occitane

Bottholi Gabriel & Evelyn/ Teuscher Chocolatier

Movado

Sunglass Hut

Librairie De France

Anne Fontaine

NBC Studios/ NBC Experience Store

Metropolitan Museum of Art Store

Dahlia

Kenneth Cole

W 49th St

Tristan & AMÉRICA

Christie's

Today Show Studio

ALDO

RA Newsstand

Aerosoles

FR — First Republic Bank

Cosi Sandwich Shop

P — Central Parking

Christie's

Exsus Travel

Dean & Deluca

Morrell Wine Bar & Restaurant

Morrell & Company Wine Store

Minamoto Kitchoan

Irene Hayes Wadley & Smythe

Kinokuniya Bookstore

Barnes & Noble

CI — Citibank

Daikichi Sushi

W 48th St

STREET LEVEL

PLAZA

ROCKEFELLER

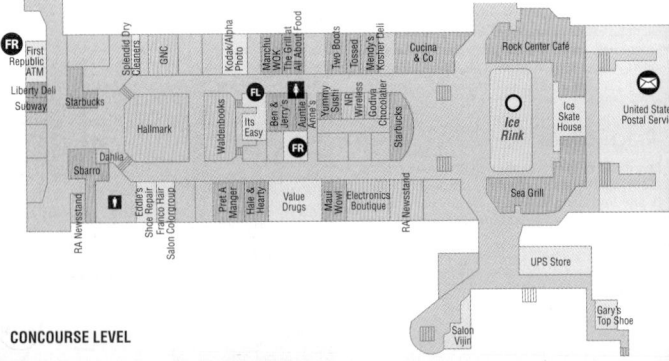

CONCOURSE LEVEL

FR — First Republic ATM

Liberty Deli

Subway

Starbucks

Splendid Dry Cleaners

GNC

Kodak/Alpha Photo

Manchu WOK

The Grillat All About Food

Two Boots

Tossed

Mendy's Kosher Deli

Cucina & Co

Rock Center Café

Hallmark

Waldenbooks

FL — Its Easy

Ben & Berry's

Aunite Anne's

FR

Yummy Sushi

NR Wireless

Godiva Chocolatier

Starbucks

Ice Rink

Ice Skate House

United States Postal Service

Dahlia

Sbarro

RA Newsstand

Eddie's Shoe Repair Franco Hair Salon Colorgroup

Pret A Manger

Hale & Hearty

Value Drugs

Maui Wowi

Electronics Boutique

RA Newsstand

Sea Grill

UPS Store

Salon Vijin

Gary's Top Shoe

General Information

NFT Map:	12
Phone:	212-632-3975
Website:	www.rockefellercenter.com
Rink Phone:	212-332-7654
Rink Website:	www.therinkatrockcenter.com
NBC Tour Phone:	212-664-3700
Top of the Rock:	www.topoftherocknyc.com

Overview

Perhaps you've been blinded five streets away by 25,000 Swarovski crystals. Or maybe you've glimpsed a gargantuan King Kong of a tree shooting seventy feet in the air and wondered how on earth such vegetation could grow in concrete. Regardless, you fall for antics, arrive in bewilderment at Rockefeller Center, and stay for the ice-skating rink, services at St. Patrick's, and the Rockettes at Radio City Music Hall.

When there's not a huge pine tree to distract you, you'll note that Rockefeller Center occupies three square blocks with a slew of retail, dining, and office facilities. Midtown corporate just ain't the same without its magic. Embodying the Art Deco architecture of the era, the center's legacy began during the Great Depression.

The Top of the Rock Observation Deck, first opened more than 70 years ago by John D. Rockefeller, has finally reopened to the masses. Enjoy jaw dropping, 360-degree views of the skyline.

Today, the Associated Press, General Electric, and NBC call Rock their 9–5. (You've seen Dean & Deluca on TV during the *Today Show*'s outdoor broadcasts.) And "30 Rock" has *Saturday Night Live* and *Late Night with Conan O'Brien*. Not bad for a tree-hugger, huh?

Where to Eat

How hungry are you? Rock Center isn't a prime dining destination, but you won't starve if you find yourself in the area. For cheaper fare, try places down in the Concourse such as Pret A Manger or Two Boots. For fancier (read: overpriced) food, try the Sea Grill (overlooking the skating rink) or the Rainbow Room on the center's 65th floor. The food isn't straight out of *Gourmet*—you're paying for the view. Tuscan Square (16 W 51st St) offers pretty decent Italian, though prices are a bit inflated here as well. Many restaurants in Rockefeller Center are open on Saturdays, but aside from the "nice" restaurants, only a few open their doors on Sundays.

Where to Shop

For all the mall-lovers out there, Rockefeller Center has its own underground version—heck, there's even a Sharper Image and a Brookstone! For original, non-commercialized goods, check out these stores in Rockefeller Center and the surrounding area:

FireZone Store and Museum • 50 Rockefeller Plaza • Official seller of FDNY merchandise.
Kinokuniya Bookstore • 10 W 49th St • Japanese-language and Asian-themed, English-language books.
Minamoto Kitchoan • 608 Fifth Ave • Authentic Japanese pastries and cakes.
La Maison Du Chocolat • 30 Rockefeller Plaza • French chocolates.
Librairie De France • 610 Fifth Ave • Foreign bookseller, including French-language texts, children's books, travel guides, and maps.
Teuscher Chocolates • 620 Fifth Ave • Swiss chocolates.

And for the practical parts of your life: Dahlia (flowers), Eddie's Shoe Repair, Kodak/Alpha Photo, and Splendid Dry Cleaners. They're all located near the entrance to the Sixth Avenue subway (Ⓑ Ⓓ Ⓕ Ⓥ). A US Post Office is on the Eastern end of Concourse near the rink and UPS is in the area perpendicular to the Sea Grill. But they, like many of the stores in the Concourse, are closed on weekends. Unless you work in Rockefeller Center, it's not likely that you'll need to use them anyway.

The Rink

To practice your double loop: The rink opens Columbus Day weekend and closes early April to make way for the Rink Bar. Skating hours are 9 am–10:30 pm Monday–Thursday, 8:30 am–midnight Friday/Saturday, and 8:30 am–10 pm on Sundays. Skating prices range from $24.50 to $26.50 for adults, depending on the day you visit. (Weekends and holidays are the most expensive times to skate.) The skating rate for children ranges from $19.50 to $21.50 per session. Skate rentals are included in the cost. Lessons are available for $30 during the week and $35 during the weekend—call 212-332-7655 for more information. With hefty skating rates and a crowded rink, better to shoot for an early weekday morning or afternoon, or very early on the weekend.

Parks & Places · **Roosevelt Island**

Overview

Once upon a time, Roosevelt Island was much like the rest of New York—populated by criminals, the sick, and the mentally ill. The difference was that they were the residents of the island's various mental institutions, hospitals, and jails, but these days this slender tract of land between Manhattan and Queens has become prime real estate for families and UN officials.

The 147-acre island, formerly known as "Welfare Island" because of its population of outcasts and the poor, was renamed after Franklin D. Roosevelt in 1973, when the island began changing its image. The first residential housing complex opened in 1975. Some of the old "monuments" remain, including the Smallpox Hospital and the Blackwell House (one of the oldest farmhouses in the city), while the Octagon Building, formerly a 19th-century mental hospital known for its deplorable conditions, is being turned into luxury condos (so yes, you're still in New York).

The island's northern tip is a popular destination for fishermen with iron gullets. It's also the home of a lighthouse designed by James Renwick, Jr., of St. Patrick's Cathedral fame. The two rehab/convalescent hospitals on the island don't offer emergency services, so if you're in need of medical attention right away, you're out of luck. The island's main drag, Main Street (where did they come up with the name?), resembles a cement-block college campus circa 1968. Just south, closer to the tram, is a newly developed stretch of condos that are fetching top dollar. Two of these buildings are residences for Memorial Sloane Kettering Cancer Center and Rockefeller and Cornell University employees.

Long time residents of Roosevelt Island take pride in their 30-year-old community, describing it as a place where people greet each other in the street and kids of all stripes play together. The housing situation on the island is becoming increasingly complicated, with many landlords looking to switch from rent-controlled status to market rates. Merchants have experienced problems too—lack of foot traffic, high rent, and high utility bills have forced some businesses to close. Those that survived are shabby and expensive. Residents flock to the Saturday morning green market under the parking garage, but for the most part prefer to shop off the island. On a more positive note, Roosevelt Island **is** a quiet respite from the chaos of Manhattan. There's lots of green space and a long promenade where you can take in the dramatic views of midtown Manhattan (hint: it is THE place to watch fireworks on July 4th.) But unless you live there, the superb view is really the only reason to stay after dark—Roosevelt Island's only bar closed in early 2005.

How to Get There

Roosevelt Island can be reached by the ⒡ train, but it's much more fun to take the tram. You can board it with a Metrocard (including an unlimited!) at 60th Street and Second Avenue in Manhattan—look for the big hulking mass drifting through the sky. It takes 4 minutes to cross and runs every 15 minutes (every 7 minutes during rush hour) 6 am–2 am, Sunday through Thursday, and 'til 3:30 am on Fridays and Saturdays. To get there by car, take the Queensboro Bridge and follow signs for the 21st Street-North exit. Go north on 21st Street and make a left on 36th Avenue. Go west on 36th Avenue and cross over the red Roosevelt Island Bridge. The only legal parking is at Motorgate Plaza at the end of the bridge at Main Street.

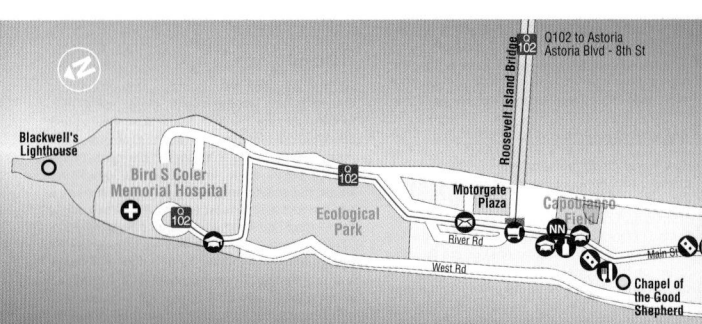

$ Banks

NN · New York National · 619 Main St

Coffee

· **Starbucks** · 455 Main St

Hospitals

· **Coler Goldwater–Coler Campus (No ER)** ·
  900 Main St [West Rd]
· **Coler Goldwater–Goldwater Campus (No ER)** ·
  1 Main St [River Rd]

O Landmarks

· **Blackwell House** · 591 Main St
· **Blackwell's Lighthouse** · n/a
· **Chapel of the Good Shepherd** · n/a
· **Smallpox Hospital** · n/a
· **Tramway** · Tramway Plz [2nd Av]

Libraries

· **Roosevelt Island** · 524 Main St [East Rd]

Liquor Stores

· **Grog Shop** · 605 Main St

Post Offices

· **Roosevelt Island** · 694 Main St [River Rd]

Restaurants

· **Trellis** · 549 Main St

Schools

· **Lillie's International Christian** · 851 Main St
· **MS 271 Building (M271)** · 645 Main St
· **PS 217 Roosevelt Island** · 645 Main St

Supermarkets

· **Gristedes** · 686 N Main St [River Rd]

Video Rental

· **Liberty Roosevelt Island** · 544 Main St [East Rd]
· **Roosevelt Island Video** · 544 Main St

Subways

F ....Roosevelt Island

Bus Lines

Q / 102 ....Main St / East and West Rds

P Parking

Parks & Places · **South Street Seaport**

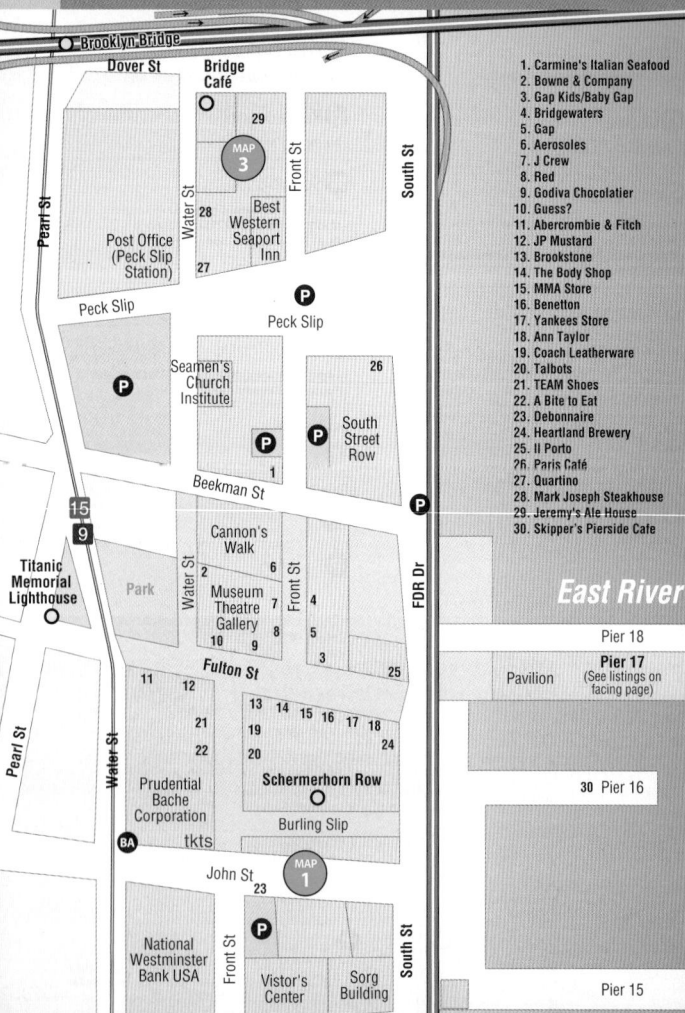

1. Carmine's Italian Seafood
2. Bowne & Company
3. Gap Kids/Baby Gap
4. Bridgewaters
5. Gap
6. Aerosoles
7. J Crew
8. Red
9. Godiva Chocolatier
10. Guess?
11. Abercrombie & Fitch
12. JP Mustard
13. Brookstone
14. The Body Shop
15. MMA Store
16. Benetton
17. Yankees Store
18. Ann Taylor
19. Coach Leatherware
20. Talbots
21. TEAM Shoes
22. A Bite to Eat
23. Debonnaire
24. Heartland Brewery
25. Il Porto
26. Paris Café
27. Quartino
28. Mark Joseph Steakhouse
29. Jeremy's Ale House
30. Skipper's Pierside Cafe

Brooklyn Bridge

Dover St

Bridge Café

Front St

South St

Pearl St

Water St

MAP 3

29

28

Best Western Seaport Inn

27

Post Office (Peck Slip Station)

Peck Slip

Peck Slip

Seamen's Church Institute

26

South Street Row

1

Beekman St

FDR Dr

East River

Titanic Memorial Lighthouse

Park

Cannon's Walk

Water St

Front St

6

Museum Theatre Gallery

10

9

8

5

4

3

Fulton St

2

25

Pier 18

Pier 17
(See listings on facing page)

Pavilion

11

12

13 14 15 16 17 18

21

19

20

24

Pearl St

Water St

22

Schermerhorn Row

Prudential Bache Corporation

Burling Slip

tkts

BA

30 Pier 16

John St

MAP 1

23

Front St

South St

National Westminster Bank USA

Vistor's Center

Sorg Building

Fletcher St

Pier 15

Long before the Upper East Side was anything but a bunch of rich country estates, the South Street Seaport was alive as the center of activity in New York. The city sprouted because of its proximity to the sea and the ease of traveling in the never-frozen harbor. Although the Seaport is now more of a mini-mall than a center of maritime commerce, there are some gems hidden on these old shipping grounds.

South Street is the origin point of the world's first steamship, the first regularly scheduled transatlantic packet (the Black Ball Line), and America's first drydock. Sailors and landlubbers alike can celebrate the history of the Seaport by visiting the fantastic South Street Seaport Museum. Follow your trip to the museum by boarding one or more of the ships permanently moored in the harbor—the *Wavertree* (a full rigged ship from Southampton, England), the *Peking* (a four-masted barque from Hamburg, Germany), and the *Ambrose* (a 20th-century lightship). If you are a bit more adventurous, take a class on or charter one of the following: the *Pioneer* (a former Pennsylvania sloop re-rigged as a schooner), the *Lettie G. Howard* (a Massachusetts fishing schooner), or the *W.O. Decker* (a wooden tugboat built in Long Island City).

Walking around the beautifully preserved and renovated 19th-century buildings on the streets surrounding Pier 17 may lead to serious hunger. Forget the food court in the Pier buildings—this should be left to the teenagers that flock here—and head to the Heartland Brewery for pub food, Red for Mexican, Mark Joseph for steaks, Quartino for organic pizza, JP Mustard for happy hour, or Sequoia for the view.

For those who are looking to shop, you will see many of the same chain stores you find across the country. A few exceptions include the Yankee Clubhouse (fun for just about anyone but Red Sox fans) and Mariposa: The Butterfly Gallery. Mariposa displays Marshall Hill's lucite panels of butterflies from around the world.

The Brooklyn Bridge looms over the whole area—the back decks of the Pier 17 Pavilion have a great view, as does the East Side Promenade, which passes underneath it. Sadly, the most authentic part of the neighborhood, the Fulton Fish Market, has moved to the Bronx, leaving only the sweet stench of seafood from two centuries past lingering in the air. After all, what you see of the Seaport now is the result of a renovation that began in the 1960s and the Fish Market was the only thing going here for a while.

If you're downtown and looking for discounted theater tickets, the Seaport TKTS booth is at the northwest corner of Front and John streets. Check the electronic board for show times and discounts, then go inside and book. At this location, matinee tickets are only sold the day before the performance. (A great way to get tickets to a hot show is by stopping here on Friday for a Saturday matinee.)

General Information

NFT Map:	1 & 3
Phone:	212-SEAPORT
Phone (museum):	212-748-8600
Museum:	12 Fulton St
	www.southstseaport.org
	Hours vary by season.
	Visit the website or call for information.
Retail:	www.southstreet seaport.com
Hours:	Mon–Sat: 10 am–9 pm,
	Sun: 11 am–8 pm
Landmarks:	Schermerhorn Row
	Bridge Café
	Brooklyn Bridge
	Titanic Memorial Lighthouse

Banks

BA · Bank of America · 175 Water St

Subways

② ③ ④ ⑤ Ⓙ Ⓜ Ⓩ
to Fulton Street

Ⓐ Ⓒ . . . . to Broadway-Nassau

Bus Lines

15 . . . . First and Second Aves

9 . . . . Ave B/East Broadway

Pier 17 Pavilion

9000 Perfumery Inc
ABCDE
Abercrombie & Fitch
Aerosoles
Alamo Flags
Ann Taylor
As Seen on TV
Bath & Body Works
Beyond The Wall
Bodies the Exhibition
The Body Shop
Bonsai Designs
Broadway Beat
Brookstone
Cartoon World
City Streets
Claire's Accessories
Coach
Debonaire
Express
Express Men
Filmline Gallery
Foot Locker
Footsies
Gamestop
Gap
Gap Kids
Godiva Chocolatier
Guess?
Inspired by Nature
J. Crew
Jewelry Mine
Lids
Mariposa: The Butterfly Gallery
Metropolitan Museum of Art Store
Neighborhoodies
New York: A View of the World
The New York Shell Shop
The NY Yankees Clubhouse Shop
Nutcracker Sweets
Paradise Candy
Purple-icious
Roy's 770 Shop
Seaport Leather
Seaport News
Seaport Watch Company
The Sharper Image Steps
Sunglass Hut & Watch Station
Talbots
TEAM
Teazeria
TKTS
United Colors of Benetton
USA Olympic Store
Van der Plas Gallery
Victoria's Secret
Waxology

Food

A Bite to Eat
Athenian Express
Bergin's Wine & Beer Garden
Cabana
Cajun Café
China Max
Haagen Dazs
Harbour Lights
Heartland Brewery
House of Crepes
IL Porto
JP Mustard
Japan Sushi Q
Juice Bar Café
Little Tokyo
MacMenamin's Irish Pub
Mrs. Field's
Murph's
Nathan's Famous
Pacific Grill
Pizza on the Pier
Pretzel Time
Red
Seaport Café
Sedutto Ice Cream
Sequoia
Simply Seafood
Subway
Tacqueria Mexicali
Uno Chicago Grill
Wine & Chill

Parks & Places · Times Square

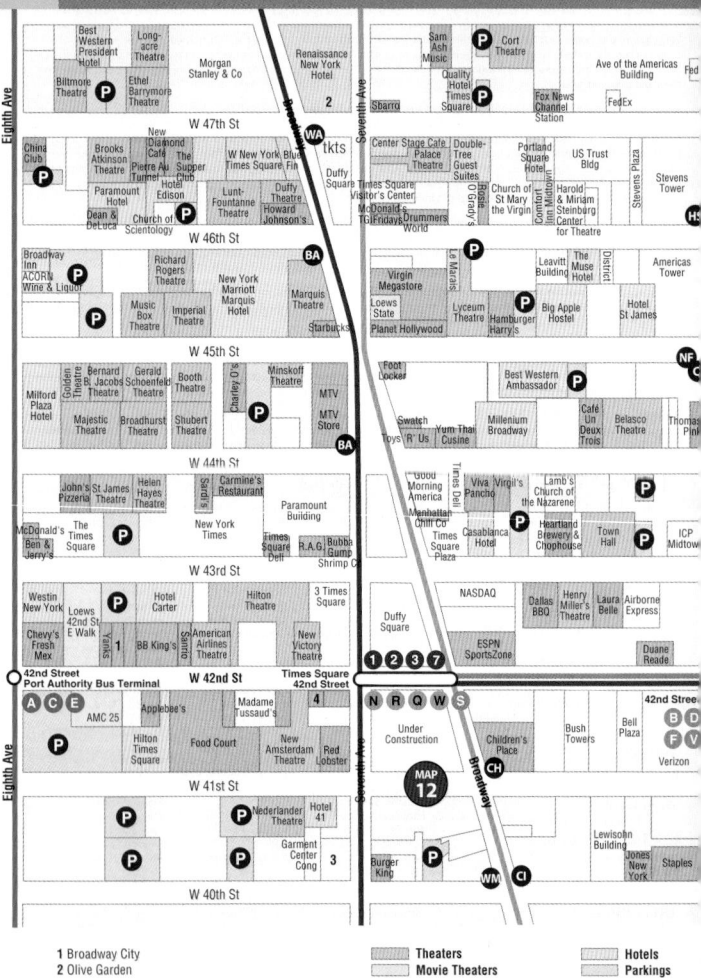

1 Broadway City
2 Olive Garden
3 Parsons School of Design
   Fashion Education Center
4 McDonald's

Theaters
Movie Theaters
Theme Restaurants/Stores

Hotels
Parkings
Other

Defined by the triangle created by 7th Avenue's intersection with Broadway, Times Square—long ago known as Long Acre Square—currently heralds an electrified Disneyfication. Theatergoers dodge and weave through the mass of humanity against a backdrop of blinding billboards and high-voltage advertisements that create a spectacle in itself. Wide-eyed tourists scour the over-stimulating skyline for where the famous New Year's ball drops, while many locals prefer to avoid the madness altogether. Best advice: wear sunglasses, especially at night.

Helpful Websites

www.timessquare.com
www.timessquarenyc.org

Transit

Take the **1** **2** **3** **7** **N** **Q** **R** **W** and **S** trains to get to the center of everything at the 42nd Street/Times Square stop.

ATMs

BA · **Bank of America** · 1515 Broadway
BA · **Bank of America** · 1535 Broadway
CH · **Chase** · 3 Times Sq
CI · **Citibank** · 1155 Sixth Ave
CI · **Citibank** · 1440 Broadway
HS · **HSBC** · 1185 Sixth Ave
NF · **North Fork** · 1166 Sixth Ave
WM · **Washington Mutual** · 1431 Broadway
WA · **Wachovia** · 1568 Broadway

Hotels

Best Western President Hotel · 234 W 48th St
Best Western Ambassador · 132 W 45th St
Big Apple Hostel · 119 W 45th St
Broadway Inn · 264 W 46th St
Casablanca Hotel · 147 W 43rd St
Comfort Inn Midtown · 129 W 46th St
Doubletree Guest Suites · 1568 Broadway
Hilton Times Square · 234 W 42nd St
Hotel 41 · 206 W 41st St
Hotel Carter · 250 W 43rd St
Hotel St James · 109 W 45th St
Milford Plaza Hotel · 270 W 45th St
Millennium Hotel Broadway · 145 W 44th St
The Muse Hotel · 130 W 46th St
New York Marriott Marquis Hotel · 1535 Broadway
Paramount Hotel · 235 W 46th St
Portland Square Hotel · 132 W 47th St
Hotel Edison · 228 W 47th St
Quality Hotel Times Square · 157 W 47th St
Renaissance New York Hotel · 714 Seventh Ave
W New York Times Square · 1567 Broadway
Westin New York · 270 W 43rd St

Movie Theaters

AMC Empire 25 · 234 W 42nd St
Loews State · 1540 Broadway
Loews 42nd St E-Walk · 247 W 42nd St

Theaters

American Airlines Theater · 227 W 42nd St
Belasco Theatre · 111 W 44th St
Bernard B. Jacobs Theatre · 242 W 45th St
Biltmore Theatre · 261 W 47th St
Booth Theatre · 222 W 45th St
Broadhurst Theatre · 235 W 44th St
Brooks Atkinson Theatre · 256 W 47th St
Cort Theatre · 138 W 48th St
Ethel Barrymore Theatre · 243 W 47th St
Gerald Schoenfeld Theatre · 236 W 45th St
Hilton Theatre · 213 W 42nd St
Harold & Miriam Steinberg Center for Theatre/ Laura Pels Theatre · 111 W 46th St
Helen Hayes Theatre · 240 W 44th St
Imperial Theatre · 249 W 45th St
John Golden Theatre · 252 W 45th St
Longacre Theatre · 220 W 48th St
Lunt-Fontanne Theatre · 205 W 46th St
Lyceum Theatre · 149 W 45th St
Majestic Theatre · 274 W 44th St
Marquis Theatre · 1535 Broadway
Minskoff Theatre · 1515 Broadway
Music Box Theatre · 239 W 45th St
Nederlander Theatre · 208 W 41st St
New Amsterdam Theatre · 214 W 42nd St
New Victory Theatre · 209 W 42nd St
Palace Theatre · 1564 Broadway
Richard Rodgers Theatre · 226 W 46th St
Shubert Theatre · 225 W 44th St
St James Theatre · 246 W 44th St
Town Hall · 123 W 43rd St

* *Cash Saving Tip: Most Broadway Theaters offer same day rush tickets for $20–25. Check individual theaters for details..*

Theme Restaurants/ Stores

Applebee's · 234 W 42nd St
BB King's Blues Club · 237 W 42nd St
Ben & Jerry's · 680 Eighth Ave
Blue Fin · 1567 Broadway
Broadway City · 241 W 42nd St
Bruegger's Bagels Bakery · 1115 Sixth Ave
Bubba Gump Shrimp Co · 1501 Broadway
Burger King · 561 Seventh Ave
Café Un Deux Trois · 123 W 44th St
Carmine's Restaurant · 200 W 44th St

Center Stage Cafe · 1568 Broadway
Charley O's · 218 W 45th St
Chevy's Fresh Mex · 243 W 42nd St
The Children's Place · 1460 Broadway
China Club 268 W 47th St
Dallas BBQ · 241 W 42nd St
Dean & DeLuca · 235 W 46th St
District · 130 W 46th St
Drummers World · 151 W 46th St
Duane Reade Pharmacy · 115 W 42nd St
ESPN Sportzone · 4 Times Sq
Food Court · 234 W 42nd St
Foot Locker · 1530 Broadway
Hamburger Harry's · 145 W 45th St
Heartland Brewery · 127 W 43rd St
John's Brick Oven Pizzeria · 260 W 44th St
Jones New York · 119 W 40th St
Laura Belle · 120 W 43rd St
Le Marais · 150 W 46th St
Manhattan Chili Co · 1500 Broadway
McDonald's · 220 W 42nd St
McDonald's · 688 4th Ave
McDonald's · 1109 Sixth Ave
McDonald's · 1560 Broadway
Modell's · 234 W 42nd St
MTV · 1515 Broadway
MTV Store · 1515 Broadway
New Diamond Café · 224 W 47th St
Olive Garden · 2 Times Square
Pierre Au Tunnel · 250 W 47th St
Planet Hollywood · 1540 Broadway
RAG · 1501 Broadway
Red Lobster · 5 Times Square
Rosie O'Grady's · 149 W 46th St
Sam Ash Music · 160 W 48th St
Sanrio · 233 W 42nd St
Sardi's · 234 W 44th St
Sbarro · 701 Seventh Ave
Staples · 1065 Sixth Ave
The Supper Club · 240 W 47th St
Swatch · 1552 Broadway
TGI Friday's · 1552 Broadway
Thomas Pink · 1155 Sixth Ave
Times Deli · 158 W 44th St
Times Square Deli · 211 W 43rd St
Toys "R" Us · 1514-1530 Broadway
Virgil's Real Barbecue · 152 W 44th St
Virgin Megastore · 1540 Broadway
Viva Pancho · 156 W 44th St
Yankee Clubhouse Shop · 245 W 42nd St
Yum Thai Cuisine · 129 W 44th St

Other

Army Recruiting Office · Want to join the Army? Opened in 1946, this Army Recruiting Office has turned more civilians into soldiers than any other recruiting station (43rd St & Broadway).
TKTS · Discounted theater tickets. Temporarily located at the Marquis Theater while Duffy Square is being renovated. More info: www.tdf.org

265

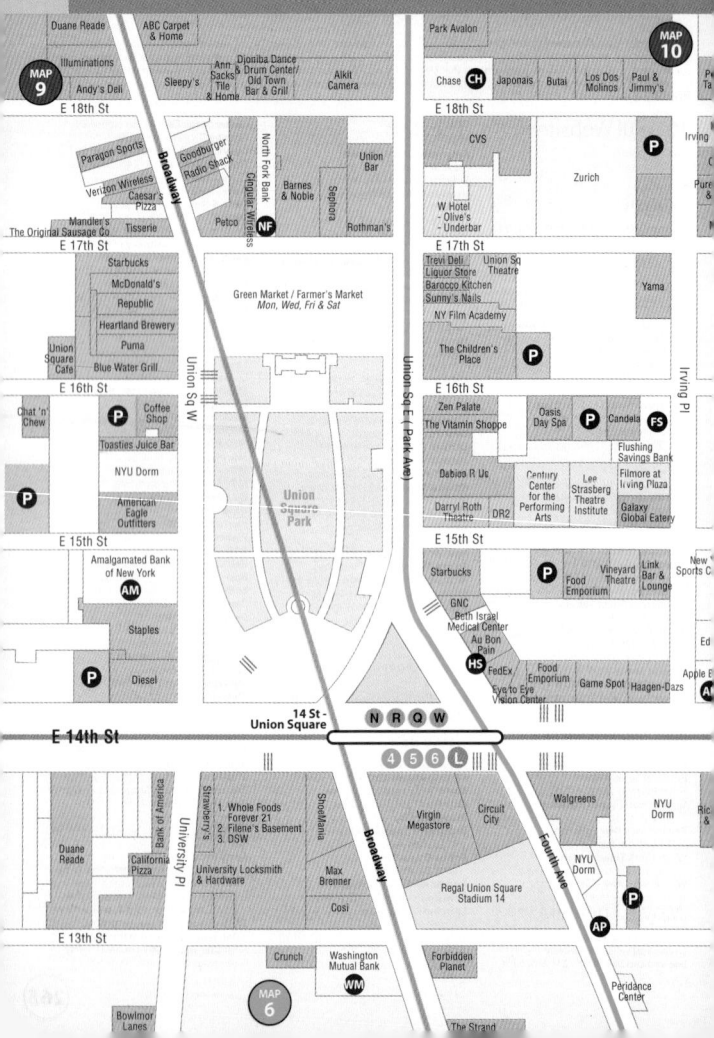

From 14th to 21st Streets, Sixth to Third Avenues, sits the nexus of downtown to midtown, dear Union Square. Once the lively backdrop for rally, burlesque, and debauchery. Now, a tame place for smokes and a turkey sandwich—and, of course, any protest opposing government that may, yawn, arise. The once posh residential nabe is evermore a four-sided strip of retail, and many of New York's finest restaurants have set up table nearby (Gotham Bar & Grill, Blue Water Grill, Gramercy Tavern, Union Square Cafe). For scholars and hermits, the legendary Strand Bookstore stakes its claim off Broadway at 12th.

Antebellum, the common once known as "The Forks" for its crossroad feel, was a site of some of the city's grandest domiciles. Fast-forward to the retail circus (known in it's heyday as "The Ladies Mile"), now devoted to big-box scenes for mass consumption. Today, Union Square is—both literally and figuratively—the page break dividing midtown's prose from downtown's verse.

From the stint between the floral sot that was the sixties and the early eighties, Union Square teemed of weed, a few needles, and a more vital, perhaps more perilous, ambience. Today, having accorded mayoral ambitions, it's been Timesquared.Proof of surrounding life is more than validated by miles of park benches that offer invaluable eye candy for those with time on their hands (check out the 25-digit clock over Virgin, 31 minutes fast), and the excellent green market where the organic, hand-raised, hand-picked, fresher than fresh, right off the farm awaits.

ATMs

AM · Amalgamated Bank of NY · 15 Union Sq
AP · Apple · 4 Irving Pl
AP · Apple · 145 Fourth Ave
BA · Bank of America · 36 E 14th St
CH · Chase · 225 Park S
FS · Flushing Savings · 33 Irving Pl
HS · HSBC · 10 Union Sq
WM · Washington Mutual · 835 Broadway

Hotels

Inn at Irving Place · 56 Irving Pl
W Hotel · 201 Park Avenue S

Stores/Restaurants

13 · 35 E 13th St
ABC Carpet & Home · 888 Broadway
Alkit Camera · 222 Park Ave S
American Eagle Outfitters · 19 Union Sq W
Andy's Deli · 873 Broadway
Angelo & Maxie's Steakhouse · 233 Park Ave S
Ann Sacks Tile & Stone · 37 E 18th St
Au Bon Pain · 6 Union Sq E
Babies"R"Us · 24 Union Sq E
Barnes & Noble · 33 E 17th St
Blue Water Grill · 31 Union Sq W
Butai · 115 E 18th St
Caesar's Pizza · 861 Broadway
California Pizza · 122 University Pl
Candela · 116 E 16th St
Casa Mono · 52 Irving Pl
Chat 'n' Chew · 10 E 16th St
The Children's Place · 36 Union Sq E
Cibar · 56 Irving Pl
Cingular Wireless · 31 E 17th St
Circuit City · 52-64 E 14th St
City Bakery · 3 W 18th St
City Crab & Seafood Co · 235 Park Ave S
Coffee Shop · 29 Union Sq W
Cosi · 841 Broadway
CVS · 215 Park Ave S
Diesel · 1 Union Sq W

Duane Reade · 873 Broadway
DSW · 40 E 14th St, 3rd fl
FedEx · 4 Union Sq E
Filene's Basement · 4 Union Sq S
Food Emporium · 10 Union Sq E
Forbidden Planet · 840 Broadway
Forever 21 · 4 Union Sq S
Galaxy Global Eatery · 15 Irving Pl
Gamespot · 107 E 14th St
Garden of Eden · 7 E 14th Street
GNC · 10 Union Sq E
Goodburger · 870 Broadway
Gotham Bar & Grill · 12 E 12th St
Gramercy Tavern · 42 E 20th St
Heartland Brewery · 35 Union Sq W
Illuminations · 873 Broadway
Japonais · 111 E 18th St
Link Bar & Lounge · 120 E 15th St
Los Dos Molinos · 119 E 18th St
Luna Park · 29 Union Sq W
Mandler's The Original Sausage Co · 26 E 17th St
Max Brenner · 841 Broadway
McDonald's · 39 Union Sq W
Mesa Grill · 102 Fifth Ave
Oasis Day Spa · 108 E 16th St
Old Town Bar & Grill · 45 E 18th St
Paragon Sports · 867 Broadway
Park Avalon · 225 Park Ave S
Paul & Jimmy's · 123 E 18th St
PC Richard & Son · 120 E 14th St
Petco · 860 Broadway
Pete's Tavern · 129 E 18th St
Puma · 33 Union Sq W
Radio Shack · 866 Broadway
Republic · 37 Union Sq W
Rothman's · 200 Park Ave S
ShoeMania · 853 Broadway
Shija Day Spa · 37 Union Sq W
Sephora · 200 Park Ave S
Sleepy's · 874 Broadway
Staples · 5-9 Union Sq W
Starbucks · 10 Union Sq E
Starbucks · 41 Union Sq W
The Strand · 828 Broadway
Strawberry's · 38 E 14th St
Tisserie · 857 Broadway
Toasties Juice Bar · 25 Union Sq W
Union Bar · 204 Park Ave S
Union Square Café · 21 E 16th St

University Locksmith & Hardware · 121 University Pl
Pure Food & Wine · 54 Irving Pl
Verizon Wireless · 859 Broadway
Virgin Megastore · 52 E 14th St
The Vitamin Shoppe · 25-30 Union Sq E
Whole Foods · 4 Union Sq S
Wiz · 17 Union Sq W
Yama · 122 E 17th St
Zen Palate · 34 Union Sq E

Entertainment

Century Center for the Performing Arts · 111 E 15th St
Classic Stage Company · 136 East 13th St
Daryl Roth Theatre/DR2 · 101 East 15th St
Djoniba Dance and Drum Centre · 37 E 18th St
Filmore at Irving Plaza · 17 Irving Pl
Lee Strasberg Theatre Institute · 115 E 15th St
Union Square Theatre · 100 E 17th St
Regal Union Square Stadium14 · 850 Broadway
Vineyard Theatre · 108 E 15th St

24-Hour Services

Duane Reade · 24 E 14th Street
Walgreens · 145 Fourth Ave

Other

Amalgamated Bank of New York · 11 Union Sq W
Beth Israel Phillips Ambulatory Center · 10 Union Sq E
Bowlmor Lanes · 110 University Pl
Carlyle Court · 25 Union Sq W
Con Edison · 4 Irving Pl
Crunch · 54 E 13th St
New York Sports Clubs · 10 Irving Pl
NY Film Academy · 100 E 17th St
The Palladium · 140 E 14th St
Peridance Center · 890 Broadway & 19th Street
Zurich · 105 E 17th St

(267)

General D
MacArthur
Plaza

FDR Dr

E 48th Street ←

873

352

First Ave

Memorial to ○
the Fallen

Japan
Society

E 47th Street ←→

Dag Hammarskjold
Plaza

Peace
Garden

Venezuela

○ Peace
Statue

E 46th Street

**East
River**

Turkey

E 45th Street

Promenade

○ Visitors
○ Entrance

Visitors Plaza

Rose
Garden

2nd
UN
Plaza

Uganda

General
Assembly

**MAP
13**

Kuwait

First UN Plaza

E 44th Street →

United Nations Plaza

International
Women's
Center

Conference
Building

E 43rd Street

Japanese
Peace Bell
Garden

FDR Dr

Ford Foundation | Tudor Park

Secretariat
Building

**TUDOR
CITY**

Fountain

Tudor City Pl

Dag Hammarskjold
Library

**Queens
Midtown
Tunnel**

E 42nd Street

Robert
Moses
Playground

To Queens

E 41st Street

495

Parks & Places · **United Nations**

General Information

Address: First Ave b/w 42nd & 48th Sts
Phone: 212-963-TOUR(8687)
Website: www.un.org
Guided Tour Hours: 9:30 am–4:45 pm (10 am–4:30 pm on weekends) except Thanksgiving Day,
                      Christmas Day, New Year's Day, and weekends during January and February.
Guided Tour Admission: $13 for adults, $9 for seniors, $8.50 for students under 30, and
                      $7 for children ages 5–14.

Overview

The United Nations Headquarters building, that giant domino teetering on the bank of the East River, opened its doors in 1951. It's here that the 191 member countries of the United Nations meet to fulfill the UN's mandate of maintaining international peace, developing friendly relations among nations, promoting development and human rights, and getting all the free f*#%ing parking they want. The UN is divided into bodies: the General Assembly, the Security Council, the Economic and Social Council, the Trusteeship Council, the Secretariat, and the International Court of Justice (located in the Hague). Specialized agencies like the World Health Organization (located in Geneva) and the UN Children's Fund (UNICEF) (located in New York) are part of the UN family.

The United Nations was founded at the end of World War II by world powers intending to create a body that would prevent war by fostering an ideal of collective security. New York was chosen to be home base when John D. Rockefeller Jr. donated $8.5 million to purchase the 18 acres the complex occupies. The UN is responsible for a lot of good—its staff and agencies have been awarded nine Nobel Peace Prizes over the years. However, the sad truth is the United Nations hasn't completely lived up to the goals and objectives of its 1945 charter. (This situation isn't helped by the bloated US doing all it can to undermine many initiatives.) Scandals involving the Oil-for-Food Programme and alleged abuses by UN troops have certainly not boosted the UN's reputation recently. However, with a new secretary general in place, there is hope that the UN can finally function as a positive global force in a world that desperately needs guidance.

This place is definitely worth a visit. The UN Headquarters complex is an international zone complete with its own security force, fire department, and post office (which issues UN stamps). It consists of four buildings: the Secretariat building (the 39-story tower), the General Assembly building, the Conference building, and the Dag Hammarskjöld Library. Once you clear what feels like airport security, you'll find yourself in the visitors' lobby where there are shops, a coffee shop, and a scattering of topical small exhibits that come and go. The guided tour is your ticket out of the lobby and into important rooms like the Security Council Chambers and the impressive and inspiring General Assembly Hall. Sometimes tour groups are allowed to briefly sit in on meetings, but don't expect to spy Ban Ki-moon, the new secretary general, roaming the halls. Take a stroll through the Peace Bell Garden (off limits to the public, but it can be seen from the inside during the guided tour). The bell, a gift from Japan in 1954, was cast from coins collected by children from 60 different countries. A bronze statue by Henry Moore, *Reclining Figure: Hand*, is located north of the Secretariat Building. The UN grounds are especially impressive when the 500 prize-winning rose bushes and 140 flowering cherry trees are in bloom.

The elegant Secretariat building is showing its age and plans for a two billion dollar renovation are underway, which means the UN will have to temporarily relocate. Where? Possibly Brooklyn, with the rest of many former Manhattanites.

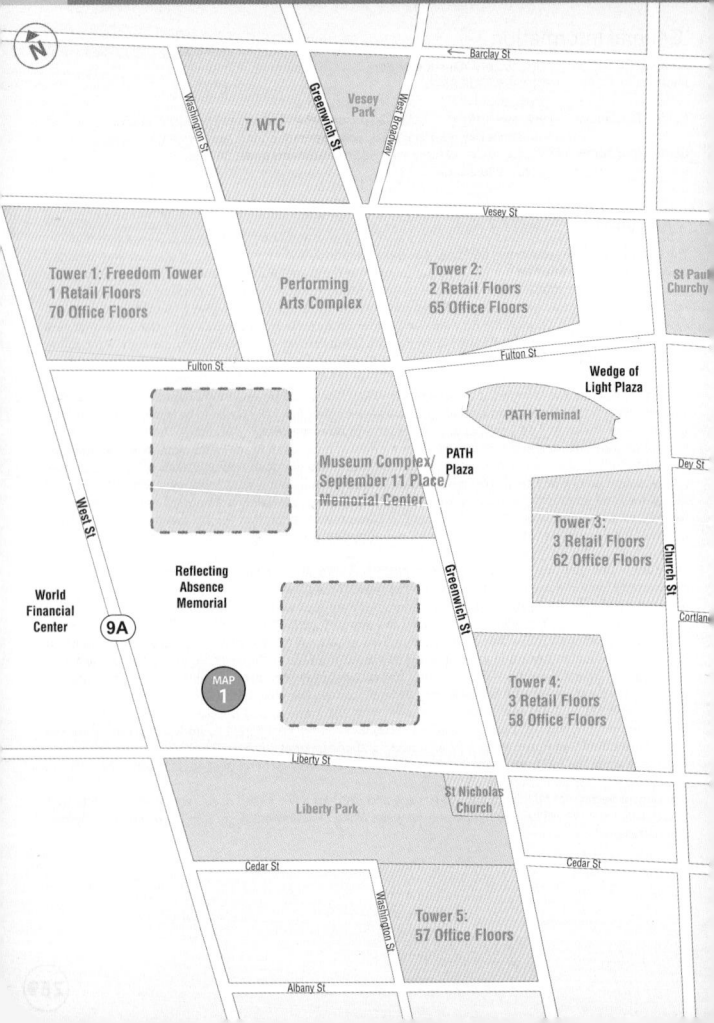

N

Barclay St

Washington St

Greenwich St

Vesey Park

West Broadway

7 WTC

Vesey St

Tower 1: Freedom Tower
1 Retail Floors
70 Office Floors

Performing
Arts Complex

Tower 2:
2 Retail Floors
65 Office Floors

St Paul
Churcl

Fulton St

Fulton St

Wedge of
Light Plaza

PATH Terminal

Museum Complex/
September 11 Place/
Memorial Center

PATH
Plaza

Dey St

Greenwich St

Tower 3:
3 Retail Floors
62 Office Floors

Church St

West St

Reflecting
Absence
Memorial

World
Financial
Center

9A

Cortlan

MAP
1

Tower 4:
3 Retail Floors
58 Office Floors

Liberty St

Liberty Park

St Nicholas
Church

Cedar St

Cedar St

Washington St

Tower 5:
57 Office Floors

Albany St

Parks & Places • **World Trade Center**

As we edge closer to a decade passing since 9/11, it's tough to not want to call your buddies over, borrow some hammers, and start filling the void still apparent in the Financial District.

Construction crews finally broke ground on the first large-scale projects in late 2006: the Freedom Tower and September 11th Memorial. To clear the area for a $2.2 billion transit hub designed by Santiago Calatrava to connect Manhattan and New Jersey and a dozen subway lines, relocating power lines is on the agenda as well. This year, these construction feats will be visually apparent, and even more so in 2009, since projected completion hovers around 2011. You can call your buddies mid-2011 if construction stalls.

Why has it taken this long? Numerous groups vied to make their vision of the rebuilding of the World Trade Center site become reality. The Port Authority originally built the buildings, and just before September 11th, they were leased to Larry Silverstein. As leaseholder, he had the right to collect insurance and redevelop the site. Created by Governor Pataki, the Lower Manhattan Development Corporation was assigned the task of overseeing the development of the site. The families of victims and the rest of the public have been vocal in expressing their desires for the rebuilding project as well.

In the fall of 2002, a single design was selected from over 400 submissions to the LMDC. Studio Daniel Libeskind's proposal, *Memory Foundations*, achieved the nearly impossible task of getting the approval of the LMDC, Port Authority, city, and state of New York. Despite the Libeskind design being accepted as the official master plan, Silverstein hired architect David Childs. Feuds over designs dissolved late in the year, and Libeskind and Childs emerged with an amicable compromise, changing the arrangement of the buildings and parks on the ground and altering the look of the Freedom Tower.

What will it look like? The spire-like Freedom Tower will climb roughly 1,800 feet in the sky. Its footprint will match the footprints of the Twin Towers at 200 by 200 feet. Boasting 2.6 million square feet of office space, restaurants, an observation deck, and broadcasting facilities for the MTVA, it will be environmentally sound and ultra-safe. If it ever gets built, that is.

And the memorial? Michael Arad designed *Reflecting Absence* as waterfalls flowing into the sunken

"footprints" of the twin towers, cascading onto the names etched in stone of those who died there. The plans also include a visitor's center designed by Norwegian firm Snohetta.

Debate still rages regarding many aspects of the project, from the height and look of the other towers to how many streets will be allowed to run through the site (many were de-mapped when the WTC was originally built). Also raging are class-action lawsuits alleging inadequate protection against toxins for workers.

Transit has been restored to pre–September 11th order, with all subway lines resuming service to the area, along with PATH service to the newly constructed PATH station.

Useful Websites

- Lower Manhattan Info provides current details about construction and future plans for the WTC site and the surrounding area: www.lowermanhattan.info

- The World Trade Center Health Registry will track the health survey of thousands of people directly exposed to the events of 9/11: www.nyc.gov/html/doh/html/wtc/index.html

- The findings of the National Commission on Terrorist Attacks Upon the United States (the 9/11 Commission): www.9-11commission.gov

- "New York New Visions" is a coalition of several groups looking at different options for rebuilding the area: www.nynv.aiga.org

- The New York Skyscraper Museum continues to add information about the WTC and downtown NYC in general; they also contributed to the historical panels placed on the viewing wall around the site: www.skyscraper.org

- A second 9/11 families group: www.911families.org

Transit · **Airlines**

Airline	Phone	JFK	EWR	LGA
Aer Lingus	800-474-7424	■		
Aeroflot	800-340-6400	■		
Aerolineas Argentinas	800-333-0276	■		
Aeromexico	800-237-6639	■		
Aerosvit Ukranian	212-661-1620	■		
Air Canada	888-247-2262	■	■	■
Air China	800-982-8802	■		
Air France	800-237-2747	■	■	
Air India	212-751-6200	■	■	
Air Jamaica	800-523-5585	■	■	
Air Plus Comet	877-999-7587	■	■	
Air Tahiti Nui	866-835-9286	■		
Air Tran	800-247-8726		■	■
Alaska Airlines	800-426-0333		■	
Alitalia	800-223-5730	■	■	
ANA (All Nippon)	800-235-9262	■	■	■
Allegro	800-903-2779	■		
American (domestic)	800-433-7300	■	■	■
American (international)	800-433-7300	■	■	■
American Eagle	800-433-7300	■	■	■
Asiana	800-227-4262	■		
ATA	800-435-9282		■	■
Austrian Airlines	800-843-0002	■		
Avianca	800-284-2622	■		
Azteca	212-289-6400	■	■	■
Biman Bangladesh	212-808-4477	■		
British Airways	800-247-9297	■	■	
BWIA	800-538-2942	■		
Cathay Pacific	800-233-2742	■	■	
Chautauqua	800-428-4322		■	■
China Airlines	800-227-5118	■		
China Eastern	866-588-0825	■		
Colgan	800-428-4322			■
Comair	800-354-9822	■	■	■
Constellation	866-484-2299	■		
Continental (domestic)	800-523-3273	■	■	
Continental (international)	800-231-0856		■	
Copa Airlines	800-359-2672	■		
Corsair (seasonal)	800-677-0720	■		
Czech Airlines	800-223-2365	■	■	
Delta (domestic)	800-221-1212	■	■	■
Delta (international)	800-241-4141	■	■	
Delta Connection	800-325-5205	■		
Delta Express	800-235-9359	■	■	■
Egyptair	800-334-6787	■		
El Al	800-223-6700	■	■	
Emirates	800-777-3999	■		
EOS	888-357-3677	■		
Etihad	888-8ETIHAD	■		
Eurofly	800-459-0581	■		
Eva Airways	800-695-1188		■	
Finnair	800-950-5000	■		
Frontier Airlines	800-432-1359		■	■
Iberia	800-772-4642	■		

Airline	Phone	JFK	EWR	LGA
Icelandair	800-223-5500	■		
Israir	877-477-2471	■		
Japan Airlines	800-525-3663	■		
Jet Blue	800-538-2583	■	■	■
KLM	800-374-7747	■	■	
Korean Air	800-438-5000	■		
Kuwait Airways	800-458-9248	■		
Lacsa	800-225-2272	■		
Lan Chile	800-735-5526	■		
Lan Ecuador	866-526-3279	■		
Lan Peru	800-735-5590	■		
LOT Polish	212-852-0240	■	■	
LTU	866-266-5588		■	
Lufthansa	800-645-3880	■	■	
Malaysia	800-582-9264		■	
Malev Hungarian	800-223-6884	■		
MaxJet	888-435-9626	■		
Mexicana	800-531-7921	■		
Miami Air (charter)	305-871-3300	■	■	
Midwest Express	800-452-2022		■	■
North American	800-371-6297	■		
Northwest (domestic)	800-225-2525	■	■	■
Northwest (international)	800-447-4747	■	■	
Olympic	800-223-1226	■		
Qantas	800-227-4500	■	■	
Royal Air Maroc	800-344-6726	■		
Royal Jordanian	212-949-0050	■		
SAS	800-221-2350	■	■	
Saudi Arabian Airlines	800-472-8342	■		
Silverjet	877-359-7458		■	
SN Brussels	516-622-2248	■		
South African Airways	800-722-9675	■	■	■
Spirit	800-772-7117			■
Sun Country	800-359-6786	■		
Swiss Airlines	877-359-7947	■	■	
TACA	800-535-8780	■		
TAM	888-235-9826	■		
Tap Air Portugal	800-221-7370		■	
Thai Airways	800-426-5204	■		
Travel Spain	800-817-6177	■		
Turkish	800-874-8875	■		
United Airlines (domestic)	800-241-6522	■	■	
United Airlines (intern'l)	800-241-6522	■	■	■
United Express	800-241-6522		■	
US Airways	800-428-4322	■	■	■
USA3000	877-872-3000		■	
Uzbekistan	212-245-1005	■		
Varig	800-468-2744	■		
Virgin Atlantic	800-862-8621	■	■	

Transit · JFK Airport

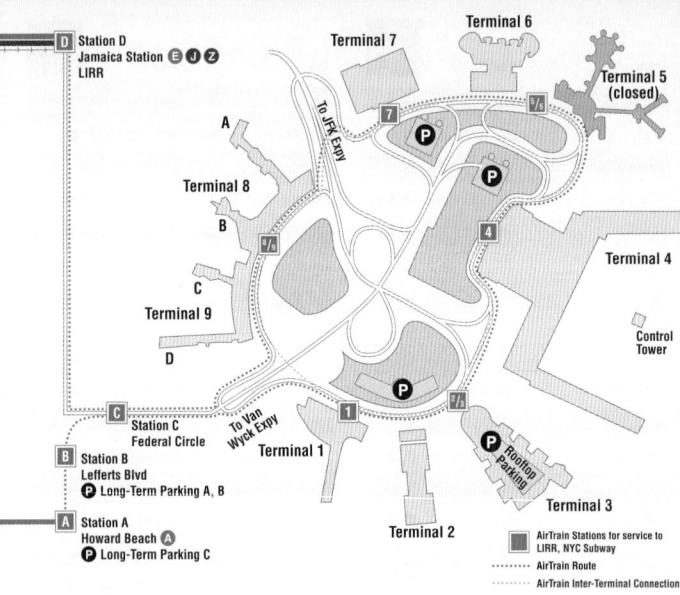

D Station D
Jamaica Station **E J Z**
LIRR

Terminal 7

Terminal 6

Terminal 5 (closed)

A

Terminal 8

B

C

Terminal 9

D

Terminal 4

Control Tower

C Station C
Federal Circle

B Station B
Lefferts Blvd
P Long-Term Parking A, B

A Station A
Howard Beach **A**
P Long-Term Parking C

To JFK Expy

To Van Wyck Expy

Terminal 1

Terminal 2

Terminal 3

Rooftop Parking

■ AirTrain Stations for service to LIRR, NYC Subway
······ AirTrain Route
······ AirTrain Inter-Terminal Connection

Airline	Terminal
Aer Lingus	4
Aeroflot	1
Aerolineas Argentinas	4
Aero Mexico	1
Aerosvit Ukrainian	4
Air Canada	7
Air China	1
Air France	1
Air India	4
Air Jamaica	4
AirPlus Comet	1
Air Tahiti Nui	4
Alitalia	1
Allegro (seasonal)	4
American	8
American Eagle	8
ANA	4
Asiana	4
Austrian Airlines	1
Avianca	4
Azteca	4
Biman Bangladesh	4
British Airways	7

Airline	Terminal
BWIA	4
Cathay Pacific	7
Cayman Airways	1
China Airlines	1
China Eastern	1
Comair	3
Constellation	4
Continental	4
Continental Express	4
Corsair (seasonal)	4
Copa Airlines	4
Czech Airlines	4
Delta	3
Egypt Air	4
El Al	4
Emirates	4
EOS	4
Etihad	4
Eurofly	4
Finnair	8
Flyglobespan	4
Harmony	4

Airline	Terminal
Iberia	7
Icelandair	7
Israir	4
Japan Airlines	1
Jet Airways	8
Jetblue(San Juan)	4
JetBlue Airways	6
KLM	4
Korean Air	1
Kuwait Airways	4
Lacsa	4
Lan Chile	4
Lan Ecuador	4
Lan Peru	4
LOT	4
LTU	4
Lufthansa	1
Malev Hungarian	8
Max Jet	4
Mexicana	4
Miami Air (charter)	4
North American	4
Northwest	4
Olympic	1

Airline	Terminal
Pakistan	4
Qantas	7
Royal Air Maroc	1
Royal Jordanian	4
Saudi Arabian Airlines	1
Singapore	4
South African	4
SN Brussels Airlines	8
Sun Country	4
Swiss International	1
TACA International	4
TAM	4
Thai Airways	4
Travel Span	4
Turkish	1
United Airlines	7
US Airways/ America West	7
USA 3000	4
US Helicopter	3
Uzbekistan	4
Varig	4
Virgin American	4
Virgin Atlantic	4
Zoom Airlines	4

General Information

Address:	JFK Expy
	Jamaica, NY 11430
Phone:	718-244-4444
Lost & Found:	718-244-4225
Website:	www.kennedyairport.com
AirTrain:	www.airtrainjfk.com
AirTrain Phone:	718-570-1048
Long Island Rail Road:	www.mta.info/lirr

Overview

Ah, JFK. It's long been a nemesis to Manhattanites due to the fact that it's the farthest of the three airports from the city. Nonetheless, more than 32 million people go through JFK every year. A $9.5 billion expansion and modernization program will transform the airport, with JetBlue taking about $900 million of that for its gigantic, 26-gate, new HQ to address the ten million of you who, in spite of JFK's distance, wake up an hour earlier to save a buck.

JetBlue's new terminal rises just behind the landmark TWA building, which you should check out if you have time to kill after getting up an hour earlier. Its bubbilicious curves make this 1950s gem a glam spaceship aptly prepared to handle any swanky NY soiree. Top that, Newark.

Rental Cars (On-Airport)

The rental car offices are all located along the Van Wyck Expressway near the entrance to the airport. Just follow the signs.
1 · **Avis** · 718-244-5406 or 800-230-4898
2 · **Budget** · 718-656-6010 or 800-527-0700
3 · **Dollar** · 718-656-2400 or 800-800-4000
5 · **Enterprise** · 718-659-1200 or 800-RENT-A-CAR
4 · **Hertz** · 718-656-7600 or 800-654-3131
6 · **National** · 718-632-8300 or 800-CAR-RENTAL

Hotels

Crown Plaza JFK · 151-20 Baisley Blvd · 718-489-1000
Comfort Inn JFK · 144-36 153rd Ln · 718-977-0001
Double Tree Club Hotel · 135-40 140th St · 718-276-2188
Holiday Inn JFK Airport · 144-02 135th Ave · 718-659-0200
Ramada Plaza Hotel · Van Wyck Expy · 718-995-9000

Car Services & Taxis

All County Express · 914-381-4223 or 800-914-4223
Classic Limousine · 631-567-5100 or 800-666-4949
Dial 7 Car & Limo Service · 212-777-7777 or 800-777-8888
Super Saver by Carmel · 800-922-7635 or 212-666-6666
Tel Aviv Limo Service · 800-222-9888 or 212-777-7777

Taxis from the airport to anywhere in Manhattan cost a flat $45 + tolls and tip, while fares to the airport are metered + tolls and tip. The SuperShuttle (800-258-3826) will drop you anywhere between Battery Park and 227th, including all hotels, for $13–$22, but be warned it could end up taking a while, depending on where your fellow passengers are going. Nevertheless, it's a good option if you want door-to-door service and have a lot of time to kill, but not a lot of cash.

How to Get There—Driving

You can take the lovely and scenic Belt Parkway straight to JFK, as long as it's not rush hour. The Belt Parkway route is about 30 miles long, even though JFK is only 15 or so miles from Manhattan. You can access the Belt by taking the Brooklyn-Battery Tunnel to the Gowanus (the best route) or by taking the Brooklyn, Manhattan, or Williamsburg Bridges to the Brooklyn-Queens Expressway to the Gowanus. If you're sick of stop-and-go highway traffic and prefer using local roads, take Atlantic Avenue in Brooklyn and drive east until you hit Conduit Avenue. Follow this straight to JFK—it's direct and fairly simple. You can get to Atlantic Avenue from any of the three downtown bridges (look at one of our maps first!). From midtown, you can take the Queens Midtown Tunnel to the Long Island Expressway to the Van Wyck Expressway S (there's never much traffic on the LIE, of course…). From uptown, you can take the Triboro Bridge to the Grand Central Parkway to the Van Wyck Expressway S. JFK also has two new AM frequencies solely devoted to keeping you abreast of all of the airport's endeavors that may affect traffic. Tune into 1630AM for general airport information and 1700AM for construction updates en route to your next flight. It might save you a sizeable headache.

How to Get There—Mass Transit

This is your chance to finish *War and Peace*. Replacing the free shuttle from the subway is the AirTrain, which will make your journey marginally smoother, but also make your wallet a little lighter. Running 24/7, you can board the AirTrain from the subway on the Ⓐ line at either the Howard Beach stop or the Ⓔ, Ⓙ, and Ⓩ lines at the Sutphin/Archer Ave-Jamaica Station stop. The ride takes around 15–25 minutes, depending on which airport terminal you need.

A one-way ride on the AirTrain sets you back $5, so a ride on the subway and then hopping the AirTrain will be a total of $7. If you're anywhere near Penn Station and your time is valuable, the LIRR to Jamaica will cost you $5 off-peak, $7 during peak times, and the journey takes roughly 20 minutes. The AirTrain portion of the trip will still cost you an additional $5 and round out your travel time to less than an hour.

If you want to give your MetroCard a workout, you can take the Ⓔ or the Ⓕ to the Turnpike/Kew Gardens stop and transfer to the 🚌. Another possibility is the ❸ or ❹ to New Lots Avenue, where you transfer to the 🚌 to JFK. The easiest and most direct option is to take a New York Airport Service Express bus (718-875-8200) from either Grand Central Station, Penn Station, or the Port Authority for $15, or you can hop on the Trans-Bridge Bus Line (800-962-9135) at Port Authority for $12. Since the buses travel on service roads, Friday afternoon is not an advisable time to try them out.

Parking

Daily rates for the Central Terminal Area lots cost $3 for the first half-hour, $6 for up to one hour, $3 for every hour after that, up to $30 per day. Long-term parking costs $15 for the first 24 hours and $5 for each 8-hour period thereafter. Be warned, though—many of the ongoing construction projects at JFK affect both their short-term and long-term lots, so be sure to allow extra time for any unpleasant surprises. For updated parking availability, call 718-244-4080.

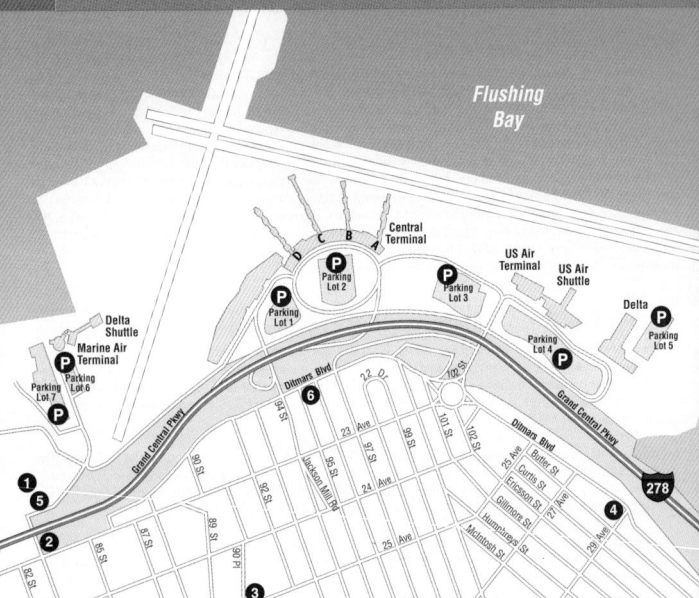

Airline	Terminal
Air Canada	A
Air Tran Airways	B
American	D
American Eagle	C
ATA	B
Colgan	US Airways
Comair	Delta
Continental	A
Continental Express	A
Delta	Delta
Delta Connection	Delta
Delta Shuttle	Marine
Frontier Airlines	B
jetBlue Airways	B
Midwest	B
Northwest	Delta
Spirit	B
United	C
United Express	C
US Airways	US Airways
US Airways Express	US Airways
US Airways Shuttle	US Airways Shuttle

General Information

Address:	LaGuardia Airport
	Flushing, NY 11371
Recorded Information:	718-533-3400
Lost & Found:	718-533-3988
Police:	718-533-3900
Website:	www.laguardiaairport.com

Overview

The reason to fly from LaGuardia (affectionately known as LGA on your baggage tags) is that it is geographically the closest airport to Manhattan and thus a cheap(er) cab ride when your delayed flight touches down at 1 in the morning. The reason not to fly to and from here is that there is no subway line (HELLO, city officials!) and the check-in areas are just too darn small to accommodate the many passengers and their many bags that crowd the terminals at just about every hour of the day.

Food is not a great option, so eat before you leave home. If you must dine, there are 5 Au Bon Pains throughout the terminals—find them as they are the most palatable choice available.

How to Get There—Driving (or directing your cabbie)

LaGuardia is mere inches away from Grand Central Parkway, which can be reached from both the Brooklyn-Queens Expressway (BQE) or from the Triboro Bridge. From Lower Manhattan, take the Brooklyn, Manhattan, or Williamsburg Bridges to the BQE to Grand Central Parkway E. From Midtown Manhattan, take FDR Drive to the Triboro to Grand Central. A potential alternate route (and moneysaver) would be to take the 59th Street Bridge to 21st Street in Queens. Once you're heading north on 21st Street, you can make a right on Astoria Boulevard and follow it all the way to 94th Street, where you can make a left and drive straight into LaGuardia. This alternate route is good if the FDR and/or the BQE is jammed, although that probably means that the 59th Street Bridge won't be much better.

How to Get There— Mass Transit

Alas, no subway line goes to LaGuardia (although there SHOULD be one running across 96th Street in Manhattan, through Astoria, and ending at LaGuardia—but that's another story). The closest the subway comes is the 🚇 🚇 🚇 🚇 Jackson Heights/ Roosevelt Avenue/74th Street stop in Queens, where you can transfer to the 🚌 or 🚌 bus bus to LaGuardia. Sound exciting? Well, it's not. A better bus to take is the 🚌, which runs across 125th Street to the airport. An even better bet would be to pay the extra few bucks and take the New York Airport Service Express Bus ($12 one-way, 718-875-8200) from Grand Central Station. It departs every 20–30 minutes and takes approximately 45 minutes; also catch it on Park Avenue between 41st and 42nd Streets, Penn Station, and the Port Authority Bus Terminal. The improbably named SuperShuttle Manhattan is a shared mini-bus that picks you up anywhere within the city limits ($13–$22 one-way, 212-258-3826). If you want a taxi, search for the "hidden" cab line tucked around Terminal D as the line is almost always shorter than the others.

How to Get There—Really

Plan ahead and call a car service to guarantee that you won't spend the morning of your flight fighting for a taxi. Nothing beats door to door service. Allstate Car and Limousine: 212-333-3333 ($30 in the am & $38 in the pm + tolls from Union Square); LimoRes: 212-777-7171 ($30 + tolls from Union Square; best to call in the morning); Dial 7: 212-777-7777 ($30 in the am & $40 in the pm + tolls from Union Square), Carmel: 212-666-6666 ($31 + tolls to LGA, $28–$35 + tolls from LGA).

Parking

Daily parking rates at LaGuardia cost $3 for the first half-hour, $6 for up to one hour, $3 for every hour thereafter, and up to $30 per day. Long-term parking is $30 for each of the first two days, then $5 for each 8-hour period thereafter (though only in Lot 3). You can use cash, credit card, or E-Z Pass to pay. Another option is independent parking lots, such as The Crowne Plaza (104-04 Ditmars Blvd, 718-457-6300 x295), Clarion Airport Parking (Ditmars Blvd & 94th St, 718-335-6713) and AviStar (23rd Ave & 90th St, 800-621-PARK). They run their own shuttle buses from their lots, and they usually charge $14–$17 per day. If all the parking garages onsite are full, follow the "P" signs to the airport exit and park in one of the off-airport locations.

Rental Cars

1 Avis • LGA		800-230-4898
2 Budget • 83-34 23rd Ave		800-527-0700
3 Dollar • 90-05 25th Ave		800-800-4000
4 Enterprise • 104-04 Ditmars Blvd		718-457-2900
5 Hertz • LGA		800-654-3131
6 National • Ditmars Blvd & 95th St		800-227-7368

Hotels

Clarion • 94-00 Ditmars Blvd • 718-335-1200
Courtyard • 90-10 Grand Central Pkwy • 718-446-4800
Crowne Plaza • 104-04 Ditmars Blvd • 718-457-6300
Eden Park Hotel • 113-10 Corona Ave • 718-699-4500
LaGuardia Marriott • 102-05 Ditmars Blvd • 718-565-8900
Paris Suites • 109-17 Horace Harding Expy • 718-760-2820
Sheraton • 135-20 39th Ave • 718-460-6666
Wyndham Garden • 100-15 Ditmars Blvd • 718-426-1500

Transit · **Newark Liberty Airport**

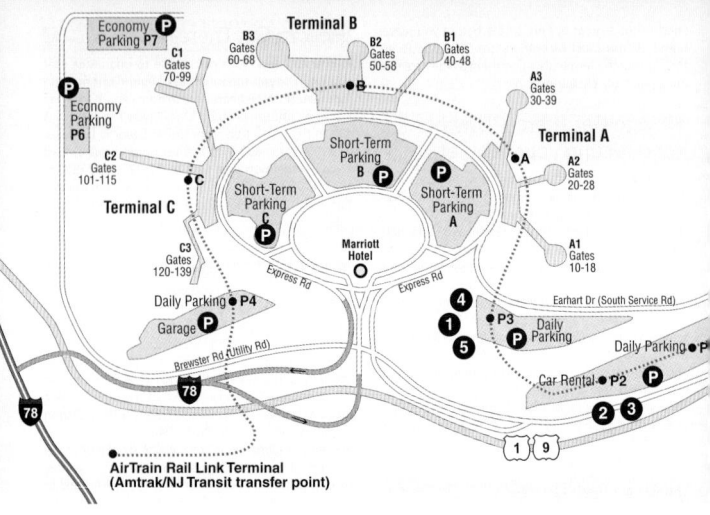

Airline	Terminal
Air Canada	A
Air France	B
Air India	B
Air Jamaica	B
Air Plus Comet (seasonal)	B
Air Tran	A
Alaska Airlines	A
Alitalia	B
America West	A
American (domestic)	A
American (international)	A/B*
American Eagle	A
British Airways	B
Casino Express (charter)	A
Chautauqua	C
Comair	B
Continental	C
Continental (Atlanta/Chicago/ Dallas/Washington DC)	A
Continental (Baton Rouge)	A
Continental (Boston)	A
Czech Airlines	B
Delta	B
Delta Express	B
El Al	B
Eva Airways	B
Express Jet – Continental	C

Airline	Terminal
Flybe British European	C
Jet Airways	B
Jet Blue	A
KLM Royal Dutch Airlines	B
L'Avion	B
LoT Polish	B
Lufthansa	B
Malaysia	B
Mexicana	B
Miami Air (Charter)**	B
Midwest	A
Northwest	B
Qantas	A
SAS	B
Silverjet	B
Singapore Airlines	B
Swiss International Air Lines	B
TAP Portugal	B
United (domestic)	A
United (international)	A/B*
United Express	A
USA3000	B
US Airways	A
US Airways Express	A
Virgin Atlantic	B

* Departs Terminal A, arrives Terminal B.

** Charter Airlines: For departure/arrival information, contact the airline or travel agent.

General Information

Address:	10 Toler Pl, Newark, NJ 07114
Phone:	888-EWR-INFO
Police/Lost & Found:	973-961-6230
Airport Information:	973-961-6000
Transportation Info:	800-AIR-RIDE (247-7533)
Radio Station:	530 AM
Website:	www.newarkairport.com

Overview

Newark Airport is easily the nicest of the three major metropolitan airports. The monorail that connects the terminals and the parking lots, the AirTrain link from Penn Station, and the diverse food court (in Terminal C), make it the city's preferred point of departure and arrival. There are also plenty of international departures, making it a great second option to the miserable experience of doing JFK.

If your flight gets delayed or you find yourself with time on your hands, check out the d-parture spa in Terminals B or C to unwind, or, if you're feeling carnivorous after your screaming match with airline personnel, Gallagher's Steakhouse (Terminal C).

How to Get There–Driving

The route to Newark Airport is easy—just take the Holland Tunnel or the Lincoln Tunnel to the New Jersey Turnpike South. You can use either Exit 14 or Exit 13A. If you want a cheaper and slightly more scenic (from an industrial standpoint) drive, follow signs for the Pulaski Skyway once you exit the Holland Tunnel. It's free, it's one of the coolest bridges in America, and it leads you to the airport just fine. If possible, check a traffic report before leaving Manhattan—sometimes there are viciously long tie-ups, especially at the Holland Tunnel. It's always worth it to see which outbound tunnel has the shortest wait.

How to Get There–Mass Transit

If you're allergic to traffic, try taking the AirTrain service from Penn Station. It's run by Amtrak ($30–$44 one-way) or NJ Transit ($14 one-way). If you use NJ Transit, choose a train that runs on the Northeast Corridor or North Jersey Coast Line with a scheduled stop for Newark Airport. If you use Amtrak, choose a train that runs on the Northeast Corridor Line with a scheduled stop for Newark Airport. The cheapest option is to take the PATH train ($1.50) to Newark Penn Station then switch to NJ Transit bus #62 ($1.25), which hits all the terminals. But just be alert at night since the area around Newark Penn Station

can be a bit shady. You can also catch direct buses departing from Port Authority Bus Terminal (with the advantage of a bus-only lane running right out of the station and into the Lincoln Tunnel), Grand Central Terminal, and Penn Station (the New York version) on Olympia for $14. The SuperShuttle will set you back $13–$22, and a taxi from Manhattan will cost you around $50.

How to Get There–Car Services

Car services are always the simplest option, although they're a bit more expensive for Newark Airport than they are for LaGuardia. Allstate Car and Limousine: 212-333-3333 ($44 in the am & $52 in the pm + tolls from Union Square); Tri-State: 212-777-7171 ($43 + tolls from Union Square; best to call in the morning); Dial 7: 212-777-7777 ($44 in the am & $49 in the pm + tolls from Union Square).

Parking

Regular parking rates are $3 for the first half-hour, $6 for up to one hour, $3 for every hour after that, and now an excessive $24 per day for the P1, P3, and P4 monorail-serviced lots. The P6 and P7 parking lots are much farther away, are only serviced by a shuttle bus, and cost $15 per day. There are some off-airport lots that you can sometimes score for $10, especially if you have a business card. Most of them are on the local southbound drag of Route 1 & 9. Valet parking costs $36 per day.

Rental Cars

1 • **Avis**	800-230-4898
2 • **Budget**	800-527-0700
3 • **Dollar**	866-434-2226
4 • **Hertz**	800-654-3131
5 • **National**	800-227-7368
6 • **Enterprise** (Off-Airport)	800-325-8007

Hotels

Marriott (On-Airport) • 973-623-0006
Courtyard Marriott • 600 Rte 1 & 9 S • 973-643-8500
Hilton • 1170 Spring St • 908-351-3900
Howard Johnson • 20 Frontage Rd • 973-344-1500
Sheraton • 128 Frontage Rd • 973-690-5500
Hampton Inn • 1128-38 Spring St • 908-355-0500
Best Western • 101 International Wy • 973-621-6200
Holiday Inn North • 160 Frontage Rd • 973-589-1000
Days Inn • 450 Rte 1 South • 973-242-0900
Ramada Inn • 550 Rte 1 S • 973-824-4000
Four Points Sheraton • 901 Spring St •
908-527-1600

(**281**)

Transit • **Bridges & Tunnels**

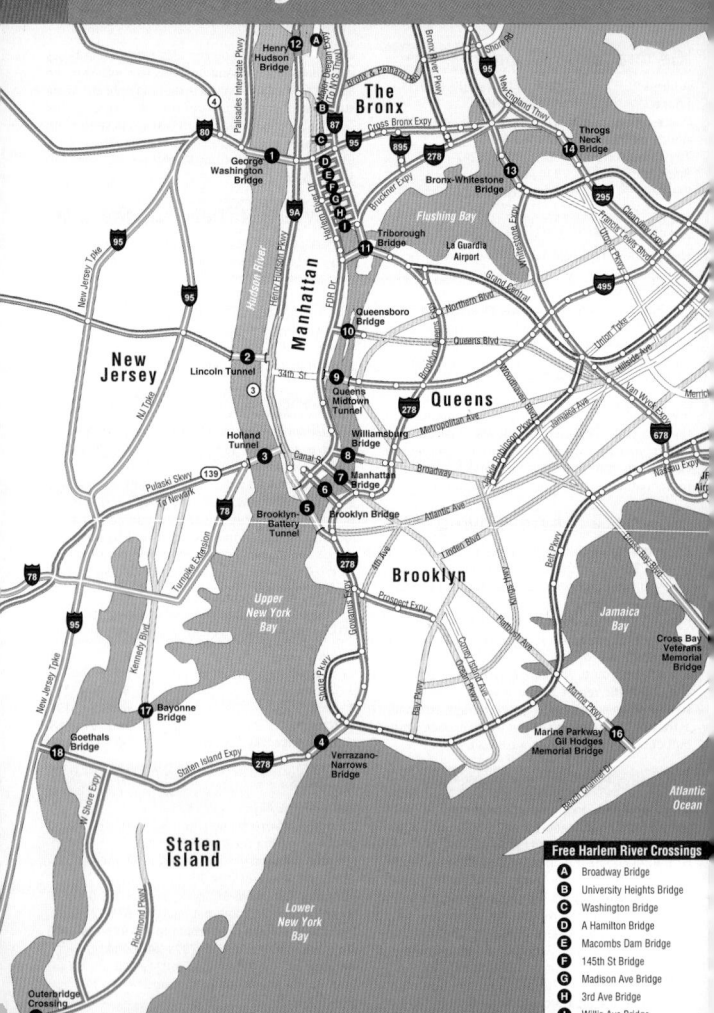

The Bronx

Henry Hudson Bridge

Throgs Neck Bridge

George Washington Bridge

Bronx-Whitestone Bridge

New Jersey

Flushing Bay

Triborough Bridge

La Guardia Airport

Manhattan

Lincoln Tunnel

Queensboro Bridge

Queens

Queens Midtown Tunnel

Holland Tunnel

Williamsburg Bridge

Manhattan Bridge

Brooklyn Bridge

Brooklyn-Battery Tunnel

Brooklyn

Upper New York Bay

Jamaica Bay

Cross Bay Veterans Memorial Bridge

Bayonne Bridge

Goethals Bridge

Marine Parkway Gil Hodges Memorial Bridge

Verrazano-Narrows Bridge

Staten Island

Lower New York Bay

Atlantic Ocean

Outerbridge Crossing

Free Harlem River Crossings

- **A** Broadway Bridge
- **B** University Heights Bridge
- **C** Washington Bridge
- **D** A Hamilton Bridge
- **E** Macombs Dam Bridge
- **F** 145th St Bridge
- **G** Madison Ave Bridge
- **H** 3rd Ave Bridge
- **I** Willis Ave Bridge

General Information

Port Authority of NY and NJ: www.panynj.gov
DOT: www.ci.nyc.ny.us/html/dot/home.html • 212-NEW-YORK
MTA: www.mta.info
EZPass: www.e-zpassny.com • 800-333-TOLL
Transportation Alternatives: www.transalt.org
Best overall site: www.nycroads.com

Overview

Since NYC is an archipelago, it's no wonder there are so many bridges and four major tunnels. Most of the bridges listed in the chart below are considered landmarks, either for their sheer beauty or because they were the first of their kind at one time. The traffic-jammed Holland Tunnel, finished in 1927, was the first vehicular tunnel connecting New Jersey and New York. King's Bridge, built between Manhattan and the Bronx in 1693, was sadly demolished in 1917. Highbridge, the oldest existing bridge in NYC (built in 1843), is no longer open to vehicles or pedestrians. Brooklyn Bridge, built in 1883, is the city's oldest functioning bridge, still open to vehicles and pedestrians alike, and is considered one of the most beautiful bridges ever built.

The '70s was a decade of neglect for city bridges. Inspections in the '80s and maintenance and refurbishment plans in the '90s/'00s have made the bridges stronger and safer than ever before. On certain holidays when the weather permits, the world's largest free-flying American flag flies from the upper arch of the New Jersey tower on the George Washington Bridge.

		Toll/EZPass peak/EZPass off-peak	# of lanes	Pedestrians/bicyclists?	# of vehicles/day (in thousands)	Original cost (in millions)	Engineer	Main span	Operated by	Opened to traffic
1	Geo. Washington Bridge	6.00/5.00/4.00 (inbound only)	14	yes	300	59	Othmar H. Ammann	4,760'	PANYNJ	10/25/31
2	Lincoln Tunnel	6.00/5.00/4.00 (inbound only)	6	no	120	75	Othmar H. Ammann / Ole Singstad	8,216'	PANYNJ	12/22/37
3	Holland Tunnel	6.00/5.00/4.00 (inbound only)	4	no	100	54	Clifford Holland / Ole Singstad	8,558'	PANYNJ	11/13/27
4	Verrazano-Narrows Bridge	* 4.50/4.00	12	no	190	320	Othmar H. Ammann	4,260'	MTA	11/21/64
5	Brooklyn-Battery Tunnel	4.50/4.00	4	no	60	90	Ole Singstad	9,117'	MTA	5/25/50
6	Brooklyn Bridge	free	6	yes	140	15	John Roebling / Washington Roebling	1,595.5'	DOT	5/24/1883
7	Manhattan Bridge	free	4	yes	150	31	Leon Moisseiff	1,470'	DOT	12/31/09
8	Williamsburg Bridge	free	8	yes	140	24.2	Leffert L. Buck	1,600'	DOT	12/19/03
9	Queens-Midtown Tunnel	4.50/4.00	4	no	80	52	Ole Singstad	6,414'	DOT	11/15/40
10	Queensboro Bridge	free	10	yes	200	20	Gustav Lindenthal	1,182'	DOT	3/30/09
11	Triborough Bridge	4.50/4.00	8/ 6/8	no	200	60.3	Othmar H. Ammann	1,380'	MTA	7/11/36
12	Henry Hudson Bridge	2.25/1.75	7	no	75	5	David Steinman	840'	MTA	12/12/36
13	Whitestone Bridge	4.50/4.00	6	no	110	20	Othmar H. Ammann	2300'	MTA	4/29/39
14	Throgs Neck Bridge	4.50/4.00	6	no	100	92	Othmar H. Ammann	1800'	MTA	1/11/61
15	Cross Bay Veterans Memorial Bridge	2.25/1.50	6	yes	20	29	n/a	3000'	MTA	5/28/70
16	Marine Parkway Gil Hodges Memorial Bridge	2.25/1.50	4	yes	25	12	Madigan and Hyland	540'	MTA	7/3/37
17	Bayonne Bridge	6.00/5.00/4.00	4	yes	20	13	Othmar H. Ammann	5,780'	PANY/NJ	11/13/31
18	Goethals Bridge	6.00/5.00/4.00	4	no	75	7.2	Othmar H. Ammann	8,600'	PANY/NJ	6/29/28
19	Outerbridge Crossing	6.00/5.00/4.00	4	no	80	9.6	Othmar H. Ammann	750'	PANY/NJ	6/29/28

* $9.00/$8.00 with EZPass to Staten Island ($6.40/4.80 for registered Staten Island residents with EZPass), $2.25 with three or more occupants—cash only. Free to Brooklyn.

Transit · **Ferries, Marinas & Heliports**

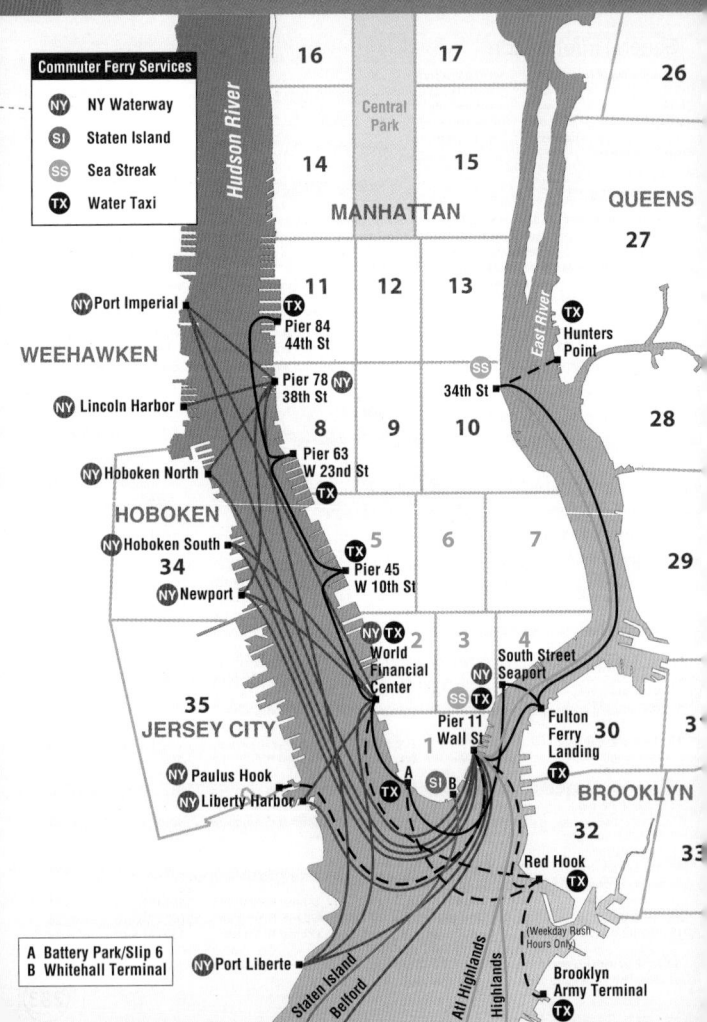

Commuter Ferry Services

- NY   NY Waterway
- Sf   Staten Island
- SS   Sea Streak
- TX   Water Taxi

16

17

26

Central Park

Hudson River

14

15

MANHATTAN

QUEENS

27

NY Port Imperial

11

TX Pier 84 44th St

TX Hunters Point

WEEHAWKEN

12

13

East River

NY Lincoln Harbor

NY Pier 78 38th St

SS 34th St

28

8

9

10

NY Hoboken North

Pier 63 W 23rd St

TX

HOBOKEN

NY Hoboken South

5

6

7

34

TX Pier 45 W 10th St

29

NY Newport

NY TX 2 World Financial Center

3

South Street Seaport

NY

35

SS TX

JERSEY CITY

Pier 11 Wall St

Fulton Ferry Landing

NY Paulus Hook

1

30

3

NY Liberty Harbor

A

Sf B

TX

BROOKLYN

32

33

Red Hook

TX

(Weekday Rush Hours Only)

A Battery Park/Slip 6
B Whitehall Terminal

NY Port Liberte

Atl Highlands
Highlands

Brooklyn Army Terminal

Staten Island
Belford

Transit · **Ferries, Marinas & Heliports**

Ferries/Boat Tours, Rentals & Charters

Name	Contact Info
Staten Island Ferry	311 · www.nyc.gov/html/dot/html/ferrybus/statfery.shtml
	This free ferry travels between Battery Park and Staten Island. On weekdays it leaves every 15–30 minutes 12 am–11:30 pm. On weekends, it leaves every hour 1:30 am–11:30 am and every half-hour at all other times.
NY Waterway	800-53-FERRY · www.nywaterway.com
	The largest ferry service in NY, NYWaterway offers many commuter routes (mostly from New Jersey), sightseeing tours. However, recent financial troubles have them closing many commuter lines.
NY Water Taxi	212-742-1969 · www.nywatertaxi.com
	Available for commuting, sightseeing, charter, and shuttles to Yankees and Mets games. Commuter tickets range between $4.50 and $6 and tours cost $20 to $25. For chartered trips or tours, call for a quote.
Sea Streak	800-BOAT-RIDE · www.seastreakusa.com
	Catamarans that go pretty fast from the Highlands in NJ to Wall Street and E 34th Street.
Circle Line	212-269-5755 · www.circleline.com
	Circle Line offers many sightseeing tours, including a visit to Ellis Island (departs from Pier 16 at South Street Seaport—$11 for adults, $4.50 for kids)
Spirit of New York	212-727-7735 · www.spiritcruises.com
	Offers lunch and dinner cruises. Prices start at $43. Leaves from Pier 62 at Chelsea Piers. Make a reservation at least one week in advance, but the earlier the better.
Loeb Boathouse	212-517-2233 ·www.centralparknyc.org
	You can rent rowboats from March through October at the Lake in Central Park, open seven days a week, weather permitting. Boat rentals cost $12 for the first hour and $3 for every additional 15 minutes (rentals also require a $30 cash deposit). The boathouse is open 10 am–5 pm, but the last boat goes out at 4:30 pm. Up to four people per boat. No reservations needed.
World Yacht Cruises	212-630-8100 or 800-498-4271 · www.worldyacht.com
	These fancy, three-hour dinner cruises start at $89.88 per person. The cruises depart from Pier 81 (41st Street) and require reservations. The cruise boards at 6 pm, sails at 7 pm, and returns at 10 pm. There's also a Sunday brunch cruise April–December that costs $61.85 per person.

Marinas/Passenger Ship Terminal

Name	Contact Info	Map
MarineMax Manhattan	212-336-7873 · www.marinemax.com	8
	Dockage at Chelsea Piers. They offer daily, weekly, and seasonal per-foot rates (there's always a waiting list).	
NY Skyports Inc	212-686-4546	10
	Located on the East River at E 23rd Street. Transient dockage costs $3 per foot.	
79th St Marina	212-496-2105	14
	This city-operated dock is filled with long-term houseboat residents. It's located at W 79th Street and the Hudson River. Open from May to October.	
Dyckman Marina	212-496-2105	25
	Transient dockage on the Hudson River at 348 Dyckman Street	
Manhattan Cruise Terminal	212-246-5450 · www.nycruise.com	11
	If Love Boat re-runs aren't enough and you decide to go on a cruise yourself, you'll leave from the Manhattan Cruise Terminal. W 55th Street at 12th Avenue. Take the West Side Highway to Piers 88-92.	
North Cove Yacht Harbor	212-786-1200 · www.thenorthcove.com	p234
	A very, very fancy place to park your yacht in Battery Park City.	

Helicopter Services

Name	Contact Info	Map
Helicopter Flight Services	212-355-0801 · www.heliny.com	3, 8
	For a minimum of $129, you can hop on a helicopter at the Downtown Manhattan Heliport at Pier 6 on the East River on weekdays, or at the W 30th Street Heliport on weekends and spend 15 minutes gazing down on Manhattan. Reservations are recommended, and there's a minimum of two passengers per flight.	
Liberty Helicopter Tours	212-967-6464 · www.libertyhelicopters.com	3, 8
	Leaves from the heliport at W 30th Street and 12th Avenue (9 am–9 pm) or the Downtown Manhattan Heliport at Pier 6 on the East River (9 am–6:30 pm). Prices start at $69, and reservations are needed only when boarding at the Seaport. Flights depart every 5–10 minutes. Minimum of four passengers per flight.	
Wall Street Helicopter	212-943-5959 · www.wallstreetheli.qpg.com	3
	Leaves from any heliport in Manhattan. Executive/corporate helicopter and twin engine aircraft charters. No sightseeing.	

285

Transit • **Driving in Manhattan**

General Information

E-ZPass Information:	800-333-TOLL
Radio Station Traffic Updates:	1010 WINS on the 1s for a 5 boroughs focus and 880 on the 8s for a suburbs focus
DOT Website:	www.ci.nyc.ny.us/html/dot/html/motorist/motorist.html
Real-Time Web Traffic Info:	www.metrocommute.com

Driving in Manhattan

Avoid it. Why drive when you can see the city so well on foot or by bus? (We don't count the subway as seeing the city, but rather as a cultural experience in and of itself.) We know that sometimes you just *have* to drive in the city, so we've made you a list of essentials.

- Great auto insurance that doesn't care if the guy who hit you doesn't have insurance and doesn't speak any English.
- Thick skin on driver, passengers, and car. Needed for the fender benders and screamed profanity from the cabbies that are ticked anyone but cabbies are on the road.
- Meditation CD to counteract cardiac arrest–inducing "almost" accidents.
- NFT. But we know you would never leave home without it.
- E-ZPass. Saves time and money. Maybe not lives, but definitely time and some money.
- New York State license plates. Even pedestrians will curse you out if you represent anywhere other than the Empire State, especially NJ or CT or Texas.
- A tiny car that can fit into a spot slightly larger than a postage stamp or tons of cash for parking garages.
- Patience with pedestrians—they own the streets of New York. Well, co-own them with the cabbies, sanitation trucks, cops, and fire engines.

The following are some tips that we've picked up over the years:

Hudson River Crossings

In the Bridge or Tunnel battle, the Bridge almost always wins. The George Washington Bridge is by far the best Hudson River crossing. It's got more lanes and better access than either tunnel with a fantastic view to boot. If you're going anywhere in the country that's north of central New Jersey, take it. However, inbound traffic on the George can back up for hours in the morning because they don't have enough toll booth operators to handle all those nuts who don't have E-ZPass. The Lincoln Tunnel is decent inbound, but check 1010 WINS if you have the chance—even though they can be horribly inaccurate and frustrating. Avoid the Lincoln like the plague during evening rush hour (starts at about 3:30 pm). If you have to take the Holland Tunnel outbound, try the Broome Street approach, but don't even bother between 5 and 7 pm on weekdays.

East River Crossings

Brooklyn

Pearl Street to the Brooklyn Bridge is the least-known approach. Only the Williamsburg Bridge has direct access (i.e. no traffic lights) to the northbound BQE in Brooklyn, and only the Brooklyn Bridge has direct access to the FDR Drive in Manhattan. Again, listen to the radio if you can, but all three bridges can be disastrous as they seem to be constantly under construction (or, in a fabulous new twist, having one lane closed by the NYPD to for some unknown (terrorism?) reason). The Williamsburg is by far the best free route into North Brooklyn, but make sure to take the outer roadway to keep your options open in case the bridge is jammed. Your best option to go anywhere else in Brooklyn is usually the Brooklyn-Battery Tunnel, which can be reached from the FDR as well as the West Side Highway. Fun fact: The water you pass was so dirty in the '50s that it used to catch fire. The tunnel is not free ($4.50), but if you followed our instructions you've

got E-ZPass anyway ($4). The bridges from south to north can be remembered as B-M-W, but they are not as cool as the cars that share the initials.

Queens

There are three options for crossing into Queens by car. The Queens Midtown Tunnel is usually miserable, since it feeds directly onto the parking lot known as the Long Island Expressway. The 59th Street Bridge (known as the Queensboro to mapmakers) is the only free crossing to Queens. The best approach to it is First Avenue to 57th Street (after that, follow the signs) or to 59th Street if you want to jump on the outer roadway that saves a ton of time and only precludes easy access to Northern Boulevard. If you're in Queens and want to go downtown in Manhattan, you can take the lower level of the 59th Street Bridge since it feeds directly onto Second Avenue, which of course goes downtown. The Triborough Bridge is usually the best option (especially if you're going to LaGuardia, Shea, Astoria for Greek food, or Flushing for dim sum). The FDR to the Triborough is good except for rush hour—then try Third Avenue to 124th Street.

Harlem River Crossings

The Triborough ($4.50) will get you to the Bronx in pretty good shape, especially if you are heading east on the Bruckner towards 95 or the Hutchinson (which will take you to eastern Westchester and Connecticut). To get to Yankee Stadium, take the Willis or the Macomb's Dam (which are both free). When you feel comfortable maneuvering the tight turns approaching the Willis, use it for all travel to Westchester and Connecticut in order to save toll money. The Henry Hudson Bridge ($2.25) will take you up to western Westchester along the Hudson, and, except for the antiquated and completely unnecessary toll plaza, is pretty good. It wins the fast and pretty prize for its beautiful surroundings. The Cross-Bronx Expressway will take years off your life. Avoid it at all costs.

Manhattan's "Highways"

There are two so-called highways in Manhattan—the Harlem River Drive/FDR Drive/East River Drive (which prohibits commercial vehicles) and the Henry Hudson Parkway/West Side Highway/Joe DiMaggio Highway. The main advantage of the FDR is that it has no traffic lights, while the West Side Highway has lights from Battery Park up through 57th Street. The main disadvantages of the FDR are (1) the potholes and (2) the narrow lanes. If there's been a lot of rain, both highways will flood, so you're out of luck (but the FDR floods first). Although the West Side Highway can fly, we would rather look at Brooklyn and Queens than Jersey, so the FDR wins.

Driving Uptown

The 96th Street transverse across Central Park is usually the best one, although if there's been a lot of rain, it will flood. If you're driving on the west side, Riverside Drive is the best route, followed next by West End Avenue. People drive like morons on Broadway, and Columbus jams up in the mid 60s before Lincoln Center and the mid 40s before the Lincoln Tunnel but it's still the best way to get all the way downtown without changing avenues. Amsterdam is a good uptown route if you can get to it. For the east side, you can take Fifth Avenue downtown to about 65th Street, whereupon you should bail out and cut over to Park Avenue for the rest of the trip. Do NOT drive on Fifth Avenue below 65th Street within a month of Christmas, and check the parade schedules before attempting it on weekends throughout the year. The 96th Street entrance to the FDR screws up First and Third Avenues going north and the 59th Street Bridge screws up Lexington and Second Avenues going downtown. Getting stuck in 59th Street Bridge traffic is one of the most frustrating things in the universe because there is absolutely no way out of it.

Driving in Midtown

Good luck! Sometimes Broadway is best because everyone's trying to get out of Manhattan, jamming up the west side (via the Lincoln Tunnel) and the east side (via the 59th Street Bridge and the Queens Midtown Tunnel). Friday nights at 9:30 pm can be a breeze, but from 10 pm to midnight, you're screwed as shows let out. The "interior" of the city is the last place to get jammed up—it's surprisingly quiet at 8 am. At 10 am, however, it's a parking lot. Those who plan to drive in Midtown on weekends from about March–October should check parade schedules for Fifth AND Sixth avenues.

The demarcation of several "THRU Streets" running east-west in Midtown has been with the city for a couple of years and folks are finally getting the hang of it. Still, it may screw you up. See the next page for more information.

Driving in the Village

People get confused walking in the village, so you can imagine how challenging driving can be in the maze of one ways and short streets. Beware. If you're coming into the Village from the northwest, 14th Street is the safest crosstown route heading east. However, going west, take 13th Street. Houston Street is under construction at a number of points along its length but it has the great benefit of direct access to FDR Drive, both getting onto it and coming off of it. If you

want to get to Houston Street from the Holland Tunnel, take Hudson Street to King Street to the Avenue of the Americas to Houston Street (this is the **only** efficient way to get to the Village from the Holland Tunnel). First Avenue is good going north and Fifth Avenue is good going south. Washington Street is the only way to make any headway southbound and Hudson Street is the only way to make any headway northbound in the West Village.

Driving Downtown

Don't do it unless you have to. Western TriBeCa is okay and so is the Lower East Side—try not to "turn in" to SoHo, Chinatown, or the Civic Center. Canal Street is a complete mess during the day (avoid it), since on its western end, everyone is trying to get to the Holland Tunnel, and on its eastern end, everyone is mistakenly driving over the Manhattan Bridge (your only other option when heading east on Canal is to turn **right** on Bowery!). Watch the potholes!

DMV Locations in Manhattan

If you're going to the DMV to get your first NY license (including drivers with other states' licenses), you'll need extensive documentation of your identity. The offices have a long list of accepted documents, but your best bet is a US passport and a Social Security card. If you don't have these things, birth certificates from the US, foreign passports, and various INS documents will be okay under certain conditions. Do not be surprised if you are turned away the first time. This trip requires great amounts of patience. Plan on spending three to six hours here. We're not kidding. This is not a lunch-hour errand.

Greenwich Street Office
11 Greenwich St
New York, NY 10004
(Cross Streets Battery Park Pl & Morris St)
M–F 8:30 am–4 pm
212-645-5550 or 718-966-6155

Harlem Office
159 E 125th St, 3rd Fl
New York, NY 10035
(Lexington and Third)
M, T, W & F 8:30 am–4 pm, Thursday 10 am–6 pm
212-645-5550 or 718-966-6155

Herald Square Office
1293-1311 Broadway, 8th Fl
New York, NY 10001
(Between W 33 & W 34th Sts)
* To exchange an out-of-state license for a New York license, you must go to License X-Press.
M–F 8:30 am–4 pm
212-645-5550 or 718-966-6155

Manhattan
License X-Press Office*
300 W 34th St
New York, NY 10001
(Between Eighth & Ninth aves)
*Service limited to license and registration renewals and out-of-state exchange. You can't get your snowmobile or boat license here, but you can surrender your license plate. Oh, and no permit renewals.
M–F 8:30 am–4 pm
212-645-5550 or 718-966-6155

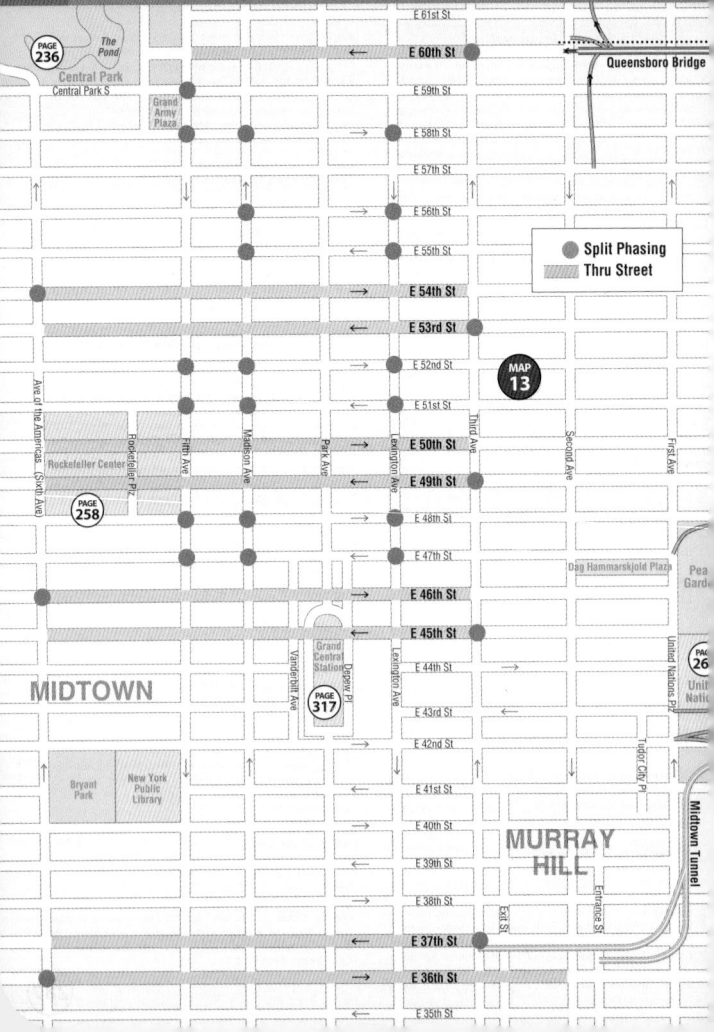

General Information

DOT Website: www.nyc.gov/html/dot/html/motorist/streetprog.html
DOT Phone: 311

Overview

In the tradition of "don't block the box" and other traffic solutions (such as randomly arresting political protesters), the city introduced "THRU Streets," a program initially tested in 2002, as a permanent fixture in Midtown in 2004. The plan was implemented on some crosstown streets in Midtown in order to reduce travel times, relieve congestion, and provide a safer environment for pedestrians and cyclists. They are still working on cleaning up the exhaust fume issue, for those concerned about said environment.

On certain streets, cars are not allowed to make turns between Sixth and Third Avenues (with the exception of Park Avenue). The regulations are in effect between 10 am and 6 pm on weekdays. The affected streets are:

> 36th & 37th Streets
> 45th & 46th Streets
> 49th & 50th Streets
> 53rd & 54th Streets
> 60th Street (between Third and Fifth Avenues)

The good news is that turns from 59th Street are permitted. Oh joy.

The above streets are easily identifiable by big, purple "THRU Streets" signs. With everything that's going on in midtown Manhattan though, you'd be forgiven for missing a sign (by us, not by the NYPD). If you happen to unwittingly find yourself on a THRU Street and can't escape on Park Avenue, you're going to have to suck it up until you get to Sixth Avenue or Third Avenue, depending on the direction you're heading. If you attempt to turn before the designated avenue, you'll find yourself with an insanely expensive ticket. Of course, if you're trying to drive crosstown, it's in your best interests to take one of these streets.

Both sides of almost every non-THRU Street in this grid have been stuck with "No Standing Except Trucks Loading and Unloading" regulations, supposedly creating up to 150 spaces for truck loading (if you were ever stuck behind a truck in morning rush hour on a THRU Street in 2004, you would rejoice at this news). Additionally, one side of each non-THRU street has been "daylighted" for 80–100 feet in advance of the intersection. We are not exactly sure how they came up with the term "daylighted," but the DOT tells us it allows space for turning vehicles.

According to the DOT, THRU Streets are working—since the program began, travel times have fallen by 25% (as people have decided to emigrate to New Zealand) and vehicle speeds have increased by an average of 33% (from 4 mph to 5.3 mph). The THRU Streets combined now carry 4,854 vehicles per hour (up from 4,187), which means that each of the THRU Streets accommodates an average of 74 additional vehicles per hour.

Split Signal Phasing

Another traffic innovation in Midtown is "split signal phasing," which allows pedestrians to cross the street without having to worry about vehicles turning in their path at about 40 non-THRU Street intersections in this same grid. Of course, this system assumes that both pedestrians and drivers follow the rules of the road. In spite of the disregard that most New Yorkers display for crossing signals, the number of pedestrian accidents in the eight-month trial period (compared to the eight months prior to implementation) fell from 81 to 74. The number of cycling accidents fell from 30 to 17. Accidents not related to pedestrians or bikes fell from 168 to 102. We don't know if this accounts for accidents caused by drivers who became confused by the pretty purple signs. We have to admit that something must be working—though there would be no accidents if no one ever left their house…

Now if the DOT and NYPD could get traffic to flow smoothly onto bridges and into tunnels, they might actually be onto something. They can save you 1.5 minutes getting crosstown, just don't try leaving the city. Ever.

Information

Department of Transportation (DOT):	311 (24 hours) or
	212-NEW-YORK (Out-of-state)
TTY Hearing-Impaired:	212-504-4115
Website:	www.ci.nyc.ny.us/html/dot/
Parking Violations Help Line:	311
TTY Automated Information	
for the Hearing Impaired:	718-802-8555
Website:	www.ci.nyc.ny.us/finance (parking ticket info)

Standing, Stopping and Parking Rules

In "No Stopping" areas, you **can't** wait in your car, drop off passengers, or load/unload.

In "No Standing" areas, you **can't** wait in your car or load/unload, but you **can** drop off passengers.

In "No Parking" areas, you **can't** wait in your car or drop off passengers, but you **can** load/unload.

Parking Meter Zones

On holidays when street cleaning rules are suspended (see calendar), the "no parking" cleaning regulations for metered parking are also suspended. You can park in these spots but have to pay the meters. Also, metered spots are still subject to rules not suspended on holidays (see below). On MLH (major legal holidays), meter rules are suspended (so no need to feed the meter).

Meters

At a broken meter, parking is allowed only up to one hour. Where a meter is missing, parking is still allowed for the maximum time on the posted sign (an hour for a one-hour meter, two hours for a two-hour meter, etc.).

Instead of old-fashioned individual meters, Midtown has "muni-meters." The machines let you purchase time-stamped slips which you stick in your windshield to show you paid. These machines accept coins, parking cards, and some (we wish it was all!) accept credit cards (for example, the machines in the theater district). In the case of a non-functional muni-meter, the one-hour time limit applies.

The DOT sells parking cards that come in $20, $50, and $100 denominations and can be used in muni-meters, municipal parking lots, and some single-space meters (look for a yellow decal). The cards can be purchased through the DOT website (www.nyc.gov/html/dot/home.html), by calling 311 (or 212-NEW-YORK if you're calling from outside the city), or by going to the Staten Island Ferry Terminal or one of the two City Stores.

As of spring 2006, you don't have to pay meters on Sunday, even if the signs say you do (unless the law changes again with the political winds).

Signs

New York City Traffic Rules state that one parking sign per block is sufficient notification. Check the entire block and read all signs carefully before you park. Then read them again.

If there is more than one sign posted for the same area, the more restrictive sign takes effect (of course). If a sign is missing on a block, the remaining posted regulations are the ones in effect.

The Blue Zone

The Blue Zone is a "No Parking" (Mon–Fri, 7 am–7 pm) area in Lower Manhattan. Its perimeter has been designated with blue paint; however, there are no individual "Blue Zone" signs posted. Any other signs posted in that area supersede Blue Zone regulations. Confused yet?

General

- All of NYC was designated a Tow Away Zone under the State's Vehicle & Traffic Law and the NYC Traffic Rules. This means that any vehicle parked or operated illegally, or with missing or expired registration or inspection stickers, may, and probably will, be towed.
- On major legal holidays, stopping, standing, and parking are permitted except in areas where stopping, standing, and parking rules are in effect seven days a week (for example, "No Standing Anytime").
- It is illegal to park in a spot where SCR are in effect, even if the street cleaner has already passed. If you sit in your car, the mermaid will usually let you stay
- Double-parking of passenger vehicles is illegal at all times, including street-cleaning days, regardless of location, purpose, or duration. Everyone, of course, does this anyway. If everyone is double parked on a certain block during street cleaning, the NYPD probably isn't ticketing. However, leave your phone number in the window in case the person you blocked feels vindictive and demand that a cop write you a ticket.
- It is illegal to park within 15 feet of either side of a fire hydrant. The painted curbs at hydrant locations do not indicate where you can park. Isn't New York great? Metermaids will tell you that each cement block on the sidewalk is five feet, so make sure you are three cement blocks from the hydrant (2.5 will not do).
- If you think you're parked legally in Manhattan, you're probably not, so go and read the signs again.
- Cops will now just write you parking tickets and mail them to you if you are parked in a bus stop; so you won't even know it's happening unless you're alert.
- There is now clearly an all-out effort to harass everyone who is insane enough to drive and/or park during the day in downtown Manhattan. Beware.

Alternate Side Parking Suspension Calendar 2008–2009 (Estimated*)

2008 Holiday	Date	Day	Rules
Labor Day	Sep 1	Mon	MLH
Rosh Hashanah	Sep 30–Oct 1	Tues–Wed	ASP
Idul-Fitr	Oct 1–3	Wed–Fri	ASP
Yom Kippur	Oct 9	Thurs	ASP
Columbus Day (Observed)	Oct 13	Mon	ASP
Succoth, 1st/2nd Day	Oct 14–15	Tues–Wed	ASP
Shemini Atzereth	Oct 21	Tues	ASP
Simchas Torah	Oct 22	Wed	ASP
Diwali	Oct 28	Tues	ASP
All Saints Day	Nov 1	Sat	ASP
Election Day	Nov 4	Tues	ASP
Veterans Day	Nov 11	Tues	ASP
Thanksgiving Day	Nov 27	Thurs	MLH
Immaculate Conception	Dec 8	Mon	ASP
Idul-Adha	Dec 8–10	Mon–Wed	ASP
Christmas Day	Dec 25	Thurs	MLH
2009 Holiday	Date	Day	Rules
New Year's Day	Jan 1	Thurs	MLH
Martin Luther King Jr's Birthday	Jan 19	Mon	ASP
Asian Lunar New Year	Jan 26	Mon	ASP
Lincoln's Birthday	Feb 12	Thurs	ASP
Presidents' Day	Feb 16	Mon	ASP
Ash Wednesday	Feb 25	Wed	ASP
Purim	Mar 10	Tues	ASP
Holy Thursday	Apr 9	Thurs	ASP
Good Friday	Apr 10	Fri	ASP
Passover (1st/2nd Day)	Apr 9–10	Thurs–Fri	ASP
Holy Thursday (Orthodox)	Apr 17	Thurs	ASP
Good Friday (Orthodox)	Apr 18	Fri	ASP
Passover (7th/8th Day)	Apr 16–17	Thurs–Fri	ASP
Solemnity of Ascension	May 21	Wed	ASP
Memorial Day	May 25	Mon	MLH
Shavuot (1st/2nd Day)	May 29–30	Fri–Sat	ASP
Independence Day	Jul 4	Sat	MLH
Feast of Assumption	Aug 15	Sat	ASP
Labor Day	Sep 7	Mon	MLH
Rosh Hashanah	Sep 19	Sat	ASP
Idul-Fitr	Sep 19–21	Sat–Mon	ASP
Yom Kippur	Sep 28	Mon	ASP
Columbus Day	Oct 12	Mon	ASP
Succoth (1st/2nd Day)	Oct 3–4	Sat–Sun	ASP
Shemini Atzereth	Oct 10	Sat	ASP
Simchas Torah	Oct 11	Sun	ASP
Diwali	Oct 17	Sat	ASP
All Saints Day	Nov 1	Sun	ASP
Election Day	Nov 3	Tues	ASP
Veterans Day	Nov 11	Wed	ASP
Thanksgiving Day	Nov 26	Thurs	MLH
Idul-Adha	Nov 27	Fri	ASP
Immaculate Conception	Dec 8	Tues	ASP
Christmas Day	Dec 25	Fri	MLH

* **Note:** We go to press before the DOT issues its official calendar. However, using various techniques, among them a Ouija Board, a chainsaw, and repeated phone calls to said DOT, we think it's pretty accurate. Nonetheless, caveat parkor.

· **Street Cleaning Rules (SCR)**

Most SCR signs are clearly marked by the "P" symbol with the broom through it. Some SCR signs are the traditional 3-hour ones ("8 am–11 am" etc.) but many others vary considerably. Check the times before you park. Then check them again.

· **Alternate Side Parking Suspended (ASP)**
"No Parking" signs in effect one day a week or on alternate days are suspended on days designated ASP; however, all "No Stopping" and "No Standing" signs remain in effect.

· **Major Legal Holiday Rules in Effect** (MLH)
"No Parking" and "No Standing" signs that are in effect fewer than seven days a week are suspended on days designated MLH in the above calendar.

· If the city finds that a neighborhood keeps its streets clean enough, it may lessen the number of street cleaning days, or even eliminate them all together. So listen to your mother and don't litter.

Tow Pounds

Manhattan
Pier 76 at W 38th St & Twelfth Ave
Monday: 7 am–11 pm,
open 24 hours: Tuesday 7 am–Sunday 6 am
212-971-0771 or 212-971-0772

Bronx
745 E 141st St b/w Bruckner Expy & East River
Monday–Friday: 8 am–9 pm, Saturday: 8 am–3 pm,
Sunday: Closed; 718-585-1385 or 718-585-1391

Brooklyn
Brooklyn Navy Yard; corner of Sands St & Navy St
Monday–Friday: 8 am–9 pm, Saturday: 8 am–4 pm,
Sunday: 12 pm–8 pm; 718-694-0696

Queens
Under the Kosciusko Bridge at 56th Rd & Laurel Hill Blvd
Monday–Friday: 8 am–6 pm, Saturday: 7 am–3 pm,
Sunday: 12 pm–8 pm; 718-786-7122, 718-786-7123, or
718-786-7136

Find out if your car was towed (and not stolen or disintegrated): 718-422-7800 or 718-802-3555 (TTY)

http://nycserv.nyc.gov/NYCServInquiry/NYCSERVMain

Once you've discovered that your car has indeed been towed, your next challenge is to find out which borough it's been towed to. This depends on who exactly towed your car—the DOT, the Marshal, etc. Don't count on the fact that since your car was parked in Manhattan that they will tow it to Manhattan—always call first.

So you've located your car, now come the particulars: If you own said towed car, you're required to present your license, registration, insurance, and payment of your fine before you can collect the impounded vehicle. If you are not the owner of the car, you can usually get it back with all of the above, if your last name matches the registration (i.e. the car belongs to a relative or spouse); otherwise, you'll need a notarized letter with the owner's signature authorizing you to take the car. The tow fee is $185, plus a $70 execution fee, plus $10–$15 for each day it's in the pound. If they've put a boot on it instead, it's still $185. You can pay with cash or debit card; if you own the car, you can also pay by credit card or certified check. We recommend bringing a wad of cash and a long Russian novel for this experience.

Transit · LIRR

General Information

New York City:	718-217-LIRR
Nassau County:	516-822-LIRR
Suffolk County:	631-231-LIRR
TTY Information (Hearing Impaired):	718-558-3022
Group Travel and Tours:	718-558-7498
	(M–F 8 pm–4 pm)
Mail & Ride:	800-649-NYNY
MTA Police Eastern Region:	718-558-3300
	or 516-733-3900
Lost & Found (M-F 7:20 am-7:20 pm):	212-643-5228
Ticket Refunds (M-F 8 am-4 pm):	718-558-3488
Ticket Machine Assistance:	877-LIRR-TSM
Hamptons Reserve Service:	718-558-8070
Website:	www.mta.info/lirr

Overview

The Long Island Railroad is the busiest railroad in North America. It has eleven lines with 124 stations stretching from Penn Station in midtown Manhattan, to the eastern tip of Long Island, Montauk Point. An estimated 81 million people ride the LIRR every year. If you enjoy traveling on overcrowded trains with intermittent air-conditioning, then the LIRR is for you. If you are going anywhere on Long Island and you don't have a car, the LIRR is your best bet. Don't be surprised if the feeling of being in a seedy bar creeps over you during evening rush—those middle-aged business men like their beer en route. Despite a recent movement to ban the sale of alcohol on LIRR station platforms and trains, for now, it's still legal to get your buzz on.

If you're not a regular LIRR user, you might find yourself taking the train to Shea Stadium for a Mets game (Port Washington Branch), Long Beach for some summer surfing (Long Beach Branch), or to Jamaica to transfer to the AirTrain to JFK (tip—the subway is cheaper). For the truly adventurous, take the LIRR all the way out to the Hamptons beach house you are visiting for the weekend (Hamptons Reserve seating is available during the summer for passengers taking 6 or more trips). Bring a book as it is a long ride.

Fares and Schedules

Fares and schedules can be obtained by calling one of the general information lines, depending on your area. They can also be found on the LIRR website. Make sure to buy your ticket before you get on the train at a ticket window or at one of the ticket vending machines in the station.

Otherwise it'll cost you an extra $4.75 to $5.50 depending on your destination. As it is a commuter railroad, the LIRR offers weekly and monthly passes, as well as ten-trip packages for on- or off-peak hours.

Pets on the LIRR

Trained service animals accompanying passengers with disabilities are permitted on LIRR trains. Other small pets are allowed on trains, but they must be confined to closed, ventilated containers.

Bikes on the LIRR

You need a permit ($5) to take your bicycle onto the Long Island Railroad. Pick one up at a ticket window or online at the LIRR website.

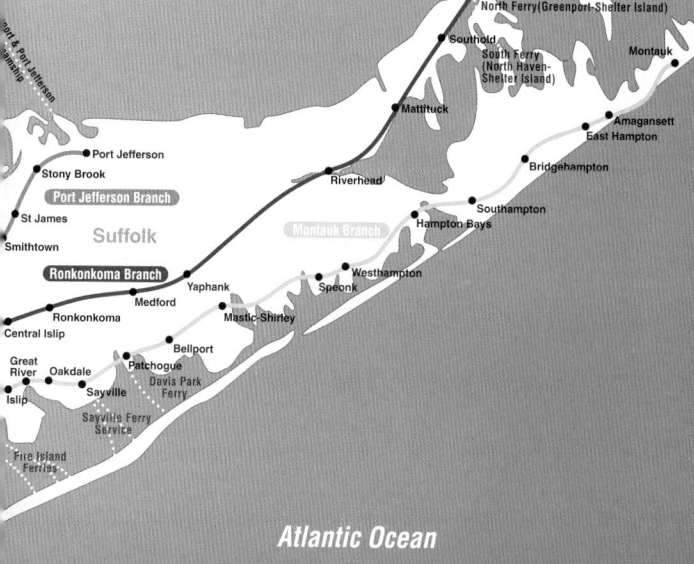

Transit · Metro-North Railroad

Key
Rail Station
Wheelchair or ADA
Accessible station
Major transit hub ● Rail Station
Connecting rail service

© 2004 Metropolitan Transportation Authority
Design: Michael Hertz Associates, NYC

HUDSON LINE
HARLEM LINE

Amtrak
to Albany

Poughkeepsie

New Hamburg

Beacon

Breakneck Ridge
Cold Spring
Garrison

Manitou

Peekskill

Cortlandt
Croton-Harmon

Ossining
Scarborough
Philipse
Manor
Tarrytown

Irvington
Ardsley-on-Hudson
Dobbs Ferry
Hastings-on-Hudson
Greystone
Glenwood
Yonkers
Ludlow
Riverdale
Spuyten Duyvil
Marble Hill
University Hts
Morris Hts
Melrose

Harlem-125 St

Grand Central Terminal
Penn Station
PATH

NEW YORK

BROOKLYN
QUEENS

DUTCHESS

Wassaic
Tenmile River
Dover Plains

Harlem Valley–Wingdale
Appalachian Trail

Pawling

Patterson

PUTNAM

Southeast
Brewster

Croton Falls
Purdy's
Golden's Bridge

Katonah
Bedford Hills
Mount Kisco

WESTCHESTER

Chappaqua
Pleasantville
Hawthorne
Mt Pleasant
North White Plains
White Plains
Hartsdale
Scarsdale

Crestwood
Tuckahoe
Bronxville
Fleetwood
Mt Vernon
West
Woodlawn
Williams Bridge
Botanical Garden
Fordham
Tremont

THE BRONX

Danbury
Branch

Danbury

Bethel

Redding

Branchville

Cannondale

Wilton

New Canaan
Branch

New Canaan

Talmadge Hill

Springdale
Glenbrook

Merritt 7

LITCHFIELD

NEW HAVEN

Houstonic River

FAIRFIELD

NEW HAVEN LINE

Waterbury
Branch

Waterbury

Naugatuck

Beacon Falls

Seymour

Ansonia

Derby–Shelton

New Haven–
Union Station

Milford

Stratford
Bridgeport

Southport
Green's Farms
Westport
East Norwalk
South Norwalk
Rowayton
Darien
Noroton Heights
Stamford
Old Greenwich
Riverside
Cos Cob
Greenwich CT
Port Chester NY
Rye
Harrison
Mamaroneck
Larchmont
New Rochelle
Pelham
Mt Vernon East

Long Island Sound

NASSAU

NYC CONNECTION ROUTE
NEW YORK CONNECTIONS

Hudson River

Long Island Sound

General Information

NYC Phone:	212-532-4900
All other areas:	800-METRO-INFO
Website:	www.mta.info/mnr
Lost and Found (Grand Central):	212-340-2555
MTA Inspector General:	800-MTA-IG4U

Overview

Metro-North is an extremely accessible and efficient railroad with three of its main lines (Hudson, Harlem, and New Haven) originating in Grand Central Station in Manhattan (42nd St & Park Ave). Those three lines east of the Hudson River, along with two lines west of the Hudson River that operate out of Hoboken, NJ (not shown on map), form the second-largest commuter railroad system in the US. Approximately 250,000 commuters use the tri-state Metro-North service each day for travel between New Jersey, New York, and Connecticut. Metro-North rail lines cover roughly 2,700 square miles of territory. The best thing about Metro-North is that it lands you at Grand Central Station, one of the city's finest pieces of architecture. On weekdays, sneak into the land of platforms via the North Passage, accessible at 47th & 48th Streets. At least for now, it's still legal to have an after work drink on Metro-North. During happy hour (starting somewhere around 3 pm), hit the bar car or buy your booze in advance on the platform at Grand Central. It might make you feel better about being a wage slave. But beware of having too happy of an hour as the bathrooms can be stinky and not all cars have them.

Fares and Schedules

Fare information is available on Metro-North's extraordinarily detailed website (along with in-depth information on each station, full timetables, and excellent maps) or at Grand Central Station. The cost of a ticket to ride varies depending on your destination so you should probably check the website before setting out. Buy advance tickets on MTA's WebTicket site for the cheapest fares. If you wait until you're on the train to pay, it'll cost you an extra $4.75–$5.50. Monthly and weekly rail passes are also available for commuters. Daily commuters save 50% on fares when they purchase a monthly travel pass.

Hours

Train frequency depends on your destination and the time of day that you're traveling. On weekdays, peak-period trains east of the Hudson River run every 20–30 minutes; off-peak trains run every 30–60 minutes; and weekend trains run hourly. Hours of operation are approximately 5 am to 3 am. Don't miss the last train out as they leave on time and wait for no one.

Bikes on Board

If you're planning on taking your two-wheeler onboard, you'll need to apply for a bicycle permit first. An application form can be found on the Metro-North website at http://mta.info/mnr/html/mnrbikepermit.htm. The $5 permit fee and application can either be mailed into the MTA, or processed right away at window 27 at Grand Central Terminal.

Common sense rules for taking bikes on board include: no bikes on escalators, no riding on the platform, and board the train after other passengers have boarded. Unfortunately there are restrictions on bicycles during peak travel times. Bicycles are not allowed on trains departing from Grand Central Terminal 7 am–9 am and 3:01 pm–8:15 pm. Bikes are not permitted on trains arriving at Grand Central 5 am–10 am and 4 pm–8 pm. Don't even think about taking your bike with you on New Year's Eve, New Year's Day, St. Patrick's Day, Mother's Day, eve of Rosh Hashanah, eve of Yom Kippur, eve of Thanksgiving, Thanksgiving Day, Christmas Eve, or Christmas Day—they're not allowed. The Friday before any long weekend is also a no-no. There's a limit of two bikes per carriage, and four bikes per train at all times. Unfortunately, the same restrictions are not imposed on passengers with 4 Vera Bradley overnight bags heading off to the country house, but that is another story.

Riders of folding bikes do not require a permit and do not have to comply with the above rules, provided that the bike is folded at all times at stations and on trains.

Pets

Only seeing-eye dogs and small pets, if restrained or confined, are allowed aboard the trains.

One-Day Getaways

Metro-North offers "One-Day Getaway" packages on its website. Packages include reduced rail fare and discounted entry to destinations along MNR lines including Bruce Museum ($20.50), Dia:Beacon ($27), Hudson River Museum/Andrus Planetarium ($14.50), Maritime Aquarium at Norwalk ($28.25), Mohegan Sun Casino ($38.25), New York Botanical Garden ($19.75), and Nyack ($14.50). WebTicket saves passengers 5% of the fare. The website also suggests one-day hiking and biking excursions.

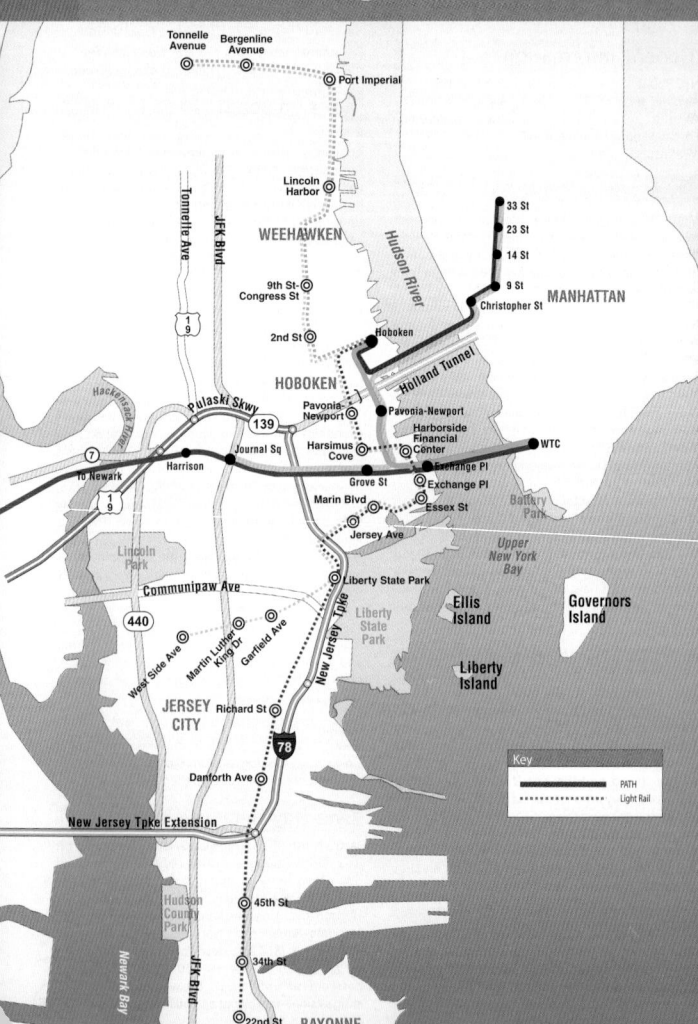

Tonnelle Avenue
Bergenline Avenue
Port Imperial

Tonnelle Ave
JFK Blvd

Lincoln Harbor

Hudson River

WEEHAWKEN

9th St-Congress St

2nd St

33 St
23 St
14 St
9 St
Christopher St

MANHATTAN

Hoboken

HOBOKEN

Holland Tunnel

Pulaski Skwy

Pavonia-Newport

Pavonia-Newport

Hackensack River

139

Journal Sq

Harsimus Cove

Harborside Financial Center

WTC

7

To Newark

Harrison

Exchange Pl

Exchange Pl

Grove St

Essex St

Marin Blvd

Battery Park

Jersey Ave

Lincoln Park

Upper New York Bay

Communipaw Ave

Liberty State Park

Ellis Island

Governors Island

440

West Side Ave

Martin Luther King Dr

Garfield Ave

Liberty State Park

Liberty Island

JERSEY CITY

Richard St

New Jersey Tpke

78

Danforth Ave

New Jersey Tpke Extension

Hudson County Park

JFK Blvd

45th St

34th St

22nd St

BAYONNE

Newark Bay

Key

————— PATH
· · · · · · · Light Rail

PATH Train

General Information
Website: www.panynj.gov/path
Phone: 800-234-7284
Police/Lost & Found: 201-216-6078

Overview

The PATH (Port Authority Trans-Hudson Corp.) is an excellent small rail system that services Newark, Jersey City, Hoboken, and Manhattan. There are a few basic lines that run directly between 33rd Street (Herald Square) in Manhattan & Hoboken, 33rd Street & Jersey City, and Newark & the WTC. Transfers between the lines are available at most stations. The PATH can be quite useful for commuters on the west side of Manhattan when the subway isn't running, say, due to a sick passenger or mysterious police investigation. Additionally, you can catch the PATH to Newark and then either jump in a cheap cab or take New Jersey Transit one stop to Newark Airport. It's a more economical option than taking a car all the way in from Manhattan, and you can take it back to the Village late at night when you've finished seeing a show at Maxwell's in Hoboken.

Check the front or the sides of incoming trains to determine their destination. Don't be fooled by the TV screens installed at stations; they occasionally announce the time of the next arrival, but as their main purpose is low-quality advertising, they are often incorrect. Also, don't assume that if a Journal Square train just passed through, the next train is going to Hoboken. Often there will be two Journal Square trains in a row, followed by two Hoboken trains. During the weekend, PATH service can be excruciatingly slow and confusing, and is best only endeavored with a seasoned rider.

Fares

The PATH costs a buck fifty one-way. Regular riders can purchase 11-trip, 20-trip, and 40-trip QuickCards, which reduce the fare per journey to $1.20–$1.36. The fare for seniors (65+) is $1 per ride. You can also use pay-per-ride MTA MetroCards for easy transition between the PATH and subway.

Hours

The PATH runs 24/7 (although a modified service operates between 11pm–6am, M–F, and 7:30pm–9 am, S, S & H). Daytime service is pretty consistent, but the night schedule for the PATH is a bit confusing, so make sure to look at the map. You may be waiting underground for up to a half an hour. During off hours the train runs on the same track through the tunnel. This allows for maintenance to be completed on the unused track.

Hudson-Bergen Light Rail

General Information
Website: http://www.mylightrail.com/
Phone: 800-772-2222

Overview

Even though it's called the Hudson-Bergen Light Rail system (HBLR, operated by NJ Transit), it actually only serves Hudson county. Bergen County residents are still waiting for their long promised connection. The HBLR has brought about some exciting changes (a.k.a. "gentrification") in Jersey City, though Bayonne remains (for the moment) totally, well…Bayonne. Currently there are 23 stops (with at least one more stop planned in Bayonne) in the system, including service to Jersey City, Hoboken, Weehawken, and Union City. Transfer at the Hoboken stop for the PATH into Manhattan.

Fares

The Light Rail is $1.90 per trip; reduced fare is 95 cents. Ten-trip tickets are $16.25, monthly passes cost $58, and monthly passes with parking are $93. Unless you have a monthly pass, you need to validate your ticket before boarding at a Ticket Validating Machine (TVM). Once validated, tickets are only valid for 90 minutes, so don't buy too far in advance. The trains and stations have random fare inspection and the fine for fare evasion is $100.

Hours

Light rail service operates between 5 am and 1:30 am. Times are approximate, check the website for exact schedules on each line.

Bikes on Board

Bikes are allowed (no permit or fee required) on board during off-peak times—weekdays from 9:30 am to 4 pm and 7 pm to 6 am, and all day Saturday, Sunday, and NJ state holidays. Bicycles have to be accompanied on the low-floor vestibule section of each rail car.

Pets

Small pets are allowed, as long as they're confined to a carry container. Service animals are permitted at all times.

(297)

Transit · **NJ Transit**

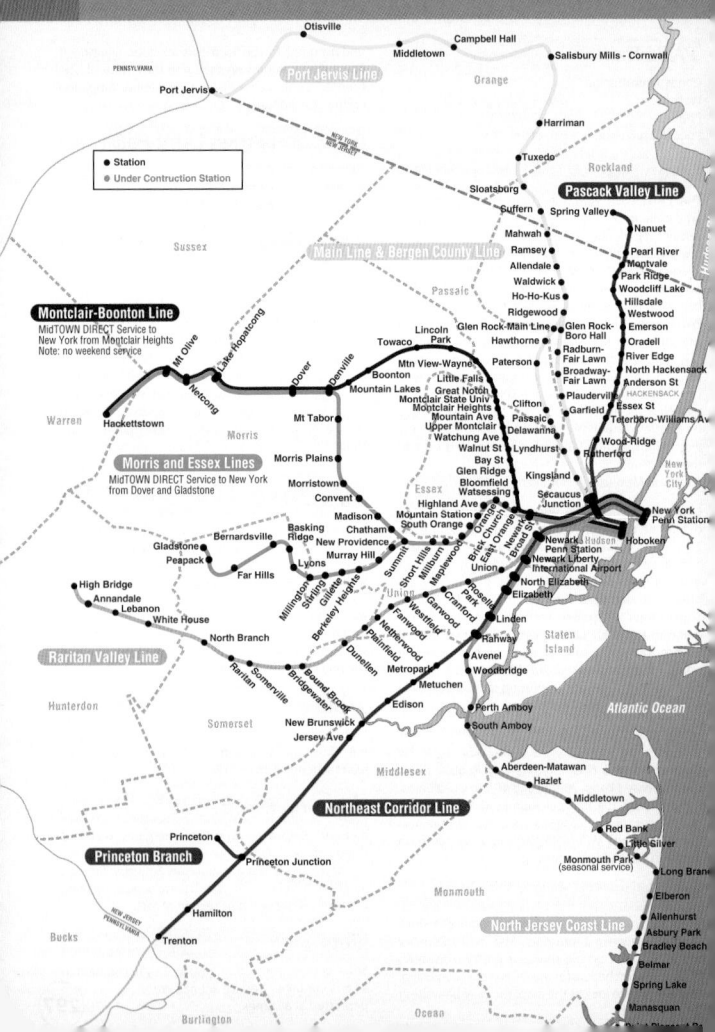

Legend
- ● Station
- ● Under Contruction Station

Port Jervis Line

Otisville
Middletown
Campbell Hall
Salisbury Mills - Cornwall

PENNSYLVANIA

Orange

Port Jervis

Harriman

Tuxedo

Rockland

Sloatsburg

Suffern · Spring Valley

Pascack Valley Line

Nanuet
Pearl River
Montvale
Park Ridge
Woodcliff Lake
Hillsdale
Westwood
Emerson
Oradell
River Edge
North Hackensack
Anderson St
HACKENSACK
Teterboro-Williams Av
Wood-Ridge

Mahwah
Ramsey
Allendale
Waldwick
Ho-Ho-Kus
Ridgewood
Glen Rock-Main Line
Glen Rock-Boro Hall
Hawthorne
Radburn-Fair Lawn
Broadway-Fair Lawn
Garfield

Main Line & Bergen County Line

Sussex

Passaic

Montclair-Boonton Line
MidTOWN DIRECT Service to
New York from Montclair Heights
Note: no weekend service

Lincoln Park
Towaco
Boonton
Mountain Lakes
Mtn View-Wayne
Little Falls
Great Notch
Montclair State Univ
Montclair Heights
Mountain Ave
Upper Montclair
Watchung Ave
Walnut St
Bay St
Glen Ridge
Bloomfield
Watsessing

Clifton
Passaic
Delawanna
Lyndhurst
Kingsland

Paterson

Essex St

Rutherford

Secaucus Junction

New York

Warren

Hackettstown
Mt Olive
Netcong
Lake Hopatcong
Dover
Denville
Mt Tabor

Morris

Morris and Essex Lines
MidTOWN DIRECT Service to New York
from Dover and Gladstone

Morris Plains
Morristown
Convent
Madison
Chatham

Essex

Bernardsville
Peapack
Gladstone

Basking Ridge
New Providence
Murray Hill
Lyons
Gillette
Stirling
Millington

Far Hills

Summit
Short Hills
Millburn
Maplewood
South Orange
Mountain Station
Highland Ave

Orange
Brick Church
East Orange
Broad St

Newark
Penn Station

Hoboken

New York
Penn Station

North Elizabeth

Newark
Liberty
International Airport

Berkeley Heights

Union

Roselle Park
Roselle
Cranford
Garwood
Westfield
Fanwood
Netherwood
Plainfield
Dunellen

Elizabeth

Linden

Rahway

Avenel

Woodbridge

Staten
Island

High Bridge
Annandale
Lebanon
White House
North Branch

Raritan Valley Line

Raritan
Somerville
Bound Brook
Bridgewater

Metropark
Metuchen
Edison

Perth Amboy

Atlantic Ocean

Hunterdon

Somerset

New Brunswick
Jersey Ave

South Amboy

Middlesex

Aberdeen-Matawan
Hazlet

Northeast Corridor Line

Middletown

Princeton
Princeton Branch

Princeton Junction

Red Bank
Little Silver
Monmouth Park
(seasonal service)
Long Branch

Hamilton

Trenton

NEW JERSEY
PENNSYLVANIA

Monmouth

Elberon
Allenhurst
Asbury Park
Bradley Beach
Belmar
Spring Lake
Manasquan

North Jersey Coast Line

Bucks

Burlington

Ocean

General Information

Address:	1 Penn Plz E
	Newark, NJ 07105
Phone:	973-491-7000 or
	800-772-2222
Website:	www.njtransit.com
Quik-Tik (monthly passes):	866-QUIK-TIK
Emergency Hotline:	973-378-6565
Newark Lost and Found:	973-491-8792
Hoboken Lost and Found:	201-714-2739
New York Lost and Found:	212-630-7389
AirTrain:	973-961-6230
Atlantic City Terminal:	609-343-7174

Overview

NJ Transit carries hundreds of thousands of New Jersey commuters to New York every morning and returns them to their suburban enclaves at the end of the day. The trains are usually clean (and immune to the weirdness that plagues the LIRR), but some lines (like the Pascack Valley Line) seem to just creep along, which can be problematic when you're trying to make a transfer before reaching the Big Apple. But with many new stations, including the renovated transfer station at Secaucus, and an expanded Light Rail system (see PATH page), NJ Transit is staying competitive with all other modes of transportation into and out of the city. NJ Transit also runs an AirTrain to Newark Airport. As the rails have been prone to power loss and broken switches lately, NJ Transit won't be competing with Japanese rail systems any time soon, but riding their rails generally beats waiting in traffic at the three measly Hudson River automobile crossings. NJ Transit also offers bus lines to Hoboken and Newark for areas not served by train lines.

Secaucus Transfer Station

The three-level train hub at Secaucus is celebrating its fifth birthday! The station cost around $450 million and took 14 years to complete. The building is dedicated to Democratic New Jersey Senator Frank R. Lautenberg, who was responsible for securing the federal funds necessary for construction. The former Secaucus Transfer Station is now officially known as the Frank R. Lautenberg Station at Secaucus Junction (which, if you want to get technical, is not actually a junction). We're certain that most commuters will adopt this name whenever referring to the station, or maybe they'll just call it "Secaucus."

For riders, the biggest advantage of the new station is that they no longer have to travel out to Hoboken to get to Penn Station. (Secaucus is just an 8-minute ride from Penn Station.) The Secaucus hub connects ten of NJ Transit's 11 rail lines, and also offers service to Newark Airport, downtown Newark, Trenton, and the Jersey Shore.

Fares and Schedules

Fares and schedules can be obtained at Hoboken, Newark, Penn Station, on NJ Transit's website, or by calling NJ Transit. If you wait to pay until you're on the train, you'll pay an extra five bucks for the privilege. NJ Transit also offers discounted monthly, weekly, weekend, and ten-trip tickets for regular commuters.

Pets

Only seeing-eye dogs and small pets in carry-on containers are allowed aboard the trains and buses.

Bikes

You can take your bicycle onboard a NJ Transit train only during off-peak hours (weekdays from 9:30 am–4 pm, and from 7 pm–5 am) and during all hours on the weekends. Bikes are not allowed on board most holidays, or the Fridays prior to any holiday weekend; however, a folding frame bicycle can be taken onboard at any time. Most NJ Transit buses participate in the "Rack'n'Roll" program, which allows you to load your bike right on to the front of the bus.

Overview

Phone: 800-USA-RAIL
Website: www.amtrak.com

General Information

Amtrak is our national train system, and while it's not particularly punctual or affordable, it *will* take you to many major northeastern cities in half a day or less. Spending a few hours on Amtrak also makes you want to move to Europe where France is now running trains at 357 mph (as opposed to 35 mph in the US). But if you plan a trip at the last minute and miss the requisite lecture on buying airline tickets or want to bring liquids with you with checking baggage, you might want to shop Amtrak's fares. Bonus: Amtrak allows you to talk on cell phones in most cars and has plugs for laptop computers at your seat.

Amtrak was created by the federal government in 1971. Today, Amtrak services 500+ stations in 46 states (Alaska, Hawaii, South Dakota, and Wyoming sadly do not have the pleasure of being serviced by Amtrak). While not being as advanced as the Eurail system, Amtrak serves over 24 million passengers a year, employs 19,000 people, still has the same décor it did in the early 1970s, and provides "contract-commuter services" for several state and regional rail lines.

Red Caps (station agents) are very helpful, especially for passengers traveling with children and strollers. The only problem is finding an available one!

Amtrak in New York

In New York City, Amtrak runs out of Pennsylvania Station, an eyesore currently located underneath Madison Square Garden. We treat the station like our annoying little brother, calling it Penn for short and avoiding it when we can. But don't despair—chances are the city you'll wind up in will have a very nice station, and, if all goes well, so will we, once the front half of the Farley Post Office is converted to a "new" Penn Station. Warning: If you hop in a cab to get to Amtrak, specify that you want to be dropped off at Eighth Avenue and 33rd Street in order to avoid LIRR and Madison Square Garden foot traffic. Don't let the cabbie argue with you, especially if you have luggage. He is just trying to make his life easier.

Popular Destinations

Many New Yorkers use Amtrak to get to Boston, Philadelphia, or Washington DC. Of course, these are the New Yorkers who are traveling on an expense account or fear the Chinatown bus service. Amtrak also runs a line up to Montreal and through western New York state (making stops in Buffalo, Rochester, Albany, etc.). Check Amtrak's website for a complete listing of all Amtrak stations.

Going to Boston

Amtrak usually runs 18 trains daily to Boston. One-way fares cost $59–$101, and the trip, which ends at South Station in downtown Boston, takes about four-and-a-half hours door-to-door. For $117 one-way, you can ride the high speed Acela ("acceleration" and "excellence" combined into one word, though perhaps "expensive" would have been more appropriate) and complete the journey in three to three-and-a-half hours—if there are not track problems.

Going to Philadelphia

About 40 Amtrak trains pass through Philadelphia every day. One-way tickets cost about $45–$60 on a regular Amtrak train; if you're really in a hurry, you can take the special "Metroliner" service for $87, which will get you there in an hour and fifteen minutes, or the Acela for $81, which takes about one hour from station to station. The cheapest rail option to Philly is actually to take NJ Transit to Trenton and then hook up with Eastern Pennsylvania's excellent SEPTA service—this will take longer, but will cost you under $25. Some commuters take this EVERY day. Thank your lucky stars you're probably not one of them.

Going to Washington DC

(Subtitle: *How Much is Your Time Worth?*)
Amtrak runs over 40 trains daily to DC and the prices vary dramatically. The cheapest trains cost $69 one-way and take just under four hours. The Acela service costs more than double at $125-$146 one-way, and delivers you to our nation's capital in less than three hours (sometimes). Worth it? Only you can say. Depending on what time of day you travel, you may be better off taking the cheaper train when the Acela will only save you 30 minutes.

A Note About Fares

While the prices quoted above for Boston, Philly, and DC destinations tend to remain fairly consistent, fares to other destinations, such as Cleveland, Chicago, etc., can vary depending on how far in advance you book your seat. For "rail sales" and other discounts, check www.amtrak.com. Military IDs will save you a bundle, so use them if you have them. Occasionally (or rarely), Amtrak offers discounts that can be found on their website under "Hot Deals."

Baggage Check (Amtrak Passengers)

A maximum of three items may be checked up to thirty minutes before departure. Up to three additional bags may be checked for a fee of $10 (two carry-on items allowed). No electronic equipment, plastic bags, or paper bags may be checked. See the "Amtrak Policies" section of their website for details.

General Information

NFT Map:	9
Address:	7th Ave & 33rd St
General Information (Amtrak):	800-872-7245
MTA Subway Stops:	❶ ❷ ❸ Ⓐ Ⓒ Ⓔ
MTA Bus Lines:	4 10 16 34
Train Lines:	LIRR, Amtrak, NJ Transit
LaGuardia Airport Bus Service:	NY Airport Service, 212-875-8200, $12
JFK Airport Bus Service:	NY Airport Service, 212-875-8200, $15
Passengers per day:	600,000

Overview

Penn Station, designed by McKim, Mead & White (New York's greatest architects), is a Beaux Arts treasure, filled with light and... oh wait, that's the one that was torn down. Penn Station is essentially a basement, complete with well-weathered leather chairs, unidentifiable dust particles, and high-cholesterol snack food. Its claim to fame is that it is the busiest Amtrak station in the country. If the government gods are with us, the plan to convert the eastern half of the Farley Post Office (also designed by McKim, Mead & White) next door to an above-ground, light-filled station will come to fruition. With bureaucracy at hand, we aren't holding our collective breath. Until then, Penn Station will go on servicing 600,000 people per day in the rat's maze under Madison Square Garden.

Penn Station services Amtrak, the LIRR, and NJ Transit trains. Amtrak, which is surely the worst national train system of any first-world country, administers the station. How is it that the Europeans have bullet trains and it still takes 3 or more hours to get from NYC to DC? While we're hoping the new station proposal will come through, will it help the crazed LIRR commuters struggling to squish down stairwells to catch the 6:05 to Ronkonkoma? We can only hope.

Dieters traveling through Penn Station should pre-pack snacks. The fast food joints are just too tempting. Donuts and ice cream and KFC, oh my! Leave yourself time to pick up some magazines and a bottle of water for your train trip. It may turn out to be longer than you think.

The plus side to Penn is that it's easy to get to from just about anywhere in the city via subway or bus. If you are just too ritzy to take the MTA (or you have an abundance of baggage), have your cab driver drop you off anywhere surrounding the station except for 7th Avenue—it is constantly jammed with tour buses and cabs trying to drop off desperately late passengers.

Terminal Shops

On the LIRR Level
Food & Drink
Auntie Anne's Soft Pretzels
Blimpie
Caruso's Pizza
Carvel
Cinnabon
Colombo Frozen Yogurt
Dunkin' Donuts
Europan Café
Haagen Dazs
Hot & Crusty
Hot Dog Stand
KFC
Knot Just Pretzels
Le Bon Café
McDonald's
Nedick's
Pizza Hut
Primo! Cappuccino
Rose Pizza and Pasta
Salad Chef/Burger Chef

Seattle Coffee Roasters
Soup King
Soup Man/Smoothie King (2)
Starbucks
Subway
TGI Friday's
Tracks Raw Bar & Grill

Other
Carlton Cards
Dreyfus Financial Center
Duane Reade
GNC
Hudson News (4)
K-Mart
Petal Pusher
Penn Books
Perfumania
Soleman—Shoe repair,
locksmith
Verizon Wireless

On the Amtrak Level
Food & Drink
Auntie Anne's Soft Pretzels (2)
Baskin Robbins
Deli
Dunkin' Donuts
Don Pepi Pizza
Houlihan's Restaurant & Bar
Nathan's/Carvel
Kabooz's Bar and Grille
Krispy Kreme Doughnuts
Penn Sushi
Pizza Hut
Primo! Cappuccino (3)
Roy Rogers
Soup Man/Smoothie King/
Sodutto Ice Cream
Zaro's Bread Basket (2)

Other
Book Corner
Duane Reade
Elegance

Gifts & Electronics
GNC
Hudson News (3)
Joseph Lawrence Jewelers
New York New York
Shoetrician—Shoe repair
and shine
Tiecoon
The Petal Pusher
Staples
Tourist Information Center
Verizon Wireless

There is a Wachovia 24-hour ATM and a PNC Bank ATM located on the Amtrak level. There is a Bank of America 24-hour ATM and a 24-hour HSBC ATM located on the LIRR level, in addition to the generic (money-thieving) ATMs located in several stores throughout the station.

Temporary Parcel/Baggage Check

The only facility for storing parcels and baggage in Penn Station is at the Baggage Check on the Amtrak level (to the left of the ticket counter). There are no locker facilities at Penn Station. The Baggage Check is open from 5:15 am until 10 pm and costs $4.50 per item for each 24-hour period.

Transit • Grand Central Terminal

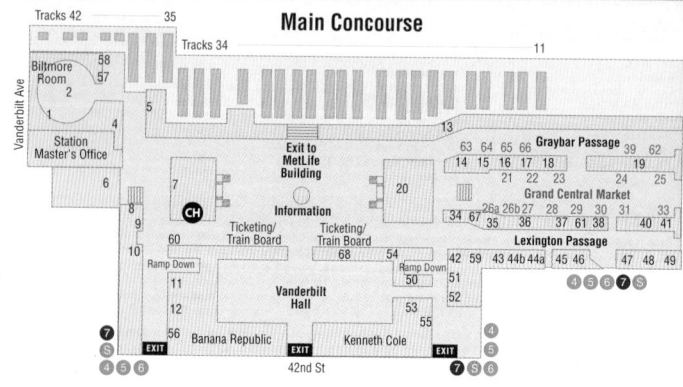

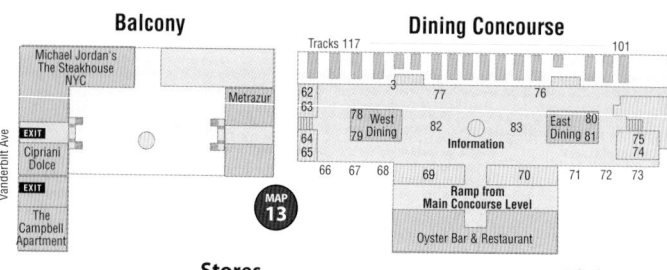

Stores

1. Eddie's Shoe Repair
2. Eastern News
3. Dahlia
4. Junior's
5. Starbucks
6. New York Transit Museum
7. Zaro's Bread Basket
8. Discovery Channel Store
9. Posman Books
10. Rite Aid
11. Central Market
12. Hot & Crusty
13. Zaro's Bread Basket
14. Oliviers & Co
15. Grande Harvest Wines
16. Cobbler & Shine
17. Stop'N Go Wireless
18. Metropolitan Museum Art Store
19. GNC
20. Hudson News
21. Greenwich Produce
22. Koglin German Hams
23. Murray's Cheese

24. Ceriello Fine Foods
25. Greenwich Produce
26a. Pescatore Seafood Company
26b. Dishes at Home
27. Li-Lac Chocolates
28. Oren's Daily Roast
29. Penzeys Spices
30. Zaro's Bread Basket
31. Wild Edibles
32. Corrado Bread & Pastry
33. Grand Central Raquet
34. Forever Silver
35. Grand Central Optical
36. Tumi
37. L'Occitane
38. Bose
39. Our Name is Mud
40. Aveda
41. Starbucks
42. Swatch
43. Origins
44a. Children's General Store
44b. Leeper Kids
45. Altitunes

46. Pink Slip
47. TOTO
48. LaCrasia Gloves & Accessories
49. Godiva Chocolatier
50. Super Runners Shop
51. Papyrus
52. Oren's Daily Roast
53. Douglas Cosmetics
54. Joon Stationary
55. Super Runners Shop
56. Neuhaus Boutique
57. Grand Central Watch Band Stand
58. Central Watch Band Stand
59. Flowers on Lexington
60. Hudson News
61. Access Artisans
62. Rosetta Stone
63. Carolyn Forsman
64. Laila Rowe
65. Canine Styles
66. Posman Books
67. Flowers on Lexington
68. Choice Foreign Currency

Dining Concourse

62. Paninoteca Italiana
63. Chirping Chicken
64. Eata Pita
65. Feng Shui
66. Mendy's Kosher Deli
67. Mendy's Kosher Dairy
68. Masa Sushi
69. Juniors
70. Zócala
71. Central Market Grill
72. Jacques-imo's To Geaux
73. Brother Jimmy's BBQ
74. Two Boots Pizza
75. Café Spice
76. Golden Krust Patties
77. New York Pretzel
78. Ciao Bella Gelateria
79. Hale and Hearty Soups
80. Zaro's Bread Basket
81. Little Pie Company
82. Dishes
83. Caffé Peppe Rosso

General Information

NFT Map:	13
Address:	42nd St & Park Ave
General Information:	212-340-2210
Lost and Found:	212-340-2555
Website:	www.grandcentralterminal.com
MTA Subway Stops:	④ ⑤ ⑥ ⑦ ⑤
MTA Bus Lines:	① ② ③ ④ 42 98 101 102 104 ⑤
Other Rail Lines:	Metro North
Newark Airport Bus Service:	Olympia, 877-8-NEWARK, $14
LaGuardia Airport Bus Service:	NY Airport Express, 718-875-8200, $12
JFK Airport Bus Service:	NY Airport Express, 718-875-8200, $15

Overview

Grand Central Terminal, designed in the Beaux Arts style by Warren & Wetmore, is by far the most beautiful of Manhattan's major terminals, and it is considered one of the most stunning terminals in the world. Its convenient location in the heart of Midtown and its refurbishments only add to its intrinsic appeal. The only downside is that the station will only get you on a train as far north as Dutchess County or as far east as New Haven via Metro North—in order to head to the Island or Jersey, you'll have to hoof it over to GCT's architecturally ugly stepsister Penn Station.

If you ever find yourself underestimating the importance of the Grand Central renovations (begun in 1996 with continued work and maintenance today), just take a peek at the ceiling toward the Vanderbilt Avenue side—the small patch of black shows how dirty the ceiling was previously. And it was really dirty...

Diners have any number of choices from Michael Jordan's The Steak House NYC or Metrazur (for those seeking fine dining) to the food court on the lower level (perfect for commuters or those intent on saving a few bucks). After hitting the raw stuff at Oyster Bar, go right outside its entrance to hear a strange audio anomaly: If you and a friend stand in opposite corners and whisper, you'll be able to hear each other clearly. You can even do some grocery shopping in the Grand Central Market on the east side of the main concourse. Alternatively, folks looking to hit the sauce may do so in 1920s grandeur in The Campbell Apartment near the Vanderbilt Avenue entrance.

Grand Central Station offers three tours: the hour-long LaSalle Tour (212-340-2345, $50 for small groups, $5/person for groups over 10, payment required in advance), the Municipal Arts Society Tour (212-935-3960, $10 suggested donation), and the Grand Central Partnership Tour (212-883-2420, free). Grand Central's website also offers a printer-friendly walking tour guide for visitors who want to wander on their own.

ATMs

Chase
Numerous generic (money-thieving) ATMs at stores throughout the station.

East Dining

Brother Jimmy's BBQ
Café Spice
Central Market Grill
Golden Krust Patties
Jaques-Imo's to Geaux
Little Pie Company
Caffé Pepe Rosso
Two Boots
Zaro's Bread Basket
Zócalo Bar and Restaurant

West Dining

Dishes
Ciao Bella Gelateria
Chirping Chicken
Eata Pita
Feng Shui
Hale and Hearty Soups
Junior's
Masa Sushi
Mendy's Kosher Dairy
Mendy's Kosher Delicatessen
New York Pretzel
Paninoteca Italiana

General Information

NFT Map:	11
Address:	41st St & 8th Ave
General Information:	212-564-8484
Kinney Garage:	212-502-2341
Website:	www.panynj.gov/CommutingTravel/bus/html/pa.html
Subway:	Ⓐ Ⓒ Ⓔ Port Authority
	❶ ❷ ❸ ❼ Ⓝ Ⓡ Ⓦ Ⓠ Ⓢ Times Square
MTA Bus Lines:	10 11 16 20 27 42 104
Newark Airport Bus Service:	Olympia, 212-964-6233, $13
LaGuardia Airport Bus Service:	NY Airport Express, 718-875-8200, $12
JFK Airport Bus Service:	NY Airport Express, 718-875-8200, $15

Overview

Devised as a solution to New York City's horrendous bus congestion, the Port Authority Bus Terminal was completed in 1950. The colossal structure consolidated midtown Manhattan's eight, separate, interstate bus stations into one convenient drop-off and pick-up point. Back in the day the Port Authority held the title of "largest bus terminal in the world," but for now we'll have to be content with merely the biggest depot in the United States. The Port Authority is located on the north and south sides of W 41st Street (b/w Eighth Ave & Ninth Ave) in a neighborhood that real-estate agents haven't yet graced with an official name. How about Greyhound Gardens?

There are plenty of things to do should you find that you've got some time to kill here. Send a postcard from the post office, donate blood at the blood bank on the main floor, use the refurbished bathrooms, bowl a few frames and have a cocktail at Leisure Time Bowl, or eat fancy French food at the ambitious sit-down restaurant, Metromarche, located in the south wing (they're really trying to class up the joint). There are also many souvenir carts, newsstands, and on-the-go restaurants, as well as a statue of beloved bus driver

Ralph Kramden located outside of the south wing. The grungiest area of the terminal is the lower bus level, which is dirty and exhaust-filled, best visited just a few minutes before you need to board your bus. The chart on the right shows which bus companies run out of the Port Authority and provides a basic description of their destinations.

If you can, avoid interstate bus rides from the Port Authority on the busiest travel days of the year. The lines are long, the people are cranky, and some of the larger bus companies hire anyone who shows up with a valid bus operator's license and their very own bus (apparently, easier to obtain than you might think). The odds of having a disastrous trip skyrocket when the driver is unfamiliar with the usual itinerary.

On Easter Sunday, Christmas Eve, or Thanksgiving, one can see all the angst-ridden sons and daughters of suburban New Jersey parents joyfully waiting in cramped, disgusting corridors for that nauseating bus ride back to Leonia or Morristown or Plainfield or wherever. A fascinating sight.

Terminal Shops

South Wing—
Lower Bus Level
Green Trees
Hudson News

South Wing—
Subway Mezzanine
Au Bon Pain
Hudson News
Music Explosion

South Wing—
Main Concourse
Metromarche
Au Bon Pain
Auntie Anne's
Casa Java
Deli Plus
Duane Reade
GNC

Jamba Juice
Hudson News
Hudson News Book Corner
Marrella Men's Hair Stylist
NY Blood Center
Radio Shack
Ruthie's Hallmark
Stop 'n Go Wireless
Strawberry
US Postal Service
Villa Pizza
World's Fare Restaurant Bar
Zaro's Bakery

South Wing—Second Floor
Café Metro
Drago Shoe Repair
Bank of America
Hudson News Book Corner
Kelly Film Express

Leisure Time Bowling
Center
McAnn's Pub
Mrs Fields Bakery Café
Munchy's Gourmet
Sak's Florist
Sweet Factory

South Wing—Fourth Floor
First Stop-Last Stop Café
Hudson News

North Wing-Lower Bus Level
Snacks-N-Wheels

North Wing—Subway
Mezzanine
Bank of America (ATM)
Green Trees
Hudson News

North Wing—Main
Concourse
Continental Airlines
Hudson News
Mrs Fields Cookies

North Wing—on 42nd
Street
Big Apple Café

North Wing—Second Floor
Bank of America (ATM)
Hudson News
Jay's Hallmark Bookstore
Tropica Juice Bar
USO

North Wing—Third Floor
Hudson News
Tropica Juice Bar

Bus Company	Phone	Area Served
Academy Bus Transportation	800-442-7272	Serves New York City, including Staten Island, Wall Street, Port Authority, and New Jersey, including Hoboken www.academybus.com
Adirondak New York & Pine Hill Trailways	800-776-7548	Serves all of New York State with coach connections throughout the US. www.trailwaysny.com
Capitol Trailways	800-333-8444	Service between Pennsylvania, Virginia, New York State, and New York City. www.capitoltrailways.com
Carl Bieber Bus	800-243-2374	Service to and from Port Authority and Wall Street in New York and Reading, Kutztown, Wescosville, Hellertown, and Easton, Pennsylvania. www.biebertourways.com
Coach USA	800-522-4514	Service between New York City and W Orange, Livingston, Morristown, E Hanover, Whippany, and Floram Park, New Jersey. www.coachusa.com
DeCamp Bus	800-631-1281	Service between New York City and New Jersey, including the Meadowlands. www.decamp.com
Greyhound Bus	800-231-2222	Serves most of the US and Canada. www.greyhound.com
Gray Line Bus	212-397-2620	Service offered throughout the US and Canada. www.grayline.com
Lakeland Bus	973-366-0600	Service between New York and New Jersey. www.lakelandbus.com
Martz Group	800-233-8604	Service between New York and Pennsylvania. www.martzgroup.com
New Jersey Transit	800-772-2222	Serves New York, New Jersey, and Philadelphia. www.njtransit.com
NY Airport Service	212-875-8200	Service between Port Authority and Kennedy and LaGuardia airports. www.nyairportservice.com
Olympia Trails	212-964-6233	Provides express bus service between Manhattan and Newark Airport. Makes stops all over New York City, including Penn Station, Grand Central, and many connections with hotel shuttles. www.olympiabus.com
Peter Pan Lines	800-343-9999	Serves the East, including Boston, New Hampshire, Maine, Philly, DC. Also goes to Canada. www.peterpanbus.com
Rockland Coaches (NY)	845-356-0877	Services New York's Port Authority, GW bridge, 44th Street, and 8th Street to and from most of Bergen County and upstate New York. www.coachusa.com/rockland
ShortLine Bus	800-631-8405	Serves the New York City airports, Atlantic City, and the Hudson Valley. www.shortlinebus.com
Suburban	732-249-1100	Offers commuter service from Central New Jersey to and from Port Authority and Wall Street. Also services between the Route 9 Corridor and New York City. www.coachusa.com/suburban
Susquehanna Trailways	800-692-6314	Service to and from New York City and Newark (Greyhound Terminal) and Summerville, New Jersey, and many stops in Central Pennsylvania, ending in Williamsport and Lock Haven. www.susquehannabus.com
Trans-Bridge Lines	610-868-6001 800-962-9135	Offers service between New York, Pennsylvania, and New Jersey, including Newark and Kennedy airports.
Red & Tan Hudson County (NJ)	908-354-3330	Serves New York City and Hudson County, New Jersey. www.coachusa.com/redandtan

General Information

NFT Map:	23
Address:	4211 Broadway & 178th St
Phone:	800-221-9903 or 212-564-8484
Website:	http://www.panynj.gov/CommutingTravel/bus/html/gwb.html
Subway:	Ⓐ (175th St), Ⓐ ❶ (181st St)
Buses:	100 98 5 4 3 9

Overview

Change is coming slowly to the George Washington Bridge Bus Terminal, though we can hope it will never lose its "lived-in" charm. The Port Authority has cleaned the station up a bit, added some needed signage, and improved the lighting, but any place with pigeons routinely wandering through the indoors can never be too chic. Hit some downtime before your bus arrives and your entertainment options are limited to people-watching, opening a new bank account, or placing bets at OTB. If you luck out and the weather's nice, though, the view of the bridge upstairs is pretty sweet.

Stores

Lower Level:
Bridge Stop Newsstand
HealthPlus Healthcare
Subway Pedestrian Walkway
NJT T Ticket Vending Machines
Port of Calls/Retail Pushcarts

Concourse:
ATM
Bridge Stop Newsstand
Dentists—Howard Bloom, DDS; Steve Kaufman DDS
E-Z Visions Travel
Food Plus Café
GW Books and Electronics
HealthPlus Healthcare
Neighborhood Trust Federal Credit Union
New York National Bank
Off-Track Betting
Pizza Palace
Terminal Barber Shop
Washington Heights Optical

Street Level:
Blockbuster Video
Rite-Aid Pharmacy
Urban Pathways—Homeless Outreach Office
Port Authority Business Outreach Center
(179th St underpass)

Bus Companies

Air Brook · 800-800-1990 · airbrook.com
To Atlantic City (Tropicana)

Astro-Eastern Bus Company ·
201-865-2230 · easternbuses.com
Trips to Florida (purchase tickets on the upper level).

Express Bus Service ·
973-881-9122 · expressbusservice.com
To Elmwood Park, Englewood, Fort Lee, Hackensack, Paramus, Paterson, River Edge, and Teaneck (all stops on Route 4).

New Jersey Transit ·
800-772-2222 · njtransit.com/sf_bu.shtml
To 60th St, Bergenfield, Bogota, Cliffside Park, Coytesville, Dumont, Edgewater (including Edgewater Commons Mall), Englewood, Englewood Cliffs, West Englewood, Fair Lawn (including the Radburn section), Fairview, Fort Lee, Glen Rock, Guttenberg, Hackensack (including NJ Bus Transfer), Hoboken, North Hackensack (Riverside Square), Irvington, Jersey City, Kearney, Leonia, Maywood, Newark, North Bergen, Paramus (including the Bergen Mall and Garden State Plaza), Paterson (including Broadway Terminal), Ridgewood, Rochelle Park, Teaneck (including Glenpointe and Holy Name Hospital), Union City, Weehawken, and West New York.

Red & Tan/Coach USA ·
201-876-9000 · coachusa.com/redandtan
To Alpine, Bergenfield, Blauvelt, Bradlees Shopping Center, Closter, Congers, Creskill, Demarest, Dumont, Emerson, Englewood, Englewood Cliffs, Grandview, Harrington Park, Haverstraw, Haworth, Hillsdale, Linwood Park, Montvale, Nanuet, (including Nanuet Shopping Mall), Nauraushaun, New City, New Milford, Northvale (including Northvale Industrial Park), Norwood, Nyack, Oradell, Orangeburg, Palisades, Park Ridge, Pearl River, Piermont, Rivervale, Rockland Lake, Rockland Psych Center, Rockleigh (including Rockleigh Industrial Park), South Nyack, Sparkill, Spring Valley, Stony Point, Tappan, Tenafly, Upper Nyack, Valley Cottage, West Haverstraw, Westwood, and Woodcliff Lake.

Saddle River Tours ·
888-778-8622 · saddlerivertours.com
To Atlantic City

Vanessa Express · 201-453-1970.
To Cliffside Park, Jersey City, North Bergen, Union City, and West New York.

General Information

NFT Map:	3
Websites:	www.chinatown-bus.com
	www.chinatown-bus.org

Overview

There are several inexpensive bus lines running from Chinatown in New York City to the respective Chinatowns in Boston, Philadelphia, Washington DC, Richmond, and Atlanta. If you're lucky, you'll catch a kung-fu movie on board, but be prepared for an '80s "classic" like Turner & Hooch. Fares usually cost $15–20 each way, and can be purchased online or in person at pick-up locations.

Cheaper than planes and trains, the Chinatown buses have become extraordinarily popular. They are in such demand that Greyhound and Amtrak have lowered their online fares to compete. That said, Chinatown buses are an infinitely more adventurous mode of transportation. The odds are high that you'll experience at least one problem during the course of your trip including, but not limited to, poor customer service, unmarked bus stops, late departures, less than ideal bus conditions, and hucking or spitting from other passengers. More pertinent problems include cancelled or delayed trips without warning, breakdowns, fires, broken bathrooms (or none at all), stolen luggage, and drop-offs on the side of the road near the highway because bus companies don't have permission to deliver passengers to central transportation hubs. Conversely, service has improved greatly in the past few years, and many people have enjoyed dirt-cheap, hassle-free experiences on the Chinatown buses. It's probably not the best choice for families, but anyone else should give it a try.

A few tips to make your trip easier: 1) MAKE SURE YOU GET ON THE RIGHT BUS. We cannot emphasize this enough. Do not be embarrassed to ask everyone on the bus which city they're going to. 2) Do not sit anywhere near the bathroom. You will smell the intense, probably illegal, cleaning products for the first half of the ride, and your fellow passengers' business for the second half. 3) If the bus isn't full, it's perfectly fine to take your luggage onboard with you if you're worried about theft. This is an especially good idea when leaving the New York stations.

Passengers should arrive at least 30 minutes prior to scheduled departure. Schedules and prices are subject to change at a moment's notice, so it's helpful to call or consult the company's website right before you leave. If you walk down East Broadway under the Manhattan Bridge, chances are people on the street will solicit you without even having to ask. Buses vary in quality from company to company and even from day to day. Fung Wah has been around the longest and is generally considered the best line, although Lucky Star is a close second. To read user reviews, visit www.chinatown-bus.com.

Bus Companies

Fung Wah Transportation Inc. •
212-925-8889 • www.fungwahbus.com
- To Boston every hour on the hour between 7 am–10 pm. From **139 Canal Street** to South Station: one-way $15, round trip $30.

Lucky Star Bus Transportation •
617-426-8801 • www.luckystarbus.com
- To Boston every hour 7 am–10 pm. From **69 Chrystie St** to South Station: one-way $15, round trip $30.

Boston Deluxe •
917-662-7552 or 646-773-3816 • www.bostondeluxe.com
- To Boston at 9 am, 12:30 pm, and 6 pm. From **1250 Broadway & 32nd St** or **88 E Broadway** to 175 Huntington Ave: one-way $15, round trip $30.
- To Hartford at 8:30 am, 12:30 pm, and 5:30 pm. From the same pick-up points to 365 Capital Ave: one-way $15, round trip $30.

Washington Deluxe • 866-BUS-NY-DC • www.washny.com
- To Washington several times a day; from **34th St & 8th Ave**. Additional departures from **Delancey & Allen Sts**, and several locations in **Williamsburg** to various locations in DC. Schedule varies by day of the week, so it's recommended that you check the website for info. One-way $20, round-trip $35.

Dragon Deluxe •
800-475-1160 or 212-966-5130 • www.dragondeluxe.com
- To Washington DC six times a day between 7:30 am and 11:30 pm. From **153 Lafayette St** or **Broadway & W 32nd St-Herald Square** to 14th & L Sts: one-way $20, round trip $35.
- To Baltimore six times a day between 7:30 am and 11:30 pm. From the same pick-up points to 5600 O'Donnell St: one-way $20, round trip $35.
- To Albany at 7:30 am and 5:30 pm. From the same pick-up points to Madison Ave (between the New York State Museum and Empire State Plaza): one-way $25, round trip $45
- To Woodbury Commons at 7:30 am and 5:30 pm. From the same pick-ups points to Woodbury Commons: one-way $15, round trip $30.

Eastern Travel • 212-244-6132 • www.easternshuttle.com
- To Washington DC 6–12 times a day between 7:30 am and 7:30 pm; From **88 E Broadway, 430 7th Ave at W 34th St**, or **5 Times Square (in front of the Ernst &Young Building)** to 715 H Street in Washington DC: one-way $20, round trip $35.
- To Baltimore 6–12 times a day between 7:30 am and 7:30 pm. From same pickup-point to 5501 O'Donnell St Cut Off: one-way $20, round trip $35.

New Century Travel • 215-627-2666 • www.2000coach.com
- To Philadelphia every hour between 7 am and 11 pm. From **88 E Broadway** or **5994 8th Ave**, Brooklyn (7 am only) to 55 N 11th St: one-way $12, round trip $20.
- To DC eight times between 7 am and 11 pm; from **88 E Broadway** to 513 H St NW: one-way $20, round trip $35.
- To Richmond at 5 pm and 1 am. From **88 E Broadway** to 2808 W Broad St: one-way $40, round-trip $60.

Today's Bus • 212-964-6334 • www.todaysbus.com
- To Philadelphia every hour between 7 am and 11 pm. From **88 E Broadway** to 1041 Race St: one-way $12, round trip $20.
- To DC 14 times a day between 7:15 am and 11 pm. From **88 E Broadway** to 6101 St NW: one-way $20, round trip $35.
- To Norfolk, VA, at 6 pm. From **13 Allen St** to 649 Newton Rd: one-way $25, round trip $40.
- To Richmond, VA, at 5 pm. From **88 E Broadway** to 5215 W Broad St: one-way $40, round trip $60.
- To Atlanta, GA, at 8 pm. From **109 E Broadway** to 5150 Buford Hwy NE: one-way $90, round trip $170.

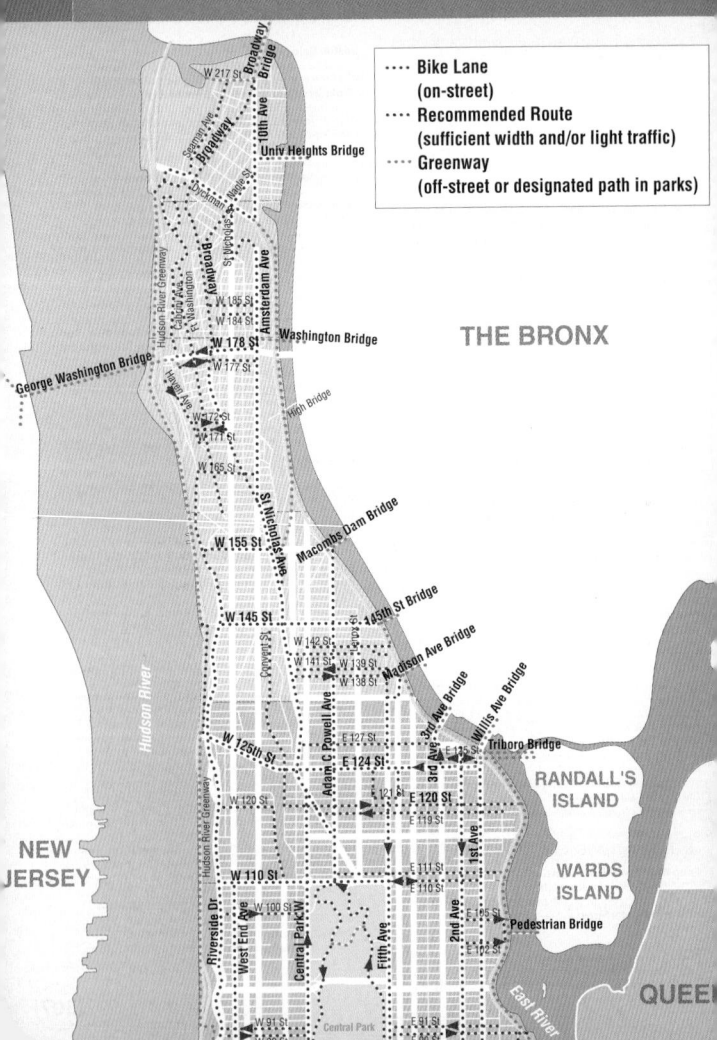

Transit · Biking & Skating in Manhattan

····· **Bike Lane**
(on-street)

····· **Recommended Route**
(sufficient width and/or light traffic)

····· **Greenway**
(off-street or designated path in parks)

THE BRONX

NEW JERSEY

RANDALL'S ISLAND

WARDS ISLAND

QUEEN

Hudson River

East River

Broadway Bridge

Univ Heights Bridge

Washington Bridge

George Washington Bridge

High Bridge

Macombs Dam Bridge

145th St Bridge

Madison Ave Bridge

3rd Ave Bridge

Willis Ave Bridge

Triboro Bridge

Pedestrian Bridge

Hudson River Greenway

Riverside Dr

West End Ave

Central Park W

Central Park

Fifth Ave

W 217 St

10th Ave

Seaman Ave

Broadway

Dyckman St

Payson Ave

St Nicholas Ave

Kappock St

Amsterdam Ave

W 185 St

W 184 St

W 178 St

W 177 St

W 172 St

W 171 St

W 165 St

W 155 St

St Nicholas Ave

W 145 St

W 142 St

W 141 St

W 139 St

W 138 St

Powell St

Broadway

Adam C Powell Ave

E 127 St

E 124 St

E 120 St

E 119 St

E 111 St

E 110 St

E 105 St

E 91 St

E 90 St

W 125 St

W 120 St

W 110 St

W 100 St

W 91 St

W 90 St

3rd Ave

2nd Ave

1st Ave

E 135 St

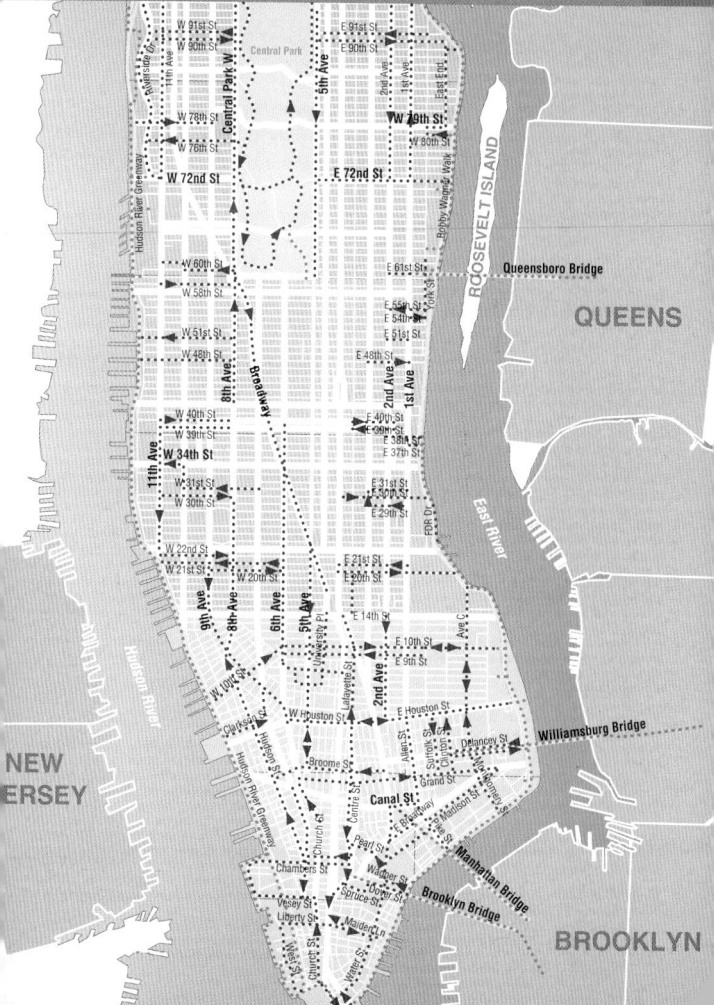

General Information

Bicycle Defense Fund:	www.bicycledefensefund.org
Bike New York, Five Borough Bike Tour:	www.bikenewyork.org
Century Road Club Association (CRCA):	www.crca.net
Department of City Planning:	www.nyc.gov/html/dcp/html/bike/home.shtml
Department of Parks & Recreation:	www.nycgovparks.org
Department of Transportation:	www.nyc.gov/html/dot/html/bicyclists/bikemain.shtml
Empire Skate Club:	www.empireskate.org
Fast & Fabulous Lesbian & Gay Bike Club:	www.fastnfab.org
Five Boro Bicycle Club:	www.5bbc.org
League of American Bicyclists:	www.bikeleague.org
New York Bicycle Coalition:	www.nybc.net
New York Cycle Club:	www.nycc.org
NYC Streets Renaissance:	www.nycstreets.org
Time's Up! Bicycle Advocacy Group:	www.times-up.org
Transportation Alternatives:	www.transalt.org

Overview

While not for the faint of heart, biking and skating around Manhattan can be one of the most efficient and exhilarating forms of transportation. Transportation Alternatives estimates that over 130,000 New Yorkers hop on a bike each day—an all-time high for the city. Manhattan is relatively flat, and the fitness and environmental advantages of using people power are incontrovertible. However, there are also some downsides, including, but not limited to, psychotic cab drivers, buses, traffic, pedestrians, pavement with potholes, glass, debris, and poor air quality. In 1994, the Bicycle Network Development Program was created to increase bicycle usage in the NYC area. Since then, many bike lanes have been created on streets and in parks (see map on previous page). These tend to be the safest places to ride, though they often get blocked by parked or standing cars. Central Park is a great place to ride, as are the newly developed paths from Battery Park that run along the Hudson River. East River Park is another nice destination for recreational riding and skating—just not after dark! In addition to bicycle rentals, Pedal Pusher Bike Shop (1306 Second Ave, 212-288-5592) offers recorded tours of Central Park, so you can learn about the park and exercise at the same time. There is also talk of creating a city wide bike rental program similar to the one that recently launched in Paris. Let's hope that New York jumps on board!

Recreational skating venues in Manhattan include Wollman and Lasker Rinks in Central Park, Chelsea Piers, Riverbank State Park (679 Riverside Drive at 145th St), and Rivergate Ice Rink (401 E 34th St). If you're looking for a place to get your skates sharpened to your own personal specifications before hitting the ice, contact Westside Skate & Stick (174 Fifth Ave, 212-228-8400), a custom pro shop for hockey and figure skaters that's by appointment only. For more information on skating venues throughout the boroughs, check out www.skatecity.com. For organized skaters, visit the Empire Skate Club at www.empireskate.org.

Bikes are sometimes less convenient than skates. Where skates can be tucked in a bag and carried onto subways, indoors, or on buses, bikes have to be locked up on the street and are always at risk of being stolen. Unfortunately, bike racks are hard to come by in NYC, so you may need to get creative on where to park. Always lock them to immovable objects and don't skimp on a cheap bike lock. With over 40,000 bikes a year stolen in NYC, the extra cost for a top-of-the-line bike lock is worth it. On the upside, bikes provide a much faster, less demanding form of transportation around the city.

Crossing the Bridges by Bike

Crossing the Brooklyn, Manhattan, or Williamsburg Bridges by bike is a great way for Brooklynites to commute to work (unless, of course, it's really windy and cold out). Riding across these bridges also makes for a great weekend outing for Manhattanites and Brooklynites alike. All bridges afford amazing views of the Manhattan and Brooklyn skylines. In the fall of 2003, the DOT estimated that nearly 4,000 cyclists crossed the East River bridges each day. It just isn't healthy to stay underground so much, so gear up and give it a go.

Brooklyn Bridge

Separate bicycle and pedestrian lanes run down the center of the bridge, with the bicycle lane on the north side and the pedestrian lane on the south. Cyclists should beware of wayfaring tourists taking photographs. We do not recommend rollerblading across the bridge—the wooden planks make for quite a bumpy ride. The bridge is quite level and, aside from the tourists and planks, fairly easy to traverse.
Brooklyn Access: Stairs to Cadman Plz E and Prospect St, ramp to Johnson & Adams Sts
Manhattan Access: Park Row and Centre St, across from City Hall Park

Manhattan Bridge

The last of the Brooklyn crossings to be outfitted with decent pedestrian and bike paths, the Manhattan Bridge bike and pedestrian paths are on separate sides of the bridge. The walking path is on the south side, and the bike path is on the north side of the bridge. The major drawback to walking across the Manhattan Bridge is that you have to climb a steep set of stairs on the Brooklyn side (not the best conditions for lugging around a stroller or suitcase). Fortunately, the bike path on the north side of the bridge is ramped on both approaches. However, be careful on Jay Street when accessing the bridge in Brooklyn due to the dangerous, fast-moving traffic.
Brooklyn Access: Jay St & Sands St
Manhattan Access: Bike Lane–Canal St & Forsyth St
Pedestrian Lane–Bowery, just south of Canal St

Williamsburg Bridge
The Williamsburg Bridge has the widest pedestrian/bike path of the three bridges to Brooklyn. The path on the north side, shared by cyclists and pedestrians, is 12 feet wide. The southern path, at eight feet wide, is also shared by bikers and walkers. Unfortunately, only one of the paths seems to be open at any give time for some illogical reason. However, during the 2005 transit strike both sides were open, and hopefully this will become the norm someday soon. As a bonus fitness feature, the steep gradient on both the Manhattan and Brooklyn sides of the bridge gives bikers and pedestrians a good workout.
Brooklyn Access: North Entrance–Driggs Ave, right by the Washington Plz
*South Entrance–*Bedford Ave b/w S 5th & S 6th Sts
Manhattan Access: Delancey St & Clinton St/Suffolk St

George Washington Bridge
Bikers get marginalized by the pedestrians on this crossway to New Jersey. The north walkway is for pedestrians only, and the south side is shared by pedestrians and bikers. Cyclists had to fight to keep their right to even bike on this one walkway, as city officials wanted to institute a "walk your bike across" rule to avoid bicycle/pedestrian accidents during construction. The bikers won the battle but are warned to "exercise extra caution" when passing pedestrians.
Manhattan Access: W 178th St & Fort Washington Ave
New Jersey Access: Hudson Ter in Fort Lee

Triborough Bridge
Biking is officially prohibited on this two-mile span that connects the Bronx, Queens, and Manhattan. Unofficially, people ride between the boroughs and over to Wards Island all the time. The bike path is quite narrow, compared to the paths on other bridges, and the lighting at night is mediocre at best. The tight path sees less pedestrian/cycling traffic than other bridges, which, paired with the insufficient lighting, gives the span a rather ominous feeling after dark. If you're worried about safety, or keen on obeying the laws, the 103rd Street footbridge provides an alternative way to reach Wards Island sans car. This pedestrian pass is open only during the warmer months, and then only during daylight hours. See page 297 for more information about the footbridge schedule.
Bronx Access: 133rd St & Cypress Ave
Manhattan Access: Ramps--124/126th Sts & First Ave Stairs–Second Ave and 124/126 Sts
Queens Access: 26th St & Hoyt Ave (beware of extremely steep stairs).

Queensboro Bridge
The north outer roadway of the Queensboro Bridge is open exclusively to bikers, 24/7, except for the day of the New York Marathon. More than 2,500 cyclists and pedestrians per day traverse the bridge. Bikers complain about safety issues on the Manhattan side of the bridge: With no direct connection from Manhattan onto the bridge's West Side, bikers are forced into an awkward five-block detour to get to Second Avenue, where they can finally access the bridge.
Manhattan Entrance: 60th St, b/w First Ave & Second Ave
Queens Entrance: Queens Plz & Crescent St

Bike Rentals (and Sales)

Metro Bicycle Stores:
• 1311 Lexington Ave & 88th St • 212-427-4450 • Map 17
• 360 W 47th St & Ninth Ave • 212-581-4500 • Map 11
• 213 W 96th St & Broadway • 212-663-7531 • Map 16
• 332 E 14th St, b/w First & Second aves • 212-228-4344 • Map 6
• 546 Sixth Ave & W 15th St • 212-255-5100 • Map 9
• 417 Canal St & Sixth Ave • 212-334-8000 • Map 2
Liberty Bicycles • 846 Ninth Ave & 55th St • 212-757-2418 • Map 11
Toga Bike Shop • 110 West End Ave & 64th St • 212-799-9625 • Map 14
Gotham Bikes • 112 W Broadway b/w Duane & Reade sts • 212-732-2453 • Map 2
Bicycle Habitat • 244 Lafayette St b/w Spring & Prince sts • 212-431-3315 • Map 6
Bicycle Heaven • 348 E 62 St b/w First & Second aves • 212-230-1919 • Map 15
Bike Works • 106 Ridge St b/w Stanton & Rivington sts • 212-388-1077 • Map 7
City Bicycles • 315 W 38th St b/w Eighth & Ninth aves • 212-563-3373 • Map 11
Eddie's Bicycles Shop • 490 Amsterdam Ave b/w 83rd & 84th sts • 212-580-2011 • Map 14
Larry and Jeff's Bicycles Plus • 1400 Third Ave b/w 79th & 80th sts • 212-794-2929 • Map 17
Pedal Pusher Bike Shop • 1306 Second Ave b/w 68th & 69th sts • 212-288-5592 • Map 15
Manhattan Bicycles • 791 Ninth Ave b/w 52nd & 53rd sts • 212-262-0111 • Map 11
New York Cyclist • 301 Cathedral Pkwy & Central Park West • 212-864-4449 • Map 16

Bikes and Mass Transit

Surprisingly, you can take your bike on trains and some buses—just make sure it's not during rush hour and you are courteous to other passengers. The subway requires you to carry your bike down staircases, use the service gate instead of the turnstile, and board at the very front or back end of the train. To ride the commuter railroads with your bike, you may need to purchase a bike permit. For appropriate contact information, see transportation pages.

Amtrak: Train with baggage car required.
LIRR: $5 permit required.
Metro-North: $5 permit required.
New Jersey Transit: No permit required.
PATH: No permit required.
New York Water Taxi: No fee or permit required
NY Waterway: $1 fee.
Staten Island Ferry: Enter at lower level.
Bus companies: Call individual companies.

Sports · Chelsea Piers

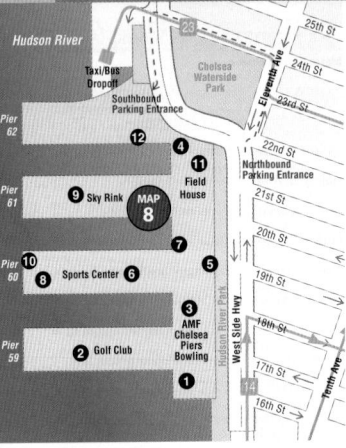

you were approaching from the north. Parking costs $12 for the first hour, $16 for two, $20 for three. Street parking in the West 20s is an excellent alternative in the evenings after 6 pm.

Facilities

Chelsea Piers is amazing. There are swimming pools, ice-skating rinks, a bowling alley, spa, restaurants, shops, batting cages—you name it. So, what's the catch? Well, it's gonna cost ya. Like Manhattan rents, only investment bankers can afford this place.

1 **Chelsea Brewing Company** · 212-336-6440. Microbrewery and restaurant. Try the amber ale, wings, nachos, and cheesy fries—all excellent.

2 **The Golf Club at Chelsea Piers** · 212-336-6410. Aside from potentially long wait times, the 250-yard driving range with 52 heated stalls and automated ball-feed (no buckets or bending over!) is pretty awesome. $25 buys you 90 balls (peak) or 147 balls (off-peak). If you don't bring your own, club hire is $4/one club, $5/two, $6/three, or $12/ten. Before 5 pm on weekdays, you can whack all the balls you want for an hour for $20 plus free club rental.

3 **300 New York** · 212-835-BOWL. A very schmancy 40-lane bowling alley equipped with video games and bar. $8/game plus $6 shoe rental.

4 **Ruthy's Bakery & Café** · 212-336-6333. Pastries and sandwiches.

5 **New York Presbyterian Sports Medicine Center** · 212-366-5100. Performance physical therapy.

6 **The Spa at Chelsea Piers** · 212-336-6780. It's not Canyon Ranch. A basic 50-minute massage is $105, a basic 50-minute facial is $105. They also have a range of scrubs, wraps, polishes, manicures, pedicures, and waxes.

7 **College Sports Television** · Street-level broadcast center accessible to the public with interactive events and activities for college sports fans.

8 **The Sports Center** · 212-336-6000. A very expensive, monster health club with a 10,000-square-foot climbing wall, a quarter-mile track, a swimming pool, and enough fitness equipment for a small army in training. If you have to ask how much the membership is, you can't afford it.

9 **Sky Rink** · 212-336-6100. Two 24/7 ice rinks mainly used for classes, training, and bar mitzvahs.

10 **The Lighthouse** · 212-336-6144. 10,000-square-foot event space for private gatherings catered by Abigail Kirsch.

11 **The Field House** · 212-336-6500. The Field House is an 80,000-square-foot building with a 23-foot climbing wall, a gymnastics training center, four batting cages, two basketball courts, and two indoor soccer fields. A season (ten games plus playoffs) of league soccer costs $230/person, league basketball costs $185/person, rock-climbing costs $18/class, and gymnastics costs $25/class.

12 **Spirit Cruise** · 866-483-3866; www.spiritofnewyork.com. Ships run out of Chelsea Piers and Weehawken, NJ. Dinner cruises are approximately $70/person, and if you're having a big function, you can rent the entire boat

General Information

Website: www.chelseapiers.com

Overview

Opened in 1910 as a popular port for trans-Atlantic ships, Chelsea Piers found itself neglected and deteriorating by the 1960s. In 1992, Roland W. Betts (fraternity brother of George W. Bush) began the plan to renovate and refurbish the piers as a gargantuan 28-acre sports and entertainment center. In 1995, Chelsea Piers re-opened its doors to the public at a final cost of $120 million—all private money. The only help from the state was a very generous 49-year lease. By 1998, Chelsea Piers was the third most popular attraction in New York City, after Times Square and the Map Room at the NY Public Library.

How to Get There

Unless you live in Chelsea, it's a real pain to get to the Piers. The closest subway is the C E to 23rd Street and Eighth Avenue, and then it's still a three-avenue block hike there. If you're lucky, you can hop a 23 bus on 23rd Street and expedite the last leg of your journey. L train commuters should get off at the Eighth Avenue stop and take the 14 bus across to the West Side Highway where you'll be dropped off at 18th Street.

If you drive, entering from the south can be a little tricky. It's pretty well signed, so keep your eyes peeled. Basically you exit right at Eleventh Avenue and 22nd Street, turn left onto 24th Street, and then make a left onto the West Side Highway. Enter Chelsea Piers the same way you would if

Unfortunately, but not surprisingly, there are no golf courses on the island of Manhattan. Thankfully, there are two driving ranges where you can at least smack the ball around until you can get to a real course, as well as a golf simulator at Chelsea Piers that lets you play a full round "at" various popular courses (Pebble Beach, St. Andrews, etc.). NYC has a number of private and public courses throughout the outer boroughs and Westchester; however, they don't even come close to satisfying the area's huge demand for courses.

Golf Courses

	Borough	Address	Phone	Par	Fee
Mosholu Golf Course	Bronx	3700 Jerome Ave	718-655-9164	9 holes, par 30	Weekend fees $17.75/early, twilight/$39.50 morning and afternoon - weekday fees $16.75-$28, non-residents add $8.
Pelham/Split Rock Golf	Bronx	870 Shore Rd	718-885-1258	18 holes, par 71	Weekend fees $17.75/early, twilight/$39.50 morning and afternoon - weekday fees $16.75-$28, non-residents add $8.
Van Cortlandt Golf Course	Bronx	Van Cortlandt Pk S & Bailey Ave	718-543-4595	18 holes, par 70	M–F/$16.75–$28; weekend $17.75/early, twilight; $39.50 morning and afternoon; non-resident add $8.
Marine Park Golf Club	Brooklyn	2880 Flatbush Ave	718-338-7149	18 holes, par 72	Weekend fees $17/early, twilight/$38 morning and afternoon–weekday fees $16–$27, non-residents add $7
Dyker Beach Golf Course	Brooklyn	86th St & Seventh Ave	718-836-9722	18 holes, par 71	Weekend fees $17/early, twilight/$38 morning and afternoon; weekday fees $16–$27, non-residents add $8
Golf Simulator	New York	Chelsea Piers Golf Club	212-336-6400		$45/hour (see previous Chelsea Piers page)
LaTourette Golf Course	Staten Island	1001 Richmond Hill Rd	718-351-1889	18 holes, par 72	M–F/$16.75–$28; weekend $17.75/early, twilight; $39.50/morning and afternoon; non-resident add $8.
Silver Lake Golf Course	Staten Island	915 Victory Blvd	718-447-5686	18 holes, par 69	M–F/$16.75–$28; weekend $17.75/early, twilight; $39.50/morning and afternoon; non-resident add $8.
South Shore Golf Course	Staten Island	200 Huguenot Ave	718-984-0101	18 holes, par 72	M–F/$16.75–$28; weekend $17.75/early, twilight; $39.50/morning and afternoon; non-resident add $8.
Clearview Golf Course	Queens	202-12 Willets Point Blvd	718-229-2570	18 holes, par 70	Weekend fees $17.75/early, twilight/$39.50 morning and afternoon–weekday fees $16.75–$28, non-residents add $8.
Douglaston Golf Course	Queens	63-20 Marathon Pkwy, Douglaston	718-428-1617	18 holes, par 67	Weekend fees $17.75/early, twilight/$39.50 morning and afternoon–weekday fees $16.75–$28, non-residents add $8.
Forest Park Golf Course	Queens	101 Forest Park Dr, Woodhaven	718-296-0999	18 holes, par 70	Weekend fees $17.75/early, twilight/$39.50 morning and afternoon–weekday fees $16.75–$28, non-residents add $8.
Kissena Park Golf Course	Queens	164-15 Booth Memorial Ave	718-939-4594	18 holes, Par 64	Weekend fees $17.75/early, twilight/$39.50 morning and afternoon–weekday fees $16.75–$28, non-residents add $8.

Driving Ranges

	Address	Phone	Fee
Brooklyn Sports Center	Brooklyn	3200 Flatbush Ave	718-253-6816	$10 for 150 balls, $12 for 285 balls
Chelsea Piers: Pier 59	Manhattan	Pier 59	212-336-6400	$20 for 118 balls, $30 for 186 balls
Randall's Island Golf	Manhattan	1 Randalls Rd	212-427-5689	$12 for 119 balls
Center Golden Bear	Queens	232-01 Northern Blvd	718-225-9187	$10 for large bucket, $7.50 for small bucket

Gyms

Gyms	Address	Phone	Map
24/7 Fitness Club	47 W 14th St	212-206-1504	6
92nd Street Y–May Center	1395 Lexington Ave	212-415-5700	17
Athletic and Swim Club at Equitable Center	787 7th Ave	212-265-3490	12
Bally Total Fitness	641 6th Ave	212-645-4565	9
Bally Total Fitness	45 E 55th St	212-688-6630	12
Bally Total Fitness	350 W 50th St	212-265-9400	11
Bally Total Fitness	139 W 32nd St	212-465-1750	9
Bally Total Fitness	1915 3rd Ave	212-369-3063	17
Battery Park Swim & Fitness Center	375 South End Ave	212-321-1117	100
Big Gym	625 W 181st St	212-568-2444	23
Bio-Fitness	244 E 84th St	212-585-4245	15
Body Strength Fitness	250 W 106th St	212-316-3338	16
Boom Fitness	1438 3rd Ave	212-879-6013	15
Boom Fitness	4 Park Ave	212-545-9590	10
Carnegie Park Swim & Health Club	200 E 94th St	212-423-0300	17
Chelsea Piers Sports Center	Chelsea Piers-Pier 60	212-336-6000	8
Chelsea Recreation Center	430 W 25th St	212-255-3705	8
Citi Fitness	244 E 14th St	212-598-9800	6
Clay	25 W 14th St	212-206-9200	6
Club 200 at Bristol Plaza	200 E 65th St	212-688-2929	15
Club 29	155 E 29th St	212-679-2299	10
Club 30	30 W 63rd St	212-247-8404	14
Crunch Fitness	25 Broadway	212-269-1067	1
Crunch Fitness	113 4th Ave	212-533-0001	6
Crunch Fitness	404 Lafayette St	212-614-0120	6
Crunch Fitness	54 E 13th St	212-475-2018	6
Crunch Fitness	623 Broadway	212-420-0507	6
Crunch Fitness	152 Christopher St	212-366-3725	5
Crunch Fitness	1109 2nd Ave	212-758-3434	13
Crunch Fitness	554 2nd Ave	212-545-9757	10
Crunch Fitness	144 W 38th St	212-869-7788	9
Crunch Fitness	162 W 83rd St	212-875-1902	14
Crunch Fitness	555 W 42nd St	212-594-8050	11
Curves	118 Water St	212-269-3600	1
Curves	36 W 34th St	212-564-8436	9
Curves	314 W 53rd St	212-245-8600	11
Curves	76 W 85th St	212-875-0800	14
Curves	274 W 145th St	212-281-2277	22
Curves	1711 1st Ave	212-410-7822	17
David Barton Gym	215 W 23rd St	212-414-2022	9
David Barton Gym	30 E 85th St	212-517-7577	15
Dolphin Fitness	94 E 4th St	212-387-9500	6
Dolphin Fitness	18 Avenue B	212-777-1001	7
Eastern Athletic	80 Leonard St	212-966-5432	3
Edge Gyms New York	403 E 91st St	212-722-0076	17
Elysium Fitness Club	117 W 72nd St	212-721-1010	14
Equinox	450 W 17th St	212-367-0863	8
Equinox Fitness	1 Park Ave	212-779-1727	10
Equinox Fitness	69 Prince St	212-334-4631	6
Equinox Fitness	521 5th Ave	212-972-8000	12
Equinox Fitness	420 Lexington Ave	212-953-2499	13
Equinox Fitness	205 E 85th St	212-439-8500	15
Equinox Fitness	2465 Broadway	212-799-1818	16
Equinox Fitness	140 E 63rd St	212-750-4900	15
Equinox Fitness	250 E 54th St	212-277-5400	13
Equinox Fitness	10 Columbus Cir	212-871-0425	12
Equinox Fitness	1633 Broadway	212-541-7000	12
Equinox Fitness	97 Greenwich Ave	212-620-0103	5
Equinox Fitness	897 Broadway	212-780-9300	9
Equinox Fitness	54 Murray St	212-566-6555	2
Equinox Fitness	14 Wall St	212-964-6688	1
Excelsior Athletic Club	301 E 57th St	212-688-5280	13

Gyms	Address	Phone	Map
The Fitness Club	11 Madison Ave	212-325-9300	9
Fitness Express Manhattan	142 W 72nd St	212-873-3377	14
Five Points Fitness	444 Broadway	212-226-4474	3
Gold's Gym	250 W 54th St	212-307-7760	12
Golds Gym	90 John St	212-227-0005	1
Gravity Fitness Center	118 W 57th St	212-245-5000	12
Hanson Fitness	795 Broadway	212-982-2233	6
Hanson Fitness	63 Greene St	212-431-7682	6
Hanson Fitness	132 Perry St	212-741-2000	5
Heartworks Health & Fitness Center	180 Maiden Ln	212-742-0110	1
The JCC in Manhattan	334 Amsterdam Ave	646-505-4444	14
John Street Fitness	80 John St	212-248-3030	1
Lenox Hill Neighborhood House	331 E 70th St	212-744-5022	15
Liberty Club MCB	200 Rector Pl	212-945-4200	100
Lift Gym	139 E 57th St	212-688-3304	13
Lucille Roberts Health Club	80 5th Ave	212-255-3999	6
Lucille Roberts Health Club	300 W 40th St	212-268-4199	12
Lucille Roberts Health Club	505 W 125th St	212-222-2522	18
Lucille Roberts Health Club	1387 St Nicholas Ave	212-927-8376	23
Lucille Roberts Health Club	143 Fulton St	212-267-3730	1
Manhattan Plaza Health Club	482 W 43rd St	212-563-7001	11
Mid City Gym	244 W 49th St	212-582-8924	12
Monterey Sports Club	175 E 96th St	212-996-8200	17
New York Athletic Club	180 Central Park S	212-247-5100	12
New York Health & Racquet Club	115 E 57th St	212-826-9650	13
New York Health & Racquet Club	110 W 56th St	212-541-7200	12
New York Health & Racquet Club	39 Whitehall St	212-269-9800	1
New York Health & Racquet Club	24 E 13th St	212-924-4600	6
New York Health & Racquet Club	20 E 50th St	212-593-1500	12
New York Health & Racquet Club	1433 York Ave	212-737-6666	15
New York Health & Racquet Club	132 E 45th St	212-986-3100	13
New York Health & Racquet Club	60 W 23rd St	212-989-2300	9
New York House & Racquet Club	62 Cooper Square	212-904-0400	6
New York Underground Fitness	440 W 57th St	212-957-4781	11
NYC Fitness	3552 Broadway	212-368-1700	21
NYSC	225 Varick St	212-645-0995	5
NYSC	885 2nd Ave	212-371-2113	13
NYSC	19 W 44th St	212-768-3535	12
NYSC	230 W 41st St	646-366-9400	12
NYSC	2311 Frederick Douglass Blvd	212-316-2500	19
NYSC	151 E 86th St	212-860-8630	17
NYSC	2527 Broadway	212-665-0009	16
NYSC	23 W 73rd St	212-496-6300	14
NYSC	61 W 62nd St	212-265-0995	14
NYSC	2162 Broadway	212-496-2444	14
NYSC	248 W 80th St	212-873-1500	14
NYSC	200 Park Ave	212-682-4440	13
NYSC	1637 3rd Ave	212-987-7200	17
NYSC	102 North End Ave	212-945-3535	100
NYSC	160 Water St	212-363-4600	1
NYSC	10 Irving Pl	212-477-1800	10
NYSC	217 Broadway	212-791-9555	3
NYSC	30 Wall St	212-482-4800	1
NYSC	50 W 34th St	212-868-0820	9
NYSC	113 E 23rd St	212-982-4400	10
NYSC	128 8th Ave	212-627-0065	8
NYSC	270 8th Ave	212-243-3400	8
NYSC	34 W 14th St	212-337-9900	6
NYSC	232 Mercer St	212-780-7407	6
NYSC	503 Broadway	212-975-6600	6
NYSC	125 7th Ave S	212-206-1500	5
NYSC	151 Reade St	212-571-1000	2

Gyms

Gyms	Address	Phone	Map
NYSC	1221 6th Ave	212-840-8240	12
NYSC	1601 Broadway	212-977-8880	12
NYSC	1657 Broadway	212-307-9400	12
NYSC	349 E 76th St	212-288-5700	15
NYSC	502 Park Ave	212-308-1010	13
NYSC	575 Lexington Ave	212-317-9400	13
NYSC	633 3rd Ave	212-661-8500	13
NYSC	131 E 31st St	212-213-1408	10
NYSC	200 Madison Ave	212-686-1144	9
NYSC	3 Park Ave	212-686-1085	10
NYSC	614 2nd Ave	212-213-5999	10
NYSC	1372 Broadway	212-575-4500	9
NYSC	1400 5th Ave	212-722-1185	19
NYSC	303 W 145th St	212-234-0016	21
Paris Health Club	752 West End Ave	212-749-3500	16
Peak Performance Sport & Fitness Center	54 W 21st St	212-229-3670	9
Printing House Fitness & Racquet Club	421 Hudson St	212-243-7600	5
Promenade Health Club	530 E 76th St	212-249-5232	15
Reebok Sports Club NY	160 Columbus Ave	212-362-6800	14
Rivergate Fitness Center	401 E 34th St	212-684-5093	10
Sheraton New York & Manhattan Health Clubs	811 7th Ave	212-841-6714	12
Sol Goldman Y	344 E 14th St	212-780-0800	6
Sports Club/LA	330 E 61st St	212-355-5100	15
Sports Club/LA	45 Rockefeller Plaza	212-218-8600	12
Steel Gym	146 W 23rd St	212-352-9876	9
Strathmore Swim & Health Club	400 E 84th St	212-396-3214	15
Strive Health and Fitness	330 E 59th St	212-486-6966	13
Synergy Fitness Clubs	227 Mulberry St	212-219-6383	6
Synergy Fitness Clubs	321 E 22nd St	212-679-7300	10
Synergy Fitness Clubs	138 W 14 St	212-414-8430	5
Synergy Fitness Clubs	2130 Broadway	212-501-9069	14
Synergy Fitness Clubs	1781 2nd Ave	212-426-0909	17
The Training Ground	118 W 72nd St	212-362-2924	14
West End Sports Club	75 West End Ave	212-265-8200	14
YMCA Harlem	180 W 135th St	212-281-4100	19
YMCA McBurney	125 W 14th St	212-741-9210	5
YMCA Vanderbilt	224 E 47th St	212-756-9600	13
YMCA West Side	5 W 63rd St	212-875-4100	14

Sports • **Swimming**

For swimming pools in Manhattan, you pretty much have two options: pay exorbitant gym fees or health club fees in order to use the private swimming facilities, or wait until the summer to share the city's free outdoor pools with openly urinating summer camp attendees. OK, so it's not that bad! Some YMCAs and YWCAs have indoor pools, and their fees are reasonable. And several of the same New York public recreation centers that have outdoor pools (and some that do not) have indoor pools for year-round swimming. Though plenty of kids use the pools, there are dedicated adult swim hours in the mornings, at lunch time, and in the evenings (pee-free if you get there early). Just don't forget to follow each pool's admittance ritual, strange as it may seem—the locker room attendants generally rule with an iron fist. And if you can wait the obligatory 30 minutes, there's an authentic local food court near the standout public pool in Red Hook (155 Bay St, Brooklyn).

Then there's the Hudson. Yes, we're serious. There are about eight races in the Hudson each year, and the water quality is tested before each race. New York City also has some great beaches for swimming, including Coney Island, Manhattan Beach, and the Rockaways. If you prefer your swimming area enclosed, check out the pool options in Manhattan:

Pools

	Address	Phone	Type	Fees	Map
All Star Fitness Center	75 West End Ave	212-265-8200	Indoor	$16/day	14
Asphalt Green	555 E 90th St	212-369-8890	Indoor	$25/day	17
Asser Levy Recreation Center	E 23rd St & Asser Levy Pl	212-447-2020	Indoor, Outdoor	Outdoor free, Indoor $75/year	10
Athletic and Swim Club at Equitable Center	787 Seventh Ave	212-265-3490	Indoor	Call for fees	12
Bally's Sports Club	139 W 32nd St	212-465-1750	Indoor	$25/day	9
Bally's Sports Club	335 Madison Ave	212-983-5320	Indoor	$25/day	12
Bally's Sports Club	350 W 50th St	212-265-9400	Indoor	$25/day	11
Battery Park Swim & Fitness Center	375 South End Ave	212-321-1117	Indoor	Call for fees	p234
Chelsea Piers Sports Center	Pier 60	212-336-6000	Indoor	$75/day	8
Chelsea Recreation Center	430 W 25th St	212-255-3705	Indoor	$75/year	8
Excelsior Athletic Club	301 E 57th St	212-688-5280	Indoor	$75/day	7
Gravity Fitness Center	118 W 57th St	212-245-5000	Indoor	$50/day	12
Hamilton Fish Recreation Center	128 Pitt St	212-387-7687	Outdoor - Summer months	Free	23
Hansborough Recreation Center	35 W 134th St	212-234-9603	Indoor	$75/year	21
Highbridge	2301 Amsterdam Ave	212-927-2400	Outdoor - Summer Months	Free	21
Holiday Inn	440 W 57th St	212-581-8100	Outdoor - Call for fees		11
Jackie Robinson Pool	85 Bradhurst Ave	212-234-9607	Outdoor - Summer months	Free	21
John Jay	E 77th St & Cherokee Pl	212-794-6566	Outdoor - Summer months	Free	15
Lasker Pool	110th St & Lenox Ave	212-534-7639	Outdoor - Summer months	Free	19
Lenox Hill Neighborhood House	331 E 70th St	212-744-5022	Indoor		15
Manhattan Plaza Health Club	482 W 43rd St	212-563-7001	Indoor - Summer months	$35/day	11
Marcus Garvey Swimming Pool	13 E 124th St	212-410-2818	Outdoor - Summer months	Free	20
New York Health & Racquet Club	110 W 56th St	212-541-7200	Indoor	$50/day or $99/month	12
New York Health & Racquet Club	115 E 57th St	212-826-9650	Indoor	$50/day or $99/month	13
New York Health & Racquet Club	132 E 45th St	212-986-3100	Indoor	$50/day or $99/month	13
New York Health & Racquet Club	1433 York Ave	212-737-6666	Indoor	$50/day or $99/month	15
New York Health & Racquet Club	20 E 50th St	212-593-1500	Indoor	$50/day or $99/month	13
New York Health & Racquet Club	24 E 13th St	212-924-4600	Indoor	$50/day or $$99/month	6
New York Health & Racquet Club	39 Whitehall St	212-269-9800	Indoor	$50/day or $99/month	1
New York Health & Racquet Club	62 Cooper Sq	212-904-0400	Indoor	$50/day or $99/month	6
New York Sports Club	1601 Broadway	212-977-8880	Indoor	$25/day	12
New York Sports Club	1637 Third Ave	212-987-7200	Indoor	$25/day	17
New York Sports Club	614 Second Ave	212-213-5999	Indoor	$25/day	10
Pelham Fritz	18 Mount Morris Park W	212-410-2818	Outdoor - Summer months	Free	19
Recreation Center 54	348 E 54th St	212-754-5411	Indoor	$75/year	13
Recreation Center 59	533 W 59th St	212-397-3159	Indoor	$75/year	11
Reebok Sports Club NY	160 Columbus Ave	212-362-6800	Indoor	$188/month	14
Riverbank State Park	679 Riverside Dr	212-694-3600	Indoor - Summer months	$2/day	21
Sheraton New York Health Club	2180 First Ave	212-621-8591	Indoor - Summer months	Free	12
Thomas Jefferson Swimming Pool	500 E 16th St	212-387-7685	Outdoor - Summer months	Free	7
Tompkins Square Mini Pool	1 Clarkson St	212-242-5228	Indoor, Outdoor	$75/year	5
Tony Dapolito Recreation Center	1 UN Plz 41st Floor	212-702-5016	Indoor	$30/day or $88/month	14
UN Plaza Health Club	1395 Lexington Ave	212-415-5700	Indoor	$30/day or $88/month	7
YMCA	180 W 135th St	212-281-4100	Indoor	$30/day or $88/month	19
YMCA	224 E 47th St	212-756-9600	Indoor	$30/day or $88/month	13
YMCA	344 E 14th St	212-780-0800	Indoor	$20/day	6

(317)

Sports · Tennis

General Information

Manhattan Parks Dept: 212-360-8131 • Website: www.nycgovparks.org
Permit Locations: The Arsenal, 830 5th Ave & 64th St; Paragon Sporting Goods Store, 867 Broadway & 18th St

Overview

There are more tennis courts on the island of Manhattan than you might think, although getting to them may be a bit more than you bargained for. Most of the public courts in Manhattan are either smack in the middle of Central Park or are on the edges of the city—such as East River Park (Map 7) and Riverside Park (Map 16). These courts in particular can make for some pretty windy playing conditions.

Tennis

Tennis	Address	Phone	Type/ # of Cts./Surface	Map
Coles Center, NYU	181 Mercer St	212-998-2020	Schools, 9 courts, Rubber	3
East River Park Tennis Courts	FDR Dr & Broome St	212-387-7678	Public, Outdoor, 12 courts, Hard	7
Midtown Tennis Club	341 Eighth Ave	212-989-8572	Private, 8 courts, Har-Tru	8
Manhattan Plz Racquet Club	450 W 43rd St	212-594-0554	Private, 5 courts, Cushioned Hard	11
Millennium UN Plaza Hotel Gym	44th & First Ave	212-758-1234	Private, 1 court, Supreme	13
River Club	447 E 52nd St	212-751-0100	Private, 2 courts, Clay	13
The Tennis Club	15 Vanderbilt Ave, 3rd Fl	212-687-3841	Private, 2 courts, Hard	13
Town Tennis Club	430 E 56th St	212-752-4059	Private, 2 courts, Clay, Hard	13
Rockefeller University	1230 York Ave	212-327-8000	Schools, 1 court, Hard	15
Sutton East Tennis Club	York Ave & 60th St	212-751-3452	Private, 8 courts, Clay, Available Oct–April.	15
Central Park Tennis Center	93rd St near West Dr	212-280-0205	Public, Outdoor, 26 Fast-Dry, 4 Hard	16
Riverside Park	Riverside Dr & W 119th St	212-978-0277	Public, Outdoor, 10 courts, Hard	16
PS 146 Ann M Short	421 E 106th St	n/a	Schools, 3 courts, Hard	17
Tower Tennis Courts	1725 York Ave	212-860-2464	Private, 2 courts, Hard	17
PS 125 Ralph Bunche	425 W 123rd St	n/a	Schools, 3 courts, Hard	18
Riverside Park	Riverside Dr & W 96th St	212-469-2006	Public, Outdoor, 10 courts, Clay	18
PS 144	134 W 122nd St	n/a	Schools, 4 courts, Hard	19
Riverbank State Park	W 145th St & Riverside Dr	212-694-3600	Public, Outdoor, 1 court, Hard	21
F Johnson Playground	W 151st St & Seventh Ave	212-234-9609	Public, Outdoor, 8 courts, Hard	22
Fort Washington Park	Hudson River & 170th St	212-304-2322	Public, Outdoor, 10 courts, Hard	23
PS 187	349 Cabrini Blvd	n/a	Schools, 4 courts, Hard	24
Columbia Tennis Center	575 W 218th St	212-942-7100	Private, 6 courts, Hard	25
Inwood Park	207th St & Seaman Ave	212-304-2381	Public, Outdoor, 9 courts, Hard	25
Roosevelt Island Racquet Club	281 Main St	212-935-0250	Private, 12 courts, Clay	p260
Randall's Island	East & Harlem Rivers	212-860-1827	Public, Outdoor, 11 courts, Hard	p254
Randall's Island Indoor Tennis	Randall's Island Park	212-427-6150	Private, 4 courts, Hard Available Oct–April.	p254

Getting a Permit

The tennis season, according to the NYC Parks Department, lasts from April 7 to November 18. Permits are good for use until the end of the season at all public courts in all boroughs, and are good for one hour of singles or two hours of doubles play. Fees are:

Juniors (17 yrs and under) $10
Senior Citizen (62 yrs and over) $20

Adults (18–61 yrs) $100
Single-play tickets $7

When it comes to yoga, New York City has it better than other places in the country, where yoga is often confined to sweaty, ping-pong-table-inhabited back rooms in makeshift recreation centers. Luckily, New Yorkers have an array of charming, airy, sometimes even glossy studios in which to practice—as well as what seems to be an infinite variety of yoga styles to choose from. You can mellow out in meditation, relax in Restorative, practice Pranayama, kick-it Kundalini style, vie for the Vinyasa vibe, jive with Jivamukti, awaken your spirit with Ashtanga, investigate Iyengar, or bend it like Bikram—just to name a few. To get

you started, here's a short list of places to try. Remember, it's always a good idea to contact studios in advance for information about their different approaches to classes, what branches of yoga they teach, class sizes, appropriate attire, cost, and schedules.

Word to the wise: You may want to begin with an introductory class wherever you land. Even seasoned yogis will want to familiarize themselves with the methods of each studio before jumping in headstand first.

Yoga

	Address	Phone	Website	Map
Kula Yoga Project	28 Warren St, 4th Fl	212-945-4460	www.kulayoga.com	2
Dance New Amsterdam	280 Broadway	212-625-8369	www.dancespace.com	3
Virayoga	580 Broadway, Ste 1109	212-334-9960	www.virayoga.com	3
Integral Yoga Institute	227 W 13th St	212-929-0586	www.integralyogany.org	5
Mahayogi Yoga Mission	228 Bleeker St	212-807-8903		5
Practice Yoga	240 W 14th St	212-255-7588	www.practiceyoga.com	5
Yamuna	132 Perry St	212-633-2143	www.yamunastudio.com	5
East West Yoga	78 Fifth Ave	212-243-5995	www.eastwestnyc.com	6
Jivamukti Yoga Center	841 Broadway	212-353-0214	www.jivamuktiyoga.com	6
Lila Yoga and Wellness	302 Bowery	212-254-2130	www.lilawellness.com	6
New York Open Center	83 Spring St	212-219-2527	www.opencenter.org	6
OM Yoga Center	826 Broadway, 6th Fl	212-254-9642	www.omyoga.com	6
Three Jewels Yoga	61 Fourth Ave	212-475-6650	www.threejewels.org	6
Yoga Mandali	560 Broadway	212-473-9001	www.yogamandali.com	6
Ashtanga Yoga Shala	295 E 8th St	212-614-9537	www.ashtangayogashala.net	7
Ramakrishnananda Classic Yoga Society	96 Ave B	646-436-7010	www.ramakrishnananda.com	7
Bikram Yoga NYC	182 Fifth Ave	212-206-9400	www.bikramyoganyc.com	9
The Breathing Project	15 W 26th St	212-979-9642	www.breathingproject.org	9
Dahn Center	37 Union Sq W	212-691-7799	www.dahnyoga.com	9
Dahn Center	830 Sixth Ave	212-725-3262	www.dahnyoga.com	9
Iyengar Yoga Institute	150 W 22nd St	212-691-9642	www.iyengarnyc.org	9
Kundalini Yoga East	873 Broadway	212-982-5959	www.kundaliniyogaeast.com	9
Laughing Lotus	59 W 19th St, 3rd Fl	212-414-2903	www.laughinglotus.com	9
Movements Afoot	151 W 30th St	212-904-1399	www.movementsafoot.com	9
Panetta Movement Center	214 W 29th St	212-239-0831	www.panettamovementcenter.com	9
Prana Mandir	143 E 59th St	212-803-5446	www.pranamandir.com	9
Shambhala Meditation Center of New York	118 W 22nd St	212-675-6544	www.ny.shambhala.org	9
Sivananda Yoga Vedanta Center	243 W 24th St	212-255-4560	www.sivananda.org	9
Universal Force Yoga	7 W 24th St	917-606-1730	www.universalforceyoga.com	9
Yoga Moves	1026 Sixth Ave	212-278-8330	www.yogamovesgyro.com	9
Yoga Works	138 Fifth Ave	212-647-9642	www.yogaworks.com	9
Dharma Yoga Center: Shri Dharma Mittra	297 Third Ave	212-889-8160	www.dharmayogacenter.com	10
NY Underground Fitness	440 W 57th St	212-957-4781	www.nyunderground fitness.com	11
Sonic Yoga	754 Ninth Ave	212-397-6344	www.sonicyoga.com	11
Bikram Yoga NYC	797 Eighth Ave	212-245-2525	www.bikramyoganyc.com	12
BR Manhattan Dahn Yoga Studio	532 Madison Ave	212-935-5777	www.dahnyoga.com	12
exhale	150 Central Park S	212-561-7400	www.exhalespa.com	12
Healthy Tao	250 W 49th St	212-586-2100	www.healthytao.com	12
Levitate Yoga	780 Eighth Ave	212-974-2288	www.levitateyoga.com	12
Yoga Works	160 E 56th St	212-935-9642	www.yogaworks.com	13
Bikram Yoga NYC	143 W 72nd St		www.bikramyoganyc.com	14
Life In Motion	2744 Broadway	212-666-0877	www.lifeinmotion.com	14
Little Yoga Space	102 W 85th St	212-501-8010	www.robinjanisyoga.com	14
Namaste Yoga	371 Amsterdam Ave	212-580-1778	www.namasteyogacenter.net	14
Practice Yoga	140 W 83rd St	212-724-4884	www.practiceyoga.com	14
Steps	2121 Broadway	212-874-2410	www.stepsnyc.com	14
World Yoga Center	265 W 72nd St	212-787-4908	www.worldyogacenter.com	14
Yoga Works	37 W 65th St, 4th Fl	212-769-9642	www.yogaworks.com	14
Bikram Yoga NYC	173 E 83rd St	212-288-9642	www.bikramyoganyc.com	15
Dahn Center	168 E 66th St	212-249-0077	www.dahnyoga.com	15
exhale	980 Madison Ave	212-561-6400	www.exhalespa.com	15
Jivamukti Yoga Studio	853 Lexington Ave	464-290-8106	www.jivamuktiyoga.com	15
MonQi Fitness	201 E 67th St	212-327-2170	www.monqifitness.com	15
New York Yoga HOT	132 E 85th St	212-717-9642	www.newyorkyoga.com	15
Yoga Works	1319 Third Ave	212-650-9642	www.yogaworks.com	15
Baby Om	250 Riverside Dr #25	212-615-6935	www.babyom.com	16
New York Yoga	1629 York Ave	212-717-9642	www.newyorkyoga.com	17
Riverside Church Wellness Center	490 Riverside Dr	212-870-6758	www.theriversidechurchny.org	18
Ta Yoga House	71 W 128th St	212-289-6363	www.ta-life.com	19

319

Whether you're looking for a new hobby or need a new atmosphere in which to booze (that isn't your 300 sq. ft. apartment), a good pool-hall is a great way to get the job done. Or perhaps you simply enjoy a hearty game of 8-ball, and it's as simple as that; in any case, an eclectic mix of options dot the island of Manhattan.

If you're in search of a laid-back, nonsense-free setting, **SoHo Billiards (Map 6)** is best. It occupies a large space with a ton of tables, cheap rates and drinks, small crowds, and a low-key, local scene. **Fat Cat Billiards (Map 5)** is another great option if you're looking for a chill setting—located underground in a dim basement, it holds 20 tables and offers an hourly rate of $4.50 (not to mention the $2 Pabst). For those of you who tire of shiny balls and green felt, there are multiple Scrabble, checkers, and chess stations scattered about—and if that's not enough, there are nightly jazz and comedy performances in the performance room.

In what appears to be a new breed of pool hall, **Slate Resaurant Bar & Billiards (Map 9)** actually has a velvet rope outside, as if to suggest there's something legitimately exclusive about it. Alas, the SoHo House it's not, although there are two levels with plenty of tables, a clean and comfy lounge setting around the bar, plenty of top-shelf liquor—and extremely loud Top-40 hits blasting on the speakers. Accordingly, the staff can have a bit of an attitude, which is more bewildering than anything else. If you're uptown, head instead to the recently renovated **East Side Billiards and Bar (Map 16)**, where in addition to the 13 tables, you can also play ping-pong. Or ditch your friends and wander into the attached video game arcade, the largest of its kind outside of Times Square (so they say). On the other hand, if you don't have any friends to begin with, think about signing up for one of the East Side seasonal pool leagues—where you not only get to compete and socialize, but receive additional discounts. Last but not least is **Amsterdam Billiards Club (Map 6)**—Manhattan's swankiest billiards parlor. With its mahogany bar, multiple fireplaces, and extensive wine list, the club is best suited for corporate events and private parties (for 20 to 500 people). It also boasts the largest co-ed league in the country and offers lessons for all skill levels.

So what are you waiting for? Turn off the latest CSI spin-off (or whatever crap you're watching), get off the couch, and give yourself a real challenge—play some pool!

Billiards

	Address	Phone	Map	Fee
128 Billiards	128 Elizabeth St	212-925-8219	3	$8 per hour per person; $12 per hour for 2 people
Fat Cat Billiards	75 Christopher St	212-675-6056	5	$5 per hour per player
Amsterdam Billiards and Bar	110 E 11th St	212-995-1314	6	$6 per person per hour
Pressure	110 University Pl	212-352-1161	6	$26 per hour
SoHo Billiards	298 Mulberry St	212-925-3753	6	$7 per hour per table
Broadway Billiard Café	10 E 21st St	212-388-1582	9	$6 per person per hour
Slate Restaurant Bar & Billiards	54 W 21st St	212-989-0096	9	$17 per hour for two players
East Side Billiard Club	163 E 86th St	212-831-7665	16	$7.50 per hour per person
Post Billiards Café	154 Post Ave	212-569-1840	25	Weekdays, $8 per hour for 2 people; weekends 10 per hour for 2 people

If you want to go bowling in Manhattan, you have four solid options. Keep in mind that there's just about no way to bowl cheaply, so if you're struggling to keep a positive balance in your bank account, you may want to find another activity or head out to New Jersey.

The best priced bowling can be found just north of historic 125th Street at **Harlem Lanes (Map 19)**. Games start at $5.50 at this two floor, 24-lane alley. Other features include a café, a sports bar, a lounge, party room (available for children's birthday parties as well as adult gatherings), and an arcade. This alley also hosts singles nights, family bowling night, and a Sunday gospel brunch.

For those looking to affordably bowl lower down on the island, hit **Leisure Time Bowl (Map 12)** where you can pay per game ($6.50 weekdays, $9.50 nights and weekends) or per lane (starting at $50/hour). Connected to the Port Authority (remember this in case you have a long wait for a bus), Leisure Time has 30 lanes, a full bar and pub menu, and two game-rooms with a new dance floor and lounge on the way. You can even make online reservations at www.leisuretimebowl.com (yes, bowling has hit the 21st century). At Chelsea Piers, you'll find the **300 New York (Map 8)**. Part of the massive AMF national chain of bowling alleys, 300 offers 40 lanes. On weekend nights, the center plays host to "Xtreme Bowling," a glow-in-the-dark "bowling party" featuring music, fog machines, and an "enhanced" rate of $8.75 per person per game. Bring your credit card to 300—you'll need it after a few short hours in the lanes.

Honestly, if you're looking for "extreme" glow-in-the-dark bowling, skip Chelsea Piers and go downtown to **Bowlmor Lanes (Map 6)**. On Monday nights, "Night Strike" is the place to be. $22 per person provides shoes and all the games you can bowl—assuming you can handle the sometimes long wait (not such a big deal since they offer free pool upstairs along with not-so-free cocktails in the lounge).

Finally, for the world's ultimate (hipster) bowling experience, head to **The Gutter (Map 29)** in Brooklyn—the borough's first new bowling alley in over fifty years. It's like a Stroh's ad from the 1980s (except the beer is fancier). It doesn't get any better than bowling on beautiful, old-school lanes and drinking tasty microbrews with your buddies.

Manhattan	Address	Phone	Map	Fees
300	Chelsea Piers, Pier 60	212-835-2695	8	$8.75/game/person. $5 for shoes.
Bowlmor Lanes	110 University Pl	212-255-8188	6	Su–Th: Before 5pm: $9.45/game; After 5pm $9.95/game; Fri-Sat: Before 5pm: $9.95/game; After 5pm: $10.95/game; Shoes: $6
Harlem Lanes	2116 Adam Clayton Powell Jr Blvd	212-678-2695	19	M–Th all day and Fr before 6pm: $5.50/game. Fr after 6 pm and weekends: $7.50/game. $4.50 for shoes.
Leisure Time	625 Eighth Ave, 2nd Fl	212-268-6909	12	Weekdays: $6.50/person/game. Weeknights and weekends: $9.50/person/game.

Brooklyn	Address	Phone	Fees
Gil Hodges Lanes	6161 Strickland Ave, Marine Park	718-763-3333	$4.50–$5.50, $3.50 for shoes
The Gutter	200 N 14th St, Williamsburg	718-387-3585	$6–$7/game/person. $2 shoe rental.
Maple Lanes	1570 60th St, Borough Park	718-331-9000	$3.50–$6.75 per game
Melody Lanes	461 37th St, Sunset Park	718-832-2695	$4.50–$6.00 per game, $3.00 for shoes
Shell Lanes	1 Bouck Ct, Coney Island	718-336-6700	$3–$5 per game, $3.25 for shoes

Queens	Address	Phone	Fees
Brunswick Woodhaven Lanes	72-25 Woodhaven Blvd, Glendale	718-896-1800	$1.25–6.50 per game, $4.50 for shoes
Cozy Bowl	98-18 Rockaway Blvd, Ozone Park	718-843-5553	$3–$6 per game, $3.50 for shoes
JIB Lanes	67-19 Parsons Blvd, Flushing	718-591-0600	$3.25 per game, $3 for shoes
Maric Lanes	19-45 49th St, Astoria	718-274-1910	$3.25–$5.50 per game, $3.50 for shoes
Whitestone Lanes	30-05 Whitestone Expy, Flushing	718-353-6300	$4–$6 per game, $3.50 for shoes
AMF 34th Avenue Lanes	69-10 34th Ave, Woodside	718-651-0440	$4–$6 per game, $4.75 for shoes

Sports · **Continental Airlines Arena**

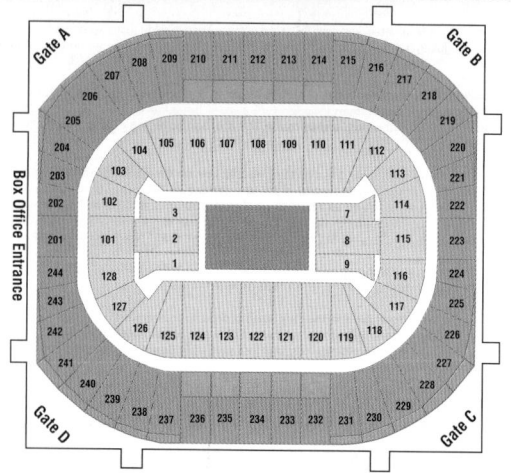

General Information

Address: East Rutherford, NJ 07073
Website: www.meadowlands.com/coarenafaq.asp
Nets: www.nba.com/nets
Ticketmaster: 212-307-7171, www.ticketmaster.com

Overview

Few sporting complexes have been less loved than Continental Airlines Arena. Cold and charmless, it's rarely succeeded as a rousing forum for sport, despite the recent success of the Devils (two Stanley Cup championships have been won here) and the Nets. The Devils moved to "The Rock" (official name: Prudential Center) in Newark in 2007, and the Nets are (probably) moving to Brooklyn sometime in the next five years (they have a deal to stay in NJ until at least 2009, and perhaps through 2013, in case Brooklyn runs Ratner out on a rail). The future of the CAA is up in the air. Will it continue to exist solely as a venue for concerts and other special events? How will the massive mall called Xanadu (no joke) being built near the arena impact it? It's all as murky as a bucketful of Meadowland's swamp water.

How to Get There—Driving

Continental Airlines Arena is only five miles from the Lincoln Tunnel. Luckily, since the fan base for the teams that play hails primarily from New Jersey, you won't have to deal with the same New York City and Long Island traffic that plagues Giants Stadium games. Additionally, attendance rates are much smaller than for football, even on the rare occasions when the Nets sell out. You can take the Lincoln Tunnel to Route 3 W to Route 120 N, or you can try either the Holland Tunnel to the New Jersey Turnpike (North) to Exit 16W, or the George Washington Bridge to the New Jersey Turnpike (South) to Exit 16W. Accessing the stadium from Exit 16W feeds you directly into the parking areas.

How to Get There—Mass Transit

The direct bus from the Port Authority Bus Terminal (NJ Transit #351) to the arena costs $9 round trip for advance-purchase tickets, and $5 each way on the bus, which accepts exact change only. Buses usually start running two hours before game time.

How to Get Tickets

The box office is open Monday to Saturday from 11 am to 6 pm and is closed Sunday, unless there is an event. For ticket information, call 201-935-3900. To purchase tickets without going to the box office, call Ticketmaster at 212-307-7171, or visit their website.

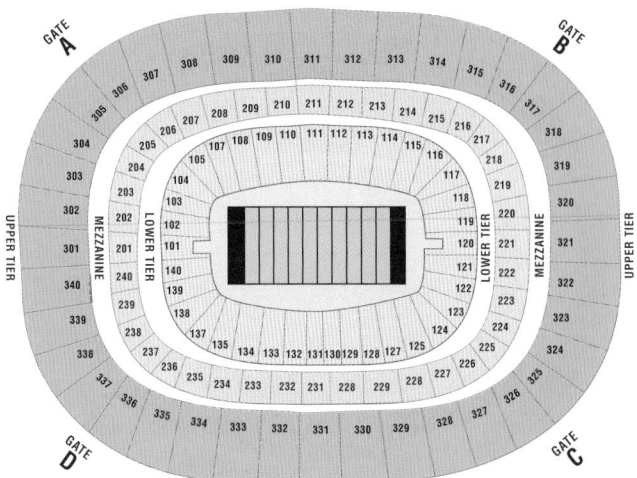

General Information

Address: East Rutherford, NJ 07073
Phone: 201-935-3900
Website: www.giantsstadium.com
Giants: www.giants.com
Jets: www.newyorkjets.com
Red Bulls: www.newyorkredbulls.com
Ticketmaster: 212-307-7171, www.ticketmaster.com

Overview

It was quite a year at the old concrete doughnut, the only stadium in the country that hosts two professional football teams. The Giants brought some much needed joy to the stadium with their incredible season. Eli and company gave the city memories to last a lifetime with their dramatic win over the undefeated Patriots in Super Bowl XLII. For the Jets things were not so hunky dory. Not only did the team stink (again), but rowdy fans at Gate D created a public relations nightmare when their caveman-like behavior was exposed for the whole world to see. Instead of shouting for a Chad Pennington TD pass, they were hootin' and hollerin' for women to take their shirts off. Classy. Still, the only way to get regular-priced tickets is to inherit them, since both teams (yup, even the lowly Jets) are sold out through the next ice age. Giants Stadium also houses Major League Soccer's Red Bulls through 2008 (for which many, many tickets are available) and is the site of several concerts and other sporting and religious events throughout the year.

How to Get There—Driving

Giants Stadium is only five miles from the Lincoln Tunnel (closer to Midtown than Shea Stadium, even), but leave early if you want to get to the game on time—remember that the Giants and the Jets are a) sold out for every game and b) have tons of fans from both Long Island and the five boroughs. You can take the Lincoln Tunnel to Route 3 W to Route 120 N, or you can try either the Holland Tunnel to the New Jersey Turnpike N to Exit 16W, or the George Washington Bridge to the New Jersey Turnpike S to Exit 16W. Accessing the stadium from Exit 16W allows direct access to parking areas. Parking costs $15 for most events.

How to Get There–Mass Transit

Less stressful than driving to Giants Stadium is taking NJ Transit Bus #351 from the Port Authority Bus Terminal directly to the stadium. Pre-paid bus trips cost $9 round trip (and $5 each way when purchased on the bus), and buses usually start running two and a half hours before kickoff.

How to Get Tickets

For the Jets and the Giants, scalpers and friends are the only options. For the Red Bulls and for concerts, you can call Ticketmaster or visit the website.

Sports · **Madison Square Garden**

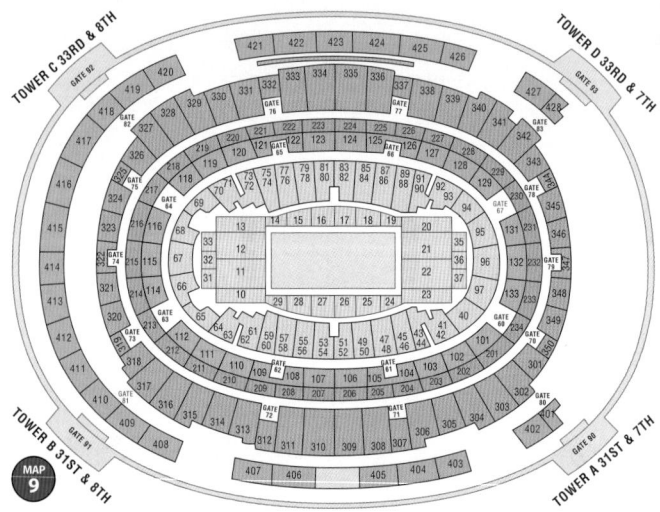

General Information

NFT Map: 9
Address: 4 Pennsylvania Plz
New York, NY 10001
Phone: 212-465-6741
Website: www.thegarden.com
Knicks: www.nyknicks.com
Liberty: www.nyliberty.com
Rangers: www.newyorkrangers.com
Ticketmaster: 212-307-7171, www.ticketmaster.com

Overview

Once resembling the Doge's Palace in Venice (c.1900), the since-relocated Altoid 'tween Seventh and Eighth Avenues atop Penn Station remains one of the legendary venues in sport, becoming so almost solely by way of the sport of boxing. It now, for good and ill, houses the NBA's Knicks (catch Spike Lee and various supermodels courtside), NHL's Rangers, The Liberty of the WNBA, St. John's University's Red Storm, as well as concerts, tennis tournaments, dog shows, political conventions, and, for those of you with 2+ years of graduate school, monster truck rallies and "professional" wrestling. There's also The Theater at Madison Square Garden for more intimate shows. Check out MSG's website for a full calendar of events.

How to Get There–Mass Transit

MSG is right above Penn Station, which makes getting there very easy. You can take the (A) (C) (E) and (1) (2) (3) lines to 34th Street and Penn Station, or the (N) (R) (Q) (W), (B) (D) (F) (V), and PATH lines to 34th Street and 6th Avenue. The Long Island Rail Road also runs right into Penn Station.

How to Get Tickets

For single seats for the Knicks and the Rangers, you can try Ticketmaster, but a better bet would be to try the "standby" line (show up a half-hour before game time and wait). You can find some decent deals online at Craigslist, Stubhub, and ebay when the Knick are riding a losing streak (which definitely has been the case in recent years). The ubiquitous ticket scalpers surrounding the Garden are a good last resort for when your rich out-of-town friends breeze in to see a game. Liberty tickets (and tickets for other events) are usually available through Ticketmaster.

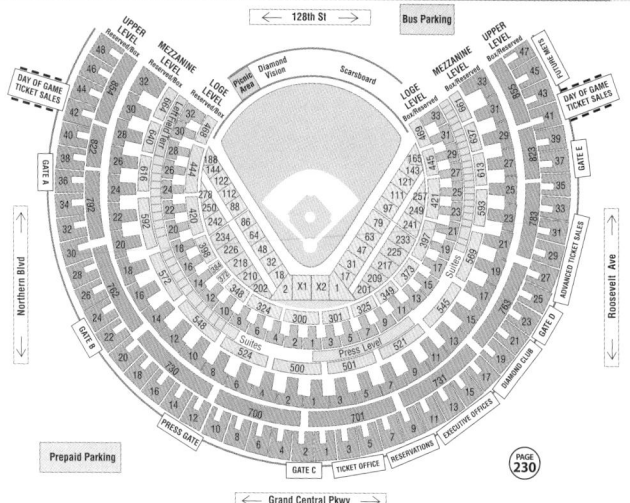

General Information

Address: 123-01 Roosevelt Ave & 126th St
Flushing, Queens

Shea Stadium/Citi Field
Box Office: 718-507-TIXX
Website: www.mets.com
Mets Clubhouse Shops: 11 W 42nd St & Roosevelt Field
Mall, Garden City, LI
Ferry: 800-BOATRIDE
or 732-872-2628

Overview

Though Mets fans would have preferred their new ballpark to be named for Jackie Robinson, Gil Hodges, or Bill Buckner, we're stuck with the purchased name of Citi Field. The team's former home, Shea Stadium (1964-2008), was named for regular guy civil servant lawyer Bill Shea who, after the Dodgers and Giants fled to the left coast, persuaded Major League Baseball to put an expansion team in New York by threatening to start a brand new baseball league which would start raiding players from their NL and AL teams with higher salaries. Shea was the first of the cookie cutter, multipurpose stadiums made to house both football and baseball, providing poor sight lines for both. With lots of foul territory, fairly deep outfield walls and cold breezes from nearby Flushing Bay whipping around its horseshoe design, Shea was not exactly a hitters ballpark, and the most successful Mets teams were centered around pitching and defense. Seating charts and other details about Citi Field are not available at press time, but since the park was built in what was once Shea's parking lot, one beloved feature of Mets home games will remain; the continual blast of low-flying airplanes heading in and out of nearby LaGuardia Airport. At one time they were seriously considering putting

a roof on the new stadium and selling advertising space that could only be seen by passengers flying overhead.

How To Get Tickets

You can order Mets tickets by phone through the Mets' box office, on the internet through the Mets' website, or at the Mets Clubhouse Shops (11 West 42nd St, the Manhattan Mall, and Roosevelt Field Mall in Garden City).

How To Get There—Driving

Yeah. Good luck trying to make the first pitch on a weekday night. But if you must, take the Triborough Bridge to the Grand Central Parkway; the Mid-Town Tunnel to the Long Island Expressway to the Grand Central; or the Brooklyn-Queens Expressway to the LIE to the Grand Central. If you want to try and avoid the highways, get yourself over to Astoria Boulevard in Queens, make a right on 108th Street, then a left onto Roosevelt Avenue.

How To Get There—Mass Transit

The good news is that the **7** train runs straight to Shea Stadium. The bad news is it's the only train that goes there. However, it will get you there and back (eventually), and the **7** is accessible from almost all the other train lines in Manhattan. Alternately, you can take the **E**, **F**, **G**, or **R** to Roosevelt Avenue and pick up the **7** there, saving about 30 minutes. Also, NY Water Taxi runs a ferry service (the "Mets Express") to Shea from the South Street Seaport, E 34th Street, and E 94th Street. The other option is the Port Washington LIRR from Penn Station, which stops at Shea on game days.

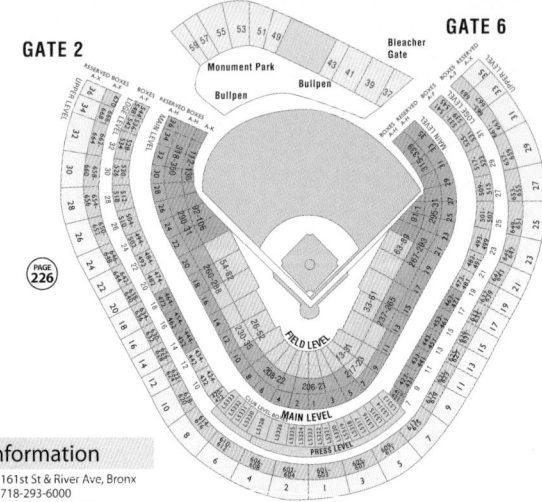

GATE 2

GATE 6

GATE 4

General Information

Address:	161st St & River Ave, Bronx
Box Office:	718-293-6000
Website:	www.yankees.com
Yankees Store:	393 Fifth Ave
Ferry:	800-53-FERRY
Ticketmaster:	212-307-7171; www.ticketmaster.com

Overview

So much to say...and yet we're tempted to say nothing at all, given the steroid controversy that (thanks to head twit Commissioner Selig) has gotten worse, especially in Yankeeland. But hope springs eternal in The Bronx, as it should, given the massive globs of revenue that the Steinbrenner clan has been able to squeeze from the World's Most Valuable Franchise.

Depending on when you read this, the Yankees have probably played their last game in Yankee Stadium 1.2 (don't forget the 1973-1975 renovation), and are settling in to brand-new-old-looking Yankee Stadium 2.0. Given the fact that the new stadium is about five feet from the old stadium, and that everything about the old stadium other than the breathtakingly-beautiful view of the field was a complete piece of crap, we're sort of excited about it (though we'd have preferred, say, Richard Meier or Rem Koolhaus as architect).

As for the team itself, if it is actually able to get out of Senate hearings and onto the field and play, things should at least be competitive, even with the departure of Joe and the Rocket. Chances are A-Rod will not duplicate his brilliant 2007 campaign, and it won't matter even if he does, because he won't get any respect until he hits .500 in at least one playoff series, so why are we even typing, really? The brightest spot will (hopefully) be young Mr. Chamberlain, who should dazzle no matter what role he plays on the pitching staff. Unless...ah, that's baseball.

How to Get There—Driving

Driving to Yankee Stadium from Manhattan isn't as bad as you might think. Your best bet is to take the Willis Avenue Bridge from either First Avenue or FDR Drive and get on the Major Deegan for about one mile until you spot the stadium exit. From the Upper West Side, follow Broadway up to 155th Street and use the Macombs Dam Bridge to cross over the river to the stadium (thus avoiding crosstown traffic). Parking (in contrast to ticket prices) is cheap, especially at lots a few blocks away from the stadium.

How to Get There—Mass Transit

Getting to the stadium by subway is easy. The **4** and **D** and the **B** (on weekdays) all run express to the stadium, and you can easily hook up with those lines at several junctions in Manhattan. It takes about 45 minutes to get to the stadium from any point in Manhattan—even less from Midtown. New York Waterway also runs a wonderful ferry (the "Yankee Clipper") from South Street Seaport, E 34th Street, and E 94th Street.

How to Get Tickets

You can purchase tickets by phone through Ticketmaster, at the box office or the Yankee store, or online through either Ticketmaster or the Yankees website. And of course the illegal scalpers who are all over the damned place.

General Information • Landmarks

Beyond the obvious crowd-pleasers, New York City landmarks are super-subjective. One person's favorite cobblestoned alley is some developer's idea of prime real estate. Bits of old New York disappear to differing amounts of fanfare and make room for whatever it is we'll be romanticizing in the future. Ain't that the circle of life? The landmarks discussed are highly idiosyncratic choices, and this list is by no means complete or even logical, but we've included an array of places, from world famous to little known, all worth visiting.

Coolest Skyscrapers

Most visitors to New York go to the top of the **Empire State Building (Map 9)**, but it's far more familiar to New Yorkers from afar—as a directional guide, or as a tip-off to obscure holidays (orange & white means it's time to celebrate ASPCA Day again!). If you want an actual view of the Empire State Building, ascend to the **Top of the Rock (Map 12)**, a.k.a. Rockefeller Center's swanky observation deck. If it's class you're looking for, the **Chrysler Building (Map 13)** has it in spades. Unfortunately, this means that only the "classiest" are admitted to the top floors. Other midtown highlights include the **Citicorp Center (Map 13)**, a building that breaks out of the boxy tower form, and the **RCA Building (Map 12)**, one of the steepest-looking skyscrapers in the city. More neck-craning excitement can be found in the financial district, including the **Woolworth Building (Map 3)**, the **American International Building (Map 1)** at 70 Pine Street (with private spire rooms accessible only to the connected), **40 Wall Street (Map 1)**, the **Bankers Trust Company Building (Map 1)**, and **20 Exchange Place (Map 1)**.

Best Bridges

The **Brooklyn Bridge (Map 3)** is undoubtedly the best bridge in New York—aesthetically, historically, and practically; you can walk or bike across on a wooden sidewalk high above the traffic. It's also worth walking across the **George Washington Bridge (Map 23)**, though it takes more time than you'd expect (trust us). The **Henry Hudson Bridge (Map 25)** expresses the tranquility of that part of the island—view it from Inwood Hill Park to see its graceful span over to Spuyten Duyvil.

Great Architecture

The Beaux Arts interior of **Grand Central Terminal (Map 13)** is full of soaring arches and skylights. Head to SoHo to see the **Singer Building (Map 6)** and other gorgeous cast-iron structures. You can find intricately carved faces and creatures on the tenement facades of the Lower East Side. The **Flatiron (Map 9)**, once among the tallest buildings in the city, remains one of the most distinctive. The **Lever House (Map 13)** and the **Seagram Building (Map 13)** redefined corporate architecture and are great examples of Modernism. Take the **Ferry to Ellis Island (Map 1)**, devoted solely to the immigrant experience, features domed ceilings and Guastavino tiled arches. The

Guggenheim (Map 17) is one of New York's most unique and distinctive buildings (apparently there's some art inside, too). **The Cathedral of St. John the Divine (Map 18)** has a very medieval vibe and is the world's largest unfinished cathedral—a much cooler destination than the eternally crowded **St. Patrick's Cathedral (Map 12)**.

Great Public Buildings

Once upon a time, the city felt that public buildings should inspire civic pride through great architecture. Head downtown to view **City Hall (Map 3)** (1812), **Tweed Courthouse (Map 3)** (1881), **Jefferson Market Courthouse (Map 5)** (1877—now a library), the **Municipal Building (Map 3)** (1914), and a host of other court-houses built in the early 20th century. **The Old Police Headquarters (Map 3)**, now a posh condo, would be a more celebrated building if it wasn't located on a little-trafficked block of Centre Street in Little Italy/Chinatown. And what are the chances a firehouse built today would have the same charm as the **Great Jones Firehouse (Map 6)**? If the guys are around outside, they're happy to let you in to look around.

Outdoor Spaces

Central Park obviously. **Madison Square Park (Map 9)** is not as well known as many other central city parks, but it is home to the Shake Shack, where you can grab a burger, a shake, and a bit of peace and quiet on the grass. For better or worse, **Washington Square Park (Map 6)** is fenced off to the masses as it gets gussied up. Look for a mid-2009 reopening when NYU students, street performers, tourists, and pot dealers will undoubtedly come flooding back to reclaim their turf. There's all kinds of interesting folk around **Tompkins Square Park (Map 7)**, which makes it ideal for people watching. In addition to **Union Square (Map 9)** housing a bunch of great statues (Gandhi, Washington, Lincoln), it also hosts an amazing farmers market (Mon, Wed, Fri, and Sat) and is close to great shopping. You can dream all you want about having a picnic at **Gramercy Park (Map 10)**, but until you score a coveted key (or become friends with Julia Roberts), you'll have to admire the greenery from the sidewalk like the rest of us. **Bryant Park (Map 12)** attracts a chi-chi lunch crowd (it's a Wi-Fi hotspot) and hosts movies in the summer. Next door, people lounge on the **New York Public Library (Map 12)** steps and reminisce about their favorite scene from *Ghostbusters*, no doubt. **Rockefeller Center (Map 12)** tends to get overrun by tourists, but it's still deserving of a visit, especially to view the Art Deco styling. **The Cloisters (Map 25)** and **Inwood Hill Park (Map 25)** are great uptown escapes. Thanks to Stuyvesant Street's diagonal path, **St. Mark's-in-the-Bowery (Map 6)** gets a nice little corner of land in front for a park, which gives a hint of its rural past. Mountainous **Marcus Garvey Park (Map 19)** in Harlem is a good destination on Sundays when the famous drum circle is in full effect.

General Information • Landmarks

Lowbrow Landmarks

The **Chinatown Ice Cream Factory (Map 3)** is worth a slog through Chinatown crowds on a hot day. Just around the corner is **Doyers Street (Map 3)**, which retains the slight air of danger from its gang war past. **CBGB's (Map 6)** is gone, but punk spirit survives (somewhat) on the nearby street corner known as **Joey Ramone Place (Map 6)**. If you're in to old-time debauchery, there are tons of classic and historic New York bars including the **Bridge Café (Map 3)**, **McSorley's (Map 6)**, Pete's Tavern **(Map 10)**, the **White Horse Tavern (Map 5)**, Chumleys **(Map 5)**, the **Ear Inn (Map 5)**, and Old Town Bar **(Map 9)**.

Lame, Bad & Overrated Landmarks

Even the most cynical New Yorker would have to admit that **Times Square (Map 12)** is a unique place, but the truth is that it's no fun to compete for sidewalk space with tourists in search of dinner at the Bubba Gump Shrimp Company. Despite the fantastic summer concert series, **South Street Seaport (Map 1)** is essentially a lame mall with some old ships parked nearby. But if potential plans for a public market come to fruition, we'll gladly brave the tourists to visit every weekend. **Madison Square Garden**

(Map 9) doesn't really deserve its status as a great sports arena. Aside from a few shining moments, the teams there usually stink, and the architecture is mostly banal. The worst part is that the gorgeous old Penn Station was torn down to make room for it. You can see pictures of the old station when you walk through the new **Penn Station (Map 9)**, which is famous not for its totally drab and depressing environs, but because of the sheer volume of traffic it handles. **The Cross Bronx Expressway (Map 23)** gets a mention as the worst highway ever.

Underrated Landmarks

Many of these get overlooked because they are uptown. **Grant's Tomb (Map 18)** was once one of New York's most famous attractions, but these days it's mostly a destination for history buffs. **The City College (Map 21)** campus is quite beautiful, and the Gothic buildings and Guastavino muck things up. Farther north, **Sylvan Terrace (Map 23)** and the **Morris- Jumel Mansion (Map 23)**, a unique block of small row houses and a revolutionary war era house, offer a truer glimpse of old New York than the Seaport or Fraunces Tavern. Memorialized in a beloved children's book, a visit to **The Little Red Lighthouse (Map 23)** will make you feel like you're on the coast of Maine and not actually standing under the George Washington Bridge.

Map 1 • Financial District

20 Exchange Place	20 Exchange Pl	Check out the cool facade with its bronze depictions of various modes of both ancient and modern transportation.
40 Wall St	40 Wall St	The tallest building in the world upon its completion in 1930…to a day, until the Chrysler went up. Oh, and Trump owns it.
American International Building	70 Pine St	Great Art Deco skyscraper.
American Stock Exchange	86 Trinity St • 212-306-1000	New York's other stock exchange.
Bankers Trust Company Building	16 Wall St	More neck-craning excitement from the NYC skyline!
Battery Maritime Building	10 South St	Ready-to-be-converted riverfront building.
Bowling Green	Broadway & State St	Watch the tourists take pics of the bull. New York's first park.
Canyon of Heroes	Broadway & City Hall Park	Markers in the sidewalk remember those honored with a ticker tape parade.
Charging Bull	Bowling Green Park	Rub his cojones for luck.
Cunard Building	25 Broadway • 212-363-9490	Former Cunard headquarters, former post office, currently a located building with great ceiling mosaics.
Customs House/Museum of the American Indian	1 Bowling Green • 212-514-3700	Stately Cass Gilbert building; check out the oval staircases.
Delmonico's Building	56 Beaver St • 212-509-3130	Once the site of THE restaurant in New York.
Equitable Building	120 Broadway • 212-490-0666	Its massiveness gave momentum to zoning laws for skyscrapers.
Ellis Island	Battery Park	Besides the museum, the main building features beautiful domed ceilings and Guastavino tiled arches.
Federal Hall	26 Wall St • 212-825-6888	Where George the First was inaugurated.
The Federal Reserve Bank	33 Liberty St • 212-720-6130	Where *Die Hard* 3 took place.
The First JP Morgan Bank	23 Wall St	Still visibly scarred from an anarchist bombing in 1920.
Liberty Plaza	Trinity Pl & Cedar St	Cool urban park (benches included).
New York Stock Exchange	20 Broad St • 212-656-5168	Where Wall Street took place.
South Street Seaport	South St • 212-732-7678	Mall with historic ships as backdrop.
St Paul's Chapel & Cemetery	Broadway & Fulton St • 212-602-0874	Old-time NYC church and cemetery.
Standard Oil Building	26 Broadway	Sweeping wall of a building overlooking Bowling Green.

Staten Island Ferry	1 Whitehall St	Grab a tall boy on board and enjoy the view.
Trinity Church	Broadway & Wall St · 212-602-0800	Formerly the tallest building in New York.
Vietnam Veterans Plaza	Coenties Slip & Water St	A nice quiet spot to contemplate our faded dreams of empire.
World Trade Center Site	Church St & Vesey St	We still can't believe what happened.

Map 2 · TriBeCa

The Dream House	275 Church St · 212-925-8270	Cool sound + light installation by LaMonte Young. Closed during summer.
Duane Park	Duane St & Hudson St	One of the nicest spots in all of New York.
Ghostbusters Firehouse	14 N Moore St	Are you the gatekeeper?
Harrison Street Row Houses	Harrison St & Greenwich St	Some old houses.
Washington Market Park	Greenwich St · 212-274-8447	One of the city's oldest marketplaces.

Map 3 · City Hall / Chinatown

African Burial Ground	Duane St & Broadway	Colonial burial ground for 20,000+ African-American slaves.
Bridge Café	279 Water St · 212-227-3344	The oldest bar in NYC. Great vibe, good food too.
Brooklyn Bridge	Chambers St & Centre St	The granddaddy of them all. Walking toward Manhattan at sunset is as good as it gets.
Chinatown Ice Cream Factory	65 Bayard · 212-608-4170	The best ice cream (ginger, black sesame, mango, red bean…), ever.
Chinatown Visitors Kiosk	Canal, Baxter, & Walker	Good meeting point. Just look out for the dragon.
City Hall	Park Row & Broadway · 212-788-6879	Beautiful and slightly less barricaded than last year.
Criminal Courthouse	100 Centre St · 212-374-4423	Imposing.
Doyers Street (Bloody Angle)	Doyers St	One of the few angled streets in New York. Has a decidedly otherworldly feel.
Eastern States Buddhist Temple	64 Mott St · 212-966-6229	The oldest Chinese Buddhist temple on the east coast.
Hall of Records/Surrogate's Court	Chambers St & Park Row	Great lobby and zodiac-themed mosaics.
Municipal Building	Chambers St & Park Row	Wonderful McKim, Mead & White masterpiece.
Not For Tourists	2 East Broadway · 212-965-8650	Where the sh** goes down!
Old Police Headquarters	240 Centre St	A beautiful building in the center of the not so beautiful Little Italy/Chinatown area.
Shearith Israel Cemetery	55 St James Pl	Oldest Jewish cemetery in New York.
Tweed Courthouse	Chambers St & Broadway	Great interior dome, but will we ever see it?
Woolworth Building	233 Broadway	A Cass Gilbert classic. The top half's being converted to condos.

Map 4 · Lower East Side

Bialystoker Synagogue	7 Bialystoker Pl · 212-475-0165	The oldest building in NY to currently house a synagogue. Once a stop on the Underground Railroad.
Eldridge Street Synagogue	12 Eldridge St	The first large-scale building constructed by Eastern European immigrants in NY.
Gouverneur Hospital	Gouverneur Slip & Water St	One of the oldest hospital buildings in the world.
Lower East Side Tenement Museum	90 Orchard St · 212-431-0233	Great illustration of turn-of-the-century (20th, that is) life.

Map 5 · West Village

Bob Dylan's One-Time Apartment	161 W 4th St	Bob Dylan lived here in the '60s.
The Cage (basketball court)	320 Sixth Ave at W 4th St	Where everybody's got game…
Chumley's	86 Bedford St · 212-675-4449	Former speakeasy under renovation; let's hope it reopens soon!
The Ear Inn	326 Spring St · 212-226-9060	Second-oldest bar in New York; great space.
Jefferson Market Courthouse	425 Sixth Ave · 212-243-4334	Now a library.
Old Homestead	56 Ninth Ave · 212-242-9040	Said to be NY's oldest steakhouse, circa 1868.
Patchin Place	W 10th St b/w Sixth Ave & Greenwich Ave	Tiny gated enclave, once home to e.e. cummings.
Stonewall Inn	53 Christopher St · 212-488-2705	Site of a very important uprising in the late '60s.
Westbeth Building	Washington St & Bethune St · 212-989-4650	Cool multifunctional arts center.
White Horse Tavern	567 Hudson St · 212-243-9260	Another old, cool bar. Dylan Thomas drank here (too much).

General Information · **Landmarks**

Map 6 · Washington Square / NYU / NoHo / SoHo

The Alamo (The Cube)	Astor Pl & Fourth Ave	Give it a spin sometime…
Asch Building (Brown Building)	23-29 Washington Pl	Site of the Triangle Shirtwaist Fire.
Bayard-Condict Building	65 Bleecker St	Louis Sullivan's only New York building.
Colonnade Row	428 Lafayette St	Remains of a very different era.
Con Edison Building	145 E 14th St	Cool top.
Cooper Union	30 Cooper Sq • 212-353-4100	Great brownstone-covered building.
Former location of CBGB & OMFUG	315 Bowery • 212-982-4052	Club is gone, but its shell remains for the time being
Gem Spa	131 Second Ave • 212-995-1866	Magazine stand that serves fantastic egg creams.
Grace Church	802 Broadway • 212-254-2000	Another old, small, comfortable church.
Great Jones Fire House	Great Jones St & Bowery	The coolest firehouse in NYC.
Joey Ramone Place	Bowery & E 2nd St	It's Joey Ramone's place. Period.
Mark Twain House	14 W 10th St	Mark Twain lived here. It's also NYC's most haunted portal.
Milano's	51 E Houston	One of our favorite bars. An utter dump.
New York Marble Cemetery	41 Second Ave	Oldest public non-sectarian cemetery in New York City.
Old Merchant's House	29 E 4th St	The merchant is now dead.
The Public Theater	425 Lafayette St • 212-260-2400	Great building, great shows.
Salmagundi Club	47 Fifth Ave • 212-255-7740	Cool building.
Singer Building	561 Broadway	Now houses Kate's Paperie; a fine building by Ernest Flagg.
Site of the Weathermen Explosion	18 W 11th St • 718-549-3200	Townhouse where the Weathermen's plans to destroy Columbia's library went awry.
St Mark's-in-the-Bowery Church	131 E 10th St • 212-674-6377	Old church with lots of community ties.
The Strand Bookstore	828 Broadway • 212-473-1452	One of a kind. All others are imitations.
Wanamaker's	Broadway & E 8th St	Once the classiest department store in the city, now houses a Kmart.
Washington Mews	University Pl (entrance)	Where horses and servants used to live. Now coveted NYU space.
Washington Square Park	Washington Sq	Dime bag, anyone?

Map 7 · East Village / Lower East Side

Charlie Parker House	151 Ave B	The Bird lived here. Great festival every summer in Tompkins Square.
General Slocum Monument	Tompkins Sq Park	Memorial to one of the worst disasters in NYC history.
Joe Strummer Mural	112 Avenue A	Ha, you think it's funny… turning rebellion into money?
Katz's Deli	205 E Houston St • 212-254-2246	Classic NY deli, interior hasn't changed in decades.
Pyramid Club	101 Ave A • 212-228-4888	Classic '80s and '90s club.
Russian and Turkish Baths	268 E 10th St • 212-473-8806	Sweat away all your urban stress.
Tompkins Square Park	Ave A & E 9th St • 212-387-7685	Home to many.
University Settlement House	184 Eldridge St • 212-674-9120	Providing a haven for lower east siders of all ages since 1886.

Map 8 · Chelsea

Chelsea Market	75 Ninth Ave	Foodies flock here. So should you.
The Frying Pan	Pier 63 • 212-989-6363	Old ship makes for amazing party digs.
General Theological Seminary	175 Ninth Ave • 212-243-5150	Oldest seminary of the Episcopal Church; nice campus.
High Line Elevated Railroad	Gansevoort to 34th St, west of Tenth Ave	Abandoned elevated railroad trestle, soon to be a park.
JA Farley Post Office	441 Eighth Ave • 212-967-2781	Another McKim, Mead & White masterpiece.
Jacob K Javits Convention Center	36th St & Eleventh Ave • 212-216-2000	IM Pei's attempt to make sense out of New York. Love the location.
Starrett-Lehigh Building	27th St & Eleventh Ave	One of the coolest factories/warehouses ever built.

Map 9 · Flatiron / Lower Midtown

Chelsea Hotel	222 W 23rd St • 212-243-3700	The scene of many, many crimes.
Empire State Building	34th St & Fifth Ave • 212-736-3100	The roof deck at night is unmatched by any other view of New York.
Flatiron Building	175 Fifth Ave • 212-633-0200	A lesson for all architects: design for the actual space.

General Information · Landmarks

Flower District	28th St b/w Sixth & Seventh Aves	Lots of flowers by day, lots of nothing by night.
Garment District	West 30s south of Herald Sq	Clothing racks by day, nothing by night. Gritty, grimy.
Macy's	151 W 34th St · 212-695-4400	13 floors of wall-to-wall tourists! Sound like fun?
Madison Square Garden	4 Penn Plz · 212-465-6000	Crappy, uninspired venue for Knicks, Rangers, Liberty, and over-the-hill rock bands.
Madison Square Park	23rd St & Broadway · 212-360-8111	One of the most underrated parks in the city. Lots of great weird sculpture.
Metropolitan Life Insurance Co	1 Madison Ave · 212-578-3700	Cool top, recently refurbished.
Penn Station	31st St & Eighth Ave	Well, the old one was a landmark, anyway…
Theodore Roosevelt Birthplace	28 E 20th St · 212-645-1242	Teddy was born here, apparently.
Tin Pan Alley	W 28th St b/w Sixth Ave & Broadway	Where all that old-timey music came from.
Union Square	14th St-Union Sq	Famous park for protests and rallys. Now bordered on all sides by chain stores.

Map 10 · Murray Hill / Gramercy

Gramercy Park	Irving Pl & 20th St	New York's only keyed park. This is where the revolution will doubtlessly start.
National Arts Club	15 Gramercy Park S · 212-477-2389	One of two beautiful buildings on Gramercy Park South.
Pete's Tavern	129 E 18th St · 212-473-7676	Where O Henry hung out. And so should you, at least once.
The Players	16 Gramercy Park S	The other cool building on Gramercy Park South.
Sniffen Court	36th St & Third Ave	Great little space.
Tammany Hall/Union Sq Theater	100 E 17th St · 212-307-4100	Once housed NYC's Democratic political machine.

Map 11 · Hell's Kitchen

The Annex/Hell's Kitchen Flea Market	W 39th St b/w Ninth Ave & Tenth Ave	Picked up where Chelsea left off.
Restaurant Row	46th St b/w Eighth & Ninth Aves	Mall. Isn't life just grand, Martha?
Theatre Row	42nd St b/w Ninth & Tenth Aves	This is that "Broadway" place that everyone keeps talking about, isn't it?

Map 12 · Midtown

Algonquin Hotel	59 W 44th St · 212-840-6800	Where snark was invented.
Broadway Dance Center	221 W 57th St, 5th Fl · 212-582-9304	The place for tap lessons
Bryant Park	42nd St & Sixth Ave	Summer movies, winter ice-skating, hook-ups year round.
Carnegie Deli	854 Seventh Ave · 212-757-2245	Serving pastrami since 1937.
Carnegie Hall	154 W 57th St · 212-247-7800	Great classic performance space. The Velvet Underground's first gig was here.
Dahesh Museum of Art	580 Madison Ave · 212-759-0606	19th–20th century academic art from Europe.
The Debt Clock	Sixth Ave & 44th St	How much Bush has borrowed—thanks again, Dubya.
Museum of Modern Art (MoMA)	11 W 53rd St · 212-708-9400	The renovation worked! Admire the beauty of architecture and art.
New York Public Library	Fifth Ave & 42nd St · 212-930-0787	A wonderful Beaux Arts building. Great park behind it. The Map Room rules.
Plaza Hotel	768 Fifth Ave · 212-759-3000	Now anyone can be Eloise with her own Plaza condo.
RCA Building	30 Rockefeller Plz	The tallest building at Rock Center, home of the famous (and pricy) Rainbow Room restaurant.
Rockefeller Center	600 Fifth Ave · 212-632-3975	Sculpture, ice skating, and a mall!
Royalton Hotel	44th St b/w Fifth & Sixth Ave · 212-869-4400	Starck + Schrager = cool.
St Patrick's Cathedral	Fifth Ave & 50th St · 212-753-2261	NYC's classic cathedral.
Times Square	42nd St-Times Sq	It looks even cooler than it does on TV!
Top of the Rock	600 Fifth Ave · 212-698-2000	Reopened after 19 years, gorgeous view of the Empire State.

Map 13 · East Midtown

Central Synagogue	123 E 55th St · 212-838-5123	NYC's oldest continuous use Jewish house of worship. Architectural gem.
Chrysler Building	405 Lexington Ave · 212-682-3070	The stuff of Art Deco dreams. Wish the Cloud Club was still there.

General Information • **Landmarks**

Citicorp Center	153 E 53rd St	How does it stand up?
Grand Central Terminal	42nd St • 212-340-2583	Another Beaux Arts masterpiece by Warren and Wetmore. Ceiling, staircases, tiles, clock, Oyster Bar, all great.
The Lever House	390 Park Ave	A great example of architectural modernism, but even better, it's so fresh and so clean!
Roosevelt Island Tram	E 59th St & Second Ave	As featured in *Spider-Man*.
Seagram Building	375 Park Ave	Or, "how to be a modernist in 3 easy steps!"
The Seven Year Itch	E 52nd St & Lexington Ave	Marilyn Monroe's lucky subway grate.
United Nations	First Ave b/w 42nd & 48th Sts • 212-963-8687	The diplomatic version of the World Cup.
Waldorf-Astoria	301 Park Ave • 212-355-3000	Great hotel, although the public spaces aren't up to the Plaza's.

Map 14 • Upper West Side (Lower)

Ansonia Hotel	2109 Broadway • 212-724-2600	Truly unique residence on Broadway.
The Dakota	Central Park W & W 72nd St	Classic Central Park West apartment building, designed by Henry J Hardenbergh.
The Dorilton	Broadway & 71st St	Cool, weird arch. Flashy facade.
Lincoln Center	Broadway & 64th St • 212-875-5456	A rich and wonderful complex. Highly recommended—movies, theater, music, opera.
The Majestic	115 Central Park W	Great brick by Chanin.
Museum of Natural History	Central Park W & 79th St • 212-769-5100	Includes the new planetarium and lots and lots of stuffed animals.
New York Historical Society	2 W 77th St • 212-873-3400	Oldest museum in New York City.
Rotunda at 79th St Boat Basin	W 79th St • 212-496-2105	Rotunda arcade arches great location.
The San Remo	Central Park W & 74th St • 212-877-0300	Emery Roth's contribution to the Upper West Side skyline.

Map 15 • Upper East Side (Lower)

Asia Society	725 Park Ave • 212-288-6400	Small-scale modernism.
Bemelmans Bar	35 E 76th St • 212-744-1600	Features lovely mural by creator of Madeline books, Ludwig Bemelmans.
Breakfast at Tiffany's Apartment Building	169 E 71st St	Where Holly Golightly and "Fred" lived in *Breakfast at Tiffany's*.
Butterfield Market	1114 Lexington Ave • 212-288-7800	UES gourmet grocer circa 1915.
Café Carlyle	35 E 76th St • 212-744-1600	Cabaret café and home of the late, great, Bobby Short.
Frick Collection	1 E 70th St • 212-288-0700	Lots of furniture.
The Jeffersons High-rise	185 E 85th St	We're movin' on up…to a dee-luxe apartment in the sky-hi.
Lascoff Apothecary	1209 Lexington Ave • 212-288-9500	Delightfully well-preserved apothecary circa 1899.
Metropolitan Museum of Art	1000 Fifth Ave • 212-535-7710	The mother of all art musuems. Check out: temple, roof garden, Clyfford Still room, baseball cards.
Mount Vernon Hotel Museum and Garden	421 E 61st St • 212-838-6878	Nice old building.
New York Society Library	53 E 79th St • 212-288-6900	A 250-year-old library. Wow!
Temple Emanu-El	1 E 65th St • 212-744-1400	Way cool building.
Whitney Museum of American Art	945 Madison Ave • 212-570-3676	It almost always has something to talk about—not the least of which is their typically controversial Biennial.

Map 16 • Upper West Side (Upper)

Fireman's Memorial	W 100th St & Riverside Dr	Memorial to fallen fire fighters.
Pomander Walk	261 W 94th St	Great little hideaway.
Soldiers and Sailors Monument	Riverside Dr & 89th St	It's been seen in *Law & Order*, along with everything else in New York.

Map 17 • Upper East Side / East Harlem

92nd Street Y	1395 Lexington Ave • 212-996-1100	Community hub for film, theater, and interesting lectures.
Cooper-Hewitt National Design Museum	2 E 91st St • 212-849-8400	Great design shows; run by the Smithsonian.

General Information · Landmarks

Glaser's Bake Shop	1670 First Ave · 212-289-2562	Best black-and-white cookies for more than a century.
Gracie Mansion	Carl Schulz Park & 88th St · 212-570-4751	Our own Buckingham Palace, and right above the FDR Drive.
Grafitti Wall of Fame	E 106th & Park Ave	This street art will blow you away.
Guggenheim Museum	1071 Fifth Ave · 212-423-3500	Wright's only building in NYC, but it's one of the best.
Henderson Place	East End Ave & E 86th St	Charming Queen Anne–style apartment houses circa 1881–82.
Jewish Museum	1109 Fifth Ave · 212-423-3200	Over 28,000 artifacts of Jewish culture and history.
Julia de Borgos Cultural Center	1680 Lexington Ave · 212-831-4333	Artistic and community hub of East Harlem.
Museo del Barrio	Fifth Ave & 104th St · 212-831-7272	NYC's only Latino museum.
Museum of the City of New York	Fifth Ave & 103rd St · 212-534-1672	Nice space, but we were excited when they were going to move to the Tweed Courthouse.
Old Municipal Asphalt Plant (Asphalt Green)	90th St & FDR Dr · 212-369-8890	Industrial architecture turned sports facility.
Papaya King	179 E 86th St · 212-369-0648	Dishing out damn good dogs since 1932.
Schaller & Weber	1654 Second Ave · 212-879-3047	A relic of old Yorkville with great German meats.
St Nicholas Russian Orthodox Cathedral	15 E 97th St	This UES cathedral, built in 1902, remains the center of Russian Orthodoxy in the US.

Map 18 · Columbia / Morningside Heights

Cathedral of St John the Divine	112th St & Amsterdam Ave · 212-316-7540	Our favorite cathedral. Completely unfinished and usually in disarray, just the way we like it.
Columbia University	116th St & Broadway · 212-854-1754	A nice little sanctuary amid the roiling masses.
Grant's Tomb	122nd St & Riverside Dr · 212-666-1640	A totally underrated experience, interesting, great grounds.
Riverside Church	490 Riverside Dr · 212-870-6700	Gothic, great views from 392-foot tower.

Map 19 · Harlem (Lower)

Alhambra Theatre and Ballroom	2116 Adam Clayton Powell Jr Blvd · 212-222-6940	Last Harlem dance hall.
Apollo Theater	253 W 125th St · 212-531-5300	Hosted James Brown's wake.
Duke Ellington Circle	110th St & Fifth Ave	Nice monument to a jazz great.
Harlem YMCA	180 W 135th St · 212-281-4100	Sidney Poitier, James Earl Jones, and Eartha Kitt have performed at this Y's "Little Theatre."
Langston Hughes Place	20 E 127th St · 212-534-5992	Where the prolific poet lived and worked 1947–1967.
Marcus Garvey Park	E 120-124th Sts & Madison Ave · 212-201-PARK	Appealingly mountainous park.
Sylvia's	328 Lenox Ave · 212-996-0660	This restaurant is worth the trip.

Map 20 · El Barrio / East Harlem

Church of Our Lady of Mt Carmel	448 E 115th St · 212-534-0681	The first Italian parish in NYC.
Harlem Courthouse	170 E 121st St	Cool.
Harlem Fire Watchtower	Marcus Garvey Park	It's tall.
Keith Haring "Crack is Wack" Mural	Second Ave & 127th St	Keith was right.
Thomas Jefferson Swimming Pool	2180 First Ave · 212-860-1383	Major pool.

Map 21 · Manhattanville / Hamilton Heights

Audubon Terrace	Broadway & W 155th St	American Academy and Institute of Arts and Letters, American Numismatic Museum, Hispanic Society of America. Pleasant, if lonely, Beaux Arts complex.
City College	Convent Ave b/w W 130th St & W 141st St · 212-650-7000	What's it doing here? Peaceful gothic campus.
Hamilton Grange National Memorial	287 Convent Ave · 212-368-9133	Elegant buildings on a serene street.
Hamilton Heights Historic District	W 141st b/w W 145th St & Convent Ave	Hamilton's old dig moved here from its original location and now facing the wrong way. Damn those Jeffersonians.
Hispanic Society Museum	613 W 155th St · 212-926-2234	Free museum (Tues–Sat) with Spanish masterpieces.
Trinity Church Cemetery's Graveyard of Heroes	3699 Broadway	Hilly, almost countryish cemetery.

Map 22 · Harlem (Upper)

The 369th Regiment Armory	2366 Fifth Ave	Home of the Harlem Hellfighters.
Abyssinian Baptist Church	132 Odell Clark Pl · 212-862-7474	NY's oldest black congregation.
The Dunbar Houses	Frederick Douglass Blvd & W 149th St	Historic multi-family houses.
St Nicholas Historic District	202 W 138th St	Beautiful neo-Georgian townhouses.

333

General Information • **Landmarks**

Map 23 • Washington Heights

Cross Bronx Expressway	n/a	Worst. Highway. Ever.
George Washington Bridge	W 178th St	Try to see it when it's lit up. Drive down from Riverdale on the Henry Hudson at night and you'll understand.
Little Red Lighthouse	under the George Washington Bridge • 212-304-2365	It's there, really!
Morris-Jumel Mansion	Edgecombe Ave & 161st St • 212-923-8008	The oldest building in New York, at least until someone changes it again.
New York Armory	216 Ft Washington Ave • 212-923-1803	World class running facility houses Track & Field Hall of Fame.
Sylvan Terrace	b/w Jumel Ter & St Nicholas Ave	The most un-Manhattanlike place in all the world.

Map 24 • Fort George / Fort Tryon

Fort Tryon Park	Ft Washington Ave	A totally beautiful and scenic park on New York's north edge.
Peter Jay Sharp Boathouse	Swindler Cove Park	See the West Bronx by boat.
Yeshiva University Main Building (Zysman Hall)	Amsterdam Ave & W 187th St • 212-960-5224	Interesting Byzantine-style building.

Map 25 • Inwood

The Cloisters	Ft Tryon Park • 212-923-3700	The Met's storehouse of medieval art. Great herb garden, nice views.
Dyckman House	4881 Broadway • 212-643-1527	Needs some work.
Henry Hudson Bridge	n/a	Affords a nice view from the Inwood Hill Park side.
Inwood Hill Park	n/a	The last natural forest and salt marsh in Manhattan!
West 215th St Steps	W 215th St	Elevation of sidewalk requires steps.

Battery Park City

The Irish Hunger Memorial	Vesey St & North End Ave	A memorial to the "The Great Irish Famine and Migration" to the US in the mid-1800s.
Manhattan Sailing Club	North Cove (Liberty St & North End Ave) • 212-786-3323	Membership required.
Mercantile Exchange	1 North End Ave	A great, big financial building in Battery Park.
Museum of Jewish Heritage	36 Battery Pl • 646-437-4200	A living memorial to the Holocaust.
Police Memorial	Liberty St & South End Ave	A fountain commemorating the career of a policeman and those killed in the line of duty.
The Real World	n/a	Tom Otterness sculptures of a tiny, whimsical society. Cooler than Smurfs.
Skyscraper Museum	39 Battery Pl • 212-968-1961	The place to go to learn what's up in New York.
Winter Garden	37 Vesey St	A cavernous marble and glass atrium.

Roosevelt Island

Blackwell House	591 Main St	Fifth-oldest wooden house in New York City.
Blackwell's Lighthouse	n/a	Built by institutionalized 19th-century convicts, just like the rest of NYC.
Chapel of the Good Shepherd	n/a	1888 Chapel given as a gift to island inmates and patients.
Smallpox Hospital	n/a	New York City's only landmarked ruin.
Tramway	Tramway Plz	As featured in Spider-Man.

Map 26 • Astoria

Astoria Park and Pool	19th St & 23rd Dr • 718-626-8621	City's oldest and largest public pool surrounded by 65 acres of waterfront parkland.
Athens Square Park	30th Ave & 30th St	You'll love it as much as the kids.
Buzzer Thirty	38-01 23rd Ave • 646-523-8582	Community arts organization with an exhibition space.
The Greater Astoria Historical Society	35-20 Broadway • 718-278-0700	Preserving the past and future of Astoria.
Kaufman Astoria Studios	34-12 36th St • 718-706-5300	The US's largest studio outside of Los Angeles sits on a 13-acre plot with 8 sound stages.
Museum of the Moving Image	36-01 35th Ave • 718-784-4520	Learn about film and television, or catch screenings of classic films.
Socrates Sculpture Park	Broadway & Vernon Blvd • 718-956-1819	Cool, gritty sculpture park with events and films.

General Information · **Landmarks**

Map 27 · Long Island City

5 Pointz/Crane Street Studios	Jackson Ave & Crane St	7 train riders will see this graffiti-covered studio building from afar; PS1 visitors should take a closer look.
Center for the Holographic Arts	45-10 Court Sq · 718-784-5065	Promotes the art of holography and/or the holography of art.
The Chocolate Factory	5-49 49th Ave · 718-482-7069	Performance space for experimental theater.
Citicorp Building	1 Court Sq	This 48-story structure is the tallest New York building outside of Manhattan.
Fisher Landau Center for Art	38-27 30th St · 718-937-0727	Temporary exhibits plus a world-class permanent collection of contemporary art.
Gantry State Park	50-50 Second St · 718-786-6385	Waterfront park and piers with breathtaking skyline views.
Hunter's Point Historic District	45th Ave b/w 21st St & 23rd St	Well-preserved homes from LIC's first heyday in the late 1800s.
Local Project	21-36 44th Rd	Non-profit performance venue and gallery space.
Long Island City Courthouse	25-10 Court Sq · 718-298-1000	Built in 1876 and rebuilt in 1904, an architectural gem.
The Noguchi Museum	9-01 33rd Rd · 718-204-7088	Showcases Noguchi's work in a converted factory with a beautiful garden.
NY Center for Media Arts	45-12 Davis St	Exhibition space for emerging artists.
PS1 Contemporary Art Center	22-25 Jackson Ave · 718-784-2084	MoMA's contemporary art space, w/ dance parties every summer since 1928.
SculptureCenter	44-19 Purves St · 718-361-1750	An artist-run nonprofit and gallery supporting experimental sculpture since 1928.
Silvercup Studios	42-22 22nd St · 718-906-2000	Former bakery is now a busy film and television studio.
The Space	42-16 West St	Organization to encourage public arts in Long Island City.

Map 28 · Greenpoint

Newton Creek Sewage Treatment Plant	Greenpoint Ave & Provost St	Take a moment to contemplate all of the famous and beautiful peoples' shit floating around in here.

Map 29 · Williamsburg

Brooklyn Brewery	79 N 11th St · 718-486-7422	Connect with your beer by witnessing its birth; free samples also encourage closeness.
City Reliquary	370 Metropolitan Ave	Artifacts from New York's vast and rich history.
Williamsburg Bridge	S 5th St & Driggs Ave	Bridge of the chosen people—Jews and well-off hipsters.

Map 30 · Brooklyn Heights / DUMBO / Downtown

Brooklyn Borough Hall	209 Joralemon St · 718-802-3700	Built in the 1840s, this Greek Revival landmark was once employed as the official City Hall of Brooklyn.
Brooklyn Bridge	Adams St & East River	If you haven't walked over it at least twice yet, you're not cool.
Brooklyn Heights Promenade	n/a	The best place to really see Manhattan. It's the view that's in all the movies.
Brooklyn Historical Society	128 Pierrepont St · 718-222-4111	Want to really learn about Brooklyn? Go here.
Brooklyn Ice Cream Factory	Fulton Ferry Pier · 718-246-3963	Expensive, old-fashioned ice cream beneath the bridge.
Brooklyn Navy Yard	Waterfront	Nation's first navy yard employed 70,000 people during WWII. Today, it houses a diverse range of businesses.
Brooklyn Tabernacle	17 Smith St · 718-783-0942	Home of the award-winning Brooklyn Tabernacle Choir.
Empire-Fulton Ferry State Park		Stunning views of the bridge.
Fulton Street Mall	Fulton St b/w Flatbush Ave & Borough Hall Plz	The shopping experience, Brooklyn style. Hot sneakers can be had for a song.
Jetsons Building	110 York St	View this sculptural roof from the Manhattan Bridge at night when it's lit with colored lights.
Junior's Restaurant	386 Flatbush Ave · 718-852-5257	For the only cheesecake worth its curds and whey. (Free pickles, great if you're preggers.)
Manhattan Bridge	n/a	Connecting Brooklyn to that other borough.
New York Transit Museum	Boerum Pl & Schermerhorn St · 718-694-1600	Everything one can say about the MTA.

Map 31 · Fort Greene / Clinton Hill

Broken Angel	Quincy St b/w Downing St & Classon St	Crazy architectural home soon to be condos. Home of Dave Chappelle's *Block Party*.
Brooklyn Academy of Music	30 Lafayette Ave · 718-636-4100	America's oldest continuously operating performing arts center. Never dull.

Brooklyn Masonic Temple	317 Clermont Ave · 718-638-1256	Its vestrymen have included Robert E. Lee and Thomas J. (Stonewall) Jackson.
Ft Greene Park	DeKalb Ave & Washington Park	Liquor store proximity is a plus on a warm afternoon when you visit this welcome chunk of green.
Lafayette Avenue Presbyterian Church	85 S Oxford St · 718-625-7515	Nationally known church with performing arts; former Underground Railroad stop.
Long Island Rail Road Station	Hanson Pl & Flatbush Ave · 718-217-5477	A low red-brick building hosting more than 20 million passengers annually. A total craphole.
Pratt Institute Power Plant	200 Willoughby Ave · 718-636-3600	This authentic steam generator gets fired up a few times a year to impress the parents. Cool.
Steiner Studios	15 Washington Ave	Film studio in the Brooklyn Navy Yard. Spike Lee's *Inside Man* was recently shot here.
Williamsburg Savings Bank Building	1 Hanson Pl	Still the tallest building in the borough and when you're lost, a sight for sore eyes.

Map 32 · BoCoCa / Red Hook

Beard Street Pier	Foot of Van Brunt St on the water	Historic 19th century warehouses, now a cluster of shops and offices.
Brooklyn Clay Retort and Fire Brick Building	76 Van Dyke St	Red Hook's first official Landmark building dates to the mid-19th century.
Gowanus Canal	n/a	Brooklyn's answer to the Seine.
Phone Booth	Huntington St & Hamilton Ave	Where hookers, pimps, and dealers call mom for money.
Red Hook Park	Richards St & Verona St	Watch futbol and eat Central American street food every Saturday from spring through fall.
Red Hook Grain Terminal	n/a	Visit just to wonder what it's doing there.
Warren Place	Warren Pl	Public housing from the 1870s.

Map 33 · Park Slope / Prospect Heights / Windsor Terrace

Brooklyn Botanic Garden	900 Washington Ave · 718-623-7200	A beautiful and peaceful spot inside and out. Cherry blossoms in spring are awe inspiring.
Brooklyn Conservatory of Music	58 Seventh Ave · 718-622-3300	This Victorian Gothic brownstone hosts performances by its students and guest artists.
Brooklyn Public Library (Central Branch)	Grand Army Plz · 718-230-2100	The building looks like a book!
Grand Army Plaza	Flatbush Ave & Plaza St	Site of John H. Duncan's Soldiers' and Sailors' Memorial Arch.
New York Puppet Library	Grand Army Plz	The Memorial Arch at Grand Army Plaza has a funky theater at the top. A must-see (Summer Saturdays only).
Park Slope Food Co-op	782 Union St · 718-622-0560	These farm-fresh-veggies will do for those in search of their peck of dirt. Rinse.

Map 34 · Hoboken

Elysian Park	n/a	On 19 June 1846, the first officially recorded, organized baseball match was played on Hoboken's Elysian Fields.
Frank Sinatra's Childhood House Location	415 Monroe St	A brick arch built by fans marks the spot where Sinatra spent his childhood.
Hoboken Historical Museum	1301 Hudson St · 201-656-2240	The zipper was invented in Hoboken.
Hoboken Terminal	1 Hudson Pl · 800-772-2222	Gorgeous Beaux Arts combination railroad and ferry terminal.
Willow Terrace	6th & 7th St b/w Willow Ave & Clinton St	Ye Olde Hoboken Towne.

Map 35 · Jersey City

Colgate Clock	30 Hudson St	The world's largest clock's dial—looks cool from Manhattan!
Harborside Shopping Complex	n/a	High-stakes shopping and banking all in one convenient complex.
Powerhouse	344 Washington St	This coal-powered railway powerhouse connected New York to New Jersey by train via Hudson River tunnels. Today the Powerhouse is being considered for residential development.
White Mana	470 Tonnele Ave	Historic diner was the "Introduction to Fast Food" at the 1939 World Fair.

General Information · **Media**

Television

1	NY1 (24-Hour News)	www.ny1.com
2	WCBS (CBS)	www.wcbstv.com
4	WNBC (NBC)	www.wnbc.com
5	WNYW (FOX)	www.fox5ny.com
7	WABC (ABC)	www.7online.com
9	WWOR (My9)	www.my9ny.com
11	WPIX (CW11)	www.cw11.trb.com
13	WNET (PBS)	www.thirteen.org
21	WLIW (Long Island Public)	www.wliw.org
25	NYC TV (Public)	www.nyc.gov/html/nycmg/
31	WPXN (Ion)	www.ionline.tv
41	WXTV (Univision)	www.univision.com
47	WNJU (Telemundo)	www.telemundo.com
49	CPTV (Conn. Public)	www.cptv.org
50	WNJN (NJ Public)	www.njn.net
55	WLNY (Syndicated TV/Movies)	www.wlnytv.com
63	WMBC (Ethnic/Religious)	www.wmbctv.com

AM Stations

570	WMCA	Religious
620	WSNR	Sports (NJ)
660	WFAN	Sports/Mets/Giants Nets/Devils
710	WOR	Talk
770	WABC	Talk/Jets
820	WNYC	Talk
880	WCBS	News/Yankees
930	WPAT	Talk/Ethnic (NJ)
970	WWDJ	Religious (NJ)
1010	WINS	News
1050	WEPN	Sports/Jets/Knicks/ Rangers
1130	WBBR	Talk/Bloomberg/ Islanders
1190	WLIB	Gospel
1280	WADO	Sports (en Espanol)/ Mets/Yankees/Jets
1330	WWRV	Religious (en Espanol)
1380	WKDM	Chinese (Mandarin)
1430	WNSW	Korean (NJ)
1480	WZRC	Cantonese
1560	WQEW	Radio Disney
1600	WWRL	Talk/NY Liberty
1660	WWRU	Korean

FM Stations

87.7	WNYZ	Top 40
88.1	WCWP	College (LI)
88.3	WBGO	Jazz (NJ)
88.7	WRHU	College (LI)
88.9	WSIA	College
89.1	WFDU	College (NJ)
89.1	WNYU	College
89.5	WSOU	College/Rock (NJ)
89.9	WKCR	College
90.3	WHCR	College
90.3	WHPC	College (LI)
90.7	WFUV	Adult Alternative
91.1	WFMU	Free-form! (NJ)
91.5	WNYE	Radio NY
92.3	WFNY	Rock
93.1	WPAT	Latin (NJ)
93.5 (Westchester)	WVIP	Caribbean
93.9	WNYC	Talk/Classical
94.7	WFME	Religious (NJ)
95.5	WPLJ (JACK)	Top 40
96.3	WQXR	Classical
96.7 (CT)	WCTZ	Adult Contemporary
97.1	WQHT	Hip-Hop/R&B
97.9	WSKQ	Latin
98.7	WRKS	Urban Adult Contemporary
99.5	WBAI	Talk
100.3	WHTZ (Z-100)	Top 40
101.1	WCBS	Pop/Rock
101.9	WQCD	Smooth Jazz
102.7	WWFS	Adult Contemporary
103.1	WBZO	Oldies (LI)
103.5	WKTU	Top 40/Dance (LI)
104.3	WAXQ	Classic Rock
105.1	WWPR	Hip-Hop/R&B
105.5	WDHA	Rock (NJ)
105.9	WCCA	Reggaeton (NJ)
106.7	WLTW	Adult Contemporary
107.1	WLIR	Rock
107.5	WBLS	Urban Adult Contemporary

Print Media

amNY	330 W 34th St, 17th Floor	212-239-5398	Free daily; pick it up at the subway.
Daily News	450 W 33rd St	212-210-2100	Daily tabloid; rival of the *Post*. Good sports.
El Diario	345 Hudson St, 13th Fl	212-807-4600	Daily; America's oldest Spanish-language newspaper.
L Magazine	20 Jay Street, Ste 207, Brooklyn	718-596-3462	Bi-weekly arts and events focus; free.
Metro NYC	44 Wall St	212-952-1500	Free daily; pick it up at the subway.
Newsday	235 Pinelawn Rd, Melville	631-843-2000	Daily; based in Long Island.
New York Magazine	444 Madison Ave, 4th Fl	212-508-0700	Broad-based upscale weekly.
New York Review of Books	1755 Broadway, 5th Fl	212-757-8070	Bi-weekly; intellectual lit review. Recommended.
New York Observer	915 Broadway, 9th Fl	212-755-2400	Weekly.
New York Post	1211 Avenue of the Americas	212-930-8000	Daily tabloid; known for its sensationalist headlines.
New York Press	333 Seventh Ave, 14th Fl	212-244-2282	Free weekly; mostly opinion/editorial.
New York Sun	105 Chambers St, 2nd Fl	212-406-2000	Daily.
New York Times	229 W 43rd St	212-556-1234	Daily; one of the world's best-known papers.
The New Yorker	4 Times Square	212-286-5400	Weekly; intellectual news, lit, and arts.
Time Out New York	475 Tenth Ave, 12th Fl	646-432-3000	Weekly; the best guide to goings-on in the city.
The Onion	536 Broadway, 10th Fl	212-627-1972	Weekly; news satire & listings.
The Village Voice	36 Cooper Sq	212-475-3300	Free, alternative weekly.
Wall Street Journal	200 Liberty St	212-416-2000	Daily; famous financial paper.

General Information · **Calendar of Events**

January

- Winter Antiques Show — Park Ave at 67th St — Selections from all over the country.
- Three Kings Day Parade — El Museo del Barrio — Features a cast of hundreds from all over the city dressed as kings or animals—camels, sheep, and donkeys (early Jan).
- Outsider Art Fair — Corner of Lafayette & Houston — Art in many forms of media from an international set. $15 admits one for one day.
- National Boat Show — Jacob Javits Convention Center — Don't go expecting a test drive (early Jan).
- Chinese New Year — Chinatown — Features dragons, performers, and parades.

February

- Empire State Building Run-Up — Empire State Building — Run until the 86th floor (0.2 miles) or heart seizure.
- The Art Show — Park Ave at 67th St — A very large art fair.
- Westminster Dog Show — Madison Square Garden — Fancy canines more well groomed than you,
- Seventh on Sixth Fall Fashion Show — Bryant Park — Weeklong celeb-studded event.
- NY Comic Con — Jacob Javits Center — Comic enthusiasts convene at the nerd mecca.

March

- International Cat Show — Madison Square Garden — Fine felines.
- St Patrick's Day Parade — Fifth Avenue — Irish pride (March 17). We recommend fleeing.
- Orchid Show — Bronx River Parkway — Brought to you by the New York Botanical Garden.
- Ringling Brothers Circus — Madison Square Garden — Greatest Show on Earth (March–April).
- Whitney Biennial — Whitney Museum — Whitney's most important American art, every other year (March–June).
- Greek Independence Day Parade — Fifth Avenue — Floats and bands representing area Greek Orthodox churches and Greek federations and organizations (Late March).
- The Armory Show — West Side Piers — Brilliant best-of-galleries show—recommended.
- New Directors/New Films — MoMA — Film festival featuring new films by emerging directors.

April

- Macy's Flower Show — Broadway and 34th St — Flowers and leather-clad vixens. Okay, just flowers really.
- Easter Parade — Fifth Avenue — Starts at 11 am, get there early (Easter Sunday).
- New York Antiquarian Book Fair — Park Ave at 67th St — 170 international booksellers exhibition.
- New York International Auto Show — Jacob Javits Convention Center — Traffic jam.
- Spring Spectacular — Radio City Music Hall — The Rockettes in bunny costumes? (Easter week).
- New York City Ballet Spring Season — Lincoln Center — Features new and classical ballet (April–June).
- Taste of Chinatown — Chinatown — $1–$2 snack stands take over the streets.

May

- Tribeca Film Festival — Various locations including Regal 16 at BPC, BMCC Chambers St, Battery Park — Festival includes film screenings, panels, lectures, discussion groups, and concerts (Early May).
- The Great Five Boro Bike Tour — Battery Park to Staten Island — Tour de NYC (first Sunday in May).
- Ninth Avenue International Food Festival — Ninth Ave from 37th to 57th Sts — Decent but overrated.
- Fleet Week — USS Intrepid — Boats and sailors from many navies (last week in May).
- New York AIDS Walk — Central Park — 10K walk whose proceeds go toward finding a cure.
- Lower East Side Festival of the Arts — Theater for the New City, 155 First Ave — Celebrating Beatniks and Pop Art (last weekend in May).
- Spring Flower Exhibition — NY Botanical Garden, Bronx — More flowers.
- Cherry Blossom Festival — Brooklyn Botanic Garden — Flowering trees and Japanese cultural events. (late April–early May).
- Martin Luther King, Jr/ 369th Regiment Parade — Fifth Avenue — Celebration of equal rights (third Sunday in May).
- Thursday Night Concert Series — South Street Seaport — Free varied concerts (May–September).

General Information · **Calendar of Events**

June

- Puerto Rican Day Parade — Fifth Avenue — Puerto Rican pride (first Sunday in June).
- Metropolitan Opera Parks Concerts — Various locations — Free performances through June and July.
- Museum Mile Festival — Fifth Avenue — Museum open-house (second Sunday in June).
- Gay and Lesbian Pride Parade — Columbus Circle, Fifth Ave & Christopher St — Commemorates the 1969 Stonewall riots (last Sunday in June).
- New York Jazz Festival — Various locations — All kinds of jazz.
- JVC Jazz Festival — Various locations — Descends from the Newport Jazz Festival.
- Mermaid Parade — Coney Island — Showcase of sea-creatures and freaks—basically, Brooklynites.
- Feast of St Anthony of Padua — Little Italy — Patron saint of expectant mothers, Portugal, seekers of lost articles, shipwrecks, Tigua Indians, and travel hostesses, among other things (Saturday before summer solstice).
- Central Park SummerStage — Central Park — Free concerts, but get there very, VERY early. (June–August).
- Bryant Park Free Summer Season — Sixth Ave at 42nd St — Free music, dance, and film (June–August).
- Midsummer Night Swing — Lincoln Center — Performances with free dance lessons (June–July).
- Big Apple Barbeque Block Party — Madison Sq Park — Outdoor jazz, endless grilled meats. 'Nuff said.
- American Crafts Festival — Lincoln Center — Celebrating quilts and such.

July

- Macy's Fireworks Display — East River — Independence Day's literal highlight (July 4).
- Washington Square Music Festival — W 4th St at LaGuardia Pl — Open-air concert (July–August).
- New York Philharmonic Concerts — Various locations — Varied programs (June–July).
- Summergarden — MoMA — Free classical concerts (July–August).
- Celebrate Brooklyn! Performing Arts Festival — Prospect Park Bandshell — Nine weeks of free outdoor events (July–August).
- Mostly Mozart — Lincoln Center — The name says it all (July–August).
- New York Shakespeare Festival — Delacorte Theater in Central Park — Two free plays every summer (June–September)—Zounds!
- Music on the Boardwalk — Coney Island — "Under the Boardwalk" not on the set list, presumably… (July–August).
- PS1 Warm Up — PS1 Contemporary Art Center — An assortment of musical performances every Saturday afternoon (July–August).
- Village Voice Siren Music Festival — Coney Island — Free outdoor show featuring renowned and emerging artists. For the alternative minded (July).

August

- Harlem Week — Harlem — Black and Latino culture. The celebration lasts all month.
- Hong Kong Dragon Boat Festival — Flushing-Meadows Park Lake, Queens — Wimpy canoes need not apply.
- The Fringe Festival — Various locations, Lower East Side — Avant-garde theater.
- US Open Tennis Championships — USTA National Tennis Center, Flushing — Final Grand Slam event of the year (August–September).
- Howl Festival — Tompkins Square Park — Counter culture meets commerce: ah, we love the East Village! Recommended.
- Lincoln Center Out of Doors — Lincoln Center — Free outdoor performances throughout the month.

September

- West Indian Day Carnival — Eastern Parkway from Utica—Grand Army Plaza, Brooklyn — Children's parade on Saturday, adult's parade on Labor Day (Labor Day Weekend).
- Richmond County Fair — 441 Clarke Ave, Staten Island — Best agricultural competitions (Labor Day).
- Wigstock — Pier 54 b/w 12th–13th Sts, west side — Celebration of drag, glamour, and artificial hair (Labor Day Weekend). Each year is rumored to be the last…
- Feast of San Gennaro — Little Italy — Plenty of greasy street food (third week in September).
- Broadway on Broadway — Times Square — Sneak peek at old and new plays.

339

General Information · **Calendar of Events**

September—*continued*

- Brooklyn BeerFest — N 11th St between Berry and Wythe, Brooklyn — Taste test of over 100 beers. Yum!
- Atlantic Antic — Brooklyn Heights — Multicultural street fair (last Sunday in September).
- New York City Opera Season — Lincoln Center — Popular and classical operas.

October

- Race for the Mayor's Cup — NY Harbor — And the winner gets to find out what he's been drinking! (September–November)
- New York Film Festival — Lincoln Center — Features film premieres (early October).
- Fall Crafts Park Avenue — Seventh Regiment Armory on Park Avenue, b/w 66th and 67th Sts — Display and sale of contemporary American crafts by 175 of the nation's finest craft artists.
- Columbus Day Parade — Fifth Avenue — Celebrating the second person to discover America (Columbus Day).
- Halloween Parade — West Village — Brings a new meaning to costumed event (October 31).
- Halloween Dog Parade — East Village — "Awwww, they're so cuuuute!"
- Fall Antique Show — Pier 92 — Look at all things you can't afford.
- Chrysanthemum and Bonsai Festival — NY Botanical Garden, Bronx — Even more flowers.
- Blessing of the Animals — St John the Divine, Morningside Heights — Where to take your gecko.
- Big Apple Circus — Lincoln Center — Step right up! (October–January)
- Hispanic Day Parade — Fifth Ave b/w 44th and 86th Sts — A celebration of Latin America's rich heritage (mid October).
- Open House NY — Various locations, all boroughs — Insider access to architecture and design landmarks (early October)—recommended.
- NY Underground Comedy — Various locations — Find undiscovered comedians before Comedy Festival Central does.
- DUMBO Art Under the Bridge Festival — Dumbo, Brooklyn — Over 600 artists open their studios to the public (late September/early October).

November

- New York City Marathon — Verrazano to Central Park — 26 miles of NYC air (first Sunday of November).
- Veteran's Day Parade — Fifth Ave from 42nd St to 79th St — Service at Eternal Light Memorial in Madison Square Park following the parade.
- Macy's Thanksgiving Day Parade — Central Park West at 79th St to Macy's — Santa starts the holiday season.
- The Nutcracker Suite — Lincoln Center — Christmas tradition (November–December).
- Singing Christmas Tree — South Street Seaport — Warning: might scare small children, family pets, and stoners (November–December).
- Christmas Spectacular — Radio City Music Hall — Rockettes star (November–January).
- A Christmas Carol — Madison Square Garden — Dickens by way of New York City (Nov–Jan).
- Origami Christmas Tree — Museum of Natural History — Hopefully not decorated with candles (Nov–Jan).

December

- Christmas Tree Lighting Ceremony — Rockefeller Center — Most enchanting spot in the city, if you don't mind sharing it with about a million others.
- Messiah Sing-In — Call 212-333-5333 — Handel would be proud.
- New Year's Eve Fireworks — Central Park — Hot cider and food available (December 31).
- New Year's Eve Ball Drop — Times Square — Welcome the new year with a freezing mob (Dec 31).
- Blessing of the Animals — Central Presbyterian Church — Where to take your other gecko (December 24).
- Menorah Lighting — Fifth Avenue — Yarmulke required.
- New Year's Eve Midnight Run — Central Park — 5k for the brave.
- John Lennon Vigil — Strawberry Fields, Central Park — Anniversary of the singer/songwriter's death. (December 9).
- Alvin Ailey American Dance Theater — New York City Center — Dance at its best.
- Holiday Window Displays — Saks Fifth Avenue, Macy's, Lord & Taylor — A New York tradition.
- Small Press Book Fair — Small Press Center — Indie publishers and self-published authors.

"New York is the concentrate of art and commerce and sport and religion and entertainment and finance, bringing to a single compact arena the gladiator, the evangelist, the promoter, the actor, the trader and the merchant." —E. B. White

Useful Phone Numbers

Emergencies:	911
General City Information:	311
City Board of Elections:	212-VOTE-NYC
Con Edison:	800-752-6633
Time Warner Cable:	212-358-0900 (Manhattan);
	718-358-0900 (Queens/
	Brooklyn);
	718-816-8686 (Staten Island)
Cablevision:	718-617-3500
Verizon:	xxx-890-1550 (add 1 and your
	local area code plus the seven
	digit number)
Police Headquarters:	646-610-5905
Public Advocate:	212-669-7200

Bathrooms

When nature calls, New York can make your life excruciatingly difficult. The city-sponsored public bathroom offerings, including dodgy subway restrooms and the sporadic experimentation with self-cleaning super sanipotties, leave a lot to be desired. Your best bet, especially in an emergency, remains bathrooms in stores and other buildings that are open to the public.

The three most popular bathroom choices for needy New Yorkers (and visitors) are Barnes & Noble, Starbucks, and any kind of fast food chain. Barnes & Noble bathrooms are essentially open to everyone (as long as you're willing to walk past countless shelves of books during your navigation to the restrooms). They're usually clean enough, but sometimes you'll find yourself waiting in line during the evening and weekends. Although Starbucks bathrooms are more prevalent, they tend to be more closely guarded (in some places you have to ask for a key) and not as clean as you'd like. Fast food restrooms are similarly unhygienic, but easy to use inconspicuously without needing to purchase anything.

For a comprehensive listing of bathrooms in NYC (including hours and even ratings), try www.allny.com (look under "NYC Bathroom Guide") and the Bathroom Diaries at www.thebathroomdiaries.com/usa/new+york.

If you're busting to go and there's no Barnes & Noble, Starbucks, or fast food joint in sight, consider the following options:

- **Public buildings**—including train stations (Grand Central, Penn Station) and malls (South Street Seaport, World Financial Center, Manhattan Mall, The Shops at Columbus Circle).
- **Government buildings**—government offices, courthouses, police stations.
- **Department stores**—Macy's, Bloomingdale's, Saks, Kmart, etc.
- **Other stores**—Old Navy, Bed Bath & Beyond, FAO Schwartz, NBA store, The Strand, etc.
- **Supermarkets**—Pathmark, Food Emporium, D'Agostino, Gristedes, Key Food, etc. You'll probably have to ask, because the restrooms in supermarkets are usually way in the back amongst the employee lockers.
- **Bars**—a good choice at night when most other places

are closed. Try to choose a busy one so as not to arouse suspicion. Most bars have those intimidating signs warning you that the restrooms are for customers only!
- **Museums**—most are closed at night, and most require an entry fee during the day. How desperate are you?
- **Colleges**—better if you're young enough to look like a student.
- **Parks**—great during the day, closed at night.
- **Hotels**—you might have to sneak past the desk though.
- **Times Square visitors centers**—1560 Broadway and 810 Seventh Avenue.
- **Places of worship**—unpredictable hours, and not all have public restrooms.
- **Subways**—how bad do you have to go? Your best bets are express stops on the IND lines, for example, 34th Street and 6th Avenue. Some stations have locked bathrooms, with keys available at the booths.
- **Gyms**—i.e. places where you have a membership.
- **Outdoor public bathrooms**—the city tries these out from time to time—see if you can find one.

Websites

www.bridgeandtunnelclub.com • Musings and explorations of New York.
www.curbed.com • Keeps track of the daily developments in New York real estate.
www.downtowninfocenter.org • Current listing of Downtown events.
www.downtownny.com • Information and map of the free Downtown Connection bus service.
www.eater.com • Restaurant gossip galore.
www.famousfatdave.com • The hungry cabbie!
www.fieldtrip.com/ny • Hundreds of suggestions for places to visit in the city.
www.forgotten-ny.com • Fascinating look at the relics of New York's past.
www.freenyc.net • Even cheapskates can have fun in the city.
www.gawker.com • A daily, guilty pleasure.
www.gothamist.com • Blog detailing various daily news and goings-on in the city.
www.hopstop.com • Get from here to there.
www.lowermanhattan.info • An excellent resource for information about what's happening in Lower Manhattan.
www.menupages.com • Menus for almost every restaurant in Manhattan.
www.midtownlunch.com • Good eats for the office set.
www.myopenbar.com • Hooray for free booze!
www.newyork.craigslist.org • Classifieds for every area, including personals, apartments, musicians, jobs, and more.
www.notfortourists.com • The ultimate NYC website.
www.nyc.gov • New York City government resources.
www.nycsubway.org • Complete history and overview of the subways.
www.nycvisit.com • The official NYC tourism site.
www.overheardinnewyork.com • Say what?
www.urbanspoon.com • Online restaurant guide.
www.vintagenytours.com • Tours by native New Yorkers.
www.vanishingnewyork.blogspot.com • Chronicling the loss of all the good stuff.

New York Timeline — a timeline of significant events in New York history (by no means complete)

1524:	Giovanni de Verrazano enters the New York harbor.
1609:	Henry Hudson explores what is now called the Hudson River.
1626:	The Dutch purchase Manhattan and New Amsterdam is founded.
1647:	Peter Stuyvesant becomes Director General of New Amsterdam.
1664:	The British capture the colony and rename it "New York."
1754:	King's College/Columbia founded.
1776:	British drive colonial army from New York and hold it for the duration of the war.
1776:	Fire destroys a third of the city.
1789:	Washington takes the Oath of Office as the first President of the United States.
1801:	Alexander Hamilton founds the *New-York Evening Post*, still published today as the *New York Post*.
1811:	The Commissioners Plan dictates a grid plan for the streets of New York.
1812:	City Hall completed.
1825:	Completion of the Erie Canal connects New York City commerce to the Great Lakes.
1835:	*New York Herald* publishes its first edition.
1835:	Great Fire destroys 600 buildings and kills 30 New Yorkers.
1854:	First Tammany Hall–supported mayor Fernando Woods elected
1859:	Central Park opens.
1863:	The Draft Riots terrorize New York for three days.
1868:	Prospect Park opens.
1871:	Thomas Nast cartoons and *New York Times* exposes lead to the end of the Tweed Ring.
1880:	The population of Manhattan reaches over 1 million.
1883:	Brooklyn Bridge opens.
1886:	The Statue of Liberty is dedicated, inspires first ticker tape parade.
1888:	The Blizzard of '88 incapacitates the city for two weeks.
1892:	Ellis Island opens; 16 million immigrants will pass through in the next 32 years.
1897:	Steeplechase Park opens, first large amusement park in Coney Island.
1898:	The City of Greater New York is founded when the five boroughs are merged.
1904:	The subway opens.
1906:	First New Year's celebration in Times Square.
1911:	Triangle Shirtwaist Fire kills 146, impels work safety movement.
1920:	A TNT-packed horse cart explodes on Wall Street, killing 30; the crime goes unsolved.
1923:	The Yankees win their first World Championship.
1929:	Stock market crashes, signaling the beginning of the Great Depression.
1929:	The Chrysler Building is completed.
1930:	The Empire State Building is built, then tallest in the world.
1927:	The Holland Tunnel opens, making it the world's longest underwater tunnel.
1931:	The George Washington Bridge is completed.
1933:	Fiorello LaGuardia elected mayor.
1934:	Robert Moses becomes Parks Commissioner.
1939:	The city's first airport, LaGuardia, opens.
1950:	United Nations opens.
1955:	Dodgers win the World Series; they move to LA two years later.
1963:	Pennsylvania Station is demolished to the dismay of many; preservation efforts gain steam
1964:	The Verrazano-Narrows Bridge is built, at the time the world's longest suspension bridge.
1965:	Malcolm X assassinated in the Audubon Ballroom.
1965:	Blackout strands hundreds of thousands during rush hour.
1969:	The Stonewall Rebellion marks beginning of the gay rights movement.
1969:	The Miracle Mets win the World Series.
1970:	Knicks win their first championship.
1970:	First New York City Marathon takes place.
1971:	World Trade Center opens.
1975:	Ford to City: Drop Dead.
1977:	Thousands arrested for various mischief during a city-wide blackout.
1977:	Ed Koch elected mayor to the first of three terms.
1987:	The Giants win the Super Bowl, their first championship in over thirty years.
1987:	Black Monday—stock market plunges.
1993:	Giuliani elected mayor.
1993:	A bomb explodes in the parking garage of the World Trade Center, killing 5.
1994:	Rangers win the Stanley Cup after a 40-year drought.
2000:	NFT publishes its first edition.
2000:	Yankees win their 26th World Championship.
2001:	The World Trade Center is destroyed in a terrorist attack; New Yorkers vow to rebuild.
2003:	Tokens are no longer accepted in subway turnstiles.
2004:	Yankees lose the LCS to the Boston Red Sox. We don't want to talk about it.
2005:	Bloomberg sees his West Side Stadium proposal quashed.
2006:	Ground is broken on the WTC memorial.
2007:	Construction begins (again) on the Second Avenue subway line.
2008:	Giants win Super Bowl XLII.

Essential New York Songs

"Sidewalks of New York" — Various, written by James Blake and Charles Lawlor, 1894

"Give My Regards to Broadway" — Various, written by George Cohan, 1904

"I'll Take Manhattan" — Various, written by Rodgers and Hart, 1925

"Puttin' on the Ritz" — Various, written by Irving Berlin, 1929

"42nd Street" — Various, written by Al Dubin and Harry Warren, 1932

"Take the A Train" — Duke Ellington, 1940

"Autumn in New York" — Frank Sinatra, 1947

"Spanish Harlem" — Ben E. King, 1961

"Car 54 Where Are You?" — Nat Hiken and John Strauss, 1961

"On Broadway" — Various, written by Weil/Mann/Leiber/Stoller, 1962

"Talkin' New York" — Bob Dylan, 1962

"Up on the Roof" — The Drifters, 1963

"59th Street Bridge Song" — Simon and Garfunkel, 1966

"I'm Waiting for My Man" — Velvet Underground, 1967

"Brooklyn Roads" — Neil Diamond, 1968

"Crosstown Traffic" — Jimi Hendrix, 1969

"Personality Crisis" — The New York Dolls, 1973

"New York State of Mind" — Billy Joel, 1976

"53rd and 3rd" — The Ramones, 1977

"Shattered" — Rolling Stones, 1978

"New York, New York" — Frank Sinatra, 1979

"Life During Wartime" — Talking Heads, 1979

"New York New York" — Grandmaster Flash and the Furious 5, 1984

"No Sleep Til Brooklyn" — Beastie Boys, 1987

"Christmas in Hollis" — Run-D.M.C., 1987

"New York" — U2, 2000

"I've Got New York" — The 6th's, 2000

"New York, New York" — Ryan Adams, 2001

"New York" — Ja Rule ft. Fat Joe, Jadakiss, 2004

Essential New York Movies

The Crowd (1928)
42nd Street (1933)
King Kong (1933)
Pride of the Yankees (1942)
Arsenic and Old Lace (1944)
Miracle on 34th Street (1947)
On the Town (1949)
On the Waterfront (1954)
The Blackboard Jungle (1955)
An Affair to Remember (1957)
The Apartment (1960)
Breakfast at Tiffany's (1961)
West Side Story (1961)
Barefoot in the Park (1967)
John & Mary (1969)
Midnight Cowboy (1969)
French Connection (1970)
Shaft (1971)
Mean Streets (1973)

Serpico (1973)
Godfather II (1974)
The Taking of Pelham One Two Three (1974)
Dog Day Afternoon (1975)
Taxi Driver (1976)
Saturday Night Fever (1977)
Superman (1978)
Manhattan (1979)
The Warriors (1979)
Fame (1980)
Escape From New York (1981)
Nighthawks (1981)
Ghostbusters (1984)
The Muppets Take Manhattan (1984)
After Hours (1985)
Crocodile Dundee (1986)
Wall Street (1987)
Moonstruck (1987)
Big (1988)

Bright Lights, Big City (1988)
Working Girl (1988)
Do the Right Thing (1989)
Last Exit to Brooklyn (1989)
When Harry Met Sally (1989)
A Bronx Tale (1993)
Kids (1995)
Men in Black (1997)
Bringing Out the Dead (1999)
The Royal Tenenbaums (2001)
Gangs of New York (2002)
Spider-Man (2002)
25th Hour (2003)
The Interpreter (2005)
Inside Man (2006)
The Devil Wears Prada (2006)
American Gangster (2007)

Essential New York Books

A Tree Grows in Brooklyn, by Betty Smith
Coming of age story set in the slums of Brooklyn.

The Bonfire of the Vanities, by Tom Wolfe
Money, class and politics undo a wealthy bond trader.

Bright Lights, Big City, by Jay McInerney
1980s yuppie and the temptations of the city.

Catcher in the Rye, by J. D. Salinger
Influential portrayal of teenage angst.

The Cricket in Times Square, by George Selden
Classic children's book.

The Death and Life of Great American Cities, by Jane Jacobs
Influential exposition on what matters in making cities work.

The Encyclopedia of New York City, by Kenneth T. Jackson, ed
Huge and definitive reference work. 2nd Edition is due in 2008.

Gotham: A History of New York City to 1898, by Edwin G. Burrows and Mike Wallace
Authoritative history of New York.

The Fuck-Up, by Arthur Nersesian
Scraping by in the East Village of the '80s.

Here is New York, by E. B. White
Reflections on the city.

House of Mirth, by Edith Wharton
Climbing the social ladder in upper crust, late 19th-century NY.

Knickerbocker's History of New York, by Washington Irving
Very early (1809) whimsical "history" of NY.

Manchild in the Promised Land, by Claude Brown
Autobiographical tale of growing up in Harlem.

The Power Broker, by Robert Caro
Biography of Robert Moses, you'll never look at the city the same way after reading it.

The Recognitions, by William Gaddis
Ever thought New Yorkers were phony? They are.

Washington Square, by Henry James
Love and marriage in upper-middle-class 1880s NY.

General Information • **For the Kids**

The Best of the Best

With all the culture the city has to offer, finding activities to amuse children is easy enough. From fencing classes to the funnest parks, our guide will provide you with great ideas for entertaining your little ones.

★ **Neatest Time-Honored Tradition:** The Central Park Carousel (830 Fifth Ave, 212-879-0244) features the largest hand-carved figures ever constructed and has been in residence in the park since 1950. $1 will buy you a memory to last forever. Open 10 am to 6 pm on weekdays and 10 am to 7 pm weekends, weather permitting.

★ **Coolest Rainy Day Activity:** The Children's Museum of the Arts (182 Lafayette St, 212-274-0986) offers activities for wee ones as young as 10 months, because its never too early to find out whether your child might be the next Picasso. Budding painters can use the open art studio; dramatic ones stage productions in the performing arts gallery; those who must touch everything delight in the creative play stations. Open Wed–Sun, 12–5 pm; Thurs, 12–6 pm.

★ **Sweetest Place to Get a Cavity:** Jacques Torres (350 Hudson St, 212-414-2462) where kids can watch cocoa beans turn into chocolate bars in the glass-encased factory-emporium. As if you needed another reason: Torres makes chocolate-covered Cheerios, and a host of other fun confections. Open Mon–Sat, 9 am–7 pm, Sun, 10 am–6 pm.

★ **Best Spots for Sledding:** Central Park's Pilgrim Hill and Cedar Hill. Kids pray for a snow day for the chance to try out this slick slope. BYO sled or toboggan.

★ **Funnest Park:** Hudson River Park Playground (Pier 51, Gansevoort St) With a beautiful view of the Hudson River, the park features several sprinklers, a winding "canal," and a boat-themed area complete with prow, mast, and captain's wheel.

★ **No Tears Hair Cuts:** Former Cozy's coiffer Jennifer Bilek (718-335-1078) offers professional in-home services, eliminating the fear of the unknown. She'll cut moms and dads, too…and offers "glamour parties" for girls ages 5–12.

★ **Best Halloween Costume Shopping:** Halloween Adventure (104 Fourth Ave, 212-673-4546) is the city's costume emporium that has every disguise you can possibly imagine, along with wigs, make-up supplies, and magic tricks to complete any child's dress-up fantasy. Open year-round.

★ **Best Place for Sunday Brunch:** Sarabeth's (945 Madison Ave, 212-570-3670) Whitney Museum outpost is significantly less crowded that the other three locations (read: you won't be waiting endlessly for a table with a hungry toddler kicking and screaming at your feet). The menu is simple and appealing to even the most finicky eaters. Open 10 am–4:30 pm.

Rainy Day Activities

When splashing in puddles has lost its novelty and ruined far too many of their designer duds:

• **American Museum of Natural History** (Central Park West at 79th St, 212-769-5100) Fantastic for kids of all ages, with something to suit every child's interest. From the larger-than-life dinosaur fossils and the realistic animal dioramas to the out-of-this-world Hayden Planetarium, all attention will be rapt. The hands-on exhibits of the Discovery Room and the IMAX theater are also worth a visit. Open 10 am–5:45 pm daily.

• **Bowlmor Lanes** (110 University Pl, 212-255-8188) Great bowling alley with a retro décor that kids will love. Bumpers are available to cut down on those pesky gutter balls. Children are welcome every day before 5 pm and all day Sunday—a popular birthday spot.

• **Brooklyn Children's Museum** (145 Brooklyn Ave, 718-735-4400) The world's first museum for children (opened in 1899) engages kids in educational hands-on activities and exhibits. Kids can learn about life in New York in the Together in the City exhibit and find out why snakes are so slimy in the Animal Outpost.

• **Staten Island Children's Museum** (1000 Richmond Ter, 718-273-2060) Offers plenty of hands-on opportunities for kids to explore everything from pirate ships to the rainforest. There's also an outdoor play space (weather permitting). Birthday parties. The museum is open Tues–Fri, 12 pm–5 pm; Sat–Sun, 10 pm–5pm.

• **Children's Museum of Manhattan** (212 W 83rd St, 212-721-1234) As soon as you arrive at the museum, sign up for some of the day's activities. While you're waiting, check out the other exhibits in the museum. There's the Word Play area designed for the younger children in your group and the Time/Warner Media Center for the older set, where kids can produce their own television shows. The museum is open Tue–Sun, 10am–5pm.

• **Intrepid Sea Air Space Museum** (Pier 86, 46th St & 12th Ave, 212-245-0072) The museum is closed until fall of 2008, while

the aircraft carrier the museum is named for undergoes refurbishment. Pier 86 is undergoing a renovation as well.

• **Little Shop of Crafts** (711 Amsterdam Ave, 212-717-6636) Great escape to bead/paint. Stay for hours.

• **Lower East Side Tenement Museum** (108 Orchard St, 212-431-0233) The museum offers insight into immigrant life in the late 19th and early 20th centuries by taking groups on tours of an historic tenement building on the Lower East Side. One tour called "Visit the Confino Family" is led by "Victoria Confino," a young girl dressed in authentic costume who teaches children about the lives of immigrants in the early 1900s. A great place to take your kids if they haven't already been there more on a school field trip.

• **The Metropolitan Museum of Art** (1000 Fifth Ave, 212-535-7710) A great museum to explore with audio guides designed specifically for children. From the armor exhibits to the Egyptian Wing, the museum offers art exhibits from all historical periods.

• **Noguchi Museum** (9-01 33rd Rd at Vernon Blvd, Long Island City, 718-204-7088) This newly renovated museum that features the works of Japanese-American artist Isamu Noguchi offers interesting tours and hands-on workshops for toddlers to teens. The fees are nominal, but you must register beforehand.

• **The Museum of Modern Art** (11 W 53rd St, 212-708-9400) Besides the kid-friendly audio guides that help make this renowned museum enjoyable for tykes, MoMA has a lot of exciting weekend family programs that get kids talking about art and film. Lots of fun hands-on programs too. Registration is a must—these programs book up fast.

• **Sydney's Playground** (66 White St, 212-431-9125) A 6,000-square-foot indoor playground featuring a bouncy house, climbing play town, and a book nook. There's also a Womb Room, a quiet, dimly lit space with a view of the play area for moms who need to quiet baby while big brother plays.

Shopping Essentials

Kid's designer couture sounds like a recipe for disaster, with threats of grass stains, paint stains, and dirt lurking around every corner. But it exists and thrives in New York City, nonetheless (e.g. Julian & Sara). buybuyBaby has nursing rooms, which are very helpful. Here's a list of shops for the best party clothes and party gifts and everything in between:

- **American Girl Place** · 609 Fifth Ave · 877-AGPLACE· dolls
- **Bambini** · 1088 Madison Ave · 212-717-6742 · European clothing
- **Bellini** · 1305 Second Ave · 212-517-9233 · furniture
- **Bombalulus** · 101 W 10th St · 212-463-0897 · unique clothing & toys
- **Bonpoint** · 1269 Madison Ave · 212-722-7720 · 811 68th St · 212-879-0900 · pricey clothing
- **Books of Wonder** · 18 W 18th St · 212- 989-3270 · books
- **Boomerang Toys** · 173 West Broadway · 212-226-7650 · infant toys
- **Bu and the Duck** · 106 Franklin St · 212-431-9226 · vintage-inspired clothing/toys
- **buybuyBABY** · 270 Seventh Ave · 917-344-1555 · furniture/clothing/toys
- **Calypso Enfant & Bebe** · 426 Broome St · 212-966-3234 · hand-made clothing
- **Catimini** · 1125 Madison Ave · 212-987-0688 · French clothing
- **The Children's General Store** · Central Passage Grand Central Terminal · 212-682-0004 · toys
- **The Children's Place** · chain clothing store
  - 1460 Broadway · 212-398-4416
  - 901 Sixth Ave · 212-268-7696
  - 173 E 86th St · 212-831-5100
  - 22 W 34th St · 212-904-1190
  - 2183 Broadway · 917-441-9807
  - 36 E 16 St · 212-529-2201
  - 600 W 181 St · 212-923-7244
  - 1164 Third Ave · 212-717-7187
  - 248 W 125th St · 212-866-9616
  - 650 Sixth Ave · 917-305-1348
  - 163 E 125th St · 212-348-3607
  - 142 Delancey St · 212-979-5071
- **Dinosaur Hill** · 306 E 9th St · 212-473-5850 · toys & clothes
- **Disney Store** · 711 Fifth Ave · 212-702-4124 · Disney merchandise
- **Discovery Channel Store** · Grand Central Station (107 E 42nd St) · 212-808-9144 · educational toys
- **East Side Kids** · 1298 Madison Ave · 212-360-5000 · shoes
- **EAT Gifts** · 1062 Madison Ave · 212-861-2544 · toys & trinkets
- **Estella** · 493 Sixth Ave · 212-255-3553 · boutique clothing
- **FAO Schwarz** · 767 Fifth Ave · 212-644-9400 · toy land
- **Funky Fresh Children's Boutique** · 9 Clinton St · 212-254-5584 · unique clothing
- **GapKids/baby Gap** · chain clothing store
  - 1 Astor Pl · 212-253-0145

- 11 Fulton St · 212-374-1051
- 1535 Third Ave · 212-423-0033
- 750 Broadway · 212-674-1877
- 2300 Broadway · 212-873-2044
- 734 Lexington Ave · 212-751-1543
- 225 Liberty St · 212-945-4090
- 1988 Broadway · 212-721-5304
- 122 Fifth Ave · 917-408-5580
- 250 W 57th St · 212-315-2250
- 657 Third Ave · 212-697-3590
- 680 Fifth Ave · 212-977-7023
- 60 W 34th St · 212-760-1268
- 1212 Sixth Ave · 212-730-1087
- 1466 Broadway · 212-382-4500
- **Geppetto's Toy Box** · 10 Christopher St · 212 620-7511 · toys
- **Granny-Made** · 381 Amsterdam Ave · 212-496-1222 · hand-made sweaters
- **Greenstone's** · hats & clothing
  - 442 Columbus Ave · 212-580-4322
  - 1184 Madison Ave · 212-427-1665
  - 1410 Second Ave · 212-794-0530
- **Gymboree** · chain clothing store
  - 1049 Third Ave · 212- 688-4044
  - 2015 Broadway · 212- 595-7662
  - 1332 Third Ave · 212-517-5548
  - 2271 Broadway · 212- 595-9071
  - 1120 Madison Ave · 212-717-6702
- **Halloween Adventure** · 104 Fourth Ave · 212-673-4546 · costumes & magic tricks
- **Hometown Kids** · 202 E 29th St · 212-381-1969 · clothes, toys, and books
- **Jacadi** · expensive French clothing
  - 1296 Madison Ave · 212-369-1616
  - 787 Madison Ave · 212-535-3200
  - 1260 Third Ave · 212-717-9292
- **Jay Kos** · boys' clothing
  - 986 Lexington Ave · 212-327-2382
  - 475 Park Ave · 212-319-2770
- **Julian & Sara** · 103 Mercer St · 212-226-1989 · European clothing
- **Just for Tykes** · 83 Mercer St · 212-274-9121 · clothing & furniture
- **KB Toys** · 901 Sixth Ave · 212-629-5386 · chain toy store
- **Karin Alexis** · 2587 Broadway · 212-769-9510 · clothing & toys
- **Kidding Around** · 60 W 15th St · 212-645-6337 · toy store
- **Kidrobot** · 126 Prince St · 212-966-6688 · toy store
- **Leeper Kids** · Grand Central Station, Lexington Terminal · 212-499-9111 · pricey clothing & toys
- **Lester's** · 1534 Second Ave · 212-734-9292 · clothing
- **Lilliput** · pricey clothing
  - 240 Lafayette St · 212-965-9201
  - 265 Lafayette St · 212-965-9567
- **Little Eric** · 1118 Madison Ave · 212-717-1513 · shoes
- **Lucky Wang** · clothing
  - 82 7th Ave · 212-229-2900

- 799 Broadway · 212-353-2850
- **Magic Windows** · 1186 Madison Ave · 212-289-0028 · clothing
- **Manhattan Dollhouse Shop** · 767 Fifth Ave (inside FAO Schwarz) · 877-DOLLHSE · dolls
- **Mary Arnold Toys** · 1010 Lexington Ave · 212-744-8510 · toys
- **Oilily** · 820 Madison Ave · 212-772-8686 · unique clothing
- **Peanut Butter and Jane** · 617 Hudson St · 212-620-7952 · clothing & toys
- **Penny Whistle Toys** · 448 Columbus Ave · 212-873-9090 · toys & trinkets
- **Planet Kids** · infant gear
  - 247 E 86th St · 212-426-2040
  - 2688 Broadway · 212-864-8705
- **Nintendo World** · 10 Rockefeller Plz · 646-459-0800 · games galore, including Pokemon
- **Promises Fulfilled** · 1592 Second Ave · 212-472-1600 · toys & trinkets
- **ShooFly** · 42 Hudson St · 212-406-3270 · shoes & accessories
- **Space Kiddets** · 26 E 22nd St · 212-420-9878 · girls' clothing
- **Spring Flowers** · shoes & clothes
  - 538 Madison Ave · 212-207-4606
  - 907 Madison Ave · 212-717-8182
  - 1050 Third Ave · 212-758-2669
- **Talbot's Kids and Babies** · clothing
  - 527 Madison Ave · 212-758-4152
  - 1523 Second Ave · 212-570-1630
- **Tannen's Magical Development Co** · 45 W 34th,Ste 608 · 212-929-4500 · magic shop
- **Tip Top Shoes** · 155 W 72nd St · 212-787-4960 · great sales for kids
- **The Scholastic Store** · 557 Broadway · 212-343-6166 · books & toys
- **Ibiza Kidz** · 61 Fourth Ave · 212-375-9984 fun clothing & shoes
- **Karin Alexis** · 2587 Broadway · 212-665-1565 · original clothing & gifts for tots
- **Tiny Doll House** · 314 E 78th St · 212-744-3719 · dolls
- **Toys R Us** · 1514 Broadway · 646-366-8800 · toy superstore
- **West Side Kids** · 498 Amsterdam Ave · 212-496-7282 · toys
- **Yoya** · clothing
  - 636 Hudson St · 646-336-6844
  - 15 Gansevoort St · 212-242-5511
- **Z'baby** · clothing
  - 100 W 72nd St · 212-579-BABY
  - 996 Lexington Ave · 212-472-BABY
- **Zitomor** · 969 Madison Ave, 3rd Fl · 212-737-5560 · toys & books

345

Outdoor *and* Educational

They can't learn *everything* from the Discovery Channel.

- **Central Park Zoo** ·
  830 Fifth Ave · 212-439-6500 ·
  Houses more than 1,400 animals, including some endangered species. Take a walk through the arctic habitat of the polar bears and penguins to the steamy tropical Rain Forest Pavilion. The Tisch Children's Zoo nearby is more suited for the younger crowd with its smaller, cuddlier animals.

- **Fort Washington Park** ·
  W 155 St to Dyckman, at the Hudson River · 212-304-2365 ·
  Call the Urban Park Rangers to arrange a tour of the little red lighthouse located at the base of the George Washington Bridge. The lighthouse affords some spectacular views—better than anything they'd see from atop Dad's shoulders. The park offers a "Junior Ranger Program" for kids, as well as a playground in Picnic Area "B."

- **Historic Richmond Town** ·
  441 Clarke Ave, Staten Island · 718-351-1611 · A 100-acre complex with over 40 points of interest and a museum that covers over three centuries of the history of Staten Island. People dressed in authentic period garb lead demonstrations and tours.

- **New York Botanical Garden** ·
  Bronx River Parkway at Fordham Road, Bronx · 718-817-8777 · 250 acres and 50 different indoor and outdoor gardens and plant exhibits to explore. The Children's Adventure Garden changes each season, and kids can dig deep and dirty in the Family Garden. Keen young botanists can join the Children's Gardening Program and get their own plot to care for.

Classes

With all of their after-school classes and camps, the children of New York City are some of the most well-rounded (and programmed) in the country. Help them beef up their college applications with some fancy extracurriculars. It's never too early…

- **92nd Street Y After-School Programs** ·
  1395 Lexington Ave, 212-415-5500 · The center provides children of all ages with tons of activities, ranging from music lessons and chess to flamenco and yoga. 92nd St is known as "the Y to beat all Ys."

- **Abrons Arts Center/Henry Street Settlement** ·
  466 Grand St, 212-598-0400 · The Arts Center offers classes and workshops for children of all ages in music, dance, theater, and visual arts.

- **Archikids** · 472 16th St, 718-768-6123 ·
  After-school classes and summer camp for children ages five and up that teach kids about architecture through hands-on building projects.

- **The Art Farm** · 419 E 91st St, 212-410-3117 ·
  "Mommy & Me" art and music classes, baking courses, and small animal care for the very young.

- **Asphalt Green** · 555 E 90th St, 212-369-8890 ·
  Swimming and diving lessons, gymnastics, team sports, and art classes. They've got it all for kids one and up.

- **Baby Moves** · 139 Perry St, 212-255-1685 ·
  A developmental play space that offers classes for infants to six year-olds in movement, music, and play.

- **The Children's Studio** · 307 E 84th St, 212-737-3344 ·
  The Studio offers hands-on courses in art, science, and yoga, with an emphasis on process and discovery.

- **Church Street School for Music and Art** ·
  74 Warren St, 212-571-7290 · This community arts center offers a variety of classes in music and art involving several different media, along with private lessons and courses for parents and children.

- **Claremont Riding Academy** · 175 W 89th St, 212-724-5100 ·
  Horseback riding lessons offered by the oldest continuously operating stable in the United States.

- **Dieu Donné Papermill** · 433 Broome St, 212-226-0573 ·
  Workshops in hand papermaking offered for children ages seven and up.

- **Greenwich House Music School** · 46 Barrow St, 212-242-4770 ·
  Group classes and private lessons in music and ballet for children of all ages.

- **Greenwich Village Center** · 219 Sullivan St, 212-254-3074 ·
  Run by the Children's Aid Society, the center provides arts and after-school classes ranging from gymnastics to origami, as well as an early childhood program and nursery school.

- **Hamilton Fish Recreation Center** · 128 Pitt St, 212-387-7687 ·
  The center offers free swimming lessons in two outdoor pools along with free after-school programs with classes like astronomy and photography.

- **Hi Art!** · 601 W 26th St, Studio 1425l, 212-362-8190 ·
  For children ages 2–12, the classes focus on the exploration of art in museums and galleries in the city and giving kids the freedom to develop what they've seen into new concepts in a spacious studio setting.

- **Institute of Culinary Education** · 50 W 23rd St, 800-522-4610 · Hands-on cooking classes.

- **Irish Arts Center** · 553 W 51st St, 212-757-3318 ·
  Introductory Irish step dancing classes for children five and up.

- **Jewish Community Center** · 334 Amsterdam Ave, 646-505-4444 · The center offers swimming lessons, team sports, and courses in arts and cooking. There's even a rooftop playground.

- **Kids at Art** · 1349 Lexington Ave, 212-410-9780 ·
  Art program that focuses on the basics in a non-competitive environment for kids ages 2–11.

- **Marshall Chess Club** · 23 W 10th St, 212-477-3716 ·
  Membership to the club offers access to weekend chess classes, summer camp, and tournaments for children ages five and up.

- **Tannen's Magic** · 45 W 34th St, Suite 608, 212-929-4500 ·
  Private magic lessons for children eight and up on weekday evenings or group lessons of three to four teens on Monday nights. Their week-long summer sleep-away camp is also very popular.

- **The Techno Team** · 160 Columbus Ave, 212-501-1425 ·
  Computer technology classes for children ages 3–12.

- **Trapeze School** · West St at Houston St, 917-797-1872 ·
  Kids ages six and up can learn how to fly through the air with the greatest of ease.

Babysitting/Nanny Services

Baby Sitter's Guild · 60 E 42nd St, 212-682-0227
Barnard Babysitting Agency · 49 Claremont Ave, 212-854-2035
My Child's Best Friend · 239 E 73rd St, 212-396-4090
New York City Explorers · 244 Fifth Ave, 212-591-2619

Where to go for more info

www.gocitykids.com
www.ny.com/kids

General Information • **Schools**

Map 1 • Financial District

Claremont Prep	41 Broad St
Downtown Little School	15 Dutch St
High School for Economics and Finance	100 Trinity Pl
High School for Leadership & Public Service	90 Trinity Pl
Millennium High	75 Broad St
UCP of NYC	80 Maiden Ln
Wildcat Academy Charter	17 Battery Pl

Map 2 • TriBeCa

Adelphi University	75 Varick St
The Art Institute of New York City	75 Varick St
Borough of Manhattan Community College	199 Chambers St
College of New Rochelle DC-37 Campus	125 Barclay St
IS 289	201 Warren St
Metropolitan College of New York	75 Varick St
Montessori	53 Beach St
New York Academy of Art	111 Franklin St
New York Law	57 Worth St
PS 150	334 Greenwich St
PS 234 Independence	292 Greenwich St
St John's University	101 Murray St
Unity Center for Urban Technologies	121 Sixth Ave
Washington Market	55 Hudson St

Map 3 • City Hall / Chinatown

French Culinary Institute	462 Broadway
M298 Pace High	100 Hester St
MS 131 Dr Sun Yat Sen	100 Hester St
Murray Bergtraum High	411 Pearl St
New York Career Institute	11 Park Pl
Pace University	1 Pace Plz
PS 001 Alfred E Smith	8 Henry St
PS 124 Yung Wing	40 Division St
PS 130 Hernando DeSoto	143 Baxter St
Ross Global Academy Charter	52 Chambers St
St James	37 St James Pl
St Joseph	1 Monroe St
Transfiguration	29 Mott St
The Transfiguration Kindergarten	10 Confucius Pl

Map 4 • Lower East Side

Beth Jacob Parochial	142 Broome St
Collaborative Academy of Science, Technology & LA	220 Henry St
Dual Language & Asian Studies High	350 Grand St
Essex Street Academy (M294)	350 Grand St
Henry Street School for International Studies (M292)	220 Henry St
High School for History and Communication	350 Grand St
JHS 056 Corlears	220 Henry St
Little Star c/o Broome Day Care	151 Broome St
Lower Manhattan Arts Academy	350 Grand St
Mesivta Tifereth Jerusalem	141 East Broadway

New Design High	350 Grand St
PS 002 Meyer London	122 Henry St
PS 042 Benjamin Altman	71 Hester St
PS 110 Florence Nightingale	285 Delancey St
PS 126 Jacob Riis	80 Catherine St
PS 134 Henrietta Szold	293 East Broadway
PS 137 John L Bernstein	293 East Broadway
PS 184M Shuang Wen	293 East Broadway
Seward Park High	350 Grand St
University Neighborhood High	200 Monroe St
University Neighborhood Middle	220 Henry St
The Urban Assembly Academy of Government and Law	350 Grand St

Map 5 • West Village

Chelsea Career and Technical Education High	131 Sixth Ave
City Country	146 W 13th St
Elisabeth Irwin High	40 Charlton St
Empire State College–State University of New York	325 Hudson St
Food/Maritime Annex (M641)	250 W Houston St
Greenwich House Music School	46 Barrow St
Greenwich Village	490 Hudson St
Home Instruction (M501)	250 W Houston St
HS 560M City as School	16 Clarkson St
Joffrey Ballet	434 Sixth Ave
Little Red School House	272 Sixth Ave
Merce Cunningham Studio	55 Bethune St
The New School for Drama	151 Bank St
Notre Dame	327 W 13th St
Our Lady of Pompeii	240 Bleecker St
Pratt Institute	144 W 14th St
PS 003 The Charrette School	490 Hudson St
PS 41 Greenwich Village	116 W 11th St
PS 721 Manhattan Occupational Training	250 W Houston St
St Joseph	111 Washington Pl
St Luke's	487 Hudson St
Village Community	272 W 10th St

Map 6 • Washington Sq / NYU / NoHo / SoHo

Alfred Adler Institute	594 Broadway
Auxiliary Services	198 Forsyth St
Benjamin N Cardozo School of Law	55 Fifth Ave
Cascades HS for Teaching and Learning (M650)	198 Forsyth St
Cooper Union	30 Cooper Sq
Eugene Lang College	65 W 11th St
Gateway	236 Second Ave
Grace Church	86 Fourth Ave
Harvey Milk High	2 Astor Pl
Hebrew Union College	1 W 4th St
Institute of Audio Research	64 University Pl
La Salle Academy	44 E 2nd St
Legacy School for Intergrated Studies	34 W 14th St

General Information · **Schools**

Little Red School House	196 Bleecker St
Milano The New School for Management and Urban Policy	72 Fifth Ave
Nativity Mission	204 Forsyth St
The New School for Jazz and Contemporary Music	55 W 13th St
New School for Social Research	65 Fifth Ave
New York Eye and Ear Institute	310 E 14th St
New York University	22 Washington Sq N
NYU Graduate School of Arts and Science	5 Washington Sq N
NYU Leonard N Stern School of Business	44 W 4th St
NYU School of Law	40 Washington Sq S
NYU Shirley M Ehrenkranz School of Social Work	1 Washington Sq N
NYU Steinhardt School of Education	82 Washington Sq E
NYU Wagner	295 Lafayette St
Parsons School of Design	66 Fifth Ave
PS 751 Career Development Center	113 E 4th St
Satellite Academy High	198 Forsyth St
St Anthony	60 MacDougal St
St George Academy	215 E 6th St
St George Elementary	215 E 6th St
St Patrick	233 Mott St
Third Street Music School Settlement	235 E 11th St
Tisch School of Arts	721 Broadway
Tisch School of Arts–Dance	111 Second Ave

Map 7 · East Village / Lower East Side

Bard High School Early College	525 E Houston St
Children's Workshop (M361)	610 E 12th St
Comelia Connelly Center for Education	220 E 4th St
East Side Community High	420 E 12th St
East Village Community	610 E 12th St
George Jackson Academy	104 St Marks Pl
Girls Preparatory Charter	333 E 4th St
Immaculate Conception	419 E 13th St
Lower East Side Prep	145 Stanton St
Manhattan Charter	100 Attorney St
Marte Valle Secondary	145 Stanton St
Mary Help of Christians	435 E 11th St
New Explorations into Science, Technology and Math	111 Columbia St
Our Lady of Sorrows	219 Stanton St
PS 015 Roberto Clemente	333 E 4th St
PS 019 Asher Levy	185 First Ave
PS 020 Anna Silver	166 Essex St
PS 034 F D Roosevelt	730 E 12th St
PS 063 William McKinley	121 E 3rd St
PS 064 Robert Simon	600 E 6th St
PS 140 Nathan Straus	123 Ridge St
PS 142 Amalia Castro	100 Attorney St
PS 188 The Island School	442 E Houston St
PS 363 Neighborhood	121 E 3rd St
PS 364 Earth School	600 E 6th St
PS 94M	442 E Houston St

St Brigid	185 E 7th St
Technology, Arts and Sciences Studio	185 First Ave
Tompkins Square Middle Extension	600 E 6th St
The Urban Assembly School of Business for Young Women	420 E 12th St

Map 8 · Chelsea

Bayard Rustin Educational Complex	351 W 18th St
Corlears	324 W 15th St
General Theological Seminary	175 Ninth Ave
Guardian Angel	193 Tenth Ave
Humanities Preparatory Academy	351 W 18th St
The James Baldwin School	351 W 18th St
The Lorge School	353 W 17th St
MS 260 Clinton School for Writers & Artists	320 W 21st St
NYC Lab HS- Collaborative Studies	333 W 17th St
NYC Lab MS-Collaborative Studies	333 W 17th St
NYC Museum School	333 W 17th St
PS 011 William T Harris	320 W 21st St
PS 033 Chelsea	281 Ninth Ave
St Columba	331 W 25th St
St Michael Academy	425 W 33rd St
Technical Career Institute	320 W 31st St

Map 9 · Flatiron / Lower Midtown

American Academy of Dramatic Arts	120 Madison Ave
Apex Technical	635 Sixth Ave
Assoc Metro Area Autistic Children	25 W 17th St
Ballet Tech	890 Broadway
The Chubb Institute	498 Seventh Ave
Community High	40 E 29th St
Fashion Institute of Technology	227 W 27th St
The Graduate Center (CUNY)	365 Fifth Ave
High School of Fashion Industries	225 W 24th St
Institute for Culinary Education	50 W 23rd St
John A Coleman	590 Sixth Ave
Learning Spring Elementary	254 W 29th St
Liberty High School Academy for Newcomers	250 W 18th St
Manhattan Village Academy	43 W 22nd St
NYU School of Continuing and Professional Studies	145 Fourth Ave
Pacific College of Oriental Medicine	915 Broadway
Phillips Beth Israel School of Nursing	776 Sixth Ave
Physical City High	55 E 25th St
Satellite Academy High	120 W 30th St
The School of Film and Television	39 W 19th St
Touro College	27 W 23rd St
Winston Preparatory	126 W 17th St
Xavier High	30 W 16th St

General Information • **Schools**

Map 10 • Murray Hill / Gramercy

The American Sign Language & English Dual Language High	225 E 23rd St
The American Sign Language & English Lower (M347)	225 E 23rd St
Baruch College	1 Bernard Baruch Wy
Baruch College Campus High	17 Lexington Ave
Churchill	301 E 29th St
Epiphany Elementary	234 E 22nd St
Friends Seminary	222 E 16th St
Health Prof & Human Svcs High	345 E 15th St
HS 413 School of the Future High	127 E 22nd St
Institute for Collaborative Education	345 E 15th St
Institute for Secondary Education	345 E 15th St
JHS 104 Simon Baruch	330 E 21st St
The Lee Strasberg Theater Institute	115 E 15th St
Manhattan Comprehensive Night and Day High	240 Second Ave
MS 255 Salk School of Science	319 E 19th St
New York Film Academy	100 E 17th St
Norman Thomas High	111 E 33rd St
NYSARC - NYC Chapter	200 Park Ave S
NYU Dental	345 E 24th St
NYU Medical Center	550 First Ave
PS 040 Augustus St-Gaudens	319 E 19th St
PS 116 Mary L Murray	210 E 33rd St
PS 226	345 E 15th St
The School of Visual Arts	209 E 23rd St
Stern College for Women of Yeshiva U	245 Lexington Ave
United Nations International	24 FDR Dr
Washington Irving High	40 Irving Pl

Map 11 • Hell's Kitchen

Alvin Ailey / Joan Weill Center for Dance	405 W 55th St
American Academy McAllister Institute	619 W 54th St
The Facing History School	525 W 50th St
Food and Finance High	525 W 50th St
High School for Environmental Studies	448 W 56th St
High School of Graphic Communication Arts	439 W 49th St
High School of Hospitality Management	525 W 50th St
Holy Cross	332 W 43rd St
Independence High (M544)	850 Tenth Ave
John Jay College	899 Tenth Ave
Manhattan Bridges High	525 W 50th St
Park West High	525 W 50th St
Professional Performing Arts High	328 W 48th St
PS 035	317 W 52nd St
PS 051 Elias Howe	520 W 45th St
PS 111 Adolph S Ochs	440 W 53rd St
PS 212 Midtown West	328 W 48th St
Sacred Heart of Jesus	456 W 52nd St
Urban Assembly School of Design & Construction	525 W 55th St
YWCA-Polly Dodge	538 W 55th St

Map 12 • Midtown

Berkeley College	3 E 43rd St
Circle in the Square Theatre	1633 Broadway
Coalition School for Social Change	220 W 58th St
Daytop Prep	54 W 40th St
The Family School West	308 W 46th St
Jacqueline Kennedy Onassis High	120 W 46th St
Katharine Gibbs	50 W 40th St
Laboratory Institute of Merchandising	12 E 53rd St
Landmark High	220 W 58th St
Lyceum Kennedy	225 W 43rd St
Practicing Law Institute	810 Seventh Ave
Repertory Company High	123 W 43rd St
St Thomas Choir	202 W 58th St
SUNY College of Optometry	33 W 42nd St
Wood Tobe-Coburn	8 E 40th St

Map 13 • East Midtown

Aaron	309 E 45th St
Amity Language Institute	124 E 40th St
The Beekman School	220 E 50th St
Cathedral High	350 E 56th St
High School of Art & Design	1075 Second Ave
Montessori Family School of Manhattan	323 E 47th St
Montessori School of New York	347 E 55th St
Neighborhood Playhouse	340 E 54th St
NY Institute of Credit	380 Lexington Ave
PS 059 Beekman Hill	228 E 57th St
Turtle Bay Music School	244 E 52nd St

Map 14 • Upper West Side (Lower)

Abraham Joshua Heschel High	20 West End Ave
American Musical and Dramatic Academy	2109 Broadway
The Anderson School	100 W 84th St
Art and Technology High	122 Amsterdam Ave
Beacon High	227 W 61st St
Beit Rabban Day	8 W 70th St
Blessed Sacrement	147 W 70th St
The Calhoun	433 West End Ave
The Calhoun Lower School	160 W 74th St
Collegiate	260 W 78th St
Ethical Culture-Fieldston	33 Central Park W
Fiorello H LaGuardia High	100 Amsterdam Ave
Fordham University	113 W 60th St
High School for Arts, Imagination & Inquiry	122 Amsterdam Ave
J G B Educ Services	15 W 65th St
JHS 044 William J O'Shea	100 W 77th St
Juilliard	60 Lincoln Ctr Plz
Law, Advocacy and Community Justice High	122 Amsterdam Ave
Louis D Brandeis High	145 W 84th St
Lucy Moses School For Music & Dance	129 W 67th St
M283 Manhattan Theatre Lab	122 Amsterdam Ave

Manhattan Day	310 W 75th St	NYU Institute of Fine Arts	1 E 78th St
Manhattan Hunter High School of Science	122 Amsterdam Ave	PS 006 Lillie D Blake	45 E 81st St
Mannes College of Music	150 W 85th St	PS 158 Bayard Taylor	1458 York Ave
Martin Luther King High	122 Amsterdam Ave	PS 183 R L Stevenson	419 E 66th St
Metropolitan Montessori	325 W 85th St	PS 290 Manhattan New School	311 E 82nd St
MS 244 Columbus Middle	100 W 77th St	Queen Sofia Spanish Institute	684 Park Ave
MS 245M The Computer School	100 W 77th St	Rabbi Arthur Schneier Park East Day	164 E 68th St
New York Academy of Sciences	250 Greenwich St	Ramaz	60 E 78th St
New York Institute of Technology	1855 Broadway	Ramaz Lower	125 E 85th St
Parkside	48 W 74th St	Ramaz Middle	114 E 85th St
Professional Children's School	132 W 60th St	Regis High	55 E 84th St
PS 009 Sarah Anderson	100 W 84th St	Rockefeller University	1230 York Ave
PS 087 William Sherman	160 W 78th St	Rudolf Steiner Lower	15 E 79th St
PS 191 Amsterdam	210 W 61st St	Rudolf Steiner Upper	15 E 78th St
PS 199 Jesse Straus	270 W 70th St	Sotheby's Institute of Art	1334 York Ave
PS 243 Center	270 W 70th St	St Ignatius Loyola	48 E 84th St
PS 811M Mickey Mantle	466 West End Ave	St Jean Baptiste High	173 E 75th St
Robert Louis Stevenson	24 W 74th St	St Stephan of Hungary	408 E 82nd St
Rodeph Sholom	7 W 83rd St	St Vincent Ferrer High	151 E 65th St
Special Music School of America (M882)	129 W 67th St	Talent Unlimited High	317 E 67th St
Urban Assembly School for Media Studies	122 Amsterdam Ave	Town School	540 E 76th St
		Ukrainian Institute of America	2 E 79th St
West End Day	255 W 71st St	Urban Academy Lab High	317 E 67th St
York Prep	40 W 68th St	Vanguard High	317 E 67th St
		Weill Cornell Medical College	525 E 68th St

Map 15 · Upper East Side (Lower)

Abraham Lincoln	12 E 79th St
All Souls	1157 Lexington Ave
Allen-Stevenson	132 E 78th St
Birch Wathen Lenox	210 E 77th St
Brearly	610 E 83rd St
Browning	52 E 62nd St
Buckley	113 E 73rd St
Caedmon	416 E 80th St
Cathedral	319 E 74th St
Chapin	100 East End Ave
Dominican Academy	44 E 68th St
East Side Middle	1458 York Ave
Eleanor Roosevelt High	411 E 76th St
Ella Baker	317 E 67th St
Episcopal	35 E 69th St
Geneva School of Manhattan	583 Park Ave
Hewitt	45 E 75th St
Hunter College	695 Park Ave
JHS 167 Robert F Wagner	220 E 76th St
Kennedy Child Study Center	151 E 67th St
Loyola	980 Park Ave
Lycée Francais de New York	505 E 75th St
Manhattan High School for Girls	154 E 70th St
Manhattan International High	317 E 67th St
Martha Graham	316 E 63rd St
Marymount	1026 Fifth Ave
Marymount Manhattan College	221 E 71st St
The McCarton School	350 E 82nd St
New York School of Interior Design	170 E 70th St

Map 16 · Upper West Side (Upper)

Abraham Joshua Heschel	270 W 89th St
Aichhorn	23 W 106th St
Alexander Robertson	3 W 95th St
The Anglo-American International	18 W 89th St
Ascension	220 W 108th St
Columbia Grammar and Prepatory	5 W 93rd St
De la Salle Academy	202 W 97th St
Dwight	291 Central Park W
Edward A Reynolds West Side High (M505)	140 W 102nd St
Holy Name of Jesus	202 W 97th St
JHS 054 Booker T Washington	103 W 107th St
Mandell Nursery-Kindergarten	127 W 94th St
Morningside Montessori	251 W 100th St
Mott Hall II	234 W 109th St
MS 246M Crossroads	234 W 109th St
MS 247M Dual Language Middle	32 W 92nd St
MS 250 West Side Collaborative	735 West End Ave
MS 256 Academic and Athletic Excellence	154 W 93rd St
MS 258 Community Action	154 W 93rd St
PS 038 Roberto Clemente	232 E 103rd St
PS 075 Emily Dickinson	735 West End Ave
PS 084 Lillian Weber	32 W 92nd St
PS 145 Bloomingdale	150 W 105th St
PS 163 Alfred E Smith	163 W 97th St
PS 165 Robert E Simon	234 W 109th St
PS 166 Richard Rodgers School of Arts and Technology	132 W 89th St

PS 333 Manhattan School for Children	154 W 93rd St
Riverside Early Learning Center	202 Riverside Dr
School for Young Performers	175 W 92nd St
The Smith School	131 W 86th St
Solomon Schechter High	1 W 91st St
St Agnes Boys	555 West End Ave
St Gregory the Great	138 W 90th St
Stephen Gaynor	148 W 90th St
The Studio School	124 W 95th St
Trinity	139 W 91st St
Upper Trevor Day	1 W 88th St
West Side Montessori	309 W 92nd St
Yeshiva Ketana of Manhattan	346 W 89th St

Map 17 · Upper East Side / East Harlem

Academy of Environmental Science Secondary High (M635)	410 E 100th St
Amber Charter	220 E 106th St
Ballet Academy East	1651 Third Ave
Bilingual Bicultural Mini	219 E 109th St
The Bilingual Bicultural School (M182)	219 E 109th St
Brick Church	62 E 92nd St
Central Park East I Elementary	1573 Madison Ave
Central Park East II (M964)	19 E 103rd St
Central Park East Secondary	1573 Madison Ave
Convent of the Sacred Heart	1 E 91st St
Cristo Rey High	112 E 106th St
Dalton	108 E 89th St
East Harlem Block	1615 Madison Ave
East Harlem School at Exodus House	309 E 103rd St
Harbor Science & Arts Charter	1 E 104th St
Heritage	1680 Lexington Ave
Horace Mann	55 E 90th St
Hunter College Elementary	71 E 94th St
Hunter College High	71 E 94th St
JHS 013 Jackie Robinson	1573 Madison Ave
La Scuola D'Italia Guglielmo M	12 E 96th St
Life Sciences Secondary	320 E 96th St
Lower Trevor Day	11 E 89th St
Manhattan Country	7 E 96th St
Mount Sinai School of Medicine	1 Gustave Levy Pl
MS 224 Manhattan East Center for Arts & Academics	410 E 100th St
National Academy School of Fine Arts	5 E 89th St
Nightingale-Bamford	20 E 92nd St
NY Center for Autism Charter	433 E 100th St
Our Lady of Good Counsel	323 E 91st St
Park East High	230 E 105th St
PS 050 Vito Marcantonio	433 E 100th St
PS 072	131 E 104th St
PS 083 Luis Munoz Rivera	219 E 109th St
PS 108 Angelo Del Toro	1615 Madison Ave
PS 146 Ann M Short	421 E 106th St
PS 169 Robert F Kennedy	110 E 88th St
PS 171 Patrick Henry	19 E 103rd St
PS 198 Isador and Ida Straus	1700 Third Ave
PS 77 Lower Lab	1700 Third Ave

Reece	180 E 93rd St
Richard R Green High School of Teaching (M570)	421 E 88th St
School of Cooperative Technical Education	321 E 96th St
Solomon Schechter	50 E 87th St
Spence	22 E 91st St
St Bernard's	4 E 98th St
St David's	12 E 89th St
St Francis de Sales	116 E 97th St
St Joseph Yorkville	420 E 87th St
Tag Young Scholars JHS (M012)	240 E 109th St
Tito Puente Educational Complex (M117)	240 E 109th St
The Trevor Day School	11 E 89th St
Young Women's Leadership High	105 E 106th St

Map 18 · Columbia / Morningside Heights

A Philip Randolph Campus High	443 W 135th St
Annunciation	461 W 131st St
Bank Street School for Children	610 W 112th St
Barnard College	3009 Broadway
Cathedral	1047 Amsterdam Ave
Columbia University	2960 Broadway
Computer School	370 W 120th St
The Cooke Center For Learning	475 Riverside Dr
Corpus Christi	535 W 121st St
High School for Math, Science and Engineering at City College	138 Convent Ave
IS 195 Roberto Clemente	625 W 133rd St
IS 223 Mott Hall	71 Convent Ave
IS 286 Renaissance Military	509 W 129th St
Jewish Theological Seminary of America	3080 Broadway
Kipp Infinity Charter	625 W 133rd St
Kipp S.T.A.R. College Preparatory (M726)	433 W 123rd St
Manhattan School of Music	120 Claremont Ave
Powell MS for Law & Social Justice	509 W 129th St
PS 036 Margaret Douglas	123 Morningside Dr
PS 125 Ralph Bunche	425 W 123rd St
PS 129 John H Finley	425 W 130th St
PS 161 Pedro A Campos	499 W 133rd St
PS 180 Hugo Newman	370 W 120th St
Riverside Church Week Day	490 Riverside Dr
The School at Columbia University	556 W 110th St
St Hilda's and St Hugh's	619 W 114th St
St Joseph's School of the Holy Family	168 Morningside Ave
Teachers College, Columbia University	525 W 120th St

Map 19 · Harlem (Lower)

Christ Crusader Academy	302 W 124th St
College of New Rochelle Rosa Parks Campus	144 W 125th St
Democracy Prep Charter	222 W 134th St
Fellowship of Learning	9 W 130th St
Frederick Douglass Academy II	215 W 114th St

General Information • **Schools**

Future Leaders Institute Charter	134 W 122nd St
Great Tomorrows USA	38 W 123rd St
Harlem Children's Zone/Promise Academy Charter M284	175 W 134th St
Harlem Children's Zone/Promise Academy II Charter	220 W 121st St
Harlem Episcopal	1330 Fifth Ave
Harlem Link Charter (M329)	134 W 122nd St
Harlem Renaissance High	22 E 128th St
Harlem Success Charter	34 W 118th St
Helene Fuld School of Nursing North	26 E 120th St
IS 275	175 W 134th St
JHS 088 Wadleigh	215 W 114th St
Kappa II	144 W 122nd St
Mount Pleasant Christian Academy	126 W 119th St
Opportunity Charter	240 W 113th St
PS 076 A Philip Randolph	220 W 121st St
PS 092 Mary M Bethune Academy	222 W 134th St
PS 133 Fred R Moore	2121 Fifth Ave
PS 149 Sojourner Truth	41 W 117th St
PS 154 Harriet Tubman	250 W 127th St
PS 162	34 W 118th St
PS 175 Henry H Garnet	175 W 134th St
PS 185 John M Langston	20 W 112th St
PS 208 Alain L Locke	21 W 111th St
PS 241 Family Academy	240 W 113th St
PS 242M GP Brown Comp	134 W 122nd St
Rice High	74 W 124th St
School of the Arts (M3SA)	215 W 114th St
Sister Clara Mohammed	102 W 116th St
Sisulu-Walker Charter	125 W 115th St
St Aloysius	223 W 132nd St
St Benedict Day Nursery & Kindergarten	21 W 124th St
Thurgood Marshall Academy	200 W 135th St
Wadleigh Secondary School for the Performing and Visual Arts	215 W 114th St

Map 20 • El Barrio / East Harlem

Academy for Health/Sciences	2351 First Ave
All Saints	52 E 130th St
Bilingual 45 RCBS (M055)	2351 First Ave
Bilingual Bicultural Art School	160 E 120th St
Children's Storefront	70 E 129th St
The Choir Academy of Harlem	2005 Madison Ave
East Harlem Tech (M02P)	2351 First Ave
Harlem Day Charter	240 E 123rd St, 4th Fl
Highway Christian Academy	132 E 111th St
HS 435 Manhattan Center Math and Science	280 Pleasant Ave
Issac Newton JHS for Science & Math (M825)	260 Pleasant Ave
JHS John S Roberts	2351 First Ave
Kappa II (M317)	144 E 128th St
King's Academy	2345 Third Ave
Leadership Village Academy Charter	315 E 113th St
Manhattan Center for Science & Math	260 Pleasant Ave
Mount Carmel-Holy Rosary	371 Pleasant Ave
New York Prep (M03Q)	315 E 113th St

NY College of Podiatric Medicine	1800 Park Ave
Our Lady Queen of Angels	232 E 113th St
PS 007 Samuel Stern	160 E 120th St
PS 030 Hernandez/Hughes	144 E 128th St
PS 057 James W Johnson	176 E 115th St
PS 079 Horan	55 E 120th St
PS 096 Joseph Lanzetta	216 E 120th St
PS 101 Draper	141 E 111th St
PS 102 Jacques Cartier	315 E 113th St
PS 112 Jose Celso Barbosa	535 E 119th St
PS 138	144 E 128th St
PS 155 William Paca	319 E 117th St
PS 206 Jose Celso Babosa	508 E 120th St
River East (M037)	508 E 120th St
St Ann	314 E 110th St
St Paul	114 E 118th St
Urban Peace Academy (M695)	2351 First Ave

Map 21 • Manhattanville / Hamilton Heights

Boricua College	3755 Broadway
Childs' Memorial Christian Academy	1763 Amsterdam Ave
City College	Convent Ave b/w W 130th St & W 141st St
Dance Theatre of Harlem	466 W 152nd St
Harlem International Community	421 W 145th St
Harlem School of the Arts	645 St Nicholas Ave
HS 685 Bread & Roses Integrated Arts High	6 Edgecombe Ave
Kappa IV (M302)	6 Edgecombe Ave
M304 Mott Hall High	6 Edgecombe Ave
The Moore Learning Center	614 W 157th St
New Heights Academy Charter	1818 Amsterdam Ave
Our Lady of Lourdes	468 W 143rd St
PS 028 Wright Brothers	475 W 155th St
PS 153 Adam C Powell	1750 Amsterdam Ave
PS 192 Jacob H Schiff	500 W 138th St
PS 325	500 W 138th St
Shabak Christian/Daly Day	459 W 152 St
St Catherine of Genoa	508 W 153rd St

Map 22 • Harlem (Upper)

East Harlem Village Academy Charter (M709)	244 W 144th St
Frederick Douglass Academy	2581 Adam Clayton Powell Jr Blvd
PS 046 Arthur Tappan	2987 Frederick Douglass Blvd
PS 123 Mahalia Jackson	301 W 140th St
PS 194 Countee Cullen	244 W 144th St
PS 197 John Russwurm	2230 Fifth Ave
PS 200 James Smith	2589 Adam Clayton Powell Jr Blvd
Resurrection	282 W 151st St
St Charles Borromeo	214 W 142nd St
St Mark the Evangelist	55 W 138th St
Thurgood Marshall Academy Lower	276 W 151st St

Map 23 • Washington Heights

Columbia University Medical Center	630 W 168th St
Columbia University School of Dental and Oral Surgery	630 W 168th St
Columbia University School of Nursing	630 W 168th St
HS 552 Gregorio Luperon High	516 W 181st St
Incarnation Elementary	570 W 175th St
Interboro	260 Audubon Ave
IS 164 Edward W Stitt	401 W 164th St
Mailman School of Public Health	722 W 168th St
Mirabel Sisters IS 90	21 Jumel Pl
The Modern School	870 Riverside Dr
MS 319 Maria Teresa	21 Jumel Pl
MS 321 Minerva	21 Jumel Pl
MS 326 Writers Today & Leaders Tomorrow	401 W 164th St
MS 328	401 W 164th St
Patria (MS 324)	21 Jumel Pl
PS 004 Duke Ellington	500 W 160th St
PS 008 Luis Belliard	465 W 167th St
PS 115 Humboldt	586 W 177th St
PS 128 Audubon	560 W 169th St
PS 173	306 Ft Washington Ave
PS 210 21st Century Academy	4111 Broadway
St Rose of Lima	517 W 164th St
St Spyridon Parochial	120 Wadsworth Ave

Map 24 • Fort George / Fort Tryon

Business & Finance High	549 Audubon Ave
City College Academy of the Arts	4600 Broadway
Community Health Academy of the Heights	511 W 182nd St
Health Careers & Sciences High	549 Audubon Ave
IS 218 Salome Ukena	4600 Broadway
IS 528 Bea Fuller Rodgers	180 Wadsworth Ave
JHS 143 Eleanor Roosevelt	511 W 182nd St
Juan Bosch Public	12 Ellwood St
Law & Public Service High	549 Audubon Ave
Media & Communications High	549 Audubon Ave
Mesivta Rabbi Samson Raphael	8593 Bennett Ave
Middle School 322	4600 Broadway
Mother Cabrini High	701 Ft Washington Ave
Our Lady Queen of Martyrs	71 Arden St
PS 005 Ellen Lurie	3703 Tenth Ave
PS 048 PO Michael J Buczek	4360 Broadway
PS 132 Juan Pablo Duarte	185 Wadsworth Ave
PS 152 Dyckman Valley	93 Nagle Ave
PS 187 Hudson Cliffs	349 Cabrini Blvd
PS 189	2580 Amsterdam Ave
St Elizabeth	612 W 187th St
Washington Heights Expeditionary Learning	511 W 182nd St
Yeshiva Rabbi SR Hirsch	91 Bennett Ave
Yeshiva University	500 W 185th St
Yeshiva University High	2540 Amsterdam Ave

Map 25 • Inwood

Amistad Dual Language	4862 Broadway
Good Shepherd	620 Isham St
JHS 052 Inwood	650 Academy St
Manhattan Christian Academy	401 W 205th St
Muscota (M314)	4862 Broadway
Northeastern Academy	532 W 215th St
PS 018	4124 Ninth Ave
PS 098 Shorac Kappock	512 W 212t St
PS Intermediate School 278	407 W 219th St
PS/IS 278 (M278)	407 W 219th St
St Jude	433 W 204th St
St Matthew Lutheran	200 Sherman Ave

Battery Park City

PS 89	201 Warren St
Stuyvesant High	345 Chambers St

Roosevelt Island

Lillie's International Christian	851 Main St
MS 271 Building (M271)	645 Main St
PS 217 Roosevelt Island	645 Main St

General Information • **Police**

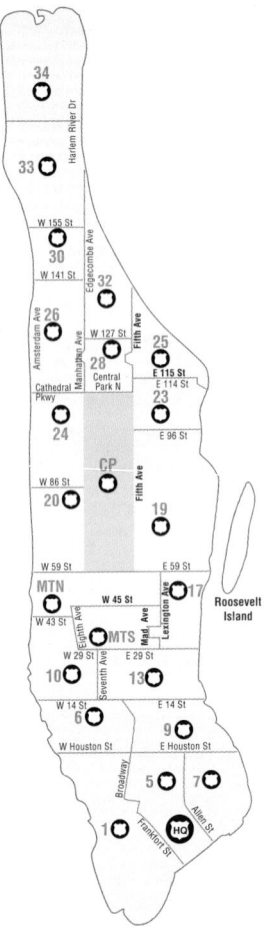

Important Phone Numbers

All Emergencies:	911
Non-Emergencies:	311
Terrorism Hot Line:	888-NYC-SAFE
Crime Stoppers:	800-577-TIPS
Crime Stoppers (Spanish):	888-57-PISTA
Sex Crimes Report Line:	212-267-RAPE
Crime Victims Hotline:	212-577-7777
Cop Shot:	800-COP-SHOT
Missing Persons Case Status:	646-610-6914
Missing Persons Squad:	212-473-2042
Operation Gun Stop:	866-GUNSTOP
Organized Crime Control Bureau Drug Line:	888-374-DRUG
Complaints (Internal Affairs):	212-741-8401
Website:	www.ci.nyc.ny.us/html/nypd/home.html

Statistics

	2006	2005	2003	2002	2001
Uniformed Personnel	37,038	39,110	37,200		
Murders	597	540	596	584	643
Rapes	1,497	1,640	1,877	2,013	1,917
Robberies	23,556	24,417	25,890	27,124	27,863
Felony Assaults	17,124	17,336	18,717	20,700	22,994
Burglaries	22,950	23,997	29,120	31,250	32,663
Grand Larcenies	46,525	47,619	46,518	45,461	46,115
Grand Larcenies (cars)	15,731	17,865	23,144	26,339	29,619

Precinct

		Phone	Map
1st Precinct	16 Ericsson Pl	212-334-0611	2
5th Precinct	19 Elizabeth St	212-334-0711	3
7th Precinct	19 1/2 Pitt St	212-477-7311	4
6th Precinct	233 W 10th St	212-741-4811	5
9th Precinct	130 Avenue C	212-477-7811	7
Mid-Town South	357 W 35th St	212-239-9811	8
10th Precinct	230 W 20th St	212-741-8211	9
13th Precinct	230 E 21st St	212-477-7411	10
Mid-Town North	306 W 54th St	212-760-8300	11
17th Precinct	167 E 51st St	212-826-3211	13
20th Precinct	120 W 82nd St	212-580-6411	14
19th Precinct	153 E 67th St	212-452-0600	15
24th Precinct	151 W 100th St	212-678-1811	16
23rd Precinct	162 E 102nd St	212-860-6411	17
26th Precinct	520 W 126th St	212-678-1311	18
28th Precinct	2271 Frederick Douglass Blvd	212-678-1611	19
32nd Precinct	250 W 135th St	212-690-6311	19
25th Precinct	120 E 119th St	212-860-6511	20
30th Precinct	451 W 151st St	212-690-8811	21
33rd Precinct	2207 Amsterdam Ave	212-927-3200	23
34th Precinct	4295 Broadway	212-927-9711	24
Central Park Precinct	86th St & Transverse Rd	212-570-4820	p236

Post Offices / Zip Codes

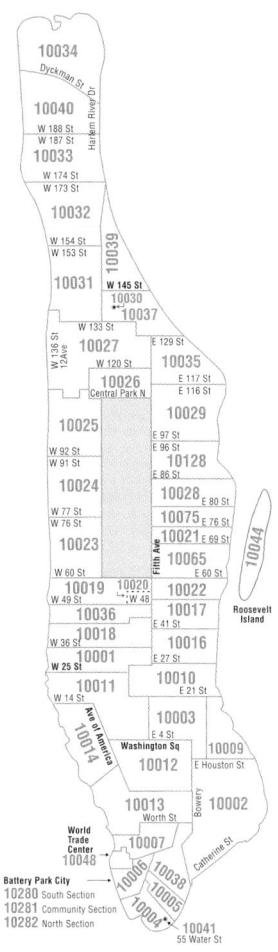

Branch	Address	Phone	Map
Canal Street	350 Canal St	212-925-3378	2
Church Street	90 Church St	212-330-5001	2
Chinatown	6 Doyers St	212-267-3510	3
Peck Slip	1 Peck Slip	212-964-1054	3
Knickerbocker	128 East Broadway	212-608-3598	4
Pitt Station	185 Clinton St	212-254-9270	4
Village	201 Varick St	212-645-0327	5
West Village	527 Hudson St	212-989-5084	5
Cooper	93 Fourth Ave	212-254-1390	6
Patchin	70 W 10th St	212-475-2534	6
Prince	124 Greene St	212-226-7868	6
Peter Stuyvesant	432 E 14th St	212-677-2112	7
Tompkins Square	244 E 3rd St	212-673-6415	7
James A Farley	421 Eighth Ave	212-330-2902	8
London Terrace	234 Tenth Ave	800-275-8777	8
Port Authority	309 W 15th St	212-645-0351	8
Empire State	19 W 33rd St	212-736-8282	9
Greeley Square	39 W 31st St	212-244-7055	9
Midtown	223 W 38th St	212-819-9604	9
Old Chelsea	217 W 18th St	212-675-0548	9
Station 138 (Macy's)	151 W 34th St	212-494-2688	9
Madison Square	149 E 23rd St	212-673-3771	10
Murray Hill	205 E 36th St	212-545-0836	10
Murray Hill Finance	115 E 34th St	212-689-1124	10
Radio City	322 W 52nd St	212-265-3672	11
Times Square	340 W 42nd St	212-502-0421	11
Bryant	23 W 43rd St	212-279-5960	12
Rockefeller Center	610 Fifth Ave	212-265-3854	12
Dag Hammarskjold	884 Second Ave	800-275-8777	13
Franklin D Roosevelt	909 Third Ave	800-275-8777	13
Grand Central Station	450 Lexington Ave	212-330-5722	13
Tudor City	5 Tudor City Pl	800-275-8777	13
Ansonia	178 Columbus Ave	212-362-1697	14
Columbus Circle	27 W 60th St	212-265-7858	14
Planetarium	127 W 83rd St	212-873-5698	14
Cherokee	1483 York Ave	212-517-8361	15
Gracie	229 E 85th St	212-988-6680	15
Lenox Hill	217 E 70th St	212-330-5561	15
Cathedral	215 W 104th St	212-662-0355	16
Park West	693 Columbus Ave	800-275-8777	16
Yorkville	1617 Third Ave	212-369-2747	17
Columbia University	534 W 112th St	800-275-8777	18
Manhattanville	365 W 125th St	212-662-1540	18
Morningside	232 W 116th St	800-275-8777	19
Oscar Garcia Rivera	153 E 110th St	212-860-1896	20
Triborough	167 E 124th St	212-534-0381	20
Hamilton Grange	521 W 146th St	212-281-1538	21
College Station	217 W 140th St	212-283-7096	21
Colonial Park	99 Macombs Pl	212-368-9849	22
Lincolnton	2266 Fifth Ave	212-281-9781	22
Audubon	511 W 165th St	212-568-2387	23
Sergeant Riayan A Tejeda	555 W 180th St	212-568-2690	23
Fort George	4558 Broadway	212-942-5266	24
Inwood Post Office	90 Vermilyea Ave	212-567-7821	25
Roosevelt Island	694 Main St	800-275-8777	p260

General Information · **Hospitals**

If you have to get to a hospital (especially in an emergency), it's best to go to the closest one. However, as a quick reference, the following is a list of the largest hospitals by neighborhood, complete with the name of its corresponding map. But no matter which hospital you drag yourself into, for heaven's sake make sure you have your insurance card.

Lower Manhattan: NYU Downtown Hospital • William & Beekman Sts, just south of the Brooklyn Bridge • [Map 3]

West Village/Chelsea: St Vincent's • Seventh Ave & 12th St [Map 5]

East Village: Beth Israel Medical Center • 14th St & Broadway/Union Square • [Map 10]

Murray Hill: Bellevue Medical Center • First Ave & 27th St [Map 10] ; NYU College of Dentistry • First Ave & 24th St [Map 10]

Hell's Kitchen/Upper West Side: St Luke's Roosevelt Hospital • 10th Ave & 58th St [Map 11]

East Side: New York Presbyterian • York Ave & 68th St [Map 15]; Lenox Hill Hospital • Lexington Ave & 77th St [Map 15]; Mt Sinai Medical Center • Madison Ave & 101st St [Map 17]

Columbia/Morningside Heights: St Luke's Hospital Center • Amsterdam Ave & 114th St [Map 18]

El Barrio: North General Hospital • Madison Ave & 125th St [Map 20]

Farther Uptown: Columbia Presbyterian Medical Center • 168th St & Broadway [Map 23]

If you have a condition that isn't immediately threatening, certain hospitals in New York specialize and excel in specific areas of medicine:

Cancer: Memorial Sloan-Kettering

Birthing Center/Labor & Delivery: St Luke's Roosevelt

Digestive Disorders: Mt Sinai

Dentistry: NYU College of Dentistry

Ear, Nose, and Throat: Mt Sinai

Eyes: New York Eye and Ear Infirmary

Geriatrics: Mt Sinai, New York Presbyterian

Heart: New York Presbyterian

Hormonal Disorders: New York Presbyterian

Kidney Disease: New York Presbyterian

Mental Health: Bellevue

Neurology: New York Presbyterian, NYU Medical Center

Orthopedics: Hospital for Special Surgery, New York Presbyterian

Pediatrics: Children's Hospital of New York Presbyterian

Psychiatry: New York Presbyterian, NYU Medical Center

Rheumatology: Hospital for Special Surgery, Hospital for Joint Diseases Orthopedic Institute, NYU Medical Center

Emergency Rooms	Address	Phone	Map
Bellevue Hospital Center	462 First Ave	212-562-1000	10
Beth Israel Medical Center	281 First Ave	212-420-2000	10
Cabrini Medical Center	227 E 19th St	212-995-6000	10
Harlem Hospital Center	506 Lenox Ave	212-939-1000	22
Hospital for Joint Diseases	301 E 17th St	212-598-6000	10
Lenox Hill	110 E 77th St	212-434-2000	15
Manhattan Eye, Ear & Throat	210 E 64th St	212-838-9200	15
Metropolitan	1901 First Ave	212-423-6262	17
Mt Sinai Medical Center	1190 Fifth Ave	212-241-6500	17
New York Eye & Ear Infirmary	310 E 14th St	212-979-4000	6
New York Presbyterian–Weill Cornell Medical Center	525 E 68th St	212-746-5454	15
New York-Presbyterian Hospital Allen Pavilion	5141 Broadway	212-932-4000	25
New York-Presbyterian Hospital/Columbia University Medical Center	622 W 168th St	212-305-2500	23
North General	1879 Madison Ave	212-423-4000	20
NYU Downtown	170 William St	212-312-5000	3
NYU Medical Center: Tisch	560 First Ave	212-263-7300	10
St Luke's	1111 Amsterdam Ave	212-523-4000	18
St Luke's Roosevelt Hospital Center	1000 Tenth Ave	212-523-4000	11
St Vincent's	170 W 12th St	212-604-7000	5
St Vincent's Midtown	415 W 51st St	212-459-8000	11
VA Hospital	423 E 23rd St	212-686-7500	10

Other Hospitals	Address	Phone	Map
Beth Israel – Phillips Ambulatory Care Center	10 Union Sq E	212-844-8000	10
Coler Goldwater–Coler Campus	900 Main St	212-848-6000	p260
Coler Goldwater–Goldwater Campus	1 Main St	212-318-8000	p260
Gouverneur	227 Madison St	212-238-7000	4
Gracie Square	420 E 76th St	212-988-4400	15
Hospital for Special Surgery	535 E 70 St	212-606-1000	15
Memorial Sloan-Kettering Cancer Center	1275 York Ave	212-639-2000	15
Renaissance Diagnostic and Treatment Center	215 W 125th St	212-932-6500	18

Beginner's mistake: Walk into the main branch of the New York Public Library at Bryant Park, and ask how to check out books. Trust us; it's happened. Recognizable for its reclining stone lions, Patience and Fortitude, the famous building is a research library with non-circulating materials that you can peruse only in the iconic building. If you want to read *War and Peace* or *The Da Vinci Code*, it's best to go to your local branch (there are 80 branch and 5 central libraries). Note: Holds take a very long time to fill, at least a week to a week and a half. If the book you need is only a 20-minute subway ride away, and you need the book now, invest the time and the $4. If it's reference material you're after, there are several specialized research libraries to help:

The Schomburg Center for Research in Black Culture (Map 22) is the nation's foremost source on African-American history. **The Science, Industry, and Business Library (Map 9)** is perhaps the newest and swankiest of all of Manhattan's libraries. **The Library for the Performing Arts (Map 14)** contains the Theatre on Film and Tape Archive. If you can give them even a semi-legitimate reason, you can watch taped performances of most Broadway shows from the past 25 years. **The Early Childhood Resource and Information Center (Map 5)** runs workshops for parenting and reading programs for children.

The aforementioned main branch of the **New York Public Library (Map 12)** (one of Manhattan's architectural treasures, designed by Carrere and Hastings in 1897) has several special collections and services, such as the Humanities and Social Sciences Library, the Map Division, Exhibition galleries, and divisions dedicated to various ethnic groups. The main branch contains 88 miles of shelves and has more than 10,000 current periodicals from almost 150 countries. Research libraries require an ACCESS card, which you can apply for at the library and which allows you to request materials in any of the reading rooms. Card sign-up can be slow, so be patient. It never hurts to bring along multiple kinds of ID, or a piece of mail if you're a new NYC resident. There's also the **Andrew Heiskell Braille and Talking Book Library (Map 9)**, designed to be barrier-free. The library contains large collections of special format materials and audio equipment for listening to recorded books and magazines. You can check out the full system online at www.nypl.org.

Library	Address	Phone	Map
115th Street	203 W 115th St	212-666-9393	19
125th St	224 E 125th St	212-534-5050	20
58th St	127 E 58th St	212-759-7358	13
67th St	328 E 67th St	212-734-1717	15
96th Street	112 E 96th St	212-289-0908	17
Aguilar	174 E 110th St	212-534-2930	20
Andrew Heiskell Braille & Talking Book Library	40 W 20th St	212-206-5400	9
Bloomingdale	150 W 100th St	212-222-8030	16
Chatham Square	3v East Broadway	212-964-6598	3
Columbus	742 Tenth Ave	212-586-5098	11
Countee Cullen	104 W 136th St	212-491-2070	22
Donnell Library Center	20 W 53rd St	212-621-0619	12
Early Childhood Resource & Information Center	66 Leroy St	212-929-0815	5
Epiphany	228 E 23rd St	212-679-2645	10
Fort Washington	535 W 179th St	212-927-3533	23
George Bruce	518 W 125th St	212-662-9727	18
Hamilton Fish Park	415 E Houston St	212-673-2290	7
Hamilton Grange	503 W 145th St	212-926-2147	21
Harlem	9 W 124th St	212-348-5620	19
Hudson Park	66 Leroy St	212-243-6876	5
Humanities & Social Sciences Library	42nd St & Fifth Ave	212-930-0830	12
Inwood	4790 Broadway	212-942-2445	25
Jefferson Market Courthouse	425 Sixth Ave	212-243-4334	5
Kips Bay	446 Third Ave	212-683-2520	10
Macomb's Bridge	2650 Adam Clayton Powell Jr Blvd	212-281-4900	22
Mid-Manhattan Library	455 Fifth Ave	212-340-0849	12
Morningside Heights Library	2900 Broadway	212-864-2530	18
Muhlenberg	209 W 23rd St	212-924-1585	9
Mulberry Street	10 Jersey St	212-966-3424	6
New Amsterdam	9 Murray St	212-732-8186	3
New York Academy of Medicine Library	1216 Fifth Ave	212-822-7200	17
New York Public Library for the Performing Arts	40 Lincoln Center Plz	212-870-1630	14
New York Society Library	53 E 79th St	212-288-6900	15
Ottendorfer	135 Second Ave	212-674-0947	6
Riverside	127 Amsterdam Ave	212-870-1810	14
Roosevelt Island	524 Main St	212-308-6243	p260
Schomburg Center for Research in Black Culture	515 Malcolm X Blvd	212-491-2200	22
Science, Industry, and Business Library	188 Madison Ave	212-592-7000	9
Seward Park	192 East Broadway	212-477-6770	4
St Agnes	444 Amsterdam Ave	212-877-4380	14
Terence Cardinal Cooke-Cathedral	560 Lexington Ave	212-752-3824	13
Tompkins Square	331 E 10th St	212-228-4747	7
Washington Heights	1000 St Nicholas Ave	212-923-6054	23
Webster	1465 York Ave	212-288 5049	15
Yorkville	222 E 79th St	212-744-5824	15

There are few cities in the world that cater to gay men as New York City does; a gay man can find anything and everything he wants, at almost any time of day, in the Big gay Apple. Some bars focus on aesthetics and atmosphere, such as **Therapy** and **Helen's**, while others like **Phoenix** and **The Cock** merely provide the space and alcohol—the rest is up to you. Some gay bars play host to particular types of men, like **Big Lug** (bears and cubs), **Chi Chiz** (men of color), and **Ninth Avenue Bistro** (leather men and the queens who love them). There are even gay bars that now offer social activities: **Climaxx** provides sports leagues and hi-def TV; **Gym** supplies the city's first gay sports bar; and **Splash** remains one of the hottest dance clubs. Be smart, be safe, and enjoy your status as a "NYC Boy."

There are more lesbian bars and parties than ever in New York City, so all you have to do is decide what night, which neighborhood and how you'll snag a girl! Although you'll find quality drinks, music, and women at **Henrietta Hudson's**, the notorious and intolerable bathroom line might discourage those lesbians who actually have a bladder. **LovergirlNYC@The Millionaire's Club** on Saturday nights boasts 500+ beautiful women, while Thursday nights at **Habibi Lounge** promise a more low-key lesbian gathering. Check out **Snapshot at Bar 13** on Tuesday nights for steamy Sapphic scenesters and musicians; **Orchid Lounge** on Sunday nights to view *The L Word* ladies (and the hotties who love them); and **Nowhere** on any night. For an up-to-the-minute list, visit www.gonycmagazine.com. And if you're not afraid of venturing out of Manhattan, check out **Chueca** in Queens—it's a lesbian bar 7 days a week! In Brooklyn, chill on the patio at **Ginger's** or the roof deck at **Cattyshack**; for an exciting Friday night dance party, head to **Sinsations at The Lab**.

Websites

The Lesbian, Gay, Bisexual & Transgender Community Center: www.gaycenter.org — Information about center programs, meetings, publications, and events.

Out & About: www.outandabout.com — Travel website for gays and lesbians including destination information, a gay travel calendar, health information, and listings of gay tour operators.

Gayellow Pages: www.gayellowpages.com — Yellow pages of gay/lesbian-owned and gay/lesbian-friendly businesses in the US and Canada.

Dyke TV: www.dyketv.org — Whether you're interested in viewing or contributing, this website has all the info you'll need.

Edwina: www.edwina.com — A NY online meeting place for gays and lesbians looking for love, lust, or just friendship.

Shescape: www.shescape.com — Hosts lesbian events at various venues in town year round.

Publications

Free at gay and lesbian venues and shops, and some street corners.

HX — Weekly magazine featuring information about bars, clubs, restaurants, events, meetings, and loads of personals. www.hx.com

Gay City News (formerly LGNY) — Newspaper for lesbian and gay New Yorkers including current local and national news items. www.gaycitynews.com

The New York Blade — NYC's only gay-owned and operated weekly newspaper featuring local and national news coverage, as well as guides to theater, nightlife, food, and local arts and entertainment. www.nyblade.com

Next Magazine – Weekly magazine that includes frisky nightlife listings, film reviews, feature articles, and more. www.nextmagazine.net.

GO NYC — Monthly magazine for the urban lesbian on the go with free arts and entertainment listings, weekly event picks, plus information on community organizations and LGBT-owned and LGBT-friendly businesses. www.gonycmagazine.com

Bookshops

Bluestockings, 172 Allen St, 212-777-6028 — Lesbian/radical bookstore and activist center with regular readings and a fair-trade café. www.bluestockings.com

Oscar Wilde: The World's Oldest Gay & Lesbian Bookshop, 15 Christopher St , 212-255-8097—Often in danger of closing, due to decreasing sales, but somehow it survives, and we're better for it. www.oscarwildebooks.com

Health Centers and Support Organizations

Callen-Lorde Community Health Center, 356 W 18th St, 212-271-7200 — Primary Care Center for GLBT New Yorkers. www.callen-lorde.org

Gay Men's Health Crisis, 119 W 24th St, 212-367-1000; Hotline: 212-807-6655 — Non-profit organization dedicated to AIDS awareness and support for those with the disease. www.gmhc.org

The Lesbian, Gay, Bisexual & Transgender Community Center, 208 W 13th, 212-620-7310 — The largest LGBT multi-service organization on the East Coast. www.gaycenter.org

Gay and Lesbian National Hotline, 212-989-0999 — Switchboard for referrals, advice, and counseling. www.glnh.org

Identity House, 39 W 14th St, Ste 205, 212-243-8181 — Offers LGBTQ counseling services, short-term therapy and/or referrals, groups, and workshops. www.identityhouse.org

Lambda Legal Defense and Education Fund, 120 Wall, St Ste 1500, 212 809-8585 — These are the people who fight the good fight in order to secure civil rights for the entire LGBT population. www.lambdalegal.org

National Gay and Lesbian Task Force, 80 Maiden, Ln Ste 1504, 212-604-9830 — This national organization creates change by building LGBT political power and de-marginalizing LGBT issues. www.ngltf.org

New York City Gay & Lesbian Anti-Violence Project, 212-714-1141 — 24-hour crisis support line for violence against LGTBH communities. www.avp.org

PFLAG, 109 E 50th St, 212-463-0629 — Parents, Families, and Friends of Lesbians and Gays meet on the second Sunday of every month 3 pm–5 pm for mutual support. www.pflagnyc.org

Lesbian and Gay Immigration Rights Task Force (LGIRTF), 350 W 31st St, Ste 505, 212-714-2904 — Advocates for changing US policy on immigration of permanent partners. www.lgirtf.org

GLAAD (Gay and Lesbian Alliance Against Defamation), 248 W 35th St, 8th fl, 212-629-3322 — These are the folks who go to bat for you in the media. www.glaad.org

OUTdancing @ Stepping Out Studios, 37 W 26th St, 646-742-9400 — The first LGBT partner dance program in the US. www.steppingoutstudios.com

LGBT Night at Leo Bar, Asia Society 725 Park Ave, 212-327-9352 — Each third Friday of the month, Asia Society partners with a different LGBT professional organization, mixing people, cocktails, and culture. Free exhibition tours included. www.asiasociety.org

Annual Events

Pride Week — Usually the last full week in June; www.hopinc.org (212-807-7433)

New York Gay and Lesbian Film Festival — Showcase of international gay and lesbian films, May/June; www.newfestival.org (212-571-2170)

Mass Blue Ribbon Ride — Replacing the old NYC to Boston AIDS ride, this version is a two-day ride across Massachusetts. The 2006 ride begins in Pittsfield and finishes in Weston, mid-August; www.massredribbonride.org (617-450-1100 or 888-MASSRIDE)

Venues — Lesbian

- **Bamboo 52** (Sun, Ladies Nite) • 344 W 52nd St • 212-315-2777 • Older, upscale *L Word* gathering. Sushi bar, too!

- **Bar 13** (Tues) • 35 E 13th St • 212-979-6677 • www.bar13.com

- **Cattyshack** • 249 Fourth Ave, Brooklyn • 718-230-5740 • www.cattyshackbklyn.com

- **Chueca Bar** • 69-04 Woodside Ave, Queens • 718-424-1171 • www.chuecabar.com • The only Latina lesbian club in NYC.

- **Cubbyhole** • 281 W 12th St • 212-243-9041 • The name says it all, but it's full of fun, flirty women!

- **Escuelita** (Fri) • 301 W 39th St • 212-631-0588 • www.enyclub.com

- **Ginger's** • 363 Fifth Ave, Park Slope • 718-788-0924 • Park Slope's hot lesbian hangout.

- **Habibi Lounge** (Thurs) • 198 Avenue A • 212-982-0932 • www.habibiloungenyc.com • This hookah bar is the place to be, 9 pm–3 am, for a relaxed, lounge-and-flirt-on-cushions evening.

- **Henrietta Hudson** • 438 Hudson St • 212-924-3347 • www.henriettahudson.com

- **Nation** (Sat, girlNation) • 12 West 45th St • 212-391-8053 • Baby dyke gathering in midtown.

- **Nowhere** • 322 E 14th St • 212-477-4744 • Welcomes both gays and lesbians—imagine that!

- **Orchid Lounge** (Sun, Wed) • 500 East 11th St • 212-254-4090 • New venue for Starlette Sundays; considered the Best Lesbian Party in NYC.

- **Rubyfruit Bar & Grill** • 531 Hudson St • 212-929-3343 • A TriBeCa institution, where mature lesbians enjoy happy hour, dinner, or drinks. Beware flannel and mullets!

- **Slipper Room** • 167 Orchard St • 212-253-7246 • www.slipperroom.com • Burlesque and drag queens abound at this LGBT-friendly bar.

- **Starbar** • 218 Avenue A • If the now-defunct Starlight and Wonder Bar had a baby, this would be their bar!

- **The Delancey** (Thurs, Unisex Salon) • 168 Delancey • 212-254-9920 • www.thedelancey.com • This lesbian party combines art and nightlife on the LES.

- **The Lab** (Fri, Sinsations) • 1428 Fulton St • 646-208-8302 • www.girlzparty.com • Indulge in wacky theme nights.

- **The Millionaire's Club** (Sat, LovergirlNYC) • 83 Worth St • 212-252-3397 • www.lovergirlnyc.com •The Big Kahuna of lesbian parties welcomes both members and non-members 10:30 pm–4 am, and includes contests, go-go dancers, and lotsa lesbians!

Venues — Gay

- **Avalon** (Sun. Nights) · 47 W 20th St · 212-807-7780 · www.avalonnewyorkcity.com
- **Barracuda** · 275 W 22nd St · 212-645-8613
- **Barrage** · 401 W 47th St · 212-586-9390
- **Big Lug** · 85 Avenue A · 212-673-1775 · www.biglugnyc.com · Perfectly named bar for bears and cubs.
- **Billie's Black** · 271 W 119th St · 212-280-2248 · www.billiesblack.com · Bar, lounge, and grill.
- **Boiler Room** · 86 E 4th St · 212-254-7536 · Internet jukebox with 100,000 selections.
- **Brite Bar** · 297 Tenth Ave · 212-279-9706 · www.britebar.com
- **Candle Bar** · 309 Amsterdam Ave · 212-874-9155 · Small, but not too small to cruise or be cruised!
- **Chi Chiz** · 135 Christopher St · 212-462-0027
- **Cleo's Ninth Avenue Salon** · 656 Ninth Ave · 212-307-1503
- **Climaxx** (Formerly Boots & Saddle) · 76 Christopher St · 212-929-9684 · www.climaxx.biz · This place has it all: go-go boys, tarot readers, sports leagues, digital jukebox, and hi-def TV.
- **The Cock** · 29 Second Ave · 212-777-6254 · The best late-night gay bar in town.
- **Cyn Lounge** (Thurs) · 216 Bedford Ave, Williamsburg · 718-384-0100 · Queers, Bears & Rears weekly party
- **Dick's Bar** · 192 Second Ave · 212-475-2071
- **The Dugout** · 185 Christopher St · 212-242-9113 · www.thedugoutny.net
- **The Duplex** · 61 Christopher St · 212-255-5438 · www.theduplex.com
- **Eagle** · 554 W 28th St · 646-473-1866 · www.eaglenyc.com
- **EasternBloc** · 505 E 6th St · 212-777-2555 · www.easternblocnyc.com · Bar for boys who crave strong drinks and stronger DJs.
- **Escuelita** · 301 W 39th St · 212-631-0588 · www.enyclub.com
- **g Lounge** · 225 W 19th St · 212-929-1085 · www.glounge.com
- **Gym** · 167 Eighth Ave · 212-337-2439 · www.gymsportsbar.com · NYC's first gay sports bar.
- **The Hangar Bar** · 115 Christopher St · 212-627-2044
- **Helen's** · 169 Eighth Ave · 212-206-0609 · www.helensnyc.com · It doesn't get much gayer than a piano bar with a singing bartender.
- **Julius'** · 159 W 10th St · 212-929-9672 · Mature men hang at this landmark bar.
- **Marie's Crisis** · 59 Grove St · 212-243-9323 · Cheapest Happy Hour in NYC.
- **Metropolitan** · 559 Lorimer St, Williamsburg · 718-599-4444

- **The Monster** · 80 Grove St · 212-924-3558 · www.manhattan-monster.com · Part cabaret, part bar, plus comedians.
- **Ninth Avenue Bistro** · 693 Ninth Ave · 212-397-8356 · Theater queens mingle with leather men.
- **Mr. Black** · 643 Broadway · 212-253-2560 · www.mrblacknyc.com · Multi-cultural dance mecca with rotating DJs.
- **No Parking** · 4168 Broadway · 212-923-8700 · Washington Heights earns another gay bar!
- **Nowhere** · 322 E 14th St · 212-477-4744 · Boys and girls welcome.
- **OW Bar** · 221 E 58th St · 212-355-3395 · www.owbar.com · Size does matter—check out the longest gay bar in NYC!
- **Pegasus** · 119 E 60th St · 212-888-4702
- **The Phoenix** · 447 E 13th St · 212-477-9979 · www.gaybarsnyc.com · No frills, no cheese, no BS.
- **Pieces Bar** · 8 Christopher St · 212-929-9291 · www.piecesbar.com
- **Posh** · 405 W 51st St · 212-957-2222
- **Pyramid Club** · 101 Avenue A · 212-228-4888 · www.thepyramidclub.com · For '80s dance nights, sans the B&T crowd.
- **Rawhide** · 212 Eighth Ave · 212-242-9332 · Leather crowd.
- **The Ritz** · 369 W 46th St · 212-333-2554 · Another bar/lounge with outdoor patio and guest DJs.
- **Secret** · 525 W 29th St · 212-268-5580 · Shh, another gay lounge.
- **Splash** (SBNY) · 50 W 17th St · 212-691-0073 · www.splashbar.com · Quintessential gay club.
- **Stonewall** · 53 Christopher St · 212-463-0950 · www.stonewall-place.com
- **Suite** · 992 Amsterdam Ave · 212-222-4600 · www.suitenyc.com · Chic bar with drag shows.
- **Xth Avenue Lounge** · 642 Tenth Ave · 212-245-9088
- **Therapy** · 348 W 52nd St · 212-397-1700 · www.therapy-nyc.com
- **Tool Box** · 1742 Second Ave · 212-348-1288
- **Townhouse** · 236 E 58th St · 212-754-4649 · www.townhouseny.com
- **Ty's** · 114 Christopher St · 212-741-9641
- **The Urge** · 33 Second Ave · 212-533-5757 · East Village lounge with 2-tier bar.
- **View Bar** · 232 Eighth Ave · 212-929-2243 · www.viewbarnyc.com
- **Vlada** · 331 West 51st St · 212-974-8030 · www.vladabar.com · Sip one of fifteen infused vodkas at this romantic and sophisticated midtown bar.
- **The Web** · 40 E 58th St · 212-308-1546 · Where the Asian boys are.
- **XES Lounge** · 157 West 24th St · 212-604-0212 · www.xesnyc.com

Map 1 · Financial District

Achira Copy Center	2 Rector St	212-227-1919
Big Apple Copy and Printing Center	115 Broadway	212-962-4282
Commerce Photo-Print	15 Dutch St	212-619-2679
DRS Imaging Services	75 Maiden Ln, 11th Fl	212-924-8680
Fedex Kinko's	100 Wall St	212-269-0024
FedEx Kinko's	110 William St	212-766-4646
Hard Copy Printing	111 John St	212-571-4141
Ikon Office Solutions	40 Broad St, Fl 24	212-376-6100
Lex Reprographic	125 Maiden Ln	212-344-9222
National Reprographics	160 Broadway	212-366-1726
Nova Offset Corporation	47 Ann St	212-349-1233
Perfect Copy Center	11 Broadway	212-425-4818
Skyline Duplication	39 Broadway	212-785-3626
Sol Speedy	26 Broadway	212-797-9400
Staples	200 Water St	212-785-9521
The UPS Store	5 Hanover Sq	212-514-7472
The UPS Store	118A Fulton St	212-406-9010
The UPS Store	64 Beaver St	212-514-7472

Map 2 · TriBeCa

21 Laminating & Binding Center	130 Church St	212-608-8870
Bestype Imaging	285 West Broadway	212-966-6886
Jean Paul Duplicating Center	275 Greenwich St	212-587-0579
Mail Boxes Etc	295 Greenwich St	212-964-5528
Shield Press	9 Lispenard St	212-431-7489
The UPS Store	305 West Broadway	212-680-3118

Map 3 · City Hall / Chinatown

Fedex Kinko's	105 Duane St	212-406-1220
Print Facility	225 Broadway	212-267-1762
Soho Reprographics	381 Broome St	212-925-7575
Staples	217 Broadway	212-346-9624
Staples	488 Broadway	212-219-1299
The UPS Store	342 Broadway	212-842-5383
Visual Arts & Photo	63E Bayard St	212-566-1328

Map 5 · West Village

Copy/Com	70A Greenwich Ave	212-924-4180
Elite Copy Center	52 Carmine St	212-691-1452
Mail Boxes Etc	511 Sixth Ave	212-924-4002
Mail Boxes Etc	302 W 12th St	212-206-6996
Mail Boxes Etc	315 Bleecker St	212-675-6310
Memory Keeper Photo	147 W 14th St	212-691-9047
Village Copy Center	520 Hudson St	212-255-6652
Village Copying Computer Center	520 Hudson St	212-255-6652

Map 6 · Washington Sq / NYU / NoHo / SoHo

4th Estate Copy Center	65 E 4th St	212-466-0871
Advanced Copy Center	552 LaGuardia Pl	212-388-1001
American Copy Center	201 E 10th St	212-505-5444
City Copies Inc	48 E 7th St	212-228-5183
East Side Copy	15 E 13th St	212-807-0465
FedEx Kinko's	21 Astor Pl	212-228-9511
First Prince Copy Center	22 Prince St	212-334-1243
King Photocopy	45 E 7th St	212-673-8481
National Reprographics	594 Broadway	212-366-7015
New University Copy	11 Waverly Pl	212-473-7369
New York Copy Center	204 E 11th St	212-673-5628
New York Copy Center	34 E 7th St	212-473-8234
Prince Street Copy	159 Prince St	212-982-7333
Source Unlimited Printing	331 E 9th St	212-473-7833
Staples	5 Union Sq W	212-929-6323
Staples	769 Broadway	646-654-6660
Unique Copy Center	252 Greene St	212-420-9198
The UPS Store	111 E 14th St	212-979-8785
The UPS Store	168 Second Ave	212-673-6313
The UPS Store	7 E 8th St	212-477-3350
The UPS Store	319 Lafayette St	212-625-0080
The Village Copier	20 E 13th St	212-924-3456

Map 7 · East Village / Lower East Side

FedEx Kinko's	250 E Houston St	212-253-9020

Map 8 · Chelsea

Empire State Blue Print	555 Eighth Ave	212-904-1933
FedEx Kinko's	655 W 34th St	212-216-2900
Mail Boxes Etc	245 Eighth Ave	212-366-4310
Staples	500 Eighth Ave	212-244-2681
The UPS Store	328 Eighth Ave	212-337-3104
The UPS Store	1 Penn Plz	212-290-8009

Map 9 · Flatiron / Lower Midtown

A Estaban & Co	132 W 36th St	212-714-2227
A-A-D United Reprographic Services	40 W 25th St	212-645-6918
AAA Wonder Copy & Printing	174 Fifth Ave	212-242-4309

General Information · **Copy Shops**

Action Letter	10 E 39th St	212-683-1607
Acu-Copy	26 W 39th St	212-944-9250
Advanced Printing NYC	263 W 38th St	212-840-8108
Alpha Business Machine	151 W 30th St	212-643-5555
Alphagraphics	253 Fifth Ave	212-889-0069
Bernie's Copy Center / Penn Graphics	242 W 30th St	212-564-9376
Beyond Printing	450 Seventh Ave	212-868-9450
BPI	34 W 17th St	212-929-6223
Century Copy Center	70 Seventh Ave	212-989-9833
Commerce Photo-Print	15 W 39th St	212-944-7810
Comzone	21 E 15th St	212-645-6428
Copy Specialists	44 E 21st St	212-533-7560
Copy Specialists	71 W 23rd St	212-689-2777
Crown Digital Imaging	262 W 38th St	212-302-8634
Digital Data Solutions	1133 Broadway	646-486-6721
Digitech Printers	150 W 30th St	212-629-6150
Document Technologies	21 W 38th St	212-395-9000
Enneso	1410 Broadway	212-686-9303
Ensof	1410 Broadway	212-686-9303
Esteban	136 W 21st St	212-989-7000
FedEx Kinko's	239 Seventh Ave	212-929-0623
FedEx Kinko's	650 Sixth Ave	646-638-9238
FedEx Kinko's	191 Madison Ave	212-685-3449
FedEx Kinko's	500 Seventh Ave	646-366-9166
FedEx Kinko's	Empire State Bldg, 350 Fifth Ave	212-279-3556
Iron Copy Center	25 E 20th St	212-529-3734
Lightning Copy	54 W 39th St	212-764-2160
Lithomatic Business Forms	233 W 18th St	212-255-6700
Longacre Copy Center	1385 Broadway	212-944-0410
Mail Boxes Etc	303 Park Ave S	212-477-0211
National Reprographics	44 W 18th St	212-366-7250
Oak Hill Graphics	18 E 39th St	212-684-4040
Perfect Copy	62 W 39th St	212-302-2002
Postnet	530 Fashion Ave	212-342-7428
Precision Photos	260 W 36th St	212-302-2770
Printability	71 W 23rd St	212-675-7800
Rainbow Photo Lab II	120 W 33rd St	212-947-1870
Sir Speedy	234 W 35th St	212-564-9320
Soho Reprographics	307 Seventh Ave	212-675-6054
Speedway Copy & Printing	224 W 35th St	212-563-1070
Splat Ink	78 W 36th St	212-268-7840
Staples	1293 Broadway	212-564-8580
Staples	Penn Station	646-674-1652
Staples	699 Sixth Ave	212-675-5698
Staples	16 E 34th St	212-683-8009
Superior Office Systems	240 W 35th St	212-695-5588
Swift Copy Printing	10 E 36th St	212-683-4900
The UPS Store	101 W 23rd St	212-529-3131
The UPS Store	130 Seventh Ave	212-989-3593
The UPS Store	243 Fifth Ave	212-213-1043
The UPS Store	244 Madison Ave	212-532-5590
The UPS Store	1357 Broadway	212-736-3255
Wholesale Copies	1 E 28th St	212-779-4065
Wonder Copy & Prinitng	174 Fifth Ave, Room 501	212-924-4953

Map 10 • Murray Hill / Gramercy

Columbia Enterprises	116 E 16th St	212-477-9363
Ever Ready Blue Print	200 Park Ave S	212-228-3131
FedEx Kinko's	257 Park Ave S	646-602-0074
Fedex Kinko's	600 Third Ave	212-599-2679
Graphics Service Bureau	370 Park Ave S	212-684-3600
Mail Boxes Etc	163 Third Ave	212-533-9100
On-Site Sourcing	443 Park Ave S Fl 3	212-252-9700
Pro-Print	424 Park Ave S	212-252-0720
Staples	345 Park Ave S	212-683-3267
Tower Copy East	370 Third Ave	212-679-3509
The UPS Store	163 Third Ave	212-533-9100
The UPS Store	388 Second Ave	212-375-8292
The UPS Store	527 Third Ave	212-683-9634
The UPS Store	163 Third Ave	212-533-9100
The UPS Store	353 Third Ave	212-481-0055

Map 11 • Hell's Kitchen

Mail Boxes Etc	331 W 57th St	212-489-8004
Mail Boxes Etc	676 Ninth Ave	212-957-9090
Rapid Copy	366 W 52nd St	212-777-3333

Map 12 • Midtown

Accurate Copy Services	250 W 57th St	212-265-4304
Advantage Reprographics	25 W 45 St	212-382-1662
Atlantic Blueprint	575 Madison Ave	212-755-3388
BPI	295 Madison Ave	212-686-2436
City Repro	939 Eighth Ave	212-247-7575
The Complete Copy Center	1271 Sixth Ave	212-757-7303
Corporate Reproductions	295 Madison Ave	212-808-0334
Deanco Press	767 Fifth Ave	212-371-2025
Discovery Copy Services	45 W 45th St	212-827-0039
Duplications Unlimited	149 W 55th St	212-247-6642

FedEx Kinko's	60 W 40th St	212-921-1060
FedEx Kinko's	233 W 54th St	212-977-2679
FedEx Kinko's	240 Central Park S	212-258-3750
FedEx Kinko's	16 E 52nd St	212-308-2679
FedEx Kinko's	1211 Sixth Ave	212-391-2679
Genie Instant Printing Center	37 W 43rd St	212-575-8258
Met Photo	1500 Broadway	212-869-6960
Metropolitan Copy	15 W 45th St	212-620-0087
Modernage Photographic Services	1150 Sixth Ave	212-227-4767
Natalia's Photo	3 W 46th St	212-997-9626
Office Depot	1441 Broadway	212-764-2465
On Press Graphics	250 W 40th St	212-278-8300
Perfection Reprographics	McGraw-Hill Bldg, 1221 Sixth Ave	212-541-9060
Pro-Print	23 W 45th St	212-354-0400
Red Rose Legal Copy Centers	18 E 41st St	646-424-1777
Servco	1150 Sixth Ave	212-575-0991
Skyline Duplication	151 W 46th St	212-302-5153
Staples	535 Fifth Ave	646-227-0585
Staples	1065 Sixth Ave	212-997-4446
Staples	57 W 57th St	212-308-0335
Staples	776 Eighth Ave	212-265-4550
The UPS Store	888C Eighth Ave	212-581-2669
The UPS Store	1514 Broadway	646-366-8867
The UPS Store	1383 Sixth Ave	212-246-4700
The Village Copier	25 W 43rd St	212-220-6143
Z Photo	136 W 44th St	212-997-9527

Map 13 • East Midtown

Copy Right Reprographics	133 E 55th St	212-319-4747
Copy Room	850 Third Ave	212-371-8600
Express Graphics	Chrysler Building (arcade level), 405 Lexington Ave	212-371-5812
EZCopying	405 Lexington Ave	212-421-7719
FedEx Kinko's	747 Third Ave	212-753-7778
FedEx Kinko's	641 Lexington Ave	212-572-9995
Fedex Kinko's	153 E 53rd St	212-753-7580
Fedex Kinko's	230 Park Ave	212-949-2534
Flynns	55 E 59th St	212-339-8700
Fromex	678 Lexington Ave	212-644-3394
Graphic Laboratory	228 E 45th St	212-682-1815
Ikon Office Solutions	950 Third Ave	212-223-3131
Lightning Copy Center	60 E 42nd St	212-682-3530
Mail Boxes Etc	1040 First Ave	212-688-8881
Metro Copy and Duplicating	222 E 45th St	212-687-6699
Midtown Copy	249 E 55th St	212-826-6030
Staples	205 E 42nd St	212-697-1591
Staples	730 Third Ave	212-867-9486
Staples	425 Park Ave	212-753-9640
Staples	575 Lexington Ave	212-644-2118
Statter	777 Third Ave	212-546-1275

The UPS Store	132 E 43rd St	212-867-0001
The UPS Store	208 E 51st St	212-753-4800
The UPS Store	954 Third Ave	212-319-1928
The Village Copier	420 Lexington Ave	212-220-6161

Map 14 • Upper West Side (Lower)

Copy USA	210 W 83rd St	212-580-8666
FedEx Kinko's	221 W 72nd St	212-362-5288
Gavin Printing	387 Amsterdam Ave	212-721-9009
IBU Copy & Copy	517 Amsterdam Ave	212-769-4484
Mail Boxes Etc	163 Amsterdam Ave	212-595-5353
Manhattan Mail Room	459 Columbus Ave	212-724-1600
Matrix Copy & Printing Services	140 W 72nd St	212-724-1309
Panda Copy	2220 Broadway	212-362-4246
Printing Express and Speed Copy Center	126 W 83rd St	212-875-1809
Staples	2248 Broadway	212-712-9617
Studio 305	313 Amsterdam Ave	212-724-8758
Upper Westside Copy Center	2054 Broadway	212-496-7500
The UPS Store	119 W 72nd St	212-496-0216
The UPS Store	366 Amsterdam Ave	212-712-2611

Map 15 • Upper East Side (Lower)

Complete Copy Center	349 E 82nd St	917-432-1139
Copy & Graphics	1388 Second Ave	212-861-1300
Copycats	968 Lexington Ave	212-734-6236
Copyland Center	335 E 65th St	212-439-8504
Copyland Center	1597 Second Ave	212-452-2906
FedEx Kinko's	1122 Lexington Ave	212-628-5500
Fromex	1247 Third Ave	212-288-8897
Mail Boxes Etc	1461 First Ave	212-734-4412
Mail Boxes Etc	954 Lexington Ave	212-288-4425
Mail Boxes Etc	1202 Lexington Ave	212-439-6104
The UPS Store	1173 Second Ave	212-832-1390
The UPS Store	1275 First Ave	212-535-3325
The UPS Store	1562 First Ave	212-861-0581
The UPS Store	1397 Second Ave	212-585-4195
Yorkville Copy Service	133 E 84th St	212-879-1410

Map 16 • Upper West Side (Upper)

Columbia Copy Center	2790 Broadway	212-865-1212
Copy Concept	216 W 103rd st	212-665-8523
Copy Door	70 W 86th St	212-362-6430
Copy Experts & Computer Center	2440 Broadway	212-875-0948

Foxy Copy	211 W 92nd St	212-724-1770
Global Copy	2578 Broadway	212-222-2679
Riverside Resumes	248 W 106th St	212-865-5800
The UPS Store	2565 Broadway	212-866-5511
The UPS Store	2753 Broadway	212-222-1202
The UPS Store	2576 Broadway	212-866-5511

Map 17 • Upper East Side / East Harlem

Copy Quest	163 E 92nd St	212-410-5055
Desktop USA	1476 Lexington Ave	212-534-9799
Kev's Copy Center	1862 Third Ave	212-828-7310
Mail Boxes Etc	1710 First Ave	212-423-5555
Staples	1280 Lexington Ave	212-426-6190
The UPS Store	217 E 86th St	212-996-7900
The UPS Store	1636 Third Ave	212-410-7814
The UPS Store	1324 Lexington Ave	212-369-6789
The Ups Store	1838 Second Ave	212-423-1826

Map 18 • Columbia / Morningside Heights

Broadway Copy Center	3062 Broadway	212-864-6501
The UPS Store	603 W 115th St	212-865-9601
The Village Copier	2872 Broadway	212-666-0600
The Village Copier	1181 Amsterdam Ave	212-666-4777

Map 19 • Harlem (Lower)

Fromex	1365 Fifth Ave	212-307-1848
Kev's Copy Center	355 Malcolm X Blvd	212-663-6003
Staples	105 W 125th St	212-864-5747
The UPS Store	2216 Frederick Douglass Blvd	212-222-8260
The UPS Store	55 W 116th St	212-876-8800

Map 20 • El Barrio / East Harlem

Copykat Information & Business Center	1785 Lexington Ave	212-534-1400
Patane Press	228 E 125th St	212-289-1440

Map 21 • Manhattanville / Hamilton Heights

Best Graphics Press	506 W 145th St	212-281-9440

Map 22 • Harlem (Upper)

Kev's Copy Center	2730 Frederick Douglass Blvd	212-926-4771

Map 23 • Washington Heights

The UPS Store	809 W 181st St	212-740-9204

Map 24 • Fort George / Fort Tryon

Staples	4320 Broadway	212-927-0467

Map 25 • Inwood

Dazlynn Office Equipment	231 Dyckman St	212-569-2050
The UPS Store	4768 Broadway	212-304-0282

The latest FedEx dropoffs are at 9:30 pm Monday–Friday at 130 Leroy (**Map 5**), 560 West 42nd Street (**Map 11**), 621 West 48th Street (**Map 11**), and 880 Third Avenue (**Map 13**). However, many Manhattan FedEx delivery trucks have a drop-off slot on the side of the truck itself, in case you're on your way to a service center at 9:15 pm and see one. Please note that locations, hours of operation, and pickup times may change. If in doubt, call 1-800-Go-FedEx or visit www.FedEx.com.

Map 1 • Financial District

FedEx Kinko's	55 Broadway	9:00pm
FedEx Kinko's	110 William St	9:00pm
FedEx Kinko's	100 William St	9:00pm
Federal Express	110 Wall St	9:00pm
Self-Service	1 New York Plaza	8:30pm
Self-Service	180 Maiden Ln	8:30pm
Self-Service	32 Old Slip	8:30pm
Self-Service	88 Pine St	8:30pm
FedEx Kinko's	100 Wall St	8:00pm
Self-Service	1 Chase Manhattan Plz	8:00pm
Self-Service	1 State St Plz	8:00pm
Self-Service	11 Broadway	8:00pm
Self-Service	125 Maiden Ln	8:00pm
Self-Service	14 Wall St	8:00pm
Self-Service	150 Broadway	8:00pm
Self-Service	17 Battery Pl	8:00pm
Self-Service	26 Broadway	8:00pm
Self-Service	4 New York Plaza	8:00pm
Self-Service	40 Exchange Pl	8:00pm
Self-Service	40 Rector St	8:00pm
Self-Service	44 Wall St	8:00pm
Self-Service	60 Wall St	8:00pm
Self-Service	7 Hanover Sq	8:00pm
Self-Service	83 Maiden Lane	8:00pm
Self-Service	90 Broad St	8:00pm
Self-Service	95 Wall St	8:00pm
Self-Service	1 Battery Park Plz	8:00pm
Self-Service	33 Liberty St	7:30pm
The MailRoom	79 Pine St	7:00pm
Self-Service	120 Broadway	7:00pm

Map 2 • TriBeCa

Self-Service	145 Hudson St	8:30pm
Self-Service	100 6th Ave	8:00pm
Self-Service	3 World Financial Center	8:00pm
Self-Service	32 Ave of The Americas	8:00pm
Mail Boxes Etc	295 Greenwich St	6:00pm
Biz Direct	130 Church St	5:30pm
Bestype Imaging	285 W Broadway	5:30pm

Map 3 • City Hall / Chinatown

FedEx Kinko's	4 Barclay St	9:00pm
Howard Shipping	33 Howard St	8:30pm
Self-Service	11 Park Pl	8:30pm
Self-Service	401 Broadway	8:30pm
Quick Global Shipping	25 Howard St	8:00pm

Global Entertainment Work	227 Grand St, 3rd Fl	8:00pm
FedEx Kinko's	105 Duane St	8:00pm
Self-Service	109 Lafayette St	8:00pm
Self-Service	434 Broadway	8:00pm
Broadway Parcel Service	383 Broadway	7:00pm
First China Express	175 Lafayette St	7:00pm
Far East Shipping Service	28 Bowery	6:30pm
WJRD	125 Canal St	6:00pm
East Express Services	88 E Broadway Rm 143	6:00pm
Self-Service	488 Broadway # 926	6:00pm
Thriftway Beekman Pharmacy	19 Beekman St	5:00pm
Self-Service	6 Doyers St	4:30pm

Map 4 • Lower East Side

Self-Service	357 Grand St	8:00pm
S+dx Computerconstruction	58 Allen St	5:30pm

Map 5 • West Village

Federal Express	130 Leroy St	9:30pm
FedEx Kinko's	229 W Fourth St	9:00pm
Self-Service	180 Varick St	8:30pm
Self-Service	350 Hudson St	8:30pm
Self-Service	375 Hudson St	8:30pm
Self-Service	201 Varick St	8:00pm
Self-Service	250 Hudson St	8:00pm
Self-Service	80 8th Ave	8:00pm
Self-Service	95 Morton St	8:00pm
Self-Service	139 Charles St	7:30pm
Self-Service	315 Hudson St	7:00pm
Mailbox Etc	302 W 12th St, Ste A	6:00pm
Village Copy & Computer	520 Hudson St	6:00pm
Mail Boxes Etc	315 Bleecker St	6:00pm
Your Neighborhood Office	332 Bleecker St	6:00pm
Mail Boxes Etc	511 Ave of the Americas	6:00pm

Map 6 • Washington Square / NYU / NoHo / SoHo

FedEx Kinko's	70 Spring St	9:00pm
FedEx Kinko's	21 Astor Pl	9:00pm
Self-Service	375 Lafayette St	8:30pm
Self-Service	799 Broadway	8:30pm

Self-Service	270 Lafayette St	8:00pm
Self-Service	580 Broadway	8:00pm
United Shipping and Package	200 E 10th St	6:30pm
First Prince Copy Center	22 Prince St	6:00pm
Ny Digital Copy Center	204 E 11th St	5:30pm
Village Postal Center	532 Laguardia Pl	5:00pm
Mail Call	341 Lafayette St	4:30pm
Self-Service	124 Greene St	4:30pm

Map 7 • East Village / Lower East Side

FedEx Kinko's	250 E Houston St	9:00pm
Keepers Packaging & Shipping	444 E 10th St	6:00pm
Ganacom Wireless Corp	139 Essex St	5:00pm
Little Village Postal	151 First Ave	5:00pm

Map 8 • Chelsea

FedEx	W 33rd St & Tenth Ave	9:00pm
Self-Service	322 8th Ave	8:00pm
Self-Service	450 W 15th St	8:00pm
Self-Service	5 Penn Plz	8:00pm
Self-Service	505 8th Ave	8:00pm
Self-Service	508 W 26th St	8:00pm
Self-Service	519 8th Ave	8:00pm
Self-Service	520 8th Ave	8:00pm
Self-Service	537 W 33rd St	8:00pm
Self-Service	538 W 34th St	8:00pm
Self-Service	545 8th Ave	8:00pm
Self-Service	75 9th Ave	8:00pm
Self-Service	547 W 27th St	7:30pm
Direct Rush Inc	356 W 37th St	6:00pm
Mail Boxes Etc	245 Eighth Ave	6:00pm
Self-Service	450 W 33rd St	6:00pm
Self-Service	111 8th Ave	5:30pm
Gr Courier	302 W 37th St Fl 2	4:30pm
Self-Service	234 10th Ave	4:30pm
Monarch Sewing USA	327 W 36th St	3:30pm

Map 9 • Flatiron / Lower Midtown

FedEx Kinko's	125 W 33rd St	9:00pm
FedEx Kinko's	157 W 35 St	9:00pm
FedEx Kinko's	1 Penn Plz	9:00pm

365

General Information · FedEx

Map 9 · Flatiron / Lower Midtown—continued

FedEx	112 W 39th St	9:00pm
FedEx Kinko's	125 Fifth Ave	9:00pm
FedEx Kinko's	1350 Broadway	9:00pm
FedEx	149 Madison Ave	9:00pm
FedEx	20 E 20th St	9:00pm
FedEx Kinko's	261 Madison Ave	9:00pm
FedEx Kinko's	350 5th Ave	9:00pm
FedEx Kinko's	4 Union Sq E	9:00pm
FedEx Kinko's	525 Seventh Ave	9:00pm
FedEx Kinko's	Eight E 23rd St	9:00pm
FedEx Kinko's	326 Seventh Ave	9:00pm
PostNet	200 W 39th St	8:00pm
FedEx Kinko's	239 Seventh Ave	8:00pm
Self-Service	1133 Broadway	8:00pm
Self-Service	121 W 27th St	8:00pm
Self-Service	1370 Broadway	8:00pm
Self-Service	207 W 25th St	8:00pm
Self-Service	21 Penn Plz	8:00pm
Self-Service	220 5th Ave	8:00pm
Self-Service	225 W 34th St	8:00pm
Self-Service	230 5th Ave	8:00pm
Self-Service	239 7th Ave	8:00pm
Self-Service	390 5th Ave	8:00pm
Self-Service	41 Madison Ave	8:00pm
Self-Service	45 W 18th St	8:00pm
Self-Service	450 7th Ave	8:00pm
Self-Service	463 7th Ave	8:00pm
Self-Service	469 7th Ave	8:00pm
Self-Service	485 7th Ave	8:00pm
Self-Service	650 Ave of The Americas	8:00pm
Self-Service	875 Ave of The Americas	8:00pm
FedEx Kinko's	500 7th Ave	7:30pm
FedEx Kinko's	650 6th Ave	7:30pm
Self-Service	132 W 31st St	7:30pm
Self-Service	1385 Broadway	7:30pm
Self-Service	5 W 37th St	7:30pm
PostNet Ny126	802 6th Ave	7:00pm
Self-Service	100 W 33rd St	7:00pm
Self-Service	1250 Broadway	7:00pm
Self-Service	1407 Broadway	7:00pm
Self-Service	28 E 28th St	7:00pm
Self-Service	37 E 28th St	7:00pm
Self-Service	50 W 34th St	7:00pm
Self-Service	699 Ave of The Americas	7:00pm
FedEx Kinko's	191 Madison Ave	6:00pm
Self-Service	1411 Broadway	6:00pm
Self-Service	16 E 34th St	6:00pm
Self-Service	276 5th Ave	6:00pm
Self-Service	330 5th Ave	6:00pm
Self-Service	366 5th Ave	6:00pm
Self-Service	217 W 18th St	5:00pm
Self-Service	233 W 18th St	5:00pm
Self-Service	5 Union Sq W	5:00pm
Self-Service	19 W 33rd St	4:30pm
Self-Service	39 W 31st St	4:30pm

Map 10 · Murray Hill / Gramercy

FedEx Kinko's	108 E 28th St	9:00pm
FedEx Kinko's	2 Park Ave	9:00pm
FedEx Kinko's	90 Park Ave	9:00pm
FedEx Kinko's	600 Third Ave	9:00pm
Self-Service	200 Park Ave S	8:15pm
FedEx Kinko's	257 Park Ave S	8:00pm
FedEx Kinko's	230 Park Ave	8:00pm
Self-Service	200 Lexington Ave	8:00pm
Self-Service	220 E 23rd St	8:00pm
Self-Service	225 Park Ave S Fl 13	8:00pm
Self-Service	3 Park Ave	8:00pm
Self-Service	475 Park Ave S	8:00pm
Self-Service	545 1st Ave	8:00pm
Self-Service	550 1st Ave	8:00pm
Self-Service	240 E 38th St	7:30pm
Backofficenyc	345 E 18th St	7:00pm
The Villager	338 First Ave	7:00pm
Self-Service	192 Lexington Ave	7:00pm
Self-Service	425 E 25th St	7:00pm
Mail Boxes Etc	303 Park Ave S	6:30pm
Baruch Copy n Mail Services	50 Lexington Ave	6:00pm
Manbi Traders	122 Lexington Ave	6:00pm
Self-Service	660 1st Ave	6:00pm
Self-Service	345 Park Ave S	5:00pm
FedEx Kinko's	600 3rd Ave	2:00pm

Map 11 · Hell's Kitchen

Federal Express	621 W 48th St	9:30pm
FedEx	560 W 42nd St	9:30pm
FedEx Kinko's	1290 Ave of the Americas	9:00pm
Self-Service	405 W 55th St	8:00pm
Self-Service	429 W 53rd St	8:00pm
Self-Service	630 9th Ave	8:00pm
Self-Service	322 W 52nd St	7:00pm
Self-Service	57 W 57th St	6:00pm
Mail Boxes Etc	676a 9th Ave	5:00pm
Self-Service	340 W 42nd St	4:30pm

Map 12 · Midtown

FedEx Kinko's	1440 Broadway	9:00pm
FedEx Kinko's	200 W 57th St	9:00pm
FedEx Kinko's	43 W 42nd St	9:00pm
FedEx Kinko's	1120 Ave of The Americas	9:00pm
Federal Express	135 W 50th St	9:00pm
FedEx Kinko's	6 W 48th St	9:00pm
FedEx Kinko's	1211 Ave of The Americas	9:00pm
FedEx Kinko's	233 W 54th St	9:00pm
FedEx Kinko's	240 Central Park S	9:00pm
Self-Service	1211 Sixth Ave	8:30pm
Self-Service	1515 Broadway	8:30pm
Self-Service	1700 Broadway	8:30pm
Self-Service	444 Madison Ave	8:30pm
Self-Service	51 W 52nd St Fl 21	8:30pm

Self-Service	590 Madison Ave	8:15pm
FedEx Kinko's	437 Madison Ave	8:00pm
FedEx Kinko's	10 E 53rd St	8:00pm
FedEx Kinko's	16 E 52nd St	8:00pm
Self-Service	10 E 40th St	8:00pm
Self-Service	1185 Ave of The Americas	8:00pm
Self-Service	120 W 45th St	8:00pm
Self-Service	1285 Ave of The Americas	8:00pm
Self-Service	1325 6th Ave	8:00pm
Self-Service	1350 Ave of The Americas	8:00pm
Self-Service	1370 Ave of The Americas	8:00pm
Self-Service	1466 Broadway	8:00pm
Self-Service	1500 Broadway	8:00pm
Self-Service	1501 Broadway	8:00pm
Self-Service	152 W 57th St	8:00pm
Self-Service	1775 Broadway	8:00pm
Self-Service	224 W 57th St	8:00pm
Self-Service	3 E 54th St	8:00pm
Self-Service	30 Rockefeller Plaza	8:00pm
Self-Service	41 W 48th St	8:00pm
Self-Service	477 Madison Ave	8:00pm
Self-Service	488 Madison Ave	8:00pm
Self-Service	500 5th Ave	8:00pm
Self-Service	530 5th Ave	8:00pm
Self-Service	555 Madison Ave	8:00pm
Self-Service	575 Madison Ave	8:00pm
Self-Service	600 Madison Ave	8:00pm
Self-Service	712 5th Ave	8:00pm
Self-Service	745 5th Ave	8:00pm
Self-Service	787 7th Ave	8:00pm
Self-Service	825 8th Ave	8:00pm
FedEx Kinko's	60 W 40th St	7:30pm
Self-Service	1095 6th Ave	7:30pm
Self-Service	156 W 56th St	7:30pm
Self-Service	335 Madison Ave	7:30pm
La Boutique	2 E 55th St	7:00pm
Self-Service	1065 6th Ave	7:00pm
Self-Service	57 W 57th St	7:00pm
FedEx Kinko's	51 E 44th St	6:30pm
FedEx Kinko's	767 Fifth Ave	6:00pm
Fifth Avenue Pack & Ship	666 5th Ave	5:30pm
Self-Service	1155 Ave of The Americas	5:00pm
Self-Service	223 W 38th St	5:00pm
Self-Service	23 W 43rd St	4:30pm
Self-Service	610 5th Ave	4:30pm

Map 13 · East Midtown

Federal Express	880 Third Ave	9:30pm
Self-Service	270 Park Ave	9:15pm
Self-Service	280 Park Ave	8:45pm
FedEx Kinko's	750 Third Ave	8:30pm
FedEx Kinko's	641 Lexington Ave	8:30pm
Self-Service	150 E 58th St	8:30pm
Self-Service	299 Park Ave	8:30pm

Self-Service	60 E 42nd St	8:15pm
FedEx Kinko's	405 Park Ave	8:00pm
FedEx Kinko's	747 3rd Ave	8:00pm
Self-Service	100 Park Ave	8:00pm
Self-Service	355 Lexington Ave	8:00pm
Self-Service	420 Lexington Ave	8:00pm
Self-Service	450 Lexington Av	8:00pm
Self-Service	55 E 59th St	8:00pm
Self-Service	630 3rd Ave	8:00pm
Self-Service	633 3rd Ave	8:00pm
Self-Service	866 United Nations Plaza	8:00pm
Self-Service	885 3rd Ave	8:00pm
Self-Service	979 3rd Ave	8:00pm
Self-Service	220 E 42nd St	7:30pm
Self-Service	353 Lexington Ave	7:30pm
FedEx Kinko's	153 E 53rd St	7:00pm
Self-Service	135 E 57th St	7:00pm
Self-Service	150 E 42nd St	7:00pm
Self-Service	211 E 43rd St	7:00pm
Self-Service	350 Park Ave	7:00pm
Self-Service	500 Park Ave	7:00pm
Self-Service	575 Lexington Ave	7:00pm
Self-Service	805 3rd Ave	7:00pm
Self-Service	909 3rd Ave	6:30pm
Self-Service	205 E 42nd St	6:00pm
Self-Service	425 Park Ave	6:00pm
Mail Boxes Etc	1040 First Ave	5:00pm
Self-Service	45 E 49th St	5:00pm

Map 14 · Upper West Side (Lower)

FedEx Kinko's	2211 Broadway	9:00pm
FedEx Kinko's	221 W 72nd St	8:00pm
Self-Service	101 West End Ave	6:30pm
Self-Service	168 Columbus Ave	6:30pm
Mail Boxes Etc	163 Amsterdam Ave	6:00pm
Manhattan MailRoom	459 Columbus Ave	6:00pm
Self-Service	127 W 83rd St	6:00pm
Self-Service	211 W 61st St	6:00pm
Self-Service	517 Amsterdam Ave	6:00pm
Self-Service	2248 Broadway	5:00pm
Self-Service	27 W 60th St	3:30pm

Map 15 · Upper East Side (Lower)

FedEx Kinko's	1122 Lexington Ave	8:30pm
Self-Service	1300 York Ave	8:30pm
Self-Service	667 Madison Ave	8:30pm
Self-Service	525 E 68th St	8:00pm
Self-Service	650 Madison Ave	7:30pm
Self-Service	695 Park Ave	7:30pm
Self-Service	1388 2nd Ave	7:00pm
Self-Service	445 E 69th St	7:00pm
Senderos	1471 Third Ave	6:00pm
Postal Express	1382 Third Ave	6:00pm

Big Apple Art Gallery	1456 Second Ave	6:00pm
Mail Boxes Etc	1461 First Ave	6:00pm
The Padded Wagon	1569 Second Ave	6:00pm
Self-Service	217 E 70th St	6:00pm
Self-Service	428 E 72nd St	6:00pm
Self-Service	968 Lexington Ave	6:00pm
Mail Boxes Etc	954 Lexington Av	5:45pm
Self-Service	425 E 61st St	5:30pm

Map 16 · Upper West Side (Upper)

Columbia Copy Center	2790 Broadway	8:00pm
Copy Experts	2440 Broadway	7:30pm
Global Copy	2578 Broadway	7:00pm
Self-Service	70 W 86th St	6:00pm
Foxy Copy	211 W 92nd St	5:00pm

Map 17 · Upper East Side / East Harlem

Self-Service	225 E 95th St	8:30pm
Self-Service	1280 Lexington Ave	8:00pm
Self-Service	1476 Lexington Ave	7:00pm
Self-Service	1 E 104th St	6:30pm
Mail Boxes Etc	1710 First Ave	6:00pm
Compu Signs Plus	1598 Third Ave	6:00pm
Self-Service	1619 3rd Ave	5:00pm
Cross County Pharmacy	1514 Madison Ave	3:00pm

Map 18 · Columbia / Morningside Heights

FedEx Kinko's	600 W 116th St	9:00pm
Self-Service	2970 Broadway	8:00pm
Self-Service	3022 Broadway	8:00pm
Self-Service	435 W 116th St	8:00pm
Self-Service	525 W 120th St	8:00pm
Self-Service	475 Riverside Dr	7:30pm

Map 19 · Harlem (Lower)

Self-Service	55 W 125th St	7:30pm
Self-Service	163 W 125th St	7:00pm

Map 20 · El Barrio / East Harlem

Self-Service	1879 Madison Ave	6:45pm

Map 21 · Manhattanville / Hamilton Heights

La Nacional	3351 Broadway	6:00pm
La Nacional	3480 Broadway	6:00pm

Map 23 · Washington Heights

Self-Service	1051 Riverside Dr	7:30pm
Doc Q Pack	2201 Amsterdam Ave	7:00pm
Self-Service	100 Haven Ave	7:00pm
Self-Service	161 Ft Washington Ave	7:00pm
Self-Service	177 Ft Washington Ave	7:00pm
Self-Service	3960 Broadway	7:00pm
Self-Service	60 Haven Ave	7:00pm
Self-Service	622 W 168th St	7:00pm
Self-Service	630 W 168th St	7:00pm
Self-Service	1150 St Nicholas Ave	6:30pm
La Nacional	1342 St Nicholas Ave	6:00pm
La Nacional	2174 Amsterdam Ave	6:00pm
La Nacional	3896 Broadway	6:00pm
Rel Express Pack	2140 Amsterdam Ave	6:00pm
La Nacional	113 Audubon Ave	6:00pm

Map 24 · Fort George / Fort Tryon

Self-Service	722 W 168th St	7:30pm
Self-Service	701 W 168th St	7:00pm
Self-Service	710 W 168th St	7:00pm
Quisqueyana Express	4468 Broadway	6:30pm
La Nacional	1443 St Nicholas Ave	6:00pm
La Nacional	151 Nagle Ave	6:00pm
La Nacional	1533 St Nicholas Ave	6:00pm

Map 25 · Inwood

Self-Service	5141 Broadway	6:00pm
Atlas Travel Group	4742 Broadway	5:00pm
La Nacional	566 W 207th St	3:00pm

Restaurants

Restaurants	Address	Phone	Map
Wo Hop	17 Mott St	212-267-2536	3
French Roast	78 W 11th St	212-533-2233	5
Around the Clock	8 Stuyvesant St	212-598-0402	6
Bamn!	37 St Marks Pl	888-400-BAMN	6
Cozy Soup & Burger	739 Broadway	212-477-5566	6
Lahore	132 Crosby St	212-965-1777	6
Veselka	144 Second Ave	212-228-9682	6
7A	109 Ave A	212-673-6583	7
Bereket Turkish Kebab House	187 E Houston St	212-475-7700	7
Odessa	119 Ave A	212-253-1470	7
Yaffa Café	97 St Marks Pl	212-674-9302	7
Empire Diner	210 Tenth Ave	212-243-2736	8
Skylight Diner	402 W 34th St	212-244-0395	8
Tick Tock Diner	481 Eighth Ave	212-268-8444	8
Kang Suh	1250 Broadway	212-564-6845	9
Kum Gang San	49 W 32nd St	212-967-0909	9
Kunjip	9 W 32nd St	212-216-9487	9
Woo Chon	8 W 36th St	212-695-0676	9
Gemini Diner	641 Second Ave	212-532-2143	10
Gramercy Restaurant	184 Third Ave	212-982-2121	10
L'Express	249 Park Ave S	212-254-5858	10
Sarge's Deli	548 Third Ave	212-679-0442	10
H&H Bagels	639 W 46th St	212-595-8000	11
Morningstar	401 W 57th St	212-246-1593	11
Big Nick's	2175 Broadway	212-362-9238	14
French Roast	2340 Broadway	212-799-1533	14
Gray's Papaya	2090 Broadway	212-799-0243	14
H&H Bagels	2239 Broadway	212-595-8003	14
Manhattan Diner	2180 Broadway	212-877-7252	14
City Diner	2441 Broadway	212-877-2720	16
La Isla Restaurant	1883 Third Ave	212-534-0002	17
Viand	300 E 86th St	212-879-9425	17
White Castle	351 E 103rd St	n/a	17
IHOP	2294 Adam Clayton Powell Jr Blvd	212-234-4747	19
Ivoire	76 E 119th St	n/a	20
Taco Mix	236 E 116 St	212-831-8147	20
New Caporal Fried Chicken	3772 Broadway	212-862-8986	21
El Malecon	4141 Broadway	212-927-3812	23
Tipico Dominicano	4177 Broadway	212-781-3900	23
Mr Seafood Market and Restaurant	3842 Ninth Ave	212-304-9440	25

Supermarkets

Supermarkets	Address	Phone	Map
Jubilee Marketplace	99 John St	212-233-0808	1
Jin Market	111 Hudson St	212-226-9310	2
Pathmark	227 Cherry St	212-227-8988	4
Key Food	52 Ave A	212-477-9063	7
Gristedes	460 Third Ave	212-251-9670	10
Gristedes	907 Eighth Ave	212-582-5873	12
Westside Market	2171 Broadway	212-595-2536	14
Gristedes	1446 Second Ave	212-535-4925	15
Gristedes	2704 Broadway	646-352-4676	16
Gristedes Mega Store	262 W 96th St	212-663-5126	16
Gristedes Mega Store	350 E 86th St	212-535-1688	17
Pathmark	300 W 145th St	212-281-3158	22
Pathmark	410 W 207th St	212-569-0600	25
Gristedes	315 South End Ave	212-233-7797	p234

Plumbers

Plumbers	Address	Phone	Map
Effective Plumbing	Multiple locations	212-545-0100	
New York Plumbing & Heating Service	Multiple locations	212-496-9191	
Roto-Rooter Plumbing	Multiple locations	212-687-1661	
Sanitary Plumbing and Heating	211 E 117th St	212-734-5000	2

Hardware Store

Hardware Store	Address	Phone	Map
HomeFront	202 E 29th St	212-545-1447	10

Copy Shops

	Address	Phone	Map
FedEx Kinko's	191 Madison Ave	212-685-3449	9
FedEx Kinko's	239 Seventh Ave	212-929-0623	9
On-Site Sourcing	443 Park Ave S Fl 3	212-252-9700	10
Discovery Copy Services	45 W 45th St	212-827-0039	12
FedEx Kinko's	233 W 54th St	212-977-2679	12
FedEx Kinko's	1211 Sixth Ave	212-391-2679	12
FedEx Kinko's	16 E 52nd St	212-308-2679	12
FedEx Kinko's	240 Central Park S	212-258-3750	12
FedEx Kinko's	60 W 40th St	212-921-1060	12
Skyline Duplication	151 W 46th St	212-302-5153	12
FedEx Kinko's	641 Lexington Ave	212-572-9995	13
FedEx Kinko's	747 Third Ave	212-753-7778	13
FedEx Kinko's	221 W 72nd St	212-362-5288	14
FedEx Kinko's	1122 Lexington Ave	212-628-5500	15
The Village Copier	2872 Broadway	212-666-0600	18

Gym

	Address	Phone	Map
James A Farley	421 Eighth Ave	212-330-2902	8

Laundromats

	Address	Phone	Map
69 Avenue C Laundromat	69 Ave C	212-388-9933	7
Classic Laundry	262 W 145th St	917-507-4865	22
106 Audubon Avenue Laundromat	106 Audubon Ave	212-795-8717	23

Veterinary

	Address	Phone	Map
Animal Emergency Clinic	1 W 15th St	212-924-3311	9
Animal Medical Center	510 E 62nd St	212-838-8100	15
Center for Veterinary Care	236 E 75th St	212-734-7480	15
Park East Animal Hospital	52 E 64th St	212-832-8417	15

Newsstands

	Map		Map
Sixth Ave & 3rd St	5	59th St & Third Ave	13
Sixth Ave (South of W 8th St)	5	First Ave & 57th St	13
Second Ave & St Marks Pl	6	72nd St & Broadway	14
St Marks Pl & Bowery	6	76th St & Broadway	14
Delancey & Essex Sts	7	Columbus Ave & 81st St	14
23rd St & Third Ave	10	79th St & York (First Ave)	15
Third Ave (34th/35th Sts)	10	First Ave & 63rd St	15
42nd St & Seventh Ave	12	Second Ave (60th/61st Sts)	15
49th St & Eighth Ave	12	86th St & Lexington Ave	17
Broadway & 50th St	12	Broadway & 116th St	18

Delivery and Messengers

	Phone
Moonlite Courier	212-473-2246
Need It Now	212-989-1919
Same Day Express	800-982-5910
Urban Express	212-855-5555

Private Investigators

	Phone
Matthew T Cloth, PI	718-449-4100
North American Investigations	800-724-8080
Sherlock Investigations	212-579-4302

Locksmiths

	Phone		Phone
A&V Locksmith	212-226-0011	East Manhattan Locksmiths	212-369-9063
Aaron-Hotz Locksmith	212-243-7166	Emergency Locksmith 24 Hours	212-231-7627
Abbey Locksmiths	212-535-2289	LockDoctors	212-935-6600
Advantage Locksmith	212-398-5500	Lockmasters Locksmith	212-690-4018
Always Ready Locksmiths	888-490-4900	Night and Day Locksmith	212-722-1017
American Locksmiths	212-888-8888	Paragon Security & Locksmith	212-620-9000
CBS Locksmith	212-410-0090	Speedway Locksmith	877-917-6500
Champion Locksmiths	212-362-7000		

General Information · **Dog Runs**

Useful websites: www.doglaw.com, www.nycparks.org, www.urbanhound.com

It's good to be a dog in New York. NYC's pooches are among the world's most pampered: they celebrate birthdays, don expensive sweaters, and prance down Fifth Avenue in weather-appropriate gear. But for the rest of us, who would rather step in dog doo than dress our pups in Burberry raincoats, there's still reason to smile. NYC is full of dog runs—both formal and informal—scattered throughout the city's parks and neighborhood community spaces. Good thing too, as the fine for having a dog off-leash can run upward of $100, and park officials are vigilant. While the city takes no active role in the management of the dog runs, it provides space to the community groups who do. These community groups are always eager for help (volunteer time or financial contributions) and may post volunteer information on park bulletin boards. It can take many years and several thousand dollars to build a dog run in New York. NYC boasts more than 40 runs, but that number doesn't seem very big when you consider that the city is home to more than one million pooches. That's not a lot of room for each dog to stretch his four legs. Each dog run is different, but pet lovers can check out www.urbanhound.com for descriptions. It's good to know, for example, that Riverside Park at 87th Street has a fountain and hose to keep dogs cool in the summer. Formal runs are probably the safest bet for pets, as most are enclosed and maintained. For safety reasons, choke or pronged collars are forbidden, and identification and rabies tags should remain on the flat collar. Most runs prohibit dogs in heat, aggressive dogs, and dogs without up-to-date shots.

There are no dog runs in Central Park, but before 9 am the park is full of people walking their dogs off-leash. While this is a strict no-no the rest of the day (and punishable by hefty fines), park officials unofficially tolerate the practice as long as dogs maintain a low profile, and are leashed immediately at 9 am.

Map · Name · Address · Comments

2 **P.S. 234** · 300 Greenwich St at Chambers St · Private run. $50/year membership. www.doglaw.com
3 **Fish Bridge Park** · Dover and Pearl Sts · Concrete-surfaced run. Features water hose, wading pool, and lock box with newspapers. www.nycgovparks.org
4 **Coleman Oval Park** · Pike & Monroe Sts · Under the Manhattan Bridge. www.nycgovparks.org
5 **West Village D.O.G. Run** · Little W 12th St · Features benches, water hose, and drink bowl. Membership costs $40 annually, but there's a waiting list. www.wvdog.org
6 **Washington Square Park** · MacDougal St at W 4th St · Located in the southwest corner of the park, this is a large, gravel-surfaced run with many spectators. This popular run gets very crowded, but is well-maintained nonetheless. www.nycgovparks.org
6 **LaGuardia Place** · Mercer St at Houston St · Private run with a membership (and a waiting list). The benefits include running water and a plastic wading pool for your dog to splash in. www.mhdra.org
6 **Union Square** · Broadway at 15th St · Crushed stone surface. www.nycgovparks.org
7 **Tompkins Square Park** · Avenue B at 10th St · New York City's first dog run (opened in 1990) is set to undergo a $150,000 restoration in 2007. Currently, toys, balls, frisbees, and dogs in heat are all prohibited. This community-centered run offers lots of shade, benches, and running water. www.firstrunfriends.org
7 **Thomas Smith Triangle** · Eleventh Ave at 23rd St · Concrete-surfaced run. www.nycgovparks.org
8 **Chelsea** · 18th St at the West Side Hwy
10 **Madison Square Park** · Madison Ave at 25th St · Medium-sized run with gravel surface and plenty of trees. www.nycgovparks.org
11 **DeWitt Clinton Park** · Eleventh Ave at 52nd & 54th Sts · Two small concrete-surfaced runs. www.nycgovparks.org
11 **Astro's Community Dog Run** · W 39th St at Tenth Ave · A private dog run (membership costs $15 a year) featuring chairs, umbrellas, fenced garden, and woodchip surface. www.hkdogrun.org
13 **E 60th Street Pavilion** · 60th St at the East River · Concrete-surfaced run. www.doglaw.com
13 **Peter Detmold Park** · Beekman Pl at 51st St · Large well-maintained run with cement and dirt surfaces and many trees. www.nycgovparks.org
13 **Robert Moses Park** · First Ave and 42nd St · Concrete surface. www.nycgovparks.org
13 **Theodore Roosevelt Park** · Central Park W at W 81st St · Gravel surface. www.nycgovparks.org
14 **Riverside Park** · Riverside Dr at 72nd St · www.nycgovparks.org
14 **Margaret Mead Park** · Columbus Ave at 81st St · www.leashline.com
15 **Balto Dog Monument** · Fifth Ave at E 67th St (Central Park)
15,17 **Carl Schurz Park** · East End Ave at 85/86th Sts · Medium-sized enclosed run with pebbled surface and separate space for small dogs. This run has benches and shady trees, and running water is available in the bathrooms. www.nycgovparks.org
16 **Riverside Park** · Riverside Dr at 87th St · Medium-sized run with gravel surface. www.nycgovparks.org
16 **Riverside Park** · Riverside Dr at 105/106th Sts · Medium-sized run with gravel surface. www.nycgovparks.org
18 **Morningside Park** · Morningside Ave b/w 114th & 119th Sts · www.nycgovparks.org
20 **Thomas Jefferson Park** · E 112th St at First Ave · Wood chip surface.
23 **J. Hood Wright Park** · Haven Ave at W 173rd St · An enclosed dirt-surfaced run. www.nycgovparks.org
24 **Fort Tryon Park/Sir William's Dog Run** · Margaret Corbin Dr, Washington Heights www.ftdog.com
25 **Inwood Hill Dog Run** · Dyckman St and Payson Ave · Gravel surface. www.nycgovparks.org
p234 **Kowsky Plaza Dog Run (Battery Park City)** · Gateway Plaza · Located near the marina, this area has small hills for your dog to run on, as well as a small fountain and bathing pool. www.bpcdogs.com
p234 **Battery Park City** · Along River Ter between Park Pl W and Murray St · Concrete-surfaced run with a view of the river. www.manhattan.about.com

Self-Storage / Van & Truck Rental

Self-Storage	Address	Phone	Map
Sofia Brothers	139 Franklin St	212-873-0700	2
Whitehall Business Archives	40 Worth St	212-587-0500	2
Manhattan Mini Storage	220 South St	800-786-7243	4
Manhattan Mini Storage	161 Varick St	212-786-7243	5
Manhattan Mini Storage	260 Spring St	800-786-7243	5
Whitehall Storage	333 Hudson St	212-675-0156	5
Whitehall Storage	303 W 10th St	212-929-3537	5
Manhattan Mini Storage	28 Second Ave	800-786-7243	6
Keepers Self Storage	444 E 10th St	212-228-6726	7
American Self Storage	500 Tenth Ave	212-714-9300	8
Bedrock Mini Storage	239 Eleventh Ave	212-255-5832	8
Chelsea Mini Storage	224 12th Ave	212-564-7735	8
Manhattan Mini Storage	541 W 29th St	212-786-7243	8
Manhattan Mini Storage	510 W 21st St	212-924-5111	8
Manhattan Mini Storage	520 W 17th St	212-786-7243	8
Manhattan Mini Storage	524 W 23rd St	800-786-7243	8
Manhattan Mini Storage	520 Eighth Ave	212-786-7243	8
Manhattan Mini Storage	531 W 21st St	212-620-7387	8
Tuck It Away	517 W 29th St	212-244-1438	8
U-haul Center of Chelsea	562 W 23rd St	212-620-4177	8
Whitehall Storage	511 W 25th St	212-989-9668	8
Manhattan Mini Storage	543 W 43rd St	212-786-7243	11
Manhattan Mini Storage	645 W 44th St	800-786-7243	11
Whitehall Storage	610 W 52nd St	212-489-1733	11
Manhattan Mini Storage	600 W 58th St	800-786-7243	14
Sofia Brothers	475 Amsterdam Ave	212-873-3600	14
Manhattan Mini Storage	420 E 62nd St	212-786-7243	15
Manhattan Mini Storage	108 W 107th St	212-531-3118	16
Hudson Self Storage	3229 Broadway	212-678-4862	18
Manhattan Mini Storage	570 Riverside Dr	800-786-7243	18
Tuck It Away	3261 Broadway	212-368-1717	18
Tuck It Away	3330 Broadway	212-694-7390	18
Tuck It Away	655 W 125th St	212-663-4784	18
Big Apple Mini Storage East	119 E 124th St	212-987-5900	19
Big Apple Mini Storage West	157 W 124th St	212-865-4899	19
Manhattan Mini Storage	400 E 110th St	212-534-8409	20
Tuck It Away	1901 Park Ave	212-368-1717	20
American Self Storage	9 W 141st St	212-283-5500	22
Extra Space Storage	58 W 143rd St	212-694-0849	22
Sofia Brothers	4396 Broadway	212-923-4300	24

Van & Truck Rental	Address	Phone	Map
Budget Truck Rental	510 W 35th St	212-465-1911	8
Budget Truck Rental	415 W 45th St	212-397-2893	11
Budget Truck Rental	220 E 117th St	212-987-3642	20
Penske	451 Tenth Ave	212-741-9800	8
U-Haul	All State Leasing, 535 W 44th St	212-643-8076	11
U-Haul	American Home Hardware & More, 590 Ninth Ave	212-581-9395	11
U-Haul	Straight Hardware, 613 Ninth Ave	212-581-9395	11
U-Haul	All State Leasing, 629 W 50th St	212-245-4929	11
U-Haul	Shell, 1599 Lexington Ave	212-426-8773	17
U-Haul	3270 Broadway	212-491-7723	18
U-Haul	Big Apple West Mini-Storage, 157 W 124th St	212-865-6804	19
U-Haul	Big Apple East Mini-Storage, 119 E 124th St	212-860-3120	20
U-Haul	1851 Park Ave	212-410-1148	20
U-Haul	562 W 23rd St	212-620-4177	8

371

If you're reading this you're probably not a tourist, and if you're not a tourist you probably don't need a hotel. However, chances are good that at some point your obnoxious friend or relative from out of state will suddenly come a-knockin', bearing news of their long-awaited arrival to the big city. "So I thought I'd stay at your place," they will suggest casually, displaying their complete ignorance of the number of square feet in an average New York apartment—and simultaneously realizing your greatest fear of playing host to someone you greatly dislike. Or there's the possibility that your place is infested with mice, bed-bugs, or pigeons and you need to escape, pronto. Or maybe you're just looking for a romantic (or slightly less than romantic) getaway without leaving the city. Whatever the case, be assured that there is a seemingly endless array of possibilities to suit all your overnight desires and needs.

Obviously, your options run from dirt cheap (that's "dirt cheap" by NYC standards) to disgustingly offensive. For those of you with money to spare and/or a respect for high status, there are the elite luxury chains—**The Ritz Carlton** (cheaper to stay at the one in Battery Park (**p 234**) than Central Park, **The Four Seasons (Map 12)** E 57th St, **The W** at Union Square **(Map 10)**, Times Square **(Map 12)**, E 39th St **(Map 10)**, and Lexington Ave at 49th St **(Map 13)**, **Le Parker Meridien (Map 12)**, **The Peninsula (Map 12)**, **The St. Regis (Map 12)**, and **The Mandarin-Oriental (Map 14)**.

Those hotels that are more unique to Manhattan include: **The Lowell (Map 15)**, a fortress of pretentiousness nestled beside Central Park, which successfully captures the feel of a snobby, high-class gentleman's club. For a similar feeling, only with a heavy dose of Renaissance Italy and a design dating back to 1882, check into **The New York Palace (Map 12)**. If you prefer more modern surroundings, the swank-tastic **Bryant Park Hotel (Map 12)** (once the landmark Radiator building before it was transformed) is a favorite amongst entertainment and fashion industry folks. Similarly, **The Regency (Map 15)**, nicknamed "Hollywood East" in the 1960s, is a must for all celeb-stalkers hangers-on alike. Meanwhile, **The Algonquin (Map 12)** offers complimentary delivery of the New Yorker, as if to suggest that they cater to a more literary crowd (maybe in the 1920s, but whether or not that's the case today is up for debate). If you're feeling fabulous, there's **The Muse Hotel (Map 12)**, located in the heart of Times Square, mere steps away from the bright lights of Broadway (*Movin' Out*, anyone?). If you're more comfortable with the old-money folks (or if you're a nostalgic member of the nouveau-riche), check out **The Carlyle (Map 15)**. Be a bit easier on your wallet and get a room at **The Excelsior Hotel (Map 14)**—it may be a tad less indulgent, but get over it, you're still right on Central Park. Yet more affordable and not an ounce less attractive is **The Hudson (Map 11)**, a chic boutique hotel from Ian Schrager. Then there's **The Shoreham (Map 12)**, which offers complimentary champagne at the front desk (so it's definitely worth a shot to pose as a guest) in addition to a fantastically retro bar, that looks like it's straight out of *A Clockwork Orange*. Last but not least, dance on over to the famous **Waldorf**

Astoria (Map 13), where the unrivaled service and $200 million in renovations more than justify the cost of staying.

There are also plenty of places to stay downtown, perfect for those of you who plan on stumbling home after a long night of bar-hopping. The sexier of these hotels include: **The Hotel Gansevoort (Map 5)**, a sleek tower of luxury, located steps away from the Meatpacking District—New York's very own version of Miami Beach! Nearby, you'll find **The Maritime Hotel (Map 10)**, which does a great impression of a cruise ship, replete with porthole-shaped windows and La Bottega, an Italian restaurant with a massive outdoor patio that feels like the deck of a Carnival liner. In trendy SoHo, you'll find **The Mercer Hotel, 60 Thompson (Map 6)**, and **The SoHo Grand (Map 2)** (there's also its sister, **The Tribeca Grand (Map 2)**, farther south)—which vary ever-so-slightly in degrees of coolness, depending on your demands. A little ways north, next to Gramercy Park, you'll find **The Inn at Irving Place (Map 10)**—things are a tad less modern at this upscale bed and breakfast (it consists of two restored 19th-century townhouses), but the Cibar lounge, the company (it's a favorite of rock and fashion royalty), and the lack of any visible sign outside are all sure to validate your sense of hip.

Let's just be honest, shall we? The truth of the matter is that you're poor. All you want is a bargain—and believe it or not, we get it. Thus, behold the most affordable splendors of the New York hotel experience: **The Gershwin Hotel (Map 9)**, **Herald Square Hotel (Map 9)**, **Super 8 Times Square (Map 12)**, **Red Roof Inn (Map 9)**, **Second Home on Second Avenue (Map 6)**, and **The Chelsea Savoy (Map 9)**.

More mid-range options include: **Hotel Thirty Thirty (Map 9)**, **The Abington Guest House (Map 5)**, **The Roger Williams Hotel (Map 9)**, **Portland Square Hotel (Map 12)**, **Comfort Inn (Map 9)**, **Clarion Hotel (Map 10)**, and **The New Yorker Hotel (Map 8)**.

Be aware that prices are generally highest during the holiday season and the summer and lowest during the off season. Not all hotels have a star rating, and those that do are sometimes inaccurate. The quoted rates will give you a pretty good idea of the quality of each hotel. Rates are ballpark and subject to change—go to one of the many travel websites (Hotels.com, Priceline, Hotwire, Travelocity, Kayak, Expedia, etc.) or individual company websites (hilton.com, spg.com, holiday-inn.com) to get the best rates. Or call the hotel and ask if they have any specials. The bottom line is that, as is the case with everything in New York, though you have plenty of options, few of them are cheap.

General Information · **Hotels**

Map 1 · Financial District

		Phone	Rate $
Exchange Hotel	129 Front St	212-742-0003	209
Gild Hall	15 Gold St	212-232-7700	429
Millenium Hilton	55 Church St	212-693-2001	449
New York Marriott Downtown	85 West St	212-385-4900	399
Wall Street Inn	9 S William St	212-747-1500	239

Map 2 · TriBeCa

Cosmopolitan Hotel	95 W Broadway	212-566-1900	195
Soho Grand	310 W Broadway	212-965-3000	474
Tribeca Grand Hotel	2 6th Ave	212-519-6600	464

Map 3 · City Hall / Chinatown

Best Western Seaport Inn	33 Peck Slip	212-766-6600	229
Hampton Inn Seaport	320 Pearl St	212-571-4400	409
Holiday Inn Downtown	138 Lafayette St	212-966-8898	314
New World Hotel	101 Bowery	212-226-5522	112
Sohotel	341 Broome St	212-226-1482	161, shared bath
Sun Hotel	140 Hester St	212-226-7070	75
Windsor Hotel	108 Forsyth St	212-226-3009	175

Map 5 · West Village

Abingdon Guest House	21 8th Ave	212-243-5384	169
Chelsea Pines Inn	317 W 14th St	212-929-1023	150
Hotel Gansevoort	18 9th Ave	212-206-6700	565
Hotel Riverview	113 Jane St	212-929-0060	46
Incentra Village House	32 8th Ave	212-206-0007	169
Liberty Inn	51 10th Ave	212-741-2333	159
Rooms to Let	83 Horatio St	212-675-5481	190
West Eleventh	278 W 11th St	212-675-7897	215

Map 6 · Washington Square / NYU / NoHo / SoHo

60 Thompson	60 Thompson St	212-431-0400	579
Howard Johnson Express Inn	135 E Houston St	212-358-8844	135
Larchmont Hotel	27 W 11th St	212-989-9333	99
Mercer Hotel	147 Mercer St	212-966-6060	595
Off Soho Suites Hotel	11 Rivington St	800-633-7646	249
Second Home on Second Avenue	221 2nd Ave	212-677-3161	105 shared / 190 private
St Marks Hotel	2 St Marks Pl	212-674-0100	120
Union Square Inn	209 E 14th St	212-614-0500	159
Washington Square Hotel	103 Waverly Pl	212-777-9515	190
White House Hotel	340 Bowery	212-477-5623	30

Map 7 · East Village / Lower East Side

East Village Bed & Coffee	110 Avenue C	917-816-0071	120
Hotel on Rivington	107 Rivington St	212-475-2600	450

Map 8 · Chelsea

Best Western Convention Center Hotel	522 W 38th St	212-405-1700	259
Chelsea International Hostel	251 W 20th St	212-647-0010	32 dorm, 75 private
Chelsea Lodge Suites	318 W 20th St	212-243-4499	195
Chelsea Star Hotel	300 W 30th St	212-244-7827	30 dorm, 99 private
Colonial House Inn	318 W 22nd St	212-243-9669	110 shared bath, 160 private bath
The Gem	449 W 36th St	212-967-7206	179
Manhattan Inn Hostel	303 W 30th St	212-629-4064	36 dorm, 110 private
New Yorker Ramada Hotel	481 8th Ave	212-971-0101	229
Vigilant Hotel	370 8th Ave	212-594-5246	140 weekly

373

General Information · **Hotels**

Map 9 · Flatiron / Lower Midtown

		Phone	Rate $
Affinia Manhattan	371 7th Ave	212-563-1800	287
Americana Inn	69 W 38th St	212-840-6700	95
The Avalon	16 E 32nd St	212-299-7000	319
Broadway Plaza Hotel	1155 Broadway	212-679-7665	259
Carlton Hotel	88 Madison Ave	212-532-4100	368
Chelsea Hotel	222 W 23rd St	212-243-3700	195
Chelsea Inn	46 W 17th St	212-645-8989	104
Chelsea Savoy Hotel	204 W 23rd St	212-929-9353	155
Comfort Inn	18 W 25th St	212-645-3990	190
Comfort Inn Manhattan	42 W 35th St	212-947-0200	289
Comfort Inn New York	442 W 36th St	212-714-6699	200
Four Points by Sheraton Chelsea	160 W 25th St	212-627-1888	304
Gershwin Hotel	7 E 27th St	212-545-8000	40 dorm, 109 private
Hampton Inn Manhattan/Chelsea	108 E 24th St	212-414-1000	329
Hampton Inn-Madison Square Garden	116 W 31st St	212-947-9700	300
Herald Square Hotel	19 W 31st St	212-279-4017	89 shared bath, 99 private bath
Holiday Inn Express-Madison Square Garden	232 W 29th St	212-695-7200	269
Hotel Chandler	12 E 31st St	212-889-6363	249
Hotel Grand Union	34 E 32nd St	212-683-5890	157
Hotel Metro	45 W 35th St	212-947-2500	225
Hotel Stanford	43 W 32nd St	212-563-1500	217
Hotel Thirty Thirty	30 E 30th St	212-689-1900	179
Inn on 23rd	131 W 23rd St	212-463-0330	229
Jolly Hotel Madison Towers	22 E 38th St	212-802-0600	247
La Quinta Inn–Manhattan	17 W 32nd St	212-736-1600	200
La Semana	25 W 24th St	212-255-5944	189
Latham Hotel	4 E 28th St	212-685-8300	79
Madison Hotel on the Park	62 Madison Ave	212-532-7373	109
Manhattan Broadway Hotel	273 W 38th St	212-921-9791	179
Morgan's Hotel	237 Madison Ave	212-686-0300	469
New York Hotel Pennsylvania	401 7th Ave	212-736-5000	209
Radisson Martinique	49 W 32nd St	212-736-3800	289
Red Roof Inn	6 W 32nd St	212-643-7100	140
Regency Inn & Suites	215 W 34th St	212-947-5050	217
Residence Inn Manhattan Times Square	1033 6th Ave	212-768-0007	329
Roger Williams Hotel	131 Madison Ave	212-448-7000	400
Senton Hotel	39 W 27th St	212-684-5800	100 shared bath, 120 private bath
Wolcott Hotel	4 W 31st St	212-268-2900	200

Map 10 · Murray Hill / Gramercy

70 Park Avenue Hotel	70 Park Ave	212-973-2400	325
Affinia Dumont	150 E 34th St	212-481-7600	279
American Dream Hostel	168 E 24th St	212-260-9779	45 dorm, 75 private
Clarion Park Avenue	429 Park Ave S	212-532-4860	240
Deauville Hotel	103 E 29th St	212-683-0990	139
Eastgate Tower	222 E 39th St	212-687-8000	234
Envoy Club	377 E 33rd St	212-481-4600	259
Gramercy Park Hotel	2 Lexington Ave	212-920-3300	545
Hotel 17	225 E 17th St	212-475-2845	128 shared bath, 201 private bath
Hotel 31	129 E 31st St	212-685-3060	133
Hotel Giraffe	365 Park Ave S	212-685-7700	359
Inn at Irving Place	56 Irving Pl	212-533-4600	484
Kitano Hotel New York	66 Park Ave	212-885-7000	332
Marcel Hotel	201 E 24th St	212-696-3800	227
Maritime Hotel	363 W 16th St	212-242-4300	395
Murray Hill East Suites	149 E 39th St	212-661-2100	210
Murray Hill Inn	143 E 30th St	212-683-6900	169
Park South Hotel	122 E 28th St	212-448-0888	259
Ramada Inn Eastside	161 Lexington Ave	212-545-1800	196
Shelburne Murray Hill	303 Lexington Ave	212-689-5200	297
W New York–The Court	130 E 39th St	212-685-1100	419
W New York–The Tuscany	120 E 39th St	212-686-1600	489
W Union Square	201 Park Ave S	212-253-9119	509
Ye Olde Carlton Arms Hotel	160 E 25th St	212-679-0680	80 shared bath, 110 private bath

Map 11 • Hell's Kitchen

		Phone	Rate $
414 Inn New York	414 W 46th St	212-399-0006	199
Belvedere Hotel	319 W 48th St	212-245-7000	327
Elk Hotel	360 W 42nd St	212-563-2864	50
Holiday Inn Midtown	440 W 57th St	212-581-8100	215
Hudson Hotel	356 W 58th St	212-554-6000	299
Skyline Hotel	725 10th Ave	212-586-3400	239
Travel Inn	515 W 42nd St	212-695-7171	300
Washington Jefferson Hotel	318 W 51st St	212-246-7550	255

Map 12 • Midtown

Algonquin Hotel	59 W 44th St	212-840-6800	399
Ameritania Hotel	230 W 54th St	212-247-5000	197
Amsterdam Court Hotel	226 W 50th St	212-459-1000	197
Best Western President Hotel	234 W 48th St	212-246-8800	285
Big Apple Hostel	119 W 45th St	212-302-2603	37 dorm, 110 private
Blakely Hotel	136 W 55th St	212-245-1800	325
Bryant Park Hotel	40 W 40th St	212-869-0100	375
Buckingham Hotel	101 W 57th St	212-246-1500	279
Carter Hotel	250 W 43rd St	212-944-6000	116
Casablanca Hotel	147 W 43rd St	212-869-1212	376
Chambers Hotel	15 W 56th St	212-974-5656	425
City Club Hotel	55 W 44th St	212-921-5500	345
Comfort Inn Midtown	129 W 46th St	212-221-2600	250
Courtyard Times Square South by Marriott	114 W 40th St	212-391-0088	329
Crowne Plaza Times Square	1605 Broadway	212-977-4000	369
Da Vinci Hotel	244 W 56th St	212-489-4100	160
Doubletree Guest Suites	1568 Broadway	212-719-1600	377
Dream	210 W 55th St	212-247-2000	279
Dylan Hotel	52 E 41st St	212-338-0500	331
Econo Lodge Times Square	302 W 47th St	212-246-1991	230
Flatotel International	135 W 52nd St	212-887-9400	331
Four Seasons Hotel	57 E 57th St	212-758-5700	755
Hampton Inn-Times Square North	851 8th Ave	212-581-4100	279
Helmsley Park Lane Hotel	36 Central Park S	212-371-4000	425
Hilton Garden Inn	790 8th Ave	212-581-7000	299
Hilton New York	1335 6th Ave	212-586-7000	319
Hilton Times Square	234 W 42nd St	212-840-8222	359
Holiday Inn Express	15 W 45th St	212-302-9088	306
Hotel 41	206 W 41st St	212-703-8600	331
Hotel Edison	228 W 47th St	212-840-5000	201
Hotel QT	125 W 45th St	212-354-2323	299
Hotel St James	109 W 45th St	212-221-3600	155
Iroquois Hotel	49 W 44th St	212-840-3080	340
Jumeirah Essex House	160 Central Park S	212-247-0300	469
Le Parker Meridien	119 W 56th St	212-245-5000	417
Library Hotel	299 Madison Ave	212-983-4500	353
The London	151 W 54th St	212-468-8856	399
Mansfield Hotel	12 W 44th St	212-277-8700	379
Marriott Courtyard Fifth Avenue	3 E 40th St	212-447-1500	299
Mayfair Hotel	242 W 49th St	212-586-0300	192
Mela	120 W 44th St	212-730-7900	329
Michelangelo	152 W 51st St	212-765-1900	395
Milford Plaza Hotel	270 W 45th St	212-869-3600	239
Millennium Broadway	145 W 44th St	212-768-4400	329
Moderne Hotel	243 W 55th St	212-397-6767	187
The Muse	130 W 46th St	212-485-2400	429
New York Inn	765 8th Ave	212-247-5400	161
New York Marriott Marquis	1535 Broadway	212-398-1900	449
New York Palace Hotel	455 Madison Ave	212-888-7000	490
Novotel New York	226 W 52nd St	212-315-0100	279
Omni Berkshire Place	21 E 52nd St	212-753-5800	469
Paramount Hotel	235 W 46th St	212-764-5500	266
Park Central Hotel	870 7th Ave	212-247-8000	279
Park Savoy Hotel	158 W 58th St	212-245-5755	125
Peninsula New York	700 5th Ave	212-956-2888	675

General Information · **Hotels**

Map 12 · Midtown —continued

		Phone	Rate $
Portland Square Hotel	132 W 47th St	212-382-0600	99 shared bath, 169 private bath
The Premier	133 W 44th St	212-789-7670	399
Quality Hotel Times Square	157 W 47th St	212-768-3700	180
Radio City Suites Hotel	142 W 49th St	212-730-0728	205
Renaissance New York Times Square	714 7th Ave	212-765-7676	359
The Ritz Carlton, Central Park	50 Central Park S	212-308-9100	645
Royalton Hotel	44 W 44th St	212-869-4400	509
Salisbury Hotel	123 W 57th St	212-246-1300	200
Sheraton Manhattan	790 7th Ave	212-581-3300	429
Sheraton New York Hotel and Towers	811 7th Ave	212-581-1000	342
Sherry Netherland Hotel	781 5th Ave	212-355-2800	449
Shoreham Hotel	33 W 55th St	212-247-6700	399
Sofitel	45 W 44th St	212-354-8844	440
St Regis	2 E 55th St	212-753-4500	750
Super 8 Times Square	59 W 46th St	212-719-2300	140
The Time	224 W 49th St	212-246-5252	279
W New York Times Square	1567 Broadway	212-930-7400	479
Warwick New York	65 W 54th St	212-247-2700	325
Wellington Hotel	871 7th Ave	212-247-3900	319
Westin New York at Times Square	270 W 43rd St	212-201-2700	400

Map 13 · East Midtown

Affinia 50	155 E 50th St	212-751-5710	306
Alex Hotel	205 E 45th St	212-867-5100	459
Bedford Hotel	118 E 40th St	212-697-4800	265
Beekman Tower Hotel	3 Mitchell Pl	212-355-7300	261
The Benjamin	125 E 50th St	212-715-2500	359
Best Western Hospitality House	145 E 49th St	212-753-8781	350
Courtyard by Marriott Midtown East	866 3rd Ave	212-644-1300	319
Crowne Plaza at the United Nations	304 E 42nd St	212-986-8800	279
Doubletree Metropolitan Hotel	569 Lexington Ave	212-752-7000	265
Fitzpatrick Grand Central Hotel	141 E 44th St	212-351-6800	239
Fitzpatrick Manhattan Hotel	687 Lexington Ave	212-355-0100	319
Grand Hyatt Hotel	109 E 42nd St	212-883-1234	329
Helmsley Middletowne Hotel	148 E 48th St	212-755-3000	324
Hotel 57	130 E 57th St	212-753-8841	259
Hotel Elysee	60 E 54th St	212-753-1066	421
Hotel Inter-Continental–The Barclay	111 E 48th St	212-755-5900	429
Hotel Lombary	111 E 56th St	212-753-8600	365
Kimberly Hotel	145 E 50th St	212-702-1600	542
Marriott New York City East Side	525 Lexington Ave	212-755-4000	349
Millenium UN Plaza	1 United Nations Plaza	212-758-1234	329
The New York Helmsley	212 E 42nd St	212-405-4300	292
Pod Hotel	230 E 51st St	212-355-0300	109 shared bath, 169 private bath
Radisson Lexington	511 Lexington Ave	212-755-4400	249
Roger Smith Hotel	501 Lexington Ave	212-755-1400	329
Roosevelt Hotel	45 E 45th St	212-661-9600	265
San Carlos Hotel	150 E 50th St	212-755-1800	307
Seton Hotel	144 E 40th St	212-889-5301	112 (shared bath), 150 (private bath)
W New York	541 Lexington Ave	212-755-1200	339
Waldorf Towers	100 E 50th St	212-355-3100	599
Waldorf-Astoria	301 Park Ave	212-355-3000	399
YMCA Vanderbilt	224 E 47th St	212-912-2500	89

Map 14 · Upper West Side (Lower)

Amsterdam Inn	340 Amsterdam Ave	212-579-7500	79 shared, 99 private bathroom
Comfort Inn Central Park West	31 W 71st St	212-721-4770	230
Country in the City	270 W 77th St	212-580-4183	204
Excelsior Hotel	45 W 81st St	212-362-9200	299
Hayden Hall Hotel	117 W 79th St	212-787-3300	229
Hotel Beacon	2130 Broadway	212-787-1100	220
Hotel Lucerne	201 W 79th St	212-875-1000	350
Hotel Riverside Studios	342 W 71st St	212-873-5999	85
Imperial Court Hotel	307 W 79th St	212-787-6600	730 weekly

General Information · **Hotels**

Inn New York City	266 W 71st St	212-580-1900	475
Mandarin Oriental New York	80 Columbus Cir	212-805-8800	925
Milburn Hotel	242 W 76th St	212-362-1006	195
On the Ave Hotel	2178 Broadway	212-362-1100	279
Phillips Club	155 W 66th St	212-835-8800	8000 monthly
Riverside Tower Hotel	80 Riverside Dr	212-877-5200	104
Trump International	1 Central Park West	212-299-1000	595
YMCA West Side	5 W 63rd St	212-875-4100	89 (shared bath)

Map 15 · Upper East Side (Lower)

Affinia Gardens	215 E 64th St	212-355-1230	359
Bentley Hotel	500 E 62nd St	212-644-6000	227
Carlyle Hotel	35 E 76th St	212-744-1600	700
Churchill Residence Suites	360 E 65th St	212-697-8970	345
Gracie Inn	502 E 81st St	212-628-1700	179
Helmsley Carlton	680 Madison Ave	212-838-3000	505
Hotel Plaza Athenee	37 E 64th St	212-734-9100	525
Lowell Hotel	28 E 63rd St	212-838-1400	665
Regency Hotel	540 Park Ave	212-759-4100	479
Surrey Hotel	20 E 76th St	212-288-3700	199

Map 16 · Upper West Side (Upper)

Central Park Hostel	19 W 103rd St	212-678-0491	dorm 30, private 89
Continental Studio	330 W 95th St	212-866-1420	30 shared, 60 private
Days Hotel Broadway	215 W 94th St	212-866-6400	186
Hostelling International New York	891 Amsterdam Ave	212-932-2300	33 dorm, 150 private
Hotel Belleclaire	250 W 77th St	212-362-7700	119 shared bath, 179 private bath
Hotel Newton	2528 Broadway	212-678-6500	139
Jazz on the Park	36 W 106th St	212-932-1600	22 shared, 65 private
Marrakech Hotel	2688 Broadway	212-222-2954	129
Morningside Inn	235 W 107th St	212-316-0055	90 shared bath, 125 private bath
West End Studios	850 West End Ave	212-662-6000	70
West Side Inn	237 W 107th St	212-866-0061	60

Map 17 · Upper East Side / East Harlem

92nd Street Y de Hirsch Residence	1395 Lexington Ave	212-415-5650	1280 monthly
Courtyard by Marriott	410 E 92nd St	212-410-6777	239
Franklin Hotel	164 E 87th St	212-369-1000	269
The Marmara-Manhattan	301 E 94th St	212-427-3100	249
Wales Hotel	1295 Madison Ave	212-876-6000	239

Map 19 · Harlem (Lower)

102 Brownstone	102 W 118th St	212-662-4223	250
Efuru Bed & Breakfast	106 W 120th St	212-961-9855	95 shared bath, 125 private bath
Fane Dumas Hotel	205 W 135th St	212-281-3400	64
YMCA of Greater NY	180 W 135th St	212-281-4100	70 (shared bathroom)

Map 21 · Manhattanville / Hamilton Heights

Alga Hotel	828 St Nicholas Ave	212-368-0700	40
Hamilton Heights Casablanca Hotel	511 W 145th St	212-491-0488	70 shared bath, 90 private bath
Hotel Caribe	515 W 145th St	212-368-9915	70 shared bath, 90 private bath
Sugar Hill Harlem Inn	460 W 141st St	917-464-3528	200

Map 22 · Harlem (Upper)

Harlem Vista Hotel	75 Macombs Pl	917-507-4140	77

Battery Park City

Embassy Suites New York City	102 North End Ave	212-945-0100	409
Ritz-Carlton New York Battery Park	2 West St	212-344-0800	495

Internet

Computerless New Yorkers harbor the theory that Kinko's raison d'etre is to make our lives more miserable. Your disk never works in the drive, or maybe the printer ran out of toner again. To add insult to injury, the overwhelmed employees are often too busy to offer immediate help. Nevertheless, it is a great comfort that—should you need to check your e-mail at 2 in the morning—those same employees are there and waiting. Several locations, including the Bryant Park address on W 40th Street **(Map 12)**, never close. That convenience comes at a hefty price, though. All Kinko's offer Internet access for 30–45 cents per minute, depending on which location you visit and which machine you use (it works out to $18–$27 per hour). For service with a personal touch (and a cup of coffee), try an alternative such as **News Bar** on West 19th **(Map 9)**. At 18 cents a minute, it's a much cheaper option.

Wi-Fi

For those with a laptop or PDA that has wireless access, there are a ton of free public Wi-Fi connections available throughout the city. The majority of the listed hotspots are maintained by private citizens, though a few are run by organizations such as the Downtown Alliance, including great spots at Bowling Green, City Hall, South Street Seaport, and the Winter Garden (www.downtownny.com/discover/wifi). More than 50 branches of the NY Public Library in Manhattan and the Bronx (and six on Staten Island) offer Wi-Fi access (www.nypl.org/branch/services/wifi.html), and the rest are sure to follow. Both www.wififreespot.com/ny.html and www.auscillate.com/wireless/manhattan are good starting points for locating a

free hotspot. If you're in downtown, park yourself anywhere in Chelsea Market or grab a veggie sandwich at **'sNice (Map 5)** to get connected gratis, or if you're feeling poetic, head with parchment (and laptop) in hand to the **Bowery Poetry Club (Map 6)**. **Think Coffee (Map 6)** offers free Wi-Fi and great espresso drinks. Although you may have to duel with caffeinated NYU students to get a space. And then there's always the ubiquitous **Cosi** which now offer free Wi-Fi at all their locations. Of course, it's always an option to simply plug in or turn on your wireless card and see what networks are available. If it doesn't offend your sense of ethics, you can often tap into other people's Wi-Fi networks for free.

With so many options that don't cost a dime, it's beyond us why you'd want to pay for a connection. There are, however, plenty of fee-based services out there. T-Mobile Hotspot subscribers ($6 per hour, $10 a day, or $40 per month/$30 per month paid annually gives you unlimited access) can find access at most Kinko's, Borders, and Starbucks. McDonald's offers Wi-Fi access at dozens of locations in Manhattan: check out www.mcdwireless.com. Free Wi-Fi is offered at Penn Station for AT&T Wireless customers. Everyone else can surf for as little as $6 per day. If you're just visiting NYC, visit www.jwire.com for a list of hotels (as well as cafes and libraries) that provide both paid and free Wi-Fi. The site offers a Hotspot Search function where you can search for locations throughout the city.

It seems plausible that recent talk of a citywide Wi-Fi network in New York could come to fruition. Philadelphia and New Orleans are already implementing plans, and New Yorkers never like to be second-best.

Internet Café	Address	Phone	Map	Wi-Fi	Computers
Cosi	54 Pine St	212-809-2674	1	■	
Cosi	55 Broad St	212-344-5000	1	■	
Dean & DeLuca Café	100 Broadway	212-577-2153	1	■	
Leonidas	74 Trinity Pl	212-233-1111	1	■	
Pecan	130 Franklin St	646-613-8293	2	■	
Blue Spoon Coffee	76 Chambers St	212-619-7230	3	■	
Caffe Del Arte	143 Mulberry St	212-219-9799	3	■	
Miro Café	474 Broadway	212-431-9391	3	■	
Universal News	484 Broadway	212-965-0730	3		■
Full City Coffee	409 Grand St	212-260-2363	4	■	
Chocolate Bar	48 Eighth Ave	212-367-7181	5	■	
Cosi	504 Sixth Ave	212-462-4188	5	■	
Grounded	28 Jane St	212-647-0943	5	■	

Internet Café	Address	Phone	Map	Wi-Fi	Computers
Le Gamin Café	522 Hudson St	212-807-7357	5	■	
Sant Ambroeus	259 W 4th	212-604-9254	5	■	
sNice	45 Eighth Ave	212-645-0310	5	■	
Aroma	36 E 4th St	212-375-0100	6	■	
Bowery Poetry Club	308 Bowery	212-614-0505	6	■	
Anyway Café	34 E 2nd St	212-533-3412	6	■	
Cosi	841 Broadway	212-614-8544	6	■	
Cyberfelds	20 E 13th St	212-647-8830	6	■	■
Housing Works Used Book Café	126 Crosby St	212-334-3324	6	■	
La Lanterna di Vittorio	129 MacDougal St	212-529-5945	6	■	
Mission Café	82 Second Ave	212-505-6616	6		■
Mr Fresh Bread	116 Second Ave	212-253-1046	6	■	
Once Upon A Tart	135 Sullivan St	212-387-8869	6	■	
Tasti D-Lite	137 Fourth Ave	212-228-5619	6		■

Internet Café	Address	Phone	Map	Wi-Fi	Computers
Tea Spot	127 MacDougal St	212-832-7768	6	■	
Think	248 Mercer St	212-228-6226	6	■	
Veniero's	342 E 11th St	212-674-7070	6	■	
Village Juice Bar	200 E 14th St	212-673-0005	6	■	
web2zone	54 Cooper Sq	212-614-7300	6	■	■
altcoffee	139 Ave A	212-529-2233	7	■	
The Bean	49 1/2 First Ave	212-353-1477	7	■	
Café Pick Me Up	145 Ave A	212-673-7231	7		
Café Pick Me Up	145 Avenue A	212-673-7231	7	■	■
Lalita Java Limited	210 E 3rd St	212-228-8448	7		
Sympathy for the Kettle	109 St Marks Pl	212-979-1650	7		
254 Snack Shop Corp	254 Tenth Ave	212-242-1202	8		
Choux Factory	316 W 23rd St	212-627-4318	8	■	
From Earth To You Gourmet Café	252 Tenth Ave	212-924-1877	8		
Antique Café	234 W 27th St	212-243-2056	9		
Antique Café	55 W 26th St	212-213-5723	9	■	
Brooklyn Bagel	319 Fifth Ave	212-532-0007	9	■	
Café Arome	138 W 32nd St	212-714-9401	9		
Café Bonjour	20 E 39th St	212-481-1224	9	■	
Café Muse	43 W 32nd St	212-290-1414	9	■	
Cosi	498 Seventh Ave	212-947-1005	9	■	
Guy & Gallard	1001 Sixth Ave	212-730-0010	9		
Guy & Gallard	180 Madison Ave	212-725-2392	9	■	
Guy & Gallard	245 W 38th St	212-302-7588	9		
Guy & Gallard	469 Seventh Ave	212-695-0006	9	■	
Guy & Gallard	475 Park Ave S	212-447-5282	9		
Guy & Gallard IV	339 Seventh Ave	212-279-7373	9	■	
Hotel Grand Union	34 E 32nd St	212-683-5890	9		■
Keko Café	121 Madison Ave	212-685-4360	9	■	
Le Gamin Café	258 W 15th St	212-929-3270	9	■	
News Bar	2 W 19th St	212-255-3996	9	■	
Subtle Tea	121 Madison Ave	212-481-4713	9	■	
Universal News	50 W 23rd St	212-647-1761	9	■	
Brasil Coffee House	161 Lexington Ave	212-213-9725	10		
Cosi	257 Park Ave S	212-598-4070	10	■	
Cosi	461 Park Ave S	212-634-3467	10		
Gregorys Coffee	327 Park Ave S	212-979-8600	10	■	
Guy & Gallard	120 E 34th St	212-684-3898	10	■	
Lady Mendl's Tea Salon	56 Irving Pl	212-533-4466	10	■	
Sunburst	206 Third Ave	212-674-1702	10	■	
The Bread Factory Café	600 Ninth Ave	212-974-8100	11	■	
The Coffee Pot	350 W 49th St	212-265-3566	11	■	
Coffee Pot	350 W 49th St	212-265-3566	11		■
Café Metro	625 Eighth Ave	212-714-9342	12	■	
City Chow	1633 Broadway	212-445-0600	12	■	
Cosi	11 W 42nd St	212-398-6662	12	■	
Cosi	1633 Broadway	212-397-9838	12	■	
Cosi	61 W 48th St	212-265-7579	12	■	
Cyber Café	250 W 49th St	212-333-4109	12	■	■
Fluffy's Café & Bakery	855 Seventh Ave	212-247-0234	12	■	
Seattle Café	1634 Broadway	212-262-4611	12	■	
Universal News	977 Eighth Ave	212-459-0932	12	■	
Cosi	38 E 45th St	212-370-0705	13	■	
Cosi	60 E 56th St	212-588-1225	13	■	
Cosi	685 Third Ave	212-697-8329	13	■	
Ing Direct	45 E 49th St	212-355-0674	13	■	■
Mambi Lounge	933 Second Ave	212-832-3500	13	■	
Manhattan Espresso HD	146 E 49th St	212-832-3010	13	■	
Beard Papa	2167 Broadway	212-799-3770	14	■	
Cosi	2160 Broadway	212-595-5616	14	■	
Lenny's Café	302 Columbus Ave	212-580-8300	14	■	
Cafe Bacio	1223 Third Ave	212-737-4730	15	■	
DT * UT	1626 Second Ave	212-327-1327	15	■	
First Avenue Coffee Shop	1433 First Ave	212-794-5246	15	■	
Gotham Coffee House	1298 Second Ave	212-717-0457	15	■	
M Rohrs	303 E 85th St	212-396-4456	15	■	■
Telegraphe Café	260 E 72nd St	212-288-1544	15	■	
Broadway Bagel	2658 Broadway	212-662-0231	16	■	
Sip	998 Amsterdam Ave	212-316-2747	16	■	
Saurin Parke Café	301 W 110th St	212-222-0683	18	■	
Society Coffee & Juice	2104 Frederick Douglass Blvd	212-222-3323	19	■	
Boma Coffee & Tea	2037 Fifth Ave	212-427-8668	20	■	
OC Bakery & Café	375 Edgecombe Ave	917-806-1664	20	■	
Astron Coffee Shop	3795 Broadway	212-368-1837	21	■	
Jou Jou	603 W 168th St	212-781-2222	23	■	
Cosi	200 Vesey St	212-571-2001	p234	■	

Eating out in New York...why do we do it? Because our kitchens are small, it's too busy, and hey, cooking is probably only 15% cheaper. Or at least that's what we tell ourselves when we're spending $81 on a hamburger (**Old Homestead Steakhouse (Map 5)**. But even those of us who love to cook can't resist the allure of some of the best and most varied cuisine in the world. For New Yorkers, eating out is simultaneously a science and an art form. Since we have so many options, we don't seem to be able to waste any meal on a haphazard choice of venue. Selecting exactly the right restaurant for an occasion is not just a matter of taste, particularly when you're preparing to splurge; it requires knowledge, logic, strategy, and even risk-assessment (is it beginning to sound like a competitive sport?). We may want a certain type of cuisine, near a subway line convenient for all parties involved, with atmosphere but not romantic, in a specific price range. And with over 25,000 options, we can always find the perfect place. Whether we're looking for a restaurant with a rare 28 from Zagat's (the culinary Bible for many New Yorkers), or we want to roll the dice with an undiscovered hole in the wall where even the Board of Health fears to tread, we will never have to settle. There is, of course, a huge drawback: we are downright spoiled. But I guess we'll just have to live with that.

Eating Old

Since New York City is a culinary hotspot with lots of big names (and wannabe big names) at work in the kitchens, it's easy to get swept up in food trends that often involve dishes that look more like art projects than meals. Many of the more experimental restaurants do merit attention, but when you're not in the mood for Parmesan cheese ice cream with pesto foam in a braised kale emulsion, you can avail yourselves of the Big Apple's time-honored stalwarts. Rub elbows with the who's who at the posh **21 Club (Map 12)** (circa 1929); dine on New American cuisine at the ancient, 213-year-old **Bridge Café (Map 3)**; slurp fresh-shucked oysters under the vaulted, tiled ceiling at Grand Central Station's **Oyster Bar (Map 13)** (circa 1913), and do not miss their desserts; sample more oysters and one of the best burgers in existence at the venerable Midtown watering hole **P.J. Clarke's (Map 13)** (since 1884); or expand your culinary horizons with calf's spleen and cheese on a roll at **Ferdinando's Focaccia (Map 32)** (circa 1904).

Eating Cheap

Eating cheap has become more stylish thanks to the recent trend of highbrow chefs and restaurateurs going lowbrow. At Danny Meyer's **Shake Shack (Map 9)**, you can grab a cheeseburger for $4 or one of their legendary Chicago Dogs (a meal in itself) for only $3.25. In addition to its brick-and-mortar location, **Daisy May's BBQ USA (Map 11)**, co-owned by Adam Perry Lang (Le Cirque, Daniel, Chanterelle), has multiple street carts throughout the city where you can fetch a hearty bowl of award-winning "Bowl'O Red" Texas-style chili for $7 and some serious 'cue. Ethnic food has always been a great friend to eaters on a budget. Vietnamese (**Cong Ly (Map 3)**), Chinese (**New Green Bo (Map 3)**, **Wo Hop (Map 3)**, **Joe's Shanghai (Map 3, 12)**, **Food Shing (Map 3)**), Middle Eastern (**Hummus Place (Map 6)**, **Gazala Place (Map 11)**), and Mexican joints (the taqueria at The Corner a.k.a. **La Esquina (Map 6)**) deserve repeat visits even if you're not trying to be frugal. And now, thanks to a new influx of hip hot dog joints, you can branch out from **Katz's Delicatessen (Map 7)**. **Papaya King (Map 11)** has kept hot dog lovers grinning since 1932. And many of us can't survive a day without at least one of the staples of NYC Jewish eats—bagels and knishes. For bagels, go with perennial winners **Ess-a-Bagel (Map 10, 13)** and **H&H Bagels (Map 11, 14)**, or try our favorites: **David's Bagels (Map 7, 10)**, **Kossar's Bialys (Map 4)**, **Absolute Bagels (Map 16)**, or the original **Tal Bagels (Map 13)**. For knishes, nothing beats the **Yonah Schimmel Knish Bakery (Map 7)**.

Eating Hip

Eating hip usually involves the food of the moment (tacos, lobster rolls, Asian street food), beautiful people (those who often look like they never eat), and some kind of exclusivity (ridiculously long waits, unpublished phone numbers, impossible-to-come-by reservations, or no reservations at all). Food snobs may warn you that the appetite that's satisfied the craving is the need to see and be seen, rather than the desire for the city's best culinary experience. That being said, the ultimate in cool dining is, of course, **Rao's (Map 20)**—or so we hear. But unless you're the Mayor, the Governor, or Woody Allen, you probably won't be getting a reservation anytime soon, so don't hold your breath. It's a similar story at the newly renovated Graydon Carter–owned, restaurant-cum-speakeasy, **The Waverly Inn (Map 5)**, where it is rumored that only A-listers have access to the secret phone number and the walk-in waits for a table can be epic (if not eternal). In the realm of destinations accessible to mere mortals with the patience of a saint, the perpetually packed gastro pub **Spotted Pig (Map 5)** tops the list; getting elbowed in the jaw every time you're about to take a bite might ruin your meal, so aim for off-hours and expect to wait anyway. Be sure to try the equally crowded, no-reservations eatery **Freemans (Map 6)**, which hides itself at the end of an alleyway; do not miss the pork chops. Take an i.v. drip to sustain you while you wait for lobster rolls at **Pearl Oyster Bar (Map 5)** and **Mary's Fish Camp (Map 5)** (where Amy Sedaris used to wait tables just for fun!). **Employees Only (Map 5)** draws trendsters who you'll find drinking and dining to the tunes of the Clash and Lou Reed

Arts & Entertainment • Restaurants

(while garter-clad waitresses wearing vintage headwear sexily saunter around), and not caring at all what the food tastes like. **Momofuku Noodle Bar (Map 7)** and its new offshoot **Momofuku Ssam Bar (Map 6)** lure in lovers of noodles and all things porky, but of course don't go to either if you're in any kind of a rush. And for those of you who have a penchant for restaurants with celebrity chefs (with celebrity tempers), and get a thrill from sitting at one of the most exclusive tables in town, pull whatever strings you've got for an evening of hip indulgence at the chef's table in the kitchen of **Gordon Ramsay at the London (Map 12)**.

Eating Late

Kang Suh's (Map 9) Korean barbeque runs all night, as well as **Bereket (Map 7)**, **Odessa (Map 7)**, **7A (Map 7)**, **Yaffa Café (Map 7)**, and a host of generic diners. **Employees Only (Map 5)** serves a special "$11 Staff Meal," available between midnight and 4 am. And, of course, **Blue Ribbon (Map 6)** is still one of the best places to eat after midnight.

Eating Pizza

Pizza constitutes a food group unto itself for New Yorkers. The coal oven spots top most lists: **Grimaldi's (Map 30)**, **Lombardi's (Map 6)**, **Luzzo's (Map 7)**, and the original **Patsy's (Map 20)** in East Harlem. The coal oven enjoys extra cachet by virtue of being illegal now, except in the aforementioned eateries where they were already in operation when legislation was passed prohibiting them. The brick oven joints, such as **John's Pizzeria (Map 5)**, **Nick's (Map 17)**, **Franny's (Map 33)**, **Slice of Harlem (Map 19)**, and **Totonno's Pizzeria Napolitano (Map 10)** never seem to slow down either. A Brooklyn favorite, the cozy, family-run **Amorina (Map 33)**, has the added benefit of spectacle—you literally watch your pizza get made a few feet away from your table. For a classic Village scene complete with live jazz, check out **Arturo's (Map 6)** on Houston Street. Pizza by the slice practically deserves its own category, but the highlights include **Patsy's (Map 20)** and **Joe's (Map 5)**.

Eating Ethnic

Spin a globe, stick your finger onto a spot blindly, and chances are you can find cuisine from that country on offer in New York. And an outstanding offering it will be. To wit: **Sammy's Roumanian (Map 6)**, **Katz's Delicatessen (Map 7)**, and **Carnegie Deli (Map 12)** (Jewish); **Shun Lee (Map 13)**, **Grand Sichuan International (Map 8, 11)**, and **Chef Ho's Peking Duck Grill (Map 17)** (Chinese); **Dawat (Map 13)**, **Tabla (Map 9)**, and **Indian Tandoor Oven (Map 15)** (Indian); **Alma (Map 32)**, **El Paso (Map 17, 20)** and **Rosa Mexicano (Map 9, 13, 14)** (Mexican); **Kang Suh (Map 9)** and **Dok Suni's (Map 7)** (Korean); **Nobu (Map 2)** and about 40 others (Japanese;) **Babbo (Map 6)**, **Felidia (Map 13)**, **Il Mulino (Map 6)**, **Sfoglia (Map 17)**, **i Trulli (Map 10)**, and countless others (Italian); **Ghenet (Map 6)** and **Zoma (Map 19)** (Ethiopian); **Eight Mile Creek (Map 6)** (Australian); **Balthazar (Map 6)**, **Chanterelle (Map 2)**, **Café D'Alsace (Map 17)**, **La Luncheonette (Map 8)**, **Jules (Map 6)**, and so many more (French); **Good World (Map 4)** and **Aquavit (Map 12)** (Scandinavian); **Heidelberg (Map 15)**, **Zum Schneider (Map 7)**, and **Hallo Berlin (Map 11)** (German); **Charles' Southern Style (Map 22)**, **Sylvia's (Map 19)**, and **Old Devil Moon (Map 7)** (Southern); **Kefi (Map 14)** and **Elias Corner (Map 26)** (Greek); **Sigiri (Map 7)** (Sri Lankan) etc. etc. etc.

Eating Meat

New York is home to arguably the world's best steakhouse, **Peter Luger's (Map 29)**. But it's competitive at the top, and clawing at Luger's heels are: the newish **Mark Joseph Steakhouse (Map 3)**, and classics like **Sparks (Map 13)**, **Palm (Map 13)**, **Smith & Wollensky (Map 13)**, **Angelo & Maxie's (Map 10)**, and the **Strip House (Map 9)**. For the Brazilian-style "all you can eat meat fest," **Churrascaria Plataforma (Map 11)** does the trick. As for hamburgers, the rankings provide material for eternal debate. Many of the favorites find their way to the top of some list or another: **P.J. Clarke (Map 13)**, **Corner Bistro (Map 5)**, **Burger Joint at Le Parker Meridien (Map 12)**, **J.G. Melon (Map 15)**, **Big Nick's (Map 14)**, and **Pastis (Map 9)**, to name a few. New on the scene is **Royale (Map 7)**, where they compliment the perfect patty with stellar fixin's, for a song. For a change of pace from your burger tour, look for evidence that we Yankees can indeed produce some damn good BBQ: **Blue Smoke (Map 10)**, **Dinosaur Bar-B-Que (Map 18)**, and **RUB BBQ (Map 9)** in Manhattan, and **Smoke Joint (Map 31)** and **Fette Sau (Map 29)** in Brooklyn (arrive early at the latter, they run out of the most popular items quickly). And wherever you go, be prepared to wash down your 'cue with some serious bourbon.

Eating Meatless

We're advanced enough here that most restaurants (except perhaps those mentioned directly above) offer at least a few items palatable to vegetarians. But don't worry, every kind of appetite gets special attention here, including non-meat-eaters. Try a whole range of vegan/macrobiotic at **Angelica Kitchen (Map 6)**, the quality Indian fare at **Pongal (Map 10)**, and, for high-end eats, **Candle 79 (Map 15)** and the vegan **Hangawi (Map 9)** (even your carnivorous friends will love it). Vegetarians have even found some of their favorite dishes in less likely places, including the stuffed peppers at the otherwise carnivorous **Rosa Mexicano (Map 9, 13, 14)**.

Eating Your Wallet

You don't have to live in this city long before realizing that while we technically use the same currency as the rest of the country, it's actually worth about half as much as elsewhere. Even the most frugal among us have found ourselves spending 100 New York dollars on a night out and thinking we got off easy. But remember that when it comes to dining out, there is no cap. You can easily spend over $150 (per person) at any number of highly regarded restaurants around town, even if you're feeling abstemious. Never mind the likes of Masa, with a $400 prix fixe. No doubt you've been just dying to try Batali's this, and Morimoto's that. But handle the decision to dine at the culinary echelon as you would (or should) handle the prospect of an open bar at your holiday office party: Know your limit (financially, emotionally, morally), and try not to do anything you'll regret in the morning. If you can keep your food down after witnessing triple digits on your share of the tab, start on the slippery slope to gastronomically induced bankruptcy at the following restaurants, which rarely disappoint: **Babbo (Map 6)**, **Per Se (Map 12)**, **Gramercy Tavern (Map 9)**, **Chanterelle (Map 2)**, **Le Bernardin (Map 12)**, **Bouley (Map 2)**, **Oceana (Map 13)**, **Union Square Café (Map 9)**, and **Daniel (Map 15)**. And remember to manage your expectations: Unless you fall in love with your waiter or waitress, the experience will not change your life. Although Per Se comes pretty damn close.

Our Favorite Restaurants

Consensus on such a crucial and personal matter is always elusive, but with a group of New Yorkers opinionated enough to produce the NFT, all we can say is, "Fughedaboutit." We've historically granted the accolade to **Blue Ribbon (Map 6)**— it's open 'til 4 am, it's where the chefs of other restaurants go, it's got fondue, it's got fried chicken, it's got great beef marrow, it's got a great vibe, great liquor, and great service. And it will always have that special place in our hearts and stomachs, but this year we're also giving a nod to a few other spots: **Sigiri (Map 7)**, a spicy Sri Lankan gem that is BYOB to boot, **Babbo (Map 6)**, well, because it's Babbo, **Fuleen Seafood (Map 3)**, the number one reason to eat lunch in Chinatown, and **Eisenberg's Sandwich Shop (Map 9)**, a classic, old-school diner counter that's still serving up egg creams and BLTs to the locals.

*Key: $: Under $10 / $$: $10–$20 / $$$: $20–$30 / $$$$: $30–$40 / $$$$$: $40+; *: Cash only / † : Accepts only American Express. / † † Accepts only Visa/Mastercard. Time refers to hour kitchen closes on weekends.*

Map 1 • Financial District

Adrienne's	54 Stone St	212-248-3838	$$	11:30 pm	Modern, thin crust pizza.
Battery Gardens	Battery Park, across from 17 State St	212-809-5508	$$$$$	10 pm	Panoramic views of NY harbor with a wood-burning fireplace.
Bayard's	1 Hanover Square	212-514-9454	$$$$	10 pm	Elegant Continental cuisine in the historic India House.
Burritoville	36 Water St	212-747-1100	$	10 pm	Takeout Mexican.
Cosi Sandwich Bar	55 Broad St	212-344-5000	$	5 pm	Sandwiches for the masses.
Cosi Sandwich Bar	54 Pine St	212-809-2674	$	4:30 pm	Sandwiches for the masses.
Daily Soup	41 John St	212-791-7687	$	3 pm	Soup!
Financier Patisserie	62 Stone St	212-344-5600	$$	9 pm	Have your cake and a light meal too.
Giovanni's Atrium	100 Washington St	212-513-4133	$$$$$	10 pm	Owner grows fresh herbs for meals!
Grotto Pizzeria	69 New St	212-809-6990	$$	7:30 pm	More quick, tasty Italian. Less nudity than that other grotto.
Heartland Brewery	93 South St	646-572-2337	$$	10 pm	Decent pub grub.
Lemongrass Grill	84 William St	212-809-8038	$$	10:30 pm	Serviceable Thai.
Les Halles	15 John St	212-285-8585	$$$	12 am	Excellent French steakhouse.
Papoo's	55 Broadway	212-809-3150	$$$$	9 pm	Good, if pricey, Italian cuisine.
Red	19 Fulton St	212-571-5900	$$	10 pm	Acceptable Mexican.
Rosario's	38 Pearl St	212-514-5454	$$	3 pm	Italian. Go for the small portions.
Roy's New York	130 Washington St	212-266-6262	$$$$	10 pm	Hawaiian fusion seafood.
Sophie's	73 New St	212-809-7755	$*	4 pm	Great cheap Cuban/Carribean.
St Maggie's Café	120 Wall St	212-943-9050	$$$	9 pm	Downtown lunch option.
Zaitzeff	72 Nassau St	212-571-7272	$$	8 pm	Quick and organic lunch.
Zeytuna	59 Maiden Ln	212-742-2436	$$	10 pm	Gourmet take-out. NFT fave.

Map 2 • TriBeCa

Acapella	1 Hudson St	212-240-0163	$$$$	10:30 pm	*Sopranos*-worthy Northern Italian cuisine.
Azafran	77 Warren St	212-284-0578	$$$	11:30 pm	Upscale tapas and Spanish dishes.
Bouley	120 W Broadway	212-964-2525	$$$$$	11:30 pm	Absolute top NYC dining. Love the apples in the foyer.
Bread Tribeca	301 Church St	212-334-8282	$$$	12 am	Country-style Italian.
Bubby's	120 Hudson St	212-219-0666	$$	12 am	Great atmosphere—good home-style eats and

					homemade pies.
Café Noir	32 Grand St	212-431-7910	$$$†	4 am	Tapas. Open 'til 4am.
Capsouto Freres	451 Washington St	212-966-4900	$$$	12 am	Excellent brunch, great space, oldish (in a good way) vibe.
Centrico	211 W Broadway	212-431-0700	$$$$	11 pm	Cha cha upscale Mexican makes you forget the ka-ching.
Chanterelle	2 Harrison St	212-966-6960	$$$$$	11 pm	Sublime French with prices to match.
City Hall	131 Duane St	212-227-7777	$$$$$	12 am	Bright, expensive, lots of suits, but still cool.
Cupping Room Café	359 W Broadway	212-925-2898	$$$	1 am	Keeps the mimosas flowing at brunch.
Danube	30 Hudson St	212-791-3771	$$$$$	11:30 pm	Excellent food with an Austrian twist. Go for the tasting menu.
Duane Park Café	157 Duane St	212-732-5555	$$$$	10:30 pm	Underrated New American.
Dylan Prime	62 Laight St	212-334-4783	$$$$$	12 am	Excellent steakhouse, great location, TriBeCa prices.
Edward's	136 W Broadway	212-233-6436	$$	1 am	Middle-of-the-road, kid's menu, mostly locals, sometimes great.
Estancia 460	460 Greenwich St	212-431-5093	$$	11 pm	Louche Argentines and brilliant french toast. Formerly Sosa Borella.
Flor de Sol	361 Greenwich St	212-366-1640	$$$	12 am	Tapas with—of course—a scene.
fresh	105 Reade St	212-406-1900	$$$$$	10:30 pm	Excellent seafood.
The Harrison	355 Greenwich St	212-274-9310	$$$$	11:30 pm	Great New American—understandably popular.
Il Giglio	81 Warren St	212-571-5555	$$$$$	11 pm	Stellar Italian. Trust us.
Ivy's Bistro	385 Greenwich St	212-343-1139	$$	11 pm	Down-to-earth neighborhood Italian.
Kitchenette	156 Chambers St	212-267-6740	$$	11 pm	Great breakfast. Try the bacon.
Kori	253 Church St	212-334-4598	$$$	10:30 pm	Korean.
Landmarc	179 W Broadway	212-343-3883	$$$$$	2 am	Modern, posh, great steaks and wines; and, of course, pricey.
Lupe's East LA Kitchen	110 6th Ave	212-966-1326	$*	12 am	Tex-Mex. Quaint.
Montrachet	239 W Broadway	212-219-2777	$$$$	11 pm	Wonderful French.
Nobu	105 Hudson St	212-219-0500	$$$$$	10:15 pm	Designer Japanese. When we have 100 titles, we'll go here.
Nobu, Next Door	105 Hudson St	212-334-4445	$$$$$	1 am	Nobu's cheaper neighbor.
Odeon	145 W Broadway	212-233-0507	$$$	2 am	We can't agree about this one, so go and make your own decision.
Pakistan Tea House	176 Church St	212-240-9800	$	4 am	The real deal. Where cabbies eat.
Palacinka	28 Grand St	212-625-0362	$$*	12 am	A tasty load of crepe. NFT fave.
Square Diner	33 Leonard St	212-925-7188	$*	9 pm	Classic neighborhood diner.
Thalassa	179 Franklin St	212-941-7661	$$$	12 am	Greek. But it's cheaper and better in Astoria.
Tribeca Grill	375 Greenwich St	212-941-3900	$$$$	11:30 pm	Are you looking at me?
Viet Café	345 Greenwich St	212-431-5888	$$$	11 pm	Glossy out of a magazine.
Walker's	16 N Moore St	212-941-0142	$$	1 am	Surprisingly good food for a pub!
Yaffa's	353 Greenwich St	212-274-9403	$$	12 am	Cooly eclectic. Food 'til 1am.
Zutto	77 Hudson St	212-233-3287	$$$	10:30 pm	Neighborhood Japanese.

Map 3 • City Hall / Chinatown

Baby O Pizza	225 Park Row	212-608-5888	$		Yo, this pizza ain't half bad.
Big Wong King	67 Mott St	212-964-0540	$*	10 pm	If you're gonna be a king, that's the kind of king to be.
Bridge Café	279 Water St	212-227-3344	$$$$$	12 am	Now extremely expensive.
Buddha Boddhai	5 Mott St	212-566-8388	$$	10 pm	Veg heads dig this place.
Cendrillon	45 Mercer St	212-343-9012	$$$$	11 pm	Flippin' Filipino. Try the young coconut pie.
Cong Ly	124 Hester St	212-343-1111	$*	10 pm	Most interesting Pho in the city.
Cup & Saucer	89 Canal St	212-925-3298	$*	5 pm	Where NFT eats. Well, just Rob.
Despana	408 Broome St	212-219-5050	$	8 pm	Excellent Spanish take-out/gourmet grocery, complete w/ bull.
Dim Sum Go Go	5 E Broadway	212-732-0797	$$	10:30 pm	New, hip, inventive dim sum; essentially, post-modern Chinese.
Drew's Place	100 Forsyth St	212-925-1343	$*	11 pm	Hip-hop sandwich shop.
East Corner Wonton	70 E Broadway	212-343-9896	$		Consistently good noodle soups.
Everest Pancake and Coffee House	22 Chatham Square	212-406-3719	$	8 pm	When the NFT office gets sick of Chinese food.
Excellent Dumpling House	111 Lafayette St	212-219-0212	$*	9 pm	Excellent dumplings, really.
Food Shing	2 E Broadway	212-219-8223	$	11 pm	Outstanding. Extra special treatment for regulars.
Freemans	End of Freeman Aly	212-420-0012	$$	11:30 pm	Taxidermy-filled hideaway with fab cocktails and delicious, rustic fare.
Fried Dumpling	106 Mosco St	212-693-1060	$*	6 pm	Five for a buck.
Fuleen Seafood	11 Division St	212-941-6888	$$$†	3 am	Chinatown gem; amazing lunch specials.
Golden Unicorn	18 E Broadway	212-941-0911	$$	11 pm	Dim sum—great for medium-sized groups.
Il Palazzo	151 Mulberry St	212-343-7000	$$$	10 pm	Excellent mid-range Italian.
Joe's Shanghai	9 Pell St	212-233-8888	$$*	11:15 pm	Great crab soup dumplings, crowded.
L'Ecole	462 Broadway	212-219-3300	$$$$	9:30 pm	The restaurant of the French Culinary Institute; new student menu every 6 weeks.

Arts & Entertainment · **Restaurants**

Key: $: Under $10 / $$: $10–$20 / $$$: $20–$30 / $$$$: $30–$40 / $$$$$: $40+; *: Cash only / †: Accepts only American Express. / † † Accepts only Visa/Mastercard. Time refers to hour kitchen closes on weekends.

Map 3 · City Hall / Chinatown—*continued*

Le Pain Quotidien	100 Grand St	212-625-9009	$$	7 pm	Excellent breads. Communal table. Euro vibe.
Mandarin Court	61 Mott St	212-608-3838	$$	11 pm	Consistently good dim sum.
Mark Joseph Steakhouse	261 Water St	212-277-0020	$$$$	11 pm	Luger's wannabe: damn close, actually, and they take plastic.
May Wah Fast Food	190 Hester St	212-925-6428	$*	10 pm	Linoleum floors, fluorescent lights, and an amazing pork chop over rice.
Mei Lai Wah Coffee House	64 Bayard St	212-925-5435	$	10 pm	The best pork buns: white, brown, and delicious.
New Green Bo Restaurant	66 Bayard St	212-625-2359	$*	12 am	Good Shanghainese. Nice alternative to Joe's.
New York Noodle Town	28 Bowery	212-349-0923	$*	4 am	Cheap Chinese soups and BBQ.
Nha Trang	87 Baxter St	212-233-5948	$$	9:30 pm	The best cheap Vietnamese.
Parigot	155 Grand St	212-274-8859	$$$	11 pm	Possibly the cutest/quaintest of all the French spots in the city.
The Paris Café	119 South St	212-240-9797	$$$	4 am	Good burgers and seafood, a bit pricey though.
Pho Viet Huong	73 Mulberry St	212-233-8988	$$	10:30 pm	Very good Vietnamese—get the salt and pepper squid.
Ping's	22 Mott St	212-602-9988	$$	12 am	Eclectic Asian seafood.
Pongsri Thai	106 Bayard St	212-349-3132	$$	11 pm	Ever wonder where district attorneys go for cheap, tasty Thai?
Positano	122 Mulberry St	212-334-9808	$$	12 am	Good northern Italian fare.
Saigon Banh Mi	138 Mott St	212-941-1541	$*	11 pm	The best Vietnamese sandwiches. Ever.
Sanur Restaurant	18 Doyers St	212-267-0088	$*	10 pm	Amazing, super cheap Malaysian.
Shing's Food Shop	Catherine St b/w Madison St & Henry St	$*	5 pm	Tasty $1.25 lunches from a street cart, perfect for surviving on an NFT salary.
Triple Eight Palace	88 E Broadway	212-941-8886	$$	8 pm	Dim sum madness under the Manhattan Bridge.
Wo Hop	17 Mott St	212-267-2536	$*	24-hrs	Chinatown mainstay.
Xin Jiang Kebab Cart	Market St b/w E Division St & East Broadway	$*		Charcoal grilled chicken hearts anyone? Get them spicy.

Map 4 · Lower East Side

88 Orchard	88 Orchard St	212-228-8880	$$††	8 pm	Bridges the gap so you don't have to walk to the East Village.
Bacaro	136 Division St	212-941-5060	$$	12 am	Venetian snack bar.
Barrio Chino	253 Broome St	212-228-6710	$$††	1 am	Started life as a tequila bar, but now more of a restaurant.
Brown Cafe	61 Hester St	212-477-2427	$$	11 pm	Sleepy hipsters congregate here for breakfast.
Congee Village	100 Allen St	212-941-1818	$$	2 am	Good neighborhood Asian.
Dumpling House	118 Eldridge St	212-625-8008	$*	9:30 pm	Famous Fat Dave recommends the sesame pancakes.
Good World	3 Orchard St	212-925-9975	$$	12 am	Excellent Scandinavian finger food.
Il Laboratorio del Gelato	95 Orchard St	212-343-9922	$*	6 pm	Mind-bogglingly incredible artisanal gelato.
Kossar's Bagels and Bialys	367 Grand St	877-4-BIALYS	$*	9 pm	Where the NFT office gets their morning bialys and bagels.
Les Enfants Terribles	37 Canal St	212-777-7518	$$$	12 am	Cozy French-African. Recommended.
Little Giant	85 Orchard St	212-226-5047	$$$$$	12 am	Quirky expensive LES newcomer.
Noah's Arc	399 Grand St	212-674-2200	$$	10 pm	Great Jewish deli.
Pho Bang	3 Pike St	212-233-3947	$*	9 pm	Vietnamese with great pho.
Sticky Rice	85 Orchard St	212-274-8208	$$	11 pm	Thai treats, Asian BBQ, BYOB, and Wi-Fi?!

Map 5 · West Village

AOC	314 Bleecker St	212-675-9463	$$$†	12 am	A fine French replacement for Grove.
Aquagrill	210 Spring St	212-274-0505	$$$$$	12 am	Excellent seafood.
August	359 Bleecker St	212-929-4774	$$$$	12 am	Bistro more like October. Crisp and rustic.
Blue Ribbon Bakery	33 Downing St	212-337-0404	$$$$	2 am	Another Blue Ribbon success.
Café Asean	117 W 10th St	212-633-0348	$$*	11 pm	Pan-Asian, via Mr. Wong.
Corner Bistro	331 W 4th St	212-242-9502	$*	3:30 am	Top NYC burgers. Open 'til 4 am.
Da Andrea	557 Hudson St	212-367-1979	$$	11 pm	Fabulous and affordable Italian.
Diablo Royale	189 W 10th St	212-620-0223	$$$	2 am	West Village taqueria and cantina—interesting crema salsas to choose from.
Ditch Plains	29 Bedford St	212-633-0202	$$$	2 am	Great for seafood or breakfast
Do Hwa	55 Carmine St	212-414-1224	$$$	11 pm	Hot-off-the-barbie Korean with friends.
Employees Only	510 Hudson St	212-242-3021	$$$$	4 am	Deco-decorated eatery with a damn good bar.
Fatty Crab	643 Hudson St	212-352-3590	$$	2 am	A new West Village favorite for Malaysian street food.

Arts & Entertainment · **Restaurants**

French Roast	78 W 11th St	212-533-2233	$$	24-hrs	Open 24 hours. French comfort food.
GoBo	401 Avenue of the Americas	212-255-3242	$$$	11 pm	Even vegans deserve a decent place to eat.
Home	20 Cornelia St	212-243-9579	$$$$	11 pm	There's no place like it.
Ivo & Lulu	558 Broome St	212-226-4399	$$*	12 am	Tiny inventive French-Caribbean (BYOB).
Joe's Pizza	7 Carmine St	212-366-1182	$*	3 am	Excellent slices.
John's Pizzeria	278 Bleecker St	212-243-1680	$$*	12:30 am	Quintessential NY pizza.
Karahi	118 Christopher St	212-965-1515	$$	10:30 pm	Authentic, delicious Indian.
Little Havana	30 Cornelia St	212-255-2212	$$$	11 pm	Cuban food cooked by the Cuban grandma you never had.
Mary's Fish Camp	64 Charles St	646-486-2185	$$$	11 pm	Amy Sedaris used to wait tables here for fun. Killer food!
Mercadito	100 7th Ave S	212-647-0410	$$$$	1 am	Inventive Mexican with great fish taco choices.
One If By Land, TIBS	17 Barrow St	212-228-0822	$$$$$	11:15 pm	Exudes romance.
Paris Commune	99 Bank St	212-929-0509	$$$	11 pm	How brunch should be.
Pastis	9 9th Ave	212-929-4844	$$$$	2:30 am	Great French vibe; LOUD.
Pearl Oyster Bar	18 Cornelia St	212-691-8211	$$$	11 pm	For all your lobster roll cravings. NFT fave.
Po	31 Cornelia St	212-645-2189	$$$$	11:30 pm	Creative Italian.
Provence	38 MacDougal St	212-475-7500	$$$	11 pm	Cute, but you don't have to spend a year here.
Souen	210 6th Ave	212-807-7421	$$$	10 pm	High-end vegetarian.
Spotted Pig	314 W 11th St	212-620-0393	$$$$	2 am	We finally got in. All great except for pig ears.
Taïm	222 Waverly Pl	212-691-1287	$$	11 pm	Gourmet falafel with mind-blowing housemade sauces.
Tea & Sympathy	108 Greenwich Ave	212-807-8329	$$$	10:30 pm	Eccentric English. Cult favorite.
Wallse	344 W 11th St	212-352-2300	$$$$	10:30 pm	Top-notch Austrian cuisine keeps the West Villagers coming back.
The Waverly Inn	16 Bank St	212-243-7900	$$$	11:45 pm	Hip, reknowned, Graydon Carter-owned café-cum-speakeasy. Good luck getting in.
Yama	38 Carmine St	212-989-9330	$$$	11:30 pm	Sushi deluxe.

Map 6 · Washington Square / NYU / NoHo / SoHo

12 Chairs	56 MacDougal St	212-254-8640	$	11 pm	Rough around the edges. Fantabulous blintzes and pirogis.
9th St Market	337 E 9th St	212-473-0242	$$	11 pm	Worth the wait for an intimate weekend brunch.
Arturo's	106 W Houston St	212-677-3820	$$	2 am	Classic NYC pizza joint. NFT pick.
Babbo	110 Waverly Pl	212-777-0303	$$$$	11:30 pm	Super Mario—eclectic Italian, fabulous wine list.
Balthazar	80 Spring St	212-965-1414	$$$	2 am	Simultaneously pretentious and amazing.
Blue Hill	75 Washington Pl	212-539-1776	$$$$$	11 pm	Wonderful food in an unexpected location.
Blue Ribbon	97 Sullivan St	212-274-0404	$$$$$	4 am	Open 'til 4 am. Everything's great.
Café Colonial	276 Elizabeth St	212-274-0044	$$	12 am	Excellent American/Brazilian.
Café Habana	17 Prince St	212-625-2001	$$$	12 am	Grilled corn + beautiful staff = amazing Cuban joint.
Eight Mile Creek	240 Mulberry St	212-431-4635	$$$	11:30 pm	Awesome Australian.
Five Points	31 Great Jones St	212-253-5700	$$$	11:30 pm	Excellent NoHo destination. Cookshop's older sibling.
Frank	88 2nd Ave	212-420-0202	$$*	2 am	Good food, great breakfast.
Ghenet	284 Mulberry St	212-343-1888	$$	11 pm	Excellent, unpretentious Ethiopian.
Hampton Chutney	68 Prince St	212-226-9996	$	9 pm	Good take-out dosas.
Hummus Place	99 MacDougal St	212-533-3089	$††	12 am	Authentic! Best hummus this side of Tel Aviv.
Il Mulino	86 W 3rd St	212-673-3783	$$$$	11 pm	Italian dining at fine Italian dining prices.
Jeollado	116 E 4th St	212-260-7696	$$*	12:30 am	Cheap sushi with REAL crabmeat.
John's of 12th Street	302 E 12th St	212-475-9531	$$*	11:30 pm	Classic Italian. Get the rollatini.
Jules	65 St Marks Pl	212-477-5560	$$$†	1 am	Small French bistro with live unimposing jazz.
La Esquina	106 Kenmare St	646-613-7100	$	12 am	Taqueria trifecta: taco stand, corner cantina, and secret subterranean abode.
Lahore	132 Crosby St	212-965-1777	$*	24-hrs	Indo-Pak deli popular with cabbies.
Mara's Homemade	342 E 6th St	212-598-1110	$$	11:30 pm	Ragin' Cajun. Recommended.
Olive's	120 Prince St	212-941-0111	$	7 pm	Killer soups/sandwiches. A must, great for take-out, too.
Paul's Palace	131 2nd Ave	212-529-3097	$*	11 pm	Burger heaven.
Pepe Rosso	149 Sullivan St	212-677-4555	$*	11 pm	Italy on a budget. Fast.
Prune	54 E 1st St	212-677-6221	$$$	11 pm	Get there early for brunch if you don't want to wait. Like, 8 am.
Sammy's Roumanian	157 Chrystie St	212-673-0330	$$$$	11 pm	An experience not to be missed.
Strip House	13 E 12th St	212-328-0000	$$$$$	12 am	Super downtown steakhouse. NFT favorite.
Temple	81 St Marks Pl	212-979-9300	$$	12 am	Cheap Korean excellence, beware of crowds.
Ukranian East Village Restaurant	140 2nd Ave	212-614-3283	$††	11 pm	Pierogis, borscht, blintzes, goulash. Comfort food.
Una Pizzeria Napoletana	349 E 12th St	212-477-9950	$$*	11 pm	100% authentic. Worth the expense.
Veselka	144 2nd Ave	212-228-9682	$	24-hrs	Pierogies absorb beer. At 4 am that's all you need to know.

Key: $: Under $10 / $$: $10–$20 / $$$: $20–$30 / $$$$: $30–$40 / $$$$$: $40+; *: Cash only / †: Accepts only American Express. / † † Accepts only Visa/Mastercard. Time refers to hour kitchen closes on weekends.

Map 7 · East Village / Lower East Side

7A	109 Avenue A	212-673-6583	$$	24-hrs	Open 24 hours. Great burgers.
Banjara	97 1st Ave	212-477-5956	$$$	12 am	Best Indian on 6th Street, hands-down.
Bereket Turkish Kebab House	187 E Houston St	212-475-7700	$*	24-hrs	Middle Eastern delights. Open late.
Big Arc Chicken	233 1st Ave	212-477-0091	$*	1 am	Cheap Middle Eastern food complete with Arabic TV.
Boca Chica	13 1st Ave	212-473-0108	$$	12 am	Excellent, fun South American.
Caracas Arepa Bar	91 E 7th St	212-228-5062	$$	10:45 pm	Authentic Venezuelan.
Clinton St Baking Company	4 Clinton St	646-602-6263	$$	11 am	Homemade buttermilk everything. LES laid back.
Dok Suni's	119 1st Ave	212-477-9506	$$$*	12 am	Excellent Korean fusion. NFT fav.
El Castillo de Jaqua	113 Rivington St	212-982-6412	$*	1 am	Great cheap Dominican.
El Sombrero	108 Stanton St	212-254-4188	$$*	3 am	Cheap margaritas. Dates back to earlier days of the LES.
Esashi	32 Avenue A	212-505-8726	$$	11:30 pm	Simple but always good neighborhood sushi.
Il Posto Accanto	190 E 2nd St	212-228-3562	$$$††	11:45 pm	Tiny, rustic Italian enoteca.
inoteca	98 Rivington St	212-614-0473	$$	3 am	Late-night tapas mafia-style.
Katz's Deli	205 E Houston St	212-254-2246	$$	2:30 am	If have what she's having!
Kuma Inn	113 Ludlow St	212-353-8866	$$*	12 am	Spicy southeast Asian tapas.
Kura Sushi	67 1st Ave	212-979-6646	$$	12:30 am	Good sushi, good atmosphere, good music.
Le Pere Pinard	175 Ludlow St	212-777-4917	$$$$†	2 am	Cool, hip, swank French bistro with lovely back patio.
Luzzo's	211 1st Ave	212-473-7447	$$	11 pm	Real coal oven. Top ten worthy.
Mama's Food Shop	200 E 3rd St	212-777-4425	$*	10 pm	Great home-cooking and take-out. NFT Pick.
Momofuku Noodle Bar	163 1st Ave	212-475-7899	$$$	12 am	Queue up for chic noodles.
Nicky's Vietnamese Sandwiches	150 E 2nd St	212-388-1088	$*	9 pm	Dirt-cheap Vietnamese treats.
Odessa	119 Avenue A	212-253-1470	$$	24-hrs	Diner. Awesome pirogies.
Old Devil Moon	511 E 12th St	212-475-4357	$$	12 am	Good southern food. Great biscuits.
Pylos	128 E 7th St	212-473-0220	$$	1 am	Delicious Greek, cool hanging-pot ceiling.
Royale	157 Ave C	212-254-6600	$$	4 am	Perfect burgers with stellar fixin's, and a deal to boot.
Schiller's Liquor Bar	131 Rivington St	212-260-4555	$$$$	3 am	Loud, good, loud, good.
Shopsin's	120 Essex St	None	$$$	3 pm	Kenny's back! Get your Blisters on My Sisters in the Essex St Market.
Sidewalk	94 Avenue A	212-473-7373	$$	24-hrs	When 7A's wait is too long…
Sigiri	91 1st Ave	212-614–9333	$$		Excellent BYBO Sri Lankan above a great beer store.
St Dymphna's	118 St Marks Pl	212-254-6636	$	12 am	A great Irish pub doesn't need shamrocks.
Takahachi	85 Avenue A	212-505-6524	$$$	12:30 am	Super-good Japanese and sushi.
Tasting Room	72 E 1st St	212-358-7831	$$$$$	11 pm	Relatively pretentious.
Teany	90 Rivington St	212-475-9190	$$*	1 am	Vegan tea room and Moby hang-out.
Yonah Schimmel's Knishery	137 E Houston St	212-477-2858	$	10 pm	Dishing delish knish since 1910.

Map 8 · Chelsea

202 Café	75 9th Ave	646-638-1173	$$	10:30 pm	Simple European eats (and fancy dishware boutique).
Better Burger Chelsea	178 8th Ave	212-989-6688	$	1 am	Ostrich burger? Check. Soy burger? Check. Antibiotic-free meat? Check.
Blue Moon Mexican Café	150 8th Ave	212-463-0560	$$$	12:30 pm	Great Mexican.
Buddakan	75 9th Ave	212-989-6699	$$$$$	12 am	NYC branch of Stephen Starr's insanely popular Philadelphia behemoth.
Burritoville	352 W 39th St	212-563-9088	$	10 pm	Takeout Mexican.
Casa Cupcake	545 9th Ave	212-465-1530	$	7 pm	Three words: sweet potato doughnuts.
Cola's Italian	148 8th Ave	212-633-8020	$$	11:30 pm	Intimate and inexpensive.
Cookshop	156 10th Ave	212-924-4440	$$	12 am	New, loft-like, local ingredient-focused eatery.
El Quinto Pino	401 W 24th St	212-206-6900	$$	12 am	Tiny, table-free tapas joint from owners of Tia Pol.
Empire Diner	210 10th Ave	212-243-2736	$$	24-hrs	A Chelsea institution. 24 hours.
Frank's Restaurant	410 W 16th St	212-243-1349	$$$$	11 pm	Noisy beef-fest.
Grand Sichuan Int'l	229 9th Ave	212-620-5200	$$	11:30 pm	Some of the best Chinese in NYC. Recommended.
Havana Chelsea	190 8th Ave	212-243-9421	$$*	10:30 pm	Great Cuban sandwiches.
La Luncheonette-Jean Francios	130 10th Ave	212-675-0342	$$$$	11:30 pm	A truly great French restaurant. Recommended.
La Taza de Oro	96 8th Ave	212-243-9946	$$*	10:30 pm	Great local Puerto Rican.
Manganaro Foods	488 9th Ave	212-563-5331	$$	7 pm	Locals-only Italian sandwich joint. Recommended.
Matsuri	369 W 16th St	212-243-6400	$$$$$	1 am	Gigantic, luxurious Japanese restaurant tucked beneath The Maritime Hotel.
Moonstruck Diner	400 W 23rd St	212-924-3709	$$	24-hrs	Not cheap as far as diners go, but generous portions.

Morimoto	88 10th Ave	212-989-8883	$$$$$	12 am	Stephen Starr's couture Japanese temple. Iron Chef-prepared cuisine.
Pepe Giallo	253 10th Ave	212-242-6055	$$	11 pm	Takeout Italian.
Pomodoro	518 9th Ave	212-239-7019	$$	10:30 pm	Takes "fast food" Italian to the next level; superb foccacia.
The Red Cat	227 10th Ave	212-242-1122	$$$$	12 am	Hip and expensive.
Sandwich Planet	534 9th Ave	212-273-9768	$	8 pm	Unlimited sandwich selection.
Skylight Diner	402 W 34th St	212-244-0395	$$	24-hrs	24-hour diner.
Soul Fixin's	371 W 34th St	212-736-1345	$$	10 pm	It would be an injustice not to include this soul food eatery.
Swich	104 8th Ave	212-488-4800	$	11 pm	You'll be "pressed" to find a cooler sandwich on the go.
Tia Pol	205 10th Ave	212-675-8805	$$	10:45 pm	Very good, very popular (crowded) tapas joint.
Tick Tock Diner	481 8th Ave	212-268-8444	$	24-hrs	24-hour diner.
Tour	102 8th Ave	212-242-7773	$$$	6 am	Embark upon a global culinary adventure—and grab a blackberry mojito along the way.
Viceroy	160 8th Ave	212-633-8484	$$$	1 am	Stargazin' American.

Map 9 • Flatiron / Lower Midtown

Ben's NY Kosher	209 W 38th St	212-398-2367	$$	8:45 pm	Deli standards, Middle Eastern and Kosher Chinese.
BLT Fish	21 W 17th St	212-691-8888	$$$$$	11:30 pm	Downstairs: New England clam shack fare. Upstairs: High-brow seafood.
Butterfield 8	5 E 38th St	212-679-0646	$$	10 pm	Walnut-paneled Murray Hill American with cool, Hitchcockian cityscape mural.
Chat 'n Chew	10 E 16th St	212-243-1616	$$	12 am	Home cookin'.
City Bakery	3 W 18th St	212-366-1414	$$	7 pm	Stellar baked goods.
Coffee Shop	29 Union Square W	212-243-7969	$$	5:30 am	Diner with a samba skew.
Craft	43 E 19th St	212-780-0880	$$$$$	11 pm	Outstanding. A top-end place worth the $.
Eisenberg's Sandwich Shop	174 5th Ave	212-675-5096	$$	11 pm	Old-school corned beef and pastrami.
Eleven Madison Park	11 Madison Ave	212-889-0905	$$$$$	11 pm	Where the elite meet to greet.
Evergreen Shanghai Restaurant	10 E 38th St	212-448-1199	$	10:30 pm	Their scallion pancakes are worth the wait, and they know it.
Gramercy Tavern	42 E 20th St	212-477-0777	$$$$$	11 pm	Expensive, but good, New American.
Hangawi	12 E 32nd St	212-213-0077	$$$$	10:30 pm	Serene Korean.
Kang Suh	1250 Broadway	212-564-6845	$$$	24-hrs	Late-night Korean. Go for the private rooms.
Koryodang	31 W 32nd St	212-967-9661	$	2 am	Bakery with mocha-filled eclairs and green tea popsicles. Yum.
Kunjip	9 W 32nd St	212-216-9487	$$	24-hrs	The best Korean food in Manhattan; try the Bo Ssam!
Le Zie 2000	172 7th Ave	212-206-8686	$$$	11:30 pm	Venetian. That means it's Italian.
Mendy's Kosher Deli	61 E 34th St	212-576-1010	$$*	8 pm	Pastrami, matzoh ball soup and knishes.
Olympic Pita	58 W 38th St	212-869-7482	$	11 pm	Boro Park favorite brings its scrumptious shawarma to Manhattan.
Republic	37 Union Square W	212-627-7172	$$	11:30 pm	Noisy noodles.
RUB BBQ	208 W 23rd St	212-524-4300	$$$	11 pm	Smokin'cue from Kansas City pit master Paul Kirk.
Salute!	270 Madison Ave	212-213-3440	$$	11 pm	Generous portions of old-world Italian cuisine.
Seoul Garden	34 W 32nd St	212-736-9002	$$	2 am	The soon tofu soup hits the spot.
Shake Shack	Madison Sq Park	212-889-6600	$	9 pm	Enjoy homemade shakes'n burgers in the park.
Tabla	11 Madison Ave	212-889-0667	$$$$$	10:30 pm	Inventive Indian-inspired American. Recommended.
Tamarind	41 E 22nd St	212-674-7400	$$$	12 am	Lovely, intimate upscale Indian.
Tocqueville	1 E 15th St	212-647-1515	$$$$$	10:30 pm	Lovely everything—and you can actually hear each other speak!
Toledo	6 E 36th St	212-696-5036	$$$	10:30 pm	Classy Spanish.
Union Square Café	21 E 16th St	212-243-4020	$$$$$	10:45 pm	Someday we'll get in and like it.
Woo Chon	8 W 36th St	212-695-0676	$$$	2 am	All-night Korean.

Map 10 • Murray Hill / Gramercy

Angelo & Maxie's	233 Park Ave S	212-220-9200	$$$	12 am	Excellent steaks, burgers, etc.
Artisanal	2 Park Ave	212-725-8585	$$$	12 am	Eat the fondue and love.
Bar Jamon	52 Irving Pl	212-253-2773	$	2 am	Pig out at this wine bar.
BLT Prime	111 E 22nd St	212-995-8500	$$$$$	11:30 pm	Steakhouse with Craft-like, a-la-carte sides.
Blue Smoke	116 E 27th St	212-447-7733	$$$$	1 am	Finger lickin' BBQ, Danny Meyer style (with downstairs jazz club).
Burger Joint	241 3rd Ave	212-228-1219	$*	2 am	$1.25 burgers and real chocolate soda? We're there!
Butai	115 E 18th St	212-387-8885	$$	12 am	Impressive Japanese cuisine.
Carl's Steaks	507 3rd Ave	212-696-5338	$	12 pm	Cheesesteaks, chickensteaks, and chili fries.
Chennai Garden	129 E 27th St	212-689-1999	$$	10 pm	Indian food that happens to be vegetarian, kosher, and very tasty.

Arts & Entertainment • **Restaurants**

Key: $: Under $10 / $$: $10–$20 / $$$: $20–$30 / $$$$: $30–$40 / $$$$$: $40+; *: Cash only / †: Accepts only American Express. / † † Accepts only Visa/Mastercard. Time refers to hour kitchen closes on weekends.

Map 10 • Murray Hill / Gramercy—continued

Chinese Mirch	120 Lexington Ave	212-532-3663	$$$	11 pm	Fiery Chinese food by way of Mumbai.
Curry Leaf	99 Lexington Ave	212-725-5558	$$$	11 pm	Best basic Indian.
El Parador Café	325 E 34th St	212-679-6812	$$$	11 pm	NY's oldest and friendliest Mexican.
Friend of a Farmer	77 Irving Pl	212-477-2188	$$$	11 pm	Chic country-cooking.
Gemini Diner	641 2nd Ave	212-532-2143	$	24-hrs	Open 24 hours. Diner.
Gramercy Restaurant	184 3rd Ave	212-982-2121	$	24-hrs	Open 24 hours. Diner.
Haandi	113 Lexington Ave	212-685-5200	$$	12 am	Stellar Pakistani grilled meats.
I Trulli	122 E 27th St	212-481-7372	$$$$$	10:30 pm	Italian. Great garden.
Jess Bakery	221 E 23rd St	212-725-4788	$	9 pm	Roast duck. Ramen Noodles. Bubbles tea. Pastries.
L'aanam	393 3rd Ave	212-686-5168	$$	11 pm	Cheap and quick Vietnamese, good—but not for serious enthusiasts.
L'Express	249 Park Ave S	212-254-5858	$$	24-hrs	Always open French diner.
La Posada	364 3rd Ave	212-213-4379	$	11 pm	Authentic Mexican burritos, tacos and enchiladas.
Latin Corner	507 3rd Ave	212-213-8364	$$	9:30 pm	Hearty Spanish cuisine. Breakfast and burgers.
Les Halles	411 Park Ave S	212-679-4111	$$$	12 am	Steak fries and French vibe.
Mark Café	125 E 23rd St	212-533-6947	$*	6 pm	Omelettes, pancakes, soups, burgers and salads.
Mee's Noodle Shop & Grill	547 2nd Ave	212-779-1596	$	11 pm	Noodles, General Tso's and sushi for cheap.
Mexico Lindo	459 2nd Ave	212-679-3665	$$$	12 am	Famous Mexican food.
Novit^ag	102 E 22nd St	212-677-2222	$$$$	11 pm	Sophisticated Italian without the pretension.
Paquitos	160 E 28th St	212-685-9815	$	11 pm	Cheap burritos, better than most.
Penelope	159 Lexington Ave	212-481-3800	$$*	11 pm	Gingham décor but oh, what a menu!
Pongal	110 Lexington Ave	212-696-9458	$$	10 pm	Possibly NY's best Indian. Vegetarian.
Pongsri Thai	311 2nd Ave	212-477-2727	$$	10:45 pm	Great, spicy Thai.
Posto	310 2nd Ave	212-716-1200	$$	12 am	Savory thin-crust pizza, salads.
Rare Bar & Grill	303 Lexington Ave	212-481-1999	$$$	12 am	Top-rated NYC burger.
Resto	111 E 29th St	212-685-5585	$$	11:30 pm	Belgian gastropub that's pretty darn great.
Rice	115 Lexington Ave	212-686-5400	$$*	11 pm	Trendy and creative Indian goodies.
Sarge's Deli	548 3rd Ave	212-679-0442	$$	24-hrs	Open 24 hours. Jewish deli.
Second Avenue Deli	162 E 33rd St	212-667-0606	$$	2 am	Reborn in a new location. Miracles do happen.
Tiffin Wallah	127 E 28th St	212-685-7301	$	3 pm	Veggie lunch buffet for a few bucks.
Totonno's Pizzeria Napolitano	462 2nd Ave	212-213-8800	$$	1 am	Manhattan wing of classic Coney Island Pizza.
Turkish Kitchen	386 3rd Ave	212-679-6633	$$$	11:30 pm	Excellent Turkish, great décor. NFT pick!
Water Club	East River at 30th St	212-683-3333	$$$$	11 pm	Romantic, good brunch on the East River.
Zen Palate	34 Union Square E	212-614-9291	$$$	11:30 pm	Dependable vegetarian.

Map 11 • Hell's Kitchen

99 Cent Pizza	569 9th Ave	212-268-1461	$*	24-hrs	Yeah it's cheap, but watch out for the crazies.
Afghan Kebab House	764 9th Ave	212-307-1612	$$	11 pm	Great kebabs.
Arriba Arriba Mexican Restaurant	762 9th Ave	212-489-0810	$$	12 am	Sangria and large Mexican lunch for $7 bucks.
Breeze	661 9th Ave	212-262-7777	$$	11:30 pm	Always great Thai/French fusion.
Burrito Box	885 9th Ave	212-489-6889	$	11:30 pm	Cheap and tasty Mexican with killer guac.
Casellula	401 W 52nd St	212-247-8137	$$$	2 am	Sophisticated wine and cheese pairings.
Chili Thai	712 9th Ave	212-265-5054		10:30pm	Tiny, friendly, and delicious.
Churruscaria Plataforma	316 W 49th St	212-245-0505	$$$$	12 am	Brazilian Feast! Don't eat all day...then come here.
Daisy May's BBQ USA	623 11th Ave	212-977-1500	$$	10 pm	Takeout BBQ and sides Mon-Fri. Plus, various Manhattan street carts!
Don Giovanni	358 W 44th St	212-581-4939	$$	2 am	One of the better cheap pies in the city.
Eatery	798 9th Ave	212-765-7080	$$	1 am	A Hell's Kitchen comfort food favorite. All delish.
Empanada Mama	763 9th Ave	212-698-9008	$	12 am	No one fries them better.
etcetera etcetera	352 W 44 St	215-399-4141	$$$$	12 am	Beautiful bar, delicious Italian food.
Gazala Place	709 9th Ave	212-245-0709	$$	10:30 pm	Brilliant Middle Eastern that also serves an appetizer platter.
Grand Sichuan Int'l	745 9th Ave	212-582-2288	$$	11 pm	Excellent weird Szechuan. Recommended.
Hallo Berlin	626 10th Ave	212-977-1944	$$	11 pm	The best wurst in the city! Check out their street cart at 54th & Fifth.
Hell's Kitchen	679 9th Ave	212-977-1588	$$$	11 pm	Haute cuisine, Mexican style. Packed.
Hudson Cafeteria	356 W 58th St	212-554-6000	$$$$$	12:30 pm	Lovely and pricey and goody.
Island Burgers 'N Shakes	766 9th Ave	212-307-7934	$$*	11 pm	Aptly named.
Joe Allen	326 W 46th St	212-581-6464	$$$	12 am	De rigueur stargazing, open late.
Little Pie Company	424 W 43rd St	212-736-4780	$	8 pm	Although dessert is the main course, you can also munch on a quiche or pot pie.
Marseille	630 9th Ave	212-333-3410	$$$$	12 am	True to the name, an expatriate's delight.
Meskerem	468 W 47th St	212-664-0520	$$	11:30 pm	Friendly and consistently good Ethiopian.

Arts & Entertainment • **Restaurants**

Morningstar	401 W 57th St	212-246-1593	$	24-hrs	French toast with ice-cream at midnight, terrible coffee.
Nizza	630 9th Ave	212-956-1800	$$	2 am	Share some fantastic antipasti: socca, tapenade, focaccette, and more.
The Nook	746 9th Ave	212-247-5500	$$$*	12 am	Delicious New American (with after-hours parties).
Old San Juan	765 9th Ave	212-262-6761	$$	11 pm	Good, Puerto Rican-Argentinean fare.
Piece of Chicken	630 9th Ave	212-582-5973	$*	10 pm	Perfect $1 chicken for addicts craving a fix.
Puttanesca	859 9th Ave	212-581-4177	$$$	1 am	Serious Italian with light-hearted prices.
Ralph's	862 9th Ave	212-581-2283	$$	11 pm	Classic Italian cuisine.
Say Cheese	649 9th Ave		$	11 pm	Incredible tomato soup compliments peach smoothies.
Shorty's	576 9th Ave	212-967-3055	$	11 pm	Philly cheese steak without the snobbery. Extra Cheez Whiz, please.
Taboon	773 10th Ave	212-713-0271	$$	11 pm	Great bang for your buck. Middle Eastern/Mediterranean.
Tout Va Bien	311 W 51st St	212-265-0190	$$$	11:30 pm	Warm, homey, pre-theater, French. NFT Pick.
Turkish Cuisine	631 9th Ave	212-397-9650	$$	12 am	Turkish food, in case you were wondering.
Vice Versa	325 W 51st St	212-399-9291	$$$	11 pm	Creative yet accessible Italian cuisine with a cool, sleek vibe.
Zen Palate	663 9th Ave	212-582-1669	$$$	10:30 pm	Dependable vegetarian.

Map 12 • Midtown

21 Club	21 W 52nd St	212-582-7200	$$$$	10 pm	Old, clubby New York.
Aquavit	13 W 54th St	212-307-7311	$$$$$	10:30 pm	Stellar dining experience: top-drawer Scandinavian.
BG	754 5th Ave	212-872-8977	$$$$	7:30 pm	Another reason to spend the whole day at Bergdorf's.
Brasserie 8 1/2	9 W 57th St	212-829-0812	$$$$	11 pm	A must for brunch. Lovely for cocktails and dinner too.
Burger Joint	119 W 56th St	212-708-7414	$*	12 am	Fancy hotel lobby leads to unexpected burger dive.
Carnegie Deli	854 7th Ave	212-757-2245	$$$*	3:30 am	Still good.
Gallagher's Steak House	228 W 52nd St	212-245-5336	$$$$	12 am	Dine on fancy steak with grizzled old New Yorkers.
Haru	205 W 43rd St	212-398-9810	$$$	11 pm	Excellent mid-range Japanese. Loud, good.
Joe's Shanghai	24 W 56th St	212-333-3868	$$	10:30 pm	Uptown version of killer dumpling factory.
La Bonne Soupe	48 W 55th St	212-586-7650	$$	11 pm	Ooh la la, the best salad dressing accompanies my soupe a l'oignon.
Le Bernardin	155 W 51st St	212-554-1515	$$$$$	11 pm	Top NYC seafood.
Metro Marche	625 8th Ave	212-239-1010	$$	12 am	Decent French at Port Authority. Not a misprint.
The Modern	9 W 53rd St	212-333-1220	$$$	11 pm	With gnocchi to die for, spend a lot and then STILL splurge on dessert.
Molyvos	871 7th Ave	212-582-7500	$$$$	11 pm	Top Greek.
Mont Blanc	315 W 48th St	212-957-0800	$$$	12 am	Classic fondue spot. Remember—drink wine, not water!
Nation Restaurant & Bar	12 W 45th St	212-391-8053	$$$	9 pm	Loud, pretentious, good.
Per Se	10 Columbus Cir	212-823-9335	$$$$$	10 pm	Divine…but you practically have to sell a kidney to afford it!
Shelly's New York	41 W 57th St	212-245-2422	$$$$	12:45 pm	Come starved, leave stuffed.
Spanky's BBQ	127 W 43rd St	212-302-9507	$$	11:30 pm	The real BBQ deal, just don't try and compare it to actual Texas BBQ.
Virgil's Real BBQ	152 W 44th St	212-921-9494	$$$	12 am	It's real.
wichcraft, Bryant Park	Sixth Ave b/w 40th St & 42nd St	212-780-0577	$$	6 pm	4 Kiosks: Sandwiches, soups, and sweets from the Craft Empire.

Map 13 • East Midtown

BLT Steak	106 E 57th St	212-752-7470	$$$$$	11:30 pm	Pricey and good, not great.
Caffé Buon Gusto	1009 2nd Ave	212-755-1476	$$	11 pm	The bread is addictive. Sop it in sauce.
Chola	232 E 58th St	212-688-4619	$$$$	11 pm	Pricey south Indian cuisine.
Cosi Sandwich Bar	60 E 56th St	212-588-1225	$	6 pm	Sandwiches for the masses.
Dawat	210 E 58th St	212-355-7555	$$$	11:15 pm	Top-end Indian.
Docks Oyster Bar	633 3rd Ave	212-986-8080	$$$	12 am	Great seafood, good atmosphere.
F&B	150 E 52nd St	212-421-8600	$	10 pm	Belgian street food that makes our carts look nasty.
Felidia	243 E 58th St	212-758-1479	$$$$	11:30 pm	Top Northern Italian.
Four Seasons	99 E 52nd St	212-754-9494	$$$$$	9:30 pm	Designer everything. Even the cotton candy.
Menchanko-tei	131 E 45th St	212-986-6805	$$	12:30 am	Japanese noodle shop.
Nikki	151 E 50th St	212-753-1144	$$$	11 pm	Eclectic Miami vice with pillows.
Oceana	55 E 54th St	212-759-5941	$$$$$	10:30 pm	Le Bernardin Jr.
Opia	130 E 57th St	212-688-3939	$$$	11 pm	Midtown spot for moules frites and steak au poivre.
Organic Harvest Café	235 E 53rd St	212 421 6444	$$	8 pm	Vegetarian.
Oyster Bar	Grand Central, Lower Level	212-490-6650	$$$	9:30 pm	Classic New York seafood joint.

389

Arts & Entertainment • **Restaurants**

Key: $: Under $10 / $$: $10–$20 / $$$: $20–$30 / $$$$: $30 –$40 / $$$$$: $40+; *: Cash only / † : Accepts only American Express. / † † Accepts only Visa/Mastercard. Time refers to hour kitchen closes on weekends.

Map 13 • East Midtown—continued

Palm	837 2nd Ave	212-687-2953	$$$$$	11 pm	Steak.
Pershing Square	90 E 42nd St	212-286-9600	$$$$	10:30 pm	Excellent food and awesome space.
PJ Clarke's	915 3rd Ave	212-317-1616	$$$	3 am	Pub grub.
Rosa Mexicano	1063 1st Ave	212-753-7407	$$$	11:30 pm	Inventive Mexican. Great guac.
Shun Lee Palace	155 E 55th St	212-371-8844	$$$$$	11:30 pm	Top-end Chinese.
Sidecar	205 E 55th St	212-317-2044	$$$	11 pm	PJ. Clarke's quieter, more refined restaurant sibling.
Smith & Wollensky	797 3rd Ave	212-753-1530	$$$$$	11 pm	Don't order the fish.
Sparks Steak House	210 E 46th St	212-687-4855	$$$$$	11:30 pm	If you can't go to Luger's.
Taksim	1030 2nd Ave	212-421-3004	$$$	11 pm	All manner of Turkish delights.
Vong	200 E 54th St	212-486-9592	$$$$$	11 pm	$38 pre-theater menu. Top Pan-Asian.
Wollensky's Grill	205 E 49th St	212-753-0444	$$$	2 am	For those who want the same food as S&W with less wait time.
Yuva	230 E 58th St	212-339-0090	$$$$	12 am	Inventive new addition to upscale Indian row.

Map 14 • Upper West Side (Lower)

'cesca	164 W 75th St	212-787-6300	$$$$	11:30 pm	Sunday Sauce worthy of a cameo in *Goodfellas*.
Artie's Deli	2290 Broadway	212-579-5959	$$	10:45 pm	Hot pastrami on rye
Asiate	80 Columbus Cir	212-805-8881	$$$$$	10 pm	Highest-end Japanese/French.
Big Nick's	2175 Broadway	212-362-9238	$$	24-hrs	Death by burger. Recommended.
Café Lalo	201 W 83rd St	212-496-6031	$$	4 am	Packed dessert and coffee destination.
Café Luxembourg	200 W 70th St	212-873-7411	$$$$	12 am	Top-end bistro.
Café Rhonda	249 Columbus Ave	212-579-9929	$$$	12 am	Pre- or post-Lincoln Center tapas.
Crumbs	321 Amsterdam Ave	212-712-9800	$	10 pm	MMM, cupcakes.
Epices du Traiteur	103 W 70th St	212-579-5904	$$$	12 am	Charming atmosphere, eclectic and flavorful food.
Fairway Café	2127 Broadway	212-595-1888	$$$	10 pm	When it's all too much.
The Firehouse	522 Columbus Ave	212-595-3139	$$	1 am	Where to go for after-softball wings.
French Roast	2340 Broadway	212-799-1533	$$	24-hrs	Open 24 hours. Good Croque Monsieur.
Gabriel's	11 W 60th St	212-956-4600	$$$	12 am	Local-draw; good all-around.
Gari	370 Columbus Ave	212-362-4816	$$$$	11:30 pm	Why UWS sushi snobs no longer have to take the cross-town bus.
Garlic Bob's	508 Columbus Ave	212-769-2627	$$	10 pm	Fab brick oven pizza and Italian entrees in dumpy setting
Good Enough to Eat	483 Amsterdam Ave	212-496-0163	$$$	11 pm	Good brunch but Sunday line starts early
Gray's Papaya	2090 Broadway	212-799-0243	$*	24-hrs	Open 24 hours. An institution.
Jacques-Imo's NYC	366 Columbus Ave	212-799-0150	$$$	11 pm	After a few hurricanes, your date may be the true Big Easy.
Jean-Luc	507 Columbus Ave	212-712-1700	$$$$$	12 am	Classy, expensive bistro.
Josie's	300 Amsterdam Ave	212-769-1212	$$$	12 am	Good vegetarian option.
Kefi	505 Columbus Ave	212-873-0200	$$$*	12 am	Greek food gets an upgrade at this amazingly affordable gem.
Kinoko	165 W 72nd St	212-580-5900	$$$	11:30 pm	All-you-can-eat sushi for $19.95.
La Caridad 78	2199 Broadway	212-874-2780	$$*	12 am	Cheap Cuban paradise.
Le Pain Quotidien	50 W 72nd St	212-712-9700	$$	7:30 pm	Great breads. Communal Table. Euro vibe.
Manhattan Diner	2180 Broadway	212-877-7252	$$	24-hrs	Diner. In Manhattan.
Nougatine	1 Central Park West	212-299-3900	$$$$$	11 pm	$24.07 prix fixe lunch!
Ouest	2315 Broadway	212-580-8700	$$$$	10 pm	Trendy upscale
Picholine	35 W 64th St	212-724-8585	$$$$	12 am	Go for the cheese.
Rain	100 W 82nd St	212-501-0776	$$$	12 am	Asian fusion with a magnificent bar.
Rosa Mexicano	61 Columbus Ave	212-977-7700	$$$$	11:30 pm	Inventive Mexican. Great guac.
Ruby Foo's Dim Sum & Sushi Palace	2182 Broadway	212-724-6700	$$$	12:30 am	Your parents will love it.
Santa Fe	73 W 71st St	212-724-0822	$$$	12 am	Calm Southwest.
Sarabeth's	423 Amsterdam Ave	212-496-6280	$$$	11 pm	Go for brunch.
Vince and Eddie's	70 W 68th St	212-721-0068	$$$	11 pm	Cozy comfort food.
Whole Foods Café	10 Columbus Cir	212-823-9600	$	10 pm	Very good and by far the cheapest eats in Time Warner Center.

Map 15 • Upper East Side (Lower)

Burger Heaven	804 Lexington Ave	212-838-3580	$	9:30 pm	'Nuff said.
Burke Bar Café	150 E 59th St	212-705-3800	$$$$	9 pm	Chef David Burke's elegant, inside-Bloomingdale's café with cheeky menu.
Burke in the Box at Bloomingdale's	150 E 59th St	212-705-3800	$	9 pm	Chef David Burke's affordable take-out eatery inside Bloomies.
Café Boulud	20 E 76th St	212-772-2600	$$$$$	11 pm	Elegant, slightly more relaxed sibling of Daniel.
Café Mingala	1393 2nd Ave	212-744-8008	$	12 am	Burmese. $5.50 lunch special!
Candle 79	154 E 79th St	212-537-7179	$$$$	10:30 pm	Upscale vegetarian cuisine in luxurious surroundings.

Arts & Entertainment · **Restaurants**

Name	Address	Phone	$	Hours	Notes
Candle Café	1307 3rd Ave	212-472-0970	$$$	10:30 pm	Delicious vegetarian café next door to Le Steak.
Donguri	309 E 83rd St	212-737-5656	$$$$$	9:45 pm	Transcendent, UES Japanese standout.
EAT	1064 Madison Ave	212-772-0022	$$$	10 pm	Great brunch spot—part of the Eli Zabar empire.
Elio's	1621 2nd Ave	212-772-2242	$$$$$	12 am	UES Italian where schmoozing with the "who's-who" goes down.
Etats-Unis	242 E 81st St	212-517-8826	$$$$$	11 pm	A jewel on the UES food map—exceptional New American.
Ethiopian Restaurant	1582 York Ave	212-717-7311	$$$	11 pm	Adequate version of a sea of mediocre Italian.
Heidelberg	1648 2nd Ave	212-628-2332	$$$$	11:30 pm	Dirndls and lederhosen serving colossal beers and sausage platters.
Indian Tandoor Oven Restaurant	175 E 83rd St	212-628-3000	$$	12 am	Delectable Indian specialties in cozy, color-draped surroundings.
Jacque's Brasserie	204 E 85th St	212-327-2272	$$$$	12 am	UES spot for tasty moules frites and Stella on tap.
JG Melon	1291 3rd Ave	212-744-0585	$$*	2:15 am	Excellent burgers. Always crowded. Open 'till 2:30 a.m.
JoJo	160 E 64th St	212-223-5656	$$$$$	11 pm	Charming French bistro.
Lexington Candy Shop/ Luncheonette	Lexington Ave	212-288-0057	$	7 pm	Charming old-time soda shop with twirly stools.
Malaga	406 E 73rd St	212-737-7659	$$$	11 pm	Sleeper Spanish joint dishing up terrific tapas and swell sangria.
Neue Galerie	1048 5th Ave	212-288-0665	$$$	9 pm	Beautiful wood-paneled surroundings for sipping Viennese coffee.
Park Avenue Café	100 E 63rd St	212-644-1900	$$$$$	11 pm	Wonderful expensive American.
Payard Patisserie & Bistro	1032 Lexington Ave	212-717-5252	$$$$	11 pm	For tea and tarts (or tarts in Ts).
Pintaile's Pizza	1577 York Ave	212-396-3479	$	9:30 pm	Tasty thin-crust stuff.
Poke	343 E 85th St	212-249-0569	$$*		BYOB sushi.

Map 16 · Upper West Side (Upper)

Name	Address	Phone	$	Hours	Notes
A	947 Columbus Ave	917-992-9662	$$$*	11 pm	French-Caribbean café. BYOB on your first date!
AIX Brasserie	2398 Broadway	212-874-7400	$$$$	11 pm	Upscale uptown French.
Alouette	2588 Broadway	212-222-6808	$$$	10:45pm	Contemporary upscale French bistro
Asiakan	710 Amsterdam Ave	212-280-8878	$$$	10:45pm	Super sushi & so hip!
Awash	947 Amsterdam Ave	212-961-1416	$$	12 am	Tasty Ethiopian.
Barney Greengrass	541 Amsterdam Ave	212-724-4707	$$$*	5 pm	Classic deli.
Bella Luna	584 Columbus Ave	212-877-2267	$$$	11 pm	Italian.
Café Con Leche	726 Amsterdam Ave	212-678-7000	$$	12 am	Cuban-Dominican haven.
Café du Soleil	2723 Broadway	212-316-5000	$$$$	11 pm	French bistro that draws locals. Nice bar.
Carmine's	2450 Broadway	212-362-2200	$$$	12 am	Large-portion Italian.
City Diner	2441 Broadway	212-877-2720	$$	24-hrs	Neighborhood joint.
Crepes on Columbus	990 Columbus Ave	212-222-0259	$$	10 pm	Savory & sweet crepes in abundance
Docks Oyster Bar	2427 Broadway	212-724-5588	$$$	12 am	Consistently good seafood.
El Malecon	764 Amsterdam Ave	212-864-5648	$	12 am	Roast chicken and a con leche
Flor de Mayo	2651 Broadway	212-663-5520	$$	12 am	Cuban-Chinese-Chicken-Chow.
Gabriela's	688 Columbus Ave	212-961-0574	$$	12 am	Cheery Mexican.
Gennaro	665 Amsterdam Ave	212-665-5348	$$$*	11 pm	Crowded Italian.
Georgia's Bake Shop	2418 Broadway	212-362-2000	$	8 pm	Great pastry, awful service but you can linger
Giovanni's	1011 Columbus Ave	212-663-7000	$$*	3 pm	Pretty good slice.
Henry's	2745 Broadway	212-866-0600	$$$	12 am	Friendly uptown joint.
Indus Valley	2636 Broadway	212 222-9222	$$$	10:45 pm	Locals rave about the food but its costs
Jerusalem Restaurant	2715 Broadway	212-865-2295	$*	12 am	Good Middle Eastern, friendly service, open late.
Krik Krak	844 Amsterdam Ave	212-222-3100	$$	11 pm	Cozy Haitian for great island meal
Lemongrass Grill	2534 Broadway	212-666-0888	$$	11:30 pm	Serviceable Thai.
Lime Leaf	2799 Broadway	212-864-5000	$$$	10:45pm	Yummy pad thai
Malaysia Grill	224 W 104th St	212-579-1333	$$	11 pm	Inexpensive Malaysian pleasure
Mary Ann's	2452 Broadway	212-877-0132	$$	11:30 pm	Good Mex, order margaritas.
Metisse	239 W 105th St	212-666-8825	$$$$	11 pm	French for blue rinse set and visiting in-laws
Metro Diner	2641 Broadway	212-866-0800	$$	1 am	Get in line for weekend brunch.
Miss Mamie's Spoonbread Too	366 W 110th St	212-865-6744	$$	10:30 pm	Soul food spectacular.
Pizzabolla	654 Amsterdam Ave	212-579-4500	$$	11 pm	Good all-rounder
Popover Cafe	551 Amsterdam Ave	212-595-8555	$$	10 pm	Kind of fun. Whatever.
Rack'n Soul	2818 Broadway	212-222-4800	$$	11 pm	Decent ribs
Restaurant Broadway	2664 Broadway	212-865-7074	$*	12 am	Great breakfast and sandwiches, good place to start the day.
Roti Roll Bombay Frankie	994 Amsterdam Ave	212-666-1500	$*	3 am	Hole in the wall rotis to soak up alcohol
Royal Kabob & Curry	2701 Broadway	212-665-4700	$$$	11 pm	Flock willingly, sitar music, and great Indian grub
Saigon Grill	620 Amsterdam Ave	212-875-9072	$$	12 am	Busy Vietnamese. Great food, dirt cheap.
Sal & Carmine's Pizza	2671 Broadway	212- 663-7651	$*	11 pm	Award-winning gem, easy to miss.
Talia's Steakhouse	668 Amsterdam Ave	212-580-3770	$$$$	2:30 am	Your basic kosher steakhouse.
Taqueria Y Fonda La Mexicana	968 Amsterdam Ave		$$		Amazing Mexican dive but eat in
Thai Market	960 Amsterdam Ave	212-200-4575	$$	11 pm	A favorite among locals.
Tokyo Pop	2728 Broadway	212-932-1000	$$$	12 am	Food is good but you'll be poorer and starving
Trattoria Pesce & Pasta	625 Columbus Ave	212-579-7970	$$$	11 pm	Italian.
Turkuaz	2637 Broadway	212-665-9541	$$	12 am	Craving gelenseksel yemekler (tradit. dish)? It's all here.

(391)

Arts & Entertainment • **Restaurants**

Key: $: Under $10 / $$: $10–$20 / $$$: $20–$30 / $$$$: $30–$40 / $$$$$: $40+; *: Cash only / †: Accepts only American Express. / †† Accepts only Visa/Mastercard. Time refers to hour kitchen closes on weekends.

Map 17 • Upper East Side / East Harlem

Bella Cucina	1293 Lexington Ave	212-289-9004	$$$	10:45 pm	Non-Zagat rated Italian with great fish specials.
Café D'Alsace	1695 2nd Ave	212-722-5133	$$$	1 am	Chic Alsatian bistro with NYC's only known beer sommelier.
Carino	1710 2nd Ave	212-860-0566	$$$	11 pm	Mama Carino's divine, home-style Sicilian kitchen.
Chef Ho's Peking Duck Grill	1720 2nd Ave	212-348-9444	$$$	11 pm	Creative gourmet-ish Chinese cuisine. Try the Banana Chicken - delicious!
Choux Factory	1685 1st Ave	212-289-2023	$	10 pm	Kona coffee and filled-to-order Japanese cream puffs.
El Paso Taqueria	1642 Lexington Ave	212-831-9831	$$	12:45 am	Real Mexican.
Elaine's	1703 2nd Ave	212-534-8103	$$$$	2 am	Ignore the naysayers! Great food and fun center-of-it-all vibe.
GK Triple A Diner	2061 3rd Ave	212-410-6950	$*	9 pm	Standard diner food.
Ithaka	308 E 86th St	212-628-9100	$$$	11 pm	Fish grilled to perfection. Live music too.
Itzocan Bistro	1575 Lexington Ave	212-423-0255	$$*	12 am	Mexi-fusion.
Jackson Hole	1270 Madison Ave	212-427-2820	$$	11 pm	Extremely large burgers.
Joy Burger Bar	1567 Lexington Ave	212-289-6222	$	11 pm	Nice addition to the nabe.
Kebap G	1830 2nd Ave	212-860-5960	$	10 pm	Bright, hip joint for Turkish-style gyros, falafel, and hummus.
La Fonda Boricua	169 E 106th St	212-410-7292	$$	9 pm	Puerto Rican home-cookin'.
La Isla Restaurant	1883 3rd Ave	212-534-0002	$*	24-hrs	Puerto Rican diner.
Luca Restaurant	1712 1st Ave	212-987-9260	$$$$$	11 pm	Northern Italian standout with loyal neighborhood following.
Nick's Restaurant & Pizzeria	1814 2nd Ave	212-987-5700	$$	11:30 pm	Piping hot, thin-crust, brick oven pizza (and pasta).
Nina's Argentinean Pizzeria	1750 2nd Ave	212-426-4627	$$††	11 pm	Italian with an Argentinean accent.
Papaya King	179 E 86th St	212-369-0648	$*	1 am	Dishing out damn good dogs since 1932.
Peri Ela	1361 Lexington Ave	212-410-4300	$$*	11 pm	Classy Turkish restaurant.
Petak's	1246 Madison Ave	212-722-7711	$$*	7 pm	Perfectly located for stocking up before a gourmet Central Park picnic.
Piatto D'Oro I	349 E 109th St	212-828-2929	$$$	10 pm	East Harlem Italian.
Pinocchio	1748 1st Ave	212-828-5810	$$$$$	10:45 pm	Itty bitty sleeper Italian with rave reviews and loyal fans.
Pintaile's Pizza	26 E 91st St	212-722-1967	$$	9:30 pm	Tasty thin-crust stuff.
Pio Pio	1746 1st Ave	212-426-5800	$$	11 pm	The Matador chicken combo will feed the whole family.
Sabora Mexico	1744 1st Ave	212-289-2641	$$††	11 pm	Small, home-cooked, cheap and delicious.
Sarabeth's	1295 Madison Ave	212-410-7335	$$$	10 pm	Good breakfast, if you can get in.
Sfoglia	1402 Lexington Ave	212-831-1402	$$$	10 pm	Exquisite and experimental Italian by 92nd Street Y.
Viand	300 E 86th St	212-879-9425	$$	24-hrs	Open all night.
White Castle	351 E 103rd St		$	24-hrs	One of three in Manhattan
Zebu Grill	305 E 92nd St	212-426-7500	$$$$$	11:30 pm	Candlelit Brazilian bistro with exposed brick and earthy wooden tables.

Map 18 • Columbia / Morningside Heights

Amir's Falafel	2911 Broadway	212-749-7500	$	11 pm	Perfect for that sudden falafel & hummus craving
Bistro Ten 18	1018 Amsterdam Ave	212-662-7600	$$$	11 pm	Excellent uptown American bistro.
Café Swish	2955 Broadway	212-222-3568	$$	11:30 pm	Fun Asian. Cook your own Swish.
Deluxe Diner	2896 Broadway	212-662-7900	$$	12 am	Hip diner with good brunch and happy hour
Dinosaur Bar-B-Que	646 W 131st St	212-694-1777	$$	12 am	Not just for rybs. Head WAY uptown.
Havana Central	2911 Broadway	212-662-8830	$$$	11:30 pm	The old West End gone Cuban. Bring earplugs.
The Heights Bar & Grill	2867 Broadway	212-866-7035	$$	12 am	Hang out on the roof with Columbia students.
Hungarian Pastry Shop	1030 Amsterdam Ave	212-866-4230	$*	11:30 pm	Exactly what it is—and excellent.
Kitchenette	1272 Amsterdam Ave	212-531-7600	$$	11 pm	Good for everything.
Koronet Pizza	2848 Broadway	212-222-1566	$*	4 am	Just one slice. Really. That's all you'll need.
Le Monde	2885 Broadway	212-531-3939	$$	1:30 am	Brasserie.
M&G Soul Food Diner	383 W 125th St	212-864-7326	$$*	12 am	A soulful diner.
Massawa	1239 Amsterdam Ave	212-663-0505	$$	11:30 pm	Neighborhood joint.
Max SoHa	1274 Amsterdam Ave	212-531-2221	$$*	12 am	The Italian genius of Max, uptown.
Mill Korean	2895 Broadway	212-666-7653	$$	10:30 pm	Great neighborhood Korean.
Ollie's	2957 Broadway	212-932-3300	$$	2 am	Only if you must.
P + W Sandwich Shop	1030 Amsterdam Ave	212-222-2245	$*	7 pm	Fresh deli meats.
Pisticci	125 La Salle St	212-932-3500	$$	11 pm	Wonderful cozy Italian.
Sezz Medi'	1260 Amsterdam Ave	212-932-2901	$$	12 am	Popular pizza/pasta place.
Symposium	544 W 113th St	212-865-1011	$$††	11 pm	Good traditional Greek.
Terrace in the Sky	400 W 119th St	212-666-9490	$$$$$	10:30 pm	Rooftop French.
Toast	3157 Broadway	212-662-1144	$$	12 am	Great diverse café menu. Recommended.

Tom's Restaurant	2880 Broadway	212-864-6137	$*	24-hrs	Diner featured regularly on Seinfeld.
Tomo Sushi	2850 Broadway	212-665-2916	$$	11 pm	Mainstream Japanese for quick sushi fix
V&T Pizzeria	1024 Amsterdam Ave	212-666-8051	$	12 am	Columbia pizza heaven.

Map 19 · Harlem (Lower)

African Kine Restaurant	256 W 116th St	212-666-9400	$	1:30 am	Senegalese.
Amy Ruth's	113 W 116th St	212-280-8779	$$	11 pm	Soul food, incredible fried chicken.
Ginger Restaurant	1400 5th Ave	212-423-1111	$$$	10:30 pm	Harlem spot dishing creative Chinese cuisine with healthy emphasis.
IHOP	2294 Adam Clayton Powell Jr Blvd	212-234-4747	$	24-hrs	Pancakes, etc.
Keur Sokhna	225 W 116th St	212-864-0081	$††	2 am	Good cheap Senegalese.
Le Baobab	120 W 116th St	212-864-4700	$	10 pm	Satisfying Senegalese.
Manna's Too	486 Lenox Ave	212-234-4488	$*	9:30 pm	Soul food buffet!
Native	161 Lenox Ave	212-665-2525	$	12 am	Excellent soul food.
Papaya King	121 W 125th St	212-665-5732	$*	9 pm	Dawgs for all you dawgs.
Piatto D'Oro II	1 E 118th St	212-722-7220	$$	11 pm	Classic Italian off-spring of East 109th Street locale.
Slice of Harlem	308 Lenox Ave	212-426-7400	$*	10 pm	Harlem brick-oven pizza. Cool.
Sylvia's	328 Lenox Ave	212-996-0660	$$$	10:30 pm	An institution. Not overrated.
Yvonne Yvonne	301 W 135th St	212-862-1223	$*	8 pm	Excellent Jamaican chicken, ribs, etc.
Zoma	2084 Frederick Douglass Blvd	212-662-0620	$$	12 am	Tasty Ethiopian in a tasteful setting.

Map 20 · El Barrio / East Harlem

A Taste of Seafood	59 E 125th St	212-831-5584	$*	10 pm	Fried fish sandwiches on white bread. Lord, have mercy!
Café Creole	2167 3rd Ave	212-876-8838	$$	12 am	Local Creole.
Camaradas	2241 1st Ave	212-348-2703	$$*	12:45 am	Spanish/Puerto Rican/tapas/music.
Caminito Steak House	1664 Park Ave	212-289-1343	$$		Just like Argentina: nice steaks and cheap wine.
Casa de los Tacos	2277 1st Ave	212-860-7389	$*	11 pm	Try an especial de la casa.
Cuchifritos	168 E 116th St	212-876-4846	$*	3 am	Puerto Rican fried treats
El Nuevo Caridad	2257 2nd Ave	212-860-8187	$	11 pm	Dominican baseball stars approve of this chicken.
El Paso Taqueria	237 E 116th St	212-860-9753	$$	11 pm	Great Mexican with fantastic daily specials.
El Tapatio Mexican Restaurant	209 E 116th St	212-876-3055	$$*	2 am	Tiny but good
Golden Crust	2085 Lexington Ave	212-722-5253	$*	9 pm	It's all about the patties.
L&T Coffee Shop	2265 1st Ave	212-348-4485	$*	6 pm	Diner.
La Hacienda	219 E 116th St	212-987-1617	$	12 am	Mex Mex.
Manna	51 E 125th St	212-360-4975	$*	8 pm	Soul food buffet by the pound.
Mojitos	227 E 116th St	212-828-8635	$$	1 am	Live music Thursday, Friday and Saturday.
Orbit East Harlem	2257 1st Ave	212-348-7818	$$$	12 am	We like it—dinner, brunch, music, etc.
Patsy's Pizzeria	2287 1st Ave	212-534-9783	$$*	11 pm	The original thin-crust pizza. Best slices take-out slices in NY.
Pee Dee Steakhouse	2006 3rd Ave	212-996-3300	$	11 pm	Grilled meats for cheap.
Polish Indian Cuisine Restaurant	2179 3rd Ave	212-410-0276	$$	11 pm	First Indian Restaurant in El Barrio.
Rao's	455 E 114th St	212-722-6709	$$$$$	11 pm	We've heard it's an institution.
Ricardo Steakhouse	2145 2nd Ave	212-289-5895	$$	11 pm	Steak, bar, outside patio with upscale vibe and valet parking.
Sandy Restaurant	2261 2nd Ave	212-348-8654	$$	2 am	Neighborhood joint. Try the lechon asado.
Taco Mix	236 E 116 St	212-831-8147	$*	24-hrs	The best tacos in El Barrio.
Treichville West African Cuisine	339 E 118th St	212-281-2900	$	4 am	West African.

Map 21 · Manhattanville / Hamilton Heights

Baton Rouge	458 W 145th St	212-281-2336	$$	12 am	Creole and Cajun.
Café Largo	3387 Broadway	212-234-1811	$$	12 pm	BYOW with quiet ambiance.
Devin's Fish & Chips	747 St Nicholas Ave	212-491-5518	$*	11:30 pm	Greasy goodness just steps from St. Nick's Pub. Recommended.
Jesus Taco	501 W 145th St	212-234-3330	$	11 pm	Tacos and burgers.
New Caporal Fried Chicken	3772 Broadway	212-862-8986	$*	24-hrs	A neighborhood institution.
Queen of Sheeba	317 W 141st St	212-862-6149	$*	10 pm	Middle Eastern.
Raw Soul	348 W 145th St	212-491-5859	$$	9 pm	All raw food, all the time.
Sunshine Jamaican Restaurant	695 St Nicholas Ave	212-368-4972	$*	9:45 pm	Delicious curried goat.

Map 22 · Harlem (Upper)

Charles' Southern-Style Kitchen	2839 Frederick Douglass Blvd	212-926-4313	$	10 pm	The fried chicken they serve in heaven.
Londel's Supper Club	2620 Frederick Douglass Blvd	212-234-6114	$$$	11 pm	Good Southern.
Margie's Red Rose	275 W 144th St	212-491-3665	$*	8:30 pm	Fried chicken heaven.
Miss Maude's	547 Lenox Ave	212-690-3100	$$		Harlem soul food.

Arts & Entertainment • **Restaurants**

Key: $: Under $10 / $$: $10–$20 / $$$: $20–$30 / $$$$: $30–$40 / $$$$$: $40+; *: Cash only / †: Accepts only American Express. / †† Accepts only Visa/Mastercard. Time refers to hour kitchen closes on weekends.

Map 23 • Washington Heights

Aqua Marina	4060 Broadway	212-928-0070	$	11 pm	Uptown Italian.
Carrot Top Pastries	3931 Broadway	212-927-4800	$	9 pm	Baked goods and coffee too!
Coogan's	4015 Broadway	212-928-1234	$$	12 am	Where med students and cops go.
Dallas BBQ	3956 Broadway	212-568-3700	$$	12 am	When you can't get to Virgil's.
El Conde Steak House	4139 Broadway	212-781-1235	$$$	1 am	Big slabs of MEAT.
El Malecon	4141 Broadway	212-927-3812	$	24-hrs	Mexican—fabulous roast chicken.
El Ranchito	4129 Broadway	212-928-0866	$$	1 am	Central America in New York!
Genesis	511 W 181st St	212-923-3030	$$	10 pm	Yummy South American cuisine a block from the 1 train.
Hispaniola	839 W 181st St	212-740-5222	$$$$	12 am	Tapas, bridge views—everything you need.
Jesse's Place	812 W 181st St	212-795-4168	$$	1 am	Neighborhood diner.
Jimmy Oro Restaurant	711 W 181st St	212-795-1414	$	11 pm	Chinese/Spanish. Huge variety.
Parrilla	3920 Broadway	212-543-9500	$$	4 am	Argentinean with cool-ass grill.
Reme Restaurant	4021 Broadway	212-923-5452	$*	8:30 pm	Comfort food.
Restaurant Tenares	2306 Amsterdam Ave	212-927-4190	$$*	8 pm	Jukebox. Brush up your Spanish standards.
Taino Restaurant	2228 Amsterdam Ave	212-543-9035	$$	11:30 pm	Neighborhood Latino w/ men constantly arguing outside.
Tipico Dominicano	4177 Broadway	212-781-3900	$	24-hrs	Family place to watch the game. Gooooooaal!

Map 24 • Fort George / Fort Tryon

107 West	811 W 187th St	212-923-3311	$$	11 pm	Salads, burgers, etc.
809 Sangria Bar	112 Dyckman St	212-304-3800	$$$	12 am	Dominican grilled meat-a-thon.
Bleu Evolution	808 W 187th St	212-928-6006	$$	11 pm	Uptown bohemian. Calm.
Caridad Restaurant	4311 Broadway	212-781-0431	$	12 am	Caribbean.
New Leaf Café	1 Margaret Corbin Dr	212-568-5323	$$$$	10 pm	Uptown haven.
Rancho Jubilee	1 Nagle Ave	212-304-0100	$$	24-hrs	Great Dominican destination.

Map 25 • Inwood

Capitol Restaurant	4933 Broadway	212-942-5090	$$*	10:00 pm	Nice neighborhood diner.
Garden Café	4961 Broadway	212-544-9480	$$		Homestyle brunch for less than 10 bucks.
Grandpa's Brick Oven Pizza	4973 Broadway	212-304-1185	$$††	2 am	Personal brick oven pies and catering.
Mamajua Café	247 Dyckman St	212-304-0140	$$$	12 am	A fusion of Spanish architecture and Taino culture.
Mr Seafood	3842 9th Ave	212-304-9440	$$*	24-hrs	Fish! Fresh! Open late!
Park Terrace Bistro	4959 Broadway	212-567-2828	$$	10:30 pm	One of the gem hidden gems of the city. Moroccan fare.
Tacos Puebla	5-22 W 207th St	212-942-1881	$*	12 am	Large portions of succulent and inexpensive Mexican food.

Battery Park City

Gigino at Wagner Park	20 Battery Pl	212-528-2228	$$$$	10 pm	Lady Liberty is your companion as you dine Italian.
Grill Room	225 Liberty St	212-945-9400	$$$$$	9 pm	Palm trees inside. Hudson river outside.
Picasso Pizza	303 South End Ave	212-321-2616	$$	10 pm	Good thin crust pizza.
PJ Clarke's	4 World Financial Ctr	212-285-1500	$$$$	12 am	New Lower Manhattan location of 120-year old burger institution.
Samantha's Fine Foods	235 South End Ave	212-945-5555	$$	9 pm	Italian take-out and catering.
Steamer's Landing	375 South End Ave	212-432-1451	$$$	10 pm	Food from Italy, from the sea, and from the farms.
Zen	311 South End Ave	212-432-3634	$$	9:30 pm	Chinese and Thai.

Roosevelt Island

Trellis	549 Main St	212-752-1517	$$	11:30 pm	Local hang out.

Map 26 • Astoria

Agnanti	19-06 Ditmars Blvd	718-545-4554	$$	12 am	Wonderful Greek/Cypriot cuisine just across from Astoria Park.
Aliada	29-19 Broadway	718-932-2240	$$	11 pm	Excellent Cypriot with deservedly famous lamb chops.
Athens Café	32-07 30th Ave	718-626-2164	$$	2 am	Catch a buzz with a frothy Café Freddo on a veranda made for people watching.
Bartolino's	34-15 Broadway	718-728-7522	$$$	11 pm	The atmo of Michael Corleone's own dining room serving Don-worthy Italian dishes.

Name	Address	Phone	Price	Hours	Notes
Chirping Chicken	30-15 Broadway	718-626-3838	$*	11 pm	Not chirping, but rather delectably roasted.
Christos Steak House	41-08 23rd Ave	718-726-8400	$$$$$	11 pm	Excellent Greek-inflected steakhouse.
Churrascaria Girassol	33-18 28th Ave	718-545-8250	$$	11 pm	Authentic Brazilian meals, including rodizio.
Dhaka Café Jhill	35-55 31st St	718-937-4200	$	11 pm	Another good spot for Bangladeshi.
Djardan	34-04 31st Ave	718-721-2694	$$††	11 pm	Bureks and other Eastern European delights.
Elias Corner	24-02 31st St	718-932-1510	$$*	11 pm	No menu, just pick your fish from the counter.
Favela	33-18 28th Ave	718-545-8250	$$	12 am	Hearty Brazilian food. Think meat, and piles of it.
Grand Café	37-01 30th Ave	718-777-7321	$$$	11 pm	Sunday brunches as fun as the people-watching.
Indigo	28-50 31st St	718-728-0050	$$	2 am	Girly cocktails, manly brews, and posh patio with retractable roof for year-round star-lit dining.
JJ's Restaurant	37-05 31st Ave	718-626-8888	$$††	12 am	Sushi-French fusion.
Jour et Nuit	28-04 Steinway St	718-204-2511	$$	1 am	Exceptional Moroccan food, very friendly staff.
Kabab Café	25-12 Steinway St	718-728-9858	$$*	11 pm	Kebabs and more cooked to order by friendly chef-owner, Ali.
La Espiga II	32-44 31st St	718-777-1993	$*	11 pm	Awesome tortas, zero atmosphere.
Latin Cabana Restaurant	34-44 Steinway St	718-729-3900	$	24-hrs	The cuban sandwich is a true work of art.
Lil Bistro 33	19-33 Ditmars Blvd	718-609-1367	$$$$	11 pm	Neighborhood café serving Asian-French cuisine.
Mombar	25-22 Steinway St	718-726-2356	$$*	10:30 pm	Egyptian food in a beautiful setting.
Neptune Diner	31-05 Astoria Blvd	718-278-4853	$$	24-hrs	Good diner, even better when you're drunk.
Original Mexican Food Deli	30-11 29th St	718-274-6936	$*	11 pm	Grab a lengua torta before siesta.
Ovelia	34-01 30th Ave	718-721-7217	$$	12 am	Swapping sentimental for sexy (and Manhattan prices).
Papa's Empanadas	25-51 Steinway St	718-726-1400	$	10 pm	Empanadas for breakfast, dessert, and everything in between.
Philoxenia	32-07 Astoria Blvd N	718-626-2000	$$	12 am	Cozy Greek spot reopened in a new location.
Poodam Thai Cuisine	44-19 Broadway	718-278-3010	$*	11 pm	Try their spicy Northern (Isaan) Thai specialties.
Rizzo's Pizza	30-13 Steinway St	718-721-9862	$*	10 pm	Yummy thin-crust square pies.
S'Agapo	34-21 34th St	718-626-0303	$$$	12 am	Popular Greek restaurant with outdoor dining for the warmer months.
Sabor Tropical	36-18 30th Ave	718-777-8506	$$	11 pm	Hearty Brazilian. Try the passionfruit mousse.
Sabry's	24-25 Steinway St	718-721-9010	$$	10 pm	Great Egyptian seafood.
Sal, Chris, and Charlie Deli	33-12 23rd Ave	718-278-9240	$$*	8 pm	They don't call them the "sandwich kings of Astoria" for nothing.
San Antonio II	36-20 Astoria Blvd S	718-777-8733	$	7:30 pm	Get a hot dog Chilean style, with guacamole, tomato, and mayo
Seven One Eight	35-01 Ditmars Blvd	718-204-5553	$$$	11 pm	Bringing vineyard French food and overpriced brunch to Queens.
Stamatis	29-12 23rd Ave	718-932-8596	$$$	1 am	Basic Athenian, octopus and other grilled fish recommended.
Telly's Taverna	28-13 23rd Ave	718-728-9056	$$	12 am	Creative specials and bang-up Greek classics.
Tokyo Japanese Restaurant	31-05 24th Ave	718-777-1880	$$	11 pm	Try the Jimmy roll.
Tony's Souvlaki Opa!	28-44 31st St	718-728-3638	$*	1 am	Greek oasis under the N train.
Trattoria L'Incontro	21-76 31st St	718-721-3532	$$$$$	11 pm	One of the city's best Italian restaurants. Seriously.
Uncle George's Greek Tavern	33-19 Broadway	718-626-0593	$	11 pm	Institutional staying power via truly boggling portions for the price.
Walima	31-06 42nd St	718-204-0707	$$	10 pm	Tasty Moroccan food from friendly owners.
Watawa	33-10 Ditmars Blvd	718-545-9596	$$	11:30 pm	Fresh, fresh sushi in a cozy Japanese setting.
Zenon	34-10 31st Ave	718-956-0133	$$*	11 pm	Cypriot taverna with some of the best meze in town.
Zlata Praha	28-48 31st St	718-721-6422	$$††	4 am	Hearty, cheap Czech food. Try the specials.

Map 27 · Long Island City

Name	Address	Phone	Price	Hours	Notes
43rd Avenue Diner / 5 Stars Punjabi	13-15 43rd Ave	718-784-7444	$$	4:30 am	Indian diner/cabbie hangout/banquet hall.
Bella Via	47-46 Vernon Blvd	718-361-7510	$$	10:30 pm	Wonderful modern Italian dishes and brick-oven pizza.
Blend	47-04 Vernon Blvd	718-729-2800	$$	11 pm	Sleek Cuban-Fusion spot. Sadly, no liquor license and no BYOB.
Bricktown Bagel Café	51-06 Vernon Blvd	718-361-2428	$	5 pm	Good bagels, decent coffee, and comfy chairs.
Brooks 1890 Restaurant	24-28 Jackson Ave	718-937-1890	$$	8 pm	If only Al Swearengen were behind the bar…
Bulgara Restaurant	37-10 11th St	718-392-5373	$$	2:30 am	Bulgarian party palace.
Café Henri	10-10 50th Ave	718-383-9315	$$	11:30 pm	BYOB French cuisine.
Cassino	47-18 Vernon Blvd	718-937-9662	$	10:30 pm	Neighborhood place for red sauce Italian.
Court Square Diner	45-30 23rd St	718-392-1222	$	24-hrs	Reliable grub available 24 hours.
Cup Diner	35-01 36th St	718-937-2322	$	10:30 pm	Diner time open 24 hours.
Dorian Café	10-01 50th Ave	718-937-1120	$	11 pm	Cozy neighborhood diner, recently revamped brunch menu.

395

Arts & Entertainment · Restaurants

Key: $: Under $10 / $$: $10–$20 / $$$: $20–$30 / $$$$: $30–$40 / $$$$$: $40+; *: Cash only / † : Accepts only American Express. / † † Accepts only Visa/Mastercard. Time refers to hour kitchen closes on weekends.

Map 27 · Long Island City—continued

El Sitio	35-55 31st St	718-278-7694	$	12 am	Cuban lunch counter with really good pressed pork sandwiches.
Halal Meat Cart	34th Ave & Steinway St				Middle Eastern hoagies.
Jackson Ave Steakhouse	12-23 Jackson Ave	718-784-1412	$$$$	11 pm	Wood-paneled steakhouse with a busy happy hour.
Junior's Café	46-18 Vernon Blvd	718-472-9694	$	11 pm	Corner bar/Italian-American restaurant popular with locals. Try the meatball sub.
Las Vegas Diner	44-62 21st St	718-482-9478	$*	9 pm	Get the mofongo.
Lucky Mojo's	516 51st Ave	718-786-RIBS	$$	11 pm	Can one place serve decent BBQ, sushi, Cajun, and Mexican, and have cheap beer to boot? Yes, it can.
Malagueta	25-35 36th Ave	718-937-4821	$$	11 pm	Great Brazilian/Euro food in a downright classy setting.
Manducatis	13-27 Jackson Ave	718-729-4602	$$$	10 pm	Classic Italian cuisine expertly prepared; a beloved neighborhood institution.
Manetta's	10-76 Jackson Ave	718-786-6171	$$	10 pm	Above-average brick oven pizza and good house-made pastas.
Masso	47-25 Vernon Blvd	718-482-8151	$$†	12 am	Simple Italian food, ridiculously bad service.
Pimenton	21-50 44th Dr	718-707-0442	$	11 pm	Great tapas, plus a garden in summer.
Queens Coffee Shop	25-15 Queens Plz N	718-786-8297	$	2 am	Get coffee, meet a recently released felon.
Riverview Restaurant	201 50th Ave	718-392-5000	$$$	11 pm	Boring food in a setting reminiscent of a hip Eastern European hotel lobby.
Roti Boti Restaurant	27-09 21st St	718-278-7888	$*	24-hrs	The late-night smut peddler of food.
Tournesol	50-12 Vernon Blvd	718-472-4355	$$$	11:30 pm	Cozy French bistro, a neighborhood gem.
Tuk Tuk	49-06 Vernon Blvd	718-472-5597	$$	10 pm	Thai for beginners.
Water's Edge	44th Dr & East River	718-482-0033	$$$$$	11:30 pm	Mom will like the American and continental cuisine with views of the skyline.

Map 28 · Greenpoint

Acapulco Deli & Restaurant	1116 Manhattan Ave	718-349-8429	$	10 pm	Authentic Mexican food with some American standards.
Amarin Café	617 Manhattan Ave	718-349-2788	$*	11 pm	Good, cheap Thai food.
Baldo's Pizza	175 Nassau Ave	718-349-7770	$$*	10 pm	Pizza; best when delivered.
Brooklyn Label	180 Franklin St	718-389-2806	$	9 pm	Scrumptious sandwiches in the stately Astral building.
Casanova	338 McGuinness Blvd	718-389-0990	$$	11 pm	Italian fare.
Christina's	853 Manhattan Ave	718-383-4382	$*	10 pm	Traditional Polish food, cheap breakfasts!
Dami's	931 Manhattan Ave	718-349-7501	$$	10 pm	Brand new Polish-American joint.
Divine Follie Café	929 Manhattan Ave	718-389-6770	$$	10 pm	Large selection of meats, pastas, and pizza.
Enid's	560 Manhattan Ave	718-349-3859	$$	10 pm	Popular brunch on weekends; also dinner weeknights.
Erb	681 Manhattan Ave	718-349-8215	$$††	11:30 pm	Try the curry noodles.
Fresca Tortilla	620 Manhattan Ave	718-389-8818	$$	11:30 pm	Cheap Mexican take-out.
God Bless Deli	818 Manhattan Ave	718-349-0605	$*	24-hrs	The only 24-hour joint in the 'hood. Cheap sandwiches and burgers.
Johnny's Café	632 Manhattan Ave	718-383-9644	$$	1 am	Home-cooked Polish standards.
Lamb & Jaffey	1073 Manhattan Ave	718-389-3638	$$$	11 pm	Classy date spot.
Lomzynianka	646 Manhattan Ave	718-389-9439	$*	9 pm	Get your kitschy Polish fix dirt cheap.
Manhattan 3 Decker	695 Manhattan Ave	718-389-6664	$$	9:30 pm	Greek and American fare.
Monsignor's	905 Lorimer St	718-963-3399	$$	11 pm	Cheap Italian.
Old Poland Restaurant	190 Nassau Ave	718-349-7775	$*	9 pm	Polish/American.
OTT	970 Manhattan Ave	718-609-2416	$$	10:30 pm	Another excellent Thai choice on Manhattan Ave.
Queen's Hideaway	222 Franklin St	718-383-2355	$$$††	10:30 pm	Home cookin' with something new every day.
Relax	68 Newell St	718-389-1665	$*	9:30 pm	Polish diner w/ good prices and excellent soups—a neighborhood favorite.
San Diego	999 Manhattan Ave	718-389-7747	$$	11 pm	Mexican kitchen.
Sapporo Haru	622 Manhattan Ave	718-389-9697	$$††	12:30 am	Fresh sushi, friendly service.
Thai Café	925 Manhattan Ave	718-383-3562	$*	11 pm	Vast menu, veg options, eat in or take out.
Valdiano	659 Manhattan Ave	718-383-1707	$$*	8:45 pm	Southern Italian.

Map 29 · Williamsburg

Acqua Santa	556 Driggs Ave	718-384-9695	$$	12 am	Bistro Italian—amazing patio.
Anna Maria Pizza	179 Bedford Ave	718-599-4550	$	4 am	A must after late-night drinking.
Baci & Abbracci	204 Grand St	718-599-6599	$$	12 am	Old-world Italian in a modern setting.
Blackbird Parlour	197 Bedford Ave	718-599-2707	$	11:30 pm	Cozy European style café with tasty sandwiches.
Bonita	338 Bedford Ave	718-384-9500	$$	12 am	Americanized Mexican in a nice atmosphere.

Bozu	296 Grand St	718-384-7770	$$††	1 am	Amazing Japanese tapas and sushi bombs.
Diner	85 Broadway	718-486-3077	$$	1 am	Amazing simple food like you've never tasted—never disappoints.
Dokebi	199 Grand St	718-782-1424	$$$	12 am	Cook your own Korean BBQ with tabletop hibachis.
Dressler	149 Broadway	718-384-6343	$$$$	12 am	So darn classy, you'll feel like you're in Park Slope.
DuMont	432 Union Ave	718-486-7717	$$	12 am	Continually changing market-fresh menu and yummy desserts.
DuMont Burger	314 Bedford Ave	718-384-6127	$$	2 am	The mini burger is even better proportioned than the original.
Fada	530 Driggs Ave	718-388-6607	$$$	1 am	Cuisine Marseillaise.
Fette Sau	354 Metropolitan Ave	718-963-3404	$$	11 pm	Enjoy pounds of meat and casks of beer in a former auto-body repair shop.
Juliette	135 N 5th St	718-388-9222	$$	1 am	Northside bistro with rooftop deck.
Kate's Brooklyn Joint	295 Berry St	718-218-7167	$$	10 pm	Fake-meat comfort food.
Marlow & Sons	81 Broadway	718-384-1441	$$$	1 am	Oysters and beer, old timey-like - go for Happy Hour
Moto	394 Broadway	718-599-6895	$$*	12 am	Triangular nook with horseshoe bar and comfort food.
Oasis	161 N 7th St.	718-218-7607	$	3 am	Cheap Middle Eastern delights right by the L, and open late.
Peter Luger Steak House	178 Broadway	718-387-7400	$$$$$*	10:45 pm	Best steak, potatoes, and spinach in this solar system.
PT	331 Bedford Ave	718-388-7438	$$$*	1 am	D.O.C's sophisticated older brother.
Raymund's Place	124 Bedford Ave	718-388-4200	$$*	11 pm	The Polish "Hooters."
Relish	225 Wythe St	718-963-4546	$$	1 am	Comfort food gone eclectic with a touch of class.
Roebling Tea Room	143 Roebling St	718-963-0760	$$$	3 am	Fancy tea eatery.
Sparky's/Egg	135 N 5th St	718-302-5151	$$*	11 pm	Organic breakfast and free range burgers.
Taco Chulo	318 Grand St	718-302-2485	$$	11 pm	Handmade, decadently pimped out tacos. Gotta love that!
Teddy's Bar and Grill	96 Berry St	718-384-9787	$††	1 am	Best bar food ever. Hipster and Polish locals unite.
Yola's Café	542 Metropolitan Ave	718-486-0757	$*	1 am	Terrific, authentic Mexican in a claustrophobic atmosphere.

Map 30 • Brooklyn Heights / DUMBO / Downtown

Bubby's	1 Main St	718-222-0666	$$	11 pm	It's all about the pie.
Curry Leaf	151 Remsen St	718-222-3900	$$	10:30 pm	Terrific Indian food.
DUMBO General Store	111 Front St	718-855-5288	$$	8 pm	Food and drink for artists.
Fascati Pizzeria	80 Henry St	718-237-1278	$*	11 pm	Excellent slice pizza.
Five Front	5 Front St	718-625-5559	$$	12 am	Tasty newcomer with a beautiful garden.
Five Guys	138 Montague St	718-797-9380	$	10 pm	Burger joint with tasty fries and free peanuts while you wait.
Grimaldi's	19 Old Fulton St	718-858-4300	$*	11:45 pm	Excellent, though not the best, NY pizza.
Hale & Hearty Soup	32 Court St	718-596-5600	$$	7 pm	Super soups.
Heights Café	84 Montague St	718-625-5555	$$$	12 am	Decent dining near the Promenade.
Henry's End	44 Henry St	718-834-1776	$$$	11 pm	Inventive, game-oriented menu.
Jack the Horse Tavern	66 Hicks St	718-852-5084	$$$$	10:30 pm	Oustanding upscale pub/New American cuisine, great feel.
Junior's Restaurant	386 Flatbush Ave	718-852-5257	$$	2 am	American with huge portions.
Miso	40 Main St	718-858-8388	$$$	11 pm	Japanese fusion cuisine.
Noodle Pudding	38 Henry St	718-625-3737	$$*	11 pm	Excellent Northern Italian fare.
Pete's Downtown	2 Water St	718-858-3510	$$	11 pm	Italian food and a view.
The Plant	25 Jay St	718-722-7541	$$	11 pm	Raw and organic foods.
Queen Ristorante	84 Court St	718-596-5954	$$$$	10:30 pm	Good white-tablecloth, bow-tied waiter Italian joint
Rice	81 Washington St	718-222-9880	$$*	11 pm	Tasty Asian for less.
River Café	1 Water St	718-522-5200	$$$$$	11 pm	Great view, but overrated.
Siggy's Good Food	76 Henry St	718-237-3199	$$††	10 pm	Vegan pal cafe.
Superfine	126 Front St	718-243-9005	$$	11 pm	Mediterranean-inspired menu, bi-level bar, local art and music. NFT pick.
Sushi California	71 Clark St	718-222-0308	$$	11 pm	Sushi Express, reasonable prices.
Thai 101	101 Montague St	718-237-2594	$$	10:30 pm	Die for this Thai.
Theresa's	80 Montague St	718-797-3996	$††	11 pm	Polish-American comfort food. Come hungry.
Toro Restaurant	1 Front St	718-625-0300	$$	12 am	Spanish-Asian fusion.

Map 31 • Fort Greene / Clinton Hill

1 Greene Sushi and Sashimi	1 Greene Ave	718-422-1000	$$	11 pm	Fresh sushi, familiar standardized setting.
67 Burger	67 Lafayette Ave	718-797-7150	$$	10 pm	Super-cool stop for a quick bite before your movie at BAM.
BAMcafé	30 Lafayette Ave	718-636-4100	$$	12 am	Café with live music weekend evenings.

Arts & Entertainment • Restaurants

Key: $: Under $10 / $$: $10–$20 / $$$: $20–$30 / $$$$: $30–$40 / $$$$$: $40+; *: Cash only / † : Accepts only American Express. / † † Accepts only Visa/Mastercard. Time refers to hour kitchen closes on weekends.

Map 31 • Fort Greene / Clinton Hill—continued

Black Iris	228 Dekalb Ave	718-852-9800	$$	11:30 pm	Middle Eastern.
Castro's Restaurant	511 Myrtle Ave	718-398-1459	$$	12 am	Burritos delivered con cervesas, if you like.
Chez Lola	387 Myrtle Ave	718-858-1484	$$$†	11 pm	French, inventive specials; a Ft. Greene favorite.
Chez Oskar	211 Dekalb Ave	718-852-6250	$$$	1 am	French cuisine in a good neighborhood bistro.
Choice Market	318 Lafayette Ave	718-230-5234	$*	9 pm	Excellent sandwiches, baked goods, burgers, etc. served w/ maddening slowness.
Grand Dakar	285 Grand Ave	718-398-8900	$$$	1 am	Friendly, insanely laid-back Senegalese.
Habana Outpost	757 Fulton St	718-858-9500	$*	12 am	Grilled corn and free movies in a solar-powered restaurant.
Ici	246 Dekalb Ave	718-789-2778	$$$	11 pm	Beautiful new addition to FG restaurant scene, and worth the splurge.
Kush	17 Putnam Ave	718-230-3471	$$	12 am	West African café and restaurant; killer short ribs.
Locanda Vini & Olii	129 Gates Ave	718-622-9202	$$	11:30 pm	Rustic but pricey neighborhood Italian. Marvelous décor.
LouLou	222 Dekalb Ave	718-246-0633	$$$	10 pm	Rustic Breton/French gem where seafood rules.
Luz	177 Vanderbilt Ave	718-246-4000	$$$	12 am	Yuppie interior with requisite brunch.
Madiba	195 Dekalb Ave	718-855-9190	$$$	12 am	South African—Bunny Chow, need we say more? Shebeen with live music.
Maggie Brown	455 Myrtle Ave	718-643-7001	$$*	12 am	Food by the fireplace; great burgers.
Mojito Restaurant	82 Washington Ave	718-797-3100	$$	10:30 pm	Classy Cuban cuisine.
Night of the Cookers	767 Fulton St	718-797-1197	$$$	12:30 am	Hip bistro with southern accents.
Olea	171 Lafayette Ave	718-643-7003	$$	12 am	Retooled Mediterenean.
Pequena	86 S Portland Ave	718-643-0000	$$*	12 am	Killer quesadillas.
Red Bamboo	271 Adelphi St	718-643-4352	$$$	3 am	Leafy patio, friendly service, veggie treats. Edamame that will make you believe.
Rice	166 Dekalb Ave	718-858-2700	$$*	11 pm	Tasty Asian for less
Ruthie's Restaurant	96 Dekalb Ave	718-246-5189	$$*	11 pm	Soul food in mega portions.
Scopello	63 Lafayette Ave	718-852-1100	$$	11 pm	Sicilian chic in stylish surroundings.
The Smoke Joint	87 S Elliot Pl	718-797-1011	$$	11 pm	BBQ with the right sauce. Holla!
Soule	920 Fulton St	718-399-7200	$$	12 am	Everything from king crab to roti to curry goat to blackened salmon. Tons of sides
Thai 101	455 Myrtle Ave	718-855-4615	$$	11 pm	Die for this thai.
Thomas Beisl	25 Lafayette Ave	718-222-5800			12 am Austrian
Zaytoons	472 Myrtle Ave	718-623-5522	$$	12 am	Above-average Middle Eastern's second outpost.

Map 32 • BoCoCa / Red Hook

Alma	187 Columbia St	718-643-5400	$$$	11 pm	Top NYC Mexican with great views of lower Manhattan.
Atlantic Chip Shop	129 Atlantic Ave	718-855-7775	$$	12 am	Heart attack on a plate.
Bar Tabac	128 Smith St	718-923-0918	$$$	3 am	Open late; fabulous frites, burgers, et al.
Bocca Lupo	391 Henry St	718-243-2522	$$$	2 am	Postmodern panini by day and (late) night. We love NYC.
Caserta Vecchia	221 Smith St	718-624-7549	$$	11 pm	Excellent, fresh brick-oven and friendly smiles; garden.
Chance	223 Smith St	718-242-1515	$$$$	12 am	Upscale Asian fusion—recommended.
Chestnut	271 Smith St	718-243-0049	$$$††	11 pm	Seasonal fare. Severely underrated.
Chicory	243 Degraw St	718-797-2121	$	10 pm	Gavin McAleer kicks major ass. Everything's great.
Cubana Café	272 Smith St	718-858-3980	$$*	11:30 pm	Colorful, authentic Cuban—lively staff.
El Nuevo Portal	217 Smith St	718-246-1416	$*	11 pm	Killer breaded steak.
Ferdinando's Focacceria Restaurant	151 Union St	718-855-1545	$*	11 pm	Sicilian specialties you won't find anywhere else! Get the panelle special.
Fragole	394 Court St	718-522-7133	$$	11:30 pm	Fresh and cozy Italian. An absolute gem.
Frankie's 457	457 Court St	718-403-0033	$$*	12 am	Fantastic meatballs. Cool space.
The Good Fork	391 Van Brunt St	718-643-6636	$$$††	10:30 pm	Yep. It's good.
The Grocery	288 Smith St	718-596-3335	$$$$$†††	11 pm	Magnificent. Reservations recommended.
Hadramout	172 Atlantic Ave	718-852-3577	$*	12 am	Great Yemeni diner—order the salta and don't fear the fenugreek foam!
Hanco's	85 Bergen St	718-858-6818	$*	9 pm	Banh Mi for people who won't trek to Sunset Park.
Hope & Anchor	347 Van Brunt St	718-237-0276	$$	1 am	Great upscale diner.
Joya	215 Court St	718-222-3484	$$*	12 am	Excellent, inexpensive, but super-noisy Thai.
Ki Sushi	122 Smith St	718-935-0575	$$	12 am	Affordable sushi in sleek surroundings
Le Petite Café	502 Court St	718-596-7060	$$	10:30 pm	Great bistro food—check out the garden.
Lucali	575 Henry St	718-858-4086	$$*	6 pm	One man makes every perfect pizza by hand.
Panino'teca 275	275 Smith St	718-237-2728	$$	12 am	Great paninis and fab cheese lasagna.
Patois	255 Smith St	718-855-1535	$$$$	11:30 pm	French bistro. Killer brunch.

Quercy	242 Court St	718-243-2151	$$$$	11 pm	Sister restaurant to La Luncheonette in Manhattan, and equally sublime.
Sam's Restaurant	238 Court St	718-596-3458	*	1 am	An Italian institution. Go for the pizza.
Saul	140 Smith St	718-935-9844	$$$	11 pm	Romantical and delicious
Sherwood Café/ Robin des Bois	195 Smith St	718-596-1609	$$*	1 am	Mellow French vibe—best croque monsieur in town.
Soul Spot	302 Atlantic Ave	718-596-9933	$$††	11 pm	American and Afro-Caribbean soul food.
Yemen Café	176 Atlantic Ave	718-834-9533	$	11 pm	More good Yemeni food, because you can never have too much lamb.
Zaytoons	283 Smith St	718-875-1880	$$	12 am	Excellent Middle Eastern pizzas and kebabs.

Map 33 • Park Slope / Prospect Heights / Windsor Terrace

12th Street Bar and Grill	1123 8th Ave	718-965-9526	$$$	11 pm	Outstanding gourmet comfort fare.
2nd Street Café	189 7th Ave	718-369-6928	$$$	12 am	Clamoring brunch crowd.
Al Di La Trattoria	248 5th Ave	718-783-4565	$$$	11 pm	Chandelier & brick-walled Italian. Super.
Anthony's	426 7th Ave	718-369-8315	$$	11 pm	New neighborhood fave for brick-oven 'za.
Applewood	501 11th St	718-768-2044		11 pm	Elegant, cheerful slow food.
Beast	638 Bergen St	718-399-6855	$$$	11:30 pm	American tapas.
Belleville	332 5th Ave	718-832-9777	$$$†	11 pm	Fab bistro French; they've perfected entrecote.
Blue Ribbon Brooklyn	280 5th Ave	718-840-0404	$$$$	4 am	The one and only!
Bogota Latin Bistro	141 5th Ave	718-230-3805	$$$	1 am	Stylish South- and Central-American restaurant.
Bonnie's Grill	278 5th Ave	718-369-9527	$$	12 am	Habit-forming contemporary diner.
Brooklyn Fish Camp	162 5th Ave	718-783-3264		11 pm	Mary's Fish Camp redux.
ChipShop	383 5th Ave	718-832-7701	$*	11 pm	Brit boys dish fish, chips, and The Beatles.
Convivium Osteria	68 5th Ave	718-857-1833	$$$$	11:30 pm	Delicious Italian with a Portuguese influence. Rustic, warm setting.
Flatbush Farm	76 St Marks Ave	718-622-3276	$$††	12 am	Local, seasonal, and delish.
Franny's	295 Flatbush Ave	718-230-0221	$$††	11:30 pm	Brilliant pizza, drop-dead fresh, NFT fave.
Kinara	473 5th Ave	718-499-3777	$$	10 pm	Large selection of vegetarian and non-vegetarian Indian dishes.
La Taqueria	72 7th Ave	718-398-4300	$	10 pm	Easy-y barato, meaning cheap. Autentico.
Mitchell's Soul Food	617 Vanderbilt Ave	718-789-3212	$*	10:30 pm	Seedy, cheap soul food.
Nana	155 5th Ave	718-230-3749	$$*	12 am	Absolutely delicious Pan-Asian.
Noo Na	565 Vanderbilt Ave	718-398-6662	$$*	2 am	Authentic Korean, finally!
Olive Vine Café	54 7th Ave	718-636-4333	$*	10:30 pm	Crispy Mediterranean pizzas.
Red Hot	349 7th Ave	718-369-0700	$$	11 pm	Fake meat for vegetarians who like to pretend they're not.
Rose Water	787 Union St	718-783-3800	$$$	11 pm	Intimate, airy Mediterranean.
Sheep Station	149 4th Ave	718-857-4337	$$*	12 am	Australian craft beers and aussie-themed food. Mate.
Stone Park Café	324 5th Ave	718-369-0082	$$$	11 pm	Already a contender for best Park Slope dining. NFT pick.
Sushi Tatsu	347 Flatbush Ave	718-638-7900	$$	11:30 pm	A breath of Japan on busy Flatbush.
Tom's	782 Washington Ave	718-636-9738	$$*	4 pm	Old-school mom-and-pop diner since 1936. A cholesterol love affair.
Watana	420 7th Ave	718-832-1611	$$	11 pm	Best Thai food on the slope. BYOB.

Map 34 • Hoboken

Amanda's	908 Washington St	201-798-0101	$$$$$	11 pm	New American. Brunch.
Arthur's Tavern	237 Washington St	201-656-5009	$$$	12 am	The best steak for the price.
Baja	104 14th St	201-653-0610	$$	11:30 pm	Good Mexican food, great sangria.
Bangkok City	335 Washington St	201-792-6613	$$	11 pm	A taste of Thai.
Biggies Clam Bar	318 Madison St	201-656-2161	$	10 pm	Boardwalk fare and perfect raw clams. Order by the dozen.
Brass Rail	135 Washington St	201-659-7074	$$$	11 pm	You can't beat the brunch deal.
Cucharamama	233 Clinton St	201-420-1700	$$$	11 pm	Great Cuban and South American.
Delfino's	500 Jefferson St	201-792-7457	$$*	10:30 pm	Pizza joint...Plus red checkered table cloths. BYO Chianti. The real thing.
East LA	508 Washington St	201-798-0052	$$	11 pm	Knock-your-socks-off margaritas and the food's not bad.
Far Side Bar & Grill	531 Washington St	201-963-7677	$$	10 pm	Hoboken's best pub food. Try the steak salad.
Frankie & Johnnie's	163 14th St	201-659-6202	$$$$$	11:30 pm	Power steakhouse. Keep an eye out for Tony Soprano.
Gaslight	400 Adams St	201-217-1400	$$	11 pm	Off the main drag, neighborhood Italian, cozy and cute. Quiz nights and comedy.
Helmer's	1036 Washington St	201-963-3333	$$$	10 pm	Old timey Bavarian joint, complete with cuckoo clocks.
Hoboken Gourmet Company	423 Washington St	201-795-0110	$$††	7 pm	Hoboken's one true café. Rustic, yummy, quirky.
Karma Kafe	505 Washington St	201-610-0900	$$	11:30 pm	Ultra-friendly Tibetan staff, hip Indian food with a wild mix of flavors.
La Isla	104 Washington St	201-659-8197	$$	10 pm	A genuine taste of Havana.
Oddfellows Restaurant	80 River St	201-656-9009	$$	11 pm	Authentic Cajun. Casual setting. Good happy hour specials.

*Key: $: Under $10 / $$: $10–$20 / $$$: $20–$30 / $$$$: $30–$40 / $$$$$: $40+; *: Cash only / † : Accepts only American Express. / † † Accepts only Visa/Mastercard. Time refers to hour kitchen closes on weekends.*

Map 34 • Hoboken—*continued*

Robongi	520 Washington St	201-222-8388	$$	11:30 pm	Consistently good sushi, friendly chefs, fun specials.
Sushi Lounge	200 Hudson St	201-386-1117	$$$	1 am	Popular, upscale sushi spot.
Trattoria Saporito	328 Washington St	201-533-1801	$$$	10:30 pm	Lacks the old-world Italian charm but has the old world taste and service. BYOB.
Zafra	301 Willow Ave	201-610-9801	$$	11 pm	Cozy with authentic Latino flavors. BYO wine—they'll magically turn it into sangria.

Map 35 • Jersey City

Amelia's Bistro	187 Warren St	201-332-2200	$$	11 pm	Try the crab cakes.
Beechwood Cafe	290 Grove St	201-985-2811	$	8:30pm	Good spot to grab a coffee.
Fatburger	286 Washington St	201-332-2244	$	10:30 pm	Pretty good burgers and shakes from the LA-based chain.
Ibby's	303 Grove St	201-432-2400	$		Mighty fine falafel.
Iron Monkey	97 Greene St	201-435-5756	$$$	2 am	Quiet, romantic atmosphere. Great rooftop terrace with full bar.
It's Greek to Me	194 Newark Ave	201-222-0844	$$	10 pm	Bad name, good gyro.
Kitchen Café	60 Sussex St	201-332-1010	$$	8 pm	The Great American breakfast.
Komegashi	103 Montgomery St	201-433-4567	$$$	10:30 pm	Authentic Japanese restaurant and sushi bar.
Komegashi Too	99 Pavonia Ave	201-533-8888	$$	11 pm	The other Komegashi.
Light Horse Tavern	199 Washington St	201-946-2028	$$$	11 pm	New American for brunch, lunch, and dinner—they have a bar, too.
Madame Claude	364 4th St	201-876-8800	$$*	11 pm	French café.
Marco and Pepe	289 Grove St	201-860-9688	$$$	11 pm	Small, painfully hip French restaurant.
Morgan Seafood	2801 John F Kennedy Blvd	201-792-2400	$$	12 am	Kickin' Egyptian coastal cuisine.
Presto's Restaurant	199 Warren St	201-433-6639	$$	9:30 pm	Italian BYOB.
Rosie Radigans	10 Exchange Pl	201-451-5566	$	10:30 pm	Excellent after work venue—terrific food, friendly bar crowd.
Saigon Café	188 Newark Ave	201-332-8711	$$	10:30 pm	Serves quality Southeast Asian cuisine.
Sri Ganesh	809 Newark Ave	201-222-3883	$*	9:30 pm	Lots and lots of dosas.
White Mana	470 Tonnele Ave	201-963-1441	$*	24-hrs	Classic diner has been slinging burgers since 1946.

Overview

If you ever get bored in New York City, you have only yourself to blame. When it comes to nightlife in particular, the only difficulty you'll have is in choosing amongst the seemingly infinite options for entertainment. New York's top weeklies—*The Village Voice* and *Time Out New York*—offer their round-ups of goings on about town, as do the e-mail newsletters such as *Flavorpill* (www.flavorpill.net), *My Open Bar* (www.myopenbar.com), *Daily Candy* (www.dailycandy.com), and *Nonsense NYC* (www.nonsensenyc.com) which each week direct you towards various concerts, multimedia events, and new bars. Over time you'll figure out which sources you trust and which venues you favor, and the explorer in you will thrive on checking out the new watering holes that seem to be sprouting like weeds downtown and in Brooklyn. For those of you who require more than a perfect drink in the ideal setting: LVHRD hosts monthly themed parties at secret locations (www.lvhrd.com). Below you'll find a few choice destinations for the key genres in evening diversion—dive bars, dance spots, music venues and much more. A word of caution: don't forget to pace yourselves.

Dive Bars

There is no shortage of dumps in this city, so we've done our best to single out the darkest and the dirtiest. A popular choice among our staff is the oh-so derelict **Mars Bar (Map 6)**—clean freaks should use the bathroom wherever they are before they get here. Other downtown favorites include **Blue & Gold (Map 6)**, **Grassroots Tavern (Map 6)**, and **Holiday Lounge (Map 6)**. On the other side of the East River, check out the **Turkey's Nest (Map 29)** in Williamsburg. And yes, there are even dives uptown. Try **Jimmy's Corner (Map 12)**, **P&G (Map 14)**, **The Subway Inn (Map 15)**, **Reif's Tavern (Map 17)**, or **1020 Bar (Map 18)**.

Best Beer Selection

When it comes to sheer beer selection, there are a number of worthy contenders. The heavily trodden **Peculier Pub (Map 6)** offers an extensive, though expensive, beer list. Visit this one on a weekday if you want to take advantage of some one-on-one time with the bartender. **The Ginger Man (Map 9)** in lower Midtown stocks over 100 kinds of bottled brew, and has over 60 options on tap. **Vol de Nuit (Map 5)** has a large number of Belgian beers and a warm but reclusive atmosphere. **Flatiron's Silver Swan (Map 9)** offers a slew of beer choices to wash down its German fare. Ditto for **Zum Schneider (Map 7)**. Hipster-fave **Otherroom (Map 5)** has a solid selection, too (and it's either beer or wine there, so don't take friends who can't live without the hard stuff). Other places to try: **Blind Tiger Ale House (Map 5)** and **The Waterfront Ale House (Map 10)**. **Heartland Brewery (Map 1, 12)** brews its own in multiple Midtown locations, but expect more of a touristy scene. **Spuyten Duyvil (Map 29)** in Williamsburg offers many rare finds among its 100-plus beers, and a great atmosphere to boot.

Outdoor Spaces

Outdoor space is a precious commodity here, so combine it with cocktails and you've got the perfect destination for city dwellers who just don't want to be cooped up on those all-too-rare temperate evenings. Truth be told, though, you'll find New Yorkers stubbornly holding court at outdoor venues in pretty much any weather short of electrical storms and sub-freezing temperatures, and they'll only retreat in those conditions when chased indoors by the staff. Take note that bars with outdoor patios have circumvented the no-smoking legislation—either a perk or a put-off, depending on your inclination. We love the aptly named **Gowanus Yacht Club (Map 32)** in Carroll Gardens. This intimate beer garden serves up cold ones with dogs and burgers in a cookout setting. Other patios to check out include **Sweet & Vicious (Map 6)**, **The Park (Map 8)**, and the **Heights Bar & Grill (Map 18)**. Other Brooklyn highlights include **The Gate (Map 33)** in Park Slope, and Williamsburg's **Pete's Candy Store (Map 29)**, **Union Pool (Map 29)**, and **Huckleberry (Map 29)**.

Best Jukebox

Personal taste factors heavily in this category of course, but here is a condensed list of NFT picks. For Manhattan: **Ace Bar (Map 7)** (indie rock/punk), **Hi-Fi (Map 7)** (a huge and diverse selection), **Lakeside Lounge (Map 7)** (a little something for everybody), **7B (Map 7)** (rock all the way), **Rudy's Bar & Grill (Map 11)** (blues), **Welcome to the Johnsons (Map 7)** (indie rock/punk). For Brooklyn: **The Charleston (Map 29)** (Williamsburg—old school), **Great Lakes (Map 33)** (Park Slope—indie rock), **The Boat (Map 32)** (Carroll Gardens—indie rock), **The Levee (Map 29)** (Williamsburg—good all around), and the **Brooklyn Social Club (Map 32)** (Carroll Gardens—country/soul goodness).

Smoker-Friendly

Despite Bloomberg's efforts to create a smoke-free New York, there are a few loopholes in the current legislation. You can still light up in cigar bars and hookah bars, bars with outdoor spaces, and privately owned establishments. Despite its total lack of ventilation, **Hudson Bar & Books (Map 5)** is a favorite destination for smokers. Smoking is also permitted at its sister uptown location, **Lexington Bar & Books (Map 15)** (jacket required). On the Upper East Side, **Club Macanudo (Map 15)** goes for a country club atmosphere. Also try **Circa Tabac (Map 2)** (cigar bar). A good number of the city's non-smoking bars will permit the act late at night, but that's entirely up to the establishment. Some have developed clever solutions; in Brooklyn at **Larry Lawrence (Map 29)**, a lofted patio allows smokers to keep an eye on the action in the bar below.

Dance Clubs

New York's old cabaret laws make it tough to find free dance spots, but they do exist (albeit often with the velvet rope scenario that may deter the impatient). We like **Lit (Map 6)**, **Good World (Map 4)**, and **Rififi (Map 6)**. If you don't mind shelling out the dough, definitely try **Capitale (Map 3)** (located in the old Bowery Savings Bank). On the weekends, entry into the swankier clubs doesn't come without paying your dues in long lines and pricey cover charges, but many of them have reduced rates on weeknights. For a less glossy crowd in and around Williamsburg, we suggest checking out the lively dance scenes at **Bembe (Map 29)**, **Black Betty (Map 29)**, and **Royal Oak (Map 29)**.

Costly Cocktails

If you don't mind spending a few extra bucks on your drinking habit, there is no shortage of options. **Bar Veloce (Map 6)**, **inoteca (Map 7)**, and the enoteca at **i Trulli (Map 10)** are heaven for oenophiles, with the added perk of flights on offer at the latter. The bar at the **Peninsula Hotel (Map 12)** boasts views nearly as staggering as its prices. Other noteworthy settings include **The Campbell Apartment (Map 13)** in Grand Central Station, and the hard-to-access **Angel's Share (Map 6)**, which also provides an unusual view from its cozy divans.

Music - Overview

New York caters to a wide array of tastes in everything, and music is no exception. From the indie rock clubs of the Lower East Side to the history-steeped jazz clubs in the Village to amateur night at the Apollo, your musical thirst can seemingly be quenched in every possible way.

Jazz, Blues, Folk and Country

There are plenty of places to see jazz in the city, starting off with classic joints like the **Village Vanguard (Map 5)**, **Birdland (Map 11)**, the **Blue Note (Map 6)**, and the **Iridium (Map 12)**, which all draw top notch talent. For a smaller (and cheaper) jazz experience, try the **Lenox Lounge (Map 19)** and **St. Nick's Pub (Map 21)** in Harlem, or the **Arthur's Tavern (Map 5)** in the Village. The **Nuyorican Poets Café (Map 7)** has frequent jazz performances. In Brooklyn, your best bet is the **BAM Café (Map 31)**. (Sadly we've lost Tonic, which hosted a rare range of jazz and world music from established and undiscovered artists.)

The big change for jazz in NYC has been the new Jazz at Lincoln Center complex in the Time Warner Center on Columbus Circle. It has three rooms: the 1,000+ seat, designed-for-jazz Rose Theater, the Allen Room, an amphitheater with a great view of the park, and the nightclub-esque Dizzy's Club Coca Cola.

The blues can make an appearance in all sorts of clubs, but **Terra Blues (Map 6)** focuses on the art form and features reliably top-notch music on an otherwise tired Bleecker

Street scene. You can even find a taste of the south in our part. For country, try **Rodeo Bar (Map 10)**, **Hank's Saloon (Map 33)**, or **Parkside Lounge (Map 7)** on Mondays. BrooklynCountryMusic.com keeps track of who's fiddlin' in Brooklyn.

Rock and Pop

It's been a tough couple of years for Manhattan rock clubs. LES favorite Luna Lounge got priced out of the scene it helped to create and moved to Brooklyn. CBGB's closed, and bizarrely moved to Las Vegas. The Continental took the Brownie's approach and stopped featuring live music. Oh, and Sin-e and Rothkos closed as well, if anyone cares. But don't despair, all is not lost. Bowery Presents, the people behind two of the best clubs in the city—**Mercury Lounge (Map 7)** and **Bowery Ballroom (Map 6)**—have added **Music Hall of Williamsburg (Map 29)** to their mini-empire. At the same time, Clear Channel-spawned Live Nation has set up a competing chain of venues, including **Rebel (Map 9)** (formerly Downtime). Whether a system of two big venue powers and a bunch of little guys develops, and whether this will benefit artists and audiences, remains to be seen. **Bowery Ballroom (Map 6)** remains the top live venue, featuring big acts but with excellent sound and a good layout. **Irving Plaza (Map 10)** is a good place to see a show as well. The **Beacon Theater (Map 14)** tends to land the biggest names, if not the newest. **Roseland (Map 12)** is billed as an intimate venue for high-profile acts, but good luck getting tickets for the Stones or anyone else of that ilk.

The best small club is **Mercury Lounge (Map 7)**, which gets great bands right before they're ready to move up to Bowery, and features a big stage and audience area (though the bar can be really cramped). As far as the rest of the Lower East Side/East Village area goes, it helps if you like your clubs to be (faux) punky basements. Try **Lit (Map 6)** or **Cake Shop (Map 7)**. In Brooklyn, try **Music Hall of Williamsburg (Map 29)**, **Union Hall (Map 33)**, **Magnetic Field (Map 32)**, **Southpaw (Map 33)**, or **Trash (Map 29)**. And **Maxwell's (Map 34)** is still your best bet in Hoboken.

Finally, a couple of great websites to check out to keep up on who's in town: OhMyRockness.com and Brooklyn-Vegan.com.

Experimental

A number of venues in New York provide a place for experimental music to get exposure. **Experimental Intermedia (Map 3)** and **Roulette (Map 2)** are fully dedicated to showcasing the avant-garde. Jon Zorn's place, **The Stone (Map 7)**, takes an experimental approach towards the performance space as well as the music, with a different artist acting as curator for an entire month, no drinks or food, and the artists taking in 100% of door proceeds. **The Kitchen (Map 8)** features experimental music in addition to film, dance, and other art forms.

Everything Else

A few places run the gamut of musical genres. **The Knitting Factory (Map 3)** can have everything from jazz to metal (and three stages to boot). **Town Hall (Map 12)** gets folksy artists one night, hot Latin tango the next, and a slew of comedy, spoken word, and other acts. **Joe's Pub (Map 6)** presents an excellent variety of musical styles and often hosts celebrated international musicians. **The Cutting Room's (Map 9)** offerings include jazz, soul, rock, vocal, and more. Keep an eye on **BAMcafé (Map 31)** for a variety of great performers.

For cabaret or piano bar, try **Don't Tell Mama (Map 11)** or **The Duplex (Map 5)**. For a more plush experience, try the **Café Carlyle (Map 15)** or **Oak Room (Map 12)** at the Algonquin Hotel. But for top cabaret talent at affordable prices, go directly to **The Metropolitan Room (Map 9)**.

If you're seeking more R&B or soul, check out the **Apollo Theater (Map 19)**, though they mostly get "oldies" acts. The Apollo's Amateur Night on Wednesday is your chance to see some up-and-comers. Both the **Bowery Poetry**

Club (Map 6) and **The Pyramid Club (Map 7)** have open mic MC'ing nights. Many dance clubs feature hip-hop DJs.

Barbes (Map 33) in Park Slope hosts a whole palette of "world music" (for lack of a better term), including Latin American, European, and traditional US styles, plus more experimental fare. For more sounds of the south, **SOB's (Map 5)** has live South American music and dancing and **Remy Lounge (Map 1)** has DJs spinning Latin pop, house, salsa, merengue, and more. **Nublu (Map 7)** is always reliable for a fun and sweaty night, especially on Wednesdays when they feature Brazilian bands and DJs.

Map 1 • Financial District

Heartland Brewery	93 South St	646-572-2337	Heartland HeartLAND HEARTLAND!
John Street Bar & Grill	17 John St	212-349-3278	Nightmarish underground nonsense.
Killarney Rose	80 Beaver St	212-422-1486	Irish pub where you can pregame for the Staten Island Ferry.
Liquid Assets	55 Church St	212-693-2001	Plush seating and soft lighting.
Papoo's	55 Broadway	212-809-3150	Popular Wall Street bar.
Ryan Maguire's Ale House	28 Cliff St	212-566-6906	Decent Irish pub.
Ryan's Sports Bar & Restaurant	46 Gold St	212-385-6044	Downtown sports bar.
Ulysses	95 Pearl St	212-482-0400	Slightly hipper downtown bar.
Whitehorse Tavern	25 Bridge St	212-668-9046	Downtown dive.

Map 2 • TriBeCa

Brandy Library	25 N Moore St	212-226-5545	Refined but cozy with lots of free tasting events.
Bubble Lounge	228 W Broadway	212-431-3433	Champagne bar.
Church Lounge	25 Walker St	212-519-6600	Luxurious space with pricey drinks and occasional live music.
Circa Tabac	32 Watts St	212-941-1781	Smoker-friendly lounge.
Lucky Strike	59 Grand St	212-941-0772	Hipsters, locals, ex-smoky.
Naked Lunch	17 Thompson St	212-343-0828	Average lounge.
Nancy Whisky Pub	1 Lispenard St	212-226-9943	Good dive.
Puffy's Tavern	81 Hudson St	212-227-3912	Suits, old timers, and hipsters.
Roulette	20 Greene St	212-219-8242	For the experimental at heart.
Soho Grand Hotel	310 W Broadway	212-965-3000	Swank sophistication.
The Tank	279 Church St	212-563-6269	Major downtown destination for experimental music.
Tribeca Tavern & Caf^ua	247 W Broadway	212-941-7671	Good enough for us.
Walker's	16 N Moore St	212-941-0142	Where old and new Tribeca neighbors mix.

Map 3 • City Hall / Chinatown

The Beekman Pub	15 Beekman St	212-732-7333	Guinness on tap and karaoke nights.
Capitale	130 Bowery	212-334-5500	Formerly the Bowery Savings Bank. Cool space.
Experimental Intermedia	224 Centre St	212-431-5127	Experimental art/performance art shows involving a variety of artistic media.
Happy Ending	302 Broome St	212-334-9676	Still taking the edge off.
Knitting Factory	74 Leonard St	212-219-3132	Great downstairs bar.
Martginetti Downstairs (Belgrade)	1 Cleveland Pl	212-680-5601	My bonus is bigger than yours. Barbour jacket required.
Metropolitan Improvement Company	3 Madison St	212 964-0422	Where the cops drink.
Milk & Honey	134 Eldridge St		Good luck finding the phone number.
The Paris Café	119 South St	212-240-9797	By far the best bar in a 10-block radius.
Winnie's	104 Bayard St	212-732-2384	Chinese gangster karaoke!

Map 4 • Lower East Side

Bacaro	136 Division St	212-941-5060	Wine and pretty snacks from Venice.
Bar 169	169 E Broadway	212-473-8866	Sometimes good, sometimes not.
Clandestino	35 Canal St	212-475-5505	Pate and wine, anyone?

403

Arts & Entertainment • **Nightlife**

Map 4 • Lower East Side—*continued*

Good World	3 Orchard St	212-925-9975	NFT staff pick for drinking after work. Nice patio.
King Size	21 Essex St	212-995-5464	Laid-back hipsters groove to funky beats.
Lolita	266 Broome St	212-966-7223	Hipster-haven.
Roots & Vine	409 Grand St	212-260-2363	Great wine bar.

Map 5 • West Village

Ara	24 9th Ave	212-242-8642	Unpretentious wine bar in a pretentious neighborhood.
Art Bar	52 8th Ave	212-727-0244	Great spaces, cool crowd.
Arthur's Tavern	57 Grove St	212-675-6879	Featuring great jazz and blues since 1937.
Automatic Slims	733 Washington St	212-645-8660	LOUD. Yes, that loud.
Duplex	61 Christopher St	212-255-5438	Everything's still fun.
The Ear Inn	326 Spring St	212-226-9060	2nd oldest bar in NYC. A great place.
Employees Only	510 Hudson St	212-242-3021	Classy cocktails for big bucks.
The Four-Faced Liar	165 W 4th St	212-366-0608	A spirited neighborhood bar with wonderfully friendly bartenders.
Gaslight Lounge	400 W 14th St	212-807-8444	Laidback atmo.
Henrietta Hudson	438 Hudson St	212-924-3347	Good lesbian vibe.
Hudson Bar and Books	636 Hudson St	212-229-2642	Like *Cheers* for a hipper, more sophisticated crowd.
Johnny's Bar	90 Greenwich Ave	212-741-5279	Occasional celeb sightings at this popular dive.
Kettle of Fish	59 Christopher St	212-414-2278	Cozy couches and darts.
Lotus	409 W 14th St	212-243-4420	Don't forget your Seven jeans.
The Otherroom	143 Perry St	212-645-9758	Surprisingly decent beer selection with great, low-key vibe.
SOB's	204 Varick St	212-243-4940	World music venue with salsa lessons on Mondays.
Stonewall Inn	53 Christopher St	212-488-2705	From the L to the GB and T, this is where it all began.
Turks and Frogs	323 W 11th St		Wine bar off the beaten track.
Village Vanguard	178 7th Ave S	212-255-4037	Classic NYC jazz venue. Not to be missed.
Vol de Nuit	148 W 4th St	212-982-3388	Belgian beers, cool vibe.
White Horse Tavern	567 Hudson St	212-243-9260	Another NYC classic.

Map 6 • Washington Square / NYU / NoHo / SoHo

Beauty Bar	231 E 14th St	212-539-1389	Just a little off the top, dahling?
Blue & Gold	79 E 7th St	212-473-8918	Another fine East Village dive.
Bowery Ballroom	6 Delancey St	212-533-2111	Great space that attracts great bands.
Bowery Poetry Club	308 Bowery	212-614-0505	Slam poetry.
Decibel	240 E 9th St	212-979-2733	Hip, underground sake bar.
Fanelli's	94 Prince St	212-226-9412	Old-time SoHo haunt. Nice tiles.
Grassroots Tavern	20 St Marks Pl	212-475-9443	That mass of fur in the corner is a cat.
Holiday Lounge	75 St Marks Pl	212-777-9637	Where to go to lose your soul.
Joe's Pub	425 Lafayette St	212-539-8776	Good acts in problematic space.
KGB	85 E 4th St	212-505-3360	Former CP HQ. Meet your comrades.
Marion's Continental	354 Bowery	212-475-7621	Classic cocktails with occasional live tunes.
Mars Bar	25 E 1st St	212-473-9842	The king of grungy bars. Recommended.
Milady's	160 Prince St	212-226-9340	The only bar of its kind in this 'hood.
Milano's	51 E Houston	212-226-8844	Grungy, narrow, awesome.
Nevada Smith's	74 3rd Ave	212-982-2591	Goooaaaaaalllllll.!
Pravda	281 Lafayette St	212-226-4944	Sophisticated lounge serving up inventive martinis.
Red Bench	107 Sullivan St	212-274-9120	Tiny, classy, quiet (sometimes).
Rififi	332 E 11th St	212-677-1027	Decent dancing.
Sweet & Vicious	5 Spring St	212-334-7915	Great outdoor space.
Webster Hall	125 E 11th St	212-353-1600	Dance club/ music venue. Amateur strip night.

Map 7 • East Village / Lower East Side

2A	25 Avenue A	212-505-2466	Great upstairs space.
7B (Horseshoe Bar)	108 Avenue B	212-473-8840	*Godfather II* shot here. What can be bad?
Ace Bar	531 E 5th St	212-979-8476	Darts, pinball, pool, and even skee-ball!
Arlene's Grocery	95 Stanton St	212-995-1652	Cheap live tunes.
Back Room	102 Norfolk St	212-228-5098	The secret room is behind a bookcase.
Barramundi	67 Clinton St	212-529-6900	Great garden in summer.
Bua	122 St Marks Pl	212-979-6276	Neighborhood bar during the week, mobs of pretty people on the weekend.
Cake Shop	152 Ludlow St	212-253-0036	Coffee, records, beer, rock shows, and a "Most Radical Jukebox."
Dark Room	165 Ludlow St	212-353-0536	For dark deeds. Ask Lindsay Lohan.
Heathers	506 E 13th St	212-254-0979	Gluten-free booze!
Hi-Fi	169 Avenue A	212-420-8392	THE best jukebox in town.
I Coppi	432 E 9th St	212-254-2263	Go with your date and an empty stomach.
Joe's Bar	520 E 6th St	212-473-9093	Classic neighborhood hangout. A favorite.
Lakeside Lounge	162 Avenue B	212-529-8463	Great jukebox, live music, décor, everything.
The Magician	118 Rivington St	212-673-7851	Hipster haven.
Mama's Bar	34 Avenue B	212-777-5729	Laid-back respite from the Avenue B craziness, with food from Mama's next door.
Manitoba's	99 Avenue B	212-982-2511	Punk scene.
Marshall Stack	66 Rivington St	212-228-4667	Winner for best bar that seemed like it would be awful.
Max Fish	178 Ludlow St	212-529-3959	Where the musicians go.

Mercury Lounge	217 E Houston St	212-260-4700	Rock venue with occasional top-notch acts.
Mona's	224 Avenue B	212-353-3780	Depressing. Recommended.
Motor City	127 Ludlow St	212-358-1595	Faux biker bar. Still good, though.
NuBlu	62 Avenue C	212-979-9925	Sexy lounge with world music, nice ambience, and outdoor porch.
Nuyorican Poet's Café	236 E 3rd St	212-505-8183	Slam poetry.
Parkside Lounge	317 E Houston St	212-673-6270	Good basic bar, live acts in the back.
The Stone	Avenue C & E 2nd St		All the front door proceeds go to the avant-garde and experimental artists, so go. Right now.
Ten Degrees	121 St Marks Pl		Cozy wine bar with live jazz on Wednesdays.
Verlaine	110 Rivington St	212-614-2494	Mellow, French-Vietnamese inspired bar with deceptively sweet cocktails.
Welcome to the Johnsons	123 Rivington St	212-420-9911	Great décor, but too crowded mostly.
Zum Schneider	107 Avenue C	212-598-1098	Get weisse, man. Prost.

Map 8 • Chelsea

Billymark's West	332 9th Ave	212-629-0118	Down and dirty dive.
Chelsea Brewing Company	Pier 59	212-336-6440	When you're done playing basketball.
Gym Sports Bar	167 8th Ave	212-337-2439	Where the boys go to watch the game…and each other.
Half King	505 W 23rd St	212-462-4300	Always the perfect drinking choice in Chelsea. Amazing brunch.
Hammerstein Ballroom	311 W 34th St	212-279-7740	Lofty rock venue.
Highline Ballroom	431 W 16th St	212-414-5994	New venue for rock, folk, dance, whatever.
The Kitchen	512 W 19th St	212-255-5793	Experimental visual and performing arts.
Molly Wee Pub	402 8th Ave	212-967-2627	You just need a pint after a trip to Penn Station.
The Park	118 10th Ave	212-352-3313	Good patio.
Red Rock West	457 W 17th St	212-366-5359	F'king loud!
West Side Tavern	360 W 23rd St	212-366-3738	Local mixture.

Map 9 • Flatiron / Lower Midtown

Avalon	660 6th Ave	212-807-7780	You gotta go at least once.
Club Shelter	20 W 39th St	646-862-6117	Dance until dawn.
Cutting Room	19 W 24th St	212-691-1900	Large, usually mellow vibe.
Live Bait	14 E 23rd St	212-353-2400	Still a great feel. A mainstay.
Merchants	112 7th Ave	212-366-7267	Good mixed space.
Metropolitan Room	34 W 22nd St	212-206-0440	Best cabaret club in the city.
Old Town Bar & Restaurant	45 E 18th St	212-529-6732	Excellent old-NY bar.
Peter McManus	152 7th Ave	212-929-9691	Refreshingly basic.
Silver Swan	41 E 20th St	212-254-3611	Beer, brats, 'n schnitzel.
Sky Bar at La Quinta	17 W 32nd St	212-736-1600	Rooftop bar with affordable drinks and a kickass view of the ESB.
Splash Bar	50 W 17th St	212-691-0073	Men dancing in waterfalls.
Under The Volcano	12 E 36th St	212-213-0093	Relaxed, subdued; large selection of tequilas.
Wakamba Cocktail Lounge	543 8th Ave	212-564-2042	Plastic palm trees and provocatively-clad barmaids.

Map 10 • Murray Hill / Gramercy

Failte Irish Whiskey Bar	531 2nd Ave	212-725-9440	Sip Guiness by the fire. Shoot a round of pool. A favorite of Irish ex-pats.
The Fillmore New York at Irving Plaza	17 Irving Pl	212-777-6800	Staple rock venue.
The Jazz Standard	116 E 27th St	212-576-2232	Solid shows. BBQ upstairs!
McSwiggan's	393 2nd Ave	212-725-8740	One of the best dive bars on the island.
Molly's	287 3rd Ave	212-889-3361	Great Irish pub with a fireplace.
Paddy Reilly's Music Bar	519 2nd Ave	212-686-1210	Sunday night means pints of Guinness and live Irish fiddlin'.
Pete's Tavern	129 E 18th St	212-473-7676	Where O Henry hung out. As should you, at least once.
Pug Uglies	257 3rd Ave	212-780-1944	Full length shuffle board table!
Revival	129 E 15th St	212-253-8061	Low maintenance beer drinking.
Rodeo	375 3rd Ave	212-683-6500	As close to a honky-tonk as you'll get, partner.
Rolf's	281 3rd Ave	212-477-4750	December holiday visit is a must for some German bier.
Waterfront Ale House	540 2nd Ave	212-696-4104	Decent local vibe.
Whiskey River	575 2nd Ave	212-679-6799	Dive bar. Neighborhood joint. Great beer selection.

Map 11 • Hell's Kitchen

Birdland	315 W 44th St	212-581-3080	Top-notch jazz.
Don't Tell Mama	343 W 46th St	212-757-0788	Good cabaret space.
House of Brews	363 W 46th St	212-245-0551	Fratty but friendly atmosphere, great beer selection.
Hudson Hotel Library	356 W 58th St	212-554-6000	Super-super-super pretentious.
Rudy's Bar & Grill	627 9th Ave	212-974-9169	Classic Hell's Kitchen. Recommended.
Vintage	753 9th Ave	212-581-4655	Ginormous martini menu. Good beers.
Xth	642 10th Ave	212-245-9088	Good local vibe.

Map 12 • Midtown

Blue Bar	59 W 44th St	212-842-6800	If you're in the mood for a Harvey Wallbanger.
China Club	268 W 47th St	212-398-3800	Think *Night at the Roxbury*.

Arts & Entertainment · **Nightlife**

Map 12 · Midtown—*continued*

Flute	205 W 54th St	212-265-5169	Munch on strawberries and cream with your bubbly.
Iridium	1650 Broadway	212-582-2121	Good mainstream jazz venue. Pricey.
Jimmy's Corner	140 W 44th St	212-221-9510	This cozy dive is the only place you should be tippling in Times Square, trust us.
Oak Room	59 W 44th St	212-840-6800	Classic and cozy cabaret.
Paramount Bar	235 W 46th St	212-764-5500	Tiny, pretentious, unavoidable.
Roseland	239 W 52nd St	212-247-0200	Big-time rock venue.
The Royalton	44 W 44th St	212-869-4400	Philippe Starck is the SH—!
Russian Vodka Room	265 W 52nd St	212-307-5835	Russian molls and cranberry vodka. Awesome.
St Andrews	120 W 44th St	212-840-8413	Great bar in the front of this restaurant.
Town Hall	123 W 43rd St	212-840-2824	Attracts great musical acts.

Map 13 · East Midtown

Blarney Stone	710 3rd Ave	212-490-0457	The only bar in purgatory.
The Campbell Apartment	Grand Central Terminal	212-953-0409	Awesome space, awesomely snooty!
Metro 53	307 E 53rd St	212-838-0007	Celebrities and suits.
Sutton Place	1015 2nd Ave	212-207-3777	Fabulous roofdeck deck is it worth the climb.

Map 14 · Upper West Side (Lower)

Beacon Theater	2124 Broadway	212-465-6500	Official venue of the Allman Bros.
Café Des Artistes	1 W 67th St	212-877-3500	Endless wine menu. Snack on hard-boiled eggs at the bar.
Dead Poet	450 Amsterdam Ave	212-595-5670	Good Irish feel.
Dublin House	225 W 79th St	212-874-9528	Great dingy Irish pub. Recommended.
Emerald Inn	205 Columbus Ave	212-874-8840	Another good Irish pub!
The Evelyn Lounge	380 Columbus Ave	212-724-2363	Candlelight upstairs, dancing downstairs.
Hi Life Bar & Grill	477 Amsterdam Ave	212-787-7199	Not a bad option for this part of town.
Jake's Dilemma	430 Amsterdam Ave	212-580-0556	Sort of okay sometimes.
P&G	279 Amsterdam Ave	212-874-8568	Depressing dive. Highly recommended.
Yogi's	2156 Broadway	212-873-9852	Cheap drinks and a country-western jukebox.

Map 15 · Upper East Side (Lower)

Accademia di Vino	1081 3rd Ave	212-888-6333	Wine bar. Laid back. Affordable. Uptown. Believe it.
The Bar at Etats-Unis	247 E 81st St	212-396-9928	Hands down the best bar eats you'll find anywhere.
Bemelmans Bar	35 E 76th St	212-744-1600	Features lovely mural by creator of Madeline books, Ludwig Bemelman.
Brandy's Piano Bar	235 E 84th St	212-650-1944	Good ol' New York vibe.
Café Carlyle	35 E 76th St	212-744-1600	Classic cabaret venue. Hellishly expensive.
Club Macanudo	26 E 63rd St	212-752-8200	A perfect environment for smokers (and non-smokers).
Feinstein's at the Regency	540 Park Ave	212-339-4095	Cabaret.
Finnegan's Wake	1361 1st Ave	212-737-3664	Standard Irish pub. Therefore, good.
Lexington Bar & Books	1020 Lexington Ave	212-717-3902	Sexy spot to sip cognac and smoke a stogie. Stupid dress code policy.
Pudding Stone's Wine Bar	1457 3rd Ave	212-717-5797	Long-countered locale to sip various vinos by the glass (or bottle).
Ryan's Daughter	350 E 85th St	212-628-2613	Free chips!
Subway Inn	143 E 60th St	212-223-8929	Sad, bad, glare, worn-out, ugh. Totally great.
Trinity Pub	299 E 84th St	212-327-4450	Low on the UES meathead scale.
Vudu	1487 2nd Ave	212-249-9540	They dance on the Upper East Side?

Map 16 · Upper West Side (Upper)

Abbey Pub	237 W 105th St	212-222-8713	Cozy Columbia hangout.
Broadway Dive	2662 Broadway	212-865-2662	Where everyone who reads this book goes.
The Ding Dong Lounge	929 Columbus Ave	212-663-2600	Downtown punk brought Uptown. Happy hour all day Tuesdays.
Dive Bar	732 Amsterdam Ave	212-749-4358	Columbia hangout.
La Negrita	999 Columbus Ave	212-961-1676	Latin-themed cocktails.
The Parlour	250 W 86th St	212-580-8923	Irish pub, two spaces, good hangout.
Sip	998 Amsterdam Ave	212-316-2747	Organic coffee by day, cool mojitos by night.
Smoke	2751 Broadway	212-864-6662	Local jazz hangout.

Map 17 · Upper East Side / East Harlem

Auction House	300 E 89th St	212-427-4458	Stylin' uptown lounge.
Cavatappo Wine Bar	1728 2nd Ave	212-426-0919	Jewel-box-sized spot to sip wine and nibble appetizers.
FB Lounge	172 E 106th St	212-410-7292	Live Latin jazz, Afrocaribbean, and world beats. Sweet.
Kinsale Tavern	1672 3rd Ave	212-348-4370	Right-off-the-boat Irish staff. Good beers.
Marty O'Brien's	1696 2nd Ave	212-722-3889	Where kilted firefighters go to enjoy pints on St. Paddy's.
Phil Hughes	1682 1st Ave	212-722-9415	An honest-to-god dive bar on the UES.
Rathbones Pub	1702 2nd Ave	212-369-7361	Basic pub.
Reif's Tavern	302 E 92nd St	212-426-0519	Dive-o-rama since 1942.
Tool Box	1742 2nd Ave	212-348-1288	Perhaps the only official gay bar on the UES.

Arts & Entertainment · **Nightlife**

Map 18 · Columbia / Morningside Heights

1020 Bar	1020 Amsterdam Ave	212-531-3468	Columbia dive. NFT pick.
Cotton Club	656 W 125th St	212-663-7980	Good, fun swingin' uptown joint.
Heights Bar & Grill	2867 Broadway	212-866-7035	Fun rooftop bar in summer.
Saurin Parke Caf^ua	301 W 110th St	212-222-0683	Caffeinated Columbia students, snacks, wine, beer.
Soundz Lounge	3155 Broadway	212-537-7660	Great sounds in semi-crowded venue.

Map 19 · Harlem (Lower)

Apollo Theater	253 W 125th St	212-531-5300	The one and only.
The Den	2150 5th Ave	212-234-3045	Welcome addition to the Harlem scene.
Lenox Lounge	288 Lenox Ave	212-427-0253	Old-time Harlem hangout, recently redone.
Moca Bar & Grill	2210 Frederick Douglass Blvd	212-665-8081	Serving up hip hop classics and R&B.

Map 20 · El Barrio / East Harlem

Café Creole	2167 3rd Ave	212-876-8838	Creole cuisine and live entertainment, satisfaction guaranteed!
Camaradas	2241 1st Ave	212-348-2703	Live music and Puerto Rican tapas.
Dexy's Lounge	2171 2nd Ave		Friendly watering hole for new uptowners.
Mojitos	227 E 116th St	212-828-8635	Good happy hour downstairs.
Orbit East Harlem	2257 1st Ave	212-348-7818	We like it—dinner, brunch, music, etc.
Ragg's Pub	101 E 119th St	212-534-9681	Irish pub in the heart of Harlem! Must be the nearby police precinct.

Map 21 · Manhattanville / Hamilton Heights

St Nick's Pub	773 St Nicholas Ave	212-283-9728	Great vibe, go for African Saturday nights.

Map 24 · Fort George / Fort Tryon

Umbrella Bar & Lounge	440 W 202nd St	212-942-5921

Map 25 · Inwood

Keenan's Bar	4878 Broadway	212-567-9016	A friendly neighborhood bar.
Piper's Kilt	4944 Broadway	212-569-7071	Irish pub and sports bar.

Battery Park City

Rise Bar	2 West St	212-344-0800	Great harbor and park views.

Map 26 · Astoria

Avenue Café	35-27 30th Ave	718-278-6967	Crêpes, frappés, good sandwiches, and transplanted Europeans.
Bohemian Hall & Beer Garden	29-19 24th Ave	718-274-4925	Nearly a century old, there's room for 500 drinkers in the garden.
Brick Café	30-95 33rd St	718-267-2735	Faux French café with lovely outdoor seating.
Café Bar	32-90 36th St	718-204-5273	Funky place for coffee or cocktails serving Mediterranean food.
Crescent Lounge	32-05 Crescent St	718-606-9705	Friendly, low-key bar with a long list of martinis and a bathroom inexplicably nicer than yours at home.
Cronin & Phelan	38-14 Broadway	718-545-8999	Open mic, live music, and karaoke! Irish you'd buy me another ale.
Fatty's Café	25-01 Ditmars Blvd	718-267-7071	Great garden.
Gilbey's of Astoria	32-01 Broadway	718-545-8567	The local yokels and cheap brews will have you saying, "Gib me's another beer."
Hell Gate Social	12-21 Astoria Blvd	718-204-8313	A decent club/lounge in an unlikely location with DJs and film screenings.
Irish Rover	37-18 28th Ave	718-278-9372	A well-loved hangout with live music, quiz nights, and Irish sports.
Mary McGuire's	38-04 Broadway	718-728-3434	Irish pub, OTB, and great burgers.
McCaffrey & Burke	28-54 31st St	718-278-9751	Dive bar complete with colorful regulars, billiards, and darts.
McCann's Pub & Grill	36-15 Ditmars Blvd	718-278-2621	Bustling Irish sports bar that attracts the young, the loud, and the thirsty.
Rapture	34-27 28th Ave	718-626-8044	Swank lounge with a Manhattan vibe, prices, and rockstar after-hours.
Rendezvous	34-13 Broadway	718-728-4268	Another lame Euro lounge.
The Sparrow	24-01 29th St	718-606-2260	A hipster outpost from the folks who brought us Tupelo.

Map 27 · Long Island City

The Cave	10-93 Jackson Ave	718-706-8783	Subterranean lounge with music and performance nights.
Domaine Bar a Vins	50-04 Vernon Blvd	718-784-2350	Great new wine bar from the people who brought you Tournesol, with oysters to boot.
Dominie's Hoek	48-17 Vernon Blvd	718-706-6531	No-frills bar with backyard patio and live music.

407

Arts & Entertainment · **Nightlife**

Map 27 · Long Island City—*continued*

LIC Bar	45-58 Vernon Blvd	718-786-5400	Vintage New York saloon with serene backyard BBQ patio and photo booth.
Lounge 47	47-10 Vernon Blvd	718-937-2044	Brady Bunch decor, solid food, nice garden.
McReilly's	46-42 Vernon Blvd	718-786-7727	Local pub with a sassy brogue and the best burgers in LIC.
PJ Leahy's	50-02 Vernon Blvd	718-472-5131	Sports bar with a flat-screen TV at every table.
Shannon Pot	45-06 Davis St	718-786-6992	Irish dive bar, nothing more, nothing less.
Sunswick Limited	35-02 35th St	718-752-0620	After the AMMI, move your image to the place with 25 beers on tap.
Water Taxi Beach Harry's	203 Borden Ave	n/a	Tropical drinks, grilled munchies, and Pabst Blue with a view from a man-made beach.

Map 28 · Greenpoint

Enid's	560 Manhattan Ave	718-349-3859	Greenpoint's finest hipster stand-by.
Europa	98 Meserole Ave	718-383-5723	Strobe light extravaganza.
Lost and Found	113 Franklin St	718-383-6000	Skee-ball, Big Buck Hunter, free hot dogs, and occasional live bands.
The Mark Bar	1025 Manhattan Ave	718-349-2340	Wide selection of beer.
Matchless	557 Manhattan Ave	718-383-5333	Rock 'n' roll trivia nights are a must.
Pencil Factory	142 Franklin St	718-609-5858	Great beer; great vibe.
Studio B	259 Banker St	718-389-1880	Fluorescent lights, eclectic bands, and DJs.
Tommy's Tavern	1041 Manhattan Ave	718-383-9699	Super-dive with live music on weekends.
Warsaw	261 Driggs Ave	718-387-0505	Brooklyn's best concert venue.

Map 29 · Williamsburg

The Abbey	536 Driggs Ave	718-599-4400	Great jukebox and staff.
Alligator Lounge	600 Metropolitan Ave	718-599-4440	Corny bar, but free pizza is free pizza.
Barcade	388 Union Ave	718-302-6464	Paradise for '80s console champions and craft-beer guzzlers.
Bembe	81 S 6th St	718-387-5389	Hookahville.
Black Betty	366 Metropolitan Ave	718-599-0243	Dark, exotic, and inviting.
Charleston	174 Bedford Ave		Still going.
Clem's	264 Grand St	718-387-9617	Classic narrow bar space and good drink specials make this a neighborhood staple.
Daddy's	437 Graham Ave	718-609-6388	Friendly hipster hideaway.
East River Bar	97 S 6th St	718-302-0511	Fun interior, patio, and live music.
Greenpoint Tavern	188 Bedford Ave	718-384-9539	Cheap beer in Styrofoam cups.
The Gutter	200 N 14th St	718-387-3585	Vintage style bowling alley with great brews on tap—what could be better?
Huckleberry Bar	588 Grand St	718-218-8555	Solid cocktails, nice garden out back.
Iona	180 Grand St	718-384-5008	Plenty of choices on tap.
Larry Lawrence	295 Grand St	718-218-7866	Laid-back bar with a lovely loft for smokers.
The Levee	212 Berry St	718-218-8787	Formerly Cokies, now a laid back vibe with free cheese balls.
Mugs Ale House	125 Bedford Ave	718-486-8232	Surprisingly good food, great beer selection, cheap.
Music Hall of Williamsburg	66 N 6th St	212-260-4700	Formerly Northsix, now Brooklyn's Bowery Ballroom.
Pete's Candy Store	709 Lorimer St	718-302-3770	Live music, trivia nights, awesome back room, and Scrabble.
Royal Oak	594 Union Ave	718-388-3884	It seems like everybody ends up here.
Savalas	285 Bedford Ave	718-599-5565	A narrow lounge, but people find space to dance.
Spuyten Duyvil	359 Metropolitan Ave	718-963-4140	Join the Belgian beer cult.
Trash	256 Grand St	718-599-1000	Punk, rock, PBR, and free tater tots.
Turkey's Nest	94 Bedford Ave	718-384-9774	Best dive in Williamsburg.
Union Pool	484 Union Ave	718-609-0484	Good starting point—or finishing point.
Zebulon	258 Wythe Ave	718-218-6934	World-fusion and jazz music with Mediterranean bar food.

Map 30 · Brooklyn Heights / DUMBO / Downtown

68 Jay Street Bar	68 Jay St	718-260-8207	Arty local bar.
Henry St Ale House	62 Henry St	718-522-4801	Cozy, dark space with good selections on tap.
Jack the Horse Tavern	66 Hicks St	718-852-5084	Oustanding upscale pub/New American cuisine, great feel.
Low Bar	81 Washington St	718-222-1569	Asian-themed basement bar.
Okeefe's	62 Court St	718-855-8751	Sports bar (large Mets following). Surprisingly decent food.
St Ann's Warehouse	38 Water St	718-254-8779	Live music, theater. Challenging entertainment.
Water Street Bar	66 Water St	718-625-9352	Roomy Irish pub.

Map 31 · Fort Greene / Clinton Hill

The Alibi	242 Dekalb Ave	718-783-8519	Real deal neighborhood bar.
BAMcafé	30 Lafayette Ave	718-636-4100	Fine food, cocktails, and live music in a classy cavernous space.
Frank's Lounge	660 Fulton St	718-625-9339	When you need to get funky.
Grand Dakar	285 Grand Ave	718-398-8900	Occasional live music; skip the jazz but check out the African sets.
Moe's	80 Lafayette Ave	718-797-9536	Laid-back friendly fun.
Reign Bar & Lounge	46 Washington Ave	718-643-7344	Posh, pricey club.
Sputnik	262 Taaffe Pl	718-398-6666	Fabulously furnished Pratt hangout.
Stonehome Wine Bar	87 Lafayette Ave	718-624-9443	Dark cave for serious oenophiles.
Thomas Beisl	25 Lafayette Ave	718-222-5800	Straight outta Vienna.

Map 32 • BoCoCa / Red Hook

Abilene	442 Court St	718-522-6900	Cozy and unpretentious. Drink specials galore.
Black Mountain Wine House	415 Union St	718-395-2614	Try the Lebanese wine!
Boat	175 Smith St	718-254-0607	Dank, dark and friendly. Nice tunes to boot.
Brazen Head	228 Atlantic Ave	718-488-0430	Cask ale, mixed crowd.
Brooklyn Inn	148 Hoyt St	718-625-9741	When you're feeling nostalgic.
Brooklyn Social	335 Smith St	718-858-7758	Old boy's lounge revamped. Cocktails still the same. NFT Pick.
Cody's Bar & Grill	154 Court St	718-852-6115	Great sports bar. Seriously.
Downtown Bar & Grill	160 Court St	718-625 2835	Gets the package games. More beers than God intended for man.
Floyd	131 Atlantic Ave	718-858-5810	Indoor bocce ball court!
Gowanus Yacht Club	323 Smith St	718-246-1321	Dogs, burgers, and beer. Love it.
Issue Project Room	232 3rd St	718-330-0313	Art and performance space next to Gowanus Canal.
Kili	81 Hoyt St	718-855-5574	Nice space and chilled vibe.
Last Exit	136 Atlantic Ave	718-222-9198	Still trying to win trivia night. $10 pails of PBR.
Magnetic Field	97 Atlantic Ave	718-834-0069	Great décor, live music on the weekends.
Montero Bar and Grill	73 Atlantic Ave	718-624-9799	A taste of what things used to be like.
Moonshine	317 Columbia St	718-422-0563	You supply the meat, they supply the grill.
PJ Hanley's	449 Court St	718-797-4057	Booze since 1874.
Red Hook Bait & Tackle	320 Van Brunt St	718-797-4892	Kitschy, comfy pub with cheap drinks and good beers on tap.
Rocky Sullivan's	34 Van Dyke St	718-246-8050	The six-point portfolio is on tap–a Red Hook must.
Sugar Lounge	147 Columbia St	718-643-2880	Hammocks, hummus, and happy people.
Sunny's	253 Conover St	718-625-8211	No longer pay-what-you-wish, but still cheap and good.
Tini Wine Bar & Café	414 Van Brunt St	718-855-4206	Wine-soaked snacking on the Red Hook waterfront.
Waterfront Ale House	155 Atlantic Ave	718-522-3794	Renowned burgers and sizable beer list.

Map 33 • Park Slope / Prospect Heights / Windsor Terrace

Bar Toto	411 11th St	718-768-4698	Great bar food.
Barbes	376 9th St	718-965-9177	Smart-looking space with eclectic entertainment. Recommended.
Beast	638 Bergen St	718-399-6855	Great, great local vibe.
Buttermilk	577 5th Ave	718-788-6297	Hippest on the block.
Canal Bar	270 3rd Ave	718-246-0011	Dive near the Gowanus, but not into it.
The Cherry Tree	65 4th Ave	718-399-1353	Rowdy Irish pub with a stately back yard.
Commonwealth	497 5th Ave	718-768-2040	So many beers, so little time.
Flatbush Farm	76 St Marks Ave	718-622-3276	Great bar, great food, great everything, really.
Fourth Avenue Pub	76 4th Ave	718-643-2273	1. Toss glass. 2. Drink fine draft beer. 3. Repeat.
Freddy's Bar and Backroom	485 Dean St	718-622-7035	Music and reading for finger-snapping hepcats.
The Gate	321 5th Ave	718-768-4329	Large outdoor area. Twenty beers on tap.
Ginger's	363 5th Ave	718-788-0924	Nice and casual for center Slope.
Good Coffeehouse Music Parlor	53 Prospect Park West	718-768-2972	Brooklyn's home for acoustic roots music.
Great Lakes	284 5th Ave	718-499-3710	Laid-back hipster dive. Great jukebox, cheap beer.
Hank's Saloon	46 3rd Ave	718-625-8003	Sweaty, hillbillyesque.
Lighthouse Tavern	243 5th Ave	718-788-8070	Don't miss Local Yokel night every Monday.
Loki Lounge	304 5th Ave	718-965-9600	Darts and billiards tone down the classic wood bar. Good music.
O'Connor's	39 5th Ave	718-783-9721	Friendly dive in need of a designer.
Pacific Standard	82 4th Ave	718-858-1951	Drinking and board games most certainly mix.
Park Slope Ale House	356 6th Ave	718-788-1756	Good pub grub and beer selection.
Patio Lounge	179 5th Ave	718-857-3477	Verdant boozing.
Puppet's Jazz Bar	294 5th Ave	718-499-2627	Jazz and wine preside in this wee club.
Soda	629 Vanderbilt Ave	718-230-8393	Nice summer drinkin' spot. NFT pick.
Southpaw	125 5th Ave	718-230-0236	Best live music in the Slope.
Timboo's	477 5th Ave	718-788-9782	Nothin' fancy—just booze, TVs and talk of gentrification.
Union Hall	702 Union St	718-638-4400	Quirky spot for indie shows and stuffed birds.

Map 34 • Hoboken

City Bistro	56 14th St	201-963-8200	Great summer scene, rooftop views to the city.
Leo's Grandezvous	200 Grand St	201-659-9467	Hoboken's Rat Pack bar. Bring a dame and have some booze.
Maxwell's	1039 Washington St	201-653-1703	A storied live music venue—if the band is good, it's worth the trek.
Oddfellows	80 River St	201-656-9009	Happening happy hour. Close to the PATH so it catches the commuter crowd.

Map 35 • Jersey City

Hamilton Park Ale House	708 Jersey Ave	201-659-9111	Relaxed *Cheers*-esque atmosphere with yummy food.
Lamp Post Bar and Grille	382 2nd St	201-222-1331	Look for the lamp post on the street to find this friendly neighborhood bar.
LITM	140 Newark Ave	201-536-5557	Artsy, laid-back lounge.
The Merchant	279 Grove St	201-200-0202	Classy bar where businessmen go to cut loose.
PJ Ryan's	172 1st St	201-239-7373	A real Irish pub—see your favorite sporting event w/ a pint.
White Star	230 Brunswick St	201-653-9234	Great bar and good eats.

We don't need to hear Liza Minelli or Frank Sinatra sing it to remember the famous line about New York City: "If I can make it there, I'll make it anywhere." A corollary of sorts might be, "If they'll make it anywhere, I can buy it there." From tasteful to tacky, classic to classless, delicious to dangerous, we've got it all: life-size stuffed animals, Ming vases, toys for, shall we say, adventurous adults, live eels, exotic spices, and even illegal fruits (but you didn't hear it here). It requires enormous self-restraint to take a walk, even just to the subway, and not buy something. And while we natives and traditionalists do occasionally lament the "mall-ification" of our fair city, we'll challenge anyone to find another place that combines convenience and quirkiness as well as this town does. You want Prada knock-offs? Chinatown. You want the real thing? Just walk north a few blocks. A real human skeleton? Cross the street. Homemade ricotta? It's practically next door. You can hunt for bargains or blow a year's salary in the blink of an eye. And even if you decide to leave your wallet at home in the interests of self-preservation, you can find endless entertainment in walking the streets and practicing the storied art of window-shopping.

Clothing and Accessories

Shopping for haute couture is no longer strictly an uptown affair, with a few high-end shops appearing in SoHo and the Meatpacking District, but the Upper East Side is still the ultimate destination for designer labels. Madison Avenue is the main artery, in the 50s, 60s, and 70s, rounded out by Fifth Avenue in the 50s and a few blocks east along 57th St. There you will find **Chanel (Map 12)**, **Burberry (Map 12)**, and all other names of that ilk. Take note, these stores still observe the age-old tradition, abandoned in most neighborhoods, of closing on Sundays. For department store shopping, try **Bloomingdale's (Maps 3, 15)** for the widest range of selection, **Macy's (Map 9)** if you're on a budget, **Lord & Taylor (Map 9)** and **Saks Fifth Avenue (Map 12)** for the classics, **Henri Bendel (Map 12)** and **Barneys (Map 15)** for trendier lines, and **Bergdorf Goodman (Map 12)** if money is no object. If you have the patience to deal with the crowds and sift through the merchandise to find bargains, **Century 21 (Map 1)** can yield great rewards of name brand clothing, shoes, make-up, accessories, and home wares at significantly discounted prices. For cheap and trendy, **H&M (Map 13, 19)** can't be beat. It's disposable clothing for the fashionistas, but be prepared to change in the aisles on crowded shopping days.

SoHo is one of the neighborhoods that's taken on features of an outdoor mall in recent years, with big chain stores taking the place of the smaller boutiques (and the few art galleries that survived the arrival of said boutiques). That said, if you can handle flocks of tourists, it's still a great place to shop because of the wide range of stores in a concentrated area (and plenty of cafés when you need to refuel). You'll find big names like **Prada (Map 6)**, whose Renzo Piano design draws as many visitors as Miuccia's clothes do. There's even the downtown branch of **Bloomingdale's (Map 3)**, a slightly hipper version of its Upper East Side big brother. In addition to the standards, you'll find many street vendors selling everything from handmade jewelry to floppy-eared children's hats. Some

of the quieter streets like Thompson, Sullivan, and Wooster appeal to the shopper who aims to avoid the chain stores. Take advantage of the fact that SoHo is densely packed and great for walking; just cruise the streets to discover hidden gems like **M0851 (Map 6)**, where you'll find elegant outwear and bags designed by a Canadian architect.

The West Village has its own enclave of hip clothing stores like **Stella McCartney (Map 5)**. Head northwest to the Meatpacking District and you can see the results of an impressive urban magic trick that transformed racks of hanging beef into racks of hanging jeans that cost $800. Check out the punk rock–inspired styles of **Alexander McQueen (Map 5)**, as well as the envelope-pushing and wallet-emptying department store **Jeffrey (Map 5)**, the subject of a reoccurring Saturday Night Live skit that's a send-up of the clerks' reputed snobbery. The other destinations for fashions from up-and-coming designers and great independent boutiques are: NoHo (the area north of Houston and east of Broadway), NoLita (north of Little Italy), and the East Village.

The Upper East Side (particularly along Madison Avenue in the East 80s) has a notable amount of designer consignment stores. **Bis Designer Resale (Map 15)** and others like it sell gently worn items from top tier designers like Chanel and Armani at a fraction of their original cost. You can also meander along "Thrift Row," a string of Upper East Side thrift shops on and near Third Avenue in the East 70s and 80s. Many of these shops, such as the **Spence-Chapin Thrift Shop (Map 17)**, carry a nice selection of designer clothing—not to mention the added bonus that the proceeds from your purchases go toward a good cause, like AIDS-related charities, cancer research, and adoption programs.

Vintage Shopping

The abundance of vintage shops—over 60 at last count—will impress any shopper, whether you're someone who's just looking for a unique piece for a special occasion or a professional stylist purchasing wardrobe for a period film. Though many vintage shops downtown have closed over the years due to astronomical rents, some holdouts deserve attention: **Fabulous Fanny's (Map 6)** in the East Village, **Frock (Map 7)** and **Edith Machinist (Map 7)** on the Lower East Side, **Screaming Mimi's (Map 6)** in NoHo, **What Comes Around Goes Around (Map 2)** in SoHo, **Family Jewels (Map 9)** and **Fisch for the Hip (Map 9)** in Chelsea. In Brooklyn, check out Williamsburg's **Beacon's Closet (Map 29)** and **Amarcord Vintage Fashion (Map 7, 29)**, and Park Slope's **Beacon's Closet (Map 33)**. You'll even find some relatively undiscovered options uptown. On the Upper East Side, check out **New York Vintage Club (Map 13)** and **Vintage Collections (Map 15)**. And don't forget the twice-yearly vintage couture and textiles auction at **Doyle New York (Map 17)**. On the Upper West Side, longtime vintage purveyor **Allan & Suzi (Map 14)** still holds court at the corner of Amsterdam and 80th Street. For you die-hards, be sure to attend the thrice-yearly Manhattan Vintage Clothing Show at the Metropolitan Pavilion, where over 75 dealers sell their vintage finery during two-day stints. And finally, there's always the Triple Pier Antiques

Show on the far West Side of Manhattan. It should go without saying that at all of the above-mentioned shops and venues, you must be prepared to pay the usual New York City premium.

Flea Markets, Street Vendors, Street Fairs & Bazaars

New Yorkers who once spent weekends perusing the eclectic finds in the asphalt lot at 26th Street and Sixth Avenue are still mourning the loss of the internationally known Annex Antique Fair & Flea Market. The good news is that many of the same vendors from Annex sell their wares at the **Annex/Hell's Kitchen Flea Market (Map 11)** on 39th Street between Ninth and Tenth Avenues. There are, of course, many other (albeit smaller) flea markets throughout the city, as well as numerous street fairs in various neighborhoods during warmer months. The best way to find them tends to be accidentally stumble upon them on an exploratory walk around town. A fantastic indoor flea market to add to your must-see list is **The Market NYC (Map 6)**, a refreshingly offbeat collection from young, local designers who aren't afraid to be truly creative. These places provide a cure for chain shopping boredom and the inevitable annoyance at seeing every third person wearing the same H&M shirt as you. Another fun option (particularly during the warmer months) is shopping street side from designers who sell their one-of-a-kind designs al fresco. You can't always identify them by name, but you can't miss their stands along Prince and Spring Streets in SoHo. Look for made-while-you-wait purses and belts, the scrap metal jewelry pieces, handmade leather-bound journals, and other singular and quirky items.

Sports

Paragon Sporting Goods (Map 9) in Union Square is hard to beat as a one-stop shop for all sports gear and accessories. They also take care of your recreational needs, with services like all-inclusive ski packages for Hunter Mountain and permitting for the NYC Parks Department tennis courts. **Sports Authority (Map 9, 13)**, **Foot Locker (Map 21, 23, 25)**, and **Modell's (Map 23)** provide a broad range of affordable sports clothing, shoes, and athletic equipment. **Blades Board & Skate (Map 14)** features groovy gear for boarding (both the wheeled and snow varieties) as well as a good selection of the latest equipment. **Everything Must Go (Map 20)**, a recently opened El Barrio skate store, carries skateboards and clothing—and has amassed a loyal neighborhood following. For the best cold weather and mountain gear, head to **Tents & Trails (Map 3)** or **Patagonia (Map 14)** (you can expect competitive prices at the former, but definitely not at the latter).

Housewares and Home Design

You can lose hours in **ABC Carpet & Home (Map 9)** just off of Union Square. Design fanatics can appreciate their ex-

otic array of furnishings (much of it antique and imported from Asia and Europe) even if they can't afford the steep prices. **Fish's Eddy (Map 9)**, **Pottery Barn (Map 13)**, and **Bed Bath & Beyond (Map 9)** offer the basics with a wide selection of styles and prices. For professional-grade kitchen supplies at the best prices around, explore the restaurant suppliers on Bowery. **Bridge Kitchenware (Map 13)** is another favorite among the city's cooks, as is the often-ignored second floor at Zabar's (Map 14). For paint, window dressings, and other home decorating supplies, try Janovic (Map 2, 5, 9, 11, 16). Prepare for sensory overload if you take on the over 200,000 square feet of commercial and residential furnishings at the **A&D Building (Map 13)**. Showrooms are open to the public, unlike at some of the smaller design ships nearby, which require business cards upon entry. Don't miss the **Conran Store (Map 13)** a few blocks away, in its quirky freestanding location under the Queensboro Bridge. And even if you can't afford the cutting edge design items, the friendly staff lets you enjoy a free game (or two) of foosball on the floor model.

Electronics

J&R (Map 3) provides most things electronic, including computers and accessories, iPods, games, cameras, music equipment, CDs, DVDs, and household appliances. **B&H (Map 8)** is the top destination for professionals and amateurs when it comes to photographic, audio, and video equipment. It's worth a visit just to witness the pure spectacle of this well-coordinated operation, as well as the outstanding selection of gear. Note that the megastore is run by Orthodox Jews who strictly observe the Sabbath and holidays, and thus you should always check the hours and days of operation (posted on their website) before heading over. Audiophiles are wonderfully served by **Stereo Exchange (Map 6)** and the jaw-dropping, price-busting **Sound by Singer (Map 9)**. Other places to shop for electronics include the **Apple Store (Map 6, 12)** and **Tekserve (Map 9)**, the (other) Apple specialists.

Food

With residents from every corner of the globe who collectively speak over 170 languages, New York couldn't help but be an exciting destination for food shopping. The offerings are as diverse as the population, whether you're looking for the best of the basics or exotic spices and other imported specialties. Two revered emporia make the Upper West Side a culinary destination—**Fairway (Maps 14, 18)** and **Zabar's (Map 14)**—and the Zabar's offshoot, **Vinegar Factory (Map 17)**, graces the Upper East. The national chain **Whole Foods (Maps 6, 9, and 14)** is multiplying, and now there's even a **Trader Joe's (Map 6)**, though only devotees can brave the crowds there. But the city's real gems come in the form of the increasing number of **Greenmarkets** (the largest is in Union Square **(Map 9)** four days a week), and the ethnic food purveyors stocked with imported goods from around the world. When it comes to Italian, Arthur Ave in the Bronx is famed for its bakeries, butcher shops, grocers, and sundry shops. The more centrally located **DiPalo Dairy (Map 3)** offers some of the best imported delicacies as well as their own celebrated fresh ricotta. For Middle Eastern specialties, **Sahadi's (Map 32)** provides the most impressive range of top quality products at prices that cannot be beat (and many of its neighbors on Atlantic Ave deserve a visit while you're in the area). Chinatown's options will overwhelm and exhaust you before they disappoint even the pickiest of shoppers, and there's even a destination for people in the market for British treats, **Myers of Keswick (Map 5)** in the West Village. We could go on and on, but we'll let you get out there to start eating and exploring your way through the city's culinary delights.

Art Supplies

Running low on Cadmium Red? Use your last stick of charcoal drawing a nude? The best art stores in NYC are scattered loosely around the SoHo area, with **Pearl Paint (Map 3)** being the most well known. Located at the corner of Mercer and Canal Streets, the store occupies a full six-story building with every type of art supply you can imagine, including a great separate frame shop out back on Lispenard. Closer to NYU and Cooper Union, you can find the best selection of paper at **New York Central Art Supply (Map 6)** on Third Avenue. **SoHo Art Materials (Map 3)** on Grand Street is a small, traditional shop that sells super premium paints and brushes for fine artists. Don't forget to check out both **Sam Flax (Map 9, 13)** and **A.I. Friedman (Map 9)** in the Flatiron area for graphic design supplies, portfolios, and gifts. Should you find yourself on the Upper East Side needing art supplies in a pinch, the fairly decent selection at **Blacker & Kooby (Map 17)** will do just fine.

As the art scene has made its way to Williamsburg, having a supply store close by is as important as a good supermarket (something folks in the 'burg are still waiting for). **Artist & Craftsman (Map 29)** on North 8th is a good bet for supplies.

*Remember to flash that student ID card if you've got it, as most art stores offer a decent discount...

Music Equipment & Instruments

New York's large and vibrant music scene supports a thriving instrument trade. To buy a new tuba or get that banjo tuned, head over to 48th Street. You'll find the largest, most well known stores, from generalist shops such as **Manny's (Map 12)** and **Sam Ash (Map 12)**, to more specialized shops like **Roberto's Woodwind Repair (Map 12)**. Just two blocks away, on 46th, drummers can make themselves at home in a store dedicated solely to their craft—**Drummer's World (Map 12)**.

If you can't take the bustle of the Times Square area and are looking for used, vintage, or just plain cool, then you'll want to shop elsewhere. Some of our favorites include: **East Village Music (Map 6)**, **First Flight (Map 7)**, **30th Street Guitars (Map 9)**, **Rogue Music (Map 9)**, and **Ludlow Guitars (Map 7)**.

For an exquisite purchase where money is no object, find the perfect grand piano at **Klavierhaus (Map 12)** or **Steinway Pianos (Map 12)**, where the salespeople pride themselves on matching even beginners with the perfect instrument for their skills and character. Also keep an eye (and an ear) out for special musical evenings at the former, and spontaneous performances at the latter.

The best remaining destination for sheet music is still the **Joseph Patelson Music House (Map 12)**.

Music for Listening

New Yorkers are still lamenting the 2006 demise of Tower Records, but fortunately there remain myriad options for music lovers who aren't satisfied with trawling the iTunes store for their fixes. Whether you just want that Top Ten hit or you are hunting for a rare LP, you have a range of destinations from which to choose. For those who like to dig, there's **Kim's Mediapolis (Map 18)**, where you're sure to find something for your record collection. For a more conventional experience, head to **J&R Music World (Map 3)** or the **Virgin Megastore (Map 6, 12)**.

The smaller stores offer more eclectic selections and usually boast a knowledgeable staff as well. Try **Other Music (Map 6)** and **Earwax (Map 29)** in Brooklyn—two stores with unique vibes. If you're still hungry for more, head to Bleecker Street to check out **Rebel Rebel (Map 5)** and **Bleecker Street Records (Map 5)**.

Shopping "Districts"

If you're fixated on a specific item, like a sausage maker or a few yards of leopard print fabric, you can shop in specialty districts around Manhattan. Brave the overwhelming selection throughout the Garment District (25th to 40th Sts, Fifth to Ninth Aves) for fabrics, buttons, zippers, ribbons, and anything else you'd need to design your own clothes. Men looking for the perfect romantic gift might want to check out the Diamond and Jewelry District (W 47th between Fifth and Sixth Aves), the world's largest market for diamonds, the Flower District (26th to 29th Sts, along and off Sixth Ave), and the Perfume District (along and off Broadway in the West 20s and 30s). Music Row (48th St between Sixth & Seventh Aves) leaves you with no excuses if you've been meaning to learn to play an instrument. The Bowery around Houston is another well-known strip where you'll find the Kitchenware District for all your culinary endeavors, the Lighting District (past Delancey St) for all your illuminating needs, and the Downtown Jewelry District (turn the corner of Bowery to Canal St) for the more unusual baubles you can't get uptown. High-end home design stores are concentrated on and around Designers Way and Decorators Way (58th and 59th Sts, between Second and Third Aves). The Flatiron District (from 14th to 34th Sts, between Sixth & Park Aves) is another home furnishing mecca. You can also take care of your photography needs where the pros do, with the city's highest concentration of stores and labs (between 5th and 6th Aves, from 18th to 22nd Sts). Sadly, Book Row (between 9th and 14th Sts) is no more. What was once an assemblage of over 25 bookstores now houses only the famous Strand Bookstore and Alabaster Bookshop, but avid readers could happily spend days browsing and purchasing in either one of them...

Map 1 • Financial District

Barclay Rex	75 Broad St	212-962-3355	For all your smoking needs.
Century 21	22 Cortlandt St	212-227-9092	Where most New Yorkers buy their underwear.
Christopher Norman Chocolates	60 New St	212-402-1243	Sweet chocolate shop.
Flowers of the World	80 Pine St	212-425-2234, 800-770-3125	Fulfill any feeling, mood, budget, or setting.
Godiva Chocolatier	33 Maiden Ln	212-809-8990	Everyone needs a fix now and then.
Radio Shack	9 Broadway	212-482-8138	Kenneth, what is the frequency?
Radio Shack	114 Fulton St	212-732-1904	Kenneth, what is the frequency?
South Street Seaport	19 Fulton St	212-SEA-PORT	Mall with historic ships as backdrop.
The World of Golf	74 Broad St	212-385-1246	Stop here on your way to Briar Cliff Manor.
Yankees Clubhouse Shop	8 Fulton St	212-514-7182	25 and counting…

Map 2 • TriBeCa

Babylicious	51 Hudson St	212-406-7440	Children's store with clothing and educational toys.
Balloon Saloon	133 W Broadway	212-227-3838	We love the name.
Bazzini	339 Greenwich St	212-334-1280	Nuts to you!
Boffi SoHo	31 Greene St	212-431-8282	Hi-end kitchen and bath design.
Canal Street Bicycles	417 Canal St	212-334-8000	Bike messenger mecca.
Duane Park Patisserie	179 Duane St	212-274-8447	Yummy!
Gotham Bikes	112 W Broadway	212-732-2453	Super helpful staff, good stuff.
Issey Miyake	119 Hudson St	212-226-0100	Flagship store of this designer.
Jack Spade	56 Greene St	212-625-1820	Barbie's got Ken, Kate's got Jack. Men's bags.
Janovic	136 Church St	212-349-0001	Top NYC paint store.
Kings Pharmacy	5 Hudson St	212-791-3100	Notary Public + discount days!
Korin Japanese Trading	57 Warren St	212-587-7021	Supplier to Japanese chefs and restaurants.
Let There Be Neon	38 White St	212-226-4883	Neon gallery and store.
Lucky Brand Dungarees	38 Greene St	212-625-0707	Lucky you.
MarieBelle's Fine Treats & Chocolates	484 Broome St	212-925-6999	Top NYC chocolatier.
New York Nautical	158 Duane St	212-962-4522	Armchair sailing.
Oliver Peoples	366 W Broadway	212-925-5400	Look as gaudy as you see.
Shoofly	42 Hudson St	212-406-3270	Dressing your child for social success.
Steven Alan	103 Franklin St	212-343-0692	Trendy designer clothing and accessories. One-of-a-kind stuff.
Urban Archaeology	143 Franklin St	212-431-4646	Retro fixtures.
We Are Nuts About Nuts	165 Church St	212-227-4695	They're nuts.
What Comes Around Goes Around	351 W Broadway	212-343-9303	LARGE, excellent collection of men's, women's, and children's vintage.
Willner Chemists	253 Broadway	212-791-0505	Free nutritional consultations for customers.

Map 3 • City Hall / Chinatown

Aji Ichiban	167 Hester St	212-925-1133	Load up on free samples from the huge selection of Asian candies and snacks.
Bangkok Center Grocery	104 Mosco St	212-732-8916	Curries, fish sauce, and other Thai products.
Catherine Street Meat Market	21 Catherine St	212-693-0494	Fresh pig deliveries every Tuesday!
The Changing Room	3 Centre St	212-226-5759	Local designers at newly opened "gallery" of sorts—must see!
Chinatown Ice Cream Factory	65 Bayard St	212-608-4170	Take home a quart of mango.
Dipalo Dairy	200 Grand St	212-226-1033	Saying cheese since 1925.
Fay Da Bakery	83 Mott St	212-791-3884	Chinese pastry and boba like nobody's business.
Fountain Pen Hospital	10 Warren St	212-964-0580	They don't take Medicaid.
GS Food Market	250 Grand St	212-274-0990	Cantonese market with fresh fish and veggies.
Hong Keung Seafood & Meat Market	75 Mulberry St	212-571-1445	Fresh seafood that you must eat today.
J&R Music & Computer World	33 Park Row	212-238-9000	Stereo, computer, and electronic equipment. Good prices.
Kate Spade	454 Broome St	212-274-1991	Purse and bag HQ. Cutesy designs.
Lung Moon Bakery	83 Mulberry St	212-349-4945	Chinese bakery.
Mitchell's Place	15 Park Pl	212-267-8156	Ca-ching for bling bling.
New Age Designer	38 Mott St	212-349-0818	Chinese emporium.
New Beef King	89 Bayard St	212-233-6612	Serious jerky.
The New York City Store	1 Centre St	212-669-8246	Fun NYC-themed stuff—subway token cufflinks, manhole cover pins, etc.
No 6	6 Centre St	212-533-3350	Notable selection of carefully selected original and reworked vintage.
Opening Ceremony	35 Howard St	212-219-2688	Expensive hipster threads for tiny bodies.
Papabubble	380 Broome St	212-966-2599	Candy labratory. Willy Wonka would be proud.

413

Arts & Entertainment • **Shopping**

Map 3 • City Hall / Chinatown—continued

Pearl Paint	308 Canal St	212-431-7932	Mecca for artists, designers, and people who just like art supplies.
Pearl River Mart	477 Broadway	212-431-4770	Chinese housewares and more.
SoHo Art Materials	127 Grand St	212-431-3938	A painter's candy store.
Tan My My Market	249 Grand St	212-966-7837	Fresh fish—some still moving.
Tent & Trails	21 Park Pl	212-227-1760	Top outfitter for gearheads.
Unimax	269 Canal St	212-925-1051	It's like 47th Street for the tattoo and piercing set.
Yellow Rat Bastard	478 Broadway	877-YELL-RAT	Filled with young street clothes and skate gear.

Map 4 • Lower East Side

Babycakes	248 Broome St	212-677-5047	A bakery dedicated solely to vegan, gluten-free goodies.
Doughnut Plant	379 Grand St	212-505-3700	Great, weird, recommended.
Hong Kong Supermarket	109 E Broadway	212-227-3388	A chance to see just how amazing food packaging can look.
il Laboratorio del Gelato	95 Orchard St	212-343-9922	Mind-bogglingly incredible artisanal gelato.
Joe's Fabric Warehouse	102 Orchard St	212-674-7089	Designer fabrics and trimmings.
Kossar's Bagels and Bialys	367 Grand St	877-4-BIALYS	Oldest bialy bakery in the US.
Mendel Goldberg Fabrics	72 Hester St	212-925-9110	Small store and selection of great fabrics.
Moishe's Kosher Bake Shop	504 Grand St	212-673-5832	Best babka, challah, hamantaschen, and rugalach.
Pippin	72 Orchard St	212-505-5159	Oodles of sparkling vintage costume jewelry.
Project 8	138 Division St	212-925-5599	Fashionable Euro-boutique.
Sweet Life	63 Hester St	212-598-0092	Gimme some CAN-DAY!
Tahir	75 Orchard St	212-253-2121	Vintage fashion with a personal touch.
Zarin Fabrics	314 Grand St	212-925-6112	Major destination in the fabric district.

Map 5 • West Village

Alexander McQueen	417 W 14th St	212-645-1797	Brit bad boy designs.
Alphabets	47 Greenwich Ave	212-229-2966	Fun miscellany store.
Bleecker Street Records	239 Bleecker St	212-255-7899	Great selection.
CO Bigelow Chemists	414 6th Ave	212-533-2700	Classic village pharmacy.
Diane von Furstenberg	874 Washington St	646-486-6440	When you have $400 burning a hole in your pocket and need a new dress.
Faicco's Pork Store	260 Bleecker St	212-243-1974	Prosciutto bread, homemade sausage, huge heros, pork heaven.
Flight 001	96 Greenwich Ave	212-989-0001	Cute hipster travel shop.
Geppetto's Toy Box	10 Christopher St	212-620-7511	Excellent toys and puppets.
Health & Harmony	470 Hudson St	212-691-3036	Small health food store with good selection and decent prices.
Jacques Torres Chocolate Haven	350 Hudson St	212-414-2462	Tastebud bliss brought to you by the Master of Chocolate.
Jeffrey	449 W 14th St	212-206-1272	Avant-garde (and wildly expensive) mini-department store.
The Leather Man	111 Christopher St	212-243-5339	No, you won't look like James Dean. But it'll help.
Little Pie Company	407 W 14th St	212-414-2324	A home-made dessert equals happiness.
Murray's Cheese Shop	254 Bleecker St	212-243-3289	We love cheese, and so does Murray's.
Mxyplyzyk	125 Greenwich Ave	800-243-9810	Great, quirky, must-have tchochkes and home décor.
Myers of Keswick	634 Hudson St	212-691-4194	Killer English sausages, pasties, etc.
O Ottomanelli's & Sons	285 Bleecker St	212-675-4217	High quality meats and the friendliest butchers in town.
Porto Rico Importing Company	201 Bleecker St	212-477-5421	Sacks of coffee beans everywhere.
Rebel Rebel Records	319 Bleecker St	212-989-0770	Small CD and LP shop with knowledgeable staff.
Scott Jordan Furniture	137 Varick St	212-620-4682	Solid hardwood furniture.
Stella McCartney	429 W 14th St	212-255-1556	Hip, animal-friendly fashion.
Vitra	29 9th Ave	212-463-5700	Sleek and modern home furnishings.

Map 6 • Washington Square / NYU / NoHo / SoHo

Apple Store SoHo	103 Prince St	212-226-3126	Don't come looking for produce.
Black Hound New York	170 2nd Ave	212-979-9505	Killer desserts. NFT favorite.
Cinema Nolita	202 Elizabeth St	212-334-9475	Great little video store.
Daily 235	235 Elizabeth St	212-334-9728	A little tchotchke store; has great journals.
East Village Cheese	40 3rd Ave	212-477-2601	Super cheap cheeses, olives, and meats. No samples!
East Village Music	85 E 4th St	212-979-8222	Excellent wares and repairs service. NFT top pick!
EMS	591 Broadway	212-966-8730	Excellent outdoor/hiking equipment and clothing.
Global Table	107 Sullivan St	212-431-5839	Quietly elegant tableware.
Grand Daisy Bakery	73 Sullivan St	212-334-9435	The best bakery, period.
Jam Paper & Envelope	135 3rd Ave	212-473-6666	And…the envelope, please.
Joe's Dairy	156 Sullivan St	212-677-8780	Homemade mozzarella fresh daily.

Kar'ikter	19 Prince St	212-274-1966	Toys for kids and adults.
Kee's Chocolates	80 Thompson St	212-334-3284	God's gift to truffle lovers.
Kiehl's	109 3rd Ave	212-677-3171	Great creams, lotions, and unguents; laughably good service.
Kim's Video	6 St Marks Pl	212-505-0311	Where to blow $100 quickly.
Lighting by Gregory	158 Bowery	212-226-1276	Bowery lighting mecca. Good ceiling fans.
Lord Willy's	223 Mott St	212-680-8888	Fab gentlemen's garb including shirts with matching pocket squares and boxers.
The Market NYC	268 Mulberry St	212-580-8995	Hip, unique designs by young, local designers.
Moishe's Bake Shop	115 2nd Ave	212-505-8555	NY's best kosher bakery.
MOMA Design Store	81 Spring St	646-613-1367	Cutting-edge, minimalist, ergonomic, offbeat, and funky everything.
Moss	150 Greene St	212-204-7100	Awesome cool stuff you can't afford! Ever!
Nancy Koltes	31 Spring St	212-219-2271	What's the thread-count?
National Wholesale Liquidators	632 Broadway	212-979-2400	They're not kidding.
New York Central Art Supply	62 3rd Ave	212-473-7705	Great selection of art, papers, and supplies.
Other Music	15 E 4th St	212-477-8150	Underground, experimental CD's, LP's, imports, and out-of-print obscurities.
Otto Tootsi Plohound	273 Lafayette St	212-431-7299	Funny name for really cool, interesting, refreshingly offbeat shoes.
Pino's Prime Meats	149 Sullivan St	212-475-8134	Old world Italian butcher. Pino's tips are priceless.
Prada	575 Broadway	212-334-8888	Big, pretentious, Rem Koolhaas-designed store!
Pylones	69 Spring St	212-431-3244	Colorful gifty things.
Saint Mark's Comics	11 St Marks Pl	212-598-9439	Important comic book store.
Stereo Exchange	627 Broadway	212-505-1111	Just-under-obscenely-priced audiophile equipment. Good for male depression.
Taschen	107 Greene St	212-226-2212	Czar of edgy, avant-garde book publishing opens first NYC outpost.
Uniqlo	546 Broadway		Cashmere, cashmere, and more cashmere—in every color!

Map 7 • East Village / Lower East Side

Alphabets	115 Avenue A	212-475-7250	Fun miscellany store.
Babeland	94 Rivington St	212-375-1701	Sex toys without the creepy vibe.
Dowel Quality Products	91 1st Ave	212-979-6045	Super-cool Indian grocery. Great beer selection, too.
Earthmatters	177 Ludlow St	212-475-4180	Organic groceries with a garden out back.
Economy Candy	108 Rivington St	212-254-1531	Candy brands from your childhood still being made and sold here!
Essex Street Market	120 Essex St	212-312-0449	Classic public market with a great combo of old-school and fresh-faced vendors.
Etherea	66 Avenue A	212-358-1126	Cool East Village record store.
Exit 9	64 Avenue A	212-228-0145	Always fun and changeable hipster gift shop (The first place to sell NFT!).
First Flight Music	174 1st Ave	212-539-1383	Good guitars and amps, spotty service.
Lancelotti	66 Avenue A	212-475-6851	Fun designer housewares, not too expensive.
Ludlow Guitars	164 Ludlow St	212-353-1775	New and used vintage guitars, accessories, and amps.
Masturbakers	511 E 12th St	212-475-0476	Erotic and custom cakes.
The Paris Apartment	70 E 1st St	917-749-5089	Romantic "Parisian" décor and stunning European flea market finds.
Russ & Daughters	179 E Houston St	212-475-4880	Fab Jewish soul food—lox, herring, sable, etc.
Saxelby Cheesemongers	120 Essex St	212-228-8204	All-American and artisinal.
Tiny Living	125 E 7th St	212-228-2748	Boutique catering to the tight squeeze of NYC living.

Map 8 • Chelsea

B&H Photo	420 9th Ave	212-444-6615	Where everyone in North America buys their cameras and film. Closed Saturdays.
Billy's Bakery	184 9th Ave	212-647-9956	Yummy homemade treats.
Brooklyn Industries	161 9th Ave	212-206-0477	A little bit of Brooklyn in the heart of Chelsea.
Buon Italia	75 9th Ave	212-633-9090	Imported Italian food.
Chelsea Market Baskets	75 9th Ave	212-727-1111	Gift baskets for all occasions.
Chelsea Wholesale Flower Market	75 9th Ave	212-620-7500	Remember, you're in Manhattan, not Westchester.
Eleni's	75 9th Ave	888-4-ELENIS	When a card won't do, iced cookies in every shape will.
Fat Witch Bakery	75 9th Ave	212-807-1335	Excellent chocolate brownies.
Find Outlet	361 W 17th St	212-243-3177	Find cheap(er) designer duds.
Gerry's	110 9th Ave	212-243-9141	Designer Men's and Women's labels on the cheap!
Kitchen Market	218 8th Ave	212-243-4433	Chiles, herbs, spices, hot sauces, salsas, and more.
Ronnybrook Milk Bar	75 9th Ave	212-741-6455	All things dairy, fresh from the Hudson Valley. Great shakes.

Arts & Entertainment • **Shopping**

Map 9 • Flatiron / Lower Midtown

17 at 17 Thrift Shop	17 W 17th St	212-727-7516	Proceeds go to Gilda's Club.
30th Street Guitars	236 W 30th St	212-868-2660	Ax heaven.
ABC Carpet & Home	888 Broadway	212-473-3000	A NYC institution for chic, even exotic, home décor and design.
Abracadabra	19 W 21st St	212-627-5194	Magic, masks, costumes—presto!
Academy Records	12 W 18th St	212-242-3000	Top Jazz/classical mecca.
Adorama Camera	42 W 18th St	212-741-0052	Good camera alternative to B&H.
Al Friedman	44 W 18th St	212-243-9000	Art supplies, frames, office furniture, and more.
Angel Street Thrift Shop	118 W 17th St	212-229-0546	Recommended thrift shop.
Ariston	110 W 17th St	212-929-4226	Excellent florist with orchids as well.
Capitol Fishing Tackle	132 W 36th St	212-929-6132	100+ year-old fishing institution.
Chelsea Flea Market	112 W 25th St		Antiqueing in the outdoors, the way God intended.
The City Quilter	133 W 25th St	212-807-0390	Quilt for success!
Cupcake Caf^ua	18 W 18th St	212-465-1538	Pretty cupcakes.
The Family Jewels	130 W 23rd St	212-633-6020	Tightly packed shop stocking yesteryear's threads for guys and gals.
Fisch For The Hip	153 W 18th St	212-228-3802	Chelsea vintage clothing boutique—well edited selection.
Fish's Eddy	889 Broadway	212-420-9020	They do dishes.
Housing Works Thrift Shop	143 W 17th St	212-366-0820	Our favorite thrift store.
Janovic	215 7th Ave	212-645-5454	Top NYC paint store.
Jazz Record Center	236 W 26th St	212-675-4480	All that jazz!
Loehmann's	101 7th Ave	212-352-0856	Join the other thousands of bargain hunters sifting through clothing piles.
Lord & Taylor	424 5th Ave	212-391-3344	Classic NYC department store.
Lush Cosmetics	1293 Broadway	212-564-9120	Fresh handmade cosmetics.
M&J Trimmings	1008 6th Ave	212-204-9595	For your DIY sewing projects.
Macy's	151 W 34th St	212-695-4400	Love the wooden escalators.
Mandler's, The Original Sausage Co	26 E 17th St	212-255-8999	Sausage emporium.
Otto Tootsi Plohound	137 5th Ave	212-460-8650	Funny name for really cool, interesting, refreshingly offbeat shoes.
Paper Presentations	23 W 18th St	212-463-7035	Relatively cheap paper and such.
Paragon Sporting Goods	867 Broadway	212-255-8036	Good all-purpose sporting goods store.
Pleasure Chest	156 7th Ave	212-242-2158	Always a great window display.
Rogue Music	251 W 30th St	212-629-5073	Used equipment you probably still can't afford.
Sam Flax	12 W 20th St	212-620-3000	Portfolios, frames, furniture, and designer gifts. NFT fave.
Space Kiddets	26 E 22nd St	212-420-9878	Bruce Lee and CBGBs onesies.
Tekserve	119 W 23rd St	212-929-3645	Apple computer sales and repairs.
Toho Shoji	990 6th Ave	212-868-7465	You made this necklace yourself? Just for me? (swoon).

Map 10 • Murray Hill / Gramercy

City Opera Thrift Shop	222 E 23rd St	212-684-5344	They always have something or other.
Foods of India	121 Lexington Ave	212-683-4419	Large selection of Indian ingredients including harder to find spices.
Homefront Kids/Kids Cuts	202 E 29th St	212-381-1966	Clothes, furniture, toys, gifts, haircuts, free gift wrap.
Housing Works Thrift Shop	157 E 23rd St	212-529-5955	Our favorite thrift store.
Kalustyan's	123 Lexington Ave	212-685-3451	Specialty foods.
La Delice Pastry Shop	372 3rd Ave	212-532-4409	Delectable pastries, buttery croissants, layer cakes.
La Mazou Cheese	370 3rd Ave	212-532-2009	Great selection of cheese and gourmet products.
Ligne Roset	250 Park Ave S	212-375-1036	Modern, sleek furniture.
Max Nass Inc.	118 E 28th St	212-679-8154	Vintage jewelry. repairs, restringing, and restoration.
Nemo Tile Company	48 E 21st St	212-505-0009	Good tile shop for small projects.
NKNY Neera Sari Palace	131 Lexington Ave	212-481-0325	Bollywood parlors for fashionistas.
Om Sari Palace	134 E 27th St	212-532-5620	Saris, bangles, earrings, sandals and accessories.
Pookie & Sebastian	541 3rd Ave	212-951-7110	Murray Hill outpost for fun, flirty, girly garb.
Quark Spy	240 E 29th St	212-683-9100	Spy shops are cool.
Shambhala	655 2nd Ave	212-213-2001	Hand crafted Jewelry, coffee and empanadas.
Todaro Bros	555 2nd Ave	212-532-0633	Home made mozzerella, pastas, high quality groceries.
Urban Angler	206 5th Ave	212-689-6400	We think it's for fishermen.

Map 11 • Hell's Kitchen

Amy's Bread	672 9th Ave	212-977-2670	Providing the heavenly smells that wake up Hell's Kitchen.
Annex/Hell's Kitchen Flea Market	W 39th St b/w Ninth Ave & Tenth Ave		Where most of the vendors from the now defunct Annex Chelsea Flea Market moved to.
Chelsea Garden Center	580 11th Ave	212-727-7100	Urban gardener's delight.

Coup de Coeur	609 9th Ave	212-586-8636	Trendy, eclectic shop with great vibes.
Delphinium	358 W 47th St	212-333-7732	For the "too lazy to make my own card" set.
Delphinium Home	653 9th Ave	212-333-3213	Everything from rubber duckies to WASP cookbooks.
Janovic	771 9th Ave	212-245-3241	Top NYC paint store.
Little Pie Company	424 W 43rd St	212-736-4780	A homemade dessert equals happiness.
Lyd	405 W 44th St	212-246-8041	The best mix of upcoming and well-loved designers.
Metro Bicycles	360 W 47th St	212-581-4500	New York's bicycle store.
Ninth Avenue International	543 9th Ave	212-279-1000	Mediterranean/Greek specialty store.
Pan Aqua Diving	460 W 43rd St	212-736-3483	SCUBA equipment and courses.
Port Authority Convenience	625 8th Ave	800-275-8777	You need it, they got it.
Poseidon Bakery	629 9th Ave	212-757-6173	Greek bakery.
Radio Shack	333 W 57th St	212-586-1909	Kenneth, what is the frequency?
Sea Breeze	541 9th Ave	212-563-7537	Bargains on fresh seafood.

Map 12 • Midtown

Apple Store	767 5th Ave	212-336-1440	Giant glass shrine houses all things Apple.
Baccarat	625 Madison Ave	212-826-4100	Top glass/crystal you can't afford.
Bergdorf Goodman	754 5th Ave	212-753-7300	Hands down—the best windows in the business.
Burberry	9 E 57th St	212-407-7100	Signature "beige plaid" purveyor.
Chanel	15 E 57th St	212-355-5050	Official outfitter of "ladies who lunch."
Colony Music	1619 Broadway	212-265-2050	Great sheet music store.
Drummer's World	151 W 46th St	212-840-3057	All-encompassing stop for drummers—from beginning to pro.
Ermenegildo Zegna	543 Madison Ave	212-421-4488	A truly stylish and classic Italian designer.
FAO Schwarz	767 5th Ave	212-644-9400	Noisy, crowded, overrated, awesome.
Felissimo	10 W 56th St	212-956-4438	Cool design store, Great townhouse.
Henri Bendel	712 5th Ave	212-247-1100	Offbeat department store specializing in the unusual and harder-to-find.
Joseph Patelson Music House	160 W 56th St	212-582-5840	Where Beethoven would shop, if he weren't dead.
Kate's Paperie	140 W 57th St	212-459-0700	Excellent stationery. NYC favorite.
Klavierhaus	211 W 58th St	212-245-4535	Unique pianos from the 19th, 20th, and 21st centuries.
Manny's Music	156 W 48th St	212-819-0576	Uptown musical instruments mecca.
Mets Clubhouse Shop	11 W 42nd St	212-768-9534	For Amazin' stuff!
Mikimoto	730 5th Ave	212-457-4600	Beautiful pearls, mostly pearls.
MoMA Design Store	44 W 53rd St	212-767-1050	Cutting-edge, minimalist, ergonomic, offbeat, and funky everything.
Museum of Arts and Design Shop	40 W 53rd St	212-956-3535	Not your average museum store.
Paul Stuart	45th St & Madison Ave	212-682-0320	Shop of choice for fancy lawyers and Wall Streeters. Great suspenders.
Petrossian Boutique	911 7th Ave	866-260-3284	Caviar and other delectables.
Roberto's Woodwind Repair Shop	146 W 46th St	212-391-1315	Saxophones, horns, clarinets, and flutes. If it blows, bring it here.
Saks Fifth Avenue	611 5th Ave	212-753-4000	Fifth Avenue mainstay with lovely holiday windows and bathrooms.
Sam Ash	160 W 48th St	212-719-2299	Musical instrument superstore.
Smythson of Bond Street	4 W 57th St	212-265-4573	High quality stationery.
Steinway and Sons	109 W 57th St	212-246-1100	Cheap knockoff pianos. Just kidding.
Takashimaya	693 5th Ave	212-350-0100	Elegant tea, furniture, accessory store. Highly recommended.
Tiffany & Co	727 5th Ave	212-755-8000	Grande dame of the little blue box.

Map 13 • East Midtown

A&D Building	150 E 58th St		Over 200,000 sq. ft. of commercial and residential furnishings. Wow.
Alkit Pro Camera	227 E 45th St	212-674-1515	Good camera shop; developing; rentals.
Bridge Kitchenware	711 3rd Ave	212-688-4220	For your inner-chef.
Buttercup Bake Shop	973 2nd Ave	212-350-4144	Move over Magnolia. Buttercup's all grown up.
Godiva Chocolatier	560 Lexington Ave	212-980-9810	Everyone needs a fix now and then.
Ideal Cheese	942 1st Ave	800-382-0109	All cheese is ideal.
Innovative Audio	150 E 58th St	212-634-4444	Quality music systems and home theaters.
New York Transit Museum	Grand Central, Main Concourse	212-878-0106	Great subway fun.
New York Vintage Club	346 E 59th St	212-207-9007	Fab vintage clothing on unexpected block.
Nicola's Specialty Emporium	997 1st Ave	212-753-9275	Italian brothers with top Italian goods.
Pottery Barn	127 E 59th St	917-369-0050	Mainstream, quality home goods.
Radio Shack	940 3rd Ave	212-750-8409	Kenneth, what's the frequency?
Sam Flax	900 3rd Ave	212-813-6666	Portfolios, frames, furniture, and designer gifts.

Arts & Entertainment • **Shopping**

Map 13 • East Midtown—*continued*

Sports Authority	845 3rd Ave	212-355-9725	Sporting goods for the masses.
Terence Conran Shop	407 E 59th St	866-755-9079	Awe-inspiring modern designs for the home. Can we live here?
The World of Golf	147 E 47th St	212-775-9398	Stop here on your way to Briar Cliff Manor.
Yankee Clubhouse Shop	110 E 59th St	212-758-7844	Any Yankee fan's paradise.
Zaro's Bread Basket	89 E 42nd St	212-292-0160	They've got bread. In baskets.

Map 14 • Upper West Side (Lower)

Allan & Suzi	416 Amsterdam Ave	212-724-7445	UWS vintage clothing and designer resale mainstay.
Alphabets	2284 Broadway	212-579-5702	Fun miscellany store.
Blades Board & Skate	156 W 72nd St	212-787-3911	One-stop shop for skateboarding and inline skating gear.
Bruce Frank	215 W 83rd St	877-232-3776	Great bead shop.
Bruno the King of Ravioli	2204 Broadway	212-580-8150	Gourmet market with a shocking specialty.
Claire's Accessories	2267 Broadway	212-877-2655	Fun for the young.
Gracious Home	1992 Broadway	212-231-7800	The definition of the word "emporium."
Grandaisy Bakery	176 W 72nd St	212-579-7222	Uptown outpost of famous Sullivan Street location.
Grom	2165 Broadway	646-290-7233	Really kickass gelato made by actual Italians.
Grom	2165 Broadway	646-290-7233	Mind-blowing gelato (and prices).
Harry's Shoes	2299 Broadway	866-442-7797	Mecca for reasonably priced footwear.
Housing Works Thrift Shop	306 Columbus Ave	212-579-7566	Our favorite thrift store.
Laytner's Linens	2270 Broadway	212-724-0180	Things that'll make you want to stay home more.
Patagonia	426 Columbus Ave	917-441-0011	Environmentally conscious store selling outstanding outdoor clothing.
Pookie & Sebastian	322 Columbus Ave	212-580-5844	Flirty tops, girly dresses, and fly jeans—for UWS chicks.
Townshop	2273 Broadway	212-787-2762	Where experts will fit you for the perfect bra.
Tumi	10 Columbus Cir	212-823-9390	When your luggage gets lost and insurance is paying.
West Side Records	233 W 72nd St	212-874-1588	Cool record store.
Yarn Co	2274 Broadway	212-787-7878	The nitty gritty for knitters in the city.
Zabar's	2245 Broadway	212-787-2000	The third gourmet shop in the "holy trinity."

Map 15 • Upper East Side (Lower)

Arthritis Thrift Shop	1383 3rd Ave	212-772-8816	Most eye-catching window displays on "Thrift Row."
Barneys New York	660 Madison Ave	212-826-8900	Museum-quality fashion (with prices to match). Recommended.
Beneath	265 E 78th St	212-288-3800	New, tiny shop with hipster brands and girly lingerie.
Bis Designer Resale	1134 Madison Ave	212-396-2760	Where you can actually afford Gucci and Prada.
Black Orchid Bookshop	303 E 81st St	212-734-5980	Mysteries are their specialty—old, new, and out-of-print.
Housing Works Thrift Shop	202 E 77th St	212-772-8461	Our favorite thrift store.
Just Bulbs	220 E 60th St	212-888-5707	Do you have any lamps? How about shades?
Kate's Paperie	1282 3rd Ave	212-396-3670	Excellent stationery. NYC favorite.
Lascoff Apothecary	1209 Lexington Ave	212-288-9500	Delightfully well-preserved apothecary, circa 1899.
Logos Bookstore	1575 York Ave	212-517-7292	Children's books, spiritual lit, and beyond.
Lyric Hi-Fi	1221 Lexington Ave	212-439-1900	Friendly, high-end stereo shop.
Martine's Chocolates too	400 E 82nd St	212-744-6289	Cute-as-a-bonbon chocolatier where decadence reigns.
Myla	20 E 69th St	212-327-2676	UES spot for sleek, incognito vibrators.
Oldies, Goldies & Moldies	1609 2nd Ave	212-737-3935	Deliciously Deco antiques and collectibles.
Orwasher's	308 E 78th St	212-288-6569	Handmade breads. Best challah on the east side.
Ottomanelli Brothers	1549 York Ave	212-772-7900	Meat chain.
Pookie & Sebastian	1488 2nd Ave	212-861-0550	Flirty tops, girly dresses, and fly jeans—for UES chicks.
Pylones	842 Lexington Ave	212-317-9822	Colorful gifty things.
Radio Shack	1477 3rd Ave	212-327-0979	Kenneth, what is the frequency?
The Shoe Box	1349 3rd Ave	212-535-9615	UES oasis for designer shoes—great department store alternative!
Steuben	667 Madison Ave	800-STEUBEN	Glass you can't afford.
Sylvia Pines Uniquities	1102 Lexington Ave	212-744-5141	Vintage jewelry and silver-framed purses fit for a flapper.
Tender Buttons	143 E 62nd St	212-758-7004	Ginormis button collection spanning old to new.
Two Little Red Hens	1652 2nd Ave	212-452-0476	Lovely cases of cakes and pies flanked by kitschy hen memorabilia.
Venture Stationers	1156 Madison Ave	212-288-7235	Great neighborhood stationers.
Vintage Collections	147 E 72nd St	212-717-7702	Lovely 2nd floor shop specializing in upscale vintage fashions.
William Poll	1051 Lexington Ave	212-288-0501	Homemade potato chips and dips with a cult following.
The Woolgathering	318 E 84th St	212-734-4747	The place to go for knitters in-the-know.
Yorkville Meat Emporium	1560 2nd Ave	212-628-5147	Hungarian specialties, fresh meat, cured pork, etc.
Zitomer	969 Madison Ave	212-737-5560	Department store with great pet gear, toy, and beauty choices.

Map 16 • Upper West Side (Upper)

Banana Republic	2360 Broadway	212-787-2064	What everyone else is wearing.
Ben & Jerry's	2722 Broadway	212-866-6237	Cherry Garcia, Phish Food, and Half Baked.
Gothic Cabinet Craft	2652 Broadway	212-678-4368	Real wood furniture!
Gourmet Garage	2567 Broadway	212-663-0656	Less greasy food than in most garages.
Health Nuts	2611 Broadway	212-678-0054	Standard health food store.
Janovic	2680 Broadway	212-531-2300	Top NYC paint store.
Joon's Fine Seafood	774 Amsterdam Ave	212-932-2942	Fresh fish market.
Metro Bicycles	231 W 96th St	212-663-7531	New York's bicycle source.
Mugi Pottery	993 Amsterdam Ave	212-866-6202	Handcrafted pottery.
New York Flowers & Plant Shed	209 W 96th St	800-753-9595	Makes you wish you had more (or any) garden space.
Planet Kids	2688 Broadway	212-864-8705	Outfitter of newborns to teens.
Regional	2607 Broadway	212-666-1915	20 regional Italian cuisines and Sunday brunch

Map 17 • Upper East Side / East Harlem

Blacker & Kooby	1204 Madison Ave	212-369-8308	Good selection of stationery, pens, and art supplies.
Blue Tree	1283 Madison Ave	212-369-BLUE	Truly unique clothing and gifts for folks who think they've seen it all.
Capezio	1651 3rd Ave	212-348-7210	Dance apparel and shoes.
Caravan 91	128 E 91st St	212-722-7282	Stationary storefront of the mobile fashion boutique on wheels.
The Children's General Store	168 E 91st St	212-426-4479	Toys, games, crafts, and all things kids love.
Ciao Bella Gelato	27 E 92nd St	212-831-5555	Try the malted milk ball gelato.
Cooper-Hewitt National Design Museum Shop	2 E 91st St		Cool design stuff.
Coup de Coeur	1628 3rd Ave	212-410-9720	Stylish boutique on not-so-stylish stretch of Third Avenue.
Doyle New York	175 E 87th St	212-427-2730	Auctioneers and appraisers, anything from jewelry and art to coins and stamps.
Eli's Vinegar Factory	431 E 91st St	212-987-0885	Gourmet market with prepared foods, cheeses, meats, seafood, and produce.
Exotic Fragrances	1645 Lexington Ave	212-410-0600	Aromatherapy for your apartment.
Glaser's Bake Shop	1670 1st Ave	212-289-2562	Best black-and-white cookies for more than a century.
Housing Works Thrift Shop	1730 2nd Ave	212-722-8306	Latest Uptown outpost of our favorite thrift shop.
Kessie & Co	163 E 87th St	212-987-1732	Vintage bric-a-brac, housewares, and clothing.
La Tropezienne	2131 1st Ave	212-860-5324	French bakery in El Barrio.
Laytner's Linens	237 E 86th St	212-996-4439	Things that'll make you want to stay home more.
MAD Vintage Couture & Designer Resale	167 E 87th St	212-427-4333	Former art gallery turned boutique.
Nellie M Boutique	1309 Lexington Ave	212-996-4410	Fun things for ladies to wear out on dates.
New York Replacement Parts	1456 Lexington Ave	212-534-0818	Plumbing supplies and bath fixtures.
Orva	155 E 86th St	212-369-3448	Ladies' discount department store.
Pickles, Olives Etc	1647 1st Ave	212-717-8966	Pickle barrel-sized shop selling pickles, olives, stuffed grape leaves, etc.
Rincon Musical	1936 3rd Ave	212-828-8604	Latino music headquarters.
Samba Bakery	165 E 106th St	212-722-8054	Some of the best French pastries in New York.
Schaller & Weber	1654 2nd Ave	212-879-3047	A relic of old Yorkville with great German meats.
Schatzie's Prime Meats	1200 Madison Ave	212-410-1555	Butcher with good prime meat and poultry.
Shatzi The Shop	243 E 86th St	212-289-1830	The saving grace of strip mall-ish, chain-hogged 86th Street.
Soccer Sport Supply	1745 1st Ave	212-427-6050	Omni soccer.
Spence-Chapin Thrift Shop	1850 2nd Ave	212-426-7643	Like the other Spence-Chapin location, but with more furniture.
Super Runners Shop	1337 Lexington Ave	212-369-6010	Brand name sneakers, apparel, and gadgets.
Tito's Plastic Covers	1642 Lexington Ave	212-369-7205	Decorate your living room like grandma.
Williams-Sonoma	1175 Madison Ave	212-289-6832	Fine cookware.

Map 18 • Columbia / Morningside Heights

Aunt Meriam's	435 W 125th St	212-531-0322	Hard to find African-American artifacts.
Book Culture	536 W 112th St	212-865-1588	NFT favorite.
El Mundo	3300 Broadway	646-548-3970	Cheap homegoods and discounted brand name apparel.
JAS Mart	2847 Broadway	212-866-4780	Japanese Asian Specialty. Japanese imports.
Kim's Mediapolis	2906 Broadway	212-864-5321	Audiovisual heaven.
Mondel Chocolates	2913 Broadway	212-864-2111	Mom-and-pop candy shop with great chocolates.
Pinkberry	2873 Broadway	212-222-0191	Overpriced La La Land froyo chain.

419

Arts & Entertainment • **Shopping**

Map 19 • Harlem (Lower)

The Body Shop	1 E 125th St	212-348-4900	Naturally inspired skin and hair care products.
Carol's Daughter	24 W 125th St		Nature-inspired skin care presented with love.
Champs	208 W 125th St	212-280-0296	Sports and street shoes and wear.
Dr Jay's Harlem NYC	256 W 125th St	212-665-7795	Inner-city urban fashions.
Grandma's Place	84 W 120th St	212-360-6776	Harlem toy boutique.
H&M	125 W 125th St	212-665-8300	Disposable fashion.
Harlem Underground Clothing	20 E 125th St	212-987-9385	Embroidered Harlem t-shirts.
Harlemade	174 Lenox Ave	212-987-2500	Clothes/gifts/art.
Hats by Bunn	2283 7th Ave	212-694-3590	Cool caps.
Hue-Man	2319 Frederick Douglass Blvd	212-665-7400	Largest African American bookstore in the country.
Jimmy Jazz	132 W 125th St	212-665-4198	Urban designers with a range of sizes.
MAC Cosmetics	202 W 125th St	212-665-0676	Beauty products in many colors and shades.
Malcolm Shabazz Harlem Market.	58 W 116th St		An open-air market for all your daishiki needs
N Boutique	114 W 116th St	212-961-1036	Hip boutique with fashion, apothecary, jewelry, footwear, and more accessories.
Nubian Heritage	2037 5th Ave	212-427-8999	Healthy organic shampoos, lotions, and more.
Settepani	196 Lenox Ave	917-492-4806	Lovely baked goods.
Studio Museum of Harlem Gift Shop	144 W 125th St	212-864-4500	Art produced by African Americans.
Xukuma	11 E 125th St	212-222-0490	Capitalize Harlem.

Map 20 • El Barrio / East Harlem

American Outlet Superstore	2226 3rd Ave	212-987-6459	Everything for your apartment
Capri Bakery	186 E 116th St	212-410-1876	Spanish El Barrio bakery.
Casa Latina Music Store	151 E 116th St	212-427-6062	El Barrio's oldest record store.
Casablanca Meat Market	127 E 110th St	212-534-7350	The line out the door every Saturday says it all.
The Children's Place	163 E 125th St	212-348-3607	Cute clothes for little ones.
Don Paco Lopez Panaderia	2129 3rd Ave	212-876-0700	Mexican bakery famous for Day of the Dead bread and Three Kings Day cake.
Eagle Tile & Home Center	2254 2nd Ave	212-423-0333	Update the tile in your kitchen or bathroom
Everything Must Go	2281 1st Ave	212-722-8203	El Barrio skateboard and clothing boutique.
Gothic Cabinet Craft	2268 3rd Ave	212-410-3508	Real wood furniture.
La Marqueta	1607 Park Ave	212-534-4900	Mainly Puerto Rican foodstuffs.
Lore Upholstery Shop	2201 3rd Ave	212-534-1025	Well Known by Madison Avenue clientele, Reupholster your sidewalk/dumpster chair.
Motherhood Maternity	163 E 125th St	212-987-8808	Casual maternity wear.
Payless Shoe Source	2143 3rd Ave	212-289-2251	Inexpensive shoes.
R&S Strauss Auto	2005 3rd Ave	212-410-6688	Power steering fluid and windshield wipers 'til 9pm!
VIM	2239 3rd Ave	212-369-5033	Street wear—jeans, sneakers, tops—for all.
Young's Fish Market	2004 3rd Ave	212-876-3427	Get it fresh or fried.

Map 21 • Manhattanville / Hamilton Heights

The Adventist Care Center	528 W 145th St	212-926-1203	Thrift store with a great selection of hats.
B-Jays USA	540 W 143rd St	212-694-3160	Every sneaker under the sun.
El Mundo	3791 Broadway	212-368-3648	Cheap homegoods and discounted brand name apparel.
Foot Locker	3549 Broadway	212-491-0927	Get your sneakers here.
SOH-Straight Out of Harlem Creative Outlet	704 St Nicholas Ave	212-234-5944	Unique gifts and crafts.
VIM	508 W 145th St	212-491-1143	Street wear—jeans, sneakers, tops—for all.

Map 22 • Harlem (Upper)

B Oyama Homme	2330 7th Ave	212-234-5128	Fashion for men.
Baskin-Robbins	2730 8th Ave	212-862-0635	31 flavors and other frozen treats.
Denim Library	2326 7th Ave	212-281-2380	Experts in denimology.
Montgomery's	2312 7th Ave	212-690-2166	Featuring one-of-a-kind fashions.
New York Public Library Shop	515 Lenox Ave	212-491-2206	Shop specializing in black history and culture.

Map 23 • Washington Heights

Baskin-Robbins	728 W 181st St	212-923-9239	31 flavors and other frozen treats.
Carrot Top Pastries	3931 Broadway	212-927-4800	Top carrot cake, muffins, chocolate cake, rugalach, and more.
The Children's Place	600 W 181st St	212-923-7244	Cute clothes for little ones.

Arts & Entertainment • Shopping

Chung Haeum	566 W 181st St	212-928-8235	Best store ever. All local artists at affordable prices.
Fever	1387 St Nicholas Ave	212-781-6232	For ladies, at night.
Foot Locker	621 W 181st St	212-568-6091	Get your sneakers here.
FootCo	1422 St Nicholas Ave	212-928-3330	Sneakers galore.
Goodwill Industries	512 W 181st St	212-923-7910	Jeans, business attire, baby and children's clothing, housewares and appliances, furniture, and more.
Modell's	606 W 181st St	212-568-3000	Generic sporting goods.
Payless Shoe Source	556 W 181st St	212-795-9183	Inexpensive shoes.
Planet Girls	3923 Broadway	212-927-0542	Cute clothes. Plants all over the store.
Santana Banana	661 W 181st St	212-568-4096	Leather shoes for men and women who are into leather.
Tribeca	655 W 181st St	212-543-3600	Trendy store for women. Good soundtrack.
VIM	561 W 181st St	212-781-8801	Street wear—jeans, sneakers, tops—for all.

Map 25 • Inwood

Carrot Top Pastries	5025 Broadway	212-569-1532	Top carrot cake, muffins, chocolate cake, rugalach, and more.
The Cloisters Museum Store	Ft Tryon Park	212-650-2277	Dark Age trinkets.
Foot Locker	146 Dyckman St	212-544-8613	There's a lot of shoe stores around here.
K&R Florist	4953 Broadway	212-942-2222	The best flower shop in the area.
Radio Shack	576 W 207th St	212-544-2180	Optimal post-nuclear-war survivor, w/ Keith Richards and cockroaches.
Radio Shack	180 Dyckman St	212-304-0364	Optimal post-nuclear-war survivor, w/ Keith Richards and cockroaches.
Tread Bike Shop	250 Dyckman St	212-544-7055	Where to fix your bike after riding through Inwood Hill Park.
VIM	565 W 207th St	212-942-7478	Street wear—jeans, sneakers, tops—for all.

Map 26 • Astoria

Candy Plum	30-98 36th St	718-721-2299	Hip clothes from new designers.
Easy Pickins	31-27 Steinway St	718-204-6200	Cheap digs for the Saturday night hoochie mama in us all.
El Mundo Discount	32-40 Steinway St	718-728-2229	Don't judge a book by its cover. Name-brand deals, high-heeled steals, tight-wad appeals.
The Furniture Market	22-08 Astoria Blvd	718-545-3935	Antiques and thrift home goods at all price points.
Jolson's Wines & Liquors	22-24 31st St	718-728-2020	Friendly, knowledgable staff and a great wine selection.
Laziza of New York Pastries	25-78 Steinway St	718-777-7676	City's best Middle Eastern baked treats.
Loveday 31	33-06 31st Ave	718-728-4057	Hip new and vintage clothes.
Martha's Country Bakery	36-21 Ditmars Blvd	718-545-9737	Best pound cake around, and everything else is good too.
Mediterranean Foods	23-18 31st St	718-721-0221	Greek groceries and prepared foods.
Rose & Joe's Italian Bakery	22-40 31st St	718-721-9422	Fresh cannolis made to order.
The Second Best	30-07 Astoria Blvd	718-204-8844	Great source for cheap secondhand furniture and knick-knacks.
Thessalikon Pastry Shop	33-21 31st Ave	718-545-8249	Famous source for takeaway trays of fabulous spanakopita.
Titan Foods	25-56 31st St	718-626-7771	The best place to shop for groceries in Astoria.
Venzini	30-64 Steinway St	718-728-2730	SoHo style, SoHo prices, but SoHo worth it.

Battery Park City

DSW Shoe Warehouse	102 North End Ave	212-945-7419	Fabulous choices for men's and women's shoes.

Map 27 • Long Island City

Art-o-Mat	46-46 Vernon Blvd		Locally themed, locally produced art and gifts. Occasional readings and events.
City Dog Lounge	49-02 Vernon Blvd	718-707-3027	Pet accessories and services.
Greenmarket	48th Ave & Vernon Blvd	212-788-7476	Local farmers and bakers, every Saturday except in winter.
Hunter's Point Wines & Spirits	47-07 Vernon Blvd	718-472-9463	Owner Paul will recommend great wines from $5 to $50. Also a well-edited liquor selection.
Mario's	47-23 Vernon Blvd	718-937-3193	Get the Italian hero with everything. It feeds two. You won't be sorry.
Newtok Video	22-42 Jackson Ave	718-784-7495	Korean, English. Is the name a joke?
Next Level Floral Design	47-30 Vernon Blvd	718-937-1155	Innovative designs that grace some of the cities' best tables.
Purple Pumpkin	47-14 Vernon Blvd	718-783-7300	Cute selection of cards and gifts for the ladies.
Slovak-Czech Varieties	10-59 Jackson Ave	718-752-2093	Everything you forgot to bring back from Prague.
Spokesman Cycles	49-04 Vernon Blvd	718-433-0405	Just what every yup-and-coming neighborhood needs.
Subdivision	48-18 Vernon Blvd	718-482-1899	Trendy clothing boutique and art gallery.
Vine Wine	12-09 Jackson Ave	718-433-2611	Expertly selected wines, almost all under $20.

Arts & Entertainment · **Shopping**

Map 28 · Greenpoint

Brooklynski	145 Driggs Ave	718-389-0901	Quirky little gifts for cool Brooklynites.
Chopin Chemists	911 Manhattan Ave	718-383-7822	Polish-speaking; useful location.
Dee & Dee	777 Manhattan Ave	718-389-0181	Mega dollar store; cheap stuff.
Film Noir	10 Bedford Ave	718-389-5773	Greenpoint's top video rental destination.
The Garden	921 Manhattan Ave	718-389-6448	Organic groceries and Polish goth chicks!
Mini Me	123 Nassau Ave	718-349-0333	Babies' and kids' clothing.
Petland Discounts	846 Manhattan Ave	718-349-8370	Shit you need for your stupid pet.
Photoplay	928 Manhattan Ave	718-383-7782	Ben's favorite Greenpoint video store.
Polam	952 Manhattan Ave	718-383-2763	Quality Polish meat market with cheap bulk pickles.
Pop's Popular Clothing	7 Franklin St	718-349-7677	Great second-hand clothing, especially jeans.
Sikorski Meat	603 Manhattan Ave	718-389-6181	Tender, salty, smoky, Polish…meat.
Steve's Meat Market	104 Nassau Ave	718-383-1780	Sausages double smoked for her pleasure.
Syrena Bakery	207 Norman Ave	718-349-0560	Very nice Polish bakery with an espresso bar and bagels.
The Thing	1001 Manhattan Ave	718-349-8234	Unusual second-hand store offers thousands of used LPs.
Uncle Louie G's	172 Greenpoint Ave	718-349-1199	So many flavors, so little time.
Wedel	772 Manhattan Ave	718-349-3933	Old School chocolate shop, straight out of Poland.
Wizard Electroland	863 Manhattan Ave	718-349-6889	Electronics store.

Map 29 · Williamsburg

Academy Records	96 N 6th St	718-218-8200	Bins and bins of new and used LPs.
Amarcord Vintage Fashion	223 Bedford Ave	718-963-4001	Well-edited vintage goodies, many pieces direct from Europe.
Artist & Craftsman	761 Metropolitan Ave	718-782-7765	Art supplies.
Beacon's Closet	88 N 11th St	718-486-0816	Rad resale with lots of gems.
Bedford Cheese Shop	229 Bedford Ave	718-599-7588	Best cheese selection in the borough.
The Brooklyn Kitchen	616 Lorimer St	718-389-2982	A primer on housewares for the Converse set.
Built By Wendy	46 N 6th St	718-384-2882	Brooklyn outpost of NYC-based independent label.
Earwax Records	218 Bedford Ave	718-486-3771	Record store with all the indie classics.
Emily's Pork Store	426 Graham Ave	718-383-7216	Broccoli rabe sausage is their specialty.
Future Perfect	115 N 6th St	718-599-6278	The coolest assemblage of cutting-edge housewares and indie furnishings.
Houndstooth	485 Driggs Ave	718-384-8705	Vintage clothing for male hipsters seeking the authorial look.
KCDC Skateshop	90 N 11th St	718-387-9006	Shop and gallery featuring locally designed gear.
The Mini-Market	218 Bedford Ave	718-302-9337	Hodge-podge of tchotchkes and fun clothes.
Model T Meats	404 Graham Ave	718-389-1553	Meat, meat, and more meat. Also, cheese.
Otte	132 N 5th St	718-302-3007	A small well-edited roster of established and emerging designers.
Passout Record Shop	131 Grand St	718-384-7273	Subversive media and in-store shows.
Pegasus	355 Bedford Ave	718-782-2842	Vintage finds at near-thrift store prices.
Roulette	188 Havemeyer St	718-218-7104	Choice vintage housewares at affordable prices.
Sound Fix	110 Bedford Ave	718-388-8090	Independent record store with a café/performance space in back.
Spoonbill & Sugartown	218 Bedford Ave	718-387-7322	Excellent indie bookstore.
Sprout	44 Grand St	718-388-4440	Contemporary home and garden store.
Spuyten Devil Grocery	132 N 5th St	718-384-1520	Belgium beer lovers' bar sells the goods in Williamsburg's mini mall.
Treehouse	430 Graham Ave	718-482-TREE	Quirky, one-of-a-kind clothing and jewelry. Plus, crafting classes!
Two Jakes	320 Wythe Ave	718-782-7780	Furniture: Mod, metal, misc.
Ugly Luggage	214 Bedford Ave	718-384-0724	Small storefront packed with antiques.
Videology	308 Bedford Ave	718-782-3468	Best video store in the 'Burg.
Yoko Devereaux	338 Broadway	718-302-1450	Hip menswear line's first retail shop.

Map 30 · Brooklyn Heights / DUMBO / Downtown

Almondine Bakery	85 Water St	718-797-5026	Pastry smells waft to the street.
Design Within Reach	76 Montague St	718-643-1015	Not really, but the stuff IS cool.
Halcyon	57 Pearl St	718-260-9299	Vinyl for DJ fanatics.
Half Pint	55 Washington St	718-875-4007	Ditch Gap Kids!
Heights Prime Meats	59 Clark St	718-237-0133	Butcher.
Jacques Torres Chocolate	66 Water St	718-875-9772	The Platonic ideal of chocolate.
Lassen & Hennigs	114 Montague St	718-875-6272	Specialty foods and deli.
Montague Street Video	143 Montague St	718-875-1715	Good selection serving the Heights.
New Balance Store	125 Court St	718-858-8550	Running sneaks and the like.
Pomme	81 Washington St	718-855-0623	Pricey imports for baby hipsters. Haircuts, too.

Recycle-A-Bicycle	35 Pearl St	718-858-2972	Bikes to the ceiling.
Stewart/Stand	165 Front St	718-407-4197	Another very cool design shop for DUMBO.
West Elm	75 Front St	718-875-7757	Cool home décor at reasonable prices.
Wonk	68 Jay St	718-596-8026	Furnish your penthouse.

Map 31 · Fort Greene / Clinton Hill

Atlantic Terminal Mall	Atlantic Ave & Flatbush Ave		Blah.
Blue Bass Vintage	431 Dekalb Ave	347-750-8935	Thrift store with wide selection and rummage sale feel.
Cake Man Raven Confectionary	708 Fulton St	718-694-2253	Get the red velvet cake!
Carol's Daughter	1 S Elliot Pl	718-596-1862	Skincare with a cult following.
Dope Jams	580 Myrtle Ave	718-622-7977	Soul, funk, hip-hop, but no dope.
Frosted Moon	154 Vanderbilt Ave	718-858-3161	Full of pretty things.
The Greene Grape	765 Fulton St	718-797-9463	Nice new wine shop.
Gureje	886 Pacific St	718-857-2522	West African flavored clothing, with a music club in the back!
Kiki's Pet Spa	239 Dekalb Ave	718-857-7272	For pet-worshippers.
Malchijah Hats	225 Dekalb Ave	718-643-3269	Beautiful and unique hats.
The Midtown Greenhouse Garden Center	115 Flatbush Ave	718-636-0020	Fully stocked with plants and gardening supplies.
My Little India	96 S Elliott Pl	718-855-5220	Furniture, candles, textiles.
Owa African Market	434 Myrtle Ave	718-643-8487	Beads galore.
Pratt Institute Bookstore	550 Myrtle Ave	718-789-1105	Art supplies, bookstore, cool stuff for students.
Sodafine	119 Grand St	718-230-3060	Hot little numbers with big price tags.
Target	139 Flatbush Ave	718-290-1109	Bull's eye!
White Elephant Gallery	572 Myrtle Ave	718-789-9423	Mindset is key. It could be treasure.
Yu Interiors	15 Greene Ave	718-237-5878	Modern furniture, bags, and candles.

Map 32 · BoCoCa / Red Hook

A Cook's Companion	197 Atlantic Ave	718-852-6901	A fantastic shop with everything for your kitchen (except the food).
Adam's Fresh Bakery by Design	144 Smith St	888-363-7374	Heaven in a cupcake.
American Beer Distributors	256 Court St	718-875-0226	International beer merchant. NFT pick.
Book Court	163 Court St	718-875-3677	The neighborhood spot for books.
Butter	389 Atlantic Ave	718-260-9033	Very cool and very expensive boutique.
Caputo's Fine Foods	460 Court St	718-855-8852	Italian gourmet specialties.
D'Amico Foods	309 Court St	718-875-5403	The best coffee in the 'hood, if not the city.
Environment337	337 Smith St	718-522-1767	Another Smith Street hit.
Exit 9	127 Smith St	718-422-7720	Quirky gifts.
Fish Tales	296 Court St	718-246-1346	The place for fish
Flight 001	132 Smith St	718-243-0001	Luggage, etc. for the pampered traveler.
Marquet Patisserie	221 Court St	718-855-1289	Mouth-watering croissants and quiches.
Mazzola Bakery	192 Union St	718-643-1719	Top bakery in CG.
Refinery	254 Smith St	718-643-7861	Great bags and accessories.
Rocketship	208 Smith St	718-797-1348	Nice selection of comic books and graphic novels.
Sahadi Importing Company	187 Atlantic Ave	718-624-4550	Middle Eastern specialty and fine foods since 1948.
Staubitz Meat Market	222 Court St	718-624-0014	Top NYC butcher.
Stinky	261 Smith St	718-522-7425	I get it! It's a cheese store!
Swallow	361 Smith St	718-222-8201	An exquisite selection of glass, jewelry, and books.

Map 33 · Park Slope / Prospect Heights / Windsor Terrace

3R Living	276 5th Ave	718-832-0951	Eco friendly and organic products and gifts.
Artesana Home	170 7th Ave	718-369-9881	Housewares better traveled than you.
Beacon's Closet	220 5th Ave	718-230-1630	Rad resale with lots of gems.
Bierkraft	191 5th Ave	718-230-7600	Cheese, chocolate, and nearly 1000 varieties of beer.
Bird	430 7th Ave	718-768-4940	Unique women's clothes and accessories; hit Baby Bird too.
Brooklyn Superhero Supply	372 5th Ave	718-499-9884	Capes, treasure maps, and bottled special powers. Also, McSweeney's publications.
Buttercup's PAW-tisserie	63 5th Ave	718-399-2228	
Clay Pot	162 7th Ave	718-788-6564	Hand-crafted gifts, jewelry.
Fabrica	619 Vanderbilt Ave	718-398-3831	Elegantly designed home furnishings.
JackRabbit Sports	151 7th Ave	718-636-9000	Mecca for runners, swimmers, and cyclists.
Leaf and Bean	83 7th Ave	718-638-5791	Coffees and teas.
Loom	115 7th Ave	718-789-0061	Irresistible gifts and housewares.
Mostly Modern	383 7th Ave	718-499-9867	Winsome wares for space-age bachelor pads.
Nancy Nancy	244 5th Ave	718-789-5262	Cards, gifts, novelties.
Rare Device	453 7th Ave	718-301-6375	Cool design shop.

Map 33 · Park Slope / Prospect Heights / Windsor Terrace—continued

Root Stock & Quade	297 7th Ave	718-832-1888	The yummiest place for flowers, plants, and bouquets.
Somethin' Else	294 5th Ave	718-768-5131	Meticulously cool music and clothes.
Stitch Therapy	176 Lincoln Pl	718-398-2020	Luxurious yarns. Plus knitting classes.
Trailer Park	77 Sterling Pl	718-623-2170	Unique and handcrafted furnishings.
Uncle Louie G's	741 Union St	718-623-6668	So many flavors, so little time.

Map 34 · Hoboken

Big Fun Toys	602 Washington St	201-714-9575	What it says.
City Paint & Hardware	130 Washington St	201-659-0061	Everything, including kitchen sinks.
Galatea	1224 Washington St	201-963-1522	Elegantly lusciously lingerie, chosen with an expert eye.
Hoboken Farmboy	127 Washington St	201-656-0581	It doesn't come much healthier. Good advice for your health needs.
Kings Fresh Ideas	333 River St	201-386-2300	Yuppie groceries for high-rise dwellers.
Kings Fresh Ideas	1212 Shipyard Ln	201-239-4060	Yuppie groceries for high-rise dwellers.
Lisa's Italian Deli	901 Park Ave	201-795-3204	Delicious heroes, large selection of Italian groceries.
Peper	1028 Washington St	201-217-1911	Hoboken's sexiest clothing. A must for your next high school reunion.
Sobsey's Produce	92 Bloomfield St	201-795-9398	Expert greengrocer. Exotic produce and gourmet foods.
Sparrow Wine and Liquor	126 Washington St	201-659-1500	Good selection of local and imported products. Staff are helpful with selections.
Sparrow Wine and Liquor	1224 Shipyard Ln	201-659-1501	Good selection of local and imported products. Staff are helpful with selections.
Tunes New & Used CDs	225 Washington St	201-653-3355	Support your local indie music store. They'll order stuff for you.
Yes I Do	312 Washington St	201-659-3300	Elegant cards, stationery, invitations, printing, and gifts.

Map 35 · Jersey City

Harborside Shopping Complex	n/a		Mall. Isn't life just grand, Martha?
Newport Center Mall	30 Mall Dr W	201-626-2025	Mall. Ah, the Jersey aesthetic…
Patel Snacks	785 Newark Ave	201-714-9676	Tasty vegetarian and vegan snacks, both sweet and savory.

Overview

If you want to see cutting-edge art, go to New York City's galleries. There are more than 500 galleries in the city, with artwork created in every conceivable medium (and of varying quality) on display. SoHo, Chelsea, DUMBO, and Williamsburg are the hot spots for gallery goers, but there are also many famous (and often more traditional) galleries and auction houses uptown, including **Christie's (Map 12)** and **Sotheby's (Map 15)**. With so much to choose from, there's almost always something that's at least *provocative*, if not actually *good*.

The scene at the upscale galleries is sometimes intimidating, especially if you look like you are on a budget. If you aren't interested in buying, they aren't interested in you being there. Some bigger galleries require appointments. Cut your teeth at smaller galleries; they aren't as scary. Also, put your name on the mailing lists. You'll get invites to openings so crowded that no one will try to pressure you into buying (and there's free wine). The Armory Show, an annual show of new art, is also a great way to see what the galleries have to offer without intimidation.

SoHo Area

Five years ago, there were still hundreds of art galleries in SoHo. Now it has practically become an outdoor mall. However, there are still some permanent artworks in gallery spaces, such as Walter De Maria's excellent *The Broken Kilometer* (Map 6) a Dia-sponsored space at 393 West Broadway, and his sublime *New York Earth Room* (Map 6). A short train down to TriBeCa will land you in LaMonte Young's awesome aural experience *Dream House* at the **MELA Foundation (Map 2)**. **Artists Space (Map 2)**, one of the first alternative art galleries in New York, is also in TriBeCa. The **HERE Arts Center (Map 5)** showcases a wide range of work and usually offers an exhibit or performance that warrants a visit

Chelsea

The commercialization of SoHo has helped make Chelsea the center of the city's gallery scene. Our recommendation is to hit at least two streets—W 24th Street between Tenth and Eleventh avenues, and W 22nd Street between Tenth and Eleventh avenues. W 24th Street is anchored by the almost-always-brilliant **Gagosian Gallery (Map 8)** and also includes the **Luhring Augustine (Map 8)**, **Charles Cowles (Map 8)**, **Mary Boone (Map 8)**, **Barbara Gladstone (Map 8)**, and **Matthew Marks (Map 8)** galleries. W 22nd Street has the architecture-friendly **Max Protech (Map 8)** gallery and the **Julie Saul (Map 8)**, **Leslie Tonkonow (Map 8)**, **Marianne Boesky (Map 8)**, **Pace Wildenstein (Map 8)**, and **Yancey Richardson (Map 8)** galleries. Also, check out the famous "artist's" bookstore **Printed Matter (Map 8)**.

Perhaps the final nail in the coffin of SoHo's art scene was **Exit Art's (Map 8)** move to 475 Tenth Avenue a couple years back. This gallery is well-known for brilliant group shows, exhibiting everything from album covers to multimedia installations, and killer openings. It's highly recommended.

Other recommendations are the Starrett-Lehigh Building (Map 8, 601 W 26th St), not only for the art but also for the great pillars, windows, and converted freight elevators, **Esso (Map 8)** for Pop Art, the **Daniel Reich Gallery (Map 8)**, and the **Jonathan LeVine Gallery (Map 8)**, which consistently features exciting artists.

Map 1 • Financial District

American Indian Community House Gallery	11 Broadway	212-598-0100
Water Street Gallery	241 Water St	212-349-9090

Map 2 • TriBeCa

A Taste of Art	147 Duane St	212-964-5493
Adelphi University	75 Varick St, 2nd Fl	212-965-8340
Anthem Gallery	41 Wooster St	347-249-4525
Apex Art	291 Church St	212-431-5270
Arcadia Fine Arts	51 Greene St	212-965-1387
Art at Format	50 Wooster St	212-941-7995
Artists Space	38 Greene St, 3rd Fl	212-226-3970
Atlantic Gallery	40 Wooster St	212-219-3183
The Atlantic Gallery	40 Wooster St, 4th Fl	212-219-3183
Brooke Alexander Editions	59 Wooster St	212-925-4338

Cheryl Hazan Gallery	35 N Moore St	212-343-8964
Cheryl Pelavin Fine Art	13 Jay St	212-925-9424
Coda Gallery	472 Broome St	212-334-0407
Dactyl Foundation for the Arts & Humanities	64 Grand St	212-696-7800
Deitch Projects	76 Grand St	212-343-7300
The Drawing Center	35 Wooster St	212-219-2166
Ethan Cohen Fine Arts	18 Jay St	212-625-1250
Gallery Gen	158 Franklin St	212-226-7717
Icosahedron Gallerie	27 N Moore St	212-966-3897
Location One	26 Greene St	212-334-3347
Mela Foundation	275 Church St, 3rd Fl	212-925-8270
The Painting Center	52 Greene St	212-343-1060
SE Feinman Fine Arts	401 Broadway	212-431-6820
SoHo Photo Gallery	15 White St	212-266-8571
Spencer Brownstone Gallery	39 Wooster St	212-334-3455
Team	83 Grand St	212-279-9219

Map 3 • City Hall / Chinatown

Animazing Art	461 Broome St	212-226-7374
Art in General	79 Walker St	212-219-0473
Broome Street Gallery	498 Broome St	212-226-6085
Canada	55 Chrystie St	212-925-4631
Christopher Henry Gallery	59 W 29th St	212-244-6004
CVZ Contemporary	446 Broadway	212-625-0408
Gallery 456	456 Broadway, 3rd Fl	212-431-9740
The Gallery at Dieu Donne Papermill	433 Broome St	212-226-0573
Globe Institute Gallery	291 Broadway	212-349-4330
Grant Gallery	7 Mercer St	212-343-2919
KS Art	73 Leonard St	212-219-9918
Ronald Feldman Fine Arts	31 Mercer St	212-226-3232
Swiss Institute Contemporary Art	495 Broadway, 3rd Fl	212-925-2035
Synagogue for the Arts	49 White St	212-966-7141

Map 4 • Lower East Side

Abrons Art Center	466 Grand St	212-498-0400
Woodward Gallery	133 Eldridge St	212-966-3411

Map 5 • West Village

14th Street Painters	110 W 14th St	212-627-9893
Akira Ikeda	17 Cornelia St, #1C	212-366-5449
Cooper Classics Collection	137 Perry St	212-929-3909
Doma	17 Perry St	212-929-4339
Franklin 54 Gallery	181 Christopher St	212-627-8690
Gavin Brown's Enterprise	620 Greenwich St	212-627-5258
Hal Katzen Gallery	459 Washington St	212-925-9777
Heller Gallery	420 W 14th St	212-414-4014
HERE	145 Sixth Ave	212-647-0202
hpgrp	32 Little W 12th St	212-727-2491
Jane Hartsook Gallery at Greenwich House Pottery	16 Jones St	212-242-4106
maccarone	96 Morton St	212-431-4977
Parkett Editions	145 Sixth Ave	212-673-2660
Plane Space	102 Charles St	917-606-1268
Pratt Manhattan Gallery	144 W 14th St, 2nd Fl	212-647-7778
Sperone Westwater	415 W 13th St	212-999-7337
Synchronicity Fine Arts	106 W 13th St	646-230-8199
Tracy Williams Ltd	313 W 4th St	212-229-2757
Westbeth Gallery	55 Bethune St	212-989-4650
White Columns	320 W 13th St	212-924-4212
Wooster Projects	418 W 15th St	212-871-6700

Map 6 • Washington Square / NYU / NoHo / SoHo

80 Washington Square East Galleries	80 Washington Sq E	212-998-5747
A/D	560 Broadway	212-966-5154
Agora Gallery Chelsea	530 W 25th St	212-226-4151
American Painting	208 E 6th St	212-254-2628
American Primitive	594 Broadway #205	212-966-1530
Andrei Kushnir/Michele Taylor	208 E 6th St	212-254-2628
Axelle Fine Arts Ltd	148 Spring St	212-226-2262
Bottom Feeders Studio Gallery	195 Chrystie St, 2nd Fl	917-974-9664
Broadway Windows	Broadway & E 10th St	212-998-5751
Bronfman Center Gallery at NYU	7 E 10th St	212-998-4114
Caldwell Snyder Gallery	451 West Broadway	212-387-0208
Campton Gallery	451 West Broadway	212-387-0208
Cecilia De Torres Ltd	140 Greene St	212-431-5869

CFM	112 Greene St	212-966-3864
David Nolan Gallery	560 Broadway	212-925-6190
Deitch Projects	18 Wooster St	212-343-7300
Dia Center for the Arts- New York Earth Room	141 Wooster St	212-473-8072
Dia Center for the Arts- The Broken Kilometer	393 West Broadway	212-989-5566
Eleanor Ettinger	119 Spring St	212-925-7474
Feature	276 Bowery	212-675-7772
Franklin Bowles Galleries	431 West Broadway	212-226-1616
Gallery Juno	568 Broadway #604B	212-431-1515
Gering & Lopez Gallery	730 Fifth Ave	646-336-7183
Gracie Mansion Fine Art	101 Second Ave	212-505-9577
Grey Art Gallery	100 Washington Sq E	212-998-6780
ISE Foundation	555 Broadway	212-925-1649
Jacques Carcanagues	21 Greene St	212-925-8110
Jamali NYC Gallery	413 W Broadway	212-966-3350
Janet Borden	560 Broadway	212-431-0166
John Szoke Editions	591 Broadway, 3rd Fl	212-219-8300
June Kelly	591 Broadway	212-226-1660
Kerrigan Cambell Art + Projects	317 E 9th St	212-505-7196
Leslie-Lohman Gay Art Foundation	26 Wooster St	212-431-2609
Louis K Meisel	141 Prince St	212-677-1340
Margarete Roeder Gallery	545 Broadway, 4th Fl	212-925-6098
Martin Lawrence	457 West Broadway	212-995-8865
Michael Ingbar Gallery of Architectural Art	568 Broadway	212-334-1100
Mimi Ferzt	81 Greene St	212-343-9377
Moss Gallery	150 Greene St	212-204-7104
Multiple Impressions	41 Wooster St	212-925-1313
Nancy Hoffman	429 West Broadway	212-966-6676
National Association of Women Artists Fifth Avenue Gallery	80 Fifth Ave #1405	212-675-1616
New York Open Center Gallery	83 Spring St	212-219-2527
New York Studio School	8 W 8th St	212-673-6466
Nolan/Eckman	560 Broadway Ste 604	212-925-6190
OK Harris Works of Art	383 West Broadway	212-431-3600
Opera Gallery	115 Spring St	212-966-6675
The Pen & Brush	16 E 10th St	212-475-3669
Peter Blum Gallery	526 W 29th St	212-343-0441
Peter Blum SoHo	99 Wooster St	212-343-0441
Peter Freeman	560 Broadway Ste 602	212-966-5154
Pomegranate Gallery	133 Greene St	212-260-4014
pop international galleries	473 West Broadway	212-533-4262
Rosenberg + Kaufman Fine Art	115 Wooster St	212-431-4838
Salmagundi Club	47 Fifth Ave	212-255-7740
Sculptors Guild	110 Greene St Ste 603	212-431-5669
Staley-Wise Gallery	560 Broadway Ste 305	212-966-6223
Storefront for Art and Architecture	97 Kenmare St	212-431-5795
Susan Teller Gallery	568 Broadway, Ste 103A	212-941-7335
Tenri Cultural Institute	43A W 13th St	212-645-2800
Terrain Gallery	141 Greene St	212-777-4490
Tobey Fine Arts	580 Broadway, Ste 902	212-431-7878
Ward-Nasse Gallery	178 Prince St	212-925-6951
Washington Square Windows	80 Washington Sq E	212-998-5751
Westwood Gallery	568 Broadway	212-925-5700
Xanadu	217 Thompson St	646-319-8597

Map 7 • East Village / Lower East Side

BlueSky/Eickholt Gallery	93 St Marks Pl	646-613-9610
Gallery Onetwentyeight	128 Rivington St	212-674-0244
MF Gallery	157 Rivington St	917-446-8681
The Phatory	618 E 9th St	212-777-7922
Rivington Arms	4 E 2nd St	646-654-3213

Map 8 • Chelsea

303 Gallery	525 W 22nd St	212-255-1121
511 Gallery	529 W 20th St	212-255-2885
ACA Galleries	529 W 20th St, 5th Fl	212-206-8080
AIR Gallery	511 W 25th St	212-255-6651
Alexander and Bonin	132 Tenth Ave	212-367-7474
Allen Sheppard Gallery	530 W 25th St	212-989-9919
Amos Eno Gallery	530 W 25th St, 6th Fl	212-226-5342
Amsterdam Whitney	511 W 25th St	212-255-9050
Andrea Meislin Gallery	526 W 26th St	212-627-2552
Andrea Rosen Gallery	525 W 24th St	212-627-6000
Andrew Edlin Gallery	529 W 20th St, 6th Fl	212-206-9723
Andrew Kreps	525 W 22nd St	212-741-8849
Anton Kern	532 W 20th St	212-367-9663
ATM Gallery	619 W 27th St	212-375-0349
Aurora Gallery	515 W 29th St, 2nd Fl	212-643-1700
Axis Gallery	453 W 17th St, 4th Fl	212-741-2582
Barbara Gladstone Gallery	515 W 24th St	212-206-9300
Barry Friedman	515 W 26th St	212-794-8950
Bellwether	134 Tenth Ave	212-929-5959
Bespoke Gallery	547 W 27th St	212-695-8201
Betty Cuningham Gallery	541 W 25th St	212-242-2772
Bitforms	529 W 20th St, 2nd Fl	212-366-6939
Blue Mountain Gallery	530 W 25th St, 4th Fl	646-486-4730
Bodhi Art	535 W 24th St	212-352-2644
Bose Pacia Modern	508 W 26th St, 11th Fl	212-989-7074
Bowery Gallery	530 W 25th St, 4th Fl	646-230-6655
Briggs Robinson Gallery	527 W 29th St	212 560-9075
Bruce Silverstein Gallery	535 W 24th St	212-627-3930
Bryce Wolkowitz Gallery	601 W 26th St #1240	212-243-8830
BUIA Gallery	541 W 23rd St	212-366-9915
Caelum Gallery	526 W 26th St, Ste 315	212-924-4161
Caren Golden Fine Art	539 W 23rd St	212-727-8304
Casey Kaplan	525 W 21st St	212-645-7335
Cavin-Morris	210 11th Ave	212-226-3768
Ceres	547 W 27th St, 2nd Fl	212-947-6100
Chambers Fine Art	210 Eleventh Ave, 2nd Fl	212-414-1169
Chapel of Sacred Mirrors/ COSM NYC	542 W 27th St	212-564-4253
Chappell Gallery	526 W 26th St, #317	212-414-2673
Charles Cowles Gallery	537 W 24th St	212-741-8999
Cheim & Read	547 W 25th St	212-242-7727
Claire Oliver Gallery	513 W 26th St	212-929-5949
Clementine Gallery	623 W 27th St	212-243-5937
Cohan and Leslie	138 Tenth Ave	212-206-8710
CRG Gallery	535 W 22nd St, 3rd Fl	212-229-2766
Cue Art Foundation	511 W 25th St	212-206-3583
Cynthia Broan Gallery	546 W 29th St	212-760-0809
D'Amelio Terras	525 W 22nd St	212-352-9460
Danese	535 W 24th St	212-223-2227
Daniel Cooney Fine Art	511 W 25th St	212-255-8158
Daniel Reich Gallery	537 W 23rd St	212-924-4949
David Krut Fine Art	526 W 26th St	212-255-3094
David Zwirner	525 W 19th St	212-727-2070
DCKT Contemporary	552 W 24th St	212-741-9955
Denise Bibro Fine Art	529 W 20th St, 4th Fl	212-647-7030
Derek Eller Gallery	615 W 27th St	212-206-6411
DFN Gallery	210 11th Ave	212-334-3400
Dillon Gallery	555 W 25th St	212-727-8700
Dinter Fine Art	547 W 27th St	212-947-2818
DJT Fine Art/Dom Taglialatella	231 Tenth Ave	212-367-0881
Dorfman Projects	529 W 20th St, 7th Fl	212-352-2272
Edition Schellmann	210 Eleventh Ave, 8th Fl	212-219-1821
Edward Thorp	210 Eleventh Ave, 6th Fl	212-691-6565
Elizabeth Dee Gallery	545 W 20th St	212-924-7545
Elizabeth Harris	529 W 20th St	212-463-9666
Esso Gallery	531 W 26th St	212-560-9728
Exit Art	475 Tenth Ave	212-966-7745
Eyebeam	540 W 21st St	212-937-6580
Feigen Contemporary	535 W 20th St	212-929-0500
First Street Gallery	526 W 26th St #915	646-336-8053

Fischbach Gallery	210 Eleventh Ave #801	212-759-2345
Flomenhaft Gallery	547 W 27th St	212-268-4952
Florence Lynch Gallery	539 W 25th St	212-924-3290
Fredericks Freiser Gallery	536 W 24th St, 6th Fl	212-633-6555
Frederieke Taylor Gallery	535 W 22nd St, 6th Fl	646-230-0992
Freight + Volume	542 W 24th St	212-989-8700
Friedrich Petzel	535 W 22nd St	212-680-9467
Gagosian Gallery	555 W 24th St	212-741-1111
Galdstone Gallery	515 W 24th St	212-206-9301
Galeria Ramis Barquet	532 W 24th St	212-675-3421
Galerie Lelong	528 W 26th St	212-315-0470
Gallery Henoch	555 W 25th St	917-305-0003
George Adams	525 W 26th St	212-564-8480
George Billis Gallery	511 W 25th St	212-645-2621
Goff and Rosenthal	537B W 23rd St	212-675-0461
GR N'Namdi Gallery	526 W 26th St	212-929-6645
Greene Naftali	526 W 26th St, 8th Fl	212-463-7770
Heidi Cho Gallery	522 W 23rd St	212-255-6783
Howard Scott	529 W 20th St, 7th Fl	646-486-7004
I-20 Gallery	557 W 23rd St	212-645-1100
InterArt Gallery	225 Tenth Ave	212-647-1811
International Poster Center	601 W 26th St	212-787-4000
International Print Center New York	526 W 26th St, Rm 824	212-989-5090
J Cacciola Galleries	531 W 25th St	212-462-4646
Jack Shainman Gallery	513 W 20th St	212-645-1701
James Cohan	533 W 26th St	212-714-9500
Jeff Bailey Gallery	511 W 25th St	212-989-0156
Jenkins Johnson Gallery	521 W 26th St	212-629-0707
Jim Kempner Fine Art	501 W 23rd St	212-206-6872
John Connelly Presents	625 W 27th St	212-337-9563
Jonathan LeVine Gallery	529 W 20th St	212-243-3822
Josee Bienvenu Gallery	529 W 20th St, 2nd Fl	212-206-7990
Julie Saul Gallery	535 W 22nd St, 6th Fl	212-627-2410
Katherine Markel Fine Arts	529 W 20th St	212-366-5368
Kent Gallery	541 W 25th St	212-627-3680
Kim Foster	529 W 20th St	212-229-0044
Kimcherova	532 W 25th St	212-929-9720
The Kitchen	512 W 19th St	212-255-5793
Klemens Gasser & Tanja Grunert	524 W 19th St, 1st Fl	212-807-9494
Klotz Sirmon Gallery	511 W 25th St	212-741-4764
Kravets/Wehby Gallery	521 W 21st St	212-352-2238
Kustera Tilton Gallery	520 W 21st St	212-989-0082
Lang Fine Art	229 Tenth Ave	212-980-2400
Larissa Goldston Gallery	530 W 25th St	212-206-7887
Lehmann Maupin	540 W 26th St	212-937-6581
Lemmons Contemporary	210 Eleventh Ave	212-337-0025
Lennon, Weinberg	514 W 25th St	212-941-0012
Leo Koenig	545 W 23rd St	212-334-9255
Leslie Tonkonow Artworks and Projects	535 W 22nd St, 6th Fl	212-255-8450
Lohin Geduld Gallery	531 W 25th St	212-675-2656
Lombard-Freid Projects	531 W 26th St	212-967-8040
Lost Art	515 W 29th St PH	212-594-5450
Lucas Schoormans	508 W 26th St #11B	212-243-3159
Luhring Augustine	531 W 24th St	212-206-9100
Luise Ross	511 W 25th St	212-343-2161
Lyons Wier Gallery	511 W 25th St #205	212-242-6220
Magnan Projects	317 Tenth Ave	212-244-2344
Margaret Thatcher Projects	511 W 25th St #404	212-675-0222
Marianne Boesky Gallery	509 W 24th St	212-680-9889
Martos Gallery	540 W 29th St	212-560-0670
Marvelli Gallery	526 W 26th St	212-627-3363
Mary Boone Gallery	541 W 24th St	212-752-2929
Mary Ryan	527 W 26th St	212-397-0669
Massimo Audiello	526 W 26th St #519	212-675-9082
Matthew Marks Gallery	523 W 24th St	212-243-0200
Max Protech	511 W 22nd St	212-633-6999
Maya Stendhal Gallery	545 W 20th St	212-366-1549
McKenzie Fine Art	511 W 25th St, 2nd Fl	212-989-5467
Medialia: Rack & Hamper Gallery	335 W 38th St, 4th Fl	212-971-0953
Metro Pictures	519 W 24th St	212-206-7100

Arts & Entertainment · **Art Galleries**

Michael Steinberg Fine Art	526 W 26th St	212-924-5770
Mike Weiss Gallery	520 W 24th St	212-691-6899
Mixed Greens	531 W 26th St	212-331-8888
Montserrat	547 W 27th St	212-268-0088
Morgan Lehman	317 Tenth Ave	212-268-6699
Moti Hasson Gallery	535 W 25th St	212-268-4444
Murray Guy	453 W 17th St	212-463-7372
MY Art Prospects	547 W 27th St 2nd Fl	212-268-7132
Nancy Margolis Gallery	523 W 25th St	212-242-3013
Neptune Fine Art & Brand X Projects	511 W 25th St	212-989-9080
New Art Center	580 Eighth Ave	212-354-2999
New Century Artists	530 W 25th St Ste 406	212-367-7072
Newman/Popiashvili Gallery	504 W 22nd St	212-274-9166
Nicole Klagsbrun Gallery	526 W 26th St #213	212-243-3335
NoHo Gallery in Chelsea	530 W 25th St, 4th Fl	212-367-7063
Pace Wildenstein	534 W 25th St	212-929-7000
Paul Kasmin Gallery	293 Tenth Ave	212-563-4474
Paul Kasmin Gallery	511 W 27th St	212-563-4474
Paul Morris Gallery	530 W 25th St	212-727-2752
Paul Rodgers/9W	529 W 20th St, 9th Fl	212-414-9810
Paul Sharpe Contemporary Art	525 W 29th St	646-613-1252
Paula Cooper Gallery	534 W 21st St	212-255-1105
Pavel Zoubok Gallery	533 W 23rd St	212-675-7490
Perry Rubenstein Gallery	527 W 23rd St	212-627-8000
Phoenix	210 Eleventh Ave, 9th Fl	212-226-8711
Pleiades Gallery	530 W 25th St	646-230-0056
Postmasters Gallery	459 W 19th St	212-727-3323
PPOW	555 W 25th St, 2nd Fl	212-647-1044
Prince Street Gallery	530 W 25th St, 4th Fl	646-230-0246
Printed Matter	195 Tenth Ave	212-925-0325
The Proposition	559 W 22nd St	212-242-0035
Qui New York/Zwicker Collective USA	601 W 26th St	212-691-2240
Randel Gallery	287 Tenth Ave, 2nd Fl	212-239-3330
Rare	521 W 26th St	212-268-1520
Reeves Contemporary	535 W 24th St, 2nd Fl	212-714-0044
Rhonda Schaller Studio	547 W 27th St	212-226-0166
Ricco/Maresca Gallery	529 W 20th St, 3rd Fl	212-627-4819
Robert Mann Gallery	210 Eleventh Ave	212-989-7600
Robert Miller	524 W 26th St	212-366-4774
Robert Steele Gallery	511 W 25th St	212-243-0165
Rush Arts Gallery & Resource Center	526 W 26th St #311	212-691-9552
Sara Meltzer Gallery	516 W 20th St	212-727-9330
Sara Tecchia Roma New York	529 W 20th St	212-741-2900
Sean Kelly Gallery	528 W 29th St	212-239-1181
Sears-Peyton Gallery	210 Eleventh Ave #802	212-966-7469
Sherry French	601 W 26th St	212-647-8867
Sikkema, Jenkins & Co	530 W 22nd St	212-929-2262
Silas Seandel Studio	551 W 22nd St	212-645-5286
Skoto Gallery	529 W 20th St	212-352-8058
SoHo 20 Chelsea	511 W 25th St Ste 605	212-367-8994
Sonnabend	536 W 22nd St	212-627-1018
Spike Gallery	547 W 20th St	212-627-4100
Stefan Stux Gallery	530 W 25th St	212-352-1600
Stellan Holm Gallery	524 W 24th St	212-627-7444
Stephen Haller	542 W 26th St	212-741-7777
Steven Kasher	521 W 23rd St	212-966-3978
Stricoff Fine Art	564 W 25th St	212-219-3977
Studio 601	511 W 25th St	212-367-7300
Sundaram Tagore Gallery	547 W 27th St	212-677-4520
Susan Inglett Gallery	534 W 22nd St	212-647-9111
SVA Main Gallery	601 W 26th St	212-592-2145
Tamar Hirschl Studio	601 W 26th St	212-255-1440
Tanya Bonakdar Gallery	521 W 21st St	212-414-4144
Thomas Erben Gallery	516 W 20th St	212-645-8701
Tony Shafrazi Gallery	544 W 26th St	212-274-9300
Van De Weghe Fine Art	521 W 23rd St	212-929-6633
Vanina Holasek Gallery	502 W 27th St	212-367-9093
Virgil De Voldere Gallery	526 W 26th St	212-343-9694
Viridian Artists	530 W 25th St, #407	212-414-4040
Von Lintel Gallery	555 W 25th St, 2nd Fl	212-242-0599

Walter Wickiser Gallery	210 Eleventh Ave	212-941-1817
White Box	525 W 26th St	212-714-2347
Yancey Richardson Gallery	535 W 22nd St	646-230-9610
Yossi Milo Gallery	525 W 25th St	212-414-0370
Yvon Lambert	564 W 25th St	212-242-3611
Zach Fuer Gallery (LFL)	530 W 24th St	212-989-7700
Zieher Smith	531 W 25th St	212-229-1088
ZONEchelsea, Center for the Arts	601 W 26th St	212-205-2177

Map 9 · Flatiron / Lower Midtown

A-forest Gallery	134 W 29th St	212-673-1168
Alp Galleries	291 Seventh Ave, 5th Fl	212-206-9108
Anna Kustera Gallery	520 W 21st St	212-989-0082
Art Center of the Graduate Center CUNY	365 Fifth Ave	212-817-7386
Christine Burgin Gallery	243 W 18th St	212-462-2668
Gallery 138	138 W 17th St	212-633-0324
Gallery ArtsIndia	206 Fifth Ave	212-725-6092
H Heather Edelman Gallery	141 W 20th St	646-230-1104
Haim Chanin Fine Arts	212 W 19th St	646-230-7200
Illustration House	110 W 25th St	212-966-9444
Marlborough Chelsea	545 W 25th St	212-541-4900
Merton D Simpson Gallery	38 W 28th St, 5th Fl	212-686-6735
Nabi Gallery	137 W 25th St	212-929-6063
NYCoo Gallery	20 W 22nd St	212-380-1149
Senior & Shopmaker	21 E 26th St	212-213-6767
Sepia International	148 W 24th St	212-645-9444
Space B	257B W 19th St	917-518-2385
Sragow	153 W 27th St, Rm 505	212-219-1793

Map 10 · Murray Hill / Gramercy

Baruch College/Sidney Mishkin Gallery	135 E 22nd St	212-802-2690
East-West Gallery	573 Third Ave	212-687-0180
Hayato New York	125 E 23rd St	212-673-7373
The National Arts Club	15 Gramercy Park S	212-475-3424
Nyehaus	15 Gramercy Park S	212-995-1785
School of Visual Arts	209 E 23rd St	212-592-2144
Swann Galleries	104 E 25th St	212-254-4710
Talwar Gallery	108 E 16th St	212-673-3096
Tepper Galleries	110 E 25th St	212-677-5300

Map 11 · Hell's Kitchen

Fountain Gallery	702 Ninth Ave	212-262-2756
Gallery MC	549 W 52nd St	212-581-1966
Hunter College/Times Square Gallery	450 W 41st St	212-772-4991
Jadite	413 W 50th St	212-315-2740

Map 12 · Midtown

AFP Galleries	595 Madison Ave	212-230-1003
Alexandre Gallery	41 E 57th St, 13th Fl	212-755-2828
Ameringer & Yohe Fine Art	20 W 57th St, 2nd Fl	212-445-0051
Art Students League of NY	215 W 57th St, 2nd Fl	212-247-4510
Austrian Cultural Forum	11 E 52nd St	212-319-5300
Babcock	724 Fifth Ave, 11th Fl	212-767-1852
Barbara Mathes	22 E 80th St	212-570-4190
Bernarducci-Meisel	37 W 57th St, 6th Fl	212-593-3757
Berwald Oriental Art	5 E 57th St	212-319-1519
Bill Hodges Gallery	24 W 57th St	212-333-2640
Bonni Benrubi	41 E 57th St, 13th Fl	212-888-6007
China 2000 Fine Art	5 E 57th St	212-588-1198
Christie's	20 Rockefeller Plz	212-636-2000
Cohen Amador	41 E 57th St	212-759-6740

D Wigmore Fine Art	730 Fifth Ave	212-581-1657
David Findlay Jr Fine Art	41 E 57th St Ste 1120	212-486-7660
DC Moore	724 Fifth Ave, 8th Fl	212-247-2111
Edwynn Houk	745 Fifth Ave, 4th Fl	212-750-7070
Forum	745 Fifth Ave, 5th Fl	212-355-4545
Franklin Parrasch	20 W 57th St	212-246-5360
Galeria Ramis Barquet	41 E 57th St, 5th Fl	212-644-9090
Galerie St Etienne	24 W 57th St Ste 802	212-245-6734
Gallery: Gertrude Stein	56 W 57th St	212-535-0600
Greenberg Van Doren Gallery	730 Fifth Ave	212-445-0444
Hammer Galleries	33 W 57th St	212-644-4400
Herbert Arnot	250 W 57th St	212-245-8287
Howard Greenberg	41 E 57th St, 14th Fl	212-334-0010
Jain Marunouchi	24 W 57th St, 6th Fl	212-969-9660
James Goodman	41 E 57th St, 8th Fl	212-593-3737
Jason McCoy	41 E 57th St	212-319-1996
Joan T Washburn	20 W 57th St, 8th Fl	212-397-6780
Julian Jadow Ceramics	37 W 57th St #601	212-757-6660
Katharina Rich Perlow	41 E 57th St, 13th Fl	212-644-7171
Kennedy Galleries	730 Fifth Ave	212-541-9600
Latincollector	37 W 57th St	212-334-7813
Laurence Miller	20 W 57th St	212-397-3930
Leo Kaplan Modern	41 E 57th St, 7th Fl	212-872-1616
Leonard Hutton	41 E 57th St, 3rd Fl	212-751-7373
Littleton & Hennessey Asian Art	724 Fifth Ave	212-586-4075
Lori Bookstein Fine Art	37 W 57th St	212-750-0949
Marian Goodman	24 W 57th St, 4th Fl	212-977-7160
Marlborough	40 W 57th St, 2nd Fl	212-541-4900
Mary Boone	745 Fifth Ave, 4th Fl	212-752-2929
Maxwell Davidson	724 Fifth Ave	212-759-7555
McKee	745 Fifth Ave, 4th Fl	212-688-5951
Michael Rosenfeld	24 W 57th St, 7th Fl	212-247-0082
Neuhoff	41 E 57th St, 4th Fl	212-838-1122
Nippon Gallery	145 W 57th St	212-581-2223
Nohra Haime	41 E 57th St, 6th Fl	212-888-3550
Pace MacGill	32 E 57th St, 9th Fl	212-759-7999
Pace Primitive	32 E 57th St, 7th Fl	212-421-3688
Pace Prints	32 E 57th St, 3rd Fl	212-421-3237
PaceWildenstein	32 E 57th St	212-421-3292
Peter Findlay	41 E 57th St, 3rd Fl	212-644-4433
The Project	37 W 57th St, 3rd Fl	212-688-1585
Projectile	37 W 57th St	212-688-1585
Reece	24 W 57th St Ste 304	212-333-5830
Rehs Galleries	5 E 57th St	212-355-5710
Rita Krauss/Meridian Gallery	41 E 57th St	212-980-2400
Scholten Japanese Art	145 W 58th St #2H	212-585-0474
Susan Sheehan	20 W 57th St, 7th Fl	212-489-3331
Tibor de Nagy	724 Fifth Ave, 12th Fl	212-262-5050
Tina Kim Fine Art	41 W 57th St, 2nd Fl	212-716-1100
UBS Art Gallery	1285 Sixth Ave	212-713-2885
Zabriskie	41 E 57th St, 4th Fl	212-752-1223

Map 13 • East Midtown

Dai Ichi Arts	249 E 48th St	212-230-1680
Gallery Korea	460 Park Ave, 6th Fl	212-759-9550
Japan Society	333 E 47th St	212-832-1155
Messineo Wyman Projects	351 E 50th St	212-414-0827
National Sculpture Society	237 Park Ave	212-764-5645
Spanierman Gallery	45 E 58th St	212-832-0208
St Peter's Lutheran Church	619 Lexington Ave	212-935-2200
Throckmorton Fine Art	145 E 57th St, 3rd Fl	212-223-1059
Trygve Lie Gallery	317 E 52nd St	212-319-0370
Ubu Gallery	416 E 59th St	212-753-4444
Wally Findlay Galleries	124 E 57th St	212-421-5390

Map 14 • Upper West Side (Lower)

Art for Healing NYC / Art for Healing Gallery	2350 Broadway	212-946-1160

Frederick Schultz Ancient Art	325 W 82nd St	212-721-6007
Littlejohn Contemporary	245 E 72nd St	212-988-4890

Map 15 • Upper East Side (Lower)

Achim Moeller Fine Art	36 E 64th St	212-644-2133
Acquavella	18 E 79th St	212-734-6300
Adam Baumgold	74 E 79th St	212-861-7338
Adelson Galleries	19 E 82nd St	212-439-6800
American Illustrators Gallery	18 E 77th St Ste 1A	212-744-5190
Andrew Roth	160A E 70th St	212-717-9067
Anita Friedman Fine Arts	980 Madison Ave	212-472-1527
Anita Shapolsky	152 E 65th St	212-452-1094
Bernard Goldberg Fine Arts	667 Madison Ave	212-813-9797
Berry-Hill	11 E 70th St	212-744-2300
Bruton	40 E 61st St	212-980-1640
CDS	76 E 79th St	212-772-9555
China Institute	125 E 65th St	212-744-8181
Conner & Rosenkranz	19 E 74th St	212-517-3710
Cook Fine Art	1063 Madison Ave	212-737-3550
Craig F Starr Associates	5 E 73rd St	212-570-1739
David Findlay Galleries	984 Madison Ave	212-249-2909
Davis & Langdale	231 E 60th St	212-838-0333
Debra Force Fine Art	14 E 73rd St Ste 4B	212-734-3636
Dickinson Roundell	19 E 66th St	212-772-8083
Ekstrom & Ekstrom	417 E 75th St	212-988-8857
Ezair	905 Madison Ave	212-628-2224
Flowers	1000 Madison Ave, 2nd Fl	212-439-1700
Francis M Naumann Fine Art	22 E 80th St	212-472-6800
Friedman & Vallois	27 E 67th St	212-517-3820
Gagosian	980 Madison Ave	212-744-2313
Galerie Rienzo	20 E 69th St #4C	212-288-2226
Gallery 71	974 Lexington Ave	212-744-7779
Gallery Schlesinger	24 E 73rd St, 2nd Fl	212-734-3600
Gemini GEL at Joni Moisant Weyl	980 Madison Ave	212-249-3324
Gerald Peters	24 E 78th St	212-628-9760
Gitterman Gallery	170 E 75th St	212-734-0868
Godel & Co	39A E 72nd St	212-288-7272
Goedhuis Contemporary	42 E 76th St	212-535-6954
Hall & Knight	21 E 67th St	212-772-2266
Hirschl & Adler Galleries	21 E 70th St	212-535-8810
Hollis Taggart Galleries	958 Madison Ave	212-628-4000
Hoorn-Ashby	766 Madison Ave, 2nd Fl	212-628-3199
Hubert Gallery	1046 Madison Ave	212-628-2922
Hunter College/Bertha & Karl Leubsdorf Gallery	E 68th St & Lexington	212-772-4991
Irena Hochman Fine Art	1100 Madison Ave	212-772-2227
Island Weiss Gallery	201 E 69th St	212-861-4608
Jacobson Howard	22 E 72nd St	212-570-2362
James Francis Trezza	39 E 78th St Ste 603	212-327-2218
James Graham & Sons	1014 Madison Ave	212-535-5767
Jan Krugier	980 Madison Ave	212-755-7288
Jane Kahan	1020 Madison Ave	212-744-1490
Janos Gat Gallery	1100 Madison Ave	212-327-0441
Kate Ganz USA	25 E 73rd St	212-535-1977
Keith De Lellis	117 1/2 E 62nd St	212-688-2050
Knoedler & Co	19 E 70th St	212-794-0550
Kouros	23 E 73rd St	212-288-5888
Kraushaar	74 E 79th St	212-288-2558
L&M Arts	45 E 78th St	212-861-0020
L'Arc En Seine	15 E 82nd St	212-585-2587
Leila Taghinia-Milani Heller Gallery	22 E 72nd St	212-249-7695
Leo Castelli	18 E 77th St	212-249-4470
Leon Tovar Gallery	16 E 71st St	212-585-2400
Linda Hyman Fine Art	44 E 67th St	212-399-0112
M&R Sayer Fine Arts	55 E 80th St, 2nd Fl	212-249-0428
M&R Sayer Fine Arts	129 E 71st St	212-517-8811
Marc Jancou Fine Art	801 Madison Ave	212-717-1700

Arts & Entertainment • Art Galleries

Mark Murray Fine Paintings	39 E 72nd St	212-585-2380
Martha Parrish & James Reinish	25 E 73rd St, 2nd Fl	212-734-7332
Mary-Anne Martin Fine Art	23 E 73rd St	212-288-2213
Megan Moynihan & Franklin Riehlman	24 E 73rd St	212-879-2545
Menconi & Schoelkopf Fine Art	13 E 69th St	212-879-8815
Meredith Ward Fine Art	60 E 66th St	212-744-7306
Michael Werner	4 E 77th St	212-988-1623
Michail-Lombardo Gallery	19 E 69th St Ste 302	212-472-2400
Michelle Rosenfeld	16 E 79th St	212-734-0900
Mitchell-Innes & Nash	1018 Madison Ave, 5th Fl	212-744-7400
MMC Gallery	221 E 71st St	212-517-0692
MME Fine Art	74 E 79th St	212-439-6600
Molly Tribal Art	49 E 78th St	212-288-0043
Paul Thiebaud Gallery	42 E 76th St	212-737-9759
Praxis International Art	25 E 73rd St, 4th Fl	212-772-9478
Questroyal Fine Art	903 Park Ave Ste 3A & B	212-744-3586
Rachel Adler Fine Art	24 E 71st St	212-308-0511
Richard Gray	1018 Madison Ave, 4th Fl	212-472-8787
Richard L Feigen & Co	34 E 69th St	212-628-0700
Schiller & Bodo	120 E 65th St	212-772-8627
Shepherd & Derom Galleries	58 E 79th St	212-861-4050
Skarstedt Fine Art	1018 Madison Ave, 3rd Fl	212-737-2060
Sotheby's	1334 York Ave	212-606-7000
Soufer	1015 Madison Ave	212-628-3225
Tilton Gallery	8 E 76th St	212-737-2221
Ukrainian Institute of America	2 E 79th St	212-288-8660
Ursus Books	981 Madison Ave	212-772-8787
Uta Scharf	42 E 76th St	212-744-3840
Vivian Horan Fine Art	35 E 67th St, 2nd Fl	212-517-9410
Wildenstein	19 E 64th St	212-879-0500
William Secord	52 E 76th St	212-249-0075
Winston Wachter Mayer Fine Art	39 E 78th St, Ste 301	212-327-2526
Yoshii	17 E 76th St, Ste 1R	212-744-5550
Zwirner & Wirth	32 E 69th St	212-517-8677

Map 17 • Upper East Side / East Harlem

Allan Stone Gallery	113 E 90th St	212-987-4997
Doyle New York	175 E 87th St	212-427-2730
Gallery at the Marmara-Manhattan	301 E 94th St	212-427-3100
Jeffrey Myers Primitive & Fine Art	12 E 86th St	212-472-0115
Neue Galerie	1048 Fifth Ave	212-628-6200
Salon 94	12 E 94th St	646-672-9212
Samson Fine Arts	1150 Fifth Ave	212-369-6677
Taller Boricua Galleries	1680 Lexington Ave	212-831-4333
Uptown Gallery	1194 Madison Ave	212-722-3677

Map 18 • Columbia / Morningside Heights

Galleries at the Interchurch Center	475 Riverside Dr	212-870-2200
Miriam & Ira D Wallach Art Gallery	116th & Broadway, 8th Fl	212-854-7288

Battery Park City

World Financial Center Courtyard Gallery	220 Vesey St	212-945-2600

Jersey City

Kearon-Hempenstall Gallery	536 Bergen Ave [Harrison Ave]	201-333-8855
New Jersey City University	2039 Kennedy Blvd [Culver Ave]	201-200-3246

The New York City book scene has taken a sharp decline in terms of diversity in recent years, with many excellent bookshops—including Coliseum Books, A Different Light, Academy, A Photographer's Place, Rizzoli SoHo, Tower Books, Brentano's, Spring Street Books, and Shortwave—all going the way of the dodo. The remaining independent stores are now the last outposts before everything interesting or alternative disappears altogether. And some of NYC's richest cultural neighborhoods—such as the East Village and the Lower East Side—don't have enough bookstores to even come close to properly serving their populations of literate hipsters. So we thought we'd take this opportunity to list some of our favorite remaining shops....

General New/Used

The Strand (Map 6) on Broadway, the largest and arguably most popular independent bookstore in town, boasts staggering range and depth in its offerings (and often the best prices around to boot). Whether you're interested in art tomes, rare first editions, foreign language texts, nonfiction works, or the latest bestseller, it's impossible to be disappointed. **Gotham Book Mart (Map 12)** remains Midtown's major literary watering hole, and **St. Mark's Bookshop (Map 6)** anchors the border between the NYU crowd and the East Village hipster contingent. Both Gotham and St. Mark's have excellent literary journal selections. **Argosy Book Store (Map 13)** on 59th Street is still a top destination for antiquarian books. Uptown, **Morningside Bookshop (Map 18)** and **Labyrinth (Map 18)** serve the Columbia area well. With four locations around the city, the punchy **Shakespeare & Company (Maps 1, 6, 10, and 15)** is a local chain that somehow manages to maintain an aura of individuality. In the West Village, **Three Lives and Co. (Map 5)** should be your destination. The **Barnes & Noble (Map 9)** in Union Square is their signature store and has a great feel. The **Housing Works Used Book Café (Map 6)** has a vintage coffeehouse feel and is one of our favorite bookstores—all of the profits go to help homeless New Yorkers living with HIV/AIDS.

Small/Used

Fortunately there are still a lot of used bookstores tucked away all over the city. **Mercer Street Books (Map 6)** serves NYU, **East Village Books (Map 7)** takes care of hipster heaven, and **Skyline (Map 9)** remains a good Chelsea destination. In Brooklyn, **Park Slope Books (Map 33)**, a.k.a. 7th Avenue Books, is a fun browse.

Travel

The city's travel book selection is possibly its greatest strength—from the **Hagstrom Map & Travel (Map 12)** near Bryant Park to several independents, such as the elegant **Complete Traveller Bookstore (Map 9)** and SoHo's **Traveler's Choice Bookstore (Map 2)**.

Art

Printed Matter (Map 8) houses one of the best collections of artists' books in the world and is highly recommended. The **New Museum of Contemporary Art Bookstore (Map 6)** also offers a brilliant selection of both artists' and art books. If you aren't on a budget and have a new coffee table to fill, try **Ursus (Map 15)** in Chelsea.

NYC/Government

The City Store (Map 3) in the Municipal Building is small but carries a solid selection (and is still the only store we've seen that sells old taxicab medallions). The **Civil Service Bookstore (Map 3)** has all the study guides you'll need when you want to change careers and start driving a bus. The **United Nations Bookshop (Map 13)** has a great range of international and governmental titles. The **New York Transit Museum (Map 12)** shop at Grand Central also has an excellent range of books on NYC.

Specialty

Books of Wonder (Map 9) in Chelsea has long been a downtown haven for children's books, and kids love that it adjoins a cupcake bakery. Two mystery shops, **They Mysterious Book Shop (Map 2)** and **Partners & Crime (Map 5)**, slake the need for whodunits. **The Drama Book Shop (Map 12)** is a great source for books on acting and the theater. **Biography Book Shop (Map 5)** speaks for itself. **Urban Center Books (Map 12)** is well known for its architecture collection. **Librairie de France (Map 12)**, located in Rockefeller Center, sells books written exclusively in (you guessed it) French. **Bluestockings (Map 7)** is an epicenter for radical and feminist literature. **Oscar Wilde Books (Map 5)** in the West Village is one of the world's largest gay and lesbian bookstores.

Readings

Anyone can read great authors, but lucky for New Yorkers, we have beaucoup chances to meet the literati, too. The four-story **Barnes & Noble (Map 9)** in Union Square regularly hosts major writers (Tom Wolfe, Nick Hornby, and former President Bill Clinton are a few of the recent guests). **Housing Works Used Book Café (Map 6)** draws some big names; Philip Gourevitch and Jonathan Lethem have discussed their tomes there in the last few years. And **McNally Robinson (Map 6)** in Nolita is another spot known for hosting great author events. Nearly all bookstores present readings, even if irregularly. Check a store's Web page for listings. Literary blogs like www.maudnewton.com list weekly events for bookworms. Even bars have taken a literary turn for the better: KGB Bar features fiction, poetry, and nonfiction readings each week (www.kgbbar.com) and One Story magazine hosts an excellent monthly reading series at Pianos (www.one-story.com). In Brooklyn, Pete's Candy Store and its weekly reading series are a good bet for your weekly dose of literature (www.petescandystore.com).

Arts & Entertainment • **Bookstores**

Map 1 • Financial District

Borders	100 Broadway	212-964-1988	Chain
Chameleon Comics	3 Maiden Ln	212-587-3411	Comics
Metropolitan Museum of Art Bookshop	12 Fulton St	212-248-0954	Specialty - Art books.
Shakespeare & Co	1 Whitehall St	212-742-7025	Chain
Strand	95 Fulton St	212-732-6070	Used; Remainders

Map 2 • TriBeCa

Barnes & Noble	97 Warren St	212-587-5389	Chain
Manhattan Books	150 Chambers St	212-385-7395	New and used textbooks.
The Mysterious Book Shop	58 Warren St	212-587-1011	Specialty - Mystery
NY Law School Bookstore	47 Worth St	212-227-7220	Specialty - Law textbooks

Map 3 • City Hall / Chinatown

Civil Service Book Shop	89 Worth St	212-226-9506	Specialty - Civil Services
Computer Book Works	78 Reade St	212-385-1616	Specialty - Computer
Ming Fay Book Store	42 Mott St	212-406-1957	Specialty - Chinese
New York City Store	1 Centre St	212-669-8246	Specialty - NYC books and municipal publications
Oriental Books Stationery & Arts	29 East Broadway	212-962-3634	Specialty - Chinese
Oriental Culture Enterprises	13 Elizabeth St	212-226-8461	Specialty - Chinese
Pace University Bookstore	41 Park Row	212-346-1605	Academic - General
World Journal Bookstore	379 East Broadway	212-226-5131	Chinese books

Map 4 • Lower East Side

Eastern Books	15 Pike St	212-964-6869	Specialty - Chinese

Map 5 • West Village

Barnes & Noble	396 Sixth Ave	212-674-8780	Chain
Biography Book Shop	400 Bleecker St	212-807-8655	Specialty - Biography
Bonnie Slotnick Cookbooks	163 W 10th St	212-989-8962	Specialty - Out of print cookbooks
Drougas Books	34 Carmine St	212-229-0079	Used, political, Eastern religious, etc.
Joanne Hendricks Cookbooks	488 Greenwich St	212-226-5731	Specialty - Wine and Cooking
Left Bank Books	304 W 4th St	212-924-5638	Used; Antiquarian
Oscar Wilde Memorial Bookshop	15 Christopher St	212-255-8097	Specialty - Gay/Lesbian
Partners & Crime Mystery Booksellers	44 Greenwich Ave	212-243-0440	Specialty - Mystery
Three Lives and Co	154 W 10th St	212-741-2069	General Interest
Time Machine	207 W 14th St	212-691-0380	Comics

Map 6 • Washington Square / NYU / NoHo / SoHo

12th Street Books & Records	11 E 12th St	212-645-4340	Used
Alabaster Bookshop	122 Fourth Ave	212-982-3550	Used
Barnes & Noble	4 Astor Pl	212-420-1322	Chain
Benjamin Cardozo School of Law Bookstore	55 Fifth Ave	212-790-0339	Academic - Law
Dashwood Books	33 Bond St	212-387-8520	Photography
East West Books	78 Fifth Ave	212-243-5994	Specialty - Spirituality; Self-Help
Forbidden Planet	840 Broadway	212-473-1576	Specialty - Fantasy/Sci-fi
Housing Works Used Book Café	126 Crosby St	212-334-3324	Used
McNally Robinson	52 Prince St	212-274-1160	General Interest
Mercer Street Books and Records	206 Mercer St	212-505-8615	Used
New Museum of Contemporary Art Bookstore	235 Bowery	212-343-0460	Art books
New York Open Center Bookstore	83 Spring St	212-219-2527	Specialty - New Age; Spiritual
New York University Book Center- Main Branch	18 Washington Pl	212-998-4667	Academic - General
New York University Book Center- Professional Bookstore	530 LaGuardia Pl	212-998-4680	Academic - Management
NYU Bookstore - Computer Store	242 Greene St	212-998-4672	Academic - Computers
Pageant Book & Print Shop	69 E 4th St	212-674-5296	Used and rare.
Scholastic Store	557 Broadway	212-343-6166	Specialty - Educational.
SF Vanni	30 W 12th St	212-675-6336	Specialty - Italian

Shakespeare & Co	716 Broadway	212-529-1330	Good local chain w/ lots of postmodern fiction.
Silver Age Comics	47 W 8th St	646-654-7054	Comics
St Mark's Bookshop	31 Third Ave	212-260-7853	General Interest.
Strand	828 Broadway	212-473-1452	Used mecca; world's messiest and best bookstore.
Surma Book & Music	11 E 7th St	212-477-0729	Specialty - Ukranian
Taschen	107 Greene St	212-226-2212	Art and photography books
Virgin Megastore	52 E 14th St	212-598-4666	Chain
Zucker Art Books	55 E 9th St	212-679-6332	Art books

Map 7 • East Village / Lower East Side

Bluestockings Bookstore Café and Activist Center	172 Allen St	212-777-6028	Specialty - Political
East Village Books and Records	99 St Marks Pl	212-477-8647	Messy pile of used stuff
Rapture Cafe & Books	200 Ave A	212-228-1177	"Indie publishers and eccentric works"
St Mark's Comics	11 St Marks Pl	212-598-9439	Specialty - Comics

Map 8 • Chelsea

Aperture Book Center	547 W 27th St	212-505-5555	Specialty - Photography
Printed Matter	195 Tenth Ave	212-925-0325	Astounding selection of artist's books; highly recommended.

Map 9 • Flatiron / Lower Midtown

Barnes & Noble	33 E 17th St	212-253-0810	Chain
Barnes & Noble	675 Sixth Ave	212-727-1227	Chain
Barnes & Noble College Bookstore	105 Fifth Ave	212-675-5500	Textbook mayhem.
Books of Wonder	16 W 18th St	212-989-3270	Top NYC children's bookstore, always has signed copies around too.
Borders	2 Penn Plz	212-244-1814	Chain
Center for Book Arts	28 W 27th St, 3rd Fl	212-481-0295	Specially - Artist/Handmade
Compleat Strategist	11 E 33rd St	212-685-3880	Specialty - Fantasy/ SciFi
Complete Traveller	199 Madison Ave	212-685-9007	Specialty - Vintage travel books
Cosmic Comics	10 E 23rd St	212-460-5322	Comics
Fashion Design Books	250 W 27th St	212-633-9646	Specialty - Fashion design
Gozlan Sefer Israel	28 W 27th St	212-725-5890	Judaica
Hudson News	Penn Station	212-971-6800	Chain
Jim Hanley's Universe	4 W 33rd St	212-268-7088	Specialty - Comics; SciFi
Koryo Books	35 W 32nd St	212-564-1844	Specialty - Korean
Levine J Co Books & Judaica	5 W 30th St	212-695-6888	Judaica
Metropolis Comics and Collectibles	873 Broadway	212-260-4147	Specialty - Comics
Penn Books	1 Penn Plz	212-239-0311	General interest
Revolution Books	9 W 19th St	212-691-3345	Specialty - Political
Rudolf Steiner Bookstore	138 W 15th St	212-242-8945	Specialty - Metaphysics
Russian Bookstore 21	174 Fifth Ave	212-924-5477	Specialty - Russian/Russia
Skyline Books	13 W 18th St	212-759-5463	Used
St Francis Friars	139 W 31st St	212-736-8500	Religious Books

Map 10 • Murray Hill / Gramercy

Baruch College Bookstore	55 Lexington Ave	646-312-4850	Academic - General
Borders	576 Second Ave	212-685-3938	Chain
Butala Emporium	108 E 28th St	212-684-4447	Indian
New York University Book Store– Health Sciences	333 E 29th St	212-998-9990	Academic - Health Sciences
Shakespeare & Co	137 E 23rd St	212-505-2021	Chain

Map 11 • Hell's Kitchen

Hudson News	Port Authority Bldg, North Wing	212-563-1030	Chain
John Jay College - Barnes & Noble	841 W 55th St	212-265-3619	Textbooks

Map 12 • Midtown

AMA Management Bookstore	1601 Broadway	212-903-8286	Specialty - Management
Barnes & Noble	555 Fifth Ave	212-697-3048	Chain
Bauman Rare Books	535 Madison Ave	212-751-0011	Antiquarian
Bookoff	14 E 41st St	212-685-1410	Used Japanese and English
Chartwell Booksellers	55 E 52nd St	212-308-0643	Specialty - books about Winston Churchill
Collector's Universe	31 W 46th St	212-398-2100	Specialty - Comics
Dahesh Heritage Fine Books	1775 Broadway, Ste 501	212-265-0600	General interest
Drama Book Shop	250 W 40th St	212-944-0595	Alas, poor Yorick…
FAO Schwarz	767 Fifth Ave	212-644-9400	Specialty - Children's
Hagstrom Map and Travel Center	51 W 43rd St	212-398-1222	Specialty - Travel/Maps
J N Bartfield-Fine Books	30 W 57th St	212-245-8890	Rare and antiquarian.
Kinokuniya	10 W 49th St	212-765-7766	Specialty - Japanese
Librarie de France	610 Fifth Ave	212-581-8810	French and Spanish books, maps, foreign-language dictionaries.
Metropolitan Museum of Art Bookshop at Rockefeller Center	15 W 49th St	212-332-1360	Specialty - Art books
Midtown Comics–Times Square	200 W 40th St	212-302-8192	Specialty - Comics
Rakuza	16 E 41st St	212-686-5560	Specialty - Japanese
Rizzoli	31 W 57th St	212-759-2424	Specialty - Art/Design
Urban Center Books	457 Madison Ave	212-935-3595	Sublime architecture & urban planning destination.
Virgin Megastore	1540 Broadway, Level B2	212-921-1020 x296	Chain

Map 13 • East Midtown

Argosy Book Store	116 E 59th St	212-753-4455	Rare and antiquarian, great selection of prints, too.
Asahiya	360 Madison Ave	212-883-0011	Specialty - Japanese
Barnes & Noble	160 E 54th St	212-750-8033	Chain
Borders	461 Park Ave	212-980-6785	Chain
Come Again	353 E 53rd St	212-308-9394	Specialty - Erotica; Gay/Lesbian
Hudson News	89 E 42nd St	212-687-0833	Chain
Martayan LAN	70 E 55th St	212-308-0018	Specialty - Rare and antiquarian maps, atlases, and books
Midtown Comics–Grand Central	459 Lexington Ave	212-302-8192	Specialty - Comics
New York Transit Museum	Grand Central, Main Concourse	212-878-0106	Specialty - NYC/Transit
Posman Books	9 Grand Central Terminal	212-983-1111	General Interest
Potterton Books	979 Third Ave	212-644-2292	Specialty - Decorative Arts/Architecture/Design
Quest Book Shop	240 E 53rd St	212-758-5521	Specialty - New Age
Richard B Arkway Books	59 E 54th St, Ste 62	212-751-8135	Specialty - Rare maps and books
United Nations Bookshop	First Ave & E 46th St	212-963-7680 800-553-3210	Good range of everything

Map 14 • Upper West Side (Lower)

Barnes & Noble	1972 Broadway	212-595-6859	Chain
Barnes & Noble	2289 Broadway	212-362-8835	Chain
Borders	10 Columbus Cir	212-823-9775	Chain
Fordham University Bookstore	113 W 60th St	212-636-6080	Academic - General
Juilliard School Bookstore	W 66th St b/w Amsterdam Ave & Broadway	212-799-5000	Academic - Music
New York Institute of Technology	1849 Broadway	212-261-1551	Specialty - Technical
Westsider	2246 Broadway	212-362-0706	Used; Antiquarian

Map 15 • Upper East Side (Lower)

Asia Society Bookstore	725 Park Ave	212-327-9217	Specialty - Asian
Blue Danube	217 E 83rd St	212-794-7099	Specialty - Hungarian
Bookberries	983 Lexington Ave	212-794-9400	General Interest

Bookstore Of The NY Psychoanalytic Institution	247 E 82nd St	212-772-8282	Specialty - Psychoanalysis
Choices Bookshop- Recovery	220 E 78th St	212-794-3858	Specialty - Self-help and recovery
Cornell University Medical College Bookstore	424 E 70th St	212-988-0400	Academic - Medical
Crawford Doyle Booksellers	1082 Madison Ave	212-288-6300	General Interest
Gotham City Comics Inc	796 Lexington Ave	212-980-0009	Comics
Hunter College Bookstore	695 Park Ave	212-650-3970	Academic - General
Imperial Fine Books	790 Madison Ave, Ste 200	212-861-6620	Antiquarian
James Cummins Book Seller	699 Madison Ave, 7th Fl	212-688-6441	Antiquarian
Locus Solus Rare Books	790 Madison Ave	212-861-9787	Rare and antiquarian.
Logos Book Store	1575 York Ave	212-517-7292	Children's books, spiritual lit, and beyond.
Metropolitan Museum of Art Bookshop	Fifth Ave & 82nd St	212-570-3894	Specialty - Art books
Shakespeare & Co	939 Lexington Ave	212-570-0201	Chain
Ursus Books	981 Madison Ave	212-772-8787	Specialty - Art
Whitney Museum of American Art Bookstore	945 Madison Ave	212-570-3614	Specialty - Art/ Artists' books

Map 16 • Upper West Side (Upper)

Funny Business Comics	212 W 92nd St	212-799-9477	Specialty - Comics
Westside Judaica	2412 Broadway	212-362-7846	Judaica

Map 17 • Upper East Side / East Harlem

Barnes & Noble	1280 Lexington Ave	212-423-9900	Chain
Barnes & Noble	240 E 86th St	212-794-1962	Chain
Corner Bookstore	1313 Madison Ave	212-831-3554	General Interest
Islamic Books & Tapes	1711 Third Ave	212-828-4038	Islamic literature
Kitchen Arts & Letters	1435 Lexington Ave	212-876-5550	Specialty - Books on food and wine

Map 18 • Columbia / Morningside Heights

Bank Street College Bookstore	610 W 112th St	212-678-1654	Academic - Education/Children
Columbia University Bookstore	2922 Broadway	212-854-4132	Academic - General
Book Culture	536 W 112th St	212-865-1588	Excellent bookstore servicing Columbia/ Barnard students.
Morningside Bookshop	2915 Broadway	212-222-3350	General Interest; New and used
Teachers College Bookstore (Columbia University Graduate School of Education)	1224 Amsterdam Ave	212-678-3920	Academic - Education

Map 19 • Harlem (Lower)

Hue-Man	2319 Frederick Douglass Blvd	212-665-7400	African-American.
Zoe Christian Bookstore	45 W 116th St	212-828-2776	Christian books

Map 20 • El Barrio / East Harlem

Jehovah jaireh	2028 Third Ave	212-426-9210	Christian

Map 21 • Manhattanville / Hamilton Heights

City College Book Store	138th St & Convent Ave	212-368-4000	General - Academic
Sisters Uptown	1942 Amsterdam Ave	212-862-3680	African-American books.

Map 23 • Washington Heights

Columbia Medical Books	3954 Broadway	212-923-2149	Academic - Medical
G W Books & Electronics	4211 Broadway	212-927-1104	General Interest
Jumel Terrace Books	426 W 160th St	212-928-9525	African-American and Mostly out of print

Map 24 • Fort George / Fort Tryon

Libreria Caliope	170 Dyckman St	212-567-3511	Spanish and English
Metropolitan Museum of Art Bookshop- Cloisters Branch	799 Ft Washington Ave	212-650-2277	Specialty - Art books

Arts & Entertainment • Bookstores

Map 25 • Inwood

| Libreria Continental | 628 W 207th St | 212-544-9004 | Specialty - Spanish |

Map 26 • Astoria

| Seaburn Books | 33-18 Broadway | 718-267-7929 | New and used. |
| Silver Age Comics | 22-55 31st St | 718-721-9691 | Comics. |

Map 27 • Long Island City

| PS1 Bookstore | 22-25 Jackson Ave | 718-784-2084 | Fabulous selection of art books. |

Map 28 • Greenpoint

Ex Libris Polish Book Gallery	140 Nassau Ave	718-349-0468	Polish.
Polish American Bookstore	648 Manhattan Ave	718-349-3756	Polish.
Polish Bookstore & Publishing	161 Java St	718-349-2738	Polish.
Polonia Book Store	882 Manhattan Ave	718-389-1684	Polish.
Word	126 Franklin St	718-383-0096	Literary fiction, non-fiction, and kids' books.

Map 29 • Williamsburg

| The Read Café | 158 Bedford Ave | 718-599-3032 | Used. |
| Spoonbill & Sugartown | 218 Bedford Ave | 718-387-7322 | Art, architecture, design, philosophy, and literature. New and used. |

Map 30 • Brooklyn Heights / DUMBO / Downtown

A&B Books	146 Lawrence St	718-596-0872	African-American books.
A&B Books	223 Duffield St	718-783-7808	General African-American books.
Barnes & Noble	106 Court St	718-246-4996	Chain.
Heights Books	109 Montague St	718-624-4876	Rare, out of print, used.
Long Island University Book Store	1 University Plz	718-858-3888	General.
St Mark's Comics	148 Montague St	718-935-0911	Comics.
Trazar's Variety Book Store	40 Hoyt St	718-797-2478	African-American books.

Map 31 • Fort Greene / Clinton Hill

Dare Books	33 Lafayette Ave	718-625-4651	General.
Pratt Bookstore	550 Myrtle Ave	718-789-1105	Art books.
Brownstone Books at BAM	30 Lafayette Ave	718-636-4136	General, specializing in film, music, and dance.

Map 32 • BoCoCa / Red Hook

Anwaar Bookstore	428 Atlantic Ave	718-875-3791	Arabic books.
Book Court	163 Court St	718-875-3677	General.
Dar Us Salam	486 Atlantic Ave	718-625-5925	Islamic books.
Freebird Books	123 Columbia St	718-643-8484	Used.
Pranga Book Store	354 Court St	718-624-2927	General new and used.
Rocketship	208 Smith St	718-797-1348	Comic books and graphic novels.

Map 33 • Park Slope / Prospect Heights / Windsor Terrace

Adam S Books	456 Bergen St	718-789-1534	General new and used.
Babbo's Books	242 Prospect Park W	718-788-3475	Used & new.
Barnes & Noble	267 Seventh Ave	718-832-9066	Chain.
Community Book Store	143 Seventh Ave	718-783-3075	General.
Park Slope Books	200 Seventh Ave	718-499-3064	Mostly used.
Seventh Avenue Books	202 Seventh Ave	718-840-0020	Used.

Arts & Entertainment · **Movie Theaters**

Multiplexes abound in NYC, though of course you should brace yourself for far steeper ticket and concession prices than in the rest of the country (with the possible exception of LA). Dinner and a movie turns out to be a rather exorbitant affair, but hey, we don't live in the Big Apple because it's cheap. And whether you're looking for the latest box office hit, or a classic from the French New Wave, there's a theater to meet your needs.

If you're after a first-run Hollywood blockbuster, we highly recommend the **AMC Loews Kips Bay (Map 10)** in Murray Hill. It has spacious theaters with large screens, big sound, comfortable seats, plenty of aisle room, and most importantly, fewer people! The **Regal Union Square 14 (Map 6)** is gargantuan, too, but movies there sell out hours or days in advance on the weekends. An IMAX theater and a cheesy '30s movie palace decorating theme make **AMC Loews Lincoln Square (Map 14)** a great place to catch a huge film, and its ideal location offers loads of after-movie options. Another great choice is the **Regal Battery Park 16 (p 202)**, but it's starting to get just as crowded as the Union Square location.

For independent or foreign films, the **Landmark Sunshine (Map 6)** has surpassed the **Angelika (Map 6)** as the superior downtown movie house. Don't get us wrong—the Angelika still presents some great movies, but the tiny screens and constant subway rumble can sometimes make you wish you'd waited for the DVD. Any list of hip venues would be incomplete without the **Two Boots Pioneer (Map 7)**, which specializes in documentaries, short films, cool film series, and festivals. If you're looking

for revivals, check the listings at the **Film Forum (Map 5)**, **BAM Rose Cinemas (Map 31)**, and the **MoMA (Map 12)**. Regular attendance at those three venues can provide an excellent education in cinema history Finally, for the truly adventurous, there's **Anthology Film Archives (Map 6)**, which plays a repertory of forgotten classics, obscure international hits, and experimental American shorts.

The most decadent and enjoyable movie experiences can be found at the theaters that feel more "New York." Sadly, the Beekman Theatre immortalized in Woody Allen's Annie Hall was demolished in 2005 to make room for a new ward for Sloan-Kettering (it's hard to argue with a cancer hospital, but film buffs can't help but wish they'd found another space for their expansion). **Clearview's Ziegfeld (Map 12)** on 54th Street is a vestige from a time long past when movie theaters were real works of art. This space is so posh with its gilding and red velvet, you'll feel like you're crossing the Atlantic on an expensive ocean liner. The **Paris Theatre (Map 12)** on 58th Street is one of our favorites in the city—it has the best balcony, hands down! Finally, if you enjoy Bollywood musicals and other Asian imports, check out **The ImaginAsian (Map 13)**. Not only does it have the best name of any theater in the city, it has some of its best films.

Oh, and don't forget to use Moviefone (777-FILM; www.moviefone.com) or Fandango (www.fandango.com) to purchase tickets in advance for crowded showtimes (opening weekends, holidays, or pretty much any night when you're trying to see a popular film).

Manhattan

	Address	Phone	Map	
AMC 19th Street	890 Broadway	212-260-8000	9	Standard multiplex.
AMC 34th Street 14	312 W 34th St	212-244-8686	8	The biggest and most comfortable of the midtown multiplexes.
AMC 72nd Street East	1230 Third Ave	212-879-1313	15	Single screen where the movies seem to play forever.
AMC 84th St 6	2310 Broadway	800-326-3264	14	Take the subway to Lincoln Square instead.
AMC Empire 25	234 W 42nd St	212-398-3939	12	Buy tickets ahead. It's Times Square.
AMC Harlem 9	2309 Frederick Douglass Blvd	212-665-8742	19	Owned by Magic Johnson. Best choice for Upper Manhattan.
AMC Lincoln Square 13	1998 Broadway	212-336-5000	14	Classy Upper West Side multiplex with IMAX.
AMC Loews Village VII	66 Third Ave	212-505-6397	6	Good-sized multiplex that keeps Union Square crowds in check.
AMC Orpheum 7	1538 Third Ave	212-505-6397	17	The Upper East Side's premier multiplex.
American Museum of Natural History IMAX	Central Park W & 79th St	212-769-5100	14	Rest your tired legs and learn something.
Angelika	18 W Houston St	212-995-2000	6	Higher profile indies play here first.
Anthology Film Archives	32 Second Ave	212-505-5181	6	Quirky retrospectives, revivals, and other rarities.
The Asia Society	725 Park Ave	212-327-9276	15	Special country-themed programs every month.
Bryant Park Summer Film Festival (outdoors)	Bryant Park, b/w 40th & 42nd Sts	212-512-5700	12	Groovy classics outdoors in sweltering summer heat.
Cinema Village	22 E 12th St	212-924-3363	6	Charming and tiny with exclusive documentaries and foreign films.
City Cinemas 1, 2, 3	1001 Third Ave	777-FILM #635	13	Ideal cure for Bloomingdale's hangover.
City Cinemas: East 86th Street	210 E 86th St	212-744-1999	17	It wouldn't be our first choice.
City Cinemas: Village East Cinemas	181 Second Ave	777-FILM #922	6	Half the theaters are gorgeous, half are dank pits.
Clearview's 62nd & Broadway	1871 Broadway	777-FILM #864	14	Popular single screen for the hip Lincoln Center crowd.
Clearview's Beekman One & Two	1271 Second Ave	212-249-4200	15	Another good choice for Upper East Siders.
Clearview's Chelsea	260 W 23rd St	212-691-5519	9	Manhattan's big, comfy, and gay multiplex.
Clearview's Chelsea West	333 W 23rd St	212-989-0060	8	Rocky Horror Fridays and Saturdays at midnight.
Clearview's First & 62nd Street	400 E 62nd St	777-FILM #957	15	You're better off taking the bus down to Kips Bay.
Clearview's Ziegfeld	141 W 54th St	777-FILM #602	12	Beloved NY classic with a gigantic screen. Don't miss.
Czech Center	1109 Madison Ave	212-288-0830	15	Czech premieres and special events.

437

Arts & Entertainment • **Movie Theaters**

Name	Address	Phone		Description
Film Forum	209 W Houston St	212-727-8110	5	Best place to pick up a film geek.
French Institute	55 E 59th St	212-355-6160	13	Talky French classics every Tuesday.
Guggenheim Museum Movie Theater	1071 Fifth Ave	212-423-3500	17	Special screenings in conjunction with current exhibitions.
IFC Center	323 Sixth Ave	212-924-7771	5	Great midnights, special events, and Manhattan exclusives.
The ImaginAsian	239 E 59th St	212-371-6682	13	Bollywood lovers unite.
Instituto Cervantes	211 E 49th St	212-308-7720	13	Spanish gems, but call to make sure there's subtitles.
Italian Academy	1161 Amsterdam Ave	212-854-2306	18	Fascinating classic film series at Columbia. Feel smart again.
Jewish Community Center in Manhattan	334 Amsterdam Ave	646-505-5708	14	Jewish premieres, previews, and festivals.
Landmark Sunshine Cinema	141 E Houston St	212-330-8182	6	High luxury indie film multiplex.
Leonard Nimoy Thalia	2537 Broadway	212-864-5400	16	A different classic movie every week. Good variety.
Lincoln Plaza Cinemas	1886 Broadway	212-757-2280	14	Uptown version of the Angelika.
Loews Kips Bay	570 Second Ave	212-447-9425	10	This multiplex is starting to show its age.
Makor	200 Hudson St	212-413-8806	2	Jewish themed films mixed with popular indies.
MOMA	11 W 53rd St	212-708-9480	12	Arty programming changes every day.
Museum of TV and Radio	25 W 52nd St	212-621-6800	12	*Gilligan's Island* on the big screen!
New Coliseum Theatre	701 W 181st St	212-740-1541	23	We love Washington Heights, but not its movie theater.
NYU Cantor Film Center	36 E 8th St	212-998-4100	6	Dirt cheap second-run blockbusters on Monday nights.
Paris Theatre	4 W 58th St	212-688-3800	12	Art house equivalent of the Ziegfeld.
Quad Cinema	34 W 13th St	212-255-8800	6	Gay-themed world premieres and second run Hollywood releases.
Regal 42nd Street E Walk	247 W 42nd St	212-50-LOEWS #572		Across the street from the Empire, but not nearly as nice.
Regal Battery Park City 16	102 North End Ave	800-326-3264 #629	p202	Beautiful downtown multiplex. Getting too crowded.
Regal Union Square Stadium 14	850 Broadway	800-326-3264 #628		Extremely crowded but fairly comfortable.
The Scandinavia House	58 Park Ave	212-779-3587	10	Scandinavian movies. Bergman and beyond.
Tribeca Cinemas	54 Varick St	212-966-8163	2	Home base of De Niro's Tribeca Film Festival.
Two Boots Pioneer Theater	155 E 3rd St	212-591-0434	7	Perpetually showing *Deep Throat* and *Easy Rider*. Good pizza.
UA 64th and 2nd	1210 Second Ave	800-326-3264 #626	15	Nice big theater with two ugly cousins.
UA East 85th Street	1629 First Ave	212-249-5100	15	Fun single screen.
Walter Reade Theater	70 Lincoln Plz	212-875-5600	14	Amazing festivals and rare screenings.
Whitney Museum Theater	945 Madison Ave	1-800-WHITNEY	15	Artist retrospectives and lectures.

Brooklyn

Name	Address	Phone		Description
BAM Rose Cinemas	30 Lafayette Ave	718-636-4100	31	Great seating and mix of first run + revivals.
Cobble Hill Cinemas	265 Court St	718-596-9113	32	Great indie destination, though theaters are small.
Ocularis	70 N 6th St	718-388-8713	29	Curated film series run out of Galapagos Art space.
Pavilion Brooklyn Heights	70 Henry St	718-596-7070	30	Intimate, classy, and just about perfect.
Pavilion Movie Theatres	188 Prospect Park W	718-369-0838	33	Nice mix of stuff right across from Propsect Park.
Regal/UA Court Street	108 Court St	718-246-7995	30	Audience-participation-friendly megaplex.
Rooftop Films	various locations	718-417-7362	n/a	Summer rooftop series—check website for locations!

Queens

Name	Address	Phone		Description
Museum of the Moving Image	36-01 35th Ave	718-784-4520	26	Excellent alternative to blockbuster crap.
UA Kaufman Studios Cinema 14	35-30 38th St	718-786-2020	26	Astoria

New Jersey

Name	Address	Phone		Description
AMC Newport Center 11	30 Mall Dr W [Thomas Gangemi Dr]	201-626-3200	35	Jersey stereotypes at their loudest and ugliest.

Arts & Entertainment • **Museums**

Make a resolution: Go to at least one museum in New York City every month. There are over 100 museums in the five boroughs, from the **Metropolitan Museum of Art (Map 15)** to the **Dyckman Farmhouse Museum (Map 25)**, an 18th-century relic in upper Manhattan. Many of these museums have special programs and lectures that are open to the public, as well as children's events and summer festivals. When you've found your favorite museums, look into membership. Benefits include free admission, guest passes, party invites, and a discount at the gift shop.

The famous Museum Miles comprises nine world-class museums along Fifth Avenue between 82nd Street and 105th Street, including the **Met (Map 15)**, and Frank Lloyd Wright's architectural masterpiece, the **Guggenheim (Map 17)**. El Museo del Barrio **(Map 17)**, devoted to early Latin American art, **The Museum of the City of New York (Map 17)**, the **Cooper-Hewitt National Design Museum (Map 17)** (housed in the Andrew Carnegie's Mansion), and the **Jewish Museum (Map 17)** are also along the mile. A few blocks off the stretch is **The Whitney Museum of American Art (Map 15)**, which showcases contemporary American artists and features the celebrated Biennial in even-numbered years.

See medieval European art at the **Cloisters (Map 25)** (also a famous picnic spot), exhibitions of up and coming African-American artists at the **Studio Museum in Harlem (Map 19)**, and PS1 **(Map 27)** (MoMA's satellite) for contemporary art. Take the kids to the **Brooklyn Children's Museum** or the **Children's Museum of Manhattan (Map 14)**. The **Lower East Side Tenement Museum (Map 4)** and the **Ellis Island Immigration Museum (Map 1)** stand as reminders of the past, while the **Hayden Planetarium (Map 14)** offers visions of the future. The treasures of the Orient are on display at the **Asia Society (Map 15)**, and coach potatoes can watch the tube all day at the **Museum of Television and Radio (Map 12)**. The **Brooklyn Museum** supplements its wide-ranging permanent collection with edgy exhibitions, performances, and other special events

Just about every museum in the city is worth a visit. Other favorites include Other favorites include the **New Museum of Contemporary Art** (Map 6) (in its spiffy new building on The Bowery), the **New-York Historical Society (Map 14)** (which focuses its exhibits on the birth of the city), the **New York Transit Museum (Map 30)**, the **Morgan Library (Map 9)** (with copies of Gutenberg's Bible on display), the **Museum of the Moving Image (Map 26)**, **The Museum of Sex (Map 9)**, **The New Museum of Contemporary Art (Map 6)** and the **Queens Museum of Art** (check out the panorama of New York City).

Manhattan

	Address	Phone	Map
American Academy of Arts & Letters	633 W 155th St	212-368-5900	21
American Folk Art Museum	45 W 53rd St	212-265-1040	12
American Geographical Society	120 Wall St	212-422-5456	1
American Institute of Graphic Arts	164 Fifth Ave	212-807-1990	9
American Museum of Natural History	Central Park W at 79th St	212-769-5100	15
American Numismatic Society	96 Fulton St	212-571-4470	1
Americas Society	680 Park Ave	212-249-8950	15
Anthology Film Archives	32 Second Ave	212-505-5181	6
Arsenal Gallery	830 Fifth Ave	212-360-8163	15
Art in General	79 Walker St	212-219-0473	3
Asia Society & Museum	725 Park Ave	212-288-6400	15
Asian American Arts Centre	26 Bowery	212-233-2154	3
Bard Graduate Center for Studies in the Decorative Arts	18 W 86th St	212-501-3000	16
Chelsea Art Museum	556 W 22nd St	212-255-0719	8
Children's Galleries for Jewish Culture	515 W 20th St	212-924-4500	8
Children's Museum of Manhattan	212 W 83rd St	212-721-1234	14
Children's Museum of the Arts	182 Lafayette St	212-274-0986	3
Children's Museum of the Native Americans	550 W 155th St	212-283-1122	21
China Institute	125 E 65th St	212-744-8181	15
The Cloisters	Ft Tryon Park	212-923-3700	25
Constitution Works	26 Wall St	212-785-1989	1
Cooper Union for the Advancement of Science and Art	7 E 7th St	212-353-4100	6
Cooper-Hewitt National Design Museum	2 E 91st St	212-849-8400	17
Czech Center	1109 Madison Ave	212-288-0830	15
Dahesh Museum of Art	580 Madison Ave	212-759-0606	12
Drawing Center	35 Wooster St	212-219-2166	2
Dyckman Farmhouse Museum	4881 Broadway	212-304-9422	25
El Museo del Barrio	1230 Fifth Ave	212-831-7272	17
Ellis Island Immigration Museum	Ellis Island, via ferry at Battery Park	212-561-4500	1

Exit Art	475 Tenth Ave	212-966-7745	8
Fraunces Tavern Museum	54 Pearl St	212-425-1778	1
Frick Collection	1 E 70th St	212-288-0700	15
Goethe-Institut	1014 Fifth Ave	212-439-8700	15
Gracie Mansion	East End Ave at 88th St	212-570-4751	17
Grant's Tomb	W 122nd St & Riverside Dr		18
Grey Art Gallery	100 Washington Sq E	212-998-6780	6
Guggenheim Museum	1071 Fifth Ave	212-423-3500	17
Hayden Planetarium	Central Park W & 79th St	212-769-5100	14
Hispanic Society Museum	613 W 155th St	212-926-2234	21
International Center of Photography (ICP)	1133 Sixth Ave	212-857-0000	12
Intrepid Sea, Air and Space Museum	Pier 86, W 46th St & 12th Ave	212-245-0072	12
Japan Society	333 E 47th St	212-832-1155	13
Jewish Museum	1109 Fifth Ave	212-423-3200	17
Lower East Side Tenement Museum	108 Orchard St	212-431-0233	4
Madame Tussauds NY	234 W 42nd St	800-246-8872	12
Merchant's House Museum	29 E 4th St	212-777-1089	6
Metropolitan Museum of Art	1000 Fifth Ave	212-535-7710	15
Morgan Library	225 Madison Ave	212-590-0300	9
Morris-Jumel Mansion	65 Jumel Ter	212-923-8008	23
Mount Vernon Hotel Museum and Garden	421 E 61st St	212-838-6878	15
Municipal Art Society	457 Madison Ave	212-935-3960	12
Museum at the Fashion Institute of Technology	Seventh Ave & 27th St	212-217-5800	9
Museum of American Finance	48 Wall St	212-908-4110	1
Museum of American Illustration	128 E 63rd St	212-838-2560	15
Museum of Arts & Design	40 W 53rd St	212-956-3535	12
The Museum of Biblical Art	1865 Broadway	212-408-1500	14
Museum of Chinese in the Americas	70 Mulberry St	212-619-4785	3
Museum of Jewish Heritage	36 Battery Pl	646-437-4200	p202
Museum of Modern Art (MoMA)	11 W 53rd St	212-708-9400	12
Museum of Sex	233 Fifth Ave	212-689-6337	9
Museum of Television and Radio	25 W 52nd St	212-621-6800	12
Museum of the City of New York	1220 Fifth Ave	212-534-1672	17
National Academy of Design	1083 Fifth Ave	212-369-4880	17
National Museum of Catholic Art & History	443 E 115th St	212-828-5209	20
National Museum of the American Indian	1 Bowling Green	212-514-3700	1
Neue Galerie	1048 Fifth Ave	212-628-6200	17
New Museum of Contemporary Art	235 Bowery	212-219-1222	6
New York City Fire Museum	278 Spring St	212-691-1303	5
New York Police Museum	100 Old Slip	212-480-3100	1
New York Public Library for the Performing Arts	40 Lincoln Center Plz	212-870-1630	14
The New York Public Library Humanities & Social Sciences Library	Fifth Ave & 42nd St	212-930-0830	12
New-York Historical Society	170 Central Park W	212-873-3400	14
Nicholas Roerich Museum	319 W 107th St	212-864-7752	16
PS1	22-25 Jackson Ave	718-784-2084	27
Rose Museum	154 W 57th St	212-247-7800	12
Rubin Museum of Art	150 W 17th St	212-620-5000	9
Scandinavia House	58 Park Ave	212-879-9779	10
School of Visual Arts Museum	209 E 23rd St	212-592-2000	10
Skyscraper Museum	39 Battery Pl	212-968-1961	p202
Sony Wonder Technology Lab	550 Madison Ave	212-833-8100	12
South Street Seaport Museum	12 Fulton St	212-748-8600	1
Sports Museum of America	26 Broadway	212-747-0900	1
Statue of Liberty Museum	Liberty Island, via ferry at Battery Park	212-363-3200	1
Studio Museum in Harlem	144 W 125th St	212-864-4500	19
Tibet House	22 W 15th St	212-807-0563	9
Ukrainian Museum	222 E 6th St	212-228-0110	6
US Archives of American Art	1285 Sixth Ave	212-399-5015	12
Whitney Museum of American Art	945 Madison Ave	212-570-3676	15

Whitney Museum of American Art at Altria	120 Park Ave	917-663-2453	13
Yeshiva University Museum	15 W 16th St	212-294-8330	24

Brooklyn

Brooklyn Children's Museum	145 Brooklyn Ave	718-735-4400	n/a
Brooklyn Historical Society	128 Pierrepont St	718-222-4111	30
Brooklyn Museum	200 Eastern Pkwy	718-638-5000	29
City Reliquary	370 Metropolitan Ave		29
Coney Island Museum	1208 Surf Ave	718-372-5159	n/a
Doll & Toy Museum of NYC	280 Cadman Plz W	718-243-0820	30
Harbor Defense Museum	230 Sheridan Loop	718-630-4349	n/a
Jewish Childrens' Museum	792 Eastern Pkwy	718-467-0600	n/a
Kurdish Library and Museum	345 Park Pl	718-783-7930	33
Museum of Contemporary African Diasporan Arts	80 Hanson Pl	718-230-0492	31
New York Aquarium	502 Surf Ave	718-265-3474	n/a
New York Transit Museum	Boerum Pl & Schermerhorn St	718-694-1600	30
The Old Stone House	First Ave b/w 3rd St & 4th St	718-768-3195	33
Simmons Collection African Arts Museum	1063 Fulton St	718-230-0933	31
Waterfront Museum	290 Conover St	718-624-4719	32
Wyckoff Farmhouse Museum	5816 Clarendon Rd	718-629-5400	n/a

Queens

Bowne House	37-01 Bowne St	718-359 0528	n/a
Fisher Landau Center for Art	38-27 30th St	718-937-0727	27
King Manor Museum	King Park, 150th St & Jamaica Ave	718-206-0545	n/a
Kingsland Homestead	Weeping Beech Park, 143-35 37th Ave	718-939-0647	n/a
Louis Armstrong Museum	34-56 107th St,	718-478-8297	n/a
The Museum for African Art (Temporary location)	36-01 43rd Ave	718-784-7700	27
Museum of the Moving Image	36-01 35th Ave	718-784-4520	26
New York Hall of Science	47-01 111th St	718-699-0005	n/a
The Noguchi Museum	9-01 33rd Rd	718-204-7088	27
PS1 Contemporary Art Center	22-25 Jackson Ave	718-784-2084	27
Queens County Farm Museum	73-50 Little Neck Pkwy	718-347-3276	n/a
Queens Museum of Art	Flushing Meadows-Corona Park	718-592-9700	n/a

New Jersey

Jersey City Museum	350 Montgomery St	201-413-0303	35

Metropolitan Museum of Art

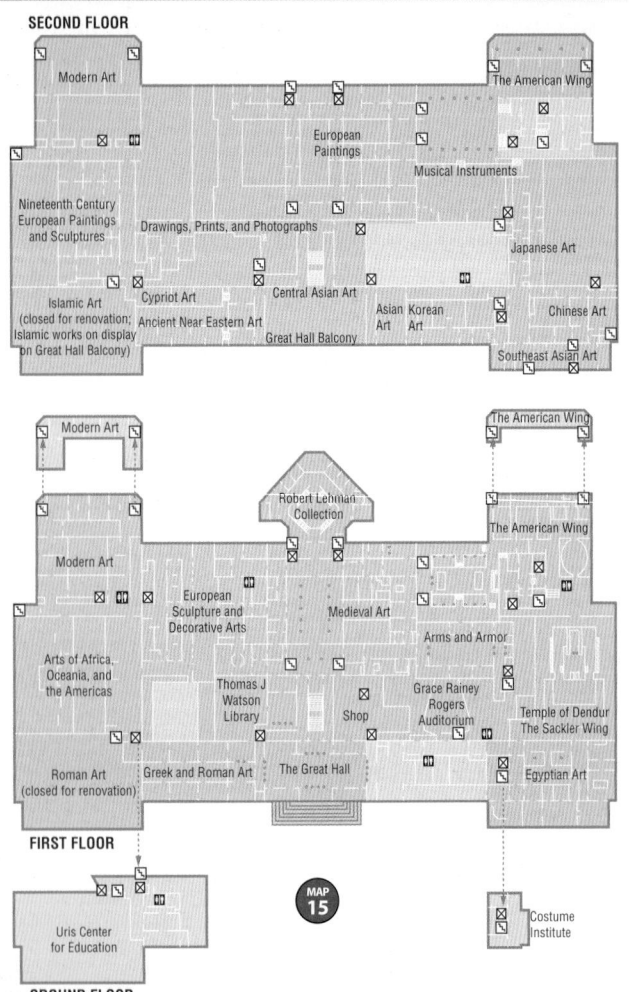

SECOND FLOOR

Modern Art

The American Wing

European Paintings

Musical Instruments

Nineteenth Century European Paintings and Sculptures

Drawings, Prints, and Photographs

Japanese Art

Islamic Art (closed for renovation; Islamic works on display on Great Hall Balcony)

Cypriot Art

Central Asian Art

Ancient Near Eastern Art

Asian Art

Korean Art

Chinese Art

Great Hall Balcony

Southeast Asian Art

Modern Art

The American Wing

Robert Lehman Collection

The American Wing

Modern Art

European Sculpture and Decorative Arts

Medieval Art

Arms and Armor

Arts of Africa, Oceania, and the Americas

Thomas J Watson Library

Shop

Grace Rainey Rogers Auditorium

Temple of Dendur The Sackler Wing

Roman Art (closed for renovation)

Greek and Roman Art

The Great Hall

Egyptian Art

FIRST FLOOR

MAP 15

Uris Center for Education

Costume Institute

GROUND FLOOR

General Information

NFT Map: 15
Address: 1000 Fifth Ave at 82nd St
Phone: 212-535-7710
Website: www.metmuseum.org
Hours: Sun, Tues–Thurs: 9:30 am–5:30 pm;
                Fri & Sat: 9:30 am–9 pm;
                Mon, New Year's Day, Christmas &
                Thanksgiving: closed. The museum
                is open on select "Holiday Mondays"
                throughout the year.
Admission: A suggested $20 donation for adults,
                $10 for students, and $15 for senior
                citizens. Admission includes the
                Main Building and The Cloisters on
                the same day. Free to members and
                children under twelve with an adult.

Overview

The Metropolitan Museum of Art is touted as the largest and most comprehensive museum in the Western
hemisphere. Established by a group of American businessmen, artists, and thinkers back in 1870, the museum was created to preserve and stimulate appreciation
for some of the greatest works of art in history.

In the first few years of its existance, the museum moved
from its original portion at 681 Fifth Avenue to the Douglas Mansion at 128 W 14th Street, and then finally to its
current Central Park location in 1880.

Calvert Vaux and Jacob Wrey Mould designed the
museum's Gothic Revival red-brick facade, which was
later remodeled in 1926 into the grand, white-col-
umned front entrance that you see today. Part of the
original facade was left intact and can still be seen from
the Robert Lehman Wing looking toward the European
Sculpture and Decorative Arts galleries.

The Met's annual attendance reaches over 4 million visitors who flock to see the more than 2 million works of
art housed in the museum's permanent collection. You
could visit the museum many times and not see more
than a small portion of the permanent collection. The
vast paintings anthology had a modest beginning in
1870 with a small donation of 174 European paintings
and has now swelled to include works spanning 5,000
years of world culture, from the prehistoric to the present and from every corner of the globe.

The Met is broken down into a series of smaller museums within each building. For instance, the American
Wing contains the most complete accumulation of
American paintings, sculpture, and decorative arts,
including period rooms offering a look at domestic life
throughout the nation's history. The Egyptian collection is the finest in the world outside of Cairo, and the
Islamic art exhibition remains unparalleled, as does the
mass of 2,500 European paintings and Impressionist
and Post-Impressionist works. The permanent gallery

of Islamic art underwent renovations in 2008, following
the 10-15 year renovation of the Greek & Roman collection. The redesigned galleries display works that have
been in storage for decades, assuring even the most
frequent visitor something fresh to check out including
the museum's newly restored, world-famous, non-gas-
guzzling **Etruscan chariot**.

Other major collections include the arms and armor,
Asian art, costumes, European sculpture and decorative
arts, medieval and Renaissance art, musical instruments,
drawings, prints, ancient antiquities from around the
world, photography, and modern art. Add to this the
many special exhibits and performances the the Met
offers throughout the year, and you have a world-class
museum with Central Park as its backyard.

This is a massive museum and seating can be difficult to find during busy weekends. When you need a
break from all of the culture, sit down for a snack in the
American Wing Café or lunch in the cafeteria. If you dip
around with a member (or become one yourself), it is
a treat to eat in the Trustees Dining Room overlooking
the park.

The Greatest Hits

You can, of course, spend countless hours at the Met.
Pick any style of art and chances are you will find a piece
here. But if you're rushed for time, check out the sublime space that houses the **Temple of Dendur** in the
Sackler Wing, the elegant **Frank Lloyd Wright Room**
in the American Wing, the fabulous **Tiffany Glass** and
Tiffany Mosaics, also in the American Wing, the **choir
screen** in the Medieval Sculpture Hall, the **Caravaggios**
and **Goyas** in the Renaissance Rooms, the **Picassos** and
Pollocks in Modern Art, and that huge **canoe** in Arts
of Africa and Oceania. For a moment of tranquility, visit
the beautiful Chinese Garden Court in the Asian galleries. When it's open, we highly recommend the **Roof
Garden**, which has killer views of Central Park as a side
dish to cocktails and conversation. When it's not, check
out seasonal specials like the **Christmas "Angel" Tree
and Neopolitan Baroque Crèche**, an annual favorite
set up in front of the medieval choir screen.

How to Get There–Mass Transit

Subway
Take the ④ ⑤ ⑥ to the 86th Street stop and walk
three blocks west to Fifth Avenue and four blocks south
to 82nd Street.

Bus
Take the ④ bus along Fifth Avenue (from uptown
locations) to 82nd Street or along Madison Avenue
(from downtown locations) to 83rd Street.

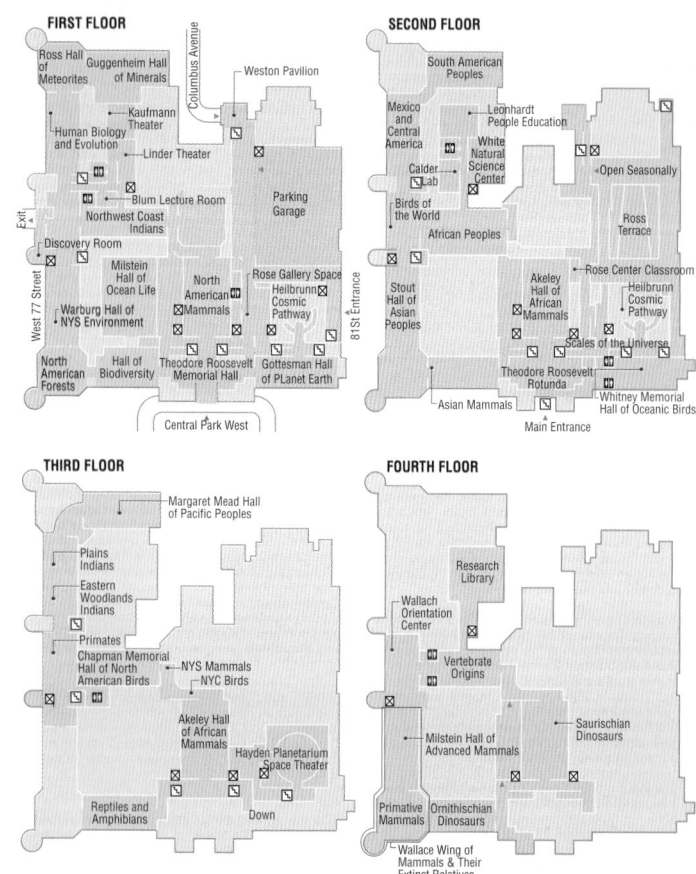

FIRST FLOOR

Ross Hall of Meteorites
Guggenheim Hall of Minerals
Columbus Avenue
Weston Pavilion
Kaufmann Theater
Human Biology and Evolution
Linder Theater
Blum Lecture Room
Northwest Coast Indians
Parking Garage
Exit
Discovery Room
West 77 Street
Milstein Hall of Ocean Life
North American Mammals
Rose Gallery Space
Heilbrunn Cosmic Pathway
Warburg Hall of NYS Environment
81ST Entrance
North American Forests
Hall of Biodiversity
Theodore Roosevelt Memorial Hall
Gottesman Hall of Planet Earth
Central Park West

SECOND FLOOR

South American Peoples
Mexico and Central America
Leonhardt People Education
White Natural Science Center
Calder Lab
Open Seasonally
Birds of the World
African Peoples
Ross Terrace
Stout Hall of Asian Peoples
Akeley Hall of African Mammals
Rose Center Classroom
Heilbrunn Cosmic Pathway
Scales of the Universe
Theodore Roosevelt Rotunda
Whitney Memorial Hall of Oceanic Birds
Asian Mammals
Main Entrance

THIRD FLOOR

Margaret Mead Hall of Pacific Peoples
Plains Indians
Eastern Woodlands Indians
Primates
Chapman Memorial Hall of North American Birds
NYS Mammals
NYC Birds
Akeley Hall of African Mammals
Hayden Planetarium Space Theater
Reptiles and Amphibians
Down

FOURTH FLOOR

Research Library
Wallach Orientation Center
Vertebrate Origins
Milstein Hall of Advanced Mammals
Saurischian Dinosaurs
Primitive Mammals
Ornithischian Dinosaurs
Wallace Wing of Mammals & Their Extinct Relatives

MAP
14

Museum of Natural History

General Information

NFT Map: 14
Address: Central Park West at 79th Street
Phone: 212-769-5100
Website: www.amnh.org
Hours: Daily, 10:00 am–5:45 pm
The Rose Center stays open until 8:45pm the first Friday of every month. Christmas & Thanksgiving: closed.
Admission: Suggested general admission is $14 for adults, $8 for children (2–12), and $10.50 for senior citizens and students. Special exhibitions, IMAX movies, and the space show are extra; packages are available. Free to members.

Overview

Admit it. You secretly TiVo the Discovery Channel and the History Channel. You've even watched one—if not several—episodes of Star Trek. Something about African beetles, famous dead guys, and the unknown universe strokes your inner Einstein. Focus your microscope on this one, smarty-pants: the American Museum of Natural History, a paradise for geeks and aspiring geeks alike, not to mention good old nature lovers. And don't worry, your TV-watching secrets are safe with us.

Decades before anyone knew what an atom was, and when relativity was just a twinkle in Einstein's eye, Albert Smith Bickmore established the AMNH. Completed in 1869, the museum held its first exhibition in the Central Park Arsenal a few years later, garnering enough respect to acquire space along classy Central Park West. Architects Calvert Vaux and J. Wrey Mould designed the new, posh building on limited Benjamins and opened it to the public in 1877. Key additions followed: The Hayden Planetarium in 1935, the Theodore Roosevelt Memorial Hall and Rotunda in 1936, and the Rose Center for Earth and Space in 2000.

As Saturday morning museum-going ritual dictates, it's going to be painfully crowded. On those days, you dodge out-of-towners, eyes wide, mouths gaping. It's much the same on weekdays with rowdy school kids on field trips. How to avoid the Excedrin-inducing atmosphere? Two words: permanent collection. The amazing series of wildlife dioramas even inspired an entire Hollywood movie (albeit not a great one, by adult standards). Don't expect to see any PETA supporters in these halls though.

When you can go at off hours, or if you feel you can brave the crowds, make a point of checking out the fascinating and often provocative special exhibits. Recent highlights have included Darwin and Water: H20=Life.

The Greatest Hits

Five floors of star-lovin', mammal-gazin', bird-watchin', fossil-fuelin' science await. Rain forest fever? Check out the Hall of Biodiversity. Didn't understand why that movie was called The Squid and The Whale? Meet the 94-foot long great blue whale and his giant squid companion at the Milstein Hall of Ocean Life. Moby teamed up with MTV2 and the Hayden Planetarium in The Rose Center for Earth and Space to produce SonicVision, an animated alternative music show that poses the question: How do you see your music? Another thought-provoking show with a celebrity element (narration by Harrison Ford) is The Search for Life: Are We Alone? For more instant thrills, check out the gigantic meteorites at the Arthur Ross Hall of Meteorites, or the five-story-tall dinosaur display in the Theodore Roosevelt Rotunda. It's the largest freestanding beast in the world. The AMNH also produces spectacular IMAX features, a great alternative to the museum's amazing but creepy taxidermy. The Hall of Gems houses the Star of India, the largest star sapphire in the world. Finally, for recreation of The Birds variety with less evil, visit The Butterfly Conservatory. Tropical butterflies flit all around you from, you guessed it, all over the world. It's enough to put TiVo on pause.

How To Get There

Subway
Take the **B** **C** to the 81st Street stop. Or take the **1** to 79th Street and walk two blocks east.

Bus
The **7** **10** and **11** all stop within a block of the museum. Take the **79** across Central Park if you are coming from the East Side.

Museum of Modern Art

General Information

NFT Map: 12
Address: 11 W 53rd St
Phone: 212-708-9400
Website: www.moma.org
Hours: Sun, Mon, Wed, Thurs, Sat: 10:30 am–5:30 pm;
Fri 10:30 am–8 pm; closed Tues, Thanksgiving,
and Christmas
Admission: $20 for adults, $16 for seniors,
$12 for students; free to members and
children under 16 accompanied by an adult

Overview

The Museum of Modern Art opened in 1929, back when impressionism and surrealism were truly modern art. SOriginally in the Heckscher Building at 730 Fifth Avenue, MoMA moved to its current address on West 53rd Street in 1932. What started out as a townhouse eventually expanded into an enormous space, with new buildings and additions in 1939 (by Phillip L. Goodwin and Edward Durell Stone), 1953 (including a sculpture garden by Phillip Johnson), 1964 (another Johnson garden), and 1984 (by Cesar Pelli). During the summer of 2002, the museum closed its Manhattan location and moved temporarily to Long Island City (MoMA's affiliate, PS1 Contemporary Art Center, is still there). After a major expansion and renovation by Yoshio Taniguchi, MoMA reopened in September 2004. Opinion varies as to the success of Taniguchi's new design, but the art is the point, right?

Wrong. Museums are one of the last great bastions of inventive, fun, not-necessarily-practical architecture. Taniguchi's design uses all available space, which, considering the price of midtown real estate, must have been a selling point for his design. Other than that, you'll have to trek up to the Guggenheim, fly off to Bilbao, or head downtown to the New Museum of Contemporary Art's new Bowery digs to see better marriages of art and design.

The re-Manhattanized museum charges $20. If crowds on a typical Saturday afternoon are any indication, the hefty entry fee is not keeping patrons away. Art lovers take note: the yearly $75 membership ($120 for a dual and $150 for a family) is the way to go. Members get a 10% discount at MoMA stores, free tickets to all film screenings, and you're free to pop in whenever you want to see your favorite Picasso (or use the restroom). For the best deal, visit the museum from 4–8 pm on Fridays, when Target sponsors free admission. The crowds aren't as bad as you might think, and you can usually slide right past the main desk and grab one of the free tickets that they scatter there.

What to See

The fourth and fifth floors are where the big names reside—Johns, Pollack, Warhol (fourth floor), Braque, Cezanne, Dali, Duchamp, Ernst, Hopper, Kandinsky, Klee, Matisse, Miro, Monet, Picasso, Rosseau, Seurat, Van Gogh, and Wyeth (fifth floor). More recent works can be found in the contemporary gallery on the second floor. Special exhibitions are featured on the third and sixth floors. The surrealist collection is outstanding, but we suspect that MoMA has only a tiny fraction of its pop art on display. Well, you can't see everything…

Moving downstairs to the third floor, it's clear that the photography collection is, as always, one of the centerpieces of the museum and is highly recommended (although the Gursky pieces are actually dotted throughout the building). The architecture and design gallery showcases a range of cool consumer items, from chairs to cars to the first Mac computers, and is one of the most popular destinations in the museum.

Recent exhibits, such as Doug Aitken's Sleepwalkers—which was the first to project film scenes onto MoMA's exterior walls—provide hope that the museum will only continue to be more innovative in the future.

Breakdown of the Space

Floor One: Lobby, Sculpture Garden, Museum Store, Restaurant
Floor Two: Contemporary Galleries, Media Gallery, Prints and Illustrated Books, Café
Floor Three: Architecture and Design, Drawing, Photography, Special Exhibitions
Floor Four: Painting and Sculpture II
Floor Five: Painting and Sculpture I, Café
Floor Six: Special Exhibitions
There are two theater levels below the first floor.

Amenities

Backpacks and large purses are not allowed in gallery spaces, and the free coat check can become messy when the check-in and check-out lines become intertwined. Leave large items (including laptops) at home.

Bathrooms and water fountains are on all floors. We don't think that there are enough of them, and the bathrooms themselves are way too small to handle the crowds.

There are three places to get food in the museum—you'll pay heavily for the convenience and Danny Meyer experience. Café 2, located on the second floor, offers "seasonal Roman fare," also known as "snooty Italian." They also have an espresso bar. Terrace 5, which overlooks the beautiful sculpture garden, has desserts, chocolates, and sandwiches, along with wine, cocktails, coffee, and tea. Both cafes open half an hour after the museum opens its doors and close half an hour before the museum closes.

For the ultimate museum dining experience, The Modern features the cuisine of Gabriel Kreuther. It has two main rooms—the Dining Room overlooks the sculpture garden, and the Bar Room is more casual and overlooks the bar. An outdoor terrace is also made available when the weather permits. The Modern serves French and New American food and features wild game menu items—sounds great if you've got a platinum card.

The Modern is open beyond museum hours, with the Dining Room closing at 10:30 pm Monday–Thursday, and 11:30 pm on Friday and Saturday. The Bar Room closes at 10:30 pm Monday–Thursday, at 11 pm on Friday and Saturday, and 9:30 pm on Sunday. There's a separate street entrance to allow diners access to The Modern after the museum closes.

On warm summer days, a gelato bar in the sculpture garden offers yummy sorbets.

So long as there are adventurous artists putting on plays in abandoned storefronts and opportunistic real estate developers knocking down beautiful old theaters to put up hotels, the New York theater scene will always be adding a few venues here and deleting a few venues there. What remains constant is that on any given night there are at least dozens, and more often hundreds, of live theater performances to be seen. And the best ones are not always the most expensive.

Broadway (theaters in the Times Square vicinity that hold at least 500 people) still has the reputation of being the place to see American theater at its finest, but the peculiar fact of the matter is that there is more much money to be gained by appealing to the infrequent theater goer than there is by trying to please the connoisseur. As a result, shows that are looked down on, if despised, by many lovers of the theater wind up selling out for years (*Mamma Mia*, anyone?), while more ambitious, artistically admired plays and musicals struggle to find an audience. Check out theater chat boards like BroadwayWorld.com and TalkinBroadway.com to see what the people who see everything have to say.

Nobody gets famous doing live theater anymore, so if you've never heard of the actor whose name is twinkling in lights (Cherry Jones, Brian Stokes Mitchell, Raul Esparza, Christine Ebersole...) chances are that person has the stage experience and acting chops to keep you enthralled for two and a half hours, unlike the big name celebrities (P. Diddy, Melanie Griffith) who make their stage acting debuts in starring roles they're not prepared for. Of course, there are also actors with extensive stage credits who come back to Broadway regularly after becoming famous. That's why we love John Lithgow, Cynthia Nixon, and Phylicia Rashad.

Many great performers work Off-Broadway (Manhattan theaters seating 100–499 people) where the writing and directing are actually more important than spectacle and scores made up of classic pop songs. Off-Off Broadway (fewer than 100 seats) is a terrific grab bag of both beginners and seasoned pros doing material that is often unlikely to draw in masses. And tickets are pretty cheap, too.

TheaterMania.com keeps an extensive list of just about every show in New York, with direct links to the websites that sell tickets. Many shows offer a limited number of inexpensive standing room and/or same-day rush tickets. A detailed directory of such offers can be found at TalkinBroadway.com.

Thousands of same-day tickets for Broadway and Off-Broadway shows are sold for 25%–50% off at the TKTS booths in Times Square (long lines) and at the South Street Seaport (short lines). They take cash and traveler's checks only. Check for hours and to see what's been recently available at www.tdf.org. Don't expect to get a bargain for the top-selling hits, but most shows use this booth at some time or another. You can also download discount coupons at Playbill.com that you can use to get seats in advance.

The dirty little secret of New York theatre is that free tickets for high-quality shows (aka not Grease, Wicked, or The Lion King etc.) are abundantly available though organizations that specialize in 'dressing the house' for productions that depend heavily on word of mouth than expensive advertising costs. By giving a yearly membership fee of around $100 to AudienceExtras.com or Play-By-Play.com, you can check your computer 24-hours a day to find free tickets (there's a per-ticket service charge of $3) for a dozen or so Off-, Off-Off-, and sometimes Broadway shows available at the last minute. That dinky little play in some church basement that you went to on a whim might wind up being the next great American classic. And if it isn't, you only spent 3 bucks.

Keep an eye out for shows by these lesser-known companies:

The young Classical theater of Harlem (www. classicaltheaterofharlem.org) has quickly earned a reputation for mounting exciting, edgy revivals of classics from Shakespeare and Brecht, as well as solid productions from more recent greats such as August Wilson and Melvin Van Peebles. A multicultural company that frequently casts against racial types, they draw a youthful audience with imaginative interpretations.

The **Mint Theater Company (Map 11)** (www.minttheater. org) specializes in reviving Broadway plays from the past they call "worthy, but neglected." In their tiny space you'll see interesting comedies and dramas from the likes of A. A. Milne, Edith Wharton, and Thomas Wolfe played traditionally with sets and costumes that really make you feel like you're watching a production from over 50 years ago.

Musicals Tonight! does the same kind of thing with forgotten musicals, only presenting them in low budgeted, but highly energized, staged readings. Nowadays most musicals revived on Broadway are revised and updated to the point where they lose their authenticity. But if you're in the mood to see what an Irving Berlin ragtime show from 1915 was really like, or if you want to see a Cole Porter tuner from the '30s with all of the dated topical references that confused audiences even back then, Musicals Tonight! serves up the past as it really was written. And check for their special concerts where Broadway understudies sing songs from the roles they are currently covering.

Broadway insiders know that Monday nights, when most shows are dark, is often the hottest night of the week for entertainment. That's when performers use their night off to partake in benefits and special events. Consistently among the best are shows from Scott Siegel's Broadway By The Year series at **Town Hall (Map 12)** (www.the-townhall-nyc.org). Each one-night concert is packed with theater and cabaret stars singing hits and obscurities introduced on Broadway in one selected year. Siegel also produces Broadway Unplugged at Town Hall, a concert of theater performers singing showtunes without amplification. The atmosphere is like a sports event, with the audience wildly cheering each naturally voiced solo.

Theaters / Performing Arts

Pearl Theatre Company (Map 6) (www.pearltheatre.org), presently located at 80 St. Mark's Place, is one of the 15 or so largest institutional theaters in New York City. Now in their 23rd year, they continue to grow as a resident company and a classical repertory, offering delights from Sheridan, Shakespeare, Aeschylus, Marivau, and Ibsen.

Now in its eighth season, Horse Trade (www.httheater.org) continues its commitment to producing a varied program of performance series, readings, workshops, and fully realized productions. Most events are performed at **The Kraine Theater (Map 6)**, which also houses the **Red Room (Map 6)** on its third floor. The theaters are also available to rent for rehearsals and performances.

HERE (Map 5) (www.here.org) not only houses two small theaters, but it also has an amazing gallery space and a cozy café/bar—perfect for pre- or post-show drinks.

In Chelsea, **The Kitchen (Map 8)** (www.thekitchen.org) literally began in the unused kitchen of the Mercer Arts Center, housed in the Broadway Central Hotel in Greenwich Village. In 1985, The Kitchen moved into its permanent home at 512 West 19th Street. The venue plays host to new performance artists blending music, dance, video, art, and spoken word.

Located in a former public school on First Avenue and 9th Street in the East Village, **P.S. 122 (Map 7)** (www.ps122.org) is a not-for-profit arts center serving New York City's dance and performance community. Shows rotate through on a regular basis, so check the website for the latest schedule. The outdoor **Delacorte Theater (Map 15)** in Central Park hosts performances only during the summer months. Tickets to the ridiculously popular and free Shakespeare in the Park performances are given away at 1 pm at the Delacorte and also at the **Public Theater (Map 6)** on the day of each performance. Hopefully, you enjoy camping because people line up for days in their tents and sleeping bags just to secure a ticket!

Just on the other side of the Manhattan Bridge in Brooklyn is the world famous Brooklyn Academy of Music. A thriving urban arts center, BAM brings domestic and international performing arts and film to Brooklyn. The center includes two theaters (**Harvey Lichtenstein Theater** and **Howard Gilman Opera House (Map 31)**), the Bam Rose Cinemas, and the BAMcafé, a restaurant and live music venue. Our favorite season is the Next Wave, an annual three-month celebration of cutting-edge dance, theater, music, and opera.

Manhattan

Broadway

Al Hirschfeld Theatre	302 W 45th St	212-239-6200	12
Ambassador Theatre	219 W 49th St	212-239-6200	12
American Airlines Theatre	227 W 42nd St	212-719-1300	12
August Wilson Theatre	245 W 52nd St	212-239-6200	12
Belasco Theatre	111 W 44th St	212-239-6200	12
Bernard B Jacobs Theatre	242 W 45th St	212-239-6200	12
Biltmore Theatre	261 W 47th St	212-239-6200	12
Booth Theatre	222 W 45th St	212-239-6200	12
Broadhurst Theatre	235 W 44th St	212-239-6200	12
Broadway Theatre	1681 Broadway	212-239-6200	12
Brooks Atkinson Theatre	256 W 47th St	212-307-4100	12
Circle in the Square Theatre	1633 Broadway	212-307-0388	12
Cort Theatre	138 W 48th St	212-239-6200	12
Ethel Barrymore Theatre	243 W 47th St	212-239-6200	12
Eugene O'Neill Theatre	230 W 49th St	212-239-6200	12
Gershwin Theatre	222 W 51st St	212-307-4100	12
Helen Hayes Theatre	240 W 44th St	212-239-6200	12
Hilton Theater	213 W 42nd St	212-556-4750	12
Imperial Theater	249 W 45th St	212-239-6200	12
John Golden Theatre	252 W 45th St	212-239-6200	12
Longacre Theatre	220 W 48th St	212-239-6200	12
Lunt-Fontanne Theatre	205 W 46th St	212-307-4100	12
Lyceum Theatre	149 W 45th St	212-239-6200	12
Majestic Theater	245 W 44th St	212-239-6200	12
Marquis Theatre	1535 Broadway	212-382-0100	12
Minskoff Theatre	200 W 45th St	212-307-4747	12
Music Box Theatre	239 W 45th St	212-239-6200	12
Nederlander Theatre	208 W 41st St	212-307-4100	12
Neil Simon Theatre	250 W 52nd St	212-307-4100	12
New Amsterdam Theatre	214 W 42nd St	212-307-4100	12
Palace Theatre	1564 Broadway	212-307-4100	12
Richard Rodgers Theatre	226 W 46th St	212-221-1211	12
Roundabout/Laura Pels Theatre	111 W 46th St	212-719-1300	12

Theaters / Performing Arts

Schoenfeld Theatre	236 W 45th St	212-239-6200	12
Shubert Theatre	225 W 44th St	212-239-6200	12
St James Theatre	246 W 44th St	212-239-6200	12
Studio 54	254 W 54th St	212-719-1300	12
Vivian Beaumont Theatre	Lincoln Center, W 65th St & Amsterdam Ave	212-362-7600	14
Walter Kerr Theatre	219 W 48th St	212-239-6200	12
Winter Garden Theatre	1634 Broadway	212-239-6200	12

Off-Broadway

37 Arts Theatre	450 W 37th St	212-307-4100	8
47th Street Theater	304 W 47th St	212-239-6200	12
Acorn Theatre	410 W 42nd St	212-714-2442	11
Actor's Playhouse	100 Seventh Ave S	212-239-6200	9
The Actors' Temple	339 W 47th St	212-239-6200	11
Astor Place Theatre	434 Lafayette St	212-254-4370	6
Atlantic Theater Company	336 W 20th St	212-691-5919	8
Barrow Street Theater	27 Barrow St	212-239-6200	5
Beckett Theatre	410 W 42nd St	212-714-2442	11
Cherry Lane Theater	38 Commerce St	212-989-2020	5
Classic Stage Co	136 E 13th St	212-677-4210	6
Connelly Theatre	220 E 4th St	212-982-2287	7
Daryl Roth Theatre	101 E 15th St	212-239-6200	10
Delacorte Theater	Central Park, W 81st St	212-539-8750	15
The Duke on 42nd Street	229 W 42nd St	212-239-6200	12
Ensemble Studio Theatre	549 W 52 St	212-247-3405	11
Harlem School of the Arts Theater	645 St Nicholas Ave	212-868-4444	21
Harold Clurman Theatre	410 W 42nd St	212-714-2442	11
HSA Theater	645 St Nicholas Ave	212-868-4444	21
Irish Repertory Theatre	132 W 22nd St	212-727-2737	9
June Havoc Theatre	312 W 36th St	212-868-4444	8
Kirk Theatre	410 W 42nd St	212-714-2442	11
Lion Theatre	410 W 42nd St	212-714-2442	11
Little Shubert Theatre	422 W 42nd St	212-239-6200	11
Lucille Lortel Theatre	121 Christopher St	212-279-4200	5
Manhattan Ensemble Theatre	55 Mercer St	212-925-1900	3
Manhattan Theatre Club	131 W 55th St	212-581-1212	12
Mazer Theater	197 East Broadway	212-239-6200	4
Minetta Lane Theatre	18 Minetta Ln	212-307-4100	6
Mitzi E Newhouse Theater	Lincoln Center, W 65th & Amsterdam Ave	212-239-6200	14
New World Stages	340 W 50th St	212-239-6200	11
New York Theatre Workshop	79 E 4th St	212-460-5475	6
Orpheum Theater	126 Second Ave	212-477-2477	6
Pearl Theatre Co	80 St Marks Pl	212-598-9802	6
Players Theatre	115 MacDougal St	212-475-1449	6
Playwrights Horizons Theater	416 W 42nd St	212-279-4200	11
The Public Theater	425 Lafayette St	212-260-2400	6
Samuel Beckett Theatre	410 W 42nd St	212-714-2442	11
Second Stage Theatre	307 W 43rd St	212-246-4422	12
Signature Theatre: Peter Norton Space	555 W 42nd St	212-244-7529	11
Snapple Theatre Center	210 W 50th St	212-307-4100	12
St Lukes Church	308 W 46th St	212-239-6200	12
Studio Theatre	410 W 42 St	212-714-2442	11
Theater at St Clement's	423 W 46th St	212-868-4444	11
Theater Ten Ten	1010 Park Ave	212-288-3246	15
TriBeCa Performing Arts Center	199 Chambers St	212-220-1460	2
Union Square Theater	100 E 17th St	212-307-4100	10
Upstairs at Studio 54	254 W 54th St	212-719-1300	12
Village Theater	158 Bleecker St	212-307-4100	6
Vineyard Theatre	108 E 15th St	212-353-0303	10
Vinnie Black's Coliseum at the Edison Hotel	221 W 46th St	212-352-3101	12
Westside Theatre	407 W 43rd St	212-239-6200	11
York Theatre at St Peter's Church	619 Lexington Ave	212-935-5820	13
The Zipper Theatre	336 W 37th St	212-563-0480	8

449

Theaters / Performing Arts

Off-Off Broadway

Theater	Address	Phone	
13th Street Theatre	50 W 13th St	212-675-6677	6
29th Street Repertory Theatre	212 W 29th St	212-465-0575	9
45th St Theater	354 W 45th St	212-279-4200	11
78th Street Theatre Lab	236 W 78th St	212-873-9050	14
Abingdon Mainstage Theatre	312 W 36th St	212-868-2055	8
Access Theater	380 Broadway, 4th Fl	212-966-1047	3
Actor's Theater Workshop	145 W 28th St	212-947-1386	8
American Place Theatre	266 W 37th St	212-594-4482	8
ArcLight Theatre	152 W 71st St	212-595-0355	14
Ars Nova Theatre	511 W 54th St	212-868-4444	11
Axis Theater	1 Sheridan Sq	212-807-9300	5
Barrow Group Arts Center	312 W 36th St	212-760-2615	8
Cedar Lake	547 W 26th St	212-244-0015	8
Center Stage, NY	48 W 21st St	212-929-2228	9
Collective: Unconscious	279 Church St	212-254-5277	1
DR2 Theatre	103 E 15th St	212-375-1110	10
Duo Theatre	62 E 4th St	212-598-4320	6
Flea Theatre	41 White St	212-226-0051	3
Gene Frankel Theatre	24 Bond St	212-777-1767	6
Gertrude Stein Repertory Theater	15 W 26th St	212-725-7254	9
HERE	145 Sixth Ave	212-647-0202	5
Hudson Guild	441 W 26th St	212-760-9800	8
Irish Arts Center	555 W 51st St	212-757-3318	11
Jewish Community Center	334 Amsterdam Ave	646-505-5700	14
Julia Miles Theater	424 W 55th St	212-765-1706	11
The Kitchen	512 W 19th St	212-255-5793	8
The Kraine Theater	85 E 4th St	212-868-4444	6
La Mama ETC	74A E 4th St	212-475-7710	6
The Looking Glass Theatre	422 W 57th St	212-307-9467	11
Manhattan Theatre Source	177 MacDougal St	212-260-4698	6
McGinn/Cazale Theatre	2162 Broadway	212-579-0528	14
Medicine Show Theatre	549 W 52nd St	212-262-4216	11
Metropolitan Playhouse	220 E 4th St, 2nd Fl	212-995-5302	7
Mint Theatre	311 W 43rd St 5th Fl	212-315-0231	11
National Black Theatre	2031 Fifth Ave	212-722-3800	19
Ohio Theater	66 Wooster St	800-965-4827	6
The Ontological Theater at St Mark's Church-in-the-Bowery	131 E 10th St	212-420-1916	6
People's Improv Theater	154 W 29th St, 2nd Fl	212-563-7488	9
Phil Bosakowski Theatre	354 W 45th St	212-352-3101	11
The Producers Club	358 W 44th St	212-315-4743	11
Producers Club II	616 Ninth Ave	212-315-4743	11
PS 122	150 First Ave	212-477-5288	7
Rattlestick Theatre	224 Waverly Pl	212-627-2556	5
The Red Room	85 E 4th St	212-868-4444	6
Repertorio EspaĐol	138 E 27th St	212-889-2850	10
Riverside Church	490 Riverside Dr	212-870-6700	18
Sanford Meisner Theatre	164 Eleventh Ave	212-206-1764	8
Soho Playhouse	15 Vandam St	212-691-1555	5
Soho Repertory Theatre	46 Walker St	212-941-8632	3
Sol Goldman Y	344 E 14th St	212-780-0800	6
St Bart's Playhouse	Park Ave & E 50th St	212-378-0248	13
Storm Theatre	145 W 46th St	212-330-8350	12
T Schreiber Studio	151 W 26th St	212-741-0209	9
TADA! Theater	15 W 28th St	212-252-1619	9
Tenement Theater	97 Orchard St	212-431-0233	4
Theater for the New City	155 First Ave	212-254-1109	7
Under St Marks	94 St Marks Pl	212-868-4444	7
Urban Stages	259 W 30th St	212-868-4444	9
West End Theatre	263 W 86th St	212-352-3101	16
Wings Theater	154 Christopher St	212-627-2961	5
WOW Café	59 E 4th St	212-777-4280	6

Performing Arts

92nd Street Y Theatre	1395 Lexington Ave	212-996-1100	17
Alice Tully Hall	Lincoln Center, 65th & Broadway	212-875-5050	14
Amato Opera	319 Bowery	212-228-8200	6
Apollo Theater	253 W 125th St	212-531-5300	19
Avery Fisher Hall	Lincoln Center, Columbus Ave at 65th St	212-875-5030	14
Baruch Performing Arts Center	55 Lexington Ave	646-312-4085	10
Beacon Theater	2124 Broadway	212-465-6500	14
Bernie West Theatre at Baruch College	17 Lexington Ave	646-312-4085	10
Carnegie Hall	154 W 57th St	212-247-7800	12
Chicago City Limits	318 W 53rd St	212-888-5233	12
City Center	131 W 55th St	212-581-7907	12
Dance Theatre Workshop	219 W 19th St	212-691-6500	9
Dicapo Opera Theatre	184 E 76th St	212-288-9438	15
French Institute	55 E 59th St	212-355-6160	13
The Gerald W Lynch Theater at John Jay College	899 Tenth Ave	212-237-8005	11
Harry DeJur Playhouse	466 Grand St	212-598-0400	4
Joyce Theater	175 Eighth Ave	212-691-9740	8
Manhattan School of Music	120 Claremont Ave	212-749-2802	18
Merkin Concert Hall	129 W 67th St	212-501-3330	14
Metropolitan Opera House	Lincoln Center, Columbus Ave at 64th St	212-362-6000	14
Miller Theater–Columbia University	200 Dodge Hall, 2960 Broadway	212-854-7799	18
New Victory Theatre	209 W 42nd St	212-239-6200	12
New York State Theatre	Lincoln Ctr, Columbus Ave at 63rd St	212-870-5570	14
Radio City Music Hall	1260 Sixth Ave	212-247-4777	12
Sylvia and Danny Kaye Playhouse	695 Park Ave	212-772-5207	15
Symphony Space	2537 Broadway	212-864-5400	16
The Theater at Madison Square Garden	2 Penn Plz	212-307-4111	9
Town Hall	123 W 43rd St	212-840-2824	12

Brooklyn

651 Arts	651 Fulton St	718-636-4181	31
Bargemusic	Fulton Ferry Landing near Brooklyn Bridge	718-624-2083	30
BRIC Studio	57 Rockwell Pl	718-855-7882	30
Brick Theatre	575 Metropolitan Ave	718-907-6189	29
Brooklyn Arts Council	55 Washington St	718-625-0080	30
Brooklyn Arts Exchange	421 Fifth Ave	718-832-0018	33
Brooklyn Conservatory of Music	58 Seventh Ave	718-622-3300	33
Brooklyn Family Theatre	1012 Eighth Ave	718-670-7205	33
Brooklyn Lyceum	227 Fourth Ave	718-857-4816	33
Charlie's Pineapple Theater Company	208 N 8th St	718-907-0577	29
Galapagos	70 N 6th St	718-782-5188	29
Gallery Players Theater	199 14th St	718-595-0547	33
Harvey Lichtenstein Theater	651 Fulton St	718-636-4100	31
The Heights Players	26 Willow Pl	718-237-2752	30
Howard Gilman Opera House	30 Lafayette Ave	718-636-4100	31
Paul Robeson Theatre	54 Greene Ave	718-783-9794	31
Puppetworks	338 Sixth Ave	718-965-3391	33
St Ann's Warehouse	38 Water St	718-254-8779	30

Queens

Astoria Performing Arts Center	31-30 33rd St	718-393-7505	26
The Chocolate Factory	5-49 49th Ave	718-482-7069	27

Understanding Your World, So You Don't Have To

Lead anchor Brandon Armstrong and the rest of the Onion team bring you, the ignorant masses, hard-hitting news, videos, and opinions you can't find anywhere else.

FREE IN PRINT WEEKLY AND ONLINE DAILY AT ONION.COM

America's Finest News Source

 the ONION

CELEBRATE BROOKLYN!

MUSIC | DANCE | WORD | FILM

PROSPECT PARK BANDSHELL

JUNE
THROUGH
AUGUST

 BRICONLINE.ORG/CB

DO MORE.

SPEND LESS.

Discover 52 restaurants. Save $10 every time.
Also available: The Bar & Lounge Deck. Do more. Spend less.

www.cityshuffle.com

Where do you go when your desire to help is larger than your zip code?

You go to Morocco, Mongolia, or 71 other countries. And when you return, your own community will benefit in ways you can't imagine.

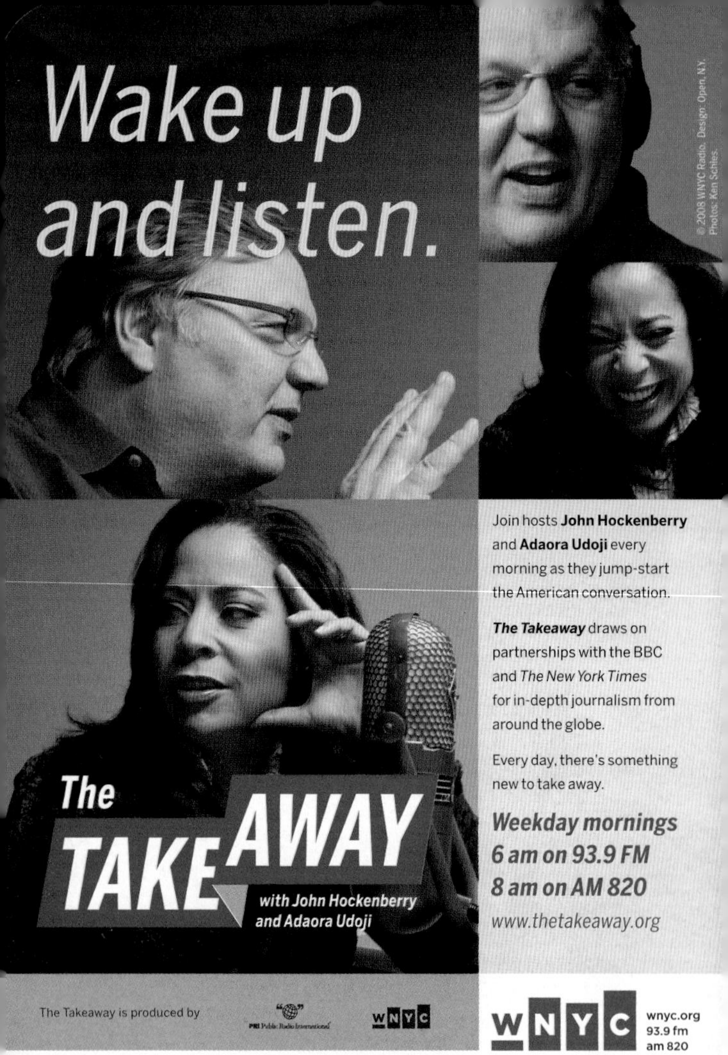

Wake up and listen.

Join hosts **John Hockenberry** and **Adaora Udoji** every morning as they jump-start the American conversation.

The Takeaway draws on partnerships with the BBC and *The New York Times* for in-depth journalism from around the globe.

Every day, there's something new to take away.

**Weekday mornings
6 am on 93.9 FM
8 am on AM 820**
www.thetakeaway.org

The TAKEAWAY
with John Hockenberry and Adaora Udoji

The Takeaway is produced by

wnyc.org
93.9 fm
am 820

© 2008 WNYC Radio. Design: Open, N.Y. Photos: Ken Schles.

Take the subway to 1904.

You'll feel like you've traveled back in time. The New York Transit Museum is housed in a historic subway station where you can board our vintage collection of subway and elevated trains and check out all the antique treasures from the world's greatest subway system.

If you have children, there are free kids' workshops every weekend. And be sure to visit the Museum Store for all kinds of collectibles and souvenirs.

And get 2-for-1 admission with this ad.

The Museum is located at the corner of Boerum Place and Schermerhorn Street in Brooklyn Heights. Take the ❷ ❸ or ❹ train to Borough Hall, then walk 2 blocks south.

For additional information and directions, call 718-694-1600. Or visit us at **www.mta.info**.

It'll be 1904 all over again.

NEW YORK TRANSIT MUSEUM

MTA Metropolitan Transportation Authority *Going your way*

www.mta.info

Street Index

Street Index

Street Index

Address Locator

Streets	Riverside	West End	Broadway	Amsterdam	Columbus	C.P.W.	Central Park
110-116	370-440		2800-2950	995-1120			
102-110	290-370	850-920	2675-2800	856-995	850-1021	419-500	
96-102	240-290	737-850	2554-2675	733-856	740-850	360-419	
90-96	180-240	620-737	2440-2554	620-733	621-740	300-360	
84-90	120-180	500-619	2321-2439	500-619	501-620	241-295	
78-84	60-120	380-499	2201-2320	380-499	381-500	239-241	
72-78	1-60	262-379	2081-2200	261-379	261-380	121-239	
66-72		122-261	1961-2079	140-260	141-260	65-115	
58-66		2-121	1791-1960	1-139	2-140	0-65	

Streets	12th Ave.	11th Ave.	Broadway	10th Ave.	9th Ave.	8th Ave.	7th Ave.	6th Ave.
52-58	710-850	741-854	1674-1791	772-889	782-907	870-992	798-921	1301-1419
46-52	600-710	625-740	1551-1673	654-770	662-781	735-869	701-797	1180-1297
40-46	480-600	503-624	1440-1550	538-653	432-662	620-734	560-701	1061-1178
34-40	360-480	405-502	Macy's-1439	430-537	431-432	480-619	442-559	1060-1061
28-34	240-360	282-404	1178-1282	314-429	314-431	362-479	322-442	815-1060
22-28	0-240	162-281	940-1177	210-313	198-313	236-361	210-321	696-814
14-22		26-161	842-940	58-209	44-197	80-235	64-209	5520-695
8-14			748-842	0-58	0-44	0-80	2-64	420-520
Houston-8			610-748					244-402